Introduction to Management Science

A Modeling and Case Studies Approach with Spreadsheets

The McGraw-Hill/Irwin Series
Operations and Decision Sciences

OPERATIONS MANAGEMENT

Bowersox, Closs, and Cooper
Supply Chain Logistics Management
First Edition

Chase, Aquilano, and Jacobs
Operations Management for Competitive Advantage
Ninth Edition

Cohen and Apte
Manufacturing Automation
First Edition

Davis, Aquilano, and Chase
Fundamentals of Operations Management
Fourth Edition

Davis and Heineke
Managing Services: Using Technology to Create Value
First Edition

Dobler and Burt
Purchasing and Supply Management
Sixth Edition

Finch
OperationsNow.com: Processes, Value, and Profitability
First Edition

Flaherty
Global Operations Management
First Edition

Fitzsimmons and Fitzsimmons
Service Management
Third Edition

Gray and Larson
Project Management
Second Edition

Harrison and Samson
Technology Management
First Edition

Hill
Manufacturing Strategy: Text & Cases
Third Edition

Hopp and Spearman
Factory Physics
Second Edition

Knod and Schonberger
Operations Management: Customer-Focused Principles
Seventh Edition

Lambert and Stock
Strategic Logistics Management
Third Edition

Leenders and Fearon
Purchasing and Supply Chain Management
Twelfth Edition

Melnyk and Swink
Value-Driven Operations Management
First Edition

Moses, Seshadri, and Yakin
HOM Operations Management Software
First Edition

Nahmias
Production and Operations Analysis
Fourth Edition

Nicholas
Competitive Manufacturing Management
First Edition

Olson
Introduction to Information Systems Project Management
First Edition

Pinedo and Chao
Operations Scheduling
First Edition

Sanderson and Uzumeri
Managing Product Families
First Edition

Schroeder
Operations Management: Contemporary Concepts
First Edition

Simchi-Levi, Kaminsky, and Simchi-Levi
Designing and Managing the Supply Chain
Second Edition

Stevenson
Operations Management
Seventh Edition

Vollmann, Berry, and Whybark
Manufacturing Planning & Control Systems
Fourth Edition

Zipkin
Foundations of Inventory Management
First Edition

BUSINESS STATISTICS

Aczel and Sounderpandian
Complete Business Statistics
Fifth Edition

ALEKS Corporation
ALEKS for Business Statistics
First Edition

Alwan
Statistical Process Analysis
First Edition

Bowerman and O'Connell
Business Statistics in Practice
Third Edition

Bryant and Smith
Practical Data Analysis: Case Studies in Business Statistics, Volumes I and II
Second Edition
Volume III
First Edition

Cooper and Schindler
Business Research Methods
Eighth Edition

Delurgio
Forecasting Principles and Applications
First Edition

Doane, Mathieson, and Tracy
Visual Statistics
Second Edition, 2.0

Doane, Mathieson, and Tracy
Visual Statistics: Statistical Process Control
First Edition, 1.0

Gitlow, Oppenheim, and Oppenheim
Quality Management: Tools and Methods for Improvement
Second Edition

Lind, Mason, and Wathen
Basic Statistics for Business and Economics
Fourth Edition

Lind, Marchal, and Mason
Statistical Techniques in Business and Economics
Eleventh Edition

Merchant, Goffinet, and Koehler
Basic Statistics Using Excel for Office 97
Second Edition

Merchant, Goffinet, and Koehler
Basic Statistics Using Excel for Office 2000
Third Edition

Neter, Kutner, Nachtsheim, and Wasserman
Applied Linear Statistical Models
Fourth Edition

Neter, Kutner, Nachtsheim, and Wasserman
Applied Linear Regression Models
Third Edition

Sahai and Kurshid
Pocket Dictionary of Statistics
First Edition

Siegel
Practical Business Statistics
Fifth Edition

Wilson and Keating
Business Forecasting
Third Edition

Zagorsky
Business Information
First Edition

QUANTITATIVE METHODS AND MANAGEMENT SCIENCE

Bonini, Hausman, and Bierman
Quantitative Analysis for Business Decisions
Ninth Edition

Hesse
Managerial Spreadsheet Modeling and Analysis
First Edition

Hillier and Hillier
Introduction to Management Science: A Modeling and Case Studies Approach with Spreadsheets
Second Edition

Introduction to Management Science

A Modeling and Case Studies Approach with Spreadsheets

Frederick S. Hillier
Stanford University

Mark S. Hillier
University of Washington

Cases developed by
Karl Schmedders
Northwestern University

Molly Stephens
Weil, Gotshal & Manges LLP

McGraw-Hill Irwin

Boston   Burr Ridge, IL   Dubuque, IA   Madison, WI   New York   San Francisco   St. Louis
Bangkok   Bogotá   Caracas   Kuala Lumpur   Lisbon   London   Madrid   Mexico City
Milan   Montreal   New Delhi   Santiago   Seoul   Singapore   Sydney   Taipei   Toronto

McGraw-Hill Higher Education

A Division of The **McGraw-Hill** Companies

INTRODUCTION TO MANAGEMENT SCIENCE:
A MODELING AND CASE STUDIES APPROACH WITH SPREADSHEETS
Published by McGraw-Hill/Irwin, a business unit of The McGraw-Hill Companies, Inc., 1221 Avenue of the Americas, New York, NY, 10020. Copyright © 2003, 2000 by The McGraw-Hill Companies, Inc. All rights reserved. No part of this publication may be reproduced or distributed in any form or by any means, or stored in a database or retrieval system, without the prior written consent of The McGraw-Hill Companies, Inc., including, but not limited to, in any network or other electronic storage or transmission, or broadcast for distance learning. Some ancillaries, including electronic and print components, may not be available to customers outside the United States.

This book is printed on acid-free paper.

domestic   4 5 6 7 8 9 0 WCK/WCK 0 9 8 7 6 5
international   3 4 5 6 7 8 9 0 WCK/WCK 0 9 8 7 6 5

ISBN 0-07-249368-2

Publisher: *Brent Gordon*
Executive editor: *Scott Isenberg*
Senior developmental editor: *Wanda J. Zeman*
Senior marketing manager: *Zina Craft*
Producer, media technology: *Todd Labak*
Project manager: *Destiny Rynne*
Production supervisor: *Debra R. Sylvester*
Cover and Interior Design: *Adam Rooke*
Supplement producer: *Matthew Perry*
Senior digital content specialist: *Brian Nacik*
Typeface: 10/12 *Times Roman*
Compositor: *Carlisle Communications, Ltd.*
Printer: *World Color Versailles*

Library of Congress Cataloging-in-Publication Data

Hillier, Frederick S.
    Introduction to management science : a modeling and case studies approach with spreadsheets / Frederick S. Hillier, Mark S. Hillier ; cases developed by Karl Schmedders, Molly Stephens.—2nd ed.
        p. cm. — (The McGraw-Hill/Irwin series. Operations and decision sciences)
    Includes index.
    ISBN 0-07-249368-2 (alk. paper)—ISBN 0-07-119554-8 (international : alk. paper)
    1. Management science. 2. Operations research. I. Hillier, Mark S. II. Title. III. McGraw-Hill/Irwin series in operations and decision sciences.
T56 .H55 2003
658.4'032—dc21   2002026551

INTERNATIONAL EDITION ISBN 0-07-119554-8
Copyright © 2003. Exclusive rights by The McGraw-Hill Companies, Inc. for manufacture and export. This book cannot be re-exported from the country to which it is sold by McGraw-Hill.
The International Edition is not available in North America.

www.mhhe.com

To our wives—Ann and Christine—for their steadfast support and to the memory of a beloved mentor, Gerald J. Lieberman, who was one of the true giants of our field

Frederick S. Hillier
Mark S. Hillier

About the Authors

Frederick S. Hillier is professor emeritus of operations research at Stanford University. Dr. Hillier is especially known for his classic, award-winning text, *Introduction to Operations Research,* co-authored with the late Gerald J. Lieberman, which has been translated into well over a dozen languages and is currently in its 7th edition. His other books include *The Evaluation of Risky Interrelated Investments, Queueing Tables and Graphs, Introduction to Stochastic Models in Operations Research,* and *Introduction to Mathematical Programming.* He received his BS in industrial engineering and doctorate specializing in operations research and management science from Stanford University. The winner of many awards in high school and college for writing, mathematics, debate, and music, he ranked first in his undergraduate engineering class and was awarded three national fellowships (National Science Foundation, Tau Beta Pi, and Danforth) for graduate study. Dr. Hillier's research has extended into a variety of areas, including integer programming, queueing theory and its application, statistical quality control, and production and operations management. He also has won a major prize for research in capital budgeting. Twice elected a national officer of professional societies, he has served in many important professional and editorial capacities. For example, he served The Institute of Management Sciences as vice president for meetings, chairman of the publications committee, associate editor of *Management Science,* and co-general chairman of an international meeting. He currently is continuing to serve as the founding series editor for the International Series in Operations Research and Management Science for Kluwer Academic Publishers. He has had visiting appointments at Cornell University, the Graduate School of Industrial Administration of Carnegie-Mellon University, the Technical University of Denmark, the University of Canterbury (New Zealand), and the Judge Institute of Management Studies at the University of Cambridge (England).

Mark S. Hillier, son of Fred Hillier, is associate professor of management science at the School of Business at the University of Washington. Dr. Hillier received his BS in engineering (plus a concentration in computer science) from Swarthmore College, and he received his MS with distinction in operations research and PhD in industrial engineering and engineering management from Stanford University. As an undergraduate, he won the McCabe Award for ranking first in his engineering class, won election to Phi Beta Kappa based on his work in mathematics, set school records on the men's swim team, and was awarded two national fellowships (National Science Foundation and Tau Beta Pi) for graduate study. During that time, he also developed a comprehensive software tutorial package, *OR Courseware,* for the Hillier-Lieberman textbook, *Introduction to Operations Research.* As a graduate student, he taught a PhD-level seminar in operations management at Stanford and won a national prize for work based on his PhD dissertation. At the University of Washington, he currently teaches courses in management science and spreadsheet modeling. He has won an MBA teaching award for his elective course in spreadsheet modeling and a universitywide teaching award for his work in teaching undergraduate classes in operations management. He also has been awarded an appointment to the Neal and Jan Dempsey Endowed Faculty Fellowship. His research interests include issues in component commonality, inventory, manufacturing, and the design of production systems. A recent paper by Dr. Hillier on component commonality won an award for best paper of 2000–2001 in *IIE Transactions.*

About the Case Writers

Karl Schmedders is associate professor in the Department of Managerial Economics and Decision Sciences at the Kellogg School of Management at Northwestern University, where he teaches quantitative methods for managerial decision making. His research interests include applications of management science in economic theory, general equilibrium theory with incomplete markets, asset pricing, and computational economics. Dr. Schmedders received his doctorate in operations research from Stanford University, where he taught both undergraduate and graduate classes in management science. Among the classes taught was a case studies course in management science and he subsequently was invited to speak at a conference sponsored by the Institute of Operations Research and Management Sciences (INFORMS) about his successful experience with this course. He received several teaching awards at Stanford, including the university's prestigious Walter J. Gores Teaching Award. He also has been named the L. G. Lavengood Professor of the Year at the Kellogg School of Management.

Molly Stephens is an associate in the corporate and securities department at Weil, Gotshal & Manges LLP in Houston, Texas. She graduated from Stanford with a BS in industrial engineering and an MS in operations research. Ms. Stephens taught public speaking in Stanford's School of Engineering and served as a teaching assistant for a case studies course in management science. As a teaching assistant, she analyzed management science problems encountered in the real world and transformed these into classroom case studies. Her research was rewarded when she won an undergraduate research grant from Stanford to continue her work and was invited to speak at INFORMS to present her conclusions regarding successful classroom case studies. Following graduation, Ms. Stephens worked at Andersen Consulting as a systems integrator, experiencing real cases from the inside, before receiving her JD degree from the University of Texas School of Law.

Preface

We have long been concerned that traditional management science textbooks have not taken the best approach in introducing business students to this exciting field. Our goal when developing the first edition of this book was to break out of the old mold and present new and innovative ways of teaching management science more effectively. We have been gratified by the favorable response to our efforts. Many reviewers and other users of the book have expressed appreciation for its various distinctive features, as well as for its clear presentation at just the right level for their business students.

Our goal for this second edition has been to build on the strengths of the first edition. Co-author Mark Hillier recently won a special teaching award for his spreadsheet modeling courses at the University of Washington while using the first edition and this experience has led to many improvements in the current edition. We also incorporated many user comments and suggestions, including requests to expand certain topics. Throughout this process, we took painstaking care to enhance the quality of the preceding edition while maintaining the distinctive orientation of the book.

This distinctive orientation is one that closely follows the recommendations in the 1996 report of the operating subcommittee of the INFORMS Business School Education Task Force, including the following extract.

> There is clear evidence that there must be a major change in the character of the (introductory management science) course in this environment. There is little patience with courses centered on algorithms. Instead, the demand is for courses that focus on business situations, include prominent non-mathematical issues, use spreadsheets, and involve model formulation and assessment more than model structuring. Such a course requires new teaching materials.

This book is designed to provide the teaching materials for such a course.

In line with the recommendations of this task force, we believe that a modern introductory management science textbook should have three key elements. As summarized in the subtitle of this book, these elements are a *modeling* and *case studies* approach with *spreadsheets*.

SPREADSHEETS

The new wave in the teaching of management science clearly is to use spreadsheets as a primary medium of instruction. Both business students and managers now live with spreadsheets, so they provide a comfortable and enjoyable learning environment. Modern spreadsheet software, including Microsoft Excel used in this book, now can be used to do real management science. For student-scale models (which include many practical real-world models), spreadsheets are a much better way of implementing management science models than traditional algebraic solvers. This means that the algebraic curtain that was so prevalent in traditional management science courses and textbooks now can be lifted.

However, with the new enthusiasm for spreadsheets, there is a danger of going overboard. Spreadsheets are not the only useful tool for performing management science analyses. Occasional modest use of algebraic and graphical analyses still have their place and we would be doing a disservice to the students by not developing their skills in these areas when appropriate. Furthermore, the book should not be mainly a spreadsheet cookbook that focuses largely on spreadsheet mechanics. Spreadsheets are a means to an end, not an end in themselves.

A MODELING APPROACH

This brings us to the second key feature of the book, a *modeling approach*. Model formulation lies at the heart of management science methodology. Therefore, we heavily emphasize the art of model formulation, the role of a model, and the analysis of model results. We primarily (but not exclusively) use a spreadsheet format rather than algebra for formulating and presenting a model.

Some instructors have many years of experience in teaching modeling in terms of formulating algebraic models (or what the INFORMS Task Force called "model structuring"). Some of these instructors feel that students should do their modeling in this way and then transfer the model to a spreadsheet simply to use the Excel Solver to solve the model. We disagree with this approach. Our experience (and the experience reported by many others) is that most business students find it more natural and comfortable to do their modeling directly in a spreadsheet. Furthermore, by using the best spreadsheet modeling techniques (as presented in this edition), formulating a spreadsheet model tends to be considerably more efficient and transparent than formulating an algebraic model.

Another break from tradition in this book (and several contemporary textbooks) is to virtually ignore the algorithms that are used to solve the models. We feel that there is no good reason why typical business students should learn the details of algorithms executed by computers. Within the time constraints of a one-term management science course, there are far more important lessons to be learned. Therefore, the focus in this book is on what we believe are these far more important lessons. High on this list is the art of modeling managerial problems on a spreadsheet.

Formulating a spreadsheet model of a real problem typically involves much more than designing the spreadsheet and entering the data. Therefore, we work through the process step by step: understand the unstructured problem, verbally develop some structure for the problem, gather the data, express the relationships in quantitative terms, and then lay out the spreadsheet model. The structured approach highlights the typical components of the model (the data, the decisions to be made, the constraints, and the measure of performance) and the different types of spreadsheet cells used for each. Consequently, the emphasis is on the modeling rather than spreadsheet mechanics.

A CASE STUDIES APPROACH

However, all this still would be quite sterile if we simply presented a long series of brief examples with their spreadsheet formulations. This leads to the third key feature of this book—a *case studies* approach. In addition to examples, essentially every chapter includes one or two case studies patterned after actual applications to convey the whole process of applying management science. In a few instances, the entire chapter revolves around a case study. By drawing the student into the story, we have designed each case study to bring that chapter's technique to life in a context that vividly illustrates the relevance of the technique for aiding managerial decision making. This storytelling, case-centered approach should make the material more enjoyable and stimulating while also conveying the practical considerations that are key factors in applying management science.

We have been pleased to have several reviewers of the first edition express particular appreciation for our case study approach. Even though this approach has received little use in other management science textbooks, we feel that it is a real key to preparing students for the practical application of management science in all its aspects. Some of the reviewers have highlighted the effectiveness of the dialogue/scenario enactment approach used in some of the case studies. Although unconventional, this approach provides a way of demonstrating the process of managerial decision making with the help of management science. It also enables previewing some key concepts in the language of management.

Except for Chapter 1, every chapter also contains full-fledged cases following the problems at the end of the chapter. These cases usually continue to employ a stimulating storytelling approach, so they can be assigned as interesting and challenging projects. Most of these cases were developed jointly by two talented case writers, Karl Schmedders (a faculty member at the Kellogg School of Management at Northwestern University) and Molly Stephens (formerly a management science consultant with Andersen Consulting). In addition, two of the cases are INFORMS teaching cases. The authors also have added some cases, including several shorter ones.

We are, of course, not the first to incorporate any of these key features into a management science textbook. However, we believe that the book currently is unique in the way that it fully incorporates all three key features together.

OTHER SPECIAL FEATURES

We also should mention some additional special features of the book that are continued from the first edition.

- Diverse examples, problems, and cases convey the pervasive relevance of management science.

- An integration of numerous management science success stories into the text (not separate boxes).

- Further descriptions of what is happening in practice.

- A strong managerial perspective.

- Review questions at the end of each section.

- A glossary at the end of each chapter.

- Partial answers to selected problems in the back of the book.

- Supplementary text material on the CD-ROM (as identified in the table of contents).

- An Excel-based software package (MS Courseware) on the CD-ROM that includes many add-ins, templates, and files (described below).

- Other helpful supplements on both the student's CD-ROM and the instructor's CD-ROM (described later).

SOFTWARE

From the First Edition

The first edition provided a comprehensive Excel-based software package called *MS Courseware* on the student's CD-ROM. This entire package is being provided again with the current edition.

This package includes Excel files that provide the live spreadsheets for all the various examples and case studies throughout the book. In addition to further investigating the examples and case studies, these spreadsheets can be used by either the student or instructor as templates to formulate and solve similar problems. The package also includes dozens of Excel templates for solving various models in the book.

Another key resource in the MS Courseware is a collection of Excel add-ins that are integrated into the corresponding chapters.

- Premium Solver for Education, including its powerful Evolutionary Solver for solving difficult optimization problems (featured in Section 10.5).

- TreePlan for generating and analyzing decision trees for decision analysis (used throughout Chapter 12).

- SensIt for performing sensitivity analysis with probabilistic systems (used mainly in Chapter 12).

- RiskSim for performing computer simulations (introduced in Chapter 15).

MS Courseware includes additional software as well.

- Microsoft Project (updated in June 2002) for constructing and analyzing a project network (featured in Chapter 8).

- Queueing Simulator for performing computer simulations of queueing systems (used in Chapter 15).

New with This Edition

We have added some exciting new software to the MS Courseware package for the current edition.

- **Crystal Ball 2000 Professional Edition.** This powerful Excel add-in greatly extends the capabilities of the standard Excel package for performing computer simulations. The new Chapter 16 is devoted to the use of Crystal Ball for computer simulations.

- **OptQuest.** Available only with the Professional Edition of Crystal Ball, this special module combines computer simulation with an advanced optimization technique. Section 16.9 focuses on the use of OptQuest.

- **CB Predictor.** This special module of the Crystal Ball package is used to apply various time-series forecasting methods. Section 13.4 features the use of this module.

- **Interactive Management Science Modules.** This innovative tool includes several modules that enable you to interactively explore certain management science techniques in depth. The modules cover techniques presented in Chapters 1, 2, 5, 13, 14, 15, and 18. In addition to the online version provided on the book's website, an offline version also is included in the MS Courseware package on the CD-ROM.

- **Solver Table.** This Excel add-in has been developed by the authors to automate sensitivity analysis in optimization problems. It is used in several chapters, including especially Chapter 5.

SOME NEW CHAPTERS

Key changes from the first edition include the addition of two completely new chapters, the expansion of previous sections into two complete chapters, and the integration of other previous material into a single chapter.

- **Chapter 3: The Art of Modeling with Spreadsheets.** This completely new chapter goes beyond anything found in other textbooks in reflecting the current state of the art in modeling with spreadsheets. Far more than an introductory primer on spreadsheet modeling, this unique chapter thoroughly discusses and illustrates such topics as (1) the step-by-step process of modeling in spreadsheets, (2) common stumbling blocks and how to get past them, (3) guidelines for building good spreadsheet models, (4) how to create spreadsheets that are easy to read, modify, and debug, (5) tips and tools for debugging a spreadsheet model, and (6) effective use of range names, shading, and so forth. The lessons in this chapter then are incorporated into the spreadsheet modeling throughout the book.

- **Chapter 9: Integer Programming.** The material on integer programming in the first edition (a section on general integer programming and a separate chapter on binary integer programming) has been combined to create a single integrated chapter.

- **Chapter 10: Nonlinear Programming.** The two sections on nonlinear programming (including separable programming) in the first edition now have been expanded into a complete chapter on the topic. Included are new elementary sections on (1) the challenges of nonlinear programming, (2) difficult nonlinear programming problems, and (3) Evolutionary Solver and genetic algorithms.

- **Chapter 11: Goal Programming.** The two sections on goal programming in the first edition have been expanded into a complete chapter on the topic. The most important addition is a new section on preemptive goal programming.

- **Chapter 16: Computer Simulation with Crystal Ball.** In response to request for more material on computer simulation, we have added this completely new second chapter (one of the longest chapters in the book) on the topic. This chapter focuses on the advanced capabilities that now are provided by the popular Excel add-in Crystal Ball. Included is complete coverage of powerful Crystal Ball features such as (1) its Distribution Gallery, (2) its Decision Table as an aid to decision making, and (3) the module OptQuest for optimizing through a series of simulation runs.

To make room for all this new material, Chapter 11 (Inventory Management with Known Demand) and Chapter 12 (Inventory Management with Uncertain Demand) in the first edition now have been transferred to the Supplements (as Chapters 18 and 19) on the CD-ROM. Since inventory management now is commonly taught in an operations management course instead of a management science course, we feel that removing this material from the text itself is appropriate.

OTHER NEW FEATURES IN THIS EDITION

We have made many other important enhancements to the second edition.

- **New Spreadsheets.** *All* the spreadsheet models throughout the book have been redesigned to reflect the current state of the art in spreadsheet modeling that is presented in Chapter 3. As one example, range names now are commonly used (often followed by the cell addresses within parentheses) to refer to ranges of cells.

- **A Reorganized Chapter on Decision Analysis.** The Decision Analysis chapter (now Chapter 12) has been completely reorganized and slightly expanded to provide a more logical flow of topics. The Excel add-ins TreePlan and SensIt now are featured. More emphasis also has been placed on sensitivity analysis.

- **A Reorganized Chapter on What-If Analysis for Linear Programming.** Chapter 5 (formerly Chapter 4) has been reorganized in a more straightforward way. A key addition has been the use of the Solver Table to perform sensitivity analysis systematically. The overall approach to what-if analysis now is a very intuitive one: (1) Begin by trying individual changes on the spreadsheet, (2) then apply the Solver Table, and (3) then refer to Excel's sensitivity report.

- **More Sensitivity Analysis.** We have increased the emphasis on sensitivity analysis, including the use of the Solver Table, in several other chapters as well.

- **Further Revisions.** Each chapter in the first edition has been carefully examined and revised as needed to update the material and increase its clarity.

- **More Cases.** We have added seven new end-of-chapter cases. To provide more variety, these cases tend to be shorter and more closely tied to the material in the chapter than the elaborate cases carried forward from the first edition.

- **Links to Articles in Interfaces.** Numerous descriptions of successful applications of management science are integrated into the text throughout the book. In each case, an article in *Interfaces* that describes the application in detail is cited. We now provide links for downloading nearly all of these articles at **www.mhhe.com/hillier2e/articles** to make it easy to pursue further reading.

- **Margin Notes.** We have inserted nearly a thousand margin notes throughout the book to clarify and highlight key points.

- **Excel Tips.** Interspersed among these margin notes are a considerable number of Excel tips (or tips for using other software efficiently).

- **Learning Objectives.** Each chapter now begins with a list of learning objectives for that chapter.

- **Two-Color Design.** An attractive new two-color design has been incorporated into this edition.

OTHER SUPPLEMENTS

An instructor's CD-ROM is being provided with this edition. This CD-ROM includes complete solutions to all problems and cases, which will be handy for cutting and pasting homework solutions. Also included is a test bank with computest that includes hundreds of multiple-choice and true-false questions. Presentation materials on PowerPoint slides also are provided. These slides include both lecture materials for nearly every chapter and all the figures (including spreadsheets) in the book.

The student's CD-ROM bundled with the book provides the entire MS Courseware package. It also includes a tutorial with sample test questions (different from those in the instructor's test bank) for self-testing quizzes on the various chapters.

A Web page will provide updates about the book, including an errata. To access this site, visit **www.mhhe.com/hillier2e.** In addition, the publisher's operations management supersite at **www.mhhe.com/pom/** links to many resources on the Internet that you might find pertinent to this book.

We welcome your comments, suggestions, and errata. We hope that you enjoy the book.

Frederick S. Hillier
Stanford University (fhillier@stanford.edu)

Mark S. Hillier
University of Washington (mhillier@u.washington.edu)

June 2002

Acknowledgments

This new edition has benefited greatly from the sage advice of many individuals. To begin, we would like to express our deep appreciation to the following individuals who provided formal reviews of the first edition and then of the manuscript for the second edition at various stages:

Kelwyn D'Souza
Hampton University

Ken Gordon
University of Colorado—Boulder

Scott E. Grasman
University of Missouri at Rolla

Samuel B. Graves
Boston College

James Grayson
Augusta State University

Harvey J. Iglarsh
Georgetown University

Murat M. Koksalan
Purdue University

Zubair Mohamed
Western Kentucky University

Jack A. Vaughan
University of Texas—El Paso

We also are grateful for the valuable input provided by many of our students as well as various other students and instructors who contacted us via e-mail.

This book has continued to be a team effort involving far more than the two coauthors. As a third co-author for the first edition, the late Gerald J. Lieberman provided important initial impetus for this project. We also are indebted to our case writers for the first edition, Karl Schmedders and Molly Stephens, for their invaluable contributions. Ann Hillier again devoted numerous long days and nights to sitting with a Macintosh, doing word processing and constructing many figures and tables. While caring for two young children, Christine Hillier also managed to devote many hours to developing solutions for new problems and preparing updates for the test bank. They all were vital members of the team.

McGraw-Hill/Irwin's editorial and production staff provided the other key members of the team, including Scott Isenberg (Executive Editor), Wanda Zeman (Senior Developmental Editor), and Destiny Rynne (Project Manager). This book is a much better product because of their guidance and hard work. It has been a real pleasure working with such a thoroughly professional staff.

Brief Contents

Contents

Introduction to Management Science

A Modeling and Case Studies Approach with Spreadsheets

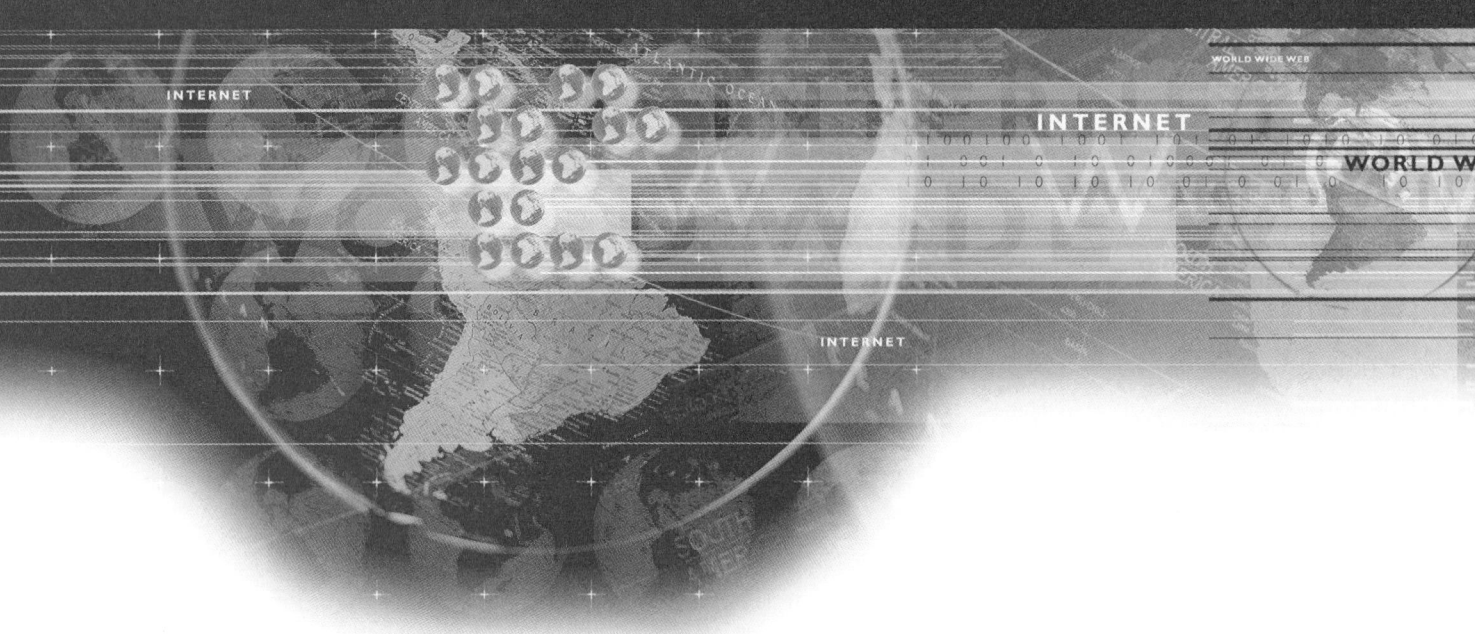

Learning objectives

After completing this chapter, you should be able to

1. Define the term *management science.*

2. Describe the nature of management science.

3. Explain what a mathematical model is.

4. Use a mathematical model to perform break-even analysis.

5. Use a spreadsheet model to perform break-even analysis.

6. Identify the kinds of annual savings that management science studies can sometimes provide.

7. Identify some special features of this book.

Chapter **One**

Introduction

Welcome to the field of *management science!* We think that it is a particularly exciting and interesting field. Exciting because management science is having a dramatic impact on the profitability of numerous business firms around the world. Interesting because the methods used to do this are so ingenious. We are looking forward to giving you a guided tour to introduce you to the special features of the field.

Some students approach a course (and textbook) about management science with a certain amount of anxiety and skepticism. The main source of the anxiety is the reputation of the field as being highly mathematical. This reputation then generates skepticism that such a theoretical approach can have much relevance for dealing with practical managerial problems. Most traditional courses (and textbooks) about management science have only reinforced these perceptions by emphasizing the mathematics of the field rather than its practical application.

Rest easy. This is not a traditional management science textbook. We realize that most readers of this book are aspiring to become managers, not mathematicians. Therefore, the emphasis throughout is on conveying what a future manager needs to know about management science. Yes, this means including a little mathematics here and there, because it is a major language of the field. The mathematics you do see will be at the level of high school algebra plus (in the later chapters) basic concepts of elementary probability theory. We think you will be pleasantly surprised by the new appreciation you gain for how useful and intuitive mathematics at this level can be. However, managers do not need to know any of the heavy mathematical theory that underlies the various techniques of management science. Therefore, the use of mathematics plays only a strictly secondary role in the book.

One reason we can deemphasize mathematics is that powerful *spreadsheet packages* now are available for applying management science. Spreadsheets provide a comfortable and familiar environment for formulating and analyzing managerial problems. The spreadsheet package takes care of applying the necessary mathematics automatically in the background with only a minimum of guidance by the user. This has begun to revolutionize the use of management science. In the past, technically trained management scientists were needed to carry out significant management science studies for management. Now spreadsheets are bringing many of the tools and concepts of management science within the reach of managers for conducting their own analyses. Although busy managers will continue to call upon management science teams to conduct major studies for them, they are increasingly becoming direct users themselves through the medium of spreadsheet packages. Therefore, since this book is aimed at future managers (and management consultants), we will emphasize the use of spreadsheets for applying management science.

What does an enlightened future manager need to learn from a management science course?

1. Gain an appreciation for the relevance and power of management science. (Therefore, we will give many examples of *actual applications* of management science and the *impact* they had on the organizations involved.)

2. Learn to recognize when management science can (and cannot) be fruitfully applied. (Therefore, we will emphasize the *kinds of problems* to which the various management science techniques can be applied.)

3. Learn how to apply the major techniques of management science to analyze a variety of managerial problems. (Therefore, we will focus largely on how spreadsheets enable many such applications with no more background in management science than provided by this book.)

4. Develop an understanding of how to interpret the results of a management science study. (Therefore, we will present many *case studies* that illustrate management science studies and how their results depend on the assumptions and data that were used.)

The objectives just described are the key teaching goals of this book.

We begin this process in the next three sections by introducing the nature of management science and the impact that it is having on many organizations. (These themes will continue throughout the remaining chapters as well.) Section 1.4 then points out some of the special features of this book that you can look forward to seeing in the subsequent chapters.

1.1 THE NATURE OF MANAGEMENT SCIENCE

What is the name *management science* (sometimes abbreviated MS) supposed to convey? It does involve *management* and *science* or, more precisely, *the science of management,* but this still is too vague. Here is a more suggestive definition.

> **Management science** is a *discipline* that attempts to *aid managerial decision making* by applying a *scientific approach* to managerial problems that involve *quantitative factors.*

Now let us see how elaborating upon each of the italicized terms in this definition conveys much more about the nature of management science.

Management Science Is a Discipline

As a discipline, management science is a whole body of knowledge and techniques that are based on a scientific foundation. For example, it is analogous in some ways to the medical field. A medical doctor has been trained in a whole body of knowledge and techniques that are based on the scientific foundations of the medical field. After receiving this training and entering practice, the doctor must diagnose a patient's illness and then choose the appropriate medical procedures to apply to the illness. The patient then makes the final decision on which medical procedures to accept. For less serious cases, the patient may choose not to consult a doctor and instead use his own basic knowledge of medical principles to treat himself. Similarly, a management scientist must receive substantial training (albeit considerably less than for a medical doctor). This training also is in a whole body of knowledge and techniques that are based on the scientific foundations of the discipline. After entering practice, the management scientist must diagnose a managerial problem and then choose the appropriate management science techniques to apply in analyzing the problem. The cognizant manager then makes the final decision as to which conclusions from this analysis to accept. For less extensive managerial problems where management science can be helpful, the manager may choose not to consult a management scientist and instead use his or her own basic knowledge of management science principles to analyze the problem.

Although it has considerably longer roots, the rapid development of the discipline began in the 1940s and 1950s. The initial impetus came early in World War II, when large numbers of scientists were called upon to apply a scientific approach to the management of the war effort for the allies. Another landmark event was the discovery in 1947 by George Dantzig of the *simplex method* for solving linear programming problems. (Linear programming is the subject of several early chapters.) Another factor that gave great impetus to the growth of the discipline was the onslaught of the computer revolution.

operations research

Management science began its rapid development during World War II with the name *operations research.*

The traditional name given to the discipline (and the one that still is widely used today outside of business schools) is **operations research.** This name was applied because the teams of scientists in World War II were doing *research* on how to manage military *operations.* The abbreviation OR also is widely used. This abbreviation often is combined with the one for management science (MS), thereby referring to the discipline as OR/MS.

One major international professional society for the discipline is the *Institute for Operations Research and the Management Sciences* (INFORMS). Headquartered in the United States, with about 12,000 members, this society holds major conferences in the United States each year plus occasional conferences elsewhere. It also publishes several prominent journals, including *Management Science, Operations Research,* and *Interfaces.* (Articles describing actual applications of management science are featured in *Interfaces,* so you will see many references to this journal throughout the book.)

In addition, there now are a few dozen member countries in the *International Federation of Operational Research Societies* (IFORS), with each member country having a national operations research society. Both Europe and Asia also have federations of operations research societies to coordinate holding international conferences and publishing international journals in those continents.

Thus, operations research/management science (OR/MS) is a truly international discipline. (We hereafter will just use the name *management science.*)

Management Science Aids Managerial Decision Making

The key word here is that management science *aids* managerial decision making. Management scientists don't make managerial decisions. Managers do. A management science study only provides an analysis and recommendations, based on the quantitative factors involved in the problem, as input to the cognizant managers. Managers must also take into account various intangible considerations that are outside the realm of management science and then use their best judgment to make the decision. Sometimes managers find that qualitative factors are as important as quantitative factors in making a decision.

A small informal management science study might be conducted by just a single individual, who may be the cognizant manager. However, management science *teams* normally are used for larger studies. (We often will use the term *team* to cover both cases throughout the book.) Such a team often includes some members who are not management scientists but who provide other types of expertise needed for the study. Although a management science team often is entirely *in-house* (employees of the company), part or all of the team may instead be *consultants* who have been hired for just the one study. Consulting firms that partially or entirely specialize in management science currently are a growing industry.

Management Science Uses a Scientific Approach

Management science is based strongly on some scientific fields, including mathematics and computer science. It also draws on the social sciences, especially economics. Since the field is concerned with the practical management of organizations, a management scientist should have solid training in business administration, including its various functional areas, as well.

To a considerable extent, a management science team will attempt to use the *scientific method* in conducting its study. This means that the team will emphasize conducting a *systematic investigation* that includes careful data gathering, developing and testing hypotheses about the problem (typically in the form of a mathematical model), and then applying sound logic in the subsequent analysis.

When conducting this systematic investigation, the management science team typically will follow the (overlapping) steps outlined and described below.

Step 1: Define the problem and gather data. In this step, the team consults with management to clearly identify the problem of concern and ascertain the appropriate objectives for the study. The team then typically spends a surprisingly large amount of time gathering relevant data about the problem with the assistance of other key individuals in the organization. A common frustration is that some key data are either very rough or completely unavailable. This may necessitate installing a new computer-based management information system.

information technology (IT)
Information technology often plays a key role in management science studies.

Fortunately, the rapid development of the **information technology (IT)** field in recent years is leading to a dramatic improvement in the quantity and quality of data that may be available to the management science (MS) team. Corporate IT now is often able to provide the computational resources and databases that are needed by the MS team. Thus, the MS team often will collaborate closely with the IT group.

Step 2: Formulate a model (typically a mathematical model) to represent the problem. Models, or approximate representations, are an integral part of everyday life. Common examples include model airplanes, portraits, globes, and so on. Similarly, models play an important role in science and business, as illustrated by models of the atom, models of genetic structure, mathematical equations describing physical laws of motion or chemical reactions, graphs, organization charts, and industrial accounting systems. Such models are invaluable for abstracting the essence of the subject of inquiry, showing interrelationships, and facilitating analysis.

Mathematical models are also approximate representations, but they are expressed in terms of mathematical symbols and expressions. Such laws of physics as $F = ma$ and $E = mc^2$ are familiar examples. Similarly, the mathematical model of a business problem is the system of equations and related mathematical expressions that describes the essence of the problem.

With the emergence of powerful spreadsheet technology, **spreadsheet models** now are widely used to analyze managerial problems. A spreadsheet model lays out the relevant data, measures of performance, interrelationships, and so forth, on a spreadsheet in an organized way that facilitates fruitful analysis of the problem. It also frequently incorporates an underlying mathematical model to assist in the analysis, but the mathematics is kept in the background so the user can concentrate on the analysis.

The *modeling process* is a creative one. When dealing with real managerial problems (as opposed to some cut-and-dried textbook problems), there normally is no single "correct" model but rather a number of alternative ways to approach the problem. The modeling process also is typically an evolutionary process that begins with a simple "verbal model" to define the essence of the problem and then gradually evolves into increasingly more complete mathematical models (perhaps in a spreadsheet format).

We further describe and illustrate such mathematical models in the next section.

Step 3: Develop a computer-based procedure for deriving solutions to the problem from the model. The beauty of a well-designed mathematical model is that it enables the use of mathematical procedures to find good solutions to the problem. These procedures usually are run on a computer because the calculations are too extensive to be done by hand. In some cases, the management science team will need to develop the procedure. In others, a standard software package already will be available for solving the model. When the mathematical model is incorporated into a spreadsheet, the spreadsheet package normally includes a Solver that usually will solve the model.

Step 4: Test the model and refine it as needed. Now that the model can be solved, the team needs to thoroughly check and test the model to make sure that it provides a sufficiently accurate representation of the real problem. A number of questions should be addressed, perhaps with the help of others who are particularly familiar with the problem. Have all the relevant factors and interrelationships in the problem been accurately incorporated into the model? Does the model seem to provide reasonable solutions? When it is applied to a past situation, does the solution improve upon what was actually done? When assumptions about costs and revenues are changed, do the solutions change in a plausible manner?

Step 5: Apply the model to analyze the problem and develop recommendations for management. The management science team now is ready to solve the model, perhaps under a variety of assumptions, in order to analyze the problem. The resulting recommendations then are presented to the managers who must make the decisions about how to deal with the problem.

If the model is to be applied repeatedly to help guide decisions on an ongoing basis, the team might also develop a **decision support system.** This is an interactive computer-based system that aids managerial decision making. The system draws current data from *databases* or *management information systems* and then solves the various versions of the model specified by the manager.

Step 6: Help to implement the team's recommendations that are adopted by management. Once management makes its decisions, the management science team normally is asked to help oversee the implementation of the new procedures. This includes providing some information to the operating management and personnel involved on the rationale for the changes that are being made. The team also makes sure that the new operating system is consistent with its recommendations as they have been modified and approved by management. If successful, the new system may be used for years to come. With this in mind, the team monitors the initial experience with the system and seeks to identify any modifications that should be made in the future.

Management Science Considers Quantitative Factors

Many managerial problems revolve around such quantitative factors as production quantities, revenues, costs, the amounts available of needed resources, and so on. By incorporating these quantitative factors into a *mathematical model* and then applying mathematical procedures to solve the model, management science provides a uniquely powerful way of analyzing such managerial problems. Although management science is concerned with the practical management of organizations, including taking into account relevant qualitative factors, its special contribution lies in this unique ability to deal with the quantitative factors.

The Special Products Company example discussed below will illustrate how management science considers quantitative factors.

Review
Questions

1. When did the rapid development of the management science discipline begin?
2. What is the traditional name given to this discipline that still is widely used outside of business schools?
3. What does a management science study provide to managers to aid their decision making?
4. Upon which scientific fields and social sciences is management science especially based?
5. What is a *decision support system?*
6. What are some common quantitative factors around which many managerial problems revolve?

1.2   AN ILLUSTRATION OF THE MANAGEMENT SCIENCE APPROACH: BREAK-EVEN ANALYSIS

The Special Products Company produces expensive and unusual gifts to be sold in stores that cater to affluent customers who already have everything. The latest new-product proposal to management from the company's Research Department is a limited edition grandfather clock. Management needs to decide whether to introduce this new product and, if so, how many of these grandfather clocks to produce. Before making this decision, a sales forecast will be obtained to estimate how many clocks can be sold. Management wishes to make the decision that will maximize the company's profit.

A cost that remains the same regardless of the production volume is referred to as a *fixed cost,* whereas a cost that varies with the production volume is called a *variable cost.*

If the company goes ahead with this product, a *fixed cost* of $50,000 would be incurred for setting up the production facilities to produce this product. (Note that this cost would *not* be incurred if management decided *not* to introduce the product since the setup then would not be done.) In addition to this fixed cost, there is a production cost that varies with the number of clocks produced. This *variable cost* is $400 per clock produced, which adds up to $400 *times* the number of clocks produced. (The cost for each additional unit produced, $400, is referred to as the *marginal cost.*) Each clock sold would generate a revenue of $900 for the company.

Expressing the Problem Mathematically

The issue facing management is to make the following decision.

Decision to be made: Number of grandfather clocks to produce (if any).

Since this number is not yet known, we introduce an algebraic variable Q to represent this quantity. Thus,

$$Q = \text{Number of grandfather clocks to produce},$$

where Q is referred to as a **decision variable.** Naturally, the value chosen for Q should not exceed the sales forecast for the number of clocks that can be sold. Choosing a value of 0 for Q would correspond to deciding not to introduce the product, in which case none of the costs or revenues described in the preceding paragraph would be incurred.

The objective is to choose the value of Q that maximizes the company's profit from this new product. The management science approach is to formulate a mathematical model to represent this problem by developing an equation that expresses the profit in terms of the decision variable Q. To get there, it is necessary first to develop equations in terms of Q for the total cost and revenue generated by the grandfather clocks.

If $Q = 0$, no cost is incurred. However, if $Q > 0$, there is both a fixed cost and a variable cost.

$$\text{Fixed cost} = \$50{,}000 \quad (\text{if } Q > 0)$$

$$\text{Variable cost} = \$400\,Q$$

Therefore, the total cost would be

$$\text{Total cost} = \begin{cases} 0 & \text{if } Q = 0 \\ \$50{,}000 + \$400Q & \text{if } Q > 0 \end{cases}$$

Since each grandfather clock sold would generate a revenue of \$900 for the company, the total revenue from selling Q clocks would be

$$\text{Total revenue} = \$900Q$$

Consequently, the profit from producing and selling Q clocks would be

$$\text{Profit} = \text{Total revenue} - \text{Total cost}$$

$$= \begin{cases} 0 & \text{if } Q = 0 \\ \$900Q - (\$50{,}000 + \$400Q) & \text{if } Q > 0 \end{cases}$$

Thus, since $\$900Q - \$400Q = \$500Q$

$$\text{Profit} = -\$50{,}000 + \$500Q \quad \text{if } Q > 0$$

Analysis of the Problem

This last equation shows that the attractiveness of the proposed new product depends greatly on the value of Q, that is, on the number of grandfather clocks that can be produced and sold. A small value of Q means a loss (negative profit) for the company, whereas a sufficiently large value would generate a positive profit for the company. For example, look at the difference between $Q = 20$ and $Q = 200$.

$$\text{Profit} = -\$50{,}000 + \$500(20) = -\$40{,}000 \quad \text{if } Q = 20$$

$$\text{Profit} = -\$50{,}000 + \$500(200) = \$50{,}000 \quad \text{if } Q = 200$$

Figure 1.1 plots both the company's total cost and total revenue for the various values of Q. Note that the cost line and the revenue line intersect at $Q = 100$. For any value of $Q < 100$, cost exceeds revenue, so the gap between the two lines represents the *loss* to the company. For any $Q > 100$, revenue exceeds cost, so the gap between the two lines now shows positive profit. At $Q = 100$, the profit is 0. Since 100 units is the production and sales volume at which the

FIGURE 1.1

Break-even analysis for the Special Products Company shows that the cost line and revenue line intersect at $Q = 100$ clocks, so this is the break-even point for the proposed new product.

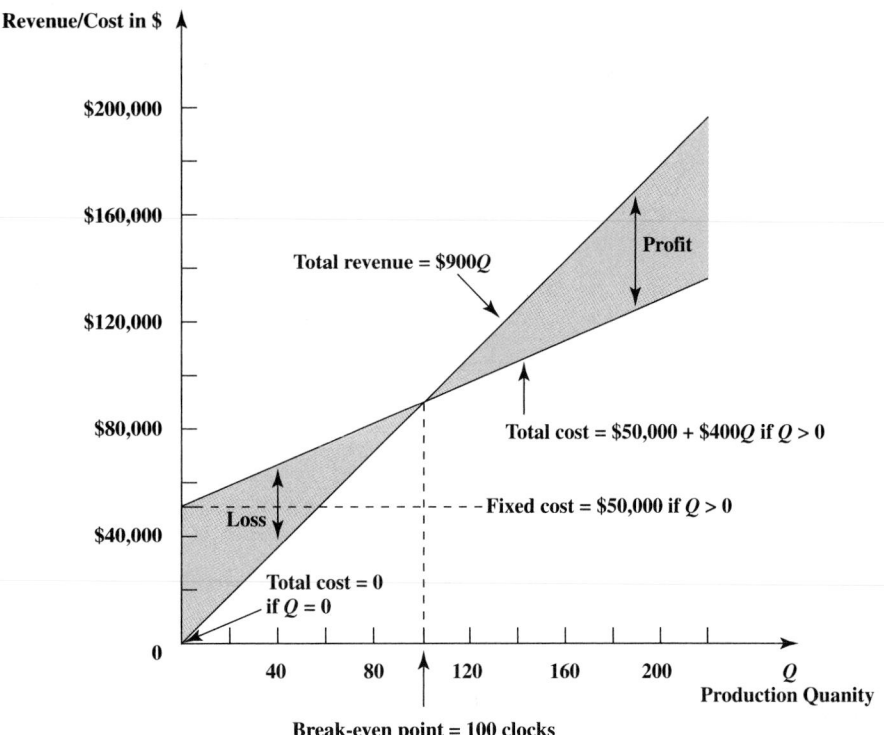

company would break even on the proposed new product, this volume is referred to as the **break-even point.** This is the point that must be exceeded to make it worthwhile to introduce the product. Therefore, the crucial question is whether the sales forecast for how many clocks can be sold is above or below the break-even point.

Figure 1.1 illustrates the *graphical procedure* for finding the break-even point. Another alternative is to use an *algebraic procedure* to solve for the point. Because the profit is 0 at this point, the procedure consists of solving the following equation for the unknown Q.

$$\text{Profit} = -\$50,000 + \$500Q = 0$$

Thus,

$$\$500Q = \$50,000$$

$$Q = \frac{\$50,000}{\$500}$$

$$Q = 100$$

A Complete Mathematical Model for the Problem

The preceding analysis of the problem made use of a basic mathematical model that consisted of the equation for profit expressed in terms of Q. However, implicit in this analysis were some additional factors that can be incorporated into a complete mathematical model for the problem.

Two of these factors concern restrictions on the values of Q that can be considered. One of these is that the number of clocks produced cannot be less than 0. Therefore,

$$Q \geq 0$$

constraints

A *constraint* in a mathematical model is an inequality or equation that expresses some restrictions on the values that can be assigned to the decision variables.

is one of the **constraints** for the complete mathematical model. Another restriction on the value of Q is that it should not exceed the number of clocks that can be sold. A sales forecast has not yet been obtained, so let the symbol s represent this currently unknown value.

s = Sales forecast (not yet available) of the number of grandfather clocks that can be sold

Consequently,

$$Q \leq s$$

parameter
The constants in a mathematical model are referred to as the *parameters* of the model.

is another constraint, where s is a **parameter** of the model whose value has not yet been chosen.

The final factor that should be made explicit in the model is the fact that management's objective is to make the decision that maximizes the company's profit from this new product. Therefore, the complete mathematical model for this problem is to find the value of the decision variable Q so as to

$$\text{Maximize profit} = \begin{cases} 0 & \text{if } Q = 0 \\ -\$50{,}000 + \$500Q & \text{if } Q > 0 \end{cases}$$

subject to

$$Q \leq s$$
$$Q \geq 0$$

objective function
The *objective function* for a mathematical model is a mathematical expression that gives the measure of performance for the problem in terms of the decision variables.

where the algebraic expression given for Profit is called the **objective function** for the model. The value of Q that solves this model depends on the value that will be assigned to the parameter s (the future forecast of the number of units that can be sold). Because the break-even point is 100, here is how the solution for Q depends on s.

Solution for Mathematical Model

$$\text{Break-even point} = \frac{\$50{,}000}{\$900 - \$400} = 100$$

If $s \leq 100$, then set $Q = 0$.

If $s > 100$, then set $Q = s$.

Therefore, the company should introduce the product and produce the number of units that can be sold *only* if this production and sales volume exceeds the break-even point.

Sensitivity Analysis of the Mathematical Model

A mathematical model is intended to be only an approximate representation of the problem. For example, some of the numbers in the model inevitably are only estimates of quantities that cannot be determined precisely at this time.

The above mathematical model is based on four numbers that are only estimates—the fixed cost of $50,000, the marginal cost of $400, the unit revenue of $900, and the sales forecast (after it is obtained). A management science study usually devotes considerable time to investigating what happens to the recommendations of the model if any of the estimates turn out to considerably miss their targets. This is referred to as **sensitivity analysis.**

sensitivity analysis
Since estimates can be wrong, *sensitivity analysis* is used to check the effect on the recommendations of a model if the estimates turn out to be wrong.

To assist you in performing sensitivity analysis on this model in a straightforward and enjoyable way, we have provided a *Break-Even Analysis* module in the *Interactive Management Science Modules* at **www.mhhe.com/hillier2e.** (All of the modules in this software package also are included on your CD-ROM.) The default model provided there is the one for the Special Products Company. Therefore, you immediately will see a replica of Figure 1.1. By following the simple directions given there, you can drag either the cost line or the revenue line to change the fixed cost, the marginal cost, or the unit revenue. This immediately enables you to see the effect on the break-even point if any of these cost or revenue numbers should turn out to have values that are somewhat different than their estimates in the model. For example, if the one deviation from the estimates is that the fixed cost turns out to be $75,000 instead of $50,000, then the break-even point becomes 150, as shown in Figure 1.2. We encourage you to try the Break-Even Analysis module to see the effect of other changes as well.

FIGURE 1.2

A screen shot of the Break-Even Analysis module in the Interactive Management Science Modules after changing the fixed cost for the Special Products Company problem from $50,000 to $75,000.

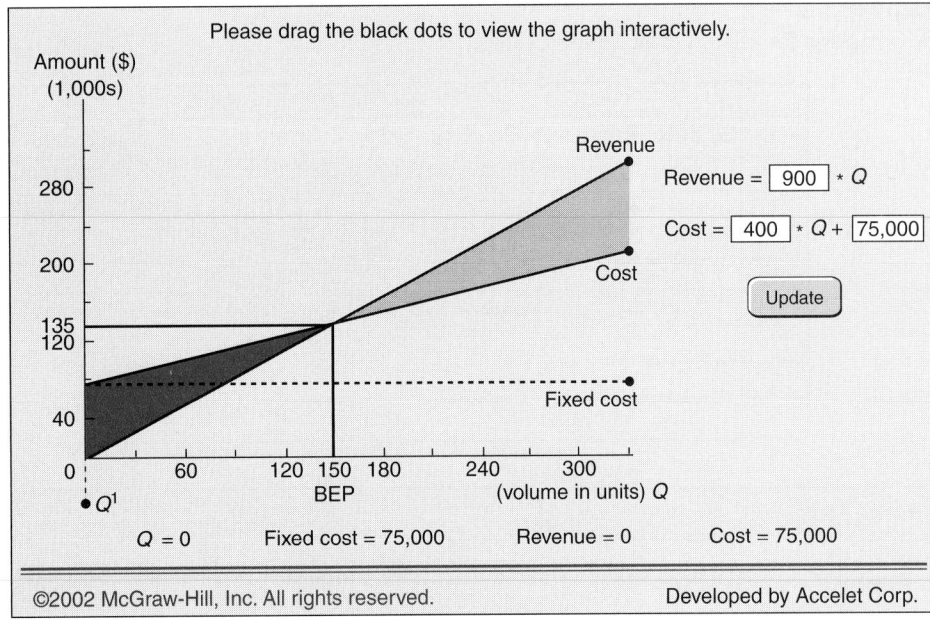

Please drag the black dots to view the graph interactively.

Amount ($) (1,000s)

Revenue

Revenue = $\boxed{900}$ * Q

Cost = $\boxed{400}$ * Q + $\boxed{75,000}$

Update

Cost

Fixed cost

Q^1

| Q = 0 | Fixed cost = 75,000 | Revenue = 0 | Cost = 75,000 |

Developed by Accelet Corp.

Spreadsheet Modeling of the Problem

You will see throughout this book that spreadsheets provide a very convenient way of using a management science approach for modeling and analyzing a wide variety of managerial problems. This certainly is true for the Special Products Company problem as well, as we now will demonstrate.

Figure 1.3 shows a spreadsheet formulation of this problem after obtaining a sales forecast that indicates 300 grandfather clocks can be sold. The data have been entered into cells C4 to C7. Cell C9 is used to record a trial value for the decision as to how many grandfather clocks to produce. As one of the many possibilities that eventually might be tried, Figure 1.3 shows the specific trial value of 200.

Excel Tip: A shortcut for defining a range name is to click on the name box (on the left of the formula bar above the spreadsheet) and type a name.

Cells F4 to F7 give the resulting total revenue, total costs, and profit (loss) by using the Excel equations shown under the spreadsheet in Figure 1.3. The Excel equations could have been written using cell references (e.g., F6 = C6*C9). However, the spreadsheet model is made clearer by naming cells (called *range names*). To define a name for a selected cell (or range of cells), choose Name\Define from the Insert menu, and type a name for the cell. These cell names then can be used in other formulas to create an equation that is easy to decipher (e.g., TotalVariableCost = MarginalCost*ProductionQuantity rather than the more cryptic F6 = C6*C9).

Excel Tip: To update formulas throughout the spreadsheet to incorporate a newly defined range name, choose Name\Apply from the Insert menu.

The lower left-hand corner of Figure 1.3 lists the names of the quantities in the spreadsheet in alphabetical order and then gives cell references where the quantities are found. Although this isn't particularly necessary for such a small spreadsheet, you should find it helpful for the larger spreadsheets found later in the book.

Excel Tip: A list of all the defined names and their corresponding cell references can be pasted into a spreadsheet by choosing Name\Paste from the Insert menu and then clicking Paste List.

This same spreadsheet is provided for you live in your MS Courseware on the CD-ROM. (All the spreadsheets in the book are included in your MS Courseware.) As you can see for yourself by bringing up and playing with the spreadsheet, it provides a straightforward way of performing sensitivity analysis on the problem. What happens if the sales forecast should have been considerably lower? What happens if some of the cost and revenue estimates are wrong? Simply enter a variety of new values for these quantities in the spreadsheet and see what happens to the profit shown in cell F7.

A spreadsheet is a convenient tool for performing sensitivity analysis.

The lower right-hand corner of Figure 1.3 introduces two useful Excel functions, the MIN(*a, b*) function and the IF(*a, b, c*) function. The equation for cell F4 uses the MIN(*a, b*) function,

FIGURE 1.3

A spreadsheet formulation of the Special Products Company problem.

	A	B	C	D	E	F
1		**Special Products Co. Break-Even Analysis**				
2						
3			**Data**			**Results**
4		Unit Revenue	$900		Total Revenue	$180,000
5		Fixed Cost	$50,000		Total Fixed Cost	$50,000
6		Marginal Cost	$400		Total Variable Cost	$80,000
7		Sales Forecast	300		Profit (Loss)	$50,000
8						
9		Production Quantity	200			

Range Name	Cell
FixedCost	C5
MarginalCost	C6
ProductionQuantity	C9
Profit	F7
SalesForecast	C7
TotalFixedCost	F5
TotalRevenue	F4
TotalVariableCost	F6
UnitRevenue	C4

	E	F
3		**Results**
4	Total Revenue	=UnitRevenue * MIN(SalesForecast, ProductionQuantity)
5	Total Fixed Cost	=IF(ProductionQuantity > 0, FixedCost, 0)
6	Total Variable Cost	=MarginalCost * ProductionQuantity
7	Profit (Loss)	=TotalRevenue − (TotalFixedCost + TotalVariableCost)

The Excel function MIN(*a, b*) gives the minimum of the numbers in the cells whose addresses are *a* and *b*.

which gives the minimum of *a* and *b*. In this case, the estimated number of grandfather clocks that will be sold is the minimum of the sales forecast and the production quantity, so

$$F4 = UnitRevenue*MIN(SalesForecast, ProductionQuantity)$$

enters the unit revenue (from cell C4) times the minimum of the sales forecast (from C7) and the production quantity (from C9) into cell F4.

Also note that the equation for cell F5 uses the IF(*a, b, c*) function, which does the following: If statement *a* is true, it uses *b;* otherwise, it uses *c*. Therefore,

IF(*a, b, c*) is one of the most widely used Excel functions.

$$F5 = IF(ProductionQuantity > 0, FixedCost, 0)$$

says to enter the fixed cost (C5) into cell F5 if the production quantity (C9) is greater than zero, but otherwise enter 0 (the fixed cost is avoided if production is not initiated).

Although the spreadsheet in Figure 1.3 enables trying a variety of trial values for the production quantity, it does not directly indicate what the production quantity should be. Figure 1.4 shows how this spreadsheet can be expanded to provide this additional guidance. As indicated by its equation at the bottom of the figure, cell F9 calculates the break-even point by dividing the fixed cost ($50,000) by the net profit per grandfather clock sold ($500), where this net profit is the unit revenue ($900) *minus* the marginal cost ($400). Since the sales forecast of 300 exceeds the break-even point of 100, this forecast has been entered into cell C9.

If desired, the complete mathematical model for break-even analysis can be *fully* incorporated into the spreadsheet by requiring that the model solution for the production quantity be entered into cell C9. This would be done by using the equation

$$C9 = IF(SalesForecast > BreakEvenPoint, SalesForecast, 0).$$

However, the disadvantage of introducing this equation is that it would eliminate the possibility of trying other production quantities that might still be of interest. For example, if management does not have much confidence in the sales forecast and wants to minimize the danger of producing more grandfather clocks than can be sold, consideration would be given to

FIGURE 1.4

An expansion of the spreadsheet in Figure 1.3 that uses the solution for the mathematical model to calculate the break-even point.

	A	B	C	D	E	F
1		**Special Products Co. Break-Even Analysis**				
2						
3			**Data**			**Results**
4		Unit Revenue	$900		Total Revenue	$270,000
5		Fixed Cost	$50,000		Total Fixed Cost	$50,000
6		Marginal Cost	$400		Total Variable Cost	$120,000
7		Sales Forecast	300		Profit (Loss)	$100,000
8						
9		Production Quantity	300		Break-Even Point	100

Range Name	Cell
BreakEvenPoint	F9
FixedCost	C5
MarginalCost	C6
ProductionQuantity	C9
Profit	F7
SalesForecast	C7
TotalFixedCost	F5
TotalRevenue	F4
TotalVariableCost	F6
UnitRevenue	C4

	E	F
3		**Results**
4	Total Revenue	=UnitRevenue * MIN(SalesForecast, ProductionQuantity)
5	Total Fixed Cost	=IF(ProductionQuantity > 0, FixedCost, 0)
6	Total Variable Cost	=MarginalCost * ProductionQuantity
7	Profit (Loss)	=TotalRevenue – (TotalFixedCost + TotalVariableCost)
8		
9	Break-Even Point	=FixedCost/(UnitRevenue – MarginalCost)

production quantities smaller than the forecast. For example, the trial value shown in cell C9 of Figure 1.3 might be chosen instead. As in any application of management science, a mathematical model can provide useful guidance but management needs to make the final decision after considering factors that may not be included in the model.

When a mathematical model is incorporated into a spreadsheet as illustrated here, it commonly is referred to as a *spreadsheet model*. You will see numerous examples of spreadsheet models throughout the book.

Review Questions

1. How do the production and sales volume of a new product need to compare to its break-even point to make it worthwhile to introduce the product?

2. What are the factors included in the complete mathematical model for the Special Products Company problem, in addition to an equation for profit?

3. What is the purpose of sensitivity analysis?

4. How can a spreadsheet be used to perform sensitivity analysis?

5. What does the MIN(*a, b*) Excel function do?

6. What does the IF(*a, b, c*) Excel function do?

1.3   THE IMPACT OF MANAGEMENT SCIENCE

Management science has had an impressive impact on improving the efficiency of numerous organizations around the world. In the process, it has made a significant contribution to increasing the productivity of the economies of various countries.

The best way to convey the impact that management science is having is to describe some *actual* applications and the benefits they have provided. Therefore, you will see many examples of actual applications throughout the book (especially in the later chapters). (These applications are highlighted by giving the names of the organizations involved in **boldface.**)

Some illustrate how a wide variety of organizations are using management science. Others are especially noteworthy applications that have won major awards.

The most prestigious prize that a practitioner of management science can win is one of the annual Franz Edelman Awards for Management Science Achievement. These awards are given for the year's best applications of management science anywhere throughout the world. The competition is sponsored jointly by the international Institute for Operations Research and the Management Sciences (INFORMS) and its College for the Practice of the Management Sciences.

Each year, several dozen entries are submitted to this competition. After an arduous review process, about six finalists are selected for awards, with approximately $10,000 going to the first-prize winner and smaller amounts to the other finalists. More important than the money is the prestige of being an award winner. An entire issue of *Interfaces* (currently the first issue of the following year) is devoted to articles describing the award-winning applications in detail.

Tables 1.1 and 1.2 provide a preview of those award-winning applications that will be discussed in subsequent chapters. The first table lists *classic* applications (conducted before

TABLE 1.1   **Some Classic Award-Winning Applications of Management Science**

Organization	Nature of Application	Issue of *Interfaces*	Chapter Where Discussed	Annual Savings
United Airlines	Schedule shift work at reservations offices and airports to meet customer needs with minimum cost	Jan.–Feb. 1986	2, 4, 13, 14	$6 million
Citgo Petroleum Corp.	Optimize refinery operations and the supply, distribution, and marketing of products	Jan.–Feb. 1987	2, 4, 7	$70 million
San Francisco Police Department	Optimally schedule and deploy police patrol officers with a computerized system	Jan.–Feb. 1989	9	$11 million
Homart Development Co.	Optimally schedule the sale of shopping malls and office buildings	Jan.–Feb. 1987	9	$40 million
AT&T	Optimize the selection of sites for telemarketing centers for AT&T business customers	Jan.–Feb. 1990	9	$406 million more sales
Amoco Oil Co.	Define and evaluate new strategies for merchandising the company's products	Dec. 1982	11	$10 million
U.S. Postal Service	Perform technical and economic analyses of options for postal automation	March–April 1987; Jan.–Feb. 1992	11, 15	$200 million
Standard Brands, Inc.	Control finished-goods inventory (safety stocks, reorder points, and order quantities) of 100 items	Dec. 1981	18	$3.8 million
IBM	Integrate a national network of spare-parts inventories to improve service support	Jan.–Feb. 1990	19	$20 million + $250 million less inventory
Hydroeléctrica Español	Apply statistical forecasting to manage a system of reservoirs used to generate hydroelectric power	Jan.–Feb. 1990	13	$2 million
Xerox Corp.	Modify the strategy for repairing customer machines to reduce response time and improve repairer productivity	Nov. 1975, Part 2	14	50% better productivity

TABLE 1.2   **Some Award-Winning Applications of Management Science since 1990**

Organization	Nature of Application	Issue of *Interfaces*	Chapter Where Discussed	Annual Savings
Procter & Gamble	Redesign the North American production and distribution system to reduce costs and improve speed to market	Jan.–Feb. 1997	6	$200 million
National Railroad of France	Develop an optimal railroad schedule and adjust train capacities daily	Jan.–Feb. 1998	7	$15 million more revenue annually
Air New Zealand	Generate minimum-cost tours of duty to cover flights and assign them to crews	Jan.–Feb. 2001	9	$6.7 million
Grantham, Mayo, Van Otterlee and Company	Construct optimal portfolios with a limited number of stocks and transactions	Jan.–Feb. 1999	9	$4 million
Sears, Roebuck	Develop a vehicle-routing and scheduling system for delivery and home service fleets	Jan.–Feb. 1999	9	$42 million
South African National Defense Force	Optimally redesign the size and shape of the defense force and its weapons systems	Jan.–Feb. 1997	9	$1.1 billion
Digital Equipment Corp.	Restructure the global supply chain of suppliers, plants, distribution centers, potential sites, and market areas	Jan.–Feb. 1995	9	$800 million
Reynolds Metals Co.	Automate a dispatching system for freight shipments from over 200 plants, warehouses, and suppliers	Jan.–Feb. 1991	9, 15	$7 million
China	Optimally select and schedule massive projects for meeting the country's future energy needs	Jan.–Feb. 1995	9	$425 million
Delta Airlines	Maximize the profit from assigning airplane types to over 2,500 domestic flights	Jan.–Feb. 1994	9	$100 million
American Airlines	Optimally assign sequences of flight legs to crews of pilots and flight attendants	Jan.–Feb. 1991	9	$20 million
IBM	Reengineer its global supply chain to respond quicker to customers while holding minimal inventory	Jan.–Feb. 2000	19	$750 million in first year
American Airlines	Design a system of fare structures, overbooking, and coordinating flights to increase revenue	Jan.–Feb. 1992	13, 19	$500 million more revenue
Merit Brass Co.	Install statistical sales forecasting and finished-goods inventory management to improve customer service	Jan.–Feb. 1993	13	Much better service
Taco Bell	Optimally schedule employees to provide desired customer service at a minimum cost	Jan.–Feb. 1998	13, 15	$13 million
L. L. Bean, Inc.	Optimally allocate telephone trunk lines, hold positions, and telephone agents to a large call center	Jan.–Feb. 1991	14	$9.5 million
New York City	Overhaul the process from when individuals are arrested until they are arraigned to reduce waiting times	Jan.–Feb. 1993	14, 15	$9.5 million
AT&T	Develop a PC-based system to guide business customers in designing their call centers	Jan.–Feb. 1993	14, 15	$750 million
Hewlett-Packard	Redesign the sizes and locations of buffers in a printer assembly line to meet production goals	Jan.–Feb. 1998	15	$280 million more revenue

1990) that still provide valuable lessons today. The second table focuses on management science studies conducted since 1990. The third column of each table indicates the issue of *Interfaces* in which each study is fully described. The fourth column shows the chapter (or chapters) of this book (including its supplements on the CD-ROM) in which the study will be discussed because it illustrates the application of that chapter's technique(s). The rightmost column indicates that these studies typically resulted in *annual savings* in the millions (often *many* millions) of dollars. Furthermore, additional benefits not recorded in the table (e.g., improved service to customers and better managerial control) sometimes were considered to be even more important than these financial benefits.

The subsequent chapters also discuss many other actual applications of management science that did not win awards. These more routine applications often provide considerably more modest benefits than the award-winning applications. However, the figures in the rightmost column of the tables do accurately reflect the dramatic impact that large, well-designed management science studies occasionally can have.

Articles published in *Interfaces* during the 1980s and 1990s also are available for viewing on the Web. Therefore, one of the features of this book's website **(www.mhhe.com/hillier2e)** is that it provides links to those articles that best describe the actual applications of management science discussed in this book, including most of those listed in Tables 1.1 and 1.2. These articles can be downloaded at **www.mhhe.com/hillier2e/articles.**

Review
Question

1. What is the order of magnitude of the annual savings that typically result from award-winning applications of management science?

1.4 SOME SPECIAL FEATURES OF THIS BOOK

The focus of this book is on teaching what an enlightened future manager needs to learn from a management science course. It is not on trying to train technical analysts. This focus has led us to include a number of special features that we hope you enjoy.

One special feature is that the entire book revolves around *modeling* as an aid to managerial decision making. This is what is particularly relevant to a manager. Although they may not use this term, all managers often engage in at least informal modeling (abstracting the essence of a problem to better analyze it), so learning more about the art of modeling is important. Since managers instigate larger management science studies done by others, they also need to be able to recognize the kinds of managerial problems where such a study might be helpful. Thus, a future manager should acquire the ability both to recognize when a management science model might be applicable and to properly interpret the results from analyzing the model. Therefore, rather than spending substantial time in this book on mathematical theory, the mechanics of solution procedures, or the manipulation of spreadsheets, the focus is on the art of model formulation, the role of a model, and the analysis of model results. A wide range of model types is considered.

Another special feature is a heavy emphasis on *case studies* to better convey these ideas in an interesting way in the context of applications. Every subsequent chapter includes at least one case study that introduces and illustrates the application of that chapter's techniques in a realistic setting. In a few instances, the entire chapter revolves around a case study. Although considerably smaller and simpler than most real studies (to maintain clarity), these case studies are patterned after actual applications requiring a major management science study. Consequently, they convey the whole process of such a study, some of the pitfalls involved, and the complementary roles of the management science team and the manager responsible for the decisions to be made.

To complement these case studies, every subsequent chapter also includes major cases at the end. These realistic cases can be used for individual assignments, team projects, or case studies in class.

The book also places heavy emphasis on conveying the diversity of application areas for the various models and techniques of management science. These application areas cut across the spectrum of the functional areas of business for a wide variety of organizations.

In addition, we try to provide you with a broad perspective about the nature of the real world of management science in practice. It is easy to lose sight of this world when cranking through textbook exercises to master the mechanics of a series of techniques. Therefore, we shift some emphasis from mastering these mechanics to seeing the big picture. The case studies, cases, and descriptions of actual applications are part of this effort. We also give further descriptions of what is happening in practice. We occasionally provide some perspectives about solving management science models, including the size of problems being solved in practice, but we do not bother you with details that you will never need to know. We indicate how widely the various models and techniques are being used. We also point out the shortcomings of some techniques and what new developments are beginning to address these shortcomings.

The last, but certainly not the least, of the special features of this book is the accompanying software. We will describe and illustrate how to use today's premier spreadsheet package, Microsoft Excel, to formulate many management science models in a spreadsheet format. Some of these models can be solved using standard Excel. However, Excel add-ins will be required to solve most of the models considered in this book.

Shrinkwrapped in the back of the book is an extensive collection of software that we collectively refer to as **MS Courseware.** Included within this collection are spreadsheet files, many add-ins for Excel, Microsoft Project, and a package of interactive Management Science Modules. Each of these is briefly described below.

MS Courseware includes numerous spreadsheet files for every chapter in this book. Each time a spreadsheet example is presented in the book, a live spreadsheet that shows the formulation and solution for the example also is available in MS Courseware. This provides a convenient reference, or even useful templates, when you set up spreadsheets to solve similar problems. Also, for many models in the book, template spreadsheet files are provided that already include all the equations necessary to solve the model. You simply enter the data for the model and the solution is immediately calculated.

Solver Table is an Excel add-in developed by the authors to automate sensitivity analysis in optimization problems. This add-in will be used in several chapters, including especially Chapter 5.

Included with standard Excel is an add-in, called Solver, which is used to solve most of the optimization models considered in the first half of this book. The standard Solver was developed by Frontline Systems, Inc. Frontline Systems also has developed several more powerful Solver packages for Excel. One of these, called Premium Solver for Education, is included within MS Courseware. A primary difference between the standard Solver and Premium Solver is that Premium Solver includes an option called Evolutionary Solver that will solve additional kinds of optimization models discussed in Chapter 10.

Also included within MS Courseware are three Excel add-ins developed by Professor Michael Middleton. TreePlan allows you to build decision trees within Excel, as covered in Chapter 12. SensIt is used to generate a number of charts useful for performing sensitivity analysis. RiskSim is a tool used to perform computer simulation, which is the topic of Chapters 15 and 16.

Decisioneering, Inc., has developed several powerful Excel add-ins that are also included within MS Courseware. Crystal Ball greatly simplifies performing Monte Carlo simulation within Excel, as covered in Chapter 16. OptQuest allows you to perform optimization within a simulation model. Finally, CB Predictor is a tool that will be useful in forecasting, as discussed in Chapter 13.

A trial version of Microsoft Project is included in MS Courseware as an aid for performing project management. This software will be utilized in Chapter 8.

As mentioned in Section 1.2, another learning aid accompanying the book is the package of Interactive Management Science Modules provided at **www.mhhe.com/hillier2e.** This innovative tool includes several modules that enable you to interactively explore several management science techniques in depth. For your convenience, an offline version of this package also is included in your MS Courseware on the CD-ROM.

Given this choice of software, we should point out that Excel is not designed for dealing with the really large management science models that occasionally arise in practice. More powerful software packages that are not based on spreadsheets, such as CPLEX or IBM's OSL, generally are used to solve such models instead. However, management science teams, not managers, primarily use these sophisticated packages (including using *modeling languages* to help input the large models). Since this book is aimed mainly at future managers rather than future management scientists, we will not have you use these packages.

To alert you to relevant material in MS Courseware, the end of each chapter has a list entitled "Learning Aids for This Chapter in Your MS Courseware."

1.5 Summary

Management science is a discipline area that attempts to aid managerial decision making by applying a scientific approach to managerial problems that involve quantitative factors. The rapid development of this discipline began in the 1940s and 1950s. The onslaught of the computer revolution has since continued to give great impetus to its growth. Further impetus now is being provided by the widespread use of spreadsheet packages, which greatly facilitate the application of management science by managers and others.

A major management science study involves conducting a systematic investigation that includes careful data gathering, developing and testing hypotheses about the problem (typically in the form of a mathematical model), and applying sound logic in the subsequent analysis. The management science team then presents its recommendations to the managers who must make the decisions about how to resolve the problem.

A major part of a typical management science study involves incorporating the quantitative factors into a mathematical model (perhaps incorporated into a spreadsheet) and then applying mathematical procedures to solve the model. Such a model uses *decision variables* to represent the quantifiable decisions to be made. An *objective function* expresses the appropriate measure of performance in terms of these decision variables. The *constraints* of the model express the restrictions on the values that can be assigned to the decision variables. The *parameters* of the model are the constants that appear in the objective function and the constraints. An example involving *break-even analysis* was used to illustrate a mathematical model.

Management science has had an impressive impact on improving the efficiency of numerous organizations around the world. In fact, many award-winning applications have resulted in annual savings in the millions, tens of millions, or even hundreds of millions of dollars.

The focus of this book is on emphasizing what an enlightened future manager needs to learn from a management science course. Therefore, the book revolves around modeling as an aid to managerial decision making. Many case studies (within the chapters) and cases (at the end of chapters) are used to better convey these ideas.

Glossary

break-even point   The production and sales volume for a product that must be exceeded to achieve a profit. (Section 1.2), *9*

constraint   An inequality or equation in a mathematical model that expresses some restrictions on the values that can be assigned to the decision variables. (Section 1.2), *9*

decision support system   An interactive computer-based system that aids managerial decision making. (Section 1.1), *7*

decision variable   An algebraic variable that represents a quantifiable decision to be made. (Section 1.2), *8*

mathematical model   An approximate representation of, for example, a business problem that is expressed in terms of mathematical symbols and expressions. (Section 1.1), *6*

model   An approximate representation of something. (Section 1.1), *6*

MS Courseware   The name of the software package that is shrinkwrapped with the book. (Section 1.4), *17*

objective function   A mathematical expression in a model that gives the measure of performance for a problem in terms of the decision variables. (Section 1.2), *10*

operations research   The traditional name for management science that still is widely used outside of business schools. (Section 1.1), *4*

parameter   One of the constants in a mathematical model. (Section 1.2), *10*

sensitivity analysis   Analysis of how the recommendations of a model might change if any of the estimates providing the numbers in the model eventually need to be corrected. (Section 1.2), *10*

spreadsheet model   An approximate representation of, for example, a business problem that is laid out on a spreadsheet in a way that facilitates analysis of the problem. (Section 1.1), *6*

Learning Aids for This Chapter in Your MS Courseware

Chapter 1 Excel Files:

Special Products Co. Example

Interactive Management Science Modules:

Module for Break-Even Analysis

Problems

1.1. Select one of the applications listed in Table 1.1. Read the article describing the application in the indicated issue of *Interfaces*. Write a one-page description of the benefits (including nonfinancial benefits) that resulted from this application of management science.

1.2. Follow the instructions of Problem 1.1 for one of the applications listed in Table 1.2.

1.3. The manager of a small firm is considering whether to produce a new product that would require leasing some special equipment at a cost of $20,000 per month. In addition to this leasing cost, a production cost of $10 would be incurred for each unit of the product produced. Each unit sold would generate $20 in revenue.

Develop a mathematical expression for the monthly profit that would be generated by this product in terms of the number of units produced and sold per month. Then determine how large this number needs to be each month to make it profitable to produce the product.

1.4. Refer to Problem 1.3. A sales forecast has been obtained that indicates that 4,000 units of the new product could be sold. This forecast is considered to be quite reliable, but there is considerable uncertainty about the accuracy of the estimates given for the leasing cost, the marginal production cost, and the unit revenue.

Use the Break-Even Analysis module in the Interactive Management Science Modules to perform the following sensitivity analysis on these estimates.

a. How large can the leasing cost be before this new product ceases to be profitable?

b. How large can the marginal production cost be before this new product ceases to be profitable?

c. How small can the unit revenue be before this new product ceases to be profitable?

1.5. Management of the Toys R4U Company needs to decide whether to introduce a certain new novelty toy for the upcoming Christmas season, after which it would be discontinued. The total cost required to produce and market this toy would be $500,000 plus $15 per toy produced. The company would receive revenue of $35 for each toy sold.

a. Assuming that every unit of this toy that is produced is sold, write an expression for the profit in terms of the number produced and sold. Then find the break-even point that this number must exceed to make it worthwhile to introduce this toy.

b. Now assume that the number that can be sold might be less than the number produced. Write an expression for the profit in terms of these two numbers.

c. Formulate a spreadsheet that will give the profit in part *b* for any values of the two numbers.

d. Write a mathematical expression for the constraint that the number produced should not exceed the number that can be sold.

1.6. A reliable sales forecast has been obtained indicating that the Special Products Company (see Section 1.2) would be able to sell 300 limited edition grandfather clocks, which appears to be enough to justify introducing this new product. However, management is concerned that this conclusion might change if more accurate estimates were available for the cost of setting up the production facilities, the marginal production cost, and the unit revenue. Therefore, before a final decision is made, management wants sensitivity analysis done on these estimates.

Use the Break-Even Analysis module in the Interactive Management Science Modules to perform the following sensitivity analysis.

a. How large can the cost of setting up the production facilities be before the grandfather clocks cease to be profitable?

b. How large can the marginal production cost be before the grandfather clocks cease to be profitable?

c. How small can the unit revenue be before the grandfather clocks cease to be profitable?

1.7. Reconsider the problem facing the management of the Special Products Company as presented in Section 1.2.

A more detailed investigation now has provided better estimates of the data for the problem. The fixed cost of initiating production of the limited edition grandfather clocks still is estimated to be $50,000, but the new estimate of the marginal cost is $500. The revenue from each grandfather clock sold now is estimated to be $700.

a. Use a graphical procedure to find the new break-even point.

b. Use an algebraic procedure to find the new break-even point.

c. State the mathematical model for this problem with the new data.

d. Incorporate this mathematical model into a spreadsheet with a sales forecast of 300. Use this spreadsheet model to find the new break-even point, and then determine the production quantity and the estimated total profit indicated by the model.

e. Suppose that management fears that the sales forecast may be overly optimistic and so does not want to consider producing more than 200 grandfather clocks. Use the spreadsheet from part *d* to determine what the production quantity should be and the estimated total profit that would result.

1.8. The Best-for-Less Corp. supplies its two retail outlets from its two plants. Plant A will be supplying 30 shipments next month. Plant B has not yet set its production schedule for next month but has the capacity to produce and ship any amount up to a maximum of 50 shipments. Retail outlet 1 has submitted its order for 40 shipments for next month. Retail outlet 2 needs a minimum of 25 shipments next month but would be happy to receive more. The production costs are the same at the two plants but the shipping costs differ. The shipping cost per shipment from each plant to each retail outlet is given below, along with a summary of the other data.

	Unit Shipping Cost		
	Retail Outlet 1	**Retail Outlet 2**	**Supply**
Plant A	$700	$400	= 30 shipments
Plant B	$800	$600	≤ 50 shipments
Needed	= 40 shipments	≥ 25 shipments	

The distribution manager, Jennifer Lopez, now needs to develop a plan for how many shipments to send from each plant to each of the retail outlets next month. Her objective is to minimize the total shipping cost.

a. Identify the individual decisions that Jennifer needs to make. For each of these decisions, define a decision variable to represent the decision.

b. Write a mathematical expression for the total shipping cost in terms of the decision variables.

c. Write a mathematical expression for each of the constraints on what the values of the decision variables can be.

d. State a complete mathematical model for Jennifer's problem.

e. What do you think Jennifer's shipping plan should be? Explain your reasoning. Then express your shipping plan in terms of the decision variables.

1.9. The Water Sports Company soon will be producing and marketing a new model line of motor boats. The production manager, Michael Jensen, now is facing a *make-or-buy decision* regarding the outboard motor to be installed on each of these boats. Based on the total cost involved, should the motors be produced internally or purchased from a vendor? Producing them internally would require an investment of $1 million in new facilities as well as a production cost of $1,600 for each motor produced. If purchased from a vendor instead, the price would be $2,000 per motor.

Michael has obtained a preliminary forecast from the company's marketing division that 3,000 boats in this model line will be sold.

a. Use spreadsheets to display and analyze Michael's two options. Which option should be chosen?

b. Michael realizes from past experience that preliminary sales forecasts are quite unreliable, so he wants to check on whether his decision might change if a more careful forecast differed significantly from the preliminary forecast. Determine a *break-even point* for the production and sales volume below which the buy option is better and above which the make option is better.

1.10. Reconsider the Special Products Company problem presented in Section 1.2.

Although the company is well qualified to do most of the work in producing the limited edition grandfather clocks, it currently lacks expertise in one key area, namely, constructing the time-keeping mechanism for the clocks. Therefore, management now is considering contracting out this part of the job to another company that has this expertise and already has some of its production facilities set up to do this kind of work. If this were done, the Special Products Company would not incur any fixed cost for initiating production of the clocks but would incur a marginal cost of $650 (including its payment to the other company) while still obtaining revenue of $900 for each clock produced and sold. However, if the company does all the production itself, all the data presented in Section 1.2 still apply. After obtaining an analysis of the sales potential, management believes that 300 grandfather clocks can be sold.

Management now wants to determine whether the *make option* (do all the production internally) or the *buy option* (contract out the production of the time-keeping mechanism) is better.

a. Use a spreadsheet to display and analyze the buy option. Show the relevant data and financial output, including the total profit that would be obtained by producing and selling 300 grandfather clocks.

b. Figure 1.4 shows the analysis for the make option. Compare these results with those from part *a* to determine which option (make or buy) appears to be better.

c. Another way to compare these two options is to find a *break-even point* for the production and sales volume, below which the buy option is better and above which the make option is better. Begin this process by developing an expression for the *difference* in profit between the make and buy options in terms of the number of grandfather clocks to produce for sale. Thus, this expression should give the *incremental profit* from choosing the make option rather than the buy option, where this incremental profit is 0 if 0 grandfather clocks are produced but otherwise is negative below the break-even point and positive above the break-even point. Using this expression as the objective function, state the overall mathematical model (including constraints) for the problem of determining whether to choose the make option and, if so, how many units of the time-keeping mechanism (one per clock) to produce.

d. Use a graphical procedure to find the break-even point described in part *c*.

e. Use an algebraic procedure to find the break-even point described in part *c*.

f. Use a spreadsheet model to find the break-even point described in part *c*. What is the conclusion about what the company should do?

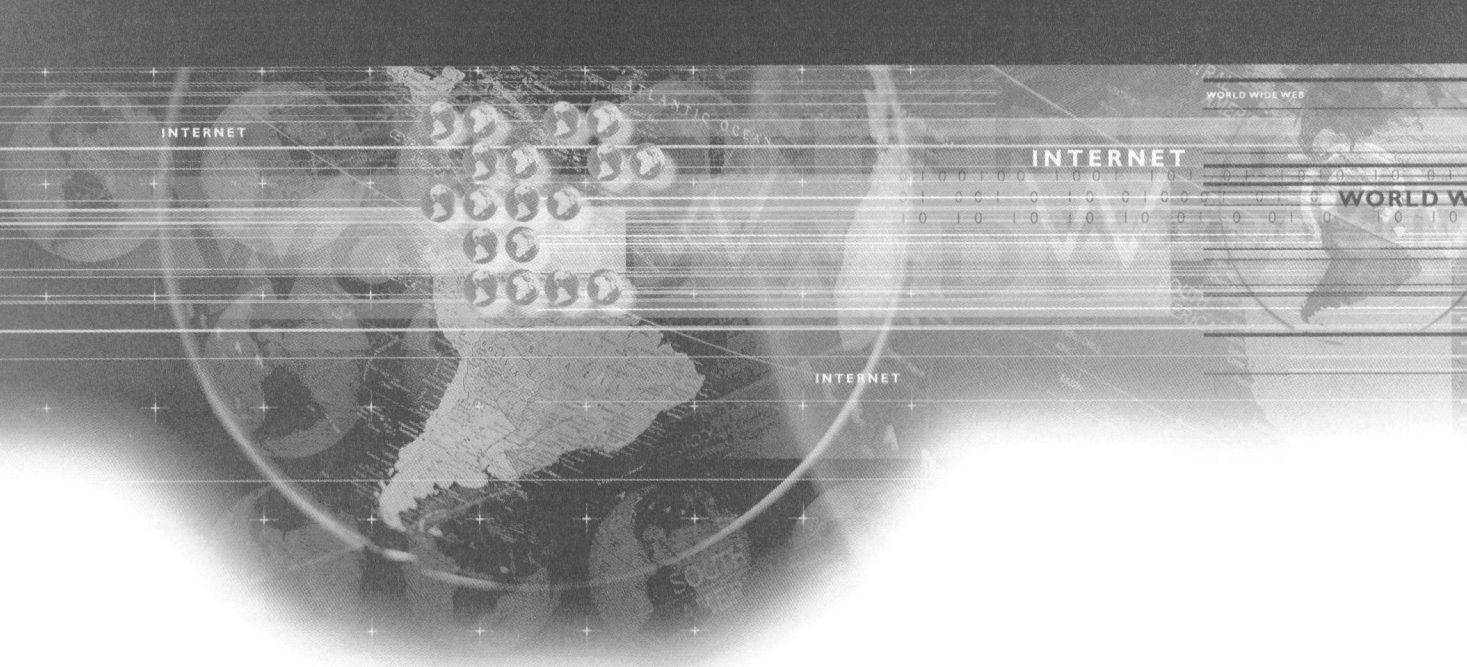

Learning objectives

After completing this chapter, you should be able to

1. Explain what linear programming is.

2. Identify the three key questions to be addressed in formulating any spreadsheet model.

3. Name and identify the purpose of the four kinds of cells used in linear programming spreadsheet models.

4. Formulate a basic linear programming model in a spreadsheet from a description of the problem.

5. Present the algebraic form of a linear programming model from its formulation on a spreadsheet.

6. Apply the graphical method to solve a two-variable linear programming problem.

7. Use Excel to solve a linear programming spreadsheet model.

Chapter **Two**

Linear Programming: Basic Concepts

The management of any organization regularly must make decisions about how to allocate its resources to various activities to best meet organizational objectives. Linear programming is a powerful problem-solving tool that aids management in making such decisions. It is applicable to both profit-making and not-for-profit organizations, as well as governmental agencies. The resources being allocated to activities can be, for example, money, different kinds of personnel, and different kinds of machinery and equipment. In many cases, a wide variety of resources must be allocated simultaneously. The activities needing these resources might be various production activities (e.g., producing different products), marketing activities (e.g., advertising in different media), financial activities (e.g., making capital investments), or some other activities. Some problems might even involve activities of *all* these types (and perhaps others), because they are competing for the same resources.

You will see as we progress that even this description of the scope of linear programming is not sufficiently broad. Some of its applications go beyond the allocation of resources. However, activities always are involved. Thus, a recurring theme in linear programming is the need to find the *best mix* of activities—which ones to pursue and at what levels.

Like the other management science techniques, linear programming uses a *mathematical model* to represent the problem being studied. The word *linear* in the name refers to the form of the mathematical expressions in this model. *Programming* does not refer to computer programming; rather, it is essentially a synonym for planning. Thus, linear programming means the *planning of activities* represented by a *linear* mathematical model.

Because it comprises a major part of management science, linear programming takes up several chapters of this book. Furthermore, many of the lessons learned about how to apply linear programming also will carry over to the application of other management science techniques.

This chapter focuses on the basic concepts of linear programming.

2.1 THREE CLASSIC APPLICATIONS OF LINEAR PROGRAMMING

To give you a perspective about the role linear programming can play in managerial decision making, we will briefly describe how it was used in three *real* situations. Each of these is a *classic* application, initiated some years ago, that has come to be regarded as a standard of excellence for future applications of linear programming. After you develop your facility with linear programming, we will refer back to each of these applications in Section 4.8, fleshing them out in more detail.

Choosing the Product Mix at Ponderosa Industrial[1]

Until its sale in 1988, **Ponderosa Industrial** was a Mexican company that produced 25 percent of the country's plywood. Like any plywood manufacturer, Ponderosa's many plywood

---

[1]Asim Roy, Emma E. DeFalomir, and Leon Lasdon, "An Optimization-Based Decision Support System for a Product Mix Problem," *Interfaces* 12, no. 2 (April 1982), pp. 26–33. This article also is available for download at **www.mhhe.com/hillier2e/articles**.

products were differentiated by thickness and by the quality of the wood used. Because they were sold in a competitive environment, the market established the prices of the products, so the prices fluctuated considerably from month to month. As a result, each product's contribution to Ponderosa's overall profit also fluctuated widely. Thus, if one product was considerably more profitable than another in one month, the reverse could well be true the following month. Therefore, a critical issue facing management each month was the choice of *product mix*— how much to produce of each product—to generate as much profit as possible. This choice was very complex, since it needed to take into account the current amounts available of various resources needed to produce the products. The six most important resources were (1) four types of logs (based on the quality of their wood) and (2) production capacities for each of the two key operations in producing plywood (the pressing operation and the polishing operation).

Linear programming finds the most profitable mix of products.

Starting in 1980, Ponderosa management used linear programming on a monthly basis to guide the product-mix decision for the upcoming month. The mathematical model for linear programming considered all relevant restrictions on this decision, including the limited amounts available of the resources required to make the products. The model was then solved to find the product mix that was feasible and yielded the *largest possible profit.* The model commonly would be solved a number of times under different scenarios for where the market was headed in order to fine-tune the product-mix decision. Linear programming also enabled management to assess whether profit could be increased further by changing any decisions on the quantities of the resources to make available for current production.

The impact of linear programming at Ponderosa was reported to be "tremendous." It led to a dramatic shift in the types of plywood products emphasized by the company. The improved product-mix decisions were credited with increasing the overall profitability of the company by 20 percent. Other contributions of linear programming included better utilization of raw material, capital equipment, and personnel.

Personnel Scheduling at United Airlines[2]

Cost control is essential for survival in the airline industry. In 1982, upper management of **United Airlines** initiated a cost-control project as part of its ensuing expansion. The goal was to improve the utilization of personnel at the airline's reservations offices and airports by matching work schedules to customer needs more closely.

At the time, United Airlines employed over 4,000 reservations sales representatives and support personnel at its 11 reservations offices and about 1,000 customer service agents at its 10 largest airports. Some were part-time, working shifts from two to eight hours; most were full-time, working 8- or 10-hour shifts. Shifts started at several different times. Each reservations office was open (by telephone) 24 hours a day, as was each of the major airports. However, the number of employees needed at each location to provide the required level of service varied greatly during the 24-hour day and might fluctuate considerably from one half-hour to the next.

Trying to design the work schedules for all the employees at a given location to meet these service requirements most efficiently is a nightmare of combinatorial considerations. Once an employee arrives, he or she will be there continuously for the entire shift (2 to 10 hours, depending on the employee), *except* for either a meal break or short rest breaks every two hours. Given the *minimum* number of employees needed on duty for *each* half-hour interval over a 24-hour day (this minimum changes from day to day over a seven-day week), *how many* employees of *each shift length* should begin work at *what start time* over *each* 24-hour day of a seven-day week? Fortunately, linear programming thrives on such combinatorial nightmares.

Actually, several management science techniques described in this book were used in the planning system developed to attack this problem. *Forecasting* (Chapter 13) and *queueing models* (Chapter 14) were both used to determine the minimum number of employees needed on duty for each half-hour interval. *Integer programming* (Chapter 9) was used to determine

[2]Thomas J. Holloran and Judson E. Bryn, "United Airlines Station Manpower Planning System," *Interfaces* 16, no. 1 (January–February 1986), pp. 39–50. This article also is available for download at **www.mhhe.com/ hillier2e/articles.**

Linear programming does
personnel scheduling to
provide the needed service
to customers at a
minimum cost.

when shifts would start. However, the core of the planning system was *linear programming,* which did all the actual scheduling to provide the needed service at the smallest possible labor cost. A new work schedule was developed each month to reflect changing conditions.

This application of linear programming was reported to have had "an overwhelming impact not only on United's management and members of the project team, but also for many who had never before heard of management science or mathematical modeling." It earned rave reviews from upper management, operating managers, and affected employees alike. For example, one manager described the scheduling system as "magical, . . . just as the (customer) lines begin to build, someone shows up for work; and just as you begin to think you're overstaffed, people start going home."

In tangible terms, this computerized planning system based on linear programming was credited with saving United Airlines more than $6 million *annually* in just direct salary and benefit costs. Other benefits included improved customer service and reduced workloads for support staff. After some updating in the early 1990s, the system is providing similar benefits today.

Planning Supply, Distribution, and Marketing at Citgo Petroleum Corporation[3]

Citgo Petroleum Corporation specializes in refining and marketing petroleum. In the mid-1980s, it had annual sales of several billion dollars, ranking it among the 150 largest industrial companies in the United States.

After several years of financial losses, Citgo was acquired in 1983 by Southland Corporation, the owner of the 7-Eleven convenience store chain (whose sales include two billion gallons of quality motor fuels annually). To turn Citgo's financial losses around, Southland created a task force composed of Southland personnel, Citgo personnel, and outside consultants. A management science consultant was appointed director of the task force and reported directly to both the president of Citgo and the chairman of the board of Southland.

During 1984 and 1985, this task force applied various management science techniques to analyze Citgo's activities in such diverse areas as refining, supply and distribution, market planning, accounts payable and receivable, inventory control, and acquisitions. It was reported that these management science applications "have changed the way Citgo does business and resulted in approximately $70 million per year profit improvement."

The bulk of this profit improvement resulted from two *linear programming systems* developed by the task force. One, called the *refinery LP system* (LP is a common abbreviation for linear programming), led to improvements in refinery yield, substantial reductions in the cost of labor, and other cost savings. The refinery LP system enabled management to operate Citgo's refinery (a major player in the profit-and-loss picture) so much more efficiently that it contributed $50 million of the $70 million profit improvement in 1985.

The other linear programming system was the Supply, Distribution, and Marketing modeling system (or simply the SDM system). Now, many years after its introduction, Citgo continues to use and benefit from this system. It is based on a special kind of linear programming model that uses a network to describe the system being studied. The model in this case provides a representation of Citgo's vast marketing and distribution network. Because it introduces some new features of linear programming, we shall return to the SDM system again in Chapters 4 and 7 after providing some more background here.

The SDM system is used to coordinate the supply, distribution, and marketing of each of Citgo's major products throughout the United States. Management uses the system to make decisions such as where to sell, what price to charge, where to buy or trade, how much to buy or

[3]Darwin Klingman, Nancy Phillips, David Steiger, Ross Wirth, and Warren Young, "The Challenges and Success Factors in Implementing an Integrated Products Planning System for Citgo," *Interfaces* 16, no. 3 (May–June 1986), pp. 1–19. Also see Darwin Klingman, Nancy Phillips, David Steiger, and Warren Young, "The Successful Deployment of Management Science throughout Citgo Petroleum Corporation," *Interfaces* 17, no. 1 (January–February 1987), pp. 4–25. These articles also are available for download at **www.mhhe.com/hillier2e/articles.**

Linear programming optimizes the supply, distribution, and marketing of each product.

trade, how much to hold in inventory, and how much to ship by each mode of transportation. Linear programming guides these decisions and when to implement them so as to minimize the total cost (or maximize the total profit) for Citgo. The SDM system also is used in "what-if" sessions, where management explores *what* would happen to the solution *if* a scenario evolves that is not assumed by the model.

The SDM system has greatly improved the efficiency of Citgo's supply, distribution, and marketing operations, enabling a huge reduction in product inventory with no drop in service levels. Soon after its introduction, the value of petroleum products being held in inventory was reduced by $116.5 million. The resulting reduction in interest expenses for borrowed capital adds roughly $14 million to Citgo's annual profits. Improvements in coordination, pricing, and purchasing decisions have been estimated to add at least another $2.5 million to annual profits.

Review Questions

1. Linear programming guided managerial decision making at Ponderosa Industrial on which critical issue facing management each month?

2. What was the impact of this application of linear programming at Ponderosa?

3. What was the goal of the described application of linear programming at United Airlines?

4. What was the impact of this application at United Airlines?

5. The SDM linear programming system at Citgo Petroleum Corp. was used to coordinate what?

6. What was the impact of this application of linear programming at Citgo?

2.2   A CASE STUDY: THE WYNDOR GLASS CO. PRODUCT-MIX PROBLEM

Jim Baker is excited. The group he heads has really hit the jackpot this time. They have had some notable successes in the past, but he feels that this one will be really special. He can hardly wait for the reaction after his memorandum reaches top management.

Jim has had an excellent track record during his seven years as manager of new product development for the Wyndor Glass Company. Although the company is a small one, it has been experiencing considerable growth largely because of the innovative new products developed by Jim's group. Wyndor's president, John Hill, has often acknowledged publicly the key role that Jim has played in the recent success of the company.

Therefore, John felt considerable confidence six months ago in asking Jim's group to develop the following new products:

- An 8-foot glass door with aluminum framing.

- A 4-foot × 6-foot double-hung, wood-framed window.

Although several other companies already had products meeting these specifications, John felt that Jim would be able to work his usual magic in introducing exciting new features that would establish new industry standards.

Now, Jim can't remove the smile from his face. They have done it.

Background

The Wyndor Glass Co. produces high-quality glass products, including windows and glass doors that feature handcrafting and the finest workmanship. Although the products are expensive, they fill a market niche by providing the highest quality available in the industry for the most discriminating buyers. The company has three plants.

Plant 1 produces aluminum frames and hardware.

Plant 2 produces wood frames.

Plant 3 produces the glass and assembles the windows and doors.

Because of declining sales for certain products, top management has decided to revamp the company's product line. Unprofitable products are being discontinued, releasing production capacity to launch the two new products developed by Jim Baker's group if management approves their release.

The 8-foot glass door requires some of the production capacity in Plants 1 and 3, but not Plant 2. The 4-foot × 6-foot double-hung window needs only Plants 2 and 3.

Management now needs to address two issues:

1. Should the company go ahead with launching these two new products?

2. If so, what should be the *product mix*—the number of units of each produced per week— for the two new products?

Management's Discussion of the Issues

Having received Jim Baker's memorandum describing the two new products, John Hill now has called a meeting to discuss the current issues. In addition to John and Jim, the meeting includes Bill Tasto, vice president for manufacturing, and Ann Lester, vice president for marketing.

Let's eavesdrop on the meeting.

John Hill (president):   Jim, Bill, Ann, thanks for coming. Jim, thanks for your good memorandum, which we all have received. These two proposed new products certainly sound promising. Tell us more about their special features. What will stand out to make customers willing to pay more for these products, given the similar products already available from other companies? Let's start with the glass door.

Jim Baker (manager of new product development):   Well, I hardly know where to begin. This glass door is loaded with special features. But there are three in particular that I think will really make the customer sit up and notice. One is that this door will have a substantially higher insulating value than any door currently on the market.

John: How is that achieved?

Jim: In three ways. First, we use dual-pane glazing. Second, we insert a new inert gas, even better than argon, between the two panes of glass. It works great. Third, we also use some special coatings and tints for solar and energy control.

John: Wonderful. The insulating value is very important to a lot of customers. Now, what are the other two features you wanted to highlight?

Jim: One is that the glass we are using provides much better protection against ultraviolet light than usual. The other is that the glass is virtually unbreakable. You would have to take a sledgehammer to the glass, and even then you would have trouble breaking it. Somebody walking into the glass, or a bird flying into it, isn't going to faze it.

John: Those are good selling points. Now, tell us about the features that would sell your new double-hung window.

Jim: Well, that's easy. First of all, this window would have all three of the special features that I have just described for the glass door. In addition, the wood finish is extremely long-lasting, and the window has a special mechanism that makes it much easier to slide than usual.

John: Wow, those are great features. But aren't we pricing ourselves out of the market by loading on all those features?

Jim: That's the best part. We've worked hard on designing these products so that they can be produced for only about a thousand dollars more than the run-of-the-mill versions of these products that other companies are putting out.

John: Terrific. Ann, how is all this going to play out in the marketplace? Are these the kinds of special features that affluent customers want?

Ann Lester (vice president for marketing):   Well, we just updated our market research on this question a few months ago. In fact, we fed Jim all our key findings. He has managed to hit all the special features for which these customers are asking. Given the kind of pricing that Jim is indicating, there is no doubt that these products would sell well. Extremely well.

John: Great. Well, Jim, it looks like you've outdone yourself this time. These should be outstanding products for the company. Congratulations!

Jim: Thank you. My group worked especially hard on this project.

John: Bill, we will want to rev up to start production of these products as soon as we can. About how much production output do you think we can achieve?

Bill Tasto (vice president for manufacturing): We do have a little available production capacity, because of the products we are discontinuing, but not a lot. We should be able to achieve a production rate of a few units per week for each of these two products.

John: Is that all?

Bill: Yes. These are complicated products requiring careful crafting. And, as I said, we don't have much production capacity available.

John: Ann, will we be able to sell several of each per week?

Ann: Easily.

John: OK, good. I would like to set the launch date for these products in six weeks. Bill and Ann, is that feasible?

Bill: Yes.

Ann: We'll have to scramble to give these products a proper marketing launch that soon. But we can do it.

John: Good. Now there's one more issue to resolve. With this limited production capacity, we need to decide how to split it between the two products. Do we want to produce the same number of both products? Or mostly one of them? Or even just produce as much as we can of one and postpone launching the other one for a little while?

Jim: It would be dangerous to hold one of the products back and give our competition a chance to scoop us.

Ann: I agree. Furthermore, launching them together has some advantages from a marketing standpoint. Since they share a lot of the same special features, we can combine the advertising for the two products. This is going to make a big splash.

The issue is to find the most profitable mix of the two new products.

John: OK. But which mixture of the two products is going to be most profitable for the company?

Bill: I have a suggestion.

John: What's that?

Bill: A couple times in the past, our Management Science Group has helped us with these same kinds of product-mix decisions, and they've done a good job. They ferret out all the relevant data and then dig into some detailed analysis of the issue. I've found their input very helpful. And this is right down their alley.

John: Yes, you're right. That's a good idea. Let's get our Management Science Group working on this issue. Bill, will you coordinate with them?

Bill: Sure.

John: And tell them that we want them to report their findings back to us within a month.

Bill: Will do.

The meeting ends.

The Management Science Group Begins Its Work

At the outset, the Management Science Group spends considerable time with Bill Tasto to clarify the general problem and specific issues that management wants addressed. A particular concern is to ascertain the appropriate objective for the problem from management's viewpoint. Bill points out that John Hill posed the issue as determining which mixture of the two products is going to be most profitable for the company.

Therefore, with Bill's concurrence, the group defines the key issue to be addressed as follows.

> **Question:** Which combination of *production rates* (the number of units produced per week) for the two new products would *maximize the total profit* from both of them?

The group also concludes that it should consider *all* possible combinations of production rates of both new products permitted by the available production capacities in the three plants. For example, one alternative (despite Jim Baker's and Ann Lester's objections) is to forgo producing one of the products for now (thereby setting its production rate equal to zero) in order to produce as much as possible of the other product. (We must not neglect the possibility that maximum profit from both products might be attained by producing none of one and as much as possible of the other.)

The Management Science Group next identifies the information it needs to gather to conduct this study:

1. Available production capacity in each of the plants.

2. How much of the production capacity in each plant would be needed by each product.

3. Profitability of each product.

Concrete data are not available for any of these quantities, so estimates have to be made. Estimating these quantities requires enlisting the help of key personnel in other units of the company.

Bill Tasto's staff develops the estimates that involve production capacities. Specifically, the staff estimates that the production facilities in Plant 1 needed for the new kind of doors will be available approximately four hours per week. (The rest of the time Plant 1 will continue with current products.) The production facilities in Plant 2 will be available for the new kind of windows about 12 hours per week. The facilities needed for both products in Plant 3 will be available approximately 18 hours per week.

The amount of each plant's production capacity actually used by each product depends on its production rate. It is estimated that each door will require one hour of production time in Plant 1 and three hours in Plant 3. For each window, about two hours will be needed in Plant 2 and two hours in Plant 3.

By analyzing the cost data and the pricing decision, the Accounting Department estimates the profit from the two products. The projection is that the profit per unit will be $300 for the doors and $500 for the windows.

Table 2.1 summarizes the data now gathered.

The Management Science Group recognizes this as being a classic **product-mix problem** (just like the one at Ponderosa Industrial described earlier). Therefore, the next step is to develop a *mathematical model*—that is, a *linear programming model*—to represent the problem so that it can be solved mathematically. The next four sections focus on how to develop this

TABLE 2.1
Data for the Wyndor Glass Co. Product-Mix Problem

	Production Time Used for Each Unit Produced		
Plant	**Doors**	**Windows**	**Available per Week**
1	1 hour	0	4 hours
2	0	2 hours	12 hours
3	3 hours	2 hours	18 hours
Unit profit	$300	$500	

model and then how to solve it to find the most profitable mix between the two products, assuming the estimates in Table 2.1 are accurate.

Review
Questions

1. What is the market niche being filled by the Wyndor Glass Co.?
2. What were the two issues addressed by management?
3. The Management Science Group was asked to help analyze which of these issues?
4. How did this group define the key issue to be addressed?
5. What information did the group need to gather to conduct its study?

2.3   FORMULATING THE WYNDOR PROBLEM ON A SPREADSHEET

Spreadsheets provide a powerful and intuitive tool for displaying and analyzing many management problems. We now will focus on how to do this for the Wyndor problem with the popular spreadsheet package Microsoft Excel.[4]

Formulating a Spreadsheet Model for the Wyndor Problem

Excel Tip: Cell shading and borders can be added either by using the borders button and the fill color button on the formatting toolbar or by choosing Cells from the Format menu and then selecting the Patterns tab and/or the Borders tab.

Excel Tip: See the margin notes near the end of Section 1.2 for several tips on adding range names.

These are the three key questions to be addressed in formulating any spreadsheet model.

Figure 2.1 displays the Wyndor problem by transferring the data in Table 2.1 onto a spreadsheet. (Columns E and F are being reserved for later entries described below.) We will refer to the cells showing the data as **data cells.** To distinguish the data cells from other cells in the spreadsheet, they are shaded light blue. The spreadsheet is made easier to interpret by using range names. The data cells in the Wyndor Glass Co. problem are given the range names Unit-Profit (C4:D4), HoursUsedPer UnitProduced (C7:D9), and HoursAvailable (G7:G9). To enter a range name, first select the range of cells, then choose Name\Define from the Insert menu and type a range name (or click in the name box on the left of the formula bar above the spreadsheet and type a name).

Three questions need to be answered to begin the process of using the spreadsheet to formulate a mathematical model (in this case, a **linear programming model**) for the problem.

1. What are the *decisions* to be made?
2. What are the *constraints* on these decisions?
3. What is the overall *measure of performance* for these decisions?

The preceding section described how Wyndor's Management Science Group spent considerable time with Bill Tasto, vice president for manufacturing, to clarify management's view of their problem. These discussions provided the following answers to these questions.

1. The decisions to be made are the *production rates* (number of units produced per week) for the two new products.

FIGURE 2.1
The initial spreadsheet for the Wyndor problem after transferring the data in Table 2.1 into data cells.

	A	B	C	D	E	F	G
1			Wyndor Glass Co. Product-Mix Problem				
2							
3			**Doors**	**Windows**			
4		Unit Profit	$300	$500			
5							Hours
6			Hours Used per Unit Produced				Available
7		Plant 1	1	0			4
8		Plant 2	0	2			12
9		Plant 3	3	2			18

[4]Other spreadsheet packages with similar capabilities also are available, and the basic ideas presented here are still applicable.

Some students find it helpful to organize their thoughts by verbally writing out their answers to the three key questions before beginning to formulate the spreadsheet model.

2. The constraints on these decisions are that the number of hours of production time used per week by the two products in the respective plants cannot exceed the number of hours available.

3. The overall measure of performance for these decisions is the *total profit* per week from the two products.

Figure 2.2 shows how these answers can be incorporated into the spreadsheet. Based on the first answer, the *production rates* of the two products are placed in cells C12 and D12 to locate them in the columns for these products just under the data cells. Since we don't know yet what these production rates should be, they are just entered as zeroes in Figure 2.2. (Actually, any trial solution can be entered, although *negative* production rates should be excluded since they are impossible.) Later, these numbers will be changed while seeking the best mix of production rates. Therefore, these cells containing the decisions to be made are called **changing cells** (or *adjustable cells*). To highlight the changing cells, they are shaded light tan and have a border. (In the spreadsheet files contained in MS Courseware, the changing cells appear in bright yellow on a color monitor.) The changing cells are given the range name UnitsProduced (C12:D12).

The changing cells contain the decisions to be made.

Using the second answer, the total number of hours of production time used per week by the two products in the respective plants is entered in cells E7, E8, and E9, just to the right of the corresponding data cells. The total number of production hours depends on the production rates of the two products, so this total is zero when the production rates are zero. With positive production rates, the total number of production hours used per week in a plant is the sum of the production hours used per week by the respective products. The production hours used by a product is the number of hours needed for *each* unit of the product *times* the number of units being produced. Therefore, when positive numbers are entered in cells C12 and D12 for the number of doors and windows to produce per week, the data in cells C7:D9 are used to calculate the total production hours per week as follows:

Production hours in Plant 1 $= 1(\text{\# of doors}) + 0(\text{\# of windows})$

Production hours in Plant 2 $= 0(\text{\# of doors}) + 2(\text{\# of windows})$

Production hours in Plant 3 $= 3(\text{\# of doors}) + 2(\text{\# of windows})$

(The colon in C7:D9 is Excel shorthand for the *range from* C7 *to* D9; that is, the entire block of cells in column C or D and in row 7, 8, or 9.) Consequently, the Excel equations for the three cells in column E are

E7 $=$ C7*C12 $+$ D7*D12

E8 $=$ C8*C12 $+$ D8*D12

E9 $=$ C9*C12 $+$ D9*D12

FIGURE 2.2

The complete spreadsheet for the Wyndor problem with an initial trial solution (both production rates equal to zero) entered into the changing cells (C12 and D12).

	A	B	C	D	E	F	G
1		**Wyndor Glass Co. Product-Mix Problem**					
2							
3			**Doors**	**Windows**			
4		Unit Profit	$300	$500			
5					Hours		Hours
6			Hours Used per Unit Produced		Used		Available
7		Plant 1	1	0	0	≤	4
8		Plant 2	0	2	0	≤	12
9		Plant 3	3	2	0	≤	18
10							
11			**Doors**	**Windows**			**Total Profit**
12		Units Produced	0	0			$0

Output cells show quantities that are calculated from the changing cells.

where each asterisk denotes multiplication. Since each of these cells provides output that depends on the changing cells (C12 and D12), they are called **output cells.**

Notice that each of the equations for the output cells involves the sum of two products. There is a function in Excel called SUMPRODUCT that will sum up the product of each of the individual terms in two different ranges of cells when the two ranges have the same number of rows and the same number of columns. Each product being summed is the product of a term in the first range and the term in the corresponding location in the second range. For example, consider the two ranges, C7:D7 and C12:D12, so that each range has one row and two columns. In this case, SUMPRODUCT (C7:D7, C12:D12) takes each of the individual terms in the range C7:D7, multiplies them by the corresponding term in the range C12:D12, and then sums up these individual products, just as shown in the first equation above. Applying the range name for UnitsProduced (C12:D12), the formula becomes SUMPRODUCT(C7:D7, UnitsProduced). Although optional with such short equations, this function is especially handy as a shortcut for entering longer equations.

The SUMPRODUCT function is used extensively in linear programming spreadsheet models.

Next, $\leq$ signs are entered in cells F7, F8, and F9 to indicate that each total value to their left cannot be allowed to exceed the corresponding number in column G. The spreadsheet still will allow you to enter trial solutions that violate the $\leq$ signs. However, these $\leq$ signs serve as a reminder that such trial solutions need to be rejected if no changes are made in the numbers in column G.

Finally, since the answer to the third question is that the overall measure of performance is the total profit from the two products, this profit (per week) is entered in cell G12, Much like the numbers in column E, it is the sum of products. Since cells C4 and D4 give the profit from *each* door and window produced, the total profit per week from these products is

$$\text{Profit} = \$300(\# \text{ of doors}) + \$500(\# \text{ of windows})$$

Hence, the equation for cell G12 is

$$\text{G12} = \text{SUMPRODUCT(C4:D4, C12:D12)}$$

Utilizing range names of TotalProfit (G12), UnitProfit (C4:D4), and UnitsProduced (C12:D12), this equation becomes

$$\text{TotalProfit} = \text{SUMPRODUCT(UnitProfit, UnitsProduced)}$$

This is a good example of the benefit of using range names for making the resulting equation easier to interpret.

TotalProfit (G12) is a special kind of output cell. It is the particular cell that is being targeted to be made as large as possible when making decisions regarding production rates. Therefore, TotalProfit (G12) is referred to as the **target cell** (or *objective cell*). The target cell is shaded a darker tan than the changing cells and is further distinguished by having a heavy border. (In the spreadsheet files contained in MS Courseware, this cell appears in orange on a color monitor.)

The target cell contains the overall measure of performance for the decisions in the changing cells.

The bottom of Figure 2.3 summarizes all the formulas that need to be entered in the Hours Used column and in the Total Profit cell. Also shown is a summary of the range names (in alphabetical order) and the corresponding cell addresses.

This completes the formulation of the spreadsheet model for the Wyndor problem.

With this formulation, it becomes easy to analyze any trial solution for the production rates. Each time production rates are entered in cells C12 and D12, Excel immediately calculates the output cells for hours used and total profit. For example, Figure 2.4 shows the spreadsheet when the production rates are set at four doors per week and three windows per week. Cell G12 shows that this yields a total profit of $2,700 per week. Also note that E7 = G7, E8 < G8, and E9 = G9, so the $\leq$ signs in column F are all satisfied. Thus, this trial solution is *feasible*. However, it would *not* be feasible to further increase both production rates, since this would cause E7 > G7 and E9 > G9.

Does this trial solution provide the best mix of production rates? Not necessarily. It might be possible to further increase the total profit by simultaneously increasing one production rate and decreasing the other. However, it is not necessary to continue using trial and error to explore such possibilities. We shall describe in Section 2.6 how the Excel Solver can be used to quickly find the best (optimal) solution.

FIGURE 2.3

The spreadsheet model for the Wyndor problem, including the formulas for the target cell TotalProfit (G12) and the other output cells in column E, where the objective is to maximize the target cell.

	A	B	C	D	E	F	G
1		**Wyndor Glass Co. Product-Mix Problem**					
2							
3			**Doors**	**Windows**			
4		Unit Profit	$300	$500			
5					Hours		Hours
6			Hours Used per Unit Produced		Used		Available
7		Plant 1	1	0	0	≤	4
8		Plant 2	0	2	0	≤	12
9		Plant 3	3	2	0	≤	18
10							
11			**Doors**	**Windows**			**Total Profit**
12		Units Produced	0	0			$0

Range Name	Cell
HoursAvailable	G7:G9
HoursUsed	E7:E9
HoursUsedPerUnitProduced	C7:D9
TotalProfit	G12
UnitProfit	C4:D4
UnitsProduced	C12:D12

	E
5	Hours
6	Used
7	=SUMPRODUCT(C7:D7, UnitsProduced)
8	=SUMPRODUCT(C8:D8, UnitsProduced)
9	=SUMPRODUCT(C9:D9, UnitsProduced)

	G
11	Total Profit
12	=SUMPRODUCT(UnitProfit, UnitsProduced)

FIGURE 2.4

The spreadsheet for the Wyndor problem with a new trial solution entered into the changing cells, UnitsProduced (C12:D12).

	A	B	C	D	E	F	G
1		**Wyndor Glass Co. Product-Mix Problem**					
2							
3			**Doors**	**Windows**			
4		Unit Profit	$300	$500			
5					Hours		Hours
6			Hours Used per Unit Produced		Used		Available
7		Plant 1	1	0	4	≤	4
8		Plant 2	0	2	6	≤	12
9		Plant 3	3	2	18	≤	18
10							
11			**Doors**	**Windows**			**Total Profit**
12		Units Produced	4	3			$2,700

This Spreadsheet Model Is a Linear Programming Model

The spreadsheet model displayed in Figure 2.3 is an example of a *linear programming* model. The reason is that it possesses all the following characteristics.

Characteristics of a Linear Programming Model on a Spreadsheet

1. Decisions need to be made on the levels of a number of activities, so *changing cells* are used to display these levels. (The two activities for the Wyndor problem are the production of the two new products, so the changing cells display the number of units produced per week for each of these products.)

2. These activity levels can have any value (including fractional values) that satisfy a number of constraints. (The production rates for Wyndor's new products are restricted only by the constraints on the number of hours of production time available in the three plants.)

3. Each **constraint** describes a restriction on the feasible values for the levels of the activities, where a constraint commonly is displayed by having an output cell on the left, a mathematical sign ($\leq$, $\geq$, or $=$) in the middle, and a data cell on the right. (Wyndor's three constraints involving hours available in the plants are displayed in Figures 2.2–2.4 by having output cells in column E, $\leq$ signs in column F, and data cells in column G.)

4. The decisions on activity levels are to be based on an overall measure of performance, which is entered in the *target cell.* The objective is to either *maximize* the target cell or *minimize* the target cell, depending on the nature of the measure of performance. (Wyndor's overall measure of performance is the total profit per week from the two new products, so this measure has been entered in the target cell G12, where the objective is to maximize this target cell.)

5. The Excel equation for each *output cell* (including the target cell) can be expressed as a SUMPRODUCT function,[5] where each term in the sum is the product of a *data cell* and a *changing cell.* (The bottom of Figure 2.3 shows how a SUMPRODUCT function is used for each output cell for the Wyndor problem.)

Characteristics 2 and 5 are key ones for differentiating a linear programming model from other kinds of mathematical models that can be formulated on a spreadsheet.

Characteristic 2 rules out situations where the activity levels need to have *integer* values. For example, such a situation would arise in the Wyndor problem if the decisions to be made were the *total* numbers of doors and windows to produce (which must be integers) rather than the numbers per week (which can have fractional values since a door or window can be started in one week and completed in the next week).

Characteristic 5 prohibits those cases where the Excel equation for an output cell cannot be expressed as a SUMPRODUCT function. To illustrate such a case, suppose that the weekly profit from producing Wyndor's new windows can be *more* than doubled by doubling the production rate because of economies in marketing larger amounts. This would mean that the Excel equation for the target cell would need to be more complicated than a SUMPRODUCT function.

Consideration of how to formulate models for these more complicated kinds of situations will be deferred to Chapters 9 and 10.

Summary of the Formulation Procedure

The procedure used to formulate a linear programming model on a spreadsheet for the Wyndor problem can be adapted to many other problems as well. Here is a summary of the steps involved in the procedure.

1. Gather the data for the problem (such as summarized in Table 2.1 for the Wyndor problem).

2. Enter the data into *data cells* on a spreadsheet.

3. Identify the decisions to be made on the levels of activities and designate *changing cells* for displaying these decisions.

4. Identify the constraints on these decisions and introduce *output cells* as needed to specify these constraints.

5. Choose the overall measure of performance to be entered into the *target cell.*

6. Use a SUMPRODUCT function to enter the appropriate value into each output cell (including the target cell).

---

[5]There also are some special situations where a SUM function can be used instead because all the numbers that would have gone into the corresponding data cells are 1's. Chapter 6 will show some examples.

This procedure does not spell out the details of how to set up the spreadsheet. There generally are alternative ways of doing this rather than a single "right" way. One of the great strengths of spreadsheets is their flexibility for dealing with a wide variety of problems.

Review
Questions

1. What are the three questions that need to be answered to begin the process of formulating a linear programming model on a spreadsheet?
2. What are the roles for the data cells, the changing cells, the output cells, and the target cell when formulating such a model?
3. What is the form of the Excel equation for each output cell (including the target cell) when formulating such a model?

2.4   THE MATHEMATICAL MODEL IN THE SPREADSHEET

A linear programming model can be formulated either as a spreadsheet model or as an algebraic model.

There are two widely used methods for formulating a linear programming model. One is to formulate it directly on a spreadsheet, as described in the preceding section. The other is to use algebra to present the model. The two versions of the model are equivalent. The only difference is whether the language of spreadsheets or the language of algebra is used to describe the model. Both versions have their advantages, and it can be helpful to be bilingual. For example, the two versions lead to different, but complementary, ways of analyzing problems like the Wyndor problem (as discussed in the next two sections). Since this book emphasizes the spreadsheet approach, we will only briefly describe the algebraic approach.

Formulating the Wyndor Model Algebraically

The reasoning for the algebraic approach is similar to that for the spreadsheet approach. In fact, except for making entries on a spreadsheet, the initial steps are just as described in the preceding section for the Wyndor problem.

1. Gather the relevant data (Table 2.1 in Section 2.2).
2. Identify the decisions to be made (the production rates for the two new products).
3. Identify the constraints on these decisions (the production time used in the respective plants cannot exceed the amount available).
4. Identify the overall measure of performance for these decisions (the total profit from the two products).
5. Convert the verbal description of the constraints and measure of performance into quantitative expressions in terms of the data and decisions (see below).

Table 2.1 indicates that the number of hours of production time available per week for the two new products in the respective plants are 4, 12, and 18. Using the data in this table for the number of hours used per door or window produced then leads to the following quantitative expressions for the constraints:

$$\text{Plant 1:} \quad (\text{\# of doors}) \qquad\qquad\qquad \leq 4$$

$$\text{Plant 2:} \qquad\qquad\qquad 2(\text{\# of windows}) \leq 12$$

$$\text{Plant 3:} \quad 3(\text{\# of doors}) + 2(\text{\# of windows}) \leq 18$$

In addition, negative production rates are impossible, so two other constraints on the decisions are

$$(\text{\# of doors}) \geq 0 \quad (\text{\# of windows}) \geq 0$$

The overall measure of performance has been identified as the total profit from the two products. Since Table 2.1 gives the unit profits for doors and windows as \$300 and \$500, respectively, the expression obtained in the preceding section for the total profit per week from these products is

$$\text{Profit} = \$300(\text{\# of doors}) + \$500(\text{\# of windows})$$

The objective is to make the decisions (number of doors and number of windows) so as to maximize this profit, subject to satisfying all the constraints identified above.

To state this objective in a compact algebraic model, we introduce algebraic symbols to represent the measure of performance and the decisions. Let

P = Profit (total profit per week from the two products, in dollars)

D = # of doors (number of the special new doors to be produced per week)

W = # of windows (number of the special new windows to be produced per week)

Substituting these symbols into the above expressions for the constraints and the measure of performance (and dropping the dollar signs in the latter expression), the linear programming model for the Wyndor problem now can be written in algebraic form as shown below.

Algebraic Model

Choose the values of D and W so as to maximize

$$P = 300D + 500W$$

subject to satisfying all the following constraints:

$$D \leq 4$$
$$2W \leq 12$$
$$3D + 2W \leq 18$$

and

$$D \geq 0 \qquad W \geq 0$$

Terminology for Linear Programming Models

Much of the terminology of algebraic models also is sometimes used with spreadsheet models. Here are the key terms for both kinds of models in the context of the Wyndor problem.

1. D and W (or C12 and D12 in Figure 2.3) are the **decision variables.**

2. $300D + 500W$ [or SUMPRODUCT (UnitProfit, UnitsProduced)] is the **objective function.**

3. P (or G12) is the *value of the objective function* (or *objective value* for short).

4. $D \geq 0$ and $W \geq 0$ (or C12 $\geq$ 0 and D12 $\geq$ 0) are called the **nonnegativity constraints** (or *nonnegativity conditions*).

5. The other constraints are referred to as **functional constraints** (or *structural constraints*).

6. The **parameters** of the model are the constants in the algebraic model (the numbers in the data cells).

7. *Any* choice of values for the decision variables (regardless of how desirable or undesirable the choice) is called a **solution** for the model.

8. A **feasible solution** is one that satisfies all the constraints, whereas an **infeasible solution** violates at least one constraint.

9. The *best* feasible solution, the one that maximizes P (or G12), is called the **optimal solution.**

Comparisons

Management scientists often use algebraic models, but managers generally prefer spreadsheet models.

So what are the relative advantages of algebraic models and spreadsheet models? An algebraic model provides a very concise and explicit statement of the problem. Sophisticated software packages that can solve huge problems generally are based on algebraic models because of both their compactness and their ease of use in rescaling the size of a problem. Management science practitioners with an extensive mathematical background find algebraic models very useful. For others, however, spreadsheet models are far more intuitive. Many very intelligent people (including many managers and business students) find algebraic models overly abstract. Spreadsheets lift this "algebraic curtain." Both managers and business students training to be managers generally live with spreadsheets, not algebraic models. Therefore, the emphasis throughout this book is on spreadsheet models.

Review
Questions

1. When formulating a linear programming model, what are the initial steps that are the same with either a spreadsheet formulation or an algebraic formulation?

2. When formulating a linear programming model algebraically, algebraic symbols need to be introduced to represent which kinds of quantities in the model?

3. What are decision variables for a linear programming model? The objective function? Nonnegativity constraints? Functional constraints?

4. What is meant by a feasible solution for the model? An optimal solution?

2.5 THE GRAPHICAL METHOD FOR SOLVING TWO-VARIABLE PROBLEMS

graphical method
The graphical method provides helpful intuition about linear programming.

Linear programming problems having only two decision variables, like the Wyndor problem, can be solved by a **graphical method**.

Although this method cannot be used to solve problems with more than two decision variables (and most linear programming problems have far more than two), it still is well worth learning. The procedure provides geometric intuition about linear programming and what it is trying to achieve. This intuition is helpful in analyzing larger problems that cannot be solved directly by the graphical method.

It is more convenient to apply the graphical method to the *algebraic version* of the linear programming model rather than the spreadsheet version. We shall illustrate the method by using the algebraic model obtained for the Wyndor problem in the preceding section. For this purpose, keep in mind that

D = Production rate for the special new doors (the number in changing cell C12 of the spreadsheet)

W = Production rate for the special new windows (the number in changing cell D12 of the spreadsheet)

Displaying Solutions as Points on a Graph

The key to the graphical method is the fact that possible solutions can be displayed as points on a two-dimensional graph that has a horizontal axis giving the value of D and a vertical axis giving the value of W. Figure 2.5 shows some sample points.

Notation: Either $(D, W) = (2, 3)$ or just $(2, 3)$ refers to the solution where $D = 2$ and $W = 3$, as well as to the corresponding point in the graph. Similarly, $(D, W) = (4, 6)$ means $D = 4$ and $W = 6$, whereas the origin $(0, 0)$ means $D = 0$ and $W = 0$.

To find the optimal solution (the best feasible solution), we first need to display graphically where the feasible solutions are. To do this, we must consider each constraint, identify the solutions graphically that are permitted by that constraint, and then combine this information to identify the solutions permitted by all the constraints.

To begin, the constraint $D \geq 0$ implies that consideration must be limited to points that lie on or to the right of the W axis in Figure 2.5. Similarly, the constraint $W \geq 0$ restricts consideration to the points on or above the D axis. Combining these two facts, the region of interest at this juncture is the one shaded in on Figure 2.6. (This region also includes *larger* values of D and W than can be shown shaded in the available space.)

FIGURE 2.5

Graph showing the points $(D, W) = (2, 3)$ and $(D, W) = (4, 6)$ for the Wyndor Glass Co. product-mix problem.

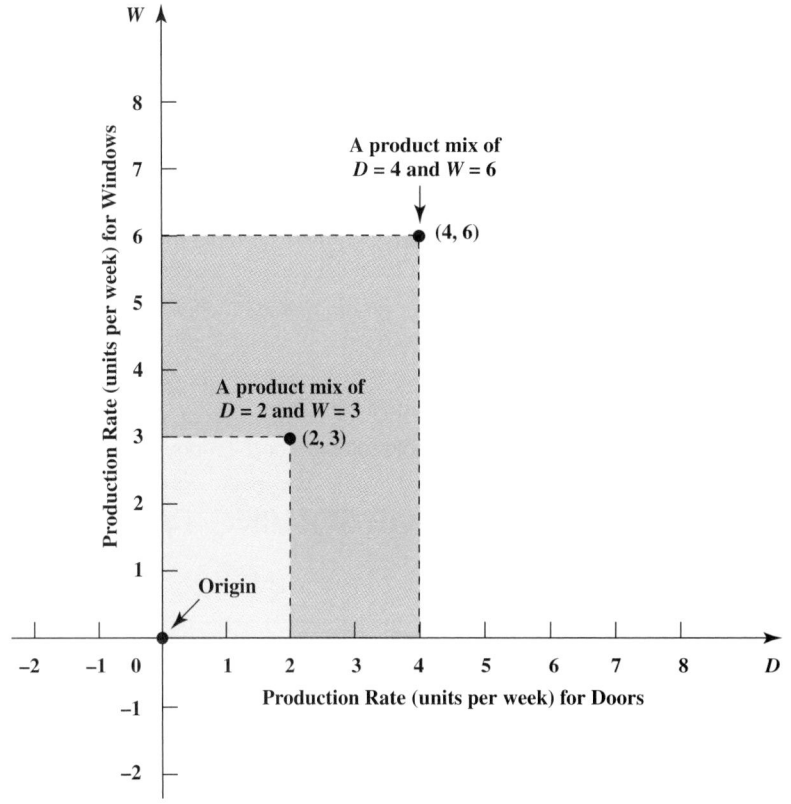

FIGURE 2.6

Graph showing that the constraints $D \geq 0$ and $W \geq 0$ rule out solutions for the Wyndor Glass Co. product-mix problem that are to the left of the vertical axis or under the horizontal axis.

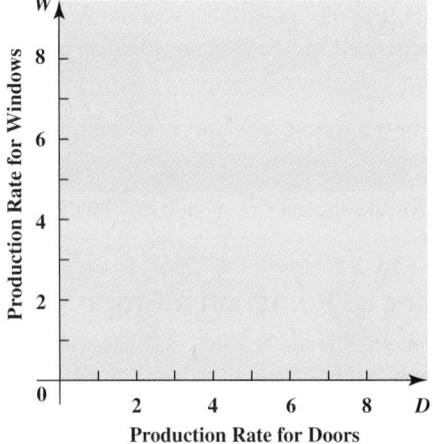

Graphing Nonnegative Solutions Permitted by Each Functional Constraint

We now will look individually at the nonnegative solutions that are permitted by each functional constraint. Later, we will combine all these constraints.

Let us begin with the first functional constraint, $D \leq 4$, which limits the usage of Plant 1 for producing the special new doors to a maximum of four hours per week. The solutions permitted by this constraint are those that lie on, or to the left of, the vertical line that intercepts the D axis at $D = 4$ (so $D = 4$ is the equation for the line). Combining this permissible region with the one given in Figure 2.6 yields the shaded region shown in Figure 2.7.

The second functional constraint, $2W \leq 12$, has a similar effect, except now the boundary of its permissible region is given by a *horizontal* line with the equation, $2W = 12$ (or $W = 6$), as

FIGURE 2.7

Graph showing that the nonnegative solutions permitted by the constraint $D \leq 4$ lie between the vertical axis and the line where $D = 4$.

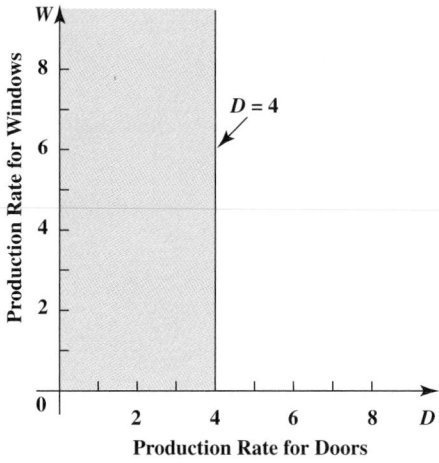

FIGURE 2.8

Graph showing that the nonnegative solutions permitted by the constraint $2W \leq 12$ must lie between the horizontal axis and the constraint boundary line whose equation is $2W = 12$.

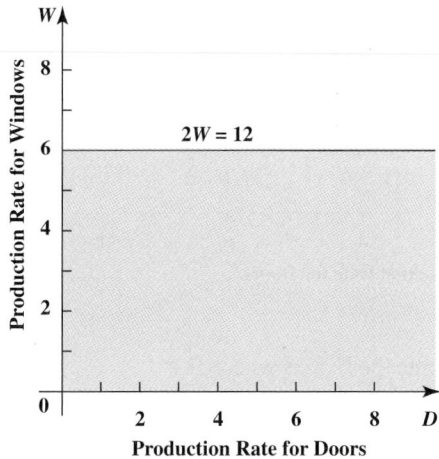

shown in Figure 2.8. The line forming the boundary of what is permitted by a constraint is sometimes referred to as a **constraint boundary line,** and its equation may be called a **constraint boundary equation.** Frequently, a *constraint boundary line* is identified by its equation.

For each of the first two functional constraints, $D \leq 4$ and $2W \leq 12$, note that the equation for the constraint boundary line ($D = 4$ and $2W = 12$, respectively) is obtained by replacing the inequality sign with an equality sign. For *any* constraint with an inequality sign (whether a functional constraint or a nonnegativity constraint), the general rule for obtaining its constraint boundary equation is to substitute an equality sign for the inequality sign.

We now need to consider one more functional constraint, $3D + 2W \leq 18$. Its constraint boundary equation

$$3D + 2W = 18$$

includes both variables, so the boundary line it represents is neither a vertical line nor a horizontal line. Therefore, the boundary line must intercept (cross through) both axes somewhere. But where?

> When a constraint boundary line is neither a vertical line nor a horizontal line, the line *intercepts* the D axis at the point on the line where $W = 0$. Similarly, the line *intercepts* the W axis at the point on the line where $D = 0$.

Hence, the constraint boundary line $3D + 2W = 18$ intercepts the D axis at the point where $W = 0$.

When $W = 0$, $3D + 2W = 18$ becomes $3D = 18$
so the intercept with the D axis is at $D = 6$

For any constraint with an inequality sign, its constraint boundary equation is obtained by replacing the inequality sign by an equality sign.

FIGURE 2.9

Graph showing that the boundary line for the constraint $3D + 2W \leq 18$ intercepts the horizontal axis at $D = 6$ and intercepts the vertical axis at $W = 9$.

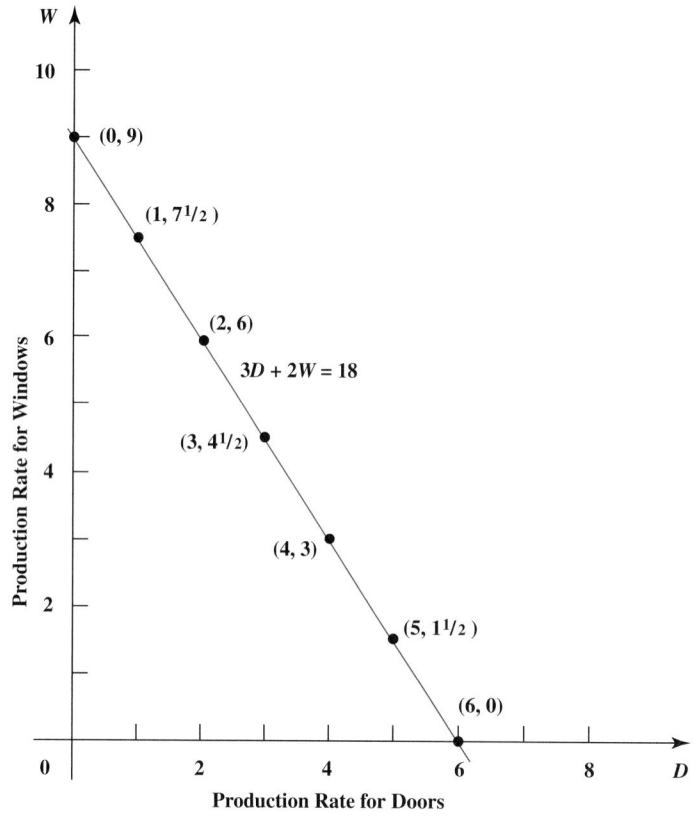

The location of a slanting constraint boundary line is found by identifying where it intercepts each of the two axes.

Similarly, the line intercepts the W axis where $D = 0$.

When $D = 0$, $\quad 3D + 2W = 18 \quad$ becomes $2W = 18$
so the intercept with the D axis is at $\qquad W = 9$

Consequently, the constraint boundary line is the line that passes through these two intercept points, as shown in Figure 2.9.

Another way to find this constraint boundary line is to change the form of the constraint boundary equation so that it expresses W in terms of D.

$$3D + 2W = 18 \quad \text{implies} \quad 2W = -3D + 18$$

so

$$W = -\frac{3}{2}D + 9$$

This form, $W = -\frac{3}{2}D + 9$, is called the **slope-intercept form** of the constraint boundary equation.

The constant term, 9, automatically is the intercept of the line with the W axis (since $W = 9$ when $D = 0$). The coefficient of D, $-\frac{3}{2}$, is the *slope* of the line.

The **slope of a line** is the change in W when D is increased by 1.

For example, consider the series of points shown on the constraint boundary line in Figure 2.9 when moving from (0,9) toward (6,0). Note how W changes by the fixed amount $-\frac{3}{2}$ each time D is increased by 1.

This derivation of the *slope-intercept form* demonstrates that the *only* numbers in the equation $3D + 2W = 18$ that determine the slope of the line are 3 and 2, the coefficients of D and W. Therefore, if the equation $3D + 2W = 18$ were to be changed *only* by changing the right-hand side (18), the slope of the new line still would be $-\frac{3}{2}$. In other words, the new line would be *parallel* to the original line. To illustrate, suppose that the new equation is $3D + 2W = 12$. Since the original line had an intercept with the W axis of $\frac{18}{2} = 9$, the new parallel line has an

Changing only the right-hand side of a constraint creates *parallel* constraint boundary lines.

FIGURE 2.10

Graph showing that changing only the right-hand side of a constraint (such as $3D + 2W \leq 18$) creates *parallel* constraint boundary lines.

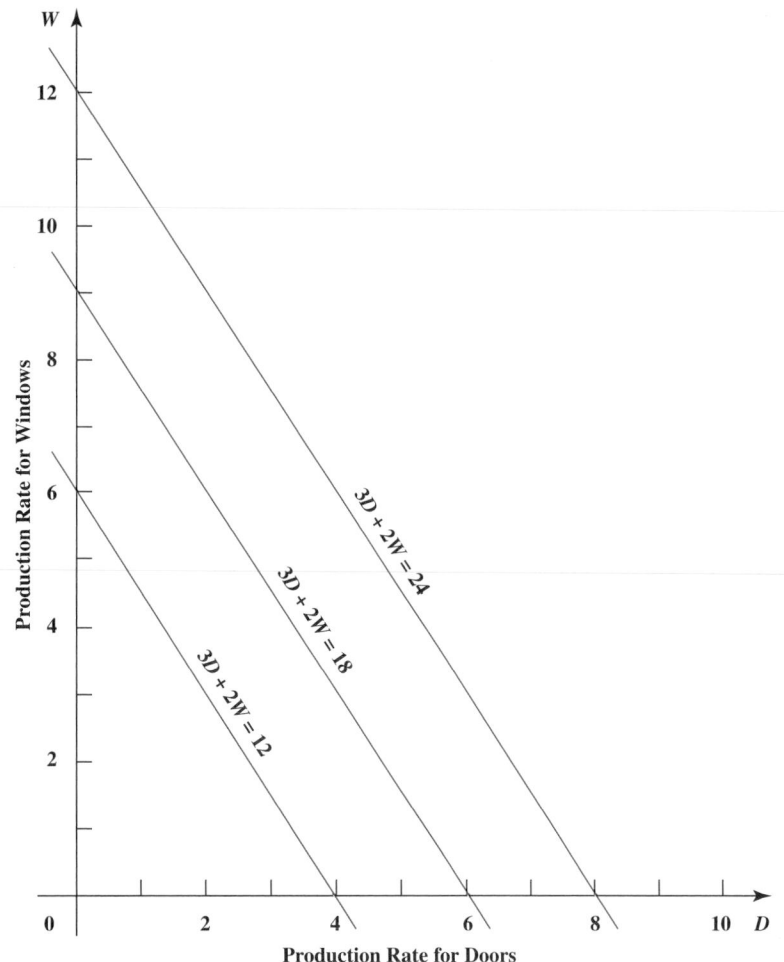

intercept of $^{12}\!/_2 = 6$, so the new line is closer to the origin, as shown in Figure 2.10. This figure also shows the parallel line for the equation, $3D + 2W = 24$, which has an intercept with the W axis of $^{24}\!/_2 = 12$, and so is further from the origin than the original line.

Checking whether (0,0) satisfies a constraint indicates which side of the constraint boundary line satisfies the constraint.

This analysis also shows that the solutions permitted by the constraint $3D + 2W \leq 18$ are those that lie on the *origin* side of the constraint boundary line $3D + 2W = 18$. The easiest way to verify this is to check whether the origin itself, $(D, W) = (0,0)$, satisfies the constraint.[6] If it does, then the permissible region lies on the side of the constraint boundary line where the origin is. Otherwise, it lies on the other side. In this case,

$$3(0) + 2(0) = 0$$

so $(D, W) = (0, 0)$ satisfies

$$3D + 2W \leq 18$$

(In fact, the origin satisfies *any* constraint with a $\leq$ sign and a positive right-hand side.) Therefore, the region permitted by this constraint is the one shown in Figure 2.11.

Graphing the Feasible Region

We now have graphed the region where solutions are permitted by the *individual* constraints in Figures 2.6, 2.7, 2.8, and 2.11. However, a feasible solution for a linear programming problem

---

[6]The one case where using the origin to help determine the permissible region does *not* work is if the constraint boundary line passes through the origin. In this case, any other point *not* lying on this line can be used just like the origin.

FIGURE 2.11

Graph showing that nonnegative solutions permitted by the constraint $3D + 2W \leq 18$ lie within the triangle formed by the two axes and this constraint's boundary line, $3D + 2W = 18$.

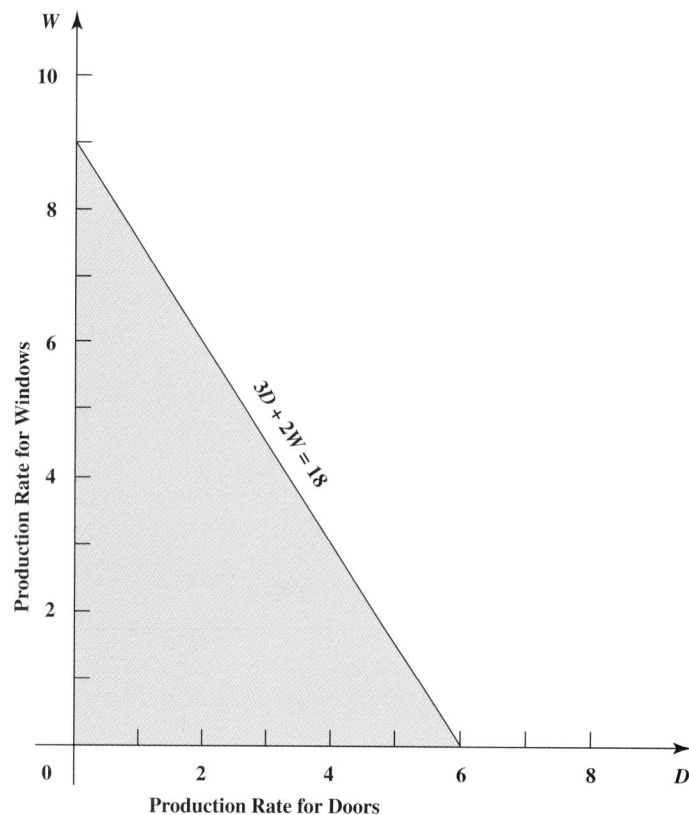

must satisfy *all* the constraints *simultaneously.* To find where these feasible solutions are located, we need to combine all the constraints in one graph and identify the points representing the solutions that are in *every* constraint's permissible region.

Figure 2.12 shows the constraint boundary line for each of the three functional constraints. We also have added arrows to each line to show which side of the line is permitted by the corresponding constraint (as identified in the preceding figures). Note that the nonnegative solutions permitted by each of these constraints lie on the side of the constraint boundary line where the origin is (or on the line itself). Therefore, the *feasible solutions* are those that lie nearer to the origin than *all three* constraint boundary lines (or on the line nearest the origin). The resulting region of feasible solutions, called the **feasible region**, is the shaded portion of Figure 2.12.

feasible region

The points in the feasible region are those that satisfy *every* constraint.

Graphing the Objective Function

Having identified the feasible region, the final step is to find which of these feasible solutions is the best one—the *optimal solution.* For the Wyndor problem, the objective happens to be to *maximize* the total profit per week from the two products (denoted by P). Therefore, we want to find the feasible solution (D, W) that makes the value of the objective function

$$P = 300D + 500W$$

as large as possible.

To accomplish this, we need to be able to locate all the points (D, W) on the graph that give a specified value of the objective function. For example, consider a value of $P = 1,500$ for the objective function. Which points (D, W) give $300D + 500W = 1,500$?

This equation is the equation of a *line.* Just as when plotting constraint boundary lines, the location of this line is found by identifying its intercepts with the two axes. When $W = 0$, this equation yields $D = 5$, and similarly, $W = 3$ when $D = 0$, so these are the two intercepts, as shown in Figure 2.13.

FIGURE 2.12
Graph showing how the feasible region is formed by the constraint boundary lines, where the arrows indicate which side of each line is permitted by the corresponding constraint.

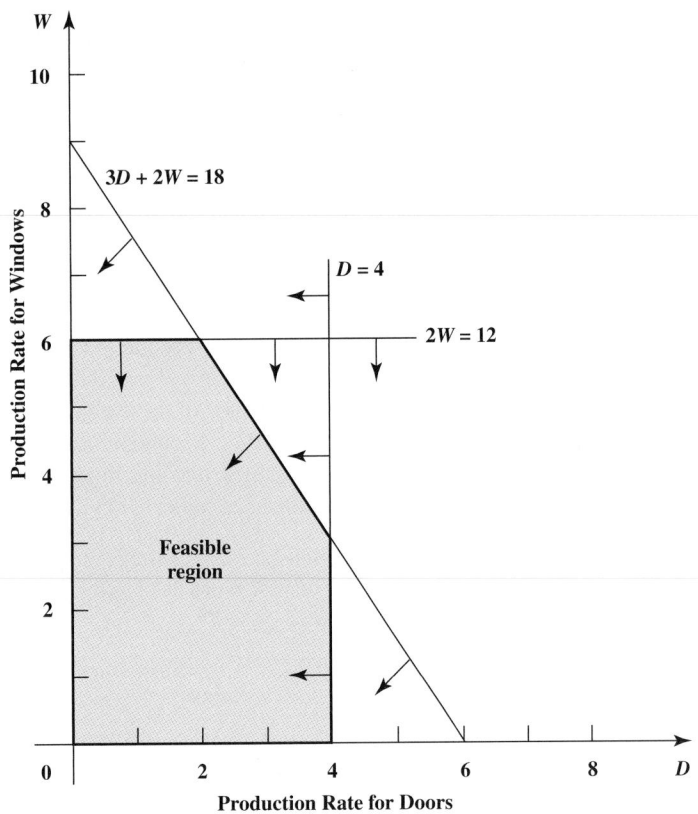

FIGURE 2.13
Graph showing the line containing all the points (D, W) that give a value of $P = 1,500$ for the objective function.

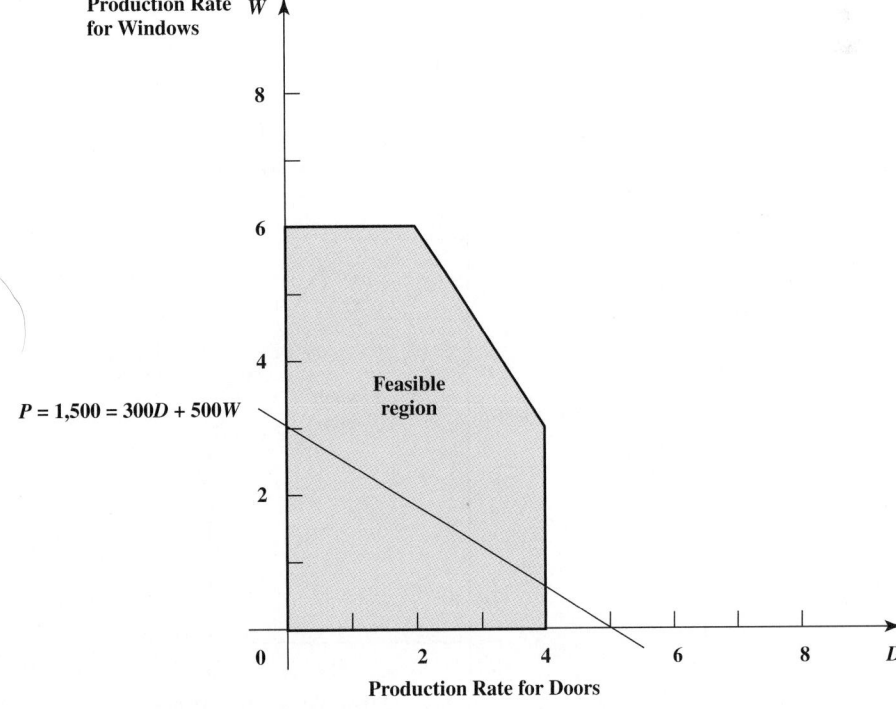

$P = 1,500$ is just one sample value of the objective function. For any other specified value of P, the points (D, W) that give this value of P also lie on a line called an *objective function line.*

> An **objective function line** is a line whose points all have the same value of the objective function.

For the objective function line in Figure 2.13, the points on this line that lie in the feasible region provide alternate ways of achieving an objective function value of $P = 1,500$. Can we do better? Let us try doubling the value of P to $P = 3,000$. The corresponding objective function line

$$300D + 500W = 3,000$$

is shown as the middle line in Figure 2.14. (Ignore the top line for the moment.) Once again, this line includes points in the feasible region, so $P = 3,000$ is achievable.

Let us pause to note two interesting features of these objective function lines for $P = 1,500$ and $P = 3,000$. First, these lines are *parallel.* Second, *doubling* the value of P from 1,500 to 3,000 also *doubles* the value of W at which the line intercepts the W axis from $W = 3$ to $W = 6$. These features are no coincidence, as indicated by the following properties.

> **Key Properties of Objective Function Lines:** All objective function lines for the same problem are *parallel.* Furthermore, the value of W at which an objective function line intercepts the W axis is *proportional* to the value of P.

To see why these properties hold, look at the *slope-intercept form* of an objective function line for the Wyndor problem:

$$W = -\frac{300}{500}D + \frac{1}{500}P$$

which reduces to

$$W = -\frac{3}{5}D + \frac{1}{500}P$$

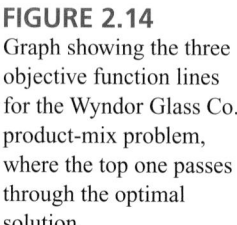

FIGURE 2.14
Graph showing the three objective function lines for the Wyndor Glass Co. product-mix problem, where the top one passes through the optimal solution.

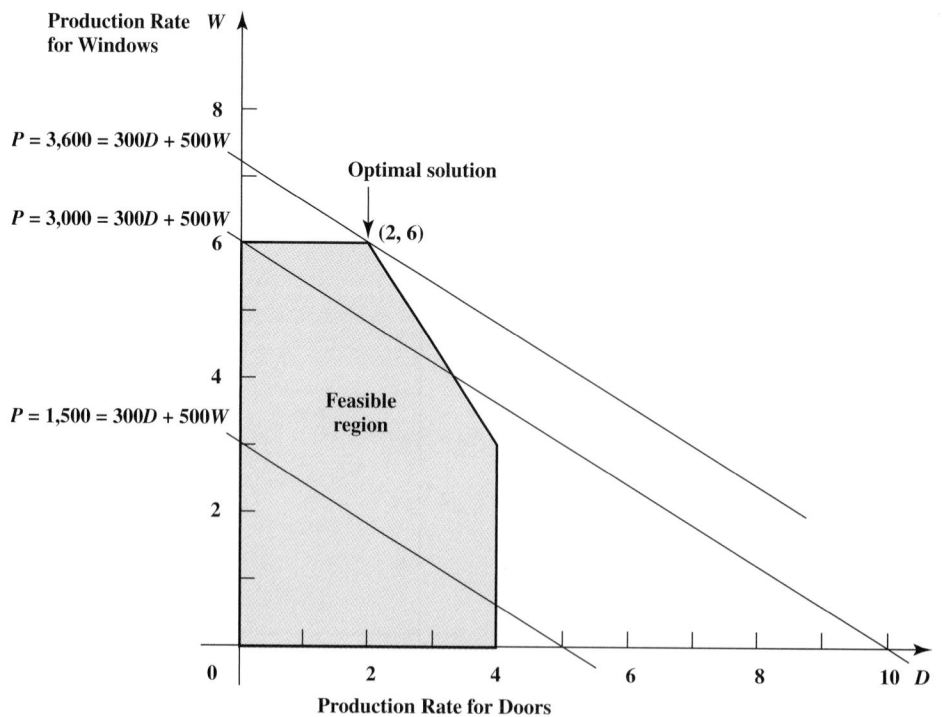

This slope-intercept form indicates that the *slope* of the lines for various values of P always is the *same*, $-3/5$, so these lines are parallel. Furthermore, this form indicates that the value of W at which a line intercepts the W axis is $\frac{1}{500} P$, so this value of W is *proportional* to P.

These key properties of objective function lines suggest the strategy to follow to find the optimal solution. We already have tried $P = 1,500$ and $P = 3,000$ in Figure 2.14 and found that their objective function lines include points in the feasible region. Increasing P again will generate another parallel objective function line farther from the origin. The objective function line of special interest is the one farthest from the origin that still includes a point in the feasible region. This is the third objective function line in Figure 2.14. The point on this line that is in the feasible region, $(D, W) = (2, 6)$, is the optimal solution since no other feasible solution has a larger value of P.

Optimal Solution

$D = 2$ (Produce 2 special new doors per week)

$W = 6$ (Produce 6 special new windows per week)

These values of D and W can be substituted into the objective function to find the value of P.

$$P = 300D + 500W = 300(2) + 500(6) = 3,600$$

A ruler (or any other straight edge) provides a convenient way of finding an optimal solution.

You can graphically implement this strategy for finding the optimal solution by using any straight edge, such as a ruler. Rotate the straight edge in the feasible region until it has the slope of the objective function lines. (You can use any objective function line, such as the $P = 1,500$ line in Figure 2.13, to obtain this slope.) Then push the straight edge with this fixed slope through the feasible region in the direction that increases P. Stop moving the straight edge at the last instant that it still passes through a point in the feasible region. This point is the optimal solution.

In addition to finding the optimal solution, another important use of the graphical method is to perform *what-if analysis* to determine what would happen to the optimal solution if any of the numbers (parameters) in the model change. The graphical approach provides key insights for answering a variety of what-if questions. We will pursue this topic further in Chapter 5.

Check out this module in the Interactive Management Science Modules to learn more about the graphical method.

The Interactive Management Science Modules (available at **www.mhhe.com/hillier2e** or in your CD-ROM) includes a module that is designed to help increase your understanding of the graphical method. This module, called *Graphical Linear Programming and Sensitivity Analysis,* enables you to immediately see the constraint boundary lines and objective function lines that result from any linear programming model with two decision variables. You also can see how the objective function lines lead you to the optimal solution. Another key feature of the module is the ease with which you can perform what-if analysis.

Summary of the Graphical Method

The graphical method can be used to solve any linear programming problem having only two decision variables. The method uses the following steps:

1. Draw the constraint boundary line for each functional constraint. Use the origin (or any point not on the line) to determine which side of the line is permitted by the constraint.

2. Find the feasible region by determining where all constraints are satisfied simultaneously.

3. Determine the slope of one objective function line. All other objective function lines will have the same slope.

4. Move a straight edge with this slope through the feasible region in the direction of improving values of the objective function. Stop at the last instant that the straight edge still passes through a point in the feasible region. This line given by the straight edge is the optimal objective function line.

5. A feasible point on the optimal objective function line is an optimal solution.

1. The graphical method can be used to solve linear programming problems with how many decision variables?

2. What do the axes represent when applying the graphical method to the Wyndor problem?

3. What is a constraint boundary line? A constraint boundary equation?

4. In the slope-intercept form of a constraint boundary equation, which part of the equation gives the *slope* of the constraint boundary line? Which part gives the point on the vertical axis where the line intercepts this axis?

5. What is the easiest way of determining which side of a constraint boundary line is permitted by the constraint?

2.6 USING EXCEL TO SOLVE LINEAR PROGRAMMING PROBLEMS

The graphical method is very useful for gaining geometric intuition about linear programming, but its practical use is severely limited by only being able to solve tiny problems with two decision variables. Another procedure that will solve linear programming problems of any reasonable size is needed. Fortunately, Excel includes a tool called **Solver** that will do this once the spreadsheet model has been formulated as described in Section 2.3. (A more powerful version of Solver, called *Premium Solver for Education* also is available in your MS Courseware.) To access Solver the first time, you need to install it by going to Excel's Add-in menu and adding Solver, after which you will find it in the Tools menu.

Excel Tip: If you select cells by clicking on them, they will first appear in the dialogue box with their cell addresses and with dollar signs (e.g., $C$9:$D$9). You can ignore the dollar signs. Solver eventually will replace both the cell addresses and the dollar signs with the corresponding range name (if a range name has been defined for the given cell addresses), but only after either adding a constraint or closing and reopening the Solver dialogue box.

Figure 2.3 in Section 2.3 shows the spreadsheet model for the Wyndor problem. The values of the decision variables (the production rates for the two products) are in the *changing cells,* UnitsProduced (C12:D12), and the value of the objective function (the total profit per week from the two products) is in the *target cell,* TotalProfit (G12). To get started, an arbitrary trial solution has been entered by placing zeroes in the changing cells. The Solver will then change these to the optimal values after solving the problem.

This procedure is started by choosing Solver in the Tools menu. The Solver dialogue box is shown in Figure 2.15.

Before the Solver can start its work, it needs to know exactly where each component of the model is located on the spreadsheet. You have the choice of typing the range names, typing in the cell addresses, or clicking on the cells in the spreadsheet. Figure 2.15 shows the result of using the first choice, so TotalProfit (rather than G12) has been entered for the target cell and UnitsProduced (rather than the range C12:D12) has been entered for the changing cells. Since the goal is to maximize the target cell, Max also has been selected.

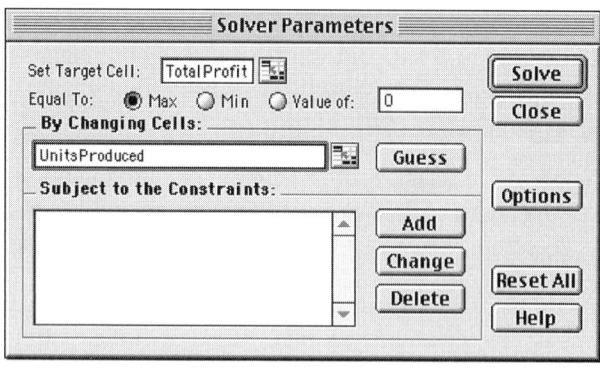

FIGURE 2.15
The Solver dialogue box after specifying which cells in Figure 2.3 are the target cell and the changing cells, plus indicating that the target cell is to be maximized.

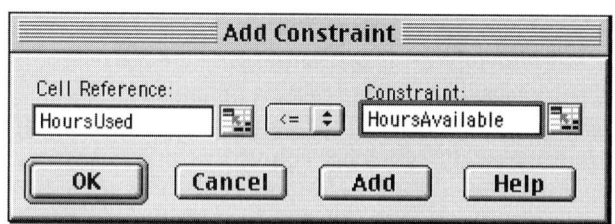

FIGURE 2.16
The Add Constraint dialogue box after specifying that cells E7, E8, and E9 in Figure 2.3 are required to be less than or equal to cells G7, G8, and G9, respectively.

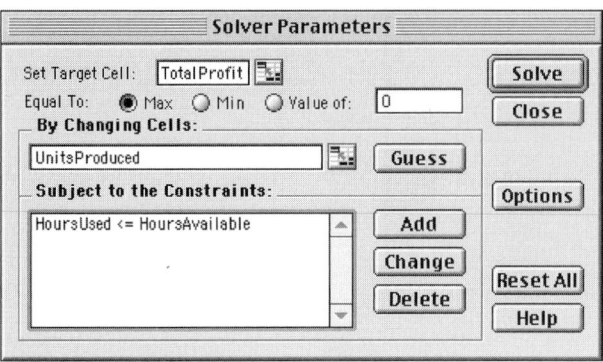

FIGURE 2.17

The Solver dialogue box after specifying the entire model in terms of the spreadsheet.

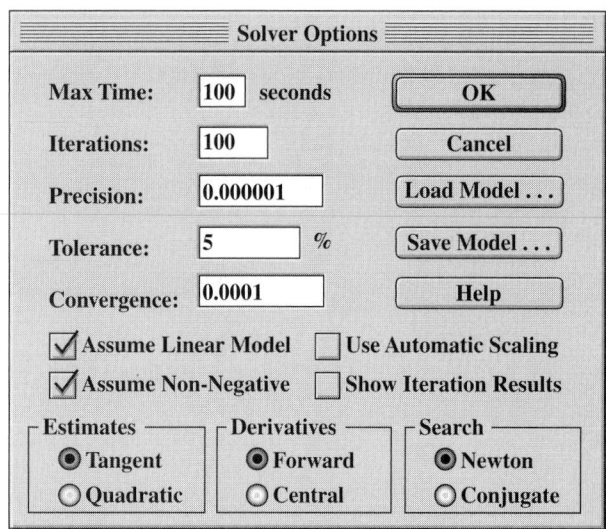

FIGURE 2.18

The Solver Options dialogue box after checking the Assume Linear Model and Assume Non-Negative options to indicate that we wish to solve a linear programming model that has nonnegativity constraints.

The Add Constraint dialogue box is used to specify all the functional constraints.

Next, the cells containing the functional constraints need to be specified. This is done by clicking on the Add button on the Solver dialogue box. This brings up the Add Constraint dialogue box shown in Figure 2.16. The $\le$ signs in cells F7, F8, and F9 of Figure 2.3 are a reminder that the cells in HoursUsed (E7:E9) all need to be less than or equal to the corresponding cells in HoursAvailable (G7:G9). These constraints are specified for the Solver by entering HoursUsed (or E7:E9) on the left-hand side of the Add Constraint dialogue box and HoursAvailable (or G7:G9) on the right-hand side. For the sign between these two sides, there is a menu to choose between $\le$, $=$, or $\ge$, so $\le$ has been chosen. This choice is needed even though $\le$ signs were previously entered in column F of the spreadsheet because the Solver only uses the constraints that are specified with the Add Constraint dialogue box.

If there were more functional constraints to add, you would click on Add to bring up a new Add Constraint dialogue box. However, since there are no more in this example, the next step is to click on OK to go back to the Solver dialogue box.

The Solver dialogue box now summarizes the complete model (see Figure 2.17) in terms of the spreadsheet in Figure 2.3. However, before asking Solver to solve the model, one more step should be taken. Clicking on the Options button brings up the dialogue box shown in Figure 2.18. This box allows you to specify a number of options about how the problem will be solved. The most important of these are the Assume Linear Model option and the Assume Non-Negative option. Be sure that both options are checked as shown in the figure. This tells Solver that the problem is a *linear* programming problem and that nonnegativity constraints are needed for the changing cells to reject negative production rates.[7] Regarding the other options, accepting the default values shown in the figure usually is fine for small problems. Clicking on the OK button then returns you to the Solver dialogue box.

The Assume Linear Model and Assume Non-Negative options specify that the problem is a linear programming problem with nonnegativity constraints.

[7]In older versions of Excel prior to Excel 97, the Assume Non-Negative option is not available, so nonnegativity constraints have to be added with the Add Constraint dialogue box. Not every linear programming model has nonnegativity constraints, but nearly all do. For the unusual model where some of the changing cells have nonnegativity constraints but others do not, these constraints should be added using the Add Constraint dialogue box rather than by choosing the Assume Non-Negative option.

FIGURE 2.19

The Solver Results dialogue box that indicates that an optimal solution has been found.

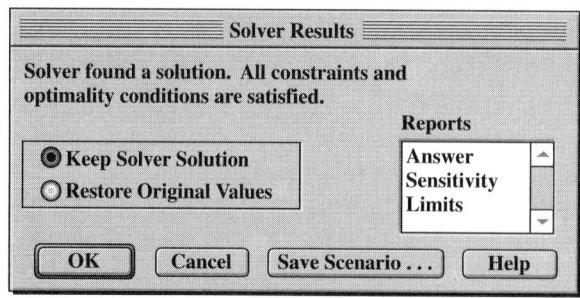

Now you are ready to click on Solve in the Solver dialogue box, which will start the solving of the problem in the background. After a few seconds (for a small problem), Solver will then indicate the results. Typically, it will indicate that it has found an optimal solution, as specified in the Solver Results dialogue box shown in Figure 2.19. If the model has no feasible solutions or no optimal solution, the dialogue box will indicate that instead by stating that "Solver could not find a feasible solution" or that "The Set Cell values do not converge." (Section 17.1 will describe how these possibilities can occur.) The dialogue box also presents the option of generating various reports. One of these (the Sensitivity Report) will be discussed in detail in Chapter 5.

After solving the model, the Solver replaces the original numbers in the changing cells with the optimal numbers, as shown in Figure 2.20. Thus, the optimal solution is to produce two doors per week and six windows per week, just as was found by the graphical method in the preceding section. The spreadsheet also indicates the corresponding number in the target cell (a total profit of $3,600 per week), as well as the numbers in the output cells HoursUsed (E7:E9).

At this point, you might want to check what would happen to the optimal solution if any of the numbers in the data cells were to be changed to other possible values. This is easy to do because Solver saves all the addresses for the target cell, changing cells, constraints, and so on when you save the file. All you need to do is make the changes you want in the data cells and then click on Solve in the Solver dialogue box again. (Chapter 5 will focus on this kind of *what-if analysis,* including how to use the Solver's Sensitivity Report to expedite the analysis.)

To assist you with experimenting with these kinds of changes, your MS Courseware includes Excel files for this chapter (as for others) that provide a complete formulation and solution of the examples here (the Wyndor problem and the one in the next section) in a spreadsheet format. We encourage you to "play" with these examples to see what happens with different data, different solutions, and so forth. You might also find these spreadsheets useful as templates for homework problems.

Review Questions

1. Which dialogue box is used to enter the addresses for the target cell and the changing cells?
2. Which dialogue box is used to specify the functional constraints for the model?
3. With the Solver Options dialogue box, which options normally need to be chosen to solve a linear programming model?

2.7 A MINIMIZATION EXAMPLE—THE PROFIT & GAMBIT CO. ADVERTISING-MIX PROBLEM

The analysis of the Wyndor Glass Co. case study in Sections 2.3 and 2.6 illustrated how to formulate and solve one type of linear programming model on a spreadsheet. The same general approach can be applied to many other problems as well. The great flexibility of linear programming and spreadsheets provides a variety of options for how to adapt the formulation of the spreadsheet model to fit each new problem. Our next example illustrates some options not used for the Wyndor problem.

FIGURE 2.20

The spreadsheet obtained after solving the Wyndor problem.

	A	B	C	D	E	F	G
1		**Wyndor Glass Co. Product-Mix Problem**					
2							
3			**Doors**	**Windows**			
4		Unit Profit	$300	$500			
5					Hours		Hours
6			Hours Used per Unit Produced		Used		Available
7		Plant 1	1	0	2	≤	4
8		Plant 2	0	2	12	≤	12
9		Plant 3	3	2	18	≤	18
10							
11			**Doors**	**Windows**			**Total Profit**
12		Units Produced	2	6			$3,600

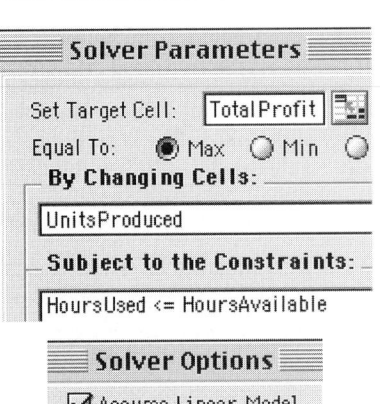

Solver Parameters

Set Target Cell: [TotalProfit]

Equal To: ● Max ○ Min ○

By Changing Cells:

UnitsProduced

Subject to the Constraints:

HoursUsed <= HoursAvailable

Solver Options

☑ Assume Linear Model
☑ Assume Non-Negative

	E
5	Hours
6	Used
7	=SUMPRODUCT(C7:D7, UnitsProduced)
8	=SUMPRODUCT(C8:D8, UnitsProduced)
9	=SUMPRODUCT(C9:D9, UnitsProduced)

	G
11	Total Profit
12	=SUMPRODUCT(UnitProfit, UnitsProduced)

Range Name	Cell
HoursAvailable	G7:G9
HoursUsed	E7:E9
HoursUsedPerUnitProduced	C7:D9
TotalProfit	G12
UnitProfit	C4:D4
UnitsProduced	C12:D12

Planning an Advertising Campaign

The Profit & Gambit Co. produces cleaning products for home use. This is a highly competitive market, and the company continually struggles to increase its small market share. Management has decided to undertake a major new advertising campaign that will focus on the following three key products:

• A spray prewash stain remover.

• A liquid laundry detergent.

• A powder laundry detergent.

This campaign will use both television and the print media. A commercial has been developed to run on national television that will feature the liquid detergent. The advertisement for the print media will promote all three products and will include cents-off coupons that consumers can use to purchase the products at reduced prices. The general goal is to increase the sales of each of these products (but especially the liquid detergent) over the next year by a significant percentage over the past year. Specifically, management has set the following goals for the campaign:

- Sales of the stain remover should increase by at least 3 percent.

- Sales of the liquid detergent should increase by at least 18 percent.

- Sales of the powder detergent should increase by at least 4 percent.

Table 2.2 shows the estimated increase in sales for each *unit* of advertising in the respective outlets. (A *unit* is a standard block of advertising that Profit & Gambit commonly purchases, but other amounts also are allowed.) The reason for -1 percent for the powder detergent in the Television column is that the TV commercial featuring the new liquid detergent will take away some sales from the powder detergent. The bottom row of the table shows the cost per unit of advertising for each of the two outlets.

Management's objective is to determine how much to advertise in each medium to meet the sales goals at a minimum total cost.

Formulating a Spreadsheet Model for This Problem

The procedure summarized at the end of Section 2.3 can be used to formulate the spreadsheet model for this problem. Each step of the procedure is repeated below, followed by a description of how it is performed here.

1. Gather the data for the problem. This has been done as presented in Table 2.2.

2. Enter the data into *data cells* on a spreadsheet. The top half of Figure 2.21 shows this spreadsheet. The data cells are in columns C and D (rows 4 and 8 to 10), as well as in cells G8:G10. Note how this particular formatting of the spreadsheet has facilitated a direct transfer of the data from Table 2.2.

3. Identify the decisions to be made on the levels of activities and designate *changing cells* for making these decisions. In this case, the activities of concern are *advertising on television* and *advertising in the print media,* so the *levels* of these activities refer to the *amount* of advertising in these media. Therefore, the decisions to be made are

    Decision 1: TV = Number of units of advertising on television

    Decision 2: PM = Number of units of advertising in the print media

The two light tan cells with light borders in Figure 2.21—C14 and D14—have been designated as the changing cells to hold these numbers:

$$\text{TV} \rightarrow \text{cell C14} \qquad \text{PM} \rightarrow \text{cell D14}$$

with AdvertisingUnits as the range name for these cells. (See the bottom of Figure 2.21 for a list of all the range names.) These are natural locations for the changing cells, since each

TABLE 2.2
Data for the Profit & Gambit Co. Advertising-Mix Problem

Product	Increase in Sales per Unit of Advertising		Minimum Required Increase
	Television	Print Media	
Stain remover	0%	1%	3%
Liquid detergent	3	2	18
Powder detergent	−1	4	4
Unit cost	$1 million	$2 million	

FIGURE 2.21

The spreadsheet model for the Profit & Gambit problem, including the formulas for the target cell TotalCost (G14) and the other output cells in column E, as well as the specifications needed to set up the Solver. The changing cells, AdvertisingUnits (C14:D14), show the optimal solution obtained by the Solver.

	A	B	C	D	E	F	G
1		**Profit & Gambit Co. Advertising-Mix Problem**					
2							
3			**Television**	**Print Media**			
4		Unit Cost ($millions)	1	2			
5							
6					Increased		Minimum
7			Increase in Sales per Unit of Advertising		Sales		Increase
8		Stain Remover	0%	1%	3%	≥	3%
9		Liquid Detergent	3%	2%	18%	≥	18%
10		Powder Detergent	-1%	4%	8%	≥	4%
11							
12							**Total Cost**
13			**Television**	**Print Media**			**($millions)**
14		Advertising Units	4	3			10

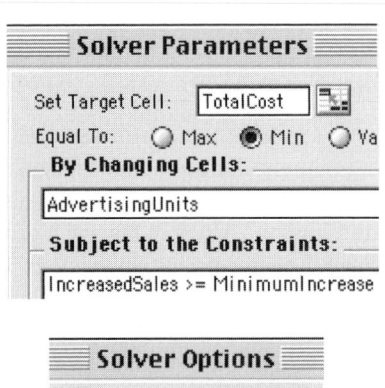

Solver Parameters

Set Target Cell: TotalCost

Equal To: ○ Max   ● Min   ○ Va

By Changing Cells:

AdvertisingUnits

Subject to the Constraints:

IncreasedSales >= MinimumIncrease

Solver Options

☑ Assume Linear Model

☑ Assume Non-Negative

	E
6	Increased
7	Sales
8	=SUMPRODUCT(C8:D8, AdvertisingUnits)
9	=SUMPRODUCT(C9:D9, AdvertisingUnits)
10	=SUMPRODUCT(C10:D10, AdvertisingUnits)

	G
12	Total Cost
13	($millions)
14	=SUMPRODUCT(UnitCost, AdvertisingUnits)

Range Name	Cells
AdvertisingUnits	C14: D14
IncreasedSales	E8: E10
IncreasedSalesPerUnitAdvertising	C8: D10
MinimumIncrease	G8: G10
TotalCost	G14
UnitCost	C4: D4

one is in the column for the corresponding advertising medium. To get started, an arbitrary trial solution (such as all zeroes) is entered into these cells. (Figure 2.21 shows the optimal solution after having already applied the Solver.)

4. Identify the constraints on these decisions and introduce *output cells* as needed to specify these constraints. The three constraints imposed by management are the goals for the increased sales for the respective products, as shown in the rightmost column of Table 2.2. These constraints are

Unlike the Wyndor problem, we need to use ≥ signs for these constraints.

Stain remover: Total increase in sales ≥ 3%

Liquid detergent: Total increase in sales ≥ 18%

Powder detergent: Total increase in sales ≥ 4%

The second and third columns of Table 2.2 indicate that the *total* increases in sales from both forms of advertising are

Total for stain remover   = 1% of PM

Total for liquid detergent   = 3% of TV + 2% of PM

Total for powder detergent = −1% of TV + 4% of PM

Consequently, since rows 8, 9, and 10 in the spreadsheet are being used to provide information about the three products, cells E8, E9, and E10 are introduced as output cells to show the total increase in sales for the respective products. In addition, $\geq$ signs have been entered in column F to remind us that the increased sales need to be at least as large as the numbers in column G. (The use of $\geq$ signs here rather than $\leq$ signs is one key difference from the spreadsheet model for the Wyndor problem in Figure 2.3.)

Unlike the Wyndor problem, the objective now is to minimize the target cell.

5. Choose the overall measure of performance to be entered into the *target cell*. Management's stated objective is to determine how much to advertise in each medium to meet the sales goals at a *minimum total cost*. Therefore, the *total cost* of the advertising is entered in the target cell TotalCost(G14). G14 is a natural location for this cell since it is in the same row as the changing cells. The bottom row of Table 2.2 indicates that the number going into this cell is

Cost = ($1 million) TV + ($2 million) PM → cell G14

6. Use a SUMPRODUCT function to enter the appropriate value into each output cell (including the target cell). Based on the above expressions for cost and total increases in sales, the SUMPRODUCT functions needed here for the output cells are those shown under the right side of the spreadsheet in Figure 2.21. Note that each of these functions involves the relevant data cells and the changing cells, AdvertisingUnits(C14, D14).

This spreadsheet model is a linear programming model, since it possesses all the characteristics of such models enumerated in Section 2.3.

Applying the Solver to This Model

The procedure for using the Excel Solver to obtain an optimal solution for this model is basically the same as described in Section 2.6. The key part of the Solver dialogue box is shown below the left-hand side of the spreadsheet in Figure 2.21. In addition to specifying the target cell and changing cells, the constraints that IncreasedSales $\geq$ MinimumIncrease have been specified in this box by using the Add Constraint dialogue box. Since the objective is to *minimize* total cost, Min also has been selected. (This is in contrast to the choice of Max for the Wyndor problem.)

The lower left-hand side of Figure 2.21 shows the options selected after clicking on the Options button in the Solver dialogue box. The Assume Linear Model option specifies that the model is a linear programming model. The Assume Non-Negative option specifies that the changing cells need nonnegativity constraints because negative values of advertising levels are not possible alternatives.

After clicking on Solve in the Solver dialogue box, the optimal solution shown in the changing cells of the spreadsheet in Figure 2.21 is obtained.

Optimal Solution

C14 = 4 (Undertake 4 units of advertising on television)

D14 = 3 (Undertake 3 units of advertising in the print media)

The target cell indicates that the total cost of this advertising plan would be $10 million.

The Mathematical Model in the Spreadsheet

When performing step 5 of the procedure for formulating a spreadsheet model, the total cost of advertising was determined to be

$$\text{Cost} = \text{TV} + 2\,\text{PM}\quad\text{(in millions of dollars)}$$

where the objective is to choose the values of TV (number of units of advertising on television) and PM (number of units of advertising in the print media) so as to minimize this cost. Step 4 identified three functional constraints:

Stain remover:	1% of PM $\geq$ 3%
Liquid detergent:	3% of TV $+\ 2\%$ of PM $\geq 18\%$
Powder detergent:	-1% of TV $+\ 4\%$ of PM $\geq$ 4%

Choosing the Assume Non-Negative option with the Solver recognized that TV and PM cannot be negative. Therefore, after dropping the percentage signs from the functional constraints, the complete mathematical model in the spreadsheet can be stated in the following succinct form.

$$\text{Minimize}\ \ \text{Cost} = \text{TV} + 2\,\text{PM}\quad\text{(in millions of dollars)}$$

subject to

Stain remover increased sales:	$\text{PM} \geq 3$
Liquid detergent increased sales:	$3\,\text{TV} + 2\,\text{PM} \geq 18$
Powder detergent increased sales:	$-\text{TV} + 4\,\text{PM} \geq 4$

and

$$\text{TV} \geq 0 \qquad \text{PM} \geq 0$$

Implicit in this statement is "Choose the values of TV and PM so as to . . . ." The term "subject to" is shorthand for "Choose these values *subject to* the requirement that the values satisfy all the following constraints."

This model is the *algebraic* version of the *linear programming* model in the spreadsheet. Note how the parameters (constants) of this algebraic model come directly from the numbers in Table 2.2. In fact, the entire model could have been formulated directly from this table.

The differences between this algebraic model and the one obtained for the Wyndor problem in Section 2.4 lead to some interesting changes in how the graphical method is applied to solve the model. To further expand your geometric intuition about linear programming, we briefly describe this application of the graphical method next.

Applying the Graphical Method

Since this linear programming model has only two decision variables, it can be solved by the graphical method described in Section 2.5. The interesting new features here are how this method adapts to *minimization* and to functional constraints with a $\geq$ sign.

Figure 2.22 shows the feasible region for this model. The three constraint boundary lines are obtained in the manner described in Section 2.5. However, the arrows indicating which side of each line satisfies that constraint now all point away from the origin. The reason is that the origin does not satisfy any functional constraint with a $\geq$ sign and a positive right-hand side.

Compare Figure 2.23 with Figure 2.14 to contrast the differences between minimization and maximization problems.

To find the *best* solution in this feasible region (one that minimizes Cost = TV + 2 PM), we first construct a sample objective function line for one specific value of the objective function that appears to be attainable, say, Cost = 15. Figure 2.23 shows that a large segment of this line passes through the feasible region. Since this is a *minimization* problem, we're looking for the *smallest* value of Cost that provides an objective function line that still passes through a point in the feasible region. The origin automatically has an objective function value of Cost = 0, so objective function lines with a positive value of Cost less than 15 will be closer to the origin than the Cost = 15 line. Therefore, we want to move from the Cost = 15 line to objective function lines closer to the origin. Figure 2.23 shows the objective function line with the smallest value of Cost (10) that still passes through a point in the feasible region. This point, (TV, PM) = (4, 3), is the optimal solution.

FIGURE 2.22
Graph showing the feasible region for the Profit & Gambit Co. advertising-mix problem, where the $\geq$ functional constraints have moved this region up and away from the origin.

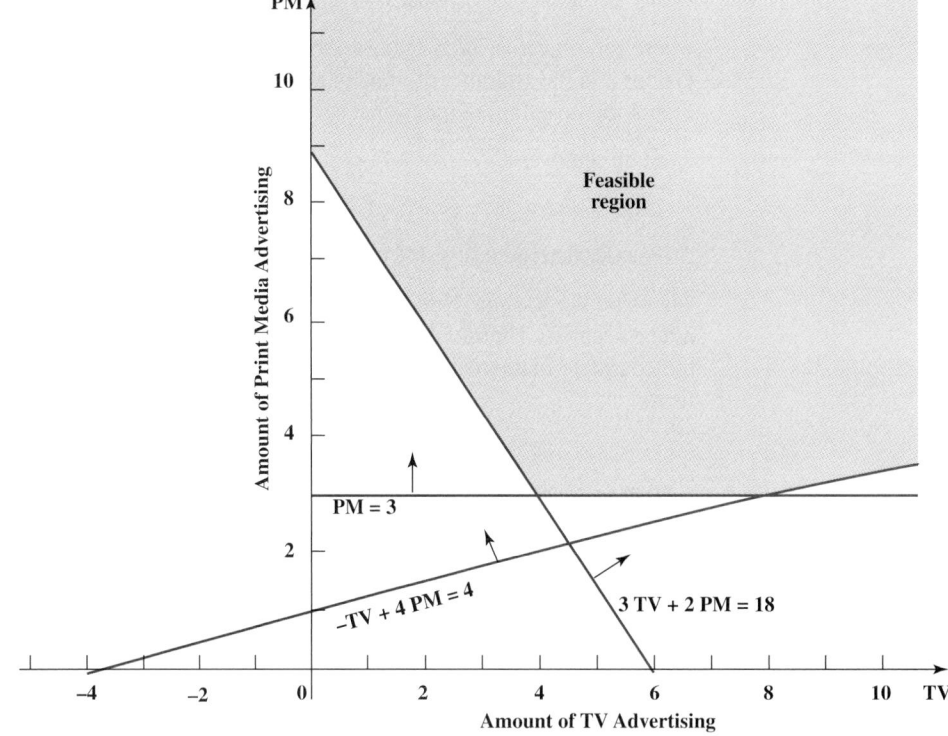

FIGURE 2.23
Graph showing two objective function lines for the Profit & Gambit Co. advertising-mix problem, where the bottom one passes through the optimal solution.

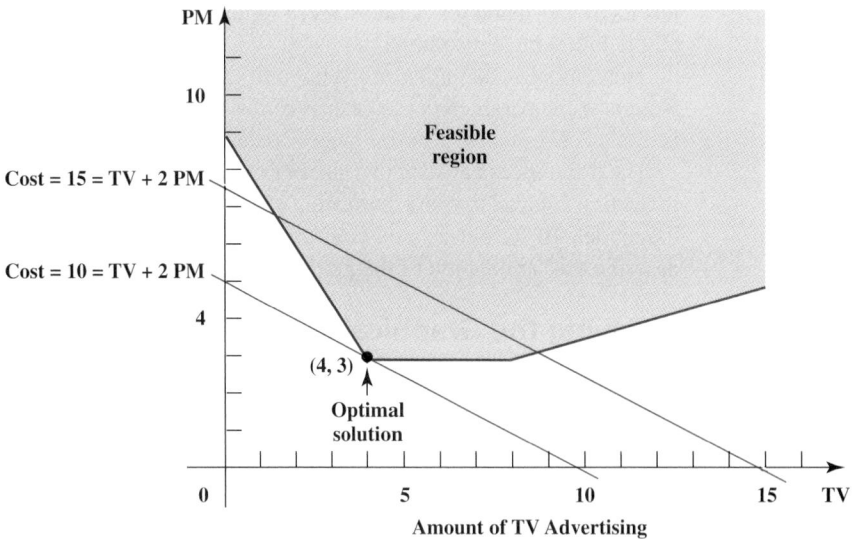

Case 5.1 will continue this example by performing what-if analysis to see what would happen to the optimal solution and the total advertising cost if management were to change its sales goals for the three products.

Review Questions

1. What kind of product is produced by the Profit & Gambit Co.?

2. Which advertising media are being considered for the three products under consideration?

3. What is management's objective for the problem being addressed?

4. What was the rationale for the placement of the target cell and the changing cells in the spreadsheet model?

5. The algebraic form of the linear programming model for this problem differs from that for the Wyndor Glass Co. problem in which two major ways?

6. Does the solution (0, 0) satisfy a ≥ functional constraint with a positive right-hand side?

7. For this minimization problem, should objective function lines passing through the feasible region be moved closer to the origin or further from the origin to reach the optimal solution?

2.8   LINEAR PROGRAMMING FROM A MANAGERIAL PERSPECTIVE

Linear programming is an invaluable aid to managerial decision making in all kinds of companies throughout the world. The emergence of powerful spreadsheet packages has helped to further spread the use of this technique. The ease of formulating and solving small linear programming models on a spreadsheet now enables some managers with a very modest background in management science to do this themselves on their own desktop.

Many linear programming studies are major projects involving decisions on the levels of many hundreds or thousands of activities. For such studies, sophisticated software packages that go beyond spreadsheets generally are used for both the formulation and solution processes. These studies normally are conducted by technically trained teams of management scientists, sometimes called operations research analysts, at the instigation of management. Management needs to keep in touch with the management science team to ensure that the study reflects management's objectives and needs. However, management generally does not get involved with the technical details of the study.

Consequently, there is little reason for a manager to know the details of how linear programming models are solved beyond the rudiments of using the Excel Solver. (Even most management science teams will use commercial software packages for solving their models on a computer rather than developing their own software.) Similarly, a manager does not need to know the technical details of how to formulate complex models, how to validate such a model, how to interact with the computer when formulating and solving a large model, how to efficiently perform what-if analysis with such a model, and so forth. Therefore, these technical details are de-emphasized in this book. A student who becomes interested in conducting technical analyses as part of a management science team should plan to take additional, more technically oriented courses in management science.

So what does an enlightened manager need to know about linear programming? A manager needs to have a good intuitive feeling for what linear programming is. One objective of this chapter is to begin to develop that intuition. That's the purpose of studying the graphical method for solving two-variable problems. It is rare to have a *real* linear programming problem with as few as two decision variables. Therefore, the graphical method has essentially no practical value for solving real problems. However, it has great value for conveying the basic notion that linear programming involves pushing up against constraint boundaries and moving objective function values in a favorable direction as far as possible. You also will see in Chapter 17 that this approach provides considerable geometric insight into how to analyze larger models by other methods.

A manager must also have an appreciation for the relevance and power of linear programming to encourage its use where appropriate. For *future* managers using this book, this appreciation is being promoted by describing *real* applications of linear programming and the resulting impact, as well as by including (in miniature form) various realistic examples and case studies that illustrate what can be done.

Certainly a manager must be able to recognize situations where linear programming is applicable. We focus on developing this skill in Chapter 4, where you will learn how to recognize the *identifying features* for each of the three major types of linear programming problems (and their mixtures).

In addition, a manager should recognize situations where linear programming should *not* be applied. Chapters 9–11 will help to develop this skill by examining the underlying assumptions of linear programming and the circumstances that violate these assumptions. These chapters also describe other approaches that *can* be applied where linear programming should not.

A manager needs to be able to distinguish between competent and shoddy studies using linear programming (or any other management science technique). Therefore, another goal of the upcoming chapters is to demystify the overall process involved in conducting a management science study, all the way from first studying a problem to final implementation of the managerial decisions based on the study. This is one purpose of the case studies throughout the book.

Finally, a manager must understand how to interpret the results of a linear programming study. He or she especially needs to understand what kinds of information can be obtained through *what-if analysis,* as well as the implications of such information for managerial decision making. Chapter 5 focuses on these issues.

Review Questions

1. Does management generally get heavily involved with the technical details of a linear programming study?

2. What is the purpose of studying the graphical method for solving problems with two decision variables when essentially all real linear programming problems have more than two?

3. List the things that an enlightened manager should know about linear programming.

2.9 Summary

Linear programming is a powerful technique for aiding managerial decision making for certain kinds of problems. The basic approach is to formulate a mathematical model called a linear programming model to represent the problem and then to analyze this model. Any linear programming model includes decision variables to represent the decisions to be made, constraints to represent the restrictions on the feasible values of these decision variables, and an objective function that expresses the overall measure of performance for the problem.

Spreadsheets provide a flexible and intuitive way of formulating and solving a linear programming model. The data are entered into data cells. Changing cells display the values of the decision variables, and a target cell shows the value of the objective function. Output cells are used to help specify the constraints. After formulating the model on the spreadsheet and specifying it further with the Solver dialogue box, the Solver is used to quickly find an optimal solution.

The graphical method can be used to solve a linear programming model having just two decision variables. This method provides considerable insight into the nature of linear programming models and optimal solutions.

Glossary

changing cells The cells in the spreadsheet that show the values of the decision variables. (Section 2.3), *31*

constraint A restriction on the feasible values of the decision variables. (Sections 2.3 and 2.4), *34*

constraint boundary equation The equation for the constraint boundary line. (Section 2.5), *39*

constraint boundary line For linear programming problems with two decision variables, the line forming the boundary of the solutions that are permitted by the constraint. (Section 2.5), *39*

data cells The cells in the spreadsheet that show the data of the problem. (Section 2.3), *30*

decision variable An algebraic variable that represents a decision regarding the level of a particular activity. The value of the decision variable appears in a changing cell on the spreadsheet. (Section 2.4), *36*

feasible region The geometric region that consists of all the feasible solutions. (Section 2.5), *42*

feasible solution A solution that simultaneously satisfies all the constraints in the linear programming model. (Section 2.4), *36*

functional constraint A constraint with a function of the decision variables on the left-hand side. All constraints in a linear programming model that are not nonnegativity constraints are called functional constraints. (Section 2.4), *36*

graphical method A method for solving linear programming problems with two decision variables on a two-dimensional graph. (Sections 2.5 and 2.7), *37*

infeasible solution A solution that violates at least one of the constraints in the linear programming model. (Section 2.4), *36*

linear programming model The mathematical model that represents a linear programming problem. (Sections 2.3 and 2.4), *30*

nonnegativity constraint A constraint that expresses the restriction that a particular decision variable must be nonnegative (greater than or equal to zero). (Sections 2.3 and 2.4), *36*

objective function   The part of a linear programming model that expresses what needs to be either maximized or minimized, depending on the objective for the problem. The value of the objective function appears in the target cell on the spreadsheet. (Section 2.4), *36*

objective function line   For a linear programming problem with two decision variables, a line whose points all have the same value of the objective function. (Section 2.5), *44*

optimal solution   The best feasible solution according to the objective function. (Section 2.4), *36*

output cells   The cells in the spreadsheet that provide output that depends on the changing cells. These cells frequently are used to help specify constraints. (Section 2.3), *32*

parameter   The parameters of a linear programming model are the constants (coefficients or right-hand sides) in the functional constraints and the objective function. Each parameter represents a quantity (e.g., the amount available of a resource) that is of importance for the analysis of the problem. (Section 2.4), *36*

product-mix problem   A type of linear programming problem where the objective is to find the most profitable mix of production levels for the products under consideration. (Section 2.2), *29*

slope-intercept form   For linear programming problems with two decision variables, the slope-intercept form of a constraint boundary equation displays both the slope of the constraint boundary line and the intercept of this line with the vertical axis. (Section 2.5), *40*

slope of a line   For a graph where the horizontal axis represents the variable x and the vertical axis represents y, the slope of a line is the change in y when x is increased by 1. (Section 2.5), *40*

solution   Any single assignment of values to the decision variables, regardless of whether the assignment is a good one or even a feasible one. (Section 2.4), *36*

Solver   The spreadsheet tool that is used to specify the model in the spreadsheet and then to obtain an optimal solution for that model. (Section 2.6), *46*

target cell   The cell in the spreadsheet that shows the overall measure of performance of the decisions. (Section 2.3), *32*

Learning Aids for This Chapter in Your MS Courseware

Chapter 2 Excel Files:

Wyndor Example
Profit & Gambit Example

Interactive Management Science Modules:

Module for Graphical Linear Programming and Sensitivity Analysis

Excel Add-ins:

Premium Solver for Education
Solver Table

Problems

We have inserted the symbol E* (for Excel) to the left of each problem or part where Excel should be used. An asterisk on the problem number indicates that at least a partial answer is given in the back of the book.

2.1.   Read the article footnoted in Section 2.1 that describes the first case study presented in that section: "Choosing the Product Mix at Ponderosa Industrial." (This article can be downloaded at **www.mhhe.com/hillier2e/articles.**)

    a. Describe the two factors that, according to the article, often hinder the use of optimization models by managers.

    b. Section 2.1 indicates without elaboration that using linear programming at Ponderosa "led to a dramatic shift in the types of plywood products emphasized by the company." Identify this shift.

    c. With the success of this application, management then was eager to use optimization for other problems as well. Identify these other problems.

2.2. Read the article footnoted in Section 2.1 that describes the second case study presented in that section: "Personnel Scheduling at United Airlines." (This article can be downloaded at **www.mhhe.com/hillier2e/articles.**)

 a. Describe how United Airlines prepared shift schedules at airports and reservations offices prior to this management science study.

 b. When this study began, the *problem definition* phase defined five specific project requirements. Identify these project requirements.

 c. Describe the flexibility built into the scheduling system to satisfy the group culture at each office. Why was this flexibility needed?

 d. Briefly describe the tangible and intangible benefits that resulted from the study.

2.3. Read the 1986 article footnoted in Section 2.1 that describes the third case study presented in that section: "Planning Supply, Distribution, and Marketing at Citgo Petroleum Corporation." (This article can be downloaded at **www.mhhe.com/hillier2e/articles.**)

 a. What happened during the years preceding this management science study that made it vastly more important to control the amount of capital tied up in inventory?

 b. What geographical area is spanned by Citgo's distribution network of pipelines, tankers, and barges? Where do they market their products?

 c. What time periods are included in the model?

 d. Which computer did Citgo use to solve the model? What were typical run times?

 e. Who are the four types of model users? How does each one use the model?

 f. List the major types of reports generated by the SDM system.

 g. What were the major implementation challenges for this study?

 h. List the direct and indirect benefits that were realized from this study.

2.4. Reconsider the Wyndor Glass Co. case study introduced in Section 2.2. Suppose that the estimates of the unit profits for the two new products now have been revised to $600 for the doors and $300 for the windows.

E* a. Formulate and solve the revised linear programming model for this problem on a spreadsheet.

 b. Formulate this same model algebraically.

 c. Use the graphical method to solve this revised model.

2.5. Reconsider the Wyndor Glass Co. case study introduced in Section 2.2. Suppose that Bill Tasto (Wyndor's vice president for manufacturing) now has found a way to provide a little additional production time in Plant 2 to the new products.

 a. Use the graphical method to find the new optimal solution and the resulting total profit if *one* additional hour per week is provided.

 b. Repeat part *a* if *two* additional hours per week are provided instead.

 c. Repeat part *a* if *three* additional hours per week are provided instead.

 d. Use these results to determine how much each additional hour per week would be worth in terms of increasing the total profit from the two new products.

E*2.6. Use the Excel Solver to do Problem 2.5.

2.7. The following table summarizes the key facts about two products, A and B, and the resources, Q, R and S, required to produce them.

Resource	Resource Usage per Unit Produced		Amount of Resource Available
	Product A	Product B	
Q	2	1	2
R	1	2	2
S	3	3	4
Profit/unit	$3,000	$2,000	

All the assumptions of linear programming hold.

E*   a. Formulate and solve a linear programming model for this problem on a spreadsheet.

b. Formulate this same model algebraically.

c. Use the graphical method to solve this model.

2.8.* This is your lucky day. You have just won a $10,000 prize. You are setting aside $4,000 for taxes and partying expenses, but you have decided to invest the other $6,000. Upon hearing this news, two different friends have offered you an opportunity to become a partner in two different entre-preneurial ventures, one planned by each friend. In both cases, this investment would involve ex-pending some of your time next summer as well as putting up cash. Becoming a *full* partner in the first friend's venture would require an investment of $5,000 and 400 hours, and your esti-mated profit (ignoring the value of your time) would be $4,500. The corresponding figures for the second friend's venture are $4,000 and 500 hours, with an estimated profit to you of $4,500. However, both friends are flexible and would allow you to come in at any *fraction* of a full part-nership you would like. If you choose a fraction of a full partnership, all the above figures given for a full partnership (money investment, time investment, and your profit) would be multiplied by this same fraction.

Because you were looking for an interesting summer job anyway (maximum of 600 hours), you have decided to participate in one or both friends' ventures in whichever combination would maximize your total estimated profit. You now need to solve the problem of finding the best com-bination.

a. Describe the analogy between this problem and the Wyndor Glass Co. problem discussed in Section 2.2. Then construct and fill in a table like Table 2.1 for this problem, identifying both the activities and the resources.

b. Identify verbally the decisions to be made, the constraints on these decisions, and the overall measure of performance for the decisions.

c. Convert these verbal descriptions of the constraints and the measure of performance into quantitative expressions in terms of the data and decisions.

E*   d. Formulate a spreadsheet model for this problem. Identify the data cells, the changing cells, and the target cell. Also show the Excel equation for each output cell expressed as a SUMPRODUCT function. Then use the Excel Solver to solve this model.

e. Indicate why this spreadsheet model is a linear programming model.

f. Formulate this same model algebraically.

g. Identify the decision variables, objective function, nonnegativity constraints, functional con-straints, and parameters in both the algebraic version and spreadsheet version of the model.

h. Use the graphical method by hand to solve this model. What is your total estimated profit?

i. Use the Graphical Linear Programming and Sensitivity Analysis module in your Interactive Management Science Modules to apply the graphical method to this model.

2.9.   You are given the following linear programming model in algebraic form, where x_1 and x_2 are the decision variables and Z is the value of the overall measure of performance.

$$\text{Maximize} \quad Z = x_1 + 2x_2$$

subject to

Constraint on resource 1: $x_1 + x_2 \leq 5$ (amount available)

Constraint on resource 2: $x_1 + 3x_2 \leq 9$ (amount available)

and

$$x_1 \geq 0 \qquad x_2 \geq 0$$

a. Identify the objective function, the functional constraints, and the nonnegativity constraints in this model.

E*   b. Incorporate this model into a spreadsheet.

c. Is $(x_1, x_2) = (3, 1)$ a feasible solution?

d. Is $(x_1, x_2) = (1, 3)$ a feasible solution?

E*   e. Use the Excel Solver to solve this model.

f. Use the graphical method by hand to solve this model.

  g. Use the Graphical Linear Programming and Sensitivity Analysis module in your Interactive Management Science Modules to apply the graphical method to this model.

2.10. You are given the following linear programming model in algebraic form, where x_1 and x_2 are the decision variables and Z is the value of the overall measure of performance.

$$\text{Maximize} \quad Z = 3x_1 + 2x_2$$

subject to

  Constraint on resource 1: $3x_1 + x_2 \leq 9$ (amount available)

  Constraint on resource 2: $x_1 + 2x_2 \leq 8$ (amount available)

and

$$x_1 \geq 0 \qquad x_2 \geq 0$$

  a. Identify the objective function, the functional constraints, and the nonnegativity constraints in this model.

E* *b.* Incorporate this model into a spreadsheet.

  c. Is $(x_1, x_2) = (2, 1)$ a feasible solution?

  d. Is $(x_1, x_2) = (2, 3)$ a feasible solution?

  e. Is $(x_1, x_2) = (0, 5)$ a feasible solution?

E* *f.* Use the Excel Solver to solve this model.

  g. Use the graphical method by hand to solve this model.

  h. Use the Graphical Linear Programming and Sensitivity Analysis module in your Interactive Management Science Modules to apply the graphical method to this model.

2.11. The Whitt Window Company is a company with only three employees that makes two different kinds of handcrafted windows: a wood-framed and an aluminum framed window. They earn \$60 profit for each wood-framed window and \$30 profit for each aluminum-framed window. Doug makes the wood frames and can make 6 per day. Linda makes the aluminum frames and can make 4 per day. Bob forms and cuts the glass and can make 48 square feet of glass per day. Each wood-framed window uses 6 square feet of glass and each aluminum-framed window uses 8 square feet of glass.

  The company wishes to determine how many windows of each type to produce per day to maximize total profit.

  a. Describe the analogy between this problem and the Wyndor Glass Co. problem discussed in Section 2.2. Then construct and fill in a table like Table 2.1 for this problem, identifying both the activities and the resources.

  b. Identify verbally the decisions to be made, the constraints on these decisions, and the overall measure of performance for the decisions.

  c. Convert these verbal descriptions of the constraints and the measure of performance into quantitative expressions in terms of the data and decisions.

E* *d.* Formulate a spreadsheet model for this problem. Identify the data cells, the changing cells, and the target cell. Also show the Excel equation for each output cell expressed as a SUMPRODUCT function. Then use the Excel Solver to solve this model.

  e. Indicate why this spreadsheet model is a linear programming model.

  f. Formulate this same model algebraically.

  g. Identify the decision variables, objective function, nonnegativity constraints, functional constraints, and parameters in both the algebraic version and spreadsheet version of the model.

  h. Use the graphical method to solve this model.

  i. A new competitor in town has started making wood-framed windows as well. This may force the company to lower the price it charges and so lower the profit made for each wood-framed window. How would the optimal solution change (if at all) if the profit per wood-framed window decreases from \$60 to \$40? From \$60 to \$20?

  j. Doug is considering lowering his working hours, which would decrease the number of wood frames he makes per day. How would the optimal solution change if he only makes 5 wood frames per day?

2.12.   The Apex Television Company has to decide on the number of 27″ and 20″ sets to be produced at one of its factories. Market research indicates that at most 40 of the 27″ sets and 10 of the 20″ sets can be sold per month. The maximum number of work-hours available is 500 per month. A 27″ set requires 20 work-hours and a 20″ set requires 10 work-hours. Each 27″ set sold produces a profit of $120 and each 20″ set produces a profit of $80. A wholesaler has agreed to purchase all the television sets produced if the numbers do not exceed the maxima indicated by the market research.

E*   *a.* Formulate and solve a linear programming model for this problem on a spreadsheet.

      b. Formulate this same model algebraically.

      c. Solve this model by using the Graphical Linear Programming and Sensitivity Analysis module in your Interactive Management Science Modules to apply the graphical method.

2.13.* You are given the following equation for a line:

$$2x_1 + x_2 = 4$$

      a. Identify the value of x_1 when $x_2 = 0$. Do the same for x_2 when $x_1 = 0$.

      b. Construct a two-dimensional graph with x_1 on the horizontal axis and x_2 on the vertical axis. Then use the information from part *a* to draw the line.

      c. Determine the numerical value of the slope of this line.

      d. Find the slope-intercept form of this equation. Then use this form to identify both the slope of the line and the intercept of the line with the vertical axis.

2.14.   Follow the instructions of Problem 2.13 for the following equation of a line.

$$2x_1 + 5x_2 = 10$$

2.15.   Follow the instructions of Problem 2.13 for the following equation of a line.

$$2x_1 - 3x_2 = 12$$

2.16.* For each of the following constraints on the decision variables x_1 and x_2, draw a separate graph to show the nonnegative solutions that satisfy this constraint.

      a. $x_1 + 3x_2 \leq 6$

      b. $4x_1 + 3x_2 \leq 12$

      c. $4x_1 + x_2 \leq 8$

      d. Now combine these constraints into a single graph to show the feasible region for the entire set of functional constraints plus nonnegativity constraints.

2.17.   For each of the following constraints on the decision variables x_1 and x_2, draw a separate graph to show the nonnegative solutions that satisfy this constraint.

      a. $10x_1 + 20x_2 \leq 40$

      b. $5x_1 + 3x_2 \geq 15$

      c. $5x_1 - x_2 \leq 15$

      d. Now combine these constraints into a single graph to show the feasible region for the entire set of functional constraints plus nonnegativity constraints.

2.18.   For each of the following constraints on the decision variables x_1 and x_2, draw a separate graph to show the nonnegative solutions that satisfy this constraint.

      a. $x_1 - x_2 \leq 2$

      b. $-3x_1 + 6x_2 \geq 3$

      c. $4x_1 - 3x_2 \geq 1$

      d. Now combine these constraints into a single graph to show the feasible region for the entire set of functional constraints plus nonnegativity constraints.

2.19.   The WorldLight Company produces two light fixtures (products 1 and 2) that require both metal frame parts and electrical components. Management wants to determine how many units of each product to produce so as to maximize profit. For each unit of product 1, one unit of frame parts and two units of electrical components are required. For each unit of product 2, three units of frame parts and two units of electrical components are required. The company has 200 units of frame parts and 300 units of electrical components. Each unit of product 1 gives a profit of $1, and each unit of product 2, up to 60 units, gives a profit of $2. Any excess over 60 units of product 2 brings no profit, so such an excess has been ruled out.

    a. Identify verbally the decisions to be made, the constraints on these decisions, and the overall measure of performance for the decisions.

    b. Convert these verbal descriptions of the constraints and the measure of performance into quantitative expressions in terms of the data and decisions.

E*   *c.* Formulate and solve a linear programming model for this problem on a spreadsheet.

    d. Formulate this same model algebraically.

    e. Solve this model by using the Graphical Linear Programming and Sensitivity Analysis module in your Interactive Management Science Modules to apply the graphical method. What is the resulting total profit?

2.20. The Primo Insurance Company is introducing two new product lines: special risk insurance and mortgages. The expected profit is $5 per unit on special risk insurance and $2 per unit on mortgages.

    Management wishes to establish sales quotas for the new product lines to maximize total expected profit. The work requirements are as follows:

	Work-Hours per Unit		Work-Hours
Department	Special Risk	Mortgage	Available
Underwriting	3	2	2,400
Administration	0	1	800
Claims	2	0	1,200

    a. Identify verbally the decisions to be made, the constraints on these decisions, and the overall measure of performance for the decisions.

    b. Convert these verbal descriptions of the constraints and the measure of performance into quantitative expressions in terms of the data and decisions.

E*   *c.* Formulate and solve a linear programming model for this problem on a spreadsheet.

    d. Formulate this same model algebraically.

    e. Solve this model by using the Graphical Linear Programming and Sensitivity Analysis module in your Interactive Management Science Modules to apply the graphical method.

2.21.* Consider the following objective function for a linear programming model with decision variables x_1 and x_2:

$$\text{Maximize} \quad \text{Profit} = 2x_1 + 3x_2$$

    a. Draw a graph that shows the corresponding objective function lines for Profit = 6, Profit = 12, and Profit = 18.

    b. Find the slope-intercept form of the equation for each of these three objective function lines. Compare the slope for these three lines. Also compare the intercept with the x_2 axis.

2.22. Using the symbol P to represent total profit, you are given the following objective function for a linear programming model with decision variables x_1 and x_2:

$$\text{Maximize} \quad P = 25x_1 + 10x_2$$

    a. Draw a graph that shows the corresponding objective function lines for $P = 100$, $P = 200$, and $P = 300$.

    b. Find the slope-intercept form of the equation for each of these three objective function lines. Compare the slope for these three lines. Also compare the intercept with the x_2 axis.

2.23. Consider the following objective function for a linear programming model with decision variables x_1 and x_2:

$$\text{Minimize Cost} = 5x_1 - x_2$$

a. Draw a graph that shows the corresponding objective function lines for Cost = 300, Cost = 200, and Cost = 100.

b. Find the slope-intercept form of the equation for each of these three objective function lines. Compare the slope for these three lines. Also compare the intercept with the x_2 axis.

2.24. Consider the following equation of a line:

$$20x_1 + 40x_2 = 400$$

a. Find the slope-intercept form of this equation.

b. Use this form to identify the slope and the intercept with the x_2 axis for this line.

c. Use the information from part *b* to draw a graph of this line.

2.25.* Find the slope-intercept form of the following equation of a line:

$$8x_1 + 5x_2 = 40$$

2.26. Find the slope-intercept form of the following equations of lines:

a. $10x_1 + 5x_2 = 20$

b. $-2x_1 + 3x_2 = 6$

c. $5x_1 - 2x_2 = 10$

2.27. Consider the following constraint on the decision variables x_1 and x_2:

$$x_1 - 2x_2 \leq 0$$

a. Write the constraint boundary equation for this constraint.

b. Find the slope-intercept form of this equation.

c. Use this form to identify the slope and the intercept with the x_2 axis for the constraint boundary line.

d. Use the information from part *c* to draw a graph of the constraint boundary line.

e. Identify which side of this line is permitted by the constraint.

2.28. You are given the following linear programming model in algebraic form, where x_1 and x_2 are the decision variables and Z is the value of the overall measure of performance.

$$\text{Maximize } Z = 20x_1 + 10x_2$$

subject to

$$x_1 - x_2 \leq 1$$
$$3x_1 + x_2 \leq 7$$

and

$$x_1 \geq 0 \qquad x_2 \geq 0$$

a. Use the graphical method to solve this model.

E* *b.* Incorporate this model into a spreadsheet and then use the Excel Solver to solve this model.

2.29.* You are given the following linear programming model in algebraic form, with x_1 and x_2 as the decision variables and constraints on the usage of four resources:

$$\text{Maximize Profit} = 2x_1 + x_2$$

subject to

$$x_2 \leq 10 \qquad \text{(resource 1)}$$
$$2x_1 + 5x_2 \leq 60 \qquad \text{(resource 2)}$$

$$x_1 + x_2 \leq 18 \qquad \text{(resource 3)}$$
$$3x_1 + x_2 \leq 44 \qquad \text{(resource 4)}$$

and

$$x_1 \geq 0 \qquad x_2 \geq 0$$

    a. Use the graphical method to solve this model.

E*   *b.* Incorporate this model into a spreadsheet and then use the Excel Solver to solve this model.

2.30.   Because of your knowledge of management science, your boss has asked you to analyze a product-mix problem involving two products and two resources. The model is shown below in algebraic form, where x_1 and x_2 are the production rates for the two products and P is the total profit.

$$\text{Maximize } P = 3x_1 + 2x_2$$

subject to

$$x_1 + x_2 \leq 8 \qquad \text{(resource 1)}$$
$$2x_1 + x_2 \leq 10 \qquad \text{(resource 2)}$$

and

$$x_1 \geq 0 \qquad x_2 \geq 0$$

    a. Use the graphical method to solve this model.

E*   *b.* Incorporate this model into a spreadsheet and then use the Excel Solver to solve this model.

2.31.   You are given the linear programming model in algebraic form shown below, where the objective is to choose the levels of two activities (x_1 and x_2) so as to maximize their total profit, subject to constraints on the amounts of three resources available.

$$\text{Maximize } \text{Profit} = 10x_1 + 20x_2$$

subject to

$$-x_1 + 2x_2 \leq 15 \qquad \text{(resource 1)}$$
$$x_1 + x_2 \leq 12 \qquad \text{(resource 2)}$$
$$5x_1 + 3x_2 \leq 45 \qquad \text{(resource 3)}$$

and

$$x_1 \geq 0 \qquad x_2 \geq 0$$

    a. Use the graphical method to solve this model.

E*   *b.* Incorporate this model into a spreadsheet and then use the Excel Solver to solve this model.

2.32.   Consider the algebraic form of a linear programming model shown below, where x_1 and x_2 are the decision variables.

$$\text{Maximize } \text{Profit} = 400x_1 + 500x_2$$

subject to

$$20x_1 + 10x_2 \leq 100$$
$$5x_1 + 10x_2 \leq 50$$
$$3x_1 - x_2 \leq 10$$
$$-x_1 + 4x_2 \leq 15$$

and

$$x_1 \geq 0 \qquad x_2 \geq 0$$

    a. Solve this model by using the graphical method by hand.

2.33.   Weenies and Buns is a food processing plant that manufactures hot dogs and hot dog buns. They grind their own flour for the hot dog buns at a maximum rate of 200 pounds per week. Each hot dog bun requires 0.1 pound of flour. They currently have a contract with Pigland, Inc., which specifies that a delivery of 800 pounds of pork product is delivered every Monday. Each hot dog requires 1/4 pound of pork product. All the other ingredients in the hot dogs and hot dog buns are in plentiful supply. Finally, the labor force at Weenies and Buns consists of five employees working full time (40 hours per week each). Each hot dog requires three minutes of labor, and each hot dog bun requires two minutes of labor. Each hot dog yields a profit of $0.20, and each bun yields a profit of $0.10.

Weenies and Buns would like to know how many hot dogs and how many hot dog buns they should produce each week so as to achieve the highest possible profit.

   a. Identify verbally the decisions to be made, the constraints on these decisions, and the overall measure of performance for the decisions.

   b. Convert these verbal descriptions of the constraints and the measure of performance into quantitative expressions in terms of the data and decisions.

E*   *c.* Formulate and solve a linear programming model for this problem on a spreadsheet.

   d. Formulate this same model algebraically.

   e. Use the graphical method to solve this model. Decide yourself whether you would prefer to do this by hand or by using the Graphical Linear Programming and Sensitivity Analysis module in your Interactive Management Science Modules.

2.34.   The Oak Works is a family-owned business that makes handcrafted dining room tables and chairs. They obtain the oak from a local tree farm, which ships them 2,500 pounds of oak each month. Each table uses 50 pounds of oak while each chair uses 25 pounds of oak. The family builds all the furniture itself and has 480 hours of labor available each month. Each table or chair requires six hours of labor. Each table nets Oak Works $400 in profit, while each chair nets $100 in profit. Since chairs are often sold with the tables, they want to produce *at least* twice as many chairs as tables.

The Oak Works would like to decide how many tables and chairs to produce so as to maximize profit.

E*   *a.* Formulate and solve a linear programming model for this problem on a spreadsheet.

   b. Formulate this same model algebraically.

   c. Use the graphical method to solve this model. Decide yourself whether you would prefer to do this by hand or by using the Graphical Linear Programming and Sensitivity Analysis module in your Interactive Management Science Modules.

2.35.   Nutri-Jenny is a weight-management center. It produces a wide variety of frozen entrees for consumption by its clients. The entrees are strictly monitored for nutritional content to ensure that the clients are eating a balanced diet. One new entree will be a "beef sirloin tips dinner." It will consist of beef tips and gravy, plus some combination of peas, carrots, and a dinner roll. Nutri-Jenny would like to determine what quantity of each item to include in the entree to meet the nutritional requirements, while costing as little as possible. The nutritional information for each item and its cost are given in the following table.

Item	Calories (per oz.)	Calories from Fat (per oz.)	Vitamin A (IU per oz.)	Vitamin C (mg per oz.)	Protein (gr. per oz.)	Cost (per oz.)
Beef tips	54	19	0	0	8	40¢
Gravy	20	15	0	1	0	35¢
Peas	15	0	15	3	1	15¢
Carrots	8	0	350	1	1	18¢
Dinner roll	40	10	0	0	1	10¢

The nutritional requirements for the entree are as follows: (1) it must have between 280 and 320 calories, (2) calories from fat should be no more than 30 percent of the total number of calories, and (3) it must have at least 600 IUs of vitamin A, 10 milligrams of vitamin C, and 30 grams of protein. Furthermore, for practical reasons, it must include at least 2 ounces of beef, and it must have at least half an ounce of gravy per ounce of beef.

E*   a. Formulate and solve a linear programming model for this problem on a spreadsheet.

  b. Formulate this same model algebraically.

2.36.   Consider the following algebraic form of a linear programming model, where the value of c_1 has not yet been ascertained.

$$\text{Maximize } Z = c_1 x_1 + x_2$$

subject to

$$x_1 + x_2 \leq 6$$
$$x_1 + 2x_2 \leq 10$$

and

$$x_1 \geq 0 \qquad x_2 \geq 0$$

Use graphical analysis to determine the optimal solution(s) for (x_1, x_2) for the various possible values of c_1 (both positive and negative).

2.37.   Consider the following algebraic form of a linear programming model, where the value of c_1 has not yet been ascertained.

$$\text{Maximize } Z = c_1 x_1 + 2x_2$$

subject to

$$4x_1 + x_2 \leq 12$$
$$x_1 - x_2 \geq 2$$

and

$$x_1 \geq 0 \qquad x_2 \geq 0$$

Use graphical analysis to determine the optimal solution(s) for (x_1, x_2) for the various possible values of c_1 (both positive and negative).

2.38.   Consider the following algebraic form of a linear programming model, where the value of k has not yet been ascertained.

$$\text{Maximize } Z = x_1 + 2x_2$$

subject to

$$-x_1 + x_2 \leq 2$$
$$x_2 \leq 3$$
$$kx_1 + x_2 \leq 2k + 3 \qquad \text{where } k \geq 0$$

and

$$x_1 \geq 0 \qquad x_2 \geq 0$$

The solution currently being used is $(x_1, x_2) = (2, 3)$. Use graphical analysis to determine the values of k such that this solution actually is optimal.

2.39.   Ralph Edmund loves steaks and potatoes. Therefore, he has decided to go on a steady diet of only these two foods (plus some liquids and vitamin supplements) for all his meals. Ralph realizes that this isn't the healthiest diet, so he wants to make sure that he eats the right quantities of the two foods to satisfy some key nutritional requirements. He has obtained the following nutritional and cost information:

Ingredient	Grams of Ingredient per Serving		Daily Requirement (grams)
	Steak	Potatoes	
Carbohydrates	5	15	≥ 50
Protein	20	5	≥ 40
Fat	15	2	≤ 60
Cost per serving	$4	$2	

Ralph wishes to determine the number of daily servings (may be fractional) of steak and potatoes that will meet these requirements at a minimum cost.

    a. Identify verbally the decisions to be made, the constraints on these decisions, and the overall measure of performance for the decisions.

    b. Convert these verbal descriptions of the constraints and the measure of performance into quantitative expressions in terms of the data and decisions.

E*   *c.* Formulate and solve a linear programming model for this problem on a spreadsheet.

    d. Formulate this same model algebraically.

    e. Use the graphical method by hand to solve this model.

    f. Use the Graphical Linear Programming and Sensitivity Analysis module in your Interactive Management Science Modules to apply the graphical method to this model.

2.40.* Your boss has asked you to use your background in management science to determine what the levels of two activities (x_1 and x_2) should be to minimize their total cost while satisfying some constraints. The algebraic form of the model is shown below.

$$\text{Minimize Cost} = 15x_1 + 20x_2$$

subject to

$$\text{Constraint 1:} \quad x_1 + 2x_2 \geq 10$$

$$\text{Constraint 2:} \quad 2x_1 - 3x_2 \leq 6$$

$$\text{Constraint 3:} \quad x_1 + x_2 \geq 6$$

and

$$x_1 \geq 0 \quad x_2 \geq 0$$

    a. Solve this model by using the Graphical Linear Programming and Sensitivity Analysis module in your Interactive Management Science Modules to apply the graphical method.

E*   *b.* Incorporate this model into a spreadsheet and then use the Excel Solver to solve this model.

2.41. Dwight is an elementary school teacher who also raises pigs for supplemental income. He is trying to decide what to feed his pigs. He is considering using a combination of pig feeds available from local suppliers. He would like to feed the pigs at minimum cost while also making sure each pig receives an adequate supply of calories and vitamins. The cost, calorie content, and vitamin content of each feed is given in the table below.

Contents	Feed Type A	Feed Type B
Calories (per pound)	800	1,000
Vitamins (per pound)	140 units	70 units
Cost (per pound)	$0.40	$0.80

Each pig requires at least 8,000 calories per day and at least 700 units of vitamins. A further constraint is that no more than 1/3 of the diet (by weight) can consist of Feed Type A, since it contains an ingredient that is toxic if consumed in too large a quantity.

a. Identify verbally the decisions to be made, the constraints on these decisions, and the overall measure of performance for the decisions.

b. Convert these verbal descriptions of the constraints and the measure of performance into quantitative expressions in terms of the data and decisions.

E* c. Formulate and solve a linear programming model for this problem on a spreadsheet.

d. Formulate this same model algebraically.

e. Use the graphical method to solve this model. What is the resulting daily cost per pig?

2.42. Reconsider the Profit & Gambit Co. problem described in Section 2.7. Suppose that the estimated data given in Table 2.2 now have been changed as shown in the table that accompanies this problem.

E* a. Formulate and solve a linear programming model on a spreadsheet for this revised version of the problem.

b. Formulate this same model algebraically.

c. Use the graphical method to solve this model.

d. What were the key changes in the data that caused your answer for the optimal solution to change from the one given in Figures 2.21 and 2.23 for the original version of the problem?

| | Increase in Sales per Unit of Advertising | | |
Product	Television	Print Media	Minimum Required Increase
Stain remover	0%	1.5%	3%
Liquid detergent	3	4	18
Powder detergent	−1	2	4
Unit cost	$1 million	$2 million	

e. Write a paragraph to the management of the Profit & Gambit Co. presenting your conclusions from the above parts. Include the potential effect of further refining the key data in the above table. Also point out the leverage that your results might provide to management in negotiating a decrease in the unit cost for either of the advertising media.

2.43. You are given the following linear programming model in algebraic form, with x_1 and x_2 as the decision variables:

$$\text{Minimize} \quad \text{Cost} = 40x_1 + 50x_2$$

subject to

$$\text{Constraint 1:} \quad 2x_1 + 3x_2 \geq 30$$

$$\text{Constraint 2:} \quad x_1 + x_2 \geq 12$$

$$\text{Constraint 3:} \quad 2x_1 + x_2 \geq 20$$

and

$$x_1 \geq 0 \qquad x_2 \geq 0$$

a. Use the graphical method to solve this model.

b. How does the optimal solution change if the objective function is changed to Cost = $40x_1 + 70x_2$?

c. How does the optimal solution change if the third functional constraint is changed to $2x_1 + x_2 \geq 15$?

E*   d. Now incorporate the original model into a spreadsheet and use the Excel Solver to solve this model.

E*   e. Use Excel to do parts *b* and *c*.

2.44. For the following algebraic form of a linear programming model, the objective is to choose the levels of two activities (x_1 and x_2) so as to minimize their total cost while satisfying some constraints.

$$\text{Minimize Cost} = 3x_1 + 2x_2$$

subject to

$$\text{Constraint 1:} \qquad x_1 + 2x_2 \leq 12$$

$$\text{Constraint 2:} \qquad 2x_1 + 3x_2 = 12$$

$$\text{Constraint 3:} \qquad 2x_1 + x_2 \geq 8$$

and

$$x_1 \geq 0 \qquad x_2 \geq 0$$

a. Use the graphical method to solve this model.

E*   b. Incorporate this model into a spreadsheet and then use the Excel Solver to solve this model.

2.45. The Learning Center runs a day camp for 6–10 year olds during the summer. Its manager, Elizabeth Reed, is trying to reduce the center's operating costs to avoid having to raise the tuition fee. Elizabeth is currently planning what to feed the children for lunch. She would like to keep costs to a minimum, but also wants to make sure she is meeting the nutritional requirements of the children. She has already decided to go with peanut butter and jelly sandwiches, and some combination of apples, milk, and/or cranberry juice. The nutritional content of each food choice and its cost are given in the table that accompanies this problem.

Food Item	Calories from Fat	Total Calories	Vitamin C (mg)	Fiber (g)	Cost (¢)
Bread (1 slice)	15	80	0	4	6
Peanut butter (1 tbsp)	80	100	0	0	5
Jelly (1 tbsp)	0	70	4	3	8
Apple	0	90	6	10	35
Milk (1 cup)	60	120	2	0	20
Cranberry juice (1 cup)	0	110	80	1	40

The nutritional requirements are as follows. Each child should receive between 300 and 500 calories, but no more than 30 percent of these calories should come from fat. Each child should receive at least 60 milligrams (mg) of vitamin C and at least 10 grams (g) of fiber.

To ensure tasty sandwiches, Elizabeth wants each child to have a minimum of 2 slices of bread, 1 tablespoon (tbsp) of peanut butter, and 1 tbsp of jelly, along with at least 1 cup of liquid (milk and/or cranberry juice).

Elizabeth would like to select the food choices that would minimize cost while meeting all these requirements.

E*   a. Formulate and solve a linear programming model for this problem on a spreadsheet.

b. Formulate this same model algebraically.

Case 2-1

Auto Assembly

Automobile Alliance, a large automobile manufacturing company, organizes the vehicles it manufactures into three families: a family of trucks, a family of small cars, and a family of midsized and luxury cars. One plant outside Detroit, Michigan, assembles two models from the family of midsized and luxury cars. The first model, the Family Thrillseeker, is a four-door sedan with vinyl seats, plastic interior, standard features, and excellent gas mileage. It is marketed as a smart buy for middle-class families with tight budgets, and each Family Thrillseeker sold generates a modest profit of $3,600 for the company. The second model, the Classy Cruiser, is a two-door luxury sedan with leather seats, wooden interior, custom features, and navigational capabilities. It is marketed as a privilege of affluence for upper-middle-class families, and each Classy Cruiser sold generates a healthy profit of $5,400 for the company.

Rachel Rosencrantz, the manager of the assembly plant, is currently deciding the production schedule for the next month. Specifically, she must decide how many Family Thrillseekers and how many Classy Cruisers to assemble in the plant to maximize profit for the company. She knows that the plant possesses a capacity of 48,000 labor-hours during the month. She also knows that it takes six labor-hours to assemble one Family Thrillseeker and 10.5 labor-hours to assemble one Classy Cruiser.

Because the plant is simply an assembly plant, the parts required to assemble the two models are not produced at the plant. Instead, they are shipped from other plants around the Michigan area to the assembly plant. For example, tires, steering wheels, windows, seats, and doors all arrive from various supplier plants. For the next month, Rachel knows that she will only be able to obtain 20,000 doors from the door supplier. A recent labor strike forced the shutdown of that particular supplier plant for several days, and that plant will not be able to meet its production schedule for the next month. Both the Family Thrillseeker and the Classy Cruiser use the same door part.

In addition, a recent company forecast of the monthly demands for different automobile models suggests that the demand for the Classy Cruiser is limited to 3,500 cars. There is no limit on the demand for the Family Thrillseeker within the capacity limits of the assembly plant.

a. Formulate and solve a linear programming model to determine the number of Family Thrillseekers and the number of Classy Cruisers that should be assembled.

Before she makes her final production decisions, Rachel plans to explore the following questions independently, except where otherwise indicated.

b. The marketing department knows that it can pursue a targeted $500,000 advertising campaign that will raise the demand for the Classy Cruiser next month by 20 percent. Should the campaign be undertaken?

c. Rachel knows that she can increase next month's plant capacity by using overtime labor. She can increase the plant's labor-hour capacity by 25 percent. With the new assembly plant capacity, how many Family Thrillseekers and how many Classy Cruisers should be assembled?

d. Rachel knows that overtime labor does not come without an extra cost. What is the maximum amount she should be willing to pay for all overtime labor beyond the cost of this labor at regular-time rates? Express your answer as a lump sum.

e. Rachel explores the option of using both the targeted advertising campaign and the overtime labor hours. The advertising campaign raises the demand for the Classy Cruiser by 20 percent, and the overtime labor increases the plant's labor-hour capacity by 25 percent. How many Family Thrillseekers and how many Classy Cruisers should be assembled using the advertising campaign and overtime labor-hours if the profit from each Classy Cruiser sold continues to be 50 percent more than for each Family Thrillseeker sold?

f. Knowing that the advertising campaign costs $500,000 and the maximum usage of overtime labor hours costs $1,600,000 beyond regular time rates, is the solution found in part *e* a wise decision compared to the solution found in part *a*?

g. Automobile Alliance has determined that dealerships are actually heavily discounting the price of the Family Thrillseekers to move them off the lot. Because of a profit-sharing agreement with its dealers, the company is not making a profit of $3,600 on the Family Thrillseeker but instead is making a profit of $2,800. Determine the number of Family Thrillseekers and the number of Classy Cruisers that should be assembled given this new discounted profit.

h. The company has discovered quality problems with the Family Thrillseeker by randomly testing Thrillseekers at the end of the assembly line. Inspectors have discovered that in over 60 percent of the cases, two of the four doors on a Thrillseeker do not seal properly. Because the percentage of defective Thrillseekers determined by the random testing is so high, the floor foreman has decided to perform quality control tests on every Thrillseeker at the end of the line. Because of the added tests, the time it takes to assemble one Family Thrillseeker has increased from 6 hours to 7.5 hours. Determine the number of units of each model that should be assembled given the new assembly time for the Family Thrillseeker.

i. The board of directors of Automobile Alliance wishes to capture a larger share of the luxury sedan market and therefore would like to meet the full demand for Classy Cruisers. They ask Rachel to determine by how much the profit of her assembly plant would decrease as compared to the profit found in part *a*. They then ask her to meet the full demand for Classy Cruisers if the decrease in profit is not more than $2,000,000.

j. Rachel now makes her final decision by combining all the new considerations described in parts *f, g,* and *h*. What are her final decisions on whether to undertake the advertising campaign, whether to use overtime labor, the number of Family Thrillseekers to assemble, and the number of Classy Cruisers to assemble?

Case 2-2

Cutting Cafeteria Costs

A cafeteria at All-State University has one special dish it serves like clockwork every Thursday at noon. This supposedly tasty dish is a casserole that contains sautéed onions, boiled sliced potatoes, green beans, and cream of mushroom soup. Unfortunately, students fail to see the special quality of this dish, and they loathingly refer to it as the Killer Casserole. The students reluctantly eat the casserole, however, because the cafeteria provides only a limited selection of dishes for Thursday's lunch (namely, the casserole).

Maria Gonzalez, the cafeteria manager, is looking to cut costs for the coming year, and she believes that one sure way to cut costs is to buy less expensive and perhaps lower quality ingredients. Because the casserole is a weekly staple of the cafeteria menu, she concludes that if she can cut costs on the ingredients purchased for the casserole, she can significantly reduce overall cafeteria operating costs. She therefore decides to invest time in determining how to minimize the costs of the casserole while maintaining nutritional and taste requirements.

Maria focuses on reducing the costs of the two main ingredients in the casserole, the potatoes and green beans. These two ingredients are responsible for the greatest costs, nutritional content, and taste of the dish.

Maria buys the potatoes and green beans from a wholesaler each week. Potatoes cost $0.40 per pound (lb), and green beans cost $1.00 per lb.

All-State University has established nutritional requirements that each main dish of the cafeteria must meet. Specifically, the dish must contain 180 grams (g) of protein, 80 milligrams (mg) of iron, and 1,050 mg of vitamin C. (There are 454 g in one lb and 1,000 mg in one g.) For simplicity when planning, Maria assumes that only the potatoes and green beans contribute to the nutritional content of the casserole.

Because Maria works at a cutting-edge technological university, she has been exposed to the numerous resources on the World Wide Web. She decides to surf the Web to find the nutritional content of potatoes and green beans. Her research yields the following nutritional information about the two ingredients:

	Potatoes	Green Beans
Protein	1.5 g per 100 g	5.67 g per 10 ounces
Iron	0.3 mg per 100 g	3.402 mg per 10 ounces
Vitamin C	12 mg per 100 g	28.35 mg per 10 ounces

(There are 28.35 g in one ounce.)

Edson Branner, the cafeteria cook who is surprisingly concerned about taste, informs Maria that an edible casserole must contain at least a six-to-five ratio in the weight of potatoes to green beans.

Given the number of students who eat in the cafeteria, Maria knows that she must purchase enough potatoes and green beans to prepare a minimum of 10 kilograms (kg) of casserole each week. (There are

1,000 g in one kg.) Again, for simplicity in planning, she assumes that only the potatoes and green beans determine the amount of casserole that can be prepared. Maria does not establish an upper limit on the amount of casserole to prepare since she knows all leftovers can be served for many days thereafter or can be used creatively in preparing other dishes.

a. Determine the amount of potatoes and green beans Maria should purchase each week for the casserole to minimize the ingredient costs while meeting nutritional, taste, and demand requirements.

Before she makes her final decision, Maria plans to explore the following questions independently, except where otherwise indicated.

b. Maria is not very concerned about the taste of the casserole; she is only concerned about meeting nutritional requirements and cutting costs. She therefore forces Edson to change the recipe to allow only for at least a one-to-two ratio in the weight of potatoes to green beans. Given the new recipe, determine the amount of potatoes and green beans Maria should purchase each week.

c. Maria decides to lower the iron requirement to 65 mg since she determines that the other ingredients, such as the onions and cream of mushroom soup, also provide iron. Determine the amount of potatoes and green beans Maria should purchase each week given this new iron requirement.

d. Maria learns that the wholesaler has a surplus of green beans and is therefore selling the green beans for a lower price of $0.50 per lb. Using the same iron requirement from part *c* and the new price of green beans, determine the amount of potatoes and green beans Maria should purchase each week.

e. Maria decides that she wants to purchase lima beans instead of green beans since lima beans are less expensive and provide a greater amount of protein and iron than green beans. Maria again wields her absolute power and forces Edson to change the recipe to include lima beans instead of green beans. Maria knows she can purchase lima beans for $0.60 per lb from the wholesaler. She also knows that lima beans contain 22.68 g of protein and 6.804 mg of iron per 10 ounces of lima beans and no vitamin C. Using the new cost and nutritional content of lima beans, determine the amount of potatoes and lima beans Maria should purchase each week to minimize the ingredient costs while meeting nutritional, taste, and demand requirements. The nutritional requirements include the reduced iron requirement from part *c*.

f. Will Edson be happy with the solution in part *e?* Why or why not?

g. An All-State student task force meets during Body Awareness Week and determines that All-State University's nutritional requirements for iron are too lax and that those for vitamin C are too stringent. The task force urges the university to adopt a policy that requires each serving of an entrée to contain at least 120 mg of iron and at least 500 mg of vitamin C. Using potatoes and lima beans as the ingredients for the dish and using the new nutritional requirements, determine the amount of potatoes and lima beans Maria should purchase each week.

Case 2-3

Staffing a Call Center

California Children's Hospital has been receiving numerous customer complaints because of its confusing, decentralized appointment and registration process. When customers want to make appointments or register child patients, they must contact the clinic or department they plan to visit. Several problems exist with this current strategy. Parents do not always know the most appropriate clinic or department they must visit to address their children's ailments. They therefore spend a significant amount of time on the phone being transferred from clinic to clinic until they reach the most appropriate clinic for their needs. The hospital also does not publish the phone numbers of all clinics and departments, and parents must therefore invest a large amount of time in detective work to track down the correct phone number. Finally, the various clinics and departments do not communicate with each other. For example, when a doctor schedules a referral with a colleague located in another department or clinic, that department or clinic al-

Source: This case is based on an actual project completed by a team of master's students in what is now the Department of Management Science and Engineering at Stanford University.

most never receives word of the referral. The parent must contact the correct department or clinic and provide the needed referral information.

In efforts to reengineer and improve its appointment and registration process, the children's hospital has decided to centralize the process by establishing one call center devoted exclusively to appointments and registration. The hospital is currently in the middle of the planning stages for the call center. Lenny Davis, the hospital manager, plans to operate the call center from 7 AM to 9 PM during the weekdays.

Several months ago, the hospital hired an ambitious management consulting firm, Creative Chaos Consultants, to forecast the number of calls the call center would receive each hour of the day. Since all appointment and registration-related calls would be received by the call center, the consultants decided that they could forecast the calls at the call center by totaling the number of appointment and registration-related calls received by all clinics and departments. The team members visited all the clinics and departments, where they diligently recorded every call relating to appointments and registration. They then totaled these calls and altered the totals to account for calls missed during data collection. They also altered totals to account for repeat calls that occurred when the same parent called the hospital many times because of the confusion surrounding the decentralized process. Creative Chaos Consultants determined the average number of calls the call center should expect during each hour of a weekday. The following table provides the forecasts.

Work Shift	Average Number of Calls
7 AM to 9 AM	40 calls per hour
9 AM to 11 AM	85 calls per hour
11 AM to 1 PM	70 calls per hour
1 PM to 3 PM	95 calls per hour
3 PM to 5 PM	80 calls per hour
5 PM to 7 PM	35 calls per hour
7 PM to 9 PM	10 calls per hour

After the consultants submitted these forecasts, Lenny became interested in the percentage of calls from Spanish speakers since the hospital services many Spanish patients. Lenny knows that he has to hire some operators who speak Spanish to handle these calls. The consultants performed further data collection and determined that, on average, 20 percent of the calls were from Spanish speakers.

Given these call forecasts, Lenny must now decide how to staff the call center during each two-hour shift of a weekday. During the forecasting project, Creative Chaos Consultants closely observed the operators working at the individual clinics and departments and determined the number of calls operators process per hour. The consultants informed Lenny that an operator is able to process an average of six calls per hour. Lenny also knows that he has both full-time and part-time workers available to staff the call center. A full-time employee works eight hours per day, but because of paperwork that must also be completed, the employee spends only four hours per day on the phone. To balance the schedule, the employee alternates the two-hour shifts between answering phones and completing paperwork. Full-time employees can start their day either by answering phones or by completing paperwork on the first shift. The full-time employees speak either Spanish or English, but none of them are bilingual. Both Spanish-speaking and English-speaking employees are paid $10 per hour for work before 5 PM and $12 per hour for work after 5 PM. The full-time employees can begin work at the beginning of the 7 AM to 9 AM shift, 9 AM to 11 AM shift, 11 AM to 1 PM shift, or 1 PM to 3 PM shift. The part-time employees work for four hours, only answer calls, and only speak English. They can start work at the beginning of the 3 PM to 5 PM shift or the 5 PM to 7 PM shift, and, like the full-time employees, they are paid $10 per hour for work before 5 PM and $12 per hour for work after 5 PM.

For the following analysis, consider only the labor cost for the time employees spend answering phones. The cost for paperwork time is charged to other cost centers.

a. How many Spanish-speaking operators and how many English-speaking operators does the hospital need to staff the call center during each two-hour shift of the day in order to answer all calls? Please provide an integer number since half a human operator makes no sense.

b. Lenny needs to determine how many full-time employees who speak Spanish, full-time employees who speak English, and part-time employees he should hire to begin on each shift. Creative Chaos Consultants advises him that linear programming can be used to do this in such a way as to minimize operating costs while answering all calls. Formulate a linear programming model of this problem.

c. Obtain an optimal solution for the linear programming model formulated in part *b* to guide Lenny's decision.

d. Because many full-time workers do not want to work late into the evening, Lenny can find only one qualified English-speaking operator willing to begin work at 1 PM. Given this new constraint, how many full-time English-speaking operators, full-time Spanish-speaking operators, and part-time operators should Lenny hire for each shift to minimize operating costs while answering all calls?

e. Lenny now has decided to investigate the option of hiring bilingual operators instead of monolingual operators. If all the operators are bilingual, how many operators should be working during each two-hour shift to answer all phone calls? As in part *a,* please provide an integer answer.

f. If all employees are bilingual, how many full-time and part-time employees should Lenny hire to begin on each shift to minimize operating costs while answering all calls? As in part *b,* formulate a linear programming model to guide Lenny's decision.

g. What is the maximum percentage increase in the hourly wage rate that Lenny can pay bilingual employees over monolingual employees without increasing the total operating costs?

h. What other features of the call center should Lenny explore to improve service or minimize operating costs?

Learning objectives

After completing this chapter, you should be able to

1. Describe the general process for modeling in spreadsheets.

2. Describe some guidelines for building good spreadsheet models.

3. Apply both the general process for modeling in spreadsheets and the guidelines in this chapter to develop your own spreadsheet model from a description of the problem.

4. Identify some deficiencies in a poorly formulated spreadsheet model.

5. Apply a variety of techniques for debugging a spreadsheet model.

Chapter **Three**

The Art of Modeling with Spreadsheets

Nearly all managers now make extensive use of spreadsheets to analyze business problems. What they are doing is *modeling* with spreadsheets.

Spreadsheet modeling is a major emphasis throughout this book. Section 1.2 in Chapter 1 introduced a spreadsheet model for performing break-even analysis. Section 2.3 in Chapter 2 described how to use spreadsheets to formulate linear programming models. Many kinds of spreadsheet models are discussed in subsequent chapters as well. However, those presentations focus mostly on the characteristics of spreadsheet models that fit the management science techniques (such as linear programming) being covered in those chapters. We devote this chapter instead to the general art of formulating spreadsheet models to fit any application.

Modeling in spreadsheets is more an art than a science. There is no systematic procedure that invariably will lead to a single correct spreadsheet model. For example, if two managers were given exactly the same business problem to analyze with a spreadsheet, their spreadsheet models would likely look quite different. There is no one right way of modeling any given problem. However, some models will be better than others.

Although no completely systematic procedure is available for modeling in spreadsheets, there is a general process that should be followed. This process has four major steps: (1) *plan* the spreadsheet model, (2) *build* the model, (3) *test* the model, and (4) *analyze* the model and its results. After introducing a case study in Section 3.1, the next section will describe this plan-build-test-analyze process in some detail and illustrate the process in the context of the case study. Section 3.2 also will discuss some ways of overcoming common stumbling blocks in the modeling process.

Unfortunately, despite its logical approach, there is no guarantee that the plan-build-test-analyze process will lead to a "good" spreadsheet model. Section 3.3 presents some guidelines for building such models. This section also uses the case study in Section 3.1 to illustrate the difference between appropriate formulations and poor formulations of a model.

Even with an appropriate formulation, the initial versions of large spreadsheet models commonly will include some small but troublesome errors, such as inaccurate references to cell addresses or typographical errors when entering equations into cells. These errors often can be difficult to track down. Section 3.4 presents some helpful ways to debug a spreadsheet model and root out such errors.

The overriding goal of this chapter is to provide a solid foundation for becoming a successful spreadsheet modeler. However, this chapter by itself will not turn you into a highly skilled modeler. Ultimately, to reach this point you also will need to study various examples of good spreadsheet models in the different areas of management science and then have lots of practice in formulating your own models. This process will continue throughout the remainder of this book.

3.1 A CASE STUDY: THE EVERGLADE GOLDEN YEARS COMPANY CASH FLOW PROBLEM

The Everglade Golden Years Company operates upscale retirement communities in certain parts of southern Florida. The company was founded in 1946 by Alfred Lee, who was in the right place at the right time to enjoy many successful years during the boom in the Florida economy as many wealthy retirees flooded into the area. Today, the company continues to be run by the Lee family, with Alfred's grandson, Sheldon Lee, as the CEO.

The past few years have been difficult ones for Everglade. The demand for retirement community housing has been light and Everglade has been unable to maintain full occupancy. However, this market has picked up recently and the future is looking brighter. Everglade has recently broken ground for the construction of a new retirement community and has more new construction planned over the next 10 years.

Julie Lee is the chief financial officer (CFO) at Everglade. She has spent the last week in front of her computer trying to come to grips with the company's imminent cash flow problem. Julie has projected Everglade's net cash flows over the next 10 years as shown in Table 3.1. With less money currently coming in than would be provided by full occupancy and with all the construction costs for the new retirement community, Everglade will have negative cash flow for the next few years. With only $1 million in cash reserves, it appears that Everglade will need to take out some loans in order to meet its financial obligations. Also, to protect against uncertainty, company policy dictates maintaining a balance of at least $500,000 in cash reserves at all times.

> With only $1 million in cash reserves and negative cash flows looming soon, loans will be needed to observe the company policy of maintaining a balance of at least $500,000 at all times.

The company's bank has offered two types of loans to Everglade. The first is a 10-year loan with interest-only payments made annually and then the entire principal repaid in a single balloon payment after 10 years. The interest rate on this long-term loan is a favorable 7 percent per year. The second option is a series of one-year loans. These loans can be taken out each year as needed, but each must be repaid (with interest) the following year. Each new loan can be used to help repay the loan for the preceding year if needed. The interest rate for these short-term loans currently is projected to be 10 percent per year.

Armed with her cash flow projections and the loan options from the bank, Julie schedules a meeting with the CEO, Sheldon Lee. Their discussion is as follows:

Julie: Well, we really seem to be in a pickle. There is no way to meet our cash flow problems without borrowing money.

Sheldon: I was afraid of that. What are our options?

Julie: I've talked to the bank, and we can take out a 10-year loan with an interest rate of 7 percent, or a series of one-year loans at a projected rate of 10 percent.

TABLE 3.1

Projected Net Cash Flows for the Everglade Golden Years Company over the Next Ten Years

Year	Projected Net Cash Flow (millions of dollars)
2003	−8
2004	−2
2005	−4
2006	3
2007	6
2008	3
2009	−4
2010	7
2011	−2
2012	10

Sheldon: Wow. That 7 percent rate sounds good. Can we just borrow all that we need using the 10-year loan?

Julie: That was my initial reaction as well. However, after looking at the cash flow projections I'm not sure the answer is so clear-cut. While we have negative cash flow for the next few years, the situation looks much brighter down the road. With a 10-year loan, we are obligated to keep the loan and make the interest payments for 10 years. The one-year loans are more flexible. We can borrow the money only in the years we need it. This way we can save on interest payments in the future.

Sheldon: Okay. I can see how the flexibility of the one-year loans could save us some money. Those loans also will look better if interest rates come down in future years.

Julie: Or they could go higher instead. There's no way to predict future interest rates, so we might as well just plan on the basis of the current projection of 10 percent per year.

Sheldon: Yes, you're right. So which do you recommend, a 10-year loan or a series of one-year loans?

Julie: Well, there's actually another option as well. We could consider a combination of the two types of loans. We could borrow some money long-term to get the lower interest rate and borrow some money short-term to retain flexibility.

The objective is to develop a financial plan that will keep the company solvent and then maximize the cash balance in 2013, after all the loans are paid off.

Sheldon: That sounds complicated. What we want is a plan that will keep us solvent throughout the 10 years and then leave us with as large a cash balance as possible at the end of the 10 years after paying off all the loans. Could you set this up on a spreadsheet to figure out the best plan?

Julie: You bet. I'll try that and get back to you.

Sheldon: Great. Let's plan to meet again next week when you have your report ready.

You'll see in the next two sections how Julie carefully develops her spreadsheet model for this cash flow problem.

Review Questions

1. What is the advantage of the long-term loan for Everglade?
2. What is the advantage of the series of short-term loans for Everglade?
3. What is the objective for the financial plan that needs to be developed?

3.2 OVERVIEW OF THE PROCESS OF MODELING WITH SPREADSHEETS

Spaghetti code is a term from computer programming. It refers to computer code that is not logically organized and thus jumps all over the place, so it is jumbled like a plate of spaghetti.

When presented with a problem like Everglade's cash flow problem, the temptation is to jump right in, launch Excel, and start entering a model. Resist this urge. Developing a spreadsheet model without proper planning inevitably leads to a model that is poorly organized and filled with "spaghetti code."

Part of the challenge of planning and developing a spreadsheet model is that there is no standard procedure to follow. It is more an art than a science. However, to provide you with some structure as you begin learning this art, we suggest that you follow the modeling process depicted in Figure 3.1.

As suggested by the figure, the four major steps in this process are to (1) plan, (2) build, (3) test, and (4) analyze the spreadsheet model. The process mainly flows in this order. However, the two-headed arrows between Build and Test indicate a recursive process where testing frequently results in returning to the Build step to fix some problems discovered during the Test step. This back and forth movement between Build and Test may occur several times until the modeler is satisfied with the model. At the same time that this back and forth movement is occurring, the modeler may be involved with further building of the model. One strategy is to begin with a small version of the model to establish its basic logic and then, after testing verifies its accuracy, to expand to a full-scale model. Even after completing the testing and then

A modeler might go back and forth between the Build and Test steps several times.

FIGURE 3.1

A flow diagram for the general plan-build-test-analyze process for modeling with spreadsheets.

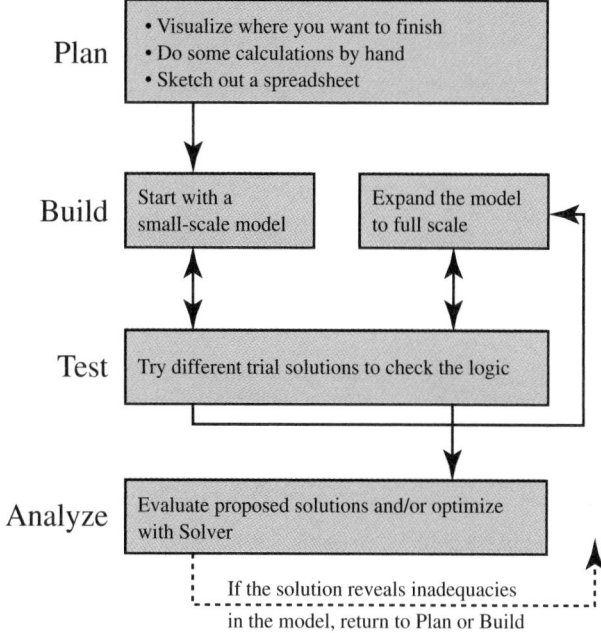

the analyzing of the model, the process may return to the Build step or even the Plan step if the Analysis step reveals inadequacies in the model.

Each of these four major steps may also include some detailed steps. For example, Figure 3.1 lists three detailed steps within the Plan step. Initially, when dealing with a fairly complicated problem, it is helpful to take some time to perform each of these detailed steps manually one at a time. However, as you become more experienced with modeling in spreadsheets, you may find yourself merging some of the detailed steps and quickly performing them mentally. An experienced modeler often is able to do some of these steps mentally, without working them out explicitly on paper. However, if you find yourself getting stuck, it is likely that you are missing a key element from one of the previous detailed steps. You then should go back a step or two and make sure that you have thoroughly completed those preceding steps.

We now describe the various components of the modeling process in the context of the Everglade cash flow problem. At the same time, we also point out some common stumbling blocks encountered while building a spreadsheet model and how these can be overcome.

Plan: Visualize Where You Want to Finish

One common stumbling block in the modeling process occurs right at the very beginning. Given a complicated situation like the one facing Julie at Everglade, sometimes it can be difficult to decide how to even get started. At this point, it can be helpful to think about where you want to end up. For example, what information should Julie provide in her report to Sheldon? What should the "answer" look like when presenting the recommended approach to the problem? What kinds of numbers need to be included in the recommendation? The answers to these questions can quickly lead you to the heart of the problem and help get the modeling process started.

The question that Julie is addressing is *which loan,* or combination of loans, to use and in *what amounts.* The long-term loan is taken in a single lump sum. Therefore, the "answer" should include a single number indicating how much money to borrow now at the long-term rate. The short-term loan can be taken in any or all of the 10 years, so the "answer" should include 10 numbers indicating how much to borrow at the short-term rate in each given year. These will be the changing cells in the spreadsheet model.

What other numbers should Julie include in her report to Sheldon? The key numbers would be the projected cash balance each year, the amount of the interest payments, and when loan payments are due. These will be output cells in the spreadsheet model.

It is important to distinguish between the numbers that represent decisions (changing cells) and those that represent results (output cells). For instance, it may be tempting to include the cash balances as changing cells. These cells clearly change depending on the decisions made. However, the cash balances are a *result* of how much is borrowed, how much is paid, and all of the other cash flows. They cannot be chosen independently but instead are a function of the other numbers in the spreadsheet. The distinguishing characteristic of changing cells (the loan amounts) is that they do not depend on anything else. They represent the independent decisions being made. They impact the other numbers, but not vice versa.

At this point, you should know what changing cells and output cells are needed.

At this stage in the process, you should have a clear idea of what the answer will look like, including what and how many changing cells are needed, and what kind of results (output cells) should be obtained.

Plan: Do Some Calculations by Hand

When building a model, another common stumbling block can arise when trying to enter a formula in one of the output cells. For example, just how does Julie keep track of the cash balances in the Everglade cash flow problem? What formulas need to be entered? There are a lot of factors that enter into this calculation, so it is easy to get overwhelmed.

If you are getting stuck at this point, it can be a very useful exercise to do some calculations by hand. Just pick some numbers for the changing cells and determine with a calculator or pencil and paper what the results should be. For example, pick some loan amounts for Everglade and then calculate the company's resulting cash balance at the end of the first couple of years. Let's say Everglade takes a long-term loan of $6 million and then adds short-term loans of $2 million in 2003 and $5 million in 2004. How much cash would the company have left at the end of 2003 and at the end of 2004?

These two quantities can be calculated by hand as follows. In 2003, Everglade has some initial money in the bank ($1 million), a negative cash flow from its business operations (−$8 million), and a cash inflow from the long-term and short-term loans ($6 million and $2 million, respectively). Thus, the ending balance for 2003 would be:

Ending balance (2003) = Starting balance	$1 million
+ Cash flow (2003)	−$8 million
+ LT loan (2003)	+ $6 million
+ ST loan (2003)	+ $2 million
	$1 million

The calculations for the year 2004 are a little more complicated. In addition to the starting balance left over from 2003 ($1 million), negative cash flow from business operations for 2004 (−$2 million), and a new short-term loan for 2004 ($5 million), the company will need to make interest payments on its 2003 loans as well as pay back the short-term loan from 2003. The ending balance for 2004 is therefore:

Ending balance (2004) = Starting balance (from end of 2003)	$1 million
+ Cash flow (2004)	−$2 million
+ ST loan (2004)	+ $5 million
−LT interest payment	−(7%)($6 million)
−ST interest payment	−(10%)($2 million)
−ST loan payback (2003)	− $2 million
	$1.38 million

Doing calculations by hand can help in a couple of ways. First, it can help clarify what formula should be entered for an output cell. For instance, looking at the by-hand calculations above, it appears that the formula for the ending balance for a particular year should be

$$\text{Ending balance} = \text{Starting balance} + \text{Cash flow} + \text{Loans} - \text{Interest payments}$$
$$- \text{Loan paybacks}.$$

Hand calculations can clarify what formulas are needed for the output cells.

It now will be a simple exercise to enter the proper cell references in the formula for the ending balance in the spreadsheet model. Second, hand calculations can help to verify the spreadsheet model. By plugging in a long-term loan of $6 million, along with short-term loans of $2 million in 2003 and $5 million in 2004, into a completed spreadsheet, the ending balances should be the same as calculated above. If they're not, this suggests an error in the spreadsheet model (assuming the hand calculations are correct).

Plan: Sketch Out a Spreadsheet

Any model typically has a large number of different elements that need to be included on the spreadsheet. For the Everglade problem, these would include some data cells (interest rates, starting balance, minimum balances, and cash flows), some changing cells (loan amounts), and a number of output cells (interest payments, loan paybacks, and ending balances). Therefore, a potential stumbling block can arise when trying to organize and lay out the spreadsheet model. Where should all the pieces fit on the spreadsheet? How do you begin putting together the spreadsheet?

Before firing up Excel and blindly entering the various elements, it can be helpful to sketch a layout of the spreadsheet. Is there a logical way to arrange the elements? A little planning at this stage can go a long way toward building a spreadsheet that is well organized. Don't bother with numbers at this point. Simply sketch out blocks on a piece of paper for the various data cells, changing cells, and output cells, and label them. Concentrate on the layout. Should a

Plan where the various blocks of data cells, changing cells, and output cells should go on the spreadsheet by sketching your layout ideas on paper.

block of numbers be laid out in a row or a column, or as a two-dimensional table? Are there common row or column headings for different blocks of cells? If so, try to arrange the blocks in consistent rows or columns so they can utilize a single set of headings. Try to arrange the spreadsheet so that it starts with the data at the top and progresses logically toward the target cell at the bottom. This will be easier to understand and follow than if the data cells, changing cells, output cells, and target cell are all scattered throughout the spreadsheet.

A sketch of a potential spreadsheet layout for the Everglade problem is shown in Figure 3.2. The data cells for the interest rates, starting balance, and minimum cash balance are at the top of the spreadsheet. All of the remaining elements in the spreadsheet then follow the same structure. The rows represent the different years (from 2003 through 2013). All the various cash inflows and outflows are then broken out in the columns, starting with the projected cash flow from the business operations (with data for each of the 10 years), continuing with the loan inflows, interest payments, and loan paybacks, and culminating with the ending balance (calcu-

FIGURE 3.2 Sketch of the spreadsheet for Everglade's cash flow problem.

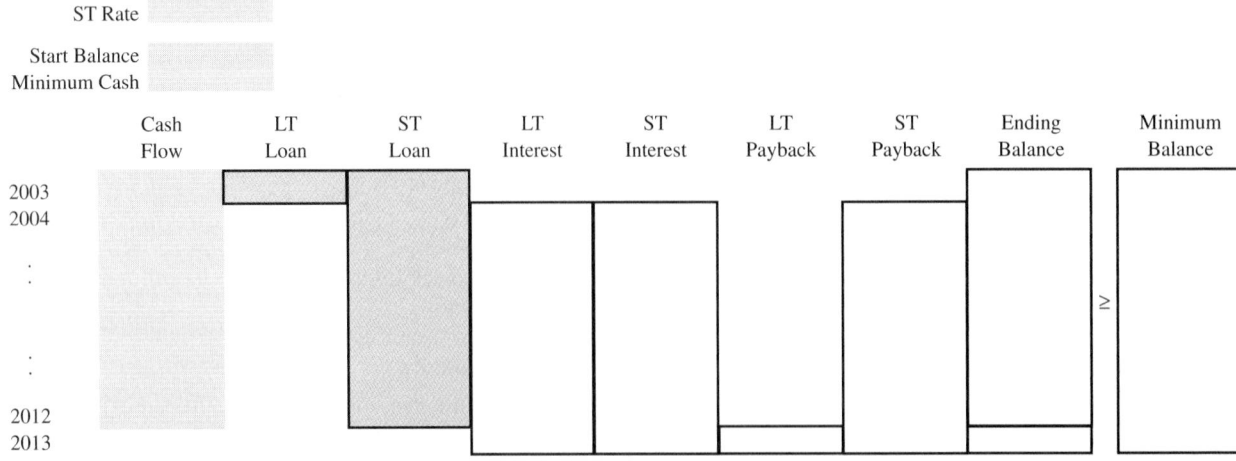

lated for each year). The long-term loan is a one-time loan (in 2003), so it is sketched as a single cell. The short-term loan can occur in any of the 10 years (2003 through 2012), so it is sketched as a block of cells. The interest payments start one year after the loans. The long-term loan is paid back 10 years later (2013).

Organizing the elements with a consistent structure, like in Figure 3.2, not only saves having to retype the year labels for each element, but also makes the model easier to understand. Everything that happens in a given year is arranged together in a single row.

It is generally easiest to start sketching the layout with the data. The structure of the rest of the model should then follow the structure of the data cells. For example, once the projected cash flows data are sketched as a vertical column (with each year in a row), then it follows that the other cash flows should be structured the same way.

There is also a logical progression to the spreadsheet. The data for the problem are located at the top and left of the spreadsheet. Then, since the cash flow, loan amounts, interest payments, and loan paybacks are all part of the calculation for the ending balance, the columns are arranged this way, with the ending balance directly to the right of all these other elements. Since Sheldon has indicated that the objective is to maximize the ending balance in 2013, this cell is designated to be the target cell.

Each year, the balance must be greater than the minimum required balance ($500,000). Since this will be a constraint in the model, it is logical to arrange the balance and minimum balance blocks of numbers adjacent to each other in the spreadsheet. You can put the $\geq$ signs on the sketch to remind yourself that these will be constraints.

> The spreadsheet in Figure 3.2 has a logical progression, starting with the data on the top left and then moving through the calculations toward the target cell on the bottom right.

Build: Start with a Small Version of the Spreadsheet

Once you've thought about a logical layout for the spreadsheet, it is finally time to open a new worksheet in Excel and start building the model. If it is a complicated model, you may want to start by building a small, readily manageable version of the model. The idea is to first make sure that you've got the logic of the model worked out correctly for the small version before expanding the model to full scale.

> Work out the logic for a small version of the spreadsheet model before expanding to full size.

For example, in the Everglade problem, we could get started by building a model for just the first two years (2003 and 2004), like the spreadsheet shown in Figure 3.3.

This spreadsheet is set up to follow the layout suggested in the sketch of Figure 3.2. The loan amounts are in columns D and E. Since the interest payments are not due until the following year, the formulas in columns F and G refer to the loan amounts from the preceding year (LTLoan, or D11, for the long-term loan, and E11 for the short-term loan). The loan payments are calculated in columns H and I. Column H is blank because the long-term loan does not need to be repaid until 2013. The short-term loan is repaid one year later, so the formula in cell I12 refers to the short-term loan taken the preceding year (cell E11). The ending balance in 2003 is the starting balance plus the sum of all the various cash flows that occur in 2003 (cells C11:I11). The ending balance in 2004 is the ending balance in 2003 (cell J11) plus the sum of all the various cash flows that occur in 2004 (cells C12:I12). All these formulas are summarized below the spreadsheet in Figure 3.3.

Building a small version of the spreadsheet works very well for spreadsheets that have a time dimension. For example, instead of jumping right into a 10-year planning problem, we can start with the simpler problem of just looking at a couple of years. Once this smaller model is working correctly, you then can expand the model to 10 years.

Even if a spreadsheet model does not have a time dimension, the same concept of starting small can be applied. For example, if certain constraints considerably complicate a problem, start by working on a simpler problem without the difficult constraints. Get the simple model working and then move on to tackle the difficult constraints. If a model has many sets of output cells, you can build up a model piece by piece by working on one set of output cells at a time, making sure each set works correctly before moving on to the next.

Test: Test the Small Version of the Model

If you do start with a small version of the model first, be sure to test this version thoroughly to make sure that all the logic is correct. It is far better to fix a problem early, while the spreadsheet

FIGURE 3.3 A small version (years 2003 and 2004 only) of the spreadsheet for the Everglade cash flow management problem.

	A	B	C	D	E	F	G	H	I	J	K	L
1		**Everglade Cash Flow Management Problem (Years 2003 and 2004)**										
2												
3		LT Rate	7%									
4		ST Rate	10%									
5					(all cash figures in millions of dollars)							
6		Start Balance	1									
7		Minimum Cash	0.5									
8												
9			Cash	LT	ST	LT	ST	LT	ST	Ending		Minimum
10		Year	Flow	Loan	Loan	Interest	Interest	Payback	Payback	Balance		Balance
11		2003	−8	6	2					1.00	≥	0.50
12		2004	−2		5	−0.42	−0.20		−2.00	1.38	≥	0.50

	F	G	H	I	J	K	L
9	LT	ST	LT	ST	Ending		Minimum
10	Interest	Interest	Payback	Payback	Balance		Balance
11					=StartBalance+SUM(C11:I11)	≥	=MinimumCash
12	= −LTRate*LTLoan	= −STRate*E11		= −E11	=J11+SUM(C12:I12)	≥	=MinimumCash

Range Name	Cell
LTLoan	D11
LTRate	C3
MinimumCash	C7
StartBalance	C6
STRate	C4

is still a manageable size, rather than later after an error has been propagated throughout a much larger spreadsheet.

Try entering numbers in the changing cells for which you know what the values of the output cells should be.

To test the spreadsheet, try entering values in the changing cells for which you know what the values of the output cells should be, and then see if the spreadsheet gives the results that you expect. For example, in Figure 3.3, if zeroes are entered for the loan amounts, then the interest payments and loan payback quantities also should be zero. If $1 million is borrowed for both the long-term loan and the short-term loan, then the interest payments the following year should be $70,000 and $100,000, respectively. (Recall that the interest rates are 7 percent and 10 percent, respectively.) If Everglade takes out a $6 million long-term loan and a $2 million short-term loan in 2003, plus a $5 million short-term loan in 2004, then the ending balances should be $1 million for 2003 and $1.38 million for 2004 (based on the calculations done earlier by hand). All these tests work correctly for the spreadsheet in Figure 3.3, so we can be fairly certain that it is correct.

Excel Tip: A shortcut for filling down or filling across to the right is to select the cell you want to copy, click on the small box in the lower right-hand corner of the selection rectangle, and drag through the cells you want to fill.

If the output cells are not giving the results that you expect, then carefully look through the formulas to see if you can determine and fix the problem. Section 3.4 will give further guidance on some ways to debug a spreadsheet model.

Build: Expand the Model to Full-Scale Size

Once a small version of the spreadsheet has been tested to make sure all the formulas are correct and everything is working properly, the model can be expanded to full-scale size. Excel's fill commands often can be used to quickly copy the formulas into the remainder of the model. For Figure 3.3, the formulas in columns F, G, I, J, and L can be copied using the Fill Down command in the Edit menu to obtain all the formulas shown in Figure 3.4. For example, selecting cells G12:G21 and choosing Fill Down will take the formula in cell G12 and copy it (after adjusting the cell address in Column E for the formula) into cells G13 through G21.

When using the fill commands, it is important to understand the difference between relative and absolute references. Consider the formula in cell G12 ($=-$STRate*E11). References to cells or ranges within a formula (like E11) are usually based upon their position relative to the cell containing the formula. Thus, E11 is two cells to the left and one cell up. This is known as a **relative reference.** When this formula is copied to a new cell, the reference is automatically adjusted to refer to the new cell that is at the same relative location (two cells to the left and one cell up). For example, the formula copied to G13 refers to cell E12, the one in G14 refers to cell E13, and so on. This is exactly what we want, since we always want the interest payment to be based on the short-term loan that was taken one year ago (two cells to the left and one cell up).

In contrast, the reference to STRate (C4) in the formula for cell G12 is called an **absolute reference.** These references do not change when they are filled into other cells. That is, wherever this formula is copied, the formula will still refer to the cell STRate (C4).

To make a relative reference, simply enter the cell address (e.g., E11). To make an absolute reference, either use a range name for the cell (e.g., STRate) or put $ signs in front of the letter and number of the cell reference (e.g., $E$11). Similarly, you can make the column absolute and the row relative (or vice versa) by putting a $ sign in front of only the letter (or number) of the cell reference. For example, if a reference to $E11 in a formula is copied to a new location, the $E will remain constant, but the row number will adjust. In the case of the formula for cell G12 in Figure 3.4, $E11 could have been used for the cell reference since column E will remain constant, but the $ sign is not necessary (and so was not used) when copying down column G since the relative location of column E (two columns to the left) always remains the same.

Excel Tip: A shortcut for changing a cell reference from relative to absolute is to press the F4 key on a PC or command-T on a Mac.

After using the Fill Down command to copy the formulas in columns F, G, I, J, and L and entering the LT loan payback into cell H21, the complete model appears as shown in Figure 3.4.

Test: Test the Full-Scale Version of the Model

Just as it was important to test the small version of the model, it needs to be tested again after it is expanded to full-scale size. The procedure is the same one followed for testing the small version, including the ideas that will be presented in Section 3.4 for debugging a spreadsheet model.

Analyze: Analyze the Model

Before using the Solver dialogue box to prepare for applying Solver, the spreadsheet in Figure 3.4 is merely an evaluative model for Everglade. It can be used to evaluate any proposed solution, including quickly determining what interest and loan payments will be required and what the resulting balances will be at the end of each year. For example, LTLoan (D11) and STLoan (E11:E20) in Figure 3.4 show one possible plan, which turns out to be unacceptable because EndingBalance (J11:J21) indicates that a negative ending balance would result in four of the years.

To optimize the model, the Solver dialogue box is used as shown in Figure 3.5 to specify the target cell, the changing cells, and the constraints. Everglade management wants to find a combination of loans that will keep the company solvent throughout the next 10 years (2003–2012) and then will leave as large a cash balance as possible in 2013 after paying off all the loans. Therefore, the target cell to be maximized is EndBalance (J21) and the changing cells are the loan amounts LTLoan (D11) and STLoan (E11:E20). To assure that Everglade maintains a minimum balance of at least $500,000 at the end of each year, the constraints for the model are EndingBalance (J11:J21) $\geq$ MinimumBalance (L11:L21).

After running Solver, the optimal solution is shown in Figure 3.5. The changing cells, LTLoan (D11) and STLoan (E11:E20) give the loan amounts in the various years. The target cell EndBalance (J21) indicates that the ending balance in 2013 will be $2.92 million.

FIGURE 3.4 A complete spreadsheet model for the Everglade cash flow management problem, including the equations entered into the target cell EndBalance (J21) and all the other output cells, to be used before calling on the Excel Solver. The entries in the changing cells, LTLoan (D11) and STLoan (E11:E20), are only a trial solution at this stage.

	A	B	C	D	E	F	G	H	I	J	K	L
1		**Everglade Cash Flow Management Problem**										
2												
3		LT Rate	7%									
4		ST Rate	10%									
5						(all cash figures in millions of dollars)						
6		Start Balance	1									
7		Minimum Cash	0.5									
8												
9			Cash	LT	ST	LT	ST	LT	ST	Ending		Minimum
10		Year	Flow	Loan	Loan	Interest	Interest	Payback	Payback	Balance		Balance
11		2003	−8	6	2					1.00	≥	0.5
12		2004	−2		5	−0.42	−0.20		−2	1.38	≥	0.5
13		2005	−4		0	−0.42	−0.50		−5	−8.54	≥	0.5
14		2006	3		0	−0.42	0		0	−5.96	≥	0.5
15		2007	6		0	−0.42	0		0	−0.38	≥	0.5
16		2008	3		0	−0.42	0		0	2.20	≥	0.5
17		2009	−4		0	−0.42	0		0	−2.22	≥	0.5
18		2010	7		0	−0.42	0		0	4.36	≥	0.5
19		2011	−2		0	−0.42	0		0	1.94	≥	0.5
20		2012	10		0	−0.42	0		0	11.52	≥	0.5
21		2013				−0.42	0	−6	0	5.10	≥	0.5

	F	G	H	I	J	K	L
9	LT	ST	LT	ST	Ending		Minimum
10	Interest	Interest	Payback	Payback	Balance		Balance
11					=StartBalance+SUM(C11:I11)	≥	=MinimumCash
12	=−LTRate*LTLoan	=−STRate*E11		=−E11	=J11+SUM(C12:I12)	≥	=MinimumCash
13	=−LTRate*LTLoan	=−STRate*E12		=−E12	=J12+SUM(C13:I13)	≥	=MinimumCash
14	=−LTRate*LTLoan	=−STRate*E13		=−E13	=J13+SUM(C14:I14)	≥	=MinimumCash
15	=−LTRate*LTLoan	=−STRate*E14		=−E14	=J14+SUM(C15:I15)	≥	=MinimumCash
16	=−LTRate*LTLoan	=−STRate*E15		=−E15	=J15+SUM(C16:I16)	≥	=MinimumCash
17	=−LTRate*LTLoan	=−STRate*E16		=−E16	=J16+SUM(C17:I17)	≥	=MinimumCash
18	=−LTRate*LTLoan	=−STRate*E17		=−E17	=J17+SUM(C18:I18)	≥	=MinimumCash
19	=−LTRate*LTLoan	=−STRate*E18		=−E18	=J18+SUM(C19:I19)	≥	=MinimumCash
20	=−LTRate*LTLoan	=−STRate*E19		=−E19	=J19+SUM(C20:I20)	≥	=MinimumCash
21	=−LTRate*LTLoan	=−STRate*E20	=−LTLoan	=−E20	=J20+SUM(C21:I21)	≥	=MinimumCash

Range Name	Cells
CashFlow	C11:C20
EndBalance	J21
EndingBalance	J11:J21
LTLoan	D11
LTRate	C3
MinimumBalance	L11:L21
MinimumCash	C7
StartBalance	C6
STLoan	E11:E20
STRate	C4

FIGURE 3.5   A complete spreadsheet model for the Everglade cash flow management problem after calling on the Excel Solver to obtain the optimal solution shown in the changing cells, LTLoan (D11) and STLoan (E11:E20). The target cell EndBalance (J21) indicates that the resulting cash balance in 2013 will be $2.92 million if all the data cells prove to be accurate.

	A	B	C	D	E	F	G	H	I	J	K	L
1		**Everglade Cash Flow Management Problem**										
2												
3		LT Rate	7%									
4		ST Rate	10%									
5						(all cash figures in millions of dollars)						
6		Start Balance	1									
7		Minimum Cash	0.5									
8												
9			Cash	LT	ST	LT	ST	LT	ST	Ending		Minimum
10		Year	Flow	Loan	Loan	Interest	Interest	Payback	Payback	Balance		Balance
11		2003	−8	6.65	0.85					0.50	≥	0.50
12		2004	−2		3.40	−0.47	−0.09		−0.85	0.50	≥	0.50
13		2005	−4		8.21	−0.47	−0.34		−3.40	0.50	≥	0.50
14		2006	3		6.49	−0.47	−0.82		−8.21	0.50	≥	0.50
15		2007	6		1.61	−0.47	−0.65		−6.49	0.50	≥	0.50
16		2008	3		0	−0.47	−0.16		−1.61	1.27	≥	0.50
17		2009	−4		3.70	−0.47	0		0	0.50	≥	0.50
18		2010	7		0	−0.47	−0.37		−3.70	2.97	≥	0.50
19		2011	−2		0	−0.47	0		0	0.50	≥	0.50
20		2012	10		0	−0.47	0		0	10.03	≥	0.50
21		2013				−0.47	0	−6.65	0	2.92	≥	0.50

	F	G	H	I	J	K	L
9	LT	ST	LT	ST	Ending		Minimum
10	Interest	Interest	Payback	Payback	Balance		Balance
11					= StartBalance+SUM(C11:I11)	≥	=MinimumCash
12	=−LTRate*LTLoan	=−STRate*E11		=−E11	=J11+SUM(C12:I12)	≥	=MinimumCash
13	=−LTRate*LTLoan	=−STRate*E12		=−E12	=J12+SUM(C13:I13)	≥	=MinimumCash
14	=−LTRate*LTLoan	=−STRate*E13		=−E13	=J13+SUM(C14:I14)	≥	=MinimumCash
15	=−LTRate*LTLoan	=−STRate*E14		=−E14	=J14+SUM(C15:I15)	≥	=MinimumCash
16	=−LTRate*LTLoan	=−STRate*E15		=−E15	=J15+SUM(C16:I16)	≥	=MinimumCash
17	=−LTRate*LTLoan	=−STRate*E16		=−E16	=J16+SUM(C17:I17)	≥	=MinimumCash
18	=−LTRate*LTLoan	=−STRate*E17		=−E17	=J17+SUM(C18:I18)	≥	=MinimumCash
19	=−LTRate*LTLoan	=−STRate*E18		=−E18	=J18+SUM(C19:I19)	≥	=MinimumCash
20	=−LTRate*LTLoan	=−STRate*E19		=−E19	=J19+SUM(C20:I20)	≥	=MinimumCash
21	=−LTRate*LTLoan	=−STRate*E20	=−LTLoan	=−E20	=J20+SUM(C21:I21)	≥	=MinimumCash

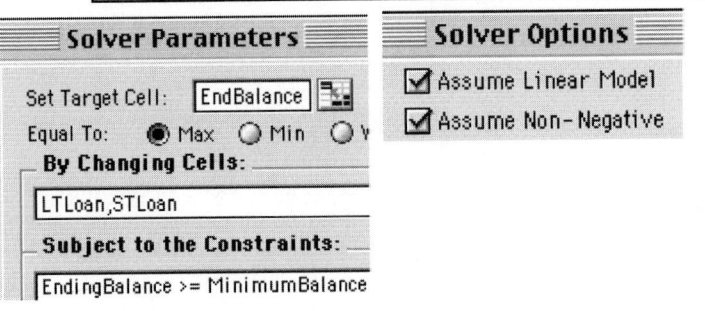

Solver Parameters

Set Target Cell: [EndBalance]

Equal To: ● Max ○ Min ○ V

By Changing Cells:

[LTLoan,STLoan]

Subject to the Constraints:

[EndingBalance >= MinimumBalance]

Solver Options

☑ Assume Linear Model
☑ Assume Non-Negative

Range Name	Cells
CashFlow	C11:C20
EndBalance	J21
EndingBalance	J11:J21
LTLoan	D11
LTRate	C3
MinimumBalance	L11:L21
MinimumCash	C7
StartBalance	C6
STLoan	E11:E20
STRate	C4

Conclusion of the Case Study

The spreadsheet model developed by Everglade's CFO, Julie Lee, is the one shown in Figure 3.5. Her next step is to submit a report to her CEO, Sheldon Lee, that recommends the plan obtained by this model.

Soon thereafter, Sheldon and Julie meet to discuss her report.

Sheldon: Thanks for your report, Julie. Excellent job. Your spreadsheet really lays everything out in a very understandable way.

Julie: Thanks. It took a little while to get the spreadsheet organized properly and to make sure it was operating correctly, but I think the time spent was worthwhile.

Sheldon: Yes, it was. You can't rush those things. But now tell me more about why you are recommending the plan shown in your spreadsheet.

Julie: OK, good. One requirement for the plan is that it must keep us solvent throughout the 10 years. You've reminded me many times about the company policy to maintain a balance of at least $500,000 in cash reserves at all times.

Sheldon: Yes, I see in column J of your spreadsheet that your plan does that. But couldn't the same thing have been accomplished by either using only a long-term loan or only using a series of short-term loans?

Julie: Yes, it could. There are various ways of taking out the loans to satisfy the company policy.

Sheldon: So why this particular plan?

Julie: Well, that's where the Excel Solver comes in to play. You'll recall that you also wanted the plan to provide the largest possible ending balance in 2013 after all the loans are paid off.

Sheldon: Yes, that's right.

Julie: Well, by making the ending balance in 2013 the target cell, the Excel Solver considers every possible plan that provides an ending balance of at least $500,000 in every year and then finds the one that maximizes this target cell. The plan it found is the one shown in my spreadsheet.

Sheldon: OK, good. That's exactly what I wanted for the plan. But how does the Excel Solver do that?

Julie: It is using a management science technique called *linear programming*.

Sheldon: Hmm, OK. Does this linear programming always work to give you the best plan?

Julie: Yes, it does as long as you set up the spreadsheet correctly. Linear programming has been around a long time and it is very reliable. That's why it is a key part of the Excel Solver.

Sheldon: Sounds good. But one thing is still bothering me.

Julie: What's that?

Sheldon: It has to do with our forecasts for the company's future cash flows. We have been assuming that the cash flows in the coming years will be the ones shown in column C of your spreadsheet. Those are good estimates, but we both know that they are only estimates. A lot of changes that we can't foresee now are likely to occur over the next 10 years. When there is a shift in the economy, or when other unexpected developments occur that impact the company, those cash flows can change a lot. How do we know if your recommended plan will still be a good one if those kinds of changes occur?

Julie: A very good question. To answer it, we should do some what-if analysis to see what would happen if those kinds of changes occur. Now that the spreadsheet is set up properly, it will be very easy to do that by simply changing some of the cash flows in column C and seeing what would happen with the current plan. You can try out any change or changes you want and immediately see the effect. Each time you change a future cash flow, you also have the option of trying out changes on short-term loan amounts to see what kind of adjustments would be needed to maintain a balance of at least $500,000 in every year.

OK, are you ready? Shall we do some what-if analysis now?

Sheldon: Let's do.

> Providing a data cell for each piece of data makes it easy to check what would happen if the correct value for a piece of data differs from its initial estimate.

Fortunately, Julie had set up the spreadsheet properly (providing a data cell for the cash flow in each of the next 10 years) to enable performing what-if analysis immediately by simply trying different numbers in some of these data cells. After spending half an hour trying different numbers, Sheldon and Julie conclude that the plan in Figure 3.5 will be a sound initial financial plan for the next 10 years, even if future cash flows deviate somewhat from current forecasts. If deviations do occur, adjustments will of course need to be made in the short-term loan amounts. At any point, Julie also will have the option of returning to the company's bank to try to arrange another long-term loan for the remainder of the 10 years at a lower interest rate than that offered for short-term loans. If so, essentially the same spreadsheet model as in Figure 3.5 can be used, along with the Excel Solver, to find the optimal adjusted financial plan for the remainder of the 10 years.

A management science technique called *computer simulation* provides another effective way of taking the uncertainty of future cash flows into account. Chapters 15 and 16 will describe this technique and Section 16.4 will be devoted to continuing the analysis of this same case study.

Review
Questions

1. What is a good way to get started with a spreadsheet model if you don't even know where to begin?
2. What are two ways in which doing calculations by hand can help you?
3. Describe a useful way to get started organizing and laying out a spreadsheet.
4. What types of values should be put into the data cells to test the model?
5. What is the difference between an absolute cell reference and a relative cell reference?

3.3   SOME GUIDELINES FOR BUILDING "GOOD" SPREADSHEET MODELS

There are many ways to set up a model on a spreadsheet. While one of the benefits of spreadsheets is the flexibility they offer, this flexibility also can be dangerous. Although Excel provides many features (such as range names, shading, borders, etc.) that allow you to create "good" spreadsheet models that are easy to understand, easy to debug, and easy to modify, it is also easy to create "bad" spreadsheet models that are difficult to understand, difficult to debug, and difficult to modify. The goal of this section is to provide some guidelines that will help you to create "good" spreadsheet models.

Enter the Data First

> All the data should be laid out on the spreadsheet before beginning to formulate the rest of the spreadsheet model.

Any spreadsheet model is driven by the data in the spreadsheet. The form of the entire model is built around the structure of the data. Therefore, it is always a good idea to enter and carefully lay out all the data before you begin to set up the rest of the model. The model structure then can conform to the layout of the data as closely as possible.

Often, it is easier to set up the rest of the model when the data are already on the spreadsheet. In the Everglade problem (see Figure 3.5), the data for the cash flows have been laid out in the first columns of the spreadsheet (B and C), with the year labels in column B and the data in cells C11:C20. Once the data are in place, the layout for the rest of the model quickly falls into place around the structure of the data. It is only logical to lay out the changing cells and output cells using the same structure, with each of the various cash flows in columns that utilize the same row labels from column B.

Now reconsider the spreadsheet model developed in Section 2.3 for the Wyndor Glass Co. problem. The spreadsheet is repeated here in Figure 3.6. The data for the Hours Used per Unit Produced have been laid out in the center of the spreadsheet in cells C7:D9. The output cells, HoursUsed (E7:E9), then have been placed immediately to the right of these data and to the left of the data on HoursAvailable(G7:G9), where the row labels for these output cells are the same as for all these data. This makes it easy to interpret the three constraints being laid out in rows 7–9 of the spreadsheet model. Next, the changing cells and target cell have been placed together in row 12 below the data, where the column labels for the changing cells are the same as for the columns of data above.

The locations of the data occasionally will need to be shifted somewhat to better accommodate the overall model. However, with this caveat, the model structure generally should conform to the data as closely as possible.

FIGURE 3.6

The spreadsheet model formulated in Section 2.3 for the Wyndor Glass Co. product-mix problem.

	A	B	C	D	E	F	G
1		**Wyndor Glass Co. Product-Mix Problem**					
2							
3			Doors	Windows			
4		Unit Profit	$300	$500			
5					Hours		Hours
6			Hours Used per Unit Produced		Used		Available
7		Plant 1	1	0	2	≤	4
8		Plant 2	0	2	12	≤	12
9		Plant 3	3	2	18	≤	18
10							
11			Doors	Windows			Total Profit
12		Units Produced	2	6			$3,600

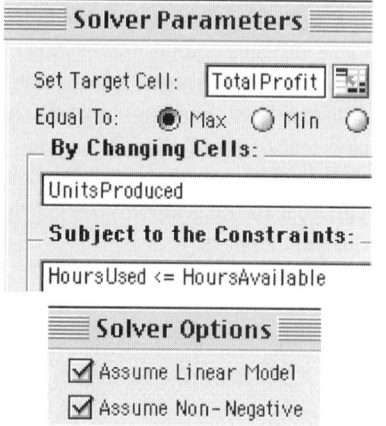

	Solver Parameters
	Set Target Cell: [Total Profit]
	Equal To: ● Max ○ Min ○
	By Changing Cells:
	[UnitsProduced]
	Subject to the Constraints:
	[HoursUsed <= HoursAvailable]

	Solver Options
	☑ Assume Linear Model
	☑ Assume Non-Negative

	E
5	Hours
6	Used
7	=SUMPRODUCT(C7:D7,UnitsProduced)
8	=SUMPRODUCT(C8:D8,UnitsProduced)
9	=SUMPRODUCT(C9:D9,UnitsProduced)

	G
11	Total Profit
12	=SUMPRODUCT(Unit Profit,UnitsProduced)

Range Name	Cells
HoursAvailable	G7:G9
HoursUsed	E7:E9
HoursUsedPerUnitProduced	C7:D9
TotalProfit	G12
UnitProfit	C4:D4
UnitsProduced	C12:D12

Organize and Clearly Identify the Data

Provide labels in the spreadsheet that clearly identify all the data.

Related data should be grouped together in a convenient format and entered into the spreadsheet with labels that clearly identify the data. For data that are laid out in tabular form, the table should have a heading that provides a general description of the data and then each row and column should have a label that will identify each entry in the table. The units of the data also should be identified. Different types of data should be well separated in the spreadsheet. However, if two tables need to use the same labels for either their rows or columns, then be consistent in making them either rows in both tables or columns in both tables.

In the Wyndor Glass Co. problem (Figure 3.6), the three sets of data have been grouped into tables and clearly labeled Unit Profit, Hours Used per Unit Produced, and Hours Available. The units of the data are identified (dollar signs are included in the unit profit data and hours are indicated in the labels of the time data). Finally, all three data tables make consistent use of rows and columns. Since the Unit Profit data have their product labels (Doors and Windows) in columns C and D, the Hours Used per Unit Produced data use this same structure. This structure also is carried through to the changing cells (Units Produced). Similarly, the data for each plant (rows 7–9) are in the rows for both the Hours Used per Unit Produced data *and* the Hours Available data. Keeping the data oriented the same way is not only less confusing, but it also makes it possible to use the SUMPRODUCT function. Recall that the SUMPRODUCT function assumes that the two ranges are exactly the same shape (i.e., the same number of rows *and* columns). If the Unit Profit data and the Units Produced data had not been oriented the same way (e.g., one in a column and the other in a row), it would not have been possible to use the SUMPRODUCT function in the Total Profit calculation.

Similarly, for the Everglade problem (Figure 3.5), the five sets of data have been grouped into cells and tables and clearly labeled ST Rate, LT Rate, Start Balance, Cash Flow, and Minimum Cash. The units of the data are identified (cells F5:I5 specify that all cash figures are in millions of dollars), and all the tables make consistent use of rows and columns (years in the rows).

Enter Each Piece of Data into One Cell Only

Every formula using the same piece of data should refer to the same single data cell.

If a piece of data is needed in more than one formula, then refer to the original data cell rather than repeating the data in additional places. This makes the model much easier to modify. If the value of that piece of data changes, it only needs to be changed in one place. You do not need to search through the entire model to find all the places where the data value appears.

For example, in the Everglade problem (Figure 3.5), there is a company policy of maintaining a cash balance of at least $500,000 at all times. This translates into a constraint for the minimum balance of $500,000 at the end of each year. Rather than entering the minimum cash position of 0.5 (in millions of dollars) into all the cells in column L, it is entered once in MinimumCash (C7) and then referred to by the cells in MinimumBalance (L11:L21). Then, if this policy were to change to, say, a minimum of $200,000 cash, the number would need to be changed in only one place.

Separate Data from Formulas

Formulas should refer to data cells for any needed numbers.

Avoid using numbers directly in formulas. Instead, enter any needed numbers into data cells and then refer to the data cells as needed. For example, in the Everglade problem (Figure 3.5), all the data (the interest rates, starting balance, minimum cash, and projected cash flows) are entered into separate data cells on the spreadsheet. When these numbers are needed to calculate the interest charges (in columns F and G), loan payments (in column H and I), ending balances (column J), and minimum balances (column L), the data cells are referred to rather than entering these numbers directly in the formulas.

Separating the data from the formulas has a couple advantages. First, all the data are visible on the spreadsheet rather than buried in formulas. Seeing all the data makes the model easier to interpret. Second, the model is easier to modify since changing data only requires modifying the corresponding data cells. You don't need to modify any formulas. This proves to be very important when it comes time to perform what-if analysis to see what the effect would be if some of the estimates in the data cells were to take on other plausible values.

Keep It Simple

Avoid the use of powerful Excel functions when simpler functions are available that are easier to interpret. As much as possible, stick to SUMPRODUCT or SUM functions. This makes the model easier to understand and also helps to ensure that the model will be linear. (Linear models are considerably easier to solve than others.) Try to keep formulas short and simple. If a complicated formula is required, break it out into intermediate calculations with subtotals. For example, in the Everglade spreadsheet, each element of the loan payments is broken out explicitly: LT Interest, ST Interest, LT Payback, and ST Payback. Some of these columns could have been combined (e.g., into two columns with LT Payments and ST Payments, or even into one column for all Loan Payments). However, this makes the formulas more complicated and also makes the model harder to test and debug. As laid out, the individual formulas for the loan payments are so simple that their values can be predicted easily without even looking at the formula. This simplifies the testing and debugging of the model.

Use Range Names

One way to refer to a block of related cells (or even a single cell) in a spreadsheet formula is to use its cell address (e.g., L11:L21 or C3). However, when reading the formula, this requires looking at that part of the spreadsheet to see what kind of information is given there. A better alternative is to assign a descriptive **range name** to the block of cells that immediately identifies what is there. (This is done by selecting the block of cells, choosing Name\Define from the Insert menu, and then typing a name.) This is especially helpful when writing a formula for an output cell. Writing the formula in terms of range names instead of cell addresses makes the formula much easier to interpret. Range names also make the description of the model in the Solver dialogue box much easier to understand.

Figure 3.5 illustrates the use of range names for the Everglade spreadsheet model. For example, consider the formula for long-term interest in cell F12. Since the long-term rate is given in cell C3 and the long-term loan amount is in cell D11, the formula for the long-term interest could have been written as $=-C3*D11$. However, by using the range name LTRate for cell C3 and the range name LTLoan for cell D11, the formula instead becomes $=-LTRate*LTLoan$, which is much easier to interpret at a glance.

On the other hand, be aware that it is easy to get carried away with defining range names. Defining too many range names can be more trouble than it is worth. For example, when related data are grouped together in a table, we recommend giving a range name only for the entire table rather than for the individual rows and columns. In general, we suggest defining range names only for each group of data cells, the changing cells, the target cell, and both sides of each group of constraints (the left-hand side and the right-hand side).

Care also should be taken to assure that it is easy to quickly identify which cells are referred to by a particular range name. Use a name that corresponds exactly to the label on the spreadsheet. For example, in Figure 3.5, columns J and L are labeled Ending Balance and Minimum Balance on the spreadsheet, so we use the range names EndingBalance and MinimumBalance. Using exactly the same name as the label on the spreadsheet makes it quick and easy to find the cells that are referred to by a range name.

When desired, a list of all the range names and their corresponding cell addresses can be pasted directly into the spreadsheet by choosing Name\Paste from the Insert menu and then clicking Paste List. Such a list (after reformatting) is included below essentially all the spreadsheets displayed in this text.

When modifying an existing model that utilizes range names, care should be taken to assure that the range names continue to refer to the correct range of cells. When inserting a row or column into a spreadsheet model, it is helpful to insert the row or column into the middle of a range rather than at the end. For example, to add another product to a product-mix model with four products, add a column between products 2 and 3 rather than after product 4. This will automatically extend the relevant range names to span across all five columns since these range names will continue to refer to everything between product 1 and product 4, including the newly inserted column for the fifth product. Similarly, deleting a row or column from the middle of a range will contract the span of the relevant range names appropriately. You can double-check the cells that are referred to by a range name by choosing that range name from the name box (on the left side of the Excel toolbar, just above the worksheet). This will highlight the cells that are referred to by the chosen range name.

Use Relative and Absolute References to Simplify Copying Formulas

Excel's fill commands provide a quick and reliable way to replicate a formula into multiple cells.

Whenever multiple related formulas will be needed, try to enter the formula just once and then use Excel's fill commands to replicate the formula. Not only is this quicker than retyping the formula, but it is also less prone to error.

We saw a good example of this when discussing the expansion of the model to full-scale size in the preceding section. Starting with the two-year spreadsheet in Figure 3.3, fill commands were used to copy the formulas in columns F, G, I, J, and L for the remaining years to create the full-scale, 10-year spreadsheet in Figure 3.4.

Using relative and absolute references for related formulas not only aids in building a model but also makes it easier to modify an existing model or template. For example, suppose that you have formulated a spreadsheet model for a product-mix problem but now wish to modify the model to add another resource. This requires inserting a row into the spreadsheet. If the output cells are written with proper relative and absolute references, then it is simple to copy the existing formulas into the inserted row.

Use Borders, Shading, and Colors to Distinguish between Cell Types

Make it easy to spot all the cells of the same type.

It is important to be able to easily distinguish between the data cells, changing cells, output cells, and target cell in a spreadsheet. One way to do this is to use different borders and cell shading for each of these different types of cells. In the text, data cells appear lightly shaded in a light blue color, changing cells are shaded light tan with a light border, output cells appear with no shading, and the target cell is shaded dark tan with a heavy border.

In the spreadsheet files in MS Courseware, data cells are light blue, changing cells are yellow, and the target cell is orange. Obviously, you may use any scheme that you like. The important thing is to be consistent, so that you can quickly recognize the types of cells. Then, when you want to examine the cells of a certain type, the color will immediately guide you there.

Show the Entire Model on the Spreadsheet

Display every element of the model on the spreadsheet rather than relying on only the Solver dialogue box to include certain elements.

The Solver uses a combination of the spreadsheet and the Solver dialogue box to specify the model to be solved. Therefore, it is possible to include certain elements of the model (such as the ≤, =, or ≥ signs and/or the right-hand sides of the constraints) in the Solver dialogue box without displaying them in the spreadsheet. However, we strongly recommend that *every* element of the model be displayed *on the spreadsheet*. Every person using or adapting the model, or referring back to it later, needs to be able to interpret the model. This is much easier to do by viewing the model on the spreadsheet than by trying to decipher it from the Solver dialogue box. Furthermore, a printout of the spreadsheet does not include information from the Solver dialogue box.

In particular, all the elements of a constraint should be displayed on the spreadsheet. For each constraint, three adjacent cells should be used for the total of the left-hand side, the ≤, =, or ≥ sign in the middle, and the right-hand side. (Note in Figure 3.5 that this was done in columns J, K, and L of the spreadsheet for the Everglade problem.) As mentioned earlier, the changing cells and target cell should be highlighted in some manner (e.g., with borders and/or cell shading). A good test is that you should not need to go to the Solver dialogue box to determine any element of the model. You should be able to identify the changing cells, the target cell, and all the constraints in the model just by looking at the spreadsheet.

A Poor Spreadsheet Model

It is certainly possible to set up a linear programming spreadsheet model without utilizing any of these ideas. Figure 3.7 shows an alternative spreadsheet formulation for the Everglade problem that violates nearly every one of these guidelines. This formulation can still be solved using Solver, which in fact yields the same optimal solution as in Figure 3.5. However, the formulation has many problems. It is not clear which cells yield the solution (borders and/or shading are not used to highlight the changing cells and target cell). Without going to the Solver dialogue box, the constraints in the model cannot be identified (the spreadsheet does not show the entire model). The spreadsheet also does not show most of the data. For example, to determine the data used for the projected cash flows, the interest rates, or the starting balance, you need to dig into the formulas in column E (the data are not separate from the formulas). If any of these data change, the actual formulas need to be modified rather than simply changing a number on the spreadsheet. Furthermore, the formulas and the model in the Solver dialogue box are difficult to interpret (range names are not utilized).

Compare Figures 3.5 and 3.7. Applying the guidelines for good spreadsheet models (as is done for Figure 3.5) results in a model that is easier to understand, easier to debug, and easier to modify. This is especially important for models that will have a long life span. If this model

FIGURE 3.7
A poor formulation of the spreadsheet model for the Everglade cash flow management problem.

	A	B	C	D	E	F
1		**A Poor Formulation of the Everglade Cash Flow Problem**				
2						
3			LT	ST	Ending	
4		Year	Loan	Loan	Balance	
5		2003	6.65	0.85	0.50	
6		2004		3.40	0.50	
7		2005		8.21	0.50	
8		2006		6.49	0.50	
9		2007		1.61	0.50	
10		2008		0	1.27	
11		2009		3.70	0.50	
12		2010		0	2.97	
13		2011		0	0.50	
14		2012		0	10.03	
15		2013			2.92	

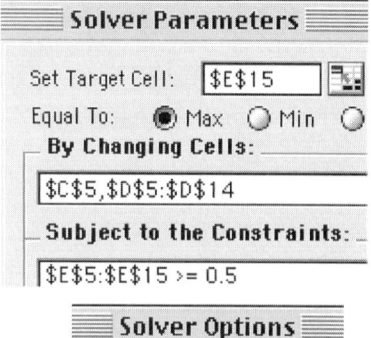

Solver Parameters

Set Target Cell: $E$15

Equal To: ⦿ Max ◯ Min ◯

By Changing Cells:
$C$5,$D$5:$D$14

Subject to the Constraints:
$E$5:$E$15 >= 0.5

Solver Options

☑ Assume Linear Model
☑ Assume Non-Negative

	E
3	Ending
4	Balance
5	=1–8+C5+D5
6	=E5–2+D6–$C$5*(0.07)–D5*(1.1)
7	=E6–4+D7–$C$5*(0.07)–D6*(1.1)
8	=E7+3+D8–$C$5*(0.07)–D7*(1.1)
9	=E8+6+D9–$C$5*(0.07)–D8*(1.1)
10	=E9+3+D10–$C$5*(0.07)–D9*(1.1)
11	=E10–4+D11–$C$5*(0.07)–D10*(1.1)
12	=E11+7+D12–$C$5*(0.07)–D11*(1.1)
13	=E12–2+D13–$C$5*(0.07)–D12*(1.1)
14	=E13+10+D14–$C$5*(0.07)–D13*(1.1)
15	=E14+D15–$C$5*(1.07)–D14*(1.1)

is going to be reused months later, the "good" model of Figure 3.5 immediately can be understood, modified, and reapplied as needed, whereas deciphering the spreadsheet model of Figure 3.7 again would be a great challenge.

<table>
<tr><td>

Review
Questions

</td><td>

1. Which part of the model should be entered first on the spreadsheet?
2. Should numbers be included in formulas or entered separately in data cells?
3. How do range names make formulas and the model in the Solver dialogue box easier to interpret? How should range names be chosen?
4. What are some ways to distinguish data cells, changing cells, output cells, and target cells on a spreadsheet?
5. How many cells are needed to completely specify a constraint on a spreadsheet?

</td></tr>
</table>

3.4   DEBUGGING A SPREADSHEET MODEL

Debugging a spreadsheet model sometimes is as challenging as debugging a computer program.

No matter how carefully it is planned and built, even a moderately complicated model usually will not be error-free the first time it is run. Often the mistakes are immediately obvious and quickly corrected. However, sometimes an error is harder to root out. Following the guidelines in Section 3.3 for developing a good spreadsheet model can make the model *much* easier to debug. Even so, much like debugging a computer program, debugging a spreadsheet model can be a difficult task. This section presents some tips and a variety of Excel features that can make debugging easier.

As a first step in debugging a spreadsheet model, test the model using the principles discussed in the first subsection on testing in Section 3.2. In particular, try different values for the changing cells for which you can predict the correct result in the output cells and see if they calculate as expected. Values of 0 are good ones to try initially because usually it is then obvious what should be in the output cells. Try other simple values, such as all 1s, where the correct results in the output cells are reasonably obvious. For more complicated values, break out a calculator and do some manual calculations to check the various output cells. Include some very large values for the changing cells to ensure that the calculations are behaving reasonably for these extreme cases.

If you have added rows or columns to the spreadsheet, make sure that each of the range names still refers to the correct cells.

If you have defined range names, be sure that they still refer to the correct cells. Sometimes they can become disjointed when you add rows or columns to the spreadsheet. To test the range names, you can either select the various range names in the name box, which will highlight the selected range in the spreadsheet, or paste the entire list of range names and their references into the spreadsheet (by choosing Name\Paste from the Insert menu and then clicking Paste List).

Carefully study each formula to be sure it is entered correctly. A very useful feature in Excel for checking formulas is the **toggle** to switch back and forth between viewing the formulas in the worksheet and viewing the resulting values in the output cells. By default, Excel shows the values that are calculated by the various output cells in the model. Typing control-~ on a PC (or command-~ on a Mac) switches the current worksheet to instead display the formulas in the output cells, as shown in Figure 3.8. Typing control-~ again switches back to the standard view of displaying the values in the output cells (like Figure 3.5).

Another useful set of features built into Excel are the **auditing tools.** Choosing Show Auditing Toolbar from the Auditing item in the Tools menu displays the Auditing Toolbar shown in Figure 3.9.

The Auditing Toolbar can be used to graphically display which cells make direct links to a given cell. For example, selecting LTLoan (D11) in Figure 3.5 and either clicking on the Trace Dependents button on the Auditing Toolbar (third from the left) or choosing Auditing\Trace Dependents from the Tools menu generates the arrows on the spreadsheet shown in Figure 3.10.

You now can immediately see that LTLoan (D11) is used in the calculation of LT Interest for every year in column F, in the calculation of LTPayback (H21), and in the calculation of the ending balance in 2003 (J11). This can be very illuminating. Think about what output cells

toggle
The toggle feature in Excel is a great way to check the formulas for the output cells.

Excel Tip: Pressing control-~ on a PC (or command-~ on a Mac) toggles the worksheet between viewing values and viewing formulas in all the output cells.

FIGURE 3.8 The spreadsheet obtained by toggling the spreadsheet in Figure 3.5 once to replace the values in the output cells by the formulas entered into those cells. Using the toggle feature in Excel once more will restore the view of the spreadsheet shown in Figure 3.5.

	A	B	C	D	E	F	G	H	I	J	K	L
1		**Everglade Cash Flow Management Problem**										
2												
3		LT Rate	0.07									
4		ST Rate	0.1									
5						(all cash figures in millions of dollars)						
6		Start Balance	1									
7		Minimum Cash	0.5									
8												
9			Cash	LT	ST	LT	ST	LT	ST	Ending		Minimum
10		Year	Flow	Loan	Loan	Interest	Interest	Payback	Payback	Balance		Balance
11		2003	−8	6.64945	0.85054		=-STRate*E11			=StartBalance+SUM(C11:I11)	>=	=MinimumCash
12		2004	−2		3.40105	=-LTRate*LTLoan	=-STRate*E12		=-E11	=J11+SUM(C12:I12)	>=	=MinimumCash
13		2005	−4		8.20662	=-LTRate*LTLoan	=-STRate*E13		=-E12	=J12+SUM(C13:I13)	>=	=MinimumCash
14		2006	3		6.49274	=-LTRate*LTLoan	=-STRate*E14		=-E13	=J13+SUM(C14:I14)	>=	=MinimumCash
15		2007	6		1.60748	=-LTRate*LTLoan	=-STRate*E15		=-E14	=J14+SUM(C15:I15)	>=	=MinimumCash
16		2008	3		0	=-LTRate*LTLoan	=-STRate*E16		=-E15	=J15+SUM(C16:I16)	>=	=MinimumCash
17		2009	−4		3.69915	=-LTRate*LTLoan	=-STRate*E17		=-E16	=J16+SUM(C17:I17)	>=	=MinimumCash
18		2010	7		0	=-LTRate*LTLoan	=-STRate*E18		=-E17	=J17+SUM(C18:I18)	>=	=MinimumCash
19		2011	−2		0	=-LTRate*LTLoan	=-STRate*E19		=-E18	=J18+SUM(C19:I19)	>=	=MinimumCash
20		2012	10		0	=-LTRate*LTLoan	=-STRate*E20		=-E19	=J19+SUM(C20:I20)	>=	=MinimumCash
21		2013				=-LTRate*LTLoan		=-LTLoan	=-E20	=J20+SUM(C21:I21)	>=	=MinimumCash

FIGURE 3.9 Excel's Auditing Toolbar. Figures 3.10 and 3.11 have been generated by using the third button from the left and the leftmost button, respectively.

FIGURE 3.10 The spreadsheet obtained by using the Excel auditing tools to trace the dependents of the LT Loan value in cell D11 of the spreadsheet in Figure 3.5.

	A	B	C	D	E	F	G	H	I	J	K	L
1		**Everglade Cash Flow Management Problem**										
2												
3		LT Rate	7%									
4		ST Rate	10%									
5						(all cash figures in millions of dollars)						
6		Start Balance	1									
7		Minimum Cash	0.5									
8												
9			Cash	LT	ST	LT	ST	LT	ST	Ending		Minimum
10		Year	Flow	Loan	Loan	Interest	Interest	Payback	Payback	Balance		Balance
11		2003	−8	6.65	0.85					0.50	≥	0.5
12		2004	−2		3.40	−0.47	−0.09		−0.85	0.50	≥	0.5
13		2005	−4		8.21	−0.47	−0.34		−3.40	0.50	≥	0.5
14		2006	3		6.49	−0.47	−0.82		−8.21	0.50	≥	0.5
15		2007	6		1.61	−0.47	−0.65		−6.49	0.50	≥	0.5
16		2008	3		0	0.47	−0.16		−1.61	1.27	≥	0.5
17		2009	−4		3.70	−0.47	0		0	0.50	≥	0.5
18		2010	7		0	−0.47	−0.37		−3.70	2.97	≥	0.5
19		2011	−2		0	−0.47	0		0	0.50	≥	0.5
20		2012	10		0	−0.47	0		0	10.03	≥	0.5
21		2013				−0.47	0	−6.65	0	2.92	≥	0.5

LTLoan should impact directly. There should be an arrow to each of these cells. If, for example, LTLoan is missing from any of the formulas in column F, the error will be immediately revealed by the missing arrow. Similarly, if LTLoan is mistakenly entered in any of the short-term loan output cells, this will show up as extra arrows.

Excel's Auditing Toolbar enables you to either trace forward or backward to see the linkages between cells.

You also can trace backward to see which cells provide the data for any given cell. These can be displayed graphically by either clicking on the Trace Precedents button on the Auditing Toolbar (the one on the far left) or choosing Auditing\Trace Precedents from the Tools menu. For example, choosing Trace Precedents for the ST Interest cell for 2004 (G12) displays the arrows shown in Figure 3.11. These arrows indicate that the ST Interest cell for 2004 (G12) refers to the ST Loan in 2003 (E11) and to STRate (C4).

When you are done, click on the Remove All Arrows button (fifth from the left) or choose Remove All Arrows from the Auditing menu item in the Tools menu.

Review Questions

1. What is a good first step for debugging a spreadsheet model?
2. How do you toggle between viewing formulas and viewing values in output cells?
3. Which Excel tool can be used to trace the dependents or precedents for a given cell?

FIGURE 3.11 The spreadsheet obtained by using the Excel auditing tools to trace the precedents of the ST Interest (2004) calculation in cell G12 of the spreadsheet in Figure 3.5.

	A	B	C	D	E	F	G	H	I	J	K	L
1		**Everglade Cash Flow Management Problem**										
2												
3		LT Rate	7%									
4		ST Rate	10%									
5						(all cash figures in millions of dollars)						
6		Start Balance	1									
7		Minimum Cash	0.5									
8												
9			Cash	LT	ST	LT	ST	LT	ST	Ending		Minimum
10		Year	Flow	Loan	Loan	Interest	Interest	Payback	Payback	Balance		Balance
11		2003	−8	6.65	0.85					0.50	≥	0.5
12		2004	−2		3.40	−0.47	−0.09		−0.85	0.50	≥	0.5
13		2005	−4		8.21	−0.47	−0.34		−3.40	0.50	≥	0.5
14		2006	3		6.49	−0.47	−0.82		−8.21	0.50	≥	0.5
15		2007	6		1.61	−0.47	−0.65		−6.49	0.50	≥	0.5
16		2008	3		0	−0.47	−0.16		−1.61	1.27	≥	0.5
17		2009	−4		3.70	−0.47	0		0	0.50	≥	0.5
18		2010	7		0	−0.47	−0.37		−3.70	2.97	≥	0.5
19		2011	−2		0	−0.47	0		0	0.50	≥	0.5
20		2012	10		0	−0.47	0		0	10.03	≥	0.5
21		2013				−0.47	0	−6.65	0	2.92	≥	0.5

3.5 Summary

There is a considerable art to modeling well with spreadsheets. This chapter focuses on providing a foundation for learning this art.

The general process of modeling in spreadsheets has four major steps: (1) plan the spreadsheet model, (2) build the model, (3) test the model, and (4) analyze the model and its results. During the planning step, it is helpful to begin by visualizing where you want to finish and then doing some calculations by hand to clarify the needed computations before starting to sketch out a logical layout for the spreadsheet. Then, when you are ready to undertake the building step, it is a good idea to start by building a small, readily manageable version of the model before expanding the model to full-scale size. This enables you to test the small version first to get all the logic straightened out correctly before expanding to a full-scale model and undertaking a final test. After completing all of this, you are ready for the analysis step, which involves applying the model to evaluate proposed solutions and perhaps using Solver to optimize the model.

Using this plan-build-test-analyze process should yield a spreadsheet model, but it doesn't guarantee that you will obtain a good one. Section 3.3 describes in detail the following guidelines for building "good" spreadsheet models:

- Enter the data first.

- Organize and clearly identify the data.

- Enter each piece of data into one cell only.

- Separate data from formulas.

- Keep it simple.

- Use range names.

- Use relative and absolute references to simplify copying formulas.

- Use borders, shading, and colors to distinguish between cell types.

- Show the entire model on the spreadsheet.

Even if all these guidelines are followed, a thorough debugging process may be needed to eliminate the errors that lurk within the initial version of the model. It is important to check whether the output cells are giving correct results for various values of the changing cells. Other items to check include whether range names refer to the appropriate cells and whether formulas have been entered into output cells correctly. Excel provides a number of useful features to aid in the debugging process. One is the ability to toggle the worksheet between viewing the results in the output cells and the formulas entered into those output cells. Several other helpful features are available from Excel's Auditing Toolbar.

Glossary

absolute reference A reference to a cell (or a column or a row) with a fixed address, as indicated either by using a range name or by placing a $ sign in front of the letter and number of the cell reference. (Section 3.2), *85*

auditing tools A set of tools provided by Excel to aid in debugging a spreadsheet model. (Section 3.4), *95*

range name A descriptive name given to a block of cells that immediately identifies what is there. (Section 3.3), *92*

relative reference A reference to a cell whose address is based upon its position relative to the cell containing the formula. (Section 3.2), *85*

toggle The act of switching back and forth between viewing the results in the output cells and viewing the formulas entered into those output cells. (Section 3.4), *95*

Learning Aids for This Chapter in Your MS Courseware

Chapter 3 Excel Files:

Everglade Case Study

Wyndor Example

An Excel Add-in:

Premium Solver for Education

Problems

We have inserted the symbol E* (for Excel) to the left of each problem or part where Excel should be used. An asterisk on the problem number indicates that at least a partial answer is given in the back of the book.

E* 3.1. Consider the Everglade cash flow problem discussed in this chapter. Suppose that extra cash is kept in an interest-bearing savings account. Assume that any cash left at the end of a year earns 3 percent interest the following year. Make any necessary modifications to the spreadsheet and re-solve. (The original spreadsheet for this problem is available on the CD-ROM.)

3.2.* The Pine Furniture Company makes fine country furniture. The company's current product lines consist of end tables, coffee tables, and dining room tables. The production of each of these tables requires 8, 15, and 80 pounds of pine wood, respectively. The tables are handmade and require one hour, two hours, and four hours, respectively. Each table sold generates $50, $100, and $220 profit, respectively. The company has 3,000 pounds of pine wood and 200 hours of labor available for the coming week's production. The chief operating officer (COO) has asked you to do some spreadsheet modeling with these data to analyze what the product mix should be for the coming week and make a recommendation.

    a. Visualize where you want to finish. What numbers will the COO need? What are the decisions that need to be made? What should the objective be?

    b. Suppose that Pine Furniture were to produce three end tables and three dining room tables. Calculate by hand the amount of pine wood and labor that would be required, as well as the profit generated from sales.

    c. Make a rough sketch of a spreadsheet model, with blocks laid out for the data cells, changing cells, output cells, and target cell.

E*   *d.* Build a spreadsheet model and then solve it.

3.3.   Reboot, Inc., is a manufacturer of hiking boots. Demand for boots is highly seasonal. In particular, the demand in the next year is expected to be 3,000, 4,000, 8,000, and 7,000 pairs of boots in quarters 1, 2, 3, and 4, respectively. With its current production facility, the company can produce at most 6,000 pairs of boots in any quarter. Reboot would like to meet all the expected demand, so it will need to carry inventory to meet demand in the later quarters. Each pair of boots sold generates a profit of $20 per pair. Each pair of boots in inventory at the end of a quarter incurs $8 in storage and capital recovery costs. Reboot has 1,000 pairs of boots in inventory at the start of quarter 1. Reboot's top management has given you the assignment of doing some spreadsheet modeling to analyze what the production schedule should be for the next four quarters and make a recommendation.

   a. Visualize where you want to finish. What numbers will top management need? What are the decisions that need to be made? What should the objective be?

   b. Suppose that Reboot were to produce 5,000 pairs of boots in each of the first two quarters. Calculate by hand the ending inventory, profit from sales, and inventory costs for quarters 1 and 2.

   c. Make a rough sketch of a spreadsheet model, with blocks laid out for the data cells, changing cells, output cells, and target cell.

E*   d. Build a spreadsheet model for quarters 1 and 2, and then thoroughly test the model.

E*   e. Expand the model to full scale and then solve it.

E* 3.4.*   The Fairwinds Development Corporation is considering taking part in one or more of three different development projects—A, B, and C—that are about to be launched. Each project requires a significant investment over the next few years and then would be sold upon completion. The projected cash flows (in millions of dollars) associated with each project are shown in the table below.

Year	Project A	Project B	Project C
1	−4	−8	−10
2	−6	−8	−7
3	−6	−4	−7
4	24	−4	−5
5	0	30	−3
6	0	0	44

Fairwinds has $10 million available now and expects to receive $6 million from other projects by the end of each year (1 through 6) that would be available for the ongoing investments the following year in projects A, B, and C. By acting now, the company may participate in each project either fully, fractionally (with other development partners), or not at all. If Fairwinds participates at less than 100 percent, then all the cash flows associated with that project are reduced proportionally. Company policy requires ending each year with a cash balance of at least $1 million.

   a. Visualize where you want to finish. What numbers are needed? What are the decisions that need to be made? What should the objective be?

   b. Suppose that Fairwinds were to participate in Project A fully and in Project C at 50 percent. Calculate by hand what the ending cash positions would be after year 1 and year 2.

   c. Make a rough sketch of a spreadsheet model, with blocks laid out for the data cells, changing cells, output cells, and target cell.

E*   d. Build a spreadsheet model for years 1 and 2, and then thoroughly test the model.

E*   e. Expand the model to full scale, and then solve it.

3.5.   Refer to the scenario described in Problem 4.12 (Chapter 4), but ignore the instructions given there. Focus instead on using spreadsheet modeling to address Web Mercantile's problem by doing the following.

   a. Visualize where you want to finish. What numbers will Web Mercantile require? What are the decisions that need to be made? What should the objective be?

   b. Suppose that Web Mercantile were to lease 30,000 square feet for all five months and then 20,000 additional square feet for the last three months. Calculate the total costs by hand.

   c. Make a rough sketch of a spreadsheet model, with blocks laid out for the data cells, changing cells, output cells, and target cell.

E* *d.* Build a spreadsheet model for months 1 and 2, and then thoroughly test the model.

E* *e.* Expand the model to full scale, and then solve it.

3.6.* Refer to the scenario described in Problem 4.14 (Chapter 4), but ignore the instructions given there. Focus instead on using spreadsheet modeling to address Larry Edison's problem by doing the following.

    a. Visualize where you want to finish. What numbers will Larry require? What are the decisions that need to be made? What should the objective be?

    b. Suppose that Larry were to hire three full-time workers for the morning shift, two for the afternoon shift, and four for the evening shift, as well as three part-time workers for each of the four shifts. Calculate by hand how many workers would be working at each time of the day and what the total cost would be for the entire day.

    c. Make a rough sketch of a spreadsheet model, with blocks laid out for the data cells, changing cells, output cells, and target cell.

E* *d.* Build a spreadsheet model and then solve it.

3.7. Refer to the scenario described in Problem 4.17 (Chapter 4), but ignore the instructions given there. Focus instead on using spreadsheet modeling to address Al Ferris's problem by doing the following.

    a. Visualize where you want to finish. What numbers will Al require? What are the decisions that need to be made? What should the objective be?

    b. Suppose that Al were to invest $20,000 each in investment *A* (year 1), investment *B* (year 2), and investment *C* (year 2). Calculate by hand what the ending cash position would be after each year.

    c. Make a rough sketch of a spreadsheet model, with blocks laid out for the data cells, changing cells, output cells, and target cell.

E* *d.* Build a spreadsheet model for years 1 through 3, and then thoroughly test the model.

E* *e.* Expand the model to full scale, and then solve it.

3.8. In contrast to the spreadsheet model for the Wyndor Glass Co. product-mix problem shown in Figure 3.6, the spreadsheet given below is an example of a poorly formulated spreadsheet model for this same problem. Referring to Section 3.3, identify the guidelines violated by the model below. Then, explain how each guideline has been violated and why the model in Figure 3.6 is a better alternative.

	A	B	C	D
1		**Wyndor Glass Co. (Poor Formulation)**		
2				
3		Doors Produced	2	
4		Windows Produced	6	
5		Hours Used (Plant 1)	2	
6		Hours Used (Plant 2)	12	
7		Hours Used (Plant 3)	18	
8		Total Profit	$3,600	

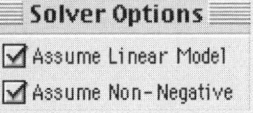

Solver Parameters

Set Target Cell: $C$8

Equal To: ◉ Max ○ Min ○

By Changing Cells:
$C$3:$C$4

Subject to the Constraints:
$C$5 <= 4
$C$6 <=12
$C$7 <=18

	B	C
5	Hours Used (Plant 1)	=1*C3+0*C4
6	Hours Used (Plant 2)	=0*C3+2*C4
7	Hours Used (Plant 3)	=3*C3+2*C4
8	Total Profit	=300*C3+500*C4

Solver Options
☑ Assume Linear Model
☑ Assume Non-Negative

E* 3.9.   Refer to the spreadsheet file named "Everglade Problem 3.9" contained on the CD-ROM. This file contains a formulation of the Everglade problem considered in this chapter. However, three errors are included in this formulation. Use the ideas presented in Section 3.4 for debugging a spreadsheet model to find the errors. In particular, try different trial values for which you can predict the correct results, use the toggle to examine all the formulas, and use the Auditing Toolbar to check precedence and dependence relationships among the various changing cells, data cells, and output cells. Describe the errors found and how you found them.

E*3.10.   Refer to the spreadsheet file named "Everglade Problem 3.10" contained on the CD-ROM. This file contains a formulation of the Everglade problem considered in this chapter. However, three errors are included in this formulation. Use the ideas presented in Section 3.4 for debugging a spreadsheet model to find the errors. In particular, try different trial values for which you can predict the correct results, use the toggle to examine all the formulas, and use the Auditing Toolbar to check precedence and dependence relationships among the various changing cells, data cells, and output cells. Describe the errors found and how you found them.

Case 3-1

Prudent Provisions for Pensions

Among its many financial products, the Prudent Financial Services Corporation (normally referred to as PFS) manages a well-regarded pension fund that is used by a number of companies to provide pensions for their employees. PFS's management takes pride in the rigorous professional standards used in operating the fund. Since the Enron collapse in late 2001 and the subsequent tightening of federal and state regulations for operating pension funds, PFS has redoubled its efforts to provide prudent management of the fund.

It is now December 2002. The total pension payments that will need to be made by the fund over the next 10 years are shown in the table below.

Year	Pension Payments ($ millions)
2003	8
2004	12
2005	13
2006	14
2007	16
2008	17
2009	20
2010	21
2011	22
2012	24

By using interest as well, PFS currently has enough liquid assets to meet all these pension payments. Therefore, to safeguard the pension fund, PFS would like to make a number of investments whose payouts would match the pension payments over the next 10 years. The only investments that PFS trusts for the pension fund are a money market fund and bonds. The money market fund pays an annual interest rate of 5 percent. The characteristics of each unit of the four bonds under consideration are shown in the table below.

	Current Price	Coupon Rate	Maturity Date	Face Value
Bond 1	$980	4%	Jan. 1, 2004	$1,000
Bond 2	920	2	Jan. 1, 2006	1,000
Bond 3	750	0	Jan. 1, 2008	1,000
Bond 4	800	3	Jan. 1, 2011	1,000

All of these bonds will be available for purchase on January 1, 2003, in as many units as desired. The coupon rate is the percentage of the face value that will be paid in interest on January 1 of each year, starting one year after purchase and continuing until (and including) the maturity date. Thus, these interest payments on January 1 of each year are in time to be used toward the pension payments for that year. Any excess interest payments will be deposited into the money market fund. To be conservative in its financial planning, PFS assumes that all the pension payments for the year occur at the beginning of the year immediately after these interest payments (including a year's interest from the money market fund) are received. The entire face value of a bond also will be received on its maturity date. Since the current price of each bond is less than its face value, the actual yield of the bond exceeds its coupon rate. Bond 3 is a zero-coupon bond, so it pays no interest but instead pays a face value on the maturity date that greatly exceeds the purchase price.

PFS would like to make the smallest possible investment (including any deposit into the money market fund) on January 1, 2003, to cover all its required pension payments through 2012. Some spreadsheet modeling needs to be done to see how to do this.

a. Visualize where you want to finish. What numbers are needed by PFS management? What are the decisions that need to be made? What should the objective be?

b. Suppose that PFS were to invest $28 million in the money market fund and purchase 10,000 units each of bond 1 and bond 2 on January 1, 2003. Calculate by hand the payments received from bonds 1 and 2 on January 1 of 2004 and 2005. Also calculate the resulting balance in the money market fund on January 1 of 2003, 2004, and 2005 after receiving these payments, making the pension payments for the year, and depositing any excess into the money market fund.

c. Make a rough sketch of a spreadsheet model, with blocks laid out for the data cells, changing cells, output cells, and target cell.

d. Build a spreadsheet model for years 2003 through 2005, and then thoroughly test the model.

e. Expand the model to consider all years through 2012, and then solve it.

Learning objectives

After completing this chapter, you should be able to

1. Recognize various kinds of managerial problems to which linear programming can be applied.

2. Describe the four major categories of linear programming problems, including their identifying features.

3. Formulate a linear programming model from a description of a problem in any of these categories.

4. Describe the difference between resource constraints and benefit constraints, including the difference in how they arise.

5. Describe fixed-requirement constraints and where they arise.

6. Identify the kinds of Excel functions that linear programming spreadsheet models use for the output cells, including the target cell.

7. Identify the four components of any linear programming model and the kind of spreadsheet cells used for each component.

8. Recognize managerial problems that can be formulated and analyzed as linear programming problems.

9. Understand the flexibility that managers have in prescribing key considerations that can be incorporated into a linear programming model.

Chapter **Four**

Linear Programming:

Formulation and Applications

Linear programming problems come in many guises. And their models take various forms. This diversity can be confusing to both students and managers, making it difficult to recognize when linear programming can be applied to address a managerial problem. Since managers instigate management science studies, the ability to recognize the applicability of linear programming is an important managerial skill. This chapter focuses largely on developing this skill.

The usual textbook approach to trying to teach this skill is to present a series of diverse examples of linear programming applications. The weakness of this approach is that it emphasizes differences rather than the common threads between these applications. Our approach will be to emphasize these common threads—the **identifying features**—that tie together linear programming problems even when they arise in very different contexts. We will describe some broad categories of linear programming problems and the identifying features that characterize them. Then we will use diverse examples, but with the purpose of illustrating and emphasizing the common threads among them.

We will focus on three key categories of linear programming problems: resource-allocation problems, cost–benefit–trade-off problems, and distribution-network problems. In each case, an important identifying feature is the nature of the restrictions on what decisions can be made, and thus the nature of the resulting functional constraints in the linear programming model. In particular, the functional constraints for each category of problems are resource constraints, benefit constraints, and fixed-requirement constraints, respectively. For each category, you will see how the basic data for a problem lead directly to a linear programming model with a certain distinctive form. Thus, model formulation becomes a by-product of proper problem formulation.

Although many linear programming problems fall completely into one of these categories, and so have only the corresponding kind of functional constraint, many others do not because they have at least a few functional constraints of one or both of the other kinds. Problems with a mixture of constraint types fall into a fourth category of linear programming problems—mixed problems.

The chapter begins with a case study that initially involves a resource-allocation problem. We then return to the case study in Section 4.5, where additional managerial considerations turn the problem into a mixed problem.

Sections 4.2, 4.3, 4.4, and 4.6 focus on the four categories of linear programming problems in turn. Section 4.7 then takes a broader look at the formulation of linear programming models from a managerial perspective. This section (along with Section 4.5) highlights the importance of having the model accurately reflect the managerial view of the problem. These (and other) sections also describe the flexibility available to managers for having the model structured to best fit their view of the important considerations.

Finally, Section 4.8 revisits the three case studies of classic applications of linear programming presented in Section 2.1. This revisit will include a discussion of some of the factors that made these applications so successful.

4.1 A CASE STUDY: THE SUPER GRAIN CORP. ADVERTISING-MIX PROBLEM

Claire Syverson, vice president for marketing of the Super Grain Corporation, is facing a daunting challenge: how to break into an already overly crowded breakfast cereal market in a big way. Fortunately, the company's new breakfast cereal—Crunchy Start—has a lot going for it: Great taste. Nutritious. Crunchy from start to finish. She can recite the litany in her sleep now. It has the makings of a winning promotional campaign.

However, Claire knows that she has to avoid the mistakes she made in her last campaign for a breakfast cereal. That had been her first big assignment since she won this promotion, and what a disaster! She thought she had developed a really good campaign. But somehow it had failed to connect with the most crucial segments of the market—young children and parents of young children. She also has concluded that it was a mistake not to include cents-off coupons in the magazine and newspaper advertising. Oh well. Live and learn.

But she had better get it right this time, especially after the big stumble last time. The company's president, David Sloan, already has impressed on her how important the success of Crunchy Start is to the future of the company. She remembers exactly how David concluded the conversation. "The company's shareholders are not happy. We need to get those earnings headed in the right direction again." Claire had heard this tune before, but she saw in David's eyes how deadly serious he is this time.

Claire often uses spreadsheets to help organize her planning. Her management science course in business school impressed upon her how valuable spreadsheet modeling can be. She regrets that she did not rely more heavily on spreadsheet modeling for the last campaign. That was a mistake that she is determined not to repeat.

Now it is time for Claire to carefully review and formulate the problem in preparation for formulating a spreadsheet model.

The Problem

Claire already has employed a leading advertising firm, Giacomi & Jackowitz, to help design a nationwide promotional campaign that will achieve the largest possible exposure for Crunchy Start. Super Grain will pay this firm a fee based on services performed (not to exceed $1 million) and has allocated an additional $4 million for advertising expenses.

Giacomi & Jackowitz has identified the three most effective advertising media for this product:

Medium 1: Television commercials on Saturday morning programs for children.

Medium 2: Advertisements in food and family-oriented magazines.

Medium 3: Advertisements in Sunday supplements of major newspapers.

The problem now is to determine which *levels* should be chosen for these *advertising activities* to obtain the most effective *advertising mix*.

To determine the *best mix of activity levels* for this particular advertising problem, it is necessary (as always) to identify the *overall measure of performance* for the problem and then the contribution of each activity toward this measure. An ultimate goal for Super Grain is to maximize its profits, but it is difficult to make a direct connection between advertising exposure and profits. Therefore, as a rough surrogate for profit, Claire decides to use *expected number of exposures* as the overall measure of performance, where each viewing of an advertisement by some individual counts as one exposure.

Giacomi & Jackowitz has made preliminary plans for advertisements in the three media. The firm also has estimated the expected number of exposures for each advertisement in each medium, as given in the bottom row of Table 4.1.

The number of advertisements that can be run in the different media are restricted by both the advertising budget (a limit of $4 million) and the planning budget (a limit of $1 million for

TABLE 4.1
Cost and Exposure Data for the Super Grain Corp. Advertising-Mix Problem

	Costs		
Cost Category	**Each TV Commercial**	**Each Magazine Ad**	**Each Sunday Ad**
Ad budget	$300,000	$150,000	$100,000
Planning budget	90,000	30,000	40,000
Expected number of exposures	1,300,000	600,000	500,000

the fee to Giacomi & Jackowitz). Another restriction is that there are only five commercial spots available for running different commercials (one commercial per spot) on children's television programs Saturday morning (medium 1) during the time of the promotional campaign. (The other two media have an ample number of spots available.)

Consequently, the three *resources* for this problem are:

Resource 1: Advertising budget ($4 million).

Resource 2: Planning budget ($1 million).

Resource 3: TV commercial spots available (5).

Table 4.1 shows how much of the advertising budget and the planning budget would be used by each advertisement in the respective media.

- The first row gives the cost per advertisement in each medium.

- The second row shows Giacomi & Jackowitz's estimates of its total cost (including overhead and profit) for designing and developing each advertisement for the respective media.[1] (This cost represents the billable fee from Super Grain.)

- The last row then gives the expected number of exposures per advertisement.

Analysis of the Problem

Claire decides to formulate and solve a linear programming model for this problem on a spreadsheet. The formulation procedure summarized at the end of Section 2.3 guides this process. Like any linear programming model, this model will have four components:

1. The data

2. The decisions

3. The constraints

4. The measure of performance

The spreadsheet needs to be formatted to provide the following kinds of cells for these components:

> Data → data cells

> Decisions → changing cells

> Constraints → output cells

> Measure of performance → target cell

Four kinds of cells are needed for these four components of a spreadsheet model.

Figure 4.1 shows the spreadsheet model formulated by Claire. Let us see how she did this by considering each of the components of the model individually.

---

[1]When presenting its estimates in this form, the firm is making two simplifying assumptions. One is that its cost for designing and developing each additional advertisement in a medium is roughly the same as for the first advertisement in that medium. The second is that its cost when working with one medium is unaffected by how much work it is doing (if any) with the other media.

FIGURE 4.1   The spreadsheet model for the Super Grain problem (Section 4.1), including the target cell TotalExposures (H13) and the other output cells BudgetSpent (F8:F9), as well as the specifications needed to set up the Solver. The changing cells NumberOfAds (C13:E13) show the optimal solution obtained by the Solver.

	A	B	C	D	E	F	G	H
1		**Super Grain Corp. Advertising-Mix Problem**						
2								
3			TV Spots	Magazine Ads	SS Ads			
4		Exposures per Ad	1,300	600	500			
5		(thousands)						
6						Budget		Budget
7			Cost per Ad ($thousands)			Spent		Available
8		Ad Budget	300	150	100	4,000	≤	4,000
9		Planning Budget	90	30	40	1,000	≤	1,000
10								
11								Total Exposures
12			TV Spots	Magazine Ads	SS Ads			(thousands)
13		Number of Ads	0	20	10			17,000
14			≤					
15		Max TV Spots	5					

Solver Parameters

Set Target Cell: [TotalExposu]

Equal To: ● Max ○ Min ○

By Changing Cells:

[NumberOfAds]

Subject to the Constraints:

BudgetSpent <= BudgetAvailable
TVSpots <= MaxTVSpots

Solver Options

☑ Assume Linear Model
☑ Assume Non-Negative

	F
6	Budget
7	Spent
8	=SUMPRODUCT(C8:E8,NumberOfAds)
9	=SUMPRODUCT(C9:E9,NumberOfAds)

	H
11	Total Exposures
12	(thousands)
13	=SUMPRODUCT(ExposuresPerAd,NumberOfAds)

Range Name	Cells
BudgetAvailable	H8: H9
BudgetSpent	F8: F9
CostPerAd	C8: E9
ExposuresPerAd	C4: E4
MaxTVSpots	C15
NumberOfAds	C13: E13
TotalExposures	H13
TVSpots	C13

The Data

One important kind of data is the information given earlier about the amounts available of the three resources for the problem (the advertising budget, the planning budget, and the commercial spots available). Table 4.1 provides the other key data for the problem. Using units of thousands of dollars, these data have been transferred directly into data cells in the spreadsheet in Figure 4.1 and given these range names: ExposuresPerAd (C4:E4), CostPerAd (C8:E9), BudgetAvailable (H8:H9), and MaxTVSpots (C15).

The Decisions

The problem has been defined as determining the most effective advertising mix among the three media selected by Giacomi & Jackowitz. Therefore, there are three decisions:

Decision 1:   TV = Number of commercials for separate spots on television.

Decision 2: M = Number of advertisements in magazines.

Decision 3:   SS = Number of advertisements in Sunday supplements.

The changing cells to hold these numbers have been placed in row 13 in the columns for these media:

$$\text{TV} \rightarrow \text{cell C13} \qquad M \rightarrow \text{cell D13} \qquad \text{SS} \rightarrow \text{cell E13}$$

These changing cells are collectively referred to by the range name NumberOfAds (C13:E13).

The Constraints

These changing cells need to be nonnegative. In addition, constraints are needed for the three resources. The first two resources are the ad budget and planning budget. The amounts available for these two budgets are shown in the range BudgetAvailable (H8:H9). As suggested by the $\leq$ signs entered into column G, the corresponding constraints are

Total spending on advertising $\leq$ 4,000   (Ad budget in \$1,000s)

Total cost of planning $\leq$ 1,000   (Planning budget in \$1,000s)

Using the data in columns C, D, and E for the resources, these totals are

Total spending on advertising = 300TV + 150M + 100SS

Total cost of planning   = 90TV + 30M + 40SS

These sums of products on the right-hand side are entered into the output cells BudgetSpent (F8:F9) by using the SUMPRODUCT functions shown in the lower right-hand side of Figure 4.1. Although the $\leq$ signs entered in column G are only cosmetic (trial solutions still can be entered in the changing cells that violate these inequalities), they will serve as a reminder later to use these same $\leq$ signs when entering the constraints in the Solver dialogue box.

The third resource is TV spots for different commercials. Five such spots are available for purchase. The number of spots used is one of the changing cells (C13). Since this cell will be used in a constraint, we assign the cell its own range name: TVSpots (C13). The maximum number of TV spots available is in the data cell MaxTVSpots (C15). Thus, the required constraint is TVSpots $\leq$ MaxTVSpots.

Excel Tip: Range names may overlap. For instance, we have used NumberOfAds to refer to the whole range of changing cells, C13:E13, and TVSpots to refer to the single cell, C13.

The Measure of Performance

Claire Syverson is using *expected number of exposures* as the overall measure of performance, so let

Exposure = Expected number of exposures (in thousands) from all the advertising

The data cells ExposuresPerAd (C4:E4) provide the expected number of exposures (in thousands) per advertisement in the respective media and the changing cells NumberOfAds (C13:E13) give the number of each type of advertisement. Therefore,

$$\text{Exposure} = 1{,}300\text{TV} + 600M + 500\text{SS}$$

$$= \text{SUMPRODUCT (ExposuresPerAd, NumberOfAds)}$$

is the formula that needs to be entered into the target cell, TotalExposures (H13).

Summary of the Formulation

The above analysis of the four components of the model has formulated the following linear programming model (in algebraic form) on the spreadsheet:

$$\text{Maximize} \quad \text{Exposure} = 1{,}300\text{TV} + 600M + 500\text{SS}$$

subject to

Ad spending:	$300\text{TV} + 150M + 100\text{SS} \le 4{,}000$	
Planning costs:	$90\text{TV} + 30M + 40\text{SS} \le 1{,}000$	
Number of television spots:	$\text{TV} \quad\quad\quad\quad \le \quad 5$	

and

$$\text{TV} \ge 0 \quad\quad M \ge 0 \quad\quad \text{SS} \ge 0$$

The difficult work of defining the problem and gathering all the relevant data in Table 4.1 leads directly to this formulation.

Solving the Model

Excel Tip: The Solver dialogue box is used to tell Solver the location on the spreadsheet of several of the elements of the model: the changing cells, the target cell, and the constraints.

To solve the spreadsheet model formulated above, some key information needs to be entered into the Solver dialogue box. The lower left-hand side of Figure 4.1 shows the needed entries: the target cell (TotalExposures), the changing cells (NumberOfAds), the objective of maximizing the target cell, and the constraints BudgetSpent ≤ BudgetAvailable and TVSpots ≤ MaxTVSpots. In addition, the lower left-hand corner of the figure shows that two Solver options need to be selected: Assume Linear Model (because the model is a linear programming model) and Assume Non-Negative (because negative levels of advertising are impossible). Clicking on the Solve button then tells the Solver to find an optimal solution for the model and display it in the changing cells.

The optimal solution given in row 13 of the spreadsheet provides the following plan for the promotional campaign:

Do not run any television commercials.

Run 20 advertisements in magazines.

Run 10 advertisements in Sunday supplements.

Since TotalExposures (H13) gives the expected number of exposures in thousands, this plan would be expected to provide 17,000,000 exposures.

Evaluation of the Adequacy of the Model

When she chose to use a linear programming model to represent this advertising-mix problem, Claire recognized that this kind of model does not provide a perfect match to this problem. However, a mathematical model is intended to be only an approximate representation of the real problem. Approximations and simplifying assumptions generally are required to have a workable model. All that is really needed is that there be a reasonably high correlation between the prediction of the model and what would actually happen in the real problem. The team now needs to check whether this criterion is satisfied.

Linear programming models allow fractional solutions.

One assumption of linear programming is that *fractional* solutions are allowed. For the current problem, this means that a fractional number (e.g., 3½) of television commercials (or of ads in magazines or Sunday supplements) should be allowed. This is technically true, since a commercial can be aired for less than a normal run, or an ad can be run in just a fraction of the usual magazines or Sunday supplements. However, one defect of the model is that it assumes that Giacomi & Jackowitz's cost for planning and developing a commercial or ad that receives only a fraction of its usual run is only that fraction of its usual cost, even though the actual cost would be the same as for a full run. Fortunately, the optimal solution obtained above was an *integer* solution (0 television commercials, 20 ads in magazines, and 10 ads in Sunday supplements), so the assumption that fractional solutions are allowed was not even needed.

Linear programming models should use SUM or SUMPRODUCT functions for the output cells, including the target cell.

Another key assumption of linear programming is that the appropriate equation for each of the output cells, including the target cell, is one that can be expressed as a SUMPRODUCT of data cells and changing cells (or occasionally just a SUM of changing cells). For the target cell (cell H13) in Figure 4.1, this implies that the expected number of exposures to be obtained from each advertising medium is *proportional* to the number of advertisements in that medium. This proportionality seems true, since each viewing of the advertisements by some individual counts as another exposure. Another implication of using a SUMPRODUCT function is that the expected number of exposures to be obtained from an advertising medium is unaffected by the number of advertisements in the other media. Again, this implication seems valid, since viewings of advertisements in different media count as separate exposures.

Although a SUMPRODUCT function is appropriate for calculating the expected number of exposures, the choice of this number for the overall measure of performance is somewhat questionable. Management's real objective is to maximize the profit generated as a result of the advertising campaign, but this is difficult to measure so *expected number of exposures* was selected to be a surrogate for profit. This would be valid if profit were proportional to the expected number of exposures. However, proportionality is only an approximation in this case because too many exposures for the same individual reach a saturation level where the impact (potential profit) from one more exposure is substantially less than for the first exposure.

To check how reasonable it is to use expected number of exposures as a surrogate for profit, Claire meets with Sid Jackowitz, one of the senior partners of Giacomi & Jackowitz. Sid indicates that the contemplated promotional campaign (20 advertisements in magazines and 10 in Sunday supplements) is a relatively modest one well below saturation levels. Most readers will only notice these ads once or twice, and a second notice is very helpful for reinforcing the first one. Furthermore, the readership of magazines and Sunday supplements is sufficiently different that the interaction of the advertising impact in these two media should be small. Consequently, Claire concludes that using expected number of exposures for the target cell in Figure 4.1 provides a reasonable approximation. (A continuation of this case study in Case 10.1 will delve into the more complicated analysis that is required in order to use profit directly as the measure of performance to be recorded in the target cell instead of making this approximation.)

Next, Claire quizzes Sid about his firm's costs for planning and developing advertisements in these media. Is it reasonable to assume that the cost in a given medium is proportional to the number of advertisements in that medium? Is it reasonable to assume that the cost of developing advertisements in one medium would not be substantially reduced if the firm had just finished developing advertisements in another medium that might have similar themes? Sid acknowledges that there is some carryover in ad planning from one medium to another, especially if both are print media (e.g., magazines and Sunday supplements), but that the carryover is quite limited because of the distinct differences in these media. Furthermore, he feels that the proportionality assumption is quite reasonable for any given medium since the amount of work involved in planning and developing each additional advertisement in the medium is nearly the same as for the first one in the medium. The total fee that Super Grain will pay Giacomi & Jackowitz will eventually be based on a detailed accounting of the amount of work done by the firm. Nevertheless, Sid feels that the cost estimates previously provided by the firm (as entered in cells C9, D9, and E9 in units of thousands of dollars) give a reasonable basis for roughly projecting what the fee will be for any given plan (the entries in the changing cells) for the promotional campaign.

Based on this information, Claire concludes that using a SUMPRODUCT function for cell F9 provides a reasonable approximation. Doing the same for cell F8 is clearly justified. Given her earlier conclusions as well, Claire decides that the linear programming model incorporated into Figure 4.1 (plus any expansions of the model needed later for the detailed planning) is a sufficiently accurate representation of the real advertising-mix problem. It will not be necessary to refine the results from this model by turning next to a more complicated kind of mathematical model (such as those to be described in Chapter 10).

Therefore, Claire sends a memorandum to the company's president, David Sloan, describing a promotional campaign that corresponds to the optimal solution from the linear programming model (no TV commercials, 20 ads in magazines, and 10 ads in Sunday supplements). She also requests a meeting to evaluate this plan and discuss whether some modifications should be made.

Management's Reaction

Soon thereafter, Claire Syverson and David Sloan meet to discuss plans for the campaign.

David Sloan (president): Thanks for your memo, Claire. The plan you outline for the promotional campaign looks like a reasonable one. However, I am surprised that it does not make any use of TV commercials. Why is that?

Claire Syverson (vice president for marketing): Well, as I described in my memo, I used a spreadsheet model to see how to maximize the number of exposures from the campaign and this turned out to be the plan that does this. I also was surprised that it did not include TV commercials, but the model indicated that introducing commercials would provide less exposures on a dollar-for-dollar basis than magazine ads and Sunday supplement ads. Don't you think it makes sense to use the plan that maximizes the number of exposures?

David: Not necessarily. Some exposures are a lot less important than others. For example, we know that middle-aged adults are not big consumers of our cereals, so we don't care very much how many of those people see our ads. On the other hand, young children are big consumers. Having TV commercials on the Saturday morning programs for children is our primary method of reaching young children. You know how important it will be to get young children to ask their parents for Crunchy Start. That is our best way of generating first-time sales. Those commercials also get seen by a lot of parents who are watching the programs with their kids. What we need is a commercial that is appealing to both parents and kids, and that gets the kids immediately bugging their parents to go buy Crunchy Start. I think that is a real key to a successful campaign.

Claire: Yes, that makes a lot of sense. In fact, I already have set some goals regarding the number of young children and the number of parents of young children that need to be reached by this promotional campaign.

David: Good. Did you include those goals in your spreadsheet model?

Claire: No, I didn't.

David: Well, I suggest that you incorporate them directly into your model. I suspect that maximizing exposures while also meeting your goals will give us a high impact plan that includes some TV commercials.

Claire: Good idea. I'll try it.

David: Are there any other factors that the plan in your memo doesn't take into account as well as you would like?

Claire: Well, yes, one. The plan doesn't take into account my budget for cents-off coupons in magazines and newspapers.

David: You should be able to add that to your model as well. Why don't you go back and see what happens when you incorporate these additional considerations?

Claire: OK, will do. You seem to have had a lot of experience with spreadsheet modeling.

David: Yes. It is a great tool as long as you maintain some healthy skepticism about what comes out of the model. No model can fully take into account everything that we must consider when dealing with managerial problems. This is especially true the first time or two you run the model. You need to keep asking, what are the missing quantitative considerations that I still should add to the model? Then, after you have made the model as complete as possible and obtained a solution, you still need to use your best managerial judgment to

The *resources* to be allocated to these activities are

Resource 1: Production capacity in Plant 1.

Resource 2: Production capacity in Plant 2.

Resource 3: Production capacity in Plant 3.

Each of the three functional constraints in the linear programming model formulated in Section 2.3 (see rows 7–9 of the spreadsheet in Figure 2.3 or 2.4) is a *resource constraint* for one of these three resources. Column E shows the amount of production capacity used in each plant and column G gives the amount available.

Table 2.1 in Section 2.2 provides the data for the Wyndor problem. You already have seen how the numbers in Table 2.1 become the parameters in the linear programming model in either its spreadsheet formulation (Section 2.3) or its algebraic form (Section 2.4).

Capital Budgeting

Financial planning is one of the most important areas of application for resource-allocation problems. The resources being allocated in this area are quite different from those for applications in the *production planning* area (such as the Wyndor Glass Co. product-mix problem), where the resources tend to be *production facilities* of various kinds. For financial planning, the resources tend to be *financial assets* such as cash, securities, accounts receivable, lines of credit, and so forth. Our specific example involves *capital budgeting,* where the resources are amounts of investment capital available at different points in time.

The Problem

The Think-Big Development Co. is a major investor in commercial real-estate development projects. It currently has the opportunity to share in three large construction projects:

Project 1: Construct a high-rise office building.

Project 2: Construct a hotel.

Project 3: Construct a shopping center.

Each project requires each partner to make investments at four different points in time: a down payment now, and additional capital after one, two, and three years. Table 4.2 shows for each project the *total* amount of investment capital required from all the partners at these four points in time. Thus, a partner taking a certain percentage share of a project is obligated to invest that percentage of each of the amounts shown in the table for the project.

All three projects are expected to be very profitable in the long run. So the management of Think-Big wants to invest as much as possible in some or all of them. Management is willing to commit all the company's investment capital currently available, as well as all additional investment capital expected to become available over the next three years. The objective is to determine the *investment mix* that will be most profitable, based on current estimates of profitability.

TABLE 4.2
Financial Data for the Projects Being Considered for Partial Investment by the Think-Big Development Co.

	Investment Capital Requirements		
Year	Office Building	Hotel	Shopping Center
0	$40 million	$80 million	$90 million
1	60 million	80 million	50 million
2	90 million	80 million	20 million
3	10 million	70 million	60 million
Net present value	$45 million	$70 million	$50 million

Since it will be several years before each project begins to generate income, which will continue for many years thereafter, we need to take into account the *time value of money* in evaluating how profitable it might be. This is done by *discounting* future cash outflows (capital invested) and cash inflows (income), and then adding discounted net cash flows, to calculate a project's *net present value*.

Based on current estimates of future cash flows (not included here except for outflows), the estimated net present value for each project is shown in the bottom row of Table 4.2. All the investors, including Think-Big, then will split this net present value in proportion to their share of the total investment.

For each project, *participation shares* are being sold to major investors, such as Think-Big, who become the partners for the project by investing their proportional shares at the four specified points in time. For example, if Think-Big takes a 10 percent share of the office building, it will need to provide $4 million now, and then $6 million, $9 million, and $1 million in 1 year, 2 years, and 3 years, respectively.

The company currently has $25 million available for capital investment. Projections are that another $20 million will become available after one year, $20 million more after two years, and another $15 million after three years. What share should Think-Big take in the respective projects to maximize the total net present value of these investments?

Formulation

This is a *resource-allocation problem.* The activities under consideration are

Activity 1: Invest in the construction of an office building.

Activity 2: Invest in the construction of a hotel.

Activity 3: Invest in the construction of a shopping center.

Thus, the decisions to be made are the levels of these activities, that is, what participation share to take in investing in each of these projects. A participation share can be expressed as either a fraction or a percentage of the entire project, so the entire project is considered to be one "unit" of that activity.

The resources to be allocated to these activities are the funds available at the four investment points. Funds not used at one point are available at the next point. (For simplicity, we will ignore any interest earned on these funds.) Therefore, the *resource constraint* for each point must reflect the cumulative funds to that point.

Resource 1: Total investment capital available now.

Resource 2: Cumulative investment capital available by the end of one year.

Resource 3: Cumulative investment capital available by the end of two years.

Resource 4: Cumulative investment capital available by the end of three years.

Since the amount of investment capital available is $25 million now, another $20 million in one year, another $20 million in two years, and another $15 million in three years, the amounts available of the resources are the following.

Amount of resource 1 available = $25 million

Amount of resource 2 available = $(25 + 20) million = $45 million

Amount of resource 3 available = $(25 + 20 + 20) million = $65 million

Amount of resource 4 available = $(25 + 20 + 20 + 15) million = $80 million

Table 4.3 shows all the data involving these resources. The rightmost column gives the amounts of resources available calculated above. The middle columns show the *cumulative* amounts of the investment capital requirements listed in Table 4.2. For example, in the Office

TABLE 4.3
Resource Data for the
Think-Big Development
Co. Investment-Mix
Problem

	Cumulative Investment Capital Required for an Entire Project			
Resource	Office Building	Hotel	Shopping Center	Amount of Resource Available
1 (Now)	$ 40 million	$ 80 million	$ 90 million	$25 million
2 (End of year 1)	100 million	160 million	140 million	45 million
3 (End of year 2)	190 million	240 million	160 million	65 million
4 (End of year 3)	200 million	310 million	220 million	80 million

Building column of Table 4.3, the second number ($100 million) is obtained by adding the first two numbers ($40 million and $60 million) in the Office Building column of Table 4.2.

The Data   As with any resource-allocation problem, three kinds of data need to be gathered. One is the amounts available of the resources, as given in the rightmost column of Table 4.3. A second is the amount of each resource needed by each project, which is given in the middle columns of this table. A third is the contribution of each project to the overall measure of performance (net present value), as given in the bottom row of Table 4.2.

The first step in formulating the spreadsheet model is to enter these data into data cells in the spreadsheet. In Figure 4.2, the data cells (and their range names) are NetPresentValue (C5:E5), CapitalRequired (C9:E12), and CapitalAvailable (H9:H12). To save space on the spreadsheet, these numbers are entered in units of millions of dollars.

The Decisions   With three activities under consideration, there are three decisions to be made.

Decision 1: OB = Participation share in the office building

Decision 2:   H = Participation share in the hotel

Decision 3: SC = Participation share in the shopping center

For example, if Think-Big management were to decide to take a one-tenth participation share (i.e., a 10 percent participation share) in each of these projects, then

OB = 0.1 = 10%

 H = 0.1 = 10%

SC = 0.1 = 10%

However, it may not be desirable to take the same participation share (expressed as either a fraction or a percentage) in each of the projects, so the idea is to choose the best combination of values of OB, H, and SC. In Figure 4.2, the participation shares (expressed as percentages) have been placed in changing cells under the data cells (row 16) in the columns for the three projects, so

OB → cell C16   H → D16   SC → cell E16

where these cells are collectively referred to by the range name ParticipationShare (C16:E16).

The Constraints   The numbers in these changing cells make sense only if they are nonnegative, so the *Assume Non-Negative* option will need to be selected in the Solver dialogue box. In addition, the four resources require resource constraints:

Total invested now ≤ 25   (millions of dollars available)

Total invested within 1 year ≤ 45   (millions of dollars available)

Total invested within 2 years ≤ 65   (millions of dollars available)

Total invested within 3 years ≤ 80   (millions of dollars available)

FIGURE 4.2   The spreadsheet model for the Think-Big problem, including the formulas for the target cell TotalNPV (H16) and the other output cells CapitalSpent (F9:F12), as well as the specifications needed to set up the Solver. The changing cells ParticipationShare (C16:E16) show the optimal solution obtained by the Solver.

	A	B	C	D	E	F	G	H
1		**Think-Big Development Co. Capital Budgeting Program**						
2								
3			Office		Shopping			
4			Building	Hotel	Center			
5		Net Present Value	45	70	50			
6		($millions)				Cumulative		Cumulative
7						Capital		Capital
8			Cumulative Capital Required ($millions)			Spent		Available
9		Now	40	80	90	25	≤	25
10		End of Year 1	100	160	140	44.76	≤	45
11		End of Year 2	190	240	160	60.58	≤	65
12		End of Year 3	200	310	220	80	≤	80
13								
14			Office		Shopping			Total NPV
15			Building	Hotel	Center			($millions)
16		Participation Share	0.00%	16.50%	13.11%			18.11

Solver Parameters

Set Target Cell: `TotalNPV`
Equal To: ● Max ○ Min ○
By Changing Cells:
`ParticipationShare`
Subject to the Constraints:
`CapitalSpent <= CapitalAvailable`

Solver Options
☑ Assume Linear Model
☑ Assume Non-Negative

Range Name	Cells
CapitalAvailable	H9:H12
CapitalRequired	C9:E12
CapitalSpent	F9:F12
ParticipationShare	C16:E16
NetPresentValue	C5:E5
TotalNPV	H16

	F
6	Cumulative
7	Capital
8	Spent
9	=SUMPRODUCT(C9:E9,ParticipationShare)
10	=SUMPRODUCT(C10:E10,ParticipationShare)
11	=SUMPRODUCT(C11:E11,ParticipationShare)
12	=SUMPRODUCT C12:E12,ParticipationShare)

	H
14	Total NPV
15	($millions)
16	=SUMPRODUCT(NetPresentValue,ParticipationShare)

The data in columns C, D, and E indicate that (in millions of dollars)

Total invested now $= \ 40 \ OB + \ 80 \ H + \ 90 \ SC$

Total invested within 1 year $= 100 \ OB + 160 \ H + 140 \ SC$

Total invested within 2 years $= 190 \ OB + 240 \ H + 160 \ SC$

Total invested within 3 years $= 200 \ OB + 310 \ H + 220 \ SC$

These totals are calculated in the output cells CapitalSpent (F9:F12) using the SUMPRODUCT function, as shown below the spreadsheet in Figure 4.2. Finally, ≤ signs are entered into column G to indicate the resource constraints that will need to be entered in the Solver dialogue box.

The Measure of Performance   The objective is to

Maximize   NPV = total *net present value* of the investments

NetPresentValue (C5:E5) shows the net present value of each entire project, while ParticipationShare (C16:E16) shows the participation share for each of the projects. Therefore, the total net present value of all the participation shares purchased in all three projects is (in millions of dollars)

$$\text{NPV} = 45 \, \text{OB} + 70 \, \text{H} + 50 \, \text{SC}$$

$$= \text{SUMPRODUCT (NetPresentValue, ParticipationShare)}$$

$$\rightarrow \text{cell H16}$$

Summary of the Formulation This completes the formulation of the linear programming model on the speadsheet, as summarized below (in algebraic form).

$$\text{Maximize} \quad \text{NPV} = 45 \, \text{OB} + 70 \, \text{H} + 50 \, \text{SC}$$

subject to

Total invested now:	$40 \, \text{OB} + 80 \, \text{H} + 90 \, \text{SC} \leq 25$
Total invested within 1 year:	$100 \, \text{OB} + 160 \, \text{H} + 140 \, \text{SC} \leq 45$
Total invested within 2 years:	$190 \, \text{OB} + 240 \, \text{H} + 160 \, \text{SC} \leq 65$
Total invested within 3 years:	$200 \, \text{OB} + 310 \, \text{H} + 220 \, \text{SC} \leq 80$

and

$$\text{OB} \geq 0 \quad \text{H} \geq 0 \quad \text{SC} \geq 0$$

where all these numbers are in units of millions of dollars.

Note that this model possesses the key *identifying feature* for resource-allocation problems, namely, each functional constraint is a *resource constraint* that has the form

$$\text{Amount of resource used} \leq \text{Amount of resource available}$$

Solving the Model The lower left-hand side of Figure 4.2 shows the entries needed in the Solver dialogue box to specify the model, along with the selection of the usual two options. The spreadsheet shows the resulting optimal solution in row 16, namely,

Invest nothing in the office building.

Invest in 16.50 percent of the hotel.

Invest in 13.11 percent of the shopping center.

TotalNPV (H16) indicates that this investment program would provide a total net present value of $18.11 million.

This amount actually is only an estimate of what the total net present value would turn out to be, depending on the accuracy of the financial data given in Table 4.2. There is some uncertainty about the construction costs for the three real estate projects, so the actual investment capital requirements for years 1, 2, and 3 may deviate somewhat from the amounts specified in this table. Because of the risk involved in these projects, the net present value for each one also might deviate from the amounts given at the bottom of the table. The next chapter describes one approach to analyzing the effect of such deviations. Chapters 15 and 16 will present another technique, called *computer simulation,* for systematically taking future uncertainties into account. Section 16.5 will focus on further analysis of this same example.

Another Look at Resource Constraints

These examples of resource-allocation problems illustrate a variety of resources: financial allocations for advertising and planning purposes, TV commercial spots available for purchase, available production capacities of different plants, and cumulative investment capital available by certain times. However, these illustrations only scratch the surface of the realm of possible resources that need to be allocated to activities in resource-allocation problems. In fact, by interpreting *resource* sufficiently broadly, *any* restriction on the decisions to be made that has the form

$$\text{Amount used} \leq \text{Amount available}$$

can be thought of as a *resource constraint*, where the thing whose amount is being measured is the corresponding "resource." Since *any* functional constraint with a ≤ sign in a linear programming model can be verbalized in this form, any such constraint can be thought of as a resource constraint.

> Hereafter, we will use **resource constraint** to refer to *any* functional constraint with a ≤ sign in a linear programming model. The constant on the right-hand side represents the *amount available* of a resource. Therefore, the left-hand side represents the *amount used* of this resource. In the algebraic form of the constraint, the coefficient (positive or negative) of each decision variable is the *resource usage per unit* of the corresponding activity.

Summary of the Formulation Procedure for Resource-Allocation Problems

The three examples illustrate that the following steps are used for any resource-allocation problem to define the specific problem, gather the relevant data, and then formulate the linear programming model.

1. Since any linear programming problem involves finding the *best mix* of levels of various activities, identify these *activities* for the problem at hand. The decisions to be made are the levels of these activities.

2. From the viewpoint of management, identify an appropriate *overall measure of performance* (commonly *profit,* or a surrogate for profit) for solutions of the problem.

3. For each activity, estimate the *contribution per unit of the activity* to this overall measure of performance.

4. Identify the *resources* that must be allocated to the activities.

5. For each resource, identify the *amount available* and then the *amount used per unit of each activity.*

6. Enter the data gathered in steps 3 and 5 into *data cells* in a spreadsheet. A convenient format is to leave two blank columns between the *activity* columns and the *amount of resource available* column.

7. Designate *changing cells* for displaying the decisions on activity levels.

8. For the two blank columns created in step 6, use the left one as a *Totals* column for *output cells* and enter ≤ signs into the right one for all the resources. In the row for each resource, use the SUMPRODUCT function to enter the *total amount used* in the Totals column.

9. Designate a *target cell* for displaying the overall measure of performance. Use a SUMPRODUCT function to enter this measure of performance.

All the functional constraints in this linear programming model in a spreadsheet are *resource constraints,* that is, constraints with a ≤ sign. This is the *identifying feature* that classifies the problem as being a resource-allocation problem.

Review
Questions

1. What is the identifying feature for a resource-allocation problem?

2. What is the form of a resource constraint?

3. What are the three kinds of data that need to be gathered for a resource-allocation problem?

4. Compare the types of activities for the three examples of resource-allocation problems.

5. Compare the types of resources for the three examples of resource-allocation problems.

4.3 COST–BENEFIT–TRADE-OFF PROBLEMS

Cost–benefit–trade-off problems have a form that is very different from resource-allocation problems. The difference arises from *managerial objectives* that are very different for the two kinds of problems.

For resource-allocation problems, limits are set on the use of various resources (including financial resources), and then the objective is to make the most effective use (according to some overall measure of performance) of these given resources.

For cost–benefit–trade-off problems, management takes a more aggressive stance, prescribing what *benefits* must be achieved by the activities under consideration (regardless of the resulting resource usage), and then the objective is to achieve all these benefits with *minimum cost*. By prescribing a *minimum acceptable level* for each kind of benefit, and then minimizing the cost needed to achieve these levels, management hopes to obtain an appropriate *trade-off* between cost and benefits. (You will see in Chapter 5 that *what-if analysis* plays a key role in providing the additional information needed for management to choose the best trade-off between cost and benefits.)

This way of formulating a problem enables management to specify minimum goals for the benefits that need to be achieved by the activities.

> **Cost–benefit–trade-off problems** are linear programming problems where the mix of levels of various activities is chosen to achieve minimum acceptable levels for various benefits at a minimum cost. The *identifying feature* is that each functional constraint is a **benefit constraint,** which has the form

$$\text{Level achieved} \geq \text{Minimum acceptable level}$$

for one of the benefits.

Interpreting *benefit* broadly, we can think of *any* functional constraint with a $\geq$ sign as a *benefit constraint.* In most cases, the *minimum acceptable level* will be prescribed by management as a policy decision, but occasionally this number will be dictated by other circumstances.

For any cost–benefit–trade-off problem, a major part of the study involves identifying all the activities and benefits that should be considered and then gathering the data relevant to these activities and benefits.

Three kinds of data are needed:

These three kinds of data are needed for any cost–benefit–trade-off problem.

1. The *minimum acceptable level* for each benefit (a managerial policy decision).

2. For each benefit, the *contribution of each activity* to that benefit (per unit of the activity).

3. The *cost* per unit of each activity.

Let's examine three examples of cost–benefit–trade-off problems.

The Profit & Gambit Co. Advertising-Mix Problem

As described in Section 2.7, the Profit & Gambit Co. will be undertaking a major new advertising campaign focusing on three cleaning products. The two kinds of advertising to be used are television and the print media. Management has established minimum goals—the minimum acceptable increase in sales for each product—to be gained by the campaign.

The problem is to determine how much to advertise in each medium to meet all the sales goals at a minimum total cost.

The activities in this cost–benefit–trade-off problem are:

An initial step in formulating any cost–benefit–trade-off problem is to identify the activities and the benefits.

Activity 1:   Advertise on television.

Activity 2:   Advertise in the print media.

The benefits being sought from these activities are:

Benefit 1: Increased sales for a spray prewash stain remover.

Benefit 2: Increased sales for a liquid laundry detergent.

Benefit 3: Increased sales for a powder laundry detergent.

Management wants these increased sales to be at least 3 percent, 18 percent, and 4 percent, respectively. As shown in Section 2.7, each benefit leads to a *benefit constraint* that incorporates the managerial goal for the *minimum acceptable level* of increase in the sales for the corresponding product, namely,

Level of benefit 1 achieved $\geq 3\%$

Level of benefit 2 achieved $\geq 18\%$

Level of benefit 3 achieved $\geq 4\%$

The data for this problem are given in Table 2.2 (Section 2.7). Section 2.7 describes how the linear programming model is formulated directly from the numbers in this table.

This example provides an interesting contrast with the Super Grain Corp. case study in Section 4.1, which led to a formulation as a resource-allocation problem. Both are advertising-mix problems, yet they lead to entirely different linear programming models. They differ because of the differences in the managerial view of the key issues in each case:

- As the vice president for marketing of Super Grain, Claire Syverson focused first on how much to spend on the advertising campaign and then set limits (an advertising budget of $4 million and a planning budget of $1 million) that led to resource constraints.

- The management of Profit & Gambit instead focused on what it wanted the advertising campaign to accomplish and then set goals (minimum required increases in sales) that led to benefit constraints.

From this comparison, we see that it is not the nature of the *application* that determines the classification of the resulting linear programming formulation. Rather, it is the nature of the *restrictions* imposed on the decisions regarding the mix of activity levels. If the restrictions involve *limits* on the usage of resources, that identifies a resource-allocation problem. If the restrictions involve *goals* on the levels of benefits, that characterizes a cost–benefit–trade-off problem. Frequently, the nature of the restrictions arise from the way management frames the problem.

However, we don't want you to get the idea that every linear programming problem falls entirely and neatly into either one type or the other. In the preceding section and this one, we are looking at *pure* resource-allocation problems and *pure* cost–benefit–trade-off problems. Although many *real* problems tend to be either one type or the other, it is fairly common to have *both* resource constraints and benefit constraints, even though one may predominate. Furthermore, we still need to consider one more category of linear programming problems (distribution-network problems) in the next section. That category will feature a third distinctive kind of constraint that sometimes arises in other problems as well. Mixed problems that combine features from these three categories are discussed and illustrated in Section 4.6.

Now, another example of a pure cost–benefit–trade-off problem.

Personnel Scheduling

One of the *real* applications of linear programming described in Section 2.1 involved a massive personnel scheduling problem at United Airlines. The resulting improvements saved the company more than $6 million annually. Part of that application concerned developing the *weekly* work schedules for customer service agents at major airports, where variations in the number of flights during different hours of the day can cause great fluctuations in the number of agents needed from one half-hour to the next.

We now will present a *greatly* simplified "textbook example" of this same kind of application. Among our simplifications, we will only consider a *daily* work schedule comprising intervals of two hours or longer. Nevertheless, the example will give you some feeling for how United Airlines approached its problem. It also will demonstrate the key role *benefit constraints* play in this kind of application.

The Problem

Union Airways is adding more flights to and from its hub airport and so needs to hire additional customer service agents. However, it is not clear just how many more should be hired.

Management recognizes the need for cost control while also consistently providing a satisfactory level of service to the company's customers, so a desirable trade-off between these two factors is being sought. Therefore, a management science team is studying how to schedule the agents to provide satisfactory service with the smallest personnel cost.

Based on the new schedule of flights, an analysis has been made of the *minimum* number of customer service agents that need to be on duty at different times of the day to provide a satisfactory level of service. These numbers are shown in the last column of Table 4.4 for the time periods given in the first column. The other entries in this table reflect one of the provisions in the company's current contract with the union that represents the customer service agents. The provision is that each agent works an eight-hour shift. The authorized shifts are

Shift 1:   6:00 AM to 2:00 PM.

Shift 2:   8:00 AM to 4:00 PM.

Shift 3:   Noon to 8:00 PM.

Shift 4:   4:00 PM to midnight.

Shift 5:   10:00 PM to 6:00 AM.

Check marks in the main body of Table 4.4 show the time periods covered by the respective shifts. Because some shifts are less desirable than others, the wages specified in the contract differ by shift. For each shift, the daily compensation (including benefits) for each agent is shown in the bottom row. The problem is to determine how many agents should be assigned to the respective shifts each day to minimize the *total* personnel cost for agents, based on this bottom row, while meeting (or surpassing) the service requirements given in the last column.

Formulation

This problem is, in fact, a pure cost–benefit–trade-off problem. To formulate the problem, we need to identify the *activities* and *benefits* involved.

Activities correspond to shifts.

The *level* of each activity is the number of agents assigned to that shift.

A *unit* of each activity is one agent assigned to that shift.

Thus, the general description of a linear programming problem as finding the *best mix of activity levels* can be expressed for this specific application as finding the *best mix of shift sizes.*

TABLE 4.4
Data for the Union Airways Personnel Scheduling Problem

Time Period	Time Periods Covered by Shift					Minimum Number of Agents Needed
	1	2	3	4	5	
6:00 AM to 8:00 AM	✓					48
8:00 AM to 10:00 AM	✓	✓				79
10:00 AM to noon	✓	✓				65
Noon to 2:00 PM	✓	✓	✓			87
2:00 PM to 4:00 PM		✓	✓			64
4:00 PM to 6:00 PM			✓	✓		73
6:00 PM to 8:00 PM			✓	✓		82
8:00 PM to 10:00 PM				✓		43
10:00 PM to midnight				✓	✓	52
Midnight to 6:00 AM					✓	15
Daily cost per agent	$170	$160	$175	$180	$195	

Benefits correspond to time periods.

For each time period, the *benefit* provided by the activities is the service that agents provide customers during that period.

The *level* of a benefit is measured by the number of agents on duty during that time period.

Once again, a careful formulation of the problem, including gathering all the relevant data, leads rather directly to a spreadsheet model. This model is shown in Figure 4.3, and we outline its formulation below.

The Data   As indicated in this figure, all the data in Table 4.4 have been entered directly into the data cells CostPerShift (C5:G5), ShiftWorksTimePeriod (C8:G17), and MinimumNeeded (J8:J17).

The Decisions   Since the activities in this case correspond to the five shifts, the decisions to be made are

S_1 = Number of agents to assign to Shift 1 (starts at 6 AM)

S_2 = Number of agents to assign to Shift 2 (starts at 8 AM)

S_3 = Number of agents to assign to Shift 3 (starts at noon)

S_4 = Number of agents to assign to Shift 4 (starts at 4 PM)

S_5 = Number of agents to assign to Shift 5 (starts at 10 PM)

The changing cells to hold these numbers have been placed in the activity columns in row 21, so

$S_1 \rightarrow$ cell C21 $S_2 \rightarrow$ cell D21   . . . $S_5 \rightarrow$ cell G21

where these cells are collectively referred to by the range name NumberWorking (C21:G21).

The Constraints   These changing cells need to be nonnegative. In addition, we need 10 *benefit constraints,* where each one specifies that the *total* number of agents serving in the corresponding time period listed in column B must be no less than the minimum acceptable number given in column J. Thus, these constraints are

Total number of agents serving 6–8 AM ≥ 48 (min. acceptable)

Total number of agents serving 8–10 AM ≥ 79 (min. acceptable)

.

.

.

Total number of agents serving midnight–6 AM ≥ 15 (min. acceptable)

Since columns C to G indicate which of the shifts serve each of the time periods, these totals are

Total number of agents serving 6–8 AM $= S_1$

Total number of agents serving 8–10 AM $= S_1 + S_2$

.

.

.

Total number of agents serving midnight–6 AM $= S_5$

These totals are calculated in the output cells TotalWorking (H8:H17) using the SUMPRODUCT functions shown below the spreadsheet in Figure 4.3.

FIGURE 4.3 The spreadsheet model for the Union Airways problem, including the formulas for the target cell TotalCost (J21) and the other output cells TotalWorking (H8:H17), as well as the specifications needed to set up the Solver. The changing cells NumberWorking (C21:G21) show the optimal solution obtained by the Solver.

	A	B	C	D	E	F	G	H	I	J
1		**Union Airways Personnel Scheduling Problem**								
2										
3			6AM–2PM	8AM–4PM	Noon–8PM	4PM–Midnight	10PM–6AM			
4			Shift	Shift	Shift	Shift	Shift			
5		Cost per Shift	$170	$160	$175	$180	$195			
6								Total		Minimum
7		Time Period		Shift Works Time Period? (1=yes, 0=no)				Working		Needed
8		6AM–8AM	1	0	0	0	0	48	≥	48
9		8AM–10AM	1	1	0	0	0	79	≥	79
10		10AM–12PM	1	1	0	0	0	79	≥	65
11		12PM–2PM	1	1	1	0	0	118	≥	87
12		2PM–4PM	0	1	1	0	0	70	≥	64
13		4PM–6PM	0	0	1	1	0	82	≥	73
14		6PM–8PM	0	0	1	1	0	82	≥	82
15		8PM–10PM	0	0	0	1	0	43	≥	43
16		10PM–12AM	0	0	0	1	1	58	≥	52
17		12AM–6AM	0	0	0	0	1	15	≥	15
18										
19			6AM–2PM	8AM–4PM	Noon–8PM	4PM–Midnight	10PM–6AM			
20			Shift	Shift	Shift	Shift	Shift			Total Cost
21		Number Working	48	31	39	43	15			$30,610

Solver Parameters

Set Target Cell: TotalCost

Equal To: ○ Max ● Min ○

By Changing Cells:

NumberWorking

Subject to the Constraints:

TotalWorking >= MinimumNeeded

Solver Options

☑ Assume Linear Model
☑ Assume Non-Negative

Range Name	Cells
CostPerShift	C5:G5
MinimumNeeded	J8:J17
NumberWorking	C21:G21
ShiftWorksTimePeriod	C8:G17
TotalCost	J21
TotalWorking	H8:H17

	H
6	Total
7	Working
8	=SUMPRODUCT(C8:G8,NumberWorking)
9	=SUMPRODUCT(C9:G9,NumberWorking)
10	=SUMPRODUCT(C10:G10,NumberWorking)
11	=SUMPRODUCT(C11:G11,NumberWorking)
12	=SUMPRODUCT(C12:G12,NumberWorking)
13	=SUMPRODUCT(C13:G13,NumberWorking)
14	=SUMPRODUCT(C14:G14,NumberWorking)
15	=SUMPRODUCT(C15:G15,NumberWorking)
16	=SUMPRODUCT(C16:G16,NumberWorking)
17	=SUMPRODUCT(C17:G17,NumberWorking)

	J
20	Total Cost
21	=SUMPRODUCT(CostPerShift,NumberWorking)

The Measure of Performance The objective is to

$$\text{Minimize} \quad \text{Cost} = \text{Total daily personnel cost for all agents}$$

Since CostPerShift (C5:G5) gives the daily cost per agent on each shift and NumberWorking (C21:G21) gives the number of agents working each shift,

$$\text{Cost} = 170S_1 + 160S_2 + 175S_3 + 180S_4 + 195S_5 \quad \text{(in dollars)}$$

$$= \text{SUMPRODUCT (CostPerShift, NumberWorking)}$$

$$\rightarrow \text{cell J21}$$

Summary of the Formulation The above steps provide the complete formulation of the linear programming model on a spreadsheet, as summarized below (in algebraic form).

$$\text{Minimize} \quad \text{Cost} = 170S_1 + 160S_2 + 175S_3 + 180S_4 + 195S_5 \quad \text{(in dollars)}$$

subject to

Total agents 6–8 AM: $\quad S_1 \quad \geq 48$

Total agents 8–10 AM: $\quad S_1 + S_2 \quad \geq 79$

.

.

.

Total agents midnight–6 AM: $\quad S_5 \geq 15$

and

$$S_1 \geq 0 \quad S_2 \geq 0 \quad S_3 \geq 0 \quad S_4 \geq 0 \quad S_5 \geq 0$$

Solving the Model The Solver now can be applied to this model by making the entries in the Solver dialogue box shown in the lower left-hand corner of Figure 4.3, along with selecting the usual two Solver options indicated in the figure. NumberWorking (C21:G21) in the spreadsheet shows the resulting optimal solution for the number of agents that should be assigned to each shift. TotalCost (J21) indicates that this plan would cost $30,610 per day.

Controlling Air Pollution

Our next example is a preview of Case 5.2 at the end of the next chapter. Rather than giving a full description of the problem and its data now, we will give a synopsis and then focus on our current theme—illustrating how *benefits* and *benefit constraints* arise to yield a *cost–benefit–trade-off problem.*

The Nori & Leets Co. is a major producer of steel in its part of the world. However, uncontrolled air pollution from the company's furnaces is endangering the health of nearby residents. The company and governmental officials together have developed stringent air quality standards for the region's airshed. These standards will require the company to reduce its annual emission rate for three main pollutants—particulate matter, sulfur oxides, and hydrocarbons—by 60 million pounds, 150 million pounds, and 125 million pounds, respectively. The company's engineers have analyzed various pollution abatement methods. On a per-unit basis, they have estimated for each method how much it would cost and how much it would reduce the emission rate for each of the three pollutants. It is clear that some mix of the pollution abatement methods will be needed to do the job. Consequently, a management science team is studying the problem of determining the *best mix* of pollution abatement methods to minimize the cost of meeting (or surpassing) the required reduction in the annual emission rates for the three pollutants.

This is a cost–benefit–trade-off problem.

The *activities* are the pollution abatement methods.

The *benefits* provided by these activities are the reductions in the emission of each of the three pollutants.

The *level* of a benefit is measured by the reduction in the annual emission rate (in units of millions of pounds) for the corresponding pollutant.

This problem has three *benefit constraints* (one for each pollutant), stated in the following form:

Particulate matter: Reduction ≥ 60

Sulfur oxides: Reduction ≥ 150

Hydrocarbons: Reduction ≥ 125

You will have an opportunity to formulate these constraints and the remainder of the linear programming model as part of Case 5.2.

It is typical in cost–benefit–trade-off problems that the prescribed minimum acceptable levels for the benefits before formulating the linear programming model are very tentative. What management really wants is the *best trade-off* between cost and benefits. But that cannot be determined until after exploring the cost consequences of a variety of benefit levels. Therefore, after obtaining an optimal solution (and its corresponding total cost) for the initial model, *what-if analysis* is used to explore how the total cost changes as changes are made in the minimum acceptable levels of the benefits. If the *marginal cost* (i.e., the rate of change in total cost) is small when benefit levels are increased, then a better trade-off would be achieved by increasing these levels. Conversely, if the marginal cost is large, then perhaps the minimum acceptable levels of benefits should be adjusted downward. Ultimately, choosing the best trade-off between cost and benefits is a *managerial judgment decision* that is guided by the information provided by *what-if analysis.*

This process of seeking the best trade-off between cost and benefits for the Nori & Leets problem is the focus of Case 5.2.

Summary of the Formulation Procedure for Cost–Benefit–Trade-off Problems

The nine steps in formulating any cost–benefit–trade-off problem follow the same pattern as presented at the end of the preceding section for resource-allocation problems, so we will not repeat them here. The main differences are that the overall measure of performance now is the total cost of the activities (or some surrogate of total cost chosen by management) in steps 2 and 3, benefits now replace resources in steps 4 and 5, and $\geq$ signs now are entered to the right of the output cells for benefits in step 8.

All the functional constraints in the resulting model are *benefit constraints,* that is, constraints with a $\geq$ sign. This is the *identifying feature* of a pure cost–benefit–trade-off problem.

Review
Questions

1. What is the difference in managerial objectives between resource-allocation problems and cost–benefit–trade-off problems?

2. What is the identifying feature of a cost–benefit–trade-off problem?

3. What is the form of a benefit constraint?

4. What are the three kinds of data that need to be gathered for a cost–benefit–trade-off problem?

5. Compare the types of activities for the three examples of cost–benefit–trade-off problems.

6. Compare the types of benefits for the three examples of cost–benefit–trade-off problems.

4.4 DISTRIBUTION-NETWORK PROBLEMS

We now come to a third category of linear programming problems—**distribution-network problems**—so called because they deal with the *distribution* of goods through a *distribution network* at minimum cost. One example described in Section 2.1 is the Supply, Distribution, and Marketing (SDM) modeling system used by Citgo Petroleum Corporation to achieve savings of $16.5 million annually.

We will focus on distribution-network problems in Chapters 6 and 7. However, we include a small example here to complete your perspective on major categories of linear programming problems.

In this example, you'll see a new type of constraint—*fixed-requirement constraints.* These constraints are an *identifying feature* of distribution-network problems. Thus, fixed-requirement constraints play the same role for distribution-network problems as do *resource constraints* for resource-allocation problems and *benefit constraints* for cost–benefit–trade-off problems. Therefore, rather than identify resources or benefits, for distribution-network problems we need to identify *requirements* and their corresponding fixed-requirement constraints.

Fixed-requirement constraints also arise in other linear programming problems, as you will see in the next two sections.

Distributing Goods through a Distribution Network

The Problem

The Big M Company produces a variety of heavy duty machines at two factories. One of its products is a large turret lathe. Orders have been received from three customers to purchase some of these turret lathes next month. These lathes will be shipped individually, and Table 4.5 shows what the cost will be for shipping each lathe from each factory to each customer. This table also shows how many lathes have been ordered by each customer and how many will be produced by each factory. The company's distribution manager now wants to determine how many machines to ship from each factory to each customer to minimize the total shipping cost.

Figure 4.4 depicts the distribution network for this problem. This network ignores the geographical layout of the factories and customers and instead lines up the two factories in one column on the left and the three customers in one column on the right. Each arrow shows one of the shipping lanes through this distribution network.

Formulation of the Problem in Linear Programming Terms

We need to identify the *activities* and *requirements* of this distribution-network problem to formulate it as a linear programming problem. In this case, two kinds of activities have been mentioned—the *production* of the turret lathes at the two factories and the *shipping* of these lathes along the various shipping lanes. However, we know the specific amounts to be produced at each factory, so no decisions need to be made about the production activities. The decisions to be made concern the levels of the *shipping activities*—how many lathes to ship through each shipping lane. Therefore, we need to focus on the shipping activities for the linear programming formulation.

TABLE 4.5
Some Data for the Big M Company Distribution-Network Problem

To	Shipping Cost for Each Lathe			
From	**Customer 1**	**Customer 2**	**Customer 3**	**Output**
Factory 1	$700	$900	$800	12 lathes
Factory 2	800	900	700	15 lathes
Order size	10 lathes	8 lathes	9 lathes	

FIGURE 4.4

The distribution network for the Big M Company problem.

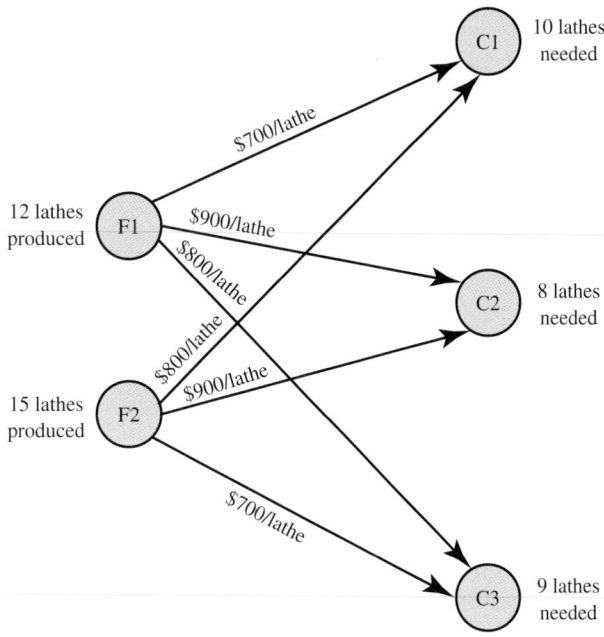

The *activities* correspond to shipping lanes, depicted by arrows in Figure 4.4.

The *level* of each activity is the number of lathes shipped through the corresponding shipping lane.

Just as any linear programming problem can be described as finding the best mix of activity levels, this one involves finding the *best mix of shipping amounts* for the various shipping lanes. The decisions to be made are

$S_{\text{F1-C1}}$ = Number of lathes shipped from Factory 1 to Customer 1

$S_{\text{F1-C2}}$ = Number of lathes shipped from Factory 1 to Customer 2

$S_{\text{F1-C3}}$ = Number of lathes shipped from Factory 1 to Customer 3

$S_{\text{F2-C1}}$ = Number of lathes shipped from Factory 2 to Customer 1

$S_{\text{F2-C2}}$ = Number of lathes shipped from Factory 2 to Customer 2

$S_{\text{F2-C3}}$ = Number of lathes shipped from Factory 2 to Customer 3

so six changing cells will be needed in the spreadsheet.

The objective is to

$$\text{Minimize} \quad \text{Cost} = \text{Total cost for shipping the lathes}$$

Using the shipping costs given in Table 4.5,

$$\text{Cost} = 700S_{\text{F1}-\text{C1}} + 900S_{\text{F1}-\text{C2}} + 800S_{\text{F1}-\text{C3}} + 800S_{\text{F2}-\text{C1}} + 900S_{\text{F2}-\text{C2}} + 700S_{\text{F2}-\text{C3}}$$

is the quantity in dollars to be entered into the target cell. (We will use a SUMPRODUCT function to do this a little later.)

The spreadsheet model also will need five constraints involving *fixed requirements.* Both Table 4.5 and Figure 4.4 show these requirements.

An initial step in formulating any distribution-network problem is to identify the activities and the fixed requirements.

Requirement 1: Factory 1 must ship 12 lathes.

Requirement 2: Factory 2 must ship 15 lathes.

Requirement 3: Customer 1 must receive 10 lathes.

Requirement 4: Customer 2 must receive 8 lathes.

Requirement 5: Customer 3 must receive 9 lathes.

Thus, there is a specific requirement associated with each of the five locations in the distribution network shown in Figure 4.4. Having one requirement for each location is a characteristic common to all distribution-network problems.

All five of these requirements can be expressed in constraint form as

$$\text{Amount provided} = \text{Required amount}$$

For example, Requirement 1 can be expressed algebraically as

$$S_{\text{F12-C1}} + S_{\text{F12-C2}} + S_{\text{F12-C3}} = 12$$

where the left-hand side gives the total number of lathes shipped from Factory 1, and 12 is the required amount to be shipped from Factory 1. Therefore, this constraint restricts $S_{\text{F1-C1}}$, $S_{\text{F1-C2}}$, and $S_{\text{F1-C3}}$ to values that sum to the required amount of 12. In contrast to the $\leq$ form for resource constraints and the $\geq$ form for benefit constraints, the constraints express *fixed requirements* that must hold with equality.

> **Fixed-requirement constraints** in a linear programming model are functional constraints that use an $=$ sign. Each such constraint can be interpreted as expressing a fixed requirement that, for some type of quantity,
>
> $$\text{Amount provided} = \text{Required amount}$$
>
> One *identifying feature* of pure distribution-network problems is that the main functional constraints in the model are fixed-requirement constraints. However, other linear programming problems sometimes include fixed-requirement constraints as well.

Formulation of the Spreadsheet Model

Careful problem *formulation needs to precede* model *formulation.*

In preparation for formulating the *model,* the *problem* has been formulated above by identifying the decisions to be made, the constraints on these decisions, and the overall measure of performance, as well as gathering all the important data displayed in Table 4.5. All this information leads to the spreadsheet model shown in Figure 4.5. The data cells include ShippingCost (C5:E6), Output (H11:H12), and OrderSize (C15:E15), incorporating all the data from Table 4.5. The changing cells are UnitsShipped (C11:E12), which give the decisions on the amounts to be shipped through the respective shipping lanes. The output cells are Total-

Here is an example where SUM functions are used for output cells instead of SUMPRODUCT functions.

ShippedOut (F11:F12) and TotalToCustomer (C13:E13), where the SUM functions entered into these cells are shown below the spreadsheet in Figure 4.5. The constraints are that Total-ShippedOut is required to equal Output and TotalToCustomer is required to equal OrderSize. These constraints have been specified on the spreadsheet and entered into the Solver dialogue box. The target cell is TotalCost (H15), where its SUMPRODUCT function gives the total shipping cost. The Solver dialogue box specifies that the objective is to minimize this cost. Finally, the figure indicates that the usual two Solver options have been selected to specify that the model is a linear programming model that has nonnegativity constraints.

UnitsShipped (C11:E12) in the spreadsheet in Figure 4.5 shows the result of applying the Solver to obtain an optimal solution for the number of lathes to ship through each shipping lane. TotalCost (H15) indicates that the total shipping cost for this shipping plan is $20,500.

To summarize, here is the algebraic form of the linear programming model that has been formulated in the spreadsheet.

Minimize $\text{Cost} = 700S_{\text{F1-C1}} + 900S_{\text{F1-C2}} + 800S_{\text{F1-C3}} + 800S_{\text{F2-C1}} + 900S_{\text{F2-C2}} + 700S_{\text{F2-C3}}$

subject to the following constraints:

FIGURE 4.5 The spreadsheet model for the Big M Company problem, including the formulas for the target cell TotalCost (H15) and the other output cells TotalShippedOut (F11:F12) and TotalToCustomer (C13:E13), as well as the specifications needed to set up the Solver. The changing cells UnitsShipped (C11:E12) show the optimal solution obtained by the Solver.

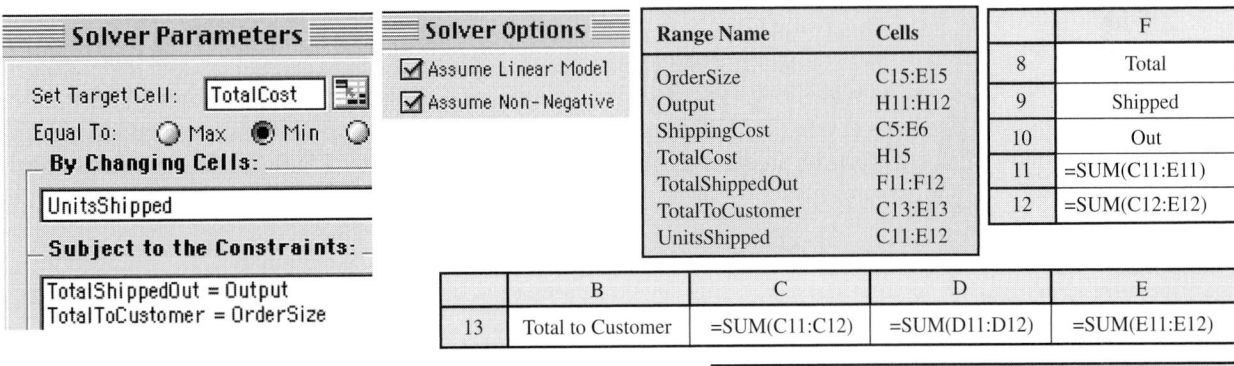

	A	B	C	D	E	F	G	H
1		**Big M Company Distribution Problem**						
2								
3		**Shipping Cost**						
4		**(per Lathe)**	Customer 1	Customer 2	Customer 3			
5		Factory 1	$700	$900	$800			
6		Factory 2	$800	$900	$700			
7								
8						Total		
9						Shipped		
10		**Units Shipped**	Customer 1	Customer 2	Customer 3	Out		Output
11		Factory 1	10	2	0	12	=	12
12		Factory 2	0	6	9	15	=	15
13		Total to Customer	10	8	9			
14			=	=	=			**Total Cost**
15		Order Size	10	8	9			**$20,500**

Solver Parameters
Set Target Cell: TotalCost
Equal To: ○ Max ● Min ○
By Changing Cells:
UnitsShipped
Subject to the Constraints:
TotalShippedOut = Output
TotalToCustomer = OrderSize

Solver Options
☑ Assume Linear Model
☑ Assume Non-Negative

Range Name	Cells
OrderSize	C15:E15
Output	H11:H12
ShippingCost	C5:E6
TotalCost	H15
TotalShippedOut	F11:F12
TotalToCustomer	C13:E13
UnitsShipped	C11:E12

	F
8	Total
9	Shipped
10	Out
11	=SUM(C11:E11)
12	=SUM(C12:E12)

	B	C	D	E
13	Total to Customer	=SUM(C11:C12)	=SUM(D11:D12)	=SUM(E11:E12)

	H
14	Total Cost
15	=SUMPRODUCT(ShippingCost,UnitsShipped)

1. *Fixed-requirement constraints:*

$$S_{F1\text{-}C1} + S_{F1\text{-}C2} + S_{F1\text{-}C3} \qquad\qquad\qquad\qquad\qquad = 12 \quad \text{(Factory 1)}$$

$$S_{F2\text{-}C1} + S_{F2\text{-}C2} + S_{F2\text{-}C3} = 15 \quad \text{(Factory 2)}$$

$$S_{F1\text{-}C1} \qquad\qquad\qquad\qquad + S_{F2\text{-}C1} \qquad\qquad = 10 \quad \text{(Customer 1)}$$

$$S_{F1\text{-}C2} \qquad\qquad\qquad\qquad + S_{F2\text{-}C2} \qquad = 8 \quad \text{(Customer 2)}$$

$$S_{F1\text{-}C3} \qquad\qquad\qquad\qquad + S_{F2\text{-}C3} = 9 \quad \text{(Customer 3)}$$

2. *Nonnegativity constraints:*

$$S_{F1\text{-}C1} \geq 0 \quad S_{F1\text{-}C2} \geq 0 \quad S_{F1\text{-}C3} \geq 0 \quad S_{F2\text{-}C1} \geq 0 \quad S_{F2\text{-}C2} \geq 0 \quad S_{F2\text{-}C3} \geq 0$$

1. Why are distribution-network problems given this name?

2. What is an identifying feature of distribution-network problems?

3. How does the form of a fixed-requirement constraint differ from that of a resource constraint? A benefit constraint?

4. What are the quantities with fixed requirements in the Big M Company problem?

4.5 CONTINUING THE SUPER GRAIN CASE STUDY

We now pick up the story of the Super Grain case study introduced in Section 4.1. As we left matters before, Super Grain's vice president for marketing, Claire Syverson, has just concluded a meeting with David Sloan (Super Grain's president) in which they discussed the planning of a promotional campaign for Crunchy Start. Prior to this meeting, a leading advertising firm, Giacomi & Jackowitz, identified the three most effective advertising media for this product. With this input, Claire formulated a linear programming spreadsheet model to determine how to divide the advertising among these three media to maximize the expected number of exposures. After seeing that the plan recommended by the spreadsheet model does not include any television advertising—which would mean the key target audiences for the campaign would not be reached well—David and Claire have decided that this first version of the spreadsheet model is inadequate.

Incorporating Additional Managerial Considerations

Therefore, David and Claire conclude that the spreadsheet model needs to be expanded to incorporate some additional considerations. In particular, since the promotional campaign is for a breakfast cereal that should have special appeal to young children, they feel that two audiences should be targeted—*young children* and *parents of young children*. (This is why one of the three advertising media recommended by Giacomi & Jackowitz is commercials on children's television programs Saturday morning.) Consequently, Claire now has set two new goals for the campaign.

Goal 1: The advertising should be seen by at least five million young children.

Goal 2: The advertising should be seen by at least five million parents of young children.

In effect, these two goals are *minimum acceptable levels* for two special *benefits* to be achieved by the advertising activities.

Benefit 1: Promoting the new breakfast cereal to young children.

Benefit 2: Promoting the new breakfast cereal to parents of young children.

Because of the way the goals have been articulated, the *level* of each of these benefits is measured by the *number of people* in the specified category that are reached by the advertising.

To enable constructing the corresponding *benefit constraints* (as described in Section 4.3), Claire asks Giacomi & Jackowitz to estimate how much each advertisement in each of the media will contribute to each benefit, as measured by the number of people reached in the specified category. These estimates are given in Table 4.6.

It is interesting to observe that management wants special consideration given to these two kinds of benefits even though the original spreadsheet model (Figure 4.1) already takes them into account to some extent. As described in Section 4.1, the *expected number of exposures* is the overall measure of performance to be maximized. This measure counts up all the times that an advertisement is seen by any individual, including all those individuals in the target audience. However, maximizing this *general* measure of performance does *not* ensure that the two *specific goals* prescribed by management (Claire Syverson) will be achieved. Claire feels that achieving these goals is essential to a successful promotional campaign. Therefore, she complements the general objective with specific benefit constraints that *do* ensure that the goals will be achieved. Having benefit constraints added to incorporate managerial goals into the model is a prerogative of management.

Benefit constraints are useful for incorporating managerial goals into the model.

TABLE 4.6

Benefit Data for the
Revised Super Grain
Corp. Advertising-Mix
Problem

	Number Reached in Target Category (in millions)			
Target Category	Each TV Commercial	Each Magazine Ad	Each Sunday Ad	Minimum Acceptable Level
Young children	1.2	0.1	0	5
Parents of young children	0.5	0.2	0.2	5

TABLE 4.7

Data for the Fixed-
Requirement Constraint
for the Revised Super
Grain Corp. Advertising-
Mix Problem

	Contribution toward Required Amount			
Requirement	Each TV Spot	Each Magazine Ad	Each Sunday Ad	Required Amount
Coupon redemption	0	$40,000	$120,000	$1,490,000

Claire has one more consideration she wants to incorporate into the model. She is a strong believer in the promotional value of *cents-off coupons* (coupons that shoppers can clip from printed advertisements to obtain a refund of a designated amount when purchasing the advertised item). Consequently, she always earmarks a major portion of her annual marketing budget for the redemption of these coupons. She still has $1,490,000 left from this year's allotment for coupon redemptions. Because of the importance of Crunchy Start to the company, she has decided to use this entire remaining allotment in the campaign promoting this cereal.

This *fixed amount* for coupon redemptions is a *fixed requirement* that needs to be expressed as a *fixed-requirement constraint.* As described in Section 4.4, the form of a fixed-requirement constraint is that, for some type of quantity,

$$\text{Amount provided} = \text{Required amount}$$

In this case, the quantity involved is the amount of money provided for the redemption of cents-off coupons. To specify this constraint in the spreadsheet, we need to estimate how much each advertisement in each of the media will contribute toward fulfilling the required amount for the quantity. Both medium 2 (advertisements in food and family-oriented magazines) and medium 3 (advertisements in Sunday supplements of major newspapers) will feature cents-off coupons. The estimates of the amount of coupon redemption per advertisement in each of these media is given in Table 4.7.

Formulation of the Revised Spreadsheet Model

Figure 4.6 shows one way of formatting the spreadsheet to expand the original spreadsheet model in Figure 4.1 to incorporate the additional managerial considerations. We outline the four components of the revised model below.

The Data

Additional data cells in NumberReachedPerAd (C11:E12), MinimumAcceptable (H11:H12), CouponRedemptionPerAd (C15:E15), and RequiredAmount (H15) give the data in Tables 4.6 and 4.7.

The Decisions

Recall that, as before, the decisions to be made are

TV = Number of commercials on television

M = Number of advertisements in magazines

SS = Number of advertisements in Sunday supplements

The changing cells to hold these numbers continue to be in NumberOfAds (C19:E19).

FIGURE 4.6 The spreadsheet model for the revised Super Grain problem (Section 4.5), including the formulas for the target cell TotalExposures (H19) and the other output cells in column F, as well as the specifications needed to set up the Solver. The changing cells NumberOfAds (C19:E19) show the optimal solution obtained by the Solver.

	A	B	C	D	E	F	G	H
1		**Super Grain Corp. Advertising-Mix Problem**						
2								
3			TV Spots	Magazine Ads	SS Ads			
4		Exposures per Ad	1,300	600	500			
5		(thousands)						
6			Cost per Ad ($thousands)			Budget Spent		Budget Available
7		Ad Budget	300	150	100	3,775	≤	4,000
8		Planning Budget	90	30	40	1,000	≤	1,000
9								
10			Number Reached per Ad (millions)			Total Reached		Minimum Acceptable
11		Young Children	1.2	0.1	0	5	≥	5
12		Parents of Young Children	0.5	0.2	0.2	5.85	≥	5
13								
14			TV Spots	Magazine Ads	SS Ads	Total Redeemed		Required Amount
15		Coupon Redemption	0	40	120	1,490		1,490
16		per Ad ($thousands)						
17								Total Exposures
18			TV Spots	Magazine Ads	SS Ads			(thousands)
19		Number of Ads	3	14	7.75			16,175
20			≤					
21		Maximum TV Spots	5					

Range Name	Cells
BudgetAvailable	H7:H8
BudgetSpent	F7:F8
CostPerAd	C7:E8
CouponRedemptionPerAd	C15:E15
ExposuresPerAd	C4:E4
MaxTVSpots	C21
MinimumAcceptable	H11:H12
NumberOfAds	C19:E19
NumberReachedPerAd	C11:E12
RequiredAmount	H15
TotalExposures	H19
TotalReached	F11:F12
TotalRedeemed	F15
TVSpots	C19

	F
6	Budget Spent
7	=SUMPRODUCT(C7:E7,NumberOfAds)
8	=SUMPRODUCT(C8:E8,NumberOfAds)
9	
10	Total Reached
11	=SUMPRODUCT(C11:E11,NumberOfAds)
12	=SUMPRODUCT(C12:E12,NumberOfAds)
13	
14	Total Redeemed
15	=SUMPRODUCT(CouponRedemptionPerAd, NumberOfAds)

	H
17	Total Exposures
18	(thousands)
19	=SUMPRODUCT(ExposuresPerAd,NumberOfAds)

The Constraints

In addition to the original constraints, we now have two benefit constraints and one fixed-requirement constraint. As specified for us (but not for the Solver) in rows 11 and 12, columns F to H, the benefit constraints are

Total number of young children reached ≥ 5 (goal 1 in millions)

Total number of parents reached ≥ 5 (goal 2 in millions)

Using the data in columns C to E of these rows,

Total number of young children reached $= 1.2TV + 0.1M + 0SS$

$= \text{SUMPRODUCT (C11:E11, NumberOfAds)}$

$\rightarrow$ cell F11

Total number of parents reached $= 0.5TV + 0.2M + 0.2SS$

$= \text{SUMPRODUCT (C12:E12, NumberOfAds)}$

$\rightarrow$ cell F12

These output cells are given the range name TotalReached (F11:F12).
The fixed-requirement constraint indicated in row 15 is that

$$\text{Total coupon redemption} = 1{,}490 \quad \text{(allotment in \$1,000s)}$$

CouponRedemptionPerAd (C15:E15) gives the number of coupons redeemed per ad, so

Total coupon redemption $= 0TV + 40M + 120SS$

$= \text{SUMPRODUCT(CouponRedemptionPerAd, NumberOfAds)}$

$\rightarrow$ cell F15

These same constraints are specified for the Solver in the Solver dialogue box, along with the original constraints, in Figure 4.6.

The Measure of Performance

The measure of performance continues to be

$$\text{Exposure} = 1{,}300TV + 600M + 500SS$$

$= \text{SUMPRODUCT (ExposuresPerAd, NumberOfAds)}$

$\rightarrow$ cell H19

so H19 is the new address for the target cell.

Summary of the Formulation

The above steps have resulted in formulating the following linear programming model (in algebraic form) on a spreadsheet.

$$\text{Maximize} \quad \text{Exposure} = 1{,}300TV + 600M + 500SS$$

subject to the following constraints:

1. *Resource constraints:*

$300TV + 150M + 100SS \leq 4{,}000$ (ad budget in \$1,000s)

$90TV + 30M + 40SS \leq 1{,}000$ (planning budget in \$1,000s)

$TV \leq 5$ (television spots available)

2. *Benefit constraints:*

$$1.2\text{TV} + 0.1M \geq 5 \quad \text{(millions of young children)}$$

$$0.5\text{TV} + 0.2M + 0.2\text{SS} \geq 5 \quad \text{(millions of parents)}$$

3. *Fixed-requirement constraint:*

$$40M + 120\text{SS} = 1{,}490 \quad \text{(coupon budget in \$1{,}000s)}$$

4. *Nonnegativity constraints:*

$$\text{TV} \geq 0 \quad M \geq 0 \quad \text{SS} \geq 0$$

Solving the Model

After making all the entries in the Solver dialogue box shown in Figure 4.6, plus selecting the usual two Solver options, the Solver finds the optimal solution given in row 19. This optimal solution provides the following plan for the promotional campaign:

Run 3 television commercials.

Run 14 advertisements in magazines.

Run 7.75 advertisements in Sunday supplements (so the eighth advertisement would appear in only 75 percent of the newspapers).

Although the expected number of exposures with this plan is only 16,175,000, versus the 17,000,000 with the first plan shown in Figure 4.1, both Claire Syverson and David Sloan feel that the new plan does a much better job of meeting all of management's goals for this campaign. They decide to adopt the new plan.

A model may need to be modified a number of times before it adequately incorporates all the important considerations.

This case study illustrates a common theme in real applications of linear programming—the continuing evolution of the linear programming model. It is common to make later adjustments in the initial version of the model, perhaps even many times, as experience is gained in using the model. Frequently, these adjustments are made to more adequately reflect some important managerial considerations.

Review Questions

1. What managerial goals needed to be incorporated into the expanded linear programming model for the Super Grain Corp. problem?

2. Which categories of functional constraints are included in the new linear programming model?

3. Why did management adopt the new plan even though it provides a smaller expected number of exposures than the original plan recommended by the original linear programming model?

4.6 MIXED PROBLEMS

Sections 4.2, 4.3, and 4.4 each described a broad category of linear programming problems—resource-allocation, cost–benefit–trade-off, and distribution-network problems. As summarized in Table 4.8, each features one of the three types of functional constraints. In fact, the *identifying feature* of a *pure* resource-allocation problem is that *all* its functional constraints are *resource constraints*. The *identifying feature* of a *pure* cost–benefit–trade-off problem is that *all* its functional constraints are *benefit constraints*. The main functional constraints in a distribution-network problem are *fixed-requirement constraints* of a certain kind.

However, as illustrated by the Super Grain case study in Section 4.5, many linear programming problems do not fall into one of these three categories. Some *almost* fit one of the categories because they have functional constraints that mostly correspond to the type indicated in Table 4.8. Others do not come close to any category because no single type of functional constraint dominates. In either case, we will refer to them as *mixed problems*.

The fourth (and final) category of linear programming problems is **mixed problems.** This category includes any problem that does not fit into one of the first three categories.

TABLE 4.8   **Types of Functional Constraints**

Type	Form*	Typical Interpretation	Main Usage
Resource constraint	LHS ≤ RHS	For some resource, Amount used ≤ Amount available	Resource-allocation problems and mixed problems
Benefit constraint	LHS ≥ RHS	For some benefit, Level achieved ≥ Minimum acceptable level	Cost–benefit–trade-off problems and mixed problems
Fixed-requirement constraint	LHS = RHS	For some quantity, Amount provided = Required amount	Distribution-network problems and mixed problems

*LHS = Left-hand side (a SUMPRODUCT function).
RHS = Right-hand side (a constant).

Some mixed problems have only two of the three types of functional constraints. Others have all three. For example, the formulation of the Super Grain Corp. problem in Section 4.5 includes two benefit constraints and one fixed-requirement constraint, in addition to the three resource constraints in the original problem.

We next give one new example of a different kind of application that further illustrates how all three types of functional constraints can arise in the same problem. This example also will illustrate a different kind of spreadsheet formulation for a linear programming model.

Reclaiming Solid Wastes

The Problem

The Save-It Company operates a reclamation center that collects four types of solid waste materials and then treats them so that they can be amalgamated (treating and amalgamating are separate processes) into a salable product. Three different grades of this product can be made, depending on the mix of the materials used. (See Table 4.9.) Although there is some flexibility in the mix for each grade, quality standards specify the minimum or maximum amount of the materials allowed in that product grade. (This minimum or maximum amount is the weight of the material expressed as a percentage of the total weight for that product grade.) For each of the two higher grades, a fixed percentage is specified for one of the materials. These specifications are given in Table 4.9 along with the cost of amalgamation and the selling price for each grade.

The reclamation center collects its solid waste materials from some regular sources and so is normally able to maintain a steady rate for treating them. Table 4.10 gives the quantities available for collection and treatment each week, as well as the cost of treatment, for each type of material.

The Save-It Co. is solely owned by Green Earth, an organization that is devoted to dealing with environmental issues; Save-It's profits are all used to help support Green Earth's activities. Green Earth has raised contributions and grants, amounting to $30,000 per week, to be

TABLE 4.9
Product Data for the Save-It Company

Grade	Specification	Amalgamation Cost per Pound	Selling Price per Pound
A	Material 1: Not more than 30% of the total Material 2: Not less than 40% of the total Material 3: Not more than 50% of the total Material 4: Exactly 20% of the total	$3.00	$8.50
B	Material 1: Not more than 50% of the total Material 2: Not less than 10% of the total Material 4: Exactly 10% of the total	2.50	7.00
C	Material 1: Not more than 70% of the total	2.00	5.50

TABLE 4.10
Solid Waste Materials
Data for the Save-It
Company

Material	Pounds/Week Available	Treatment Cost per Pound	Additional Restrictions
1	3,000	$3.00	1. For each material, at least half of
2	2,000	6.00	the pounds/week available
3	4,000	4.00	should be collected and treated.
4	1,000	5.00	2. $30,000 per week should be
			used to treat these materials.

used exclusively to cover the entire treatment cost for the solid waste materials. The board of directors of Green Earth has instructed the management of Save-It to divide this money among the materials in such a way that *at least half* of the amount available of each material is actually collected and treated. These additional restrictions are listed in Table 4.10.

Within the restrictions specified in Tables 4.9 and 4.10, management wants to allocate the materials to product grades so as to maximize the total weekly profit (total sales income *minus* total amalgamation cost).

Formulation of the Problem in Linear Programming Terms

This is a *mixed* linear programming problem. To formulate it, we need to identify all the *activities, resources, benefits,* and *fixed requirements* lurking within it. The key to identifying the activities lies in management's goal to find the *best allocation of materials to product grades.* Each combination of a material and a product grade requires a decision: How much of that material should go into that product grade? This amount becomes the *level* of an *activity.*

> Each *activity* corresponds to the treatment of one solid waste material preparing it for amalgamation into one product grade.
> The *level* of this activity is the *amount* of the material treated preparatory to amalgamation into the product grade.

Thus, the decisions to be made are the number of pounds of each type of material to allocate to each product grade per week.

There are many constraints on these decisions because of limited resources, prescribed benefits, and fixed requirements, as summarized below.

Limited Resources: The four solid waste materials, where the amounts available are given in the second column of Table 4.10. In addition, the limited usages of materials 1 and 3 specified in the second column of Table 4.9 are interpreted as limited resources that lead to resource constraints.

Prescribed Benefits: The collection and treatment of each solid waste material is a benefit, where the minimum acceptable level (half of what is available) is prescribed on the right side of Table 4.10. In addition, the second column of Table 4.9 specifies minimum acceptable usages of material 2, so these are interpreted as prescribed benefits.

Fixed Requirements:

1. The fixed usages of material 4 specified in the second column of Table 4.9.

2. The fixed amount of money to be used for treating the solid waste materials, as specified on the right side of Table 4.10.

Management's objective is to maximize the *total weekly profit* from all three product grades, so this is the overall measure of performance for the problem. It is calculated by subtracting the total amalgamation cost from the total sales income. The contributions and grants of $30,000 per week specifically for treating the solid waste materials completely cover the treatment costs, so these costs are not included in calculating profit. The only cost considered, therefore, is the amalgamation cost. Thus, for each product grade, the profit per pound is obtained by subtracting the amalgamation cost given in the third column of Table 4.9 from the selling price in the fourth column.

Formulation of the Spreadsheet Model

As always, there is no single "right" way to format the spreadsheet for the formulation of the model for this problem. Since this problem is larger and more complicated than the previous examples, there are even more reasonable possibilities than usual in this case. For example, one possibility is to adopt the approach shown in Figure 4.6 of having separate rows of the spreadsheet used for the resource constraints, the benefit constraints, and the fixed-requirement constraints. However, we feel that the formulation shown in Figure 4.7 is preferable in this case because it is more compact and intuitive. We outline this formulation below.

The Data   Tables 4.9 and 4.10 provide all the data for this problem. The numbers in the last two columns of Table 4.9 have been entered into the data cells UnitAmalgCost (C4:E4) and UnitSellingPrice (C5:E5). The data in the second and third columns of Table 4.10 have been entered into the data cells AmountAvailable (M12:M15) and UnitTreatmentCost (G12:G15). The minimum treatment quantities specified by the first additional restriction in this table are in MinimumToTreat (I12:I15). The $30,000 for the second additional restriction is entered in FundsAvailable (K6). Finally, the percentages for the specifications in the second column of Table 4.9 are in MixturePercents (L19:L28).

FIGURE 4.7   The spreadsheet model for the Save-It Co. problem, including the formulas for the target cell TotalProfit (D20) and the other output cells, as well as the specifications needed to set up the Solver. The changing cells MaterialAllocation (C12:E15) show the optimal solution obtained by the Solver.

	A	B	C	D	E	F	G	H	I	J	K	L	M
1		**Save-It Company Reclamation Problem**											
2													
3			Grade A	Grade B	Grade C								
4		Unit Amalg. Cost	$3.00	$2.50	$2.00		Total Treatment Cost				$30,000		
5		Unit Selling Price	$8.50	$7.00	$5.50						=		
6		Unit Profit	$5.50	$4.50	$3.50		Treatment Funds Available				$30,000		
7													
8													
9			**Material Allocation**				Unit				Total		
10			(pounds of material used for each product grade)				Treatment		Minimum		Material		Amount
11			Grade A	Grade B	Grade C		Cost		to Treat		Treated		Available
12		Material 1	412.28	2,587.72	0		$3		1,500	≤	3,000	≤	3,000
13		Material 2	859.65	517.54	0		$6		1,000	≤	1,377.19	≤	2,000
14		Material 3	447.37	1,552.63	0		$4		2,000	≤	2,000	≤	4,000
15		Material 4	429.82	517.54	0		$5		500	≤	947.37	≤	1,000
16		Total Products	2,149.12	5,175.44	0.00								
17												Mixture	
18							**Mixture Specifications**					Percents	
19							Grade A, Material 1	412.28	≤		644.74	30% of Grade A	
20			Total Profit	$35,110			Grade A, Material 2	859.65	≥		859.65	40% of Grade A	
21							Grade A, Material 3	447.37	≤		1,074.56	50% of Grade A	
22							Grade A, Material 4	429.82	=		429.82	20% of Grade A	
23													
24							Grade B, Material 1	2,587.72	≤		2,587.72	50% of Grade B	
25							Grade B, Material 2	517.54	≥		517.54	10% of Grade B	
26							Grade B, Material 4	517.54	=		517.54	10% of Grade B	
27													
28							Grade C, Material 1	0.00	≤		0.00	70% of Grade C	

FIGURE 4.7 *(Continued)*

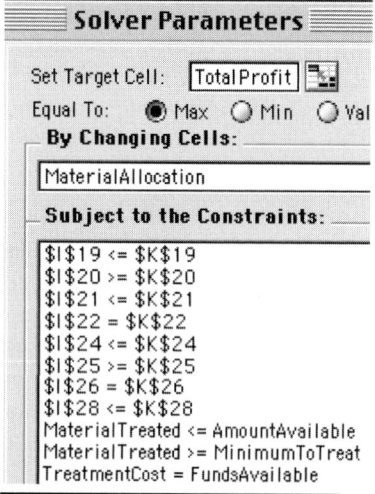

	J	K
4	Total Treatment Cost	=SUMPRODUCT(MaterialTreated,UnitTreatmentCost)

	B	C	D	E
6	Unit Profit	=C5-C4	=D5-D4	=E5-E4

	I	J	K	L	M
9			Total		
10	Minimum		Material		Amount
11	to Treat		Treated		Available
12	1,500	≤	=SUM(C12:E12)	≤	3,000
13	1,000	≤	=SUM(C13:E13)	≤	2,000
14	2,000	≤	=SUM C14:E14)	≤	4,000
15	500	≤	=SUM(C15:E15)	≤	1,000

	H	I	J	K	L	M
19	Grade A, Material 1	=C12	≤	=L19*GradeA	0.3	of Grade A
20	Grade A, Material 2	=C13	≥	=L20*GradeA	0.4	of Grade A
21	Grade A, Material 3	=C14	≤	=L21*GradeA	0.5	of Grade A
22	Grade A, Material 4	=C15	=	=L22*GradeA	0.2	of Grade A
23						
24	Grade B, Material 1	=D12	≤	=L24*GradeB	0.5	of Grade B
25	Grade B, Material 2	=D13	≥	=L25*GradeB	0.1	of Grade B
26	Grade B, Material 4	=D15	=	=L26*GradeB	0.1	of Grade B
27						
28	Grade C, Material 1	=E12	≤	=L28*GradeC	0.7	of Grade C

	B	C	D	E
16	Total Products	=SUM(C12:C15)	=SUM(D12:D15)	=SUM(E12:E15)

	C	D
20	Total Profit	=SUMPRODUCT(Unit Profit,TotalProducts)

The Decisions The 12 decisions to be made are

x_{A1} = Number of pounds of Material 1 allocated to Product Grade A per week

x_{A2} = Number of pounds of Material 2 allocated to Product Grade A per week

.

.

.

x_{C4} = Number of pounds of Material 4 allocated to Product Grade C per week

The 12 changing cells to hold these numbers have been organized in the table with the range name MaterialAllocation (C12:E15).

The Constraints In addition to the nonnegativity constraints, there are 17 functional constraints that need to be specified in both the spreadsheet and the Solver dialogue box. Eight of these use output cells MaterialTreated (K12:K15) that calculate the total number of pounds of the respective materials collected and treated for amalgamation per week. These calculations are

Total (Material 1) $= x_{A1} + x_{B1} + x_{C1} = $ SUM(C12:E12) $\rightarrow$ cell K12

Total (Material 2) $= x_{A2} + x_{B2} + x_{C2} = $ SUM(C13:E13) $\rightarrow$ cell K13

Total (Material 3) $= x_{A3} + x_{B3} + x_{C3} = $ SUM(C14:E14) $\rightarrow$ cell K14

Total (Material 4) $= x_{A4} + x_{B4} + x_{C4} = $ SUM(C15:E15) $\rightarrow$ cell K15

The eight constraints then are MaterialTreated (K12:K15) $\geq$ MinimumToTreat (I12:I15) (benefit constraints based on the first additional restriction of Table 4.10) and MaterialTreated (K12:K15) $\leq$ AmountAvailable (M12:M15) (resource constraints based on the second column of this same table).

The second additional restriction in Table 4.10 uses the output cell TreatmentCost (K4) and the data cell FundsAvailable (K6) to form the following fixed-requirement constraint:

$$\text{TreatmentCost} = \text{FundsAvailable}$$

where

$$\text{TreatmentCost} = \text{SUMPRODUCT(UnitTreatmentCost, MaterialTreated)}.$$

Finally, the eight constraints specified in the second column of Table 4.9 need to be incorporated into the spreadsheet model. This is done by using the box in rows 19–28. The numbers in column I are entered directly from the corresponding changing cells, so I19 = C12, I20 = C13, . . . , I29 = E12. Each number in column K is the percentage indicated in column L of the total for that grade given in cell GradeA (C16), GradeB (D16), or GradeC (E16). For example, the constraint for row 19 needs to specify that

$$x_{A1} \leq 0.3 \ (\text{Total for Grade A})$$

where

Total for Grade A $= x_{A1} + x_{A2} + x_{A3} + x_{A4}$

which is done by requiring that

$$\text{I19} \leq \text{K19}$$

where

K19 = L19 $\times$ GradeA

L19 = 0.3

GradeA = SUM(C12:C15)

(The formulas shown on the bottom of Figure 4.7 spell out all the details for these eight constraints.)

The Measure of Performance   The unit profit for each product grade is calculated in the output cells UnitProfit (C6:E6), where C6 = C5 − C4, D6 = D5 − D4, and E6 = E5 − E4. The total amount of each product produced is calculated in the output cells TotalProducts (C16:E16), where C16 = SUM(C12:C15), D16 = SUM(D12:D15), and E16 = SUM(E12:E15). Therefore, since the overall measure of performance is the *total weekly profit* from all three product grades, the equation for the target cell TotalProfit (D20) is

$$\text{TotalProfit} = \text{SUMPRODUCT(UnitProfit, TotalProducts)}$$

Summary of the Formulation   The complete formulation developed above for the linear programming model in the spreadsheet now can be summarized (in algebraic form) as follows:

Maximize   Profit $= 5.5 \ (x_{A1} + x_{A2} + x_{A3} + x_{A4}) + 4.5(x_{B1} + x_{B2} + x_{B3} + x_{B4})$
$$+ \ 3.5 \ (x_{C1} + x_{C2} + x_{C3} + x_{C4})$$

subject to the following constraints:

1. *Mixture specifications* (second column of Table 4.9):

$$x_{A1} \leq 0.3(x_{A1} + x_{A2} + x_{A3} + x_{A4}) \quad \text{(Grade A, Material 1)}$$

$$x_{A2} \geq 0.4(x_{A1} + x_{A2} + x_{A3} + x_{A4}) \quad \text{(Grade A, Material 2)}$$

$$x_{A3} \leq 0.5(x_{A1} + x_{A2} + x_{A3} + x_{A4}) \quad \text{(Grade A, Material 3)}$$

$$x_{A4} = 0.2(x_{A1} + x_{A2} + x_{A3} + x_{A4}) \quad \text{(Grade A, Material 4)}$$

$$x_{B1} \leq 0.5(x_{B1} + x_{B2} + x_{B3} + x_{B4}) \quad \text{(Grade B, Material 1)}$$

$$x_{B2} \geq 0.1(x_{B1} + x_{B2} + x_{B3} + x_{B4}) \quad \text{(Grade B, Material 2)}$$

$$x_{B4} = 0.1(x_{B1} + x_{B2} + x_{B3} + x_{B4}) \quad \text{(Grade B, Material 4)}$$

$$x_{C1} \leq 0.7(x_{C1} + x_{C2} + x_{C3} + x_{C4}) \quad \text{(Grade C, Material 1)}$$

2. *Availability of materials* (second column of Table 4.10):

$$x_{A1} + x_{B1} + x_{C1} \leq 3{,}000 \quad \text{(Material 1)}$$

$$x_{A2} + x_{B2} + x_{C2} \leq 2{,}000 \quad \text{(Material 2)}$$

$$x_{A3} + x_{B3} + x_{C3} \leq 4{,}000 \quad \text{(Material 3)}$$

$$x_{A4} + x_{B4} + x_{C4} \leq 1{,}000 \quad \text{(Material 4)}$$

3. *Restriction on amounts treated* (right side of Table 4.10):

$$x_{A1} + x_{B1} + x_{C1} \geq 1{,}500 \quad \text{(Material 1)}$$

$$x_{A2} + x_{B2} + x_{C2} \geq 1{,}000 \quad \text{(Material 2)}$$

$$x_{A3} + x_{B3} + x_{C3} \geq 2{,}000 \quad \text{(Material 3)}$$

$$x_{A4} + x_{B4} + x_{C4} \geq 500 \quad \text{(Material 4)}$$

4. *Restriction on treatment cost* (right side of Table 4.10):

$$3(x_{A1} + x_{B1} + x_{C1}) + 6(x_{A2} + x_{B2} + x_{C2})$$
$$+ 4(x_{A3} + x_{B3} + x_{C3}) + 5(x_{A4} + x_{B4} + x_{C4}) = 30{,}000$$

5. *Nonnegativity constraints:*

$$x_{A1} \geq 0 \qquad x_{A2} \geq 0 \qquad \ldots \qquad x_{C4} \geq 0$$

Solving the Model Applying the Solver to the spreadsheet model formulated in Figure 4.7 gives the optimal solution shown in the changing cells (C12:E15) for the number of pounds of each type of material allocated to each product grade per week. The resulting total weekly profit is given in the target cell TotalProfit (D20) as $35,110.

Some Observations about This Example

In comparison with other linear programming examples in this book, the above model is a rather large one. It has 12 decision variables and 17 functional constraints, including eight resource constraints, six benefit constraints, and three fixed-requirement constraints. Nevertheless, most real linear programming problems are much larger.

When dealing with large linear programming models of the size commonly found in practice, practitioners usually do not attempt to enter the model one number at a time on a spreadsheet. Instead, a *mathematical programming modeling language* commonly is used to efficiently generate the model from existing databases.

The Save-It Co. problem is an example of a **blending problem.** Blending problems are a special type of *mixed* linear programming problem where the objective is to find the best way of blending ingredients into final products to meet certain specifications. Some of the earliest applications of linear programming were for *gasoline blending,* where various petroleum ingredients were blended to obtain various grades of gasoline. Other blending problems involve such final products as steel, fertilizer, animal feed, and so on.

However, mixed linear programming problems arise in many other contexts as well.

Summary of the Formulation Procedure for Mixed Linear Programming Problems

The procedure for formulating mixed problems is similar to those for the other three categories of linear programming problems. However, each of these other categories features just one of the three types of functional constraints (resource constraints, benefit constraints, and fixed-requirement constraints), whereas mixed problems can include all three types. The following summary for mixed problems includes separate steps for dealing with these different types of functional constraints.

1. Since any linear programming problem involves finding the *best mix* of levels of various activities, identify these *activities* for the problem at hand. The decisions to be made are the *levels* of these activities.

2. From the viewpoint of management, identify an appropriate *overall measure of performance* for solutions of the problem.

3. For each activity, estimate the *contribution per unit* of the activity to this overall measure of performance.

4. Identify any *resources* that must be allocated to the activities (as described in Section 4.2). For each one, identify the *amount available* and then the *amount used per unit of each activity.*

5. Identify any *benefits* to be obtained from the activities (as described in Section 4.3). For each one, identify the *minimum acceptable level* prescribed by management and then the *benefit contribution per unit of each activity.*

6. Identify any *fixed requirements* that, for some type of quantity, the amount provided must equal a required amount (as described in Section 4.4). For each fixed requirement, identify the *required amount* and then the *contribution toward this required amount per unit of each activity.*

7. Enter the data gathered in steps 3–6 into *data cells* in a spreadsheet.

8. Designate *changing cells* for displaying the decisions on activity levels.

9. Use *output cells* to specify the constraints on resources, benefits, and fixed requirements.

10. Designate a *target cell* for displaying the overall measure of performance.

Review
Questions

1. What types of functional constraints can appear in a mixed linear programming problem?
2. The Save-It Co. problem is an example of what special type of mixed linear programming problem?

4.7 MODEL FORMULATION FROM A MANAGERIAL PERSPECTIVE

Both the measure of performance and the constraints in a model need to reflect the managerial view of the problem.

Formulating and analyzing a linear programming model provides information to help managers make their decisions. That means the model must accurately reflect the managerial view of the problem:

- The overall *measure of performance* must capture what management wants accomplished.

- When management limits the amounts of resources that will be made available to the activities under consideration, these limitations should be expressed as *resource constraints.*

- When management establishes minimum acceptable levels for benefits to be gained from the activities, these managerial goals should be incorporated into the model as *benefit constraints.*

- If management has fixed requirements for certain quantities, then *fixed-requirement constraints* are needed.

With the help of spreadsheets, some managers now are able to formulate and solve small linear programming models themselves. However, larger linear programming models generally are formulated by *management science teams,* not managers. When this is done, the management science team must thoroughly understand the managerial view of the problem. This requires clear communication with management from the very beginning of the study and maintaining effective communication as new issues requiring managerial guidance are identified. Management needs to clearly convey its view of the problem and the important issues involved. A manager cannot expect to obtain a helpful linear programming study without making clear just what help is wanted.

Linear programming studies need strong managerial input and support.

You will gain a greater appreciation for the importance of clear communication between the management science team and management when you become involved with real applications of linear programming. As is necessary in any textbook, the examples in this chapter are far smaller, simpler, and more clearly spelled out than is typical of real applications. Many real studies require formulating complicated linear programming models involving hundreds or thousands of decisions and constraints. In these cases, there usually are many ambiguities about just what should be incorporated into the model. Strong managerial input and support are vital to the success of a linear programming study for such complex problems.

When dealing with huge real problems, there is no such thing as "the" correct linear programming model for the problem. The model continually evolves throughout the course of the study. Early in the study, various techniques are used to test initial versions of the model to identify the errors and omissions that inevitably occur when constructing such a large model. This testing process is referred to as **model validation.**

Once the basic formulation has been validated, there are many reasonable variations of the model that might be used. Which variation to use depends on such factors as the assumptions about the problem that seem most reasonable, the estimates of the parameters of the model that seem most reliable, and the degree of detail desired in the model.

In large linear programming studies, a good approach is to begin with a relatively simple version of the model and then use the experience gained with this model to evolve toward more elaborate models that more nearly reflect the complexity of the real problem. This process of **model enrichment** continues only as long as the model remains reasonably easy to solve. It must be curtailed when the study's results are needed by management. Managers often need to curb the natural instinct of management science teams to continue adding "bells and whistles" to the model rather than winding up the study in a timely fashion with a less elegant but adequate model.

When managers study the output of the current model, they often detect some undesirable characteristics that point toward needed model enrichments. These enrichments frequently take the form of new *benefit constraints* to satisfy some managerial goals not previously articulated. (Recall that this is what happened in the Super Grain case study.)

Even though many reasonable variations of the model could be used, an *optimal solution* can be solved for only with respect to one specific version of the model at a time. This is why *what-if analysis* is such an important part of a linear programming study. After obtaining an optimal solution with respect to one specific model, management will have many what-if questions:

What-if analysis addresses some key questions that remain after formulating and solving a model.

- What if the estimates of the parameters in the model are incorrect?

- How do the conclusions change if different plausible assumptions are made about the problem?

- What happens when certain managerial options are pursued that are not incorporated into the current model?

The next chapter is devoted primarily to describing how what-if analysis addresses these and related issues, as well as how managers use this information.

Because managers *instigate* management science studies, they need to know enough about linear programming models and their formulation to be able to recognize managerial problems to which linear programming can be applied. Furthermore, since managerial input is so important for linear programming studies, managers need to understand the kinds of managerial concerns that can be incorporated into the model. Developing these two skills have been the most important goals of this chapter.

Review Questions

1. A linear programming model needs to reflect accurately whose view of the problem?
2. Who generally formulates large linear programming models?
3. What line of communication is vital in a linear programming study?
4. What is meant by *model validation?*
5. What is meant by the process of *model enrichment?*
6. Why is what-if analysis an important part of a linear programming study?

4.8 CLASSIC APPLICATIONS OF LINEAR PROGRAMMING, REVISITED

In Section 2.1, we described three representative *real* applications of linear programming and the resulting impact on the companies involved. Now that you have progressed through Chapters 2–4, we can tell you more about these applications. For each, we will discuss the following features:

1. The type of linear programming problem considered (relative to the categories described in this chapter).

2. The size of the problem.

3. Some factors that helped make this application so successful.

You may find it helpful to review each of these case studies in Section 2.1 before picking up the continuing story below.

Choosing the Product Mix at Ponderosa Industrial

Recall the critical issue facing the management of Ponderosa Industrial: choosing the most profitable mix of lumber to produce on a monthly basis. The volatility of the market prices for these products made this an especially difficult problem with a great impact on profitability.

This problem is similar to the Wyndor Glass Co. problem described in Sections 2.2 and 4.2. Both are *product-mix problems.* Both have *resources* that must be allocated to the production of various products. In both cases, these resources include certain kinds of *production capacities.* And in both cases, these resources lead to *resource constraints* in the linear programming model.

However, as is the case when comparing real applications to textbook examples, the Ponderosa problem is far more complicated than the Wyndor problem. Instead of the two decision variables and three functional constraints for Wyndor, the Ponderosa linear programming model has 90 decisions to be made and 45 functional constraints. Furthermore, whereas the Wyndor problem is a *resource-allocation problem,* the Ponderosa problem does not fit purely into this category. The Ponderosa model includes a considerable number of *fixed-requirement constraints* that express fixed relationships between the components of the products. And its model also includes some *benefit constraints* that ensure that the production and sale of certain products will not fall below minimum acceptable levels needed to satisfy the company's customers. Therefore, the Ponderosa problem falls into the *mixed* category described in Section 4.6.

Two factors helped make the Ponderosa application successful. One is that they implemented a financial planning system with a *natural-language* user interface, with the optimization codes operating in the background. Using natural language rather than mathematical symbols to display the components of the linear programming model and its output made the process understandable to the managers making the product-mix decisions. You have already seen examples of the natural-language approach in this chapter when using Excel to formulate linear programming models in a spreadsheet format with names for the activities, resources, benefits, and fixed requirements of a problem. Reporting to management in the language of managers is a key ingredient for the successful application of linear programming.

The other success factor was that the optimization system used was *interactive*. After obtaining an optimal solution for one version of the model, this feature enabled managers to ask a variety of what-if questions and receive immediate responses. Better decisions can result from exploring other plausible scenarios—a process that gave managers more confidence that their decisions would perform well under most foreseeable circumstances.

In any application, this ability to respond quickly to management's needs and queries through what-if analysis (whether interactive or not) is a vital part of a linear programming study.

Personnel Scheduling at United Airlines

As described in Section 2.1, linear programming has been used by United Airlines to design the weekly work schedule for all the employees (dozens or hundreds of them) at each of its regional reservations offices and at each of its major airports. The objective is to minimize the labor cost while meeting the service requirements for each half-hour time period in each 24-hour day of the week.

Although the details about the linear programming model have not been published, it is clear that the basic approach used is the one illustrated by the Union Airways example in Section 4.3. The main functional constraints are *benefit constraints* that ensure that the number of employees on duty during each time period will not fall below minimum acceptable levels. Therefore, the model is basically a *cost–benefit–trade-off problem.*

However, the Union Airways example only has five decisions to be made. By contrast, the United Airlines model for some of the locations scheduled involves over 20,000 decisions! The difference is that a real application must consider a myriad of important details that can be ignored in a textbook example. For example, the United Airlines model takes into account such things as the meal and break assignment times for each employee scheduled, differences in shift lengths for different employees, and days off over a weekly schedule, among other scheduling details.

The most important success factor in this application was "the support of operational managers and their staffs." Since these are the people who implement scheduling procedures, nothing much could be accomplished to improve these procedures without gaining their cooperation and support. This was a lesson learned by experience, because the management science team initially failed to establish a good line of communication with the operating managers, who then resisted the team's initial recommendations. The team leaders described their mistake as follows: "The cardinal rule for earning the trust and respect of operating managers and support staffs—'getting them involved in the development process'—had been violated." The team then worked much more closely with the operating managers—with outstanding results.

Planning Supply, Distribution, and Marketing at Citgo Petroleum Corporation

Section 2.1 describes how the application of management science techniques, including especially linear programming, literally turned around the fortunes of Citgo Petroleum Corporation during the mid-1980s. For example, one linear programming system (the Supply, Distribution, and Marketing modeling system) coordinated the supply, distribution, and marketing of each major product through Citgo's vast marketing and distribution network.

This linear programming model is of the same type as the model for the Big M Company problem in Section 4.4. Both are *distribution-network problems*.

However, the Big M Company model involves just six decisions to be made and five fixed-requirement constraints. By contrast, the Citgo model for each major product involves about 15,000 decisions and 3,000 fixed-requirement constraints!

When dealing with such huge models, it is inevitable that many errors will creep into the initial model. Therefore, it is extremely important to conduct a thorough process of *model validation* to test and correct the model. Citgo's management science team reported that when they checked their initial model for data errors and inconsistencies, the paper log of error messages generated was about an inch thick! After thorough model validation was completed, each new application of the working model typically would generate fewer than 10 error and warning messages about bad or questionable numbers that needed checking.

Some of the factors that contributed to the success of this application of linear programming were the same as for the two preceding companies discussed. Like Ponderosa Industrial, one factor was developing output reports in the language of managers to really meet their needs. These output reports are designed to be easy for managers to understand and use, and they address the issues that are important to management. Also like Ponderosa, another factor was enabling management to respond quickly to the dynamics of the industry by using the linear programming system extensively in what-if sessions. As in so many applications of linear programming, what-if analysis proved more important than the initial optimal solution obtained for one version of the model.

Much like the United Airlines application, another success factor was the enthusiastic support of operational managers during the development and implementation of this linear programming system.

However, the most important success factor was the unlimited support provided the management science task force by top management, ranging right up to the chief executive officer and the chairman of the board of Citgo's parent company, Southland Corporation. (We mentioned in Section 2.1 that the director of the task force, an eminent management science consultant, reported directly to both the president of Citgo and the chairman of the board of Southland.) This backing by top management included strong financial and organizational support.

When discussing both this linear programming system and other applications of management science implemented by the task force, team members described the financial support of top management as follows:

> The total cost of the systems implemented, $20–$30 million, was the greatest obstacle to this project. However, because of the information explosion in the petroleum industry, top management realized that numerous information systems were essential to gather, store, and analyze data. The incremental cost of adding management science technologies to these computers and systems was small, in fact very small in light of the enormous benefits they provided.

The organizational support provided by top management took a variety of forms. One example was the creation and staffing of the position of Senior Vice President of Operations Coordination to evaluate and coordinate recommendations based on the model which spanned organizational boundaries.

Review Questions

1. Compare the three applications of linear programming regarding which category (resource-allocation, cost–benefit–trade-off, distribution-network, or mixed problem) each fits.
2. Compare these applications regarding the number of decisions to be made.
3. What were the factors that helped make the Ponderosa application successful?
4. What were the factors that helped make the United Airlines application successful?
5. What were the factors that helped make the Citgo application successful?

4.9 Summary

Functional constraints with a ≤ sign are called *resource constraints,* because they require that the *amount used* of some resource must be *less than or equal to* the *amount available* of that resource. The identifying feature of *resource-allocation problems* is that all their functional constraints are resource constraints.

Functional constraints with a ≥ sign are called *benefit constraints,* since their form is that the *level achieved* for some benefit must be *greater than or equal to* the *minimum acceptable level* for that benefit. Frequently, benefit constraints express goals prescribed by management. If every functional constraint is a benefit constraint, then the problem is a *cost–benefit–trade-off problem.*

Functional constraints with an = sign are called *fixed-requirement constraints,* because they express the fixed requirement that, for some quantity, the *amount provided* must be *equal to* the *required amount.* One identifying feature of *distribution-network problems* is that their main functional constraints are fixed-requirement constraints with a certain form.

Linear programming problems that do not fit into any of these three categories are called *mixed problems.*

In many real applications, management science teams formulate and analyze large linear programming models to help guide managerial decision making. Such teams need strong managerial input and support to help ensure that their work really meets management's needs.

Glossary

benefit constraint   A functional constraint with a ≥ sign. The left-hand side is interpreted as the level of some benefit that is achieved by the activities under consideration, and the right-hand side is the minimum acceptable level for that benefit. (Section 4.3), *121*

blending problem   A type of mixed linear programming problem where the objective is to find the best way of blending ingredients into final products to meet certain specifications. (Section 4.6), *142*

cost–benefit–trade-off problem   A type of linear programming problem involving the trade-off between the total cost of the activities under consideration and the benefits to be achieved by these activities. Its identifying feature is that each functional constraint in the linear programming model is a benefit constraint. (Section 4.3), *121*

distribution-network problem   A type of linear programming problem concerned with the optimal distribution of goods through a distribution network. Its main functional constraints are fixed-requirement constraints. (Section 4.4), *128*

fixed-requirement constraint   A functional constraint with an = sign. The left-hand side represents the amount provided of some type of quantity, and the right-hand side represents the required amount for that quantity. (Section 4.4), *130*

identifying feature   A feature of a model that identifies the category of linear programming problem it represents. (Chapter introduction), *105*

mixed problem   Any linear programming problem that does not fit into any of the other three categories (resource-allocation problems, cost–benefit–trade-off problems, and distribution-network problems). (Section 4.6), *136*

model enrichment   The process of using experience with a model to identify and add important details that will provide a better representation of the real problem. (Section 4.7), *144*

model validation   The process of checking and testing a model to develop a valid model. (Section 4.7), *144*

resource-allocation problem   A type of linear programming problem concerned with allocating resources to activities. Its identifying feature is that each functional constraint in its model is a resource constraint. (Section 4.2), *113*

resource constraint   A functional constraint with a ≤ sign. The left-hand side represents the amount of some resource that is used by the activities under consideration, and the right-hand side represents the amount available of that resource. (Section 4.2), *113, 120*

Learning Aids for This Chapter in Your MS Courseware

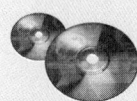

Chapter 4 Excel Files:

Super Grain Example

Think-Big Example

Union Airways Example

Big M Example

Revised Super Grain Example

Save-It Example

An Excel Add-in:

Premium Solver for Education

Problems

We have inserted the symbol E* to the left of each problem (or its parts) where Excel should be used (unless your instructor gives you contrary instructions). An asterisk on the problem number indicates that at least a partial answer is given in the back of the book.

4.1.   Reconsider the Super Grain Corp. case study as presented in Section 4.1. The advertising firm, Giacomi & Jackowitz, now has suggested a fourth promising advertising medium—radio commercials—to promote the company's new breakfast cereal, Crunchy Start. Young children are potentially major consumers of this cereal, but parents of young children (the major potential purchasers) often are too busy to do much reading (so may miss the company's advertisements in magazines and Sunday supplements) or even to watch the Saturday morning programs for children where the company's television commercials are aired. However, these parents do tend to listen to the radio during the commute to and from work. Therefore, to better reach these parents, Giacomi & Jackowitz suggests giving consideration to running commercials for Crunchy Start on nationally syndicated radio programs that appeal to young adults during typical commuting hours.

   Giacomi & Jackowitz estimates that the cost of developing each new radio commercial would be $50,000, and that the expected number of exposures per commercial would be 900,000. The firm has determined that 10 spots are available for different radio commercials, and each one would cost $200,000 for a normal run.

E*   *a.* Formulate and solve a spreadsheet model for the revised advertising-mix problem that includes this fourth advertising medium. Identify the data cells, the changing cells, and the target cell. Also show the Excel equation for each output cell expressed as a SUMPRODUCT function.

   b. Indicate why this spreadsheet model is a linear programming model.

   c. Express this model in algebraic form.

4.2.*   Consider a resource-allocation problem having the following data:

Resource	Resource Usage per Unit of Each Activity		Amount of Resource Available
	1	2	
1	2	1	10
2	3	3	20
3	2	4	20
Contribution per unit	$20	$30	

Contribution per unit = profit per unit of the activity.

E*   *a.* Formulate a linear programming model for this problem on a spreadsheet.

E*   *b.* Use the spreadsheet to check the following solutions: $(x_1, x_2) = (2, 2), (3, 3), (2, 4), (4, 2), (3, 4), (4, 3)$. Which of these solutions are feasible? Which of these feasible solutions has the best value of the objective function?

   c. Use the Solver to find an optimal solution.

   d. Express this model in algebraic form.

   e. Use the graphical method to solve this model.

4.3.   Consider a resource-allocation problem having the following data.

Resource	Resource Usage per Unit of Each Activity			Amount of Resource Available
	1	2	3	
A	30	20	0	500
B	0	10	40	600
C	20	20	30	1,000
Contribution per unit	$50	$40	$70	

Contribution per unit = profit per unit of the activity.

E*   *a.* Formulate and solve a linear programming model for this problem on a spreadsheet.

    b. Express this model in algebraic form.

E*4.4. Consider a resource-allocation problem having the following data:

Resource	Resource Usage per Unit of Each Activity				Amount of Resource Available
	1	**2**	**3**	**4**	
P	3	5	−2	4	400
Q	4	−1	3	2	300
R	6	3	2	−1	400
S	−2	2	5	3	300
Contribution per unit	$11	$9	$8	$9	

Contribution per unit = profit per unit of the activity.

    a. Formulate a linear programming model for this problem on a spreadsheet.

    b. Make five guesses of your own choosing for the optimal solution. Use the spreadsheet to check each one for feasibility and, if feasible, for the value of the objective function. Which feasible guess has the best objective function value?

    c. Use the Solver to find an optimal solution.

4.5.* The Omega Manufacturing Company has discontinued the production of a certain unprofitable product line. This act created considerable excess production capacity. Management is considering devoting this excess capacity to one or more of three products, products 1, 2, and 3. The available capacity of the machines that might limit output is summarized in the following table:

Machine Type	Available Time (in Machine-Hours per Week)
Milling machine	500
Lathe	350
Grinder	150

The number of machine-hours required for each unit of the respective products is as follows:

Productivity Coefficient (in Machine-Hours per Unit)

Machine Type	Product 1	Product 2	Product 3
Milling machine	9	3	5
Lathe	5	4	0
Grinder	3	0	2

    The Sales Department indicates that the sales potential for products 1 and 2 exceeds the maximum production rate and that the sales potential for product 3 is 20 units per week. The unit profit would be $50, $20, and $25, respectively, for products 1, 2, and 3. The objective is to determine how much of each product Omega should produce to maximize profit.

    a. Indicate why this is a resource-allocation problem by identifying both the activities and the limited resources to be allocated to these activities.

    b. Identify verbally the decisions to be made, the constraints on these decisions, and the overall measure of performance for the decisions.

    c. Convert these verbal descriptions of the constraints and the measure of performance into quantitative expressions in terms of the data and decisions.

E*   *d.* Formulate a spreadsheet model for this problem. Identify the data cells, the changing cells, the target cell, and the other output cells. Also show the Excel equation for each output cell expressed as a SUMPRODUCT function. Then use the Excel Solver to solve the model.

    e. Summarize the model in algebraic form.

4.6. Ed Butler is the production manager for the Bilco Corporation, which produces three types of spare parts for automobiles. The manufacture of each part requires processing on each of two machines, with the following processing times (in hours):

	Part		
Machine	A	B	C
1	0.02	0.03	0.05
2	0.05	0.02	0.04

Each machine is available 40 hours per month. Each part manufactured will yield a unit profit as follows:

	Part		
	A	B	C
Profit	$50	$40	$30

Ed wants to determine the mix of spare parts to produce to maximize total profit.

a. Identify both the activities and the resources for this resource-allocation problem.

E* b. Formulate a linear programming model for this problem on a spreadsheet.

E* c. Make three guesses of your own choosing for the optimal solution. Use the spreadsheet to check each one for feasibility and, if feasible, for the value of the objective function. Which feasible guess has the best objective function value?

E* d. Use the Solver to find an optimal solution.

e. Express the model in algebraic form.

E*4.7. Consider the following algebraic formulation of a resource-allocation problem with three resources, where the decisions to be made are the levels of three activities (A_1, A_2, and A_3).

$$\text{Maximize} \quad \text{Profit} = 20A_1 + 40A_2 + 30A_3$$

subject to

Resource 1: $3A_1 + 5A_2 + 4A_3 \le 400$ (amount available)

Resource 2: $A_1 + A_2 + A_3 \le 100$ (amount available)

Resource 3: $A_1 + 3A_2 + 2A_3 \le 200$ (amount available)

and

$$A_1 \ge 0 \qquad A_2 \ge 0 \qquad A_3 \ge 0$$

Formulate and solve the spreadsheet model for this problem.

4.8. Consider a cost–benefit–trade-off problem having the following data:

Benefit	Benefit Contribution per Unit of Each Activity		Minimum Acceptable Level
	1	2	
1	5	3	60
2	2	2	30
3	7	9	126
Unit cost	$60	$50	

E*   a. Formulate a linear programming model for this problem on a spreadsheet.

E*   b. Use the spreadsheet to check the following solutions: $(x_1, x_2) = (7, 7), (7, 8), (8, 7), (8, 8), (8, 9), (9, 8)$. Which of these solutions are feasible? Which of these feasible solutions has the best value of the objective function?

E*   c. Use the Solver to find an optimal solution.

      d. Express the model in algebraic form.

      e. Use the graphical method to solve this model.

E*4.9.   Consider a cost–benefit–trade-off problem having the following data:

Benefit	Benefit Contribution per Unit of Each Activity				Minimum Acceptable Level
	1	2	3	4	
P	2	−1	4	3	80
Q	1	4	−1	2	60
R	3	5	4	−1	110
Unit cost	$400	$600	$500	$300	

a. Formulate a linear programming model for this problem on a spreadsheet.

b. Make five guesses of your own choosing for the optimal solution. Use the spreadsheet to check each one for feasibility and, if feasible, for the value of the objective function. Which feasible guess has the best objective function value?

c. Use the Solver to find an optimal solution.

4.10.*   Fred Jonasson manages a family-owned farm. To supplement several food products grown on the farm, Fred also raises pigs for market. He now wishes to determine the quantities of the available types of feed (corn, tankage, and alfalfa) that should be given to each pig. Since pigs will eat any mix of these feed types, the objective is to determine which mix will meet certain nutritional requirements at a *minimum cost*. The number of units of each type of basic nutritional ingredient contained within a kilogram of each feed type is given in the following table, along with the daily nutritional requirements and feed costs:

Nutritional Ingredient	Kilogram of Corn	Kilogram of Tankage	Kilogram of Alfalfa	Minimum Daily Requirement
Carbohydrates	90	20	40	200
Protein	30	80	60	180
Vitamins	10	20	60	150
Cost (¢)	84	72	60	

E*   a. Formulate a linear programming model for this problem on a spreadsheet.

E*   b. Use the spreadsheet to check if $(x_1, x_2, x_3) = (1, 2, 2)$ is a feasible solution and, if so, what the daily cost would be for this diet. How many units of each nutritional ingredient would this diet provide daily?

E*   c. Take a few minutes to use a trial-and-error approach with the spreadsheet to develop your best guess for the optimal solution. What is the daily cost for your solution?

E*   d. Use the Solver to find an optimal solution.

      e. Express the model in algebraic form.

4.11.   Maureen Laird is the chief financial officer for the Alva Electric Co., a major public utility in the Midwest. The company has scheduled the construction of new hydroelectric plants 5, 10, and 20 years from now to meet the needs of the growing population in the region served by the company. To cover the construction costs, Maureen needs to invest some of the company's money now to meet these future cash flow needs. Maureen may purchase only three kinds of financial assets, each of which costs $1 million per unit. Fractional units may be purchased. The assets produce income 5, 10, and 20 years from now, and that income is needed to cover minimum cash flow requirements in those years, as shown in the following table.

	Income per Unit of Asset			
Year	Asset 1	Asset 2	Asset 3	Minimum Cash Flow Required
5	$2 million	$1 million	$0.5 million	$400 million
10	0.5 million	0.5 million	1 million	100 million
20	0	1.5 million	2 million	300 million

Maureen wishes to determine the mix of investments in these assets that will cover the cash flow requirements while minimizing the total amount invested.

E*   *a.* Formulate a linear programming model for this problem on a spreadsheet.

E*   *b.* Use the spreadsheet to check the possibility of purchasing 100 units of asset 1, 100 units of asset 2, and 200 units of asset 3. How much cash flow would this mix of investments generate 5, 10, and 20 years from now? What would be the total amount invested?

E*   *c.* Take a few minutes to use a trial-and-error approach with the spreadsheet to develop your best guess for the optimal solution. What is the total amount invested for your solution?

E*   *d.* Use the Solver to find an optimal solution.

   e. Summarize the model in algebraic form.

4.12. Web Mercantile sells many household products through an online catalog. The company needs substantial warehouse space for storing its goods. Plans now are being made for leasing warehouse storage space over the next five months. Just how much space will be required in each of these months is known. However, since these space requirements are quite different, it may be most economical to lease only the amount needed each month on a month-by-month basis. On the other hand, the additional cost for leasing space for additional months is much less than for the first month, so it may be less expensive to lease the maximum amount needed for the entire five months. Another option is the intermediate approach of changing the total amount of space leased (by adding a new lease and/or having an old lease expire) at least once but not every month.

   The space requirement and the leasing costs for the various leasing periods are as follows:

Month	Required Space (Square Feet)	Leasing Period (Months)	Cost per Sq. Ft. Leased
1	30,000	1	$ 65
2	20,000	2	100
3	40,000	3	135
4	10,000	4	160
5	50,000	5	190

The objective is to minimize the total leasing cost for meeting the space requirements.

   a. Indicate why this is a cost–benefit–trade-off problem by identifying both the activities and the benefits being sought from these activities.

   b. Identify verbally the decisions to be made, the constraints on these decisions, and the overall measure of performance for the decisions.

   c. Convert these verbal descriptions of the constraints and the measure of performance into quantitative expressions in terms of the data and decisions.

E*   *d.* Formulate a spreadsheet model for this problem. Identify the data cells, the changing cells, the target cell, and the other output cells. Also show the Excel equation for each output cell expressed as a SUMPRODUCT function. Then use the Excel Solver to solve the model.

   e. Summarize the model in algebraic form.

E*4.13. Consider the following algebraic formulation of a cost–benefit–trade-off problem involving three benefits, where the decisions to be made are the levels of four activities (A_1, A_2, A_3, and A_4):

$$\text{Minimize} \quad \text{Cost} = 2A_1 + A_2 - A_3 + 3A_4$$

subject to

Benefit 1: $3A_1 + 2A_2 - 2A_3 + 5A_4 \geq 80$ (minimum acceptable level)

Benefit 2: $\quad A_1 - \quad A_2 \quad\quad + \quad A_4 \geq 10$ (minimum acceptable level)

Benefit 3: $\quad A_1 + \quad A_2 - \quad A_3 + 2A_4 \geq 30$ (minimum acceptable level)

and

$$A_1 \geq 0 \qquad A_2 \geq 0 \qquad A_3 \geq 0 \qquad A_4 \geq 0$$

Formulate and solve the spreadsheet model for this problem.

4.14. Larry Edison is the Director of the Computer Center for Buckly College. He now needs to schedule the staffing of the center. It is open from 8 AM until midnight. Larry has monitored the usage of the center at various times of the day and determined that the following number of computer consultants are required:

Time of Day	Minimum Number of Consultants Required to Be on Duty
8 AM–noon	6
Noon–4 PM	8
4 PM–8 PM	12
8 PM–midnight	6

Two types of computer consultants can be hired: full-time and part-time. The full-time consultants work for eight consecutive hours in any of the following shifts: morning (8 AM–4 PM), afternoon (noon–8 PM), and evening (4 PM–midnight). Full-time consultants are paid $14 per hour.

Part-time consultants can be hired to work any of the four shifts listed in the table. Part-time consultants are paid $12 per hour.

An additional requirement is that during every time period, there must be at least two full-time consultants on duty for every part-time consultant on duty.

Larry would like to determine how many full-time and part-time consultants should work each shift to meet the above requirements at the minimum possible cost.

a. Which category of linear programming problem does this problem fit? Why?

E* *b.* Formulate and solve a linear programming model for this problem on a spreadsheet.

c. Summarize the model in algebraic form.

4.15.* The Medequip Company produces precision medical diagnostic equipment at two factories. Three medical centers have placed orders for this month's production output. The following table shows what the cost would be for shipping each unit from each factory to each of these customers. Also shown are the number of units that will be produced at each factory and the number of units ordered by each customer.

	Unit Shipping Cost			
From \ To	Customer 1	Customer 2	Customer 3	Output
Factory 1	$600	$800	$700	400 units
Factory 2	400	900	600	500 units
Order size	300 units	200 units	400 units	

A decision now needs to be made about the shipping plan for how many units to ship from each factory to each customer.

a. Which category of linear programming problem does this problem fit? Why?

E* b. Formulate and solve a linear programming model for this problem on a spreadsheet.

c. Summarize this formulation in algebraic form.

4.16. The Fagersta Steelworks currently is working two mines to obtain its iron ore. This iron ore is shipped to either of two storage facilities. When needed, it then is shipped on to the company's steel plant. The diagram below depicts this distribution network, where M1 and M2 are the two mines, S1 and S2 are the two storage facilities, and P is the steel plant. The diagram also shows the monthly amounts produced at the mines and needed at the plant, as well as the shipping cost and the maximum amount that can be shipped per month through each shipping lane.

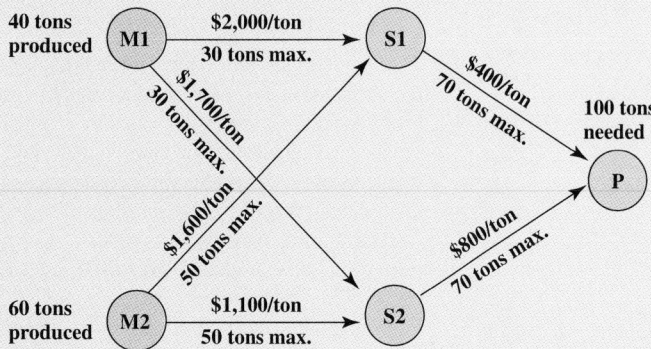

Management now wants to determine the most economical plan for shipping the iron ore from the mines through the distribution network to the steel plant.

a. Identify all the requirements that will need to be expressed in fixed-requirement constraints.

E* b. Formulate and solve a linear programming model for this problem on a spreadsheet.

c. Express this model in algebraic form.

4.17.* Al Ferris has $60,000 that he wishes to invest now in order to use the accumulation for purchasing a retirement annuity in five years. After consulting with his financial advisor, he has been offered four types of fixed-income investments, which we will label as investments *A, B, C,* and *D.*

Investments *A* and *B* are available at the beginning of each of the next five years (call them years 1 to 5). Each dollar invested in *A* at the beginning of a year returns $1.40 (a profit of $0.40) two years later (in time for immediate reinvestment). Each dollar invested in *B* at the beginning of a year returns $1.70 three years later.

Investments *C* and *D* will each be available at one time in the future. Each dollar invested in *C* at the beginning of year 2 returns $1.90 at the end of year 5. Each dollar invested in *D* at the beginning of year 5 returns $1.30 at the end of year 5.

Al wishes to know which investment plan maximizes the amount of money that can be accumulated by the beginning of year 6.

a. Although this is not a distribution-network problem, all its functional constraints can be expressed as fixed-requirement constraints. To do this, let A_t, B_t, C_t, and D_t be the amounts invested in investments *A, B, C,* and *D,* respectively, at the beginning of year *t* for each *t* where the investment is available and will mature by the end of year 5. Also let R_t be the number of available dollars *not* invested at the beginning of year *t* (and so available for investment in a later year). Thus, the amount invested at the beginning of year *t plus* R_t must equal the number of dollars available for investment at that time. Write such an equation in terms of the relevant variables above for the beginning of each of the five years to obtain the five fixed-requirement constraints for this problem.

b. Formulate a complete linear programming model for this problem in algebraic form.

E* c. Formulate and solve this model on a spreadsheet.

4.18. The Metalco Company desires to blend a new alloy of 40 percent tin, 35 percent zinc, and 25 percent lead from several available alloys having the following properties:

Property	Alloy				
	1	2	3	4	5
Percentage of tin	60	25	45	20	50
Percentage of zinc	10	15	45	50	40
Percentage of lead	30	60	10	30	10
Cost ($/lb)	22	20	25	24	27

The objective is to determine the proportions of these alloys that should be blended to produce the new alloy at a minimum cost.

    a. Identify all the requirements that will need to be expressed in fixed-requirement constraints.

E*   *b.* Formulate and solve a linear programming model for this problem on a spreadsheet.

    c. Express this model in algebraic form.

4.19. The Weigelt Corporation has three branch plants with excess production capacity. Fortunately, the corporation has a new product ready to begin production, and all three plants have this capability, so some of the excess capacity can be used in this way. This product can be made in three sizes—large, medium, and small—that yield a net unit profit of $420, $360, and $300, respectively. Plants 1, 2, and 3 have the excess capacity to produce 750, 900, and 450 units per day of this product, respectively, regardless of the size or combination of sizes involved.

    The amount of available in-process storage space also imposes a limitation on the production rates of the new product. Plants 1, 2, and 3 have 13,000, 12,000, and 5,000 square feet, respectively, of in-process storage space available for a day's production of this product. Each unit of the large, medium, and small sizes produced per day requires 20, 15, and 12 square feet, respectively.

    Sales forecasts indicate that if available, 900, 1,200, and 750 units of the large, medium, and small sizes, respectively, would be sold per day.

    At each plant, some employees will need to be laid off unless most of the plant's excess production capacity can be used to produce the new product. To avoid layoffs if possible, management has decided that the plants should use the same percentage of their excess capacity to produce the new product.

    Management wishes to know how much of each of the sizes should be produced by each of the plants to maximize profit.

E*   *a.* Formulate and solve a linear programming model for this mixed problem on a spreadsheet.

    b. Express the model in algebraic form.

4.20.* A cargo plane has three compartments for storing cargo: front, center, and back. These compartments have capacity limits on both *weight* and *space,* as summarized below:

Compartment	Weight Capacity (Tons)	Space Capacity (Cubic Feet)
Front	12	7,000
Center	18	9,000
Back	10	5,000

Furthermore, the weight of the cargo in the respective compartments must be the same proportion of that compartment's weight capacity to maintain the balance of the airplane.

    The following four cargoes have been offered for shipment on an upcoming flight as space is available:

Cargo	Weight (Tons)	Volume (Cubic Feet/Ton)	Profit ($/Ton)
1	20	500	320
2	16	700	400
3	25	600	360
4	13	400	290

Any portion of these cargoes can be accepted. The objective is to determine how much (if any) of each cargo should be accepted and how to distribute each among the compartments to maximize the total profit for the flight.

E*   *a.* Formulate and solve a linear programming model for this mixed problem on a spreadsheet.

      b. Express the model in algebraic form.

4.21.   Comfortable Hands is a company that features a product line of winter gloves for the entire family—men, women, and children. They are trying to decide what mix of these three types of gloves to produce.

        Comfortable Hands's manufacturing labor force is unionized. Each full-time employee works a 40-hour week. In addition, by union contract, the number of full-time employees can never drop below 20. Nonunion, part-time workers also can be hired with the following union-imposed restrictions: (1) each part-time worker works 20 hours per week and (2) there must be at least two full-time employees for each part-time employee.

        All three types of gloves are made out of the same 100 percent genuine cowhide leather. Comfortable Hands has a long-term contract with a supplier of the leather and receives a 5,000-square-foot shipment of the material each week. The material requirements and labor requirements, along with the *gross profit* per glove sold (not considering labor costs), are given in the following table.

Glove	Material Required (Square Feet)	Labor Required (Minutes)	Gross Profit (per Pair)
Men's	2	30	$ 8
Women's	1.5	45	10
Children's	1	40	6

        Each full-time employee earns $13 per hour, while each part-time employee earns $10 per hour. Management wishes to know what mix of each of the three types of gloves to produce per week, as well as how many full-time and part-time workers to employ. They would like to maximize their *net profit*—their gross profit from sales minus their labor costs.

E*   *a.* Formulate and solve a linear programming model for this problem on a spreadsheet.

      b. Summarize this formulation in algebraic form.

E*4.22.   Oxbridge University maintains a powerful mainframe computer for research use by its faculty, Ph.D. students, and research associates. During all working hours, an operator must be available to operate and maintain the computer, as well as to perform some programming services. Beryl Ingram, the director of the computer facility, oversees the operation.

        It is now the beginning of the fall semester and Beryl is confronted with the problem of assigning different working hours to her operators. Because all the operators are currently enrolled in the university, they are available to work only a limited number of hours each day.

        There are six operators (four undergraduate students and two graduate students). They all have different wage rates because of differences in their experience with computers and in their programming ability. The following table shows their wage rates, along with the maximum number of hours that each can work each day.

Operators	Wage Rate	Maximum Hours of Availability				
		Mon.	Tue.	Wed.	Thurs.	Fri.
K. C.	$10.00/hour	6	0	6	0	6
D. H.	$10.10/hour	0	6	0	6	0
H. B.	$9.90/hour	4	8	4	0	4
S. C.	$9.80/hour	5	5	5	0	5
K. S.	$10.80/hour	3	0	3	8	0
N. K.	$11.30/hour	0	0	0	6	2

        Each operator is guaranteed a certain minimum number of hours per week that will maintain an adequate knowledge of the operation. This level is set arbitrarily at 8 hours per week for the undergraduate students (K.C., D.H., H.B., and S.C.) and 7 hours per week for the graduate students (K. S. and N. K.).

The computer facility is to be open for operation from 8 AM to 10 PM Monday through Friday with exactly one operator on duty during these hours. On Saturdays and Sundays, the computer is to be operated by other staff.

Because of a tight budget, Beryl has to minimize cost. She wishes to determine the number of hours she should assign to each operator on each day. Formulate and solve a spreadsheet model for this problem.

4.23.   Slim-Down Manufacturing makes a line of nutritionally complete, weight-reduction beverages. One of its products is a strawberry shake that is designed to be a complete meal. The strawberry shake consists of several ingredients. Some information about each of these ingredients is given below.

Ingredient	Calories from Fat (per tbsp.)	Total Calories (per tbsp.)	Vitamin Content (mg/tbsp.)	Thickeners (mg/tbsp.)	Cost (¢/tbsp.)
Strawberry flavoring	1	50	20	3	10
Cream	75	100	0	8	8
Vitamin supplement	0	0	50	1	25
Artificial sweetener	0	120	0	2	15
Thickening agent	30	80	2	25	6

The nutritional requirements are as follows. The beverage must total between 380 and 420 calories (inclusive). No more than 20 percent of the total calories should come from fat. There must be at least 50 milligrams (mg) of vitamin content. For taste reasons, there must be at least two tablespoons (tbsp.) of strawberry flavoring for each tbsp. of artificial sweetener. Finally, to maintain proper thickness, there must be exactly 15 mg of thickeners in the beverage.

Management would like to select the quantity of each ingredient for the beverage that would minimize cost while meeting the above requirements.

a. Identify the requirements that lead to resource constraints, to benefit constraints, and to fixed-requirement constraints.

E*   *b.* Formulate and solve a linear programming model for this problem on a spreadsheet.

c. Summarize this formulation in algebraic form.

4.24.   Joyce and Marvin run a day care for preschoolers. They are trying to decide what to feed the children for lunches. They would like to keep their costs down, but they also need to meet the nutritional requirements of the children. They have already decided to go with peanut butter and jelly sandwiches, and some combination of graham crackers, milk, and orange juice. The nutritional content of each food choice and its cost are given in the table below.

Food Item	Calories from Fat	Total Calories	Vitamin C (mg)	Protein (g)	Cost (¢)
Bread (1 slice)	10	70	0	3	5
Peanut butter (1 tbsp.)	75	100	0	4	4
Strawberry jelly (1 tbsp.)	0	50	3	0	7
Graham cracker (1 cracker)	20	60	0	1	8
Milk (1 cup)	70	150	2	8	15
Juice (1 cup)	0	100	120	1	35

The nutritional requirements are as follows. Each child should receive between 400 and 600 calories. No more than 30 percent of the total calories should come from fat. Each child should consume at least 60 milligrams (mg) of vitamin C and 12 grams (g) of protein. Furthermore, for practical reasons, each child needs exactly 2 slices of bread (to make the sandwich), at least twice as much peanut butter as jelly, and at least 1 cup of liquid (milk and/or juice).

Joyce and Marvin would like to select the food choices for each child that minimize cost while meeting the above requirements.

a. Identify the requirements that lead to resource constraints, to benefit constraints, and to fixed-requirement constraints.

E*   b. Formulate and solve a linear programming model for this problem on a spreadsheet.

c. Express the model in algebraic form.

Case 4-1

Fabrics and Fall Fashions

From the 10th floor of her office building, Katherine Rally watches the swarms of New Yorkers fight their way through the streets infested with yellow cabs and the sidewalks littered with hot dog stands. On this sweltering July day, she pays particular attention to the fashions worn by the various women and wonders what they will choose to wear in the fall. Her thoughts are not simply random musings; they are critical to her work since she owns and manages TrendLines, an elite women's clothing company.

Today is an especially important day because she must meet with Ted Lawson, the production manager, to decide upon next month's production plan for the fall line. Specifically, she must determine the quantity of each clothing item she should produce given the plant's production capacity, limited resources, and demand forecasts. Accurate planning for next month's production is critical to fall sales since the items produced next month will appear in stores during September and women generally buy the majority of the fall fashions when they first appear in September.

She turns back to her sprawling glass desk and looks at the numerous papers covering it. Her eyes roam across the clothing patterns designed almost six months ago, the lists of material requirements for each pattern, and the lists of demand forecasts for each pattern determined by customer surveys at fashion shows. She remembers the hectic and sometimes nightmarish days of designing the fall line and presenting it at fashion shows in New York, Milan, and Paris. Ultimately, she paid her team of six designers a total of $860,000 for their work on her fall line. With the cost of hiring runway models, hair stylists, and make-up artists; sewing and fitting clothes; building the set; choreographing and rehearsing the show; and renting the conference hall, each of the three fashion shows cost her an additional $2,700,000.

She studies the clothing patterns and material requirements. Her fall line consists of both professional and casual fashions. She determined the price for each clothing item by taking into account the quality and cost of material, the cost of labor and machining, the demand for the item, and the prestige of the TrendLines brand name.

The fall professional fashions include:

Clothing Item	Material Requirements	Price	Labor and Machine Cost
Tailored wool slacks	3 yards of wool 2 yards of acetate for lining	$300	$160
Cashmere sweater	1.5 yards of cashmere	450	150
Silk blouse	1.5 yards of silk	180	100
Silk camisole	0.5 yard of silk	120	60
Tailored skirt	2 yards of rayon 1.5 yards of acetate for lining	270	120
Wool blazer	2.5 yards of wool 1.5 yards of acetate for lining	320	140

The fall casual fashions include:

Clothing Item	Material Requirements	Price	Labor and Machine Cost
Velvet pants	3 yards of velvet 2 yards of acetate for lining	$350	$175
Cotton sweater	1.5 yards of cotton	130	60
Cotton miniskirt	0.5 yard of cotton	75	40
Velvet shirt	1.5 yards of velvet	200	160
Button-down blouse	1.5 yards of rayon	120	90

She knows that for the next month, she has ordered 45,000 yards of wool, 28,000 yards of acetate, 9,000 yards of cashmere, 18,000 yards of silk, 30,000 yards of rayon, 20,000 yards of velvet, and 30,000 yards of cotton for production. The prices of the materials are listed below.

Material	Price per Yard
Wool	$ 9.00
Acetate	1.50
Cashmere	60.00
Silk	13.00
Rayon	2.25
Velvet	12.00
Cotton	2.50

Any material that is not used in production can be sent back to the textile wholesaler for a full refund, although scrap material cannot be sent back to the wholesaler.

She knows that the production of both the silk blouse and cotton sweater leaves leftover scraps of material. Specifically, for the production of one silk blouse or one cotton sweater, 2 yards of silk and cotton, respectively, are needed. From these 2 yards, 1.5 yards are used for the silk blouse or the cotton sweater and 0.5 yard is left as scrap material. She does not want to waste the material, so she plans to use the rectangular scrap of silk or cotton to produce a silk camisole or cotton miniskirt, respectively. Therefore, whenever a silk blouse is produced, a silk camisole is also produced. Likewise, whenever a cotton sweater is produced, a cotton miniskirt is also produced. Note that it is possible to produce a silk camisole without producing a silk blouse and a cotton miniskirt without producing a cotton sweater.

The demand forecasts indicate that some items have limited demand. Specifically, because the velvet pants and velvet shirts are fashion fads, TrendLines has forecasted that it can sell only 5,500 pairs of velvet pants and 6,000 velvet shirts. TrendLines does not want to produce more than the forecasted demand because once the pants and shirts go out of style, the company cannot sell them. TrendLines can produce less than the forecasted demand, however, since the company is not required to meet the demand. The cashmere sweater also has limited demand because it is quite expensive, and TrendLines knows it can sell at most 4,000 cashmere sweaters. The silk blouses and camisoles have limited demand because many women think silk is too hard to care for, and TrendLines projects that it can sell at most 12,000 silk blouses and 15,000 silk camisoles.

The demand forecasts also indicate that the wool slacks, tailored skirts, and wool blazers have a great demand because they are basic items needed in every professional wardrobe. Specifically, the demand is 7,000 pairs of wool slacks and 5,000 wool blazers. Katherine wants to meet at least 60 percent of the demand for these two items to maintain her loyal customer base and not lose business in the future. Although the demand for tailored skirts could not be estimated, Katherine feels she should make at least 2,800 of them.

a. Ted is trying to convince Katherine not to produce any velvet shirts since the demand for this fashion fad is quite low. He argues that this fashion fad alone accounts for $500,000 of the fixed design and other costs. The net contribution (price of clothing item − materials cost − labor cost) from selling the fashion fad should cover these fixed costs. Each velvet shirt generates a net contribution of $22. He argues that given the net contribution, even satisfying the maximum demand will not yield a profit. What do you think of Ted's argument?

b. Formulate and solve a linear programming problem to maximize profit given the production, resource, and demand constraints.

Before she makes her final decision, Katherine plans to explore the following questions independently, except where otherwise indicated.

c. The textile wholesaler informs Katherine that the velvet cannot be sent back because the demand forecasts show that the demand for velvet will decrease in the future. Katherine can therefore get no refund for the velvet. How does this fact change the production plan?

d. What is an intuitive economic explanation for the difference between the solutions found in parts *b* and *c?*

e. The sewing staff encounters difficulties sewing the arms and lining into the wool blazer since the blazer pattern has an awkward shape and the heavy wool material is difficult to cut and sew. The increased labor time to sew a wool blazer increases the labor and machine cost for each blazer by $80. Given this new cost, how many of each clothing item should TrendLines produce to maximize profit?

f. The textile wholesaler informs Katherine that since another textile customer canceled his order, she can obtain an extra 10,000 yards of acetate. How many of each clothing item should TrendLines now produce to maximize profit?

g. TrendLines assumes that it can sell every item that was not sold during September and October in a big sale in November at 60 percent of the original price. Therefore, it can sell all items in unlimited quantity during the November sale. (The previously mentioned upper limits on demand only concern the sales during September and October.) What should the new production plan be to maximize profit?

Case 4-2

New Frontiers

Rob Richman, president of AmeriBank, takes off his glasses, rubs his eyes in exhaustion, and squints at the clock in his study. It reads 3 AM. For the last several hours, Rob has been poring over AmeriBank's financial statements from the last three quarters of operation. AmeriBank, a medium-sized bank with branches throughout the United States, is headed for dire economic straits. The bank, which provides transaction, savings, investment, and loan services, has been experiencing a steady decline in its net income over the past year, and trends show that the decline will continue. The bank is simply losing customers to nonbank and foreign bank competitors.

AmeriBank is not alone in its struggle to stay out of the red. From his daily industry readings, Rob knows that many American banks have been suffering significant losses because of increasing competition from nonbank and foreign bank competitors offering services typically in the domain of American banks. Because the nonbank and foreign bank competitors specialize in particular services, they are able to better capture the market for those services by offering less expensive, more efficient, more convenient services. For example, large corporations now turn to foreign banks and commercial paper offerings for loans, and affluent Americans now turn to money-market funds for investment. Banks face the daunting challenge of distinguishing themselves from nonbank and foreign bank competitors.

Rob has concluded that one strategy for distinguishing AmeriBank from its competitors is to improve services that nonbank and foreign bank competitors do not readily provide: transaction services. He has decided that a more convenient transaction method must logically succeed the automatic teller machine, and he believes that electronic banking over the Internet allows this convenient transaction method. Over the Internet, customers are able to perform transactions on their desktop computers either at home or work. The explosion of the Internet means that many potential customers understand and use the World Wide Web. He therefore feels that if AmeriBank offers Web banking (as the practice of Internet banking is commonly called), the bank will attract many new customers.

Before Rob undertakes the project to make Web banking possible, however, he needs to understand the market for Web banking and the services AmeriBank should provide over the Internet. For example, should the bank only allow customers to access account balances and historical transaction information over the Internet, or should the bank develop a strategy to allow customers to make deposits and withdrawals over the Internet? Should the bank try to recapture a portion of the investment market by continuously running stock prices and allowing customers to make stock transactions over the Internet for a minimal fee?

Because AmeriBank is not in the business of performing surveys, Rob has decided to outsource the survey project to a professional survey company. He has opened the project up for bidding by several survey companies and will award the project to the company that is willing to perform the survey for the least cost. Rob provided each survey company with a list of survey requirements to ensure that Ameri Bank receives the needed information for planning the Web banking project.

Because different age groups require different services, AmeriBank is interested in surveying four different age groups. The first group encompasses customers who are 18 to 25 years old. The bank assumes that this age group has limited yearly income and performs minimal transactions. The second group encompasses customers who are 26 to 40 years old. This age group has significant sources of income, performs many transactions, requires numerous loans for new houses and cars, and invests in various securities. The third group encompasses customers who are 41 to 50 years old. These customers typically have the same level of income and perform the same number of transactions as the second age group, but the bank assumes that these customers are less likely to use Web banking since they have not become as comfortable with the explosion of computers or the Internet. Finally, the fourth group encompasses customers who are 51 years of age and over. These customers commonly crave security and require continuous information on retirement funds. The bank believes that it is highly unlikely that customers in this age group will use Web banking, but the bank desires to learn the needs of this age group for the future. AmeriBank wants to interview 2,000 customers with at least 20 percent from the first age group, at least 27.5 percent from the second age group, at least 15 percent from the third age group, and at least 15 percent from the fourth age group.

Rob understands that the Internet is a recent phenomenon and that some customers may not have heard of the World Wide Web. He therefore wants to ensure that the survey includes a mix of customers who know the Internet well and those that have less exposure to the Internet. To ensure that AmeriBank obtains the correct mix, he wants to interview at least 15 percent of customers from the Silicon Valley where Internet use is high, at least 35 percent of customers from big cities where Internet use is medium, and at least 20 percent of customers from small towns where Internet use is low.

Sophisticated Surveys is one of three survey companies competing for the project. It has performed an initial analysis of these survey requirements to determine the cost of surveying different populations. The costs per person surveyed are listed in the following table:

| | Age Group | | | |
Region	18 to 25	26 to 40	41 to 50	51 and over
Silicon Valley	$4.75	$6.50	$6.50	$5.00
Big cities	5.25	5.75	6.25	6.25
Small towns	6.50	7.50	7.50	7.25

Sophisticated Surveys explores the following options cumulatively.

a. Formulate a linear programming model to minimize costs while meeting all survey constraints imposed by AmeriBank.

b. If the profit margin for Sophisticated Surveys is 15 percent of cost, what bid will it submit?

c. After submitting its bid, Sophisticated Surveys is informed that it has the lowest cost but that Ameri Bank does not like the solution. Specifically, Rob feels that the selected survey population is not representative enough of the banking customer population. Rob wants at least 50 people of each age group surveyed in each region. What is the new bid made by Sophisticated Surveys?

d. Rob feels that Sophisticated Surveys oversampled the 18-to-25-year-old population and the Silicon Valley population. He imposes a new constraint that no more than 600 individuals can be surveyed from the 18-to-25-year-old population and no more than 650 individuals can be surveyed from the Silicon Valley population. What is the new bid?

e. When Sophisticated Surveys calculated the cost of reaching and surveying particular individuals, the company thought that reaching individuals in young populations would be easiest. In a recently completed survey, however, Sophisticated Surveys learned that this assumption was wrong. The new costs for surveying the 18-to-25-year-old population are listed below:

Region	Cost per Person
Silicon Valley	$6.50
Big cities	6.75
Small towns	7.00

Given the new costs, what is the new bid?

f. To ensure the desired sampling of individuals, Rob imposes even stricter requirements. He fixes the exact percentage of people that should be surveyed from each population. The requirements are listed next.

Population	Percentage of People Surveyed
18 to 25	25%
26 to 40	35
41 to 50	20
51 and over	20
Silicon Valley	20
Big cities	50
Small towns	30

By how much would these new requirements increase the cost of surveying for Sophisticated Surveys? Given the 15 percent profit margin, what would Sophisticated Surveys bid?

Case 4-3

Assigning Students to Schools

The Springfield School Board has made the decision to close one of its middle schools (sixth, seventh, and eighth grades) at the end of this school year and reassign all of next year's middle school students to the three remaining middle schools. The school district provides busing for all middle school students who must travel more than approximately a mile, so the school board wants a plan for reassigning the students that will minimize the total busing cost. The annual cost per student for busing from each of the six residential areas of the city to each of the schools is shown in the following table (along with other basic data for next year), where 0 indicates that busing is not needed and a dash indicates an infeasible assignment.

					Busing Cost per Student		
Area	Number of Students	Percentage in 6th Grade	Percentage in 7th Grade	Percentage in 8th Grade	School 1	School 2	School 3
1	450	32	38	30	$300	$ 0	$700
2	600	37	28	35	—	400	500
3	550	30	32	38	600	300	200
4	350	28	40	32	200	500	—
5	500	39	34	27	0	—	400
6	450	34	28	38	500	300	0
				School capacity:	900	1,100	1,000

The school board also has imposed the restriction that each grade must constitute between 30 and 36 percent of each school's population. The above table shows the percentage of each area's middle school population for next year that falls into each of the three grades. The school attendance zone boundaries can be drawn so as to split any given area among more than one school, but assume that the percentages shown in the table will continue to hold for any partial assignment of an area to a school.

You have been hired as a management science consultant to assist the school board in determining how many students in each area should be assigned to each school.

a. Formulate and solve a linear programming model for this problem.

b. What is your resulting recommendation to the school board?

After seeing your recommendation, the school board expresses concern about all the splitting of residential areas among multiple schools. They indicate that they "would like to keep each neighborhood together."

c. Adjust your recommendation as well as you can to enable each area to be assigned to just one school. (Adding this restriction may force you to fudge on some other constraints.) How much does this increase the total busing cost? (This line of analysis will be pursued more rigorously in Case 9.4.)

The school board is considering eliminating some busing to reduce costs. Option 1 is to only eliminate busing for students traveling 1 to 1.5 miles, where the cost per student is given in the table as $200. Option 2 is to also eliminate busing for students traveling 1.5 to 2 miles, where the estimated cost per student is $300.

d. Revise the model from part *a* to fit Option 1, and solve. Compare these results with those from part *b,* including the reduction in total busing cost.

e. Repeat part *d* for Option 2.

The school board now needs to choose among the three alternative busing plans (the current one or Option 1 or Option 2). One important factor is busing costs. However, the school board also wants to place equal weight on a second factor: the inconvenience and safety problems caused by forcing students to travel by foot or bicycle a substantial distance (more than a mile, and especially more than 1.5 miles). Therefore, they want to choose a plan that provides the best trade-off between these two factors.

f. Use your results from parts *b, d,* and *e* to summarize the key information related to these two factors that the school board needs to make this decision.

g. Which decision do you think should be made? Why?

Note: This case will be continued in later chapters (Cases 5.4 and 9.4), so we suggest that you save your analysis, including your basic spreadsheet model.

Case 4-4

Kuwait's al-Manakh Stock Market

The Kuwait al-Manakh Stock Market crash in 1982 resulted in outstanding debts of some $94 billion and left the country in a state of economic panic. The Kuwaiti judicial system faced the near impossible task of assigning criminal and financial liability among the 6,000 investors caught in a web of 29,000 "bounced" postdated checks and IOUs associated with the bankruptcies and business failures.

Postdated checks and IOUs, written on behalf of speculative Kuwaiti investors and traders, funded the market's boom and led to its dramatic crash. Developing a method to disentangle the web of outstanding debt could save many years, and nearly $10 billion in court and attorney fees. In addition, the disentanglement would "net out" offsetting debts and reduce the magnitude of the total outstanding debt resulting from the crash, thereby reducing the negative impact of the market crash on the economy.

The government of Kuwait recognized that this complex web had to be disentangled quickly, fairly, and in a way most beneficial to the economy. His Excellency Shaikh Ali Al-Khalifa Al-Sabah, Minister of Finance and Oil of Kuwait, turned to the Kuwait Institute for Scientific Research for help.

EVENTS LEADING UP TO THE CREATION OF THE AL-MANAKH STOCK EXCHANGE

The al-Manakh Stock Market was established in 1979 by Kuwaiti trading companies and speculative investors to take the place of the very tightly controlled official stock market of Kuwait (KSE). After the KSE had undergone a major crash in 1977, permanent government controls were put in place to control Kuwait's highly speculative investors, who were motivated by high liquidity coupled with poor returns on Kuwaiti investments abroad as a result of volatile exchange rates. Oil-rich Kuwaitis had few places to invest their money other than in the country's stock market, but as the KSE began to boom, speculative traders entered the market, and the rapid speculative growth eventually caused the KSE to crash. Speculators writing postdated checks for investments that they could not afford meant that the market's boom was supported by funds that did not exist. Once out of control, when one investor defaulted, a chain re-

Source: This is one of the INFORMS Teaching Cases that have been prepared to provide material for class discussion. This particular case was prepared by Sam Ridesec under the supervision of Professor Peter Bell, Richard Ivey School of Business, the University of Western Ontario, Canada. Copyright 1998, by The Institute for Operations Research and the Management Sciences. Reproduced by permission of INFORMS, the copyright owner.

action of bankruptcies was inevitable since investors could not honor their checks and IOUs because their accounts receivable and expected market returns were needed to fund these debts.

After the crash, the complicated puzzle of unpayable debts led to the bottom falling out of the KSE and produced a widespread panic in the Kuwaiti economy. As a result, the government bailed out creditors at a cost of $525 million. Tight government controls, including new laws severely restricting the use of post-dated checks on the KSE, were established following this crash to curb further speculative trading.

EVENTS LEADING UP TO THE AL-MANAKH CRASH

The Kuwaiti government owned nearly half of the country's share-holding companies, and with very few investment opportunities other than oil, wealthy Kuwaitis had few investment alternatives at home. After a third major oil hike in 1979, wealthy Kuwaitis enjoyed a time of prosperity. Public spending and the demand for places to invest money rose. This increase in liquidity combined with few investment alternatives led to another speculative bubble. Since returns on foreign investments were poor, investors looked at the al-Manakh Stock Exchange as a place where they could carry out the speculative trading that had occurred on the KSE prior to the 1977 crash.

The al-Manakh exchange was unregulated, and in the absence of government regulation or supervision, the use of postdated checks soared along with stock prices. Traders created numerous Gulf companies in neighboring Arab states solely for speculative purposes to avoid domestic regulations governing new companies. Investors poured money anywhere they could. At the peak of the stock market's explosion, 3.5 billion shares were traded, or more than four times the 837 million of the KSE. A 100 percent increase in stock value within a few weeks was not surprising to the 6,000 individuals and corporations feverishly trading in the al-Manakh market.

By 1982, the al-Manakh exchange was out of control. Untrained and uncertified brokers were trading worthless securities at astronomical P/E ratios. With a complicated mesh of postdated checks being traded to fund the explosion, traders used crude and often illegal methods of settlement. The inevitable crash left traders in a complicated puzzle of postdated checks and IOUs, making it difficult to determine who was responsible for each trade. Traders faced the disastrous implications of having written postdated checks against funds that they expected to receive in the future, from the sale of stocks at a profit before the postdated checks came due.

THE CRASH

In August 1982, the bubble burst when one of the largest of the 18 major trading companies defaulted on its debts. During the month, traded shares fell from 602 to 72 million as securities traded in the market lost 60 to 98 percent of their value.

The crash was a huge shock to the Kuwaiti economy. Initially, neither the central bank nor the government knew the magnitude of the crash and the resulting outstanding debt. Traders were left with worthless stocks in defunct Gulf companies as well as a web of two-way IOU notes and postdated checks.

First calculations of the resulting outstanding debt after the crash produced a figure of $94 billion, or 4.3 times the Kuwaiti gross domestic product. The majority of this figure was the sum of the face value of nearly 29,000 postdated checks. In addition, 95 percent of the total outstanding debt involved only 18 traders who were caught in a mesh of entangled debt responsibilities.

ATTEMPTS TO RECTIFY THE SITUATION

In late 1982, the government took some steps to attempt to contain the damage. It established a clearinghouse with the purpose of collecting, matching, verifying, and systematizing the financial accounts of individuals and brokers, and set aside a $1.7 billion trust fund to compensate small investors (losses less than $1.7 million). Finally, an arbitration panel was established to effect settlements, and to sanction and finalize settlements reached voluntarily between traders.

Unfortunately, the government's initial strategy of forcing traders to pay their debts as part of the solution did not work. Many traders had become insolvent and few were willing to meet their accounts payable before collecting their receivables, especially when their accounts receivable were needed to pay off their debts. This problem, and the fact that a resolution did not seem to be arising in the near future, led the Kuwaiti government to form the Corporation for the Settlement of Company Forward Share Transactions. This company established a special task force made up of A. A. Eliman (San Francisco State University), M. Girgis (LTC Techno-Economics Research Group, Inc.), and S. Kotob (Kuwait

Institute for Scientific Research). Under the supervision of the Kuwaiti minister of oil and finance, the task force began the high priority task of untangling traders and settling debts.

APPRECIATING THE TRADERS' ENTANGLEMENT

Figure 1 illustrates the example of four entangled traders. Each trader had some assets, (potentially) an uncollected receivable from each other trader, and (potentially) an unpaid payable to each other trader.

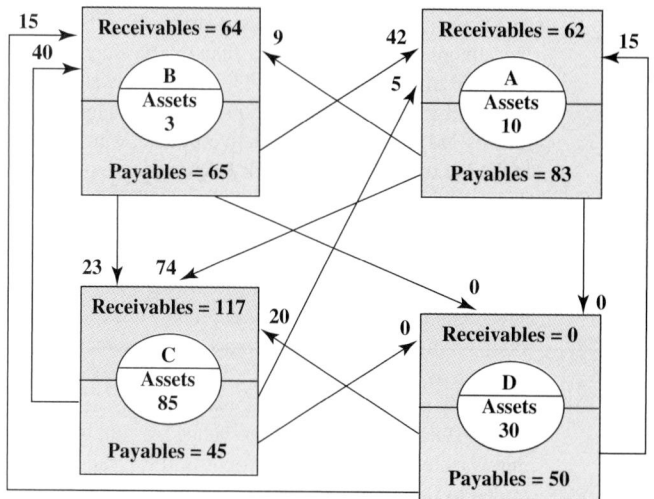

Each trader's assets were further broken down into four asset classes. These were, in order of decreasing risk, cash and KSE shares, real estate, receivables from other entangled traders, and shares of Gulf companies. For the example, consider the four traders' assets to be as follows:

	Trader			
	A	**B**	**C**	**D**
Cash and KSE shares	1	0.6	15	5
Real estate	4	1.2	24	7
Receivables from solvents	3	0.2	27	3
Shares of Gulf companies	2	1	19	15
Total assets	10	3	85	30

In this situation, three of the traders (A, B, and D) could not determine how much of their debt they could pay before knowing what portion of their receivables they would collect from the other entangled traders. Therefore, one can appreciate how the situation could not be resolved without outside intervention to decide who could and should pay what and to whom. In addition, there was the issue of how the different asset types were to be treated and in what proportion they were to be paid.

The task force first defined the debt settlement ratio (DSR):

$$DSR = Minimum \left[\frac{Assets + Actual\ receivables}{Payables}, 1 \right]$$

In order to determine the portion of debt that could be honored by each trader, the task force set out a series of equations to determine each trader's DSR that was dependent on actual receivables: Computing each trader's DSR would essentially require first determining the payments that each trader would make. A further problem with this method was the necessity to restrict the payments from solvent traders to the amount they actually owed. The task force, however, was able to use DSRs as a method of trader classification without knowing what portion of actual receivables would be collected (Figure 2).

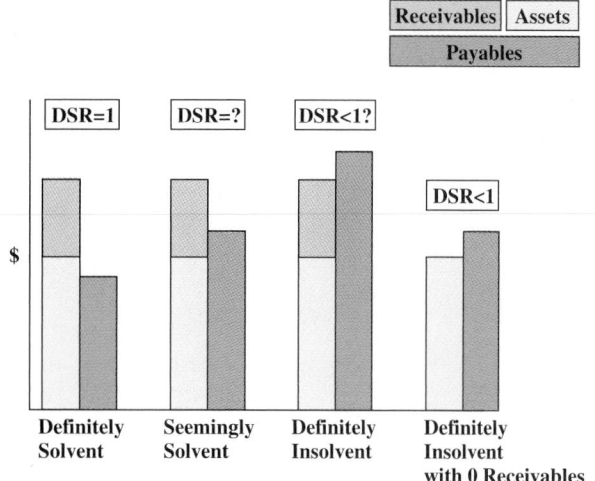

A METHOD FOR DISENTANGLING THE TRADERS

After considering the dilemma faced in determining the traders' DSRs, the task force realized that determining DSRs would actually disentangle the traders, since each intertrader payment would have to be calculated to determine traders' actual receivables. However, the rationale behind these payments needed to be decided. What should these payments accomplish? What possible settlement options were the fairest and/or the most beneficial to the economy?

Possible payment disentanglement rationales considered included attempting to:

- Limit the number of bankruptcies.

- Pay off as many solvent creditors as possible.

- Achieve the largest possible total payments to all creditors.

- Maximize the sum of insolvents' DSRs.

- Minimize insolvents' deficits (assets + receivables − payables).

- Determine DSRs that were least susceptible to further deterioration in asset value.

- Determine DSRs while keeping the DSRs of the largest 18 insolvent traders equal.

The task force also needed to consider the following factors:

- All traders had to be treated equally and in accordance with the strengths and weaknesses of their financial portfolios, al-Manakh stock trading, and their choice of trade cohorts.

- Maximizing the ability for traders to pay their debts in full would minimize the negative effect of the crash on the economy.

- A trader's DSR could not be higher than one, since that would imply that the trader would be paying out more than the amount owed.

- By Kuwaiti law, debts to multiple creditors had to be paid in equal proportion of the amount owed to each creditor.

- All solvent traders should honor their payables in cash (even if this required them to liquidate other assets).

- The disentanglement solution must prevent traders who actually owed money from making net gains.

The task force had many decisions to make to arrive at an equitable solution that would disentangle the web of debts and "net out" the actual loss to the economy. If a credible solution could not be found, each of the 29,000 postdated checks and IOUs would require three court cases to settle: a criminal case, a commercial case, and a bankruptcy case. The outcome of this legal process would send many Kuwaiti entrepreneurs to jail, including many with strong political and social ties; would cost the government some $380 million; and would require the judicial system to increase capacity 18-fold for five years. Most importantly, the Kuwaiti economy's state of panic and recession would not improve until the situation was resolved. Time was of the essence.

a. Address the following issues:

1. Determine a method of allocating payments between traders using the example given in the case, while ignoring the asset breakdown.

2. How should the total payments be allocated among asset classes?

b. Discuss the following questions:

1. What management science tools can be used to help resolve this problem?

2. What is the advantage of a model-based approach over a legal or political procedure?

3. What is the most appropriate and fair rationale (or objective) to guide disentangling payments?

4. What constraints must be taken into account?

5. How should different assets be treated?

Learning objectives

After completing this chapter, you should be able to

1. Explain what is meant by *what-if analysis.*

2. Summarize the benefits of what-if analysis.

3. Enumerate the different kinds of changes in the model that can be considered by what-if analysis.

4. Describe how the spreadsheet formulation of the problem can be used to perform any of these kinds of what-if analysis.

5. Use the Solver Table to systematically investigate the effect of changing either one or two data cells to various other trial values.

6. Find how much any single coefficient in the objective function can change without changing the optimal solution.

7. Evaluate simultaneous changes in objective function coefficients to determine whether the changes are small enough that the original optimal solution must still be optimal.

8. Predict how the value in the target cell would change if a small change were to be made in the right-hand side of one or more of the functional constraints.

9. Find how much the right-hand side of a single functional constraint can change before this prediction becomes no longer valid.

10. Evaluate simultaneous changes in right-hand sides to determine whether the changes are small enough that this prediction must still be valid.

Chapter Five

What-If Analysis for Linear Programming

Chapters 2 and 4 have described and illustrated how to formulate a linear programming model on a spreadsheet to represent a variety of managerial problems, and then how to use the Solver to find an optimal solution for this model. You might think that this would finish our story about linear programming: Once the manager learns the optimal solution, she would immediately implement this solution and then turn her attention to other matters. However, this is not the case. The enlightened manager demands much more from linear programming, and linear programming has much more to offer her—as you will discover in this chapter.

An optimal solution is only optimal with respect to a particular mathematical model that provides only a rough representation of the real problem. A manager is interested in much more than just finding such a solution. The purpose of a linear programming study is to help guide management's final decision by providing insights into the likely consequences of pursuing various managerial options under a variety of assumptions about future conditions. Most of the important insights are gained while conducting analysis *after* finding an optimal solution for the original version of the basic model. This analysis is commonly referred to as **what-if analysis** because it involves addressing some questions about *what* would happen to the optimal solution *if* different assumptions were made about future conditions. Spreadsheets play a central role in addressing these *what-if questions*.

This chapter focuses on the types of information provided by what-if analysis and why it is valuable to managers. The first section provides an overview. Section 5.2 returns to the Wyndor Glass Co. product-mix case study (Section 2.2) to describe the what-if analysis that is needed in this situation. The subsequent sections then flesh out the picture in the context of this case study.

5.1 THE IMPORTANCE OF WHAT-IF ANALYSIS TO MANAGERS

The examples and problems in the preceding chapters on linear programming have provided the data needed to determine precisely all the numbers that should go into the data cells for the spreadsheet formulation of the linear programming model. (Recall that these numbers are referred to as the **parameters of the model.**) Real applications seldom are this straightforward. Substantial time and effort often are needed to track down the needed data. Even then, it may be possible to develop only rough estimates of the parameters of the model.

In real applications, many of the numbers in the model may be only rough estimates.

For example, in the Wyndor case study, two key parameters of the model are the coefficients in the objective function that represent the unit profits of the two new products. These parameters were estimated to be $300 for the doors and $500 for the windows. However, what these unit profits actually will turn out to be depends on many factors—the costs of raw materials, production, shipping, advertising, and so on, as well as such things as the market reception to the new products and the amount of competition encountered. Some of these factors cannot be estimated with real accuracy until long after the linear programming study has been completed and the new products have been on the market for some time.

Therefore, before Wyndor's management makes a decision on the product mix, it will want to know what the effect would be if the unit profits turn out to differ significantly from the estimates. For example, would the optimal solution change if the unit profit for the doors turned out to be $200 instead of the estimate of $300? How inaccurate can the estimate be in either direction before the optimal solution changes?

Such questions are addressed in Section 5.3 when only one estimate is inaccurate. Section 5.4 will address similar questions when multiple estimates are inaccurate.

What happens to the optimal solution if an error is made in estimating a parameter of the model?

If the optimal solution will remain the same over a wide range of values for a particular coefficient in the objective function, then management will be content with a fairly rough estimate for this coefficient. On the other hand, if even a small error in the estimate would change the optimal solution, then management will want to take special care to refine this estimate. Management sometimes will get involved directly in adjusting such estimates to its satisfaction.

Here then is a summary of the first benefit of what-if analysis:

1. Typically, many of the parameters of a linear programming model are only *estimates* of quantities (e.g., unit profits) that cannot be determined precisely at this time. What-if analysis reveals how close each of these estimates needs to be to avoid obtaining an erroneous optimal solution, and therefore pinpoints the **sensitive parameters** (those parameters where extra care is needed to refine their estimates because even small changes in their values can change the optimal solution).

Several sections describe how what-if analysis provides this benefit for the most important parameters. Sections 5.3 and 5.4 do this for the coefficients in the objective function (these numbers appear in the spreadsheet in the row for the unit contribution of each activity toward the overall measure of performance). Sections 5.5 and 5.6 do the same for the *right-hand sides of the functional constraints* (these are the numbers that typically are in the right-hand column of the spreadsheet just to the right of the ≤, ≥, or = signs).

Businesses operate in a dynamic environment. Even when management is satisfied with the current estimates and implements the corresponding optimal solution, conditions may change later. For example, suppose that Wyndor's management is satisfied with $300 as the estimate of the unit profit for the doors, but increased competition later forces a price reduction that reduces this unit profit. Does this change the optimal product mix? The what-if analysis shown in Section 5.3 immediately indicates in advance which new unit profits would leave the optimal product mix unchanged, which can help guide management in its new pricing decision. Furthermore, if the optimal product mix is unchanged, then there is no need to solve the model again with the new coefficient. Avoiding solving the model again is no big deal for the tiny two-variable Wyndor problem, but it is extremely welcome for real applications that may have hundreds or thousands of constraints and variables. In fact, for such large models, it may not even be practical to re-solve the model repeatedly to consider the many possible changes of interest.

What happens to the optimal solution if conditions change in the future?

Thus, here is the second benefit of what-if analysis:

2. If conditions change after the study has been completed (a common occurrence), what-if analysis leaves signposts that indicate (without solving the model again) whether a resulting change in a parameter of the model changes the optimal solution.

Again, several subsequent sections describe how what-if analysis does this.

These sections focus on studying how changes in the parameters of a linear programming model affect the optimal solution. This type of what-if analysis commonly is referred to as **sensitivity analysis,** because it involves checking how *sensitive* the optimal solution is to the value of each parameter. Sensitivity analysis is a vital part of what-if analysis.

However, rather than being content with the passive sensitivity analysis approach of checking the effect of parameter estimates being inaccurate, what-if analysis often goes further to take a proactive approach. An analysis may be made of various possible managerial actions that would result in changes to the model.

A prime example of this proactive approach arises when certain parameters of the model represent *managerial policy decisions* rather than quantities that are largely outside the control of management. For example, for the Wyndor product-mix problem, the right-hand sides of the three functional constraints (4, 12, 18) represent the number of hours of production time in the three respective plants being made available per week for the production of the two new products. Management can change these three resource amounts by altering the production levels for the old products in these plants. Therefore, after learning the optimal solution, management will want to know the impact on the profit from the new products if these resource amounts are changed in certain ways. One key question is how much this profit can be increased by increasing the available production time for the new products in just one of the plants. Another is how much this profit can be increased by simultaneously making helpful changes in the available production times in all the plants. If the profit from the new products can be increased enough to more than compensate for the profit lost by decreasing the production levels for certain old products, management probably will want to make the change.

What happens if managerial policy decisions change?

We now can summarize the third benefit of what-if analysis:

3. When certain parameters of the model represent managerial policy decisions, what-if analysis provides valuable guidance to management regarding the impact of altering these policy decisions.

Sections 5.5 and 5.6 will explore this benefit further.

What-if analysis sometimes goes even further in providing helpful guidance to management, such as when analyzing alternate scenarios for how business conditions might evolve. However, this chapter will focus on the three benefits summarized above.

Review
Questions

1. What are the *parameters* of a linear programming model?
2. How can inaccuracies arise in the parameters of a model?
3. What does what-if analysis reveal about the parameters of a model that are only estimates?
4. Is it always inappropriate to make only a fairly rough estimate for a parameter of a model? Why?
5. How is it possible for the parameters of a model to be accurate initially and then become inaccurate at a later date?
6. How does what-if analysis help management prepare for changing conditions?
7. What is meant by *sensitivity analysis?*
8. For what kinds of managerial policy decisions does what-if analysis provide guidance?

5.2   CONTINUING THE WYNDOR CASE STUDY

We now return to the case study introduced in Section 2.2 involving the Wyndor Glass Co. product-mix problem.

To review briefly, recall that the company is preparing to introduce two exciting new products:

- An 8-foot glass door with aluminum framing.

- A 4-foot $\times$ 6-foot double-hung wood-framed window.

To analyze which mix of the two products would be most profitable, the company's Management Science Group introduced two decision variables:

D = Production rate of this new kind of door

W = Production rate of this new kind of window

where this rate measures the number of units produced per week. Three plants will be involved in the production of these products. Based on managerial decisions regarding how much these plants will continue to be used to produce current products, the number of hours of production time per week being made available in plants 1, 2, and 3 for the new products is 4, 12, and 18, respectively. After obtaining rough estimates that the profit per unit will be $300 for the doors and $500 for the windows, the Management Science Group then formulated the linear programming model shown in Figure 5.1, where the objective is to choose the values of D and W in the changing cells UnitsProduced (C12:D12) so as to maximize the total profit (per week) given in the target cell TotalProfit (G12). Applying the Solver to this model yielded the optimal solution shown on this spreadsheet and summarized as follows.

Optimal Solution

$D = 2$	(Produce 2 doors per week.)
$W = 6$	(Produce 6 windows per week.)
Profit $= 3,600$	(The estimated total weekly profit is \$3,600.)

However, this optimal solution assumes that all the estimates that provide the parameters of the model (as shown in the UnitProfit (C4:D4), HoursUsedPerUnitProduced (C7:D9), and HoursAvailable (G7:G9) data cells) are accurate.

The head of the Management Science Group, Lisa Taylor, now is ready to meet with management to discuss the group's recommendation that the above product mix be used.

FIGURE 5.1

The spreadsheet model and its optimal solution for the original Wyndor problem before beginning what-if analysis.

	A	B	C	D	E	F	G
1		**Wyndor Glass Co. Product-Mix Problem**					
2							
3			Doors	Windows			
4		Unit Profit	$300	$500			
5					Hours		Hours
6			Hours Used per Unit Produced		Used		Available
7		Plant 1	1	0	2	≤	4
8		Plant 2	0	2	12	≤	12
9		Plant 3	3	2	18	≤	18
10							
11			Doors	Windows			Total Profit
12		Units Produced	2	6			$3,600

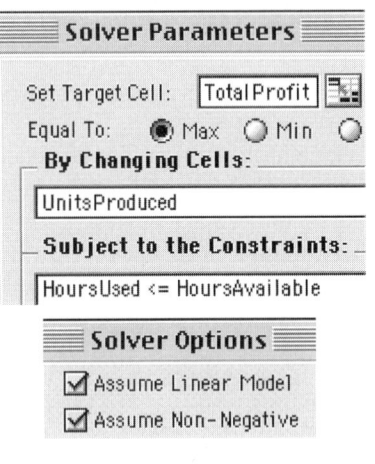

Solver Parameters

Set Target Cell: TotalProfit

Equal To: ⦿ Max ○ Min ○

By Changing Cells:

UnitsProduced

Subject to the Constraints:

HoursUsed <= HoursAvailable

Solver Options

☑ Assume Linear Model

☑ Assume Non-Negative

	E
5	Hours
6	Used
7	=SUMPRODUCT(C7:D7, UnitsProduced)
8	=SUMPRODUCT(C8:D8, UnitsProduced)
9	=SUMPRODUCT(C9:D9, UnitsProduced)

	G
11	Total Profit
12	=SUMPRODUCT(UnitProfit, UnitsProduced)

Range Name	Cells
DoorsProduced	C12
HoursAvailable	G7:G9
HoursUsed	E7:E9
HoursUsedPerUnitProduced	C7:D9
TotalProfit	G12
UnitProfit	C4:D4
UnitsProduced	C12:D12
WindowsProduced	D12

Management's Discussion of the Recommended Product Mix

John Hill (president): Thanks for your preliminary report, Lisa. It appears that your group has done a fine study as usual.

Lisa Taylor (head of Management Science Group):   Thank you. All the members of the group made important contributions. However, we're not done yet. I asked for this meeting so we could explore what questions you and Bill would like us to pursue further. In particular, I am especially concerned that we weren't able to better pin down just what the numbers should be to go into our model. If any of these estimates are very far off, it could change what the product mix should be.

John: That concerns me also. Bill, you've been coordinating with Lisa's group. Which estimates do you think are the shakiest?

Bill Tasto (vice president for manufacturing): Without question, the estimates of the unit profits for the two products. The other numbers are pretty solid. We have a good handle on how many hours of production time will be needed in each plant to produce a unit of either product. Also, we already have made our preliminary decisions on how many hours of production time per week will be made available in each plant for these new products.

John: How were the estimates of the unit profits obtained?

Lisa: We got a tentative pricing decision on the new products from Ann Lester. Then we asked the Accounting Department, with some help from Bill's and Ann's staffs, to analyze the cost data for producing and marketing these products. However, since the products haven't gone into production yet, all they could do is analyze the data from similar current products and then try to project what the changes would be for these new products. They gave us some numbers, but said they were pretty rough. They would need to do a lot more work to pin down the numbers better.

John: We may need to ask them to do that. To determine whether we have to do that, we first have to find out if a correction in the estimate of the unit profit for either product is likely to change what the product mix should be. Do you have a way of checking how far off one of these estimates can be without changing the optimal product mix?

The allowable range for a unit profit indicates how far its estimate can be off without affecting the optimal product mix.

Lisa: Yes, we do. We can quickly find what we call the *allowable range* for each unit profit. As long as the true value of the unit profit is within this allowable range, and the other unit profit is correct, the optimal product mix will not change. If this range is pretty wide, you don't need to worry about refining the estimate of the unit profit. However, if the range is quite narrow, then it is important to pin down the estimate more closely.

John: OK. Clearly we want you to get this allowable range for each unit profit for us. But we also want to know what happens if both estimates are off.

Lisa: Yes, we can provide a way of checking whether the optimal product mix might change for any new combination of unit profits you think might be the true one.

John: Great. That's what we need. There's also one more thing.

Lisa: What's that?

John: Bill gave you the numbers for how many hours of production time we're making available per week in the three plants for these new products. I noticed you used these numbers on your spreadsheet.

Lisa: Yes. They're the right-hand sides of our constraints. Is something wrong with these numbers?

John: No, not at all. I just wanted to let you know that we haven't made a final decision on whether these are the numbers we want to use. We would like your group to provide us with some analysis of what the effect would be if we change any of those numbers. How much more profit could we get from the new products for each additional hour of production time per week we provide in one of the plants? That sort of thing. Then, to decide what to do, we would compare this additional profit with the profit we would lose by cutting back on the production of current products.

Lisa: Yes, we can get that analysis to you right away also.

John: We might also be interested in making simultaneous changes in the available production hours for two or three of the plants.

Lisa: No problem. We'll give you information about that as well.

John: Wonderful. We'll look forward to getting your final report.

Summary of Management's What-If Questions

Here is a summary of John Hill's what-if questions that Lisa and her group will be addressing in the coming sections.

1. What happens if the estimate of the unit profit of one of Wyndor's new products is inaccurate? (Section 5.3)

2. What happens if the estimates of the unit profits of both of Wyndor's new products are inaccurate? (Section 5.4)

3. What happens if a change is made in the number of hours of production time per week being made available to Wyndor's new products in one of the plants? (Section 5.5)

4. What happens if simultaneous changes are made in the number of hours of production time per week being made available to Wyndor's new products in all the plants? (Section 5.6)

Review
Questions

1. Which estimates of the parameters in the linear programming model for the Wyndor problem are most questionable?

2. Which numbers in this model represent tentative managerial decisions that management might want to change after receiving the Management Science Group's analysis?

5.3 THE EFFECT OF CHANGES IN ONE OBJECTIVE FUNCTION COEFFICIENT

Section 5.1 began by discussing the fact that many of the parameters of a linear programming model typically are only *estimates* of quantities that cannot be determined precisely at the time. What-if analysis (or *sensitivity analysis* in particular) reveals how close each of these estimates needs to be to avoid obtaining an erroneous optimal solution.

We focus in this section on how sensitivity analysis does this when the parameters involved are *coefficients in the objective function*. (Recall that each of these coefficients gives the *unit contribution* of one of the activities toward the overall measure of performance.) In the process, we will address the first of the what-if questions posed by Wyndor management in the preceding section.

Question 1: What happens if the estimate of the unit profit of one of Wyndor's new products is inaccurate?

To start this process, first consider the question of what happens if the estimate of $300 for the unit profit for Wyndor's new kind of door is inaccurate. To address this question, let

P_D = Unit profit for the new kind of door

= Cell C4 in the spreadsheet (see Figure 5.1)

Although $P_D = \$300$ in the current version of Wyndor's linear programming model, we now want to explore how much larger or how much smaller P_D can be and still have $(D, W) = (2, 6)$ as the optimal solution. In other words, how much can the estimate of $300 for the unit profit for these doors be off before the model will give an erroneous optimal solution?

Using the Spreadsheet to Do Sensitivity Analysis

Click on the Solve button again and the spreadsheet immediately reveals the effect of changing any values in the data cells.

One of the great strengths of a spreadsheet is the ease with which it can be used interactively to perform various kinds of what-if analysis, including the sensitivity analysis being considered in this section. Once the Solver has been set up to obtain an optimal solution, you can immediately find out what would happen if one of the parameters of the model were to be changed to some other value. All you have to do is make this change on the spreadsheet and then click on the Solve button again.

To illustrate, Figure 5.2 shows what would happen if the unit profit for doors were to be decreased from $P_D = \$300$ to $P_D = \$200$. Comparing with Figure 5.1, there is no change at all in the optimal solution. In fact, the *only* changes in the new spreadsheet are the new value of P_D in cell C4 and a decrease of $200 in the total profit shown in cell G12 (because each of the two doors produced per week provides $100 less profit). Because the optimal solution does not change, we now know that the original estimate of $P_D = \$300$ can be considerably *too high* without invalidating the model's optimal solution.

But what happens if this estimate is *too low* instead? Figure 5.3 shows what would happen if P_D were to be increased to $P_D = \$500$. Again, there is no change in the optimal solution.

Because the original value of $P_D = \$300$ can be changed considerably in either direction without changing the optimal solution, P_D is said to be *not a sensitive parameter*. It is not necessary to pin down this estimate with great accuracy to have confidence that the model is providing the correct optimal solution.

This may be all the information that is needed about P_D. However, if there is a good possibility that the true value of P_D will turn out to be outside this broad range from $200 to $500, further investigation would be desirable. How much higher or lower can P_D be before the optimal solution would change?

Figure 5.4 demonstrates that the optimal solution would indeed change if P_D were increased all the way up to $P_D = \$1,000$. Thus, we now know that this change occurs somewhere between $500 and $1,000 during the process of increasing P_D.

FIGURE 5.2

The revised Wyndor problem where the estimate of the unit profit for doors has been decreased from $P_D = \$300$ to $P_D = \$200$, but no change occurs in the optimal solution.

	A	B	C	D	E	F	G
1		**Wyndor Glass Co. Product-Mix Problem**					
2							
3			Doors	Windows			
4		Unit Profit	$200	$500			
5					Hours		Hours
6			Hours Used per Unit Produced		Used		Available
7		Plant 1	1	0	2	≤	4
8		Plant 2	0	2	12	≤	12
9		Plant 3	3	2	18	≤	18
10							
11			Doors	Windows			Total Profit
12		Units Produced	2	6			$3,400

FIGURE 5.3

The revised Wyndor problem where the estimate of the unit profit for doors has been increased from $P_D = \$300$ to $P_D = \$500$, but no change occurs in the optimal solution.

	A	B	C	D	E	F	G
1		**Wyndor Glass Co. Product-Mix Problem**					
2							
3			Doors	Windows			
4		Unit Profit	$500	$500			
5					Hours		Hours
6			Hours Used per Unit Produced		Used		Available
7		Plant 1	1	0	2	≤	4
8		Plant 2	0	2	12	≤	12
9		Plant 3	3	2	18	≤	18
10							
11			Doors	Windows			Total Profit
12		Units Produced	2	6			$4,000

FIGURE 5.4

The revised Wyndor problem where the estimate of the unit profit for doors has been increased from $P_D = \$300$ to $P_D = \$1,000$, which results in a change in the optimal solution.

	A	B	C	D	E	F	G
1		**Wyndor Glass Co. Product-Mix Problem**					
2							
3			Doors	Windows			
4		Unit Profit	$1,000	$500			
5					Hours		Hours
6			Hours Used per Unit Produced		Used		Available
7		Plant 1	1	0	4	≤	4
8		Plant 2	0	2	6	≤	12
9		Plant 3	3	2	18	≤	18
10							
11			Doors	Windows			Total Profit
12		Units Produced	4	3			$5,500

Using the Solver Table to Do Sensitivity Analysis Systematically

To pin down just when the optimal solution will change, we could continue selecting new values of P_D at random. However, a better approach is to systematically consider a range of values of P_D. An Excel add-in developed by the authors, called the *Solver Table,* is designed to perform just this sort of analysis. It is available to you in your MS Courseware.

The Solver Table is used to show the results in the changing cells and/or certain output cells for various trial values in a data cell. For each trial value in the data cell, Solver is called on to re-solve the problem.

To use the Solver Table, first expand the original spreadsheet (Figure 5.1) to make a table with headings as shown in Figure 5.5. In the first column of the table (cells B19:B28), list the trial values for the data cell (the unit profit for doors), except leave the first row (cell B18) blank. The headings of the next columns specify which output will be evaluated. For each of these columns, use the first row of the table (cells C18:E18) to write an equation that refers to the relevant changing cell or output cell. In this case, the cells of interest are DoorsProduced (C12), WindowsProduced (D12), and TotalProfit (G12), so the equations for C18:E18 are those shown in Figure 5.5.

Next, select the entire table by clicking and dragging from cells B18 through E28, and then choose the Solver Table from the Tools menu. In the Solver Table dialogue box (as shown at the bottom of Figure 5.5), indicate the column input cell (C4), which refers to the data cell that is being changed in the first column of the table. Nothing is entered for the row input cell because no row is being used to list the trial values of a data cell in this case.

The Solver Table re-solves the problem for a whole range of values of a data cell.

Excel Tip: When filling in the first column of a Solver Table with the trial values for the data cell of interest, skip the first row to leave room in the other columns for the equations referring to the changing cells and/or output cells of interest.

FIGURE 5.5

Expansion of the spreadsheet in Figure 5.1 to prepare for using the Solver Table to show the effect of systematically varying the estimate of the unit profit for doors in the Wyndor problem.

	A	B	C	D	E	F	G
1		**Wyndor Glass Co. Product-Mix Problem**					
2							
3			Doors	Windows			
4		Unit Profit	$300	$500			
5					Hours		Hours
6			Hours Used per Unit Produced		Used		Available
7		Plant 1	1	0	2	≤	4
8		Plant 2	0	2	12	≤	12
9		Plant 3	3	2	18	≤	18
10							
11			Doors	Windows			Total Profit
12		Units Produced	2	6			$3,600
13							
14							Select
15							these cells
16		Unit Profit	Optimal Units Produced		Total		(B18:E28)
17		for Doors	Doors	Windows	Profit		before
18			2	6	$3,600		choosing
19		$100					the Solver
20		$200					Table.
21		$300					
22		$400					
23		$500					
24		$600					
25		$700					
26		$800					
27		$900					
28		$1,000					

	C	D	E
16	Optimal Units Produced		Total
17	Doors	Windows	Profit
18	=DoorsProduced	=WindowsProduced	=TotalProfit

Range Name	Cells
DoorsProduced	C12
TotalProfit	G12
WindowsProduced	D12

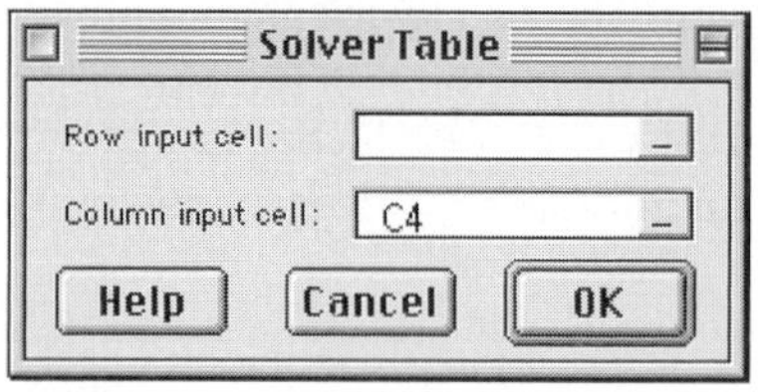

Solver Table

Row input cell:

Column input cell: C4

Help   Cancel   OK

Excel Tip: The Solver Table add-in can be installed either by simply opening the Solver Table file in MS Courseware or by using the installer included in MS Courseware.

The Solver Table shown in Figure 5.6 is then generated automatically by clicking on the OK button. For each trial value listed in the first column of the table for the data cell of interest, Excel re-solves the problem using Solver and then fills in the corresponding values in the other columns of the table. (The numbers in the first row of the table come from the original solution in the spreadsheet before changing the original value in the data cell.)

The table reveals that the optimal solution remains the same all the way from $P_D = \$100$ (and perhaps lower) to $P_D = \$700$, but that a change occurs somewhere between $700 and $800. We next could systematically consider values of P_D between $700 and $800 to determine more

FIGURE 5.6

An application of the Solver Table that shows the effect of systematically varying the estimate of the unit profit for doors in the Wyndor problem.

	B	C	D	E
16	Unit Profit	Optimal Units Produced		Total
17	for Doors	Doors	Windows	Profit
18		2	6	$3,600
19	$100	2	6	$3,200
20	$200	2	6	$3,400
21	$300	2	6	$3,600
22	$400	2	6	$3,800
23	$500	2	6	$4,000
24	$600	2	6	$4,200
25	$700	2	6	$4,400
26	$800	4	3	$4,700
27	$900	4	3	$5,100
28	$1,000	4	3	$5,500

FIGURE 5.7

Part of the sensitivity report generated by the Excel Solver for the original Wyndor problem (Figure 5.1), where the last three columns enable identifying the allowable ranges for the unit profits for doors and windows.

The allowable range for a coefficient in the objective function is the range of values for this coefficient over which the optimal solution for the original model remains optimal.

The sensitivity report generated by the Excel Solver reveals the allowable range for each coefficient in the objective function.

Adjustable Cells

Cell	Name	Final Value	Reduced Cost	Objective Coefficient	Allowable Increase	Allowable Decrease
$C$12	DoorsProduced	2	0	300	450	300
$D$12	WindowsProduced	6	0	500	1E+30	300

closely where the optimal solution changes. However, here is a shortcut. The range of values of P_D over which $(D, W) = (2, 6)$ remains as the optimal solution is referred to as the **allowable range for an objective function coefficient**, or just the **allowable range** for short. Upon request, the Excel Solver will provide a report called the *sensitivity report* that, after a couple of simple calculations, reveals exactly what this allowable range is.

Using the Sensitivity Report to Find the Allowable Range

As was shown in Figure 2.19, when the Solver gives the message that it has found a solution, it also gives on the right a list of three reports that can be provided. By selecting the second one (labeled Sensitivity), you will obtain the sensitivity report.

Figure 5.7 shows the relevant part of this report for the Wyndor problem. The Final Value column indicates the optimal solution. The next column gives the *reduced costs*. (We will not discuss these reduced costs because the information they provide can also be obtained more directly from the allowable ranges.) The next three columns provide the information needed to identify the *allowable range* for each coefficient in the objective function. The Objective Coefficient column gives the current value of each coefficient, and then the next two columns give the *allowable increase* and the *allowable decrease* from this value to remain within the allowable range.

For example, consider P_D, the coefficient of D in the objective function. Since D is the production rate for these special doors, the Doors row in the table provides the following information (without the dollar sign) about P_D:

Current value of P_D: 300

Allowable increase in P_D: 450   So $P_D \leq 300 + 450 = 750$

Allowable decrease in P_D: 300   So $P_D \geq 300 - 300 = 0$

Allowable range for P_D: $0 \leq P_D \leq 750$

Therefore, if P_D is changed from its current value (without making any other change in the model), the current solution $(D, W) = (2, 6)$ will remain optimal so long as the new value of P_D is within this allowable range.

FIGURE 5.8

The two dashed lines that pass through solid constraint boundary lines are the objective function lines when P_D (the unit profit for doors) is at an endpoint of its allowable range, $0 \le P_D \le 750$, since either line or any objective function line in between still yields $(D, W) = (2, 6)$ as an optimal solution for the Wyndor problem.

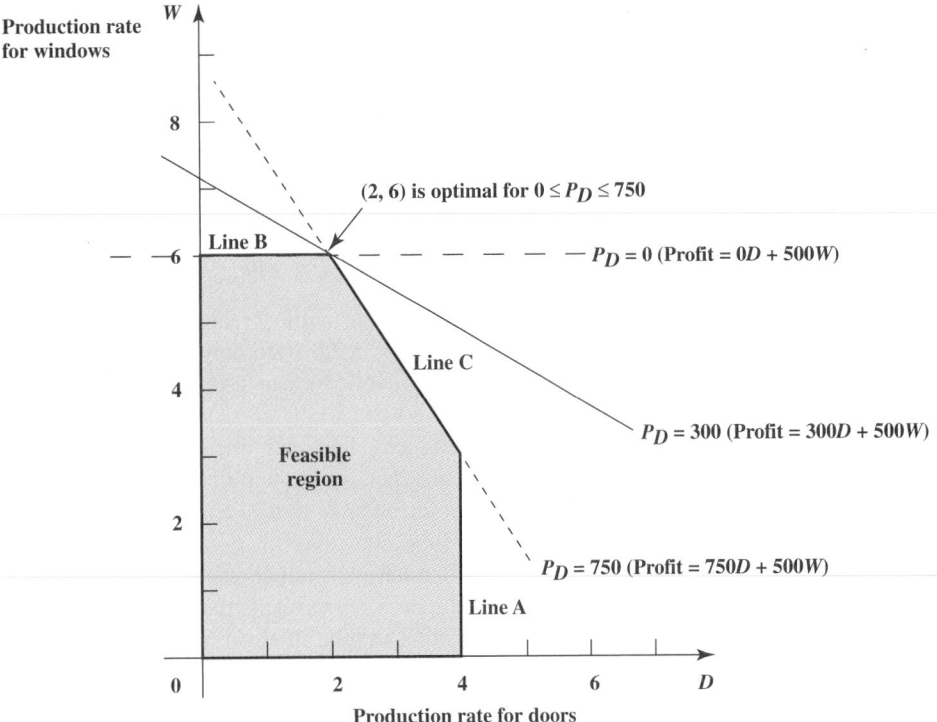

Figure 5.8 provides graphical insight into this allowable range. For the original value of $P_D = 300$, the solid line in the figure shows the slope of the objective function line passing through $(2, 6)$. At the lower end of the allowable range, when $P_D = 0$, the objective function line that passes through $(2, 6)$ now is line B in the figure, so every point on the line segment between $(0, 6)$ and $(2, 6)$ is an optimal solution. For any value of $P_D < 0$, the objective function line will have rotated even further so that $(0, 6)$ becomes the only optimal solution. At the upper end of the allowable range, when $P_D = 750$, the objective function line that passes through $(2, 6)$ becomes line C, so every point on the line segment between $(2, 6)$ and $(4, 3)$ becomes an optimal solution. For any value of $P_D > 750$, the objective function line is even steeper than line C, so $(4, 3)$ becomes the only optimal solution.

Check out this module in the Interactive Management Science Modules to gain graphical insight into the allowable range.

The module called *Graphical Linear Programming and Sensitivity Analysis* in the Interactive Management Science Modules (available at **www.mhhe.com/hillier2e/** or in your CD-ROM) is designed to help you perform this kind of graphical analysis. After you enter the model for the original Wyndor problem, the module provides you with the graph shown in Figure 5.8 (without the dashed lines). You then can simply drag one end of the objective function line up or down to see how far you can increase or decrease P_D before $(D, W) = (2, 6)$ will no longer be optimal.

Conclusion: The allowable range for P_D is $0 \le P_D \le 750$, because $(D, W) = (2, 6)$ remains optimal over this range but not beyond. (When $P_D = 0$ or $P_D = 750$, there are multiple optimal solutions, but $(D, W) = (2, 6)$ still is one of them.) With the range this wide around the original estimate of \$300 ($P_D = 300$) for the unit profit for doors, we can be quite confident of obtaining the correct optimal solution for the true unit profit even though the discussion in Section 5.2 indicates that this estimate is fairly rough.

The sensitivity report also can be used to find the allowable range for the unit profit for Wyndor's other new product. In particular, let

P_W = Unit profit for Wyndor's new kind of window

= Cell D4 in the spreadsheet

Referring to the Windows row of the sensitivity report (Figure 5.7), this row indicates that the allowable decrease in P_W is 300 (so $P_W \ge 500 - 300 = 200$) and the allowable increase is

1E + 30. What is meant by 1E+30? This is shorthand in Excel for 10^{30} (1 with 30 zeroes after it). This tremendously huge number is used by Excel to represent *infinity*. Therefore, the allowable range of P_W is obtained from the sensitivity report as follows:

Current value of P_W:	500	
Allowable increase in P_W:	Unlimited	So P_W has no upper limit
Allowable decrease in P_W:	300	So $P_W \geq 500 - 300 = 200$
Allowable range:	$P_W \geq 200$	

The allowable range is quite wide for both objective function coefficients. Thus, even though $P_D = \$300$ and $P_W = \$500$ were only rough estimates of the true unit profit for the doors and windows, respectively, we can still be confident that we have obtained the correct optimal solution.

We are not always so lucky. For some linear programming problems, even a small change in the value of certain coefficients in the objective function can change the optimal solution. Such coefficients are referred to as *sensitive parameters*. The sensitivity report will immediately indicate which of the objective function coefficients (if any) are sensitive parameters. These are parameters that have a small allowable increase and/or a small allowable decrease. Hence, extra care should be taken to refine these estimates.

Once this has been done and the final version of the model has been solved, the allowable ranges continue to serve an important purpose. As indicated in Section 5.1, the second benefit of what-if analysis is that if conditions change after the study has been completed (a common occurrence), what-if analysis leaves signposts that indicate (without solving the model again) whether a resulting change in a parameter of the model changes the optimal solution. Thus, if weeks, months, or even years later, the unit profit for one of Wyndor's new products changes substantially, its allowable range indicates immediately whether the old optimal product mix still is the appropriate one to use. Being able to draw an affirmative conclusion without reconstructing and solving the revised model is extremely helpful for any linear programming problem, but especially so when the model is a large one.

> A parameter is considered sensitive if even a small change in its value can change the optimal solution.

Review Questions

1. What is meant by the *allowable range* for a coefficient in the objective function?

2. What is the significance if the true value for a coefficient in the objective function turns out to be so different from its estimate that it lies outside its allowable range?

3. In Excel's sensitivity report, what is the interpretation of the Objective Coefficient column? The Allowable Increase column? The Allowable Decrease column?

5.4 THE EFFECT OF SIMULTANEOUS CHANGES IN OBJECTIVE FUNCTION COEFFICIENTS

The coefficients in the objective function typically represent quantities (e.g., unit profits) that can only be estimated because of considerable uncertainty about what their true values will turn out to be. The allowable ranges described in the preceding section deal with this uncertainty by focusing on just one coefficient at a time. In effect, the allowable range for a particular coefficient assumes that the original estimates for all the other coefficients are completely accurate so that this coefficient is the only one whose true value may differ from its original estimate.

In actuality, the estimates for *all* the coefficients (or at least more than one of them) may be inaccurate simultaneously. The crucial question is whether this is likely to result in obtaining the wrong optimal solution. If so, greater care should be taken to refine these estimates as much as possible, at least for the more crucial coefficients. On the other hand, if what-if analysis reveals that the anticipated errors in estimating the coefficients are unlikely to affect the optimal solution, then management can be reassured that the current linear programming model and its results are providing appropriate guidance.

This section focuses on how to determine, without solving the problem again, whether the optimal solution might change if certain changes occur simultaneously in the coefficients of the objective function (due to their true values differing from their estimates). In the process, we will address the second of Wyndor management's what-if questions.

Question 2: What happens if the estimates of the unit profits of both of Wyndor's new products are inaccurate?

Using the Spreadsheet for This Analysis

Once again, the quickest and easiest way to address this kind of question is to simply try out different estimates on the spreadsheet formulation of the model and see what happens each time when clicking on the Solve button.

In this case, the optimal product mix indicated by the model is heavily weighted toward producing the windows (6 per week) rather than the doors (only 2 per week). Since there is equal enthusiasm for both new products, management is concerned about this imbalance. Therefore, Ann Lester (vice president for marketing) has raised a what-if question. What would happen if the estimate of the unit profit for the doors ($300) were too low and the corresponding estimate for the windows ($500) were too high? The estimates could easily be off in these directions (as could be checked with considerable additional investigation). If this were the case, would this lead to a more balanced product mix being the most profitable one?

This question can be answered in a matter of seconds simply by substituting new estimates of the unit profits in the original spreadsheet in Figure 5.1 and clicking on the Solve button. Figure 5.9 shows that new estimates of $450 for doors and $400 for windows causes no change at all in the solution for the optimal product mix. (The total profit does change, but this occurs only because of the changes in the unit profits.) Would even larger changes in the estimates of unit profits finally lead to a change in the optimal product mix? Figure 5.10 shows that this does happen, yielding a relatively balanced product mix of $(D, W) = (4, 3)$, when estimates of $600 for doors and $300 for windows are used.

Using Two-Dimensional Solver Tables for This Analysis

Unlike a *one-way* Solver Table (as in Figure 5.6) which shows results for trial values in a *single* data cell, a *two-way* Solver Table shows results for trial values in *two* data cells.

A *two-way* Solver Table provides a way of systematically investigating the effect if the estimates of both unit profits are inaccurate. This kind of Solver Table shows the results in a single output cell for various trial values in two data cells. Therefore, it can be used to show how TotalProfit (G12) in Figure 5.1 varies over a range of trial values in the two data cells, UnitProfit (C4:D4). For each pair of trial values in these data cells, Solver is called on to re-solve the problem.

FIGURE 5.9
The revised Wyndor problem where the estimates of the unit profits for doors and windows have been changed to $P_D = \$450$ and $P_W = \$400$, respectively, but no change occurs in the optimal solution.

	A	B	C	D	E	F	G
1		**Wyndor Glass Co. Product-Mix Problem**					
2							
3			Doors	Windows			
4		Unit Profit	$450	$400			
5					Hours		Hours
6			Hours Used per Unit Produced		Used		Available
7		Plant 1	1	0	2	≤	4
8		Plant 2	0	2	12	≤	12
9		Plant 3	3	2	18	≤	18
10							
11			Doors	Windows			Total Profit
12		Units Produced	2	6			$3,300

To create a two-way Solver Table for the Wyndor problem, expand the original spreadsheet (Figure 5.1) to make a table with column and row headings as shown in rows 16–21 of the spreadsheet in Figure 5.11. In the upper left-hand corner of the table (C17), write an equation that refers to the target cell (=TotalProfit). In the first column of the table (column C, below the equation in cell C17), insert various trial values for the first data cell of interest (the unit

FIGURE 5.10

The revised Wyndor problem where the estimates of the unit profits for doors and windows have been changed to $600 and $300, respectively, which results in a change in the optimal solution.

	A	B	C	D	E	F	G
1		**Wyndor Glass Co. Product-Mix Problem**					
2							
3			Doors	Windows			
4		Unit Profit	$600	$300			
5					Hours		Hours
6			Hours Used per Unit Produced		Used		Available
7		Plant 1	1	0	4	≤	4
8		Plant 2	0	2	6	≤	12
9		Plant 3	3	2	18	≤	18
10							
11			Doors	Windows			Total Profit
12		Units Produced	4	3			$3,300

FIGURE 5.11

Expansion of the spreadsheet in Figure 5.1 to prepare for using a two-dimensional Solver Table to show the effect on total profit of systematically varying the estimates of the unit profits of doors and windows for the Wyndor problem.

	A	B	C	D	E	F	G	H	I
1		**Wyndor Glass Co. Product-Mix Problem**							
2									
3			Doors	Windows					
4		Unit Profit	$300	$500					
5					Hours		Hours		
6			Hours Used per Unit		Used		Available		
7		Plant 1	1	0	2	≤	4		
8		Plant 2	0	2	12	≤	12		
9		Plant 3	3	2	18	≤	18		Select
10									these cells (C17:H21)
11			Doors	Windows			Total Profit		before
12		Units Produced	2	6			$3,600		choosing
13									the Solver
14									Table.
15									
16		**Total Profit**		Unit Profit for Windows					
17			$3,600	$100	$200	$300	$400	$500	
18			$300						
19		Unit Profit	$400						
20		for Doors	$500						
21			$600						

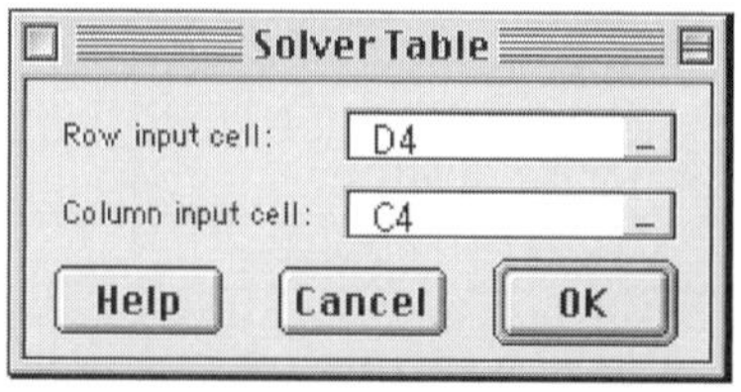

		C
17		= TotalProfit

Range Name	Cell
TotalProfit	G12

Solver Table

Row input cell: D4

Column input cell: C4

[Help] [Cancel] [OK]

profit for doors). In the first row of the table (row 17, to the right of the equation in cell C17), insert various trial values for the second data cell of interest (the unit profit for windows).

Next, select the entire table (C17:H21) and choose Solver Table from the Tools menu (after having installed this Excel add-in provided in your MS Courseware). In the Solver Table dialogue box (shown at the bottom of Figure 5.11), indicate which data cells are being changed simultaneously. The column input cell C4 refers to the data cell whose various trial values are listed in the first column of the table (C18:C21), while the row input cell refers to the data cell whose various trial values are listed in the first row of the table (D17:H17).

The Solver Table shown in Figure 5.12 is then generated automatically by clicking on the OK button. For each pair of trial values for the two data cells, Excel re-solves the problem using Solver and then fills in the total profit in the corresponding spot in the table. (The number in C17 comes from the target cell in the original spreadsheet before the original values in the two data cells have been changed.)

Although a two-way Solver Table is limited to showing results in a single cell of the table for each combination of trial values in two data cells, the & symbol can be used to show results from multiple cells of the original spreadsheet in this single cell.

Unlike a one-way Solver Table that can show the results of *multiple* changing cells and/or output cells for various trial values of a single data cell, a two-way Solver Table is limited to showing the results in a *single* cell for each pair of trial values in the two data cells of interest. However, there is a trick using the & symbol that enables the Solver Table to show the results from multiple changing cells and/or output cells within a single cell of the table. We utilize this trick in the Solver Table shown in Figure 5.13 to show the results for *both* changing cells DoorsProduced (C12) and WindowsProduced (D12) for each pair of trial values for UnitProfit (C4:D4). The key formula is in cell C25:

$$C25 = \text{"(" \& DoorsProduced \& ", " \& WindowsProduced \& ")"}$$

FIGURE 5.12

A two-dimensional application of the Solver Table that shows the effect on total profit of systematically varying the estimates of the unit profits of doors and windows for the Wyndor problem.

	B	C	D	E	F	G	H
16	**Total Profit**		Unit Profit for Windows				
17		$3,600	$100	$200	$300	$400	$500
18		$300	$1,500	$1,800	$2,400	$3,000	$3,600
19	Unit Profit	$400	$1,900	$2,200	$2,600	$3,200	$3,800
20	for Doors	$500	$2,300	$2,600	$2,900	$3,400	$4,000
21		$600	$2,700	$3,000	$3,300	$3,600	$4,200

FIGURE 5.13

A two-dimensional application of the Solver Table that shows the effect on the optimal solution of systematically varying the estimates of the unit profits of doors and windows for the Wyndor problem.

	B	C	D	E	F	G	H
24	**Units Produced (Doors, Windows)**		Unit Profit for Windows				
25		(2,6)	$100	$200	$300	$400	$500
26		$300	(4,3)	(4,3)	(2,6)	(2,6)	(2,6)
27	Unit Profit	$400	(4,3)	(4,3)	(2,6)	(2,6)	(2,6)
28	for Doors	$500	(4,3)	(4,3)	(4,3)	(2,6)	(2,6)
29		$600	(4,3)	(4,3)	(4,3)	(4,3)	(2,6)

	C
25	= "(" & DoorsProduced & "," & WindowsProduced & ")"

Range Name	Cell
DoorsProduced	C12
WindowsProduced	D12

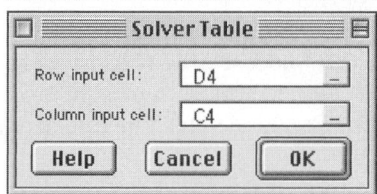

Solver Table
Row input cell: D4
Column input cell: C4
Help   Cancel   OK

Solver Table Selection: C25:H29

Excel Tip: Any text that you would like a formula to display (such as the parentheses and commas in the formula in C25 of Figure 5.13) must be enclosed within quotation marks.

The & character tells Excel to concatenate, so the result will be a left parenthesis, followed by the value in DoorsProduced (C12), then a comma and the contents in WindowsProduced (D12), and finally a right parenthesis. If DoorsProduced=2 and WindowsProduced=6, the result is (2, 6). Thus, the results from *both* changing cells are displayed within a *single* cell of the table.

After the usual preliminaries in entering the information shown in rows 24–25 and columns B–C of Figure 5.13, along with the formula in C25, clicking on the OK button automatically generates the entire Solver Table. Cells D26:H29 show the optimal solution for the various combinations of trial values for the unit profits of the doors and windows. The upper right-hand corner (cell H26) of this Solver Table gives the optimal solution of $(D, W) =$ (2, 6) when using the original unit-profit estimates of $300 for doors and $500 for windows. Moving down from this cell corresponds to increasing this estimate for doors, while moving to the left amounts to decreasing the estimate for windows. (The cells when moving up or to the right of H18 are not shown because these changes would only increase the attractiveness of $(D, W) =$ (2, 6) as the optimal solution.) Note that $(D, W) =$ (2, 6) continues to be the optimal solution for all the cells near H18. This indicates that the original estimates of unit profit would need to be very inaccurate indeed before the optimal product mix would change. Although the estimates are fairly rough, management is confident that they are not that inaccurate. Therefore, there is no need to expend the considerable effort that would be needed to refine the estimates.

What-if analysis shows that there is no need to refine Wyndor's estimates of the unit profits for doors and windows.

At this point, it continues to appear that $(D, W) =$ (2, 6) is the best product mix for initiating the production of the two new products (although additional what-if questions remain to be addressed in subsequent sections). However, we also now know from Figure 5.13 that as conditions change in the future, if the unit profits for both products change enough, it may be advisable to change the product mix later. We still need to leave clear signposts behind to signal when a future change in the product mix should be considered, as described next.

Gleaning Additional Information from the Sensitivity Report

The preceding section described how the data in the sensitivity report enable finding the allowable range for an individual coefficient in the objective function when that coefficient is the only one that changes from its original value. These same data (the allowable increase and allowable decrease in each coefficient) also can be used to analyze the effect of *simultaneous* changes in these coefficients. Here is how.

A sum ≤ 100 percent guarantees that the original optimal solution is still optimal.

The 100 Percent Rule for Simultaneous Changes in Objective Function Coefficients: If simultaneous changes are made in the coefficients of the objective function, calculate for each change the percentage of the allowable change (increase or decrease) for that coefficient to remain within its allowable range. If the *sum* of the percentage changes does *not* exceed 100 percent, the original optimal solution definitely will still be optimal. (If the sum *does* exceed 100 percent, then we cannot be sure.)

This rule does not spell out what happens if the sum of the percentage changes *does* exceed 100 percent. The consequence depends on the directions of the changes in the coefficients. Exceeding 100 percent may or may not change the optimal solution, but so long as 100 percent is not exceeded, the original optimal solution *definitely will* still be optimal.

Keep in mind that we can safely use the entire allowable increase or decrease in a single objective function coefficient only if none of the other coefficients have changed at all. With simultaneous changes in the coefficients, we focus on the *percentage* of the allowable increase or decrease that is being used for each coefficient.

To illustrate, consider the Wyndor problem again, along with the information provided by the sensitivity report in Figure 5.7. Suppose conditions have changed after the initial study, and the unit profit for doors (P_D) has increased from $300 to $450 while the unit profit for windows (P_W) has decreased from $500 to $400. The calculations for the 100 percent rule then are

P_D: \$300 → \$450

$$\text{Percentage of allowable increase} = 100\left(\frac{450 - 300}{450}\right)\% = 33\tfrac{1}{3}\%$$

P_W: \$500 → \$400

$$\text{Percentage of allowable decrease} = 100\left(\frac{500 - 400}{300}\right)\% = 33\tfrac{1}{3}\%$$

$$\text{Sum} = \overline{66\tfrac{2}{3}\%}$$

Since the sum of the percentages does not exceed 100 percent, the original optimal solution $(D, W) = (2, 6)$ definitely is still optimal, just as we found earlier in Figure 5.9.

Now suppose conditions have changed even further, so P_D has increased from \$300 to \$600 while P_W has decreased from \$500 to \$300. The calculations for the 100 percent rule now are

P_D: \$300 → \$600

$$\text{Percentage of allowable increase} = 100\left(\frac{600 - 300}{450}\right)\% = 66\tfrac{2}{3}\%$$

P_W: \$500 → \$300

$$\text{Percentage of allowable decrease} = 100\left(\frac{500 - 300}{300}\right)\% = 66\tfrac{2}{3}\%$$

$$\text{Sum} = \overline{133\tfrac{1}{3}\%}$$

Since the sum of the percentages now exceeds 100 percent, the 100 percent rule says that we can no longer guarantee that $(D, W) = (2, 6)$ is still optimal. In fact, we found earlier in both Figures 5.10 and 5.13 that the optimal solution has changed to $(D, W) = (4, 3)$.

These results suggest how to find just where the optimal solution changes while P_D is being increased and P_W is being decreased in this way. Since 100 percent is midway between 66⅔ percent and 133⅓ percent, the sum of the percentage changes will equal 100 percent when the values of P_D and P_W are midway between their values in the above cases. In particular, $P_D = $ \$525 is midway between \$450 and \$600 and $P_W = $ \$350 is midway between \$400 and \$300. The corresponding calculations for the 100 percent rule are

P_D: \$300 → \$525

$$\text{Percentage of allowable increase} = 100\left(\frac{525 - 300}{450}\right)\% = 50\%$$

P_W: \$500 → \$350

$$\text{Percentage of allowable decrease} = 100\left(\frac{500 - 350}{300}\right)\% = 50\%$$

$$\text{Sum} = \overline{100\%}$$

Although the sum of the percentages equals 100 percent, the fact that it does not *exceed* 100 percent guarantees that $(D, W) = (2, 6)$ is still optimal. Figure 5.14 shows graphically that *both* (2, 6) and (4, 3) are now optimal, as well as all the points on the line segment connecting these two points. However, if P_D and P_W were to be changed any further from their original values (so that the sum of the percentages exceeds 100 percent), the objective function line would be rotated so far toward the vertical that $(D, W) = (4, 3)$ would become the only optimal solution.

Here is an example where the original optimal solution is still optimal even though the sum exceeds 100 percent.

At the same time, keep in mind that having the sum of the percentages of allowable changes exceed 100 percent does not automatically mean that the optimal solution will change. For example, suppose that the estimates of both unit profits are halved. The resulting calculations for the 100 percent rule are

FIGURE 5.14

When the estimates of the unit profits for doors and windows change to $P_D =$ \$525 and $P_W =$ \$350, which lies at the edge of what is allowed by the 100 percent rule, the graphical method shows that $(D, W) = (2, 6)$ still is an optimal solution, but now every other point on the line segment between this solution and $(4, 3)$ also is optimal.

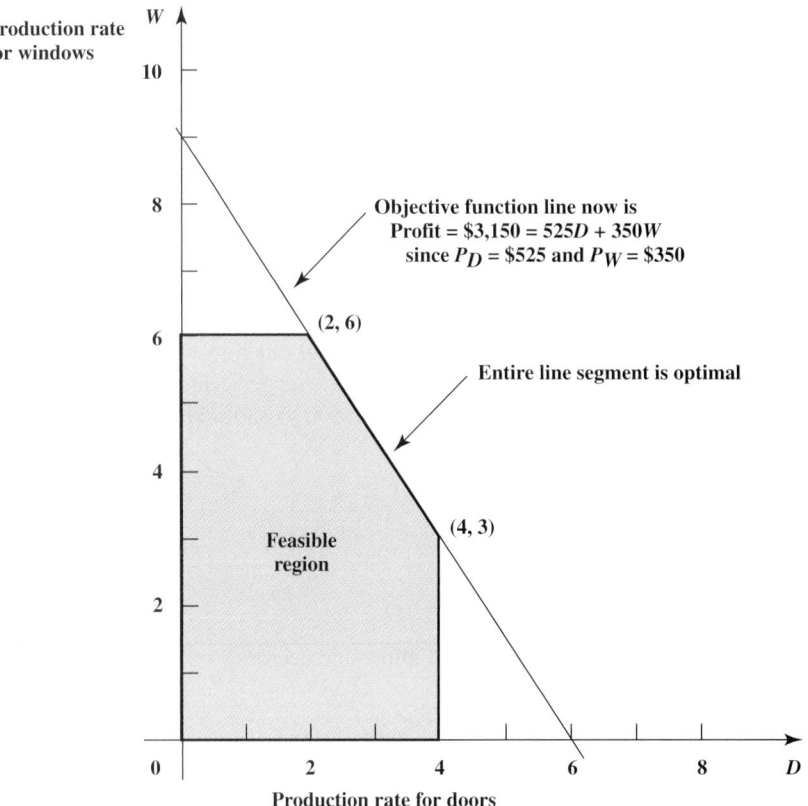

P_D: \$300 → \$150

$$\text{Percentage of allowable decrease} = 100\left(\frac{300 - 150}{300}\right)\% = 50\%$$

P_W: \$500 → \$250

$$\text{Percentage of allowable decrease} = 100\left(\frac{500 - 250}{300}\right)\% = 83\%$$

$$\text{Sum} = \overline{133\%}$$

Even though this sum exceeds 100 percent, Figure 5.15 shows that the original optimal solution is still optimal. In fact, the objective function line has the same slope as the original objective function line (the solid line in Figure 5.8). This happens whenever *proportional changes* are made to all the unit profits, which will automatically lead to the same optimal solution.

Comparisons

You now have seen three approaches to investigating what happens if simultaneous changes occur in the coefficients of the objective function: (1) try out changes directly on a spreadsheet, (2) use a two-way Solver Table, and (3) apply the 100 percent rule.

The spreadsheet approach is a good place to start, especially for less experienced modelers, because it is simple and quick. If you are only interested in checking one specific set of changes in the coefficients, you can immediately see what happens after making the changes in the spreadsheet.

More often, there will be numerous possibilities for what the true values of the coefficients will turn out to be, because of uncertainty in the original estimates of these coefficients. The Solver Table is useful for systematically checking a variety of possible changes in one or two objective function coefficients. Trying out representative possibilities on the spreadsheet may provide all the insight that is needed. Perhaps the optimal solution for the original model will

FIGURE 5.15

When the estimates of the unit profits for doors and windows change to $P_D =$ $150 and $P_W =$ $250 (half their original values), the graphical method shows that the optimal solution still is $(D, W) = (2, 6)$, even though the 100 percent rule says that the optimal solution might change.

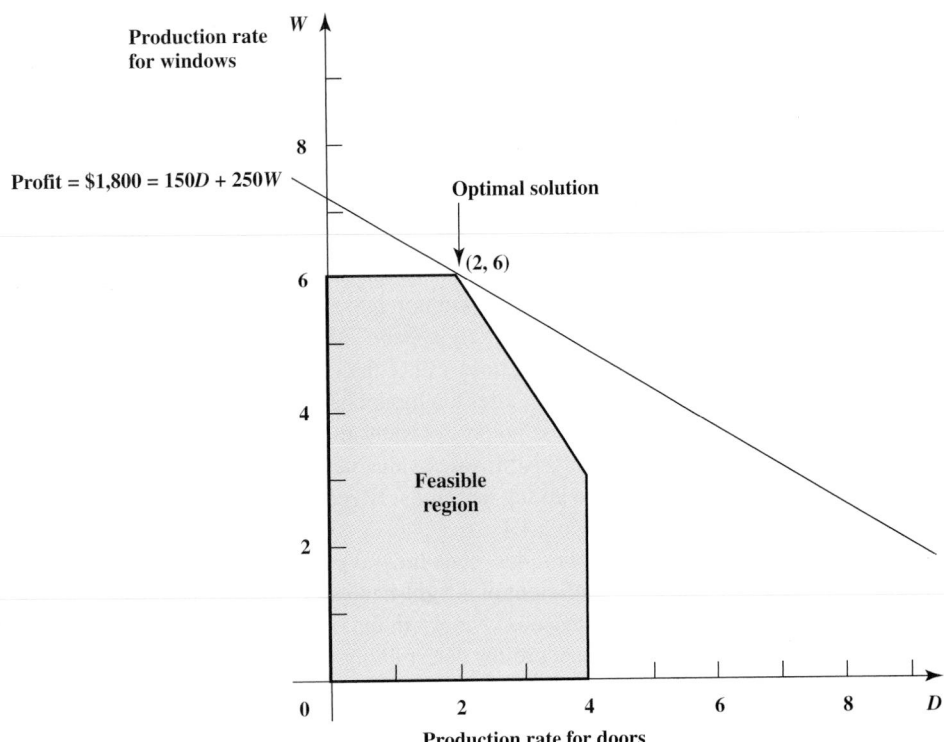

remain optimal over nearly all these possibilities, so this solution can be confidently used. Or perhaps it will become clear that the original estimates need to be refined before selecting a solution.

When the spreadsheet approach and/or Solver Table does not provide a clear conclusion, the 100 percent rule can usefully complement this approach in the following ways:

- The 100 percent rule can be used to determine just how large the changes in the objective function coefficients need to be before the original optimal solution may no longer be optimal.

- When the model has a large number of decision variables (as is common for real problems), it may become impractical to use the spreadsheet approach to systematically try out a variety of simultaneous changes in many or all of the coefficients in the objective function because of the huge number of representative possibilities. The Solver Table can only be used to systematically check possible changes in—at most—two coefficients at a time. However, by dividing each coefficient's allowable increase or allowable decrease by the number of decision variables, the 100 percent rule immediately indicates how much each coefficient can be safely changed without invalidating the current optimal solution.

- After completing the study, if conditions change in the future that cause some or all of the coefficients in the objective function to change, the 100 percent rule quickly indicates whether the original optimal solution must remain optimal. If the answer is affirmative, there is no need to take all the time that may be required to reconstruct the (revised) spreadsheet model. The time saved can be very substantial for large models.

Review Questions

1. In the 100 percent rule for simultaneous changes in objective function coefficients, what are the percentage changes that are being considered?

2. In this 100 percent rule, if the sum of the percentage changes does not exceed 100 percent, what does this say about the original optimal solution?

3. In this 100 percent rule, if the sum of the percentage changes exceeds 100 percent, does this mean that the original optimal solution is no longer optimal?

5.5   THE EFFECT OF SINGLE CHANGES IN A CONSTRAINT

We now turn our focus from the coefficients in the objective function to the effect of changing the functional constraints. The changes might occur either in the coefficients on the left-hand sides of the constraints or in the values of the right-hand sides.

We might be interested in the effect of such changes for the same reason we are interested in this effect for objective function coefficients, namely, that these parameters of the model are only *estimates* of quantities that cannot be determined precisely at this time so we want to determine the effect if these estimates are inaccurate.

When the right-hand sides represent managerial policy decisions, what-if analysis provides guidance regarding the effect of altering these decisions.

However, a more common reason for this interest is the one discussed at the end of Section 5.1, namely, that the right-hand sides of the functional constraints may well represent *managerial policy decisions* rather than quantities that are largely outside the control of management. Therefore, after the model has been solved, management will want to analyze the effect of altering these policy decisions in a variety of ways to see if these decisions can be improved. What-if analysis provides valuable guidance to management in determining the effect of altering these policy decisions. (Recall that this was cited as the third benefit of what-if analysis in Section 5.1.)

This section describes how to perform what-if analysis when making changes in just one spot (a coefficient or a right-hand side) of a single constraint. The next section then will deal with simultaneous changes in the constraints.

The procedure for determining the effect if a single change is made in a constraint is the same regardless of whether the change is in a coefficient on the left-hand side or in the value on the right-hand side. (The one exception is that the Excel sensitivity report provides information about changes in the right-hand side but does not do so for the left-hand side.) Therefore, we will illustrate the procedure by making changes in a right-hand side.

In particular, we return to the Wyndor case study to address the third what-if question posed by Wyndor management in Section 5.2.

Question 3: What happens if a change is made in the number of hours of production time per week being made available to Wyndor's new products in one of the plants?

The number of hours available in each plant is the value of the right-hand side for the corresponding constraint, so we want to investigate the effect of changing this right-hand side for one of the plants. With the original optimal solution, $(D, W) = (2, 6)$, only 2 of the 4 available hours in plant 1 are used, so changing this number of available hours (barring a large decrease) would have no effect on either the optimal solution or the resulting total profit from the two new products. However, it is unclear what would happen if the number of available hours in either plant 2 or plant 3 were to be changed. Let's start with plant 2.

Using the Spreadsheet for This Analysis

Referring back to Section 5.2, Figure 5.1 shows the spreadsheet model for the original Wyndor problem before beginning what-if analysis. The optimal solution is $(D, W) = (2, 6)$ with a total profit of $3,600 per week from the two new products. Cell G8 shows that 12 hours of production time per week are being made available for the new products in plant 2.

To see what happens if a specific change is made in this number of hours, all you need to do is substitute the new number in cell G8 and click on the Solve button again. For example, Figure 5.16 shows the result if the number of hours is increased from 12 to 13. The corresponding optimal solution in C12:D12 gives a total profit of $3,750. Thus, the resulting change in profit would be

$$\text{Incremental profit} = \$3,750 - \$3,600$$

$$= 150$$

Since this increase in profit is obtained by adding just one more hour in Plant 2, it would be interesting to see the effect of adding several more hours. Figure 5.17 shows the effect of

FIGURE 5.16

The revised Wyndor problem where the hours available in plant 2 per week have been increased from 12 (as in Figure 5.1) to 13, which results in an increase of $150 in the total profit per week from the two new products.

	A	B	C	D	E	F	G
1		**Wyndor Glass Co. Product-Mix Problem**					
2							
3			Doors	Windows			
4		Unit Profit	$300	$500			
5					Hours		Hours
6			Hours Used per Unit Produced		Used		Available
7		Plant 1	1	0	1.66667	≤	4
8		Plant 2	0	2	13	≤	13
9		Plant 3	3	2	18	≤	18
10							
11			Doors	Windows			Total Profit
12		Units Produced	1.667	6.5			$3,750

FIGURE 5.17

A further revision of the Wyndor problem in Figure 5.16 to further increase the hours available in plant 2 from 13 to 18, which results in a further increase in total profit of $750 (which is the $150 per hour added in plant 2).

	A	B	C	D	E	F	G
1		**Wyndor Glass Co. Product-Mix Problem**					
2							
3			Doors	Windows			
4		Unit Profit	$300	$500			
5					Hours		Hours
6			Hours Used per Unit Produced		Used		Available
7		Plant 1	1	0	0	≤	4
8		Plant 2	0	2	18	≤	18
9		Plant 3	3	2	18	≤	18
10							
11			Doors	Windows			Total Profit
12		Units Produced	0	9			$4,500

adding five more hours. Comparing Figure 5.17 to Figure 5.16, the additional profit from providing five more hours would be

$$\text{Incremental profit} = \$4,500 - \$3,750$$

$$= \$750 \text{ from adding 5 hours}$$

$$= \$150 \text{ per hour added}$$

So far, each additional hour provided in plant 2 adds $150 to profit.

Would adding even more hours increase profit even further? Figure 5.18 shows what would happen if a total of 20 hours per week were made available to the new products in plant 2. Both the optimal solution and the total profit are the same as in Figure 5.17, so increasing from 18 to 20 hours would not help. (The reason is that the 18 hours available in plant 3 prevent producing more than 9 windows per week, so only 18 hours can be used in plant 2.) Thus, it appears that 18 hours is the maximum that should be considered for plant 2.

Now management needs to consider the trade-off between adding production time for the new products and decreasing it for other products.

However, the fact that the total profit from the two new products can be increased substantially by increasing the number of hours per week made available to the new products from 12 to 18 does not mean that these additional hours should be provided automatically. The production time made available for these two new products can be increased only if it is decreased for other products. Therefore, management will need to assess the disadvantages of decreasing the production time for any other products (including both lost profit and less tangible disadvantages) before deciding whether to increase the production time for the new products. This

FIGURE 5.18

A further revision of the Wyndor problem in Figure 5.17 to further increase the hours available in plant 2 from 18 to 20, which results in no change in total profit because the optimal solution cannot make use of these additional hours.

	A	B	C	D	E	F	G
1		**Wyndor Glass Co. Product-Mix Problem**					
2							
3			Doors	Windows			
4		Unit Profit	$300	$500			
5					Hours		Hours
6			Hours Used per Unit Produced		Used		Available
7		Plant 1	1	0	0	≤	4
8		Plant 2	0	2	18	≤	20
9		Plant 3	3	2	18	≤	18
10							
11			Doors	Windows			Total Profit
12		Units Produced	0	9			$4,500

analysis also might lead to *decreasing* the production time made available to the two new products in one or more of the plants.

Using the Solver Table for This Analysis

A Solver Table can be used to systematically determine the effect of making various changes in one of the parameters in a constraint. In Figure 5.19, we use the Solver Table to show how the changing cells and total profit change as the number of available hours in plant 2 range between 4 and 20. The trial values considered for this number are listed in the first column of the table (B19:B35). The output cells of interest are the DoorsProduced (C12), WindowsProduced (D12), and TotalProfit (G12), so equations referring to these cells are entered in the first row of the table (C18:E18). Running the Solver Table (with the column input cell as G8, the hours available in plant 2) then fills in the values in the body of the table (C19:E35). We also have calculated in column F the incremental profit, that is, the additional profit that was obtained by adding the last hour to the time available in plant 2.

An interesting pattern is apparent in the incremental profit column. Starting at 12 hours available at plant 2 (the current allotment), each additional hour allocated yields an additional $150 in profit (up to 18 hours). Similarly, if hours are taken away from plant 2, each hour lost causes a loss of $150 profit (down to six hours). This rate of change in the profit for increases or decreases in the right-hand side of a constraint is known as the *shadow price*.

In general, the shadow price for a constraint reveals the rate at which the target cell can be increased by increasing the right-hand side of that constraint. This remains valid as long as the right-hand side is within its allowable range.

> Given an optimal solution and the corresponding value of the objective function for a linear programming model, the **shadow price** for a functional constraint is the *rate* at which the value of the objective function can be increased by increasing the right-hand side of the constraint by a small amount.

However, the shadow price of $150 for the plant 2 constraint is valid only within a range of values near 12 (in particular, between 6 hours and 18 hours). If the number of available hours is increased beyond 18 hours, then the incremental profit drops to zero. If the available hours are reduced below six hours, then profit drops at a faster rate of $250 per hour. Therefore, letting RHS denote the value of the right-hand side, the shadow price of $150 is valid for

$$6 \leq \text{RHS} \leq 18$$

In contrast to the allowable ranges for objective function coefficients described in Section 5.3, this allowable range focuses on a right-hand side and the corresponding shadow price.

This range is known as the **allowable range for the right-hand side** (or just **allowable range** for short).

> The **allowable range for the right-hand side** of a functional constraint is the range of values for this right-hand side over which this constraint's shadow price remains valid.

FIGURE 5.19

An application of the Solver Table that shows the effect of varying the number of hours of production time being made available per week in plant 2 for Wyndor's new products.

	A	B	C	D	E	F	G
1		**Wyndor Glass Co. Product-Mix Problem**					
2							
3			Doors	Windows			
4		Unit Profit	$300	$500			
5					Hours		Hours
6			Hours Used per Unit Produced		Used		Available
7		Plant 1	1	0	2	≤	4
8		Plant 2	0	2	12	≤	12
9		Plant 3	3	2	18	≤	18
10							
11			Doors	Windows			Total Profit
12		Units Produced	2	6			$3,600
13							
14							
15							
16		Time Available in	Optimal Units Produced		Total	Incremental	
17		Plant 2 (hours)	Doors	Windows	Profit	Profit	
18			2	6	$3,600		
19		4	4	2	$2,200		Select these cells (B18:E35) before choosing the Solver Table.
20		5	4	2.5	$2,450	$250	
21		6	4	3	$2,700	$250	
22		7	3.667	3.5	$2,850	$150	
23		8	3.333	4	$3,000	$150	
24		9	3	4.5	$3,150	$150	
25		10	2.667	5	$3,300	$150	
26		11	2.333	5.5	$3,450	$150	
27		12	2	6	$3,600	$150	
28		13	1.667	6.5	$3,750	$150	
29		14	1.333	7	$3,900	$150	
30		15	1	7.5	$4,050	$150	
31		16	0.667	8	$4,200	$150	
32		17	0.333	8.5	$4,350	$150	
33		18	0	9	$4,500	$150	
34		19	0	9	$4,500	$0	
35		20	0	9	$4,500	$0	

	C	D	E
16	Optimal Units Produced		Total
17	Doors	Windows	Profit
18	=DoorsProduced	=WindowsProduced	=TotalProfit

	F
16	Incremental
17	Profit
18	
19	
20	=E20-E19
21	=E21-E20
22	=E22-E21
23	=E23-E22

Solver Table

Row input cell: _____

Column input cell: [G8]

[Help] [Cancel] [OK]

Range Name	Cell
DoorsProduced	C12
TotalProfit	G12
WindowsProduced	D12

Using the Sensitivity Report to Obtain the Key Information

As illustrated above, it is straightforward to use the Solver Table to calculate the *shadow price* for a functional constraint, as well as to find (or at least closely approximate) the *allowable range* for the right-hand side of this constraint over which the shadow price remains valid. However, this same information also can be obtained immediately from Solver's sensitivity report for all the functional constraints. Figure 5.20 shows the full sensitivity report provided by the Solver for the original Wyndor problem after obtaining the optimal solution given in Figure 5.1. The top half is the part already shown in Figure 5.7 for finding allowable ranges for the objective function coefficients. The bottom half focuses on the functional constraints, including providing the shadow prices for these constraints in the fourth column. The first three columns remind us that (1) the output cells for these constraints in Figure 5.1 are cells E7 to E9, (2) these cells give the number of production hours used per week in the three plants, and (3) the final values in these cells are 2, 12, and 18 (as shown in column E of Figure 5.1). (We will discuss the last three columns a little later.)

The shadow price given in the fourth column for each constraint tells us how much the value of the objective function [target cell (G12) in Figure 5.1] would increase if the right-hand side of that constraint (cell G7, G8, or G9) were to be increased by 1. Conversely, it also tells us how much the value of the objective function would *decrease* if the right-hand side were to be decreased by 1. The shadow price for the Plant 1 constraint is 0, because this plant already is using less hours (2) than are available (4) so there would be no benefit to making an additional hour available. However, plants 2 and 3 are using all the hours available to them for the two new products (with the product mix given by the changing cells). Thus, it is not surprising that the shadow prices indicate that the target cell would increase if the hours available in either plant 2 or plant 3 were to be increased.

The shadow prices reveal the relationship between profit and the amount of production time made available in the plants.

To express this information in the language of management, the value of the objective function for this problem [target cell (G12) in Figure 5.1] represents the *total profit* in dollars per week from the two new products under consideration. The right-hand side of each functional constraint represents the number of hours of production time being made available per week for these products in the plant that corresponds to this constraint. Therefore, the shadow price for a functional constraint informs management as to how much the total profit from the two new products could be increased for each additional hour of production time made available to these products per week in the corresponding plant. Conversely, the shadow price indicates how much this profit would decrease for each reduction of an hour of production time in that plant. This interpretation of the shadow price remains valid as long as the change in the number of hours of production time is not very large.

Here is how to find the allowable ranges for the right-hand sides from the sensitivity report.

Specifically, this interpretation of the shadow price remains valid as long as the number of hours of production time remains within its *allowable range.* The Solver's sensitivity report provides all the data needed to identify the allowable range of each functional constraint. Refer back to the bottom of this report given in Figure 5.20. The final three columns enable calculating this range. The "Constraint R.H. Side" column indicates the original value of the

FIGURE 5.20

The complete sensitivity report generated by the Excel Solver for the original Wyndor problem as formulated in Figure 5.1.

Adjustable Cells

Cell	Name	Final Value	Reduced Cost	Objective Coefficient	Allowable Increase	Allowable Decrease
$C$12	DoorsProduced	2	0	300	450	300
$D$12	WindowsProduced	6	0	500	1E+30	300

Constraints

Cell	Name	Final Value	Shadow Price	Constraint R. H. Side	Allowable Increase	Allowable Decrease
$E$7	Plant 1 Used	2	0	4	1E+30	2
$E$8	Plant 2 Used	12	150	12	6	6
$E$9	Plant 3 Used	18	100	18	6	6

right-hand side before any change is made. Adding the number in the "Allowable Increase" column to this original value then gives the upper endpoint of the allowable range. Similarly, subtracting the number in the "Allowable Decrease" column from this original value gives the lower endpoint. Using the fact that 1E + 30 represents infinity (∞), these calculations of the allowable ranges are shown below, where a subscript has been added to each RHS to identify the constraint involved.

Plant 1 constraint: $4 - 2 \leq RHS_1 \leq 4 + \infty$,   so $2 \leq RHS_1$ (no upper limit)

Plant 2 constraint: $12 - 6 \leq RHS_2 \leq 12 + 6$,   so $6 \leq RHS_2 \leq 18$

Plant 3 constraint: $18 - 6 \leq RHS_3 \leq 18 + 6$,   so $12 \leq RHS_3 \leq 24$

In the case of the plant 2 constraint, Figure 5.21 provides graphical insight into why $6 \leq RHS_2 \leq 18$ is the range of validity for the shadow price. The optimal solution for the original problem, $(D, W) = (2, 6)$, lies at the intersection of line B and line C. The equation for line B is $2W = 12$ because this is the constraint boundary line for the plant 2 constraint ($2W \leq 12$). However, if the value of this right-hand side ($RHS_2 = 12$) is changed, line B will either shift upward (for a larger value of RHS_2) or downward (for a smaller value of RHS_2). As line B shifts, the boundary of the feasible region shifts accordingly and the optimal solution continues to lie at the intersection of the shifted line B and line C—provided the shift in line B is not so large that this intersection is no longer feasible. Each time RHS_2 is increased (or decreased) by 1, this intersection shifts enough to increase (or decrease) Profit by the amount of the shadow price ($150). Figure 5.21 indicates that this intersection remains feasible (and so optimal) as RHS_2 increases from 12 to 18, because the feasible region expands upward as line B shifts upward. However, for values of RHS_2 larger than 18, this intersection is no longer feasible because it gives a negative value of D (the production rate for doors). Thus, each increase of 1 above 18 no longer increases Profit by the amount of the shadow price. Similarly, as RHS_2 decreases from 12 to 6, this intersection remains feasible (and so optimal) as line B shifts down

FIGURE 5.21

A graphical interpretation of the allowable range, $6 \leq RHS_2 \leq 18$, for the right-hand side of Wyndor's plant 2 constraint.

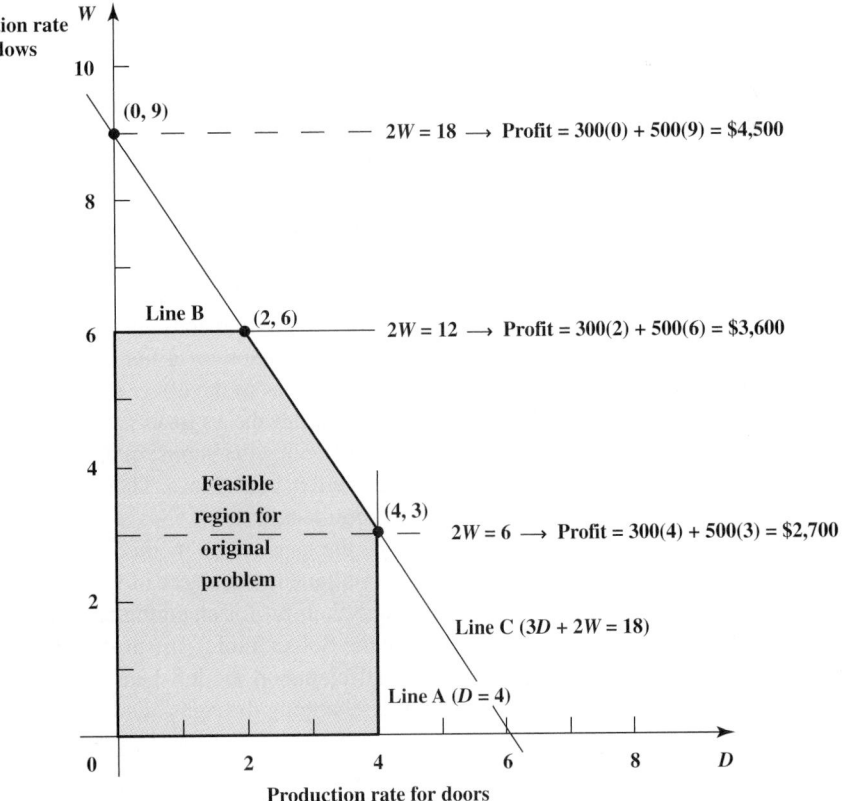

accordingly. However, for values of RHS_2 less than 6, this intersection is no longer feasible because it violates the plant 1 constraint ($D \leq 4$) whose boundary line is line A. Hence, each decrease of 1 below 6 no longer decreases Profit by the amount of the shadow price. Consequently, $6 \leq RHS \leq 18$ is the allowable range over which the shadow price is valid.

Summary

Recall again that the right-hand side of each functional constraint represents the number of hours of production time per week in the corresponding plant that is being made available to the two new products. The *shadow price* for each constraint reveals how much the total profit from these new products would increase for each additional hour of production time made available in the corresponding plant for these products. This interpretation of the shadow price remains valid as long as the number of hours remains within its *allowable range*. Therefore, each shadow price can be applied by management to evaluate a change in its original decision regarding the number of hours as long as the new number is within the corresponding allowable range. This evaluation also would need to take into account how the change in the number of hours made available to the new products would impact the production rates and profits for the company's other products.

Review
Questions

1. Why might it be of interest to investigate the effect of making changes in a functional constraint?

2. Why might it be possible to alter the right-hand side of a functional constraint?

3. What is meant by a *shadow price?*

4. How can a shadow price be found by using the spreadsheet? By using the Solver Table? By using Solver's sensitivity report?

5. Why are shadow prices of interest to managers?

6. Can shadow prices be used to determine the effect of *decreasing* rather than increasing the right-hand side of a functional constraint?

7. What does a shadow price of 0 tell a manager?

8. Which columns of the Solver's sensitivity report are used to find the allowable range for the right-hand side of a functional constraint?

9. Why are these allowable ranges of interest to managers?

5.6 THE EFFECT OF SIMULTANEOUS CHANGES IN THE CONSTRAINTS

The preceding section described how to perform what-if analysis to investigate the effect of changes in a single spot of a constraint. We now turn our consideration to the effect of simultaneous changes in the constraints.

Managerial policy decisions involving right-hand sides frequently are interrelated, so changes in these decisions should be considered simultaneously.

The need to consider these simultaneous changes arises frequently. There may be considerable uncertainty about the estimates for a number of the parameters in the functional constraints, so questions will arise as to the effect if the true values of the parameters simultaneously deviate significantly from the estimates. Since the right-hand sides of the constraints often represent managerial policy decisions, questions will arise about what would happen if some of these decisions were to be changed. These decisions frequently are interrelated and so need to be considered simultaneously.

We outline next how the usual three methods for performing what-if analysis can be applied to considering simultaneous changes in the constraints. The third one (using Solver's sensitivity report) is only helpful for changing right-hand sides. For the first two (using the spreadsheet and using the Solver Table), the procedure is the same regardless of whether the changes are in the coefficients on the left-hand sides or in the right-hand sides of the constraints (or both). Since changing the right-hand sides is the more important case, we will focus on this case.

In particular, we now will deal with the last of Wyndor management's what-if questions.

Question 4: What happens if simultaneous changes are made in the number of hours of production time per week being made available to Wyndor's new products in all the plants?

In particular, after seeing that the plant 2 constraint has the largest shadow price (150), versus a shadow price of 100 for the plant 3 constraint, management now is interested in exploring a specific type of simultaneous change in these production hours. By shifting the production of one of the company's current products from plant 2 to plant 3, it is possible to increase the number of production hours available to the new products in plant 2 by decreasing the number of production hours available in plant 3 by the same amount. Management wonders what would happen if these simultaneous changes in production hours were made.

Using the Spreadsheet for This Analysis

According to the shadow prices, the effect of shifting one hour of production time per week from plant 3 to plant 2 would be as follows.

RHS_2: $12 \rightarrow 13$ Change in total profit $=$ Shadow price $=$ $150

RHS_3: $18 \rightarrow 17$ Change in total profit $= -$Shadow price $= \underline{-100}$

Net increase in total profit $=$ $50

We now are checking to see whether the shadow prices remain valid for evaluating such large simultaneous changes in the right-hand sides.

However, we don't know if these shadow prices remain valid if *both* right-hand sides are changed by this amount.

A quick way to check this is to substitute the new right-hand sides into the original spreadsheet in Figure 5.1 and click on the Solve button again. The resulting spreadsheet in Figure 5.22 shows that the net increase in total profit (from $3,600 to $3,650) is indeed $50, so the shadow prices are valid for these particular simultaneous changes in right-hand sides.

How long will these shadow prices remain valid if we continue shifting production hours from plant 3 to plant 2? We could continue checking this by substituting other combinations of right-hand sides into the spreadsheet and re-solving each time. However, a more systematic way of doing this is to use the Solver Table as described below.

Using the Solver Table for This Analysis

Since it can become tedious, or even impractical, to use the spreadsheet to investigate a large number of simultaneous changes in the right-hand sides, let us see how a Solver Table (provided in your MS Courseware) can be used to do this analysis more systematically.

FIGURE 5.22

The revised Wyndor problem where column G in Figure 5.1 has been changed by shifting one of the hours available in plant 3 to plant 2 and then re-solving.

	A	B	C	D	E	F	G
1		**Wyndor Glass Co. Product-Mix Problem**					
2							
3			Doors	Windows			
4		Unit Profit	$300	$500			
5					Hours		Hours
6			Hours Used per Unit Produced		Used		Available
7		Plant 1	1	0	1.33333	≤	4
8		Plant 2	0	2	13	≤	13
9		Plant 3	3	2	17	≤	17
10							
11			Doors	Windows			Total Profit
12		Units Produced	1.333	6.5			$3,650

We could use a two-way Solver Table to investigate how the profit and optimal production rates vary for different combinations of the number of hours available in plant 2 and plant 3. However, in this case we aren't interested in *all* combinations of hours in the two plants, but rather only those combinations that involve a simple *shifting* of available hours from plant 3 to plant 2. For this analysis, we will see that a one-way Solver Table is sufficient.

For each hour reduced in plant 3, an additional hour is made available in plant 2. Thus, the number of available hours in plant 2 is a function of the number of available hours in plant 3. In particular, since there are 30 total hours available at the two plants ($RHS_2 + RHS_3 = 30$), the number of available hours in plant 2 (RHS_2) is

$$RHS_2 = 30 - RHS_3$$

By entering a formula into one data cell in terms of another one, the one-way Solver Table is able to investigate interrelated trial values in both data cells.

Figure 5.23 shows the Wyndor Glass Co. spreadsheet with the data cell for the number of available hours in plant 2 replaced by the above formula. Because of this formula, whenever the number of available hours in plant 3 is reduced, the number of available hours in plant 2 will automatically increase by the same amount. Now a one-way Solver Table can be used to investigate various numbers of available hours in plant 3 (with the corresponding automatic adjustment made to the available hours at plant 2). The trial values for the number of hours available in plant 3 are shown in the Solver Table at the bottom of the spreadsheet in Figure 5.23 (C20:C26). We are interested in the output cells DoorsProduced (C12), WindowsProduced (D12), and TotalProfit (G12), so equations referring to these cells are entered in the first row of the table (D19:F19). Running the Solver Table (with the column input cell as G9, the hours available in plant 3) then fills in the values in the body of the table (D20:F26). We have calculated the incremental profit (in column G) for each hour shifted from plant 3 to plant 2.

Again there is a pattern to the incremental profit. For each hour shifted from plant 3 to plant 2 (up to 3 hours), an additional profit of $50 is achieved. However, if more than 3 hours are shifted, the incremental profit becomes $-\$250$. Thus, it appears worthwhile to shift up to 3 available hours from plant 3 to plant 2, but no more.

Although a one-way Solver Table is limited to enumerating trial values for only one data cell, you have just seen how such a Solver Table still can systematically investigate a large number of simultaneous changes in two data cells by entering a formula for the second data cell in terms of the first one. The two data cells considered above happened to be right-hand sides of constraints, but either or both could have been coefficients on the left-hand side instead. It is even possible to enter formulas for multiple data cells in terms of the one whose trial values are being enumerated. Furthermore, by using the two-way Solver Table, trial values can be enumerated simultaneously for two data cells, with the possibility of entering formulas for additional data cells in terms of these two.

Gleaning Additional Information from the Sensitivity Report

Despite the versatility of the Solver Table, it cannot handle a number of important cases. The most important one is where management wants to explore various possibilities for changing its policy decisions that correspond to changing several right-hand sides simultaneously in a variety of ways. Although the spreadsheet can be used to see the effect of any combination of simultaneous changes, it can take an exorbitant amount of time to systematically investigate a large number of simultaneous changes in right-hand sides in this way. Fortunately, Solver's sensitivity report provides valuable information for guiding such an investigation. In particular, there is a *100 percent rule* (analogous to the one presented in Section 5.4) that uses this information to conduct this kind of investigation.

Recall that the 100 percent rule described in Section 5.4 is used to investigate simultaneous changes in *objective function coefficients*. The new 100 percent rule presented next investigates simultaneous changes in *right-hand sides* in a similar way.

The data needed to apply the new 100 percent rule for the Wyndor problem are given by the last three columns in the bottom part of the sensitivity report in Figure 5.20. Keep in mind that we can safely use the entire allowable decrease or increase from the current value of a right-hand side only if none of the other right-hand sides are changed at all. With simultaneous changes in the right-hand sides, we focus for each change on the *percentage* of the allowable

FIGURE 5.23 By inserting a formula into cell G8 that keeps the total number of hours available in plant 2 and plant 3 equal to 30, this one-dimensional application of the Solver Table shows the effect of shifting more and more of the hours available from plant 3 to plant 2.

	A	B	C	D	E	F	G	H
1		**Wyndor Glass Co. Product-Mix Problem**						
2								
3			Doors	Windows				
4		Unit Profit	$300	$500				
5					Hours		Hours	
6			Hours Used per Unit Produced		Used		Available	
7		Plant 1	1	0	2	≤	4	Total (Plants 2 & 3)
8		Plant 2	0	2	12	≤	12	30
9		Plant 3	3	2	18	≤	18	
10								
11			Doors	Windows			Total Profit	
12		Units Produced	2	6			$3,600	
13								
14								
15								
16								
17		Time Available in	Time Available in	Optimal Units Produced		Total	Incremental	
18		Plant 2 (hours)	Plant 3 (hours)	Doors	Windows	Profit	Profit	
19				2	6	$3,600		Select these cells (C19:F26), before choosing the Solver Table.
20		12	18	2	6	$3,600		
21		13	17	1.333	6.5	$3,650	$50	
22		14	16	0.667	7	$3,700	$50	
23		15	15	0	7.5	$3,750	$50	
24		16	14	0	7	$3,500	-$250	
25		17	13	0	6.5	$3,250	-$250	
26		18	12	0	6	$3,000	-$250	

Solver Table

Row input cell: [   ]

Column input cell: [G9]

[Help] [Cancel] [OK]

Range Name	Cells
DoorsProduced	C12
TotalProfit	G12
WindowsProduced	D12

	G	H
5	Hours	
6	Available	
7	4	Total (Plants 2 & 3)
8	=H8-G9	30
9	18	

	B	C	D	E	F	G
17	Time Available in	Time Available in	Optimal Units Produced		Total	Incremental
18	Plant 2 (hours)	Plant 3 (hours)	Doors	Windows	Profit	Profit
19			=DoorsProduced	=WindowsProduced	=TotalProfit	
20	=$H$8-C20	18	2	6	$3,600	
21	=$H$8-C21	17	1.333	6.5	$3,650	=F21-F20
22	=$H$8-C22	16	0.667	7	$3,700	=F22-F21
23	=$H$8-C23	15	0	7.5	$3,750	=F23-F22
24	=$H$8-C24	14	0	7	$3,500	=F24-F23
25	=$H$8-C25	13	0	6.5	$3,250	=F25-F24
26	=$H$8-C26	12	0	6	$3,000	=F26-F25

decrease or increase that is being used. As detailed below, the 100 percent rule basically says that we can safely make the simultaneous changes only if the *sum* of these percentages does not exceed 100 percent.

This 100 percent rule reveals whether the simultaneous changes in the right-hand sides are small enough to guarantee that the shadow prices are still valid.

The 100 Percent Rule for Simultaneous Changes in Right-Hand Sides: The shadow prices remain valid for predicting the effect of simultaneously changing the right-hand sides of some of the functional constraints as long as the changes are not too large. To check whether the changes are small enough, calculate for each change the percentage of the allowable change (decrease or increase) for that right-hand side to remain within its allowable range. If the *sum* of the percentage changes does *not* exceed 100 percent, the shadow prices definitely will still be valid. (If the sum *does* exceed 100 percent, then we cannot be sure.)

To illustrate this rule, consider again the simultaneous changes (shifting one hour of production time per week from plant 3 to plant 2) that led to Figure 5.22. The calculations for the 100 percent rule in this case are

RHS_2: $12 \rightarrow 13$

$$\text{Percentage of allowable increase} = 100\left(\frac{13 - 12}{6}\right) = 16\tfrac{2}{3}\%$$

RHS_3: $18 \rightarrow 17$

$$\text{Percentage of allowable decrease} = 100\left(\frac{18 - 17}{6}\right) = 16\tfrac{2}{3}\%$$

$$\text{Sum} = \overline{33\tfrac{1}{3}\%}$$

Since the sum of $33\tfrac{1}{3}$ percent is less than 100 percent, the shadow prices definitely are valid for predicting the effect of these changes, as was illustrated with Figure 5.22.

The fact that $33\tfrac{1}{3}$ percent is one-third of 100 percent suggests that the changes can be three times as large as above without invalidating the shadow prices. To check this, let us apply the 100 percent rule with these larger changes.

RHS_2: $12 \rightarrow 15$

$$\text{Percentage of allowable increase} = \left(\frac{15 - 12}{6}\right)\% = 50\%$$

RHS_3: $18 \rightarrow 15$

$$\text{Percentage of allowable decrease} = \left(\frac{18 - 15}{6}\right)\% = 50\%$$

$$\text{Sum} = \overline{100\%}$$

Because the sum does *not exceed* 100 percent, the shadow prices are still valid, but these are the largest changes in the right-hand sides that can provide this guarantee. In fact, Figure 5.23 demonstrated that the shadow prices become invalid for larger changes.

Review Questions

1. Why might it be of interest to investigate the effect of making simultaneous changes in the functional constraints?

2. How can the spreadsheet be used to investigate simultaneous changes in the functional constraints?

3. What are the capabilities of the Solver Table for investigating simultaneous changes in the functional constraints?

4. Why might a manager be interested in considering simultaneous changes in right-hand sides?

5. What is the 100 percent rule for simultaneous changes in right-hand sides?

6. What are the data needed to apply the 100 percent rule for simultaneous changes in right-hand sides?

7. What is guaranteed if the sum of the percentages of allowable changes in the right-hand sides does not exceed 100 percent?

8. What is the conclusion if the sum of the percentages of allowable changes in the right-hand sides does exceed 100 percent?

5.7 Summary

What-if analysis is analysis done *after* finding an optimal solution for the original version of the basic model. This analysis provides important insights to help guide managerial decision making. This chapter describes how this is done when the basic model is a linear programming model. The spreadsheet for the model, the Solver Table provided in your MS Courseware, and the sensitivity report generated by the Excel Solver all play a central role in this process.

The coefficients in the objective function typically represent quantities that can only be roughly estimated when the model is formulated. Will the optimal solution obtained from the model be the correct one if the true value of one of these coefficients is significantly different from the estimate used in the model? The spreadsheet can be used to quickly check specific changes in the coefficient. The Solver Table enables the systematic investigation of many trial values for this coefficient. For a broader investigation, the *allowable range* for each coefficient identifies the interval within which the true value must lie, in order for this solution to still be the correct optimal solution. These ranges are easily calculated from the data in the sensitivity report provided by the Excel Solver.

What happens if there are significant inaccuracies in the estimates of two or more coefficients in the objective function? Specific simultaneous changes can be checked with the spreadsheet. A two-way Solver Table can systematically investigate various simultaneous changes in two coefficients. To go further, the *100 percent rule for simultaneous changes in objective function coefficients* provides a convenient way of checking whole ranges of simultaneous changes, again by using the data in the Solver's sensitivity report.

What-if analysis usually extends to considering the effect of changes in the functional constraints as well. Occasionally, changes in the coefficients of these constraints will be considered because of the uncertainty in their original estimates. More frequently, the changes considered will be in the right-hand sides of the constraints. The right-hand sides frequently represent managerial policy decisions. In such cases, *shadow prices* provide valuable guidance to management about the potential effects of altering these policy decisions. The shadow price for each constraint is easily found by using the spreadsheet, the Solver Table, or the sensitivity report.

Shadow price analysis can be validly applied to investigate possible changes in right-hand sides as long as these changes are not too large. The *allowable range* for each right-hand side indicates just how far it can be changed, assuming no other changes are made. If, in fact, other changes are made as well, the *100 percent rule for simultaneous changes in right-hand sides* enables checking whether the changes definitely are not too large. The Solver's sensitivity report provides the key information needed to find each allowable range or to apply this 100 percent rule. Both the spreadsheet and the Solver Table also can sometimes be used to help investigate these simultaneous changes.

Glossary

allowable range for an objective function coefficient The range of values for a particular coefficient in the objective function over which the optimal solution for the original model remains optimal. (Section 5.3), *180*

allowable range for the right-hand side The range of values for the right-hand side of a functional constraint over which this constraint's shadow price remains valid. (Section 5.5), *192*

parameters of the model The parameters of a linear programming model are the constants (coefficients or right-hand sides) in the functional constraints and the objective function. (Section 5.1), *171*

sensitive parameter A parameter is considered sensitive if even a small change in its value can change the optimal solution. (Section 5.1), *172*

sensitivity analysis The part of what-if analysis that focuses on individual parameters of the model. It involves checking how sensitive the optimal solution is to the value of each parameter. (Section 5.1), *172*

shadow price The shadow price for a functional constraint is the rate at which the optimal value of the objective function can be increased by increasing the right-hand side of the constraint by a small amount. (Section 5.5), *192*

what-if analysis Analysis that addresses questions about what would happen to the optimal solution if different assumptions were made about future conditions. (Chapter introduction), *171*

Learning Aids for This Chapter in Your MS Courseware

Chapter 5 Excel Files:

Wyndor Example
Profit & Gambit Example

Excel Add-ins:

Premium Solver for Education
Solver Table

Interactive Management Science Modules:

Module for Graphical Linear Programming and Sensitivity Analysis

Problems

We have inserted the symbol E* to the left of each problem (or its parts) where Excel should be used (unless your instructor gives you contrary instructions). An asterisk on the problem number indicates that at least a partial answer is given in the back of the book.

5.1.* One of the products of the G.A. Tanner Company is a special kind of toy that provides an estimated unit profit of $3. Because of a large demand for this toy, management would like to increase its production rate from the current level of 1,000 per day. However, a limited supply of two subassemblies (A and B) from vendors makes this difficult. Each toy requires two subassemblies of type A, but the vendor providing these subassemblies would only be able to increase its supply rate from the current 2,000 per day to a maximum of 3,000 per day. Each toy requires only one subassembly of type B, but the vendor providing these subassemblies would be unable to increase its supply rate above the current level of 1,000 per day.

Because no other vendors currently are available to provide these subassemblies, management is considering initiating a new production process internally that would simultaneously produce an equal number of subassemblies of the two types to supplement the supply from the two vendors. It is estimated that the company's cost for producing one subassembly of each type would be $2.50 more than the cost of purchasing these subassemblies from the two vendors. Management wants to determine both the production rate of the toy and the production rate of each pair of subassemblies (one A and one B) that would maximize the total profit.

Viewing this problem as a resource-allocation problem, one of the company's managers has organized its data as follows:

Resource	Resource Usage per Unit of Each Activity		Amount of Resource Available
	Produce Toys	Produce Subassemblies	
Subassembly A	2	−1	3,000
Subassembly B	1	−1	1,000
Unit profit	$3	−$2.50	

E* *a.* Formulate and solve a spreadsheet model for this problem.

E* *b.* Since the stated unit profits for the two activities are only estimates, management wants to know how much each of these estimates can be off before the optimal solution would change. Begin exploring this question for the first activity (producing toys) by using the spreadsheet and Solver to manually generate a table that gives the optimal solution and total profit as the unit profit for this activity increases in 50¢ increments from $2.00 to $4.00. What conclusion can be drawn about how much the estimate of this unit profit can differ in each direction from its original value of $3.00 before the optimal solution would change?

E* *c.* Repeat part *b* for the second activity (producing subassemblies) by generating a table as the unit profit for this activity increases in 50¢ increments from −$3.50 to −$1.50 (with the unit profit for the first activity fixed at $3).

E* *d.* Use the Solver Table to systematically generate all the data requested in parts *b* and *c*, except use 25¢ increments instead of 50¢ increments. Use these data to refine your conclusions in parts *b* and *c*.

E*   *f.* Use Excel's sensitivity report to find the allowable range for the unit profit of each activity.

E*   *g.* Use a two-dimensional Solver Table to systematically generate the total profit as the unit profits of the two activities are changed simultaneously as described in parts *b* and *c*.

h. Use the information provided by Excel's sensitivity report to describe how far the unit profits of the two activities can change simultaneously before the optimal solution might change.

5.2.   Consider a resource-allocation problem having the following data:

| Resource | Resource Usage per Unit of Each Activity | | Amount of Resource Available |
	1	2	
1	1	2	10
2	1	3	12
Unit profit	$2	$5	

The objective is to determine the number of units of each activity to undertake so as to maximize the total profit.

While doing what-if analysis, you learn that the estimates of the unit profits are accurate only to within ± 50 percent. In other words, the ranges of *likely values* for these unit profits are $1 to $3 for activity 1 and $2.50 to $7.50 for activity 2.

E*   *a.* Formulate a spreadsheet model for this problem based on the original estimates of the unit profits. Then use the Solver to find an optimal solution and to generate the sensitivity report.

E*   *b.* Use the spreadsheet and Solver to check whether this optimal solution remains optimal if the unit profit for activity 1 changes from $2 to $1. From $2 to $3.

E*   *c.* Also check whether the optimal solution remains optimal if the unit profit for activity 1 still is $2 but the unit profit for activity 2 changes from $5 to $2.50. From $5 to $7.50.

E*   *d.* Use the Solver Table to systematically generate the optimal solution and total profit as the unit profit of activity 1 increases in 20¢ increments from $1 to $3 (without changing the unit profit of activity 2). Then do the same as the unit profit of activity 2 increases in 50¢ increments from $2.50 to $7.50 (without changing the unit profit of activity 1). Use these results to estimate the allowable range for the unit profit of each activity.

e. Use the Graphical Linear Programming and Sensitivity Analysis module in your Interactive Management Science Modules to estimate the allowable range for the unit profit of each activity.

f. Use the sensitivity report to find the allowable range for the unit profit of each activity. Then use these ranges to check your results in parts *b–e*.

E*   *g.* Use a two-dimensional Solver Table to systematically generate the optimal solution as the unit profits of the two activities are changed simultaneously as described in part *d*.

h. Use the Graphical Linear Programming and Sensitivity Analysis module to interpret the results in part *g* graphically.

E*5.3.   Consider the Big M Co. problem presented in Section 4.4, including the spreadsheet in Figure 4.5 showing its formulation and optimal solution.

There is some uncertainty about what the unit costs will be for shipping through the various shipping lanes. Therefore, before adopting the optimal solution in Figure 4.5, management wants additional information about the effect of inaccuracies in estimating these unit costs.

Use the Excel Solver to generate the sensitivity report preparatory to addressing the following questions.

a. Which of the unit shipping costs given in Table 4.5 has the smallest margin for error without invalidating the optimal solution given in Figure 4.5? Where should the greatest effort be placed in estimating the unit shipping costs?

    b. What is the allowable range for each of the unit shipping costs?

    c. How should the allowable range be interpreted to management?

    d. If the estimates change for more than one of the unit shipping costs, how can you use the sensitivity report to determine whether the optimal solution might change?

E*5.4.*   Consider the Union Airways problem presented in Section 4.3, including the spreadsheet in Figure 4.3 showing its formulation and optimal solution.

    Management is about to begin negotiations on a new contract with the union that represents the company's customer service agents. This might result in some small changes in the daily costs per agent given in Table 4.4 for the various shifts. Several possible changes listed below are being considered separately. In each case, management would like to know whether the change might result in the solution in Figure 4.3 no longer being optimal. Answer this question in parts *a* to *e* by using the spreadsheet and Solver directly. If the optimal solution changes, record the new solution.

    a. The daily cost per agent for shift 2 changes from $160 to $165.

    b. The daily cost per agent for shift 4 changes from $180 to $170.

    c. The changes in parts *a* and *b* both occur.

    d. The daily cost per agent increases by $4 for shifts 2, 4, and 5, but decreases by $4 for shifts 1 and 3.

    e. The daily cost per agent increases by 2 percent for each shift.

    f. Use the Solver to generate the sensitivity report for this problem. Suppose that the above changes are being considered later without having the spreadsheet model immediately available on a computer. Show in each case how the sensitivity report can be used to check whether the original optimal solution must still be optimal.

    g. For each of the five shifts in turn, use the Solver Table to systematically generate the optimal solution and total cost when the only change is that the daily cost per agent on that shift increases in $3 increments from $15 less than the current cost up to $15 more than the current cost.

E*5.5.*   Consider the Think-Big Development Co. problem presented in Section 4.2, including the spreadsheet in Figure 4.2 showing its formulation and optimal solution. In parts *a–g,* use the spreadsheet and Solver to check whether the optimal solution would change and, if so, what the new optimal solution would be, if the estimates in Table 4.2 of the net present values of the projects were to be changed in each of the following ways. (Consider each part by itself.)

    a. The net present value of project 1 (a high-rise office building) increases by $200,000.

    b. The net present value of project 2 (a hotel) increases by $200,000.

    c. The net present value of project 1 decreases by $5 million.

    d. The net present value of project 3 (a shopping center) decreases by $200,000.

    e. All three changes in parts *b, c,* and *d* occur simultaneously.

    f. The net present values of projects 1, 2, and 3 change to $46 million, $69 million, and $49 million, respectively.

    g. The net present values of projects 1, 2, and 3 change to $54 million, $84 million, and $60 million, respectively.

    h. Use the Solver to generate the sensitivity report for this problem. For each of the above parts, suppose that the change occurs later without having the spreadsheet model immediately available on a computer. Show in each case how the sensitivity report can be used to check whether the original optimal solution must still be optimal.

    i. For each of the three projects in turn, use the Solver Table to systematically generate the optimal solution and the total net present value when the only change is that the net present value of that project increases in $1 million increments from $5 million less than the current value up to $5 million more than the current value.

5.6.   Ken and Larry, Inc., supplies its ice cream parlors with three flavors of ice cream: chocolate, vanilla, and banana. Due to extremely hot weather and a high demand for its products, the company has run short of its supply of ingredients: milk, sugar, and cream. Hence, they will not be able to fill all the orders received from their retail outlets, the ice cream parlors. Due to these circumstances, the company has decided to choose the amount of each flavor to produce that will maximize total profit, given the constraints on the supply of the basic ingredients.

The chocolate, vanilla, and banana flavors generate, respectively, $1.00, $0.90, and $0.95 of profit per gallon sold. The company has only 200 gallons of milk, 150 pounds of sugar, and 60 gallons of cream left in its inventory. The linear programming formulation for this problem is shown below in algebraic form.

Let

C = Gallons of chocolate ice cream produced

V = Gallons of vanilla ice cream produced

B = Gallons of banana ice cream produced

Maximize   Profit = $1.00C + 0.90V + 0.95B$

subject to

Milk: $0.45C + 0.50V + 0.40B \leq 200$ gallons

Sugar: $0.50C + 0.40V + 0.40B \leq 150$ pounds

Cream: $0.10C + 0.15V + 0.20B \leq 60$ gallons

and

$C \geq 0$ $V \geq 0$ $B \geq 0$

This problem was solved using the Excel Solver. The spreadsheet (already solved) and the sensitivity report are shown below. (Note: The numbers in the sensitivity report for the milk constraint are missing on purpose, since you will be asked to fill in these numbers in part *f*.)

	A	B	C	D	E	F	G
1		Chocolate	Vanilla	Banana			
2	Unit Profit	$1.00	$0.90	$0.95			
3							
4	Resource	Resources Used per Gallon Produced			Used		Available
5	Milk	0.45	0.5	0.4	180	≤	200
6	Sugar	0.5	0.4	0.4	150	≤	150
7	Cream	0.1	0.15	0.2	60	≤	60
8							
9		Chocolate	Vanilla	Banana			Total Profit
10	Gallons Produced	0	300	75			$341.25

Adjustable Cells

Cell	Name	Final Value	Reduced Cost	Objective Coefficient	Allowable Increase	Allowable Decrease
$C$10	Gallons Produced Chocolate	0	−0.0375	1	0.0375	1E+30
$D$10	Gallons Produced Vanilla	300	0	0.9	0.05	0.0125
$E$10	Gallons Produced Banana	75	0	0.95	0.0214	0.05

Constraints

Cell	Name	Final Value	Shadow Price	Constraint R. H. Side	Allowable Increase	Allowable Decrease
$F$5	Milk Used					
$F$6	Sugar Used	150	1.875	150	10	30
$F$7	Cream Used	60	1	60	15	3.75

For each of the following parts, answer the question as specifically and completely as possible without solving the problem again with the Excel Solver. Note: Each part is independent (i.e., any change made to the model in one part does not apply to any other parts).

a. What is the optimal solution and total profit?

b. Suppose the profit per gallon of banana changes to $1.00. Will the optimal solution change and what can be said about the effect on total profit?

c. Suppose the profit per gallon of banana changes to 92¢. Will the optimal solution change and what can be said about the effect on total profit?

d. Suppose the company discovers that three gallons of cream have gone sour and so must be thrown out. Will the optimal solution change and what can be said about the effect on total profit?

e. Suppose the company has the opportunity to buy an additional 15 pounds of sugar at a total cost of $15. Should it do so? Explain.

f. Fill in all the sensitivity report information for the milk constraint, given just the optimal solution for the problem. Explain how you were able to deduce each number.

5.7.　David, LaDeana, and Lydia are the sole partners and workers in a company that produces fine clocks. David and LaDeana are each available to work a maximum of 40 hours per week at the company, while Lydia is available to work a maximum of 20 hours per week.

The company makes two different types of clocks: a grandfather clock and a wall clock. To make a clock, David (a mechanical engineer) assembles the inside mechanical parts of the clock while LaDeana (a woodworker) produces the hand-carved wood casings. Lydia is responsible for taking orders and shipping the clocks. The amount of time required for each of these tasks is shown next.

Task	Time Required	
	Grandfather Clock	Wall Clock
Assemble clock mechanism	6 hours	4 hours
Carve wood casing	8 hours	4 hours
Shipping	3 hours	3 hours

Each grandfather clock built and shipped yields a profit of $300, while each wall clock yields a profit of $200.

The three partners now want to determine how many clocks of each type should be produced per week to maximize the total profit.

a. Formulate a linear programming model in algebraic form for this problem.

b. Use the Graphical Linear Programming and Sensitivity Analysis module in your Interactive Management Science Modules to solve the model. Then use this module to check if the optimal solution would change if the unit profit for grandfather clocks were changed from $300 to $375 (with no other changes in the model). Then check if the optimal solution would change if, in addition to this change in the unit profit for grandfather clocks, the estimated unit profit for wall clocks also changed from $200 to $175.

E*　c. Formulate and solve the original version of this model on a spreadsheet.

E*　d. Use the Excel Solver to check the effect of the changes specified in part b.

E*　e. Use the Solver Table to systematically generate the optimal solution and total profit as the unit profit for grandfather clocks is increased in $20 increments from $150 to $450 (with no change in the unit profit for wall clocks). Then do the same as the unit profit for wall clocks is increased in $20 increments from $50 to $350 (with no change in the unit profit for grandfather clocks). Use this information to estimate the allowable range for the unit profit of each type of clock.

E*　f. Use a two-dimensional Solver Table to systematically generate the optimal solution (similar to Figure 5.13) as the unit profits for the two types of clocks are changed simultaneously as specified in part e, except use $50 increments instead of $20 increments.

E*　g. For each of the three partners in turn, use the Excel Solver to determine the effect on the optimal solution and the total profit if that partner alone were to increase his or her maximum number of work hours available per week by 5 hours.

E*   h. Use the Solver Table to systematically generate the optimal solution and the total profit when the only change is that David's maximum number of hours available to work per week changes to each of the following values: 35, 37, 39, 41, 43, 45. Then do the same when the only change is that LaDeana's maximum number of hours available to work per week changes in the same way. Then do the same when the only change is that Lydia's maximum number of hours available to work per week changes to each of the following values: 15, 17, 19, 21, 23, 25.

E*   i. Generate the Excel sensitivity report and use it to determine the allowable range for the unit profit for each type of clock and the allowable range for the maximum number of hours each partner is available to work per week.

       j. To increase the total profit, the three partners have agreed that one of them will slightly increase the maximum number of hours available to work per week. The choice of which one will be based on which one would increase the total profit the most. Use the sensitivity report to make this choice. (Assume no change in the original estimates of the unit profits.)

       k. Explain why one of the shadow prices is equal to zero.

       l. Can the shadow prices in the sensitivity report be validly used to determine the effect if Lydia were to change her maximum number of hours available to work per week from 20 to 25? If so, what would be the increase in the total profit?

       m. Repeat part *l* if, in addition to the change for Lydia, David also were to change his maximum number of hours available to work per week from 40 to 35.

       n. Use graphical analysis to verify your answer in part *m*.

E*5.8.* Reconsider Problem 5.1. After further negotiations with each vendor, management of the G.A. Tanner Company has learned that either of them would be willing to consider increasing their supply of their respective subassemblies over the previously stated maxima (3,000 subassemblies of type A per day and 1,000 of type B per day) if the company would pay a small premium over the regular price for the extra subassemblies. The size of the premium for each type of subassembly remains to be negotiated. The demand for the toy being produced is sufficiently high that 2,500 per day could be sold if the supply of subassemblies could be increased enough to support this production rate. Assume that the original estimates of unit profits given in Problem 5.1 are accurate.

       a. Formulate and solve a spreadsheet model for this problem with the original maximum supply levels and the additional constraint that no more than 2,500 toys should be produced per day.

       b. Without considering the premium, use the spreadsheet and Solver to determine the shadow price for the subassembly A constraint by solving the model again after increasing the maximum supply by one. Use this shadow price to determine the maximum premium that the company should be willing to pay for each subassembly of this type.

       c. Repeat part *b* for the subassembly B constraint.

       d. Estimate how much the maximum supply of subassemblies of type A could be increased before the shadow price (and the corresponding premium) found in part *b* would no longer be valid by using the Solver Table to generate the optimal solution and total profit (excluding the premium) as the maximum supply increases in increments of 100 from 3,000 to 4,000.

       e. Repeat part *d* for subassemblies of type B by using the Solver Table as the maximum supply increases in increments of 100 from 1,000 to 2,000.

       f. Use the Solver's sensitivity report to determine the shadow price for each of the subassembly constraints and the allowable range for the right-hand side of each of these constraints.

E*5.9. Reconsider the model given in Problem 5.2. While doing what-if analysis, you learn that the estimates of the right-hand sides of the two functional constraints are accurate only to within ± 50 percent. In other words, the ranges of *likely values* for these parameters are 5 to 15 for the first right-hand side and 6 to 18 for the second right-hand side.

       a. After solving the original spreadsheet model, determine the shadow price for the first functional constraint by increasing its right-hand side by one and solving again.

       b. Use the Solver Table to generate the optimal solution and total profit as the right-hand side of the first functional constraint is incremented by 1 from 5 to 15. Use this table to estimate the allowable range for this right-hand side, that is, the range over which the shadow price obtained in part *a* is valid.

       c. Repeat part *a* for the second functional constraint.

       d. Repeat part *b* for the second functional constraint where its right-hand side is incremented by 1 from 6 to 18.

    e. Use the Solver's sensitivity report to determine the shadow price for each functional constraint and the allowable range for the right-hand side of each of these constraints.

5.10.   Consider a resource-allocation problem having the following data:

	Resource Usage per Unit of Each Activity		
Resource	1	2	Amount of Resource Available
1	1	3	8
2	1	1	4
Unit profit	$1	$2	

The objective is to determine the number of units of each activity to undertake so as to maximize the total profit.

    a. Use the graphical method to solve this model.

    b. Use graphical analysis to determine the shadow price for each of these resources by solving again after increasing the amount of the resource available by one.

E*   *c.* Use the spreadsheet model and the Solver instead to do parts *a* and *b*.

E*   *d.* For each resource in turn, use the Solver Table to systematically generate the optimal solution and the total profit when the only change is that the amount of that resource available increases in increments of 1 from 4 less than the original value up to 6 more than the original value. Use these results to estimate the allowable range for the amount available for each resource.

E*   *e.* Use the Solver's sensitivity report to obtain the shadow prices. Also use this report to find the range for the amount of each resource available over which the corresponding shadow price remains valid.

    f. Describe why these shadow prices are useful when management has the flexibility to change the amounts of the resources being made available.

5.11.   Follow the instructions of Problem 5.10 for a resource-allocation problem that again has the objective of maximizing total profit and that has the following data:

	Resource Usage per Unit of Each Activity		
Resource	1	2	Amount of Resource Available
1	1	0	4
2	1	3	15
3	2	1	10
Unit profit	$3	$2	

E*5.12.*   Consider the Super Grain Corp. case study as presented in Section 4.1, including the spreadsheet in Figure 4.1 showing its formulation and optimal solution. Use the Excel Solver to generate the sensitivity report. Then use this report to independently address each of the following questions.

    a. How much could the total expected number of exposures be increased for each additional $1,000 added to the advertising budget?

    b. Your answer in part *a* would remain valid for how large of an increase in the advertising budget?

c. How much could the total expected number of exposures be increased for each additional $1,000 added to the planning budget?

d. Your answer in part *c* would remain valid for how large of an increase in the planning budget?

e. Would your answers in parts *a* and *c* definitely remain valid if *both* the advertising budget and planning budget were increased by $100,000 each?

f. If only $100,000 can be added to *either* the advertising budget or the planning budget, where should it be added to do the most good?

g. If $100,000 must be *removed* from either the advertising budget or the planning budget, from which budget should it be removed to do the least harm?

E*5.13. Follow the instructions of Problem 5.12 for the continuation of the Super Grain Corp. case study as presented in Section 4.5 including the spreadsheet in Figure 4.6 showing its formulation and optimal solution.

E*5.14. Consider the Union Airways problem presented in Section 4.3, including the spreadsheet in Figure 4.3 showing its formulation and optimal solution.

Management now is considering increasing the level of service provided to customers by increasing one or more of the numbers in the rightmost column of Table 4.4 for the minimum number of agents needed in the various time periods. To guide them in making this decision, they would like to know what impact this change would have on total cost.

Use the Excel Solver to generate the sensitivity report in preparation for addressing the following questions.

a. Which of the numbers in the rightmost column of Table 4.4 can be increased without increasing total cost? In each case, indicate how much it can be increased (if it is the only one being changed) without increasing total cost.

b. For each of the other numbers, how much would the total cost increase per increase of 1 in the number? For each answer, indicate how much the number can be increased (if it is the only one being changed) before the answer is no longer valid.

c. Do your answers in part *b* definitely remain valid if all the numbers considered in part *b* are simultaneously increased by 1?

d. Do your answers in part *b* definitely remain valid if all 10 numbers are simultaneously increased by 1?

e. How far can all 10 numbers be simultaneously increased by the same amount before your answers in part *b* may no longer be valid?

Case 5-1

Selling Soap

Reconsider the Profit & Gambit Co. advertising-mix problem presented in Section 2.7. Recall that a major advertising campaign is being planned that will focus on three key products: a stain remover, a liquid detergent, and a powder detergent. Management has made the following policy decisions about what needs to be achieved by this campaign.

• Sales of the stain remover should increase by at least 3 percent.

• Sales of the liquid detergent should increase by at least 18 percent.

• Sales of the powder detergent should increase by at least 4 percent.

The spreadsheet in Figure 2.21 shows the linear programming model that was formulated for this problem. The minimum required increases in the sales of the three products are given in the data cells MinimumIncrease (G8:G10). The changing cells AdvertisingUnits (C14:D14) indicate that an optimal solution for the model is to undertake four units of advertising on television and three units of advertising in the print media. The target cell TotalCost (G14) shows that the total cost for this advertising campaign would be $10 million.

After receiving this information, Profit & Gambit management now wants to analyze the trade-off between the total advertising cost and the resulting benefits achieved by increasing the sales of the three products. Therefore, a management science team (you) has been given the assignment of developing the information that management will need to analyze this trade-off and decide whether it should change any of its policy decisions regarding the required minimum increases in the sales of the three products. In particular, management needs some detailed information about how the total advertising cost would change if it were to change any or all of these policy decisions.

a. For each of the three products in turn, use graphical analysis to determine how much the total advertising cost would change if the required minimum increase in the sales of that product were to be increased by 1 percent (without changing the required minimum increases for the other two products).

b. Use the spreadsheet shown in Figure 2.21 (available on the CD-ROM) to obtain the information requested in part *a*.

c. For each of the three products in turn, use the Solver Table (available on the CD-ROM) to determine how the optimal solution for the model and the resulting total advertising cost would change if the required minimum increase in the sales of that product were to be systematically varied over a range of values (without changing the required minimum increases for the other two products). In each case, start the range of values at 0 percent and increase by 1 percent increments up to double the original minimum required increase.

d. Use the Solver to generate the sensitivity report and indicate how the report is able to provide the information requested in part *a*. Also use the report to obtain the allowable range for the required minimum increase in the sales of each product. Interpret how each of these allowable ranges relates to the results obtained in part *c*.

e. Suppose that all the original numbers in MinimumIncrease (G8:G10) were to be increased simultaneously by the same amount. How large can this amount be before the shadow prices provided by the sensitivity report may no longer be valid?

f. Below is the beginning of a memorandum from the management science team to Profit & Gambit management that is intended to provide management with the information it needs to perform its trade-off analysis. Write the rest of this memorandum based on a summary of the results obtained in the preceding parts. Present your information in clear, simple terms that use the language of management. Avoid technical terms such as shadow prices, allowable ranges, and so forth.

MEMORANDUM

To: Profit & Gambit management
From: The Management Science Team
Subject: The trade-off between advertising expenditures and increased sales

As instructed, we have been continuing our analysis of the plans for the major new advertising campaign that will focus on our spray prewash stain remover, our liquid formulation laundry detergent, and our powder laundry detergent.

Our recent report presented our preliminary conclusions on how much advertising to do in the different media to meet the sales goals at a minimum total cost:

Allocate $4 million to advertising on television.

Allocate $6 million to advertising in the print media.

Total advertising cost: $10 million.

We estimate that the resulting increases in sales will be

Stain remover: 3 percent increase in sales

Liquid detergent: 18 percent increase in sales

Powder detergent: 8 percent increase in sales.

(concluded)

You had specified that these increases should be at least 3 percent, 18 percent, and 4 percent, respectively, so we have met the minimum levels for the first two products and substantially exceeded it for the third.

However, you also indicated that your decisions on these minimum required increases in sales (3 percent, 18 percent, and 4 percent) had been tentative ones. Now that we have more specific information on what the advertising costs and the resulting increases in sales will be, you plan to reevaluate these decisions to see if small changes might improve the trade-off between advertising cost and increased sales.

To assist you in reevaluating your decisions, we now have analyzed this trade-off for each of the three products. Our best estimates are the following.

Case 5-2

Controlling Air Pollution

As introduced in Section 4.3, the Nori & Leets Co. is one of the major producers of steel in its part of the world. It is located in the city of Steeltown and is the only large employer there. Steeltown has grown and prospered along with the company, which now employs nearly 50,000 residents. Therefore, the attitude of the townspeople always has been, "What's good for Nori & Leets is good for the town." However, this attitude is now changing; uncontrolled air pollution from the company's furnaces is ruining the appearance of the city and endangering the health of its residents.

A recent stockholders' revolt resulted in the election of a new enlightened board of directors for the company. These directors are determined to follow socially responsible policies, and they have been discussing with Steeltown city officials and citizens' groups what to do about the air pollution problem. Together they have worked out stringent air quality standards for the Steeltown airshed.

The three main types of pollutants in this airshed are particulate matter, sulfur oxides, and hydrocarbons. The new standards require that the company reduce its annual emission of these pollutants by the amounts shown in the following table.

Pollutant	Required Reduction in Annual Emission Rate (million pounds)
Particulates	60
Sulfur oxides	150
Hydrocarbons	125

The board of directors has instructed management to have the engineering staff determine how to achieve these reductions in the most economical way.

The steelworks have two primary sources of pollution, namely, the blast furnaces for making pig iron and the open-hearth furnaces for changing iron into steel. In both cases, the engineers have decided that the most effective abatement methods are (1) increasing the height of the smokestacks,[1] (2) using filter devices (including gas traps) in the smokestacks, and (3) including cleaner, high-grade materials among the fuels for the furnaces. Each of these methods has a technological limit on how heavily it can be used (e.g., a maximum feasible increase in the height of the smokestacks), but there also is considerable flexibility for using the method at a fraction of its technological limit.

The next table shows how much emissions (in millions of pounds per year) can be eliminated from each type of furnace by fully using any abatement method to its technological limit.

---

[1]Subsequent to this study, this particular abatement method has become a controversial one. Because its effect is to reduce ground-level pollution by spreading emissions over a greater distance, environmental groups contend that this creates more acid rain by keeping sulfur oxides in the air longer. Consequently, the U.S. Environmental Protection Agency adopted new rules to remove incentives for using tall smokestacks.

Reduction in Emission Rate from the Maximum Feasible Use of an Abatement Method

Pollutant	Taller Smokestacks		Filters		Better Fuels	
	Blast Furnaces	Open-Hearth Furnaces	Blast Furnaces	Open-Hearth Furnaces	Blast Furnaces	Open-Hearth Furnaces
Particulates	12	9	25	20	17	13
Sulfur oxides	35	42	18	31	56	49
Hydrocarbons	37	53	28	24	29	20

For purposes of analysis, it is assumed that each method also can be less fully used to achieve any fraction of the abatement capacities shown in this table. Furthermore, the fractions can be different for blast furnaces and open-hearth furnaces. For either type of furnace, the emission reduction achieved by each method is not substantially affected by whether or not the other methods also are used.

After these data were developed, it became clear that no single method by itself could achieve all the required reductions. On the other hand, combining all three methods at full capacity on both types of furnaces (which would be prohibitively expensive if the company's products are to remain competitively priced) is much more than adequate. Therefore, the engineers concluded that they would have to use some combination of the methods, perhaps with fractional capacities, based on their relative costs. Furthermore, because of the differences between the blast and the open-hearth furnaces, the two types probably should not use the same combination.

An analysis was conducted to estimate the total annual cost that would be incurred by each abatement method. A method's annual cost includes increased operating and maintenance expenses, as well as reduced revenue due to any loss in the efficiency of the production process caused by using the method. The other major cost is the start-up cost (the initial capital outlay) required to install the method. To make this one-time cost commensurable with the ongoing annual costs, the time value of money was used to calculate the annual expenditure that would be equivalent in value to this start-up cost.

This analysis led to the total annual cost estimates given in the following table for using the methods at their full abatement capacities.

Total Annual Cost from the Maximum Feasible Use of an Abatement Method

Abatement Method	Blast Furnaces	Open-Hearth Furnaces
Taller smokestacks	$8 million	$10 million
Filters	7 million	6 million
Better fuels	11 million	9 million

It also was determined that the cost of a method being used at a lower level is roughly proportional to the fraction of the abatement capacity (given in the preceding table) that is achieved. Thus, for any given fraction achieved, the total annual cost would be roughly that fraction of the corresponding quantity in the cost table.

The stage now is set to develop the general framework of the company's plan for pollution abatement. This plan needs to specify which types of abatement methods will be used and at what fractions of their abatement capacities for (1) the blast furnaces and (2) the open-hearth furnaces.

You have been asked to head a management science team to analyze this problem. Management wants you to begin by determining which plan would minimize the total annual cost of achieving the required reductions in annual emission rates for the three pollutants.

a. Identify verbally the components of a linear programming model for this problem.

b. Display the model on a spreadsheet.

c. Obtain an optimal solution and generate the sensitivity report.

Management now wants to conduct some what-if analysis with your help. Since the company does not have much prior experience with the pollution abatement methods under consideration, the cost estimates given in the third table are fairly rough, and each one could easily be off by as much as 10 percent in either direction. There also is some uncertainty about the values given in the second table, but less so than for the third table. By contrast, the values in the first table are policy standards and so are prescribed constants.

However, there still is considerable debate about where to set these policy standards on the required reductions in the emission rates of the various pollutants. The numbers in the first table actually are preliminary values tentatively agreed upon before learning what the total cost would be to meet these standards. Both the city and company officials agree that the final decision on these policy standards should be based on the *trade-off* between costs and benefits. With this in mind, the city has concluded that each 10 percent increase in the policy standards over the current values (all the numbers in the first table) would be worth $3.5 million to the city. Therefore, the city has agreed to reduce the company's tax payments to the city by $3.5 million for *each* 10 percent increase in the policy standards (up to 50 percent) that is accepted by the company.

Finally, there has been some debate about the *relative* values of the policy standards for the three pollutants. As indicated in the first table, the required reduction for particulates now is less than half of that for either sulfur oxides or hydrocarbons. Some have argued for decreasing this disparity. Others contend that an even greater disparity is justified because sulfur oxides and hydrocarbons cause considerably more damage than particulates. Agreement has been reached that this issue will be reexamined after information is obtained about which trade-offs in policy standards (increasing one while decreasing another) are available without increasing the total cost.

d. Identify the parameters of the linear programming model that should be classified as *sensitive parameters*. Make a resulting recommendation about which parameters should be estimated more closely, if possible.

e. Analyze the effect of an inaccuracy in estimating each cost parameter given in the third table. If the true value were 10 percent *less* than the estimated value, would this change the optimal solution? Would it change if the true value were 10 percent *more* than the estimated value? Make a resulting recommendation about where to focus further work in estimating the cost parameters more closely.

f. For each pollutant, specify the rate at which the total cost of an optimal solution would change with any small change in the required reduction in the annual emission rate of the pollutant. Also specify how much this required reduction can be changed (up or down) without affecting the rate of change in the total cost.

g. For each unit change in the policy standard for particulates given in the first table, determine the change in the opposite direction for sulfur oxides that would keep the total cost of an optimal solution unchanged. Repeat this for hydrocarbons instead of sulfur oxides. Then do it for a simultaneous and equal change for both sulfur oxides and hydrocarbons in the opposite direction from particulates.

h. Letting θ denote the percentage increase in all the policy standards given in the first table, use the Solver Table to systematically find an optimal solution and the total cost for the revised linear programming problem for each $\theta = 10, 20, 30, 40, 50$. Considering the tax incentive offered by the city, use these results to determine which value of θ (including the option of $\theta = 0$) should be chosen by the company to minimize its total cost of both pollution abatement and taxes.

i. For the value of θ chosen in part *h,* generate the sensitivity report and repeat parts *f* and *g* so that the decision makers can make a final decision on the *relative* values of the policy standards for the three pollutants.

Case 5-3

Farm Management

The Ploughman family owns and operates a 640-acre farm that has been in the family for several generations. The Ploughmans always have had to work hard to make a decent living from the farm and have had to endure some occasional difficult years. Stories about earlier generations overcoming hardships due to droughts, floods, and so forth, are an important part of the family history. However, the Ploughmans enjoy their self-reliant lifestyle and gain considerable satisfaction from continuing the family tradition of successfully living off the land during an era when many family farms are being abandoned or taken over by large agricultural corporations.

John Ploughman is the current manager of the farm, while his wife Eunice runs the house and manages the farm's finances. John's father, Grandpa Ploughman, lives with them and still puts in many hours working on the farm. John and Eunice's older children, Frank, Phyllis, and Carl, also are given heavy chores before and after school.

The entire family can produce a total of 4,000 person-hours' worth of labor during the winter and spring months and 4,500 person-hours during the summer and fall. If any of these person-hours are not needed, Frank, Phyllis, and Carl will use them to work on a neighboring farm for $5/hour during the winter and spring months and $5.50/hour during the summer and fall.

The farm supports two types of livestock, dairy cows and laying hens, as well as three crops: soybeans, corn, and wheat. (All three are cash crops, but the corn also is a feed crop for the cows and the wheat also is used for chicken feed.) The crops are harvested during the late summer and fall. During the winter months, John, Eunice, and Grandpa make a decision about the mix of livestock and crops for the coming year.

Currently, the family has just completed a particularly successful harvest that has provided an investment fund of $20,000 that can be used to purchase more livestock. (Other money is available for ongoing expenses, including the next planting of crops.) The family currently has 30 cows valued at $35,000 and 2,000 hens valued at $5,000. They wish to keep all this livestock and perhaps purchase more. Each new cow would cost $1,500, and each new hen would cost $3.

Over a year's time, the value of a herd of cows will decrease by about 10 percent and the value of a flock of hens will decrease by about 25 percent due to aging.

Each cow will require two acres of land for grazing and 10 person-hours of work per month, while producing a net annual cash income of $850 for the family. The corresponding figures for each hen are no significant acreage, 0.05 person-hours per month, and an annual net cash income of $4.25. The chicken house can accommodate a maximum of 5,000 hens, and the size of the barn limits the herd to a maximum of 42 cows.

For each acre planted in each of the three crops, the following table gives the number of person-hours of work that will be required during the first and second halves of the year, as well as a rough estimate of the crop's net value (in either income or savings in purchasing feed for the livestock).

Data per Acre Planted

	Soybeans	Corn	Wheat
Winter and spring, person-hours	1.0	0.9	0.6
Summer and fall, person-hours	1.4	1.2	0.7
Net value	$70	$60	$40

To provide much of the feed for the livestock, John wants to plant at least one acre of corn for each cow in the coming year's herd and at least 0.05 acre of wheat for each hen in the coming year's flock.

John, Eunice, and Grandpa now are discussing how much acreage should be planted in each of the crops and how many cows and hens to have for the coming year. Their objective is to maximize the family's monetary worth at the end of the coming year (the *sum* of the net income from the livestock for the coming year *plus* the net value of the crops for the coming year *plus* what remains from the investment fund *plus* the value of the livestock at the end of the coming year *plus* income from working on a neighboring farm *minus* living expenses of $40,000 for the year).

a. Identify verbally the components of a linear programming model for this problem.

b. Display the model on a spreadsheet.

c. Obtain an optimal solution and generate the sensitivity report. What does the model predict regarding the family's monetary worth at the end of the coming year?

d. Find the allowable range for the net value per acre planted for each of the three crops.

The above estimates of the net value per acre planted in each of the three crops assumes good weather conditions. Adverse weather conditions would harm the crops and greatly reduce the resulting value. The scenarios particularly feared by the family are a drought, a flood, an early frost, *both* a drought and an early frost, and *both* a flood and an early frost. The estimated net values for the year under these scenarios are shown next.

	Net Value per Acre Planted		
Scenario	**Soybeans**	**Corn**	**Wheat**
Drought	−$10	−$15	0
Flood	15	20	$10
Early frost	50	40	30
Drought and early frost	−15	−20	−10
Flood and early frost	10	10	5

e. Find an optimal solution under each scenario after making the necessary adjustments to the linear programming model formulated in part *b*. In each case, what is the prediction regarding the family's monetary worth at the end of the year?

f. For the optimal solution obtained under each of the six scenarios (including the good weather scenario considered in parts *a–d*), calculate what the family's monetary worth would be at the end of the year if each of the other five scenarios occurs instead. In your judgment, which solution provides the best balance between yielding a large monetary worth under good weather conditions and avoiding an overly small monetary worth under adverse weather conditions?

Grandpa has researched what the weather conditions were in past years as far back as weather records have been kept and obtained the following data.

Scenario	**Frequency**
Good weather	40%
Drought	20
Flood	10
Early frost	15
Drought and early frost	10
Flood and early frost	5

With these data, the family has decided to use the following approach to making its planting and livestock decisions. Rather than the optimistic approach of assuming that good weather conditions will prevail (as done in parts *a–d*), the *average* net value under all weather conditions will be used for each crop (weighting the net values under the various scenarios by the frequencies in the above table).

g. Modify the linear programming model formulated in part *b* to fit this new approach.

h. Repeat part *c* for this modified model.

i. Use a shadow price obtained in part *h* to analyze whether it would be worthwhile for the family to obtain a bank loan with a 10 percent interest rate to purchase more livestock now beyond what can be obtained with the $20,000 from the investment fund.

j. For each of the three crops, use the sensitivity report obtained in part *h* to identify how much latitude for error is available in estimating the net value per acre planted for that crop without changing the optimal solution. Which two net values need to be estimated most carefully? If both estimates are incorrect simultaneously, how close do the estimates need to be to guarantee that the optimal solution will not change? Use a two-dimensional Solver Table to systematically generate the optimal monetary worth as these two net values are varied simultaneously over ranges that go up to twice as far from the estimates as needed to guarantee that the optimal solution will not change.

This problem illustrates a kind of situation that is frequently faced by various kinds of organizations. To describe the situation in general terms, an organization faces an uncertain future where any one of a number of scenarios may unfold. Which one will occur depends on conditions that are outside the control of the organization. The organization needs to choose the levels of various activities, but the unit contribution of each activity to the overall measure of performance is greatly affected by which scenario unfolds. Under these circumstances, what is the best mix of activities?

k. Think about specific situations outside of farm management that fit this description. Describe one.

Case 5-4

Assigning Students to Schools (Revisited)

Reconsider Case 4.3. The Springfield School Board still has the policy of providing busing for all middle school students who must travel more than approximately a mile. Another current policy is to allow splitting residential areas among multiple schools if this will reduce the total busing cost. (This latter policy will be reversed in Case 9.4.) However, before adopting a busing plan based on part *a* of Case 4.3, the school board now wants to conduct some what-if analysis.

a. If you have not already done so for part *a* of Case 4.3, formulate and solve a linear programming model for this problem on a spreadsheet.

b. Use the Solver to generate the sensitivity report.

One concern of the school board is the ongoing road construction in area 6. These construction projects have been delaying traffic considerably and are likely to affect the cost of busing students from area 6, perhaps increasing costs as much as 10 percent.

c. Use the sensitivity report to check how much the busing cost from area 6 to school 1 can increase (assuming no change in the costs for the other schools) before the current optimal solution would no longer be optimal. If the allowable increase is less than 10 percent, use the Solver to find the new optimal solution with a 10 percent increase.

d. Repeat part *c* for school 2 (assuming no change in the costs for the other schools).

e. Now assume that the busing cost from area 6 would increase by the same percentage for all the schools. Use the sensitivity report to determine how large this percentage can be before the current optimal solution might no longer be optimal. If the allowable increase is less than 10 percent, use the Solver to find the new optimal solution with a 10 percent increase.

The school board has the option of adding portable classrooms to increase the capacity of one or more of the middle schools for a few years. However, this is a costly move that the board would only consider if it would significantly decrease busing costs. Each portable classroom holds 20 students and has a leasing cost of $2,500 per year. To analyze this option, the school board decides to assume that the road construction in area 6 will wind down without significantly increasing the busing costs from that area.

f. For each school, use the corresponding shadow price from the sensitivity report to determine whether it would be worthwhile to add any portable classrooms.

g. For each school where it is worthwhile to add any portable classrooms, use the sensitivity report to determine how many could be added before the shadow price would no longer be valid (assuming this is the only school receiving portable classrooms).

h. If it would be worthwhile to add portable classrooms to more than one school, use the sensitivity report to determine the combinations of the number to add for which the shadow prices definitely would still be valid. Then use the shadow prices to determine which of these combinations is best in terms of minimizing the total cost of busing students and leasing portable classrooms. Use the Solver for finding the corresponding optimal solution for assigning students to schools.

i. If part *h* was applicable, modify the best combination of portable classrooms found there by adding one more to the school with the most favorable shadow price. Use the Solver to find the corresponding optimal solution for assigning students to schools and to generate the corresponding sensitivity report. Use this information to assess whether the plan developed in part *h* is the best one available for minimizing the total cost of busing students and leasing portables. If not, find the best plan.

Learning objectives

After completing this chapter, you should be able to

1. Describe the characteristics of transportation problems.

2. Formulate a spreadsheet model for a transportation problem from a description of the problem.

3. Do the same for some variants of transportation problems.

4. Give the name of two algorithms that can solve huge transportation problems that are well beyond the scope of the Excel Solver.

5. Identify several areas of application of transportation problems and their variants.

6. Describe the characteristics of assignment problems.

7. Identify the relationship between assignment problems and transportation problems.

8. Formulate a spreadsheet model for an assignment problem from a description of the problem.

9. Do the same for some variants of assignment problems.

10. Give the name of an algorithm that can solve huge assignment problems that are well beyond the scope of the Excel Solver.

Chapter **Six**

Transportation and Assignment Problems

You have seen in the preceding chapters just how useful linear programming can be to an enlightened manager in dealing with a wide variety of problems. You will continue to broaden your horizons in this chapter about the breadth of applicability of linear programming. The focus will be on two related special types of linear programming problems that are so important that they have been given their own names, namely, *transportation problems* and *assignment problems*. Both fall into the third category of linear programming problems introduced in Chapter 4—distribution-network problems.

Transportation problems received this name because many of their applications involve determining how to transport goods optimally. However, you will see that some of their important applications have nothing to do with transportation.

Assignment problems are best known for applications involving assigning people to tasks. However, they have a variety of other applications as well.

Following a case study, the initial sections of this chapter describe the characteristics of transportation problems and their variants, illustrate the formulation of spreadsheet models for such problems, and survey a variety of applications. The subsequent sections then do the same for assignment problems.

6.1 A CASE STUDY: THE P & T COMPANY DISTRIBUTION PROBLEM

Douglas Whitson is concerned. Costs have been escalating and revenues have not been keeping pace. If this trend continues, shareholders are going to be very unhappy with the next earnings report. As CEO of the P & T Company, he knows that the buck stops with him. He's got to find a way to bring costs under control.

Douglas suddenly picks up the telephone and places a call to his distribution manager, Richard Powers.

Douglas (CEO): Richard. Douglas Whitson here.

Richard (distribution manager): Hello, Douglas.

Douglas: Say, Richard. I've just been looking over some cost data and one number jumped out at me.

Richard: Oh? What's that?

Douglas: The shipping costs for our peas. $178,000 last season! I remember it running under $100,000 just a few years ago. What's going on here?

Richard: Yes, you're right. Those costs have really been going up. One factor is that our shipping volume is up a little. However, the main thing is that the fees charged by the truckers we've been using have really shot up. We complained. They said something about their new contract with the union representing their drivers pushed their costs up substantially. And their insurance costs are up.

Douglas: Have you looked into changing truckers?

Richard: Yes. In fact, we've already selected new truckers for the upcoming growing season.

Douglas: Good. So your shipping costs should come down quite a bit next season?

Richard: Well, my projection is that they should run about $165,000.

Douglas: Ouch. That's still too high.

Richard: That seems to be the best we can do.

Douglas: Well, let's approach this from another angle. You're shipping the peas from our three canneries to all four of our warehouses?

Richard: That's right.

Douglas: How do you decide how much each cannery will ship to each warehouse?

Richard: We have a standard strategy that we've been using for many years.

Douglas: Does this strategy minimize your total shipping cost?

Richard: I think it does a pretty good job of that.

There is a technique for generating a shipping plan that minimizes the total shipping cost.

Douglas: But does it use an algorithm to generate a shipping plan that is guaranteed to minimize the total shipping cost?

Richard: No, I can't say it does that. Is there a way of doing that?

Douglas: Yes. I understand there is a management science technique for doing that. This is something I learned when I interviewed that new MBA graduate we hired last month, Kim Baker. Kim thought this technique could be directly applicable to our company. We hired Kim to help us incorporate some of the best techniques being taught in business schools these days. I think we should have Kim look at your shipping plan and see if she can improve upon it.

Richard: Sounds reasonable.

Douglas: OK, good. I would like you to coordinate with Kim and report back to me soon.

Richard: Will do.

The conversation ends quickly.

Background

The P & T Company is a small family-owned business. It receives raw vegetables, processes and cans them at its canneries, and then distributes the canned goods for eventual sale.

One of the company's main products is canned peas. The peas are prepared at three canneries (near Bellingham, Washington; Eugene, Oregon; and Albert Lea, Minnesota) and then shipped by truck to four distributing warehouses in the western United States (Sacramento, California; Salt Lake City, Utah; Rapid City, South Dakota; and Albuquerque, New Mexico), as shown in Figure 6.1.

The Company's Current Approach

For many years, the company has used the following strategy for determining how much output should be shipped from each of the canneries to meet the needs of each of the warehouses.

Current Shipping Strategy

1. Since the cannery in Bellingham is furthest from the warehouses, ship its output to its nearest warehouse, namely, the one in Sacramento, with any surplus going to the warehouse in Salt Lake City.

2. Since the warehouse in Albuquerque is furthest from the canneries, have its nearest cannery (the one in Albert Lea) ship its output to Albuquerque, with any surplus going to the warehouse in Rapid City.

3. Use the cannery in Eugene to supply the remaining needs of the warehouses.

For the upcoming harvest season, an estimate has been made of the output from each cannery, and each warehouse has been allocated a certain amount from the total supply of peas. This information is given in Table 6.1.

Applying the current shipping strategy to the data in Table 6.1 gives the shipping plan shown in Table 6.2. The shipping costs per truckload for the upcoming season are shown in Table 6.3.

FIGURE 6.1

Location of the canneries and warehouses for the P & T Co. problem.

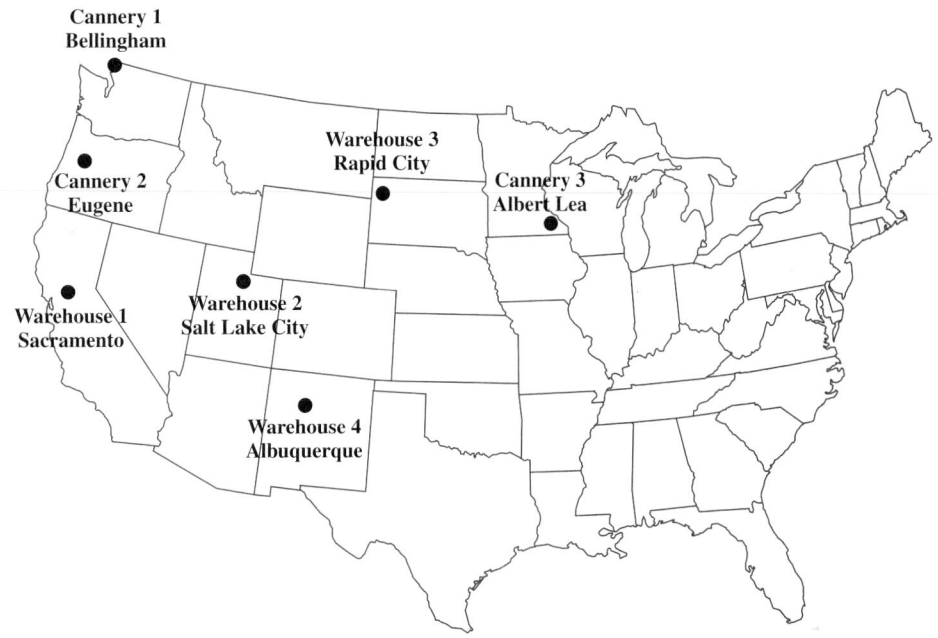

TABLE 6.1
Shipping Data for the P & T Co.

Cannery	Output		Warehouse	Allocation
Bellingham	75 truckloads		Sacramento	80 truckloads
Eugene	125 truckloads		Salt Lake City	65 truckloads
Albert Lea	100 truckloads		Rapid City	70 truckloads
			Albuquerque	85 truckloads
Total	300 truckloads			
			Total	300 truckloads

TABLE 6.2
Current Shipping Plan for the P & T Co.

	Warehouse			
To From	Sacramento	Salt Lake City	Rapid City	Albuquerque
Cannery				
Bellingham	75	0	0	0
Eugene	5	65	55	0
Albert Lea	0	0	15	85

TABLE 6.3

Shipping Costs per Truckload for the P & T Co.

	Warehouse			
To From **Cannery**	**Sacramento**	**Salt Lake City**	**Rapid City**	**Albuquerque**
Bellingham	$464	$513	$654	$867
Eugene	352	416	690	791
Albert Lea	995	682	388	685

Combining the data in Tables 6.2 and 6.3 yields the total shipping cost under the current plan for the upcoming season:

$$\text{Total shipping cost} = 75(\$464) + 5(\$352) + 65(\$416) + 55(\$690) + 15(\$388) + 85(\$685)$$
$$= \$165,595$$

Kim Baker now is reexamining the current shipping strategy to see if she can develop a new shipping plan that would reduce the total shipping cost to an absolute minimum.

The Management Science Approach

Kim immediately recognizes that this problem is just a classic example of a *transportation problem.* Formulating the problem in this way is straightforward. Furthermore, software is readily available for quickly finding an optimal solution on a desktop computer. This enables Kim to return to management the next day with a new shipping plan that would reduce the total shipping cost by over $13,000.

This story will unfold in the next section after we provide more background about transportation problems.

Review
Questions

1. What is the specific concern being raised by the CEO of the P & T Co. in this case study?
2. What is Kim Baker being asked to do?

6.2   CHARACTERISTICS OF TRANSPORTATION PROBLEMS

The Model for Transportation Problems

To describe the model for transportation problems, we need to use terms that are considerably less specific than for the P & T Co. problem. Transportation problems in general are concerned (literally or figuratively) with distributing *any* commodity from *any* group of supply centers, called **sources,** to *any* group of receiving centers, called **destinations,** in such a way as to minimize the total distribution cost. The correspondence in terminology between the specific application to the P & T Co. problem and the general model for any transportation problem is summarized in Table 6.4.

As indicated by the fourth and fifth rows of the table, each source has a certain **supply** of units to distribute to the destinations, and each destination has a certain **demand** for units to

TABLE 6.4

Terminology for a Transportation Problem

P & T Co. Problem	General Model
Truckloads of canned peas	Units of a commodity
Canneries	Sources
Warehouses	Destinations
Output from a cannery	Supply from a source
Allocation to a warehouse	Demand at a destination
Shipping cost per truckload from a cannery to a warehouse	Cost per unit distributed from a source to a destination

A transportation problem is concerned with sending supplies from sources to meet the demands at destinations.

be received from the sources. The model for a transportation problem makes the following assumption about these supplies and demands.

The Requirements Assumption: Each source has a fixed *supply* of units, where this entire supply must be distributed to the destinations. Similarly, each destination has a fixed *demand* for units, where this entire demand must be received from the sources.

This assumption that there is no leeway in the amounts to be sent or received means that there needs to be a balance between the total supply from all sources and the total demand at all destinations.

The Feasible Solutions Property: A transportation problem will have feasible solutions if and only if the *sum* of its supplies *equals* the *sum* of its demands.

Fortunately, these sums are equal for the P & T Co. since Table 6.1 indicates that the supplies (outputs) sum to 300 truckloads and so do the demands (allocations).

In some real problems, the supplies actually represent *maximum* amounts (rather than fixed amounts) to be distributed. Similarly, in other cases, the demands represent maximum amounts (rather than fixed amounts) to be received. Such problems do not fit the model for a transportation problem because they violate the *requirements assumption,* so they are *variants* of a transportation problem. Fortunately, it is relatively straightforward to formulate a spreadsheet model for such variants that the Excel Solver can still solve, as will be illustrated in Section 6.3.

The next section will describe how some problems that violate the requirements assumption can still be formulated and solved.

The last row of Table 6.4 refers to a cost per unit distributed. This reference to a *unit cost* implies the following basic assumption for any transportation problem.

The Cost Assumption: The cost of distributing units from any particular source to any particular destination is *directly proportional* to the number of units distributed. Therefore, this cost is just the *unit cost* of distribution *times* the *number of units distributed.*

The supplies, demands, and unit costs provide all the data for a transportation problem.

The only data needed for a transportation problem model are the supplies, demands, and unit costs. These are the *parameters of the model.* All these parameters for the P & T Co. problem are shown in Table 6.5. This table (including the description implied by its column and row headings) summarizes the model for the problem.

The Model: Any problem (whether involving transportation or not) fits the model for a transportation problem if it (1) can be described completely in terms of a table like Table 6.5 that identifies all the sources, destinations, supplies, demands, and unit costs, and (2) satisfies both the *requirements assumption* and the *cost assumption.* The objective is to minimize the total cost of distributing the units.

Therefore, formulating a problem as a transportation problem only requires filling out a table in the format of Table 6.5. It is not necessary to write out a formal mathematical model (even though we will do this for demonstration purposes later).

The Big M Company distribution-network problem presented in Section 4.4 is another example of a transportation problem. In this example, the company's two factories need to ship

TABLE 6.5 **The Data for the P & T Co. Problem Formulated as a Transportation Problem**

Destination (Warehouse):	Unit Cost				
	Sacramento	Salt Lake City	Rapid City	Albuquerque	Supply
Source (Cannery)					
Bellingham	$464	$513	$654	$867	75
Eugene	352	416	690	791	125
Albert Lea	995	682	388	685	100
Demand	80	65	70	85	

turret lathes to three customers and the objective is to determine how to do this so as to minimize the total shipping cost. Table 4.5 presents the data for this problem in the same format as Table 6.5, where the factories are the sources, their outputs are the supplies, the customers are the destinations, and their order sizes are the demands.

Using Excel to Formulate and Solve Transportation Problems

Section 4.4 describes the formulation of the spreadsheet model for the Big M Company problem. We now will do the same for the P & T Co. problem.

The decisions to be made are the number of truckloads of peas to ship from each cannery to each warehouse. The constraints on these decisions are that the total amount shipped from each cannery must equal its output (the supply) and the total amount received at each warehouse must equal its allocation (the demand). The overall measure of performance is the total shipping cost, so the objective is to minimize this quantity.

This information leads to the spreadsheet model shown in Figure 6.2. All the data provided in Table 6.5 are displayed in the following data cells: UnitCost (D5:G7), Supply (J12:J14), and

FIGURE 6.2 A spreadsheet formulation of the P & T Co. problem as a transportation problem, including the target cell TotalCost (J17) and the other output cells TotalShipped (H12:H14) and TotalReceived (D15:G15), as well as the specifications needed to set up the model. The changing cells ShipmentQuantity (D12:G14) show the optimal shipping plan obtained by the Solver.

	A	B	C	D	E	F	G	H	I	J
1		**P & T Co. Distribution Problem**								
2										
3		**Unit Cost**			Destination (Warehouse)					
4				Sacramento	Salt Lake City	Rapid City	Albuquerque			
5		Source	Bellingham	$464	$513	$654	$867			
6		(Cannery)	Eugene	$352	$416	$690	$791			
7			Albert Lea	$995	$682	$388	$685			
8										
9										
10		**Shipment Quantity**			Destination (Warehouse)					
11		**(Truckloads)**		Sacramento	Salt Lake City	Rapid City	Albuquerque	Total Shipped		Supply
12		Source	Bellingham	0	20	0	55	75	=	75
13		(Cannery)	Eugene	80	45	0	0	125	=	125
14			Albert Lea	0	0	70	30	100	=	100
15			Total Received	80	65	70	85			
16				=	=	=	=			Total Cost
17			Demand	80	65	70	85			$152,535

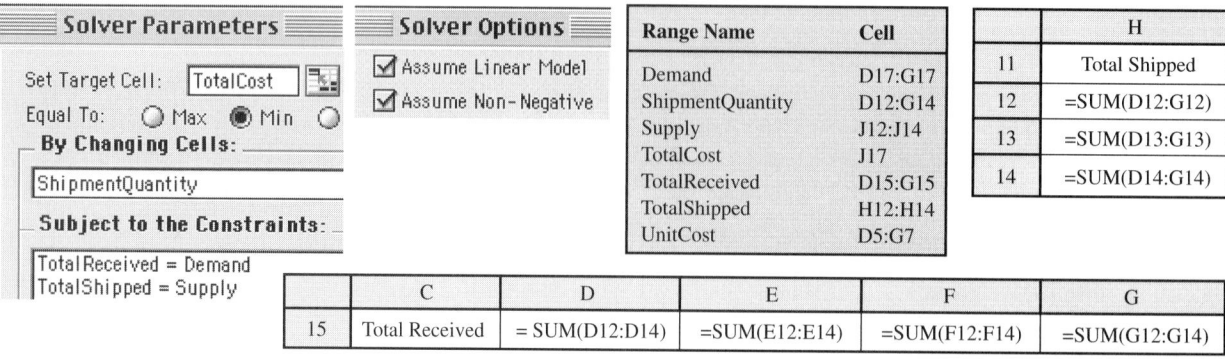

Solver Parameters

Set Target Cell: TotalCost
Equal To: ○ Max ● Min ○
By Changing Cells:
ShipmentQuantity
Subject to the Constraints:
TotalReceived = Demand
TotalShipped = Supply

Solver Options
☑ Assume Linear Model
☑ Assume Non-Negative

Range Name	Cell
Demand	D17:G17
ShipmentQuantity	D12:G14
Supply	J12:J14
TotalCost	J17
TotalReceived	D15:G15
TotalShipped	H12:H14
UnitCost	D5:G7

	H
11	Total Shipped
12	=SUM(D12:G12)
13	=SUM(D13:G13)
14	=SUM(D14:G14)

	C	D	E	F	G
15	Total Received	= SUM(D12:D14)	=SUM(E12:E14)	=SUM(F12:F14)	=SUM(G12:G14)

	J
16	Total Cost
17	=SUMPRODUCT(UnitCost,ShipmentQuantity)

This spreadsheet model of a transportation problem uses two separate tables to display the unit cost data and the changing cells (the shipment quantities), with the same row and column labels for both tables. The constraints are specified next to the changing cells.

Demand (D17:G17). The decisions on shipping quantities are given by the changing cells, ShippingQuantity (D12:G14). The output cells are TotalShipped (H12:H14) and Total Received (D15:G15), where the SUM functions entered into these cells are shown near the bottom of Figure 6.2. The constraints, TotalShipped (H12:H14) = Supply (J12:J14) and Total Received (D15:G15) = Demand (D17:G17), have been specified on the spreadsheet and entered into the Solver dialogue box. The target cell is TotalCost (J17), where its SUMPRODUCT function is shown in the lower right-hand corner of Figure 6.2. The Solver dialogue box specifies that the objective is to minimize this target cell. One of the selected Solver options (Assume Non-Negative) specifies that all shipment quantities must be nonnegative. The other one (Assume Linear Model) indicates that this transportation problem is also a linear programming problem (as described later in this section).

To begin the process of solving the problem, any value (such as 0) can be entered in each of the changing cells. After clicking on the Solve button, the Solver will use the simplex method to solve the transportation problem and determine the best value for each of the decision variables. This optimal solution is shown in ShippingQuantity (D12:G14) in Figure 6.2, along with the resulting value $152,535 in the target cell TotalCost (J17).

The Network Representation of a Transportation Problem

A nice way to visualize a transportation problem graphically is to use its *network representation.* This representation ignores the geographical layout of the sources and destinations. Instead, it simply lines up all the sources in one column on the left (where S_1 is the symbol for Source 1, etc.) and all the destinations in one column on the right (where D_1 is the symbol for Destination 1, etc.). Figure 6.3 shows the network representation of the P & T Co. problem, where the numbering of the sources (canneries) and destinations (warehouses) is that given in Figure 6.1. The arrows show the possible routes for the truckloads of canned peas, where the number next to each arrow is the shipping cost (in dollars) per truckload for that route. Since the figure also includes the supplies and demands, it includes all the data provided by Table 6.5. Therefore, this network representation provides an alternative way of summarizing the model for a transportation problem model.

Since the Big M Company problem presented in Section 4.4 also is a transportation problem, it too has a network representation like the one in Figure 6.3, as shown in Figure 4.4.

For transportation problems larger than the P & T Co. problem, it is not very convenient to draw the entire network and display all the data. Consequently, the network representation is mainly a visualization device.

Recall that Section 4.4 described distribution-network problems as a major category of linear programming problems that involve the distribution of goods through a distribution network. The networks in both Figure 4.4 and Figure 6.3 are a simple type of distribution network

Transportation problems are a special type of network-distribution problem, which is one of the major types of linear programming problems.

FIGURE 6.3
The network representation of the P & T Co. transportation problem shows all the data in Table 6.5 graphically.

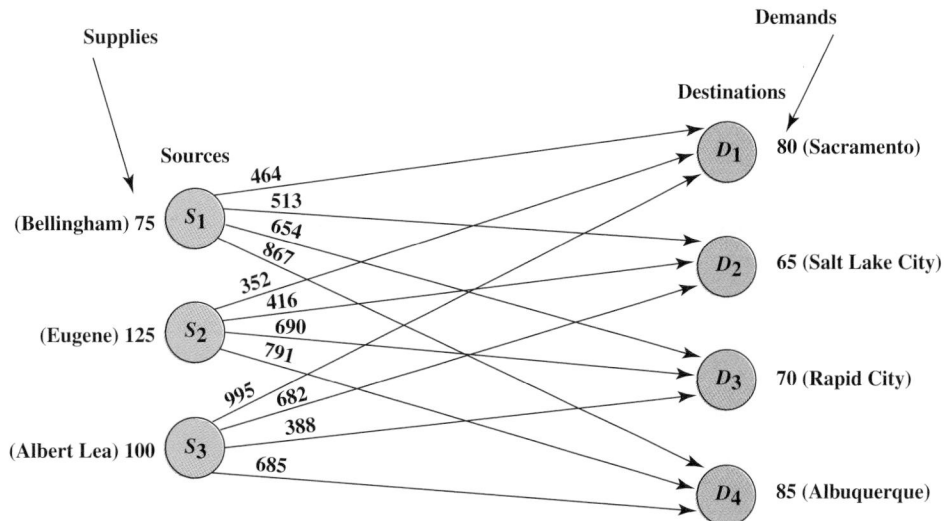

where every shipping lane goes directly from a source to a destination. Consequently, transportation problems are a special type of distribution-network problem.

In Chapter 7, you will see many more network representations of other distribution-network problems.

The Transportation Problem Is a Linear Programming Problem

To demonstrate that the P & T Co. problem (or any other transportation problem) is, in fact, a linear programming problem, let us formulate its mathematical model in algebraic form.

Using the numbering of canneries and warehouses given in Figure 6.1, let x_{ij} be the number of truckloads to be shipped from Cannery i to Warehouse j for each $i = 1, 2, 3$ and $j = 1, 2, 3, 4$. The objective is to choose the values of these 12 decision variables (the x_{ij}) so as to

Minimize $Cost = 464x_{11} + 513x_{12} + 654x_{13} + 867x_{14} + 352x_{21} + 416x_{22} + 690x_{23}$
$+ 791x_{24} + 995x_{31} + 682x_{32} + 388x_{33} + 685x_{34}$

subject to the constraints

$$
\begin{aligned}
x_{11} + x_{12} + x_{13} + x_{14} &&&&&&&= 75 \\
x_{21} + x_{22} + x_{23} + x_{24} &&&&&&&= 125 \\
x_{31} + x_{32} + x_{33} + x_{34} &&&&&&&= 100 \\
x_{11} && + x_{21} && + x_{31} &&&= 80 \\
x_{12} && + x_{22} && + x_{32} &&&= 65 \\
x_{13} && + x_{23} && + x_{33} &&&= 70 \\
x_{14} && + x_{24} && + x_{34} &&&= 85
\end{aligned}
$$

and

$$x_{ij} \geq 0 \qquad (i = 1, 2, 3; j = 1, 2, 3, 4)$$

This is indeed a linear programming problem.

The P & T Co. always ships *full* truckloads of canned peas since anything less would be uneconomical. This implies that each x_{ij} should have an *integer* value (0, 1, 2, . . .). To avoid obtaining an optimal solution for our model that has *fractional* values for any of the decision variables, we could add another set of constraints specifying that each x_{ij} must have an integer value. This would convert our linear programming problem into an *integer programming* problem, which is more difficult to solve. (We will discuss integer programming problems in Chapter 9.) Fortunately, this conversion is not necessary because of the following property of transportation problems.

This property ensures that an optimal solution normally will have integer values, so there is no need to add constraints that require this. (Because of rounding error, Excel occasionally will return a noninteger value very close to the correct integer value, but you can safely make the change to the integer value.)	**Integer Solutions Property:** As long as all its supplies and demands have integer values, any transportation problem with feasible solutions is guaranteed to have an optimal solution with integer values for all its decision variables. Therefore, it is not necessary to add constraints to the model that restrict these variables to only have integer values.

When dealing with transportation problems, practitioners typically do not bother to write out the complete linear programming model in algebraic form since all the essential information can be presented much more compactly in a table like Table 6.5 or in the corresponding spreadsheet model.

Before leaving this linear programming model though, take a good look at the left-hand side of the functional constraints. Note that every coefficient is either 0 (so the variable is deleted) or 1. Also note the distinctive pattern for the locations of the coefficients of 1, including the fact that each variable has a coefficient of 1 in exactly two constraints. These distinctive features of the coefficients play a key role in being able to solve transportation problems extremely efficiently.

Solving Transportation Problems

Because transportation problems are a special type of linear programming problem, they can be solved by the *simplex method* (the procedure used by the Excel Solver to solve linear programming problems). However, because of the very distinctive pattern of coefficients in its functional constraints noted above, it is possible to greatly *streamline* the simplex method to solve transportation problems far more quickly. This streamlined version of the simplex method is called the **transportation simplex method.** It sometimes can solve large transportation problems more than 100 times faster than the regular simplex method. However, it is only applicable to transportation problems.

Just like a transportation problem, other *distribution-network problems* also have a similar distinctive pattern of coefficients in their functional constraints. Therefore, the simplex method can be greatly streamlined in much the same way as for the transportation simplex method to solve *any* distribution-network problem (including any transportation problem) very quickly. This streamlined method is called the **network simplex method.**

Linear programming software often includes the network simplex method, and may include the transportation simplex method as well. When only the network simplex method is available, it provides an excellent alternative way of solving transportation problems. In fact, the network simplex method has become quite competitive with the transportation simplex method in recent years.

After obtaining an optimal solution, *what-if analysis* generally is done for transportation problems in much the same way as described in Chapter 5 for other linear programming problems. Either the transportation or network simplex method can readily obtain the allowable range for each coefficient in the objective function. Dealing with changes in right-hand sides (supplies and demands) is more complicated now because of the requirement that the sum of the supplies must equal the sum of the demands. Thus, each change in a supply must be accompanied by a corresponding change in a demand (or demands), and vice versa.

Because the Excel Solver is not intended to solve the really large linear programming problems that often arise in practice, it simply uses the simplex method to solve transportation problems as well as other distribution-network problems encountered in this book (and considerably larger ones as well), so we will continue to use the Solver (or Premium Solver) and thereby forgo any use of the transportation simplex method or network simplex method.

> Either the transportation simplex method or the network simplex method can be used to solve huge transportation problems that are beyond the scope of the simplex method used by the Excel Solver.

Completing the P & T Co. Case Study

We now can summarize the end of the story of how the P & T Co. was able to substantially improve on the current shipping plan shown in Table 6.2, which has a total shipping cost of $165,595.

You already have seen how Kim Baker was able to formulate this problem as a *transportation problem* simply by filling out the table shown in Table 6.5. The corresponding formulation on a spreadsheet was shown in Figure 6.2. Applying the Solver then gave the optimal solution shown in ShipmentQuantity (D12:G14).

Note that this optimal solution is not an intuitive one. Of the 75 truckloads being supplied by Bellingham, 55 of them are being sent to Albuquerque, even though this is far more expensive ($867 per truckload) than to any other warehouse. However, this sacrifice for Cannery 1 enables low-cost shipments for both Canneries 2 and 3. Although it would be difficult to find this optimal solution manually, the simplex method in the Excel Solver finds it readily.

As given in the target cell TotalCost (J17), the total shipping cost for this optimal shipping plan is

> Even though the current shipping plan intuitively seemed to be the best one available, solving the spreadsheet model reduced the total shipping cost by about 8 percent.

$$\text{Total shipping cost} = 20(\$513) + 55(\$867) + 80(\$352) + 45(\$416) + 70(\$388) \\ + 30(\$685)$$

$$= \$152,535$$

a reduction of $13,060 from the current shipping plan. Richard Powers is pleased to report this reduction to his CEO, Douglas Whitson, who congratulates him and Kim Baker for achieving this significant savings.

An Award-Winning Application of a Transportation Problem

Except for its small size, the P & T Co. problem is typical of the problems faced by many corporations that must ship goods from their manufacturing plants to their customers.

For example, consider an award-winning management science study conducted at **Procter & Gamble** (as described in the January–February 1997 issue of *Interfaces*). Prior to the study, the company's supply chain consisted of hundreds of suppliers, over 50 product categories, over 60 plants, 15 distribution centers, and over 1,000 customer zones. However, as the company moved toward global brands, management realized that it needed to consolidate plants to reduce manufacturing expenses, improve speed to market, and reduce capital investment. Therefore, the study focused on redesigning the company's production and distribution system for its North American operations. The result was a reduction in the number of North American plants by almost 20 percent, saving over $200 million in pretax costs per year.

A major part of the study revolved around formulating and solving transportation problems for individual product categories. For each option regarding the plants to keep open, and so forth, solving the corresponding transportation problem for a product category shows what the distribution cost would be for shipping the product category from those plants to the distribution centers and customer zones. Numerous such transportation problems were solved in the process of identifying the best new production and distribution system. (The article describing this application of management science can be downloaded at **www.mhhe.com/hillier2e/articles.**)

This application of management science required solving numerous transportation problems with dozens of sources and over a thousand destinations, but savings of over $200 million per year were achieved.

Review *Questions*

1. Give a one-sentence description of transportation problems.
2. What data are needed for the model of a transportation problem?
3. What needs to be done to formulate a problem as a transportation problem?
4. What is required for a transportation problem to have feasible solutions?
5. Under what circumstances will a transportation problem automatically have an optimal solution with integer values for all its decision variables?
6. Name two algorithms that can solve transportation problems much faster than the general simplex method.

6.3 MODELING VARIANTS OF TRANSPORTATION PROBLEMS

The P & T Co. problem is an example of a transportation problem where everything fits immediately. Real life is seldom this easy. Linear programming problems frequently arise that are *almost* transportation problems, but one or more features do not quite fit. Here are the features that we will consider in this section.

1. The sum of the supplies *exceeds* the sum of the demands, so each supply represents a *maximum* amount (not a *fixed* amount) to be distributed from that source.

2. The sum of the supplies is *less* than the sum of the demands, so each demand represents a *maximum* amount (not a *fixed* amount) to be received at that destination.

3. A destination has both a *minimum* demand and a *maximum* demand, so any amount between these two values can be received.

4. Certain source–destination combinations cannot be used for distributing units.

5. The objective is to maximize the total profit associated with distributing units rather than to minimize the total cost.

For each of these features, it is possible to reformulate the problem in a clever way to make it fit the format for transportation problems. When this is done with a really big problem (say, one with many hundreds or thousands of sources and destinations), it is extremely helpful because either the transportation simplex method or network simplex method can solve the problem in this format *much* faster (perhaps more than 100 times faster) than the simplex method can solve the general linear programming formulation.

However, when the problem is *not* really big, the simplex method still is capable of solving the general linear programming formulation in a reasonable period of time. Therefore, a basic software package (such as the Excel Solver) that includes the simplex method but not the transportation simplex method or network simplex method can be applied to such problems without trying to force them into the format for a transportation problem. This is the approach we

Spreadsheet models that aren't quite transportation problems because they have at least one of the above features can still be solved by the Excel Solver.

will use. In particular, this section illustrates the formulation of spreadsheet models for *variants* of transportation problems that have some of the features listed above.

Our first example focuses on features 1 and 4. A second example will illustrate the other features.

Example 1: Assigning Plants to Products

The Better Products Company has decided to initiate the production of four new products, using three plants that currently have excess production capacity. The products require a comparable production effort per unit, so the available production capacity of the plants is measured by the number of units of any product that can be produced per day, as given in the rightmost column of Table 6.6. The bottom row gives the required production rate (number of units produced per day) to meet projected sales. Each plant can produce any of these products, *except* that Plant 2 *cannot* produce Product 3. However, the variable costs per unit of each product differ from plant to plant, as shown in the main body of the table.

The issue is to decide which plants should produce which products.

Management now needs to make a decision about which plants should produce which products. *Product splitting,* where the same product is produced in more than one plant, is permitted. (We shall return to this same example in Section 6.7 to consider the option where product splitting is prohibited, which requires a different kind of formulation.)

Formulation of a Spreadsheet Model

This problem is almost a transportation problem. In fact, after substituting conventional terminology (supply, demand, etc.) for the column and row headings in Table 6.6, this table basically fits the formulation for a transportation problem, as shown in Table 6.7. But there are two ways in which this problem deviates from a transportation problem.

One (minor) deviation is that a transportation problem requires a unit cost for *every* source–destination combination, but Plant 2 cannot produce Product 3, so no unit cost is available for this particular combination. The other deviation is that the sum of the supplies (75 + 75 + 45 = 195) *exceeds* the sum of the demands (20 + 30 + 30 + 40 = 120) in Table 6.7. Thus, as the *feasible solutions property* (Section 6.2) indicates, the transportation problem represented by Table 6.7 would have no feasible solutions. The *requirements assumption* (Section 6.2) specifies that the entire supply from each source must be used.

TABLE 6.6
Data for the Better Products Co. Problem

		Unit Cost				Capacity Available
Product:		1	2	3	4	
Plant						
1		$41	$27	$28	$24	75
2		40	29	—	23	75
3		37	30	27	21	45
Required production		20	30	30	40	

TABLE 6.7
The Data for the Better Products Co. Problem Formulated as a Variant of a Transportation Problem

	Unit Cost				Supply
Destination (Product): 1	2	3	4		
Source (Plant)					
1	$41	$27	$28	$24	75
2	40	29	—	23	75
3	37	30	27	21	45
Demand	20	30	30	40	

It is not necessary now to use the entire supply from each source.

In reality, these supplies in Table 6.7 represent production capacities that will not need to be fully used to meet the sales demand for the products. Thus, these supplies are *upper bounds* on the amounts to be used.

The spreadsheet model for this problem, shown in Figure 6.4, has the same format as the one in Figure 6.2 for the P & T Co. transportation problem with two key differences. First, because Plant 2 cannot produce Product 3, a dash is inserted into cell E5 and the constraint that E12 = 0 is included in the Solver dialogue box. Second, because the supplies are upper bounds, cells H11:H13 have ≤ signs instead of = signs and the corresponding constraints in the Solver dialogue box are ProducedAtPlant (G11:G13) ≤ Capacity (I11:I13).

Using the Excel Solver then gives the optimal solution shown in the changing cells DailyProduction (C11:F13) for the production rate of each product at each plant. This solution minimizes the cost of distributing 120 units of production from the total supply of 195 to meet the total demand of 120 at the four destinations (products). The total cost given in the target cell TotalCost (I16) is $3,260 per day.

FIGURE 6.4 A spreadsheet formulation of the Better Products Co. problem as a variant of a transportation problem, including the target cell TotalCost (I16) and the other output cells ProducedAtPlant (G11:G13) and ProductsProduced (C14:F14), as well as the specifications needed to set up the model. The changing cells DailyProduction (C11:F13) show the optimal production plan obtained by the Solver.

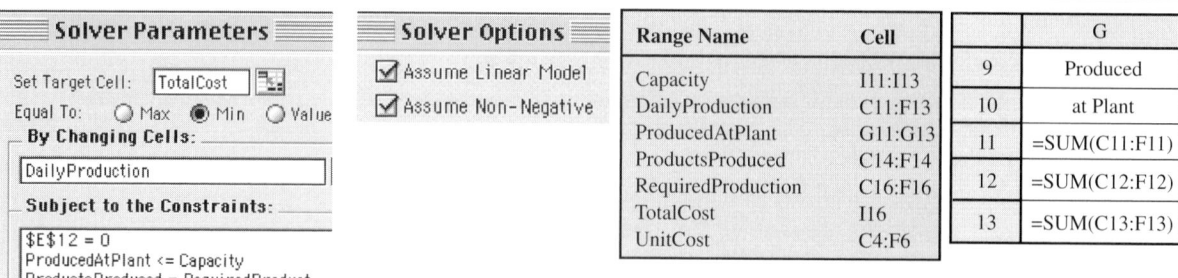

	A	B	C	D	E	F	G	H	I
1		**Better Products Co. Production Planning Problem**							
2									
3		**Unit Cost**	Product 1	Product 2	Product 3	Product 4			
4		Plant 1	$41	$27	$28	$24			
5		Plant 2	$40	$29	–	$23			
6		Plant 3	$37	$30	$27	$21			
7									
8									
9							Produced		
10		**Daily Production**	Product 1	Product 2	Product 3	Product 4	at Plant		Capacity
11		Plant 1	0	30	30	0	60	≤	75
12		Plant 2	0	0	0	15	15	≤	75
13		Plant 3	20	0	0	25	45	≤	45
14		Products Produced	20	30	30	40			
15			=	=	=	=			Total Cost
16		Required Production	20	30	30	40			$3,260

Solver Parameters

Set Target Cell: TotalCost
Equal To: ○ Max ● Min ○ Value
By Changing Cells:
DailyProduction
Subject to the Constraints:
$E$12 = 0
ProducedAtPlant <= Capacity
ProductsProduced = RequiredProduct...

Solver Options

☑ Assume Linear Model
☑ Assume Non-Negative

Range Name	Cell
Capacity	I11:I13
DailyProduction	C11:F13
ProducedAtPlant	G11:G13
ProductsProduced	C14:F14
RequiredProduction	C16:F16
TotalCost	I16
UnitCost	C4:F6

	G
9	Produced
10	at Plant
11	=SUM(C11:F11)
12	=SUM(C12:F12)
13	=SUM(C13:F13)

	B	C	D	E	F
14	Products Produced	=SUM(C11:C13)	=SUM(D11:D13)	=SUM(E11:E13)	=SUM(F11:F13)

	I
15	Total Cost
16	=SUMPRODUCT(UnitCost, DailyProduction)

Example 2: Choosing Customers

The Nifty Company specializes in the production of a single product, which it produces in three plants. The product is doing very well, so the company currently is receiving more purchase requests than it can fill. Plans have been made to open an additional plant, but it will not be ready until next year.

For the coming month, four potential customers (wholesalers) in different parts of the country would like to make major purchases. Customer 1 is the company's best customer, so his full order will be met. Customers 2 and 3 also are valued customers, so the marketing manager has decided that, at a minimum, at least a third of their order quantities should be met. However, she does not feel that Customer 4 warrants special consideration, and so is unwilling to guarantee any minimum amount for this customer. There will be enough units produced to go somewhat above these minimum amounts.

Due largely to substantial variations in shipping costs, the net profit that would be earned on each unit sold varies greatly, depending on which plant is supplying which customer. Therefore, the final decision on how much to send to each customer (above the minimum amounts established by the marketing manager) will be based on maximizing profit.

The unit profit for each combination of a plant supplying a customer is shown in Table 6.8. The rightmost column gives the number of units that each plant will produce for the coming month (a total of 20,000). The bottom row shows the order quantities that have been requested by the customers (a total of 30,000). The next-to-last row gives the minimum amounts that will be provided (a total of 12,000), based on the marketing manager's decisions described above.

Decisions need to be made regarding how much to sell to each customer and what shipping plan to use.

The marketing manager needs to determine how many units to sell to each customer (observing these minimum amounts) and how many units to ship from each plant to each customer to maximize profit.

Formulation of a Spreadsheet Model

This problem is almost a transportation problem, since the plants can be viewed as *sources* and the customers as *destinations,* where the production quantities are the *supplies* from the sources.

If this were fully a transportation problem, the purchase quantities would be the *demands* for the destinations. However, this does not work here because the *requirements assumption* (Section 6.2) says that the demand must be a *fixed* quantity to be received from the sources. Except for Customer 1, all we have here are *ranges* for the purchase quantities between the minimum and the maximum given in the last two rows of Table 6.8. In fact, one objective is to solve for the most desirable values of these purchase quantities.

We now have a range for how much each customer must receive.

Figure 6.5 shows the spreadsheet model for this variant of a transportation problem. Instead of a demand row below the changing cells, we instead have both a minimum row and a maximum row. The corresponding constraints in the Solver dialogue box are TotalShipped (C17:F17) ≤ MaxPurchase (C19:F19) and TotalShipped (C17:F17) ≥ MinPurchase (C15:F15), along with the usual supply constraints. Since the objective is to maximize the total profit rather than minimize the total cost, the Solver dialogue box specifies that the target cell TotalProfit (I17) is to be maximized.

TABLE 6.8
Data for the Nifty Co. Problem

	Customer:	1	2	3	4	Production Quantity
			Unit Profit			
Plant						
1		$55	$42	$46	$53	8,000
2		37	18	32	48	5,000
3		29	59	51	35	7,000
Minimum purchase		7,000	3,000	2,000	0	
Requested purchase		7,000	9,000	6,000	8,000	

FIGURE 6.5 A spreadsheet formulation of the Nifty Co. problem as a variant of a transportation problem, including the target cell TotalProfit (I17) and the other output cells TotalProduction (G11:G13) and TotalShipped (C17:F17), as well as the specifications needed to set up the model. The changing cells Shipment (C11:F13) show the optimal shipping plan obtained by the Solver.

	A	B	C	D	E	F	G	H	I
1		**Nifty Co. Product-Distribution Problem**							
2									
3		**Unit Profit**	Customer 1	Customer 2	Customer 3	Customer 4			
4		Plant 1	$55	$42	$46	$53			
5		Plant 2	$37	$18	$32	$48			
6		Plant 3	$29	$59	$51	$35			
7									
8									
9							Total		Production
10		**Shipment**	Customer 1	Customer 2	Customer 3	Customer 4	Production		Quantity
11		Plant 1	7,000	0	1,000	0	8,000	=	8,000
12		Plant 2	0	0	0	5,000	5,000	=	5,000
13		Plant 3	0	6,000	1,000	0	7,000	=	7,000
14									
15		Min Purchase	7,000	3,000	2,000	0			
16			≤	≤	≤	≤			Total Profit
17		Total Shipped	7,000	6,000	2,000	5,000			$1,076,000
18			≤	≤	≤	≤			
19		Max Purchase	7,000	9,000	6,000	8,000			

Solver Parameters

Set Target Cell: [TotalProfit]

Equal To: ● Max ○ Min ○ Val

By Changing Cells:

[Shipment]

Subject to the Constraints:

TotalProduction = ProductionQuantity
TotalShipped <= MaxPurchase
TotalShipped >= MinPurchase

Solver Options

☑ Assume Linear Model
☑ Assume Non-Negative

Range Name	Cell
MaxPurchase	C19:F19
MinPurchase	C15:F15
ProductionQuantity	I11:I13
Shipment	C11:F13
TotalProduction	G11:G13
TotalProfit	I17
TotalShipped	C17:F17
UnitProfit	C4:F6

	G
9	Total
10	Production
11	=SUM(C11:F11)
12	=SUM(C12:F12)
13	=SUM(C13:F13)

	B	C	D	E	F
17	Total Shipped	=SUM(C11:C13)	=SUM(D11:D13)	=SUM(E11:E13)	=SUM(F11:F13)

	I
16	Total Profit
17	=SUMPRODUCT(UnitProfit,Shipment)

After clicking on the Solve button, the optimal solution shown in Figure 6.5 is obtained. Cells TotalShipped (C17:F17) indicate how many units to sell to the respective customers. The changing cells Shipment (C11:F13) show how many units to ship from each plant to each customer. The resulting total profit of $1.076 million is given in the target cell TotalProfit (I17).

Review Questions

1. What needs to be done to formulate the spreadsheet model for a variant of a transportation problem where each supply from a source represents a maximum amount rather than a fixed amount to be distributed from that source?

2. What needs to be done to formulate the spreadsheet model for a variant of a transportation problem where the demand for a destination can be anything between a specified minimum amount and a specified maximum amount?

6.4   SOME OTHER APPLICATIONS OF VARIANTS OF TRANSPORTATION PROBLEMS

You now have seen examples illustrating three areas of application of transportation problems and their variants:

1. Shipping goods (the P & T Co. problem).

2. Assigning plants to products (the Better Products Co. problem).

3. Choosing customers (the Nifty Co. problem).

You will further broaden your horizons in this section by seeing examples illustrating some (but far from all) other areas of application.

Distributing Natural Resources

Metro Water District is an agency that administers water distribution in a large geographic region. The region is fairly arid, so the district must purchase and bring in water from outside the region. The sources of this imported water are the Colombo, Sacron, and Calorie rivers. The district then resells the water to users in its region. Its main customers are the water departments of the cities of Berdoo, Los Devils, San Go, and Hollyglass.

It is possible to supply any of these cities with water brought in from any of the three rivers, with the exception that no provision has been made to supply Hollyglass with Calorie River water. However, because of the geographic layouts of the aqueducts and the cities in the region, the cost to the district of supplying water depends upon both the source of the water and the city being supplied. The variable cost per acre foot of water for each combination of river and city is given in Table 6.9.

> Decisions need to be made regarding how much water to take from each river and how much to send from each river to each city.

Using units of 1 million acre feet, the bottom row of the table shows the amount of water needed by each city in the coming year (a total of 12.5). The rightmost column shows the amount available from each river (a total of 16).

Since the total amount available exceeds the total amount needed, management wants to determine how much water to take from each river, and then how much to send from each river to each city. The objective is to minimize the total cost of meeting the needs of the four cities.

Formulation and Solution

> It is not necessary to use the entire available supply from each river.

Figure 6.6 shows a spreadsheet model for this variant of a transportation problem. Because Hollyglass cannot be supplied with Calorie River water, the Solver dialogue box includes the constraint that F13 = 0. The amounts available in column I represent maximum amounts rather than fixed amounts, so ≤ signs are used for the corresponding constraints, TotalFromRiver (G11:G13) ≤ Available (I11:I13).

The Excel Solver then gives the optimal solution shown in Figure 6.6. The cells Total-FromRiver (G11:G13) indicate that the entire available supply from the Colombo and Sacron rivers should be used whereas only 1.5 million acre feet of the 5 million acre feet available from the Calorie River should be used. The changing cells WaterDistribution (C11:F13) provide the plan for how much to send from each river to each city. The total cost is given in the target cell TotalCost (I17) as $1.975 billion.

TABLE 6.9
Water Resources Data for Metro Water District

| | Cost per Acre Foot | | | | |
	Berdoo	Los Devils	San Go	Hollyglass	Available
Colombo River	$160	$130	$220	$170	5
Sacron River	140	130	190	150	6
Calorie River	190	200	230	—	5
Needed	2	5	4	1.5	(million acre feet)

FIGURE 6.6 A spreadsheet formulation of the Metro Water District problem as a variant of a transportation problem, including the target cell TotalCost (I17) and the other output cells TotalFromRiver (G11:G13) and TotalToCity (C14:F14), as well as the specifications needed to set up the model. The changing cells WaterDistribution (C11:F13) show the optimal solution obtained by the Solver.

	A	B	C	D	E	F	G	H	I
1		**Metro Water District Distribution Problem**							
2									
3		**Unit Cost ($millions)**	Berdoo	Los Devils	San Go	Hollyglass			
4		Colombo River	160	130	220	170			
5		Sacron River	140	130	190	150			
6		Calorie River	190	200	230	–			
7									
8									
9		**Water Distribution**					Total		
10		**(million acre-feet)**	Berdoo	Los Devils	San Go	Hollyglass	from River		Available
11		Colombo River	0	5	0	0	5	≤	5
12		Sacron River	2	0	2.5	1.5	6	≤	6
13		Calorie River	0	0	1.5	0	1.5	≤	5
14		Total to City	2	5	4	1.5			
15			=	=	=	=			Total Cost
16		Needed	2	5	4	1.5			($millions)
17									1,975

Solver Parameters

Set Target Cell: `TotalCost`

Equal To: ○ Max ● Min ○

By Changing Cells:

`WaterDistribution`

Subject to the Constraints:

```
$F$13 = 0
TotalFromRiver <= Available
TotalToCity = Needed
```

Solver Options

☑ Assume Linear Model
☑ Assume Non-Negative

Range Name	Cell
Available	I11:I13
Needed	C16:F16
TotalCost	I17
TotalFromRiver	G11:G13
TotalToCity	C14:F14
UnitCost	C4:F6
WaterDistribution	C11:F13

	G
9	Total
10	from River
11	=SUM(C11:F11)
12	=SUM(C12:F12)
13	=SUM(C13:F13)

	B	C	D	E	F
14	Total to City	=SUM(C11:C13)	=SUM(D11:D13)	=SUM(E11:E13)	=SUM(F11:F13)

	I
15	Total Cost
16	($millions)
17	=SUMPRODUCT(UnitCost,WaterDistribution)

Production Scheduling

The Northern Airplane Company builds commercial airplanes for various airline companies around the world. The last stage in the production process is to produce the jet engines and then to install them (a very fast operation) in the completed airplane frame. The company has been working under some contracts to deliver a considerable number of airplanes in the near future, and the production of the jet engines for these planes must now be scheduled for the next four months.

To meet the contracted dates for delivery, the company must supply engines for installation in the quantities indicated in the second column of Table 6.10. Thus, the cumulative number of engines produced by the end of months 1, 2, 3, and 4 must be at least 10, 25, 50, and 70, respectively.

TABLE 6.10 Production Scheduling Data for the Northern Airplane Company Problem

Month	Scheduled Installations	Maximum Production		Unit Cost of Production		Unit Cost of Storage
		Regular Time	Overtime	Regular Time	Overtime	
1	10	20	10	$1.08 million	$1.10 million	$15,000
2	15	30	15	1.11 million	1.12 million	15,000
3	25	25	10	1.10 million	1.11 million	15,000
4	20	5	10	1.13 million	1.15 million	

The facilities that will be available for producing the engines vary according to other production, maintenance, and renovation work scheduled during this period. The resulting monthly differences in the maximum number of engines that can be produced during *regular time* hours (no overtime) are shown in the third column of Table 6.10, and the additional numbers that can be produced during *overtime* hours are shown in the fourth column. The cost of producing each one on either regular time or overtime is given in the fifth and sixth columns.

Because of the variations in production costs, it may well be worthwhile to produce some of the engines a month or more before they are scheduled for installation, and this possibility is being considered. The drawback is that such engines must be stored until the scheduled installation (the airplane frames will not be ready early) at a storage cost of $15,000 per month (including interest on expended capital) for each engine,[1] as shown in the rightmost column of Table 6.10.

The objective is to determine a production schedule that will minimize the total cost.

The production manager wants a schedule developed for the number of engines to be produced in each of the four months so that the total of the production and storage costs will be minimized.

Formulation and Solution

Figure 6.7 shows the formulation of this problem as a variant of a transportation problem. The *sources* of the jet engines are their production on *regular time* (RT) and on *overtime* (OT) in each of the four months. Their *supplies* are obtained from the third and fourth columns of Table 6.10. The *destinations* for these engines are their installation in each of the four months, so their *demands* are given in the second column of Table 6.10.

It is not possible to install an engine in some month prior to its production, so the Solver dialogue box includes constraints that the number installed must be zero in each of these cases. Similarly, dashes are inserted into the UnitCost table for these cases. Otherwise, the unit costs given in this table (in units of $1 million) are obtained by combining the unit cost of production from the fifth or sixth column of Table 6.10 with any storage costs ($0.015 million per unit per month stored). (The equations entered into UnitCost (D13:G20) are shown after the spreadsheet in Figure 6.7.) Since the quantities in MaxProduction (J25:J32) represent the maximum amounts that can be produced, they are preceded by ≤ signs in column I. The corresponding supply constraints, Produced (H25:H32) ≤ MaxProduction (J25:J32), are included in the Solver dialogue box along with the usual demand constraints.

Like the preceding example, having ≤ signs rather than = signs for the supply constraints makes this problem only a *variant* of a transportation problem.

The changing cells UnitsProduced (D25:G32) show an optimal solution for this problem. Table 6.11 summarizes the key features of this solution. Overtime is used only once (in month 3). Despite the hefty costs incurred by storing engines, extra engines are produced in the first and third months to be stored for installation later. Even month 2 produces enough engines that five will remain in storage for installation in month 3, despite the fact that production costs are higher in month 2 than in month 3. Thus, a human scheduler would have difficulty in finding this schedule. However, the Excel Solver has no difficulty in balancing all the factors involved

[1]For modeling purposes, it is being assumed that this storage cost is incurred at the end of the month for just those engines that are being held over into the next month. Thus, engines that are produced in a given month for installation in the same month are assumed to incur no storage cost.

FIGURE 6.7   A spreadsheet formulation of the Northern Airplane Co. problem as a variant of a transportation problem, including the target cell TotalCost (J36) and the other output cells UnitCost (D13:G20), Produced (H25:H32), and Installed (D33:G33), as well as the specifications needed to set up the model. The changing cells UnitsProduced (D25:G32) display the optimal production schedule obtained by the Solver.

	A	B	C	D	E	F	G	H	I	J
1		**Northern Airplane Co. Production-Scheduling Problem**								
2										
3		**Production Cost**		Regular			**Storage Cost**			
4		**($millions)**		Time	Overtime		**($millions per month)**			
5			Month 1	1.08	1.10		0.015			
6			Month 2	1.11	1.12					
7			Month 3	1.10	1.11					
8			Month 4	1.13	1.15					
9										
10										
11		**Unit Cost**			Month Installed					
12		**($millions)**		1	2	3	4			
13			1 (RT)	1.080	1.095	1.110	1.125			
14			1 (OT)	1.100	1.115	1.130	1.145			
15			2 (RT)	–	1.110	1.125	1.140			
16		Month	2 (OT)	–	1.120	1.135	1.150			
17		Produced	3 (RT)	–	–	1.100	1.115			
18			3 (OT)	–	–	1.110	1.125			
19			4 (RT)	–	–	–	1.130			
20			4 (OT)	–	–	–	1.150			
21										
22										
23					Month Installed					Maximum
24		**Units Produced**		1	2	3	4	Produced		Production
25			1 (RT)	10	5	5	0	20	≤	20
26			1 (OT)	0	0	0	0	0	≤	10
27			2 (RT)	0	10	0	0	10	≤	30
28		Month	2 (OT)	0	0	0	0	0	≤	15
29		Produced	3 (RT)	0	0	10	15	25	≤	25
30			3 (OT)	0	0	10	0	10	≤	10
31			4 (RT)	0	0	0	5	5	≤	5
32			4 (OT)	0	0	0	0	0	≤	10
33			Installed	10	15	25	20			
34				=	=	=	=			Total Cost
35		Scheduled Installations		10	15	25	20			($millions)
36										77.4

to reduce the total cost to an absolute minimum, which turns out to be $77.4 million (as shown in the target cell TotalCost [J36]) in this case.

Designing School Attendance Zones

The Middletown School District is opening a third high school and thus needs to redraw the boundaries for the areas of the city that will be assigned to the respective schools.

FIGURE 6.7   *(continued)*

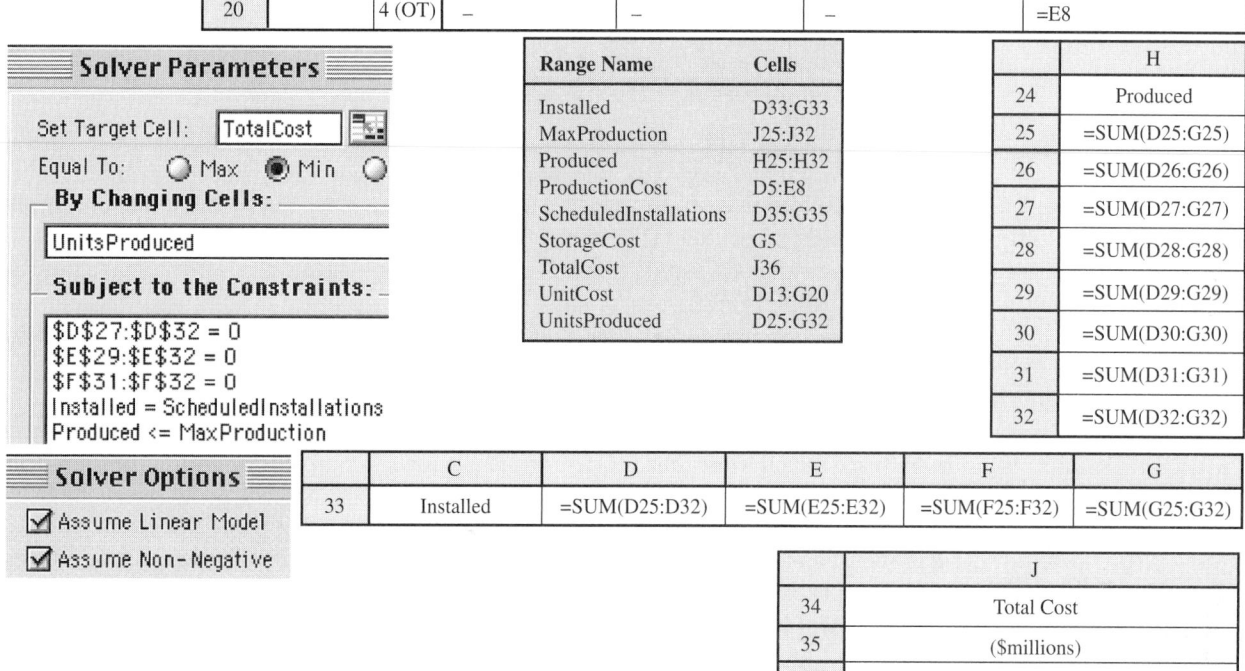

	B	C	D	E	F	G
11	**Unit Cost**			Month Installed		
12	**($millions)**		1	2	3	4
13		1 (RT)	=D5	=D5+StorageCost	=D5+2*StorageCost	=D5+3*StorageCost
14		1 (OT)	=E5	=E5+StorageCost	=E5+2*StorageCost	=E5+3*StorageCost
15		2 (RT)	–	=D6	=D6+StorageCost	=D6+2*StorageCost
16	Month	2 (OT)	–	=E6	=E6+StorageCost	=E6+2*StorageCost
17	Produced	3 (RT)	–	–	=D7	=D7+StorageCost
18		3 (OT)	–	–	=E7	=E7+StorageCost
19		4 (RT)	–	–	–	=D8
20		4 (OT)	–	–	–	=E8

Solver Parameters

Set Target Cell: [TotalCost]

Equal To: ○ Max   ● Min   ○

By Changing Cells:

[UnitsProduced]

Subject to the Constraints:

$D$27:$D$32 = 0
$E$29:$E$32 = 0
$F$31:$F$32 = 0
Installed = ScheduledInstallations
Produced <= MaxProduction

Solver Options

☑ Assume Linear Model
☑ Assume Non-Negative

Range Name	Cells
Installed	D33:G33
MaxProduction	J25:J32
Produced	H25:H32
ProductionCost	D5:E8
ScheduledInstallations	D35:G35
StorageCost	G5
TotalCost	J36
UnitCost	D13:G20
UnitsProduced	D25:G32

	H
24	Produced
25	=SUM(D25:G25)
26	=SUM(D26:G26)
27	=SUM(D27:G27)
28	=SUM(D28:G28)
29	=SUM(D29:G29)
30	=SUM(D30:G30)
31	=SUM(D31:G31)
32	=SUM(D32:G32)

	C	D	E	F	G
33	Installed	=SUM(D25:D32)	=SUM(E25:E32)	=SUM(F25:F32)	=SUM(G25:G32)

	J
34	Total Cost
35	($millions)
36	=SUMPRODUCT(UnitCost,UnitsProduced)

TABLE 6.11
Optimal Production Schedule for the Northern Airplane Co.

Month	Production	Installations	Stored
1 (RT)	20	10	10
2 (RT)	10	15	5
3 (RT)	25	25	5
3 (OT)	10	0	10
4 (RT)	5	20	0

For preliminary planning, the city has been divided into nine tracts with approximately equal populations. (Subsequent detailed planning will divide the city further into over 100 smaller tracts.) The main body of Table 6.12 shows the approximate distance between each tract and school. The rightmost column gives the number of high school students in each tract next year. (These numbers are expected to grow slowly over the next several years.) The last two rows show the minimum and maximum number of students each school should be assigned.

The school district management has decided that the appropriate objective in setting school attendance zone boundaries is to minimize the *average distance* that students must travel to

The objective is to minimize the average distance that students must travel to school.

TABLE 6.12

Data for the Middletown School District Problem

	Distance (Miles) to School			
	School: 1	2	3	Number of High School Students
Tract				
1	2.2	1.9	2.5	500
2	1.4	1.3	1.7	400
3	0.5	1.8	1.1	450
4	1.2	0.3	2.0	400
5	0.9	0.7	1.0	500
6	1.1	1.6	0.6	450
7	2.7	0.7	1.5	450
8	1.8	1.2	0.8	400
9	1.5	1.7	0.7	500
Minimum enrollment	1,200	1,100	1,000	
Maximum enrollment	1,800	1,700	1,500	

school. At this preliminary stage, they want to determine how many students from each tract should be assigned to each school to achieve this objective, while also satisfying the enrollment constraints at each school indicated by the bottom two rows of Table 6.12.

Formulation and Solution

Minimizing the average distance that students must travel is equivalent to *minimizing the sum of the distances* that individual students must travel. Therefore, adopting the latter objective, this is just a variant of a transportation problem where the unit costs are distances.

Because each school has both a minimum and maximum enrollment, we proceed just as in the Nifty Co. example (Section 6.3) to provide two rows of data cells below the changing cells that specify these minimum and maximum amounts in the spreadsheet model shown in Figure 6.8. The corresponding constraints are included in the Solver dialogue box along with the usual supply constraints. Clicking on the Solve button then gives the optimal solution shown in the changing cells NumberOfStudents (C17:E25).

This optimal solution gives the following plan:

Assign tracts 2 and 3 to school 1.

Assign tracts 1, 4, and 7 to school 2.

Assign tracts 6, 8, and 9 to school 3.

Split tract 5, with 350 students assigned to school 1 and 150 students assigned to school 2.

As indicated in the target cell TotalDistance (H30), the total distance traveled to school by all the students is 3,530 miles (an average of 0.872 mile per student).

Meeting Energy Needs Economically

The Energetic Company needs to make plans for the *energy systems* for a new building.

The *energy needs* in the building fall into three categories: (1) electricity, (2) heating water, and (3) heating space in the building. The daily requirements for these three categories (all measured in the same units) are 20 units, 10 units, and 30 units, respectively.

The three possible *sources of energy* to meet these needs are electricity, natural gas, and a solar heating unit that can be installed on the roof. The size of the roof limits the largest possible solar heater to providing 30 units per day. However, there is no limit to the amount of electricity and natural gas available.

Electricity needs can be met only by purchasing electricity. Both other energy needs (water heating and space heating) can be met by any of the three sources of energy or a combination thereof.

FIGURE 6.8   A spreadsheet formulation of the Middletown School District problem as a variant of a transportation problem, including the target cell TotalDistance (H30) and the other output cells TotalFromTract (F17:F25) and TotalAtSchool (C29:E29), as well as the specifications needed to set up the model. The changing cells NumberOfStudents (C17:E25) show the optimal zoning plan obtained by the Solver.

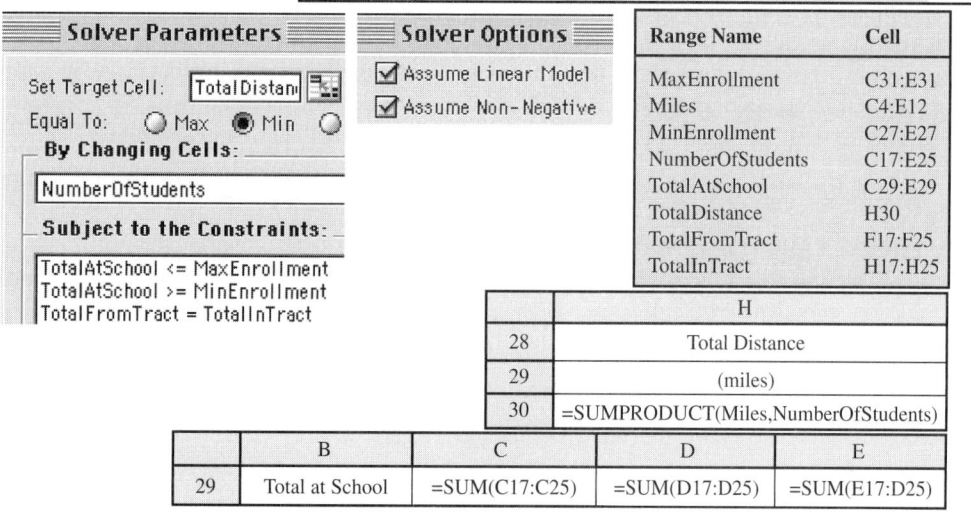

	A	B	C	D	E	F	G	H
1		**Middletown School District Zoning Problem**						
2								
3		**Distance (Miles)**	School 1	School 2	School 3			
4		Tract 1	2.2	1.9	2.5			
5		Tract 2	1.4	1.3	1.7			
6		Tract 3	0.5	1.8	1.1			
7		Tract 4	1.2	0.3	2			
8		Tract 5	0.9	0.7	1			
9		Tract 6	1.1	1.6	0.6			
10		Tract 7	2.7	0.7	1.5			
11		Tract 8	1.8	1.2	0.8			
12		Tract 9	1.5	1.7	0.7			
13								
14								
15		**Number of**				Total		Total
16		**Students**	School 1	School 2	School 3	from Tract		in Tract
17		Tract 1	0	500	0	500	=	500
18		Tract 2	400	0	0	400	=	400
19		Tract 3	450	0	0	450	=	450
20		Tract 4	0	400	0	400	=	400
21		Tract 5	350	150	0	500	=	500
22		Tract 6	0	0	450	450	=	450
23		Tract 7	0	450	0	450	=	450
24		Tract 8	0	0	400	400	=	400
25		Tract 9	0	0	500	500	=	500
26								
27		Min Enrollment	1,200	1,100	1,000			
28			≤	≤	≤			Total Distance
29		Total at School	1,200	1,500	1,350			(Miles)
30			≤	≤	≤			3,530
31		Max Enrollment	1,800	1,700	1,500			

Range Name	Cell
MaxEnrollment	C31:E31
Miles	C4:E12
MinEnrollment	C27:E27
NumberOfStudents	C17:E25
TotalAtSchool	C29:E29
TotalDistance	H30
TotalFromTract	F17:F25
TotalInTract	H17:H25

	F
15	Total
16	from Tract
17	=SUM(C17:E17)
18	=SUM(C18:E18)
19	=SUM(C19:E19)
20	=SUM(C20:E20)
21	=SUM(C21:E21)
22	=SUM(C22:E22)
23	=SUM(C23:E23)
24	=SUM(C24:E24)
25	=SUM(C25:E25)

	H
28	Total Distance
29	(miles)
30	=SUMPRODUCT(Miles,NumberOfStudents)

	B	C	D	E
29	Total at School	=SUM(C17:C25)	=SUM(D17:D25)	=SUM(E17:D25)

TABLE 6.13
Cost Data for the
Energetic Co. Problem

	Unit Cost		
Energy Need:	Electricity	Water Heating	Space Heating
Source of Energy			
Electricity	$400	$500	$600
Natural gas	—	600	500
Solar heater	—	300	400

The objective is to minimize the total cost of meeting all the energy needs.

The unit costs for meeting these energy needs from these sources of energy are shown in Table 6.13. The objective of management is to minimize the total cost of meeting all the energy needs.

Formulation and Solution

Figure 6.9 shows the formulation of this problem as a variant of a transportation problem. The changing cells DailyEnergyUse (D12:F14) show the resulting optimal solution for how many units of each energy source should be used to meet each energy need. The target cell TotalCost (I18) gives the total cost as $24,000 per day.

Choosing a New Site Location

One of the most important decisions that the management of many companies must face is where to locate a major new facility. The facility might be a new factory, a new distribution center, a new administrative center, or some other building. The new facility might be needed because of expansion. In other cases, the company may be abandoning an unsatisfactory location.

There generally are several attractive potential sites from which to choose. Increasingly, in today's global economy, the potential sites may extend across national borders.

Shipping costs are a prime consideration in deciding where to locate a new factory, so solving transportation problems becomes a key part of the analysis.

There are a number of important factors that go into management's decision. One of them is *shipping costs.* For example, when evaluating a potential site for a new factory, management needs to consider the impact of choosing this site on the cost of shipping goods from *all* the factories (including the new factory at this site) to the distribution centers. By locating the new factory near some distribution centers that are far from all the current factories, the company can obtain low shipping costs for the new factory and, at the same time, substantially reduce the shipping costs from the current factories as well. Management needs to know what the *total* shipping cost would be, following an optimal shipping plan, for each potential site for the new factory.

A similar question may arise regarding the total cost of shipping some raw material from its various sources to all the factories (including the new one) for each potential site for the new factory.

A transportation problem (or a variant) often provides the appropriate way of formulating such questions. Solving this formulation for each potential site then provides key input to management, who must evaluate both this information and other relevant considerations in making its final selection of the site.

The case study presented in the next section illustrates this kind of application.

Review Questions

1. What are the areas of application illustrated in this section for variants of transportation problems?
2. What is the objective of management for the Metro Water District problem?
3. What are the sources and destinations in the formulation of the Northern Airplane Co. production scheduling problem?
4. What plays the role of unit costs in the Middletown School District problem?
5. What is the objective of management for the Energetic Co. problem?

FIGURE 6.9

A spreadsheet formulation of the Energetic Co. problem as a variant of a transportation problem, including the target cell TotalCost (I18) and the other output cells TotalUsed (G12:G14) and TotalSupplied (D15:F15), as well as the specifications needed to set up the model. The changing cells DailyEnergyUse (D12:F14) give the optimal energy-sourcing plan obtained by the Solver.

	A	B	C	D	E	F	G	H	I
1	**Energetic Co. Energy-Sourcing Problem**								
2									
3					**Energy Need**				
4		**Unit Cost ($/day)**		Electricity	Water Heating	Space Heating			
5		Source	Electricity	400	500	600			
6		of Energy	Natural Gas	–	600	500			
7			Solar Heater	–	300	400			
8									
9									
10		**Daily Energy Use**			**Energy Need**		Total		
11		Source		Electricity	Water Heating	Space Heating	Used		
12		of Energy	Electricity	20	0	0	20		
13			Natural Gas	0	0	10	10		Max Solar
14			Solar Heater	0	10	20	30	≤	30
15			Total Supplied	20	10	30			
16				=	=	=			Total Cost
17			Demand	20	10	30			($/day)
18									24,000

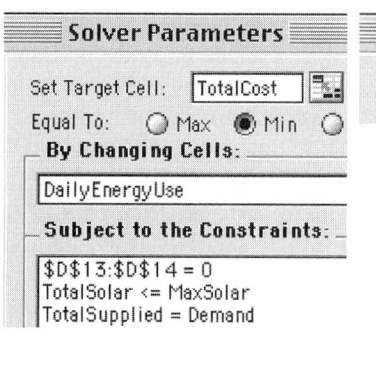

Solver Parameters

Set Target Cell: `TotalCost`

Equal To: ○ Max   ● Min   ○

By Changing Cells:

`DailyEnergyUse`

Subject to the Constraints:

`$D$13:$D$14 = 0`
`TotalSolar <= MaxSolar`
`TotalSupplied = Demand`

Solver Options

☑ Assume Linear Model
☑ Assume Non-Negative

Range Name	Cells
DailyEnergyUse	D12:F14
Demand	D17:F17
MaxSolar	I14
TotalCost	I18
TotalSolar	G14
TotalSupplied	D15:F15
TotalUsed	G12:G14
UnitCost	D5:F7

	G
10	Total
11	Used
12	=SUM(D12:F12)
13	=SUM(D13:F13)
14	=SUM(D14:F14)

	C	D	E	F
15	Total Supplied	=SUM(D12:D14)	=SUM(E12:E14)	=SUM(F12:F14)

	I
16	Total Cost
17	($/day)
18	=SUMPRODUCT(UnitCost,DailyEnergyUse)

6.5   A CASE STUDY: THE TEXAGO CORP. SITE SELECTION PROBLEM

The Texago Corporation is a large, fully integrated petroleum company based in the United States. The company produces most of its oil in its own oil fields and then imports the rest of what it needs from the Middle East. An extensive distribution network is used to transport the oil to the company's refineries and then to transport the petroleum products from the refineries to Texago's distribution centers. The locations of these various facilities are given in Table 6.14.

TABLE 6.14
Location of Texago's Current Facilities

Type of Facility	Locations
Oil fields	1. Several in Texas 2. Several in California 3. Several in Alaska
Refineries	1. Near New Orleans, Louisiana 2. Near Charleston, South Carolina 3. Near Seattle, Washington
Distribution centers	1. Pittsburgh, Pennsylvania 2. Atlanta, Georgia 3. Kansas City, Missouri 4. San Francisco, California

TABLE 6.15
Potential Sites for Texago's New Refinery and Their Main Advantages

Potential Site	Main Advantages
Near Los Angeles, California	1. Near California oil fields. 2. Ready access from Alaska oil fields. 3. Fairly near San Francisco distribution center.
Near Galveston, Texas	1. Near Texas oil fields. 2. Ready access from Middle East imports. 3. Near corporate headquarters.
Near St. Louis, Missouri	1. Low operating costs. 2. Centrally located for distribution centers. 3. Ready access to crude oil via the Mississippi River.

Texago is continuing to increase its market share for several of its major products. Therefore, management has made the decision to expand its output by building an additional refinery and increasing its imports of crude oil from the Middle East. The crucial remaining decision is where to locate the new refinery.

The addition of the new refinery will have a great impact on the operation of the entire distribution system, including decisions on how much crude oil to transport from each of its sources to each refinery (including the new one) and how much finished product to ship from each refinery to each distribution center. Therefore, the three key factors for management's decision on the location of the new refinery are

1. The cost of transporting the oil from its sources to all the refineries, including the new one.

2. The cost of transporting finished product from all the refineries, including the new one, to the distribution centers.

3. Operating costs for the new refinery, including labor costs, taxes, the cost of needed supplies (other than crude oil), energy costs, the cost of insurance, and so on. (Capital costs are not a factor since they would be essentially the same at any of the potential sites.)

Management has set up a task force to study the issue of where to locate the new refinery. After considerable investigation, the task force has determined that there are three attractive potential sites. These sites and the main advantages of each are spelled out in Table 6.15.

Three sites—Los Angeles, Galveston, and St. Louis—are candidates for the location of the new refinery, so the issue now is to choose one of them.

Gathering the Necessary Data

The task force needs to gather a large amount of data, some of which requires considerable digging, in order to perform the analysis requested by management.

Management wants all the refineries, including the new one, to operate at full capacity. Therefore, the task force begins by determining how much crude oil each refinery would need brought in annually under these conditions. Using units of 1 million barrels, these needed amounts are shown on the left side of Table 6.16. The right side of the table shows the current

TABLE 6.16
Production Data for Texago Corp.

Refinery	Crude Oil Needed Annually (Million Barrels)	Oil Fields	Crude Oil Produced Annually (Million Barrels)
New Orleans	100	Texas	80
Charleston	60	California	60
Seattle	80	Alaska	100
New site	120		
		Total	240
Total	360	Needed imports = 360 − 240 = 120	

TABLE 6.17
Cost Data for Shipping Crude Oil to a Texago Refinery

	Cost per Unit Shipped to Refinery or Potential Refinery (Millions of Dollars per Million Barrels)					
	New Orleans	Charleston	Seattle	Los Angeles	Galveston	St. Louis
Source						
Texas	2	4	5	3	1	1
California	5	5	3	1	3	4
Alaska	5	7	3	4	5	7
Middle East	2	3	5	4	3	4

TABLE 6.18
Cost Data for Shipping Finished Product to a Distribution Center

	Cost per Unit Shipped to Distribution Center (Millions of Dollars)			
	Pittsburgh	Atlanta	Kansas City	San Francisco
Refinery				
New Orleans	6.5	5.5	6	8
Charleston	7	5	4	7
Seattle	7	8	4	3
Potential Refinery				
Los Angeles	8	6	3	2
Galveston	5	4	3	6
St. Louis	4	3	1	5
Number of units needed	100	80	80	100

annual output of crude oil from the various oil fields. These quantities are expected to remain stable for some years to come. Since the refineries need a total of 360 million barrels of crude oil, and the oil fields will produce a total of 240 million barrels, the difference of 120 million barrels will need to be imported from the Middle East.

Since the amounts of crude oil produced or purchased will be the same regardless of which location is chosen for the new refinery, the task force concludes that the associated production or purchase costs (exclusive of shipping costs) are not relevant to the site selection decision. On the other hand, the costs for transporting the crude oil from its source to a refinery are very relevant. These costs are shown in Table 6.17 for both the three current refineries and the three potential sites for the new refinery.

Also very relevant are the costs of shipping the finished product from a refinery to a distribution center. Letting one unit of finished product correspond to a refinery's production from 1 million barrels of crude oil, these costs are given in Table 6.18. The bottom row of the table shows the number of units of finished product needed by each distribution center.

The final key body of data involves the *operating costs* for a refinery at each potential site. Estimating these costs requires site visits by several members of the task force to collect detailed

TABLE 6.19
Estimated Operating Costs for a Texago Refinery at Each Potential Site

Site	Annual Operating Cost (Millions of Dollars)
Los Angeles	620
Galveston	570
St. Louis	530

For each of the three potential sites, the task force needs to consider the total costs for all the refineries (including the new one) of shipping both the crude oil and the finished product, as well as the operating costs for the new refinery.

information about local labor costs, taxes, and so forth. Comparisons then are made with the operating costs of the current refineries to help refine these data. In addition, the task force gathers information on one-time site costs for land, construction, and other expenses and amortizes these costs on an equivalent uniform annual cost basis. This process leads to the estimates shown in Table 6.19.

Analysis (Six Applications of a Transportation Problem)

Armed with these data, the task force now needs to develop the following key financial information for management:

1. Total shipping cost for crude oil with each potential choice of a site for the new refinery.

2. Total shipping cost for finished product with each potential choice of a site for the new refinery.

For both types of costs, once a site is selected, an optimal shipping plan will be determined and then followed. Therefore, to find either type of cost with a *potential* choice of a site, it is necessary to solve for the optimal shipping plan given that choice and then calculate the corresponding cost.

The task force recognizes that the problem of finding an optimal shipping plan for a given choice of a site is just a transportation problem. In particular, for shipping crude oil, Figure 6.10 shows the spreadsheet model for this transportation problem, where the entries in the data cells come directly from Tables 6.16 and 6.17. The entries for the *New Site* column (cells G5:G8) will come from one of the last three columns of Table 6.17, depending on which potential site currently is being evaluated. At this point, before entering this column and clicking on the Solve button, a trial solution of 0 for each of the shipment quantities has been entered into the changing cells ShipmentQuantity (D13:G16).

Figures 6.11, 6.12, and 6.13 all use the same spreadsheet model for a transportation problem that is shown in Figure 6.10.

These same changing cells in Figures 6.11, 6.12, and 6.13 show the optimal shipping plan for each of the three possible choices of a site. The target cell TotalCost (J20) gives the resulting total annual shipping cost in millions of dollars. In particular, if Los Angeles were to be chosen as the site for the new refinery (Figure 6.11), the total annual cost of shipping crude oil in the optimal manner would be $880 million. If Galveston were chosen instead (Figure 6.12), this cost would be $920 million, whereas it would be $960 million if St. Louis were chosen (Figure 6.13).

The analysis of the cost of shipping finished product is similar. Figure 6.14 shows the spreadsheet model for this transportation problem, where rows 5–7 come directly from the first three rows of Table 6.18. The *New Site* row would be filled in from one of the next three rows of Table 6.18, depending on which potential site for the new refinery is currently under evaluation. Since the units for finished product leaving a refinery are equivalent to the units for crude oil coming in, the data in Supply (J13:J16) come from the left side of Table 6.16.

Figures 6.15, 6.16, and 6.17 all use the same spreadsheet model for a transportation problem that is shown in Figure 6.14.

The changing cells ShipmentQuantity (D13:G16) in Figures 6.15, 6.16, and 6.17 show the optimal plan for shipping finished product for each of the sites being considered for the new refinery. The target cell TotalCost (J20) in Figure 6.15 indicates that the resulting total annual cost for shipping finished product if the new refinery were in Los Angeles is $1.57 billion. Similarly, this total cost would be $1.63 billion if Galveston were the chosen site (Figure 6.16) and $1.43 billion if St. Louis were chosen (Figure 6.17).

FIGURE 6.10   The basic spreadsheet formulation for the Texago transportation problem for shipping crude oil from the oil fields to the refineries, including the new refinery at a site still to be selected. The target cell is TotalCost (J20) and the other output cells are TotalShipped (H13:H16) and TotalReceived (D17:G17). Before entering the data for a new site and then clicking on the Solve button, a trial solution of 0 has been entered into each of the changing cells ShipmentQuantity (D13:G16).

	A	B	C	D	E	F	G	H	I	J
1	**Texago Corp. Site-Selection Problem (Shipping to Refineries)**									
2										
3					**Refineries**					
4		**Unit Cost ($millions)**		New Orleans	Charleston	Seattle	New Site			
5			Texas	2	4	5				
6		Oil	California	5	5	3				
7		Fields	Alaska	5	7	3				
8			Middle East	2	3	5				
9										
10										
11		**Shipment Quantity**			**Refineries**					
12		**(millions of barrels)**		New Orleans	Charleston	Seattle	New Site	Total Shipped		Supply
13			Texas	0	0	0	0	0	=	80
14		Oil	California	0	0	0	0	0	=	60
15		Fields	Alaska	0	0	0	0	0	=	100
16			Middle East	0	0	0	0	0	=	120
17			Total Received	0	0	0	0			
18				=	=	=	=			Total Cost
19			Demand	100	60	80	120			($millions)
20										0

Solver Parameters

Set Target Cell: [TotalCost]

Equal To: ○ Max ● Min ○

By Changing Cells:

[ShipmentQuantity]

Subject to the Constraints:

TotalReceived = Demand
TotalShipped = Supply

Solver Options

☑ Assume Linear Model
☑ Assume Non-Negative

Range Name	Cells
Demand	D19:G19
ShipmentQuantity	D13:G16
Supply	J13:J16
TotalCost	J20
TotalReceived	D17:G17
TotalShipped	H13:H16
UnitCost	D5:G8

	H
12	Total Shipped
13	=SUM(D13:G13)
14	=SUM(D14:G14)
15	=SUM(D15:G15)
16	=SUM(D16:G16)

	C	D	E	F	G
17	Total Received	=SUM(D13:D16)	=SUM(E13:E16)	=SUM(F13:F16)	=SUM(G13:G16)

	J
18	Total Cost
19	($millions)
20	=SUMPRODUCT(UnitCost,ShipmentQuantity)

For each of the three alternative sites, two separate spreadsheet models have been used for planning the shipping of crude oil and the shipping of finished product. However, another option would have been to combine all this planning into a single spreadsheet model for each site and then to simultaneously optimize the plans for the two types of shipments. This would essentially involve combining Figure 6.11 with Figure 6.15, Figure 6.12 with Figure 6.16, and Figure 6.13 with Figure 6.17, and then using the sum of the shipping costs for the pair of transportation problems as

FIGURE 6.11   The changing cells ShipmentQuantity (D13:G16) give Texago management an optimal plan for shipping crude oil if Los Angeles is selected as the new site for the refinery in column G of Figure 6.10.

	A	B	C	D	E	F	G	H	I	J
1	**Texago Corp. Site-Selection Problem (Shipping to Refineries, Including Los Angeles)**									
2										
3					**Refineries**					
4		**Unit Cost ($millions)**		New Orleans	Charleston	Seattle	Los Angeles			
5			Texas	2	4	5	3			
6		Oil	California	5	5	3	1			
7		Fields	Alaska	5	7	3	4			
8			Middle East	2	3	5	4			
9										
10										
11		**Shipment Quantity**			**Refineries**					
12		**(millions of barrels)**		New Orleans	Charleston	Seattle	Los Angeles	Total Shipped		Supply
13			Texas	40	0	0	40	80	=	80
14		Oil	California	0	0	0	60	60	=	60
15		Fields	Alaska	0	0	80	20	100	=	100
16			Middle East	60	60	0	0	120	=	120
17			Total Received	100	60	80	120			
18				=	=	=	=			Total Cost
19			Demand	100	60	80	120			($millions)
20										880

FIGURE 6.12   The changing cells ShipmentQuantity (D13:G16) give Texago management an optimal plan for shipping crude oil if Galveston is selected as the new site for a refinery in column G of Figure 6.10.

	A	B	C	D	E	F	G	H	I	J
1	**Texago Corp. Site-Selection Problem (Shipping to Refineries, Including Galveston)**									
2										
3					**Refineries**					
4		**Unit Cost ($millions)**		New Orleans	Charleston	Seattle	Galveston			
5			Texas	2	4	5	1			
6		Oil	California	5	5	3	3			
7		Fields	Alaska	5	7	3	5			
8			Middle East	2	3	5	3			
9										
10										
11		**Shipment Quantity**			**Refineries**					
12		**(millions of barrels)**		New Orleans	Charleston	Seattle	Galveston	Total Shipped		Supply
13			Texas	20	0	0	60	80	=	80
14		Oil	California	0	0	0	60	60	=	60
15		Fields	Alaska	20	0	80	0	100	=	100
16			Middle East	60	60	0	0	120	=	120
17			Total Received	100	60	80	120			
18				=	=	=	=			Total Cost
19			Demand	100	60	80	120			($millions)
20										920

FIGURE 6.13   The changing cells ShipmentQuantity (D13:G16) give Texago management an optimal plan for shipping crude oil if St. Louis is selected as the new site for a refinery in column G of Figure 6.10.

	A	B	C	D	E	F	G	H	I	J
1			Texago Corp. Site-Selection Problem (Shipping to Refineries, Including St. Louis)							
2										
3						Refineries				
4			Unit Cost ($millions)	New Orleans	Charleston	Seattle	St. Louis			
5			Texas	2	4	5	1			
6		Oil	California	5	5	3	4			
7		Fields	Alaska	5	7	3	7			
8			Middle East	2	3	5	4			
9										
10										
11			Shipment Quantity			Refineries				
12			(millions of barrels)	New Orleans	Charleston	Seattle	St. Louis	Total Shipped		Supply
13			Texas	0	0	0	80	80	=	80
14		Oil	California	0	20	0	40	60	=	60
15		Fields	Alaska	20	0	80	0	100	=	100
16			Middle East	80	40	0	0	120	=	120
17			Total Received	100	60	80	120			
18				=	=	=	=			Total Cost
19			Demand	100	60	80	120			($millions)
20										960

the target cell to be minimized. This would have the advantage of showing all the shipment planning for a given site on a single spreadsheet. At the end of the chapter, Case 6-2 will continue this Texago case study by considering a situation where this kind of combined spreadsheet model is needed to find the best overall shipping plan for each possible choice of a site.

The Message to Management

The task force now has completed its financial analysis of the three alternative sites for the new refinery. Table 6.20 shows all the major *variable* costs (costs that vary with the decision) on an annual basis that would result from each of the three possible choices for the new site. The second column summarizes what the total annual cost of shipping crude oil to all refineries (including the new one) would be for each alternative (as already given in Figures 6.11, 6.12, and 6.13). The third column repeats the data in Figures 6.15, 6.16, and 6.17 on the total annual cost of shipping finished product from the refineries to the distribution centers. The fourth column shows the estimated operating costs for a refinery at each potential site, as first given in Table 6.19.

Adding across these three columns gives the total variable cost for each alternative.

Conclusion: From a purely financial viewpoint, St. Louis is the best site for the new refinery. This site would save the company about $200 million annually as compared to the Galveston alternative and about $150 million as compared to the Los Angeles alternative.

However, as with any site selection decision, management must consider a wide variety of factors, including some nonfinancial ones. (For example, remember that one important advantage of the Galveston site is that it is close to corporate headquarters.) Furthermore, if ways can be found to reduce some of the costs in Table 6.20 for either the Los Angeles or Galveston sites, this might change the financial evaluation substantially. Management also must consider whether there are any cost trends or trends in the marketplace that might alter the picture in the future.

FIGURE 6.14 The basic spreadsheet formulation for the Texago transportation problem for shipping finished product from the refineries (including the new one at a site still to be selected) to the distribution centers. The target cell is TotalCost (J20) and the other output cells are TotalShipped (H13:H16) and TotalReceived (D17:G17). Before entering the data for a new site and then clicking on the Solve button, a trial solution of 0 has been entered into each of the changing cells ShipmentQuantity (D13:G16).

	A	B	C	D	E	F	G	H	I	J
1			**Texago Corp. Site-Selection Problem (Shipping to D. C.'s)**							
2										
3						**Distribution Center**				
4			**Unit Cost ($millions)**	Pittsburgh	Atlanta	Kansas City	San Francisco			
5			New Orleans	6.5	5.5	6	8			
6		Refineries	Charleston	7	5	4	7			
7			Seattle	7	8	4	3			
8			New Site							
9										
10										
11		**Shipment Quantity**				**Distribution Center**				
12		**(millions of barrels)**		Pittsburgh	Atlanta	Kansas City	San Francisco	Total Shipped		Supply
13			New Orleans	0	0	0	0	0	=	100
14		Refineries	Charleston	0	0	0	0	0	=	60
15			Seattle	0	0	0	0	0	=	80
16			New Site	0	0	0	0	0	=	120
17			Total Received	0	0	0	0			
18				=	=	=	=			Total Cost
19			Demand	100	80	80	100			($millions)
20										0

Solver Parameters

Set Target Cell: TotalCost

Equal To: ○ Max ● Min ○

By Changing Cells:

ShipmentQuantity

Subject to the Constraints:

TotalReceived = Demand
TotalShipped = Supply

Solver Options

☑ Assume Linear Model
☑ Assume Non-Negative

Range Name	Cells
Demand	D19:G19
ShipmentQuantity	D13:G16
Supply	J13:J16
TotalCost	J20
TotalReceived	D17:G17
TotalShipped	H13:H16
UnitCost	D5:G8

	H
12	Total Shipped
13	=SUM(D13:G13)
14	=SUM(D14:G14)
15	=SUM(D15:G15)
16	=SUM(D16:G16)

	C	D	E	F	G
17	Total Received	=SUM(D13:D16)	=SUM(E13:E16)	=SUM(F13:F16)	=SUM(G13:G16)

	J
18	Total Cost
19	($millions)
20	=SUMPRODUCT(UnitCost,ShipmentQuantity)

FIGURE 6.15   The changing cells ShipmentQuantity (D13:G16) give Texago management an optimal plan for shipping finished product if Los Angeles is selected as the new site for a refinery in rows 8 and 16 of Figure 6.14.

	A	B	C	D	E	F	G	H	I	J
1		**Texago Corp. Site-Selection Problem (Shipping to D. C.'s When Choose Los Angeles)**								
2										
3					**Distribution Center**					
4		**Unit Cost ($millions)**		Pittsburgh	Atlanta	Kansas City	San Francisco			
5			New Orleans	6.5	5.5	6	8			
6		Refineries	Charleston	7	5	4	7			
7			Seattle	7	8	4	3			
8			Los Angeles	8	6	3	2			
9										
10										
11		**Shipment Quantity**			**Distribution Center**					
12		**(millions of barrels)**		Pittsburgh	Atlanta	Kansas City	San Francisco	Total Shipped		Supply
13			New Orleans	80	20	0	0	100	=	100
14		Refineries	Charleston	0	60	0	0	60	=	60
15			Seattle	20	0	0	60	80	=	80
16			Los Angeles	0	0	80	40	120	=	120
17			Total Received	100	80	80	100			
18				=	=	=	=			Total Cost
19			Demand	100	80	80	100			($millions)
20										1,570

FIGURE 6.16   The changing cells ShipmentQuantity (D13:G16) give Texago management an optimal plan for shipping finished product if Galveston is selected as the new site for a refinery in rows 8 and 16 of Figure 6.14.

	A	B	C	D	E	F	G	H	I	J
1		**Texago Corp. Site-Selection Problem (Shipping to D. C.'s When Choose Galveston)**								
2										
3					**Distribution Center**					
4		**Unit Cost ($millions)**		Pittsburgh	Atlanta	Kansas City	San Francisco			
5			New Orleans	6.5	5.5	6	8			
6		Refineries	Charleston	7	5	4	7			
7			Seattle	7	8	4	3			
8			Galveston	5	4	3	6			
9										
10										
11		**Shipment Quantity**			**Distribution Center**					
12		**(millions of barrels)**		Pittsburgh	Atlanta	Kansas City	San Francisco	Total Shipped		Supply
13			New Orleans	100	0	0	0	100	=	100
14		Refineries	Charleston	0	60	0	0	60	=	60
15			Seattle	0	0	0	80	80	=	80
16			Galveston	0	20	80	20	120	=	120
17			Total Received	100	80	80	100			
18				=	=	=	=			Total Cost
19			Demand	100	80	80	100			($millions)
20										1,630

FIGURE 6.17   The changing cells ShipmentQuantity (D13:G16) give Texago management an optimal plan for shipping finished product if St. Louis is selected as the new site for a refinery in rows 8 and 16 of Figure 6.14.

	A	B	C	D	E	F	G	H	I	J
1		**Texago Corp. Site-Selection Problem (Shipping to D. C.'s When Choose St. Louis)**								
2										
3					**Distribution Center**					
4		**Unit Cost ($millions)**		Pittsburgh	Atlanta	Kansas City	San Francisco			
5			New Orleans	6.5	5.5	6	8			
6		Refineries	Charleston	7	5	4	7			
7			Seattle	7	8	4	3			
8			St. Louis	4	3	1	5			
9										
10										
11		**Shipment Quantity**			**Distribution Center**					
12		**(millions of barrels)**		Pittsburgh	Atlanta	Kansas City	San Francisco	Total Shipped		Supply
13			New Orleans	100	0	0	0	100	=	100
14		Refineries	Charleston	0	60	0	0	60	=	60
15			Seattle	0	0	0	80	80	=	80
16			St. Louis	0	20	80	20	120	=	120
17			Total Received	100	80	80	100			
18				=	=	=	=			Total Cost
19			Demand	100	80	80	100			($millions)
20										1,430

TABLE 6.20
Annual Variable Costs Resulting from the Choice of Each Site for the New Texago Refinery

Site	Total Cost of Shipping Crude Oil	Total Cost of Shipping Finished Product	Operating Cost for New Refinery	Total Variable Cost
Los Angeles	$880 million	$1.57 billion	$620 million	$3.07 billion
Galveston	920 million	1.63 billion	570 million	3.12 billion
St. Louis	960 million	1.43 billion	530 million	2.92 billion

After careful consideration, Texago management tentatively chooses the St. Louis site. (This story continues in Case 6-2, where the task force is asked to analyze the option of enlarging the capacity of the new refinery before the final decision is made on its site.)

Review Questions

1. What are the three key factors for management's decision on the location of the new refinery?

2. Why do shipping costs to and from the *current* refineries need to be considered along with those for the new refinery?

3. Why did the Texago task force find it necessary to solve six transportation problems instead of just one?

4. What else must Texago management consider in addition to the financial analysis based on solving six transportation problems?

6.6   CHARACTERISTICS OF ASSIGNMENT PROBLEMS

We now turn to another special type of linear programming problem called *assignment problems*. As the name suggests, this kind of problem involves making *assignments*. Frequently, these are assignments of people to jobs. Thus, many applications of the assignment problem involve aiding managers in matching up their personnel with tasks to be performed. Other applications might instead involve assigning machines, vehicles, or plants to tasks.

We begin with an example.

An Example: The Sellmore Company Problem

The marketing manager of the Sellmore Company will be holding the company's annual sales conference soon for sales regional managers and personnel. To assist in the administration of the conference, he is hiring four temporary employees (Ann, Ian, Joan, and Sean), where each will handle one of the following four tasks:

1. Word processing of written presentations.

2. Computer graphics for both oral and written presentations.

3. Preparation of conference packets, including copying and organizing written materials.

4. Handling of advance and on-site registrations for the conference.

He now needs to decide which person to assign to each task.

Although each temporary employee has at least the minimal background necessary to perform any of the four tasks, they differ considerably in how efficiently they can handle the different types of work. Table 6.21 shows how many hours each would need for each task. The rightmost column gives the hourly wage based on the background of each employee.

Formulation of a Spreadsheet Model

Figure 6.18 shows a spreadsheet model for this problem. Table 6.21 is entered at the top. Combining these required times and wages gives the cost (cells D15:G18) for each possible assignment of a temporary employee to a task, using equations shown at the bottom of Figure 6.18. This *cost table* is just the way that any assignment problem is displayed. The objective is to determine which assignments should be made to minimize the sum of the associated costs.

The values of 1 in Supply (J24:J27) indicate that each person (assignee) listed in column C must perform exactly one task. The values of 1 in Demand (D30:G30) indicate that each task must be performed by exactly one person. These requirements then are specified in the constraints given in the Solver dialogue box.

Each of the changing cells Assignment (D24:G27) is given a value of 1 when the corresponding assignment is being made, and a value of 0 otherwise. Therefore, the Excel equation for the target cell, TotalCost = SUMPRODUCT(Cost, Assignment), gives the total cost for the assignments being made. The Solver dialogue box specifies that the objective is to minimize this target cell.

The changing cells in Figure 6.18 show the optimal solution obtained after clicking on the Solve button. This solution is

Assign Ann to prepare conference packets.

Assign Ian to do the computer graphics.

Assign Joan to handle registrations.

Assign Sean to do the word processing.

The total cost given in cell J30 is $1,957.

Sidebar notes:

Decisions need to be made regarding which person to assign to each task.

Using Cost (D15:G18), the objective is to minimize the total cost of the assignments.

A value of 1 in a changing cell indicates that the corresponding assignment is being made, whereas 0 means that the assignment is not being made.

Excel Tip: When solving an assignment problem, rounding errors occasionally will cause Excel to return a noninteger value very close to 0 (e.g., 1.23 E-10, meaning 0.000000000123) or very close to 1 (e.g., 0.9999912). To make the spreadsheet cleaner, you may replace these "ugly" representations by their proper value of 0 or 1 in the changing cells.

TABLE 6.21
Data for the Sellmore Co. Problem

Temporary Employee	Required Time per Task (Hours)				Hourly Wage
	Word Processing	Graphics	Packets	Registrations	
Ann	35	41	27	40	$14
Ian	47	45	32	51	12
Joan	39	56	36	43	13
Sean	32	51	25	46	15

FIGURE 6.18 A spreadsheet formulation of the Sellmore Co. problem as an assignment problem, including the target cell TotalCost (J30) and the other output cells Cost (D15:G18), TotalAssignments (H24:H27), and TotalAssigned (D28:G28), as well as the specifications needed to set up the model. The values of 1 in the changing cells Assignment (D24:G27) show the optimal plan obtained by the Solver for assigning the people to the tasks.

	A	B	C	D	E	F	G	H	I	J
1	**Sellmore Co. Assignment Problem**									
2										
3					**Task**					
4		**Required Time**		Word					Hourly	
5		**(Hours)**		Processing	Graphics	Packets	Registrations		Wage	
6			Ann	35	41	27	40		$14	
7		Assignee	Ian	47	45	32	51		$12	
8			Joan	39	56	36	43		$13	
9			Sean	32	51	25	46		$15	
10										
11										
12					**Task**					
13				Word						
14		**Cost**		Processing	Graphics	Packets	Registrations			
15			Ann	$490	$574	$378	$560			
16		Assignee	Ian	$564	$540	$384	$612			
17			Joan	$507	$728	$468	$559			
18			Sean	$480	$765	$375	$690			
19										
20										
21					**Task**					
22		**Assignment**		Word				Total		
23				Processing	Graphics	Packets	Registrations	Assignments		Supply
24			Ann	0	0	1	0	1	=	1
25		Assignee	Ian	0	1	0	0	1	=	1
26			Joan	0	0	0	1	1	=	1
27			Sean	1	0	0	0	1	=	1
28			Total Assigned	1	1	1	1			
29				=	=	=	=			Total Cost
30			Demand	1	1	1	1			$1,957

	B	C	D	E	F	G
13			Word			
14	**Cost**		Processing	Graphics	Packets	Registrations
15		Ann	=D6*I6	=E6*I6	=F6*I6	=G6*I6
16	Assignee	Ian	=D7*I7	=E7*I7	=F7*I7	=G7*I7
17		Joan	=D8*I8	=E8*I8	=F8*I8	=G8*I8
18		Sean	=D9*I9	=E9*I9	=F9*I9	=G9*I9

	H
22	Total
23	Assignments
24	=SUM(D24:G24)
25	=SUM(D25:G25)
26	=SUM(D26:G26)
27	=SUM(D27:G27)

Solver Parameters

Set Target Cell: TotalCost
Equal To: ○ Max ● Min ○
By Changing Cells:
Assignment
Subject to the Constraints:
TotalAssigned = Demand
TotalAssignments = Supply

Solver Options
☑ Assume Linear Model
☑ Assume Non-Negative

	J
29	Total Cost
30	=SUMPRODUCT(Cost,Assignment)

Range Name	Cells
Assignment	D24:G27
Cost	D15:G18
Demand	D30:G30
HourlyWage	I6:I9
RequiredTime	D6:G9
Supply	J24:J27
TotalAssigned	D28:G28
TotalAssignments	H24:H27
TotalCost	J30

	C	D	E	F	G
28	Total Assigned	=SUM(D24:D27)	=SUM(E24:E27)	=SUM(F24:F27)	=SUM(G24:G27)

The Model for Assignment Problems

Any assignment problem can be described in the following general terms. Given a set of **tasks** to be performed and a set of **assignees** who are available to perform these tasks, the problem is to determine which assignee should be assigned to each task.

To fit the model for an assignment problem, the following assumptions need to be satisfied:

1. The number of assignees and the number of tasks are the same.

2. Each assignee is to be assigned to exactly *one* task.

3. Each task is to be performed by exactly *one* assignee.

4. There is a cost associated with each combination of an assignee performing a task.

5. The objective is to determine how all the assignments should be made to minimize the total cost.

The first three assumptions are fairly restrictive. Many potential applications do not quite fit these assumptions. However, these *variants* of assignment problems still can be solved by the Excel Solver, as we will describe in Section 6.7.

Excel Tip: The spreadsheet model for any assignment problem needs to include constraints like those shown in Figure 6.18 in order to enforce assumptions 2 and 3.

When the assumptions are satisfied, all that needs to be done to formulate a problem as an assignment problem is to (1) identify the assignees and tasks and (2) construct a **cost table** that gives the cost associated with each combination of an assignee performing a task. Figure 6.18 illustrates how to display this formulation on a spreadsheet. The spreadsheet model for any assignment problem will include constraints to enforce assumptions 2 and 3. In Figure 6.18, these constraints are TotalAssignments (H24:H27) = Supply (J24:J27) and TotalAssigned (D28:G28) = Demand (D30:G30), where values of 1 are entered in the data cells Supply (J24:J27) and Demand (D30:G30).

The Network Representation of an Assignment Problem

In addition to a cost table, the *network representation* provides an alternative way of displaying an assignment problem. Figure 6.19 shows the network representation of the Sellmore Co. assignment problem, where all the assignees are lined up in order on the left and all the tasks are lined up in order on the right. The arrows show the possible assignments, where exactly four arrows are to be chosen—one emanating from each assignee and one leading to each task. The number next to each arrow gives the cost if that particular assignment is chosen.

FIGURE 6.19

The network representation of the Sellmore Co. assignment problem shows all the possible assignments and their costs graphically.

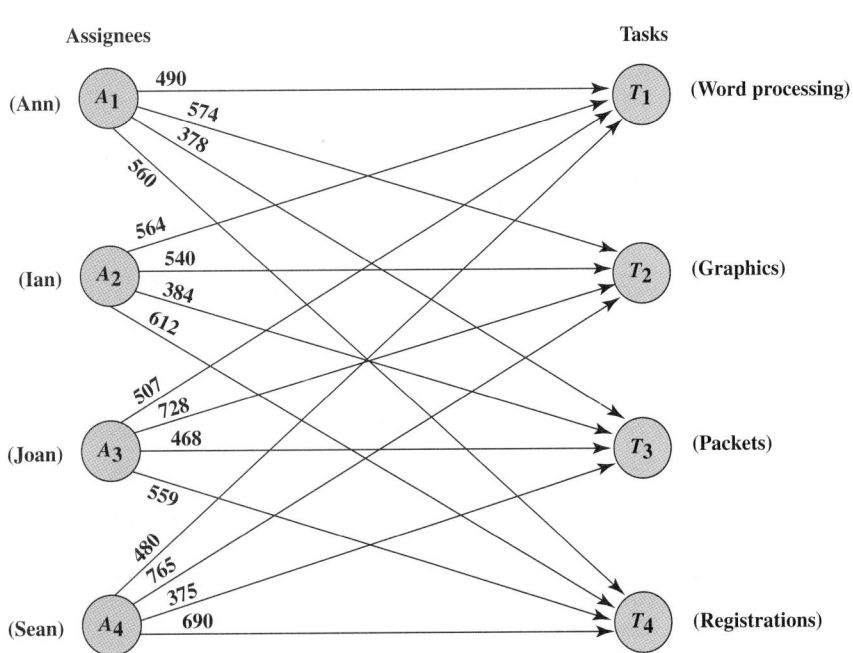

This network representation provides a way of visualizing an assignment problem graphically. You also will see in the next chapter that this representation shows the relationship between assignment problems and other linear programming problems of the *distribution-network type*.

The Assignment Problem Is a Special Type of Transportation Problem

Did you happen to notice that the network representation in Figure 6.19 is strikingly similar to the network representation for a transportation problem shown in Figure 6.3? Look and see.

This similarity is no coincidence. The assignment problem is, in fact, just a special type of transportation problem where the *sources* now are *assignees* and the *destinations* now are *tasks*. Furthermore, as illustrated by the Sellmore Co. assignment problem in Figure 6.18, every source has a supply of 1 (since each assignee is to be assigned to exactly one task) and every destination has a demand of 1 (since each task is to be performed by exactly one assignee).

Therefore, all the characteristics of transportation problems described in Section 6.2 also apply to assignment problems.

> *The assignees and tasks of an assignment problem are analogous to the sources and destinations of a transportation problem.*

Solving Assignment Problems

The Excel Solver uses the simplex method to solve any kind of linear programming problem, including both transportation problems and assignment problems and their variants. This works fine for problems of the size considered in this book (or even considerably larger).

However, as discussed in Section 6.2, either the *transportation simplex method* or the *network simplex method* provides a far more efficient way of solving big transportation problems. Consequently, since the assignment problem is a special type of transportation problem, these same algorithms can be used to solve big assignment problems quickly.

Nevertheless, even these special algorithms do not provide the fastest way of solving assignment problems. There are much faster algorithms available that have been designed specifically to solve assignment problems. The most famous of these is called the **Hungarian method.** In practice, one of these special algorithms normally would be used to solve large assignment problems. Although the Excel Solver does not have *special-purpose algorithms* such as the Hungarian method for efficiently solving special types of linear programming problems, other linear programming software packages are available that do.

> *Although not available with the Excel Solver, special-purpose algorithms (such as the Hungarian method) can be used to solve very large assignment problems.*

Review Questions

1. Give a one-sentence description of assignment problems.
2. What assumptions about *assignees* and *tasks* need to hold for a problem to be an assignment problem?
3. What needs to be done to formulate a problem as an assignment problem?
4. What are the sources, destinations, supplies, and demands when an assignment problem is described as a special kind of transportation problem?
5. Name an algorithm that has been designed specifically just to solve assignment problems very quickly.

6.7 MODELING VARIANTS OF ASSIGNMENT PROBLEMS

Variants of assignment problems frequently arise because they have one or more features that do not quite fit all the assumptions enumerated in the preceding section for the model of an assignment problem. The features we will consider are the following:

1. Certain assignees are unable to perform certain tasks.
2. Although each assignee will perform exactly one task, there are more tasks than assignees, so some tasks will not be done.
3. Although each task will be performed by exactly one assignee, there are more assignees than tasks, so some assignees will not perform any task.

4. Each assignee can be assigned to perform more than one task simultaneously.

5. Each task can be performed jointly by more than one assignee.

For each of these features, there is a clever way of reformulating the problem to make it fit the format for an assignment problem, which then enables using an extremely efficient special-purpose algorithm (such as the *Hungarian method*). However, this isn't necessary except on problems that are much larger than any considered in this book. Therefore, we instead will formulate a spreadsheet model in the most straightforward way and solve it with the Excel Solver.

Three examples are presented below to illustrate the above features. The first example focuses on features 1 and 2. The second combines feature 4 with a variation of feature 3. The third deals with feature 5.

To illuminate the close relationships between transportation problems and assignment problems, the second and third examples are based on earlier examples of variants of transportation problems.

Example 1: Assigning Machines to Locations

The Job Shop Company has purchased three new machines of different types. There are five available locations in the shop where a machine could be installed. Some of these locations are more desirable than others for particular machines because of their proximity to work centers that will have a heavy work flow to and from these machines. (There will be no work flow *between* the new machines.) Therefore, the objective is to assign the new machines to the available locations to minimize the total cost of materials handling. The estimated cost per hour of materials handling involving each of the machines is given in Table 6.22 for the respective locations. Location 2 is not considered suitable for machine 2, so no cost is given for this case.

Formulation of a Spreadsheet Model

As it stands, this is almost an assignment problem, since the machines can be viewed as *assignees* to be assigned to locations as the *tasks*. However, it does not quite qualify because assumption 1 for the assignment problem model is violated (we have two more locations than machines), as are assumption 3 (two locations will not be filled by a machine) and assumption 4 (we do not have a cost associated with assigning machine 2 to location 2).

Figure 6.20 shows a spreadsheet model for this variant of an assignment problem. Because location 2 cannot be used for machine 2, the Solver dialogue box includes the constraint that $D12 = 0$. The usual supply constraints, TotalAssignments (H11:H13) = Supply (J11:J13), ensure that each machine will be assigned to exactly one location. The fact that two locations will not be used is taken into account by using a $\leq$ sign in the demand constraints, TotalAssigned (C14:G14) $\leq$ Demand (C16:G16).

The changing cells Assignment (C11:G13) with a value of 1 show the assignments being made in the optimal solution after clicking on the Solve button. Since none of these cells for locations 2 and 5 have a value of 1, a machine will not be placed in either of these locations. The target cell TotalCost (J17) indicates that the total cost for this optimal solution is $31 per hour.

Where should the new machines be located to minimize the total cost of materials handling?

Since machines are being assigned to locations, this is like an assignment problem, but with three minor differences.

A $\leq$ sign is used in the demand constraints instead of an $=$ sign because two of the locations will not be assigned a machine.

TABLE 6.22
Materials-Handling Cost Data for the Job Shop Co. Problem

		Cost per Hour				
Location:		1	2	3	4	5
Machine						
1		$13	$16	$12	$14	$15
2		15	—	13	20	16
3		4	7	10	6	7

FIGURE 6.20 A spreadsheet formulation of the Job Shop Co. problem as a variant of an assignment problem, including the target cell TotalCost (J17) and the other output cells TotalAssignments (H11:H13) and Total Assigned (C14:G14), as well as the specifications needed to set up the model. The values of 1 in the changing cells Assignment (C11:G13) show the optimal plan obtained by the Solver for assigning the machines to the locations.

	A	B	C	D	E	F	G	H	I	J
1		**Job Shop Co. Machine-Location Problem**								
2										
3		Cost ($/hour)	Location 1	Location 2	Location 3	Location 4	Location 5			
4		Machine 1	13	16	12	14	15			
5		Machine 2	15	–	13	20	16			
6		Machine 3	4	7	10	6	7			
7										
8										
9								Total		
10		Assignment	Location 1	Location 2	Location 3	Location 4	Location 5	Assignments		Supply
11		Machine 1	0	0	0	1	0	1	=	1
12		Machine 2	0	0	1	0	0	1	=	1
13		Machine 3	1	0	0	0	0	1	=	1
14		Total Assigned	1	0	1	1	0			
15			≤	≤	≤	≤	≤			Total Cost
16		Demand	1	1	1	1	1			($/hour)
17										31

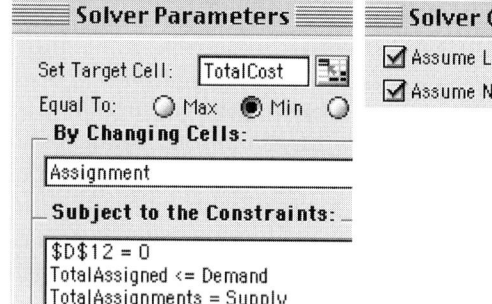

Solver Parameters

Set Target Cell: `TotalCost`

Equal To: ○ Max ● Min ○

By Changing Cells:

`Assignment`

Subject to the Constraints:

```
$D$12 = 0
TotalAssigned <= Demand
TotalAssignments = Supply
```

Solver Options

☑ Assume Linear Model
☑ Assume Non-Negative

Range Name	Cell
Assignment	C11:G13
Cost	C4:G6
Demand	C16:G16
Supply	J11:J13
TotalAssigned	C14:G14
TotalAssignments	H11:H13
TotalCost	J17

	H
9	Total
10	Assignments
11	=SUM(C11:G11)
12	=SUM(C12:G12)
13	=SUM(C13:G13)

	B	C	D	E	F	G
14	Total Assigned	=SUM(C11:C13)	=SUM(D11:D13)	=SUM(E11:E13)	=SUM(F11:F13)	=SUM(G11:G13)

	J
15	Total Cost
16	($/hour)
17	=SUMPRODUCT(Cost,Assignment)

Example 2: Assigning Plants to Products

Reconsider Example 1 in Section 6.3, where the Better Products Co. needs to assign three plants to produce four new products. The relevant data are given in Table 6.6.

As described in Section 6.3, management had permitted *product splitting* (where the same product is produced in more than one plant). However, there are some *hidden costs* associated with product splitting that are not reflected in Table 6.6, including extra setup, distribution, and administration costs. Therefore, management now has decided to have the problem analyzed again under the additional restriction that *product splitting is prohibited.*

New Problem Statement: Given the data in Table 6.6, minimize the total cost of assigning each plant to at least one new product where each product is to be produced in only one plant (no product splitting). Since there are three plants and four new products, two plants will produce one new product and a third plant will produce two. Only plants 1 and 2 have the capacity to produce two products.

Formulation of a Spreadsheet Model

This now is almost an assignment problem; plants need to be assigned to products, and each product is to be produced by exactly one plant.

Since we want to assign plants to products, the plants can be viewed as *assignees* and the products as the *tasks* to be performed for this variant of an assignment problem. Figure 6.21 shows the resulting spreadsheet model.

The data from Table 6.6 are given at the top. However, the unit costs given in cells C4:F6 are not the appropriate costs for the cost table for a variant of an assignment problem. To construct the appropriate cost table, we must determine each cost associated with assigning a plant to *all* the required production of a product. The corresponding unit cost shown in rows 4–6 is the cost of producing only one unit rather than the entire required (daily) production given in row 8. Therefore, we must multiply this unit cost by the required (daily) production to obtain the total (daily) cost of the assignment. For example, consider the assignment of Plant 1 to product 1.

Cost of Plant 1 producing one unit of product 1   = $41

Required (daily) production of product 1   = 20 units

Total (daily) cost of assigning Plant 1 to product 1 = 20 ($41)

                                                 = $820

Cost(C12:F14) gives the total (daily) assignment costs, calculated in this way (see the equations at the bottom of the figure), for each combination of assigning a plant to a product.

Since Plant 2 cannot produce product 3, the Solver dialogue box includes the constraint that E20 = 0. Either Plant 1 or Plant 2 (but not both) needs to be chosen to produce a second product, so these two plants are given a supply of 2 in cells I19:I20. A ≤ sign is then used for the corresponding supply constraints, G19:G20 ≤ I19:I20. However, the supply constraint for Plant 3 and the demand constraints are the usual ones for an assignment problem.

After clicking on the Solve button, the optimal solution shown in the changing cells Assignment (C19:F21) is obtained, namely, Plant 1 produces products 2 and 3, Plant 2 produces product 1, and Plant 3 produces product 4. The target cell TotalCost (I24) gives the total daily cost of $3,290 for this production plan.

It is interesting to compare this solution with the one given in DailyProduction (C11:F13) of Figure 6.4 when product splitting was permitted. Note that the assignments for plants 2 and 3 in Figure 6.4 are quite different than here. The total cost calculated for the production plan shown in that figure is $3,260 per day, or $30 per day less than for the plan in Figure 6.21.

However, the formulation of the original problem (product splitting permitted) as a variant of a transportation problem does not take into account *hidden costs* of product splitting (extra setup, distribution, and administration costs), which probably are considerably more than $30 per day. Therefore, management adopted the production plan based on this new formulation (product splitting prohibited) as a variant of an assignment problem.

Example 3: Designing School Attendance Zones

Now refer back to Section 6.4 for the problem faced by the management of the Middletown School District in designing school attendance zones. Table 6.12 gives the data for the problem and Figure 6.8 shows its formulation as a variant of a transportation problem.

The optimal solution obtained from this formulation has two problems that concern management. One is that this solution splits tract 5 between two schools (schools 1 and 2). Each tract is a cohesive neighborhood that has always stayed together in attending the same school prior to high school. The school district superintendent and the school board are in agreement that it would be much better to continue to keep each neighborhood (including tract 5) together in assigning it to a single school. The second problem with the solution is that it assigns the smallest number of students (1,200) to the school with the largest capacity (school 1, with a capacity of 1,800 students). Although this is marginally acceptable (the school board has chosen 1,200 as the minimum number of students it would allow to be assigned to school 1), a more even allocation of students to the schools would be preferable.

FIGURE 6.21 In contrast to Figure 6.4, product splitting is not allowed, so the Better Products Co. problem becomes a variant of an assignment problem. The target cell is TotalCost (I24) and the other output cells are Cost (C12:F14), Total Assignments (G19:G21), and Total Assigned (C22:F22), where the equations entered into these cells are shown below the spreadsheet. The values of 1 in the changing cells Assignment (C19:F21) display the optimal production plan obtained by the Solver.

	A	B	C	D	E	F	G	H	I
1		**Better Products Co. Production Planning Problem (Revised)**							
2									
3		**Unit Cost**	Product 1	Product 2	Product 3	Product 4			
4		Plant 1	$41	$27	$28	$24			
5		Plant 2	$40	$29	–	$23			
6		Plant 3	$37	$30	$27	$21			
7									
8		Required Production	20	30	30	40			
9									
10									
11		**Cost ($/day)**	Product 1	Product 2	Product 3	Product 4			
12		Plant 1	$820	$810	$840	$960			
13		Plant 2	$800	$870	–	$920			
14		Plant 3	$740	$900	$810	$840			
15									
16									
17							Total		
18		**Assignment**	Product 1	Product 2	Product 3	Product 4	Assignments		Supply
19		Plant 1	0	1	1	0	2	≤	2
20		Plant 2	1	0	0	0	1	≤	2
21		Plant 3	0	0	0	1	1	=	1
22		Total Assigned	1	1	1	1			
23			=	=	=	=			Total Cost
24		Demand	1	1	1	1			$3,290

Solver Parameters

Set Target Cell: [TotalCost]
Equal To: ○ Max ● Min ○
By Changing Cells:
[Assignment]
Subject to the Constraints:
$E$20 = 0
$G$19:$G$20 <= $I$19:$I$20
$G$21 = $I$21
TotalAssigned = Demand

Solver Options
☑ Assume Linear Model
☑ Assume Non-Negative

	B	C	D	E	F
11	**Cost ($/day)**	Product 1	Product 2	Product 3	Product 3
12	Plant 1	=C4*C$8	=D4*D$8	=E4*E$8	=F4*F$8
13	Plant 2	=C5*C$8	=D5*D$8	–	=F5*F$8
14	Plant 3	=C6*C$8	=D6*D$8	=E6*E$8	=F6*F$8

Range Name	Cell
Assignment	C19:F21
Cost	C12:F14
Demand	C24:F24
RequiredProduction	C8:F8
Supply	I19:I21
TotalAssigned	C22:F22
TotalAssignments	G19:G21
TotalCost	I24
UnitCost	C4:F6

	G
17	Total
18	Assignments
19	=SUM(C19:F19)
20	=SUM(C20:F20)
21	=SUM(C21:F21)

	I
23	Total Cost
24	=SUMPRODUCT(Cost,Assignment)

	B	C	D	E	F
22	Total Assigned	=SUM(C19:C21)	=SUM(D19:D21)	=SUM(E19:E21)	=SUM(F19:F21)

Therefore, the school district management has decided to prohibit splitting any tract between schools. To provide a relatively even allocation of students to schools, management also will require that exactly three tracts be assigned to each school.

> *New Problem Statement:* Given the data in Table 6.12, minimize the total distance that all students must travel to school when each tract is assigned entirely to one school (no tract splitting) and each school is assigned exactly three tracts.

This now is almost an assignment problem since each tract needs to be assigned to exactly one school. The difference is that three tracts are being assigned to each school.

Formulation of a Spreadsheet Model

Since tracts are being assigned to schools, this problem can be interpreted as a variant of an assignment problem where the tracts are the *assignees* and the schools are the *tasks*. It is only a variant because each school is to be assigned exactly three tracts, whereas assumption 3 for the assignment problem model specifies that each task is to be performed by exactly *one* assignee. Therefore, in the spreadsheet model shown in Figure 6.22, each task (school) is given

FIGURE 6.22   In contrast to Figure 6.8, tract splitting is no longer allowed, so the Middletown School District problem becomes a variant of an assignment problem. The target cell is TotalDistance (H30) and the other output cells are TotalAssignments (F18:F26), TotalAssigned (C27:E27), and (in units of miles) Cost (I5:K13), where the equations entered into these cells are shown after the spreadsheet. The values of 1 in the changing cells Assignment (C18:E26) show the optimal zoning plan found by the Solver.

	A	B	C	D	E	F	G	H	I	J	K
1		**Middletown School District Zoning Problem (Revised)**									
2											
3		**Distance**				Number of		**Cost**			
4		**(Miles)**	School 1	School 2	School 3	Students		**(Miles)**	School 1	School 2	School 3
5		Tract 1	2.2	1.9	2.5	500		Tract 1	1,100	950	1,250
6		Tract 2	1.4	1.3	1.7	400		Tract 2	560	520	680
7		Tract 3	0.5	1.8	1.1	450		Tract 3	225	810	495
8		Tract 4	1.2	0.3	2	400		Tract 4	480	120	800
9		Tract 5	0.9	0.7	1	500		Tract 5	450	350	500
10		Tract 6	1.1	1.6	0.6	450		Tract 6	495	720	270
11		Tract 7	2.7	0.7	1.5	450		Tract 7	1,215	315	675
12		Tract 8	1.8	1.2	0.8	400		Tract 8	720	480	320
13		Tract 9	1.5	1.7	0.7	500		Tract 9	750	850	350
14											
15											
16						Total					
17		**Assignment**	School 1	School 2	School 3	Assignments		Supply			
18		Tract 1	0	1	0	1	=	1			
19		Tract 2	1	0	0	1	=	1			
20		Tract 3	1	0	0	1	=	1			
21		Tract 4	0	1	0	1	=	1			
22		Tract 5	1	0	0	1	=	1			
23		Tract 6	0	0	1	1	=	1			
24		Tract 7	0	1	0	1	=	1			
25		Tract 8	0	0	1	1	=	1			
26		Tract 9	0	0	1	1	=	1			
27		Total Assigned	3	3	3						
28			=	=	=			Total Distance			
29		Demand	3	3	3			(Miles)			
30								3,560			

FIGURE 6.22 *(continued)*

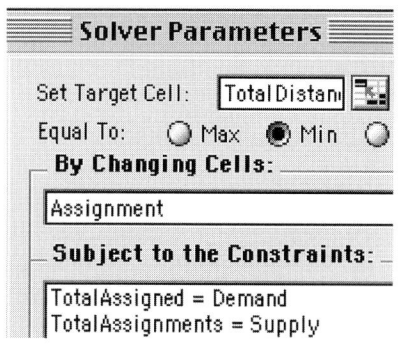

	H	I	J	K
3	**Cost**			
4	**(Miles)**	School 1	School 2	School 3
5	Tract 1	=C5*F5	=D5*F5	=E5*F5
6	Tract 2	=C6*F6	=D6*F6	=E6*F6
7	Tract 3	=C7*F7	=D7*F7	=E7*F7
8	Tract 4	=C8*F8	=D8*F8	=E8*F8
9	Tract 5	=C9*F9	=D9*F9	=E9*F9
10	Tract 6	=C10*F10	=D10*F10	=E10*F10
11	Tract 7	=C11*F11	=D11*F11	=E11*F11
12	Tract 8	=C12*F12	=D12*F12	=E12*F12
13	Tract 9	=C13*F13	=D13*F13	=E13*F13

	F
16	Total
17	Assignments
18	=SUM(C18:E18)
19	=SUM(C19:E19)
20	=SUM(C20:E20)
21	=SUM(C21:E21)
22	=SUM(C22:E22)
23	=SUM(C23:E23)
24	=SUM(C24:E24)
25	=SUM(C25:E25)
26	=SUM(C26:E26)

	H
28	Total Distance
29	(Miles)
30	=SUMPRODUCT(Cost,Assignment)

	B	C	D	E
27	Total Assigned	=SUM(C18:C26)	=SUM(D18:D26)	=SUM(E18:E26)

Range Name	Cell
Assignment	C18:E26
Cost	I5:K13
Demand	C29:E29
Distance	C5:E13
NumberOfStudents	F5:F13
Supply	H18:H26
TotalAssigned	C27:E27
TotalAssignments	F18:F26
TotalDistance	H30

Since the "cost" of assigning a tract to a school is being measured by the total distance that students must travel, the distance to the school needs to be multiplied by the number of students in the tract.

a demand of 3 rather than 1. Otherwise, the constraints for this model are the same as for an assignment problem.

The objective for an assignment problem is to minimize the total cost of all the assignments made, but now *cost* is being measured in terms of the total *distance* that students travel. Therefore, the cost of assigning any tract to a particular school is the number of students in that tract *times* the distance to that school per student, where both of these quantities are given in the table called Distance (C5:E13) in Figure 6.22. To illustrate, consider the cost of assigning tract 1 to school 1.

Distance from tract 1 to school 1   = 2.2 miles

Number of students in tract 1   = 500

Cost of assigning tract 1 to school 1 = 500(2.2 miles)

                = 1,100 miles

The table called Cost (I5:K13) shows the costs calculated in this way for all the combinations of tracts and schools, using the equations given for these cells.

The changing cells Assignment (C18:E26) show the optimal assignments of tracts to schools obtained by clicking on the Solve button. As indicated in the target cell TotalDistance (H30), the resulting total distance traveled to school by all the students is 3,560 miles. This amounts to an average of 0.879 mile per student.

This plan is very similar to the one obtained in Section 6.4 (see Figure 6.8) when tract splitting was permitted. The only difference is that the earlier plan splits tract 5, with 150 of its 500 students assigned to school 2 rather than to school 1, thereby reducing the distance traveled to school for each of these 150 students from 0.9 mile to 0.7 mile. However, the school district management feels that this small saving in distance traveled does not justify separating these 150 students from their neighbors who had always gone to school with them. Therefore, management adopted the new plan.

As this example and the preceding one illustrate, management often needs to have modifications made in the original model of the problem to better consider managerial concerns.

Review
Questions

1. When formulating a spreadsheet model for a variant of an assignment problem where certain assignees are unable to perform certain tasks, how is this feature formulated in the model?
2. If an assignee will perform more than one task, how is this feature formulated in the spreadsheet model?
3. If a task will be performed jointly by more than one assignee, how is this feature formulated in the spreadsheet model?

6.8 Summary

Transportation problems and assignment problems (and their variants) are special types of linear programming problems that have a variety of important applications.

A transportation problem is concerned (literally or figuratively) with distributing a commodity from its *sources* to some *destinations*. Each source has a fixed supply and each destination has a fixed demand for the commodity. A basic assumption is that the cost of distribution from each source to each destination is directly proportional to the amount distributed. Formulating a transportation problem requires identifying the unit costs of distribution, the supplies, and the demands.

Given a set of *tasks* to be performed and a set of *assignees* who are available to perform the tasks (one assignee per task), an assignment problem deals with the question of which assignee should be assigned to each task so as to minimize the total cost of performing all the tasks. The assignees can be people, machines, vehicles, plants, and so on, so there are many applications. The formulation of the problem requires constructing a *cost table* that gives the cost for each possible assignment of an assignee to a task.

A variety of features that do not quite fit either the transportation problem format or the assignment problem format also can be readily formulated in a spreadsheet model.

The overriding goal of this chapter has been to enable you to recognize when a problem you might face as a future manager can be formulated and analyzed as a transportation or assignment problem, or as a variant of one of these problem types.

Glossary

assignees   The entities (people, machines, vehicles, plants, etc.) that are to perform the tasks when formulating a problem as an assignment problem. (Section 6.6) *253*

cost table   The table that summarizes the formulation of an assignment problem by giving the cost for each possible assignment of an assignee to a task. (Section 6.6) *253*

demand at a destination   The number of units that need to be received by this destination from the sources. (Section 6.2) *222*

destinations   The receiving centers for a transportation problem. (Section 6.2) *222*

Hungarian method   An algorithm designed specifically to solve assignment problems very efficiently. (Section 6.6) *254*

network simplex method   A streamlined version of the simplex method for solving distribution-network problems, including transportation and assignment problems, very efficiently. (Section 6.2) *227*

sources   The supply centers for a transportation problem. (Section 6.2) *222*

supply from a source   The number of units to be distributed from this source to the destinations. (Section 6.2) *222*

tasks   The jobs to be performed by the assignees when formulating a problem as an assignment problem. (Section 6.6) *253*

transportation simplex method   A streamlined version of the simplex method for solving transportation problems very efficiently. (Section 6.2) *227*

Learning Aids for This Chapter in Your MS Courseware

Chapter 6 Excel Files:

P & T Case Study

Better Products Example

Nifty Example

Metro Example

Northern Airplane Example

Middletown Example

Energetic Example

Texago Case Study (6 spreadsheets)

Sellmore Example

Job Shop Example

Revised Better Products Example

Revised Middletown Example

An Excel Add-in:

Premium Solver for Education

Problems

We have inserted the symbol E* to the left of each problem (or its parts) where Excel should be used (unless your instructor gives you contrary instructions). An asterisk on the problem number indicates that at least a partial answer is given in the back of the book.

6.1.   Consider the transportation problem having the following data:

		Unit Cost ($)		
Destination:	**1**	**2**	**3**	**Supply**
Source				
1	9	6	8	4
2	7	12	10	3
3	6	7	6	2
Demand	4	2	3	

    a. Draw the network representation of this problem.

E*   *b.* Display the problem on a spreadsheet and then use the Excel Solver to obtain an optimal solution.

6.2.   Consider the transportation problem having the following data:

		Unit Cost ($)			
Destination:	**1**	**2**	**3**	**4**	**Supply**
Source					
1	3	7	6	4	5
2	2	4	3	2	2
3	4	3	8	5	3
Demand	3	3	2	2	

    a. Draw the network representation of this problem.

E*   *b.* Display the problem on a spreadsheet and then use the Excel Solver to obtain an optimal solution.

6.3.   The Cost-Less Corp. supplies its four retail outlets from its four plants. The shipping cost per shipment from each plant to each retail outlet is given below.

		Unit Shipping Cost		
Retail Outlet:	**1**	**2**	**3**	**4**
Plant				
1	$500	$600	$400	$200
2	200	900	100	300
3	300	400	200	100
4	200	100	300	200

Plants 1, 2, 3, and 4 make 10, 20, 20, and 10 shipments per month, respectively. Retail outlets 1, 2, 3, and 4 need to receive 20, 10, 10, and 20 shipments per month, respectively.

The distribution manager, Randy Smith, now wants to determine the best plan for how many shipments to send from each plant to the respective retail outlets each month. Randy's objective is to minimize the total shipping cost.

    a. Formulate this problem as a transportation problem by constructing a table that identifies all the sources, supplies, destinations, demands, and unit costs.

E*   *b.* Display the transportation problem on a spreadsheet and then use the Excel Solver to obtain an optimal solution.

6.4.   The Childfair Company has three plants producing child push chairs that are to be shipped to four distribution centers. Plants 1, 2, and 3 produce 12, 17, and 11 shipments per month, respectively. Each distribution center needs to receive 10 shipments per month. The distance from each plant to the respective distribution centers is given below:

	Distance to Distribution Center (Miles)			
	1	**2**	**3**	**4**
Plant				
1	800	1,300	400	700
2	1,100	1,400	600	1,000
3	600	1,200	800	900

The freight cost for each shipment is $100 plus 50 cents/mile.

How much should be shipped from each plant to each of the distribution centers to minimize the total shipping cost?

   a. Formulate this problem as a transportation problem by constructing a table that identifies all the sources, supplies, destinations, demands, and unit costs.

E*   *b.* Display the transportation problem on a spreadsheet and then use the Excel Solver to obtain an optimal solution.

E*6.5.*   Tom would like 3 pints of home brew today and an additional 4 pints of home brew tomorrow. Dick is willing to sell a maximum of 5 pints total at a price of $3.00/pint today and $2.70/pint tomorrow. Harry is willing to sell a maximum of 4 pints total at a price of $2.90/pint today and $2.80/pint tomorrow.

Tom wishes to know what his purchases should be to minimize his cost while satisfying his thirst requirements. Formulate and solve a spreadsheet model for this problem.

E*6.6.   The Versatech Corporation has decided to produce three new products. Five branch plants now have excess product capacity. The unit manufacturing cost of the first product would be $31, $29, $32, $28, and $29 in plants 1, 2, 3, 4, and 5, respectively. The unit manufacturing cost of the second product would be $45, $41, $46, $42, and $43 in plants 1, 2, 3, 4, and 5, respectively. The unit manufacturing cost of the third product would be $38, $35, and $40 in plants 1, 2, and 3, respectively, whereas plants 4 and 5 do not have the capability for producing this product. Sales forecasts indicate that 600, 1,000, and 800 units of products 1, 2, and 3, respectively, should be produced per day. Plants 1, 2, 3, 4, and 5 have the capacity to produce 400, 600, 400, 600, and 1,000 units daily, respectively, regardless of the product or combinations of products involved. Assume that any plant having the capability and capacity to produce them can produce any combination of the products in any quantity.

Management wishes to know how to allocate the new products to the plants to minimize total manufacturing cost. Formulate and solve a spreadsheet model for this problem.

E*6.7.   Suppose that England, France, and Spain produce all the wheat, barley, and oats in the world. The world demand for wheat requires 125 million acres of land devoted to wheat production. Similarly, 60 million acres of land are required for barley and 75 million acres of land are required for oats. The total amount of land available for these purposes in England, France, and Spain is 70 million acres, 110 million acres, and 80 million acres, respectively. The number of hours of labor needed in England, France, and Spain, respectively, to produce an acre of wheat is 18, 13, and 16; to produce an acre of barley is 15, 12, and 12; and to produce an acre of oats is 12, 10, and 16. The labor cost per hour in England, France, and Spain, respectively, for producing wheat is $9.00, $7.20, and $9.90; for producing barley is $8.10, $9.00, and $8.40; and for producing oats is $6.90, $7.50, and $6.30. The problem is to allocate land use in each country so as to meet the world food requirements and minimize the total labor cost. Formulate and solve a spreadsheet model for this problem.

E*6.8.   A contractor, Susan Meyer, has to haul gravel to three building sites. She can purchase as much as 18 tons at a gravel pit in the north of the city and 14 tons at one in the south. She needs 10, 5, and 10 tons at sites 1, 2, and 3, respectively. The purchase price per ton at each gravel pit and the hauling cost per ton are given in the following table.

Pit	Hauling Cost per Ton at Site			Price per Ton
	1	**2**	**3**	
North	$30	$60	$50	$100
South	60	30	40	120

Susan wishes to determine how much to haul from each pit to each site to minimize the total cost for purchasing and hauling gravel. Formulate and solve a spreadsheet model for this problem.

E*6.9.   Reconsider the P & T Co. case study presented in Sections 6.1 and 6.2. Refer to the spreadsheet in Figure 6.2, which shows the formulation as a transportation problem and displays an optimal solution. You now learn that one or more of the unit costs in the data cells UnitCost (D5:G7) may change slightly before shipments begin.

   Use the Excel Solver to generate the sensitivity report for this problem. Use this report to determine the allowable range for each of the unit costs. What do these allowable ranges tell P & T management?

E*6.10.   Reconsider the Metro Water District problem presented in Section 6.4. Refer to the spreadsheet in Figure 6.6, which shows the formulation as a variant of a transportation problem and displays an optimal solution.

   The numbers given in the data cells are only estimates that may be somewhat inaccurate, so management now wishes to do some what-if analysis. Use the Excel Solver to generate the sensitivity report. Then use this report to address the following questions. (In each case, assume that the indicated change is the only change in the model.)

   a. Would the optimal solution in Figure 6.6 remain optimal if the cost per acre foot of shipping Calorie River water to San Go were actually $200 rather than $230?

   b. Would this solution remain optimal if the cost per acre foot of shipping Sacron River water to Los Devils were actually $160 rather than $130?

   c. Must this solution remain optimal if the costs considered in parts *a* and *b* were simultaneously changed from their original values to $215 and $145, respectively?

   d. Suppose that the supply from the Sacron River and the demand at Hollyglass are decreased simultaneously by the same amount. Must the shadow prices for evaluating these changes remain valid if the decrease were 0.5 million acre feet?

E*6.11.   Reconsider the Metro Water District problem presented in Section 6.4, including the data given in Table 6.9.

   The numbers in this table for the amount of water needed by the respective cities actually represent the absolute minimum that each city must have. Each city would like to have as much as 2 million additional acre feet beyond this minimum amount.

   Since the amount of water available exceeds the sum of these minimum amounts by 3.5 million acre feet, Metro management has decided to distribute this additional water to the cities as well. The decisions on how much additional water the respective cities will receive beyond meeting their minimum needs will be based on minimizing Metro's total cost. Management wants to know which plan for distributing water from the rivers to the cities will achieve this objective. Formulate and solve a spreadsheet model for this problem.

E*6.12.   The Onenote Co. produces a single product at three plants for four customers. The three plants will produce 60, 80, and 40 units, respectively, during the next week. The firm has made a commitment to sell 40 units to customer 1, 60 units to customer 2, and at least 20 units to customer 3. Both customers 3 and 4 also want to buy as many of the remaining units as possible. The net profit associated with shipping a unit from plant *i* for sale to customer *j* is given by the following table:

Plant	Customer			
	1	**2**	**3**	**4**
1	$800	$700	$500	$200
2	500	200	100	300
3	600	400	300	500

Management wishes to know how many units to sell to customers 3 and 4 and how many units to ship from each of the plants to each of the customers to maximize profit. Formulate and solve a spreadsheet model for this problem.

E*6.13. The Move-It Company has two plants building forklift trucks that then are shipped to three distribution centers. The production costs are the same at the two plants, and the cost of shipping each truck is shown below for each combination of plant and distribution center:

	Distribution Center		
	1	**2**	**3**
Plant			
A	$800	$700	$400
B	600	800	500

A total of 60 forklift trucks are produced and shipped per week. Each plant can produce and ship any amount up to a maximum of 50 trucks per week, so there is considerable flexibility on how to divide the total production between the two plants so as to reduce shipping costs. However, each distribution center must receive exactly 20 trucks per week.

Management's objective is to determine how many forklift trucks should be produced at each plant, and then what the overall shipping pattern should be to minimize total shipping cost. Formulate and solve a spreadsheet model for this problem.

E*6.14. Redo Problem 6.13 when any distribution center may receive any quantity between 10 and 30 forklift trucks per week in order to further reduce total shipping cost, provided only that the total shipped to all three distribution centers must still equal 60 trucks per week.

E*6.15. The Build-Em-Fast Company has agreed to supply its best customer with three widgits during *each* of the next three weeks, even though producing them will require some overtime work. The relevant production data are as follows:

	Maximum Production		Production Cost per Unit,
Week	**Regular Time**	**Overtime**	**Regular Time**
1	2	2	$300
2	3	2	500
3	1	2	400

The cost per unit produced with overtime for each week is $100 more than for regular time. The cost of storage is $50 per unit for each week it is stored. There is already an inventory of two widgits on hand currently, but the company does not want to retain any widgits in inventory after the three weeks.

Management wants to know how many units should be produced in each week to minimize the total cost of meeting the delivery schedule. Formulate and solve a spreadsheet model for this problem.

E*6.16. The MJK Manufacturing Company must produce two products in sufficient quantity to meet contracted sales in each of the next three months. The two products share the same production facilities, and each unit of both products requires the same amount of production capacity. The available production and storage facilities are changing month by month, so the production capacities, unit production costs, and unit storage costs vary by month. Therefore, it may be worthwhile to overproduce one or both products in some months and store them until needed.

For each of the three months, the initialed columns of the following table give the maximum number of units of the two products combined that can be produced on regular time (RT) and on overtime (OT). For each of the two products, the subsequent columns give (1) the number of units needed for the contracted sales, (2) the cost (in thousands of dollars) per unit produced on regular time, (3) the cost (in thousands of dollars) per unit produced on overtime, and (4) the cost (in thousands of dollars) of storing each extra unit that is held over into the next month. In each case, the numbers for the two products are separated by a slash /, with the number for product 1 on the left and the number for product 2 on the right.

Month	Maximum Combined Production		Sales	Product 1/Product 2		Unit Cost of Storage ($1,000s)
				Unit Cost of Production ($1,000s)		
	RT	OT		RT	OT	
1	10	3	5/3	15/16	18/20	1/2
2	8	2	3/5	17/15	20/18	2/1
3	10	3	4/4	19/17	22/22	

The production manager wants a schedule developed for the number of units of each of the two products to be produced on regular time and, if regular time production capacity is used up, on overtime in each of the three months. The objective is to minimize the total of the production and storage costs while meeting the contracted sales for each month. There is no initial inventory, and no final inventory is desired after the three months.

Formulate and solve a spreadsheet model for this problem.

6.17. Consider the transportation problem having the following data:

Destination:	1	2	3	4	Supply
	Unit Cost ($)				
Source					
1	7	4	1	4	1
2	4	6	7	2	1
3	8	5	4	6	1
4	6	7	6	3	1
Demand	1	1	1	1	

a. What property ensures that this problem has feasible solutions?

b. What property ensures that this problem has an optimal solution with values of 0 or 1 for all the shipment amounts?

c. Explain how this problem can be interpreted to be an assignment problem.

d. Draw the network representation of this assignment problem.

E*   e. Display the problem on a spreadsheet and then use the Excel Solver to obtain an optimal solution.

6.18. Consider the assignment problem having the following cost table:

	Job		
	1	2	3
Person			
A	$5	$7	$4
B	3	6	5
C	2	3	4

The optimal solution is A-3, B-1, C-2, with a total cost of $10.

a. Draw the network representation of this problem.

E*   b. Formulate this problem on a spreadsheet and then use the Excel Solver to obtain the optimal solution identified above.

6.19. Consider the assignment problem having the following cost table:

	Task			
	1	**2**	**3**	**4**
Assignee				
A	$8	$6	$5	$7
B	6	5	3	4
C	7	8	4	6
D	6	7	5	6

    a. Draw the network representation of this assignment problem.

E*   *b.* Formulate this problem on a spreadsheet and then use the Excel Solver to obtain an optimal solution.

6.20. Four cargo ships will be used for shipping goods from one port to four other ports (labeled 1, 2, 3, 4). Any ship can be used for making any one of these four trips. However, because of differences in the ships and cargoes, the total cost of loading, transporting, and unloading the goods for the different ship–port combinations varies considerably, as shown in the following table:

	Port			
	1	**2**	**3**	**4**
Ship				
1	$500	$400	$600	$700
2	600	600	700	500
3	700	500	700	600
4	500	400	600	600

The objective is to assign the four ships to four different ports in such a way as to minimize the total cost for all four shipments.

    a. Describe how this problem fits into the format for an assignment problem.

E*   *b.* Formulate and solve this problem on a spreadsheet.

E*6.21. Reconsider Problem 6.6. Suppose that the sales forecasts have been revised downward to 240, 400, and 320 units per day of products 1, 2, and 3, respectively. Thus, each plant now has the capacity to produce all that is required of any one product. Therefore, management has decided that each new product should be assigned to only one plant and that no plant should be assigned more than one product (so that three plants are each to be assigned one product, and two plants are to be assigned none). The objective is to make these assignments so as to minimize the *total* cost of producing these amounts of the three products. Formulate and solve a spreadsheet model for this problem.

6.22.* The coach of an age group swim team needs to assign swimmers to a 200-yard medley relay team to send to the Junior Olympics. Since most of his best swimmers are very fast in more than one stroke, it is not clear which swimmer should be assigned to each of the four strokes. The five fastest swimmers and the best times (in seconds) they have achieved in each of the strokes (for 50 yards) are

Stroke	Carl	Chris	David	Tony	Ken
Backstroke	37.7	32.9	33.8	37.0	35.4
Breaststroke	43.4	33.1	42.2	34.7	41.8
Butterfly	33.3	28.5	38.9	30.4	33.6
Freestyle	29.2	26.4	29.6	28.5	31.1

The coach wishes to determine how to assign four swimmers to the four different strokes to minimize the sum of the corresponding best times.

    a. Describe how this problem fits into the format for a variant of an assignment problem even though it does not involve costs. What plays the role of costs?

E*   *b.* Formulate and solve this problem on a spreadsheet.

E*6.23.   Reconsider Problem 6.8. Now suppose that trucks (and their drivers) need to be hired to do the hauling, where each truck can only be used once to haul gravel from a single pit to a single site. Enough trucks are available to haul all the gravel that can be purchased at each site. Each truck can haul five tons, and the cost per truck is five times the hauling cost per ton given earlier. Only full trucks are to supply each site.

    Formulate and solve a spreadsheet model for this problem.

E*6.24.   Reconsider Problem 6.13. Now distribution centers 1, 2, and 3 must receive exactly 10, 20, and 30 units per week, respectively. For administrative convenience, management has decided that each distribution center will be supplied totally by a single plant, so that one plant will supply one distribution center and the other plant will supply the other two distribution centers. The choice of these assignments of plants to distribution centers is to be made solely on the basis of minimizing total shipping cost.

    Formulate and solve a spreadsheet model for this problem.

Case 6-1

Shipping Wood to Market

Alabama Atlantic is a lumber company that has three sources of wood and five markets to be supplied. The annual availability of wood at sources 1, 2, and 3 is 15, 20, and 15 million board feet, respectively. The amount that can be sold annually at markets 1, 2, 3, 4, and 5 is 11, 12, 9, 10, and 8 million board feet, respectively.

In the past, the company has shipped the wood by train. However, because shipping costs have been increasing, the alternative of using ships to make some of the deliveries is being investigated. This alternative would require the company to invest in some ships. Except for these investment costs, the shipping costs in thousands of dollars per million board feet by rail and by water (when feasible) would be the following for each route:

Source	Unit Cost by Rail ($1,000s) to Market					Unit Cost by Ship ($1,000s) to Market				
	1	2	3	4	5	1	2	3	4	5
1	61	72	45	55	66	31	38	24	—	35
2	69	78	60	49	56	36	43	28	24	31
3	59	66	63	61	47	—	33	36	32	26

The capital investment (in thousands of dollars) in ships required for each million board feet to be transported annually by ship along each route is given as follows:

Source	Unit Investment for Ships ($1,000s) to Market				
	1	2	3	4	5
1	275	303	238	—	285
2	293	318	270	250	265
3	—	283	275	268	240

Considering the expected useful life of the ships and the time value of money, the equivalent uniform annual cost of these investments is one-tenth the amount given in the table. The objective is to determine the overall shipping plan that minimizes the total equivalent uniform annual cost (including shipping costs).

You are the head of the management science team that has been assigned the task of determining this shipping plan for each of the following three options.

Option 1: Continue shipping exclusively by rail.

Option 2: Switch to shipping exclusively by water (except where only rail is feasible).

Option 3: Ship by either rail or water, depending on which is less expensive for the particular route.

Present your results for each option. Compare.

Finally, consider the fact that these results are based on current shipping and investment costs, so that the decision on the option to adopt now should take into account management's projection of how these costs are likely to change in the future. For each option, describe a scenario of future cost changes that would justify adopting that option now.

Case 6-2

Continuation of the Texago Case Study

Reconsider the case study presented in Section 6.5 involving the Texago Corp. site selection problem.

Texago management has tentatively chosen St. Louis as the site of the new refinery. However, management now is addressing the question of what the capacity of the new refinery should be.

While analyzing the site selection problem, the task force was told to assume that the new refinery would have the capacity to process 120 million barrels of crude oil per year. As indicated in Table 6.16, this then would increase the total capacity of all the corporation's refineries from 240 million barrels to 360 million barrels. According to marketing forecasts, Texago will be able to sell all its finished product once this new capacity becomes available, but no more. Therefore, the choice of 120 million barrels as the capacity of the new refinery would enable all the corporation's refineries to operate at full capacity while also fully meeting the forecasted demand for Texago's products.

However, to prepare for possible future increases in demand beyond the current forecasts, management now wants to also consider the option of enlarging the plans for the new refinery so that it would have the capacity to process 150 million barrels of crude oil annually. Although this would force the corporation's refineries collectively to operate below full capacity by 30 million barrels for awhile, the extra capacity then would be available later if Texago were to continue to increase its market share. This might be well worthwhile since the capital and operating costs incurred by enlarging the plans for the new refinery would be far less (perhaps 40 percent less) than constructing and operating another refinery later to process only 30 million barrels of crude oil per year. Furthermore, management feels that this extra capacity might be needed within a few years.

The extra capital costs needed to increase the capacity of the new refinery by 30 million barrels is estimated to be $1.2 billion. The cost of carrying this extra capital would be about $100 million per year, depending on future interest rates. If some of this extra capacity were used at the new refinery, the total operating cost for the refinery would be somewhat larger than the amount shown in Table 6.19, but decreasing the production rate by the same amount at another refinery would decrease its total operating cost by a comparable amount. Since the operating cost per million barrels of crude oil processed is roughly the same at all the refineries, including the new one, the total operating cost for processing 360 million barrels should not be substantially affected by the allocation of this work to the refineries. However, management feels that having some flexibility for where to allocate this work might permit a substantial reduction in the cost of shipping crude oil and finished product. Since Table 6.20 indicates that the total annual shipping cost for crude oil and finished product would be $2.92 billion with St. Louis as the site for the refinery, management hopes that substantial reductions can be achieved in this way.

Figures 6.13 and 6.17 show the optimal shipping plans for crude oil and finished product, respectively, when the new refinery is in St. Louis and has a capacity of processing 120 million barrels of crude oil per year. Management now is asking the task force to analyze the situation under the option of increasing this capacity to 150 million barrels. In particular, management wants the following questions addressed. Under the new option, how should the shipping plan for crude oil in Figure 6.13 change and how much reduction in the total shipping cost would be achieved? How should the shipping plan for finished product in Figure 6.17 change and how much reduction in the total shipping cost would be achieved? Finally, assuming that the differences in operating costs shown in Table 6.19 would continue to apply under the new option, would the financial comparison of the three sites given in Table 6.20 be altered substantially if this option were to be adopted?

As the head of the task force, you have decided to lead the way in executing the following steps with the new option.

a. Formulate and solve a spreadsheet model to find an optimal plan for shipping 360 million barrels of crude oil per year from the oil fields to the refineries, including the new one in St. Louis, where the amount of crude oil each refinery will receive (up to its capacity) is based on minimizing the total annual cost for these shipments. (**Hint:** You can save some time in this and subsequent parts by using the live spreadsheets for the Texago case study in this chapter's Excel files as a starting point.) Compare the resulting total annual cost for these shipments with the results obtained in Figure 6.13 under the original assumption of a smaller refinery in St. Louis.

b. Assume that the plan found in part *a* (including its specification of how much crude oil each refinery will receive) will be used. On this basis, formulate and solve a spreadsheet model to find an optimal plan for shipping finished product from the refineries to the distribution centers. Compare the resulting total annual cost for these shipments with the results obtained in Figure 6.17. Also calculate the total annual cost of shipping both crude oil and finished product under this plan and compare it with the corresponding total of $2.39 billion obtained from Table 6.20.

c. You realize that the cost of shipping final product tends to be somewhat larger than the cost of shipping crude oil. Therefore, rather than having the decisions regarding the amount of crude oil each refinery will receive and process be dictated by minimizing the total annual cost of shipping crude oil (as in parts *a* and *b*), you decide to check what would happen if these decisions were based on minimizing the total annual cost of shipping final product instead. Formulate and solve a spreadsheet model to find an optimal plan for shipping final product from the refineries (including the new one in St. Louis) to the distribution centers, where the allocation of the 360 million barrels of crude oil per year to the refineries is based on minimizing the total annual cost for these shipments. Compare the resulting total annual cost for these shipments with the results obtained in part *b* and in Figure 6.17.

d. Assume that the plan found in part *c* (including its specification regarding how much crude oil each refinery will receive and process) will be used. On this basis, formulate and solve a spreadsheet model to find an optimal plan for shipping crude oil from the oil fields to the refineries. Compare the resulting total annual cost for these shipments with the results obtained in part *a* and in Figure 6.13. Also calculate the total annual cost of shipping both crude oil and finished product under this plan and compare it with the corresponding total obtained in part *b* and in Table 6.20.

e. You realize that, so far, you have been *suboptimizing* the overall problem by optimizing only one part of the problem at a time, so now it is time to get down to serious business. Formulate a single spreadsheet model that simultaneously considers the shipping of 360 million barrels of crude oil per year from the oil fields to the refineries (including the new one in St. Louis) and the shipping of final product from the refineries to the distribution centers. Use the objective of minimizing the grand total of all these shipping costs. Since the refineries collectively have a capacity of processing 390 million barrels of crude oil per year, the decisions regarding the amount of crude oil each refinery will receive and process (up to each refinery's capacity) also are to be based on this same objective. Solve the model and compare the resulting total of all the shipping costs with the corresponding total calculated in parts *b* and *d* and in Table 6.20.

f. Repeat part *e* if the new refinery (with a capacity of processing 150 million barrels of crude oil per year) were to be placed in Los Angeles instead of St. Louis. Then repeat it again if Galveston were to be selected as the site instead of St. Louis. Using the operating costs given in Table 6.19 for the three sites, construct a table like Table 6.20 to show the new financial comparison between the sites. (Although the operating costs will be larger than given in Table 6.19 if the new refinery processes more than 120 million barrels of crude oil per year, management has instructed the task force to assume that the differences in operating costs shown in Table 6.19 would continue to apply, so the differences in the total variable costs in the table being constructed would still be valid.)

g. You now are ready to submit all your results (including your spreadsheets) to management. Write an accompanying memorandum that presents your recommendations.

Case 6-3

Project Pickings

Tazer, a pharmaceutical manufacturing company, entered the pharmaceutical market 12 years ago with the introduction of six new drugs. Five of the six drugs were simply permutations of existing drugs and therefore did not sell very heavily. The sixth drug, however, addressed hypertension and was a huge success. Since Tazer had a patent on the hypertension drug, it experienced no competition, and profits from the hypertension drug alone kept Tazer in business.

During the past 12 years, Tazer continued a moderate amount of research and development, but it never stumbled upon a drug as successful as the hypertension drug. One reason is that the company never had the motivation to invest heavily in innovative research and development. The company was riding the profit wave generated by its hypertension drug and did not feel the need to commit significant resources to finding new drug breakthroughs.

Now Tazer is beginning to fear the pressure of competition. The patent for the hypertension drug expires in five years,[1] and Tazer knows that once the patent expires, generic drug manufacturing companies will swarm into the market like vultures. Historical trends show that generic drugs decrease sales of branded drugs by 75 percent.

Tazer is therefore looking to invest significant amounts of money in research and development this year to begin the search for a new breakthrough drug that will offer the company the same success as the hypertension drug. Tazer believes that if the company begins extensive research and development now, the probability of finding a successful drug shortly after the expiration of the hypertension patent will be high.

As head of research and development at Tazer, you are responsible for choosing potential projects and assigning project directors to lead each of the projects. After researching the needs of the market, analyzing the shortcomings of current drugs, and interviewing numerous scientists concerning the promising areas of medical research, you have decided that your department will pursue five separate projects, which are listed below:

Project Up: Develop a more effective antidepressant that does not cause serious mood swings.

Project Stable: Develop a drug that addresses manic-depression.

Project Choice: Develop a less intrusive birth control method for women.

Project Hope: Develop a vaccine to prevent HIV infection.

Project Release: Develop a more effective drug to lower blood pressure.

For each of the five projects, you are only able to specify the medical ailment the research should address since you do not know what compounds will exist and be effective without research.

You also have five senior scientists to lead the five projects. You know that scientists are very temperamental people and will only work well if they are challenged and motivated by the project. To ensure that the senior scientists are assigned to projects they find motivating, you have established a bidding system for the projects. You have given each of the five scientists 1,000 bid points. They assign bids to each project, giving a higher number of bid points to projects they most prefer to lead.

The following table provides the bids from the five senior scientists for the five individual projects:

Project	Dr. Kvaal	Dr. Zuner	Dr. Tsai	Dr. Mickey	Dr. Rollins
Project Up	100	0	100	267	100
Project Stable	400	200	100	153	33
Project Choice	200	800	100	99	33
Project Hope	200	0	100	451	34
Project Release	100	0	600	30	800

You decide to evaluate a variety of scenarios you think are likely.

---

[1]In general, patents protect inventions for 17 years. In 1995, GATT legislation extending the protection given by new pharmaceutical patents to 20 years became effective. The patent for Tazer's hypertension drug was issued prior to the GATT legislation, however. Thus, the patent only protects the drug for 17 years.

a. Given the bids, you need to assign one senior scientist to each of the five projects to maximize the preferences of the scientists. What are the assignments?

b. Dr. Rollins is being courted by Harvard Medical School to accept a teaching position. You are fighting desperately to keep her at Tazer, but the prestige of Harvard may lure her away. If this were to happen, the company would give up the project with the least enthusiasm. Which project would not be done?

c. You do not want to sacrifice any project since researching only four projects decreases the probability of finding a breakthrough new drug. You decide that either Dr. Zuner or Dr. Mickey could lead two projects. Under these new conditions with just four senior scientists, which scientists will lead which projects to maximize preferences?

d. After Dr. Zuner was informed that she and Dr. Mickey are being considered for two projects, she decided to change her bids. Dr. Zuner's new bids for each of the projects are the following:

Project Up: 20

Project Stable: 450

Project Choice: 451

Project Hope: 39

Project Release: 40

Under these new conditions with just four senior scientists, which scientists will lead which projects to maximize preferences?

e. Do you support the assignments found in part *d*? Why or why not?

f. Now you again consider all five scientists. You decide, however, that several scientists cannot lead certain projects. In particular, Dr. Mickey does not have experience with research on the immune system, so he cannot lead Project Hope. His family also has a history of manic-depression, and you feel that he would be too personally involved in Project Stable to serve as an effective project leader. Dr. Mickey therefore cannot lead Project Stable. Dr. Kvaal also does not have experience with research on the immune system and cannot lead Project Hope. In addition, Dr. Kvaal cannot lead Project Release because he does not have experience with research on the cardiovascular system. Finally, Dr. Rollins cannot lead Project Up because her family has a history of depression and you feel she would be too personally involved in the project to serve as an effective leader. Because Dr. Mickey and Dr. Kvaal cannot lead two of the five projects, they each have only 600 bid points. Dr. Rollins has only 800 bid points because she cannot lead one of the five projects. The following table provides the new bids of Dr. Mickey, Dr. Kvaal, and Dr. Rollins:

Project	Dr. Mickey	Dr. Kvaal	Dr. Rollins
Project Up	300	86	Can't lead
Project Stable	Can't lead	343	50
Project Choice	125	171	50
Project Hope	Can't lead	Can't lead	100
Project Release	175	Can't lead	600

Which scientists should lead which projects to maximize preferences?

g. You decide that Project Hope and Project Release are too complex to be led by only one scientist. Therefore, each of these projects will be assigned two scientists as project leaders. You decide to hire two more scientists in order to staff all projects: Dr. Arriaga and Dr. Santos. Because of religious reasons, neither of them want to lead Project Choice and so they assign 0 bid points to this project. The following table lists all projects, scientists, and their bids.

Project	Kvaal	Zuner	Tsai	Mickey	Rollins	Arriaga	Santos
Up	86	0	100	300	Can't lead	250	111
Stable	343	200	100	Can't lead	50	250	1
Choice	171	800	100	125	50	0	0
Hope	Can't lead	0	100	Can't lead	100	250	333
Release	Can't lead	0	600	175	600	250	555

Which scientists should lead which projects to maximize preferences?

h. Do you think it is wise to base your decision in part *g* only on an optimal solution for a variant of an assignment problem?

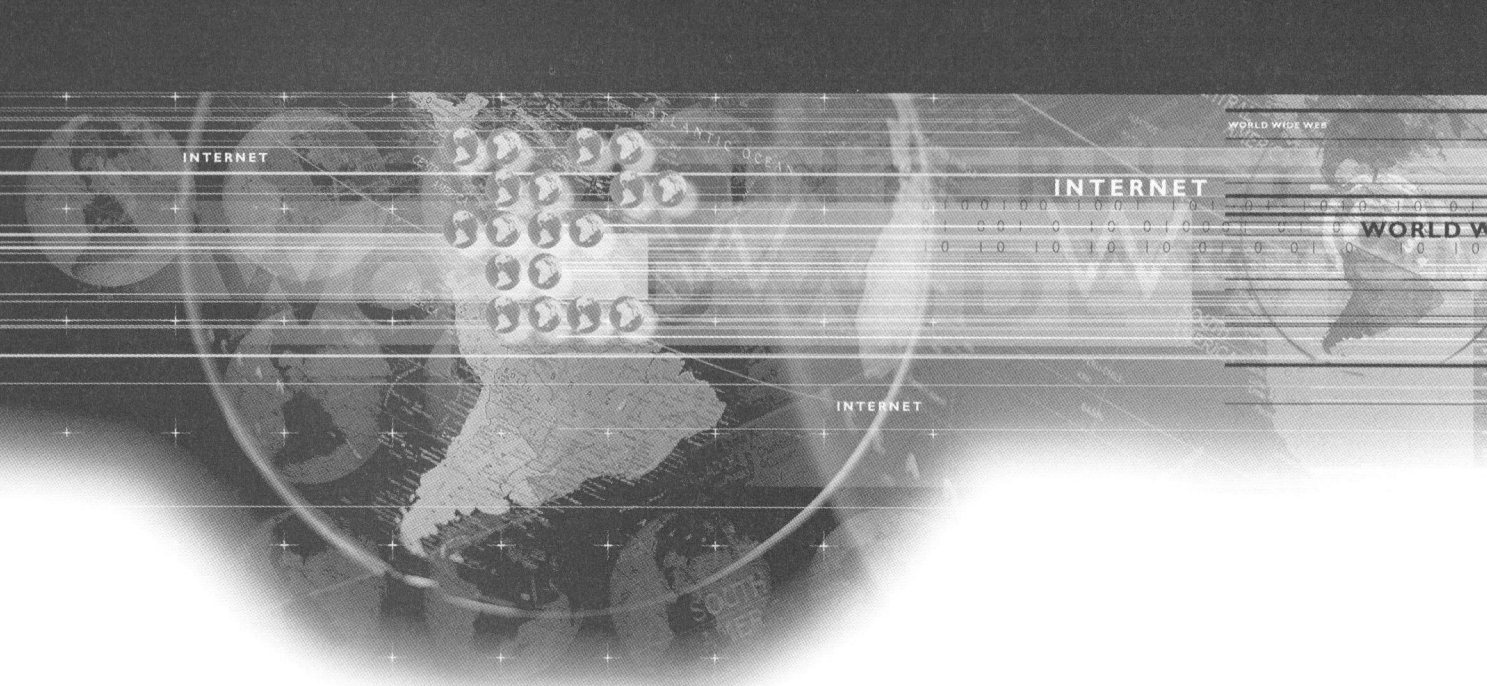

Learning objectives

After completing this chapter, you should be able to

1. Formulate network models for various types of network optimization problems.

2. Describe the characteristics of minimum-cost flow problems, maximum flow problems, shortest path problems, and minimum spanning-tree problems.

3. Identify some areas of application for these types of problems.

4. Identify several categories of network optimization problems that are special types of minimum-cost flow problems.

5. Formulate and solve a spreadsheet model for a minimum-cost flow problem, a maximum flow problem, or a shortest path problem from a description of the problem.

6. Use a simple algorithm to solve small minimum spanning-tree problems.

Chapter **Seven**

Network Optimization Problems

Networks arise in numerous settings and in a variety of guises. Transportation, electrical, and communication networks pervade our daily lives. Network representations also are widely used for problems in such diverse areas as production, distribution, project planning, facilities location, resource management, and financial planning—to name just a few examples. In fact, a network representation provides such a powerful visual and conceptual aid for portraying the relationships between the components of systems that it is used in virtually every field of scientific, social, and economic endeavor.

One of the most exciting developments in management science in recent years has been the unusually rapid advance in both the methodology and application of network optimization problems. A number of algorithmic breakthroughs have had a major impact, as have ideas from computer science concerning data structures and efficient data manipulation. Consequently, algorithms and software now are available and are being used to solve huge problems on a routine basis that would have been completely intractable a couple of decades ago.

As one example of this usage, consider the **National Railroad of France,** which transports over 50 million passengers per year through its vast rail network. As described in the January–February 1998 issue of *Interfaces,* this company uses advanced network optimization techniques both to develop a schedule that best matches the preferences of its customers and to adjust the capacity of its trains on a daily basis to better fit capacity to demand. These techniques are credited with increasing revenue by $15 million per year as well as substantially reducing operating costs and improving service for travelers. This application of management science won the prestigious first prize among the 1997 Franz Edelman Awards for Management Science Achievement.

This chapter presents the network optimization problems that have been particularly helpful in dealing with managerial issues. We focus on the nature of these problems and their applications rather than on the technical details and the algorithms used to solve the problems.

Many network optimization problems actually are special types of *linear programming* problems. For example, both of the special types of linear programming problems discussed in the preceding chapter—transportation problems and assignment problems—also have network representations, presented in Figures 6.3 and 6.19.

Section 7.1 discusses an especially important type of network optimization problem called a *minimum-cost flow problem.* Minimum-cost flow problems are the special type of linear programming problem referred to in Section 4.4 as a *distribution-network problem.*

Section 7.3 presents *maximum flow problems,* which are concerned with such issues as how to maximize the flow of goods through a distribution network. Section 7.2 lays the groundwork by introducing a case study of a maximum flow problem.

Section 7.4 considers *shortest path problems.* In their simplest form, the objective is to find the shortest route between two locations.

Section 7.5 discusses *minimum spanning-tree problems,* which are concerned with minimizing the cost of providing connections between all users of a system. This is the only network optimization problem considered in this chapter (or the preceding chapter) that is not, in fact, a special type of linear programming problem.

7.1 MINIMUM-COST FLOW PROBLEMS

Section 4.4 described distribution-network problems as a major type of linear programming problem that deals with the distribution of goods through a *distribution network* at minimum cost. The term *distribution-network problem* is, in fact, just another name for *minimum-cost flow problem*. (We will use the latter, more common name hereafter.)

An Example: The Distribution Unlimited Co. Problem

The Distribution Unlimited Co. has two factories producing a product that needs to be shipped to two warehouses. Here are some details.

Factory 1 is producing 80 units.

Factory 2 is producing 70 units.

Warehouse 1 needs 60 units.

Warehouse 2 needs 90 units.

(Each unit corresponds to a full truckload of the product.)

Figure 7.1 shows the distribution network available for shipping this product, where F1 and F2 are the two factories, W1 and W2 are the two warehouses, and DC is a distribution center. The arrows show feasible shipping lanes. In particular, there is a rail link from factory 1 to warehouse 1 and another from factory 2 to warehouse 2. (Any amounts can be shipped along these rail links.) In addition, independent truckers are available to ship up to 50 units from each factory to the distribution center, and then to ship up to 50 units from the distribution center to each warehouse. (Whatever is shipped to the distribution center must subsequently be shipped on to the warehouses.)

The objective is to minimize the total shipping cost through the distribution network.

The shipping costs differ considerably among these shipping lanes. The cost per unit shipped through each lane is shown above the corresponding arrow in Figure 7.2.

Management's objective is to determine the shipping plan (how many units to ship along each shipping lane) that will minimize the total shipping cost.

Except for its very small size, this problem is a typical *minimum-cost flow problem*. As described in Section 4.4, a full-fledged linear programming model can be formulated in algebraic form to represent such a problem. However, there is no need to develop such a lengthy formulation. A network such as Figure 7.2 provides a simpler and more intuitive formulation.

To make the network less crowded, the problem usually is presented even more compactly, as shown in Figure 7.3. The number in square brackets next to the location of each facility indicates the net number of units (outflow minus inflow) generated there. Thus, the number of

FIGURE 7.1

The distribution network for the Distribution Unlimited Co. problem, where each feasible shipping lane is represented by an arrow.

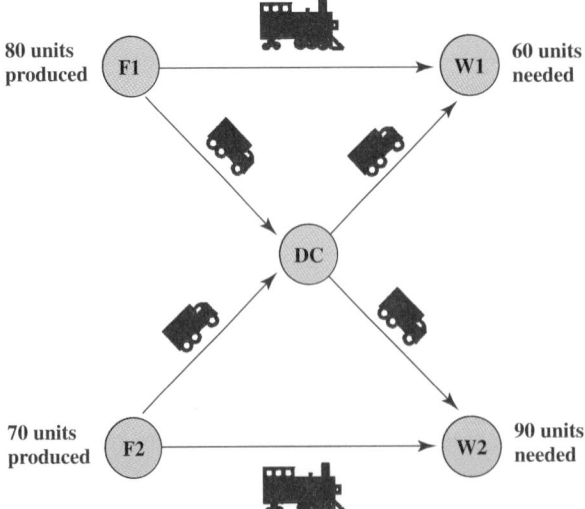

units terminating at each warehouse is shown as a negative number. The number at the distribution center is 0 since the number of units leaving *minus* the number of units arriving must equal 0. The number on top of each arrow shows the unit shipping cost along that shipping lane. Any number in square brackets underneath an arrow gives the maximum number of units that can be shipped along that shipping lane. (The absence of a number in square brackets underneath an arrow implies that there is no limit on the shipping amount there.) This network provides a complete representation of the problem, including all the necessary data, so it constitutes a *network model* for this minimum-cost flow problem.

Figure 7.3 illustrates how a minimum-cost flow problem can be completely depicted by a network.

Since this is such a tiny problem, you probably can see what the optimal solution must be. (Try it.) This solution is shown in Figure 7.4, where the shipping amount along each shipping lane is given in parentheses there. (To avoid confusion, we delete the unit shipping costs and shipping capacities in this figure.) Combining these shipping amounts with the unit shipping costs given in Figures 7.2 and 7.3, the total shipping cost for this solution is

$$\text{Total shipping cost} = 30(\$700) + 50(\$300) + 50(\$400) + 50(\$200)$$
$$+ 50(\$400) + 20(\$900)$$
$$= \$104,000$$

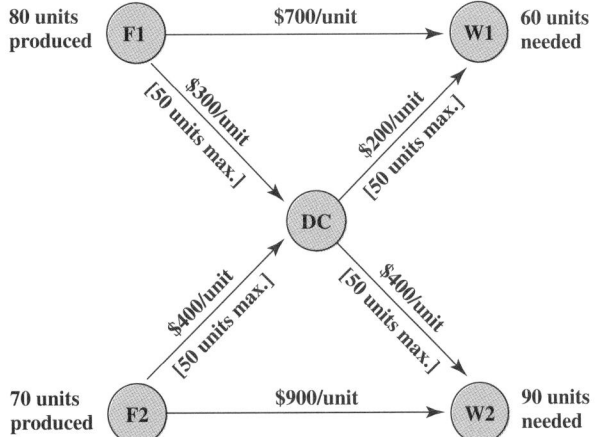

FIGURE 7.2
The data for the distribution network for the Distribution Unlimited Co. problem.

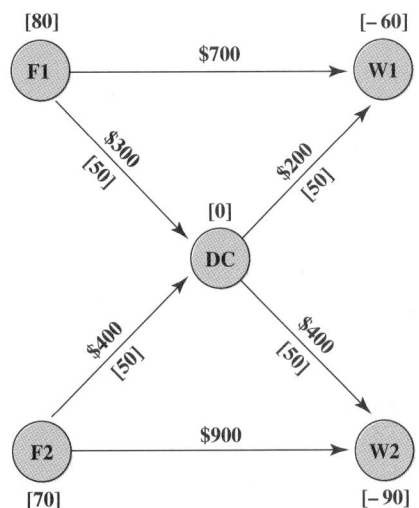

FIGURE 7.3
A network model for the Distribution Unlimited Co. problem as a minimum-cost flow problem.

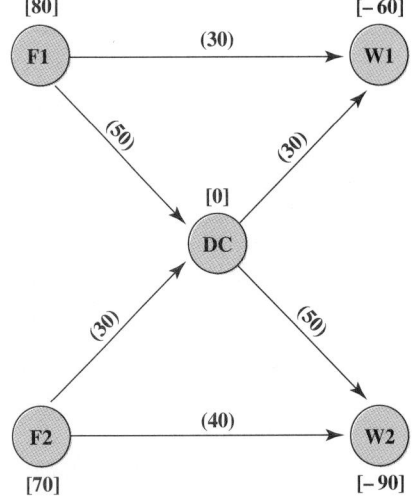

FIGURE 7.4
The optimal solution for the Distribution Unlimited Co. problem, where the shipping amounts are shown in parentheses over the arrows.

General Characteristics

This example possesses all the general characteristics of any minimum-cost flow problem. Before summarizing these characteristics, here is the terminology you will need.

Terminology

1. The model for any minimum-cost flow problem is represented by a *network* with flow passing through it.

2. The circles in the network are called **nodes.**

A supply node has net flow going out whereas a demand node has net flow coming in.

3. Each node where the net amount of flow generated (outflow minus inflow) is a fixed *positive* number is a **supply node.** (Thus, F1 and F2 are the supply nodes in Figure 7.3.)

4. Each node where the net amount of flow generated is a fixed *negative* number is a **demand node.** (Consequently, W1 and W2 are the demand nodes in the example.)

5. Any node where the net amount of flow generated is fixed at *zero* is a **transshipment node.** (Thus, DC is the transshipment node in the example.) Having the amount of flow out of the node equal the amount of flow into the node is referred to as **conservation of flow.**

6. The arrows in the network are called **arcs.**

7. The maximum amount of flow allowed through an arc is referred to as the **capacity** of that arc.

Using this terminology, the general characteristics of minimum-cost flow problems (the model for this type of problem) can be described in terms of the following assumptions.

Assumptions of a Minimum-Cost Flow Problem

1. *At least one* of the nodes is a *supply node.*

2. *At least one* of the other nodes is a *demand node.*

3. All the remaining nodes are *transshipment nodes.*

Since the arrowhead on an arc indicates the direction in which flow is allowed, a pair of arcs pointing in opposite directions is used if flow can occur in both directions.

4. Flow through an arc is only allowed in the direction indicated by the arrowhead, where the maximum amount of flow is given by the *capacity* of that arc. (If flow can occur in both directions, this would be represented by a pair of arcs pointing in opposite directions.)

5. The network has enough arcs with sufficient capacity to enable all the flow generated at the *supply nodes* to reach all the *demand nodes.*

6. The cost of the flow through each arc is *proportional* to the amount of that flow, where the cost per unit flow is known.

The objective is to minimize the total cost of supplying the demand nodes.

7. The objective is to minimize the total cost of sending the available supply through the network to satisfy the given demand. (An alternative objective is to maximize the total profit from doing this.)

A *solution* for this kind of problem needs to specify how much flow is going through each arc. To be a *feasible* solution, the amount of flow through each arc cannot exceed the capacity of that arc and the net amount of flow generated at each node must equal the specified amount for that node. The following property indicates when the problem will have feasible solutions.

The Feasible Solutions Property: Under the above assumptions, a minimum-cost flow problem will have feasible solutions if and only if the sum of the supplies from its supply nodes *equals* the sum of the demands at its demand nodes.

Note that this property holds for the Distribution Unlimited Co. problem, because the sum of its supplies is $80 + 70 = 150$ and the sum of its demands is $60 + 90 = 150$.

For many applications of minimum-cost flow problems, management desires a solution with *integer* values for all the flow quantities (e.g., integer numbers of *full* truckloads along each shipping lane). The model does not include any constraints that require this for feasible solutions. Fortunately, such constraints are not needed because of the following property.

Integer Solutions Property: As long as all its supplies, demands, and arc capacities have integer values, any minimum-cost flow problem with feasible solutions is guaranteed to have an optimal solution with integer values for all its flow quantities.

See in Figure 7.2 that this property holds for the Distribution Unlimited Co. problem. All the supplies (80 and 70), demands (60 and 90), and arc capacities (50) have integer values. Therefore, all the flow quantities in the optimal solution given in Figure 7.4 (30 three times, 50 two times, and 40) have integer values. This ensures that only full truckloads will be shipped into and out of the distribution center. (Remember that each unit corresponds to a full truckload of the product.)

Now let us see how to obtain an optimal solution for the Distribution Unlimited Co. problem by formulating a spreadsheet model and then applying the Excel Solver.

Using Excel to Formulate and Solve Minimum-Cost Flow Problems

Figure 7.5 shows a spreadsheet model that is based directly on the network representation of the problem in Figure 7.3. The arcs are listed in columns B and C, along with their capacities (unless unlimited) in column F and their costs per unit flow in column G. The changing cells Ship (D4:D9) show the flow amounts through these arcs and the target cell TotalCost (D11) provides the total cost of this flow by using the equation

$$D11 = SUMPRODUCT(Ship,UnitCost)$$

FIGURE 7.5

A spreadsheet model for the Distribution Unlimited Co. minimum-cost flow problem, including the target cell TotalCost (D11) and the other output cells NetFlow (J4:J8), as well as the equations entered into these cells and the other specifications needed to set up the model. The changing cells Ship (D4:D9) show the optimal shipping quantities through the distribution network obtained by the Solver.

	A	B	C	D	E	F	G	H	I	J	K	L
1		**Distribution Unlimited Co. Minimum Cost Flow Problem**										
2												
3		**From**	**To**	**Ship**		**Capacity**	**Unit Cost**		**Nodes**	**Net Flow**		**Supply/Demand**
4		F1	W1	30			$700		F1	80	=	80
5		F1	DC	50	≤	50	$300		F2	70	=	70
6		DC	W1	30	≤	50	$200		DC	0	=	0
7		DC	W2	50	≤	50	$400		W1	-60	=	-60
8		F2	DC	30	≤	50	$400		W2	-90	=	-90
9		F2	W2	40			$900					
10												
11			**Total Cost**	$110,000								

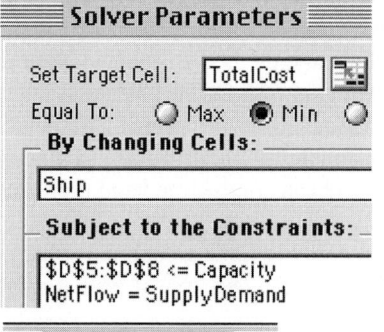

Range Name	Cells
Capacity	F5:F8
From	B4:B9
NetFlow	J4:J8
Nodes	I4:I8
Ship	D4:D9
SupplyDemand	L4:L8
To	C4:C9
TotalCost	D11
UnitCost	G4:G9

	J
3	**Net Flow**
4	=SUMIF(From,I4,Ship)-SUMIF(To,I4,Ship)
5	=SUMIF(From,I5,Ship)-SUMIF(To,I5,Ship)
6	=SUMIF(From,I6,Ship)-SUMIF(To,I6,Ship)
7	=SUMIF(From,I7,Ship)-SUMIF(To,I7,Ship)
8	=SUMIF(From,I8,Ship)-SUMIF(To,I8,Ship)

	C	D
11	**Total Cost**	=SUMPRODUCT(Ship,UnitCost)

Capacity constraints like these are needed in any minimum-cost flow problem that has any arcs with limited capacity.

Any minimum-cost flow problem needs net flow constraints like this for every node.

Excel Tip: SUMIF(A, B, C) adds up each entry in the range C for which the corresponding entry in range A equals B. This function is especially useful in network problems for calculating the net flow generated at a node.

The first set of constraints in the Solver dialogue box, D5:D8 ≤ Capacity (F5:F8), ensures that the arc capacities are not exceeded.

Similarly, Column I lists the nodes, column J calculates the actual net flow generated at each node (given the flows in the changing cells), and column L specifies the net amount of flow that needs to be generated at each node. Thus, the second set of constraints in the Solver dialogue box is NetFlow (J4:J8) = SupplyDemand (L4:L8), requiring that the actual net amount of flow generated at each node must equal the specified amount.

The equations entered into NetFlow (J4:J8) use the difference of two SUMIF functions to calculate the net flow (outflow minus inflow) generated at each node. In each case, the first SUMIF function calculates the flow leaving the node and the second one calculates the flow entering the node. For example, consider the F1 node (I4). SUMIF(From,I4,Ship) sums each individual entry in Ship (D4:D9) if that entry is in a row where the entry in From (B4:B9) is the same as in I4. Since I4 = F1 and the only rows that have F1 in the From column are rows 4 and 5, the sum in the Ship column is only over these same rows, so this sum is D4 + D5. Similarly, SUMIF(To,I4,Ship) sums each individual entry in Ship (D4:D9) if that entry is in a row where the entry in To (C4:C9) is the same as in I4. However, F1 never appears in the To column, so this sum is 0. Therefore, the overall equation for J4 yields J4 = D4 + D5 = 30 + 50 = 80, which is the net flow generated at the F1 node.

While it appears more complicated to use the SUMIF function rather than just entering J4 = D4 + D5, J5 = D8 + D9, J6 = D6 + D7 − D5 − D8, and so on, it is actually simpler. The SUMIF formula only needs to be entered once (in cell J4). It can then be copied down into the remaining cells in NetFlow (J5:J8). For a problem with many nodes, this is much quicker and (perhaps more significantly) less prone to error. In a large problem, it is all too easy to miss an arc when determining which cells in the Ship column to add and subtract to calculate the net flow for a given node.

The first Solver option selected (Assume Linear Model) acknowledges that this is still a linear programming problem (in a streamlined form). The second option (Assume Non-Negative) specifies that the flow amounts cannot be negative.

Clicking on the Solve button gives the optimal solution shown in Ship (D4:D9). This is the same solution as displayed in Figure 7.4.

Solving Large Minimum-Cost Flow Problems More Efficiently

Because minimum-cost flow problems are a special type of linear programming problem, and the *simplex method* can solve any linear programming problem, it also can solve any minimum-cost flow problem in the standard way. For example, the Excel Solver uses the simplex method to solve this type (or any other type) of linear programming problem. This works fine for small problems, like the Distribution Unlimited Co. problem, and for considerably larger ones as well. Therefore, the approach illustrated in Figure 7.5 will serve you well for any minimum-cost flow problem encountered in this book and for many that you will encounter subsequently.

However, we should mention that a different approach is sometimes needed in practice to solve really big problems. Because of the special form of minimum-cost flow problems, it is possible to greatly *streamline* the simplex method to solve them far more quickly. In particular, rather than going through all the algebra of the simplex method, it is possible to execute the same steps far more quickly by working directly with the network for the problem.

This streamlined version of the simplex method is called the **network simplex method.** (As you may recall our mentioning in Section 6.2, the network simplex method also can be used to solve transportation problems.) The network simplex method can solve some huge problems that are much too large for the simplex method.

Like the simplex method, the network simplex method not only finds an optimal solution but also can be a valuable aid to managers in conducting the kinds of what-if analyses described in Chapter 5.

The network simplex method can solve much larger minimum-cost flow problems (sometimes with millions of nodes and arcs) than can the simplex method used by the Excel Solver.

Many companies now use the network simplex method to solve their minimum-cost flow problems. Some of these problems are huge, with many tens of thousands of nodes and arcs. Occasionally, the number of arcs will even be far larger, perhaps into the millions.

Although the Excel Solver does not, other commercial software packages for linear programming commonly include the network simplex method.

An important advance in recent years has been the development of excellent *graphical interfaces* for modeling minimum-cost flow problems. These interfaces make the design of the model and the interpretation of the output of the network simplex method completely visual and intuitive with no mathematics involved. This is very helpful for managerial decision making.

Some Applications

Probably the most important kind of application of minimum-cost flow problems is to the operation of a distribution network, such as the one depicted in Figures 7.1–7.4 for the Distribution Unlimited Co. problem. (This is why minimum-cost flow problems were referred to as distribution-network problems in Section 4.4.) As summarized in the first row of Table 7.1, this kind of application always involves determining a plan for shipping goods from their *sources* (factories, etc.) to *intermediate storage facilities* (as needed) and then on to the *customers.*

However, the distribution network often is much more complicated than the one shown in Figures 7.1–7.4. For example, consider the distribution network for the **International Paper Company** (as described in the March–April 1988 issue of *Interfaces*). This company is the world's largest manufacturer of pulp, paper, and paper products, as well as a major producer of lumber and plywood. It also either owns or has rights over about 20 million acres of woodlands. The supply nodes in its distribution network are these woodlands in their various locations. However, before the company's goods can eventually reach the demand nodes (the customers), they must pass through a long sequence of transshipment nodes. A typical path through the distribution network is

$$\text{woodlands} \rightarrow \text{woodyards} \rightarrow \text{sawmills}$$

$$\rightarrow \text{paper mills} \rightarrow \text{converting plants}$$

$$\rightarrow \text{warehouses} \rightarrow \text{customers}$$

Solving its minimum-cost flow problem saved Citgo at least $16.5 million annually.

Another example of a complicated distribution network is the one for the **Citgo Petroleum Corporation** described in Section 2.1. Applying a minimum-cost flow problem formulation to improve the operation of this distribution network saved Citgo at least $16.5 million annually.

For some applications of minimum-cost flow problems, all the transshipment nodes are *processing facilities* rather than intermediate storage facilities. This is the case for *solid waste management,* as indicated in Table 7.1. Here, the flow of materials through the network begins at the sources of the solid waste, then goes to the facilities for processing these waste materials into a form suitable for landfill, and then sends them on to the various landfill locations. However, the objective still is to determine the flow plan that minimizes the total cost, where the cost now is for both shipping and processing.

In other applications, the *demand nodes* might be processing facilities. For example, in the third row of Table 7.1, the objective is to find the minimum-cost plan for obtaining supplies from various possible vendors, storing these goods in warehouses (as needed), and then shipping the supplies to the company's processing facilities (factories, etc.).

TABLE 7.1   **Typical Kinds of Applications of Minimum-Cost Flow Problems**

Kind of Application	Supply Nodes	Transshipment Nodes	Demand Nodes
Operation of a distribution network	Sources of goods	Intermediate storage facilities	Customers
Solid waste management	Sources of solid waste	Processing facilities	Landfill locations
Operation of a supply network	Vendors	Intermediate warehouses	Processing facilities
Coordinating product mixes at plants	Plants	Production of a specific product	Market for a specific product
Cash flow management	Sources of cash at a specific time	Short-term investment options	Needs for cash at a specific time

The July–August 1987 issue of *Interfaces* describes how, even back then, microcomputers were being used by **Marshalls, Inc.** (an off-price retail chain), to deal with a minimum-cost flow problem this way. In this application, Marshalls was optimizing the flow of freight from vendors to processing centers and then on to retail stores. Some of its networks had over 20,000 arcs. (The articles describing this application and the ones at the International Paper Company and Citgo Petroleum Corporation can be downloaded at **www.mhhe.com/hillier2e/articles.**)

The next kind of application in Table 7.1 (coordinating product mixes at plants) illustrates that arcs can represent something other than a shipping lane for a physical flow of materials. This application involves a company with several plants (the supply nodes) that can produce the same products but at different costs. Each arc from a supply node represents the production of one of the possible products at that plant, where this arc leads to the transshipment node that corresponds to this product. Thus, this transshipment node has an arc coming in from each plant capable of producing this product, and then the arcs leading out of this node go to the respective customers (the demand nodes) for this product. The objective is to determine how to divide each plant's production capacity among the products so as to minimize the total cost of meeting the demand for the various products.

The last application in Table 7.1 (cash flow management) illustrates that different nodes can represent some event that occurs at different times. In this case, each supply node represents a specific time (or time period) when some cash will become available to the company (through maturing accounts, notes receivable, sales of securities, borrowing, etc.). The supply at each of these nodes is the amount of cash that will become available then. Similarly, each demand node represents a specific time (or time period) when the company will need to draw on its cash reserves. The demand at each such node is the amount of cash that will be needed then. The objective is to maximize the company's income from investing the cash between each time it becomes available and when it will be used. Therefore, each transshipment node represents the choice of a specific short-term investment option (e.g., purchasing a certificate of deposit from a bank) over a specific time interval. The resulting network will have a succession of flows representing a schedule for cash becoming available, being invested, and then being used after the maturing of the investment.

Special Types of Minimum-Cost Flow Problems

There are five important categories of network problems that turn out to be special types of minimum-cost flow problems.

One is the *transportation problems* discussed in the early part of the preceding chapter. Figure 6.3 in Section 6.2 shows the network representation of a typical transportation problem. In our current terminology, the sources and destinations of a transportation problem are the supply nodes and demand nodes, respectively. Thus, a transportation problem is just a minimum-cost flow problem without any transshipment nodes and without any capacity constraints on the arcs (all of which go directly from a supply node to a demand node).

A second category is the *assignment problems* discussed in Section 6.6. Recall that this kind of problem involves assigning a group of assignees to a group of tasks where each assignee is to perform a single task. The network representation of a typical assignment problem is displayed in Figure 6.19 in Section 6.6. We also pointed out in that section that an assignment problem can be viewed as a special type of transportation problem whose sources are the assignees and whose destinations are the tasks. This then makes the assignment problem also a special type of minimum-cost flow problem with the characteristics described in the preceding paragraph. In addition, each assignee is a supply node with a supply of 1 and each task is a demand node with a demand of 1.

A transshipment problem is just a minimum-cost flow problem that has unlimited capacities for all its arcs.

A third special type of minimum-cost flow problem is **transshipment problems.** This kind of problem is just like a transportation problem except for the additional feature that the shipments from the sources (supply nodes) to the destinations (demand nodes) might also pass through intermediate transfer points (transshipment nodes) such as distribution centers. Like a transportation problem, there are no capacity constraints on the arcs. Consequently, any minimum-cost flow problem where each arc can carry any desired amount of flow is a transshipment problem. For example, if the data in Figure 7.2 were altered so that any amounts (within the ranges of the supplies and demands) could be shipped into and out of the distribution center, the Distribution Unlimited Co. would become just a transshipment problem.[1]

Because of their close relationship to a general minimum-cost flow problem, we will not discuss transshipment problems further.

The other two important special types of minimum-cost flow problems are *maximum flow problems* and *shortest path problems,* which will be described in Sections 7.3 and 7.4 after presenting a case study of a maximum flow problem in the next section.

In case you are wondering why we are bothering to point out that these five kinds of problems are special types of minimum-cost flow problems, here is one very important reason. It means that the *network simplex method* can be used to solve large problems of any of these types that might be difficult or impossible for the simplex method to solve. It is true that other efficient *special-purpose algorithms* also are available for each of these kinds of problems (such as the *transportation simplex method* for the transportation problem). However, recent implementations of the network simplex method have become so powerful that it now provides an excellent alternative to these other algorithms in most cases. This is especially valuable when the available software package includes the network simplex method but not another relevant special-purpose algorithm. Furthermore, even after finding an optimal solution, the network simplex method can continue to be helpful in aiding managerial what-if sessions along the lines discussed in Chapter 5.

> The network simplex method can be used to solve huge problems of any of these five special types.

Review Questions

1. Name and describe the three kinds of nodes in a minimum-cost flow problem.
2. What is meant by the *capacity* of an arc?
3. What is the usual objective for a minimum-cost flow problem?
4. What property is necessary for a minimum-cost flow problem to have feasible solutions?
5. What is the integer solutions property for minimum-cost flow problems?
6. What is the name of the streamlined version of the simplex method that is designed to solve minimum-cost flow problems very efficiently?
7. What are a few typical kinds of applications of minimum-cost flow problems?
8. Name five important categories of network optimization problems that turn out to be special types of minimum-cost flow problems.

7.2   A CASE STUDY: THE BMZ CO. MAXIMUM FLOW PROBLEM

What a day! First being called into his boss's office and then receiving an urgent telephone call from the company president himself. Fortunately, he was able to reassure them that he has the situation under control.

Although his official title is Supply Chain Manager for the BMZ Company, Karl Schmidt often tells his friends that he really is the company's *crisis manager.* One crisis after another. The supplies needed to keep the production lines going haven't arrived yet. Or the supplies have arrived but are unusable because they are the wrong size. Or an urgent shipment to a key customer has been delayed. This current crisis is typical. One of the company's most important distribution centers—the one in Los Angeles—urgently needs an increased flow of shipments from the company.

Karl was chosen for this key position because he is considered a rising young star. Having just received his MBA degree from a top American business school four years ago, he is the youngest member of upper-level management in the entire company. His business school training in the latest management science techniques has proven invaluable in improving supply chain management throughout the company. The crises still occur, but the frequent chaos of past years has been eliminated.

Karl has a plan for dealing with the current crisis. This will mean calling on management science once again.

---

[1]Be aware that a minimum-cost flow problem that does have capacity constraints on the arcs is sometimes referred to as a *capacitated transshipment problem.* We will not use this terminology.

Background

The BMZ Company is a European manufacturer of luxury automobiles. Although its cars sell well in all the developed countries, its exports to the United States are particularly important to the company.

BMZ has a well-deserved reputation for providing excellent service. One key to maintaining this reputation is having a plentiful supply of automobile replacement parts readily available to the company's numerous dealerships and authorized repair shops. These parts are mainly stored in the company's distribution centers and then delivered promptly when needed. One of Karl Schmidt's top priorities is avoiding shortages at these distribution centers.

The company has several distribution centers in the United States. However, the closest one to the Los Angeles center is over 1,000 miles away in Seattle. Since BMZ cars are becoming especially popular in California, it is particularly important to keep the Los Angeles center well supplied. Therefore, the fact that supplies there are currently dwindling is a matter of real concern to BMZ top management—as Karl learned forcefully today.

Most of the automobile replacement parts are produced at the company's main factory in Stuttgart, Germany, along with the production of new cars. It is this factory that has been supplying the Los Angeles center with spare parts. Some of these parts are bulky, and very large numbers of certain parts are needed, so the total volume of the supplies has been relatively massive—over 300,000 cubic feet of goods arriving monthly. Now a much larger amount will be needed over the next month to replenish the dwindling inventory.

The Problem

The problem is to maximize the flow of automobile replacement parts from the factory in Stuttgart, Germany, to the distribution center in Los Angeles.

Karl needs to execute a plan quickly for shipping as much as possible from the main factory to the distribution center in Los Angeles over the next month. He already has recognized that this is a *maximum flow problem*—a problem of maximizing the flow of replacement parts from the factory to this distribution center.

The factory is producing far more than can be shipped to this one distribution center. Therefore, the limiting factor on how much can be shipped is the limited capacity of the company's distribution network.

This distribution network is depicted in Figure 7.6, where the nodes labeled ST and LA are the factory in Stuttgart and the distribution center in Los Angeles, respectively. There is a rail head at the factory, so shipments first go by rail to one of three European ports: Rotterdam

FIGURE 7.6
The BMZ Co. distribution network from its main factory in Stuttgart, Germany, to a distribution center in Los Angeles.

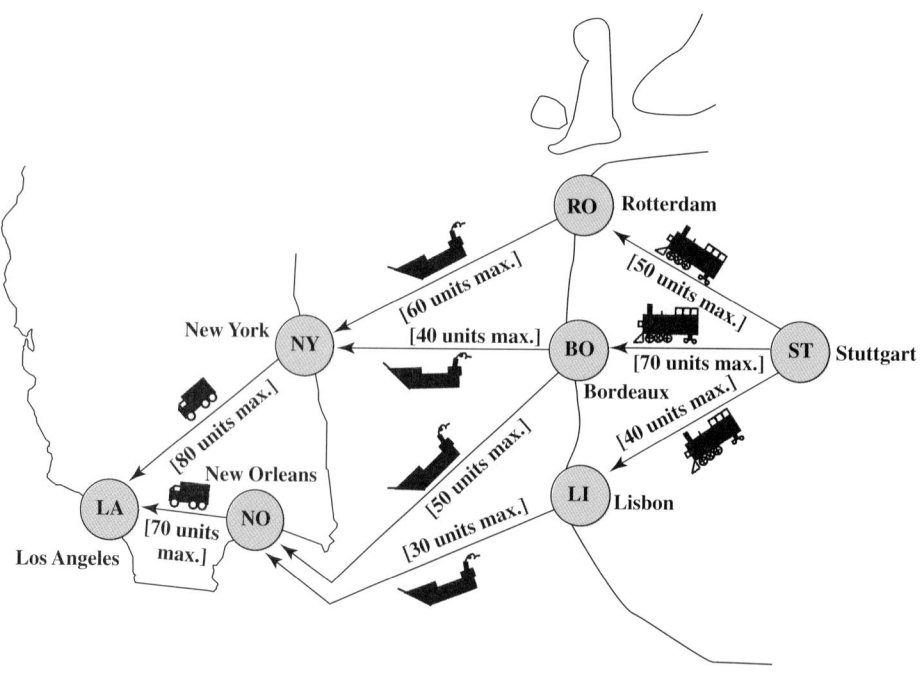

(node RO), Bordeaux (node BO), and Lisbon (node LI). They then go by ship to ports in the United States, either New York (node NY) or New Orleans (node NO). Finally, they are shipped by truck from these ports to the distribution center in Los Angeles.

The organizations operating these railroads, ships, and trucks are independently owned companies that ship goods for numerous firms. Because of prior commitments to their regular customers, these companies are unable to drastically increase the allocation of space to any single customer on short notice. Therefore, the BMZ Co. is only able to secure a limited amount of shipping space along each shipping lane over the next month. The amounts available are given in Figure 7.6, using units of *hundreds of cubic meters*. (Since each unit of 100 cubic meters is a little over 3,500 cubic feet, these are large volumes of goods that need to be moved.)

Model Formulation

Figure 7.7 shows the *network model* for this maximum flow problem. Rather than showing the geographical layout of the distribution network, this network simply lines up the nodes (representing the cities) in evenly spaced columns. The arcs represent the shipping lanes, where the capacity of each arc (given in square brackets under the arc) is the amount of shipping space available along that shipping lane. The objective is to determine how much flow to send through each arc (how many units to ship through each shipping lane) to maximize the total number of units flowing from the factory in Stuttgart to the distribution center in Los Angeles.

Figure 7.8 shows the corresponding spreadsheet model for this problem when using the format introduced in Figure 7.5. The main difference from the model in Figure 7.5 is the change in the objective. Since we are no longer minimizing the total cost of the flow through the network, column G in Figure 7.5 can be deleted in Figure 7.8. The target cell MaxFlow (D14) in Figure 7.8 now needs to give the total number of units flowing from Stuttgart to Los Angeles. Thus, the equations at the bottom of the figure include D14 = I4, where I4 gives the net flow leaving Stuttgart to go to Los Angeles. As in Figure 7.5, the equations in Figure 7.8 entered into NetFlow (I4:I10) again use the difference of two SUMIF functions to calculate the net flow generated at each node. Since the objective is to maximize the flow shown in MaxFlow (D14), the Solver dialogue box specifies that this target cell is to be maximized. After clicking on the Solve button, the optimal solution shown in the changing cells Ship (D4:D12) is obtained for the amount that BMZ should ship through each shipping lane.

In contrast to the spreadsheet model in Figure 7.5, which *minimizes* TotalCost (D11), the spreadsheet model in Figure 7.8 *maximizes* the target cell MaxFlow (D14).

FIGURE 7.7

A network model for the BMZ Co. problem as a maximum flow problem, where the number in square brackets below each arc is the capacity of that arc.

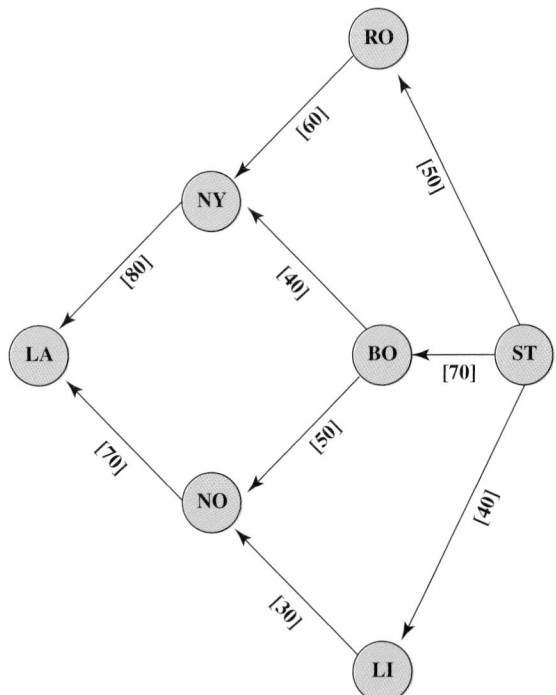

FIGURE 7.8 A spreadsheet model for the BMZ Co. maximum flow problem, including the equations entered into the target cell MaxFlow (D14) and the other output cells NetFlow (I4:I10), as well as the other specifications needed to set up the model. The changing cells Ship (D4:D12) show the optimal shipping quantities through the distribution network obtained by the Solver.

	A	B	C	D	E	F	G	H	I	J	K
1		**BMZ Co. Maximum Flow Problem**									
2											
3		**From**	**To**	**Ship**		**Capacity**		**Nodes**	**Net Flow**		**Supply/Demand**
4		Stuttgart	Rotterdam	50	≤	50		Stuttgart	150		
5		Stuttgart	Bordeaux	70	≤	70		Rotterdam	0	=	0
6		Stuttgart	Lisbon	30	≤	40		Bordeaux	0	=	0
7		Rotterdam	New York	50	≤	60		Lisbon	0	=	0
8		Bordeaux	New York	30	≤	40		New York	0	=	0
9		Bordeaux	New Orleans	40	≤	50		New Orleans	0	=	0
10		Lisbon	New Orleans	30	≤	30		Los Angeles	-150		
11		New York	Los Angeles	80	≤	80					
12		New Orleans	Los Angeles	70	≤	70					
13											
14			**Maximum Flow**	150							

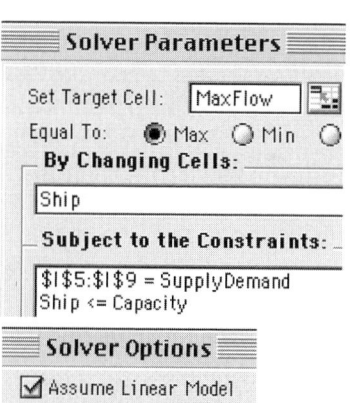

Solver Parameters

Set Target Cell: `MaxFlow`
Equal To: ● Max ○ Min ○
By Changing Cells:
`Ship`
Subject to the Constraints:
`$I$5:$I$9 = SupplyDemand`
`Ship <= Capacity`

Solver Options
☑ Assume Linear Model
☑ Assume Non-Negative

Range Name	Cells
Capacity	F4:F12
From	B4:B12
MaxFlow	D14
NetFlow	I4:I10
Nodes	H4:H10
Ship	D4:D12
SupplyDemand	K5:K9
To	C4:C12

	I
3	**Net Flow**
4	=SUMIF(From,H4,Ship)-SUMIF(To,H4,Ship)
5	=SUMIF(From,H5,Ship)-SUMIF(To,H5,Ship)
6	=SUMIF(From,H6,Ship)-SUMIF(To,H6,Ship)
7	=SUMIF(From,H7,Ship)-SUMIF(To,H7,Ship)
8	=SUMIF(From,H8,Ship)-SUMIF(To,H8,Ship)
9	=SUMIF(From,H9,Ship)-SUMIF(To,H9,Ship)
10	=SUMIF(From,H10,Ship)-SUMIF(To,H10,Ship)

	C	D
14	**Maximum Flow**	=I4

However, Karl is not completely satisfied with this solution. He has an idea for doing even better. This will require formulating and solving another maximum flow problem. (This story continues in the middle of the next section.)

Review Questions

1. What is the current crisis facing the BMZ Co.?

2. When formulating this problem in network terms, what is flowing through BMZ's distribution network? From where to where?

3. What is the objective of the resulting maximum flow problem?

7.3 MAXIMUM FLOW PROBLEMS

Like a minimum-cost flow problem, a maximum flow problem is concerned with *flow through a network.* However, the objective now is different. Rather than minimizing the cost of the flow, the objective now is to find a flow plan that maximizes the amount flowing through the network. This is how Karl Schmidt was able to find a flow plan that maximizes the number of units of automobile replacement parts flowing through BMZ's distribution network from its factory in Stuttgart to the distribution center in Los Angeles.

General Characteristics

Except for the difference in objective (maximize flow versus minimize cost), the characteristics of the maximum flow problem are quite similar to those for the minimum-cost flow problem. However, there are some minor differences, as we will discuss after summarizing the assumptions.

Assumptions of a Maximum Flow Problem

1. All flow through the network originates at one node, called the **source,** and terminates at one other node, called the **sink.** (The source and sink in the BMZ problem are the factory and the distribution center, respectively.)

2. All the remaining nodes are *transshipment nodes.* (These are nodes RO, BO, LI, NY, and NO in the BMZ problem.)

3. Flow through an arc is only allowed in the direction indicated by the arrowhead, where the maximum amount of flow is given by the *capacity* of that arc. At the *source,* all arcs point away from the node. At the *sink,* all arcs point into the node.

The objective is to find a flow plan that maximizes the flow from the source to the sink.

4. The objective is to maximize the total amount of flow from the source to the sink. This amount is measured in either of two equivalent ways, namely, either the amount *leaving the source* or the amount *entering the sink.* (Cells D14 and I4 in Figure 7.8 use the amount leaving the source.)

The source and sink of a maximum flow problem are analogous to the supply nodes and demand nodes of a minimum-cost flow problem. These are the only nodes in both problems that do not have conservation of flow (flow out equals flow in). Like the supply nodes, the source *generates flow.* Like the demand nodes, the sink *absorbs flow.*

However, there are two differences between these nodes in a minimum-cost flow problem and the corresponding nodes in a maximum flow problem.

One difference is that, whereas supply nodes have fixed supplies and demand nodes have fixed demands, the source and sink do not. The reason is that the objective is to maximize the flow leaving the source and entering the sink rather than fixing this amount.

Although a maximum flow problem has only a single source and a single sink, variants with multiple sources and sinks also can be solved, as illustrated below.

The second difference is that, whereas the number of supply nodes and the number of demand nodes in a minimum-cost flow problem may be *more than one,* there can be *only one* source and *only one* sink in a maximum flow problem. However, variants of maximum flow problems that have multiple sources and sinks can still be solved by the Excel Solver, as you now will see illustrated by the BMZ case study introduced in the preceding section.

Continuing the Case Study with Multiple Supply Points and Multiple Demand Points

Here is Karl Schmidt's idea for how to improve upon the flow plan obtained at the end of Section 7.2 (as given in column D of Figure 7.8).

The company has a second, smaller factory in Berlin, north of its Stuttgart factory, for producing automobile parts. Although this factory normally is used to help supply distribution centers in northern Europe, Canada, and the northern United States (including one in Seattle), it also is able to ship to the distribution center in Los Angeles. Furthermore, the distribution center in Seattle has the capability of supplying parts to the customers of the distribution center in Los Angeles when shortages occur at the latter center.

In this light, Karl now has developed a better plan for addressing the current inventory shortages in Los Angeles. Rather than simply maximizing shipments from the Stuttgart factory to Los Angeles, he has decided to maximize shipments from both factories to the distribution centers in both Los Angeles and Seattle.

Figure 7.9 shows the network model representing the expanded distribution network that encompasses both factories and both distribution centers. In addition to the nodes shown in Figures 7.6 and 7.7, node BE is the second, smaller factory in Berlin; nodes HA and BN are additional ports used by this factory in Hamburg and Boston, respectively; and node SE is the distribution center in Seattle. As before, the arcs represent the shipping lanes, where the number in square

FIGURE 7.9

A network model for the expanded BMZ Co. problem as a variant of a maximum flow problem, where the number in square brackets below each arc is the capacity of that arc.

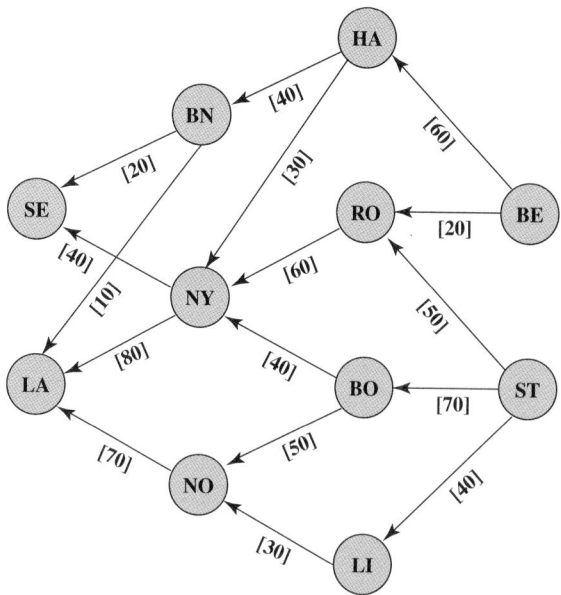

brackets below each arc is the capacity of that arc, that is, the maximum number of units that can be shipped through that shipping lane over the next month.

The corresponding spreadsheet model is displayed in Figure 7.10. The format is the same as in Figure 7.8. However, the target cell MaxFlow (D21) now gives the total flow from Stuttgart and Berlin, so D21 = I4 + I5 (as shown by the equation for this target cell given at the bottom of the figure).

The changing cells Ship (D4:D19) in this figure show the optimal solution obtained for the number of units to ship through each shipping lane over the next month. Comparing this solution with the one in Figure 7.8 shows the impact of Karl Schmidt's decision to expand the distribution network to include the second factory and the distribution center in Seattle. As indicated in column I of the two figures, the number of units going to Los Angeles directly has been increased from 150 to 160, in addition to the 60 units going to Seattle as a backup for the inventory shortage in Los Angeles. This plan solved the crisis in Los Angeles and won Karl commendations from top management.

Some Applications

The applications of maximum flow problems and their variants are somewhat similar to those for minimum-cost flow problems described in the preceding section when management's objective is to *maximize flow* rather than to *minimize cost.* Here are some typical kinds of applications.

1. Maximize the flow through a distribution network, as for the BMZ Co. problem.

2. Maximize the flow through a company's supply network from its vendors to its processing facilities.

3. Maximize the flow of oil through a system of pipelines.

4. Maximize the flow of water through a system of aqueducts.

5. Maximize the flow of vehicles through a transportation network.

Solving Very Large Problems

The expanded BMZ network in Figure 7.9 has 11 nodes and 16 arcs. However, the networks for most real applications are considerably larger, and occasionally vastly larger. As the number of nodes and arcs grows into the hundreds or thousands, the formulation and solution approach illustrated in Figures 7.8 and 7.10 quickly becomes impractical.

Fortunately, management scientists have other techniques available for formulating and solving huge problems with many tens of thousands of nodes and arcs. One technique is to re-

FIGURE 7.10   A spreadsheet model for the expanded BMZ Co. problem as a variant of a maximum flow problem with sources in both Stuttgart and Berlin and sinks in both Los Angeles and Seattle. Using the target cell MaxFlow (D21) to maximize the total flow from the two sources to the two sinks, the Solver yields the optimal shipping plan shown in the changing cells Ship (D4:D19).

	A	B	C	D	E	F	G	H	I	J	K
1		**BMZ Co. Expanded Maximum Flow Problem**									
2											
3		**From**	**To**	**Ship**		**Capacity**		**Nodes**	**Net Flow**		**Supply/Demand**
4		Stuttgart	Rotterdam	40	≤	50		Stuttgart	140		
5		Stuttgart	Bordeaux	70	≤	70		Berlin	80		
6		Stuttgart	Lisbon	30	≤	40		Hamburg	0	=	0
7		Berlin	Rotterdam	20	≤	20		Rotterdam	0	=	0
8		Berlin	Hamburg	60	≤	60		Bordeaux	0	=	0
9		Rotterdam	New York	60	≤	60		Lisbon	0	=	0
10		Bordeaux	New York	30	≤	40		Boston	0	=	0
11		Bordeaux	New Orleans	40	≤	50		New York	0	=	0
12		Lisbon	New Orleans	30	≤	30		New Orleans	0	=	0
13		Hamburg	New York	30	≤	30		Los Angeles	-160		
14		Hamburg	Boston	30	≤	40		Seattle	-60		
15		New Orleans	Los Angeles	70	≤	70					
16		New York	Los Angeles	80	≤	80					
17		New York	Seattle	40	≤	40					
18		Boston	Los Angeles	10	≤	10					
19		Boston	Seattle	20	≤	20					
20											
21			**Maximum Flow**	220							

Solver Parameters

Set Target Cell: [MaxFlow]
Equal To: ● Max ○ Min ○
By Changing Cells:
[Ship]
Subject to the Constraints:
$I$6:$I$12 = SupplyDemand
Ship <= Capacity

Solver Options
☑ Assume Linear Model
☑ Assume Non-Negative

Range Name	Cells
Capacity	F4:F19
From	B4:B19
MaxFlow	D21
NetFlow	I4:I14
Nodes	H4:H14
Ship	D4:D19
SupplyDemand	K6:K12
To	C4:C19

	I
3	**Net Flow**
4	=SUMIF(From,H4,Ship)-SUMIF(To,H4,Ship)
5	=SUMIF(From,H5,Ship)-SUMIF(To,H5,Ship)
6	=SUMIF(From,H6,Ship)-SUMIF(To,H6,Ship)
7	=SUMIF(From,H7,Ship)-SUMIF(To,H7,Ship)
8	=SUMIF(From,H8,Ship)-SUMIF(To,H8,Ship)
9	=SUMIF(From,H9,Ship)-SUMIF(To,H9,Ship)
10	=SUMIF(From,H10,Ship)-SUMIF(To,H10,Ship)
11	=SUMIF(From,H11,Ship)-SUMIF(To,H11,Ship)
12	=SUMIF(From,H12,Ship)-SUMIF(To,H12,Ship)
13	=SUMIF(From,H13,Ship)-SUMIF(To,H13,Ship)
14	=SUMIF(From,H14,Ship)-SUMIF(To,H14,Ship)

	C	D
21	**Maximum Flow**	=I4+I5

formulate a variant of a maximum flow problem so that an extremely efficient special-purpose algorithm for maximum flow problems still can be applied. Another is to reformulate the problem to fit the format for a minimum-cost flow problem so that the network simplex method can be applied. These special algorithms are available in some software packages, but not in the Excel Solver. Thus, if you should ever encounter a maximum flow problem or a variant that is beyond the scope of the Excel Solver (which won't happen in this book), rest assured that it probably can be formulated and solved in another way by a qualified management scientist.

1. How does the objective of a maximum flow problem differ from that for a minimum-cost flow problem?

2. What are the *source* and the *sink* for a maximum flow problem? For each, in what direction do all their arcs point?

3. What are the two equivalent ways in which the total amount of flow from the source to the sink can be measured?

4. The source and sink of a maximum flow problem are different from the supply nodes and demand nodes of a minimum-cost flow problem in what two ways?

5. What are a few typical kinds of applications of maximum flow problems?

7.4 SHORTEST PATH PROBLEMS

The most common applications of shortest path problems are for what the name suggests—finding the *shortest path* between two points. Here is an example.

An Example: The Littletown Fire Department Problem

Littletown is a small town in a rural area. Its fire department serves a relatively large geographical area that includes many farming communities. Since there are numerous roads throughout the area, many possible routes may be available for traveling to any given farming community from the fire station. Since time is of the essence in reaching a fire, the fire chief wishes to determine in advance the *shortest path* from the fire station to each of the farming communities.

Figure 7.11 shows the road system connecting the fire station to one of the farming communities, including the mileage along each road. Can you find which route from the fire station to the farming community minimizes the total number of miles?

Model Formulation for the Littletown Problem

Figure 7.12 gives the network representation of this problem, which ignores the geographical layout and the curves in the roads. This network model is the usual way of representing a short-

The objective is to find the shortest route from the fire station to the farming community.

FIGURE 7.11
The road system between the Littletown Fire Station and a certain farming community, where A, B, . . . , H are junctions and the number next to each road shows its distance in miles.

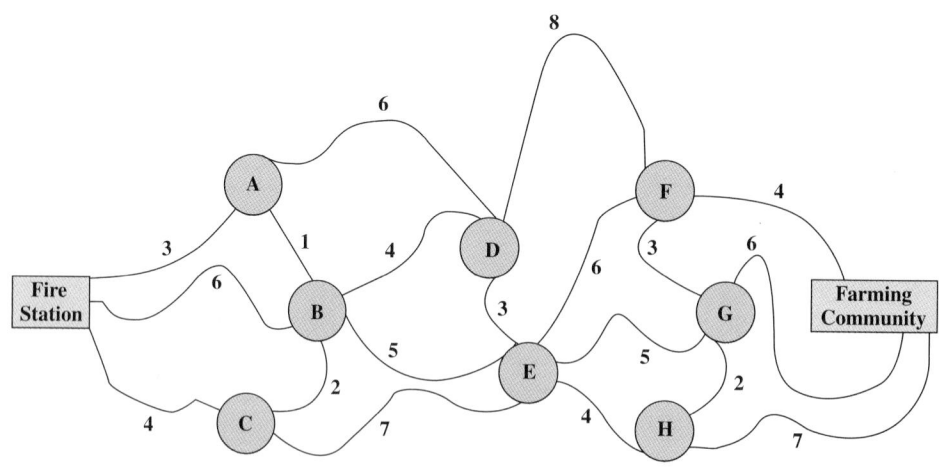

FIGURE 7.12
The network representation of Figure 7.11 as a shortest path problem.

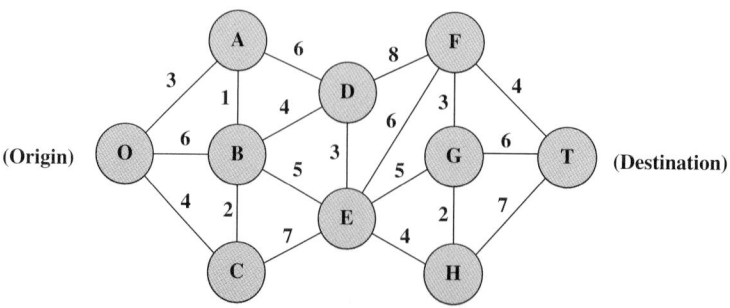

In a shortest path problem, travel goes from the origin to the destination through a series of links (such as roads) that connect pairs of nodes (junctions) in the network.

est path problem. The junctions now are nodes of the network, where the fire station and farming community are two additional nodes labeled as O (for *origin*) and T (for *destination*), respectively. Since travel (flow) can go in either direction between the nodes, the lines connecting the nodes now are referred to as **links**[2] instead of *arcs*. A link between a pair of nodes allows travel in either direction, whereas an arc allows travel in only the direction indicated by an arrowhead, so the lines in Figure 7.12 need to be links instead of arcs. (Notice that the links do not have an arrowhead at either end.)

Have you found the shortest path from the origin to the destination yet? (Try it now before reading further.) It is

$$O \rightarrow A \rightarrow B \rightarrow E \rightarrow F \rightarrow T$$

with a total distance of 19 miles.

This problem (like any shortest path problem) can be thought of as a special kind of minimum-cost flow problem (Section 7.1) where the *miles traveled* now are interpreted to be the *cost* of flow through the network. A trip from the fire station to the farming community is interpreted to be a flow of 1 on the chosen path through the network, so minimizing the cost of this flow is equivalent to minimizing the number of miles traveled. The fire station is considered to be the one supply node, with a supply of 1 to represent the start of this trip. The farming community is the one demand node, with a demand of 1 to represent the completion of this trip. All the other nodes in Figure 7.12 are transshipment nodes, so the net flow generated at each is 0.

This spreadsheet model is like one for a minimum-cost flow problem with no arc capacity constraints except that distances replace unit costs and travel on a chosen path is interpreted as a flow of 1 through this path.

Figure 7.13 shows the spreadsheet model that results from this interpretation. The format is basically the same as for the minimum-cost flow problem formulated in Figure 7.5, except now there are no arc capacity constraints and the unit cost column is replaced by a column of distances in miles. The flow quantities given by the changing cells OnRoute (D4:D27) are 1 for each arc that is on the chosen path from the fire station to the farming community and 0 otherwise. The target cell TotalDistance (D29) gives the total distance of this path in miles. (See the equation for this cell at the bottom of the figure.) Columns B and C together list all the vertical links in Figure 7.12 twice, once as a downward arc and once as an upward arc, since either direction might be on the chosen path. The other links are only listed as left-to-right arcs, since this is the only direction of interest for choosing a shortest path from the origin to the destination.

Column K shows the net flow that needs to be generated at each of the nodes. Using the equations at the bottom of the figure, each column I cell then calculates the *actual* net flow at that node by adding the flow out and subtracting the flow in. The corresponding constraints, Nodes (H4:H13) = SupplyDemand (K4:K13), are specified in the Solver dialogue box.

The solution shown in OnRoute (D4:D27) is the optimal solution obtained after clicking on the Solve button. It is exactly the same as the shortest path given earlier.

Just as for minimum-cost flow problems and maximum flow problems, special algorithms are available for solving large shortest path problems very efficiently, but these algorithms are not included in the Excel Solver. Using a spreadsheet formulation and the Solver is fine for problems of the size of the Littletown problem and somewhat larger, but you should be aware that vastly larger problems can still be solved by other means.

General Characteristics

Except for more complicated variations beyond the scope of this book, all shortest path problems share the characteristics illustrated by the Littletown problem. Here are the basic assumptions.

Assumptions of a Shortest Path Problem

1. You need to choose a path through the network that starts at a certain node, called the **origin,** and ends at another certain node, called the **destination.**

2. The lines connecting certain pairs of nodes commonly are *links* (which allow travel in either direction), although arcs (which only permit travel in one direction) also are allowed.

---

[2]Another name sometimes used is *undirected arc,* but we will not use this terminology.

FIGURE 7.13 A spreadsheet model for the Littletown Fire Department shortest path problem, including the equations entered into the target cell TotalDistance (D29) and the other output cells SupplyDemand (K4:K13). The values of 1 in the changing cells OnRoute (D4:D27) reveal the optimal solution obtained by the Solver for the shortest path (19 miles) from the fire station to the farming community.

	A	B	C	D	E	F	G	H	I	J	K
1		**Littletown Fire Department Shortest Path Problem**									
2											
3		**From**	**To**	**On Route**		**Distance**		**Nodes**	**Net Flow**		**Supply/Demand**
4		Fire St.	A	1		3		Fire St.	1	=	1
5		Fire St.	B	0		6		A	0	=	0
6		Fire St.	C	0		4		B	0	=	0
7		A	B	1		1		C	0	=	0
8		A	D	0		6		D	0	=	0
9		B	A	0		1		E	0	=	0
10		B	C	0		2		F	0	=	0
11		B	D	0		4		G	0	=	0
12		B	E	1		5		H	0	=	0
13		C	B	0		2		Farm Com.	-1	=	-1
14		C	E	0		7					
15		D	E	0		3					
16		D	F	0		8					
17		E	D	0		3					
18		E	F	1		6					
19		E	G	0		5					
20		E	H	0		4					
21		F	G	0		3					
22		F	Farm Com.	1		4					
23		G	F	0		3					
24		G	H	0		2					
25		G	Farm Com.	0		6					
26		H	G	0		2					
27		H	Farm Com.	0		7					
28											
29			**Total Distance**	19							

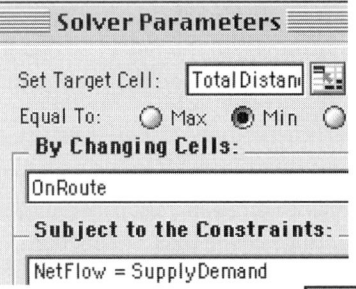

Solver Parameters

Set Target Cell: TotalDistan

Equal To: ○ Max ● Min ○

By Changing Cells:

OnRoute

Subject to the Constraints:

NetFlow = SupplyDemand

Solver Options

☑ Assume Linear Model
☑ Assume Non-Negative

Range Name	Cells
Distance	F4:F27
From	B4:B27
NetFlow	I4:I13
Nodes	H4:H13
OnRoute	D4:D27
SupplyDemand	K4:K13
To	C4:C27
TotalDistance	D29

	I
3	**Net Flow**
4	=SUMIF(From,H4,OnRoute)-SUMIF(To,H4,OnRoute)
5	=SUMIF(From,H5,OnRoute)-SUMIF(To,H5,OnRoute)
6	=SUMIF(From,H6,OnRoute)-SUMIF(To,H6,OnRoute)
7	=SUMIF(From,H7,OnRoute)-SUMIF(To,H7,OnRoute)
8	=SUMIF(From,H8,OnRoute)-SUMIF(To,H8,OnRoute)
9	=SUMIF(From,H9,OnRoute)-SUMIF(To,H9,OnRoute)
10	=SUMIF(From,H10,OnRoute)-SUMIF(To,H10,OnRoute)
11	=SUMIF(From,H11,OnRoute)-SUMIF(To,H11,OnRoute)
12	=SUMIF(From,H12,OnRoute)-SUMIF(To,H12,OnRoute)
13	=SUMIF(From,H13,OnRoute)-SUMIF(To,H13,OnRoute)

	C	D
29	**Total Distance**	=SUMPRODUCT(OnRoute,Distance)

3. Associated with each link (or arc) is a nonnegative number called its **length.** (Be aware that the drawing of each link in the network typically makes no effort to show its true length other than giving the correct number next to the link.)

4. The objective is to find the shortest path (the path with the minimum total length) from the origin to the destination.

The objective is to find the shortest path from the origin to the destination.

Some Applications

Not all applications of shortest path problems involve minimizing the distance traveled from the origin to the destination. In fact, they might not even involve travel at all. The links (or arcs) might instead represent activities of some other kind, so choosing a path through the network corresponds to selecting the best sequence of activities. The numbers giving the "lengths" of the links might then be, for example, the costs of the activities, in which case the objective would be to determine which sequence of activities minimizes the total cost.

Here are three categories of applications.

1. Minimize the total *distance* traveled, as in the Littletown example.

2. Minimize the total *cost* of a sequence of activities, as in the example that follows in the subsection below.

3. Minimize the total *time* of a sequence of activities, as in the example involving the Quick Company on page 294.

An Example of Minimizing Total Cost

Sarah has just graduated from high school. As a graduation present, her parents have given her a car fund of $21,000 to help purchase and maintain a certain three-year-old used car for college. Since operating and maintenance costs go up rapidly as the car ages, Sarah's parents tell her that she will be welcome to trade in her car on another three-year-old car one or more times during the next three summers if she determines that this would minimize her total net cost. They also inform her that they will give her a new car in four years as a college graduation present, so she should definitely plan to trade in her car then. (These are pretty nice parents!)

Table 7.2 gives the relevant data for *each* time Sarah purchases a three-year-old car. For example, if she trades in her car after two years, the next car will be in ownership year 1 during her junior year, and so forth.

Sarah needs a schedule for trading in her car that will minimize her total net cost.

When should Sarah trade in her car (if at all) during the next three summers to minimize her total net cost of purchasing, operating, and maintaining the car(s) over her four years of college?

Figure 7.14 shows the network formulation of this problem as a shortest path problem. Nodes 1, 2, 3, and 4 are the end of Sarah's first, second, third, and fourth years of college, respectively. Node 0 is now, before starting college. Each arc from one node to a second node corresponds to the activity of purchasing a car at the time indicated by the first of these two nodes and then trading it in at the time indicated by the second node. Sarah begins by purchasing a car now, and she ends by trading in a car at the end of year 4, so node 0 is the *origin* and node 4 is the *destination*.

The number of arcs on the path chosen from the origin to the destination indicates how many times Sarah will purchase and trade in a car. For example, consider the path

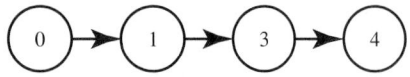

	Operating and Maintenance Costs for Ownership Year				Trade-in Value at End of Ownership Year			
Purchase Price	1	2	3	4	1	2	3	4
$12,000	$2,000	$3,000	$4,500	$6,500	$8,500	$6,500	$4,500	$3,000

TABLE 7.2
Sarah's Data Each Time She Purchases a Three-Year-Old Car

FIGURE 7.14

Formulation of the problem of when Sarah should trade in her car as a shortest path problem. The node labels measure the number of years from now. Each arc represents purchasing a car and then trading it in later.

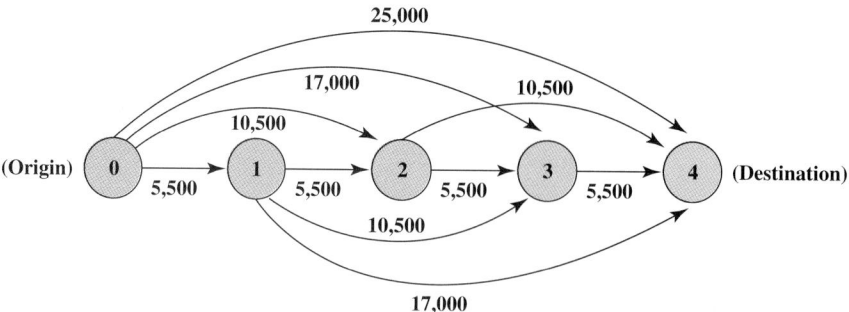

This corresponds to purchasing a car now, then trading it in at the end of year 1 to purchase a second car, then trading in the second car at the end of year 3 to purchase a third car, and then trading in this third car at the end of year 4.

Since Sarah wants to minimize her total net cost from now (node 0) to the end of year 4 (node 4), each arc length needs to measure the net cost of that arc's cycle of purchasing, maintaining, and trading in a car. Therefore,

Arc length = Purchase price + Operating and maintenance costs − Trade-in value

For example, consider the arc from node 1 to node 3. This arc corresponds to purchasing a car at the end of year 1, operating and maintaining it during ownership years 1 and 2, and then trading it in at the end of ownership year 2. Consequently,

$$\text{Length of arc from } ① \text{ to } ③ = 12{,}000 + 2{,}000 + 3{,}000 - 6{,}500$$
$$= 10{,}500 \quad \text{(in dollars)}$$

> The sum of the arc lengths on any path through this network gives the total net cost of the corresponding plan for trading in cars.

The arc lengths calculated in this way are shown next to the arcs in Figure 7.14. Adding up the lengths of the arcs on any path from node 0 to node 4 then gives the total net cost for that particular plan for trading in cars over the next four years. Therefore, finding the shortest path from the origin to the destination identifies the plan that will minimize Sarah's total net cost.

> The target cell now is TotalCost instead of TotalDistance.

Figure 7.15 shows the corresponding spreadsheet model, formulated in just the same way as for Figure 7.13 except that distances are now costs. Thus, the target cell TotalCost (D23) now gives the total cost that is to be minimized. The changing cells OnRoute (D12:D21) in the figure display the optimal solution obtained after having clicked on the Solve button. Since values of 1 indicate the path being followed, the shortest path turns out to be

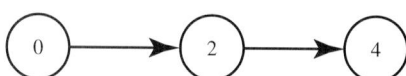

Trade in the first car at the end of Year 2.

Trade in the second car at the end of Year 4.

The length of this path is 10,500 + 10,500 = 21,000, so Sarah's total net cost is $21,000, as given by the target cell. Recall that this is exactly the amount in Sarah's car fund provided by her parents. (These are *really* nice parents!)

An Example of Minimizing Total Time

The Quick Company has learned that a competitor is planning to come out with a new kind of product with great sales potential. Quick has been working on a similar product that had been scheduled to come to market in 20 months. However, research is nearly complete and Quick's management now wishes to rush the product out to meet the competition.

There are four nonoverlapping phases left to be accomplished, including the remaining research (the first phase) that currently is being conducted at a normal pace. However, each phase can instead be conducted at a priority or crash level to expedite completion. These are the only levels that will be considered for the last three phases, whereas both the normal level

FIGURE 7.15   A spreadsheet model that formulates Sarah's problem as a shortest path problem where the objective is to minimize the total cost instead of the total distance. The bottom of the figure shows the equations entered in the target cell TotalCost (D23) and the other output cells Cost (E12:E21) and NetFlow (H12:H16). After applying the Solver, the values of 1 in the changing cells OnRoute (D12:D21) identify the shortest (least expensive) path for scheduling trade-ins.

	A	B	C	D	E	F	G	H	I	J
1		**Sarah's Car Purchasing Problem**								
2										
3			Operating &	Trade-in Value at End	Purchase					
4			Maint. Cost	of Year	Price					
5		Year 1	$2,000	$8,500	$12,000					
6		Year 2	$3,000	$6,500						
7		Year 3	$4,500	$4,500						
8		Year 4	$6,500	$3,000						
9										
10										
11		**From**	**To**	**On Route**	**Cost**		**Nodes**	**Net Flow**		**Supply/Demand**
12		Year 0	Year 1	0	$5,500		Year 0	1	=	1
13		Year 0	Year 2	1	$10,500		Year 1	0	=	0
14		Year 0	Year 3	0	$17,000		Year 2	0	=	0
15		Year 0	Year 4	0	$25,000		Year 3	0	=	0
16		Year 1	Year 2	0	$5,500		Year 4	-1	=	-1
17		Year 1	Year 3	0	$10,500					
18		Year 1	Year 4	0	$17,000					
19		Year 2	Year 3	0	$5,500					
20		Year 2	Year 4	1	$10,500					
21		Year 3	Year 4	0	$5,500					
22										
23			**Total Cost**	$21,000						

Range Name	Cells
Cost	E12:E21
From	B12:B21
NetFlow	H12:H16
Nodes	G12:G16
OnRoute	D12:D21
OpMaint1	C5
OpMaint2	C6
OpMaint3	C7
OpMaint4	C8
PurchasePrice	E5
SupplyDemand	J12:J16
To	C12:C21
TotalCost	D23
TradeIn1	D5
TradeIn2	D6
TradeIn3	D7
TradeIn4	D8

	E
11	**Cost**
12	=PurchasePrice+OpMaint1-TradeIn1
13	=PurchasePrice+OpMaint1+OpMaint2-TradeIn2
14	=PurchasePrice+OpMaint1+OpMaint2+OpMaint3-TradeIn3
15	=PurchasePrice+OpMaint1+OpMaint2+OpMaint3+OpMaint4-TradeIn4
16	=PurchasePrice+OpMaint1-TradeIn1
17	=PurchasePrice+OpMaint1+OpMaint2-TradeIn2
18	=PurchasePrice+OpMaint1+OpMaint2+OpMaint3-TradeIn3
19	=PurchasePrice+OpMaint1-TradeIn1
20	=PurchasePrice+OpMaint1+OpMaint2-TradeIn2
21	=PurchasePrice+OpMaint1-TradeIn1

	H
11	**Net Flow**
12	=SUMIF(From,G12,OnRoute)-SUMIF(To,G12,OnRoute)
13	=SUMIF(From,G13,OnRoute)-SUMIF(To,G13,OnRoute)
14	=SUMIF(From,G14,OnRoute)-SUMIF(To,G14,OnRoute)
15	=SUMIF(From,G15,OnRoute)-SUMIF(To,G15,OnRoute)
16	=SUMIF(From,G16,OnRoute)-SUMIF(To,G16,OnRoute)

	C	D
23	**Total Cost**	=SUMPRODUCT(OnRoute,Cost)

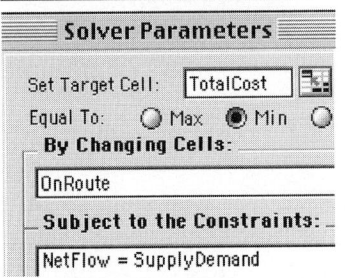

Solver Parameters

Set Target Cell: `TotalCost`

Equal To: ○ Max ● Min ○

By Changing Cells:

`OnRoute`

Subject to the Constraints:

`NetFlow = SupplyDemand`

Solver Options

☑ Assume Linear Model
☑ Assume Non-Negative

and these two levels will be considered for the first phase. The times required at these levels are shown in Table 7.3.

Management now has allocated $30 million for these four phases. The cost of each phase at the levels under consideration is shown in Table 7.4.

The objective is to minimize the total time for the project.

Management wishes to determine at which level to conduct each of the four phases to minimize the total time until the product can be marketed, subject to the budget restriction of $30 million.

Figure 7.16 shows the network formulation of this problem as a shortest path problem. Each node indicates the situation at that point in time. Except for the destination, a node is identified by two numbers:

1. The number of phases completed.

2. The number of millions of dollars left for the remaining phases.

The origin is *now,* when 0 phases have been completed and the entire budget of $30 million is left. Each arc represents the choice of a particular level of effort (identified in parentheses below the arc) for that phase. The *time* (in months) required to perform the phase with this level of effort then is the *length* of the arc (shown above the arc). Time is chosen as the measure of arc length because the objective is to minimize the total time for all four phases. Summing the arc lengths for any particular path through the network gives the total time for the plan corresponding to that path. Therefore, the shortest path through the network identifies the plan that minimizes total time.

The sum of the arc lengths on any path through this network gives the total time of the corresponding plan for preparing the new product.

All four phases have been completed as soon as any one of the four nodes with a first label of 4 has been reached. So why doesn't the network just end with these four nodes rather than hav-

		Remaining		Design of	Initiate Production
	Level	Research	Development	Manufacturing System	and Distribution
TABLE 7.3	Normal	5 months	—	—	—
Time Required for the	Priority	4 months	3 months	5 months	2 months
Phases of Preparing	Crash	2 months	2 months	3 months	1 month
Quick Co.'s New Product					

		Remaining		Design of	Initiate Production
	Level	Research	Development	Manufacturing System	and Distribution
TABLE 7.4	Normal	$3 million	—	—	—
Cost for the Phases of	Priority	6 million	$6 million	$9 million	$3 million
Preparing Quick Co.'s	Crash	9 million	9 million	12 million	6 million
New Product					

FIGURE 7.16

Formulation of the Quick Co. problem as a shortest path problem. Except for the dummy destination, the arc labels indicate, first, the number of phases completed and, second, the amount of money left (in millions of dollars) for the remaining phases. Each arc length gives the time (in months) to perform that phase.

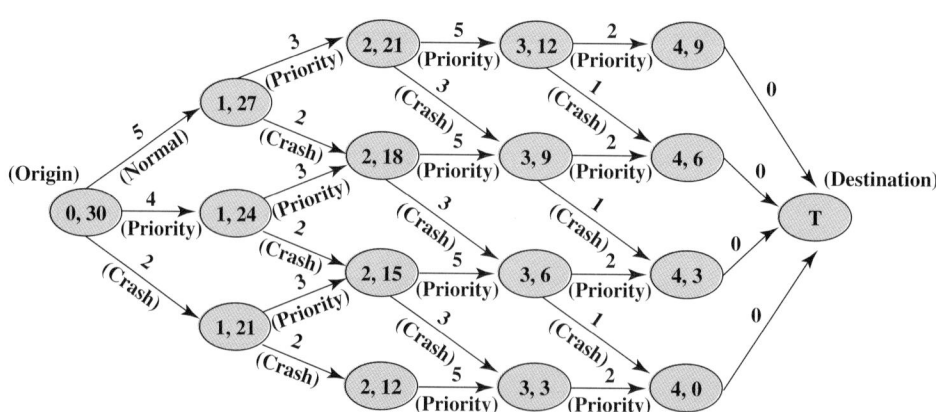

ing an arc coming out of each one? The reason is that a shortest path problem is required to have only a single destination. Consequently, a dummy destination is added at the right-hand side.

> When real travel through a network can end at more than one node, an arc with length 0 is inserted from each of these nodes to a **dummy destination** so that the network will have just a single destination.

Since each of the arcs into the dummy destination has length 0, this addition to the network does not affect the total length of a path from the origin to its ending point.

The target cell now is TotalTime instead of TotalDistance.

Figure 7.17 displays the spreadsheet model for this problem. Once again, the format is the same as in Figures 7.13 and 7.15, except now the quantity of concern in column F and the target cell TotalTime (D32) is time rather than distance or cost. Since the Solve button has already been

FIGURE 7.17   A spreadsheet model that formulates the Quick Co. problem as a shortest path problem where the objective is to minimize the total time instead of the total distance, so the target cell is TotalTime (D32). The other output cells are NetFlow (I4:I20). The values of 1 in the changing cells OnRoute (D4:D30) reveal the shortest (quickest) path obtained by the Solver.

	A	B	C	D	E	F	G	H	I	J	K
1		**Quick Co. Product Development Scheduling Problem**									
2											
3		**From**	**To**	**On Route**		**Time**		**Nodes**	**Net Flow**		**Supply/Demand**
4		(0, 30)	(1, 27)	0		5		(0, 30)	1	=	1
5		(0, 30)	(1, 24)	0		4		(1, 27)	0	=	0
6		(0, 30)	(1, 21)	1		2		(1, 24)	0	=	0
7		(1, 27)	(2, 21)	0		3		(1, 21)	0	=	0
8		(1, 27)	(2, 18)	0		2		(2, 21)	0	=	0
9		(1, 24)	(2, 18)	0		3		(2, 18)	0	=	0
10		(1, 24)	(2, 15)	0		2		(2, 15)	0	=	0
11		(1, 21)	(2, 15)	1		3		(2, 12)	0	=	0
12		(1, 21)	(2, 12)	0		2		(3, 12)	0	=	0
13		(2, 21)	(3, 12)	0		5		(3, 9)	0	=	0
14		(2, 21)	(3, 9)	0		3		(3, 6)	0	=	0
15		(2, 18)	(3, 9)	0		5		(3, 3)	0	=	0
16		(2, 18)	(3, 6)	0		3		(4, 9)	0	=	0
17		(2, 15)	(3, 6)	0		5		(4, 6)	0	=	0
18		(2, 15)	(3, 3)	1		3		(4, 3)	0	=	0
19		(2, 12)	(3, 3)	0		5		(4, 0)	0	=	0
20		(3, 12)	(4, 9)	0		2		(T)	-1	=	-1
21		(3, 12)	(4, 6)	0		1					
22		(3, 9)	(4, 6)	0		2					
23		(3, 9)	(4, 3)	0		1					
24		(3, 6)	(4, 3)	0		2					
25		(3, 6)	(4, 0)	0		1					
26		(3, 3)	(4, 0)	1		2					
27		(4, 9)	(T)	0		0					
28		(4, 6)	(T)	0		0					
29		(4, 3)	(T)	0		0					
30		(4, 0)	(T)	1		0					
31											
32			**Total Time**	10							

(continued)

FIGURE 7.17 *(continued)*

Range Name	Cells
From	B4:B30
NetFlow	I4:I20
Nodes	H4:H20
OnRoute	D4:D30
SupplyDemand	K4:K20
Time	F4:F30
To	C4:C30
TotalTime	D32

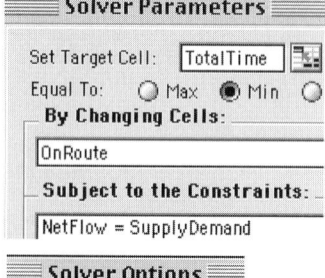

Solver Parameters

Set Target Cell: TotalTime

Equal To: ○ Max ● Min ○

By Changing Cells:

OnRoute

Subject to the Constraints:

NetFlow = SupplyDemand

Solver Options

☑ Assume Linear Model
☑ Assume Non-Negative

	I
3	**Net Flow**
4	=SUMIF(From,H4,OnRoute)-SUMIF(To,H4,OnRoute)
5	=SUMIF(From,H5,OnRoute)-SUMIF(To,H5,OnRoute)
6	=SUMIF(From,H6,OnRoute)-SUMIF(To,H6,OnRoute)
7	=SUMIF(From,H7, OnRoute)-SUMIF(To,H7,OnRoute)
8	=SUMIF(From,H8,OnRoute)-SUMIF(To,H8,OnRoute)
9	=SUMIF(From,H9,OnRoute)-SUMIF(To,H9,OnRoute)
10	=SUMIF(From,H10,OnRoute)-SUMIF(To,H10,OnRoute)
11	=SUMIF(From,H11,OnRoute)-SUMIF(To,H11,OnRoute)
12	=SUMIF(From,H12,OnRoute)-SUMIF(To,H12,OnRoute)
13	=SUMIF(From,H13,OnRoute)-SUMIF(To,H13,OnRoute)
14	=SUMIF(From,H14,OnRoute)-SUMIF(To,H14,OnRoute)
15	=SUMIF(From,H15,OnRoute)-SUMIF(To,H15,OnRoute)
16	=SUMIF(From,H16,OnRoute)-SUMIF(To,H16,OnRoute)
17	=SUMIF(From,H17,OnRoute)-SUMIF(To,H17,OnRoute)
18	=SUMIF(From,H18,OnRoute)-SUMIF(To,H18,OnRoute)
19	=SUMIF(From,H19,OnRoute)-SUMIF(To,H19,OnRoute)
20	=SUMIF(From,H20,OnRoute)-SUMIF(To,H20,OnRoute)

	C	D
32	**Total Time**	=SUMPRODUCT(OnRoute,Time)

TABLE 7.5

The Optimal Solution Obtained by the Excel Solver for Quick Co.'s Shortest Path Problem

Phase	Level	Time	Cost
Remaining research	Crash	2 months	$ 9 million
Development	Priority	3 months	6 million
Design of manufacturing system	Crash	3 months	12 million
Initiate production and distribution	Priority	2 months	3 million
Total		10 months	$30 million

clicked, the changing cells OnRoute (D4:D30) indicate which arcs lie on the path that minimizes the total time. Thus, the shortest path is

with a total length of 2 + 3 + 3 + 2 + 0 = 10 months, as given by TotalTime (D32). The resulting plan for the four phases is shown in Table 7.5. Although this plan does consume the entire budget of $30 million, it reduces the time until the product can be brought to market from the originally planned 20 months down to just 10 months.

Given this information, Quick's management now must decide whether this plan provides the best trade-off between time and cost. What would be the effect on total time of spending a few million more dollars? What would be the effect of reducing the spending somewhat instead? It is easy to provide management with this information as well by quickly solving some shortest path problems that correspond to budgets different from $30 million. The ultimate decision regarding which plan provides the best time–cost trade-off then is a judgment decision that only management can make.

Review
Questions

1. What are the origin and the destination in the Littletown Fire Department example?

2. What is the distinction between an arc and a link?

3. What are the supply node and the demand node when a shortest path problem is interpreted as a minimum-cost flow problem? With what supply and demand?

4. What are three measures of the length of a link (or arc) that lead to three categories of applications of shortest path problems?

5. What is the objective for Sarah's shortest path problem?

6. When does a dummy destination need to be added to the formulation of a shortest path problem?

7. What kind of trade-off does the management of the Quick Co. need to consider in making its final decision about how to expedite its new product to market?

7.5   MINIMUM SPANNING-TREE PROBLEMS

Starting with only the nodes for a network, the problem now is to design the network by deciding which links it should have.

This chapter focuses on problems with *network representations.* Thus far, the networks already have been complete with both nodes and links (or arcs).

We now turn our attention to a different kind of problem where the objective is to *design the network.* The nodes are given, but we must decide which links to give to the network. Specifically, each *potential link* has a cost (different for different links) for inserting it into the network. We are required to insert enough links to provide a path between *every pair of nodes.* The objective is to do this in a way that minimizes the total cost of the links.

Such a problem is referred to as a *minimum spanning-tree problem,* as illustrated by the following example.

An Example: The Modern Corp. Problem

Management of the Modern Corporation has decided to have a state-of-the-art *fiber-optic network* installed to provide high-speed communications (data, voice, and video) between its major centers.

The nodes in Figure 7.18 show the geographical layout of the corporation's major centers (which include corporate headquarters, a supercomputer facility, and a research park, as well as production and distribution centers). The dashed lines are the potential locations of fiber-optic cables. (Other cables between pairs of centers also are possible but have been ruled out as uneconomical.) The number next to each dashed line gives the cost (in millions of dollars) if that particular cable is chosen for installation.

Any pair of centers does not need to have a cable directly connecting them in order to take full advantage of the fiber-optic technology for high-speed communications between these centers. All that is necessary is to have a series of cables that connect the centers.

FIGURE 7.18
A display of Modern Corp.'s major centers (the nodes), the possible locations for fiber-optic cables (the dashed lines), and the cost in millions of dollars for those cables (the numbers).

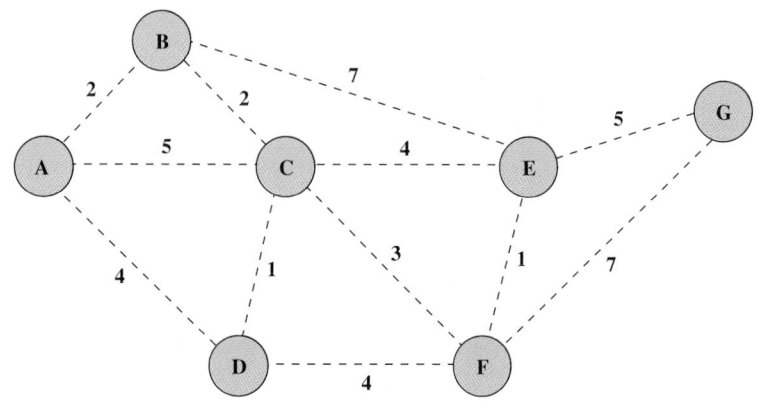

FIGURE 7.19

The fiber-optic network that provides the optimal solution for Modern Corp.'s minimum spanning-tree problem.

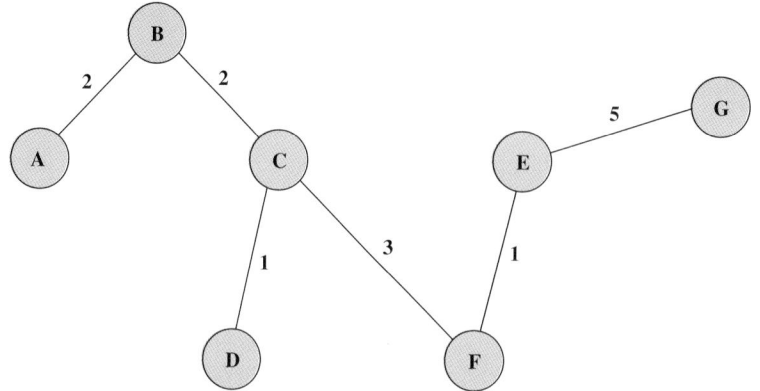

Management wants to minimize the total cost of installing fiber-optic cables that will provide high-speed communications between every pair of the corporation's major centers.

The problem is to determine which cables should be installed to minimize the total cost of providing high-speed communications between *every* pair of centers. This is, in fact, a *minimum spanning-tree problem.*

The optimal solution for this problem is shown in Figure 7.19, where the links in this network correspond to the possible cables in Figure 7.18 that should be chosen for installation. (Note that there is indeed a path between every pair of centers.) The resulting cost of this fiber-optic network is

$$\text{Total cost} = 2 + 2 + 1 + 3 + 1 + 5 = 14 \qquad (\$14 \text{ million})$$

Any other design of the network that connects every pair of centers would cost at least $1 million more.

What is the reason for the strange name, *minimum spanning-tree problem?* Here is the explanation. In the terminology of network theory, the network in Figure 7.19 is a **tree** because it does not have any paths that begin and end at the same node without backtracking (i.e., no paths that cycle). It also is a **spanning tree** because it is a tree that provides a path between every pair of nodes (so it spans all the nodes). Finally, it is a **minimum spanning tree** because it *minimizes* the total cost among all spanning trees.

General Characteristics

Just as for Modern Corp.'s problem, every minimum spanning-tree problem satisfies the following assumptions.

Assumptions of a Minimum Spanning-Tree Problem

1. You are given the *nodes* of a network but *not* the *links*. Instead, you are given the *potential links* and the positive *cost* (or a similar measure) for each if it is inserted into the network.

2. You wish to design the network by inserting enough links to satisfy the requirement that there be a path between *every pair* of nodes.

3. The objective is to satisfy this requirement in a way that minimizes the total cost of doing so.

The objective is to minimize the total cost of inserting links that will provide a path between every pair of nodes.

An optimal solution for this problem always is a *spanning tree.* Here is an easy way to recognize a spanning tree.

> The number of links in a spanning tree always is one less than the number of nodes. Furthermore, each node is directly connected by a single link to at least one other node.

See that this description fits the spanning tree in Figure 7.19, where there are six links and seven nodes (all directly connected to at least one other node). Remove any one of these links and assumption 2 above would be violated (no spanning tree). (Check this.) Incur the needless extra cost of adding another link instead (without removing one) and you again no longer have a spanning tree. (Check that adding any unused link from Figure 7.18 into Figure 7.19 would create a path that begins and ends at the same node without backtracking, which violates the definition of a tree.)

Finally, we should point out that, in contrast to transportation, assignment, maximum flow, and shortest path problems, a minimum spanning-tree problem is *not* a special type of minimum-cost flow problem. (It is not even a special type of linear programming problem.) Furthermore, it cannot be solved by the Excel Solver.

That is the bad news. The good news is that you can solve it very easily by the algorithm described below without even using a computer.

A Remarkably Simple Algorithm

Starting with no links in the network, each step of the algorithm selects one new link to insert from the list of potential links. As described below, the algorithm continues in this way until every node is touched by a link, at which point the selected nodes form a minimum spanning tree.

Algorithm for a Minimum Spanning-Tree Problem

1. Choice of the first link: Select the *cheapest* potential link.

2. Choice of the next link: Select the *cheapest* potential link between a node that already is touched by a link and a node that does not yet have such a link.

3. Repeat step 2 over and over until every node is touched by a link (perhaps more than one). At that point, an optimal solution (a minimum spanning tree) has been obtained.

(*Tie breaking:* Ties for the *cheapest* potential link may be broken arbitrarily without affecting the optimality of the final solution. However, ties in step 2 signal that there may also be (but need not be) other optimal solutions that would be obtained by breaking ties in another way.)

Application of the Algorithm to the Modern Corp. Problem

Now let us apply this algorithm to Modern Corp.'s minimum spanning-tree problem as displayed in Figure 7.18.

Among all the potential links (the dashed lines), the one between node C and node D ties with the one between node E and node F as the cheapest (a cost of 1). Therefore, for step 1, we need to select one of these two potential links to be the first link inserted into the network. Breaking the tie arbitrarily, let us select the one between node C and node D (the other will be chosen later), as shown next.

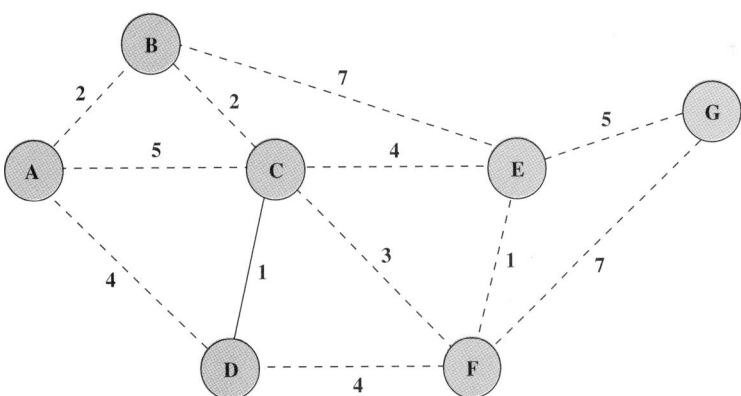

Since nodes C and D already are touched by a link, we are listing all the potential links between one of these nodes and one of the others. The cheapest of these potential links will be added to the network.

Next, we apply step 2 for the first time. The two nodes that are touched by a link are nodes C and D, so we need to compare the costs of the potential links between either of these nodes and a node that does not yet have a touching link. These potential links and their costs are

C ------ B : Cost = 2   C ------ F : Cost = 3

C ------ A : Cost = 5   D ------ A : Cost = 4

C ------ E : Cost = 4   D ------ F : Cost = 4

Since the cheapest of these is the one between node C and node B, with a cost of 2, it is selected to be the next link inserted into the network, as displayed below.

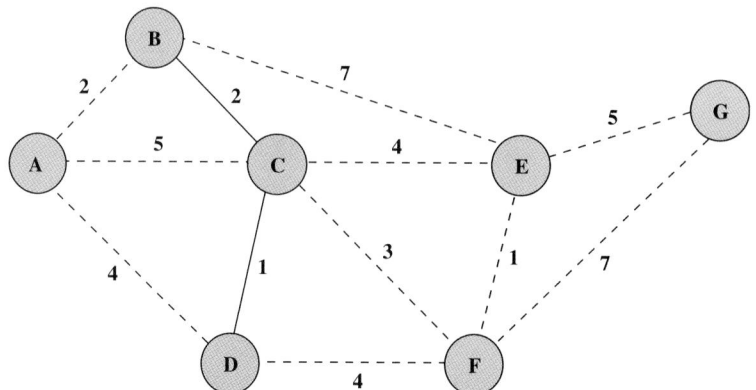

Now, nodes B, C, and D each are touched by a link (or two links in the case of node C), so the next execution of step 2 requires comparing the costs of the potential links between one of these nodes and one of the others.

The cheapest of these is the potential link between node B and node A, so it becomes the next link added to the network.

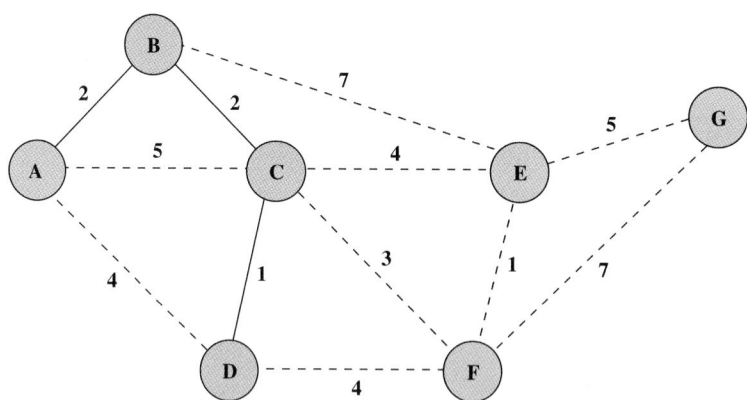

Nodes A, B, C, and D now all have touching links, so we next compare the costs of the potential links between one of these nodes and one of the others. (Actually, none of these potential links involve node A, since it does not have any potential links that go to a node that is not yet touched by a link.)

| C------E | : Cost = 4 | D------F | : Cost = 4 |
| C------F | : Cost = 3 | B------E | : Cost = 7 |

The cheapest is the potential link between node C and node F, so it is added next.

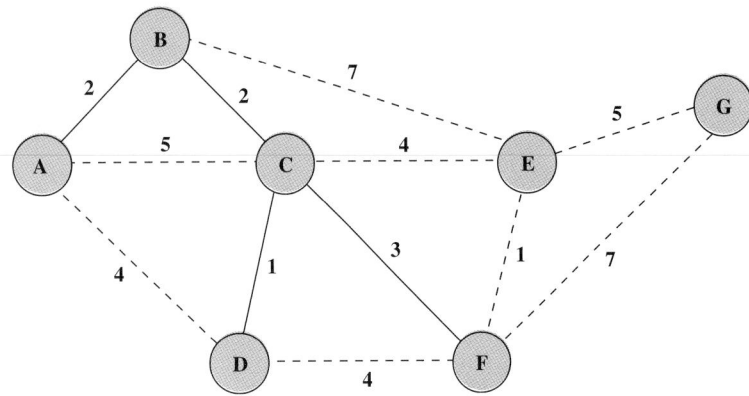

All but nodes E and G now are touched by a link. Therefore, the only potential links that need to be considered next are between either node E or G and one of the other nodes.

C ------ E   : Cost = 4   F ------ E   : Cost = 1

B ------ E   : Cost = 7   F ------ G   : Cost = 7

The cheapest by far is the potential link between node F and node E, so it finally gets inserted into the network. (Remember that this potential link was tied to be the initial link in step 1.)

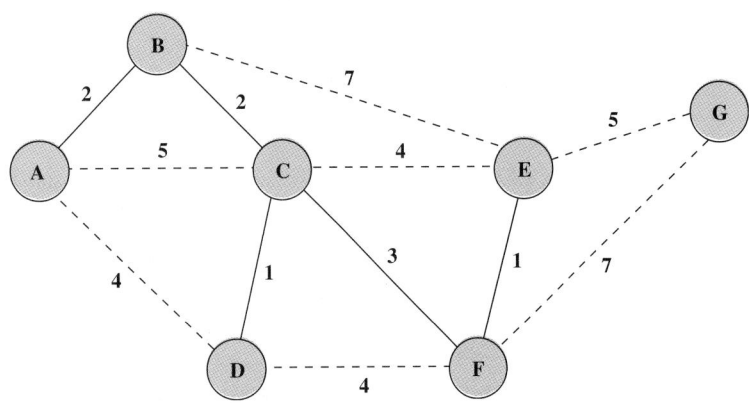

Since node G now is the only node untouched by a link, the only potential links to consider next are those between this node and the others.

F ------ G   : Cost = 7   E ------ G   : Cost = 5

The cheaper one is the potential link between node E and node G, so we insert it into the network.

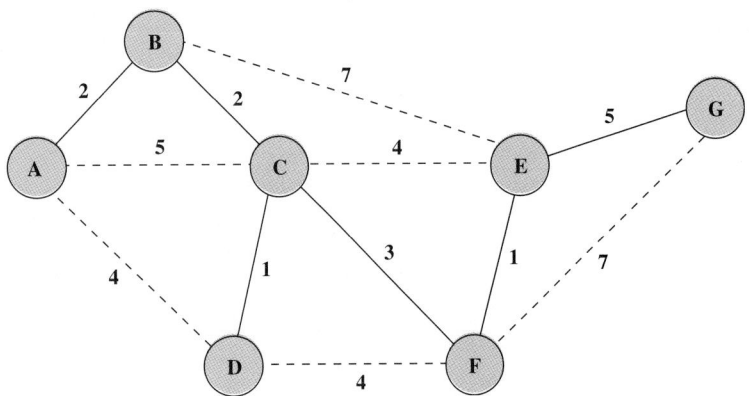

The solid lines show where the fiber-optic cables should be installed for a total cost of $14 million. Any other plan would cost at least $1 million more.

Every node now is touched by a link, so the algorithm is done and this is our optimal solution. All the links that have been inserted into the network form a *minimum spanning tree* with a total cost of 2 + 2 + 1 + 3 + 1 + 5 = 14 ($14 million). All the remaining potential links (dashed lines) are rejected because the inserted links provide a path between every pair of nodes.

Notice that this optimal solution is the same as the one given in Figure 7.19. (There is only one optimal solution for this particular problem.)

What would have happened if the tie had been broken the other way in step 1 by selecting the potential link between node E and node F to be the initial link inserted into the network instead of the potential link between node C and node D? Go ahead and check this out by cranking through the algorithm from this point. You will find that exactly the same links get selected, but in a different order from before.

This algorithm is referred to as a **greedy algorithm** because it simply grabs the most favorable choice (the cheapest potential link) at each step without worrying about the effect of this choice on subsequent decisions. It is remarkable that such a quick and simple-minded procedure still is guaranteed to find an optimal solution. Rejoice this time, but beware. Greedy algorithms normally will not necessarily find optimal solutions for other management science problems.

Some Applications

In this age of the information superhighway, applications similar to the Modern Corp. example have become increasingly important. However, minimum spanning-tree problems have several other types of applications as well.

1. Design of telecommunication networks (computer networks, leased-line telephone networks, cable television networks, etc.).

2. Design of a lightly used transportation network to minimize the total cost of providing the links (rail lines, roads, etc.).

3. Design of a network of high-voltage electrical power transmission lines.

4. Design of a network of wiring on electrical equipment (e.g., a digital computer system) to minimize the total length of the wire.

5. Design of a network of pipelines to connect a number of locations.

Review Questions

1. In a minimum spanning-tree problem, what part of the network is given and what part remains to be designed?

2. What kind of network is being designed in the Modern Corp. example?

3. In the terminology of network theory, what is a tree? A spanning tree? A minimum spanning tree?

4. What is an easy way to recognize a spanning tree?

5. What is the objective of a minimum spanning-tree problem?

6. Is a minimum spanning-tree problem a special type of minimum-cost flow problem?

7. What kind of algorithm will solve a minimum spanning-tree problem (but very few other management science problems)?

8. What are a few types of applications of minimum spanning-tree problems?

7.6 Summary

Networks of some type arise in a wide variety of contexts. Network representations are very useful for portraying the relationships and connections between the components of systems. Each component is represented by a point in the network called a *node,* and then the connections between components (nodes) are represented by lines called *arcs* (for one-way travel) or *links* (for two-way travel).

Frequently, a flow of some type must be sent through a network, so a decision needs to be made about the best way to do this. The kinds of network optimization models introduced in this chapter provide a powerful tool for making such decisions.

The model for minimum-cost flow problems plays a central role among these network optimization models, both because it is so broadly applicable and because it can be readily solved. The Excel Solver solves spreadsheet formulations of reasonable size, and the network simplex method can be used to solve larger problems, including huge problems with tens of thousands of nodes and arcs. A minimum-cost flow problem typically is concerned with optimizing the flow of goods through a network from their points of origin (the *supply nodes*) to where they are needed (the *demand nodes*). The objective is to minimize the total cost of sending the available supply through the network to satisfy the given demand. One typical application (among several) is to optimize the operation of a distribution network.

Special types of minimum-cost flow problems include transportation problems and assignment problems (discussed in the preceding chapter) as well as two prominent types introduced in this chapter: maximum flow problems and shortest path problems.

Given the limited capacities of the arcs in the network, the objective of a maximum flow problem is to maximize the total amount of flow from a particular point of origin (the *source*) to a particular terminal point (the *sink*). For example, this might involve maximizing the flow of goods through a company's supply network from its vendors to its processing facilities.

A shortest path problem also has a beginning point (the *origin*) and an ending point (the *destination*), but now the objective is to find a path from the origin to the destination that has the minimum total *length*. For some applications, length refers to distance, so the objective is to minimize the total distance traveled. However, some applications instead involve minimizing either the total cost or the total time of a sequence of activities.

Whereas all these models are concerned with optimizing the operation of an existing network, minimum spanning-tree problems are a prominent example of a model for optimizing the design of a new network. In this case, the nodes are given, but decisions need to be made on which links to insert into the network. The objective is to minimize the total cost of the links while providing a path between every pair of nodes. For example, this is management's usual objective when designing a modern telecommunication network to link a company's various centers.

Glossary

arc   A channel through which flow may occur from one node to another, shown as an arrow between the nodes pointing in the direction in which flow is allowed. (Section 7.1), *278*

capacity of an arc   The maximum amount of flow allowed through the arc. (Section 7.1), *278*

conservation of flow   Having the amount of flow out of a node equal the amount of flow into that node. (Section 7.1), *278*

demand node   A node where the net amount of flow generated (outflow minus inflow) is a fixed negative number, so that flow is absorbed there. (Section 7.1), *278*

destination   The node at which travel through the network is assumed to end for a shortest path problem. (Section 7.4), *291*

dummy destination   A fictitious destination introduced into the formulation of a shortest path problem with multiple possible termination points to satisfy the requirement that there be just a single destination. (Section 7.4), *297*

greedy algorithm   An algorithm that simply grabs the most favorable choice at each step without worrying about the effect of this choice on subsequent decisions. (Section 7.5), *304*

length of a link or arc   The number (typically a distance, a cost, or a time) associated with including the link or arc in the selected path for a shortest path problem. (Section 7.4), *293*

link   A channel through which flow may occur in either direction between a pair of nodes, shown as a line between the nodes. (Section 7.4), *291*

minimum spanning tree   One among all spanning trees that minimizes total cost. (Section 7.5), *300*

network simplex method   A streamlined version of the simplex method for solving minimum-cost flow problems very efficiently. (Section 7.1), *280*

node   A junction point of a network, shown as a labeled circle. (Section 7.1), *278*

origin   The node at which travel through the network is assumed to start for a shortest path problem. (Section 7.4), *291*

sink   The node for a maximum flow problem at which all flow through the network terminates. (Section 7.3), *287*

source   The node for a maximum flow problem at which all flow through the network originates. (Section 7.3), *287*

spanning tree   A tree that provides a path between every pair of nodes. (Section 7.5), *300*

supply node   A node where the net amount of flow generated (outflow minus inflow) is a fixed positive number. (Section 7.1), *278*

transshipment node   A node where the amount of flow out equals the amount of flow in. (Section 7.1), *278*

transshipment problem   A special type of minimum-cost flow problem where there are no capacity constraints on the arcs. (Section 7.1), *282*

tree   A network that does not have any paths that begin and end at the same node without backtracking. (Section 7.5), *300*

Learning Aids for This Chapter in Your MS Courseware

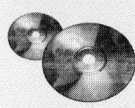

Chapter 7 Excel Files:

Distribution Unlimited Example
BMZ Example
Expanded BMZ Example

Littletown Fire Department Example
Sarah Example
Quick Example

An Excel Add-in:

Premium Solver for Education

Problems

We have inserted the symbol E* to the left of each problem (or its parts) where Excel should be used (unless your instructor gives you contrary instructions). An asterisk on the problem number indicates that at least a partial answer is given in the back of the book.

7.1.* Consider the transportation problem having the following data.

	Destination			
	1	**2**	**3**	**Supply**
Source				
1	6	7	4	40
2	5	8	6	60
Demand	30	40	30	

    a. Formulate a network model for this problem as a minimum-cost flow problem by drawing a network similar to Figure 7.3.

E* *b.* Formulate and solve a spreadsheet model for this problem in the format used for transportation problems in Chapter 6.

E* *c.* Formulate and solve a spreadsheet model for this problem in the format of a minimum-cost flow problem.

7.2. The Makonsel Company is a fully integrated company that both produces goods and sells them at its retail outlets. After production, the goods are stored in the company's two warehouses until needed by the retail outlets. Trucks are used to transport the goods from the two plants to the warehouses, and then from the warehouses to the three retail outlets.

Using units of full truckloads, the following table shows each plant's monthly output, its shipping cost per truckload sent to each warehouse, and the maximum amount that it can ship per month to each warehouse.

	Unit Shipping Cost		Shipping Capacity		
To **From**	**Warehouse 1**	**Warehouse 2**	**Warehouse 1**	**Warehouse 2**	**Output**
Plant 1	$425	$560	125	150	200
Plant 2	510	600	175	200	300

For each retail outlet (RO), the next table shows its monthly demand, its shipping cost per truckload from each warehouse, and the maximum amount that can be shipped per month from each warehouse.

		Unit Shipping Cost			Shipping Capacity		
To **From**	**RO1**	**RO2**	**RO3**	**RO1**	**RO2**	**RO3**
Warehouse 1	$470	$505	$490	100	150	100
Warehouse 2	390	410	440	125	150	75
Demand	150	200	150	150	200	150

Management now wants to determine a distribution plan (number of truckloads shipped per month from each plant to each warehouse and from each warehouse to each retail outlet) that will minimize the total shipping cost.

a. Draw a network that depicts the company's distribution network. Identify the supply nodes, transshipment nodes, and demand nodes in this network.

b. Formulate a network model for this problem as a minimum-cost flow problem by inserting all the necessary data into the network drawn in part *a*. (Use the format depicted in Figure 7.3 to display these data.)

E*   c. Formulate and solve a spreadsheet model for this problem.

7.3.   The Audiofile Company produces boomboxes. However, management has decided to subcontract out the production of the speakers needed for the boomboxes. Three vendors are available to supply the speakers. Their price for each shipment of 1,000 speakers is shown below.

Vendor	Price
1	$22,500
2	22,700
3	22,300

Each shipment would go to one of the company's two warehouses. In addition to the price for each shipment, each vendor would charge a shipping cost for which it has its own formula based on the mileage to the warehouse. These formulas and the mileage data are shown below.

Vendor	Charge per Shipment	Warehouse 1	Warehouse 2
1	$300 + 40¢/mile	1,600 miles	400 miles
2	$200 + 50¢/mile	500 miles	600 miles
3	$500 + 20¢/mile	2,000 miles	1,000 miles

Whenever one of the company's two factories needs a shipment of speakers to assemble into the boomboxes, the company hires a trucker to bring the shipment in from one of the warehouses. The cost per shipment is given below, along with the number of shipments needed per month at each factory.

	Unit Shipping Cost	
	Factory 1	**Factory 2**
Warehouse 1	$200	$700
Warehouse 2	400	500
Monthly demand	10	6

Each vendor is able to supply as many as 10 shipments per month. However, because of shipping limitations, each vendor is only able to send a maximum of six shipments per month to each warehouse. Similarly, each warehouse is only able to send a maximum of six shipments per month to each factory.

Management now wants to develop a plan for each month regarding how many shipments (if any) to order from each vendor, how many of those shipments should go to each warehouse, and then how many shipments each warehouse should send to each factory. The objective is to minimize the sum of the purchase costs (including the shipping charge) and the shipping costs from the warehouses to the factories.

a. Draw a network that depicts the company's supply network. Identify the supply nodes, transshipment nodes, and demand nodes in this network.

b. This problem is only a *variant* of a minimum-cost flow problem because the supply from each vendor is a *maximum* of 10 rather than a fixed amount of 10. However, it can be converted to a full-fledged minimum-cost flow problem by adding a dummy demand node that receives (at zero cost) all the unused supply capacity at the vendors. Formulate a network model for this minimum-cost flow problem by inserting all the necessary data into the network drawn in part *a* supplemented by this dummy demand node. (Use the format depicted in Figure 7.3 to display these data.)

E* c. Formulate and solve a spreadsheet model for the company's problem.

7.4.* Consider Figure 7.9 (in Section 7.3), which depicts the BMZ Co. distribution network from its factories in Stuttgart and Berlin to the distribution centers in both Los Angeles and Seattle. This figure also gives in brackets the maximum amount that can be shipped through each shipping lane.

In the weeks following the crisis described in Section 7.2, the distribution center in Los Angeles has successfully replenished its inventory. Therefore, Karl Schmidt (the supply chain manager for the BMZ Co.) has concluded that it will be sufficient hereafter to ship 130 units per month to Los Angeles and 50 units per month to Seattle. (One unit is a hundred cubic meters of automobile replacement parts.) The Stuttgart factory (node ST in the figure) will allocate 130 units per month and the Berlin factory (node BE) will allocate 50 units per month out of their total production to cover these shipments. However, rather than resuming the past practice of supplying the Los Angeles distribution center from only the Stuttgart factory and supplying the Seattle distribution center from only the Berlin factory, Karl has decided to allow either factory to supply either distribution center. He feels that this additional flexibility is likely to reduce the total shipping cost.

The following table gives the shipping cost per unit through each of these shipping lanes.

To From	LI	BO	RO	HA	NO	NY	BN	LA	SE
Node									
ST	$3,200	$2,500	$2,900	—	—	—	—	—	—
BE	—	—	$2,400	$2,000	—	—	—	—	—
LI	—	—	—	—	$6,100	—	—	—	—
BO	—	—	—	—	$6,800	$5,400	—	—	—
RO	—	—	—	—	—	$5,900	—	—	—
HA	—	—	—	—	—	$6,300	$5,700	—	—
NO	—	—	—	—	—	—	—	$3,100	—
NY	—	—	—	—	—	—	—	$4,200	$4,000
BN	—	—	—	—	—	—	—	$3,400	$3,000

Unit Shipping Cost to Node

Karl wants to determine the shipping plan that will minimize the total shipping cost.

a. Formulate a network model for this problem as a minimum-cost flow problem by inserting all the necessary data into the distribution network shown in Figure 7.9. (Use the format depicted in Figure 7.3 to display these data.)

E*   *b.* Formulate and solve a spreadsheet model for this problem.

       c. What is the total shipping cost for this optimal solution?

7.5. Reconsider Problem 7.4. Suppose now that, for administrative convenience, management has decided that all 130 units per month needed at the distribution center in Los Angeles must come from the Stuttgart factory (node ST) and all 50 units per month needed at the distribution center in Seattle must come from the Berlin factory (node BE). For each of these distribution centers, Karl Schmidt wants to determine the shipping plan that will minimize the total shipping cost.

       a. For the distribution center in Los Angeles, formulate a network model for this problem as a minimum-cost flow problem by inserting all the necessary data into the distribution network shown in Figure 7.6. (Use the format depicted in Figure 7.3 to display these data.)

E*   *b.* Formulate and solve a spreadsheet model for the problem formulated in part *a.*

       c. For the distribution center in Seattle, draw its distribution network emanating from the Berlin factory at node BE.

       d. Repeat part *a* for the distribution center in Seattle by using the network drawn in part *c.*

E*   *e.* Formulate and solve a spreadsheet model for the problem formulated in part *d.*

       f. Add the total shipping costs obtained in parts *b* and *e.* Compare this sum with the total shipping cost obtained in part *c* of Problem 7.4 (as given in the back of the book).

7.6. Consider the maximum flow problem formulated in Figures 7.7 and 7.8 for the BMZ case study. Redraw Figure 7.7 and insert the optimal shipping quantities (cells D4:D12 in Figure 7.8) in parentheses above the respective arcs. Examine the capacities of these arcs. Explain why these arc capacities ensure that the shipping quantities in parentheses must be an optimal solution because the maximum flow cannot exceed 150.

E*7.7.* Formulate and solve a spreadsheet model for the maximum flow problem shown below, where node A is the source, node F is the sink, and the arc capacities are the numbers in square brackets shown next to the arcs.

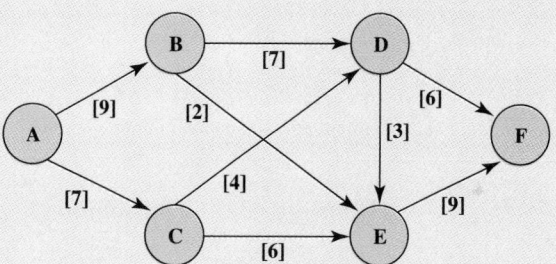

7.8. The diagram depicts a system of aqueducts that originate at three rivers (nodes R1, R2, and R3) and terminate at a major city (node T), where the other nodes are junction points in the system.

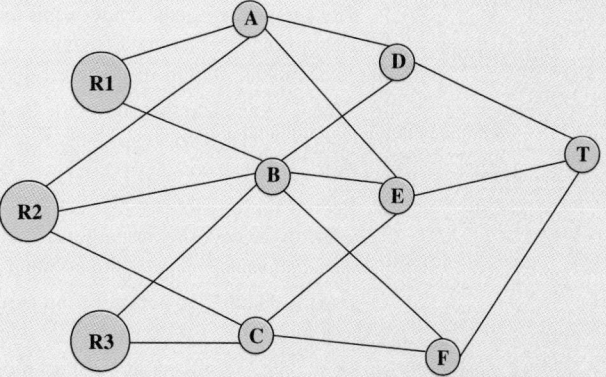

    Using units of thousands of acre feet, the following tables show the maximum amount of water that can be pumped through each aqueduct per day.

To From	A	B	C
R1	75	65	—
R2	40	50	60
R3	—	80	70

To From	D	E	F
A	60	45	—
B	70	55	45
C	—	70	90

To From	T
D	120
E	190
F	130

The city water manager wants to determine a flow plan that will maximize the flow of water to the city.

a. Formulate this problem as a maximum flow problem by identifying a source, a sink, and the transshipment nodes, and then drawing the complete network that shows the capacity of each arc.

E*   *b.* Formulate and solve a spreadsheet model for this problem.

7.9.   Refer back to Table 6.14, which gives the location of Texago Corporation's three oil fields, three refineries, and four distribution centers. In addition to these locations, Texago also imports oil from the Middle East and has opened a new refinery in St. Louis.

A major strike involving the transportation industries now has sharply curtailed Texago's capacity to ship oil from the four oil fields to the four refineries and to ship petroleum products from the refineries to the distribution centers. Using units of thousands of barrels of crude oil (and its equivalent in refined products), the following tables show the maximum number of units that can be shipped per day from each oil field to each refinery and from each refinery to each distribution center.

	Refinery			
Oil Field	New Orleans	Charleston	Seattle	St. Louis
Texas	11	7	2	8
California	5	4	8	7
Alaska	7	3	12	6
Middle East	8	9	4	15

	Distribution Center			
Refinery	Pittsburgh	Atlanta	Kansas City	San Francisco
New Orleans	5	9	6	4
Charleston	8	7	9	5
Seattle	4	6	7	8
St. Louis	12	11	9	7

The Texago management now wants to determine a plan for how many units to ship from each oil field to each refinery and from each refinery to each distribution center that will maximize the total number of units reaching the distribution centers.

a. Draw a rough map that shows the location of Texago's oil fields, refineries, and distribution centers. Add arrows to show the flow of crude oil and then petroleum products through this distribution network.

b. Redraw this distribution network by lining up all the nodes representing oil fields in one column, all the nodes representing refineries in a second column, and all the nodes representing distribution centers in a third column. Then add arcs to show the possible flow.

c. Use the distribution network from part *b* to formulate a network model for Texago's problem as a variant of a maximum flow problem.

E*   *d.* Formulate and solve a spreadsheet model for this problem.

E*7.10.   Reconsider the Littletown Fire Department problem presented in Section 7.4 and depicted in Figure 7.11. Due to maintenance work on the one-mile road between nodes A and B, a detour currently must be taken that extends the trip between these nodes to four miles.

Formulate and solve a spreadsheet model for this revised problem to find the new shortest path from the fire station to the farming community.

7.11. You need to take a trip by car to another town that you have never visited before. Therefore, you are studying a map to determine the shortest route to your destination. Depending on which route you choose, there are five other towns (call them A, B, C, D, E) through which you might pass on the way. The map shows the mileage along each road that directly connects two towns without any intervening towns. These numbers are summarized in the following table, where a dash indicates that there is no road directly connecting these two towns without going through any other towns.

	Miles between Adjacent Towns					
Town	**A**	**B**	**C**	**D**	**E**	**Destination**
Origin	40	60	50	—	—	—
A		10	—	70	—	—
B			20	55	40	—
C				—	50	—
D					10	60
E						80

a. Formulate a network model for this problem as a shortest path problem by drawing a network where nodes represent towns, links represent roads, and numbers indicate the length of each link in miles.

E*   b. Formulate and solve a spreadsheet model for this problem.

c. Use part *b* to identify your shortest route.

d. If each number in the table represented your *cost* (in dollars) for driving your car from one town to the next, would the answer in part *c* now give your minimum-cost route?

e. If each number in the table represented your *time* (in minutes) for driving your car from one town to the next, would the answer in part *c* now give your minimum-time route?

7.12.* At a small but growing airport, the local airline company is purchasing a new tractor for a tractor-trailer train to bring luggage to and from the airplanes. A new mechanized luggage system will be installed in three years, so the tractor will not be needed after that. However, because it will receive heavy use, so that the running and maintenance costs will increase rapidly as it ages, it may still be more economical to replace the tractor after one or two years. The following table gives the total net discounted cost associated with purchasing a tractor (purchase price minus trade-in allowance, plus running and maintenance costs) at the end of year i and trading it in at the end of year j (where year 0 is now).

		j	
	1	**2**	**3**
i			
0	$8,000	$18,000	$31,000
1		10,000	21,000
2			12,000

Management wishes to determine at what times (if any) the tractor should be replaced to minimize the total cost for the tractor(s) over three years.

a. Formulate a network model for this problem as a shortest path problem.

E*   b. Formulate and solve a spreadsheet model for this problem.

7.13. One of Speedy Airlines's flights is about to take off from Seattle for a nonstop flight to London. There is some flexibility in choosing the precise route to be taken, depending upon weather conditions. The following network depicts the possible routes under consideration, where SE and LN are Seattle and London, respectively, and the other nodes represent various intermediate locations.

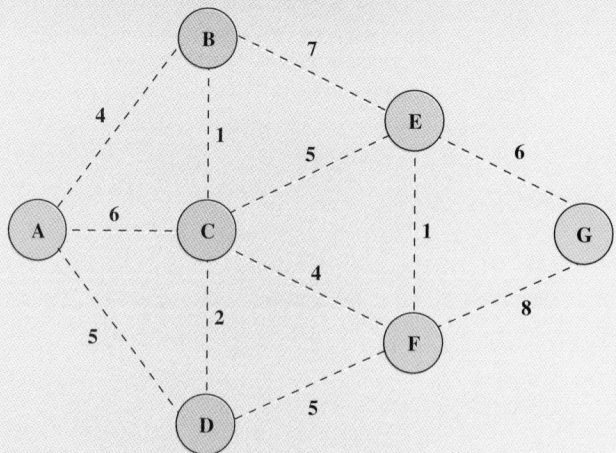

The winds along each arc greatly affect the flying time (and so the fuel consumption). Based on current meteorological reports, the flying times (in hours) for this particular flight are shown next to the arcs. Because the fuel consumed is so expensive, the management of Speedy Airlines has established a policy of choosing the route that minimizes the total flight time.

    a. What plays the role of distances in interpreting this problem to be a shortest path problem?

E*   *b.* Formulate and solve a spreadsheet model for this problem.

7.14.   Reconsider the Modern Corp. problem presented in Section 7.5. When the algorithm for a minimum spanning-tree problem was applied to this problem, there was a tie at step 1 for choosing the first link. This tie was broken arbitrarily by selecting the potential link between node C and node D.

        Now break the tie the other way by selecting the potential link between node E and node F to be the first link and then reapply the rest of the algorithm. Show each step. (You again should obtain the minimum spanning tree shown in Figure 7.19.)

7.15.*   Use the greedy algorithm presented in Section 7.5 to find a minimum spanning tree for a network with the following nodes and with the links still to be chosen. The dashed lines between pairs of nodes represent *potential* links and the number next to each dashed line represents the cost (in thousands of dollars) of inserting that link into the network.

7.16.   Use the greedy algorithm presented in Section 7.5 to find a minimum spanning tree for a network with the following nodes and with the links still to be chosen. The dashed lines between pairs of nodes represent *potential* nodes and the number next to each dashed line represents the cost (in millions of dollars) of inserting that link into the network.

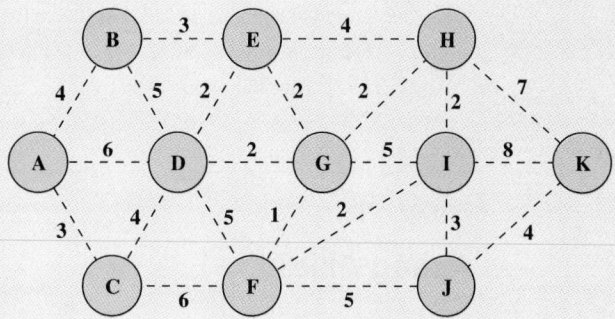

7.17. The Wirehouse Lumber Company will soon begin logging eight groves of trees in the same general area. Therefore, it must develop a system of dirt roads that makes each grove accessible from every other grove. The distance (in miles) between every pair of groves is as follows:

				Distance between Pairs of Groves				
Grove	1	2	3	4	5	6	7	8
1	—	1.3	2.1	0.9	0.7	1.8	2.0	1.5
2	1.3	—	0.9	1.8	1.2	2.6	2.3	1.1
3	2.1	0.9	—	2.6	1.7	2.5	1.9	1.0
4	0.9	1.8	2.6	—	0.7	1.6	1.5	0.9
5	0.7	1.2	1.7	0.7	—	0.9	1.1	0.8
6	1.8	2.6	2.5	1.6	0.9	—	0.6	1.0
7	2.0	2.3	1.9	1.5	1.1	0.6	—	0.5
8	1.5	1.1	1.0	0.9	0.8	1.0	0.5	—

Management now wants to determine between which pairs of groves the roads should be constructed to connect all groves with a minimum total length of road.

a. Describe how this problem fits the network description of a minimum spanning-tree problem.

b. Use the greedy algorithm presented in Section 7.5 to solve the problem.

7.18. The Premiere Bank soon will be hooking up computer terminals at each of its branch offices to the computer at its main office, using special phone lines with telecommunications devices. The phone line from a branch office need not be connected directly to the main office. It can be connected indirectly by being connected to another branch office that is connected (directly or indirectly) to the main office. The only requirement is that every branch office be connected by some route to the main office.

The charge for the special phone lines is $100 times the number of miles involved, where the distance (in miles) between every pair of offices is as follows:

			Distance between Pairs of Offices			
	Main	Branch 1	Branch 2	Branch 3	Branch 4	Branch 5
Main office	—	190	70	115	270	160
Branch 1	190	—	100	110	215	50
Branch 2	70	100	—	140	120	220
Branch 3	115	110	140	—	175	80
Branch 4	270	215	120	175	—	310
Branch 5	160	50	220	80	310	—

Management wishes to determine which pairs of offices should be directly connected by special phone lines in order to connect every branch office (directly or indirectly) to the main office at a minimum total cost.

   a. Describe how this problem fits the network description of a minimum spanning-tree problem.

   b. Use the greedy algorithm presented in Section 7.5 to solve the problem. What is the total cost for the special phone lines?

Case 7-1

Aiding Allies

Commander Votachev steps into the cold October night and deeply inhales the smoke from his cigarette, savoring its warmth. He surveys the destruction surrounding him—shattered windows, burning buildings, torn roads—and smiles. His two years of work training revolutionaries east of the Ural Mountains has proven successful; his troops now occupy seven strategically important cities in the Russian Federation: Kazan, Perm, Yekaterinburg, Ufa, Samara, Saratov, and Orenburg. His siege is not yet over, however. He looks to the west. Given the political and economic confusion in the Russian Federation at this time, he knows that his troops will be able to conquer Saint Petersburg and Moscow shortly. Commander Votachev will then be able to rule with the wisdom and control exhibited by his communist predecessors Lenin and Stalin.

Across the Pacific Ocean, a meeting of the top security and foreign policy advisors of the United States is in progress at the White House. The president has recently been briefed about the communist revolution masterminded by Commander Votachev and is determining a plan of action. The president reflects upon a similar October long ago in 1917, and he fears the possibility of a new age of radical Communist rule accompanied by chaos, bloodshed, escalating tensions, and possibly nuclear war. He therefore decides that the United States needs to respond and to respond quickly. Moscow has requested assistance from the United States military, and the president plans to send troops and supplies immediately.

The president turns to General Lankletter and asks him to describe the preparations being taken in the United States to send the necessary troops and supplies to the Russian Federation.

General Lankletter informs the president that along with troops, weapons, ammunition, fuel, and supplies, aircraft, ships, and vehicles are being assembled at two port cities with airfields: Boston and Jacksonville. The aircraft and ships will transfer all troops and cargo across the Atlantic Ocean to the Eurasian continent. The general hands the president a list of the types of aircraft, ships, and vehicles being assembled along with a description of each type. The list is shown below.

Transportation Type	Name	Capacity	Speed
Aircraft	C-141 Starlifter	150 tons	400 miles per hour
Ship	Transport	240 tons	35 miles per hour
Vehicle	Palletized Load System Truck	16,000 kilograms	60 miles per hour

All aircraft, ships, and vehicles are able to carry both troops and cargo. Once an aircraft or ship arrives in Europe, it stays there to support the armed forces.

The president then turns to Tabitha Neal, who has been negotiating with the NATO countries for the last several hours to use their ports and airfields as stops to refuel and resupply before heading to the Russian Federation. She informs the president that the following ports and airfields in the NATO countries will be made available to the U.S. military.

Ports	Airfields
Napoli	London
Hamburg	Berlin
Rotterdam	Istanbul

The president stands and walks to the map of the world projected on a large screen in the middle of the room. He maps the progress of troops and cargo from the United States to three strategic cities in the Russian Federation that have not yet been seized by Commander Votachev. The three cities are Saint Petersburg, Moscow, and Rostov. He explains that the troops and cargo will be used both to defend the Russian cities and to launch a counter attack against Votachev to recapture the cities he currently occupies. (The map is shown at the end of the case.)

The president also explains that all Starlifters and transports leave Boston or Jacksonville. All transports that have traveled across the Atlantic must dock at one of the NATO ports to unload. Palletized load system trucks brought over in the transports will then carry all troops and materials unloaded from the ships at the NATO ports to the three strategic Russian cities not yet seized by Votachev. All Starlifters that have traveled across the Atlantic must land at one of the NATO airfields for refueling. The planes will then carry all troops and cargo from the NATO airfields to the three Russian cities.

a. Draw a network showing the different routes troops and supplies may take to reach the Russian Federation from the United States.

b. Moscow and Washington do not know when Commander Votachev will launch his next attack. Leaders from the two countries therefore have agreed that troops should reach each of the three strategic Russian cities as quickly as possible. The president has determined that the situation is so dire that cost is no object—as many Starlifters, transports, and trucks as are necessary will be used to transfer troops and cargo from the United States to Saint Petersburg, Moscow, and Rostov. Therefore, no limitations exist on the number of troops and amount of cargo that can be transferred between any cities.

The president has been given the following information about the length of the available routes between cities.

From	To	(Kilometers)
Boston	Berlin	7,250 km
Boston	Hamburg	8,250
Boston	Istanbul	8,300
Boston	London	6,200
Boston	Rotterdam	6,900
Boston	Napoli	7,950
Jacksonville	Berlin	9,200
Jacksonville	Hamburg	9,800
Jacksonville	Istanbul	10,100
Jacksonville	London	7,900
Jacksonville	Rotterdam	8,900
Jacksonville	Napoli	9,400
Berlin	Saint Petersburg	1,280
Hamburg	Saint Petersburg	1,880
Istanbul	Saint Petersburg	2,040
London	Saint Petersburg	1,980
Rotterdam	Saint Petersburg	2,200
Napoli	Saint Petersburg	2,970
Berlin	Moscow	1,600
Hamburg	Moscow	2,120
Istanbul	Moscow	1,700
London	Moscow	2,300
Rotterdam	Moscow	2,450
Napoli	Moscow	2,890
Berlin	Rostov	1,730
Hamburg	Rostov	2,470
Istanbul	Rostov	990
London	Rostov	2,860
Rotterdam	Rostov	2,760
Napoli	Rostov	2,800

Given the distance and the speed of the transportation used between each pair of cities, how can the president most quickly move troops from the United States to each of the three strategic Russian cities? Highlight the path(s) on the network. How long will it take troops and supplies to reach Saint Petersburg? Moscow? Rostov?

c. The president encounters only one problem with his first plan: he has to sell the military deployment to Congress. Under the War Powers Act, the president is required to consult with Congress before introducing troops into hostilities or situations where hostilities will occur. If Congress does not give authorization to the president for such use of troops, the president must withdraw troops after 60 days. Congress also has the power to decrease the 60-day time period by passing a concurrent resolution.

The president knows that Congress will not authorize significant spending for another country's war, especially when voters have paid so much attention to decreasing the national debt. He therefore decides that he needs to find a way to get the needed troops and supplies to Saint Petersburg, Moscow, and Rostov at the minimum cost.

Each Russian city has contacted Washington to communicate the number of troops and supplies the city needs at a minimum for reinforcement. After analyzing the requests, General Lankletter has converted the requests from numbers of troops, gallons of gasoline, and so on, to tons of cargo for easier planning. The requirements are listed below.

City	Requirements
Saint Petersburg	320,000 tons
Moscow	440,000 tons
Rostov	240,000 tons

Both in Boston and Jacksonville, there are 500,000 tons of the necessary cargo available. When the United States decides to send a plane, ship, or truck between two cities, several costs occur: fuel costs, labor costs, maintenance costs, and appropriate port or airfield taxes and tariffs. These costs are listed next.

From	To	Cost
Boston	Berlin	$50,000 per Starlifter
Boston	Hamburg	$30,000 per transport
Boston	Istanbul	$55,000 per Starlifter
Boston	London	$45,000 per Starlifter
Boston	Rotterdam	$30,000 per transport
Boston	Napoli	$32,000 per transport
Jacksonville	Berlin	$57,000 per Starlifter
Jacksonville	Hamburg	$48,000 per transport
Jacksonville	Istanbul	$61,000 per Starlifter
Jacksonville	London	$49,000 per Starlifter
Jacksonville	Rotterdam	$44,000 per transport
Jacksonville	Napoli	$56,000 per transport
Berlin	Saint Petersburg	$24,000 per Starlifter
Hamburg	Saint Petersburg	$3,000 per truck
Istanbul	Saint Petersburg	$28,000 per Starlifter
London	Saint Petersburg	$22,000 per Starlifter
Rotterdam	Saint Petersburg	$3,000 per truck
Napoli	Saint Petersburg	$5,000 per truck
Berlin	Moscow	$22,000 per Starlifter
Hamburg	Moscow	$4,000 per truck
Istanbul	Moscow	$25,000 per Starlifter
London	Moscow	$19,000 per Starlifter
Rotterdam	Moscow	$5,000 per truck
Napoli	Moscow	$5,000 per truck
Berlin	Rostov	$23,000 per Starlifter
Hamburg	Rostov	$7,000 per truck
Istanbul	Rostov	$2,000 per Starlifter
London	Rostov	$4,000 per Starlifter
Rotterdam	Rostov	$8,000 per truck
Napoli	Rostov	$9,000 per truck

The president faces a number of restrictions when trying to satisfy the requirements. Early winter weather in northern Russia has brought a deep freeze with much snow. Therefore, General Lankletter is opposed to sending truck convoys in the area. He convinces the president to supply Saint Petersburg only through the air. Moreover, the truck routes into Rostov are quite limited, so that from each port, at most 2,500 trucks can be sent to Rostov. The Ukrainian government is very sensitive about American airplanes flying through its air space. It restricts the U.S. military to at most 200 flights from Berlin to Rostov and to at most 200 flights from London to Rostov. (The U.S. military does not want to fly around the Ukraine and is thus restricted by the Ukrainian limitations.)

How does the president satisfy each Russian city's military requirements at minimum cost? Highlight the path to be used between the United States and the Russian Federation on the network.

d. Once the president releases the number of planes, ships, and trucks that will travel between the United States and the Russian Federation, Tabitha Neal contacts each of the American cities and NATO countries to indicate the number of planes to expect at the airfields, the number of ships to expect at the docks, and the number of trucks to expect traveling across the roads. Unfortunately, Tabitha learns that several additional restrictions exist that cannot be immediately eliminated. Because of airfield congestion and unalterable flight schedules, only a limited number of planes may be sent between any two cities. These plane limitations are given below.

From	To	Maximum Number of Airplanes
Boston	Berlin	300
Boston	Istanbul	500
Boston	London	500
Jacksonville	Berlin	500
Jacksonville	Istanbul	700
Jacksonville	London	600
Berlin	Saint Petersburg	500
Istanbul	Saint Petersburg	0
London	Saint Petersburg	1,000
Berlin	Moscow	300
Istanbul	Moscow	100
London	Moscow	200
Berlin	Rostov	0
Istanbul	Rostov	900
London	Rostov	100

In addition, because some countries fear that citizens will become alarmed if too many military trucks travel the public highways, they object to a large number of trucks traveling through their countries. These objections mean that a limited number of trucks are able to travel between certain ports and Russian cities. These limitations are listed below.

From	To	Maximum Number of Trucks
Rotterdam	Moscow	600
Rotterdam	Rostov	750
Hamburg	Moscow	700
Hamburg	Rostov	500
Napoli	Moscow	1,500
Napoli	Rostov	1,400

Tabitha learns that all shipping lanes have no capacity limits due to the American control of the Atlantic Ocean.

The president realizes that due to all the restrictions, he will not be able to satisfy all the reinforcement requirements of the three Russian cities. He decides to disregard the cost issue and instead to maximize the total amount of cargo he can get to the Russian cities. How does the president maximize the total amount of cargo that reaches the Russian Federation? Highlight the path(s) used between the United States and the Russian Federation on the network.

e. Even before all American troops and supplies had reached Saint Petersburg, Moscow, and Rostov, infighting among Commander Votachev's troops about whether to make the next attack against Saint Petersburg or against Moscow split the revolutionaries. Troops from Moscow easily overcame the vulnerable revolutionaries. Commander Votachev was imprisoned, and the next step became rebuilding the seven cities razed by his armies.

The president's top priority is to help the Russian government to re-establish communications between the seven Russian cities and Moscow at minimum cost. The price of installing communication lines between any two Russian cities varies given the cost of shipping wire to the area, the level of destruction in the area, and the roughness of the terrain. Luckily, a city is able to communicate with all others if it is connected only indirectly to every other city. Saint Petersburg and Rostov are already connected to Moscow, so if any of the seven cities is connected to Saint Petersburg or Rostov, it will also be connected to Moscow. The cost of replacing communication lines between two given cities for which this is possible is shown below.

Where should communication lines be installed to minimize the total cost of re-establishing communications between Moscow and all seven Russian cities?

Between	Cost to Re-establish Communication Lines
Saint Petersburg and Kazan	$210,000
Saint Petersburg and Perm	185,000
Saint Petersburg and Ufa	225,000
Moscow and Ufa	310,000
Moscow and Samara	195,000
Moscow and Orenburg	440,000
Moscow and Saratov	140,000
Rostov and Saratov	200,000
Rostov and Orenburg	120,000
Kazan and Perm	150,000
Kazan and Ufa	105,000
Kazan and Samara	95,000
Perm and Yekaterinburg	85,000
Perm and Ufa	125,000
Yekaterinburg and Ufa	125,000
Ufa and Samara	100,000
Ufa and Orenburg	75,000
Saratov and Samara	100,000
Saratov and Orenburg	95,000

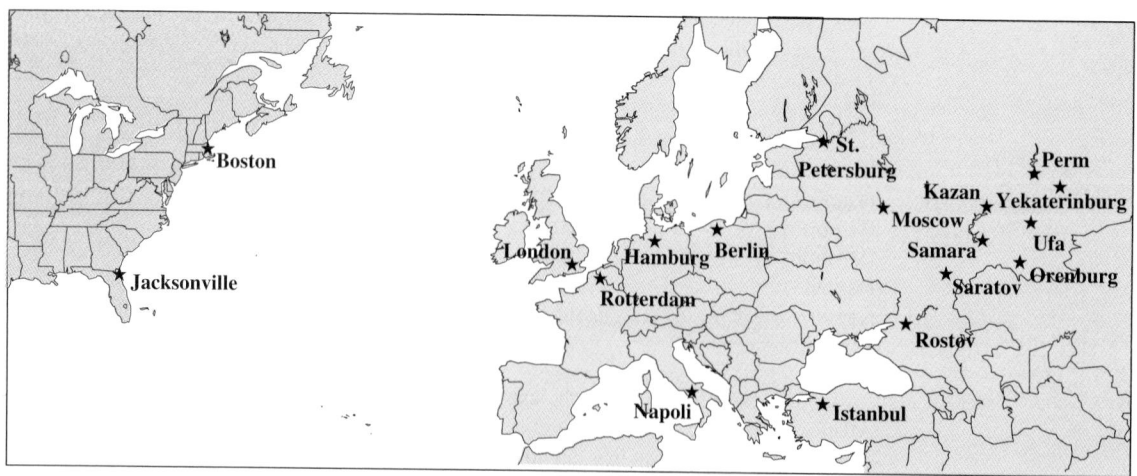

Case 7-2

Money in Motion

Jake Nguyen runs a nervous hand through his once finely combed hair. He loosens his once perfectly knotted silk tie. And he rubs his sweaty hands across his once immaculately pressed trousers. Today has certainly not been a good day.

Over the past few months, Jake had heard whispers circulating from Wall Street—whispers from the lips of investment bankers and stockbrokers famous for their outspokenness. They had whispered about a coming Japanese economic collapse—whispered because they had believed that publicly vocalizing their fears would hasten the collapse.

And, today, their very fears have come true. Jake and his colleagues gather around a small television dedicated exclusively to the Bloomberg channel. Jake stares in disbelief as he listens to the horrors taking place in the Japanese market. And the Japanese market is taking the financial markets in all other East Asian countries with it on its tailspin. He goes numb. As manager of Asian foreign investment for Grant Hill Associates, a small West Coast investment boutique specializing in currency trading, Jake bears personal responsibility for any negative impacts of the collapse. And Grant Hill Associates will experience negative impacts.

Jake had not heeded the whispered warnings of a Japanese collapse. Instead, he had greatly increased the stake Grant Hill Associates held in the Japanese market. Because the Japanese market had performed better than expected over the past year, Jake had increased investments in Japan from $2.5 million to $15 million only one month ago. At that time, one dollar was worth 80 yen.

No longer. Jake realizes that today's devaluation of the yen means that one dollar is worth 125 yen. He will be able to liquidate these investments without any loss in yen, but now the dollar loss when converting back into U.S. currency would be huge. He takes a deep breath, closes his eyes, and mentally prepares himself for serious damage control.

Jake's meditation is interrupted by a booming voice calling for him from a large, corner office. Grant Hill, the president of Grant Hill Associates, yells, "Nguyen, get the hell in here!"

Jake jumps and looks reluctantly toward the corner office hiding the furious Grant Hill. He smooths his hair, tightens his tie, and walks briskly into the office.

Grant Hill meets Jake's eyes upon his entrance and continues yelling, "I don't want one word out of you, Nguyen! No excuses; just fix this debacle! Get all of our money out of Japan! My gut tells me this is only the beginning! Get the money into safe U.S. bonds! NOW! And don't forget to get our cash positions out of Indonesia and Malaysia ASAP with it!"

Jake has enough common sense to say nothing. He nods his head, turns on his heels, and practically runs out of the office.

Safely back at his desk, Jake begins formulating a plan to move the investments out of Japan, Indonesia, and Malaysia. His experiences investing in foreign markets have taught him that when playing with millions of dollars, *how* he gets money out of a foreign market is almost as important as *when* he gets money out of the market. The banking partners of Grant Hill Associates charge different transaction fees for converting one currency into another one and wiring large sums of money around the globe.

And now, to make matters worse, the governments in East Asia have imposed very tight limits on the amount of money an individual or a company can exchange from the domestic currency into a particular foreign currency and withdraw it from the country. The goal of this dramatic measure is to reduce the outflow of foreign investments out of those countries to prevent a complete collapse of the economies in the region. Because of Grant Hill Associates's cash holdings of 10.5 billion Indonesian rupiahs and 28 million Malaysian ringgits, along with the holdings in yen, it is not clear how these holdings should be converted back into dollars.

Jake wants to find the most cost-effective method to convert these holdings into dollars. On his company's website, he always can find on-the-minute exchange rates for most currencies in the world (see Table 1).

TABLE 1   Currency Exchange Rates

From \ To	Yen	Rupiah	Ringgit	U.S. Dollar	Canadian Dollar	Euro	Pound	Peso
Japanese yen	1	50	0.04	0.008	0.01	0.0064	0.0048	0.0768
Indonesian rupiah		1	0.0008	0.00016	0.0002	0.000128	0.000096	0.001536
Malaysian ringgit			1	0.2	0.25	0.16	0.12	1.92
U.S. dollar				1	1.25	0.8	0.6	9.6
Canadian dollar					1	0.64	0.48	7.68
European euro						1	0.75	12
English pound							1	16
Mexican peso								1

The table states that, for example, 1 Japanese yen equals 0.008 U.S. dollars. By making a few phone calls, he discovers the transaction costs his company must pay for large currency transactions during these critical times (see Table 2).

TABLE 2   Transaction Cost (Percent)

From \ To	Yen	Rupiah	Ringgit	U.S. Dollar	Canadian Dollar	Euro	Pound	Peso
Yen	—	0.5	0.5	0.4	0.4	0.4	0.25	0.5
Rupiah		—	0.7	0.5	0.3	0.3	0.75	0.75
Ringgit			—	0.7	0.7	0.4	0.45	0.5
U.S. dollar				—	0.05	0.1	0.1	0.1
Canadian dollar					—	0.2	0.1	0.1
Euro						—	0.05	0.5
Pound							—	0.5
Peso								—

Jake notes that exchanging one currency for another one results in the same transaction cost as a reverse conversion. Finally, Jake finds out the maximum amounts of domestic currencies his company is allowed to convert into other currencies in Japan, Indonesia, and Malaysia (see Table 3).

TABLE 3   Transaction Limits in Equivalent of 1,000 Dollars

From \ To	Yen	Rupiah	Ringgit	U.S. Dollar	Canadian Dollar	Euro	Pound	Peso
Yen	—	5,000	5,000	2,000	2,000	2,000	2,000	4,000
Rupiah	5,000	—	2,000	200	200	1,000	500	200
Ringgit	3,000	4,500	—	1,500	1,500	2,500	1,000	1,000

a. Formulate Jake's problem as a minimum-cost flow problem, and draw the network for his problem. Identify the supply and demand nodes for the network.

b. Which currency transactions must Jake perform to convert the investments from yens, rupiahs, and ringgits into U.S. dollars to ensure that Grant Hill Associates has the maximum dollar amount after all transactions have occurred? How much money does Jake have to invest in U.S. bonds?

c. The World Trade Organization forbids transaction limits because they promote protectionism. If no transaction limits exist, what method should Jake use to convert the Asian holdings from the respective currencies into dollars?

d. In response to the World Trade Organization's mandate forbidding transaction limits, the Indonesian government introduces a new tax to protect its currency that leads to a 500 percent increase in transaction costs for transactions of rupiahs. Given these new transaction costs but no transaction limits, what currency transactions should Jake perform to convert the Asian holdings from the respective currencies into dollars?

e. Jake realizes that his analysis is incomplete because he has not included all aspects that might influence his planned currency exchanges. Describe other factors that Jake should examine before he makes his final decision.

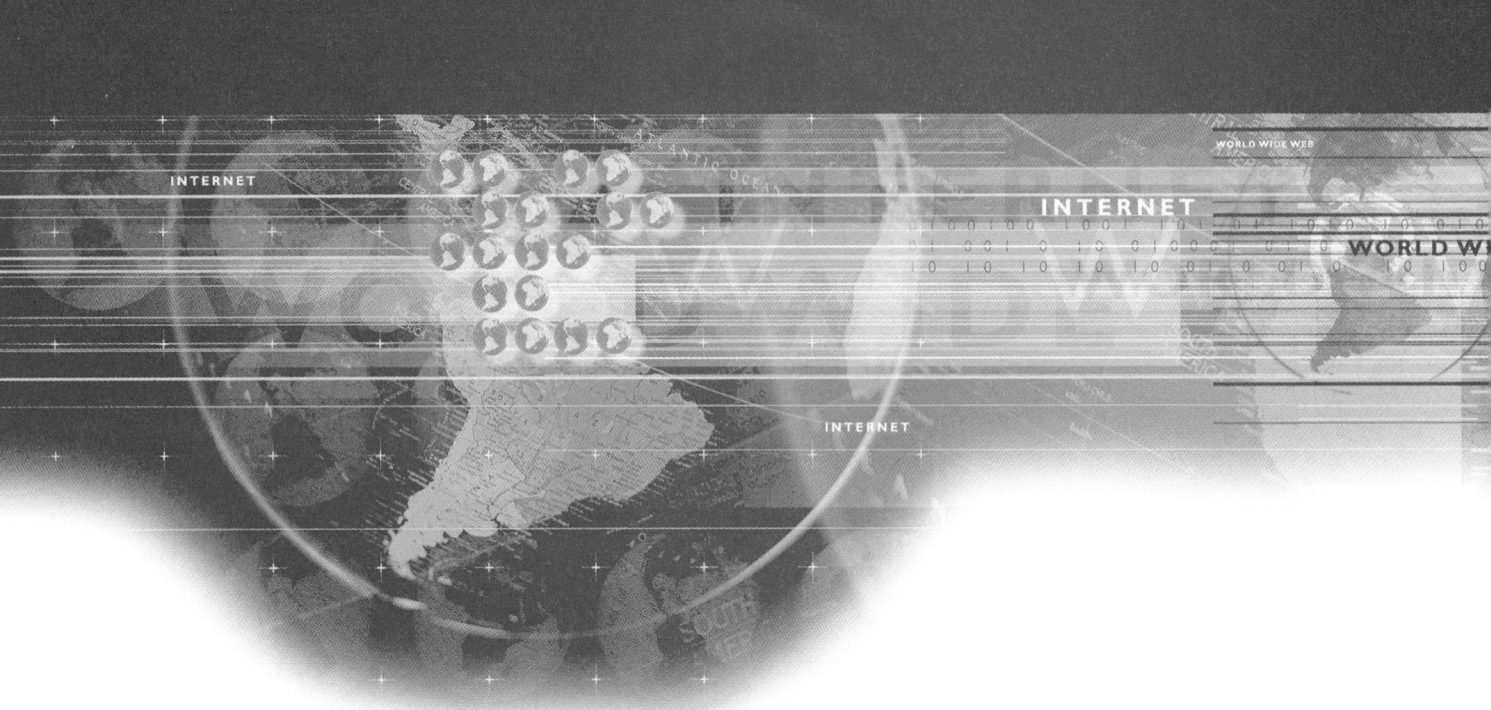

Learning objectives

After completing this chapter, you should be able to

1. Describe the kind of help that PERT/CPM can provide a project manager.

2. Identify the types of information needed to construct a project network for PERT/CPM.

3. Use this information to construct a project network for a particular project.

4. Use a project network to develop a complete schedule, including both the earliest and latest times when each activity should start and finish.

5. Identify the critical bottleneck activities where any delays must be avoided to prevent delaying project completion.

6. Find an approximate probability of completing a project by the deadline.

7. Find the least expensive way of expediting a project to meet a target completion date.

8. Use a systematic procedure to help plan, schedule, and control project costs.

9. Provide an evaluation of PERT/CPM from a managerial perspective.

10. Identify some kinds of extensions to PERT/CPM that now are becoming available.

Chapter **Eight**

PERT/CPM Models for Project Management

One of the most challenging jobs that any manager can take on is the management of a large-scale project that requires coordinating numerous activities throughout the organization. A myriad of details must be considered in planning how to coordinate all these activities, in developing a realistic schedule, and then in monitoring the progress of the project.

Fortunately, two closely related management science techniques, **PERT** (*program evaluation and review technique*) and **CPM** (*critical path method*), are available to assist the project manager in carrying out these responsibilities. These techniques make heavy use of *networks* (as introduced in the preceding chapter) to help plan and display the coordination of all the activities. They also normally use a *software package* to deal with all the data needed to develop schedule information and then to monitor the progress of the project. *Project management software,* such as MS Project in your MS Courseware, now is widely available for these purposes.

PERT and CPM have been widely used for a variety of projects, including the following types:

1. Construction of a new plant.

2. Research and development of a new product.

3. NASA space exploration projects.

4. Movie productions.

5. Building of a ship.

6. Government-sponsored projects for developing a new weapons system.

7. Relocation of a major facility.

8. Maintenance of a nuclear reactor.

9. Installation of a management information system.

10. Conducting of an advertising campaign.

PERT and CPM were independently developed in the late 1950s. Ever since, they have been among the most widely used management science techniques.

The original versions of PERT and CPM had some important differences, as we will point out later in the chapter. However, they also had a great deal in common, and the two techniques have gradually merged further over the years. In fact, today's software packages often include all the important options from both original versions.

Consequently, practitioners now commonly use the two names interchangeably, or combine them into the single acronym **PERT/CPM** as we often will do. We will make the distinction between them only when we are describing an option that was unique to one of the original versions.

The next section introduces a case study that will carry through the chapter to illustrate the various options for analyzing projects provided by PERT/CPM.

8.1 A CASE STUDY: THE RELIABLE CONSTRUCTION CO. PROJECT

The Reliable Construction Company has just made the winning bid of $5.4 million to construct a new plant for a major manufacturer. The manufacturer needs the plant to go into operation within a year. Therefore, the contract includes the following provisions:

The deadline is in 47 weeks, with a penalty for missing it and a bonus for finishing within 40 weeks.

- A *penalty* of $300,000 if Reliable has not completed construction by the deadline 47 weeks from now.

- To provide additional incentive for speedy construction, a *bonus* of $150,000 to be paid to Reliable if the plant is completed within 40 weeks.

Reliable is assigning its best construction manager, David Perty, to this project to help ensure that it stays on schedule. Mr. Perty has earned the confidence of management through many years of exemplary performance with the company. He began as a carpenter fresh out of community college and soon became the youngest foreman in the company, so he knows the construction business from the ground up. While a foreman, he went back to college part time at night to earn his business degree. It was an arduous schedule that stretched out over five years, but he found that he enjoyed his business major and was good at it. His favorite course was a graduate-level elective in project management, and it was there that he thoroughly learned the techniques of PERT/CPM. Immediately after earning his business degree with honors, Mr. Perty was promoted to construction manager. He has been serving the company in this capacity now for 14 years, and rumors have it that he may be next in line to move into top management in a year when the retirement of the company president will cause some shuffling of the top positions. Although Mr. Perty would welcome this opportunity, he does not feel any hurry to move up. Despite its many stresses, he thoroughly enjoys the challenges of being a construction manager, including the opportunities to apply the latest project management techniques.

The construction manager, David Perty, will focus his initial planning on meeting the deadline of 47 weeks.

Mr. Perty is very pleased to receive this latest assignment as the project manager for such an important project. He looks forward to the challenge of bringing the project in on schedule, and perhaps earning a promotion in the process. However, since he is doubtful that it will be feasible to finish within 40 weeks without incurring excessive costs, he has decided to focus his initial planning on meeting the deadline of 47 weeks.

He will need to arrange for a number of crews to perform the various construction activities at different times. Table 8.1 shows his list of the various **activities.** The third column provides important additional information for coordinating the scheduling of the crews.

For any given activity, its **immediate predecessors** (as given in the third column of Table 8.1) are those activities that must be completed by no later than the start time of the given activity. (Similarly, the given activity is called an **immediate successor** of each of its immediate predecessors.)

TABLE 8.1
Activity List for the Reliable Construction Co. Project

Activity	Activity Description	Immediate Predecessors	Estimated Duration (Weeks)
A	Excavate	—	2
B	Lay the foundation	A	4
C	Put up the rough wall	B	10
D	Put up the roof	C	6
E	Install the exterior plumbing	C	4
F	Install the interior plumbing	E	5
G	Put up the exterior siding	D	7
H	Do the exterior painting	E, G	9
I	Do the electrical work	C	7
J	Put up the wallboard	F, I	8
K	Install the flooring	J	4
L	Do the interior painting	J	5
M	Install the exterior fixtures	H	2
N	Install the interior fixtures	K, L	6

For example, the top entries in this column indicate that

1. Excavation does not need to wait for any other activities.

2. Excavation must be completed before starting to lay the foundation.

3. The foundation must be completely laid before starting to put up the rough wall, and so on.

When a given activity has *more than one* immediate predecessor, all must be finished before the activity can begin.

In order to schedule the activities, Mr. Perty consults with each of the crew foremen to develop an estimate of how long each activity should take when it is done in the normal way. These estimates are given in the rightmost column of Table 8.1.

Adding up these times gives a grand total of 79 weeks, which is far beyond the deadline for the project. Fortunately, some of the activities can be done in parallel, which substantially reduces the project completion time.

Here are the key questions that will be addressed in the following sections.

Given all the information in Table 8.1, Mr. Perty now wants to develop answers to the following questions.

1. How can the project be displayed graphically to better visualize the flow of the activities? (Section 8.2)

2. What is the total time required to complete the project if no delays occur? (Section 8.3)

3. When do the individual activities need to start and finish (at the latest) to meet this project completion time? (Section 8.3)

4. When can the individual activities start and finish (at the earliest) if no delays occur? (Section 8.3)

5. Which are the critical bottleneck activities where any delays must be avoided to prevent delaying project completion? (Section 8.3)

6. For the other activities, how much delay can be tolerated without delaying project completion? (Section 8.3)

7. Given the uncertainties in accurately estimating activity durations, what is the probability of completing the project by the deadline (47 weeks)? (Section 8.4)

8. If extra money is spent to expedite the project, what is the least expensive way of attempting to meet the target completion time (40 weeks)? (Section 8.5)

9. How should ongoing costs be monitored to try to keep the project within budget? (Section 8.6)

Being a regular user of PERT/CPM, Mr. Perty knows that this technique will provide invaluable help in answering these questions (as you will see in the sections indicated in parentheses above).

Review
Questions

1. What are the financial terms in the contract that the Reliable Construction Co. has just won?

2. What is the deadline that Mr. Perty is focusing on meeting?

3. What is meant by an *immediate predecessor* of an activity? An *immediate successor?*

4. What are the three types of information that Mr. Perty gathered regarding the project?

8.2   USING A NETWORK TO VISUALLY DISPLAY A PROJECT

The preceding chapter describes how valuable *networks* can be to represent and help analyze many kinds of problems. In much the same way, networks play a key role in dealing with projects. They enable showing the relationships between the activities and placing everything into perspective. They then are used to help analyze the project and answer the kinds of questions raised at the end of the preceding section.

Project Networks

A network used to represent a project is called a **project network.** A project network consists of a number of **nodes** (typically shown as small circles or rectangles) and a number of **arcs** (shown as arrows) that lead from some node to another. (If you have not previously studied Chapter 7, where nodes and arcs are discussed extensively, just think of them as the names given to the small circles or rectangles and to the arrows in the network.)

As Table 8.1 indicates, there are three types of information needed to describe a project.

1. Activity information: Break down the project into its individual activities (at the desired level of detail).

2. Precedence relationships: Identify the immediate predecessor(s) for each activity.

3. Time information: Estimate the duration of each activity.

The project network needs to convey all this information. There are two alternative types of project networks available for doing this.

One type is the **activity-on-arc (AOA) project network,** where each activity is represented by an *arc.* A node is used to separate an activity (an outgoing arc) from each of its immediate predecessors (an incoming arc). The sequencing of the arcs thereby shows the precedence relationships between the activities.

The second type is the **activity-on-node (AON) project network,** where each activity is represented by a *node.* The arcs then are used just to show the precedence relationships between the activities. In particular, the node for each activity with immediate predecessors has an arc coming in from each of these predecessors.

The original versions of PERT and CPM used AOA project networks, so this was the conventional type for some years. However, AON project networks have some important advantages over AOA project networks for conveying exactly the same information.

1. AON project networks are considerably easier to construct than AOA project networks.

2. AON project networks are easier to understand than AOA project networks for inexperienced users, including many managers.

3. AON project networks are easier to revise than AOA project networks when there are changes in the project.

For these reasons, AON project networks have become increasingly popular with practitioners. It appears somewhat likely that they will become the conventional type to use. Therefore, we now will focus solely on AON project networks.

Figure 8.1 shows the project network for Reliable's project.[1] Referring also to the third column of Table 8.1, note how there is an arc leading to each activity from each of its immediate predecessors. Because activity A has no immediate predecessors, there is an arc leading from the **start node** to this activity. Similarly, since activities M and N have no immediate successors, arcs lead from these activities to the **finish node.** Therefore, the project network nicely displays at a glance all the precedence relationships between all the activities (plus the start and finish of the project). Based on the rightmost column of Table 8.1, the number next to the node for each activity then records the estimated duration (in weeks) of that activity.

For projects of this size and larger, it is not always straightforward to construct the project network from the activity list. In case you have trouble doing this, we have included a supplement to this chapter on your CD-ROM that outlines and illustrates a systematic procedure for constructing the project network.

In real applications, software commonly is used to construct the project network. We next describe how MS Project (in your MS Courseware) does this for Reliable's project.

---

[1]Although project networks often are drawn from left to right, we go from top to bottom to better fit on the printed page.

FIGURE 8.1

The project network for the Reliable Construction Co. project.

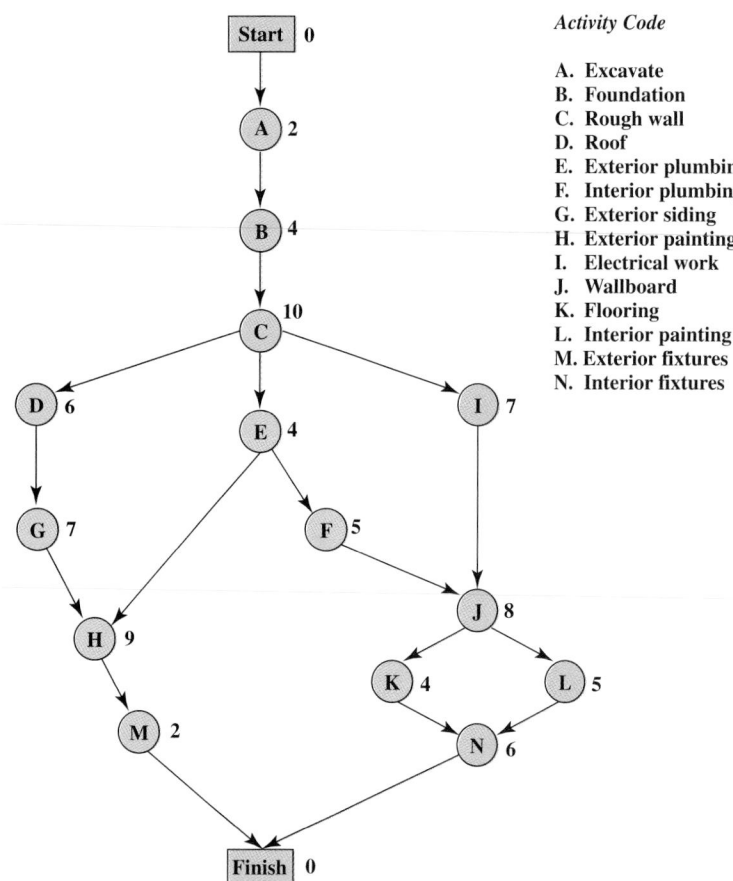

Activity Code

A. **Excavate**
B. **Foundation**
C. **Rough wall**
D. **Roof**
E. **Exterior plumbing**
F. **Interior plumbing**
G. **Exterior siding**
H. **Exterior painting**
I. **Electrical work**
J. **Wallboard**
K. **Flooring**
L. **Interior painting**
M. **Exterior fixtures**
N. **Interior fixtures**

Using MS Project

The first step with MS Project is to enter the information in the activity list (Table 8.1). Choose the View menu and then select its option called Table. From the resulting submenu, choose the option called Entry to bring up the table needed to enter the information. This table is displayed in Figure 8.2 for Reliable's project. You enter the task (activity) names, the duration of each, a starting date for the first activity, and the immediate predecessors of each, as shown in the figure. The program automatically builds up the rest of the table (including the chart on the right) as you enter this information.

The default duration is in units of days, but we have changed the units to weeks here. Such a change can be made by choosing Options under the Tools menu and then changing "Duration is entered in" under the Schedule options.

The default date format is a calendar date (e.g., 1/2/03). This can be changed by choosing Options from the Tools menu and then changing the Date Format option under the View options. We have chosen to count time from time 0. Thus, the start time for the first activity is given as W1/1, which is shorthand for Week 1, day 1. A five-day work week is assumed. For example, since the duration of the first activity is two weeks, its finish time is given as W2/5 (Week 2, day 5).

The chart on the right is referred to as a **Gantt chart.** This kind of chart is a popular one in practice for displaying a project schedule, because the bars nicely show the scheduled start and finish times for the respective activities. (This figure assumes that the project begins at the beginning of a calendar year.) The arrows show the precedence relationships between the activities. For example, since both activities 5 and 7 are immediate predecessors of activity 8, there are arrows from both activities 5 and 7 leading to activity 8.

This project entry table can be returned to at any time by choosing Table:Entry in the View menu.

FIGURE 8.2   The spreadsheet used by MS Project for entering the activity list for the Reliable Construction Co. project. On the right is a Gantt chart showing the project schedule.

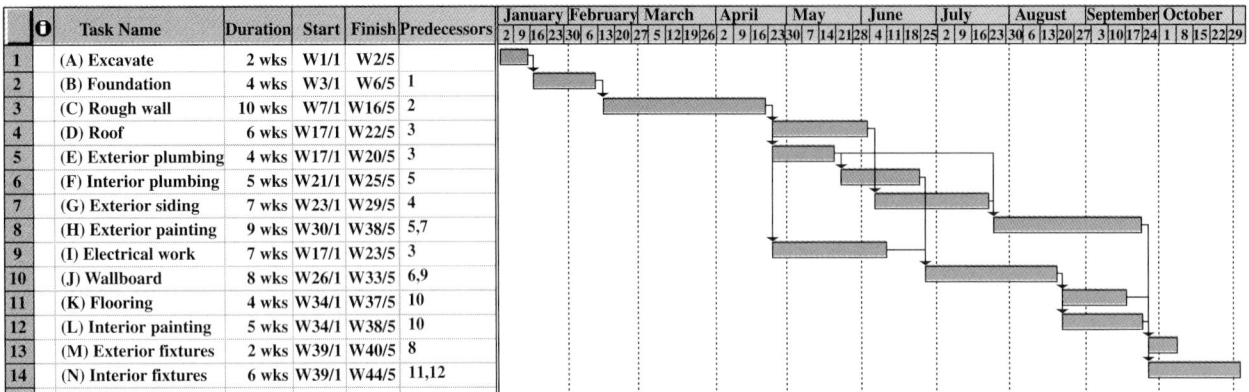

	❶	Task Name	Duration	Start	Finish	Predecessors
1		(A) Excavate	2 wks	W1/1	W2/5	
2		(B) Foundation	4 wks	W3/1	W6/5	1
3		(C) Rough wall	10 wks	W7/1	W16/5	2
4		(D) Roof	6 wks	W17/1	W22/5	3
5		(E) Exterior plumbing	4 wks	W17/1	W20/5	3
6		(F) Interior plumbing	5 wks	W21/1	W25/5	5
7		(G) Exterior siding	7 wks	W23/1	W29/5	4
8		(H) Exterior painting	9 wks	W30/1	W38/5	5,7
9		(I) Electrical work	7 wks	W17/1	W23/5	3
10		(J) Wallboard	8 wks	W26/1	W33/5	6,9
11		(K) Flooring	4 wks	W34/1	W37/5	10
12		(L) Interior painting	5 wks	W34/1	W38/5	10
13		(M) Exterior fixtures	2 wks	W39/1	W40/5	8
14		(N) Interior fixtures	6 wks	W39/1	W44/5	11,12

FIGURE 8.3

Reliable's project network as constructed with MS Project.

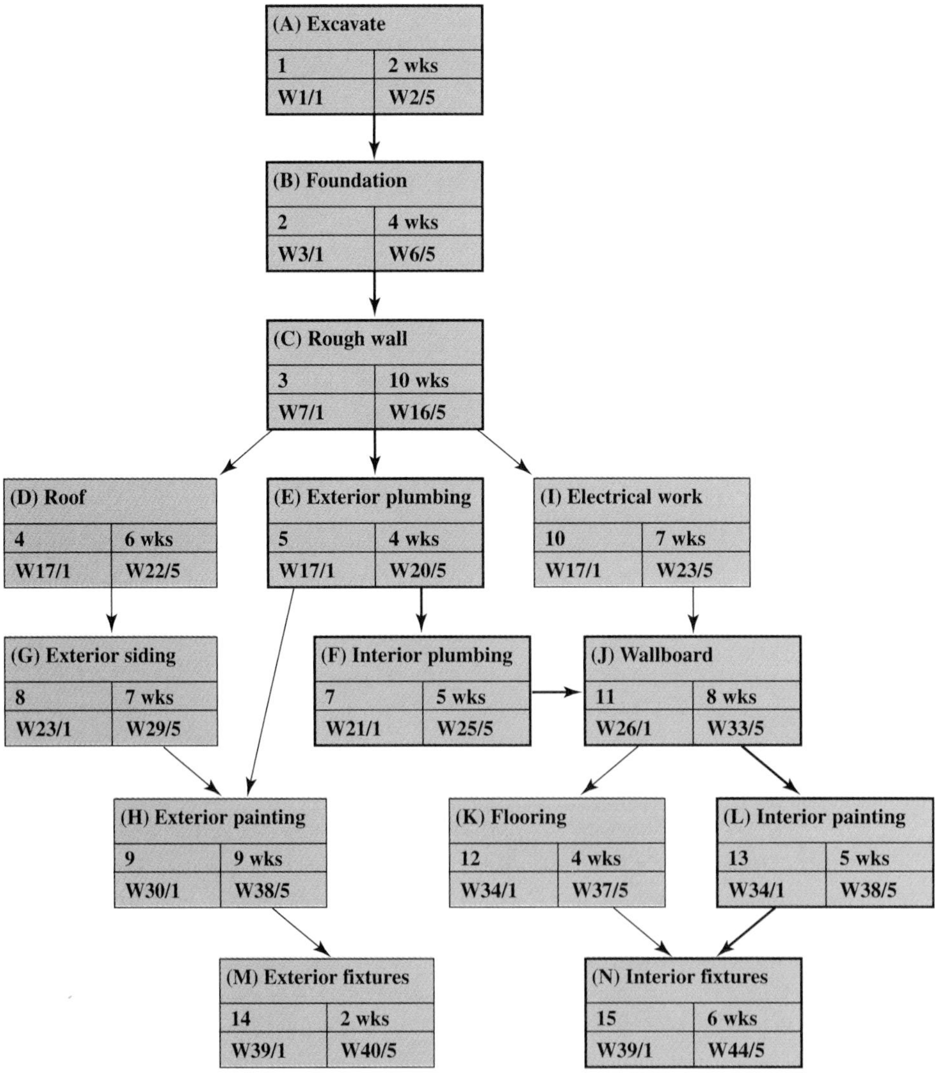

(A) Excavate	
1	2 wks
W1/1	W2/5

(B) Foundation	
2	4 wks
W3/1	W6/5

(C) Rough wall	
3	10 wks
W7/1	W16/5

(D) Roof	
4	6 wks
W17/1	W22/5

(E) Exterior plumbing	
5	4 wks
W17/1	W20/5

(I) Electrical work	
10	7 wks
W17/1	W23/5

(G) Exterior siding	
8	7 wks
W23/1	W29/5

(F) Interior plumbing	
7	5 wks
W21/1	W25/5

(J) Wallboard	
11	8 wks
W26/1	W33/5

(H) Exterior painting	
9	9 wks
W30/1	W38/5

(K) Flooring	
12	4 wks
W34/1	W37/5

(L) Interior painting	
13	5 wks
W34/1	W38/5

(M) Exterior fixtures	
14	2 wks
W39/1	W40/5

(N) Interior fixtures	
15	6 wks
W39/1	W44/5

You can choose between various views with the view toolbar down the left side of the screen. The Gantt Chart view is the default. The PERT Chart view shows the project network. This view initially lines all the activity boxes up in a row, but they can be moved as desired by dragging the boxes with the mouse. Figure 8.3 shows this project network after placing the activity boxes in the same locations as the corresponding nodes in Figure 8.1 (except no boxes are included now for the start and finish of the project). Note that each box provides considerable information about the activity. After giving its name, the second row shows the activity number and duration. The last row then gives the scheduled start and finish times.

Subsequent displays of the output of MS Project are shown in the MS Project file in your MS Courseware.

MS Project also provides additional information of the types described in some of the subsequent sections. We will point this out as it arises. However, rather than continuing to display the form of the output in the upcoming sections, we will show it in the MS Project file for this chapter in your MS Courseware.

Review Questions

1. What three types of information does a project network need to convey?
2. What is the difference between an activity-on-arc (AOA) project network and an activity-on-node (AON) project network? Which type is being used here?
3. What do the bars in a Gantt chart show?

8.3 SCHEDULING A PROJECT WITH PERT/CPM

At the end of Section 8.1, we mentioned that Mr. Perty, the project manager for the Reliable Construction Co. project, wants to answer a series of questions and so will use PERT/CPM as the best method for obtaining answers. His first question has been answered in the preceding section. Here are the five questions that will be answered in this section.

Question 2: What is the total time required to complete the project if no delays occur?

Question 3: When do the individual activities need to start and finish (at the latest) to meet this project completion time?

Question 4: When can the individual activities start and finish (at the earliest) if no delays occur?

Question 5: Which are the critical bottleneck activities where any delays must be avoided to prevent delaying project completion?

Question 6: For the other activities, how much delay can be tolerated without delaying project completion?

The project network in Figure 8.1 enables answering all these questions by providing two crucial pieces of information, namely, the *order* in which certain activities must be performed and the (estimated) *duration* of each activity. We begin by focusing on Questions 2 and 5.

The Critical Path

How long should the project take? We noted earlier that summing the durations of all the activities gives a grand total of 79 weeks. However, this isn't the answer to the question because some of the activities can be performed (roughly) simultaneously.

What is relevant instead is the *length* of each *path* through the network.

A **path** through a project network is one of the routes following the arrows (arcs) from the start node to the finish node. The **length of a path** is the *sum* of the (estimated) *durations* of the activities on the path.

The six paths through the project network in Figure 8.1 are given in Table 8.2, along with the calculations of the lengths of these paths. The path lengths range from 31 weeks up to 44 weeks for the longest path (the fourth one in the table).

TABLE 8.2

The Paths and Path Lengths through Reliable's Project Network

Path	Length (Weeks)
Start→A→B→C→D→G→H→M→Finish	$2 + 4 + 10 + 6 + 7 + 9 + 2 = 40$
Start→A→B→C→E→H→M→Finish	$2 + 4 + 10 + 4 + 9 + 2 = 31$
Start→A→B→C→E→F→J→K→N→Finish	$2 + 4 + 10 + 4 + 5 + 8 + 4 + 6 = 43$
Start→A→B→C→E→F→J→L→N→Finish	$2 + 4 + 10 + 4 + 5 + 8 + 5 + 6 = 44$
Start→A→B→C→I→J→K→N→Finish	$2 + 4 + 10 + 7 + 8 + 4 + 6 = 41$
Start→A→B→C→I→J→L→N→Finish	$2 + 4 + 10 + 7 + 8 + 5 + 6 = 42$

So given these path lengths, what do you think should be the (estimated) *project duration* (the total time required for the project)? Let us reason it out.

The project duration cannot be shorter than any of the path lengths.

Since the activities on any given path must be done one after another with no overlap, the project duration cannot be *shorter* than the path length. However, the project duration can be *longer* because some activity on the path with multiple immediate predecessors might have to wait longer for an immediate predecessor *not* on the path to finish than for the one on the path. For example, consider the second path in Table 8.2 and focus on activity H. This activity has two immediate predecessors, one (activity G) *not* on the path and one (activity E) that is. After activity C finishes, only 4 more weeks are required for activity E but 13 weeks will be needed for activity D and then activity G to finish. Therefore, the project duration must be considerably longer than the length of the second path in the table.

However, the project duration will not be longer than one particular path. This is the *longest path* through the project network. The activities on this path can be performed sequentially without interruption. (Otherwise, this would not be the longest path.) Therefore, the time required to reach the finish node equals the length of this path. Furthermore, all the shorter paths will reach the finish node no later than this.

Here is the key conclusion.

> The (estimated) *project duration* equals the *length of the longest path* through the project network. This longest path is called the **critical path.** (If more than one path tie for the longest, they all are critical paths.)

Thus, for the Reliable Construction Co. project, we have

$$\text{Critical path: Start} \rightarrow A \rightarrow B \rightarrow C \rightarrow E \rightarrow F \rightarrow J \rightarrow L \rightarrow N \rightarrow \text{Finish}$$
$$\text{(Estimated) project duration} = 44 \text{ weeks}$$

The activities on the critical path are the bottleneck activities. Any delays there will delay project completion.

We now have answered Mr. Perty's Questions 2 and 5 given at the beginning of the section. If no delays occur, the total time required to complete the project should be about 44 weeks. Furthermore, the activities on this critical path are the critical bottleneck activities where any delays in their completion must be avoided to prevent delaying project completion. This is valuable information for Mr. Perty since he now knows that he should focus most of his attention on keeping these particular activities on schedule in striving to keep the overall project on schedule. Furthermore, if he decides to reduce the duration of the project (remember that bonus for completion within 40 weeks), these are the main activities where changes should be made to reduce their durations.

For small project networks like Figure 8.1, finding all the paths and determining the longest path is a convenient way to identify the critical path. However, this is not an efficient procedure for larger projects. PERT/CPM uses a considerably more efficient procedure instead.

Not only is this PERT/CPM procedure very efficient for larger projects, it also provides much more information than is available from finding all the paths. In particular, it answers *all five* of Mr. Perty's questions listed at the beginning of the section rather than just two. These answers provide the key information needed to schedule all the activities and then to evaluate the consequences should any activities slip behind schedule.

The components of this procedure are described in the remainder of this section.

Scheduling Individual Activities

The PERT/CPM scheduling procedure begins by addressing Question 4: When can the individual activities start and finish (at the earliest) if no delays occur? Having no delays means that (1) the *actual* duration of each activity turns out to be the same as its *estimated* duration and (2) each activity begins as soon as all its immediate predecessors are finished. The starting and finishing times of each activity if no delays occur anywhere in the project are called the **earliest start time** and the **earliest finish time** of the activity. These times are represented by the symbols

ES and EF denote the start time and finish time for an activity if no delays occur anywhere in the project.

$\mathbf{ES}$ = Earliest start time for a particular activity

$\mathbf{EF}$ = Earliest finish time for a particular activity

where

$$EF = ES + \text{(estimated) duration of the activity}$$

Rather than assigning calendar dates to these times, we will use the convention of counting the number of time periods (weeks for Reliable's project) from when the project started. Thus,

$$\text{Starting time for project} = 0$$

Since activity A starts Reliable's project, we have

$$\text{Activity A:}\quad \text{ES} = 0$$

$$\text{EF} = 0 + \text{duration (2 weeks)}$$

$$= 2$$

where the duration (in weeks) of activity A is given in Figure 8.1 as the boldfaced number next to this activity. Activity B can start as soon as activity A finishes, so

$$\text{Activity B:}\quad \text{ES} = \text{EF for activity A}$$

$$= 2$$

$$\text{EF} = 2 + \text{duration (4 weeks)}$$

$$= 6$$

This calculation of ES for activity B illustrates our first rule for obtaining ES.

If an activity has only a *single* immediate predecessor, then

$$\text{ES for the activity} = \text{EF for the immediate predecessor}$$

This rule (plus the calculation of each EF) immediately gives ES and EF for activity C, then for activities D, E, I, and then for activities G, F as well. Figure 8.4 shows ES and EF for each of these activities to the right of its node. For example,

FIGURE 8.4

Earliest start time (ES) and earliest finish time (EF) values for the initial activities in Figure 8.1 that have only a single immediate predecessor.

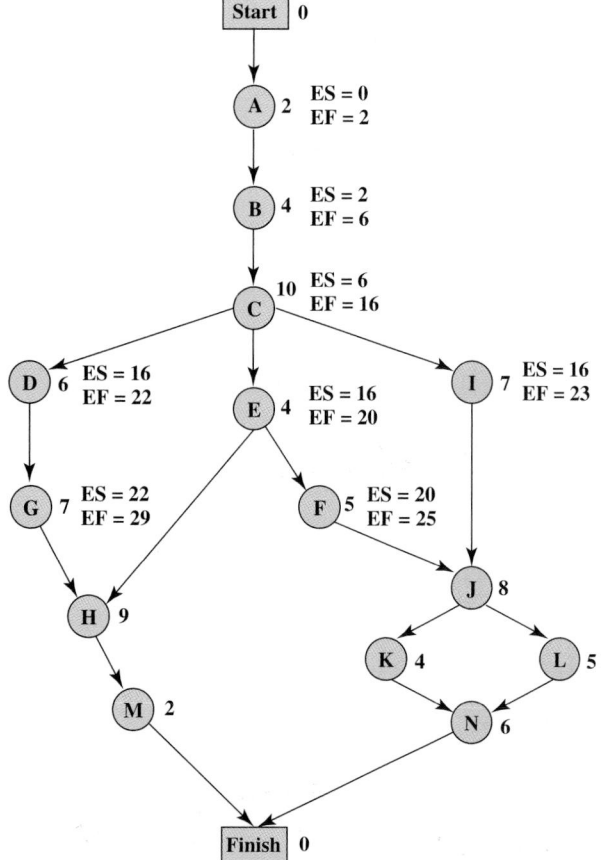

$$\text{Activity G:} \quad \text{ES} = \text{EF for activity D}$$

$$= 22$$

$$\text{EF} = 22 + \text{duration (7 weeks)}$$

$$= 29$$

which means that this activity (putting up the exterior siding) should start 22 weeks and finish 29 weeks after the start of the project.

Now consider activity H, which has *two* immediate predecessors, activities G and E. Activity H must wait to start until *both* activities G and E are finished, which gives the following calculation.

Immediate predecessors of activity H:

$$\text{Activity G has EF} = 29$$

$$\text{Activity E has EF} = 20$$

$$\text{Larger EF} = 29$$

Therefore,

$$\text{ES for activity H} = \text{Larger EF above}$$

$$= 29$$

This calculation illustrates the general rule for obtaining the earliest start time for any activity.

Earliest Start Time Rule

The earliest start time rule provides ES for an activity as soon as ES and EF have been calculated for each of its immediate predecessors.

The earliest start time of an activity is equal to the *largest* of the earliest finish times of its immediate predecessors. In symbols,

$$\text{ES} = \text{Largest EF of the immediate predecessors}$$

When the activity has only a single immediate predecessor, this rule becomes the same as the first rule given earlier. However, it also allows any larger number of immediate predecessors as well. Applying this rule to the rest of the activities in Figure 8.4 (and calculating each EF from ES) yields the complete set of ES and EF values given in Figure 8.5.

Note that Figure 8.5 also includes ES and EF values for the start and finish nodes. The reason is that these nodes are conventionally treated as *dummy activities* that require no time. For the start node, $\text{ES}=0=\text{EF}$ automatically. For the finish node, the earliest start time rule is used to calculate ES in the usual way, as illustrated next.

Immediate predecessors of the finish node:

$$\text{Activity M has EF} = 40$$

$$\text{Activity N has EF} = 44$$

$$\text{Larger EF} = 44$$

Therefore,

$$\text{ES for the finish node} = \text{Larger EF above}$$

$$= 44$$

$$\text{EF for the finish node} = 44 + 0 = 44$$

EF for the finish node indicates when the project should be completed if everything stays on schedule.

This last calculation indicates that the project should be completed in 44 weeks if everything stays on schedule according to the start and finish times for each activity given in Figure 8.5. (This answers Question 2.) Mr. Perty now can use this schedule to inform the crew responsible for each activity as to when it should plan to start and finish its work.

Here is a summary of the overall procedure for obtaining such a schedule for any project.

FIGURE 8.5

Earliest start time (ES) and earliest finish time (EF) values for all the activities (plus the start and finish nodes) of the Reliable Construction Co. project.

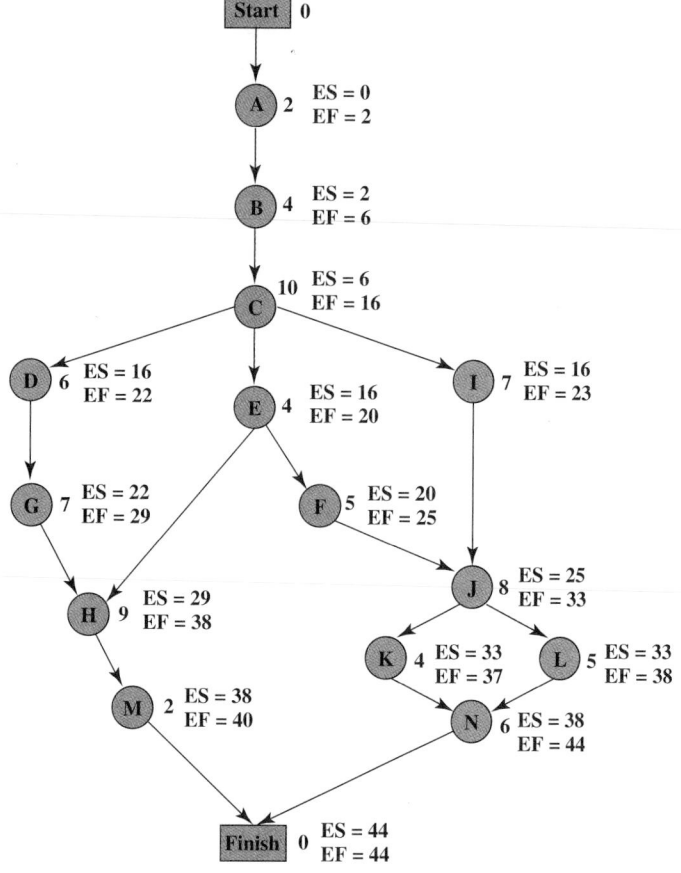

Procedure for Obtaining Earliest Times for All Activities

1. For each activity that starts the project (including the start node), set its earliest start time as ES = 0.

2. For each activity whose ES value has just been obtained, calculate its earliest finish time as

$$EF = ES + \text{(estimated) duration of the activity}$$

3. For each new activity whose immediate predecessors now have EF values, obtain its ES by applying the *earliest start time rule.* Then apply step 2 to calculate its EF.

4. Repeat step 3 over and over again until ES and EF have been obtained for *all* activities (including the finish node).

This procedure starts with the initial activities and then works forward in time to find ES and EF for each subsequent activity in turn.

This process of starting with the initial activities and working *forward* in time toward the final activities is referred to as making a **forward pass** through the network.

Keep in mind that the schedule obtained from this procedure assumes that the *actual* duration of each activity will turn out to be the same as its *estimated* duration. What happens if some activity takes longer than expected? Would this delay project completion? Perhaps, but not necessarily. It depends on which activity and the length of the delay.

The next part of the procedure focuses on determining how much later than indicated in Figure 8.5 an activity can start or finish without delaying project completion.

Later Schedules That Avoid Delaying Project Completion

Having found *earliest* start and finish times for each activity, we next want to answer Question 3 by finding the *latest* start and finish times that will still enable completing the project in 44 weeks.

The **latest start time for an activity** is the latest possible time that it can start without delaying the completion of the project (so the finish node still is reached at its earliest finish time), assuming no subsequent delays in the project. The **latest finish time** has the corresponding definition with respect to finishing the activity.

In symbols,

LS and LF denote the latest time an activity can start and finish, respectively, without delaying the completion of the project.

$$\textbf{LS} = \text{Latest start time for a particular activity}$$

$$\textbf{LF} = \text{Latest finish time for a particular activity}$$

where

$$\text{LS} = \text{LF} - \text{(estimated) duration of the activity}$$

To find LF, we have the following rule.

Latest Finish Time Rule

The latest finish time rule provides LF for an activity as soon as LS and LF have been calculated for each of its immediate successors.

The latest finish time of an activity is equal to the *smallest* of the latest start times of its immediate successors. In symbols,

$$\text{LF} = \text{Smallest LS of the immediate successors}$$

Since an activity's immediate successors cannot start until the activity finishes, this rule is saying that the activity must finish in time to enable *all* its immediate successors to begin by their latest start times.

For example, consider activity M in Figure 8.1. Its only immediate successor is the finish node. This node must be reached by time 44 to complete the project within 44 weeks, so we begin by assigning values to this node as follows.

$$\text{Finish node:} \quad \text{LF} = \text{its EF} = 44$$

$$\text{LS} = 44 - 0 = 44$$

Now we can apply the latest finish time rule to activity M.

$$\text{Activity M:} \quad \text{LF} = \text{LS for the finish node}$$

$$= 44$$

$$\text{LS} = 44 - \text{duration (2 weeks)}$$

$$= 42$$

(Since activity M is one of the activities that together complete the project, we also could have automatically set its LF equal to the earliest finish time of the finish node without applying the latest finish time rule.)

Since activity M is the only immediate successor of activity H, we now can apply the latest finish time rule to the latter activity.

$$\text{Activity H:} \quad \text{LF} = \text{LS for activity M}$$

$$= 42$$

$$\text{LS} = 42 - \text{duration (9 weeks)}$$

$$= 33$$

This procedure starts with the final activities and then works backward in time to find LF and LS for each preceding activity in turn.

Note that the procedure being illustrated above is to start with the final activities and work *backward* in time toward the initial activities. Thus, in contrast to the *forward pass* used to find earliest start and finish times, we now are making a **backward pass** through the network, as summarized below.

Procedure for Obtaining Latest Times for All Activities

1. For each of the activities that together complete the project (including the finish node), set its latest finish time (LF) equal to the earliest finish time of the finish node.

2. For each activity whose LF value has just been obtained, calculate its latest start time as

$$LS = LF - \text{(estimated) duration of the activity}$$

3. For each new activity whose immediate successors now have LS values, obtain its LF by applying the *latest finish time rule.* Then apply step 2 to calculate its LS.

4. Repeat step 3 over and over again until LF and LS have been obtained for *all* activities (including the start node).

Figure 8.6 shows the results of applying this procedure to its conclusion. For example, consider activity C, which has three immediate successors.

Immediate successors of activity C:

$$\text{Activity D has LS} = 20$$

$$\text{Activity E has LS} = 16$$

$$\text{Activity I has LS} = 18$$

$$\text{Smallest LS} = 16$$

Therefore,

$$\text{LF for activity C} = \text{Smallest LS above}$$

$$= 16$$

Mr. Perty now knows that the schedule given in Figure 8.6 represents his "last chance schedule." Even if an activity starts and finishes as late as indicated in the figure, he still will be able to avoid delaying project completion beyond 44 weeks as long as there is no subsequent slippage in the schedule. However, to allow for unexpected delays, he would prefer to stick instead

FIGURE 8.6

Latest start time (LS) and latest finish time (LF) for all the activities (plus the start and finish nodes) of the Reliable Construction Co. project.

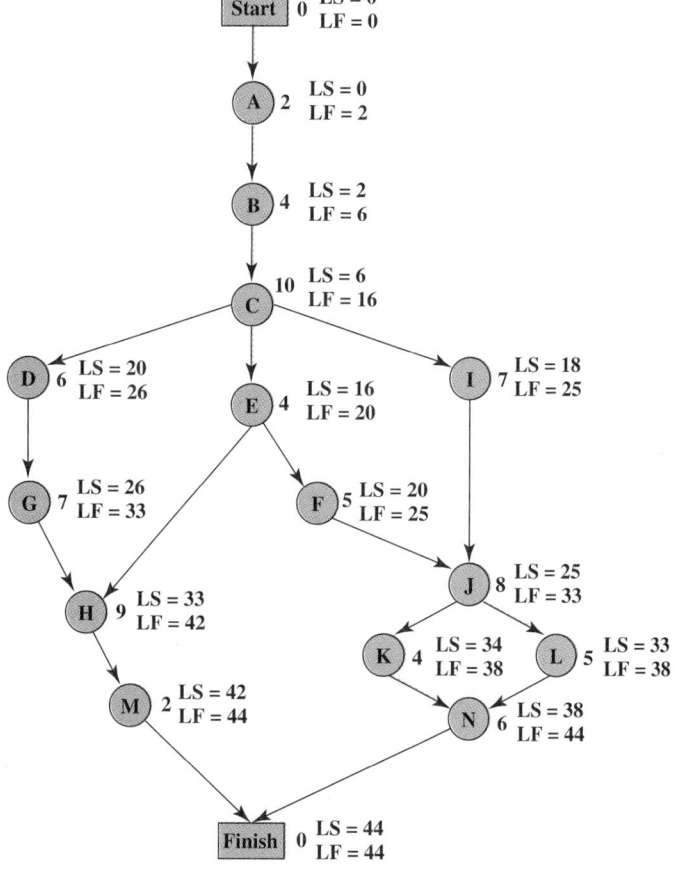

to the *earliest time schedule* given in Figure 8.5 whenever possible in order to provide some slack in parts of the schedule.

If the start and finish times in Figure 8.6 for a particular activity are later than the corresponding earliest times in Figure 8.5, then this activity has some slack in the schedule. The last part of the PERT/CPM procedure for scheduling a project is to identify this slack and then to use this information to find the *critical path*. (This will answer both Questions 5 and 6.)

Identifying Slack in the Schedule

To identify slack, it is convenient to combine the latest times in Figure 8.6 and the earliest times in Figure 8.5 into a single figure. Using activity M as an example, this is done by displaying the information for each activity as follows.

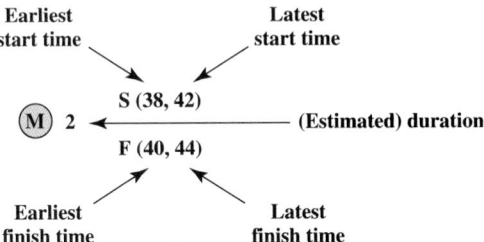

(Note that the S or F in front of each parenthesis will remind you of whether these are start times or finish times.) Figure 8.7 displays this information for the entire project.

This figure makes it easy to see how much slack each activity has.

FIGURE 8.7

The complete project network showing ES and LS (in the upper parentheses next to the node) and EF and LF (in the lower parentheses next to the node) for each activity of the Reliable Construction Co. project. The darker arrows show the critical path through the project network.

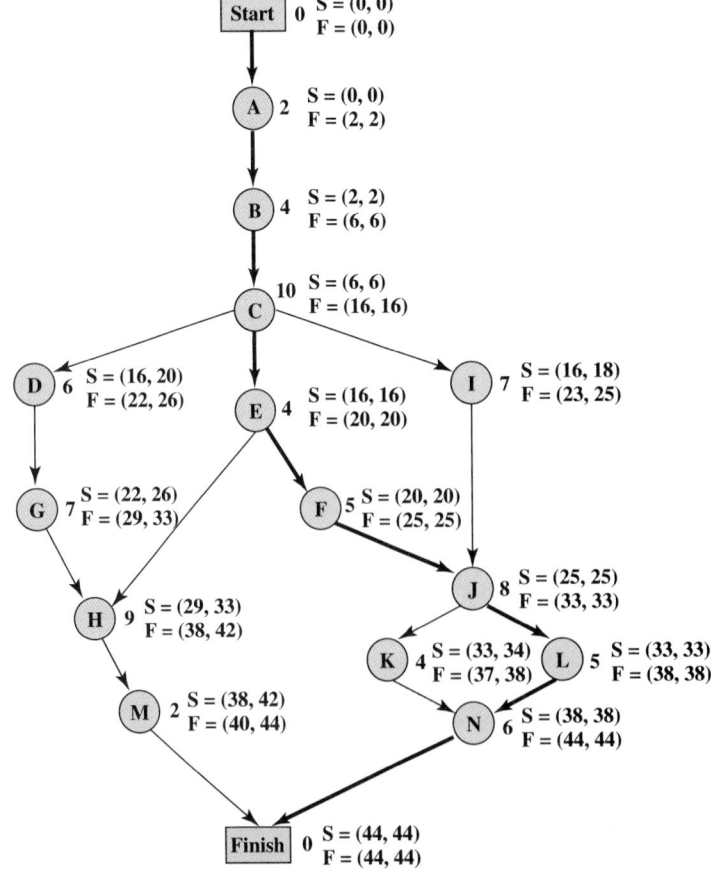

An activity's slack indicates how long it can be delayed without delaying the completion of the project.

The **slack for an activity** is the difference between its latest finish time and its earliest finish time. In symbols,

$$\text{Slack} = \text{LF} - \text{EF}$$

(Since LF − EF = LS − ES, either difference actually can be used to calculate slack.)

For example,

$$\text{Slack for activity M} = 44 - 40 = 4$$

This indicates that activity M can be delayed up to 4 weeks beyond the earliest time schedule without delaying the completion of the project at 44 weeks. This makes sense since the project is finished as soon as both activities M and N are completed and the earliest finish time for activity N (44) is 4 weeks later than for activity M (40). As long as activity N stays on schedule, the project still will finish at 44 weeks if any delays in starting activity M (perhaps due to preceding activities taking longer than expected) and in performing activity M do not cumulate more than 4 weeks.

Table 8.3 shows the slack for each of the activities. Note that some of the activities have *zero slack,* indicating that any delays in these activities will delay project completion. This is how PERT/CPM identifies the critical path(s).

The activities on a critical path should be monitored with special care to keep the project on schedule.

Each activity with *zero slack* is on a *critical path* through the project network such that any delay along this path will delay project completion.

Thus, the critical path is

$$\text{Start} \to A \to B \to C \to E \to F \to J \to L \to N \to \text{Finish}$$

just as we found by a different method at the beginning of the section. This path is highlighted in Figure 8.7 by the darker arrows. It is the activities on this path that Mr. Perty must monitor with special care to keep the project on schedule.

Review

Now let us review Mr. Perty's questions at the beginning of the section and see how all of them have been answered by the PERT/CPM scheduling procedure.

Question 2: What is the total time required to complete the project if no delays occur? This is the earliest finish time at the finish node (EF=44 weeks), as given at the bottom of Figures 8.5 and 8.7.

TABLE 8.3
Slack for Reliable's Activities

Activity	Slack (LF — EF)	On Critical Path?
A	0	Yes
B	0	Yes
C	0	Yes
D	4	No
E	0	Yes
F	0	Yes
G	4	No
H	4	No
I	2	No
J	0	Yes
K	1	No
L	0	Yes
M	4	No
N	0	Yes

Question 3: When do the individual activities need to start and finish (at the latest) to meet this project completion time? These times are the latest start times (LS) and latest finish times (LF) given in Figures 8.6 and 8.7. These times provide a "last chance schedule" to complete the project in 44 weeks if no further delays occur.

Question 4: When can the individual activities start and finish (at the earliest) if no delays occur? These times are the earliest start times (ES) and earliest finish times (EF) given in Figures 8.5 and 8.7. These times usually are used to establish the initial schedule for the project. (Subsequent delays may force later adjustments in the schedule.)

Question 5: Which are the critical bottleneck activities where any delays must be avoided to prevent delaying project completion? These are the activities on the critical path shown by the darker arrows in Figure 8.7. Mr. Perty needs to focus most of his attention on keeping these particular activities on schedule in striving to keep the overall project on schedule.

Question 6: For the other activities, how much delay can be tolerated without delaying project completion? These tolerable delays are the positive slacks given in the middle column of Table 8.3.

Using a Computer to Answer These Questions

If you prefer to use a spreadsheet to do the work involved in answering these questions, Figure 8.8 shows how this can be done. The top half gives the answers. To obtain these answers, you need to enter the appropriate equations into the various cells (as shown in the bottom half of the figure) by applying the logic described in this section. The column E equations are directly based on the *earliest start time rule*. Column F uses the formula that EF = ES + Duration of the activity, where the duration of all the activities is given by Time (D4:D17). Similarly, column G uses the formula that LS = LF − Duration of the activity. Column H directly applies the *latest finish time rule*. Column I uses the formula that Slack = LF − EF. Column J answers *Yes* if Slack = 0 and *No* otherwise.

Using a spreadsheet may be more trouble than it is worth in this case, but it has a couple of advantages.

It may take longer to set up the spreadsheet and enter all the equations than to mentally perform all the calculations directly on the project network. However, if you don't trust your arithmetic, Excel can be relied on to do that part of the job correctly. The spreadsheet also displays the results in a nice format.

MS Project can quickly generate Reliable's schedule, as displayed in an MS Project file in your MS Courseware.

After having entered the *project entry table* (Figure 8.2), you can use MS Project to generate a table similar to the top half of Figure 8.8 by choosing Table:Schedule under the View menu. As shown in the MS Project file for this chapter in your MS Courseware, this table labels ES, EF, LS, and LF as Start, Finish, Late Start, and Late Finish, respectively. Each of these times is displayed in the same format as in Figures 8.2 and 8.3. The table also shows two quantities, called *free slack* and *total slack,* for each activity. When multiple activities on the same path have the same slack, *free slack* only shows this slack once for the last of these activities. *Total slack* is what we (and others) have called slack. The critical path is identified by referring back to Figure 8.3 and identifying the path with the broader arrows. (With a color monitor and printer, the critical path is shown in red.)

Review Questions

1. What is meant by the following terms: (*a*) a path through the project network; (*b*) the length of a path; and (*c*) a critical path?
2. What needs to happen in order to meet a schedule based on earliest start times and earliest finish times?
3. What does the earliest start time rule say?
4. What is a forward pass through the project network?
5. Why is a schedule based on latest start times and latest finish times a "last chance schedule"?
6. What does the latest finish time rule say?
7. How does a backward pass through the project network differ from a forward pass?
8. What is the significance of a critical path for the project manager?
9. What are two methods of finding a critical path through the project network?

FIGURE 8.8 The equations in the bottom half show how to develop the schedule for the Reliable Construction Co. project on a spreadsheet.

	A	B	C	D	E	F	G	H	I	J
1		**Reliable Construction Co. Project Scheduling Problem**								
2										
3		**Activity**	**Description**	**Time**	**ES**	**EF**	**LS**	**LF**	**Slack**	**Critical?**
4		A	Excavate	2	0	2	0	2	0	Yes
5		B	Foundation	4	2	6	2	6	0	Yes
6		C	Rough Wall	10	6	16	6	16	0	Yes
7		D	Roof	6	16	22	20	26	4	No
8		E	Exterior Plumbing	4	16	20	16	20	0	Yes
9		F	Interior Plumbing	5	20	25	20	25	0	Yes
10		G	Exterior Siding	7	22	29	26	33	4	No
11		H	Exterior Painting	9	29	38	33	42	4	No
12		I	Electrical Work	7	16	23	18	25	2	No
13		J	Wallboard	8	25	33	25	33	0	Yes
14		K	Flooring	4	33	37	34	38	1	No
15		L	Interior Painting	5	33	38	33	38	0	Yes
16		M	Exterior Fixtures	2	38	40	42	44	4	No
17		N	Interior Fixtures	6	38	44	38	44	0	Yes
18										
19					**Project Duration**	44				

	E	F	G	H	I	J
3	**ES**	**EF**	**LS**	**LF**	**Slack**	**Critical?**
4	0	=ES+Time	=LF-Time	=MIN(G5)	=LF-EF	=IF(Slack=0,"Yes","No")
5	=MAX(F4)	=ES+Time	=LF-Time	=MIN(G6)	=LF-EF	=IF(Slack=0,"Yes","No")
6	=MAX(F5)	=ES+Time	=LF-Time	=MIN(G7,G8,G12)	=LF-EF	=IF(Slack=0,"Yes","No")
7	=MAX(F6)	=ES+Time	=LF-Time	=MIN(G10)	=LF-EF	=IF(Slack=0,"Yes","No")
8	=MAX(F6)	=ES+Time	=LF-Time	=MIN(G9,G11)	=LF-EF	=IF(Slack=0,"Yes","No")
9	=MAX(F8)	=ES+Time	=LF-Time	=MIN(G13)	=LF-EF	=IF(Slack=0,"Yes","No")
10	=MAX(F7)	=ES+Time	=LF-Time	=MIN(G11)	=LF-EF	=IF(Slack=0,"Yes","No")
11	=MAX(F8,F10)	=ES+Time	=LF-Time	=MIN(G16)	=LF-EF	=IF(Slack=0,"Yes","No")
12	=MAX(F6)	=ES+Time	=LF-Time	=MIN(G13)	=LF-EF	=IF(Slack=0,"Yes","No")
13	=MAX(F9,F12)	=ES+Time	=LF-Time	=MIN(G14,G15)	=LF-EF	=IF(Slack=0,"Yes","No")
14	=MAX(F13)	=ES+Time	=LF-Time	=MIN(G17)	=LF-EF	=IF(Slack=0,"Yes","No")
15	=MAX(F13)	=ES+Time	=LF-Time	=MIN(G17)	=LF-EF	=IF(Slack=0,"Yes","No")
16	=MAX(F11)	=ES+Time	=LF-Time	=ProjectDuration	=LF-EF	=IF(Slack=0,"Yes","No")
17	=MAX(F14,F15)	=ES+Time	=LF-Time	=ProjectDuration	=LF-EF	=IF(Slack=0,"Yes","No")
18						
19	**Project Duration**	=MAX(EF)				

Range Name	Cells
Activity	B4:B17
Critical?	J4:J17
Description	C4:C17
EF	F4:F17
ES	E4:E17
LF	H4:H17
LS	G4:G17
ProjectDuration	F19
Slack	I4:I17
Time	D4:D17

8.4 DEALING WITH UNCERTAIN ACTIVITY DURATIONS

Now we come to the next of Mr. Perty's questions posed at the end of Section 8.1.

Question 7: Given the uncertainties in accurately estimating activity durations, what is the probability of completing the project by the deadline (47 weeks)?

Recall that Reliable will incur a large penalty ($300,000) if this deadline is missed. Therefore, Mr. Perty needs to know the probability of meeting the deadline. If this probability is not very high, he will need to consider taking costly measures (using overtime, etc.) to shorten the duration of some of the activities.

It is somewhat reassuring that the PERT/CPM scheduling procedure in the preceding section obtained an estimate of 44 weeks for the project duration. However, Mr. Perty understands very well that this estimate is based on the assumption that the *actual* duration of each activity will turn out to be the same as its *estimated* duration for at least the activities on the critical path. Since the company does not have much prior experience with this kind of project, there is considerable uncertainty about how much time actually will be needed for each activity. In reality, the duration of each activity is a *random variable* having some probability distribution.

The original version of PERT took this uncertainty into account by using three different types of estimates of the duration of an activity to obtain basic information about its probability distribution, as described below.

> There often is considerable uncertainty about what the duration of an activity will be.

The PERT Three-Estimate Approach

Applying the **PERT three-estimate approach,** the three estimates to be obtained for each activity are

   Most likely estimate (m) = Estimate of the most likely value of the duration

   Optimistic estimate (o) = Estimate of the duration under the most favorable conditions

   Pessimistic estimate (p) = Estimate of the duration under the most unfavorable conditions

The intended location of these three estimates with respect to the probability distribution is shown in Figure 8.9.

Thus, the optimistic and pessimistic estimates are meant to lie at the extremes of what is possible, whereas the most likely estimate provides the highest point of the probability distribution. PERT also assumes that the *form* of the probability distribution is a *beta distribution* (which has a shape like that in the figure) in order to calculate the *mean* and *variance* of the probability distribution. As Figure 8.9 illustrates, a beta distribution provides a reasonable shape for a distribution of activity times, including having two endpoints (o and p) and a single highest point (m) that correspond to the definitions of the three time estimates.

   Let

$$\mu = \text{Mean of the probability distribution in Figure 8.9}$$

$$\sigma^2 = \text{Variance of the probability distribution in Figure 8.9}$$

Thus, if the activity were to be performed numerous times and the duration recorded each time, μ would be essentially the *average* of these durations and σ^2 would be a measure of the *variability* of these durations. If $\sigma^2 = 0$, then all the durations would be exactly the same (no variability), whereas a large value of σ^2 indicates a lot of variability in the durations. The *standard deviation* σ (the square root of σ^2) also helps to measure the variability. Many of the durations would be spread out over the interval between ($\mu - \sigma$) and ($\mu + \sigma$), but some would be further from μ than this. However, for most probability distributions such as the beta distribution, essentially all the durations would lie inside the interval between ($\mu - 3\sigma$) and ($\mu + 3\sigma$). (For example, for a normal distribution, 99.73 percent of the distribution lies inside

FIGURE 8.9

Model of the probability distribution of the duration of an activity for the PERT three-estimate approach: m = most likely estimate, o = optimistic estimate, and p = pessimistic estimate.

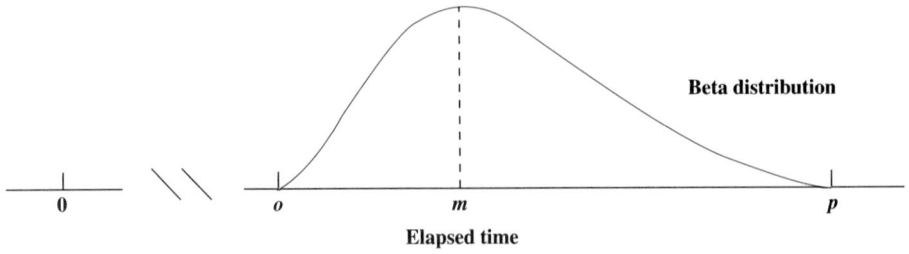

The spread between the optimistic and pessimistic estimates is roughly 6 standard deviations.

this interval.) In other words, the spread between the smallest and largest durations (essentially $p - o$) would be roughly 6σ. Therefore, an approximate formula for σ^2 is

$$\sigma^2 = \left(\frac{p - o}{6}\right)^2$$

Similarly, an approximate formula for μ is

$$\mu = \frac{o + 4m + p}{6}$$

Intuitively, this formula is placing most of the weight on the *most likely estimate* and then small equal weights on the other two estimates.

We should mention here that these formulas for estimating μ and σ^2 have become somewhat controversial in recent years. As discussed further in Section 8.7, some research studies have questioned the accuracy of these estimates and suggested alternative estimation procedures. However, for the time being, these formulas continue to be part of the standard PERT procedure.

MS Project provides the option of calculating μ for each activity with the above formula. Choosing Table:PA_PERT Entry under the View menu enables entering the three types of estimates for the respective activities (where the most likely estimate is labeled as the expected duration). Choosing Toolbars:PERT Analysis under the View menu then enables a toolbar that allows doing various types of analysis with these estimates. Using the Calculate PERT option on this toolbar recalculates Duration with the above formula to obtain μ. Another option is to show the Gantt charts based on each of the three kinds of estimates.

MS Project includes the option of using the three-estimate approach, as displayed in an MS Project file in your MS Courseware.

Mr. Perty now has contacted the foreman of each crew that will be responsible for one of the activities to request that these three estimates be made of the duration of the activity. The responses are shown in the first four columns of Table 8.4.

For example, the three estimates for activity C are

$$\text{Activity C:} \qquad o = 6 \qquad m = 9 \qquad p = 18$$

Therefore, applying the above formulas, the mean and variance of the duration of this activity are approximately

$$\mu = \frac{6 + 4(9) + 18}{6} = 10$$

$$\sigma^2 = \left(\frac{18 - 6}{6}\right)^2 = 4$$

TABLE 8.4

Expected Value and Variance of the Duration of Each Activity for Reliable's Project

Activity	Optimistic Estimate, o	Most Likely Estimate, m	Pessimistic Estimate, p	Mean, $\mu = \dfrac{o + 4m + p}{6}$	Variance, $\sigma^2 = \left(\dfrac{p - o}{6}\right)^2$
A	1	2	3	2	$\frac{1}{9}$
B	2	3½	8	4	1
C	6	9	18	10	4
D	4	5½	10	6	1
E	1	4½	5	4	$\frac{4}{9}$
F	4	4	10	5	1
G	5	6½	11	7	1
H	5	8	17	9	4
I	3	7½	9	7	1
J	3	9	9	8	1
K	4	4	4	4	0
L	1	5½	7	5	1
M	1	2	3	2	$\frac{1}{9}$
N	5	5½	9	6	$\frac{4}{9}$

TABLE 8.5

The Paths and Path Lengths through Reliable's Project Network When the Duration of Each Activity Equals Its Pessimistic Estimate

Path	Length (weeks)
Start→A→B→C→D→G→H→M→Finish	3 + 8 + 18 + 10 + 11 + 17 + 3 = 70
Start→A→B→C→E→H→M→Finish	3 + 8 + 18 + 5 + 17 + 3 = 54
Start→A→B→C→E→F→J→K→N→Finish	3 + 8 + 18 + 5 + 10 + 9 + 4 + 9 = 66
Start→A→B→C→E→F→J→L→N→Finish	3 + 8 + 18 + 5 + 10 + 9 + 7 + 9 = 69
Start→A→B→C→I→J→K→N→Finish	3 + 8 + 18 + 9 + 9 + 4 + 9 = 60
Start→A→B→C→I→J→L→N→Finish	3 + 8 + 18 + 9 + 9 + 7 + 9 = 63

Note that the value of the mean (μ) is not the same as the most likely estimate (m). This is not unusual (the possibility of *much* higher durations here pushes the mean up), but μ generally is at least fairly close to *m*.

The last two columns of Table 8.4 show the approximate mean and variance of the duration of each activity, calculated in this same way. In this example, all the means happen to be the same as the estimated duration obtained in Table 8.1 of Section 8.1. Therefore, if all the activity durations were to equal their means, the duration of the project still would be 44 weeks, or 3 weeks before the deadline. (See Figure 8.7 for the critical path requiring 44 weeks.)

However, this piece of information is not very reassuring to Mr. Perty. He knows that the durations fluctuate around their means. Consequently, it is inevitable that the duration of some activities will be larger than the mean, perhaps even nearly as large as the pessimistic estimate, which could greatly delay the project.

To check the *worst case scenario,* Mr. Perty reexamines the project network with the duration of each activity set equal to the *pessimistic estimate* (as given in the fourth column of Table 8.4). Table 8.5 shows the six paths through this network (as given previously in Table 8.2) and the length of each path using the pessimistic estimates. The fourth path, which was the critical path in Figure 8.7, now has increased its length from 44 weeks to 69 weeks. However, the length of the first path, which originally was 40 weeks (as given in Table 8.2), now has increased all the way up to 70 weeks. Since this is the longest path, it is the critical path with pessimistic estimates, which would give a project duration of 70 weeks.

The next step is to estimate the probability of meeting the deadline of 47 weeks, which requires making three simplifying approximations.

Given this dire (albeit unlikely) worst case scenario, Mr. Perty realizes that it is far from certain that the deadline of 47 weeks will be met. But what is the probability of doing so?

PERT/CPM makes three *simplifying approximations* to help calculate this probability.

Three Simplifying Approximations

To calculate the probability that *project duration* will be no more than 47 weeks, it is necessary to obtain the following information about the probability distribution of project duration.

Probability Distribution of Project Duration

1. What is the *mean* (denoted by μ_p) of this distribution?

2. What is the *variance* (denoted by σ_p^2) of this distribution?

3. What is the *form* of this distribution?

Recall that project duration equals the *length* (total elapsed time) of the *longest path* through the project network. However, just about any of the six paths listed in Table 8.5 can turn out to be the longest path (and so the critical path), depending on what the duration of each activity turns out to be between its optimistic and pessimistic estimates. Since dealing with all these paths would be complicated, PERT/CPM focuses on just the following path.

The mean critical path is obtained by assuming that the duration of each activity will equal its mean and then applying the procedure for finding a critical path described in the preceding section.

The **mean critical path** is the path through the project network that would be the critical path if the duration of each activity were to equal its *mean.*

To find Reliable's mean critical path, note again that the mean durations listed in the fifth column of Table 8.4 happen to equal the estimated durations given in the rightmost column of Table 8.1 for every activity. Therefore, in this case, the critical path based on mean durations is the same as the one based on estimated durations that was found in the preceding section. Thus, the mean critical path is

$$\text{Start} \rightarrow A \rightarrow B \rightarrow C \rightarrow E \rightarrow F \rightarrow J \rightarrow L \rightarrow N \rightarrow \text{Finish}$$

as highlighted in Figure 8.7.

Simplifying Approximation 1: Assume that the *mean critical path* will turn out to be the longest path through the project network. This is only a rough approximation since the assumption occasionally does not hold in the usual case where some of the activity durations do not equal their means. Fortunately, when the assumption does not hold, the true longest path commonly is not much longer than the mean critical path (as illustrated in Table 8.5).

Although this approximation will enable us to calculate μ_p, we need one more approximation to obtain σ_p^2.

Simplifying Approximation 2: Assume that the durations of the activities on the mean critical path are *statistically independent.* Thus, the three estimates of the duration of an activity would never change after learning the durations of some of the other activities. This assumption should hold if the activities are performed truly independently of each other. However, the assumption becomes only a rough approximation if the circumstances that cause the duration of one activity to deviate from its mean also tend to cause similar deviations for some other activities.

We now have a simple method for computing μ_p and σ_p^2.

Calculation of μ_p and σ_p^2: Because of simplifying approximation 1, the *mean* of the probability distribution of project duration is approximately

μ_p = Sum of the *means* of the durations for the activities on the mean critical path

Because of both simplifying approximations 1 and 2, the *variance* of the probability distribution of project duration is approximately

> Table 8.6 lists *only* the activities on the mean critical path and then sums their means and variances separately to obtain μ_p and σ_p^2.

σ_p^2 = Sum of the *variances* of the durations for the activities on the mean critical path

Since the means and variances of the durations for all the activities of Reliable's project already are given in Table 8.4, we only need to record these values for the activities on the mean critical path, as shown in Table 8.6. Summing the second column and then summing the third column give

$$\mu_p = 44 \qquad \sigma_p^2 = 9$$

Now we just need an approximation for the *form* of the probability distribution of project duration.

Simplifying Approximation 3: Assume that the form of the probability distribution of project duration is the *normal distribution,* which has the bell shape illustrated in Figure 8.10. By using simplifying approximations 1 and 2, there is some statistical theory (one version of the central limit theorem) that justifies this assumption as being a reasonable approximation if the number

TABLE 8.6

Calculation of μ_p and σ_p^2 for Reliable's Project

Activities on Mean Critical Path	Mean	Variance
A	2	1/9
B	4	1
C	10	4
E	4	4/9
F	5	1
J	8	1
L	5	1
N	6	4/9
Project duration	$\mu_p = 44$	$\sigma_p^2 = 9$

FIGURE 8.10

The three simplifying approximations lead to the probability distribution of the duration of Reliable's project being approximated by the normal distribution shown here. The shaded area is the portion of the distribution that meets the deadline of 47 weeks.

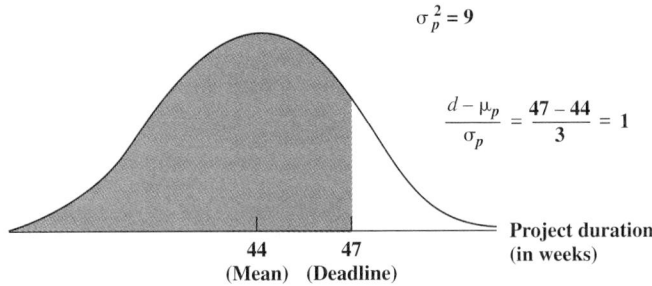

$$\sigma_p^2 = 9$$

$$\frac{d - \mu_p}{\sigma_p} = \frac{47 - 44}{3} = 1$$

Project duration (in weeks)

44 (Mean) 47 (Deadline)

of activities on the mean critical path is not too small (say, at least five). The approximation becomes better as this number of activities increases.

Now we are ready to determine (approximately) the probability of completing Reliable's project within 47 weeks.

Approximating the Probability of Meeting the Deadline

Let

d = Deadline for the project

= 47 weeks

$P(T \le d)$ = Probability that the project duration (T) does not exceed the deadline (given the three simplifying approximations)

To find $P(T \le d)$, first calculate the *standard deviation* of project duration as

$$\sigma_p = \sqrt{\sigma^2} = \sqrt{9} = 3$$

and then compute

$$\frac{d - \mu_p}{\sigma_p} = \frac{47 - 44}{3} = 1$$

= Number of standard deviations by which d exceeds μ_p

Finally, use this latter number to read off the corresponding value of $P(T \le d)$ in Table 8.7, so

$$P(T \le d) = 0.84$$

(This table is an abbreviation of the table for the normal distribution given in Appendix A.)

TABLE 8.7

Approximate Probability of Meeting a Project Deadline

$\dfrac{d - \mu_p}{\sigma_p}$	$P(T \le d)$	$\dfrac{d - \mu_p}{\sigma_p}$	$P(T \le d)$
−3.0	0.0014	0	0.50
−2.5	0.0062	0.25	0.60
−2.0	0.023	0.5	0.69
−1.75	0.040	0.75	0.77
−1.5	0.067	1.0	0.84
−1.25	0.11	1.25	0.89
−1.0	0.16	1.5	0.933
−0.75	0.23	1.75	0.960
−0.5	0.31	2.0	0.977
−0.25	0.40	2.5	0.9938
0	0.50	3.0	0.9986

Beware that this approach usually overstates the true probability of meeting the project deadline somewhat.

Warning: This $P(T \leq d)$ is only a rough approximation of the true probability of meeting the project deadline. Furthermore, because of simplifying approximation 1, it usually overstates the true probability somewhat. Therefore, the project manager should view $P(T \leq d)$ as only providing rough guidance on the best odds of meeting the deadline without taking new costly measures to try to reduce the duration of some activities.

Because this $P(T \leq d)$ is only a rough approximation of the true probability of meeting the project deadline, another prominent management science technique (computer simulation) often is used to obtain a better approximation. We will return to this same example in Chapter 16 to describe how this is done.

To assist you in carrying out the PERT/CPM procedure for calculating $P(T \leq d)$, we have provided an Excel template (labeled PERT) in this chapter's Excel files in your MS Courseware. Figure 8.11 illustrates the use of this template for Reliable's project. The data for the problem are entered in the cells shaded light blue in the spreadsheet. After entering data, the results immediately appear in the other sections. In particular, by entering the three time estimates for each activity, the spreadsheet will automatically calculate the corresponding estimates for the mean and variance in columns G and H. Next, by specifying the mean critical path (by entering * in column F for each activity on the mean critical path) and the deadline (in cell K12), the spreadsheet automatically calculates the mean and variance of the length of the mean critical path (in cells K7:K8) along with the probability that the project

FIGURE 8.11   This Excel template in your MS Courseware enables efficient application of the PERT three-estimate approach, as illustrated here for Reliable's project.

	A	B	C	D	E	F	G	H	I	J	K
1		**Template for PERT Three-Estimate Approach**									
2											
3				Time Estimates		On Mean					
4		Activity	o	m	p	Critical Path	μ	σ^2			
5		A	1	2	3	*	2	0.1111		Mean Critical	
6		B	2	3.5	8	*	4	1		Path	
7		C	6	9	18	*	10	4		μ	44
8		D	4	5.5	10		6	1		σ^2	9
9		E	1	4.5	5	*	4	0.4444			
10		F	4	4	10	*	5	1		$P(T \leq d) =$	0.8413
11		G	5	6.5	11		7	1		where	
12		H	5	8	17		9	4		$d =$	47
13		I	3	7.5	9		7	1			
14		J	3	9	9	*	8	1			
15		K	4	4	4		4	0			
16		L	1	5.5	7	*	5	1			
17		M	1	2	3		2	0.1111			
18		N	5	5.5	9	*	6	0.4444			

Range Name	Cells
Activity	B5:B18
ActivityMean	G5:G18
ActivityVariance	H5:H18
CompletionProbability	K10
CriticalPathMean	K7
CriticalPathVariance	K8
d	K12
m	D5:D18
o	C5:C18
OnMeanCriticalPath	F5:F18
p	E5:E18

	G	H
4	μ	σ^2
5	=IF(o=" "," ",(o+4*m+p)/6)	=IF(o=" "," ",((p–o)/6)^2)
6	=IF(o=" "," ",(o+4*m+p)/6)	=IF(o=" "," ",((p–o)/6)^2)
7	=IF(o=" "," ",(o+4*m+p)/6)	=IF(o=" "," ",((p–o)/6)^2)
8	=IF(o=" "," ",(o+4*m+p)/6)	=IF(o=" "," ",((p–o)/6)^2)
9	:	:
10	:	:

	J	K
5		Mean Critical
6		Path
7	μ	=SUMIF(OnMeanCriticalPath,"*",ActivityMean)
8	σ^2	=SUMIF(OnMeanCriticalPath,"*",ActivityVariance)
9		
10	$P(T \leq d) =$	=NORMDIST(d,CriticalPathMean,SQRT(CriticalPathVariance),1)

will be completed by the deadline (in cell K10). (If you are not sure which path is the mean critical path, the mean length of *any* path can be checked by entering a * for each activity on that path in column F. After checking every candidate, the path with the longest mean length in cell K7 then is the mean critical path.)

There is a significant chance of missing the deadline with the current plan.

Realizing that $P(T \leq d) = 0.84$ is probably an optimistic approximation, Mr. Perty is somewhat concerned that he may have perhaps only a 60 to 80 percent chance of meeting the deadline with the current plan. Therefore, rather than taking the significant chance of the company incurring the late penalty of $300,000, he decides to investigate what it would cost to reduce the project duration down to about 40 weeks. If the *time–cost trade-off* for doing this is favorable, the company might then be able to earn the bonus of $150,000 for finishing within 40 weeks.

You will see this story unfold in the next section.

Review Questions

1. What are the names of the three estimates in the PERT three-estimate approach?
2. Where are these three estimates meant to be located in the probability distribution of the duration of an activity?
3. What simplifying approximation is made about which path will be the longest path through the project network?
4. What simplifying approximation is made about the relationship between the durations of different activities?
5. What is the formula for the mean (μ_p) of the probability distribution of project duration?
6. What is the formula for the variance (σ_p^2) of the probability distribution of project duration?
7. What simplifying approximation is made about the form of the probability distribution of project duration?
8. The approximation obtained for the probability of meeting the project deadline is likely to be on which side (higher or lower) of the true probability?

8.5 CONSIDERING TIME–COST TRADE-OFFS

Mr. Perty now wants to investigate how much extra it would cost to reduce the expected project duration down to 40 weeks (the deadline for the company earning a bonus of $150,000 for early completion). Therefore, he is ready to address the next of his questions posed at the end of Section 8.1.

Question 8: If extra money is spent to expedite the project, what is the least expensive way of attempting to meet the target completion time (40 weeks)?

Mr. Perty remembers that CPM provides an excellent procedure for using *linear programming* to investigate such *time–cost trade-offs,* so he will use this approach again to address this question.

We begin with some background.

Time–Cost Trade-Offs for Individual Activities

The first key concept for this approach is that of *crashing.*

Crashing an activity refers to taking special costly measures to reduce the duration of an activity below its normal value. These special measures might include using overtime, hiring additional temporary help, using special time-saving materials, obtaining special equipment, and so forth. **Crashing the project** refers to crashing a number of activities to reduce the duration of the project below its normal value.

The goal is to reduce the anticipated duration of the project down to a desired level.

The **CPM method of time–cost trade-offs** is concerned with determining how much (if any) to crash each of the activities to reduce the anticipated duration of the project down to a desired value.

The data necessary for determining how much to crash a particular activity are given by the *time–cost graph* for the activity. Figure 8.12 shows a typical time–cost graph. Note the two key points on this graph labeled *normal* and *crash.*

FIGURE 8.12

A typical time–cost graph for an activity.

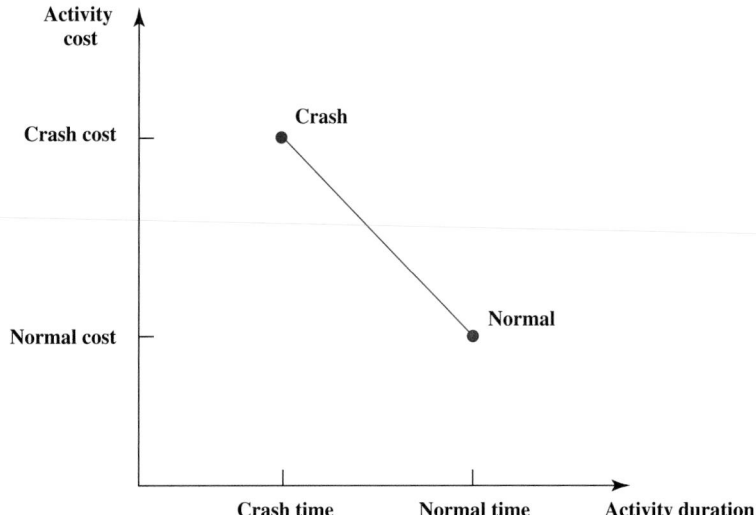

The **normal point** on the time–cost graph shows the time (duration) and cost of the activity when it is performed in the normal way. The **crash point** shows the time and cost when the activity is *fully crashed;* that is, it is fully expedited with no cost spared to reduce its duration as much as possible.

The options for each activity are to be at its crash point, its normal point, or somewhere on the line segment between these two points.

For most applications, it is assumed that *partially crashing* the activity at any level will give a combination of time and cost that will lie somewhere on the line segment between these two points. (For example, this assumption says that *half* of a full crash will give a point on this line segment that is midway between the normal and crash points.) This simplifying approximation reduces the necessary data gathering to estimating the time and cost for just two situations: *normal conditions* (to obtain the normal point) and a *full crash* (to obtain the crash point).

Using this approach, Mr. Perty has his staff and crew foremen working on developing these data for each of the activities of Reliable's project. For example, the foreman of the crew responsible for putting up the wallboard indicates that adding two temporary employees and using overtime would enable him to reduce the duration of this activity from eight weeks to six weeks, which is the minimum possible. Mr. Perty's staff then estimates the cost of fully crashing the activity in this way as compared to following the normal eight-week schedule, as shown below.

Activity J (Put up the wallboard)

Normal point: Time = 8 weeks, Cost = $430,000

Crash point: Time = 6 weeks, Cost = $490,000

Maximum reduction in time = 8 − 6 = 2 weeks

$$\text{Crash cost per week saved} = \frac{\$490,000 - \$430,000}{2}$$

$$= \$30,000$$

Table 8.8 gives the corresponding data obtained for all the activities.

Which Activities Should Be Crashed?

Summing the *normal cost* and *crash cost* columns of Table 8.8 gives

Sum of normal costs = $4.55 million

Sum of crash costs   = $6.15 million

Recall that the company will be paid $5.4 million for doing this project. (This figure excludes the $150,000 bonus for finishing within 40 weeks and the $300,000 penalty for not finishing

TABLE 8.8
Time–Cost Trade-Off Data for the Activities of Reliable's Project

Activity	Time (weeks)		Cost		Maximum Reduction in Time (weeks)	Crash Cost per Week Saved
	Normal	Crash	Normal	Crash		
A	2	1	$180,000	$ 280,000	1	$100,000
B	4	2	320,000	420,000	2	50,000
C	10	7	620,000	860,000	3	80,000
D	6	4	260,000	340,000	2	40,000
E	4	3	410,000	570,000	1	160,000
F	5	3	180,000	260,000	2	40,000
G	7	4	900,000	1,020,000	3	40,000
H	9	6	200,000	380,000	3	60,000
I	7	5	210,000	270,000	2	30,000
J	8	6	430,000	490,000	2	30,000
K	4	3	160,000	200,000	1	40,000
L	5	3	250,000	350,000	2	50,000
M	2	1	100,000	200,000	1	100,000
N	6	3	330,000	510,000	3	60,000

within 47 weeks.) This payment needs to cover some *overhead costs* in addition to the costs of the activities listed in the table, as well as provide a reasonable profit to the company. When developing the (winning) bid of $5.4 million, Reliable's management felt that this amount would provide a reasonable profit as long as the total cost of the activities could be held fairly close to the normal level of about $4.55 million. Mr. Perty understands very well that it is now his responsibility to keep the project as close to both budget and schedule as possible.

As found previously in Figure 8.7, if all the activities are performed in the normal way, the anticipated duration of the project would be 44 weeks (if delays can be avoided). If *all* the activities were to be *fully crashed* instead, then a similar calculation would find that this duration would be reduced to only 28 weeks. But look at the prohibitive cost ($6.15 million) of doing this! Fully crashing all activities clearly is not an option that can be considered.

However, Mr. Perty still wants to investigate the possibility of partially or fully crashing just a few activities to reduce the anticipated duration of the project down to 40 weeks.

The problem: What is the least expensive way of crashing some activities to reduce project duration to the specified level (40 weeks)?

Marginal cost analysis finds the least expensive way to reduce project duration one week at a time.

One way of solving this problem is **marginal cost analysis,** which uses the last column of Table 8.8 (along with Figure 8.7 in Section 8.3) to determine the least expensive way to reduce project duration one week at a time. The easiest way to conduct this kind of analysis is to set up a table like Table 8.9 that lists all the paths through the project network and the current length of each of these paths. To get started, this information can be copied directly from Table 8.2.

Since the fourth path listed in Table 8.9 has the longest length (44 weeks), the only way to reduce project duration by a week is to reduce the duration of the activities on this particular path by a week. Comparing the crash cost per week saved given in the last column of Table 8.8 for these activities, the smallest cost is $30,000 for activity J. (Note that activity I with this same cost is not on this path.) Therefore, the first change is to crash activity J enough to reduce its duration by a week.

This change results in reducing the length of each path that includes activity J (the third, fourth, fifth, and sixth paths in Table 8.9) by a week, as shown in the second row of Table 8.10. Because the fourth path still is the longest (43 weeks), the same process is repeated to find the least expensive activity to shorten on this path. This again is activity J, since the next-to-last column in Table 8.8 indicates that a maximum reduction of two weeks is allowed for this activity. This second reduction of a week for activity J leads to the third row of Table 8.10.

At this point, the fourth path still is the longest (42 weeks), but activity J cannot be shortened any further. Among the other activities on this path, activity F now is the least expensive to shorten ($40,000 per week) according to the last column of Table 8.8. Therefore, this activ-

TABLE 8.9

The Initial Table for Starting Marginal Cost Analysis of Reliable's Project

		Length of Path					
Activity to Crash	Crash Cost	ABCDGHM	ABCEHM	ABCEFJKN	ABCEFJLN	ABCIJKN	ABCIJLN
		40	31	43	44	41	42

TABLE 8.10

The Final Table for Performing Marginal Cost Analysis on Reliable's Project

		Length of Path					
Activity to Crash	Crash Cost	ABCDGHM	ABCEHM	ABCEFJKN	ABCEFJLN	ABCIJKN	ABCIJLN
		40	31	43	44	41	42
J	$30,000	40	31	42	43	40	41
J	30,000	40	31	41	42	39	40
F	40,000	40	31	40	41	39	40
F	40,000	40	31	39	40	39	40

ity is shortened by a week to obtain the fourth row of Table 8.10, and then (because a maximum reduction of two weeks is allowed) is shortened by another week to obtain the last row of this table.

The longest path (a tie between the first, fourth, and sixth paths) now has the desired length of 40 weeks, so we don't need to do any more crashing. (If we did need to go further, the next step would require looking at the activities on all three paths to find the least expensive way of shortening all three paths by a week.) The total cost of crashing activities J and F to get down to this project duration of 40 weeks is calculated by adding the costs in the second column of Table 8.10—a total of $140,000. Figure 8.13 shows the resulting project network.

Since $140,000 is slightly less than the bonus of $150,000 for finishing within 40 weeks, it might appear that Mr. Perty should proceed with this solution. However, he actually concludes that he probably should not crash the project at all, as we will discuss at the end of the section. (Meanwhile, be mulling over why his conclusion makes sense because of the preceding section on dealing with uncertain activity durations.)

Figure 8.13 shows that reducing the durations of activities F and J to their crash times has led to now having *three* critical paths through the network. The reason is that, as we found earlier from the last row of Table 8.10, the three paths tie for being the longest, each with a length of 40 weeks.

Linear programming provides a more efficient alternative to marginal cost analysis for large projects.

With larger networks, marginal cost analysis can become quite unwieldy. A more efficient procedure would be desirable for large projects.

For these reasons, the standard CPM procedure is to apply *linear programming* instead (commonly with a customized software package).

Using Linear Programming to Make Crashing Decisions

The problem of finding the least expensive way of crashing activities can be rephrased in a form more familiar to linear programming as follows.

Restatement of the problem: Consider the total cost of the project, including the extra cost of crashing activities. The problem then is to minimize this total cost, subject to the constraint that project duration must be less than or equal to the time desired by the project manager.

FIGURE 8.13

The project network if activities J and F are fully crashed (with all other activities normal) for Reliable's project. The darker arrows show the various critical paths through the project network.

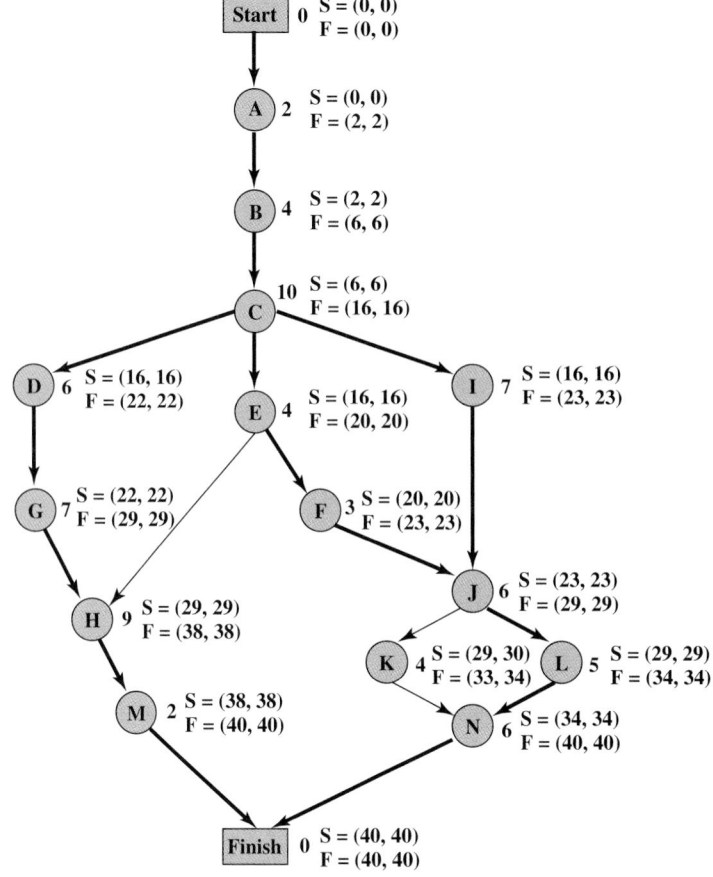

The decisions to be made are the following:

These decisions will appear in the changing cells.

1. The start time of each activity.

2. The reduction in the duration of each activity due to crashing.

3. The finish time of the project (must not exceed 40 weeks).

Figure 8.14 shows how this problem can be formulated as a linear programming model on a spreadsheet. The decisions to be made are shown in the changing cells, StartTime (I6:I19), TimeReduction (J6:J19), and ProjectFinishTime (I22). Columns B to H correspond to the columns in Table 8.8. As the equations in the bottom half of the figure indicate, columns G and H are calculated in a straightforward way. The equations for column K express the fact that the finish time for each activity is its start time *plus* its normal time *minus* its time reduction due to crashing. The equation entered into the target cell TotalCost (I24) adds all the normal costs plus the extra costs due to crashing to obtain the total cost.

The last set of constraints in the Solver dialogue box, TimeReduction (J6:J19) ≤ Max-TimeReduction (G6:G19), specifies that the time reduction for each activity cannot exceed its maximum time reduction given in column G. The two preceding constraints, ProjectFinish-Time (I22) ≥ MFinish (K18) and ProjectFinishTime (I22) ≥ NFinish (K19), indicate that the project cannot finish until each of the two immediate predecessors (activities M and N) finish. The constraint that ProjectFinishTime (I22) ≤ MaxTime (K22) is a key one that specifies that the project must finish within 40 weeks.

The constraints involving StartTime (I6:I19) all are *start-time constraints* that specify that an activity cannot start until each of its immediate predecessors have finished. For example, the first constraint shown, BStart (I7) ≥ AFinish (K6), says that activity B cannot start until activity A (its immediate predecessor) finishes. When an activity has more than one immediate predecessor, there is one such constraint for each of them. To illustrate, activity H has both activities E and G as immediate predecessors. Consequently, activity H has two start-time constraints, HStart (I13) ≥ EFinish (K10) and HStart (I13) ≥ GFinish (K12).

Although the start-time constraints allow a delay in starting an activity, an optimal solution would not allow this to happen for any activity on a critical path.

You may have noticed that the ≥ form of the *start-time constraints* allows a delay in starting an activity after all its immediate predecessors have finished. Although such a delay is feasible in the model, it cannot be optimal for any activity on a critical path since this needless delay would increase the total cost (by necessitating additional crashing to meet the project duration constraint). Therefore, an optimal solution for the model will not have any such delays, except possibly for activities not on a critical path.

Columns I and J in Figure 8.14 show the optimal solution obtained after having clicked on the Solve button. (Note that this solution involves one delay—activity K starts at 30 even though its only immediate predecessor, activity J, finishes at 29—but this doesn't matter since activity K is not on a critical path.) This solution corresponds to the one displayed in Figure 8.13 that was obtained by marginal cost analysis.

Mr. Perty's Conclusions

Mr. Perty always keeps a sharp eye on the bottom line. Therefore, when his staff brings him the above plan for crashing the project to try to reduce its duration from about 44 weeks to about 40 weeks, he first looks at the estimated total cost of $4.69 million. Since the estimated total cost without any crashing is $4.55 million, the additional cost from the crashing would be about $140,000. This is $10,000 less than the bonus of $150,000 that the company would earn by finishing within 40 weeks.

FIGURE 8.14   The spreadsheet displays the application of the CPM method of time–cost trade-offs to Reliable's project, where columns I and J show the optimal solution obtained by using the Excel Solver with the entries shown in the Solver Parameters dialogue box.

	A	B	C	D	E	F	G	H	I	J	K
1		**Reliable Construction Co. Project Scheduling Problem with Time–Cost Trade-Offs**									
2											
3							Maximum	Crash Cost			
4			**Time**		**Cost**		Time	per Week	Start	Time	Finish
5		Activity	Normal	Crash	Normal	Crash	Reduction	Saved	Time	Reduction	Time
6		A	2	1	$180,000	$280,000	1	$100,000	0	0	2
7		B	4	2	$320,000	$420,000	2	$50,000	2	0	6
8		C	10	7	$620,000	$860,000	3	$80,000	6	0	16
9		D	6	4	$260,000	$340,000	2	$40,000	16	0	22
10		E	4	3	$410,000	$570,000	1	$160,000	16	0	20
11		F	5	3	$180,000	$260,000	2	$40,000	20	2	23
12		G	7	4	$900,000	$1,020,000	3	$40,000	22	0	29
13		H	9	6	$200,000	$380,000	3	$60,000	29	0	38
14		I	7	5	$210,000	$270,000	2	$30,000	16	0	23
15		J	8	6	$430,000	$490,000	2	$30,000	23	2	29
16		K	4	3	$160,000	$200,000	1	$40,000	30	0	34
17		L	5	3	$250,000	$350,000	2	$50,000	29	0	34
18		M	2	1	$100,000	$200,000	1	$100,000	38	0	40
19		N	6	3	$330,000	$510,000	3	$60,000	34	0	40
20											
21											Max Time
22							Project Finish Time		40	≤	40
23											
24								Total Cost	$4,690,000		

continued

FIGURE 8.14 *(continued)*

	G	H
3	Maximum	Crash Cost
4	Time	per Week
5	Reduction	Saved
6	=NormalTime-CrashTime	=(CrashCost-NormalCost)/MaxTimeReduction
7	=NormalTime-CrashTime	=(CrashCost-NormalCost)/MaxTimeReduction
8	=NormalTime-CrashTime	=(CrashCost-NormalCost)/MaxTimeReduction
9	=NormalTime-CrashTime	=(CrashCost-NormalCost)/MaxTimeReduction
10	:	:
11	:	:

Range Name	Cells
AFinish	K6
AStart	I6
BFinish	K7
BStart	I7
CFinish	K8
CrashCost	F6:F19
CrashCostPerWeekSaved	H6:H19
CrashTime	D6:D19
CStart	I8
DFinish	K9
DStart	I9
EFinish	K10
EStart	I10
FFinish	K11
FinishTime	K6:K19
FStart	I11
GFinish	K12
GStart	I12
HFinish	K13
HStart	I13
IFinish	K14
IStart	I14
JFinish	K15
JStart	I15
KFinish	K16
KStart	I16
LFinish	K17
LStart	I17
MaxTime	K22
MaxTimeReduction	G6:G19
MFinish	K18
MStart	I18
NFinish	K19
NormalCost	E6:E19
NormalTime	C6:C19
NStart	I19
ProjectFinishTime	I22
StartTime	I6:I19
TimeReduction	J6:J19
TotalCost	I24

Solver Parameters

Set Target Cell: [TotalCost]

Equal To: ○ Max ● Min ○ Value

By Changing Cells:

[StartTime,TimeReduction,ProjectFinis]

Subject to the Constraints:

```
BStart >= AFinish     IStart >= CFinish
CStart >= BFinish     JStart >= FFinish
DStart >= CFinish     JStart >= IFinish
EStart >= CFinish     KStart >= JFinish
FStart >= EFinish     LStart >= JFinish
GStart >= DFinish     MStart >= HFinish
HStart >= EFinish     NStart >= KFinish
HStart >= GFinish     NStart >= LFinish
ProjectFinishTime <= MaxTime
ProjectFinishTime >= MFinish
ProjectFinishTime >= NFinish
TimeReduction <= MaxTimeReduction
```

Solver Options

☑ Assume Linear Model

☑ Assume Non-Negative

	K
4	Finish
5	Time
6	=StartTime+NormalTime-TimeReduction
7	=StartTime+NormalTime-TimeReduction
8	=StartTime+NormalTime-TimeReduction
9	=StartTime+NormalTime-TimeReduction
10	:
11	:

	H	I
24	Total Cost	=SUM(NormalCost)+SUMPRODUCT(CrashCostPerWeekSaved,TimeReduction)

The CPM method of time–cost trade-offs ignores the considerable uncertainty in activity times, so the predicted project duration under any crashing plan may miss the actual duration by a considerable amount.

It is sometimes useful to postpone a decision on crashing an activity until near its start time. Information on how well the project schedule is progressing can then influence this decision.

However, Mr. Perty knows from long experience what we discussed in the preceding section, namely, that there is considerable uncertainty about how much time actually will be needed for each activity and so for the overall project. Recall that the PERT three-estimate approach led to having a *probability distribution* for project duration. Without crashing, this probability distribution has a *mean* of 44 weeks but such a large *variance* that there is even a substantial probability (roughly 0.2) of not even finishing within 47 weeks (which would trigger a penalty of $300,000). With the new crashing plan reducing the mean to 40 weeks, there is as much chance that the actual project duration will turn out to exceed 40 weeks as being within 40 weeks. Why spend an extra $140,000 to obtain a 50 percent chance of earning the bonus of $150,000?

Conclusion 1: The plan for crashing the project only provides a 50 percent chance of actually finishing the project within 40 weeks, so the extra cost of the plan ($140,000) is not justified. Therefore, Mr. Perty rejects any crashing at this stage.

Mr. Perty does note that the two activities that had been proposed for crashing (F and J) come about halfway through the project. Therefore, if the project is well ahead of schedule before reaching activity F, then implementing the crashing plan almost certainly would enable finishing the project within 40 weeks. Furthermore, Mr. Perty knows that it would be good for the company's reputation (as well as a feather in his own cap) to finish this early.

> **Conclusion 2:** The extra cost of the crashing plan can be justified if it almost certainly would earn the bonus of $150,000 for finishing the project within 40 weeks. Therefore, Mr. Perty will hold the plan in reserve to be implemented if the project is running well ahead of schedule before reaching activity F.

Mr. Perty is more concerned about the possibility that the project will run so far behind schedule that the penalty of $300,000 will be incurred for not finishing within 47 weeks. If this becomes likely without crashing, Mr. Perty sees that it probably can be avoided by crashing activity J (at a cost of $30,000 per week saved) and, if necessary, crashing activity F as well (at a cost of $40,000 per week saved). This will hold true as long as these activities remain on the critical path (as is likely) after the delays have occurred.

> **Conclusion 3:** The extra cost of part or all of the crashing plan can be easily justified if it likely would make the difference in avoiding the penalty of $300,000 for not finishing the project within 47 weeks. Therefore, Mr. Perty will hold the crashing plan in reserve to be partially or wholly implemented if the project is running far behind schedule before reaching activity F or activity J.

In addition to carefully monitoring the schedule as the project evolves (and making a later decision about any crashing), Mr. Perty will be closely watching the costs to try to keep the project within budget. The next section describes how he plans to do this.

Review Questions

1. What are some ways of crashing an activity?
2. What are the two key points in a time–cost graph for an activity? What do these points show?
3. Does crashing an activity always reduce the duration of the project? Why?
4. What are the costs being examined when performing marginal cost analysis on a project?
5. What are the decisions to be made when using linear programming to make crashing decisions?
6. In the linear programming formulation, describe in words what each starting time constraint is saying.
7. Why did Mr. Perty decide to reject the proposed plan for crashing the project even though the extra cost of the plan is less than the bonus for early completion of the project?

8.6 SCHEDULING AND CONTROLLING PROJECT COSTS

Any good project manager like Mr. Perty carefully plans and monitors both the *time* and *cost* aspects of the project. Both schedule and budget are important.

Sections 8.3 and 8.4 have described how PERT/CPM deals with the *time* aspect in developing a schedule and taking uncertainties in activity or project durations into account. Section 8.5 then placed an equal emphasis on time and cost by describing the CPM method of time–cost trade-offs.

Mr. Perty now is ready to turn his focus to *costs* by addressing the last of his questions posed at the end of Section 8.1.

> **Question 9:** How should ongoing costs be monitored to try to keep the project within budget?

Mr. Perty recalls that the PERT/CPM technique known as PERT/Cost is specifically designed for this purpose.

> **PERT/Cost** is a systematic procedure (normally computerized) to help the project manager plan, schedule, and control project costs.

The PERT/Cost procedure begins with the hard work of developing an estimate of the cost of each activity when it is performed in the planned way (including any crashing). At this stage, Mr. Perty does not plan on any crashing, so the estimated costs of the activities in Reliable's project are given in the normal cost column of Table 8.8 in the preceding section. These costs

TABLE 8.11
The Project Budget for
Reliable's Project

Activity	Estimated Duration (weeks)	Estimated Cost	Cost per Week of Its Duration
A	2	$180,000	$ 90,000
B	4	320,000	80,000
C	10	620,000	62,000
D	6	260,000	43,333
E	4	410,000	102,500
F	5	180,000	36,000
G	7	900,000	128,571
H	9	200,000	22,222
I	7	210,000	30,000
J	8	430,000	53,750
K	4	160,000	40,000
L	5	250,000	50,000
M	2	100,000	50,000
N	6	330,000	55,000

then are displayed in the *project budget* shown in Table 8.11. This table also includes the estimated duration of each activity (as already given in Table 8.1, Figures 8.1–8.8, and the normal time column of Table 8.8). Dividing the cost of each activity by its duration gives the amount in the rightmost column of Table 8.11.

> **Assumption:** A common assumption when using PERT/Cost is that the costs of performing an activity are incurred at a constant rate throughout its duration. Mr. Perty is making this assumption, so the estimated cost during each week of an activity's duration is given by the rightmost column of Table 8.11.

When applying PERT/Cost to larger projects with numerous activities, it is common to combine each group of related activities into a "work package." Both the project budget and the schedule of project costs (described below) then are developed in terms of these work packages rather than the individual activities. Mr. Perty has chosen not to do this since his project has only 14 activities.

Scheduling Project Costs

PERT/Cost provides a weekly schedule of expenses so that the project manager can monitor whether the project is staying within budget.

Mr. Perty needs to know how much money is required to cover project expenses week by week. PERT/Cost provides this information by using the rightmost column of Table 8.11 to develop a weekly schedule of expenses when the individual activities begin at their earliest start times. Then, to indicate how much flexibility is available for delaying expenses, PERT/Cost does the same thing when the individual activities begin at their latest start times instead.

To do this, this chapter's Excel files in your MS Courseware include an Excel template (labeled PERT Cost) for generating a project's schedule of costs for up to 45 time periods. (MS Project generates basically the same information by choosing Table:Cost and then Reports under the View menu, and next choosing the Costs . . . option and selecting the Cash Flow report.) Figure 8.15 shows this Excel template (including the equations entered into its output cells) for the beginning of Reliable's project, based on earliest start times (column E) as first obtained in Figure 8.5, where Columns B, C, and D come directly from Table 8.11. Figure 8.16 jumps ahead to show this same template for weeks 17 to 25. Since activities D, E, and I all have earliest start times of 16 (16 weeks after the commencement of the project), they all start in week 17, while activities F and G commence later during the period shown. Columns W through AE give the weekly cost (in dollars) of each of these activities, as obtained from column F (see Figure 8.15), for the duration of the activity (given by column C). Row 21 shows the sum of the weekly activity costs for each week.

Row 22 of this template gives the total project cost from week 1 on up to the indicated week. For example, consider week 17. Prior to week 17, activities A, B, and C all have been completed but no other activities have begun, so the total cost for the first 16 weeks (from the third

FIGURE 8.15   This Excel template in your MS Courseware enables efficient application of the PERT/Cost procedure, as illustrated here for the beginning of Reliable's project when using earliest start times.

	A	B	C	D	E	F	G	H	I	J
1		**Template for PERT/Cost**								
2										
3			Estimated							
4			Duration	Estimated	Start	Cost Per Week	Week	Week	Week	Week
5		Activity	(weeks)	Cost	Time	of Its Duration	1	2	3	4
6		A	2	$180,000	0	$90,000	$90,000	$90,000	$0	
7		B	4	$320,000	2	$80,000	$0	$0	$80,000	
8		C	10	$620,000	6	$62,000	$0	$0	$0	...
9		D	6	$260,000	16	$43,333	$0	$0	$0	
10		E	4	$410,000	16	$102,500	$0	$0	$0	
11		F	5	$180,000	20	$36,000	$0	$0	$0	
12		G	7	$900,000	22	$128,571	$0	$0	$0	...
13		H	9	$200,000	29	$22,222	$0	$0	$0	
14		I	7	$210,000	16	$30,000	$0	$0	$0	
15		J	8	$430,000	25	$53,750	$0	$0	$0	
16		K	4	$160,000	33	$40,000	$0	$0	$0	...
17		L	5	$250,000	33	$50,000	$0	$0	$0	
18		M	2	$100,000	38	$50,000	$0	$0	$0	
19		N	6	$330,000	38	$55,000	$0	$0	$0	
20										
21						Weekly Project Cost	$90,000	$90,000	$80,000	...
22						Cumulative Project Cost	$90,000	$180,000	$260,000	...

	F	G	H
4	Cost Per Week	Week	Week
5	of Its Duration	1	2
6	=EstimatedCost/EstimatedDuration	=IF(AND(Week>StartTime,Week<=StartTime+EstimatedDuration),CostPerWeek,0)	...
7	=EstimatedCost/EstimatedDuration	=IF(AND(Week>StartTime,Week<=StartTime+EstimatedDuration),CostPerWeek,0)	...
8	=EstimatedCost/EstimatedDuration	=IF(AND(Week>StartTime,Week<=StartTime+EstimatedDuration),CostPerWeek,0)	...
9	:	:	
10	:	:	

	F	G	H	I	J
21	Weekly Project Cost	=SUM(G6:G19)	=SUM(H6:H19)	=SUM(I6:I19)	...
22	Cumulative Project Cost	=G21	=G22+H21	=H22+I21	...

Range Name	Cells
Activity	B6:B19
CostPerWeek	F6:F19
CumulativeProjectCost	G22:AY22
EstimatedCost	D6:D19
EstimatedDuration	C6:C19
StartTime	E6:E19
Week	G5:AY5
WeeklyProjectCost	G21:AY21

column of Table 8.11) are $180,000 + $320,000 + $620,000 = $1,120,000. Adding the weekly project cost for week 17 then gives $1,120,000 + $175,833 = $1,295,833.

Thus, Figure 8.16 (and its extension to earlier and later weeks) shows Mr. Perty just how much money he will need to cover each week's expenses, as well as the cumulative amount, assuming the project can stick to the earliest start time schedule.

FIGURE 8.16   This spreadsheet extends the template in Figure 8.15 to weeks 17 to 25.

	A	B	E	W	X	Y	Z	AA	AB	AC	AD	AE
1	**Template for PERT/Cost**											
2												
3												
4			Start	Week	Week	Week	Week	Week	Week	Week	Week	Week
5		Activity	Time	17	18	19	20	21	22	23	24	25
6		A	0	$0	$0	$0	$0	$0	$0	$0	$0	$0
7		B	2	$0	$0	$0	$0	$0	$0	$0	$0	$0
8		C	6	$0	$0	$0	$0	$0	$0	$0	$0	$0
9		D	16	$43,333	$43,333	$43,333	$43,333	$43,333	$43,333	$0	$0	$0
10		E	16	$102,500	$102,500	$102,500	$102,500	$0	$0	$0	$0	$0
11		F	20	$0	$0	$0	$0	$36,000	$36,000	$36,000	$36,000	$36,000
12		G	22	$0	$0	$0	$0	$0	$0	$128,571	$128,571	$128,571
13		H	29	$0	$0	$0	$0	$0	$0	$0	$0	$0
14		I	16	$30,000	$30,000	$30,000	$30,000	$30,000	$30,000	$30,000	$0	$0
15		J	25	$0	$0	$0	$0	$0	$0	$0	$0	$0
16		K	33	$0	$0	$0	$0	$0	$0	$0	$0	$0
17		L	33	$0	$0	$0	$0	$0	$0	$0	$0	$0
18		M	38	$0	$0	$0	$0	$0	$0	$0	$0	$0
19		N	38	$0	$0	$0	$0	$0	$0	$0	$0	$0
20												
21				$175,833	$175,833	$175,833	$175,833	$109,333	$109,333	$194,571	$164,571	$164,571
22				$1,295,833	$1,471,667	$1,647,500	$1,823,333	$1,932,667	$2,042,000	$2,236,571	$2,401,143	$2,565,714

Next, PERT/Cost uses the same procedure to develop the corresponding information when each activity begins at its *latest* start times instead. These latest start times were first obtained in Figure 8.6 and are repeated here in column E of Figure 8.17. The rest of this figure then is generated in the same way as for Figure 8.16. For example, since activity D has a latest start time of 20 (versus an earliest start time of 16), its weekly cost of $43,333 now begins in week 21 rather than week 17. Similarly, activity G has a latest start time of 26, so it has no entries for the weeks considered in this figure.

Figure 8.17 (and its extension to earlier and later weeks) tells Mr. Perty what his weekly and cumulative expenses would be if he were to postpone each activity as long as possible without delaying project completion (assuming no unexpected delays occur). Comparing row 22 of Figures 8.16 and 8.17 indicates that fairly substantial *temporary* savings can be achieved by such postponements, which is very helpful if the company is incurring cash shortages. (However, such postponements would only be used reluctantly since they would remove any latitude for avoiding a delay in the completion of the project if any activities were to incur unexpected delays.)

To better visualize the comparison between row 22 of Figures 8.16 and 8.17, it is helpful to graph these two rows together over all 44 weeks of the project, as shown in Figure 8.18. Since the earliest start times and latest start times are the same for the first three activities (A, B, C), which encompass the first 16 weeks, the cumulative project cost is the same for the two kinds of start times over this period. After week 16, we obtain two distinct cost curves by plotting the values in row 22 of Figures 8.16 and 8.17 (and their extensions to later weeks). Since sticking to either earliest start times or latest start times leads to project completion at the end of 44 weeks, the two cost curves come together again at that point with a total project cost of $4.55 million. The dots on either curve are the points at which the weekly project costs change.

Naturally, the start times and activity costs that led to Figure 8.18 are only estimates of what actually will transpire. However, the figure provides a *best forecast* of cumulative project costs

Postponing activities to their latest start times also postpones the costs of these activities, which is helpful when cash is short, but this also increases the risk of missing the scheduled project completion date.

FIGURE 8.17   The application of the PERT/Cost procedure to weeks 17 to 25 of Reliable's project when using latest start times.

	A	B	E	W	X	Y	Z	AA	AB	AC	AD	AE
1		**Template for PERT/Cost**										
2												
3												
4			Start	Week	Week	Week	Week	Week	Week	Week	Week	Week
5		Activity	Time	17	18	19	20	21	22	23	24	25
6		A	0	$0	$0	$0	$0	$0	$0	$0	$0	$0
7		B	2	$0	$0	$0	$0	$0	$0	$0	$0	$0
8		C	6	$0	$0	$0	$0	$0	$0	$0	$0	$0
9		D	20	$0	$0	$0	$0	$43,333	$43,333	$43,333	$43,000	$43,333
10		E	16	$102,500	$102,500	$102,500	$102,500	$0	$0	$0	$0	$0
11		F	20	$0	$0	$0	$0	$36,000	$36,000	$36,000	$36,000	$36,000
12		G	26	$0	$0	$0	$0	$0	$0	$0	$0	$0
13		H	33	$0	$0	$0	$0	$0	$0	$0	$0	$0
14		I	18	$0	$0	$30,000	$30,000	$30,000	$30,000	$30,000	$30,000	$30,000
15		J	25	$0	$0	$0	$0	$0	$0	$0	$0	$0
16		K	34	$0	$0	$0	$0	$0	$0	$0	$0	$0
17		L	33	$0	$0	$0	$0	$0	$0	$0	$0	$0
18		M	42	$0	$0	$0	$0	$0	$0	$0	$0	$0
19		N	38	$0	$0	$0	$0	$0	$0	$0	$0	$0
20												
21				$102,500	$102,500	$132,500	$132,500	$109,333	$109,333	$109,333	$109,333	$109,333
22				$1,222,500	$1,325,000	$1,457,500	$1,590,000	$1,699,333	$1,808,667	$1,918,000	$2,027,333	$2,136,667

FIGURE 8.18
The schedule of cumulative project costs when all activities begin at their earliest start times (the top cost curve) or at their latest start times (the bottom cost curve).

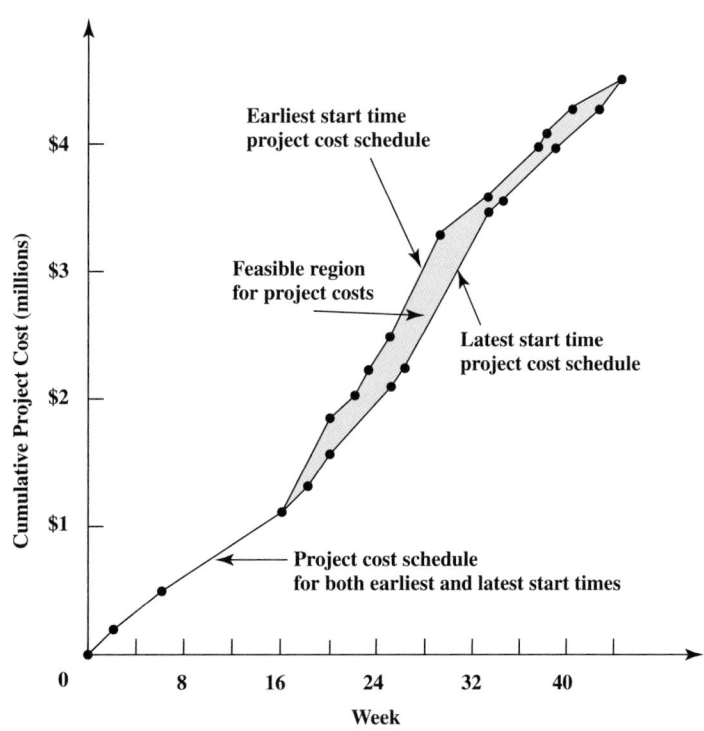

week by week when following a work schedule based on either earliest or latest start times. If either of these work schedules is selected, this best forecast then becomes a *budget* to be followed as closely as possible. A budget in the shaded area between the two cost curves also can be obtained by selecting a work schedule that calls for beginning each activity somewhere between its earliest and latest start times. The only *feasible* budgets for scheduling project completion at the end of week 44 (without any crashing) lie in this shaded area or on one of the two cost curves.

Figure 8.18 shows the only feasible week-by-week budgets that will not delay project completion.

Reliable Construction Co. has adequate funds to cover expenses until payments are received. Therefore, Mr. Perty has selected a work schedule based on earliest start times to provide the best chance for prompt completion. (He is still nervous about the significant probability of incurring the penalty of $300,000 for not finishing within 47 weeks.) Consequently, his budget is provided by the top cost curve in Figure 8.18.

Controlling Project Costs

Once the project is under way, Mr. Perty will need to monitor actual costs carefully and take corrective action as needed to avoid serious cost overruns. One important way of monitoring costs is to compare actual costs to date with his budget provided by the top curve in Figure 8.18.

However, since deviations from the planned work schedule may occur, this method of monitoring costs is not adequate by itself. For example, suppose that individual activities have been costing more than budgeted, but delays have prevented some activities from beginning when scheduled. These delays might cause the total cost to date to be less than the budgeted cumulative project cost, thereby giving the illusion that project costs are well under control. Furthermore, regardless of whether the cost performance of the project as a whole seems satisfactory, Mr. Perty needs information about the cost performance of individual activities to identify trouble spots where corrective action is needed.

Therefore, PERT/Cost periodically generates a report that focuses on the cost performance of the individual activities. To illustrate, Table 8.12 shows the report that Mr. Perty received after the completion of week 22 (halfway through the project schedule). The first column lists the activities that have at least begun by this time. The next column gives the budgeted total cost of each activity (as given previously in the third column of Table 8.11). The third column indicates what percentage of the activity now has been completed. Multiplying the second and third columns then gives the fourth column, which thereby represents the budgeted value of the work completed on the activity.

The PERT/Cost report gives the cost overrun to date of each activity, which identifies the trouble spots where corrective action is needed.

The fourth column is the one that Mr. Perty wants to compare to the *actual cost* to date given in the fifth column. Subtracting the fourth column from the fifth gives the *cost overrun* to date of each activity, as shown in the rightmost column. (A negative number in the cost overrun column indicates a *cost underrun*.)

Mr. Perty pays special attention in the report to the activities that are not yet completed, since these are the ones that he can still affect. (He used earlier reports to monitor activities A, B, C, and E while they were under way, which led to meeting the total budget for these four activities.) Activity D is barely over budget (less than 3 percent), but Mr. Perty is very concerned

TABLE 8.12
PERT/Cost Report after Week 22 of Reliable's Project

Activity	Budgeted Cost	Percent Completed	Value Completed	Actual Cost to Date	Cost Overrun to Date
A	$ 180,000	100%	$ 180,000	$ 200,000	$20,000
B	320,000	100	320,000	330,000	10,000
C	620,000	100	620,000	600,000	−20,000
D	260,000	75	195,000	200,000	5,000
E	410,000	100	410,000	400,000	−10,000
F	180,000	25	45,000	60,000	15,000
I	210,000	50	105,000	130,000	25,000
Total	$2,180,000		$1,875,000	$1,920,000	$45,000

about the large cost overruns to date for activities F and I. Therefore, he next will investigate these two activities and work with the foremen involved to improve their cost performances.

Note in the bottom row of Table 8.12 that the cumulative project cost after week 22 is $1.92 million. This is considerably less than Mr. Perty's *budgeted* cumulative project cost of $2.042 million given in cell AB22 of Figure 8.16. Without any further information, this comparison would suggest an excellent cost performance for the project so far. However, the real reason for being under budget is that the current activities all are behind schedule and so have not yet incurred some expenses that had been scheduled to occur earlier. Fortunately, the PERT/Cost report provides valuable additional information that paints a truer picture of cost performance to date. By focusing on individual activities rather than the overall project, the report identifies the current trouble spots (activities F and I) that require Mr. Perty's immediate attention. Thus, the report enables him to take corrective action while there is still time to reverse these cost overruns.

Review
Questions

1. What is the purpose of PERT/Cost?
2. How does the PERT/Cost procedure begin?
3. What assumption is commonly made about how the cost of performing an activity is spread over the duration of the activity?
4. What is a work package?
5. Which two work schedules does PERT/Cost use as a basis for developing cost schedules?
6. What two types of information about project cost are provided for each time period by a PERT/Cost schedule of costs?
7. What information does a PERT/Cost report provide about the cost performance of each activity?
8. Why is a PERT/Cost report needed when the project manager already can evaluate the cost performance of the overall project by comparing the actual cost to date with the budgeted cumulative cost?

8.7   AN EVALUATION OF PERT/CPM FROM A MANAGERIAL PERSPECTIVE

PERT/CPM has stood the test of time. Despite being more than 40 years old, it continues to be one of the most widely used techniques of management science. It is a standard tool of project managers.

The Value of PERT/CPM

Much of the value of PERT/CPM derives from the basic framework it provides for planning a project. Recall its planning steps: (1) identify the activities that are needed to carry out the project; (2) estimate how much time will be needed for each activity; (3) determine the activities that must immediately precede each activity; and (4) develop the project network that visually displays the relationships between the activities. The discipline of going through these steps forces the needed planning to be done.

The scheduling information generated by PERT/CPM also is vital to the project manager. When can each activity begin if there are no delays? How much delay in an activity can be tolerated without delaying project completion? What is the critical path of activities where no delay can be tolerated? What is the effect of uncertainty in activity times? What is the probability of meeting the project deadline under the current plan? PERT/CPM provides the answers.

PERT/CPM also assists the project manager in other ways. Schedule and budget are key concerns. The CPM method of time–cost trade-offs enables investigating ways of reducing the duration of the project at an additional cost. PERT/Cost provides a systematic procedure for planning, scheduling, and controlling project costs.

In many ways, PERT/CPM exemplifies the application of management science at its finest. Its modeling approach focuses on the key features of the problem (activities, precedence relationships, time, and cost) without getting mired down in unimportant details. The resulting

PERT/CPM addresses the issues that are important to management.

model (a project network and an optional linear programming formulation) are easy to understand and apply. It addresses the issues that are important to management (planning, scheduling, dealing with uncertainty, making time–cost trade-offs, and controlling costs). It assists the project manager in dealing with these issues in useful ways and in a timely manner.

Using the Computer

PERT/CPM continues to evolve to meet new needs. At its inception over 40 years ago, it was largely executed manually. The project network sometimes was spread out over the walls of the project manager. Recording changes in the plan became a major task. Communicating changes to crew foremen and subcontractors was cumbersome. The computer has changed all of that.

Project management software now is a standard tool for project managers.

For many years now, PERT/CPM has become highly computerized. There has been a remarkable growth in the number and power of software packages for PERT/CPM that run on personal computers or workstations. *Project management software* (for example, Microsoft Project) now is a standard tool for project managers.[2] This has enabled applications to numerous projects that each involve many millions of dollars and perhaps even thousands of activities. Possible revisions in the project plan now can be investigated almost instantaneously. Actual changes and the resulting updates in the schedule, and so forth, are recorded virtually effortlessly. Communications to all parties involved through computer networks and telecommunication systems also have become quick and easy.

Nevertheless, PERT/CPM still is not a panacea. It has certain major deficiencies for some applications. We briefly describe each of these deficiencies below along with how it is being addressed through research on improvements or extensions to PERT/CPM.

Approximating the Means and Variances of Activity Durations

The PERT three-estimate approach described in Section 8.4 provides a straightforward procedure for approximating the mean and variance of the probability distribution of the duration of each activity. Recall that this approach involved obtaining a most likely estimate, an optimistic estimate, and a pessimistic estimate of the duration. Given these three estimates, simple formulas were given for approximating the mean and variance. The means and variances for the various activities then were used to estimate the probability of completing the project by a specified time.

Better methods now are available for approximating the mean and variance of activity durations.

Unfortunately, considerable subsequent research has shown that this approach tends to provide a pretty rough approximation of the mean and variance. Part of the difficulty lies in aiming the optimistic and pessimistic estimates at the *end points* of the probability distribution. These end points correspond to very rare events (the best and worst that could ever occur) that typically are outside the estimator's realm of experience. The accuracy and reliability of such estimates are not as good as for points that are not at the extremes of the probability distribution. For example, research has demonstrated that much better estimates can be obtained by aiming them at the 10 percent and 90 percent points of the probability distribution. The optimistic and pessimistic estimates then would be described in terms of having 1 chance in 10 of doing better or 1 chance in 10 of doing worse. The middle estimate also can be improved by aiming it at the 50 percent point (the median value) of the probability distribution.

Revising the definitions of the three estimates along these lines leads to considerably more complicated formulas for the mean and variance of the duration of an activity. However, this is no problem since the analysis is computerized anyway. The important consideration is that much better approximations of the mean and variance are obtained in this way.[3]

---

[2]For information on 46 software packages for project management, see M. Elliott, "Buyer's Guide: Project Management Software," *IIE Solutions,* March 2001, pp. 45–52.

[3]For further information, see, for example, D. L. Keefer and W. A. Verdini, "Better Estimation of PERT Activity Time Parameters," *Management Science* 39 (September 1993), pp. 1086–91. Also see A. H.-L. Lau, H.-S. Lau, and Y. Zhang, "A Simple and Logical Alternative for Making PERT Time Estimates," *IIE Transactions* 28 (March 1996), pp. 183–92.

Approximating the Probability of Meeting the Deadline

Of all the assumptions and simplifying approximations made by PERT/CPM, one is particularly controversial. This is simplifying approximation 1 in Section 8.4, which assumes that the *mean critical path* will turn out to be the longest path through the project network. This approximation greatly simplifies the calculation of the approximate probability of completing the project by a specified deadline. Unfortunately, in reality, there usually is a significant chance, and sometimes a very substantial chance, that some other path or paths will turn out to be longer than the mean critical path. Consequently, the calculated probability of meeting the deadline usually overstates the true probability somewhat. PERT/CPM provides no information on the likely size of the error. (Research has found that the error often is modest, but can be very large.) Thus, the project manager who relies on the calculated probability can be badly misled.

Considerable research has been conducted to develop more accurate (albeit more complicated) analytical approximations of this probability. Of special interest are methods that provide both upper and lower bounds on the probability.[4]

> Computer simulation can provide a better approximation of the probability of meeting a project deadline, as illustrated in Section 16.3 for Reliable's project.

Another alternative is to use the technique of computer simulation described in Chapters 15 and 16 to approximate this probability. This appears to be the most commonly used method in practice (when any is used) to improve upon the PERT/CPM approximation. We describe in Section 16.3 how this would be done for the Reliable Construction Co. project.

Dealing with Overlapping Activities

Another key assumption of PERT/CPM is that an activity cannot begin until all its immediate predecessors are completely finished. Although this may appear to be a perfectly reasonable assumption, it too is sometimes only a rough approximation of reality.

For example, in the Reliable Construction Co. project, consider activity H (do the exterior painting) and its immediate predecessor, activity G (put up the exterior siding). Naturally, this painting cannot begin until the exterior siding is there on which to paint. However, it certainly is possible to begin painting on one wall while the exterior siding still is being put up to form the other walls. Thus, activity H actually can begin before activity G is completely finished. Although careful coordination is needed, this possibility to overlap activities can significantly reduce project duration below that predicted by PERT/CPM.

> PDM provides ways of dealing with overlapping activities that are not available with PERT/CPM.

The **precedence diagramming method (PDM)** has been developed as an extension of PERT/CPM to deal with such overlapping activities.[5] PDM provides four options for the relationship between an activity and any one of its immediate predecessors.

Option 1: The activity cannot begin until the immediate predecessor has been in progress a certain amount of time.

Option 2: The activity cannot finish until a certain amount of time after the immediate predecessor has finished.

Option 3: The activity cannot finish until a certain amount of time after the immediate predecessor has started.

Option 4: The activity cannot begin until a certain amount of time after the immediate predecessor has finished. (Rather than overlapping the activities, note that this option creates a lag between them such as, for example, waiting for the paint to dry before beginning the activity that follows painting.)

---

[4]See, for example, J. Kamburowski, "Bounding the Distribution of Project Duration in PERT Networks," *Operations Research Letters* 12 (July 1992), pp. 17–22. Also see T. Iida, "Computing Bounds on Project Duration Distributions for Stochastic PERT Networks," *Naval Research Logistics* 47 (October 2000), pp. 559–80.

[5]For an introduction to PDM, see pp. 136–44 in A. B. Badiru and P. S. Pulat, *Comprehensive Project Management: Integrating Optimization Models, Management Principles, and Computers* (Englewood Cliffs, NJ: Prentice-Hall, 1995).

Alternatively, the *certain amount of time* mentioned in each option also can be expressed as a certain percentage of the work content of the immediate predecessor.

After incorporating these options, PDM can be used much like PERT/CPM to determine earliest start times, latest start times, and the critical path and to investigate time–cost trade-offs, and so on.

Although it adds considerable flexibility to PERT/CPM, PDM is neither as well known nor as widely used as PERT/CPM. This should gradually change.

Incorporating the Allocation of Resources to Activities

PERT/CPM assumes that each activity has available all the resources (money, personnel, equipment, etc.) needed to perform the activity in the normal way (or on a crashed basis). In actuality, many projects have only limited resources for which the activities must compete. A major challenge in planning the project then is to determine how the resources should be allocated to the activities.

PERT/CPM does not consider the issue of how to allocate resources to activities.

Once the resources have been allocated, PERT/CPM can be applied in the usual way. However, it would be far better to combine the allocation of the resources with the kind of planning and scheduling done by PERT/CPM so as to strive simultaneously toward a desired objective. For example, a common objective is to allocate the resources so as to minimize the duration of the project.

Much research has been conducted (and is continuing) to develop the methodology for simultaneously allocating resources and scheduling the activities of a project. This subject is beyond the scope of this book, but considerable reading is available elsewhere.[6]

The Future

Despite its deficiencies, PERT/CPM undoubtedly will continue to be widely used for the foreseeable future. It provides the project manager with most of what he or she wants: structure, scheduling information, tools for controlling schedule (latest start times, slacks, the critical path, etc.) and controlling costs (PERT/Cost), as well as the flexibility to investigate time–cost trade-offs.

Even though some of the approximations involved with the PERT three-estimate approach are questionable, these inaccuracies ultimately may not be too important. Just the process of developing estimates of the duration of activities encourages effective interaction between the project manager and subordinates that leads to setting mutual goals for start times, activity durations, project duration, and so forth. Striving together toward these goals may make them self-fulfilling prophecies despite inaccuracies in the underlying mathematics that led to these goals.

Similarly, possibilities for a modest amount of overlapping of activities need not invalidate a schedule generated by PERT/CPM, despite its assumption that no overlapping can occur. Actually having a small amount of overlapping may just provide the slack needed to compensate for the "unexpected" delays that inevitably seem to slip into a schedule.

Even when needing to allocate resources to activities, just using common sense in this allocation and then applying PERT/CPM should be quite satisfactory for some projects.

PERT/CPM continues to be a vital tool for project managers, but useful improvements and extensions also are becoming available.

Nevertheless, it is unfortunate that the kinds of improvements and extensions to PERT/CPM described in this section have not been incorporated much into practice to date. Old comfortable methods that have proven their value are not readily discarded, and it takes awhile to learn about and gain confidence in new better methods. However, we anticipate that these improvements and extensions gradually will come into more widespread use as they prove their value as well. We also expect that the recent and current extensive research on techniques for project management and scheduling (much of it in Europe) will continue and will lead to further improvements in the future.

---

[6]See, for example, ibid., pp. 162–209. Also see L. Özdamar and G. Ulusay, "A Survey on the Resource-Constrained Project Scheduling Problem," *IIE Transactions* 27 (October 1995), pp. 574–86, as well as S. S. Erenguc, T. Ahn, and D. G. Conway, "The Resource Constrained Project Scheduling Problem with Multiple Crashable Modes: An Exact Solution Method," *Naval Research Logistics* 48 (March 2001), pp. 107–27.

Review
Questions

1. What are some important managerial issues in managing a project that PERT/CPM addresses?
2. What have been some benefits from changing from the original manual execution of PERT/CPM to its computer implementation in more recent years?
3. In the PERT three-estimate approach, what has research shown regarding how the accuracy of the optimistic and pessimistic estimates is affected by the choice of the points at which these estimates are aimed in the probability distribution of the duration of the activity involved?
4. What is an alternative technique for improving the PERT/CPM approximation of the probability that the project will meet its deadline?
5. What is the name of a method for extending PERT/CPM to permit activities and their immediate predecessors to overlap?
6. What does PERT/CPM assume about the availability of the resources needed to perform each activity in the normal way?
7. Beyond the estimates themselves, what is an additional benefit of conducting the process of developing estimates of the duration of activities?
8. Considering that PERT/CPM has become such a well-established management science technique, are new improvements and extensions still being developed?

8.8 Summary

Ever since their inception in the late 1950s, PERT (program evaluation and review technique) and CPM (critical path method) have been used extensively to assist project managers in planning, scheduling, and controlling their projects. Over time, these two techniques gradually have merged, so PERT/CPM today refers to the combined version that includes all the various options of either of the original techniques.

The application of PERT/CPM begins by breaking the project down into its individual activities, identifying the immediate predecessors of each activity, and estimating the duration of each activity. The next step is to construct a project network to visually display all this information. The type of network that is becoming increasingly popular for this purpose is the activity-on-node (AON) project network, where each activity is represented by a node.

PERT/CPM then generates scheduling information for the project manager, including the earliest start time, the latest start time, and the slack for each activity. It also identifies the critical path of activities such that any delay along this path will delay project completion. Since the critical path is the longest path through the project network, its length determines the duration of the project, assuming all activities remain on schedule.

However, it is difficult for all activities to remain on schedule because there frequently is considerable uncertainty about what the duration of an activity will turn out to be. The PERT three-estimate approach addresses this situation by obtaining three different kinds of estimates (most likely, optimistic, and pessimistic) for the duration of each activity. This information is used to approximate the mean and variance of the probability distribution of this duration. It then is possible to approximate the probability that the project will be completed by the deadline.

The CPM method of time–cost trade-offs enables the project manager to investigate the effect on total cost of changing the estimated duration of the project to various alternative values. The data needed for this activity are the time and cost for each activity when it is done in the normal way and then when it is fully crashed (expedited). Either marginal cost analysis or linear programming can be used to determine how much (if any) to crash each activity to minimize the total cost of meeting any specified deadline for the project.

The PERT/CPM technique called PERT/Cost provides the project manager with a systematic procedure for planning, scheduling, and controlling project costs. It generates a complete schedule for what the project costs should be in each time period when activities begin at either their earliest start times or latest start times. It also generates periodic reports that evaluate the cost performance of the individual activities, including identifying those where cost overruns are occurring.

PERT/CPM does have some important deficiencies. These include questionable approximations made when estimating the mean and variance of activity durations as well as when estimating the probability that the project will be completed by the deadline. Another deficiency is that it does not allow an activity to begin until all its immediate predecessors are completely finished, even though some overlap is sometimes possible. In addition, PERT/CPM does not address the important issue of how to allocate limited resources to the various activities.

Nevertheless, PERT/CPM has stood the test of time in providing project managers with most of the help they want. Furthermore, much progress is being made in developing improvements and extensions to PERT/CPM (such as the precedence diagramming method for dealing with overlapping activities) that address these deficiencies.

Glossary

activity A distinct task that needs to be performed as part of a project. (Section 8.1), *324*

activity-on-arc (AOA) project network A project network where each activity is represented by an arc (arrow). (Section 8.2), *326*

activity-on-node (AON) project network A project network where each activity is represented by a node (small circle or rectangle) and the arcs (arrows) show the precedence relationships between the activities. (Section 8.2), *326*

arc An arrow in the project network. (Section 8.2), *326*

backward pass The process of moving backward through the project network to determine the latest finish time and latest start time of each activity. (Section 8.3), *334*

CPM An acronym for critical path method, a technique for assisting project managers with carrying out their responsibilities. (Introduction), *323*

CPM method of time–cost trade-offs A method of investigating the trade-off between the total cost of a project and its duration when various levels of crashing are used to reduce the duration. (Section 8.5), *346*

crash point The point on the time–cost graph for an activity that shows the time (duration) and cost when the activity is fully crashed; that is, it is fully expedited with no cost spared to reduce its duration as much as possible. (Section 8.5), *347*

crashing an activity Taking special costly measures to reduce the duration of an activity below its normal value. (Section 8.5), *346*

crashing the project Crashing a number of activities to reduce the duration of the project below its normal value. (Section 8.5), *346*

critical path The longest path through the project network, so the activities on this path are the critical bottleneck activities where any delays in their completion must be avoided to prevent delaying project completion. (Section 8.3), *330*

earliest finish time for an activity The time at which this activity will finish if there are no delays anywhere in the project. (Section 8.3), *330*

earliest start time for an activity The time at which this activity will begin if there are no delays anywhere in the project. (Section 8.3), *330*

EF Abbreviation for the earliest finish time of an activity. (Section 8.3), *330*

ES Abbreviation for the earliest start time of an activity. (Section 8.3), *330*

finish node The node (small rectangle) in the project network that represents the finish of the project. (Section 8.2), *326*

forward pass The process of moving forward through the project network to determine the earliest start time and earliest finish time of each activity. (Section 8.3), *333*

Gantt chart A chart that uses bars to show the scheduled start and finish times of the various activities of a project. (Section 8.2), *327*

immediate predecessor The immediate predecessors of a given activity are those activities that must be completed by no later than the start time of the given activity. (Section 8.1), *324*

immediate successor Given the immediate predecessors of an activity, this activity then becomes the immediate successor of each of these immediate predecessors. (Section 8.1), *334*

latest finish time for an activity The latest possible time that this activity can finish without delaying project completion (assuming no subsequent delays in the project). (Section 8.3), *334*

latest start time for an activity The latest possible time that this activity can start without delaying project completion (assuming no subsequent delays in the project). (Section 8.3), *334*

length of a path The sum of the (estimated) durations of the activities on the path. (Section 8.3), *329*

LF Abbreviation for the latest finish time of an activity. (Section 8.3), *334*

LS Abbreviation for the latest start time of an activity. (Section 8.3), *334*

marginal cost analysis A method of using the marginal cost of crashing individual activities on the current critical path to determine the least expensive way of reducing project duration to a desired level. (Section 8.5), *348*

mean critical path The path through the project network that would be the critical path if the duration of each activity were to equal its mean. (Section 8.4), *342*

most likely estimate An estimate of the most likely value of the duration of an activity. (Section 8.4), *340*

node A small circle or rectangle that serves as a junction point in the project network. (Section 8.2), *326*

normal point The point on the time–cost graph for an activity that shows the time (duration) and cost of the activity when it is performed in the normal way. (Section 8.5), *347*

optimistic estimate An estimate of the duration of an activity under the most favorable conditions. (Section 8.4), *340*

path A path through a project network is one of the routes following the arrows (arcs) from the start node to the finish node. (Section 8.3), *329*

PERT An acronym for program evaluation and review technique, a technique for assisting project managers with carrying out their responsibilities. (Introduction), *323*

PERT/Cost A systematic procedure (normally computerized) to help the project manager plan, schedule, and control project costs. (Section 8.6), *353*

PERT/CPM The merger of the two techniques originally known as PERT and CPM. (Introduction), *323*

PERT three-estimate approach An approach to dealing with uncertainties in activity times by

obtaining three different kinds of estimates (most likely, optimistic, and pessimistic) for the duration of each activity. (Section 8.4), *340*
pessimistic estimate An estimate of the duration of an activity under the most unfavorable conditions. (Section 8.4), *340*
precedence diagramming method (PDM) An extension of PERT/CPM that deals with overlapping activities. (Section 8.7), *361*
project network A network used to visually display a project. (Section 8.2), *326*

slack for an activity The amount of time that this activity can be delayed without delaying project completion (assuming no subsequent delays in the project); it is calculated as the difference between the latest finish time and the earliest finish time for the activity. (Section 8.3), *337*
start node The node (small rectangle) in the project network that represents the start of the project. (Section 8.2), *326*

Learning Aids for This Chapter in Your MS Courseware

Chapter 8 Excel Files:

Reliable Example (Project Schedule)
Template for PERT Three-Estimate Approach (labeled PERT)
Reliable Example (CPM Method of Time–Cost Trade-Offs)
Template for PERT/Cost (labeled PERT Cost)
Reliable's ES Schedule of Costs
Reliable's LS Schedule of Costs

Special Software:

MS Project

MS Project Files:

Reliable's Schedule
Reliable's Three-Estimate Data
Reliable's Schedule of Costs Based on Earliest Start Times (last 8 weeks)

An Excel Add-in:

Premium Solver for Education

Supplement to Chapter 8 on the CD-ROM:

The Procedure for Constructing a Project Network

Problems

To the left of the problems (or their parts), we have inserted an E whenever Excel can be helpful. An asterisk on this symbol indicates that it definitely should be used (unless your instructor gives you contrary instructions). Your instructor might also suggest that you use MS Project on some of the problems. An asterisk on the problem number indicates that at least a partial answer is given in the back of the book.

8.1. Christine Phillips is in charge of planning and coordinating next spring's sales management training program for her company. Christine has listed the following activity information for this project:

Activity	Activity Description	Immediate Predecessors	Estimated Duration (Weeks)
A	Select location	—	2
B	Obtain speakers	—	3
C	Make speaker travel plans	A, B	2
D	Prepare and mail brochure	A, B	2
E	Take reservations	D	3

a. Construct the project network for this project.
b. Find all the paths and path lengths through this project network. Which of these paths is a critical path?

      c. Find the earliest times, latest times, and slack for each activity. Use this information to determine which of the paths is a critical path.

      d. It is now one week later, and Christine is ahead of schedule. She has already selected a location for the sales meeting, and all the other activities are right on schedule. Will this shorten the length of the project? Why or why not?

8.2.*   Reconsider Problem 8.1. Christine has done more detailed planning for this project and so now has the following expanded activity list:

Activity	Activity Description	Immediate Predecessors	Estimated Duration (weeks)
A	Select location	—	2
B	Obtain keynote speaker	—	1
C	Obtain other speakers	B	2
D	Make speaker travel plans for keynote speaker	A, B	2
E	Make travel plans for other speakers	A, C	3
F	Make food arrangements	A	2
G	Negotiate hotel rates	A	1
H	Prepare brochure	C, G	1
I	Mail brochure	H	1
J	Take reservations	I	3
K	Prepare handouts	C, F	4

      Follow the instructions for Problem 8.1 with this expanded activity list.

8.3.   Consider a project with the following activity list.

Activity	Immediate Predecessors	Estimated Duration (months)
A	—	1
B	A	2
C	B	4
D	B	3
E	B	2
F	C	3
G	D, E	5
H	F	1
I	G, H	4
J	I	2
K	I	3
L	J	3
M	K	5
N	L	4

      a. Construct the project network for this project.

      b. Find the earliest start time and earliest finish time for each activity.

      c. Find the latest start time and latest finish time for each activity.

      d. Find the slack for each activity. Which of the paths is a critical path?

8.4.   You and several friends are about to prepare a lasagna dinner. The tasks to be performed, their immediate predecessors, and their estimated durations are as follows:

Task	Task Description	Tasks That Must Precede	Time (minutes)
A	Buy the mozzarella cheese*	—	30
B	Slice the mozzarella	A	5
C	Beat 2 eggs	—	2
D	Mix eggs and ricotta cheese	C	3
E	Cut up onions and mushrooms	—	7
F	Cook the tomato sauce	E	25
G	Boil large quantity of water	—	15
H	Boil the lasagna noodles	G	10
I	Drain the lasagna noodles	H	2
J	Assemble all the ingredients	I, F, D, B	10
K	Preheat the oven	—	15
L	Bake the lasagna	J, K	30

*There is none in the refrigerator.

a. Construct the project network.

b. Find all the paths and path lengths through this project network. Which of these paths is a critical path?

c. Find the earliest start time and earliest finish time for each activity.

d. Find the latest start time and latest finish time for each activity.

e. Find the slack for each activity. Which of the paths is a critical path?

f. Because of a phone call, you were interrupted for 6 minutes when you should have been cutting the onions and mushrooms. By how much will the dinner be delayed? If you use your food processor, which reduces the cutting time from 7 to 2 minutes, will the dinner still be delayed?

8.5.* Ken Johnston, the data processing manager for Stanley Morgan Bank, is planning a project to install a new management information system. He now is ready to start the project and wishes to finish in 20 weeks. After identifying the 14 separate activities needed to carry out this project, as well as their precedence relationships and estimated durations (in weeks), Ken has constructed the following project network:

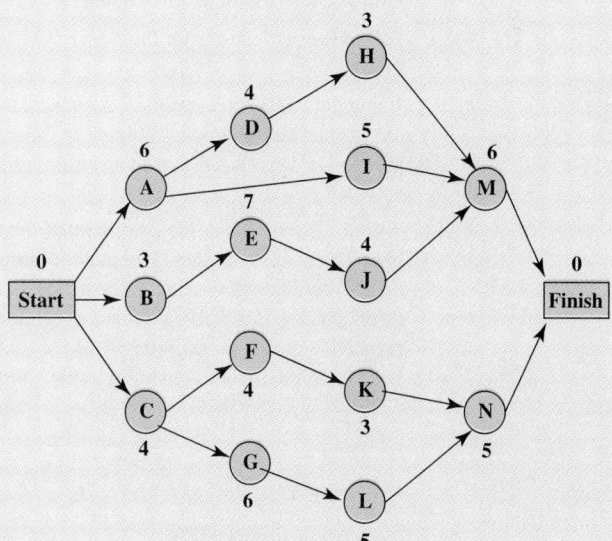

a. Find all the paths and path lengths through this project network. Which of these paths is a critical path?

b. Find the earliest times, latest times, and slack for each activity. Will Ken be able to meet his deadline if no delays occur?

c. Use the information from part *b* to determine which of the paths is a critical path. What does this tell Ken about which activities he should focus most of his attention on for staying on schedule?

d. Use the information from part *b* to determine what the duration of the project would be if the only delay is that activity I takes 2 extra weeks. What if the only delay is that activity H takes 2 extra weeks? What if the only delay is that activity J takes 2 extra weeks?

8.6. You are given the following information about a project consisting of six activities:

Activity	Immediate Predecessors	Estimated Duration (months)
A	—	5
B	—	1
C	B	2
D	A, C	4
E	A	6
F	D, E	3

a. Construct the project network for this project.

b. Find the earliest times, latest times, and slack for each activity. Which of the paths is a critical path?

c. If all other activities take the estimated amount of time, what is the maximum duration of activity D without delaying the completion of the project?

8.7. Reconsider the Reliable Construction Co. case study introduced in Section 8.1, including the complete project network obtained in Figure 8.7 at the end of Section 8.3. Note that the estimated durations of the activities in this figure turn out to be the same as the mean durations given in Table 8.4 (Section 8.4) when using the PERT three-estimate approach.

Now suppose that the *pessimistic* estimates in Table 8.4 are used instead to provide the estimated durations in Figure 8.7. Find the new earliest times, latest times, and slacks for all the activities in this project network. Also identify the critical path and the total estimated duration of the project. (Table 8.5 provides some clues.)

8.8.* Follow the instructions for Problem 8.7 except use the *optimistic* estimates in Table 8.4 instead.

8.9. Follow the instructions for Problem 8.7 except use the *crash times* given in Table 8.8 (Section 8.5) instead.

8.10.* Using the PERT three-estimate approach, the three estimates for one of the activities of a project are as follows: optimistic estimate = 30 days, most likely estimate = 36 days, pessimistic estimate = 48 days. What are the resulting estimates of the mean and variance of the duration of the activity?

8.11. Alfred Lowenstein is the president of the Research Division for Better Health, Inc., a major pharmaceutical company. His most important project coming up is the development of a new drug to combat AIDS. He has identified 10 groups in his division that will need to carry out different phases of this research-and-development project. Referring to the work to be done by the respective groups as activities A, B, . . ., J, the precedence relationships for when these groups need to do their work are shown in the following project network.

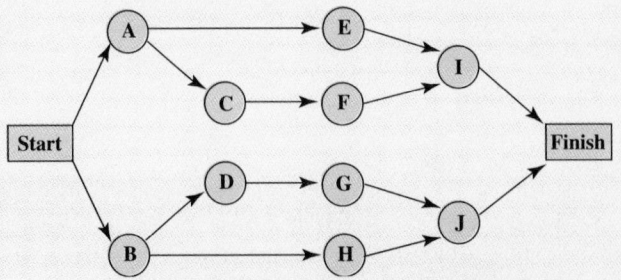

To beat the competition, Better Health's CEO has informed Alfred that he wants the drug ready within 22 months if possible.

Alfred knows very well that there is considerable uncertainty about how long each group will need to do its work. Using the PERT three-estimate approach, the manager of each group has provided a most likely estimate, an optimistic estimate, and a pessimistic estimate of the duration of that group's activity. Using PERT formulas, these estimates now have been converted into estimates of the mean and variance of the probability distribution of the duration of each group's activity, as given in the following table (after rounding to the nearest integer).

Activity	Duration (months)	
	Estimated Mean	Estimated Variance
A	4	5
B	6	10
C	4	8
D	3	6
E	8	12
F	4	6
G	3	5
H	7	14
I	5	8
J	5	7

a. Find the mean critical path for this project.

b. Use this mean critical path and Table 8.7 to find the approximate probability that the project will be completed within 22 months.

c. Now consider the other three paths through this project network. For each of these paths, use Table 8.7 to find the approximate probability that the path will be completed within 22 months.

d. What should Alfred tell his CEO about the likelihood that the drug will be ready within 22 months?

E*8.12. Reconsider Problem 8.11. For each of the 10 activities, here are the three estimates that led to the estimates of the mean and variance of the duration of the activity (rounded to the nearest integer) given in the table for Problem 8.11.

Activity	Time Required (Months)		
	Optimistic Estimate	Most Likely Estimate	Pessimistic Estimate
A	1.5	2	15
B	2	3.5	21
C	1	1.5	18
D	0.5	1	15
E	3	5	24
F	1	2	16
G	0.5	1	14
H	2.5	3.5	25
I	1	3	18
J	2	3	18

(Note how the great uncertainty in the duration of these research activities causes each pessimistic estimate to be several times larger than either the optimistic estimate or the most likely estimate.)

Now use the Excel template in your MS Courseware (as depicted in Figure 8.11) to help you carry out the instructions for Problem 8.11. In particular, enter the three estimates for each activity and the template immediately will display the estimates of the means and variances of the activity durations. After indicating each path of interest, the template also will display the approximate probability that the path will be completed within 22 months.

8.13. Bill Fredlund, president of Lincoln Log Construction, is considering placing a bid on a building project. Bill has determined that five tasks would need to be performed to carry out the project. Using the PERT three-estimate approach, Bill has obtained the estimates in the table below for how long these tasks will take. Also shown are the precedence relationships for these tasks.

	Time Required (Weeks)			
Task	Optimistic Estimate	Most Likely Estimate	Pessimistic Estimate	Immediate Predecessors
A	3	4	5	—
B	2	2	2	A
C	3	5	6	B
D	1	3	5	A
E	2	3	5	B, D

There is a penalty of $500,000 if the project is not completed in 11 weeks. Therefore, Bill is very interested in how likely it is that his company could finish the project in time.

    a. Construct the project network for this project.

E   *b.* Find the estimate of the mean and variance of the duration of each activity.

E   *c.* Find the mean critical path.

E   *d.* Find the approximate probability of completing the project within 11 weeks.

    e. Bill has concluded that the bid he would need to make to have a realistic chance of winning the contract would earn Lincoln Log Construction a profit of about $250,000 if the project is completed within 11 weeks. However, because of the penalty for missing this deadline, his company would lose about $250,000 if the project takes more than 11 weeks. Therefore, he wants to place the bid only if he has at least a 50 percent chance of meeting the deadline. How would you advise him?

8.14.* Sharon Lowe, vice president for marketing for the Electronic Toys Company, is about to begin a project to design an advertising campaign for a new line of toys. She wants the project completed within 57 days in time to launch the advertising campaign at the beginning of the Christmas season.

Sharon has identified the six activities (labeled A, B, . . . F) needed to execute this project. Considering the order in which these activities need to occur, she also has constructed the following project network.

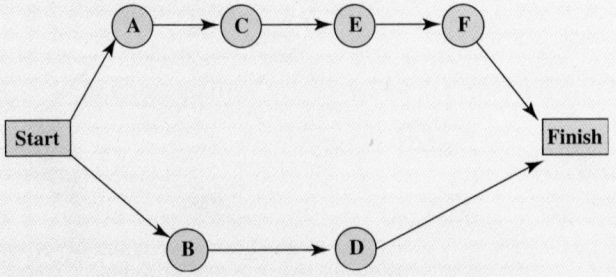

Using the PERT three-estimate approach, Sharon has obtained the following estimates of the duration of each activity.

	Time Required (days)		
Activity	**Optimistic Estimate**	**Most Likely Estimate**	**Pessimistic Estimate**
A	12	12	12
B	15	21	39
C	12	15	18
D	18	27	36
E	12	18	24
F	2	5	14

E   *a.* Find the estimate of the mean and variance of the duration of each activity.

   b. Find the mean critical path.

E   *c.* Use the mean critical path to find the approximate probability that the advertising campaign will be ready to launch within 57 days.

E   *d.* Now consider the other path through the project network. Find the approximate probability that this path will be completed within 57 days.

   e. Since these paths do not overlap, a better estimate of the probability that the project will finish within 57 days can be obtained as follows. The project will finish within 57 days if *both* paths are completed within 57 days. Therefore, the approximate probability that the project will finish within 57 days is the *product* of the probabilities found in parts *c* and *d*. Perform this calculation. What does this answer say about the accuracy of the standard procedure used in part *c?*

8.15.   The Lockhead Aircraft Co. is ready to begin a project to develop a new fighter airplane for the U.S. Air Force. The company's contract with the Department of Defense calls for project completion within 100 weeks, with penalties imposed for late delivery.

   The project involves 10 activities (labeled A, B, . . ., J), where their precedence relationships are shown in the following project network.

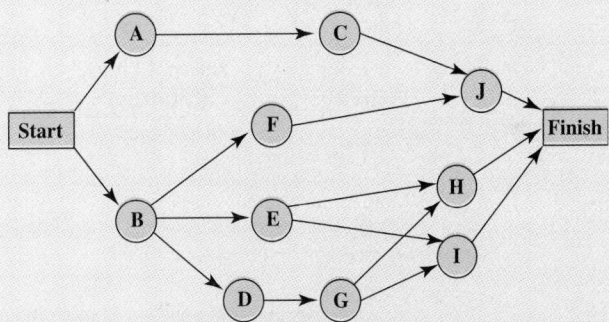

   Using the PERT three-estimate approach, the usual three estimates of the duration of each activity have been obtained as given below.

	Time Required (Weeks)		
Activity	**Optimistic Estimate**	**Most Likely Estimate**	**Pessimistic Estimate**
A	28	32	36
B	22	28	32
C	26	36	46
D	14	16	18
E	32	32	32
F	40	52	74
G	12	16	24
H	16	20	26
I	26	34	42
J	12	16	30

E   *a.* Find the estimate of the mean and variance of the duration of each activity.

      b. Find the mean critical path.

E   *c.* Find the approximate probability that the project will finish within 100 weeks.

      d. Is the approximate probability obtained in part *c* likely to be higher or lower than the true value?

8.16.   Label each of the following statements about the PERT three-estimate approach as true or false, and then justify your answer by referring to specific statements (with page citations) in the chapter.

      a. Activity durations are assumed to be no larger than the optimistic estimate and no smaller than the pessimistic estimate.

      b. Activity durations are assumed to have a normal distribution.

      c. The mean critical path is assumed to always require the minimum elapsed time of any path through the project network.

8.17.   The Tinker Construction Company is ready to begin a project that must be completed in 12 months. This project has four activities (A, B, C, D) with the project network shown below.

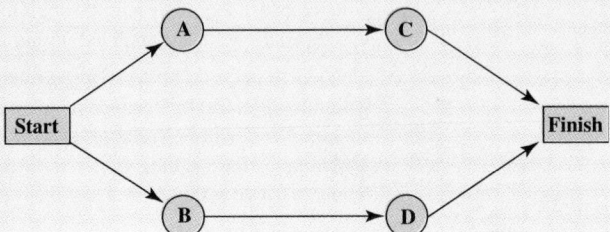

The project manager, Sean Murphy, has concluded that he cannot meet the deadline by performing all these activities in the normal way. Therefore, Sean has decided to use the CPM method of time–cost trade-offs to determine the most economical way of crashing the project to meet the deadline. He has gathered the following data for the four activities.

Activity	Normal Time (Months)	Crash Time (Months)	Normal Cost	Crash Cost
A	8	5	$25,000	$40,000
B	9	7	20,000	30,000
C	6	4	16,000	24,000
D	7	4	27,000	45,000

Use marginal cost analysis to solve the problem.

8.18.   Reconsider the Tinker Construction Co. problem presented in Problem 8.17. While in college, Sean Murphy took a management science course that devoted a month to linear programming, so Sean has decided to use linear programming to analyze this problem.

      a. Consider the upper path through the project network. Formulate a two-variable linear programming model (in algebraic form) for the problem of how to minimize the cost of performing this sequence of activities within 12 months. Use the graphical method to solve this model.

      b. Repeat part *a* for the lower path through the project network.

      c. Combine the models in parts *a* and *b* into a single complete linear programming model (in algebraic form) for the problem of how to minimize the cost of completing the project within 12 months. What must an optimal solution for this model be?

E*   *d.* Formulate and solve a spreadsheet model in the format of Figure 8.14 for this problem.

E*   *e.* Check the effect of changing the deadline by re-solving this model with a deadline of 11 months and then with a deadline of 13 months.

8.19.   Reconsider the Electronic Toys Co. problem presented in Problem 8.14. Sharon Lowe is concerned that there is a significant chance that the vitally important deadline of 57 days will not be met. Therefore, to make it virtually certain that the deadline will be met, she has decided to crash the project, using the CPM method of time–cost trade-offs to determine how to do this in the most economical way.

Sharon now has gathered the data needed to apply this method, as given below.

Activity	Normal Time (Days)	Crash Time (Days)	Normal Cost	Crash Cost
A	12	9	$210,000	$270,000
B	23	18	410,000	460,000
C	15	12	290,000	320,000
D	27	21	440,000	500,000
E	18	14	350,000	410,000
F	6	4	160,000	210,000

The normal times are the estimates of the means obtained from the original data in Problem 8.14. The mean critical path gives an estimate that the project will finish in 51 days. However, Sharon knows from the earlier analysis that some of the pessimistic estimates are far larger than the means, so the project duration might be considerably longer than 51 days. Therefore, to better ensure that the project will finish within 57 days, she has decided to require that the estimated project duration based on means (as used throughout the CPM analysis) must not exceed 47 days.

a. Consider the lower path through the project network. Use marginal cost analysis to determine the most economical way of reducing the length of this path to 47 days.

b. Repeat part *a* for the upper path through the project network. What is the total crashing cost for the optimal way of decreasing estimated project duration to 47 days?

E*   c. Formulate and solve a spreadsheet model that fits linear programming for this problem.

8.20.* Good Homes Construction Company is about to begin the construction of a large new home. The company's president, Michael Dean, is currently planning the schedule for this project. Michael has identified the five major activities (labeled A, B, . . ., E) that will need to be performed according to the following project network.

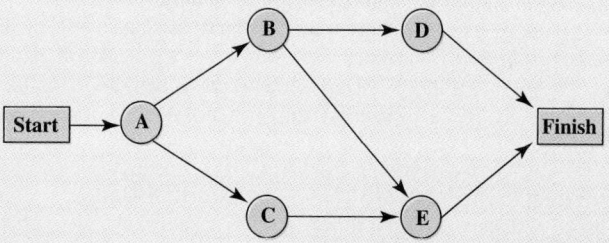

He also has gathered the following data about the normal point and crash point for each of these activities.

Activity	Normal Time (Weeks)	Crash Time (Weeks)	Normal Cost	Crash Cost
A	3	2	$54,000	$60,000
B	4	3	62,000	65,000
C	5	2	66,000	70,000
D	3	1	40,000	43,000
E	4	2	75,000	80,000

These costs reflect the company's direct costs for the material, equipment, and direct labor required to perform the activities. In addition, the company incurs indirect project costs such as supervision and other customary overhead costs, interest charges for capital tied up, and so forth. Michael estimates that these indirect costs run $5,000 per week. He wants to minimize the overall cost of the project. Therefore, to save some of these indirect costs, Michael concludes that he should shorten the project by doing some crashing to the extent that the crashing cost for each additional week saved is less than $5,000.

a. To prepare for analyzing the effect of crashing, find the earliest times, latest times, and slack for each activity when they are done in the normal way. Also identify the corresponding critical path(s) and project duration.

b. Use marginal cost analysis to determine which activities should be crashed and by how much to minimize the overall cost of the project. Under this plan, what is the duration and cost of each activity? How much money is saved by doing this crashing?

E*   c. Now formulate a spreadsheet model that fits linear programming and repeatedly solve it to do part b by shortening the deadline one week at a time from the project duration found in part a.

E*8.21.*   21st Century Studios is about to begin the production of its most important (and most expensive) movie of the year. The movie's producer, Dusty Hoffmer, has decided to use PERT/CPM to help plan and control this key project. He has identified the eight major activities (labeled A, B, . . ., H) required to produce the movie. Their precedence relationships are shown in the project network below.

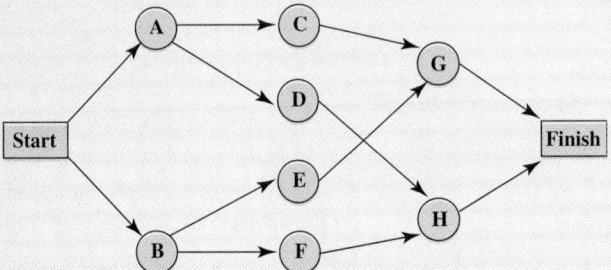

Dusty now has learned that another studio also will be coming out with a blockbuster movie during the middle of the upcoming summer, just when his movie was to be released. This would be very unfortunate timing. Therefore, he and the top management of 21st Century Studios have concluded that they must accelerate production of their movie and bring it out at the beginning of the summer (15 weeks from now) to establish it as *the* movie of the year. Although this will require substantially increasing an already huge budget, management feels that this will pay off in much larger box office earnings both nationally and internationally.

Dusty now wants to determine the least costly way of meeting the new deadline 15 weeks hence. Using the CPM method of time–cost trade-offs, he has obtained the following data.

Activity	Normal Time (weeks)	Crash Time (weeks)	Normal Cost (millions)	Crash Cost (millions)
A	5	3	$20	$30
B	3	2	10	20
C	4	2	16	24
D	6	3	25	43
E	5	4	22	30
F	7	4	30	48
G	9	5	25	45
H	8	6	30	44

Formulate and solve a spreadsheet model that fits linear programming for this problem.

E*8.22.   Reconsider the Lockhead Aircraft Co. problem presented in Problem 8.15 regarding a project to develop a new fighter airplane for the U.S. Air Force. Management is extremely concerned that current plans for this project have a substantial likelihood (roughly a probability of 0.5) of missing the deadline imposed in the Department of Defense contract to finish within 100 weeks. The company has a bad record of missing deadlines, and management is worried that doing so again would jeopardize obtaining future contracts for defense work. Furthermore, management would like to avoid the hefty penalties for missing the deadline in the current contract. Therefore, the decision has been made to crash the project using the CPM method of time–cost trade-offs to determine how to do this in the most economical way. The data needed to apply this method are given below.

Activity	Normal Time (Weeks)	Crash Time (Weeks)	Normal Cost (Millions)	Crash Cost (Millions)
A	32	28	$160	$180
B	28	25	125	146
C	36	31	170	210
D	16	13	60	72
E	32	27	135	160
F	54	47	215	257
G	17	15	90	96
H	20	17	120	132
I	34	30	190	226
J	18	16	80	84

These normal times are the rounded estimates of the means obtained from the original data in Problem 8.15. The corresponding mean critical path provides an estimate that the project will finish in 100 weeks. However, management understands well that the high variability of activity durations means that the actual duration of the project may be much longer. Therefore, the decision is made to require that the estimated project duration based on means (as used throughout the CPM analysis) must not exceed 92 weeks.

Formulate and solve a spreadsheet model that fits linear programming for this problem.

8.23. Reconsider Problem 8.20 involving the Good Homes Construction Co. project to construct a large new home. Michael Dean now has generated the plan for how to crash this project (as given as an answer in the back of the book). Since this plan causes all three paths through the project network to be critical paths, the earliest start time for each activity also is its latest start time.

Michael has decided to use PERT/Cost to schedule and control project costs.

a. Find the earliest start time for each activity and the earliest finish time for the completion of the project.

b. Construct a table like Table 8.11 to show the budget for this project.

c. Construct a table like Figure 8.16 (by hand) to show the schedule of costs based on earliest times for each of the eight weeks of the project.

E* d. Now use the corresponding Excel template in your MS Courseware to do parts *b* and *c* on a single spreadsheet.

e. After four weeks, activity A has been completed (with an actual cost of $65,000) and activity B has just now been completed (with an actual cost of $55,000), but activity C is just 33 percent completed (with an actual cost to date of $44,000). Construct a PERT/Cost report after week 4. Where should Michael concentrate his efforts to improve cost performances?

8.24.* The P-H Microchip Co. needs to undertake a major maintenance and renovation program to overhaul and modernize its facilities for wafer fabrication. This project involves six activities (labeled A, B, . . ., F), with the precedence relationships shown in the following network.

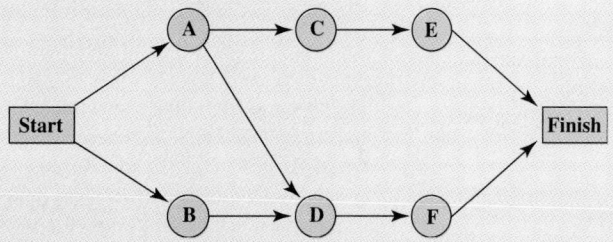

The estimated durations and costs of these activities are shown on the next page.

Activity	Estimated Duration (Weeks)	Estimated Cost
A	6	$420,000
B	2	180,000
C	4	540,000
D	5	360,000
E	7	590,000
F	9	630,000

  a. Find the earliest times, latest times, and slack for each activity. What is the earliest finish time for the completion of the project?

E* *b.* Use the Excel template for PERT/Cost in your MS Courseware to display the budget and schedule of costs based on earliest start times for this project on a single spreadsheet.

E* *c.* Repeat part *b* except based on latest start times.

  d. Use these spreadsheets to draw a figure like Figure 8.18 to show the schedule of cumulative project costs when all activities begin at their earliest start times or at their latest start times.

  e. After four weeks, activity B has been completed (with an actual cost of $200,000), activity A is 50 percent completed (with an actual cost to date of $200,000), and activity D is 50 percent completed (with an actual cost to date of $210,000). Construct a PERT/Cost report after week 4. Where should the project manager focus her attention to improve cost performance?

8.25. Reconsider Problem 8.5 involving a project at Stanley Morgan Bank to install a new management information system. Ken Johnston already has obtained the earliest times, latest times, and slack for each activity. He now is getting ready to use PERT/Cost to schedule and control the costs for this project. The estimated durations and costs of the various activities are given in the following table.

Activity	Estimated Duration (Weeks)	Estimated Cost
A	6	$180,000
B	3	75,000
C	4	120,000
D	4	140,000
E	7	175,000
F	4	80,000
G	6	210,000
H	3	45,000
I	5	125,000
J	4	100,000
K	3	60,000
L	5	50,000
M	6	90,000
N	5	150,000

E* *a.* Use the Excel template for PERT/Cost in your MS Courseware to display the budget and schedule of costs based on earliest start times for this project on a single spreadsheet.

E* *b.* Repeat part *a* except based on latest start times.

  c. Use these spreadsheets to draw a figure like Figure 8.18 to show the schedule of cumulative project costs when all activities begin at their earliest start times or at their latest start times.

  d. After eight weeks, activities A, B, and C have been completed with actual costs of $190,000, $70,000, and $150,000, respectively. Activities D, E, F, G, and I are under way, with the percent completed being 40 percent, 50 percent, 60 percent, 25 percent, and 20 percent, respectively. Their actual costs to date are $70,000, $100,000, $45,000, $50,000, and $35,000, respectively. Construct a PERT/Cost report after week 8. Which activities should Ken Johnston investigate to try to improve their cost performances?

Case 8-1

Steps to Success

Janet Richards fixes her eyes on those of her partner Gilbert Baker and says firmly, "Alright. Let's do it."

And with those words, InterCat, a firm founded by Janet and Gilbert that specializes in the design and maintenance of Internet catalogues for small consumer businesses, will be going public. InterCat employs 30 individuals, with the majority of them computer programmers. Many of the employees have followed the high-technology market very closely and have decided that since high-technology firms are more understood and valued in the United States than in other countries, InterCat should issue its stock only in the United States. Five million shares of InterCat stock will comprise this new issue.

The task the company has ahead of itself is certainly daunting. Janet and Gilbert know that many steps have to be completed in the process of making an initial public offering. They also know that they need to complete the process within 28 weeks because they need the new capital fairly soon to ensure that InterCat has the resources to capture valuable new business from its competitors and continue growing. They also value a speedy initial public offering because they believe that the window of opportunity for obtaining a good stock price is presently wide open—the public is wild about shopping on the Internet, and few companies offering Web page design services have gone public.

Because the 28-week deadline is breathing down their necks, Janet and Gilbert decide to map the steps in the process of making an initial public offering. They list each major activity that needs to be completed, the activities that directly precede each activity, the time needed to complete each activity, and the cost of each activity. This list is shown below.

Activity	Immediate Predecessors	Time (Weeks)	Cost
Evaluate the prestige of each potential underwriter.		3	$ 8,000
Select a syndicate of underwriters.	Evaluate the prestige of each potential underwriter.	1.5	4,500
Negotiate the commitment of each member of the syndicate.	Select a syndicate of underwriters.	2	9,000
Negotiate the spread* for each member of the syndicate.	Select a syndicate of underwriters.	3	12,000
Prepare the registration statement, including the proposed financing and information about the firm's history, existing business, and plans for the future.	Negotiate both the commitment and spread for each member of the syndicate.	5	50,000
Submit the registration statement to the Securities and Exchange Commission (SEC).	Prepare the registration statement.	1	1,000
Make presentations to institutional investors and develop the interest of potential buyers.	Submit the registration statement to the SEC.	6	25,000
Distribute the preliminary prospectus, affectionately termed the red herring.	Submit the registration statement to the SEC.	3	15,000
Calculate the issue price.	Submit the registration statement to the SEC.	5	12,000
Receive deficiency memorandum from the SEC.	Submit the registration statement to the SEC.	3	0
Amend the registration statement and resubmit it to the SEC.	Receive deficiency memorandum from the SEC.	1	6,000
Receive registration confirmation from the SEC.	Amend the registration statement and resubmit it to the SEC.	2	0
Confirm that the new issue complies with the "blue sky" laws of each state.	Make presentations to institutional investors and develop the interest of potential buyers. Distribute the preliminary prospectus, affectionately termed the red herring. Calculate the issue price. Receive registration confirmation from the SEC.	1	5,000
Appoint a registrar.	Receive registration confirmation from the SEC.	3	12,000
Appoint a transfer agent.	Receive registration confirmation from the SEC.	3.5	13,000
Issue final prospectus that includes the final offer price and any amendments to all purchasers offered securities through the mail.	Confirm that the new issue complies with the "blue sky" laws of each state. Appoint a registrar and transfer agent.	4.5	40,000
Phone interested buyers.	Confirm that the new issue complies with the "blue sky" laws of each state. Appoint a registrar and transfer agent.	4	9,000

*The spread is the payment an underwriter receives for services.

Janet and Gilbert present the list of steps to the employees of InterCat. The head of the finance department, Leslie Grey, is fresh out of business school. She remembers the various project management tools she has learned in business school and suggests that Janet and Gilbert use PERT/CPM analysis to understand where their priorities should lie.

a. Draw the project network for completing the initial public offering of InterCat stock. How long is the initial public offering process? What are the critical steps in the process?

b. How would the change in the following activities affect the time to complete the initial public offering? Please evaluate each change independently.

    i. Some members of the syndicate are playing hardball. Therefore, the time it takes to negotiate the commitment of each member of the syndicate increases from two to three weeks.

    ii. The underwriters are truly math geniuses. Therefore, the time it takes to calculate the issue price decreases to four weeks.

    iii. Whoa! The SEC found many deficiencies in the initial registration statement. The underwriters must therefore spend 2.5 weeks amending the statement and resubmitting it to the SEC.

    iv. The new issue does not comply with the "blue sky" laws of a handful of states. The time it takes to edit the issue for each state to ensure compliance increases to four weeks.

c. Janet and Gilbert hear through the grapevine that their most fierce competitor, Soft Sales, is also planning to go public. They fear that if InterCat does not complete its initial public offering before Soft Sales, the price investors are willing to pay for InterCat stock will drop since investors will perceive Soft Sales to be a stronger, more organized company. Janet and Gilbert therefore decide that they want to complete the process of issuing new stock within 22 weeks. They think such a goal is possible if they throw more resources—workers and money—into some activities. They list the activities that can be shortened, the time the activity will take when it is fully shortened, and the cost of shortening the activity this much. They also conclude that partially shortening each activity listed below is possible and will give a time reduction and cost proportional to the amounts when fully shortened.

Activity	Time (Weeks)	Cost
Evaluate the prestige of each potential underwriter.	1.5	$14,000
Select a syndicate of underwriters.	0.5	8,000
Prepare the registration statement, including the proposed financing and information about the firm's history, existing business, and plans for the future.	4	95,000
Make presentations to institutional investors and develop the interest of potential buyers.	4	60,000
Distribute the preliminary prospectus, affectionately termed the red herring.	2	22,000
Calculate the issue price.	3.5	31,000
Amend the registration statement and resubmit it to the SEC.	0.5	9,000
Confirm that the new issue complies with the "blue sky" laws of each state.	0.5	8,300
Appoint a registrar.	1.5	19,000
Appoint a transfer agent.	1.5	21,000
Issue final prospectus that includes the final offer price and any amendments to all purchasers offered securities through the mail.	2	99,000
Phone interested buyers.	1.5	20,000

How can InterCat meet the new deadline set by Janet and Gilbert at minimum cost?

d. Janet and Gilbert learn that the investment bankers are two-timing scoundrels! They are also serving as lead underwriters for the Soft Sales new issue! To keep the deal with InterCat, the bankers agree to let Janet and Gilbert in on a little secret. Soft Sales has been forced to delay its public issue because the company's records are disorganized and incomplete. Given this new information, Janet and Gilbert decide that they can be more lenient on the initial public offering timeframe. They want to complete the process of issuing new stock within 24 weeks instead of 22 weeks. Assume that the cost and time to complete the appointment of the registrar and transfer agent are the same as in part *c*. How can InterCat meet this new deadline set by Janet and Gilbert at minimum cost?

Case 8-2

"School's Out Forever . . ."

Alice Cooper

Brent Bonnin begins his senior year of college filled with excitement and a twinge of fear. The excitement stems from his anticipation of being done with it all—professors, exams, problem sets, grades, group meetings, all-nighters . . . The list could go on and on. The fear stems from the fact that he is graduating in December and has only four months to find a job.

Brent is a little unsure about how he should approach the job search. During his sophomore and junior years, he had certainly heard seniors talking about their strategies for finding the perfect job, and he knows that he should first visit the Campus Career Planning Center to devise a search plan.

On September 1, the first day of school, he walks through the doors of the Campus Career Planning Center and meets Elizabeth Merryweather, a recent graduate overflowing with energy and comforting smiles. Brent explains to Elizabeth that since he is graduating in December and plans to begin work in January, he wants to leave all of November and December open for interviews. Such a plan means that by October 31 he has to have all his preliminary materials, such as cover letters and résumés, submitted to the companies where he wants to work.

Elizabeth recognizes that Brent has to follow a very tight schedule, if he wants to meet his goal within the next 60 days. She suggests that the two of them sit down together and decide the major milestones that need to be completed in the job search process. Elizabeth and Brent list the 19 major milestones. For each of the 19 milestones, they identify the other milestones that must be accomplished directly before Brent can begin this next milestone. They also estimate the time needed to complete each milestone. The list is shown below.

Milestone	Milestones Directly Preceding Each Milestone	Time to Complete Each Milestone
A. Complete and submit an online registration form to the career center.	None.	2 days (This figure includes the time needed for the career center to process the registration form.)
B. Attend the career center orientation to learn about the resources available at the center and the campus recruiting process.	None.	5 days (This figure includes the time Brent must wait before the career center hosts an orientation.)
C. Write an initial résumé that includes all academic and career experiences.	None.	7 days
D. Search the Internet to find job opportunities available outside of campus recruiting.	None.	10 days
E. Attend the company presentations hosted during the fall to understand the cultures of companies and to meet with company representatives.	None.	25 days
F. Review the industry resources available at the career center to understand the career and growth opportunities available in each industry. Take a career test to understand the career that provides the best fit with your skills and interests. Contact alumni listed in the career center directories to discuss the nature of a variety of jobs.	*A* Complete and submit an online registration form to the career center. *B* Attend the career center orientation.	7 days

(continued)

Milestone	Milestones Directly Preceding Each Milestone	Time to Complete Each Milestone
G. Attend a mock interview hosted by the career center to practice interviewing and to learn effective interviewing styles.	A Complete and submit an online registration form to the career center. B Attend the career center orientation. Write the initial résumé.	4 days (This figure includes the time that elapses between the day that Brent signs up for the interview and the day that the interview takes place.)
H. Submit the initial résumé to the career center for review.	A Complete and submit an online registration form to the career center. B Attend the career center orientation. C Write the initial résumé	2 days (This figure includes the time the career center needs to review the résumé.)
I. Meet with a résumé expert to discuss improvements to the initial résumé.	H Submit the initial résumé to the career center for review.	1 day
J. Revise the initial résumé.	I Meet with a résumé expert to discuss improvements.	4 days
K. Attend the career fair to gather company literature, speak to company representatives, and submit résumés.	J Revise the initial résumé.	1 day
L. Search campus job listings to identify the potential jobs that fit your qualifications and interests.	F Review the industry resources, take the career test, and contact alumni.	5 days
M. Decide which jobs you will pursue given the job opportunities you found on the Internet, at the career fair, and through the campus job listings.	D Search the Internet. Search the L campus job listings. Attend the K career fair.	3 days
N. Bid to obtain job interviews with companies that recruit through the campus career center and have open interview schedules.*	M Decide which jobs you will pursue.	3 days
O. Write cover letters to seek jobs with companies that either do not recruit through the campus career center or recruit through the campus career center but have closed interview schedules.** Tailor each cover letter to the culture of each company.	M Decide which jobs you will pursue. E Attend company presentations.	10 days
P. Submit the cover letters to the career center for review.	O Write the cover letters.	4 days (This figure includes the time the career center needs to review the cover letters.)
Q. Revise the cover letters.	P Submit the cover letters to the career center for review.	4 days
R. For the companies that are not recruiting through the campus career center, mail the cover letter and résumé to the company's recruiting department.	Q Revise the cover letters.	6 days (This figure includes the time needed to print and package the application materials and the time needed for the materials to reach the companies.)
S. For the companies that recruit through the campus career center but that hold closed interview schedules, drop the cover letter and résumé at the career center.	Q Revise the cover letters.	2 days (This figure includes the time needed to print and package the application materials.)

*An open interview schedule occurs when the company does not select the candidates that it wants to interview. Any candidate may interview, but since the company has only a limited number of interview slots, interested candidates must bid points (out of their total allocation of points) for the interviews. The candidates with the highest bids win the interview slots.

**Closed interview schedules occur when a company requires candidates to submit their cover letters, résumés, and test scores so that the company is able to select the candidates it wants to interview.

In the evening after his meeting with Elizabeth, Brent meets with his buddies at the college coffee house to chat about their summer endeavors. Brent also tells his friends about the meeting he had earlier with Elizabeth. He describes the long to-do list he and Elizabeth developed and says that he is really worried about keeping track of all the major milestones and getting his job search organized. One of his friends reminds him of the cool management science class they all took together in the first semester of Brent's junior year and how they had learned about some techniques to organize large projects. Brent remembers this class fondly since he was able to use a number of the methods he studied in that class in his last summer job.

a. Draw the project network for completing all milestones before the interview process. If everything stays on schedule, how long will it take Brent until he can start with the interviews? What are the critical steps in the process?

b. Brent realizes that there is a lot of uncertainty in the times it will take him to complete some of the milestones. He expects to get really busy during his senior year, in particular since he is taking a demanding course load. Also, students sometimes have to wait quite a while before they get appointments with the counselors at the career center. In addition to the list estimating the most likely times that he and Elizabeth wrote down, he makes a list of optimistic and pessimistic estimates of how long the various milestones might take.

Milestone	Optimistic Estimate (Days)	Pessimistic Estimate (Days)
A	1	4
B	3	10
C	5	14
D	7	12
E	20	30
F	5	12
G	3	8
H	1	6
I	1	1
J	3	6
K	1	1
L	3	10
M	2	4
N	2	8
O	3	12
P	2	7
Q	3	9
R	4	10
S	1	3

How long will it take Brent to get everything done under the worst-case scenario? How long will it take if all his optimistic estimates are correct?

c. Determine the mean critical path for Brent's job search process. What is the variance of the project duration?

d. Give a rough estimate of the probability that Brent will be done within 60 days.

e. Brent realizes that he has made a serious mistake in his calculations so far. He cannot schedule the career fair to fit his schedule. Brent read in the campus newspaper that the fair has been set 24 days from today on September 25th. Draw a revised project network that takes into account this complicating fact.

f. What is the mean critical path for the new network? What is the probability that Brent will complete his project within 60 days?

Learning objectives

After completing this chapter, you should be able to

1. Explain how integer programming differs from linear programming.

2. Describe how general integer programming problems arise.

3. Formulate a general integer programming model from a description of the problem.

4. Describe how binary decision variables are used to represent yes-or-no decisions.

5. Use binary decision variables to formulate constraints for mutually exclusive alternatives and contingent decisions.

6. Formulate a binary integer programming model from a description of the problem.

7. List some areas where important applications of binary integer programming are occurring.

8. Describe the role of auxiliary binary variables.

9. Formulate basic binary integer programming models where auxiliary binary variables are needed.

Chapter **Nine**

Integer Programming

Integer programming extends linear programming to require integer solutions.

This chapter introduces another important management science technique, called *integer programming,* that is closely related to linear programming. In fact, the kind of model that integer programming uses to represent managerial problems is identical to a linear programming model, except that it has the additional restriction that some or all of the decision variables must have integer values $(0, 1, 2, \ldots)$.

One of the characteristics of a linear programming model is that the decision variables are allowed to have any values, including fractional values (e.g., $2\frac{3}{4}$ or 4.1353), that satisfy the various constraints. A decision variable might turn out to have an integer value in the optimal solution but, in most cases,[1] this will be only a coincidence.

In some applications, the decision variables will make sense *only* if they have integer values. For example, it may be necessary to assign people, machines, or vehicles to activities in integer quantities, so the decision variables representing these quantities need to be *integer variables* (variables restricted to integer values). This is a common kind of situation that integer programming addresses.

Integer programming problems fall into two broad categories. One is *general integer programming,* which allows at least some of the integer variables to have *any* integer values that satisfy the functional and nonnegativity constraints of the model. The other is *binary integer programming,* which restricts the integer variables to just two values, either 0 or 1. These 0-1 variables, called *binary variables,* provide great flexibility for modeling managerial problems involving a number of interrelated *yes-or-no decisions.* Each yes-or-no decision would involve some managerial option in which there are only two possible choices: yes, go ahead with this option, or no, decline this option. A binary decision variable then is assigned a value of 1 for choosing yes and a value of 0 for choosing no. A binary integer programming model will consider many such options simultaneously (with a binary decision variable for each one), where the overall objective is to choose the best combination of options.

Binary (0-1) variables are used to represent yes-or-no decisions.

Section 9.1 focuses on general integer programming. The remainder of the chapter then is devoted to binary integer programming, including a case study, a survey of some of its applications, and two sections on the formulation of binary integer programming models. In addition, a supplement to this chapter entitled *Some Perspectives on Solving Binary Integer Programming Problems* is provided on the CD-ROM.

9.1 GENERAL INTEGER PROGRAMMING

A general integer programming problem is simply a variation of a linear programming problem where some or all of the decision variables are **integer variables** (variables that are restricted to integer values). In most cases, these integer variables are allowed to have any integer values that satisfy the functional and nonnegativity constraints. (Restricting certain integer variables to the values 0 and 1 is allowed but, in contrast to binary programming, at least some of the integer variables don't have this restriction.) Such problems are quite common.

---

[1]The one exception is that, as mentioned in Sections 6.2 and 7.1, certain special types of linear programming problems possess an integer solutions property that guarantees an optimal solution with integer values.

For example, consider the linear programming model formulated for the Wyndor Glass Co. product-mix problem in Chapter 2. This would have been a general integer programming model if the two decision variables, D and W, had represented the total production quantity of doors and windows, respectively, instead of the production rates. Because these production quantities would need to be whole numbers, D and W would have to be restricted to integer values.

One example of an actual application of general integer programming is provided by the first-prize winner of the 1988 Franz Edelman Award for Management Science Achievement. This prestigious prize was awarded for a management science study done for the **San Francisco Police Department,** as described in the January–February 1989 issue of *Interfaces.* This study resulted in the development of a computerized system for optimally scheduling and deploying police patrol officers. The new system provided annual savings of $11 million, an annual $3 million increase in traffic citation revenues, and a 20 percent improvement in response times. The main decision variables in the mathematical model were the number of officers to schedule to go on duty at each of the shift start times. Since this number had to be an integer, these decision variables were restricted to having integer values.

Here is another example where integer decision variables arise.

An Example: The TBA Airlines Problem

TBA Airlines is a small regional company that specializes in short flights in small airplanes. The company has been doing well and management has decided to expand its operations.

The basic issue facing management now is whether to purchase more small airplanes to add some new short flights or to start moving into the national market by purchasing some large airplanes for new cross-country flights (or both). Many factors will go into management's final decision, but the most important one is which strategy is likely to be most profitable.

The first row of Table 9.1 shows the estimated net annual profit (inclusive of capital recovery costs) from each type of airplane purchased. The second row gives the purchase cost per airplane and also notes that the total amount of capital available for airplane purchases is $100 million. The third row records the fact that management does not want to purchase more than two small airplanes because of limited possibilities for adding lucrative short flights, whereas they have not specified a maximum number for large airplanes (other than that imposed by the limited capital available).

How many airplanes of each type should be purchased to maximize the total net annual profit?

Since only two decisions need to be made, this question can be addressed graphically. Before turning to a spreadsheet, we will use this approach first to add graphical insight into the comparisons between linear programming and integer programming.

A Linear Programming Formulation of the TBA Airlines Problem

Let us begin analyzing this problem by attempting to use a linear programming formulation. To apply the graphical method, we will formulate the model in algebraic form.

The decisions to be made are

S = Number of small airplanes to purchase

L = Number of large airplanes to purchase

TABLE 9.1
Data for the TBA
Airlines Problem

	Small Airplane	Large Airplane	Capital Available
Net annual profit per airplane	$1 million	$5 million	
Purchase cost per airplane	$5 million	$50 million	$100 million
Maximum purchase quantity	2	No maximum	

FIGURE 9.1

Applying the graphical method to the linear programming model for the TBA Airlines problem yields $(S, L) = (2, 1.8)$ as the optimal solution. Rounding $L = 1.8$ down then gives $(2, 1)$ as a feasible integer solution.

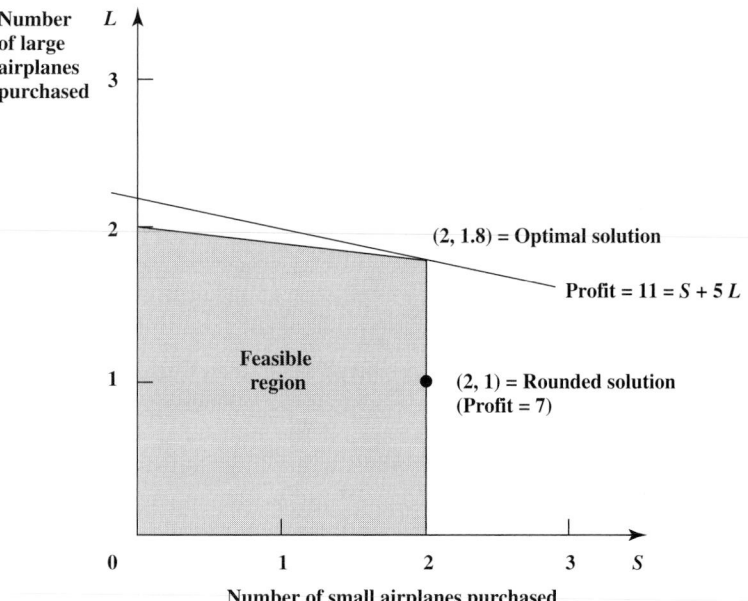

The constraints on these decisions are the limited capital available and the maximum purchase quantity of small airplanes (along with nonnegativity constraints). The objective is to maximize the total net annual profit. Therefore, using units of millions of dollars, the data in Table 9.1 provide the following linear programming model:

$$\text{Maximize} \quad \text{Profit} = S + 5L$$

subject to

$$5S + 50L \leq 100$$
$$S \quad \leq \quad 2$$

and

$$S \geq 0 \qquad L \geq 0$$

Applying the graphical method, Figure 9.1 shows the optimal solution for this model, namely,

$S = 2$:   Purchase 2 small airplanes

$L = 1.8$:   Purchase 1.8 large airplanes

for a total net profit of $11 million.

It is, of course, impossible for the company to purchase a fractional number of airplanes, so this solution is of little use for the real problem. About all we can do with it is round down the fractional value (1.8) to obtain the following *rounded solution:*

$S = 2$:   Purchase 2 small airplanes

$L = 1$:   Purchase 1 large airplane

Rounding an optimal linear programming solution may not give an optimal integer solution.

for a total net annual profit of $7 million. However, there is no guarantee that this rounded solution is the *optimal integer solution.* (In fact, you soon will see that it is far from optimal.)

What we need to do is add constraints to the model that restrict the values of the decision variables to *integer values* and then solve for the optimal solution for this *integer programming model.* This is exactly what we will do after highlighting the assumption of linear programming that is being violated by this problem.

The TBA Airlines Problem Violates the Divisibility Assumption of Linear Programming

One of the basic assumptions of linear programming is the following.

> **Divisibility Assumption of Linear Programming:** Decision variables in a linear programming model are allowed to have *any* values, including *fractional* values, that satisfy the functional and nonnegativity constraints. Thus, these variables are *not* restricted to just integer values. Since each decision variable represents the level of some activity, it is being assumed that the activities can be run at *fractional levels*. If this assumption is violated because the real problem requires that the decision variables have integer values, then *integer programming* should be used instead of linear programming.

For the TBA Airlines problem, the activities involve the purchase of airplanes of different types, so the level of each activity is the number of airplanes of that type purchased. Since the number purchased must have an integer value, the divisibility assumption is violated.

There are some applications where linear programming can be used as a reasonable approximation even though the divisibility assumption is violated. This would be the case, for example, when the variable values are very big and, because of inevitable imprecision in the model, there is a bit of flexibility to violate the constraints slightly. Rounding then becomes a perfectly practical procedure. Thus, if the value of a variable were, say, $L = 101.8$, it should be fine to simply round it to the nearest integer, $L = 102$.

However, with $L = 1.8$ in the TBA Airlines problem, it is a different story. Rounding to $L = 2$ would require spending $10 million more capital than is available, which is unacceptable to TBA management. Therefore, we now abandon linear programming and turn to integer programming to deal with this problem.

An Integer Programming Formulation of the TBA Airlines Problem

The integer programming formulation of this problem is exactly the same as the linear programming formulation except for one crucial difference—constraints are added that require the decision variables to have integer values. Therefore, the algebraic form of the integer programming model is

$$\text{Maximize} \quad \text{Profit} = S + 5L$$

subject to

$$5S + 50L \leq 100$$
$$S \qquad \leq \quad 2$$

and

$$S \geq 0 \qquad L \geq 0$$

$$S, L \text{ are integers}$$

The original linear programming model, without the addition of the last row above, is referred to as the **LP relaxation** of this integer programming problem. Its feasible region shown in Figure 9.1 is reproduced as the shaded region in Figure 9.2.

However, the only feasible solutions for the integer programming problem are the *integer solutions* (shown as dots in Figure 9.2) that lie within this shaded region, namely, $(0, 0)$, $(1, 0)$, $(2, 0)$, $(0, 1)$, $(1, 1)$, $(2, 1)$, and $(0, 2)$. The *optimal solution* (i.e., the best of these seven feasible solutions) can be found by the following convenient method.

This graphical method is the same as for linear programming except the last step.

> **Graphical Method for Integer Programming:** When an integer programming problem has just two decision variables, its optimal solution can be found by applying the *graphical method for linear programming* (see Section 2.5) with just one change at the end. Thus, we begin as usual by graphing the feasible region for the LP relaxation, determining the slope of objective function lines, and moving a straight edge with this slope through this feasible region in the direction of improving values of the objective function. However, rather than stopping at the last instant that the straight edge still passes through this feasible region, we now stop at the last

FIGURE 9.2

Applying the graphical method for integer programming to the TBA Airlines problem yields $(S, L) = (0, 2)$ as the optimal solution.

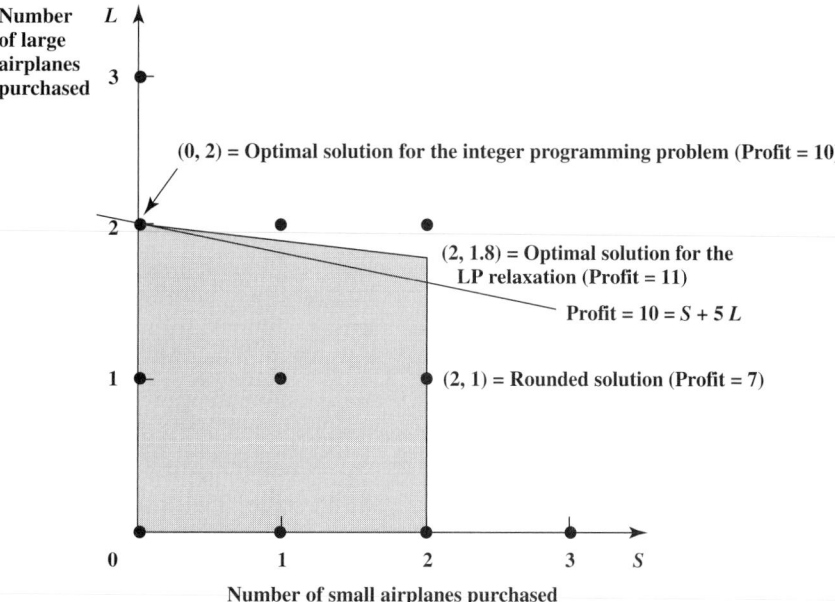

Number of large airplanes purchased L

(0, 2) = Optimal solution for the integer programming problem (Profit = 10)

(2, 1.8) = Optimal solution for the LP relaxation (Profit = 11)

Profit = 10 = $S + 5L$

(2, 1) = Rounded solution (Profit = 7)

Number of small airplanes purchased S

instant that the straight edge passes through an integer point that lies within this feasible region. This integer point is the optimal solution.

Figure 9.2 shows the result of applying this method to the TBA Airlines problem. When Profit = 0, the objective function line passes through the integer point (0, 0). When Profit (in millions of dollars) is increased in turn to 1, 2, 5, 6, and 7, the objective function line moves up to pass through the integer points (1, 0), (2, 0), (0, 1), (1, 1), and (2, 1), respectively. Finally, when Profit is increased to 10, the objective function line passes through the last feasible point (0, 2). Therefore, the optimal solution is

$S = 0$:   Purchase no small airplanes

$L = 2$:   Purchase 2 large airplanes

for a total net annual profit of $10 million.

Note in Figure 9.2 how far away this optimal solution is from the optimal solution for the LP relaxation. We cannot reach the former solution simply by rounding the latter one, or even by moving to any of the four dots shown in Figure 9.2 that are closest to the latter solution. Therefore, first finding the optimal solution for the LP relaxation has done us little good in finding the optimal solution for the real problem, the integer programming problem.

Another interesting feature of this example is how markedly inferior the rounded solution in Figure 9.2 is to the optimal solution for the integer programming problem. Although the latter solution yields a total net annual profit of $10 million, the rounded solution would only provide $7 million per year. Rounding cannot be relied on to find an optimal solution, or even a good feasible integer solution. In fact, on bigger problems where a number of variables have fractional values, it may not be at all obvious how to round the variables to obtain *any* feasible integer solution. To guarantee finding an optimal solution, a procedure designed for this purpose should be used instead. We now turn to such a procedure.

Rounding has some serious drawbacks.

Formulating and Solving Spreadsheet Models for Integer Programming Problems

The spreadsheet procedure for integer programming is exactly the same as for linear programming except for adding one step when specifying the constraints in the Solver dialogue box. This extra step is that you also need to include the constraints that the decision variables (changing cells) need to be integer.

FIGURE 9.3

A spreadsheet model for the TBA Airlines integer programming problem where the changing cells, UnitsProduced (C12:D12), show the optimal airplane purchases obtained by the Solver, and the target cell, TotalProfit (G12), gives the resulting total profit in millions of dollars.

	A	B	C	D	E	F	G
1		**TBA Airlines Airplane Purchasing Problem**					
2							
3			Small Airplane	Large Airplane			
4		Unit Profit ($millions)	1	5			
5							
6					Capital		Capital
7			Capital per Unit Produced		Spent		Available
8		Capital ($millions)	5	50	100	≤	100
9							
10							Total Profit
11			Small Airplane	Large Airplane			($millions)
12		Units Produced	0	2			10
13			≤				
14		Maximum Small Airplanes	2				

	E
6	Capital
7	Spent
8	= SUMPRODUCT(CapitalPerUnitProduced,UnitsProduced)

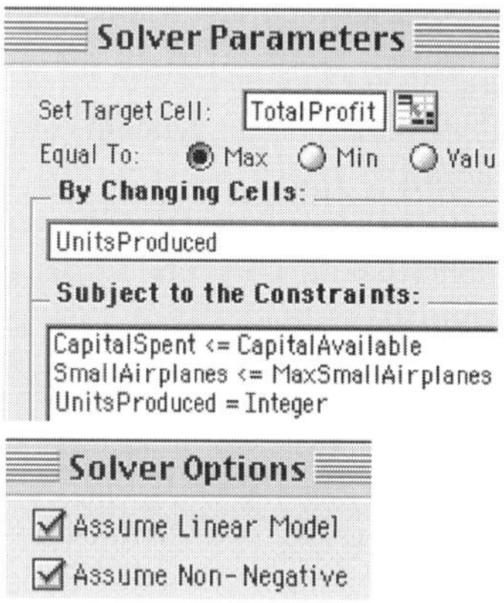

	G
10	Total Profit
11	($millions)
12	= SUMPRODUCT(UnitProfit,UnitsProduced)

Solver Parameters

Set Target Cell: [TotalProfit]

Equal To: ● Max ○ Min ○ Valu

By Changing Cells:

[UnitsProduced]

Subject to the Constraints:

```
CapitalSpent <= CapitalAvailable
SmallAirplanes <= MaxSmallAirplanes
UnitsProduced = Integer
```

Solver Options

☑ Assume Linear Model
☑ Assume Non-Negative

Range Name	Cells
CapitalAvailable	G8
CapitalPerUnitProduced	C8:D8
CapitalSpent	E8
MaxSmallAirplanes	C14
SmallAirplanes	C12
TotalProfit	G12
UnitProfit	C4:D4
UnitsProduced	C12:D12

Excel Tip: To constrain a range of changing cells to be integer, choose the range of cells in the left-hand side of the Add Constraint dialogue box and choose int from the pop-up menu. Clicking OK then enters the constraint that these cells = integer in the Solver dialogue box.

The Excel Solver or Premium Solver can handle a few dozen integer variables and sometimes many more.

Figure 9.3 shows how this is done for the TBA problem. Except for the third line of constraints in the Solver dialogue box, this entire formulation fits the linear programming formulation of the problem. The constraints that the changing cells need to be integer are added in the Add Constraint dialogue box. Choose the range of these cells (C12:D12) as the left-hand side and then choose int from the pop-up menu between the left-hand and right-hand side.[2]

These changing cells in Figure 9.3 show the optimal solution, $(S, L) = (0, 2)$, obtained after clicking on the Solve button.

Algorithms for solving integer programming models (including the one in the Excel Solver) are not nearly as efficient as those for linear programming. This is the reason why a linear programming model (with rounding of the optimal solution) is sometimes used to approximate an integer programming model when this is considered a reasonable approximation. However, the Excel Solver or Premium Solver is sometimes able to solve an integer programming model with well over 100 variables, depending on the difficulty of the problem.

---

[2] On most versions of Excel, Solver will automatically fill in "integer" in the right-hand side of the Add Constraint dialogue box after choosing int from the pop-up menu. A bug in some versions of Excel (e.g., most Macintosh versions) leaves the right-hand side of the Add Constraint dialogue box blank and then gives an error message if you click OK. Typing "integer" into the right-hand side before clicking OK is a workaround for this bug.

The best commercial software (not using spreadsheets) occasionally has been successful in solving very large integer programming models ranging into the thousands of integer variables. This is an area of continuing research and progress.

Types of Integer Programming Problems

The TBA Airlines problem illustrates a situation where *all* the decision variables are required to have integer values. Some other applications will have a variety of decision variables where only *some* of them will have this restriction.

> **Pure integer programming** problems are those where all the decision variables must be integers. **Mixed integer programming** problems only require some of the variables (the "integer variables") to have integer values so the divisibility assumption holds for the rest (the "continuous variables").

Many applications of integer programming (either pure or mixed) further restrict the integer variables to just the two values, 0 or 1.

> **Binary variables** are variables whose only possible values are 0 and 1. **Binary integer programming** problems are those where all the decision variables restricted to integer values are further restricted to be binary variables. (We hereafter will use the abbreviation **BIP** for *binary integer programming*.) Such problems can be further categorized as either **pure BIP problems** or **mixed BIP problems,** depending on whether *all* the decision variables or only *some* of them are binary variables.

(Integer programming problems which have integer variables that are not restricted to the values 0 and 1 may be referred to as **general integer programming** problems to differentiate them from BIP problems, whereas the term **integer programming** encompasses both general integer programming and BIP.)

BIP problems are somewhat less difficult to solve than general integer programming problems with the same number of integer variables, but they still are far more difficult than linear programming problems of comparable size. The supplement to this chapter on the CD-ROM (*Some Perspectives on Solving Binary Integer Programming Problems*) discusses some of the difficulties and pitfalls involved in solving large BIP problems. One pitfall especially emphasized is that simply rounding an optimal solution for the LP relaxation is a particularly dangerous shortcut with BIP problems.

Since binary variables only provide two choices, they are ideally suited to be the decision variables when dealing with **yes-or-no decisions.** In such a decision, the only two possible choices are yes and no, so the binary decision variable is assigned a value of 1 for choosing yes and a value of 0 for choosing no. Here are some examples of yes-or-no decisions.

1. Should we undertake a particular fixed project?

2. Should we make a particular fixed investment?

3. Should we locate a facility in a particular site?

Applications of BIP for dealing with such decisions are so important that we devote the remainder of this chapter to this subject, beginning with a case study.

Excel Tip: Even when a changing cell is constrained to be integer, rounding errors occasionally will cause Excel to return a noninteger value very close to an integer (e.g., 1.23E-10, meaning 0.0000000000123). To make the spreadsheet cleaner, you may replace these "ugly" representations by their proper integer values in the changing cells.

Excel Tip: In the Solver Options, the Tolerance setting (5 percent by default) causes Solver to stop solving an integer programming problem when it finds a feasible solution whose objective function value is within the Tolerance of being optimal. This is useful to speed up solving large problems. For smaller problems (e.g., homework problems), the Tolerance should be set to 0 to guarantee finding an optimal solution.

Binary variables are ideal decision variables for yes-or-no decisions.

Review
Questions

1. Why might a decision variable need to be restricted to integer values?

2. How does an integer programming model differ from a linear programming model?

3. What is the divisibility assumption of linear programming?

4. What is the LP relaxation of an integer programming problem?

5. How does the graphical method for integer programming differ from the graphical method for linear programming?

6. Can an optimal solution for an integer programming problem always be found by rounding the optimal solution for its LP relaxation?

7. What is the distinction between pure and mixed integer programming?

8. What are binary integer programming problems? How do they arise?

9.2 A CASE STUDY: THE CALIFORNIA MANUFACTURING CO. PROBLEM

"OK, Steve here is the situation. With our growing business, we are strongly considering building a new factory. Maybe even two. The factory needs to be close to a large, skilled labor force, so we are looking at Los Angeles and San Francisco as the potential sites. We also are considering building one new warehouse. Not more than one. This warehouse would make sense in saving shipping costs only if it is in the same city as the new factory. Either Los Angeles or San Francisco. If we decide not to build a new factory at all, we definitely don't want the warehouse either. Is this clear, so far?"

"Yes, Armando, I understand," Steve Chan responds. "What are your criteria for making these decisions?"

"Well, all the other members of top management have joined me in addressing this issue," Armando Ortega replies. "We have concluded that these two potential sites are very comparable on nonfinancial grounds. Therefore, we feel that these decisions should be based mainly on financial considerations. We have $10 million of capital available for this expansion and we want it to go as far as possible in improving our bottom line. Which feasible combination of investments in factories and warehouses in which locations will be most profitable for the company in the long run? In your language, we want to maximize the total net present value of these investments."

What is the most profitable combination of investments?

"That's very clear. It sounds like a classical management science problem."

"That's why I called you in, Steve. I would like you to conduct a quick management science study to determine the most profitable combination of investments. I also would like you to take a look at the amount of capital being made available and its effect on how much profit we can get from these investments. The decision to make $10 million available is only a tentative one. That amount is stretching us, because we now are investigating some other interesting project proposals that would require quite a bit of capital, so we would prefer to use less than $10 million on these particular investments if the last few million don't buy us much. On the other hand, this expansion into either Los Angeles or San Francisco, or maybe both of these key cities, is our number one priority. It will have a real positive impact on the future of this company. So we are willing to go out and raise some more capital if it would give us a lot of bang for the buck. Therefore, we would like you to do some what-if analysis to tell us what the effect would be if we were to change the amount of capital being made available to anything between $5 million and $15 million."

"Sure, Armando, we do that kind of what-if analysis all the time. We refer to it as sensitivity analysis because it involves checking how sensitive the outcome is to the amount of capital being made available."

"Good. Now, Steve, I need your input within the next couple weeks. Can you do it?"

"Well, Armando, as usual, the one question is whether we can gather all the necessary data that quickly. We'll need to get good estimates of the net present value of each of the possible investments. I'll need a lot of help in digging out that information."

"I thought you would say that. I already have my staff working hard on developing those estimates. I can get you together with them this afternoon."

"Great. I'll get right on it."

As president of the California Manufacturing Company, Armando Ortega has had many similar conversations in the past with Steve Chan, the company's top management scientist. Armando is confident that Steve will come through for him again.

Background

The California Manufacturing Company is a diversified company with several factories and warehouses throughout California, but none yet in Los Angeles or San Francisco. Because the company is enjoying increasing sales and earnings, management feels that the time may be ripe to expand into one or both of those prime locations. A basic issue is whether to build a new factory in either Los Angeles or San Francisco, or perhaps even in both cities. Management also is considering building at most one new warehouse, but will restrict the choice of location to a city where a new factory is being built.

TABLE 9.2

Data for the California Manufacturing Co. Problem

Decision Number	Yes-or-No Question	Decision Variable	Net Present Value (Millions)	Capital Required (Millions)
1	Build a factory in Los Angeles?	x_1	$8	$6
2	Build a factory in San Francisco?	x_2	5	3
3	Build a warehouse in Los Angeles?	x_3	6	5
4	Build a warehouse in San Francisco?	x_4	4	2

Capital available: $10 million

TABLE 9.3   **Binary Decision Variables for the California Manufacturing Co. Problem**

Decision Number	Decision Variable	Possible Value	Interpretation of a Value of 1	Interpretation of a Value of 0
1	x_1	0 or 1	Build a factory in Los Angeles	Do not build this factory
2	x_2	0 or 1	Build a factory in San Francisco	Do not build this factory
3	x_3	0 or 1	Build a warehouse in Los Angeles	Do not build this warehouse
4	x_4	0 or 1	Build a warehouse in San Francisco	Do not build this warehouse

The decisions to be made are listed in the second column of Table 9.2 in the form of yes-or-no questions. In each case, giving an answer of yes to the question corresponds to the decision to make the investment to build the indicated facility (a factory or a warehouse) in the indicated location (Los Angeles or San Francisco). The capital required for the investment is given in the rightmost column, where management has made the tentative decision that the total amount of capital being made available for all the investments is $10 million. (Note that this amount is inadequate for some of the combinations of investments.) The fourth column shows the estimated *net present value* (net long-run profit considering the time value of money) if the corresponding investment is made. (The net present value is 0 if the investment is not made.) Much of the work of Steve Chan's management science study (with substantial help from the president's staff) goes into developing these estimates of the net present values. As specified by the company's president, Armando Ortega, the objective now is to find the feasible combination of investments that maximizes the total net present value.

Introducing Binary Decision Variables for the Yes-or-No Decisions

As summarized in the second column of Table 9.2, the problem facing management is to make four interrelated *yes-or-no decisions.* To formulate a mathematical model for this problem, Steve Chan needs to introduce a decision variable for each of these decisions. Since each decision has just two alternatives, choose yes or choose no, the corresponding decision variable only needs to have two values (one for each alternative). Therefore, Steve uses a *binary variable,* whose only possible values are 0 and 1, where 1 corresponds to the decision to choose yes and 0 corresponds to choosing no.

These decision variables are shown in the second column of Table 9.3. The final two columns give the interpretation of a value of 1 and 0, respectively.

Dealing with Interrelationships between the Decisions

Recall that management wants no more than one new warehouse to be built. In terms of the corresponding decision variables, x_3 and x_4, this means that no more than one of these variables is allowed to have the value 1. Therefore, these variables must satisfy the constraint

$$x_3 + x_4 \leq 1$$

as part of the mathematical model for the problem.

These two alternatives (build a warehouse in Los Angeles or build a warehouse in San Francisco) are referred to as **mutually exclusive alternatives** because choosing one of these

With a group of mutually exclusive alternatives, only one of the corresponding binary decision variables can equal 1.

alternatives excludes choosing the other. Groups of two or more mutually exclusive alternatives arise commonly in BIP problems. For each such group where at most one of the alternatives can be chosen, the constraint on the corresponding binary decision variables has the form shown above, namely, the sum of these variables must be *less than or equal to* 1. For some groups of mutually exclusive alternatives, management will exclude the possibility of choosing *none* of the alternatives, in which case the constraint will set the sum of the corresponding binary decision variables *equal* to 1.

The California Manufacturing Co. problem also has another important kind of restriction. Management will allow a warehouse to be built in a particular city only if a factory also is being built in that city. For example, consider the situation for Los Angeles (LA).

If decide no, do not build a factory in LA (i.e., if choose $x_1 = 0$),
  then cannot build a warehouse in LA (i.e., must choose $x_3 = 0$).

If decide yes, do build a factory in LA (i.e., if choose $x_1 = 1$),
  then can either build a warehouse in LA or not (i.e., can choose either $x_3 = 1$ or 0).

How can these interrelationships between the factory and warehouse decisions for LA be expressed in a constraint for a mathematical model? The key is to note that, for either value of x_1, the permissible value or values of x_3 are less than or equal to x_1. Since x_1 and x_3 are binary variables, the constraint

$$x_3 \leq x_1$$

forces x_3 to take on a permissible value given the value of x_1.

Exactly the same reasoning leads to

$$x_4 \leq x_2$$

as the corresponding constraint for San Francisco. Just as for Los Angeles, this constraint forces having no warehouse in San Francisco ($x_4 = 0$) if a factory will not be built there ($x_2 = 0$), whereas going ahead with the factory there ($x_2 = 1$) leaves open the decision to build the warehouse there ($x_4 = 0$ or 1).

One yes-or-no decision is contingent on another yes-or-no decision if the first one is allowed to be yes only if the other one is yes.

For either city, the warehouse decision is referred to as a **contingent decision,** because the decision depends on a prior decision regarding whether to build a factory there. In general, one yes-or-no decision is said to be contingent on another yes-or-no decision if it is allowed to be yes *only if* the other is yes. As above, the mathematical constraint expressing this relationship requires that the binary variable for the former decision must be less than or equal to the binary variable for the latter decision.

The rightmost column of Table 9.2 reveals one more interrelationship between the four decisions, namely, that the amount of capital expended on the four facilities under consideration cannot exceed the amount available ($10 million). Therefore, the model needs to include a constraint that requires

Capital expended $\leq \$10$ million

How can the amount of capital expended be expressed in terms of the four binary decision variables? To start this process, consider the first yes-or-no decision (build a factory in Los Angeles?). Combining the information in the rightmost column of Table 9.2 and the first row of Table 9.3,

$$\text{Capital expended on factory in Los Angeles} = \begin{cases} \$6 \text{ million} & \text{if } x_1 = 1 \\ 0 & \text{if } x_1 = 0 \end{cases}$$

$$= \$6 \text{ million } \textit{times } x_1$$

By the same reasoning, the amount of capital expended on the other three investment opportunities (in units of millions of dollars) is $3x_2$, $5x_3$, and $2x_4$, respectively. Consequently,

Capital expended $= 6x_1 + 3x_2 + 5x_3 + 2x_4$ (in millions of dollars)

Therefore, the constraint becomes

$$6x_1 + 3x_2 + 5x_3 + 2x_4 \leq 10$$

The BIP Model

As indicated by Armando Ortega in his conversation with Steve Chan, management's objective is to find the feasible combination of investments that *maximizes* the total net present value of these investments. Thus, the value of the objective function should be

$$\text{NPV} = \text{Total net present value}$$

If the investment is made to build a particular facility (so that the corresponding decision variable has a value of 1), the estimated net present value from that investment is given in the fourth column of Table 9.2. If the investment is not made (so the decision variable equals 0), the net present value is 0. Therefore, continuing to use units of millions of dollars,

$$\text{NPV} = 8x_1 + 5x_2 + 6x_3 + 4x_4$$

is the quantity to enter into the target cell to be maximized.

Incorporating the constraints developed in the preceding subsection, the complete BIP model then is shown in Figure 9.4. The format is basically the same as for linear programming models. The one key difference arises when using the Solver dialogue box. Each of the decision variables (cells C18:D18 and C16:D16) is constrained to be binary. This is accomplished in the Add Constraint dialogue box by choosing each range of variables as the left-hand side and then choosing bin from the pop-up menu. [Note that early versions of Excel do not include the bin option. In these versions, binary variables can still be specified by constraining the variables to be integer (by choosing int), and then adding two further sets of constraints that specify that each of these variables must be greater than or equal to zero *and* less than or equal to one.] The other constraints shown in the Solver dialogue box (see the lower left-hand side of Figure 9.4) have been made quite intuitive by using the suggestive range names given in the lower right-hand side of the figure. For convenience, the equations entered into the output cells in E12 and D20 use a SUMPRODUCT function that includes C17:D17 and either C11:D11 or C5:D5 because the blanks or ≤ signs in these rows are interpreted as zeroes by the Solver.

Note how helpful the range names are for interpreting this BIP spreadsheet model.

The Excel Solver gives the optimal solution shown in C18:D18 and C16:D16 of the spreadsheet, namely, build factories in *both* Los Angeles and San Francisco, but do not build any warehouses. The target cell (D20) indicates that the total net present value from building these two factories is estimated to be $13 million.

Performing Sensitivity Analysis

Now that Steve Chan has used the BIP model to determine what should be done when the amount of capital being made available to these investments is $10 million, his next task is to perform sensitivity analysis on this amount. Recall that Armando Ortega wants him to determine what the effect would be if this amount were changed to anything else between $5 million and $15 million.

In Chapter 5, we described three different methods of performing sensitivity analysis on a linear programming spreadsheet model when there is a change in a constraint: using trial and error with the spreadsheet, applying the Solver Table, or referring to the Excel sensitivity report. The first two of these can be used on integer programming problems in exactly the same way as for linear programming problems. The third method, however, does not work. The sensitivity report is not available for integer programming problems (choosing it results in an error message). This is because the concept of a shadow price and allowable range no longer applies. In contrast to linear programming, the objective function values for an integer programming problem do not change in a predictable manner when the right-hand side of a constraint is changed.

The Excel sensitivity report is *not* available for integer programming problems.

Trial-and-error and/or the Solver Table can be used to perform sensitivity analysis for integer programming problems. See Section 5.3 for more details on using the Solver Table.

It is straightforward to determine the impact of changing the amount of available capital by trial and error. Simply try different values in the data cell CapitalAvailable (G12) and click Solve in the Solver. However, a more systematic way to perform this analysis is to use an Excel add-in in your MS Courseware called the *Solver Table.* The Solver Table works for integer programming models in exactly the same way as it does for linear programming models (as described in Section 5.3 in the subsection entitled *Using the Solver Table to Do Sensitivity Analysis Systematically*).

FIGURE 9.4

A spreadsheet formulation of the BIP model for the California Manufacturing Co. case study where the changing cells BuildFactory? (C18:D18) and BuildWarehouse? (C16:D16) give the optimal solution obtained by using the Excel Solver.

	A	B	C	D	E	F	G
1		California Manufacturing Co. Facility Location Problem					
2							
3		**NPV ($millions)**	LA	SF			
4		Warehouse	6	4			
5							
6		Factory	8	5			
7							
8		**Capital Required**					
9		**($millions)**	LA	SF			
10		Warehouse	5	2	Capital		Capital
11					Spent		Available
12		Factory	6	3	9	≤	10
13							
14					Total		Maximum
15		**Build?**	LA	SF	Warehouses		Warehouses
16		Warehouse	0	0	0	≤	1
17			≤	≤			
18		Factory	1	1			
19							
20		Total NPV ($millions)		$13			

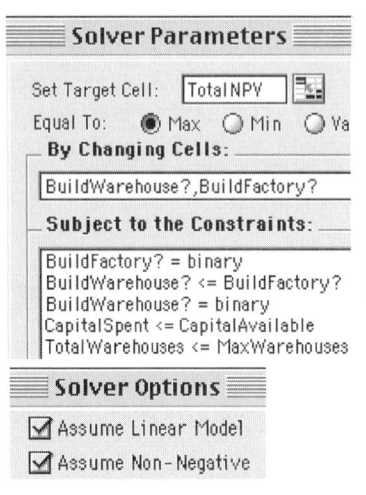

Solver Parameters

Set Target Cell: TotalNPV

Equal To: ● Max ○ Min ○ Va

By Changing Cells:

BuildWarehouse?,BuildFactory?

Subject to the Constraints:

BuildFactory? = binary
BuildWarehouse? <= BuildFactory?
BuildWarehouse? = binary
CapitalSpent <= CapitalAvailable
TotalWarehouses <= MaxWarehouses

Solver Options

☑ Assume Linear Model
☑ Assume Non-Negative

	E
10	Capital
11	Spent
12	= SUMPRODUCT(CapitalRequired,Build?)
13	
14	Total
15	Warehouses
16	= SUM(BuildWarehouse?)

Range Name	Cells
Build?	C16:D18
BuildWarehouse?	C16:D16
BuildFactory?	C18:D18
CapitalAvailable	G12
CapitalRequired	C10:D12
CapitalSpent	E12
MaxWarehouses	G16
NPV	C4:D6
TotalNPV	D20
TotalWarehouses	E16

	C	D
20	Total NPV ($millions)	=SUMPRODUCT(NPV,Build?)

After expanding the original spreadsheet (Figure 9.4) to make room, the Solver Table has been used to generate the results shown in Figure 9.5 by executing the following steps. In the first row of the table, enter formulas that refer to all the changing cells or output cells of interest. In this case, these are all the changing cells (C16, D16, C18, D18) and the target cell, TotalNPV (D20). The trial values for CapitalAvailable (G12) are entered in the first column of the table (B26:B36). Then, select the entire table (B25:G36) and choose Solver Table from the

FIGURE 9.5

An application of the Solver Table that shows the effect on the optimal solution and the resulting total net present value of systematically varying the amount of capital being made available for these investments.

	B	C	D	E	F	G	H
23	Capital Available	Warehouse	Warehouse	Factory	Factory	Total NPV	
24	($millions)	in LA?	in SF?	in LA?	in SF?	($millions)	
25		0	0	1	1	13	
26	5	0	1	0	1	9	
27	6	0	1	0	1	9	
28	7	0	1	0	1	9	Select the entire table (B25:G36), before choosing Solver Table from the Tools menu.
29	8	0	1	0	1	9	
30	9	0	0	1	1	13	
31	10	0	0	1	1	13	
32	11	0	1	1	1	17	
33	12	0	1	1	1	17	
34	13	0	1	1	1	17	
35	14	1	0	1	1	19	
36	15	1	0	1	1	19	

	B	C	D	E	F	G
23	Capital Available	Warehouse	Warehouse	Factory	Factory	Total NPV
24	($millions)	in LA?	in SF?	in LA?	in SF?	($millions)
25		=C16	=D16	=C18	=D18	=TotalNPV

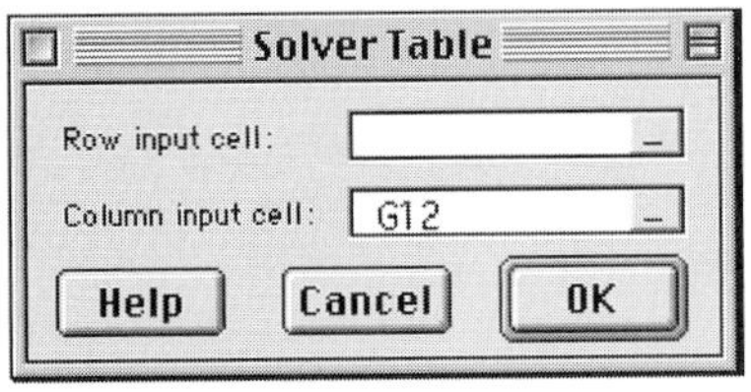

Solver Table

Row input cell: _____

Column input cell: G12

[Help] [Cancel] [OK]

Range Name	Cell
TotalNPV	D20

Tools menu. The column input cell is chosen as G12 (the CapitalAvailable data cell) since this is the data cell that is being varied in the first column of the table. Clicking OK then causes the Solver Table to re-solve the problem for all the trial values for CapitalAvailable (G12) in the first column of the table and fill in the corresponding results in the other columns of the table.

Sensitivity analysis also could be performed on any of the other data cells—NPV (C4:D6), CapitalRequired (C10:D12), and MaxWarehouses (G16)—in a similar way with the Solver Table (or by using trial and error with the spreadsheet). However, a careful job was done in developing good estimates of the net present value of each of the possible investments, and there is little uncertainty in the values entered in the other data cells, so Steve Chan decides that further sensitivity analysis is not needed.

Management's Conclusion

Steve Chan's report is delivered to Armando Ortega within the two-week deadline. The report recommends the plan presented in Figure 9.4 (build a factory in both Los Angeles and San Francisco but no warehouses) if management decides to stick with its tentative decision to make $10 million of capital available for these investments. One advantage of this plan is that it only uses $9 million of this capital, which frees up $1 million of capital for other project proposals currently being investigated. The report also highlights the results shown in Figure 9.5 while emphasizing two points. One is that a heavy penalty would be paid (a reduction in the total net present value from $13 million to $9 million) if the amount of capital being made available were to be reduced below $9 million. The other is that *increasing* the amount of capital being made available by just $1 million (from $10 million to $11 million) would enable a substantial increase of $4 million in the total net present value (from $13 million to $17 million). However, a much larger further increase in the amount of capital being made available (from $11 million to $14 million) would be needed to enable a considerably smaller further increase in the total net present value (from $17 million to $19 million).

Armando Ortega deliberates with other members of top management before making a decision. It is quickly concluded that increasing the amount of capital being made available all the way up to $14 million would be stretching the company's financial resources too dangerously to justify the relatively small payoff. However, there is considerable discussion of the pros and cons of the two options of using either $9 million or $11 million of capital. Because of the large payoff from the latter option (an additional $4 million in total net present value), management finally decides to adopt the plan presented in row 32 of Figure 9.5. Thus, the company will build new factories in both Los Angeles and San Francisco as well as a new warehouse in San Francisco, with an estimated total net present value of $17 million. However, because of the large capital requirements of this plan, management also decides to defer building the warehouse until the two factories are completed so that their profits can help finance the construction of the warehouse.

Review Questions

1. What are the four interrelated decisions that need to be made by the management of the California Manufacturing Co.?
2. Why are binary decision variables appropriate to represent these decisions?
3. What is the objective specified by management for this problem?
4. What are the mutually exclusive alternatives in this problem? What is the form of the resulting constraint in the BIP model?
5. What are the contingent decisions in this problem? For each one, what is the form of the resulting constraint in the BIP model?
6. What is the tentative managerial decision on which sensitivity analysis needs to be performed?

9.3 SOME OTHER APPLICATIONS

Just as in the California Manufacturing Co. case study, managers frequently face yes-or-no decisions. Therefore, binary integer programming (BIP) is widely used to aid in these decisions.

We now will introduce various types of yes-or-no decisions. We also will mention some examples of actual applications where binary integer programming was used to address these decisions.

Each of these applications is fully described in an article in the journal *Interfaces*. In each case, we will mention the specific issue in which the article appears in case you want to read further. Most of these articles also are available for downloading from the Internet. For links to their Web pages, log on to **www.mhhe.com/hillier2e/articles.**

Investment Analysis

In Section 4.2, the example of the Think-Big Development Co. investing in commercial real-estate development projects illustrates how linear programming can be used to make capital budgeting decisions about how much to invest in various projects. However, as the California Manufacturing Co. case study demonstrates, some capital budgeting decisions do not involve *how much* to invest but, rather, *whether* to invest a fixed amount. Specifically, the four decisions in the case study were whether to invest the fixed amount of capital required to build a certain kind of facility (factory or warehouse) in a certain location (Los Angeles or San Francisco).

Management often faces decisions about whether to make fixed investments (those where the amount of capital required has been fixed in advance). Should we acquire a certain subsidiary being spun off by another company? Should we purchase a certain source of raw materials? Should we add a new production line to produce a certain input item ourselves rather than continuing to obtain it from a supplier?

In general, capital budgeting decisions about fixed investments are yes-or-no decisions of the following type.

Each yes-or-no decision:

Should we make a certain fixed investment?

$$\text{Its decision variable} = \begin{cases} 1, & \text{if yes} \\ 0, & \text{if no} \end{cases}$$

The July–August 1990 issue of *Interfaces* describes how the **Turkish Petroleum Refineries Corporation** used BIP to analyze capital investments worth tens of millions of dollars to expand refinery capacity and conserve energy.

A rather different example that still falls somewhat into this category is described in the January–February 1997 issue of *Interfaces*. A major management science study was conducted for the top military management of the **South African National Defense Force** to upgrade its capabilities with a smaller budget. The "investments" under consideration in this case were acquisition costs and ongoing expenses that would be required to provide specific types of military capabilities. A mixed BIP model was formulated to choose those specific capabilities that would maximize the overall effectiveness of the Defense Force while satisfying a budget constraint. The model had over 16,000 variables (including 256 binary variables) and over 5,000 functional constraints. The resulting optimization of the size and shape of the defense force provided savings of over $1.1 billion per year as well as vital nonmonetary benefits. The impact of this study won it the prestigious first prize among the 1996 Franz Edelman Awards for Management Science Achievement.

The January–February 1999 issue of *Interfaces* presents another award-winning application of a mixed BIP model to investment analysis. This particular model has been used by the investment firm **Grantham, Mayo, Van Otterloo and Company** to construct many quantitatively managed portfolios representing over $8 billion in assets. In each case, a portfolio has been constructed that is close (in terms of sector and security exposure) to a target portfolio but with a far smaller and more manageable number of distinct stocks. A binary variable is used to represent each yes-or-no decision as to whether a particular stock should be included in the portfolio and then a separate continuous variable represents the amount of the stock to include. Given a current portfolio that needs to be rebalanced, it is desirable to reduce transaction costs by minimizing the number of transactions needed to obtain the final portfolio, so binary variables also are included to represent the yes-or-no decisions as to whether to make the transactions to change the amounts of individual stocks being held. The inclusion of this consideration in the model has reduced the annual cost of trading the portfolios being managed by at least $4 million.

> This BIP application saved over $1.1 billion per year.

Site Selection

In this global economy, many corporations are opening up new plants in various parts of the world to take advantage of lower labor costs, and so on. Before selecting a site for a new plant, many potential sites may need to be analyzed and compared. (The California Manufacturing Co. case study had just two potential sites for each of two kinds of facilities.) Each of the potential sites involves a yes-or-no decision of the following type.

Each yes-or-no decision:

Should a certain site be selected for the location of a certain new facility?

$$\text{Its decision variable} = \begin{cases} 1, & \text{if yes} \\ 0, & \text{if no} \end{cases}$$

In many cases, the objective is to select the sites so as to minimize the total cost of the new facilities that will provide the required output.

As described in the January–February 1990 issue of *Interfaces*, **AT&T** used a BIP model to help dozens of its customers select the sites for their telemarketing centers. The model minimizes labor, communications, and real-estate costs while providing the desired level of coverage by the centers. In one year alone (1988), this approach enabled 46 AT&T customers to make their yes-or-no decisions on site locations swiftly and confidently, while committing to $375 million in annual network services and $31 million in equipment sales from AT&T.

We next describe an important type of problem for many corporations where site selection plays a key role.

Designing a Production and Distribution Network

Manufacturers today face great competitive pressure to get their products to market more quickly as well as to reduce their production and distribution costs. Therefore, any corporation that distributes its products over a wide geographical area (or even worldwide) must pay continuing attention to the design of its production and distribution network.

This design involves addressing the following kinds of yes-or-no decisions.

Should a certain plant remain open?

Should a certain site be selected for a new plant?

Should a certain distribution center remain open?

Should a certain site be selected for a new distribution center?

If each market area is to be served by a single distribution center, then we also have another kind of yes-or-no decision for each combination of a market area and a distribution center.

Should a certain distribution center be assigned to serve a certain market area?

For each of the yes-or-no decisions of any of these kinds,

$$\text{Its decision variable} = \begin{cases} 1, & \text{if yes} \\ 0, & \text{if no} \end{cases}$$

Ault Foods Limited (July–August 1994 issue of *Interfaces*) used this approach to design its production and distribution center. Management considered 10 sites for plants, 13 sites for distribution centers, and 48 market areas. This application of BIP was credited with saving the company $200,000 per year.

Digital Equipment Corporation (January–February 1995 issue of *Interfaces*) provides another example of an application of this kind. At the time, this large multinational corporation was serving one-quarter million customer sites, with more than half of its $14 billion annual revenues coming from 81 countries outside the United States. Therefore, this application involved restructuring the corporation's entire *global supply chain,* consisting of its suppliers, plants, distribution centers, potential sites, and market areas all around the world. The restructuring generated annual cost reductions of $500 million in manufacturing and $300 million in logistics, as well as a reduction of over $400 million in required capital assets.

BIP was used to restructure the corporation's entire global supply chain, saving over $800 million per year.

Dispatching Shipments

Once a production and distribution network has been designed and put into operation, daily operating decisions need to be made about how to send the shipments. Some of these decisions again are yes-or-no decisions.

For example, suppose that trucks are being used to transport the shipments and each truck typically makes deliveries to several customers during each trip. It then becomes necessary to select a route (sequence of customers) for each truck, so each candidate for a route leads to the following yes-or-no decision.

A yes-or-no decision can involve whether to select a combination of options simultaneously.

Should a certain route be selected for one of the trucks?

$$\text{Its decision variable} = \begin{cases} 1, & \text{if yes} \\ 0, & \text{if no} \end{cases}$$

The objective would be to select the routes that would minimize the total cost of making all the deliveries.

Various complications also can be considered. For example, if different truck sizes are available, each candidate for selection would include both a certain route and a certain truck size. Similarly, if timing is an issue, a time period for the departure also can be specified as part of the yes-or-no decision. With both factors, each yes-or-no decision would have the form shown below.

Should all the following be selected simultaneously for a delivery run:

1. A certain route,

2. A certain size of truck, and

3. A certain time period for the departure?

$$\text{Its decision variable} = \begin{cases} 1, & \text{if yes} \\ 0, & \text{if no} \end{cases}$$

Here are a few of the companies that use BIP to help make these kinds of decisions. A Michigan-based retail chain called **Quality Stores** (March–April 1987 issue of *Interfaces*) makes the routing decisions for its delivery trucks this way, thereby saving about $450,000 per year. **Air Products and Chemicals, Inc.** (December 1983 issue of *Interfaces*) saves approximately $2 million annually (about 8 percent of its prior distribution costs) by using this approach to produce its daily delivery schedules. The **Reynolds Metals Co.** (January–February 1991 issue of *Interfaces*) achieves savings of over $7 million annually with an automated dispatching system based partially on BIP for its freight shipments from over 200 plants, warehouses, and suppliers. **Sears, Roebuck and Company** (January–February 1999 issue of *Interfaces*) achieves over $42 million in annual savings by using extensions of BIP to assign routes to its delivery and home-service fleets.

Scheduling Interrelated Activities

We all schedule interrelated activities in our everyday lives, even if it is just scheduling when to begin our various homework assignments. So, too, managers must schedule various kinds of interrelated activities. When should we begin production for various new orders? When should we begin marketing various new products? When should we make various capital investments to expand our production capacity?

For any such activity, the decision about when to begin can be expressed in terms of a series of yes-or-no decisions, with one of these decisions for each of the possible time periods in which to begin, as shown below.

Should a certain activity begin in a certain time period?

$$\text{Its decision variable} = \begin{cases} 1, & \text{if yes} \\ 0, & \text{if no} \end{cases}$$

Since a particular activity can begin in only one time period, the choice of the various time periods provides a group of *mutually exclusive alternatives,* so the decision variable for only one time period can have a value of 1.

For example, this approach was used to schedule the building of a series of seven office buildings on the property adjacent to **Texas Stadium** (home of the Dallas Cowboys) over a seven-year planning horizon. In this case, the model had 49 binary decision variables, seven for each office building corresponding to each of the seven years in which its construction could begin. This application of BIP was credited with increasing the profit by $6.3 million. (See the October 1983 issue of *Interfaces.*)

A somewhat similar application on a vastly larger scale occurred in **China** (January–February 1995 issue of *Interfaces*). China was facing at least $240 billion in new investments over a 15-year horizon to meet the energy needs of its rapidly growing economy. Shortages of coal and electricity required developing new infrastructure for transporting coal and transmitting electricity, as well as building new dams and plants for generating thermal, hydro, and nuclear power. Therefore, the Chinese State Planning Commission and the World Bank collaborated in developing a huge mixed BIP model to guide the decisions on which projects to approve and when to undertake them over the 15-year planning period to minimize the total discounted

This BIP application involved scheduling $240 billion in new investments over 15 years.

cost. It is estimated that this application of management science is saving China about $6.4 billion over the 15 years.

Scheduling Asset Divestitures

This next application actually is another example of the preceding one (scheduling interrelated activities). However, rather than dealing with such activities as constructing office buildings or investing in hydroelectric plants, the activities now are *selling* (divesting) *assets* to generate income. The assets can be either *financial* assets, such as stocks and bonds, or *physical* assets, such as real estate. Given a group of assets, the problem is to determine when to sell each one to maximize the net present value of total profit from these assets while generating the desired income stream.

In this case, each yes-or-no decision has the following form.

Should a certain asset be sold in a certain time period?

$$\text{Its decision variable} = \begin{cases} 1, & \text{if yes} \\ 0, & \text{if no} \end{cases}$$

One company that deals with these kinds of yes-or-no decisions is **Homart Development Company** (January–February 1987 issue of *Interfaces*), which ranks among the largest commercial land developers in the United States. One of its most important strategic issues is scheduling divestiture of shopping malls and office buildings. At any particular time, well over 100 assets will be under consideration for divestiture over the next 10 years. Applying BIP to guide these decisions is credited with adding $40 million of profit from the divestiture plan.

Airline Applications

The airline industry is an especially heavy user of management science throughout its operations. For example, one large consulting firm spun off by American Airlines employs several hundred management science professionals solely to focus on the problems of companies involved with transportation, including especially airlines. We will mention here just two of the applications that specifically use BIP.

One is the *fleet assignment problem.* Given several different types of airplanes available, the problem is to assign a specific type to each flight leg in the schedule so as to maximize the total profit from meeting the schedule. The basic trade-off is that if the airline uses an airplane that is too small on a particular flight leg, it will leave potential customers behind, while if it uses an airplane that is too large, it will suffer the greater expense of the larger airplane to fly empty seats.

For each combination of an airplane type and a flight leg, we have the following yes-or-no decision.

Should a certain type of airplane be assigned to a certain flight leg?

$$\text{Its decision variable} = \begin{cases} 1, & \text{if yes} \\ 0, & \text{if no} \end{cases}$$

This huge integer programming model with 60,000 variables provides annual savings of $100 million.

Delta Air Lines (January–February 1994 issue of *Interfaces*) flies over 2,500 domestic flight legs every day, using about 450 airplanes of 10 different types. It uses a huge integer programming model (about 40,000 functional constraints, 20,000 binary variables, and 40,000 general integer variables) to solve its fleet assignment problem each time a change is needed. This application saves Delta approximately $100 million per year.

A fairly similar application is the *crew scheduling problem.* Here, rather than assigning airplane types to flight legs, we are instead assigning sequences of flight legs to crews of pilots and flight attendants. Thus, for each feasible sequence of flight legs that leaves from a crew base and returns to the same base, the following yes-or-no decision must be made.

Should a certain sequence of flight legs be assigned to a crew?

$$\text{Its decision variable} = \begin{cases} 1, & \text{if yes} \\ 0, & \text{if no} \end{cases}$$

The objective is to minimize the total cost of providing crews that cover each flight leg in the schedule.

American Airlines (July–August 1989 and January–February 1991 issues of *Interfaces*) achieves annual savings of over $20 million by using BIP to solve its crew scheduling problem on a monthly basis.

This approach also is being used extensively by airline companies headquartered outside the United States. For example, **Air New Zealand** (January–February 2001 issue of *Interfaces*) saves approximately $6.7 million per year by using BIP to optimize crew scheduling.

A full-fledged formulation example of this type will be presented at the end of Section 9.5.

Review
Questions

1. How is the binary decision variable defined for each yes-or-no decision?

2. What is the nature of each yes-or-no decision for capital budgeting with fixed investment proposals?

3. What is the nature of each yes-or-no decision when applying BIP to site selection?

4. What kinds of yes-or-no decisions involving site selection also arise when designing a company's production and distribution network?

5. How can the assignment of routes to delivery trucks be posed as yes-or-no decisions?

6. How much is China estimated to be saving by applying BIP to guide the decisions on which projects to approve and when to undertake them over a 15-year planning period?

7. What is the form of each yes-or-no decision when scheduling asset divestitures?

8. What are two kinds of applications of BIP in the airline industry?

9.4 SOME OTHER FORMULATION POSSIBILITIES WITH BINARY VARIABLES

The two preceding sections give various examples of how yes-or-no decisions can arise. Each such decision is represented by a *binary decision variable* in a BIP model.

In addition to any such binary decision variables, other binary variables sometimes are introduced simply to help formulate the model. Here is the terminology to distinguish between the two kinds of binary variables.

> A **binary decision variable** is a binary variable that represents a yes-or-no decision. An **auxiliary binary variable** is an additional binary variable that is introduced into the model, not to represent a yes-or-no decision, but simply to help formulate the model as a (pure or mixed) BIP problem. Auxiliary binary variables will be denoted by $y_1, y_2, \ldots$.

This section illustrates three of the ways in which auxiliary binary variables can play a crucial role in being able to formulate the model to fit a standard problem so that the model can be solved. To facilitate focusing on the role of the auxiliary binary variables, all three examples are variations of the familiar Wyndor Glass Co. problem introduced in Section 2.2 and formulated as a linear programming model on a spreadsheet in Section 2.3. To further refresh your memory, Figure 9.6 shows the graphical solution originally developed in Section 2.5 for this problem, where the symbol P represents the weekly profit in dollars.

This original Wyndor problem has no yes-or-no decisions and so no binary decision variables. However, each variation presented below introduces a complication that can be overcome by using auxiliary binary variables to formulate a model that can be readily solved. (Because the Wyndor problem has only two decision variables, we will be able to use graphical analysis to help introduce and analyze each variation before showing how auxiliary binary variables can be used with any number of decision variables.)

Variation 1: Wyndor with Setup Costs for Initiating Production

Now suppose that the following two changes are made in the original problem.

> **Change 1 for variation 1:** For each product, producing any units requires incurring a substantial one-time *setup cost* for setting up the production facilities for the entire production run for this product. These setup costs are $700 for doors and $1,300 for windows. Otherwise, each door and window still contributes $300 and $500, respectively, to profit.

FIGURE 9.6

This graph summarizes the presentation in Section 2.5 of the application of the graphical method to the original Wyndor problem.

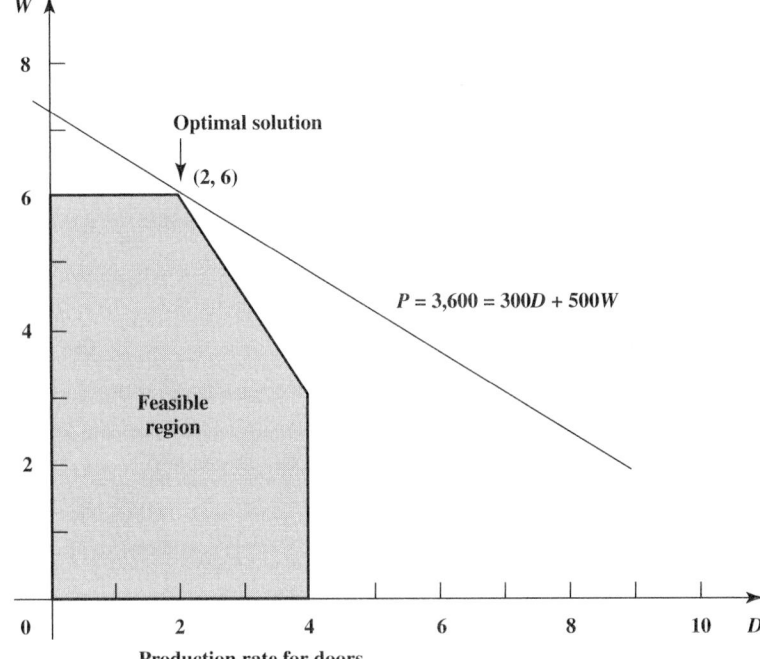

TABLE 9.4

Net Profit ($) for Variation 1 of the Wyndor Problem

	Net Profit ($)	
Number of Units Produced	**Doors**	**Windows**
0	0 (300) − 0 = 0	0 (500) − 0 = 0
1	1 (300) − 700 = −400	1 (500) − 1,300 = −800
2	2 (300) − 700 = −100	2 (500) − 1,300 = −300
3	3 (300) − 700 = 200	3 (500) − 1,300 = 200
4	4 (300) − 700 = 500	4 (500) − 1,300 = 700
5	Not feasible	5 (500) − 1,300 = 1,200
6	Not feasible	6 (500) − 1,300 = 1,700

Change 2 for variation 1: The production runs for these products will be ended after one week, so D and W in the original model now represent the *total* number of doors and windows produced, respectively, rather than production rates. Therefore, these two variables need to be restricted to integer values.

Table 9.4 shows the resulting net profit from producing any feasible quantity for either product. Note that the large setup cost for either product makes it unprofitable to produce less than three units of that product.

The dots in Figure 9.7 show the feasible solutions for this problem. By adding the appropriate entries in Table 9.4, the figure also shows the calculation of the total net profit P for each of the corner points. The optimal solution turns out to be

$$(D, W) = (0, 6) \quad \text{with} \quad P = 1,700$$

By contrast, the original solution

$$(D, W) = (2, 6) \quad \text{with} \quad P = 1,600$$

now gives a smaller value of P. The reason that this original solution (which gave $P = 3,600$ for the original problem) is no longer optimal is that the setup costs reduce the total net profit so much:

$$P = 3,600 − 700 − 1,300 = 1,600$$

FIGURE 9.7

The dots are the feasible solutions for variation 1 of the Wyndor problem. Also shown is the calculation of the total net profit P (in dollars) for each corner point from the net profits given in Table 9.4.

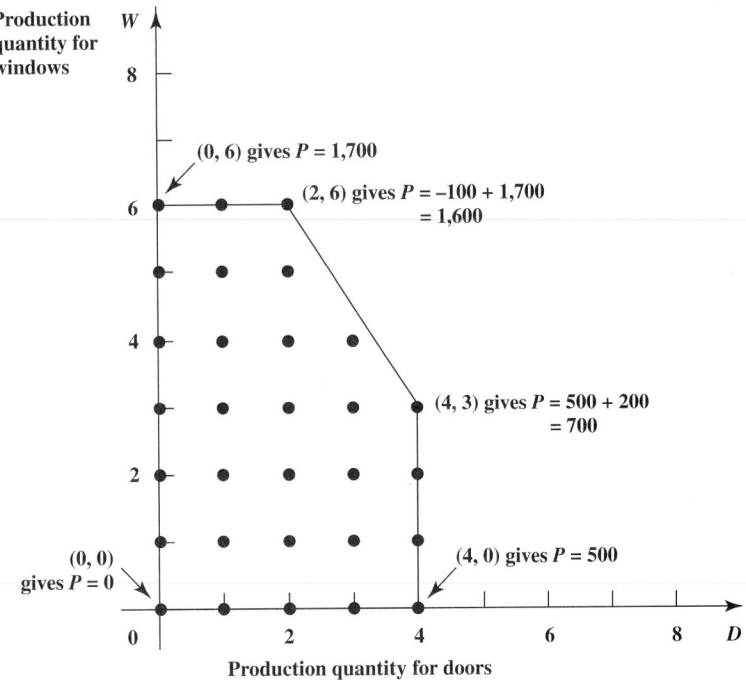

Therefore, the graphical method for linear programming can no longer be used to find the optimal solution for this new problem with setup costs.

How can we formulate a model for this problem so that it fits a standard kind of model that can be solved by an available algorithm? Table 9.4 shows that the net profit for either product is no longer *directly proportional* to the number of units produced. Therefore, as it stands, the problem no longer fits either linear or integer programming. Before, for the original problem without setup costs, the objective function was simply $P = 300D + 500W$. Now we need to subtract from this expression each setup cost *if* the corresponding product will be produced, but we should not subtract the setup cost if the product will not be produced. There appears to be no way to fit such an objective function to the requirements of linear programming (or the equivalent requirements of integer programming). This is where *auxiliary binary variables* come to the rescue.

Formulation with Auxiliary Binary Variables

For each setup cost, there are just two possibilities. Either it will be incurred or it will not. A binary variable has just two values. Therefore, we can introduce an *auxiliary binary variable* for each setup cost and associate each value of the binary variable with one of the two possibilities for the setup cost. In particular, let

These auxiliary binary variables enable subtracting each setup cost only if the setup is performed.

$$y_1 = \begin{cases} 1, & \text{if perform the setup to produce doors} \\ 0, & \text{if not} \end{cases}$$

$$y_2 = \begin{cases} 1, & \text{if perform the setup to produce windows} \\ 0, & \text{if not} \end{cases}$$

Therefore, the objective function now can be written as

$$P = 300D + 500W - 700y_1 - 1{,}300y_2$$

which fits the format for integer programming.

Since a setup is required to produce the corresponding product, these auxiliary binary variables can be related directly to the production quantities as follows.

$$y_1 = \begin{cases} 1, & \text{if } D > 0 \text{ can hold (can produce doors)} \\ 0, & \text{if } D = 0 \text{ must hold (cannot produce doors)} \end{cases}$$

$$y_2 = \begin{cases} 1, & \text{if } W > 0 \text{ can hold (can produce windows)} \\ 0, & \text{if } W = 0 \text{ must hold (cannot produce windows)} \end{cases}$$

We need to include constraints in the model that will ensure that these relationships will hold. (An algorithm solving the model only recognizes the objective function and the constraints, not the definitions of the variables.)

So what are the constraints of the model for variation 1? We still need all the constraints of the original model. We also need constraints that D and W are integers (because of change 2) and that y_1 and y_2 are binary. In addition, we need some ordinary linear programming constraints that will ensure the following relationships:

If $y_1 = 0$, then $D = 0$.

If $y_2 = 0$, then $W = 0$.

(If $y_1 = 1$ or $y_2 = 1$, no restrictions are placed on D or W other than those already imposed by the other constraints.)

It is possible with Excel to use the IF function to represent this relationship between y_1 and D and between y_2 and W.[3] Unfortunately, the IF function does not fit into a linear programming (or integer programming) format. Consequently, the Excel Solver has difficulty solving spreadsheet models that use this function. This is why another formulation with ordinary linear programming constraints is needed instead to express these relationships.

Since the other constraints impose bounds on D and W of $0 \le D \le 4$ and $0 \le W \le 6$, here are some ordinary linear programming constraints that ensure these relationships.

$$D \le 4\,y_1$$

$$W \le 6\,y_2$$

These constraints force the model to refuse production if the corresponding setup is not performed.

Note that setting $y_1 = 0$ gives $D \le 0$, which forces the nonnegative D to be $D = 0$, whereas setting $y_1 = 1$ gives $D \le 4$, which allows all the values of D already allowed by the other constraints. Then check that the same conclusions apply for W when setting $y_2 = 0$ and $y_2 = 1$.

It was not necessary to choose 4 and 6 for the respective coefficients of y_1 and y_2 in these two constraints. Any coefficients *larger* than 4 and 6 would have the same effect. You just need to avoid *smaller* coefficients, since this would impose undesired restrictions on D and W when $y_1 = 1$ and $y_2 = 1$.

On larger problems, it is sometimes difficult to determine the smallest acceptable coefficients for these auxiliary binary variables. Therefore, it is common to formulate the model by just using a reasonably large number (say, 99 in this case) that is safely larger than the smallest acceptable coefficient.

Figure 9.8 shows one way of formulating this model when using the number 99. The format for the first 14 rows is the same as for the original problem, so the difference arises in rows 15–17 of the spreadsheet. The values of the auxiliary binary variables, y_1 and y_2, appear in the new changing cells, Setup? (C17:D17). The bottom of the figure identifies the equations entered into the output cells in row 16, C16 = 99*C17 and D16 = 99*D17. Consequently, the constraints, UnitsProduced (C14:D14) $\le$ OnlyIfSetup (C16:D16), impose the relationships that $D \le 99y_1$ and $W \le 99y_2$.

The changing cells in this spreadsheet show the optimal solution obtained after applying the Excel Solver. Thus, this solution is to not produce any doors ($y_1 = 0$ and $D = 0$) but to perform the setup to enable producing 6 windows ($y_2 = 1$ and $W = 6$) to obtain a net profit of $1,700.

Note that this optimal solution does indeed satisfy the requirements that $D = 0$ must hold when $y_1 = 0$ and that $W > 0$ can hold when $y_2 = 1$. The constraints do permit performing a setup to produce a product and then not producing any units ($y_1 = 1$ with $D = 0$ or $y_2 = 1$ with $W = 0$), but the objective function causes an optimal solution automatically to avoid this fool-

---

[3]This is not straightforward since, for example, in the case where y_1 is not equal to 0 in the IF function, D needs to be set equal to a cell that is constrained to equal the changing cell holding the value of D.

FIGURE 9.8

A spreadsheet model for variation 1 of the Wyndor problem, where the Excel Solver gives the optimal solution shown in the changing cells, UnitsProduced (C14:D14) and Setup? (C17:D17).

	A	B	C	D	E	F	G	H
1		**Wyndor Glass Co. Product-Mix with Setup Costs**						
2								
3			Doors	Windows				
4		Unit Profit	$300	$500				
5		Setup Cost	$700	$1,300				
6								
7					Hours		Hours	
8			Hours Used per Unit Produced		Used		Available	
9		Plant 1	1	0	0	≤	4	
10		Plant 2	0	2	12	≤	12	
11		Plant 3	3	2	12	≤	18	
12								
13			Doors	Windows				
14		Units Prod'd	0	6				
15			≤	≤			Production Profit	$3,000
16		Only If Setup	0	99			−Total Setup Cost	$1,300
17		Setup?	0	1			Total Profit	$1,700

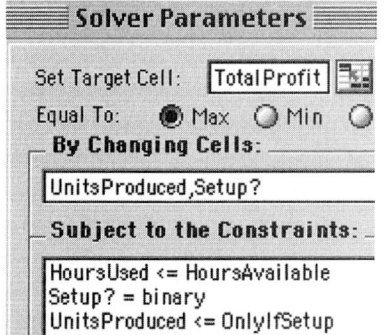

Solver Parameters

Set Target Cell: `TotalProfit`

Equal To: ● Max   ○ Min   ○

By Changing Cells:

`UnitsProduced,Setup?`

Subject to the Constraints:

```
HoursUsed <= HoursAvailable
Setup? = binary
UnitsProduced <= OnlyIfSetup
```

Solver Options

☑ Assume Linear Model
☑ Assume Non-Negative

Range Name	Cells
HoursAvailable	G9:G11
HoursUsed	E9:E11
HoursUsedPerUnitProduced	C9:D11
OnlyIfSetup	C16:D16
ProductionProfit	H15
Setup?	C17:D17
SetupCost	C5:D5
TotalProfit	H17
TotalSetupCost	H16
UnitProfit	C4:D4
UnitsProduced	C14:D14

	E
7	Hours
8	Used
9	=SUMPRODUCT(C9:D9,UnitsProduced)
10	=SUMPRODUCT(C10:D10,UnitsProduced)
11	=SUMPRODUCT(C11:D11,UnitsProduced)

	B	C	D
16	Only If Setup	=99*C17	=99*D17

	G	H
15	Production Profit	=SUMPRODUCT(UnitProfit,UnitsProduced)
16	−Total Setup Cost	=SUMPRODUCT(SetupCost,Setup?)
17	Total Profit	=ProductionProfit − TotalSetupCost

ish option of incurring the setup cost for no purpose. None of this would have been possible without introducing the auxiliary binary variables y_1 and y_2.

Variation 2: Wyndor with Mutually Exclusive Products

Instead of the changes in variation 1, suppose now that the only change from the original Wyndor problem is the following.

Change for variation 2: The two potential new products (doors and windows) would compete for the same customers. Therefore, management has decided not to produce both of them together. At most one can be chosen for production, so

We now must choose between the two products.

$$\text{either} \quad D = 0 \quad \text{or} \quad W = 0 \quad \text{(or both)}$$

Thus, we now are dealing with *mutually exclusive products.*

Figure 9.9 shows the feasible region for this problem, namely, the line segment from $(0, 0)$ to $(4, 0)$ and the line segment from $(0, 0)$ to $(0, 6)$. These are the only solutions from the feasible region for the original problem for which either $x_1 = 0$ or $x_2 = 0$. For this tiny problem, it can be seen from the figure that the feasible solution that maximizes P (i.e., the optimal solution) is

$$(D, W) = (0, 6) \quad \text{with} \quad P = 3,000$$

Linear or integer programming models require that every constraint must be satisfied, so either-or restrictions need to be reformulated to fit this format.

Linear or integer programming models do not permit an *either-or-restriction* such as *either $D = 0$ or $W = 0$*. How can we rewrite this restriction in a standard form to fit such a model so that the model can be solved by available algorithms (including those in the Excel Solver)?

As illustrated by the case study in Section 9.2, if D and W were binary variables, we would only need to rewrite the restriction that the two products are mutually exclusive alternatives as $D + W \leq 1$. However, D and W represent production rates that can take on various values besides 0 and 1, so this constraint does not work.

Now watch auxiliary binary variables come to the rescue again.

Formulation with Auxiliary Binary Variables

For each product, there are just two possibilities regarding the decision of whether it can be produced. Either it can or it cannot. Therefore, we can associate each of the two values of an auxiliary binary variable with one of these possibilities. Specifically, let the auxiliary binary variables be

$$y_1 = \begin{cases} 1, & \text{if } D > 0 \text{ can hold (can produce doors)} \\ 0, & \text{if } D = 0 \text{ must hold (cannot produce doors)} \end{cases}$$

$$y_2 = \begin{cases} 1, & \text{if } W > 0 \text{ can hold (can produce windows)} \\ 0, & \text{if } W = 0 \text{ must hold (cannot produce windows)} \end{cases}$$

FIGURE 9.9

The dark line segments show the feasible solutions for variation 2 of the Wyndor problem.

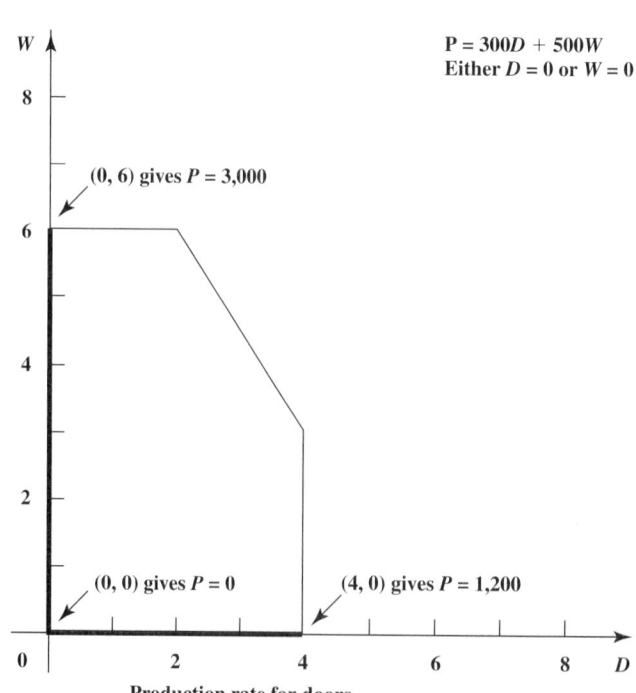

The relationships between y_1 and D, as well as between y_2 and W, are identical to the ones for variation 1. Therefore, Figure 9.10 demonstrates that the analogous constraints involving these variables, UnitsProduced (C13:D13) $\leq$ OnlyIfProduce (C15:D15) and Produce? (C16:D16) = binary, can be used to ensure that these relationships hold. To make the products mutually exclusive, we now add the usual kind of constraint for mutually exclusive alternatives with regard to these two binary variables,

$$y_1 + y_2 \leq 1$$

which gives the constraint, TotalProduced (E16) $\leq$ MaximumToProduce (G16), in the spreadsheet model. This forces either C16 = 0 or D16 = 0 (or both).

FIGURE 9.10

A spreadsheet model for variation 2 of the Wyndor problem, where the Excel Solver provides the optimal solution shown in the changing cells, UnitsProduced (C13:D13) and Produce? (C16:D16).

	A	B	C	D	E	F	G
1		**Wyndor Glass Co. with Mutually Exclusive Products**					
2							
3			Doors	Windows			
4		Unit Profit	$300	$500			
5							
6					Hours		Hours
7			Hours Used per Unit Produced		Used		Available
8		Plant 1	1	0	0	$\leq$	4
9		Plant 2	0	2	12	$\leq$	12
10		Plant 3	3	2	12	$\leq$	18
11							
12			Doors	Windows			
13		Units Produced	0	6			
14			$\leq$	$\leq$	Total		Maximum
15		Only If Produce	0	99	Produced		to Produce
16		Produce?	0	1	1	$\leq$	1
17							
18							Total Profit
19							$3,000

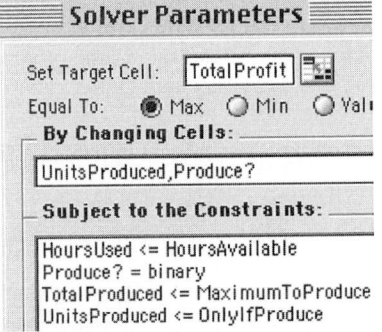

Solver Parameters

Set Target Cell: TotalProfit

Equal To: ● Max ○ Min ○ Val
By Changing Cells:

UnitsProduced,Produce?

Subject to the Constraints:

HoursUsed <= HoursAvailable
Produce? = binary
TotalProduced <= MaximumToProduce
UnitsProduced <= OnlyIfProduce

Range Name	Cells
HoursAvailable	G8:G10
HoursUsed	E8:E10
HoursUsedPerUnitProduced	C8:D10
MaximumToProduce	G16
OnlyIfProduce	C15:D15
Produce?	C16:D16
TotalProduced	E16
TotalProfit	G19
UnitProfit	C4:D4
UnitsProduced	C13:D13

	E
6	Hours
7	Used
8	=SUMPRODUCT(C8:D8,UnitsProduced)
9	=SUMPRODUCT(C9:D9,UnitsProduced)
10	=SUMPRODUCT(C10:D10,UnitsProduced)

	B	C	D
15	Only If Produce	=99*C16	=99*D16

Solver Options

☑ Assume Linear Model
☑ Assume Non-Negative

	E
14	Total
15	Produced
16	=SUM(Produce?)

	G
18	Total Profit
19	=SUMPRODUCT(UnitProfit,UnitsProduced)

These are the only new constraints needed along with the constraints of the original model. Since D and W now have their original definitions as *production rates* (change 2 for variation 1 no longer applies), these variables do not need to have integer values, so the model in Figure 9.10 is a mixed BIP model.

In contrast to variation 1, there are no extra costs associated with any values of y_1 and y_2. The original objective function, without y_1 and y_2, still applies, as indicated by the equation entered into the target cell TotalProfit (G19).

The Excel Solver gives the optimal solution shown in the changing cells, namely, the windows are the product chosen to be produced, and then they are produced at the maximum rate ($W = 6$) allowed by the original constraints.

For such a small problem, we were able to find this optimal solution from Figure 9.9 without introducing auxiliary binary variables. However, auxiliary binary variables become necessary when dealing with larger problems. For example, if this pair of mutually exclusive products is just part of a larger group of products under consideration, then the larger model would need to add the constraints involving y_1 and y_2.

You will see this same approach included again in the first example of the next section when there are *three* potential new products and *at most two* can be chosen to be produced.

Variation 3: Wyndor with Either-Or Constraints

Now suppose that the only change from the original Wyndor problem is the one spelled out below.

We now must choose between two plants to help produce the doors and windows.

Change for variation 3: The company has just opened a new plant (plant 4) that is similar to plant 3, so the new plant can perform the same operations as plant 3 to help produce the two new products (doors and windows). However, for administrative reasons, management wants just one of the plants to be chosen to work on these products. The plant chosen should be the one that provides the most profitable product mix.

Table 9.5 gives the data for this problem. This table is identical to Table 2.1 for the original problem except for the addition of the data for plant 4. Although the hours of production time are different for plants 3 and 4 (because of differences in the types of production facilities being used), the costs of the operations for each product are essentially the same for the two plants. Therefore, the unit profits in the last row of the table are unaffected by the choice of which plant to use for these products.

The data for plant 4 indicate that if this plant is chosen, then we must satisfy the constraint

$$2D + 4W \leq 28$$

when solving for the most profitable product mix. However, if plant 3 is chosen instead, then this constraint is irrelevant and we must instead satisfy the original constraint for plant 3,

$$3D + 2W \leq 18$$

A pair of either-or constraints allows either one to be chosen as the one that must be satisfied and then the other one can be ignored.

In other words, the relevant restriction is the following pair of **either-or constraints:**

$$\text{Either} \quad 3D + 2W \leq 18$$

$$\text{Or} \quad 2D + 4W \leq 28$$

TABLE 9.5
Data for Variation 3 of the Wyndor Problem

Plant	Production Time Used for Each Unit Produced (Hours)		Production Time Available per Week (Hours)
	Doors	*Windows*	
1	1	0	4
2	0	2	12
3	3	2	18
4	2	4	28
Unit profit	$300	$500	

Choosing one of these two constraints as the one that must be satisfied corresponds to choosing one of the two plants to help produce the doors and windows. The choice of which plant depends on which one allows the largest total profit when considering all the constraints of the model.

Figure 9.11 shows the effect of these two choices. If plant 3 were chosen to help produce these two products (so $3D + 2W \le 18$ is relevant but $2D + 4W \le 28$ is not), then we would have the linear programming problem on the left side of the figure. Since this problem is identical to the original Wyndor problem shown in Figure 9.6, the best available solution would be

$$(D, W) = (2, 6) \quad \text{with} \quad P = 3{,}600$$

However, if plant 4 were chosen instead (so $2D + 4W \le 28$ is relevant but $3D + 2W \le 18$ is not), then we would have the linear programming problem on the right side of the figure. The best available solution for this problem would be

$$(D, W) = (4, 5) \quad \text{with} \quad P = 3{,}700$$

Since $P = 3{,}700$ is larger than $P = 3{,}600$, the largest possible weekly profit is \$3,700, which is only obtainable by choosing plant 4 instead of plant 3 to help produce the two new products.

Despite its either-or constraints, we have just managed to solve the complete model for variation 3 by solving and comparing two linear programming problems. However, solving larger models with several pairs of either-or constraints in this way would require solving and comparing numerous linear programming problems. We would much prefer to be able to apply a standard algorithm (such as those used by the Excel Solver) just once to solve the model.

Unfortunately, the model for variation 3 is not a linear programming model, since either-or constraints are not allowed in linear or integer programming. In fact, this model does not fit the format for *any* kind of standard model. Therefore, we cannot use a standard algorithm once to find an optimal solution for this model in its current form.

How can we reformulate this model into a standard format where a standard algorithm can be used one time to find an optimal solution? Once again, auxiliary binary variables come to the rescue.

Either-or constraints need to be reformulated to fit the format of linear or integer programming models.

FIGURE 9.11

These two graphs for variation 3 of the Wyndor problem show the linear programming problem and its optimal solution that would result if the plant chosen to help produce the two new products were (*a*) plant 3 or (*b*) plant 4.

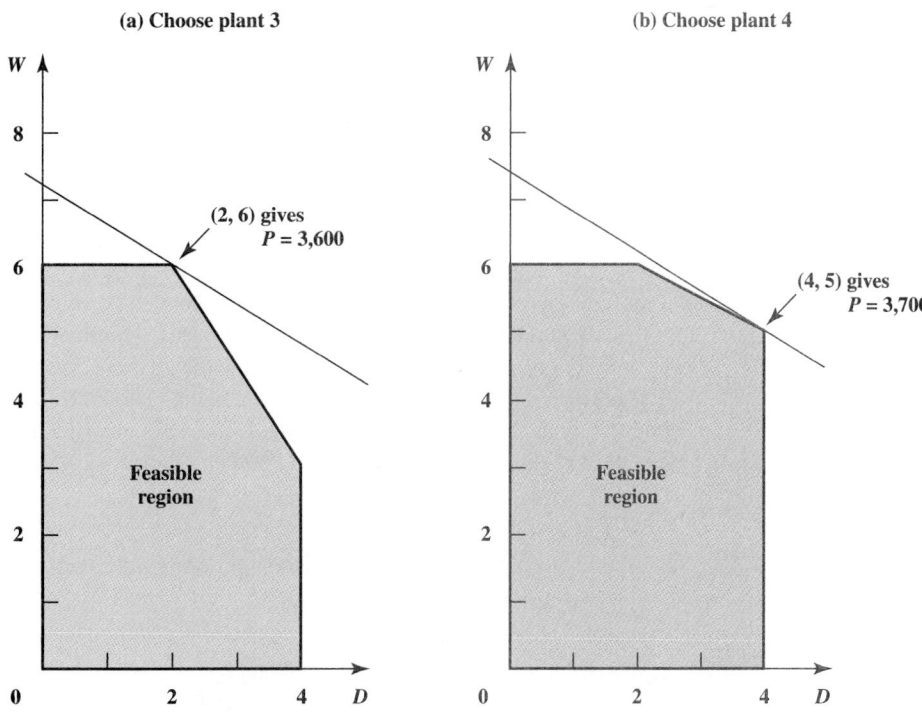

Formulation with an Auxiliary Binary Variable

This one auxiliary binary variable is all that is needed to fit the model into the format of a mixed BIP model.

There are just two possibilities: either $3D + 2W \leq 18$ must hold (due to choosing plant 3) or $2D + 4W \leq 28$ must hold (due to choosing plant 4). Therefore, we can introduce an auxiliary binary variable y to indicate which possibility is chosen by defining y as

$$y = \begin{cases} 1, & \text{if } 2D + 4W \leq 28 \text{ must hold (choose plant 4)} \\ 0, & \text{if } 3D + 2W \leq 18 \text{ must hold (choose plant 3)} \end{cases}$$

This definition is enforced by introducing an extremely large positive number (we will use 99 again) and then making the following changes in the model.

	Replace	by
Either	$3D + 2W \leq 18$	$3D + 2W \leq 18 + 99y$
Or	$2D + 4W \leq 28$	$2D + 4W \leq 28 + 99(1 - y)$
		y is binary

To see why these new constraints work, check what happens when $y = 0$.

$y = 0$	gives	$3D + 2W \leq 18$
	and	$2D + 4W \leq 28 + 99$ (a relatively huge number)

so

$3D + 2W \leq 18$ must hold

but $\quad 2D + 4W \leq 28$ does not need to hold

Since the other constraints in the model prevent $2D + 4W$ from being much larger than 28, having $y = 0$ give $2D + 4W \leq 28 + 99$ has the same effect as eliminating this constraint from the model. Similarly,

$y = 1$	gives	$3D + 2W \leq 18 + 99$ (a relatively huge number)
	and	$2D + 4W \leq 28$

so

$3D + 2W \leq 18$ does not need to hold

but $\quad 2D + 4W \leq 28$ must hold

Again, adding 99 to the right-hand side of $3D + 2W \leq 18$ is equivalent to eliminating the constraint.

Figure 9.12 shows how this approach can be incorporated into a spreadsheet model. An additional changing cell (E16) displays the value of y. As indicated in the figure by the equations entered into cells G10 and G11, these cells give the modified right-hand sides of the plants 3 and 4 constraints that result from the value of y. With the constraints included in the Solver dialogue box, we now have a mixed BIP model that can be solved by the Excel Solver.

Clicking on the Solve button causes the Solver to simultaneously choose the value of y and the production rates (D and W) that maximize the total profit given in the target cell TotalProfit (H14). Since $y = 1$ in this optimal solution, plant 4 should be chosen to help produce the new products, with $D = 4$ and $W = 5$. This choice of plant provides a weekly profit of \$3,700 rather than the \$3,600 obtainable by choosing plant 3 instead.

Review Questions

1. What is the distinction between a binary decision variable and an auxiliary binary variable?

2. Why is a linear programming formulation no longer valid for a product-mix problem when there are setup costs for initiating production?

3. How can an auxiliary binary variable be defined in terms of whether a setup is performed to initiate the production of a certain product?

4. What is meant by *mutually exclusive products*?

FIGURE 9.12

A spreadsheet model for variation 3 of the Wyndor problem, where the Excel Solver gives the optimal solution shown in the changing cells, UnitsProduced (C14:D14) and WhichPlantToUse? (E16).

	A	B	C	D	E	F	G	H
1		**Wyndor Glass Co. Problem with Either–Or Constraints**						
2								
3			Doors	Windows				
4		Unit Profit	$300	$500				
5							Modified	
6					Hours		Hours	Hours
7			Hours Used per Unit Produced		Used		Available	Available
8		Plant 1	1	0	4	≤	4	4
9		Plant 2	0	2	10	≤	12	12
10		Plant 3	3	2	22	≤	117	18
11		Plant 4	2	4	28	≤	28	28
12								
13			Doors	Windows				
14		Units Prod'd	4	5			Total Profit	$3,700
15								
16		Which Plant to Use? (0=Plant 3, 1=Plant 4)			1			

Solver Parameters

Set Target Cell: [Total Profit]

Equal To: ● Max ○ Min ○ Value

By Changing Cells:

[UnitsProduced,WhichPlantToUse?]

Subject to the Constraints:

[HoursUsed <= ModifiedHoursAvailable
WhichPlantToUse? = binary]

Range Name	Cells
HoursAvailable	H8:H11
HoursUsed	E8:E11
HoursUsedPerUnitProduced	C8:D11
ModifiedHoursAvailable	G8:G11
TotalProfit	H14
UnitProfit	C4:D4
UnitsProduced	C14:D14
WhichPlantToUse?	E16

Solver Options

☑ Assume Linear Model

☑ Assume Non-Negative

	E	F	G
5			Modified
6	Hours		Hours
7	Used		Available
8	=SUMPRODUCT(C8:D8,UnitsProduced)	≤	=H8
9	=SUMPRODUCT(C9:D9,UnitsProduced)	≤	=H9
10	=SUMPRODUCT(C10:D10,UnitsProduced)	≤	=H10+99*WhichPlantToUse?
11	=SUMPRODUCT(C11:D11,UnitsProduced)	≤	=H11+99*(1-WhichPlantToUse?)

	G	H
14	Total Profit	=SUMPRODUCT(UnitProfit,UnitsProduced)

5. How can an auxiliary binary variable be defined in terms of whether to allow the production of a certain product?

6. How does an either-or constraint arise in variation 3 of the Wyndor problem?

7. When two individual constraints are paired together as either-or constraints, how can an auxiliary binary variable be defined in terms of which one of these individual constraints is chosen as the one that must hold?

9.5 SOME FORMULATION EXAMPLES

We now present a series of examples that illustrate a variety of formulation techniques with binary variables, including those discussed in the preceding sections. For the sake of clarity, these examples have been kept very small. In actual applications, these formulations typically would be just a small part of a vastly larger model.

Example 1: Imposing Managerial Restrictions

The Research and Development Division of the Good Products Company has developed three possible new products. However, to avoid undue diversification of the company's product line, management has imposed the following restriction:

> **Restriction 1:** From the three possible new products, *at most two* should be chosen to be produced.

Each of these products can be produced in either of two plants. For administrative reasons, management has imposed a second restriction in this regard:

> **Restriction 2:** Just one of the two plants should be chosen to be the sole producer of the new products.

The production cost per unit of each product would be essentially the same in the two plants. However, because of differences in their production facilities, the number of hours of production time needed per unit of each product might differ between the two plants. These data are given in Table 9.6 along with other relevant information, including marketing estimates of the number of units of each product that could be sold per week if it is produced. According to management, the objective is to choose the products, the plant, and the production rates of the chosen products so as to maximize the total profit.

In some ways, this problem resembles a standard *product-mix problem* such as the Wyndor Glass Co. case study described in Section 2.2. In fact, if we changed the problem by dropping the two restrictions *and* by requiring each unit of a product to use the production hours given in Table 9.6 in *both plants* (so the two plants now perform different operations needed by the products), it would become just such a problem. In particular, let x_1, x_2, and x_3 be the production rates of the respective products. Displaying the values of these decision variables in changing cells UnitsProduced (C12:E12), the spreadsheet model then would become the one shown in rows 1–13 and 15 of Figure 9.13 if column H and the other rows were omitted except for TotalProfit (H21). MaximumSales (C15:E15) provides upper bounds on the production rates for the three products, so

$$x_1 \le 7, \qquad x_2 \le 5, \qquad x_3 \le 9$$

are needed as constraints in the model.

For the real problem, however, restriction 1 necessitates adding to the model the constraint:

No more than two of the decision variables (x_1, x_2, x_3) can have a value greater than zero.

TABLE 9.6
Data for Example 1 (The Good Products Co. Problem)

		Production Time Used for Each Unit Produced (Hours)			Production Time Available per Week (Hours)
		Product 1	Product 2	Product 3	
Plant					
	1	3	4	2	30
	2	4	6	2	40
Unit profit		5	7	3	(thousands of dollars)
Sales potential		7	5	9	(units per week)

FIGURE 9.13 A spreadsheet formulation of the mixed BIP model for the Good Products Co. problem, where the Excel Solver provides the optimal solution given in the changing cells, UnitsProduced (C12:E12), Produce? (C17:E17), and WhichPlantToUse? (E21).

	A	B	C	D	E	F	G	H	I
1		**Good Products Co. with Managerial Restrictions**							
2									
3			Product 1	Product 2	Product 3				
4		Unit Profit ($thousands)	5	7	3				
5								Modified	
6						Hours		Hours	Hours
7			Hours Used per Unit Produced			Used		Available	Available
8		Plant 1	3	4	2	34.5	≤	129	30
9		Plant 2	4	6	2	40	≤	40	40
10									
11			Product 1	Product 2	Product 3				
12		Units Produced	5.5	0	9				
13			≤	≤	≤				
14		Only If Produce	7	0	9				
15		Maximum Sales	7	5	9	Total		Maximum	
16						Produced		to Produce	
17		Produce?	1	0	1	2	≤	2	
18									
19								Total Profit	
20								($thousands)	
21		Which Plant to Use? (0=Plant 1, 1=Plant 2)			1			54.5	

Solver Parameters

Set Target Cell: TotalProfit

Equal To: ● Max ○ Min ○ Value

By Changing Cells:

UnitsProduced,Produce?,WhichPlantT

Subject to the Constraints:

HoursUsed <= ModifiedHoursAvailable
Produce? = binary
TotalProduced <= MaximumToProduce
UnitsProduced <= OnlyIfProduce
WhichPlantToUse? = binary

Solver Options

☑ Assume Linear Model
☑ Assume Non-Negative

Range Name	Cells
HoursAvailable	I8:I9
HoursUsed	F8:F9
HoursUsedPerUnitProduced	C8:E9
MaximumSales	C15:E15
MaximumToProduce	H17
ModifiedHoursAvailable	H8:H9
OnlyIfProduce	C14:E14
Produce?	C17:E17
TotalProduced	F17
TotalProfit	H21
UnitProfit	C4:E4
UnitsProduced	C12:E12
WhichPlantToUse?	E21

	F
15	Total
16	Produced
17	=SUM(Produce?)

	B	C	D	E
14	Only If Produce	=C15*C17	=D15*D17	=E15*E17

	F	G	H
5			Modified
6	Hours		Hours
7	Used		Available
8	=SUMPRODUCT(C8:E8,UnitsProduced)	≤	=I8+99*WhichPlantToUse?
9	=SUMPRODUCT(C9:E9,UnitsProduced)	≤	=I9+99*(1-WhichPlantToUse?)

	H
19	Total Profit
20	($thousands)
21	=SUMPRODUCT(UnitProfit,UnitsProduced)

This constraint does not fit into a linear or integer programming format, so the key question is how to convert it to such a format so that a corresponding algorithm can be used to solve the overall model. If the decision variables were binary variables, then the constraint would be expressed in this format as $x_1 + x_2 + x_3 \leq 2$. However, with *continuous* decision variables, a more complicated approach involving the introduction of auxiliary binary variables is needed.

Restriction 2 necessitates replacing the first two functional constraints ($3x_1 + 4x_2 + 2x_3 \leq 30$ and $4x_1 + 6x_2 + 2x_3 \leq 40$) by the restriction

$$\text{Either} \quad 3x_1 + 4x_2 + 2x_3 \leq 30$$

$$\text{Or} \quad 4x_1 + 6x_2 + 2x_3 \leq 40$$

must hold, where the choice of which constraint must hold corresponds to the choice of which plant will be used to produce the new products. Variation 3 of the Wyndor problem in the preceding section illustrated how such either-or constraints can be converted to a linear or integer programming format, again with the help of an auxiliary binary variable.

Formulation with Auxiliary Binary Variables

Review the formulation for variation 2 of the Wyndor problem to see how to deal with restriction 1.

Except for involving more products and choices, restriction 1 is similar to the restriction imposed in variation 2 of the Wyndor problem in the preceding section. For variation 2, there were just *two* new products, and the restriction was that *at most one* could be chosen to be produced. Following the formulation approach used there, we can deal with restriction 1 by introducing *three* auxiliary binary variables (y_1, y_2, y_3) with the interpretation that

$$y_j = \begin{cases} 1, & \text{if } x_j > 0 \text{ can hold (can produce product } j) \\ 0, & \text{if } x_j = 0 \text{ must hold (cannot produce product } j) \end{cases}$$

for $j = 1, 2, 3$. To enforce this interpretation in the model, we replace the constraints on the maximum production rates of the three products—$x_1 \leq 7$, $x_2 \leq 5$, and $x_3 \leq 9$—by the new constraints,

$$x_1 \leq 7y_1, \qquad x_2 \leq 5y_2, \qquad x_3 \leq 9y_3$$

Therefore, $y_1 = 1$ allows any feasible value of x_1, whereas $y_1 = 0$ forces $x_1 = 0$, and both y_2 and y_3 have the same effect on x_2 and x_3, respectively. We also add the constraints,

$$y_1 + y_2 + y_3 \leq 2$$

$$y_j \text{ is binary}, \qquad \text{for } j = 1, 2, 3$$

Review the formulation for variation 3 of the Wyndor problem to see how to deal with restriction 2.

Consequently, when these constraints force choosing at most two of the y_j to equal 1, this amounts to choosing at most two of the new products as the ones that can be produced.

To deal with restriction 2, we use the same approach as for variation 3 of the Wyndor problem in the preceding section. Therefore, we introduce another auxiliary binary variable y_4 with the interpretation that

$$y_4 = \begin{cases} 1, & \text{if } 4x_1 + 6x_2 + 2x_3 \leq 40 \text{ must hold (choose plant 2)} \\ 0, & \text{if } 3x_1 + 4x_2 + 2x_3 \leq 30 \text{ must hold (choose plant 1)} \end{cases}$$

This interpretation is enforced by adding the constraints

$$3x_1 + 4x_2 + 2x_3 \leq 30 + 99y_4$$

$$4x_1 + 6x_2 + 2x_3 \leq 40 + 99(1 - y_4)$$

$$y_4 \text{ is binary}$$

Both column H and rows 13–21 of Figure 9.13 show how all of this can be incorporated into the spreadsheet model in an intuitive way. The additional changing cells, Produce? (C17:E17) and WhichPlantToUse? (E21), give the values of the four auxiliary binary variables, so all four cells are constrained to be binary. The constraint that TotalProduced (F17) $\leq$ MaximumToProduce (H17) forces choosing at most two of the new products to be produced. The equations entered into OnlyIfProduce (C14:E14)—as shown at the bottom of the figure—give the values of

$7y_1$, $5y_2$, and $9y_3$, so the constraints that UnitsProduced (C12:E12) $\leq$ OnlyIfProduce (C14:E14) force the production rate of a product to be 0 in row 12 if the decision has been made in row 17 not to produce that product. With the equations that are shown for ModifiedHours Available (H8:H9), the constraints that HoursUsed (F18:F19) $\leq$ ModifiedHoursAvailable (H8:H9) correspond to the algebraic constraints given at the end of the preceding paragraph.

The spreadsheet model now is a mixed BIP model, with three continuous decision variables [UnitsProduced (C12:E12)] and four auxiliary binary variables [Produce? (C17:E17) and WhichPlantToUse? (E21)], so now the problem is formulated in a form that can be solved. Using the Excel Solver gives the optimal solution shown in the changing cells in Figure 9.13, namely, choose products 1 and 3 to produce, choose plant 2 for the production, and choose the production rates of 5½ units per week for product 1 and 9 units per week for product 3. The resulting total profit given in the target cell TotalProfit (H21) is $54,500 per week.

Example 2: Violating Proportionality

The Supersuds Corporation is developing its marketing plans for next year's new products. For three of these products, the decision has been made to purchase a total of five TV spots for commercials on national television networks. Each spot will feature a single product. Therefore, the problem on which we will focus is how to allocate the five spots to these three products, with a maximum of three spots (and a minimum of zero) for each product.

Table 9.7 shows the estimated impact of allocating zero, one, two, or three spots to each product. This impact is measured in terms of the *profit* from the *additional sales* that would result from the spots, considering also the cost of producing the commercial and purchasing the spots. The objective is to allocate five spots to the products so as to maximize the total profit.

This problem is small enough that it can be solved easily by trial and error. (The optimal solution is to allocate two spots to product 1, no spots to product 2, and three spots to product 3.) However, we will show one formulation with auxiliary binary variables for illustrative purposes. Such a formulation would become necessary if this small problem needed to be incorporated into a larger model involving the allocation of resources to marketing activities for all the corporation's new products.

A Formulation with Auxiliary Binary Variables

A natural formulation would be to let

x_1 = Number of TV spots allocated to product 1

x_2 = Number of TV spots allocated to product 2

x_3 = Number of TV spots allocated to product 3

P = Total profit (in millions of dollars)

Without a fixed unit profit for each additional TV spot allocated to the same product, we can't use a SUMPRODUCT function to obtain the total profit, so this doesn't fit integer programming yet.

The contribution of each of these integer decision variables (x_1, x_2, x_3) to P then would be given by the corresponding column in Table 9.7. However, each column indicates that profit is *not* proportional to the number of TV spots allocated to that product. Therefore, we cannot write a legitimate objective function in terms of these decision variables to fit integer programming. Using the algebraic form, the best that we can do with these decision variables is to formulate

TABLE 9.7
Data for Example 2 (the Supersuds Corp. Problem)

	Profit (Millions)		
Number of TV Spots	**Product 1**	**Product 2**	**Product 3**
0	0	0	0
1	$1	0	−$1
2	3	$2	2
3	3	3	4

an incomplete integer programming model (not a *binary* integer programming model) that includes all the needed constraints but not an objective function.

$$\text{Maximize } P = ?$$

subject to

$$x_1 \leq 3$$

$$x_2 \leq 3$$

$$x_3 \leq 3$$

$$x_1 + x_2 + x_3 = 5$$

and

$$x_1 \geq 0 \qquad x_2 \geq 0 \qquad x_3 \geq 0$$

$$x_1, x_2, x_3 \text{ are integers}$$

Now see what happens when we introduce nine auxiliary binary variables with the following interpretations:

$$y_{11} = \begin{cases} 1, & \text{if } x_1 = 1 \\ 0, & \text{otherwise} \end{cases} \quad y_{12} = \begin{cases} 1, & \text{if } x_1 = 2 \\ 0, & \text{otherwise} \end{cases} \quad y_{13} = \begin{cases} 1, & \text{if } x_1 = 3 \\ 0, & \text{otherwise} \end{cases}$$

$$y_{21} = \begin{cases} 1, & \text{if } x_2 = 1 \\ 0, & \text{otherwise} \end{cases} \quad y_{22} = \begin{cases} 1, & \text{if } x_2 = 2 \\ 0, & \text{otherwise} \end{cases} \quad y_{23} = \begin{cases} 1, & \text{if } x_2 = 3 \\ 0, & \text{otherwise} \end{cases}$$

$$y_{31} = \begin{cases} 1, & \text{if } x_3 = 1 \\ 0, & \text{otherwise} \end{cases} \quad y_{32} = \begin{cases} 1, & \text{if } x_3 = 2 \\ 0, & \text{otherwise} \end{cases} \quad y_{33} = \begin{cases} 1, & \text{if } x_3 = 3 \\ 0, & \text{otherwise} \end{cases}$$

For example, look at the definitions of y_{11}, y_{12}, and y_{13}. These definitions imply that

$$(y_{11}, y_{12}, y_{13}) = (0, 0, 0) \qquad \text{if} \qquad x_1 = 0$$

$$(y_{11}, y_{12}, y_{13}) = (1, 0, 0) \qquad \text{if} \qquad x_1 = 1$$

$$(y_{11}, y_{12}, y_{13}) = (0, 1, 0) \qquad \text{if} \qquad x_1 = 2$$

$$(y_{11}, y_{12}, y_{13}) = (0, 0, 1) \qquad \text{if} \qquad x_1 = 3$$

These four alternative values of x_1 are the only possible values. Since these alternative values are mutually exclusive alternatives, y_1, y_2, and y_3 need to satisfy the constraints

$$y_{11} + y_{12} + y_{13} \leq 1$$

$$y_{11}, y_{12}, y_{13} \text{ are binary}$$

Selecting values of y_{11}, y_{12}, and y_{13} that satisfy these constraints is equivalent to selecting a value of x_1 that satisfies the constraints

$$x_1 \leq 3$$

$$x_1 \geq 0$$

$$x_1 \text{ is integer}$$

In just the same way, the other auxiliary binary variables need to satisfy the constraints

$$y_{21} + y_{22} + y_{23} \leq 1$$

$$y_{31} + y_{32} + y_{33} \leq 1$$

$$y_{21}, y_{22}, y_{23}, y_{31}, y_{32}, y_{33} \text{ are binary}$$

Selecting values of these variables that satisfy these constraints is equivalent to selecting values of x_2 and x_3 that satisfy the constraints

$$x_2 \leq 3$$
$$x_3 \leq 3$$
$$x_2 \geq 0, \qquad x_3 \geq 0$$
$$x_2, x_3 \text{ are integers}$$

With these auxiliary binary variables, we now will be able to formulate a BIP model for the problem.

Therefore, we now can formulate a model for the Supersuds problem in terms of these auxiliary binary variables by including the above constraints on these variables. We also need to add a constraint that will ensure that the original constraint,

$$x_1 + x_2 + x_3 = 5$$

still will hold. The key here is to note that the definitions of the auxiliary binary variables imply that

$$x_1 = y_{11} + 2y_{12} + 3y_{13}$$
$$x_2 = y_{21} + 2y_{22} + 3y_{23}$$
$$x_3 = y_{31} + 2y_{32} + 3y_{33}$$

Therefore, the original constraint can be replaced by the constraint

$$y_{11} + 2y_{12} + 3y_{13} + y_{21} + 2y_{22} + 3y_{23} + y_{31} + 2y_{32} + 3y_{33} = 5$$

Finally, we come to the whole reason for bothering with all of this, namely, that the auxiliary binary variables enable us to formulate a legitimate objective function. Using monetary units of millions of dollars, the three profit columns of Table 9.7 respectively indicate that

$$\text{Profit from product 1} = y_{11} + 3y_{12} + 3y_{13}$$
$$\text{Profit from product 2} = 2y_{22} + 3y_{23}$$
$$\text{Profit from product 3} = -y_{31} + 2y_{32} + 4y_{33}$$

Therefore, adding these three profits, the total profit is

$$P = y_{11} + 3y_{12} + 3y_{13} + 2y_{22} + 3y_{23} - y_{31} + 2y_{32} + 4y_{33}$$

Consequently, the complete BIP model for the Supersuds problem can be formulated on a spreadsheet as shown in Figure 9.14, where the changing cells Solution (D11:F13) display the values of the auxiliary binary variables. Clicking on the Solve button then provides the optimal solution shown in these changing cells in the figure, namely,

$y_{11} = 0$	$y_{12} = 1$	$y_{13} = 0$	so	$x_1 = 2$	(allocate 2 TV spots to product 1)
$y_{21} = 0$	$y_{22} = 0$	$y_{23} = 0$	so	$x_2 = 0$	(allocate 0 TV spots to product 2)
$y_{31} = 0$	$y_{32} = 0$	$y_{33} = 1$	so	$x_3 = 3$	(allocate 3 TV spots to product 3)

which yields a profit of $P = 7$ ($7 million), according to the target cell TotalProfit (I13). The number of TV spots being allocated to the respective products is shown in NumberOfSpots (D18:F18).

Example 3: Airline Crew Scheduling

Southwestern Airways needs to assign its crews to cover all its upcoming flights. We will focus on the problem of assigning three crews based in San Francisco (SFO) to the 11 flights shown in Figure 9.15. These same flights are listed in the first column of Table 9.8. The other 12 columns show the 12 feasible sequences of flights for a crew. (The numbers in each column indicate the order of the flights.) Exactly three of the sequences need to be chosen (one per crew) in such a way that every flight is covered. (It is permissible to have more than one crew

FIGURE 9.14

A spreadsheet formulation of the BIP model for the Supersuds problem, where the optimal solution obtained by the Excel Solver is given in Solution (D11:F13), which yields NumberOfSpots (D18:F18).

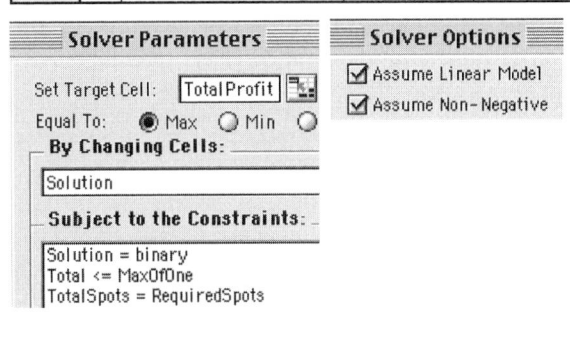

	A	B	C	D	E	F	G	H	I
1		**Supersuds Corp. Marketing Plan**							
2									
3		**Profit**							
4		**($millions)**		Product 1	Product 2	Product 3			
5		Number	1	1	0	-1			
6		of	2	3	2	2			
7		Spots	3	3	3	4			
8									
9									
10		**Solution**		Product 1	Product 2	Product 3			Total
11		Number	1	0	0	0			Profit
12		of	2	1	0	0			($millions)
13		Spots	3	0	0	1			7
14			Total	1	0	1			
15				≤	≤	≤			
16		Max Of One		1	1	1	Total		Required
17							Spots		Spots
18		Number of Spots		2	0	3	5	=	5

Range Name	Cells
MaxOfOne	D16:F16
NumberOfSpots	D18:F18
Profit	D5:F7
RequiredSpots	I18
Solution	D11:F13
Total	D14:F14
TotalProfit	I13
TotalSpots	G18

	I
10	Total
11	Profit
12	($millions)
13	=SUMPRODUCT(Profit,Solution)

	C	D	E	F
14	Total	=SUM(D11:D13)	=SUM(E11:E13)	=SUM(F11:F13)

	C	D	E
18	Number of Spots	=SUMPRODUCT(C11:C13,D11:D13)	=SUMPRODUCT(C11:C13,E11:E13)

	G
16	Total
17	Spots
18	=SUM(NumberOfSpots)

on a flight, where the extra crews would fly as passengers, but union contracts require that the extra crews still be paid for their time as if they were working.) The cost of assigning a crew to a particular sequence of flights is given (in thousands of dollars) in the bottom row of the table. The objective is to minimize the total cost of the three crew assignments that cover all the flights.

FIGURE 9.15
The arrows show the 11 Southwestern Airways flights that need to be covered by the three crews based in San Francisco.

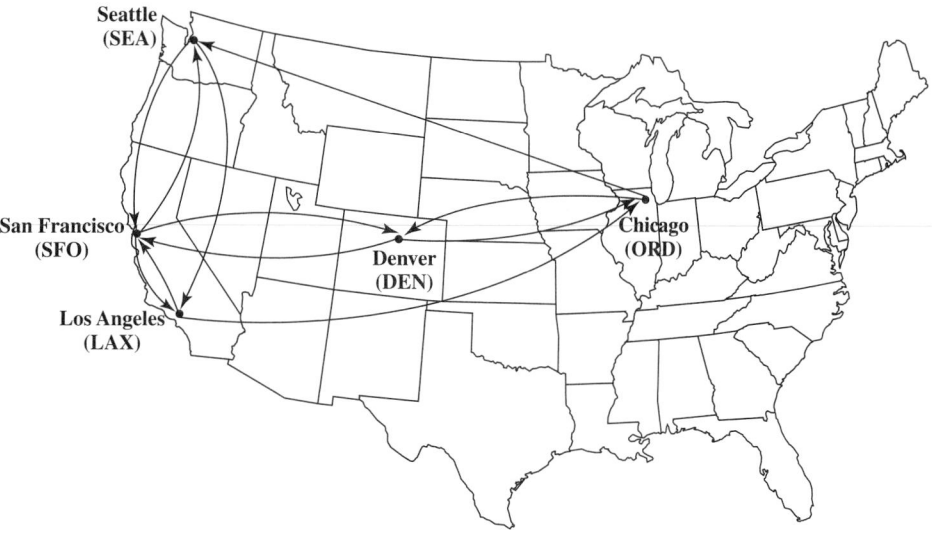

TABLE 9.8
Data for Example 3 (the Southwestern Airways Problem)

Flight	Feasible Sequence of Flights											
	1	2	3	4	5	6	7	8	9	10	11	12
1. San Francisco to Los Angeles (SFO–LAX)	1			1			1			1		
2. San Francisco to Denver (SFO–DEN)		1			1			1			1	
3. San Francisco to Seattle (SFO–SEA)			1			1			1			1
4. Los Angeles to Chicago (LAX–ORD)				2			2		3	2		3
5. Los Angeles to San Francisco (LAX–SFO)	2					3				5	5	
6. Chicago to Denver (ORD–DEN)				3	3				4			
7. Chicago to Seattle (ORD–SEA)							3	3		3	3	4
8. Denver to San Francisco (DEN–SFO)		2		4	4				5			
9. Denver to Chicago (DEN–ORD)					2			2			2	
10. Seattle to San Francisco (SEA–SFO)			2				4	4				5
11. Seattle to Los Angeles (SEA–LAX)						2			2	4	4	2
Cost, $1,000s	2	3	4	6	7	5	7	8	9	9	8	9

Formulation with Binary Variables

With 12 feasible sequences of flights, we have 12 yes-or-no decisions:

Should sequence j be assigned to a crew? $(j = 1, 2, \ldots, 12)$

Therefore, we use 12 binary variables to represent these respective decisions:

$$x_j = \begin{cases} 1, & \text{if sequence } j \text{ is assigned to a crew} \\ 0, & \text{otherwise} \end{cases}$$

FIGURE 9.16   A spreadsheet formulation of the BIP model for the Southwestern Airways crew scheduling problem, where FlySequence (C22:N22) shows the optimal solution obtained by the Excel Solver. The list of flight sequences under consideration is given in cells A25:D37.

	A	B	C	D	E	F	G	H	I	J	K	L	M	N	O	P	Q
1		**Southwestern Airways Crew Scheduling Problem**															
2																	
3								Flight Sequence									
4			1	2	3	4	5	6	7	8	9	10	11	12			
5		Cost ($thousands)	2	3	4	6	7	5	7	8	9	9	8	9			At
6																	Least
7		**Includes Segment?**													Total		One
8		SFO–LAX	1	0	0	1	0	0	1	0	0	1	0	0	1	≥	1
9		SFO–DEN	0	1	0	0	1	0	0	1	0	0	1	0	1	≥	1
10		SFO–SEA	0	0	1	0	0	1	0	0	1	0	0	1	1	≥	1
11		LAX–ORD	0	0	0	1	0	0	1	0	1	1	0	1	1	≥	1
12		LAX–SFO	1	0	0	0	0	1	0	0	0	1	1	0	1	≥	1
13		ORD–DEN	0	0	0	1	1	0	0	0	1	0	0	0	1	≥	1
14		ORD–SEA	0	0	0	0	0	0	1	1	0	1	1	1	1	≥	1
15		DEN–SFO	0	1	0	1	1	0	0	0	1	0	0	0	1	≥	1
16		DEN–ORD	0	0	0	0	1	0	0	1	0	0	1	0	1	≥	1
17		SEA–SFO	0	0	1	0	0	0	1	1	0	0	0	1	1	≥	1
18		SEA–LAX	0	0	0	0	0	1	0	0	1	1	1	1	1	≥	1
19																	
20															Total		Number
21			1	2	3	4	5	6	7	8	9	10	11	12	Sequences		of Crews
22		Fly Sequence?	0	0	1	1	0	0	0	0	0	0	1	0	3	≤	3
23																	
24														Total Cost ($thousands)		18	

25		**Flight Sequence Key**
26	1	SFO-LAX
27	2	SFO-DEN-SFO
28	3	SFO-SEA-SFO
29	4	SFO-LAX-ORD-DEN-SFO
30	5	SFO-DEN-ORD-DEN-SFO
31	6	SFO-SEA-LAX-SFO
32	7	SFO-LAX-ORD-SEA-SFO
33	8	SFO-DEN-ORD-SEA-SFO
34	9	SFO-SEA-LAX-ORD-DEN-SFO
35	10	SFO-LAX-ORD-SEA-LAX-SFO
36	11	SFO-DEN-ORD-SEA-LAX-SFO
37	12	SFO-SEA-LAX-ORD-SEA-SFO

Solver Parameters

Set Target Cell: `TotalCost`

Equal To: ○ Max   ● Min   ○

By Changing Cells:

`FlySequence?`

Subject to the Constraints:

```
FlySequence? = binary
Total >= AtLeastOne
TotalSequences <= NumberOfCrews
```

Solver Options

☑ Assume Linear Model
☑ Assume Non-Negative

Range Name	Cells
AtLeastOne	Q8:Q18
Cost	C5:N5
FlySequence	C22:N22
IncludesSegment?	C8:N18
NumberOfCrews	Q22
Total	O8:O18
TotalCost	Q24
TotalSequences	O22

	O
7	Total
8	=SUMPRODUCT(C8:N8,FlySequence?)
9	=SUMPRODUCT(C9:N9,FlySequence?)
10	=SUMPRODUCT(C10:N10,FlySequence?)
11	=SUMPRODUCT(C11:N11,FlySequence?)
12	=SUMPRODUCT(C12:N12,FlySequence?)
13	=SUMPRODUCT(C13:N13,FlySequence?)
14	=SUMPRODUCT(C14:N14,FlySequence?)
15	=SUMPRODUCT(C15:N15,FlySequence?)
16	=SUMPRODUCT(C16:N16,FlySequence?)
17	=SUMPRODUCT(C17:N17,FlySequence?)
18	=SUMPRODUCT(C18:N18,FlySequence?)
19	
20	Total
21	Sequences
22	=SUM(FlySequence?)

	P	Q
24	Total Cost ($thousands)	=SUMPRODUCT(Cost,FlySequence?)

The most interesting part of this formulation is the nature of each constraint that ensures that a corresponding flight is covered. For example, consider the last flight in Table 9.8 (Seattle to Los Angeles). Five sequences (namely, sequences 6, 9, 10, 11, and 12) include this flight. Therefore, at least one of these five sequences must be chosen. The resulting constraint is

$$x_6 + x_9 + x_{10} + x_{11} + x_{12} \geq 1$$

BIP problems whose constraints have this form are called *set covering problems.*

Using similar constraints for the other 10 flights, Figure 9.16 shows a spreadsheet formulation of the complete BIP model for this problem. The Excel Solver provides the optimal solution shown in Flysequence (C22:N22). In terms of the x_j variables, this solution is

$x_3 = 1$ (assign sequence 3 to a crew)

$x_4 = 1$ (assign sequence 4 to a crew)

$x_{11} = 1$ (assign sequence 11 to a crew)

and all other $x_j = 0$, for a total cost of $18,000 as given by TotalCost (Q24). (Another optimal solution is $x_1 = 1$, $x_5 = 1$, $x_{12} = 1$, and all other $x_j = 0$.)

Many airlines are solving huge BIP models of this kind.

As discussed at the end of Section 9.3, airline crew scheduling has become one important application of BIP in recent years. Problems involving thousands of possible flight sequences now are being solved by using models similar to the one shown above but with thousands of binary variables rather than just a dozen.

Review Questions

1. How does restriction 1 for Example 1 relate to the restriction imposed in variation 2 of the Wyndor problem in the preceding section?

2. After introducing auxiliary binary variables for Example 1, what constraint on these variables forces choosing at most two of the possible new products as the ones that can be produced?

3. When using the natural (integer) decision variables (x_1, x_2, x_3) defined for Example 2, why is it not possible to write a legitimate objective function in terms of these decision variables to fit integer programming?

4. What are the groups of mutually exclusive alternatives that arise when introducing the auxiliary binary variables for Example 2?

5. For Example 3, there is a constraint for each flight to ensure that this flight is covered by a crew. Describe the mathematical form of this constraint. Then explain in words what this constraint is saying.

9.6 Summary

The *divisibility assumption* of linear programming allows the decision variables to have any values, including fractional values, that satisfy the functional and nonnegativity constraints. When this assumption is violated because some or all of the variables need to be restricted to integer values, then *integer programming* should be used instead. The Excel Solver can readily solve integer programming problems of reasonable size.

Managers frequently must make yes-or-no decisions, where the only two possible choices are yes, go ahead with a particular option, or no, decline this option. A binary integer programming (BIP) model considers many options simultaneously, with a binary decision variable for each option. Mixed BIP models include some continuous decision variables as well.

Many companies have saved millions of dollars by formulating and solving BIP models for such diverse applications as capital budgeting, site selection, designing of production and distribution networks, dispatching of shipments, scheduling of interrelated activities, scheduling of asset divestitures, and various airline applications.

In addition to binary decision variables, *auxiliary binary variables* sometimes can be very useful in helping reformulate a model that cannot be solved into a BIP model that is readily solvable. For example, these variables can be used to deal with (1) setup costs for initiating production, (2) mutually exclusive products, and (3) either-or constraints.

Section 9.5 presents a series of examples that illustrate a variety of formulation techniques with binary variables.

Glossary

auxiliary binary variable A binary variable that is introduced into the model, not to represent a yes-or-no decision, but simply to help formulate the model as a (pure or mixed) BIP problem. (Section 9.4), *401*

binary decision variable A binary variable that represents a yes-or-no decision by assigning a value of 1 for choosing yes and a value of 0 for choosing no. (Section 9.4), *401*

binary integer programming Integer programming where all the integer variables are further restricted to be binary variables. (Section 9.1), *389*

binary variable A variable whose only possible values are 0 and 1. (Section 9.1), *389*

BIP Abbreviation for binary integer programming. (Section 9.1), *389*

contingent decision A yes-or-no decision is a contingent decision if it can be yes only if a certain other yes-or-no decision is yes. (Section 9.2), *392*

divisibility assumption A basic assumption of linear programming that allows the decision variables to have any values, including fractional values, that satisfy the functional and nonnegativity constraints. (Section 9.1), *386*

either-or constraints A pair of constraints such that either one can be chosen to be observed and then the other one would be ignored. (Section 9.4), *408*

general integer programming Integer programming where at least some of the integer variables can have any integer values that satisfy the functional and nonnegativity constraints rather than being restricted to the values 0 and 1. (Section 9.1), *389*

graphical method for integer programming A method for solving integer programming

problems that have only two decision variables by graphing the problem on a two-dimensional graph. (Section 9.1), *386*

integer programming A variation of linear programming that has the additional restriction that some or all of the decision variables must have integer values. Encompasses both general integer programming and binary integer programming. (Section 9.1), *389*

integer variable A variable that is allowed to have only integer values. (Section 9.1), *383*

LP relaxation The linear programming problem obtained by deleting from the current integer programming problem the constraints that require at least some of the decision variables to have integer values. (Section 9.1), *386*

mixed BIP problem A BIP problem where some of the variables are restricted to be binary variables but the rest have no special restriction. (Section 9.1), *389*

mixed integer programming Integer programming where only some of the decision variables are required to have integer values. (Section 9.1), *389*

mutually exclusive alternatives A group of alternatives where choosing any one alternative excludes choosing any of the others. (Section 9.2), *391*

pure BIP problem A BIP problem where all the variables are restricted to be binary variables. (Section 9.1), *389*

pure integer programming Integer programming where all the decision variables are required to have integer values. (Section 9.1), *389*

yes-or-no decision A decision whose only possible choices are (1) yes, go ahead with a certain option, or (2) no, decline this option. (Section 9.1), *389*

Learning Aids for This Chapter in Your MS Courseware

Chapter 8 Excel Files:

TBA Airlines Example
California Mfg. Case Study
Three Variants of Wyndor Example
Good Products Example
Supersuds Example
Southwestern Airways Example

Excel Add-ins:

Premium Solver for Education
Solver Table

Supplement to This Chapter on the CD-ROM:

Some Perspectives on Solving Binary Integer Programming Problems

Problems

To the left of the problems (or their parts), we have inserted an E* whenever Excel should be used (unless your instructor gives you contrary instructions). An asterisk on the problem number indicates that at least a partial answer is given in the back of the book.

9.1. Vincent Cardoza is the owner and manager of a machine shop that does custom order work. This Wednesday afternoon, he has received calls from two customers who would like to place rush orders. One is a trailer hitch company that would like some custom-made heavy-duty tow bars. The other is a mini-car-carrier company that needs some customized stabilizer bars. Both customers would like as many as possible by the end of the week (two working days). Since both products would require the use of the same two machines, Vincent needs to decide and inform the customers this afternoon about how many of each product he will agree to make over the next two days.

Each tow bar requires 3.2 hours on machine 1 and 2 hours on machine 2. Each stabilizer bar requires 2.4 hours on machine 1 and 3 hours on machine 2. Machine 1 will be available for 16 hours over the next two days and machine 2 will be available for 15 hours. The profit for each tow bar produced would be $130 and the profit for each stabilizer bar produced would be $150.

Vincent now wants to determine the mix of these production quantities that will maximize the total profit.

a. Formulate an integer programming model in algebraic form for this problem.

b. Use the graphical method for integer programming to solve this model.

E*   *c.* Formulate and solve the model on a spreadsheet.

9.2. Pawtucket University is planning to buy new copier machines for its library. Three members of its Management Science Department are analyzing what to buy. They are considering two different models: Model A, a high-speed copier, and Model B, a lower speed but less expensive copier. Model A can handle 20,000 copies a day and costs $6,000. Model B can handle 10,000 copies a day but only costs $4,000. They would like to have at least six copiers so that they can spread them throughout the library. They also would like to have at least one high-speed copier. Finally, the copiers need to be able to handle a capacity of at least 75,000 copies per day. The objective is to determine the mix of these two copiers that will handle all these requirements at minimum cost.

E*   *a.* Formulate and solve a spreadsheet model for this problem.

b. Formulate this same model in algebraic form.

c. Use the graphical method for integer programming to solve this model.

9.3.* Consider the following algebraic form of an integer programming model:

$$\text{Maximize} \qquad \text{Profit} = 5x_1 + x_2$$

subject to

$$-x_1 + 2x_2 \le 4$$
$$x_1 - x_2 \le 1$$
$$4x_1 + x_2 \le 12$$

and

$$x_1 \ge 0 \qquad x_2 \ge 0$$

$$x_1, x_2 \text{ are integers}$$

a. Use the graphical method for integer programming to solve this model.

b. Use the graphical method for linear programming to solve the LP relaxation of the model. Round this solution to the *nearest* integer solution and check whether it is feasible. Then enumerate *all* the rounded solutions by rounding this solution for the LP relaxation in *all* possible ways (i.e., by rounding each noninteger value both up and down). For each rounded solution, check for feasibility and, if feasible, calculate Profit. Are any of these feasible rounded solutions optimal for the integer programming model?

9.4. Follow the instructions of Problem 9.3 for the following algebraic form of an integer programming model:

$$\text{Maximize} \qquad \text{Profit} = 220x_1 + 80x_2$$

subject to

$$5x_1 + 2x_2 \leq 16$$
$$2x_1 - x_2 \leq 4$$
$$-x_1 + 2x_2 \leq 4$$

and

$$x_1 \geq 0 \qquad x_2 \geq 0$$
$$x_1, x_2 \text{ are integers}$$

9.5.* Northeastern Airlines is considering the purchase of new long-, medium-, and short-range jet passenger airplanes. The purchase price would be $67 million for each long-range plane, $50 million for each medium-range plane, and $35 million for each short-range plane. The board of directors has authorized a maximum commitment of $1.5 billion for these purchases. Regardless of which airplanes are purchased, air travel of all distances is expected to be sufficiently large that these planes would be utilized at essentially maximum capacity. It is estimated that the net annual profit (after capital recovery costs are subtracted) would be $4.2 million per long-range plane, $3 million per medium-range plane, and $2.3 million per short-range plane.

It is predicted that enough trained pilots will be available to the company to crew 30 new airplanes. If only short-range planes were purchased, the maintenance facilities would be able to handle 40 new planes. However, each medium-range plane is equivalent to 1⅓ short-range planes, and each long-range plane is equivalent to 1⅔ short-range planes in terms of their use of the maintenance facilities.

The information given here was obtained by a preliminary analysis of the problem. A more detailed analysis will be conducted subsequently. However, using the preceding data as a first approximation, management wishes to know how many planes of each type should be purchased to maximize profit.

E* *a.* Formulate and solve a spreadsheet model for this problem.

b. Formulate this model in algebraic form.

9.6. Reconsider Problem 6.8 involving a contractor (Susan Meyer) who needs to arrange for hauling gravel from two pits to three building sites.

Susan now needs to hire the trucks (and their drivers) to do the hauling. Each truck can only be used to haul gravel from a single pit to a single site. In addition to the hauling and gravel costs specified in Problem 6.8, there now is a fixed cost of $50 associated with hiring each truck. A truck can haul five tons, but it is not required to go full. For each combination of pit and site, there now are two decisions to be made: the number of trucks to be used and the amount of gravel to be hauled.

a. Formulate a mixed integer programming model in algebraic form for this problem.

E* *b.* Formulate and solve this model on a spreadsheet.

9.7. Reconsider the California Manufacturing Co. case study presented in Section 9.2. The mayor of San Diego now has contacted the company's president, Armando Ortega, to try to persuade him to build a factory and perhaps a warehouse in that city. With the tax incentives being offered the company, Armando's staff estimates that the net present value of building a factory in San Diego would be $7 million and the amount of capital required to do this would be $4 million. The net present value of building a warehouse there would be $5 million and the capital required would be $3 million. (This option will only be considered if a factory also is being built there.)

Armando has asked Steve Chan to revise his previous management science study to incorporate these new alternatives into the overall problem. The objective still is to find the feasible combination of investments that maximizes the total net present value, given that the amount of capital available for these investments is $10 million.

a. Formulate a BIP model in algebraic form for this problem.

E* *b.* Formulate and solve this model on a spreadsheet.

9.8. Select one of the actual applications of BIP by a company mentioned in Section 9.3. Read the article describing the application in the referenced issue of *Interfaces*. (Most of the articles are available for downloading from the Internet and links to their web pages are provided at **www.mhhe.com/hillier2e/articles.**) Write a two-page summary of the application and its benefits.

9.9.* A young couple, Eve and Steven, want to divide their main household chores (marketing, cooking, dishwashing, and laundering) between them so that each has two tasks but the total time they spend on household duties is kept to a minimum. Their efficiencies on these tasks differ, where the time each would need to perform the task is given by the following table:

	Time Needed per Week (Hours)			
	Marketing	**Cooking**	**Dish Washing**	**Laundry**
Eve	4.5	7.8	3.6	2.9
Steven	4.9	7.2	4.3	3.1

    a. Formulate a BIP model in algebraic form for this problem.

E*   *b.* Formulate and solve this model on a spreadsheet.

9.10. A real-estate development firm, Peterson and Johnson, is considering five possible development projects. Using units of millions of dollars, the following table shows the estimated long-run profit (net present value) that each project would generate, as well as the amount of investment required to undertake the project.

	Development Project				
	1	**2**	**3**	**4**	**5**
Estimated profit (millions)	$1	$ 1.8	$ 1.6	$0.8	$1.4
Capital required (millions)	6	12	10	4	8

The owners of the firm, Dave Peterson and Ron Johnson, have raised $20 million of investment capital for these projects. Dave and Ron now want to select the combination of projects that will maximize their total estimated long-run profit (net present value) without investing more than $20 million.

    a. Formulate a BIP model in algebraic form for this problem.

E*   *b.* Formulate and solve this model on a spreadsheet.

E*   *c.* Perform sensitivity analysis on the amount of investment capital made available for the development projects by using the Solver Table to solve the model with the following amounts of investment capital (in millions of dollars): 16, 18, 20, 22, 24, 26, 28, and 30. Include both the changing cells and the target cell as output cells in the Solver Table.

E*9.11. The board of directors of General Wheels Co. is considering seven large capital investments. Each investment can be made only once. These investments differ in the estimated long-run profit (net present value) that they will generate as well as in the amount of capital required, as shown by the following table:

Investment Opportunity	Estimated Profit (Millions)	Capital Required (Millions)
1	$17	$43
2	10	28
3	15	34
4	19	48
5	7	17
6	13	32
7	9	23

The total amount of capital available for these investments is $100 million. Investment opportunities 1 and 2 are mutually exclusive, and so are 3 and 4. Furthermore, neither 3 nor 4 can be undertaken unless one of the first two opportunities is undertaken. There are no such restrictions on investment opportunities 5, 6, and 7. The objective is to select the combination of capital investments that will maximize the total estimated long-run profit (net present value).

    a. Formulate and solve a BIP model on a spreadsheet for this problem.

    b. Perform sensitivity analysis on the amount of capital made available for the investment opportunities by using the Solver Table to solve the model with the following amounts of capital (in millions of dollars): 80, 90, 100, 110, . . ., and 200. Include both the changing cells and the target cell as output cells in the Solver Table.

E*9.12. Reconsider Problem 6.22, where a swim team coach needs to assign swimmers to the different legs of a 200-yard medley relay team. Formulate and solve a BIP model on a spreadsheet for this problem. Identify the groups of mutually exclusive alternatives in this formulation.

E*9.13.* The Research and Development Division of the Progressive Company has been developing four possible new product lines. Management must now make a decision as to which of these four products actually will be produced and at what levels. Therefore, a management science study has been requested to find the most profitable product mix.

    A substantial cost is associated with beginning the production of any product, as given in the first row of the following table. Management's objective is to find the product mix that maximizes the total profit (total net revenue minus start-up costs).

	Product			
	1	**2**	**3**	**4**
Start-up cost	$50,000	$40,000	$70,000	$60,000
Marginal revenue	70	60	90	80

Let the continuous decision variables x_1, x_2, x_3, and x_4 be the total number of units produced of products 1, 2, 3, and 4, respectively. Management has imposed the following policy constraints on these variables:

1. No more than two of the products can be produced.

2. Either product 3 or 4 can be produced only if either product 1 or 2 is produced.

3. Either $5x_1 + 3x_2 + 6x_3 + 4x_4 \leq 6{,}000$
   or $4x_1 + 6x_2 + 3x_3 + 5x_4 \leq 6{,}000$
   Use auxiliary binary variables to formulate and solve a mixed BIP model on a spreadsheet for this problem.

E*9.14. The Toys-R-4-U Company has developed two new toys for possible inclusion in its product line for the upcoming Christmas season. Setting up the production facilities to begin production would cost $50,000 for toy 1 and $80,000 for toy 2. Once these costs are covered, the toys would generate a unit profit of $10 for toy 1 and $15 for toy 2.

    The company has two factories that are capable of producing these toys. However, to avoid doubling the start-up costs, just one factory would be used, where the choice would be based on maximizing profit. For administrative reasons, the same factory would be used for both new toys if both are produced.

    Toy 1 can be produced at the rate of 50 per hour in factory 1 and 40 per hour in factory 2. Toy 2 can be produced at the rate of 40 per hour in factory 1 and 25 per hour in factory 2. Factories 1 and 2, respectively, have 500 hours and 700 hours of production time available before Christmas that could be used to produce these toys.

    It is not known whether these two toys would be continued after Christmas. Therefore, the problem is to determine how many units (if any) of each new toy should be produced before Christmas to maximize the total profit. Formulate and solve a mixed BIP model on a spreadsheet for this problem.

E*9.15. The Fly-Right Airplane Company builds small jet airplanes to sell to corporations for use by their executives. To meet the needs of these executives, the company's customers sometimes order a custom design of the airplanes being purchased. When this occurs, a substantial start-up cost is incurred to initiate the production of these airplanes.

    Fly-Right has recently received purchase requests from three customers with short deadlines. However, because the company's production facilities already are almost completely tied up filling previous orders, it will not be able to accept all three orders. Therefore, a decision now needs to be made on the number of airplanes the company will agree to produce (if any) for each of the three customers.

The relevant data are given in the table below. The first row gives the start-up cost required to initiate the production of the airplanes for each customer. Once production is under way, the marginal net revenue (which is the purchase price minus the marginal production cost) from each airplane produced is shown in the second row. The third row gives the percentage of the available production capacity that would be used for each airplane produced. The last row indicates the maximum number of airplanes requested by each customer (but less will be accepted).

	Customer 1	Customer 2	Customer 3
Start-up cost	$3 million	$2 million	0
Marginal net revenue	$2 million	$3 million	$0.8 million
Capacity used per plane	20%	40%	20%
Maximum order	3 planes	2 planes	5 planes

Fly-Right now wants to determine how many airplanes to produce for each customer (if any) to maximize the company's total profit (total net revenue minus start-up costs). Formulate and solve a spreadsheet model with both integer variables and binary variables for this problem.

E*9.16. Reconsider the Fly-Right Airplane Co. problem introduced in Problem 9.15. A more detailed analysis of the various cost and revenue factors now has revealed that the potential profit from producing airplanes for each customer cannot be expressed simply in terms of a start-up cost and a fixed marginal net revenue per airplane produced. Instead, the profits are given by the following table.

	Profit (Millions)		
Airplanes Produced	Customer 1	Customer 2	Customer 3
0	0	0	0
1	−$1	$1	$1
2	2	5	3
3	4		5
4			6
5			7

Use auxiliary binary variables to formulate and solve a BIP model on a spreadsheet for this new version of the problem.

E*9.17.* Reconsider Problem 4.5, where the management of the Omega Manufacturing Company is considering devoting excess production capacity to one or more of three products. (See the Partial Answers to Selected Problems in Appendix B in the back of the book for the optimal solution for Problem 4.5.) Management now has decided to add the restriction that no more than two of the three prospective products should be produced. Use auxiliary binary variables to formulate and solve a mixed BIP model on a spreadsheet for this new version of the problem.

9.18. Consider the following algebraic form of an integer nonlinear programming model:

$$\text{Maximize} \quad \text{Profit} = 4x_1^2 - x_1^3 + 10x_2^2 - x_2^4$$

subject to

$$x_1 + x_2 \le 3$$

and

$$x_1 \ge 0 \qquad x_2 \ge 0$$

$$x_1 \text{ and } x_2 \text{ are integers}$$

a. Reformulate this model in algebraic form as a pure BIP model with six binary variables.

E* *b.* Display and solve this model on a spreadsheet.

c. Reexpress the optimal solution obtained in part *b* in terms of the variables, x_1 and x_2, for the original model.

E*9.19.* Consider the following special type of shortest path problem (discussed in Section 7.4) where the nodes are in columns and the only paths considered always move forward one column at a time.

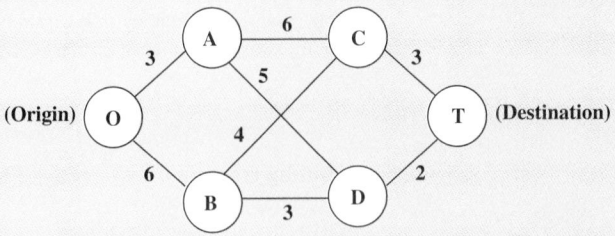

The numbers along the links represent distances (in miles), and the objective is to find the shortest path from the origin to the destination.

This problem also can be formulated as a BIP model involving both mutually exclusive alternatives and contingent decisions. Formulate and solve this BIP model on a spreadsheet. Identify the constraints for (1) mutually exclusive alternatives and (2) contingent decisions.

E*9.20. Speedy Delivery provides two-day delivery service of large parcels across the United States. Each morning at each collection center, the parcels that have arrived overnight are loaded onto several trucks for delivery throughout the area. Since the competitive battlefield in this business is speed of delivery, the parcels are divided among the trucks according to their geographical destinations to minimize the average time needed to make the deliveries.

On this particular morning, the dispatcher for the Blue River Valley Collection Center, Sharon Lofton, is hard at work. Her three drivers will be arriving in less than an hour to make the day's deliveries. There are nine parcels to be delivered, all at locations many miles apart. As usual, Sharon has loaded these locations into her computer. She is using her company's special software package, a decision support system called Dispatcher. The first thing Dispatcher does is use these locations to generate a considerable number of attractive possible routes for the individual delivery trucks. These routes are shown in the following table (where the numbers in each column indicate the order of the deliveries), along with the estimated time required to traverse the route.

Delivery Location	Attractive Possible Route									
	1	2	3	4	5	6	7	8	9	10
A	1				1				1	
B		2		1		2			2	2
C			3	3			3		3	
D	2					1		1		
E				2	2	3				
F		1			2					
G	3						1	2		3
H				1		3				1
I		3			4		2			
Time (in hours)	6	4	7	5	4	6	5	3	7	6

Dispatcher is an interactive system that shows these routes to Sharon for her approval or modification. (For example, the computer may not know that flooding has made a particular route infeasible.) After Sharon approves these routes as attractive possibilities with reasonable time estimates, Dispatcher next formulates and solves a BIP model for selecting three routes that minimize their total time while including each delivery location on exactly one route.

Using the data in the table, demonstrate how Dispatcher can formulate and solve this BIP model on a spreadsheet.

E*9.21. An increasing number of Americans are moving to a warmer climate when they retire. To take advantage of this trend, Sunny Skies Unlimited is undertaking a major real-estate development project. The project is to develop a completely new retirement community (to be called Pilgrim Haven) that will cover several square miles. One of the decisions to be made is where to locate the two fire stations that have been allocated to the community. For planning purposes, Pilgrim Haven has been divided into five tracts, with no more than one fire station to be located in any given tract. Each station is to respond to *all* the fires that occur in the tract in which it is located as well as in the other tracts that are assigned to this station. Thus, the decisions to be made consist of (1) the tracts to receive a fire station and (2) the assignment of each of the other tracts to one of the fire stations. The objective is to minimize the overall average of the *response times* to fires.

The following table gives the average response time to a fire in each tract (the columns) if that tract is served by a station in a given tract (the rows). The bottom row gives the forecasted average number of fires that will occur in each of the tracts per day.

Assigned Station Located in Tract	Response Times (Minutes) to Fire in Tract				
	1	2	3	4	5
1	5	12	30	20	15
2	20	4	15	10	25
3	15	20	6	15	12
4	25	15	25	4	10
5	10	25	15	12	5
Average frequency of fires per day	2	1	3	1	3

Formulate and solve a BIP model on a spreadsheet for this problem. Identify any constraints that correspond to mutually exclusive alternatives or contingent decisions.

9.22. Reconsider Problem 9.21. The management of Sunny Skies Unlimited now has decided that the decision regarding the locations of the fire stations should be based mainly on costs.

The cost of locating a fire station in a tract is $200,000 for tract 1, $250,000 for tract 2, $400,000 for tract 3, $300,000 for tract 4, and $500,000 for tract 5. Management's objective now is the following:

Determine which tracts should receive a station to minimize the total cost of stations while ensuring that each tract has at least one station close enough to respond to a fire in no more than 15 minutes (on the average).

In contrast to the original problem, note that the total number of fire stations is no longer fixed. Furthermore, if a tract without a station has more than one station within 15 minutes, it is no longer necessary to assign this tract to just one of these stations.

a. Formulate the algebraic form of a pure BIP model with five binary variables for this problem.

E* *b.* Display and solve this model on a spreadsheet.

Case 9-1

Capacity Concerns

Bentley Hamilton throws the business section of *The New York Times* onto the conference room table and watches as his associates jolt upright in their overstuffed chairs.

Mr. Hamilton wants to make a point.

He throws the front page of the *The Wall Street Journal* on top of *The New York Times* and watches as his associates widen their eyes once heavy with boredom.

Mr. Hamilton wants to make a big point.

He then throws the front page of the *Financial Times* on top of the newspaper pile and watches as his associates dab the fine beads of sweat off their brows.

Mr. Hamilton wants his point indelibly etched into his associates' minds.

"I have just presented you with three leading financial newspapers carrying today's top business story," Mr. Hamilton declares in a tight, angry voice. "My dear associates, our company is going to hell in a hand basket! Shall I read you the headlines? From *The New York Times,* 'CommuniCorp stock drops to lowest in 52 weeks.' From *The Wall Street Journal,* 'CommuniCorp loses 25 percent of the pager market in only one year.' Oh, and my favorite, from the *Financial Times,* 'CommuniCorp cannot Communi-Cate: CommuniCorp stock drops because of internal communications disarray.' How did our company fall into such dire straits?"

Mr. Hamilton throws a transparency showing a line sloping slightly upward onto the overhead projector. "This is a graph of our productivity over the last 12 months. As you can see from the graph, productivity in our pager production facility has increased steadily over the last year. Clearly, productivity is not the cause of our problem."

Mr. Hamilton throws a second transparency showing a line sloping steeply upward onto the overhead projector. "This is a graph of our missed or late orders over the last 12 months." Mr. Hamilton hears an audible gasp from his associates. "As you can see from the graph, our missed or late orders have increased steadily and significantly over the past 12 months. I think this trend explains why we have been losing market share, causing our stock to drop to its lowest level in 52 weeks. We have angered and lost the business of retailers, our customers who depend upon on-time deliveries to meet the demand of consumers."

"Why have we missed our delivery dates when our productivity level should have allowed us to fill all orders?" Mr. Hamilton asks. "I called several departments to ask this question."

"It turns out that we have been producing pagers for the hell of it!" Mr. Hamilton says in disbelief. "The marketing and sales departments do not communicate with the manufacturing department, so manufacturing executives do not know what pagers to produce to fill orders. The manufacturing executives want to keep the plant running, so they produce pagers regardless of whether the pagers have been ordered. Finished pagers are sent to the warehouse, but marketing and sales executives do not know the number and styles of pagers in the warehouse. They try to communicate with warehouse executives to determine if the pagers in inventory can fill the orders, but they rarely receive answers to their questions."

Mr. Hamilton pauses and looks directly at his associates. "Ladies and gentlemen, it seems to me that we have a serious internal communications problem. I intend to correct this problem immediately. I want to begin by installing a companywide computer network to ensure that all departments have access to critical documents and are able to easily communicate with each other through e-mail. Because this intranet will represent a large change from the current communications infrastructure, I expect some bugs in the system and some resistance from employees. I therefore want to phase in the installation of the intranet."

Mr. Hamilton passes the following time line and requirements chart to his associates (IN = intranet).

Month 1	Month 2	Month 3	Month 4	Month 5
IN education	Install IN in sales	Install IN in manufacturing	Install IN in warehouse	Install IN in marketing

Department	Number of Employees
Sales	60
Manufacturing	200
Warehouse	30
Marketing	75

Mr. Hamilton proceeds to explain the time line and requirements chart. "In the first month, I do not want to bring any department onto the intranet; I simply want to disseminate information about it and get buy-in from employees. In the second month, I want to bring the sales department onto the intranet since the sales department receives all critical information from customers. In the third month, I want to bring the manufacturing department onto the intranet. In the fourth month, I want to install the intranet at the warehouse, and in the fifth and final month, I want to bring the marketing department onto the intranet. The requirements chart under the time line lists the number of employees requiring access to the intranet in each department."

Mr. Hamilton turns to Emily Jones, the head of Corporate Information Management. "I need your help in planning for the installation of the intranet. Specifically, the company needs to purchase servers for the internal network. Employees will connect to company servers and download information to their own desktop computers."

Mr. Hamilton passes Emily the following chart detailing the types of servers available, the number of employees each server supports, and the cost of each server.

Type of Server	Number of Employees Server Supports	Cost of Server
Standard Intel Pentium PC	Up to 30 employees	$ 2,500
Enhanced Intel Pentium PC	Up to 80 employees	5,000
SGI Workstation	Up to 200 employees	10,000
Sun Workstation	Up to 2,000 employees	25,000

"Emily, I need you to decide what servers to purchase and when to purchase them to minimize cost and to ensure that the company possesses enough server capacity to follow the intranet implementation timeline," Mr. Hamilton says. "For example, you may decide to buy one large server during the first month to support all employees, or buy several small servers during the first month to support all employees, or buy one small server each month to support each new group of employees gaining access to the intranet."

"There are several factors that complicate your decision," Mr. Hamilton continues. "Two server manufacturers are willing to offer discounts to CommuniCorp. SGI is willing to give you a discount of 10 percent off each server purchased, but only if you purchase servers in the first or second month. Sun is willing to give you a 25 percent discount off all servers purchased in the first two months. You are also limited in the amount of money you can spend during the first month. CommuniCorp has already allocated much of the budget for the next two months, so you only have a total of $9,500 available to purchase servers in months 1 and 2. Finally, the manufacturing department requires at least one of the three more powerful servers. Have your decision on my desk at the end of the week."

a. Emily first decides to evaluate the number and type of servers to purchase on a month-to-month basis. For each month, formulate an integer programming problem to determine which servers Emily should purchase in that month to minimize costs in that month and support the new users given your results for the preceding months. How many and which types of servers should she purchase in each month? How much is the total cost of the plan?

b. Emily realizes that she could perhaps achieve savings if she bought a larger server in the initial months to support users in the final months. She therefore decides to evaluate the number and type of servers to purchase over the entire planning period. Formulate an integer programming problem to determine which servers Emily should purchase in which months to minimize total cost and support all new users. How many and which types of servers should she purchase in each month? How much is the total cost of the plan?

c. Why is the answer using the first method different from that using the second method?

d. Are there other costs for which Emily is not accounting in her problem formulation? If so, what are they?

e. What further concerns might the various departments of CommuniCorp have regarding the intranet?

Case 9-2

Assigning Art

It had been a dream come true for Ash Briggs, a struggling artist living in the San Francisco Bay area. He had made a trip to the corner grocery store late one Friday afternoon to buy some milk, and, on impulse, he had also purchased a California lottery ticket. One week later, he was a multimillionaire.

Ash did not want to squander his winnings on materialistic, trivial items. Instead he wanted to use his money to support his true passion: art. Ash knew all too well the difficulties of gaining recognition as an artist in this post-industrial, technological society where artistic appreciation is rare and financial support even rarer. He therefore decided to use the money to fund an exhibit of up-and-coming modern artists at the San Francisco Museum of Modern Art.

Ash approached the museum directors with his idea, and the directors became excited immediately after he informed them that he would fund the entire exhibit in addition to donating $1 million to the museum. Celeste McKenzie, a museum director, was assigned to work with Ash in planning the exhibit. The exhibit was slated to open one year from the time Ash met with the directors, and the exhibit pieces would remain on display for two months.

Ash began the project by combing the modern art community for potential artists and pieces. He presented a list (see next page) of artists, their pieces, and the price of displaying each piece[4] to Celeste.

Ash possesses certain requirements for the exhibit. He believes the majority of Americans lack adequate knowledge of art and artistic styles, and he wants the exhibit to educate Americans. Ash wants visitors to become aware of the collage as an art form, but he believes collages require little talent. He therefore decides to include only one collage. Additionally, Ash wants viewers to compare the delicate lines in a three-dimensional wire mesh sculpture to the delicate lines in a two-dimensional computer-generated drawing. He therefore wants at least one wire-mesh sculpture displayed if a computer-generated drawing is displayed. Alternatively, he wants at least one computer-generated drawing displayed if a wire-mesh sculpture is displayed. Furthermore, Ash wants to expose viewers to all painting styles, but he wants to limit the number of paintings displayed to achieve a balance in the exhibit between paintings and other art forms. He therefore decides to include at least one photo-realistic painting, at least one cubist painting, at least one expressionist painting, at least one watercolor painting, and at least one oil painting. At the same time, he wants the number of paintings to be no greater than twice the number of other art forms.

Ash wants all his own paintings included in the exhibit since he is sponsoring the exhibit and since his paintings celebrate the San Francisco Bay area, the home of the exhibit.

Ash possesses personal biases for and against some artists. Ash is currently having a steamy affair with Candy Tate, and he wants both of her paintings displayed. Ash counts both David Lyman and Rick Rawls as his best friends, and he does not want to play favorites among these two artists. He therefore decides to display as many pieces from David Lyman as from Rick Rawls and to display at least one piece from each of them. Although Ziggy Lite is very popular within art circles, Ash believes Ziggy makes a mockery of art. Ash will therefore only accept one display piece from Ziggy, if any at all.

Celeste also possesses her own agenda for the exhibit. As a museum director, she is interested in representing a diverse population of artists, appealing to a wide audience, and creating a politically correct exhibit. To advance feminism, she decides to include at least one piece from a female artist for every two pieces included from a male artist. To advance environmentalism, she decides to include either one or both of the pieces "Aging Earth" and "Wasted Resources." To advance Native American rights, she decides to include at least one piece by Bear Canton. To advance science, she decides to include at least one of the following pieces: "Chaos Reigns," "Who Has Control?," "Beyond," and "Pioneers."

Celeste also understands that space is limited at the museum. The museum only has enough floor space for four sculptures and enough wall space for 20 paintings, collages, and drawings.

Finally, Celeste decides that if "Narcissism" is displayed, "Reflection" should also be displayed since "Reflection" also suggests narcissism.

Please explore the following questions independently except where otherwise indicated.

a. Ash decides to allocate $4 million to fund the exhibit. Given the pieces available and the specific requirements from Ash and Celeste, formulate and solve a binary integer programming problem to maximize the number of pieces displayed in the exhibit without exceeding the budget. How many pieces are displayed? Which pieces are displayed?

b. To ensure that the exhibit draws the attention of the public, Celeste decides that it must include at least 20 pieces. Formulate and solve a binary integer programming problem to minimize the cost of the exhibit while displaying at least 20 pieces and meeting the requirements set by Ash and Celeste. How much does the exhibit cost? Which pieces are displayed?

---

[4]The display price includes the cost of paying the artist for loaning the piece to the museum, transporting the piece to San Francisco, constructing the display for the piece, insuring the piece while it is on display, and transporting the piece back to its origin.

Artist	Piece	Description of Piece	Price
Colin Zweibell	"Perfection"	A wire-mesh sculpture of the human body	$300,000
	"Burden"	A wire-mesh sculpture of a mule	250,000
	"The Great Equalizer"	A wire-mesh sculpture of a gun	125,000
Rita Losky	"Chaos Reigns"	A series of computer-generated drawings	400,000
	"Who Has Control?"	A computer-generated drawing intermeshed with lines of computer code	500,000
	"Domestication"	A pen-and-ink drawing of a house	400,000
	"Innocence"	A pen-and-ink drawing of a child	550,000
Norm Marson	"Aging Earth"	A sculpture of trash covering a larger globe	700,000
	"Wasted Resources"	A collage of various packaging materials	575,000
Candy Tate	"Serenity"	An all-blue watercolor painting	200,000
	"Calm before the Storm"	A painting with an all-blue watercolor background and a black watercolor center	225,000
Robert Bayer	"Void"	An all-black oil painting	150,000
	"Sun"	An all-yellow oil painting	150,000
David Lyman	"Storefront Window"	A photo-realistic painting of a jewelry store display window	850,000
	"Harley"	A photo-realistic painting of a Harley-Davidson motorcycle	750,000
Angie Oldman	"Consumerism"	A collage of magazine advertisements	400,000
	"Reflection"	A mirror (considered a sculpture)	175,000
	"Trojan Victory"	A wooden sculpture of a condom	450,000
Rick Rawls	"Rick"	A photo-realistic self-portrait (painting)	500,000
	"Rick II"	A cubist self-portrait (painting)	500,000
	"Rick III"	An expressionist self-portrait (painting)	500,000
Bill Reynolds	"Beyond"	A science fiction oil painting depicting Mars colonization	650,000
	"Pioneers"	An oil painting of three astronauts aboard the space shuttle	650,000
Bear Canton	"Wisdom"	A pen-and-ink drawing of an Apache chieftain	250,000
	"Superior Powers"	A pen-and-ink drawing of a traditional Native American rain dance	350,000
	"Living Land"	An oil painting of the Grand Canyon	450,000
Helen Row	"Study of a Violin"	A cubist painting of a violin	400,000
	"Study of a Fruit Bowl"	A cubist painting of a bowl of fruit	400,000
Ziggy Lite	"My Namesake"	A collage of Ziggy cartoons	300,000
	"Narcissism"	A collage of photographs of Ziggy Lite	300,000
Ash Briggs	"All That Glitters"	A watercolor painting of the Golden Gate Bridge	50,000*
	"The Rock"	A watercolor painting of Alcatraz	50,000*
	"Winding Road"	A watercolor painting of Lombard Street	50,000*
	"Dreams Come True"	A watercolor painting of the San Francisco Museum of Modern Art	50,000*

*Ash does not require personal compensation, and the cost for moving his pieces to the museum from his home in San Francisco is minimal. The cost of displaying his pieces therefore only includes the cost of constructing the display and insuring the pieces.

    c. An influential patron of Rita Losky's work who chairs the museum's board of directors learns that Celeste requires at least 20 pieces in the exhibit. He offers to pay the minimum amount required on top of Ash's $4 million to ensure that exactly 20 pieces are displayed in the exhibit and that all of Rita's pieces are displayed. How much does the patron have to pay? Which pieces are displayed?

Case 9-3

Stocking Sets

Daniel Holbrook, an expediter at the local warehouse for Furniture City, sighed as he moved boxes and boxes of inventory to the side to reach the shelf where the particular item he needed was located. He dropped to his hands and knees and squinted at the inventory numbers lining the bottom row of the shelf. He did not find the number he needed. He worked his way up the shelf until he found the number matching the number on the order slip. Just his luck! The item was on the top row of the shelf! Daniel walked back through the warehouse to find a ladder, stumbling over boxes of inventory littering his path. When he finally climbed the ladder to reach the top shelf, his face crinkled in frustration. Not again! The item he needed was not in stock! All he saw above the inventory number was an empty space covered with dust!

Daniel trudged back through the warehouse to make the dreaded phone call. He dialed the number of Brenda Sims, the saleswoman on the kitchen showroom floor of Furniture City, and informed her that the particular light fixture the customer had requested was not in stock. He then asked her if she wanted him to look for the rest of the items in the kitchen set. Brenda told him that she would talk to the customer and call him back.

Brenda hung up the phone and frowned. Mr. Davidson, her customer, would not be happy. Ordering and receiving the correct light fixture from the regional warehouse would take at least two weeks.

Brenda then paused to reflect upon business during the last month and realized that over 80 percent of the orders for kitchen sets could not be filled because items needed to complete the sets were not in stock at the local warehouse. She also realized that Furniture City was losing customer goodwill and business because of stockouts. The furniture megastore was gaining a reputation for slow service and delayed deliveries, causing customers to turn to small competitors that sold furniture directly from the showroom floor.

Brenda decided to investigate the inventory situation at the local warehouse. She walked the short distance to the building next door and gasped when she stepped inside the warehouse. What she saw could only be described as chaos. Spaces allocated for some items were overflowing into the aisles of the warehouse while other spaces were completely bare. She walked over to one of the spaces overflowing with inventory to determine what item was overstocked. She could not believe her eyes! The warehouse had at least 30 rolls of pea-green wallpaper! No customer had ordered pea-green wallpaper since 1973!

Brenda marched over to Daniel demanding an explanation. Daniel said that the warehouse had been in such a chaotic state since his arrival one year ago. He said the inventory problems occurred because management had a policy of stocking every furniture item on the showroom floor in the local warehouse. Management only replenished inventory every three months, and when inventory was replenished, management ordered every item regardless of whether it had been sold. Daniel also said that he had tried to make management aware of the problems with overstocking unpopular items and understocking popular items, but management would not listen to him because he was simply an expediter.

Brenda understood that Furniture City required a new inventory policy. Not only was the megastore losing money by making customers unhappy with delivery delays, but it was also losing money by wasting warehouse space. By changing the inventory policy to stock only popular items and replenish them immediately when sold, Furniture City would ensure that the majority of customers would receive their furniture immediately and that the valuable warehouse space would be utilized effectively.

Brenda needed to sell her inventory policy to management. Using her extensive sales experience, she decided that the most effective sales strategy would be to use her kitchen department as a model for the new inventory policy. She would identify all kitchen sets comprising 85 percent of customer orders. Given the fixed amount of warehouse space allocated to the kitchen department, she would identify the items Furniture City should stock to satisfy the greatest number of customer orders. She would then calculate the revenue from satisfying customer orders under the new inventory policy, using the bottom line to persuade management to accept her policy.

Brenda analyzed her records over the past three years and determined that 20 kitchen sets were responsible for 85 percent of the customer orders. These 20 kitchen sets were composed of up to eight features in a variety of styles. Brenda listed each feature and its popular styles.

Brenda then created a table (given on page 436) showing the 20 kitchen sets and the particular features composing each set. To simplify the table, she used the codes shown in parentheses below to represent the particular feature and style. For example, kitchen set 1 consists of floor tile T2, wallpaper W2, light fixture L4, cabinet C2, countertop O2, dishwasher D2, sink S2, and range R2. Notice that sets 14 through 20 do not contain dishwashers.

Floor Tile	Wallpaper	Light Fixtures	Cabinets
(T1) White textured tile	(W1) Plain ivory paper	(L1) One large rectangular frosted fixture	(C1) Light solid wood cabinets
(T2) Ivory textured tile	(W2) Ivory paper with dark brown pinstripes	(L2) Three small square frosted fixtures	(C2) Dark solid wood cabinets
(T3) White checkered tile with blue trim	(W3) Blue paper with marble texture	(L3) One large oval frosted fixture	(C3) Light-wood cabinets with glass doors
(T4) White checkered tile with light yellow trim	(W4) Light yellow paper with marble texture	(L4) Three small frosted globe fixtures	(C4) Dark-wood cabinets with glass doors

Countertops	Dishwashers	Sinks	Ranges
(O1) Plain light-wood countertops	(D1) White energy-saving dishwasher	(S1) Sink with separate hot and cold water taps	(R1) White electric oven
(O2) Stained light-wood countertops	(D2) Ivory energy-saving dishwasher	(S2) Divided sink with separate hot and cold water taps and garbage disposal	(R2) Ivory electric oven
(O3) White lacquer-coated countertops		(S3) Sink with one hot and cold water tap	(R3) White gas oven
(O4) Ivory lacquer-coated countertops		(S4) Divided sink with one hot and cold water tap and garbage disposal	(R4) Ivory gas oven

Brenda knew she had only a limited amount of warehouse space allocated to the kitchen department. The warehouse could hold 50 square feet of tile and 12 rolls of wallpaper in the inventory bins. The inventory shelves could hold two light fixtures, two cabinets, three countertops, and two sinks. Dishwashers and ranges are similar in size, so Furniture City stored them in similar locations. The warehouse floor could hold a total of four dishwashers and ranges.

Every kitchen set always includes exactly 20 square feet of tile and exactly five rolls of wallpaper. Therefore, 20 square feet of a particular style of tile and five rolls of a particular style of wallpaper are required for the styles to be in stock.

a. Formulate and solve a binary integer programming problem to maximize the total number of kitchen sets (and thus the number of customer orders) Furniture City stocks in the local warehouse. Assume that when a customer orders a kitchen set, all the particular items composing that kitchen set are replenished at the local warehouse immediately.

b. How many of each feature and style should Furniture City stock in the local warehouse? How many different kitchen sets are in stock?

c. Furniture City decides to discontinue carrying nursery sets, and the warehouse space previously allocated to the nursery department is divided between the existing departments at Furniture City. The kitchen department receives enough additional space to allow it to stock both styles of dishwashers and three of the four styles of ranges. How does the optimal inventory policy for the kitchen department change with this additional warehouse space?

d. Brenda convinces management that the kitchen department should serve as a testing ground for future inventory policies. To provide adequate space for testing, management decides to allocate all the space freed by the nursery department to the kitchen department. The extra space means that the kitchen department can store not only the dishwashers and ranges from part c, but also all sinks, all countertops, three of the four light fixtures, and three of the four cabinets. How much does the additional space help?

e. How would the inventory policy be affected if the items composing a kitchen set could not be replenished immediately? Under what conditions is the assumption of immediate replenishment nevertheless justified?

	T1	T2	T3	T4	W1	W2	W3	W4	L1	L2	L3	L4	C1	C2	C3	C4	O1	O2	O3	O4	D1	D2	S1	S2	S3	S4	R1	R2	R3	R4
Set 1		X				X						X		X						X		X		X				X		
Set 2		X																		X		X				X		X		
Set 3	X				X								X			X	X				X								X	
Set 4			X				X		X		X		X		X				X		X		X		X		X			X
Set 5										X						X		X		X	X	X		X			X			X
Set 6		X		X		X			X				X										X		X					
Set 7	X						X			X		X			X		X	X										X		
Set 8		X			X						X		X		X							X			X	X			X	
Set 9		X			X					X					X			X	X		X	X	X	X					X	
Set 10	X				X				X								X				X					X				
Set 11			X			X					X			X			X					X						X	X	
Set 12		X							X						X			X			X		X				X		X	
Set 13				X				X				X	X				X		X					X					X	
Set 14				X				X	X			X	X												X		X			
Set 15			X				X			X			X						X											
Set 16			X				X				X			X	X				X							X				
Set 17	X							X				X								X			X	X				X		
Set 18		X					X		X		X		X			X				X				X						
Set 19		X						X										X												X
Set 20		X					X																							X

Case 9–4

Assigning Students to Schools (Revisited)

Reconsider Case 4.3. The Springfield School Board now has made the decision to prohibit the splitting of residential areas among multiple schools. Thus, each of the six areas must be assigned to a single school.

a. Formulate and solve a BIP model for this problem under the current policy of providing busing for all middle school students who must travel more than approximately a mile.

b. Referring to part *c* of Case 4.3, determine how much the total busing cost increases because of the decision to prohibit the splitting of residential areas among multiple schools.

c, d, e, f. Repeat parts *d, e, f, g* of Case 4.3 under the new school board decision to prohibit splitting of residential areas among multiple schools.

Learning objectives

After completing this chapter, you should be able to

1. Describe how a nonlinear programming model differs from a linear programming model.

2. Recognize when a nonlinear programming model is needed to represent a problem.

3. Formulate a nonlinear programming model from a description of the problem.

4. Construct nonlinear formulas needed for nonlinear programming models.

5. Distinguish between nonlinear programming problems that should be easy to solve and those that may be difficult (if not impossible) to solve.

6. Use the Excel Solver to solve simple types of nonlinear programming problems.

7. Combine the Excel Solver with the Solver Table to attempt to solve some more difficult nonlinear programming problems.

8. Use Evolutionary Solver to attempt to solve some difficult nonlinear programming problems.

9. Recognize when the separable programming technique is applicable to enable using linear programming with a nonlinear objective function.

10. Apply the separable programming technique when applicable.

Chapter **Ten**

Nonlinear Programming

The previous chapters have introduced you to a wide variety of management science models, including various types of linear programming and integer programming models. However, one characteristic shared by all these linear programming and integer programming models is that they all are *linear models,* that is, models where all the functions (mathematical relationships) involved are linear.

When formulating a linear model in a spreadsheet, this means that the Excel functions being used to express the formulas in output cells include only sums (e.g., C1 + C2, or SUM(C1:C2), or C1 − C2) or products of a number (or data cell) and a changing cell (e.g., 2*C4 or the SUMPRODUCT of data cells with changing cells). If any output cell includes the multiplication or division of changing cells (e.g., C4*C5 or C3/C6 or C4^2) or uses almost any Excel function other than SUM or SUMPRODUCT (such as ROUND, ABS, IF, MAX, MIN, SQRT, etc.), then the resulting model will typically not be linear.

Table 10.1 gives various examples of formulas that could be entered into output cells when the data cells are in column D and the changing cells are in column C. The formulas on the left are all linear while those on the right are not. The first four examples in each column are quite similar. Can you see why the formulas on the left are linear while those on the right are not? The key to seeing this distinction is that a linear formula permits any calculations that involve only the data cells but restricts each changing cell to having only the most basic arithmetic operations: addition or subtraction and multiplication or division by a constant.

> A formula automatically becomes nonlinear if it ever multiplies or divides a changing cell by another changing cell or if it assigns an exponent (other than 1) to any changing cell.

Despite the versatility of linear models, managers occasionally encounter problems where such a model does not quite fit because at least one of the formulas that needs to be entered into output cells is not linear. In most cases, this occurs because the formula for the target cell needs to be nonlinear, and this is the case that we will focus on in this chapter. If the model is a linear programming model except for having at least one nonlinear formula for an output cell (such as the target cell), then it is called a *nonlinear programming* model.

Formulating and solving nonlinear programming models often is considerably more challenging than formulating and solving linear programming models. However, these challenges

TABLE 10.1

Examples of Linear and Nonlinear Formulas in a Spreadsheet When the Data Cells Are in Column D and the Changing Cells Are in Column C

Linear Formulas	Nonlinear Formulas
SUMPRODUCT(D4:D6, C4:C6)	SUMPRODUCT(C4:C6, C1:C3)
[(D1 + D2)/D3]* C4	[(C1 + C2)/C3]* D4
IF(D2 >= 2, 2*C3, 3*C4)	IF(C2 >=2, 2*C3, 3*C4)
SUMIF(D1:D6, 4, C1:C6)	SUMIF(C1:C6, 4, D1:D6)
SUM(D4:D6)	ROUND(C1)
2*C1 + 3*C4 + C6	MAX(C1, 0)
C1 + C2 + C3	MIN(C1, C2)
	ABS(C1)
	SQRT(C1)
	C1* C2
	C1 / C2
	C1^2

Note: Data cells are in D1:D6; changing cells are in C1:C6.

frequently can be overcome, sometimes in relatively straightforward ways. Rest easy. This chapter focuses on the relatively straightforward types of nonlinear programming which require only reasonably routine spreadsheet modeling and the application of the Excel Solver (in some cases) or the Premium Solver (in other cases). This is all a manager (or future manager) needs to know about nonlinear programming. A management science specialist should be called on to deal with more difficult types of nonlinear programming.

Because of the close relationship between linear and nonlinear programming, it is sometimes unclear which technique should be used to analyze a managerial problem. This occurs for problems where the appropriate formula for the target cell is nonlinear but is reasonably close to being linear. In this case, one alternative is to use a linear approximation for the formula so that linear programming can be applied. The advantage is greater ease of formulating and solving the model. Since a model is intended to be only an idealized representation of the real problem, this alternative is reasonable if the linear approximation is a good one. However, the major advantage of using nonlinear programming instead is the greater precision it provides in seeking the best solution for the real problem. When the appropriate nonlinear programming model is not an overly difficult one to formulate and solve, it makes good sense to use this model. If desired, a linear programming model still can be used to perform some quick preliminary analysis, including some what-if analysis, but the greater precision of nonlinear programming should not be foregone lightly for the final analysis.

Section 10.1 discusses the challenges encountered when using nonlinear programming. Fortunately, there are some "easy" types of nonlinear programming problems that arise fairly frequently. Two such types are presented in Sections 10.2 and 10.3. Section 10.4 then describes how some "difficult" nonlinear programming problems still can be solved by applying the Excel Solver (or Premium Solver) multiple times with different starting solutions. However, the Excel Solver is unable to solve some other nonlinear programming problems. Therefore, Premium Solver provides an additional procedure called *Evolutionary Solver* for coping with such problems. Evolutionary Solver is described in Section 10.5.

> Nonlinear programming often provides greater precision than linear programming for analyzing managerial problems.

10.1 THE CHALLENGES OF NONLINEAR PROGRAMMING

In almost every respect, a nonlinear programming model is indistinguishable from a linear programming model. In both cases, decisions need to be made regarding the levels of a number of activities, where these activity levels can have any value (including a fractional value) that satisfies a number of constraints. The decisions regarding activity levels are to be based on an overall measure of performance. When the model is formulated in a spreadsheet, the changing cells display the activity levels, output cells help to represent the constraints, and the target cell shows the overall measure of performance.

The only way to distinguish a nonlinear programming model from a linear programming model is to examine the formulas entered into the output cells. It is a nonlinear programming model if one or more of these formulas is nonlinear instead of linear. Commonly, such a model has only one nonlinear formula, and it is the one entered into the target cell.

Despite such a small difference in the *appearance* of the two kinds of models, their *application* differs in three major ways.

> A nonlinear programming model has the same appearance as a linear programming model except for having a nonlinear formula in at least one output cell (commonly the target cell).

- Nonlinear programming is used to model *nonproportional relationships* between activity levels and the overall measure of performance, whereas linear programming assumes a proportional relationship.

- Constructing the nonlinear formula(s) needed for a nonlinear programming model is considerably more difficult than developing the linear formulas used in linear programming.

- Solving a nonlinear programming model is often much more difficult (if it is possible at all) than solving a linear programming model.

As these comparisons indicate, using nonlinear programming instead of linear programming raises some new challenges. Let us examine these challenges a little more closely.

The Challenge of Nonproportional Relationships

When either a linear programming model or a nonlinear programming model is formulated in a spreadsheet, the target cell needs to show the overall measure of performance that results from the activity levels that are displayed in the changing cells. However, nonlinear programming uses a more complicated relationship between the activity levels and the overall measure of performance than does linear programming.

In the case of linear programming, this relationship is assumed to be a particularly simple one. To illustrate, consider again the Wyndor Glass Co. problem introduced in Section 2.2 and formulated in Section 2.3. The activities for this problem are the production of the special new doors and the special new windows, where the levels of these activities are

$$D = \text{Number of doors to be produced per week}$$

$$W = \text{Number of windows to be produced per week}$$

The overall measure of performance is the total weekly profit obtained from the production and sale of these doors and windows. The unit profit has been estimated to be \$300 for each door and \$500 for each window. The graphs in Figure 10.1 show the resulting relationship between the level of each activity (D and W) and the contribution of that activity to the overall measure of performance. The straight line in each graph shows a **proportional relationship** because the weekly profit from each product is *proportional* to the production rate for that product. These straight lines also indicate that the objective function

$$\text{Profit} = \$300D + \$500W$$

is *linear*. The fact that this formula being entered into the target cell is linear helps to make the overall model a linear programming model.

As illustrated by the Wyndor Glass Co. problem, *every* linear programming problem assumes a proportional relationship between each activity and the overall measure of performance. This key assumption can be summarized as follows.

> **Proportionality Assumption of Linear Programming:** The contribution of each activity to the value of the objective function is *proportional* to the level of the activity.[1] In other words, the term

FIGURE 10.1
Profit graphs for the Wyndor Glass Co. that show the weekly profit from each product versus the production rate for that product.

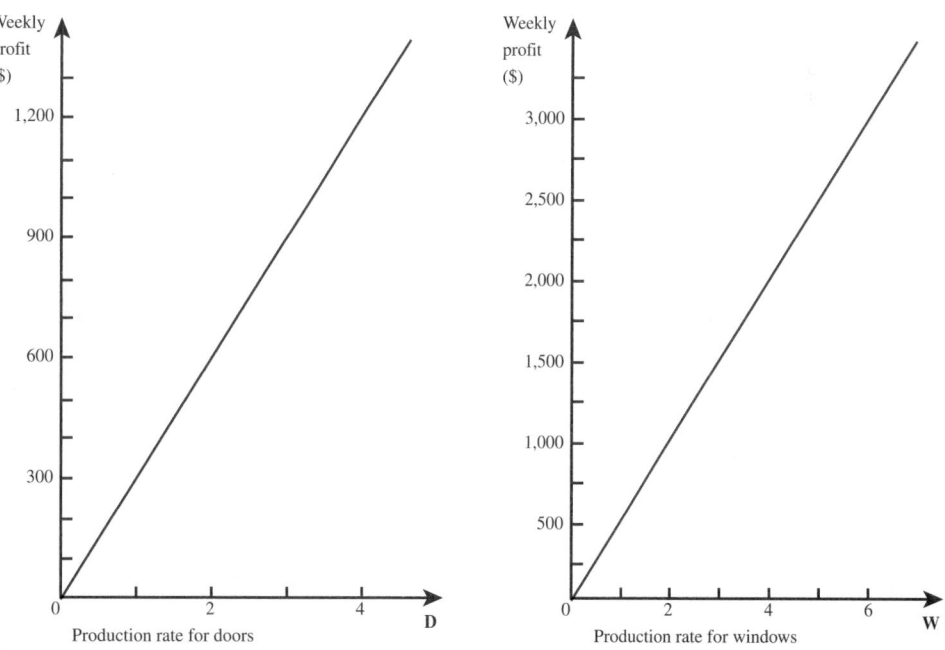

[1] The same assumption also is made about the contribution of each activity to the left-hand side of each functional constraint, but we are focusing in this chapter on how to deal with a lack of proportionality in the objective function.

in the objective function involving this activity consists of a coefficient times a decision variable, where the coefficient is the contribution per unit of this activity and the decision variable is the level of this activity. (For example, for each product in the Wyndor Glass Co. problem, the coefficient is the product's unit profit and the decision variable is the production rate for the product.)

Nonlinear programming problems arise when this assumption is violated. This occurs whenever any activity has a **nonproportional relationship** with the overall measure of performance because the contribution of the activity to this measure of performance is *not proportional* to the level of the activity.

> Nonlinear programming problems arise when the proportionality assumption of linear programming is violated.

Figure 10.2 shows four examples of different types of nonproportional relationships. (For definiteness, these graphs assume that the overall measure of performance is profit, but any other measure to be maximized also could be used.)

The first of these examples, shown in Figure 10.2(a), illustrates a profit graph with *decreasing marginal returns.*

Consider any activity where a graph of its profit versus the level of the activity is plotted. Suppose that the *slope* (steepness) of the graph never increases but sometimes decreases as the level of the activity increases. Then the activity is said to have **decreasing marginal returns.**

Similarly, in problems where the objective is to minimize the total cost of the activities, an activity is said to have decreasing marginal returns if the slope of its *cost graph* never decreases but sometimes *increases* as the level of the activity increases.[2]

FIGURE 10.2

Examples of profit graphs with nonproportional relationships: *(a)* decreasing marginal returns; *(b)* piecewise linear with decreasing marginal returns; *(c)* decreasing marginal returns except for discontinuities; and *(d)* increasing marginal returns.

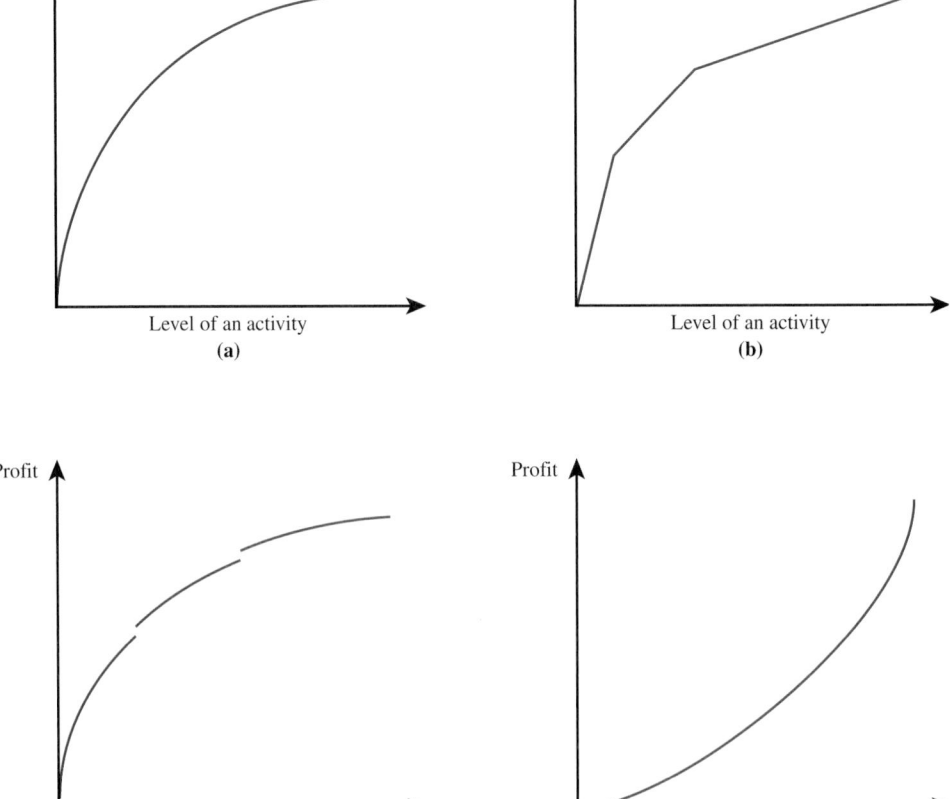

[2]Using mathematical terminology, a profit graph with decreasing marginal returns is said to be a *concave function*, whereas a cost graph with decreasing marginal returns is said to be a *convex function*. We are using the more suggestive economic term, decreasing marginal returns, to cover both cases (including for functions of multiple decision variables).

Since frequently it is difficult to continue increasing profit at the same rate as the level of an activity keeps getting pushed higher and higher, activities with decreasing marginal returns are fairly common. For example, it may be necessary to lower the price of a product to increase its sales. Alternatively, if the price is held constant, the marketing costs may need to go up more than proportionally to attain increases in the level of sales. (The next section begins with an example in which marketing costs behave in this way.) Decreasing marginal returns also occur when less efficient facilities and personnel need to be used to increase the level of an activity.

Figure 10.2(b) illustrates a profit graph that is **piecewise linear** because it consists of a sequence of connected line segments. As the level of the activity increases, the slope of the profit graph remains the same within each line segment but then decreases at the kink where the next line segment begins. Since the slope never increases as the level of the activity increases but does decrease at the kinks, this profit graph also fits the definition of having decreasing marginal returns. This kind of graph might occur, for example, because overtime needs to be used to increase the level of the activity beyond the first kink, and then even more expensive weekend overtime is needed to increase the level beyond the second kink.

Figure 10.2(c) provides an example of a nonproportional relationship that does not quite have decreasing marginal returns. The reason it does not is that there are spots called **discontinuities** where the profit graph is disconnected because it suddenly jumps up or down. Such discontinuities could occur, for example, because quantity discounts for purchasing a component of a product become available when the production level for the product rises above certain thresholds.

Having activities with decreasing marginal returns is not the only way in which the proportionality assumption can be violated. For example, another way is to have activities with *increasing* marginal returns, as illustrated by Figure 10.2(d). In this case, the slope of the profit graph never decreases but sometimes *increases* as the level of the activity increases. (Similarly, a *cost graph* exhibits increasing marginal returns if its slope never increases but sometimes *decreases* as the level of the activity increases.) This can occur because of the greater efficiencies sometimes achieved at higher levels of an activity.

Profit graphs are used when the overall objective is to maximize the total profit from all the activities. However, *cost graphs* are needed instead when the overall objective is to *minimize* the total cost of all the activities. An activity can violate the proportionality assumption in the same ways that are illustrated in Figure 10.2 if its cost graph has any of the shapes shown in Figure 10.3. For each case, note how this cost graph bends in the opposite way from the corresponding profit graph in Figure 10.2. Thus, an increasing slope in the cost graph reflects decreasing marginal returns, whereas a decreasing slope reflects increasing marginal returns. (The same conclusion applies to graphs where the objective is to *minimize* some overall measure of performance other than total cost.)

Figures 10.2 and 10.3 illustrate only some of the possible nonproportional relationships. For example, an activity might have *neither* decreasing marginal returns nor increasing marginal returns because the slope of its graph sometimes decreases and sometimes increases as the level of the activity increases.

In addition, sometimes there are interactions between activities that cause (or help to cause) the objective function to be nonlinear. To illustrate, consider the Wyndor Glass Co. problem again. Suppose now that a major advertising campaign will be required to market either new product if it is produced by itself, but that the same single campaign can be used to effectively promote both products if both are produced. Because a major cost is saved for the second product, their joint profit is somewhat more than the sum of their individual profits when each is produced by itself. In particular, the appropriate objective function is, say,

$$\text{Profit} = \$300D + \$500W + \$100DW$$

where DW denotes the *product* of D and W. Because of the cross-product term, $\$100DW$, this objective function is nonlinear even though, when either D or W is fixed at some value, the proportionality assumption still holds for the other product.

When there are interactions between activities, the total profit from all the activities sometimes will still have decreasing marginal returns. (The common technical term for this is that the objective function is *concave*.) The intuitive interpretation of decreasing marginal returns

Many activities have decreasing marginal returns.

An activity has increasing marginal returns if its efficiency increases as the level of the activity is increased.

Even when the proportionality assumption is satisfied, interactions between activities still can lead to a nonlinear programming model.

FIGURE 10.3
Examples of cost graphs with nonproportional relationships: (*a*) decreasing marginal returns; (*b*) piecewise linear with decreasing marginal returns; (*c*) decreasing marginal returns except for discontinuities; and (*d*) increasing marginal returns. Each cost graph bends in the opposite way from the corresponding profit graph in Figure 10.2.

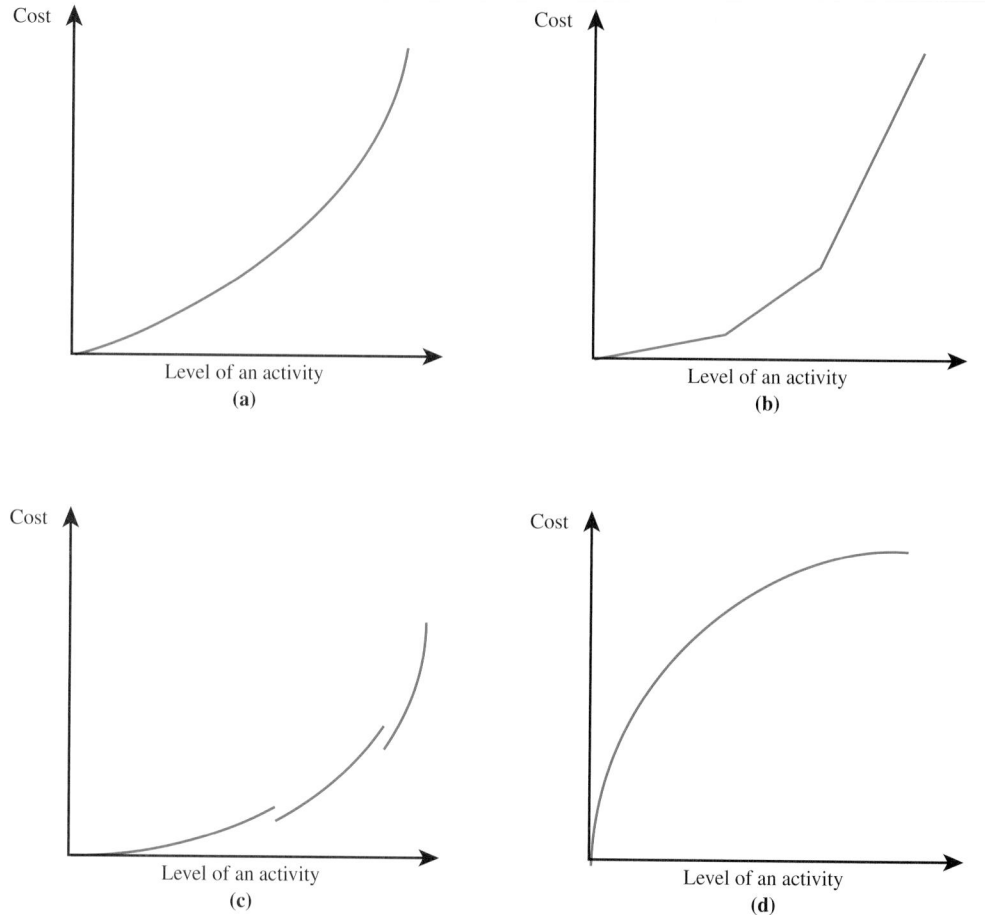

(a profit graph that never bends up but sometimes bends down) continues to apply here. We will not bother with the complex technical definition that is needed in this case.

The Challenge of Constructing Nonlinear Formulas

For a linear programming model, it is relatively simple to construct the formula that needs to be entered into the target cell by using a SUMPRODUCT function. For example, when the target cell gives the total profit from all the activities (as for the Wyndor Glass Co. problem), each product being summed is simply the product of the unit profit for an activity (as given in a data cell) and the level of that activity (as given in a changing cell).

Considerably more work is needed for a nonlinear programming problem. Even when there are no interactions between activities, it is necessary to construct a nonlinear formula for each activity that represents the contribution of that activity to the objective function that needs to be entered into the target cell. For example, when the objective is to maximize total profit, the nonlinear formula for each activity needs to correspond to the profit graph for that activity.

One useful method for fitting a nonlinear formula to a graph begins by assuming a general form for the formula. For a profit graph with decreasing marginal returns, it is common to assume a quadratic form, such as

This quadratic form for a profit graph (or a cost graph) is widely used.

$$\text{Profit from an activity} = a x^2 + b x + c$$

where x is the level of the activity and a is a *negative* constant. Another possibility is to assume a logarithmic form, like

$$\text{Profit from an activity} = a \ln(x) + b$$

where $\ln(x)$ is called the natural logarithm of x.

FIGURE 10.4

An example of an activity for which prior data are available on the profit versus the level of the activity, so Excel's curve fitting method can be applied.

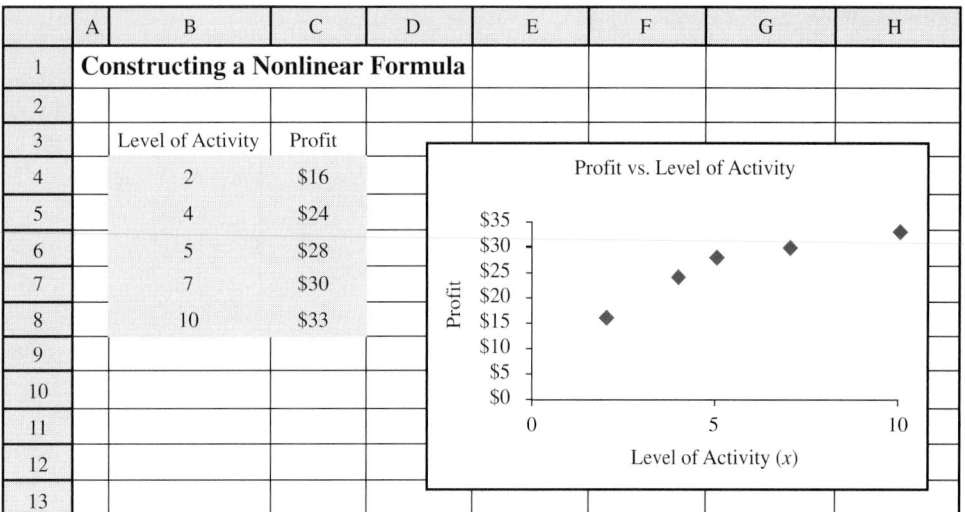

In either case, the next step is to find the appropriate values of the parameters (e.g., *a, b,* and *c*). Excel has a built-in **curve fitting method** to find the values of the parameters that best fit the data. For example, suppose that prior data (or at least estimates) are available on the profit that would be achieved at several levels of the activity, as shown in the spreadsheet in Figure 10.4.

The first step in applying the curve fitting method in Excel is to graph the profit data (profit versus level of the activity), using an X–Y scatter chart. Next, select the graph by clicking on it and then choose "Add Trendline" from the Chart menu. This brings up the dialogue box shown on the left side of Figure 10.5. Use this dialogue box to choose the *form* of the equation that you want Excel to fit to the data. For example, to fit a quadratic equation to the data, choose Polynomial with Order 2.

The order of a polynomial is the highest exponent used in the polynomial. For a quadratic equation, the order is 2.

Next, click on the Options tab. This shows the dialogue box shown on the right side of Figure 10.5. Choose the option to "Display equation on chart" and click OK. Excel then chooses the parameters for the equation of the chosen form that most closely fits the graphed data. For example, the quadratic equation that most closely matches the data in Figure 10.4 is

$$\text{Profit} = -0.3002\, x^2 + 5.661\, x + 6.1477$$

This equation is shown and plotted directly on the graph of profit versus activity level, as shown in Figure 10.6.

FIGURE 10.5

The Add Trendline dialogue box that is used to perform the curve fitting method in Excel. The "Type" tab is used to enter the form of the equation. The "Options" tab includes the option to display the equation on the chart.

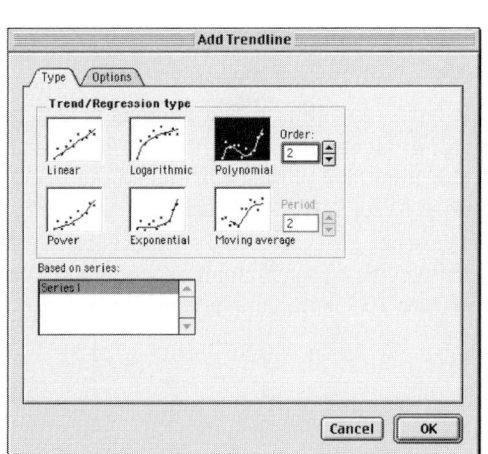
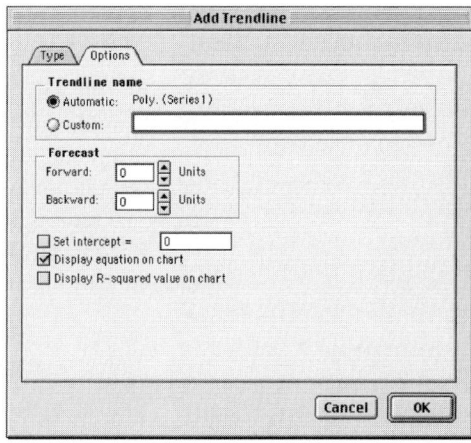

FIGURE 10.6

The quadratic equation found by Excel that most closely matches the profit versus level of activity data for the example introduced in Figure 10.4.

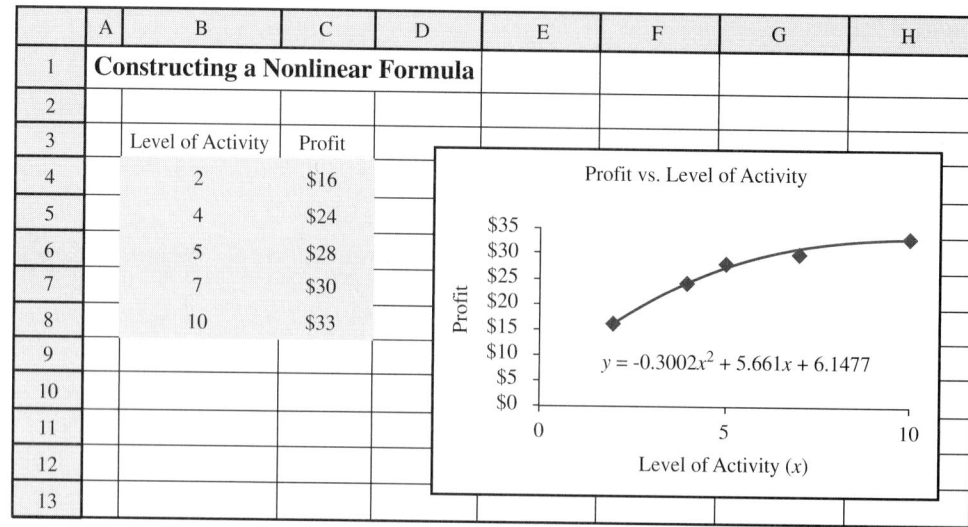

	A	B	C	D	E	F	G	H
1	**Constructing a Nonlinear Formula**							
2								
3		Level of Activity	Profit					
4		2	$16					
5		4	$24					
6		5	$28					
7		7	$30					
8		10	$33					
9								
10								
11								
12								
13								

Chart: Profit vs. Level of Activity

$$y = -0.3002x^2 + 5.661x + 6.1477$$

The quadratic form provides at least a reasonable approximation for many profit graphs, so it is used often. However, it is prudent to check whether the approximation actually is a reasonable one for any particular activity. This is done by estimating the profit that would be obtained by the activity at several different levels in addition to the data being used by the curve fitting method, and then checking whether the profit at these other levels is reasonably close to what is given by the formula. If it is not, one alternative is to collect more data and reapply the curve fitting method to seek a better overall fit. Another alternative is to adopt a different form for the formula (e.g., logarithmic) and then to apply the corresponding curve fitting method.

The Challenge of Solving Nonlinear Programming Models

It is easy to solve linear programming models with either the Excel Solver or a variety of other software packages. Very large problems are solved routinely every day. In fact, the most advanced software packages now are successfully solving amazingly huge problems. Furthermore, the solution obtained is guaranteed to be optimal.

Despite excellent progress in recent years, life is not nearly this good when dealing with nonlinear programming models. They often are much more difficult to solve than linear programming models. Furthermore, even when a solution is obtained, it sometimes cannot be guaranteed to be optimal.

Fortunately, some types of nonlinear programming models are relatively easy to solve. Cases (*a*) and (*b*) in Figure 10.2 (when maximizing) or in Figure 10.3 (when minimizing) are examples of "easy" types of nonlinear programming models, namely, types where the activities have decreasing marginal returns. As long as all the activities fit either case (except for any that still satisfy the proportionality assumption), formulating the model in a spreadsheet is not especially difficult and the Excel Solver can readily solve the model if it is not unusually large. The next section focuses on case (*a*) and Section 10.3 considers case (*b*).

Although some nonlinear programming models can be very difficult to solve, those that have decreasing marginal returns generally are relatively easy.

Unfortunately, other types of nonlinear programming tend to be more difficult. For example, even though case (*c*) in Figures 10.2 and 10.3 has decreasing marginal returns except at the discontinuities in the graph, the presence of such discontinuities for any of the activities makes it uncertain that the Excel Solver will successfully solve the model. Having increasing marginal returns, as in case (*d*), also can create serious complications.

Far more complicated nonlinear programming models can be constructed than any of those suggested by Figures 10.2 and 10.3. For example, consider the following model in algebraic form.

Maximize   Profit $= 0.5x^5 - 6x^4 + 24.5x^3 - 39x^2 + 20x$

subject to

$$x \leq 5$$

$$x \geq 0$$

FIGURE 10.7

An example of a complicated nonlinear programming model where the Excel Solver obtains three different final solutions when it starts with three different initial solutions.

	A	B	C	D	E
1	**Solver Solution**				
2	**(Starting with $x = 0$)**				
3					
4					Maximum
5		$x =$	0.371	$\leq$	5
6					
7		Profit = $0.5x^5-6x^4+24.5x^3-39x^2+20x$			
8		=	\$3.19		

	A	B	C	D	E
1	**Solver Solution**				
2	**(Starting with $x = 3$)**				
3					
4					Maximum
5		$x =$	3.126	$\leq$	5
6					
7		Profit = $0.5x^5-6x^4+24.5x^3-39x^2+20x$			
8		=	\$6.13		

	A	B	C	D	E
1	**Solver Solution**				
2	**(Starting with $x = 4.7$)**				
3					
4					Maximum
5		$x =$	5.000	$\leq$	5
6					
7		Profit = $0.5x^5-6x^4+24.5x^3-39x^2+20x$			
8		=	\$0.00		

	B	C
7	Profit =	Profit = $0.5x^5-6x^4+24.5x^3-39x^2+20x$
8		=0.5* x^5-6*x^4+24.5*x^3-39*x^2+20*x

Range Name	Cell
Maximum	E5
x	C5
Profit	C8

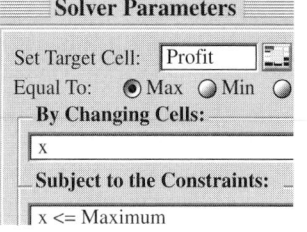

Solver Parameters

Set Target Cell: [Profit]

Equal To: ● Max ○ Min ○

By Changing Cells:

[x]

Subject to the Constraints:

[x <= Maximum]

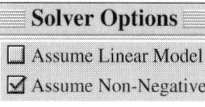

Solver Options

☐ Assume Linear Model

☑ Assume Non-Negative

FIGURE 10.8

The profit graph for the example considered in Figure 10.7.

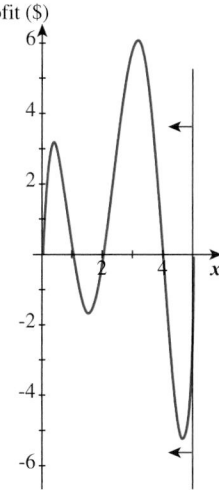

Profit (\$)

When maximizing, the standard Excel Solver only climbs to a local maximum and stops. This local maximum may or may not be the global maximum.

In this case, there is only a single activity, where x represents the level of this activity. Furthermore, there is only a single functional constraint ($x \leq 5$) in addition to the nonnegativity constraint. Nevertheless, Figure 10.7 demonstrates what a difficult time the Excel Solver has in attempting to cope with this problem. The model is straightforward to formulate in a spreadsheet, with x (C5) as the changing cell and Profit (C8) as the target cell. (Note that the Solver option, Assume Linear Model, is *not* chosen in this case because this is not a linear programming model.) When $x = 0$ is entered as the initial value in the changing cell, the left spreadsheet in Figure 10.7 shows that Solver then indicates that $x = 0.371$ is the optimal solution with Profit = \$3.19. However, if $x = 3$ is entered as the initial value instead, as in the middle spreadsheet in Figure 10.7, Solver obtains $x = 3.126$ as the optimal solution with Profit = \$6.13. Trying still another initial value of $x = 4.7$ in the right spreadsheet, Solver now indicates an optimal solution of $x = 5$ with Profit \$0. What is going on here?

Plotting the profit graph for such a complicated objective function is a difficult task, but doing so in Figure 10.8 does help to explain Solver's difficulties with this problem. Starting at $x = 0$, the profit graph does indeed climb to a peak at $x = 0.371$, as reported in the left spreadsheet of Figure 10.7. Starting at $x = 3$ instead, the graph climbs to a peak at $x = 3.126$, which is the solution found in the middle spreadsheet. Using the right spreadsheet's starting solution of $x = 4.7$, the graph climbs until it reaches the boundary imposed by the $x \leq 5$ constraint, so $x = 5$ is the peak in that direction. These three peaks are referred to as the **local maxima** (or *local optima*) because each one is a maximum of the graph within a local neighborhood of that point. However, only the largest of these local maxima is the **global maximum,** that is, the highest point on the entire graph. Thus, the middle spreadsheet in Figure 10.7 did succeed in finding the optimal solution at $x = 3.126$ with Profit = \$6.13.

The algorithm used by the Excel Solver to solve nonlinear programming problems can be thought of as a mountain climbing procedure. It starts at the initial solution entered into the changing cells and then begins climbing that mountain until it reaches the peak (or is blocked from climbing further by reaching the boundary imposed by the constraints). The procedure terminates when it reaches this peak (or boundary) and reports this solution. It has no way of detecting whether there is a taller mountain somewhere else on the profit graph.

When the target cell is to be minimized instead of maximized, this algorithm reverses direction and climbs down until it reaches the lowest point in that valley (or is blocked by a boundary). Once again, it has no way of detecting whether there is a lower valley somewhere else on the cost graph.

A nonlinear programming problem needs to have decreasing marginal returns to guarantee that the solution obtained by the Excel Solver actually is optimal.

The reason that having decreasing marginal returns for all the activities (except any with a proportional relationship) is an easy type of nonlinear programming problem is that the profit graph (when maximizing) has only one mountain. Therefore, a local maximum at the peak of the mountain (or a boundary) also is a global maximum, so the solution obtained by the Excel Solver is guaranteed to be optimal. For example, the profit graph based on a quadratic form in Figure 10.6 has decreasing marginal returns, so it has only a single mountain and its peak (which happens to be at $x = 9.43$) is the global maximum. Similarly, when minimizing a cost graph with decreasing marginal returns, there is only one valley so the local minimum at the bottom (or a boundary) also is a global minimum.

Figure 10.7 suggests that one way of dealing with more difficult problems that may have multiple local optima is to apply the Excel Solver repeatedly with a variety of starting solutions and then adopt the best of the final solutions obtained. Although this will not guarantee finding a globally optimal solution, it often will provide a good chance of finding at least a very good solution. Therefore, this is a reasonable approach for some relatively small problems, particularly when a systematic procedure is used to provide a comprehensive cross-section of starting solutions. Solver Table in your MS Courseware is a useful tool for systematically providing starting solutions when only one or two decision variables are being changed simultaneously. Section 10.4 describes this kind of approach to problems that may have multiple local optima.

However, this kind of approach is not very practical for problems with a large number of decision variables, since a huge number of starting solutions would be required to provide a comprehensive cross-section for such problems. What is needed is an algorithm that occasionally will "jump" from the current mountain to another more promising mountain on the profit graph so that the algorithm is likely to eventually reach the tallest mountain on its own regardless of which starting solution is entered into the changing cells. Premium Solver (available in your MS Courseware) provides such an algorithm called *Evolutionary Solver.* Although Evolutionary Solver has its limitations as well, it provides an excellent complement to the Excel Solver for attempting to cope with many nonlinear programming problems. Evolutionary Solver and its use are described in Section 10.5.

Review *Questions*

1. What are the features of linear programming models that are shared by nonlinear programming models?

2. How does the appearance of a nonlinear programming model differ from that of a linear programming model?

3. In what three major ways does the application of nonlinear programming models differ from that of linear programming models?

4. What is the proportionality assumption of linear programming that is violated by nonlinear programming problems?

5. When an activity has decreasing marginal returns, how does the slope of its profit graph behave?

6. What could cause the profit graph of an activity to be piecewise linear with decreasing marginal returns?

7. What is a common assumption about the form of the formula for the profit of an activity when applying a curve fitting method?

8. What are the types of nonlinear programming models that are relatively easy to solve?

9. When it is given a starting solution, how does the Excel Solver then proceed to attempt to solve a maximization problem with multiple local maxima?

10. What can be done to give the Excel Solver a better chance of obtaining an optimal solution (or at least a very good solution) for a maximization problem with multiple local maxima?

10.2 NONLINEAR PROGRAMMING WITH DECREASING MARGINAL RETURNS

In this section, we will focus on nonlinear programming problems having the following characteristics.

1. The same constraints as for a linear programming model.

2. A nonlinear objective function.

3. Each activity that violates the proportionality assumption of linear programming has *decreasing marginal returns* (as defined in the preceding section and illustrated in Figures 10.2[a] and 10.3[a]).

The Excel Solver can readily solve such problems because the solution it obtains is guaranteed to be optimal for this type of problem.

This is a particularly simple type of nonlinear programming problem. The Excel Solver can readily solve such problems if they are not unusually large.

For some problems of this type, the objective function will include cross-product terms involving the product of two or more decision variables. In this case, whenever all but one of the decision variables are fixed at particular values, the effect on the value of the objective function of increasing the one decision variable must still satisfy either proportionality or decreasing marginal returns for the third characteristic to hold. (The precise mathematical description of the third characteristic is that an objective function being maximized is required to be *concave* whereas an objective function being minimized is required to be *convex.*)

As discussed in the preceding section, it is fairly common for an activity to provide less and less return as the level of the activity is increased, so the activity has decreasing marginal returns. Consequently, nonlinear programming problems with decreasing marginal returns arise fairly frequently. We will go through two examples in some detail to illustrate how this happens and then describe how to formulate and solve such a problem.

In some cases, when the nonlinear objective function is reasonably close to being linear, a linear programming model will be used as an approximation to perform the preliminary analysis and then a more precise nonlinear programming model will be used to do the detailed analysis. This is what is happening below as the story of the Wyndor Glass Co. case study continues to unfold.

Continuation of the Wyndor Glass Co. Case Study

As described in Section 2.2, the Wyndor Glass Co. produces high-quality glass products, where different parts of the production are performed in three plants. It now is launching two new products (a special kind of door and a special kind of window), where the anticipated profit has been estimated to be $300 per door and $500 per window. Section 2.3 discusses how these estimates of the unit profits, along with information regarding constraints, have led to the formulation of a linear programming model whose objective function to be maximized is Profit = $300D + $500W, where D and W are the number of doors and windows to be produced per week, respectively.

To refresh your memory, Figure 10.9 shows the spreadsheet model that was formulated in Section 2.3 for this problem. Having clicked on the Solve button, the changing cells UnitsProduced (C12:D12) give the optimal solution, $(D, W) = (2, 6)$, and the target cell TotalProfit (G12) indicates that this will yield a weekly profit of $3,600, according to the model.

This model assumes that the profit from either of these new products would be *proportional* to the production rate for the product. However, this is a questionable assumption. Therefore, before making a final decision on the production rates, Wyndor management wants a more precise analysis to be done, as described in the following conversation between two members of management.

John Hill (Wyndor president): How are your marketing plans coming along for the launch of our two new products, Ann?

Ann Lester (Wyndor vice president for marketing): Pretty well. I have a much better handle on what needs to be done now.

John: Will it be very expensive?

Ann : That depends on what sales volume we need to generate. Our market research indicates that we would be able to sell small numbers of the new doors and windows with virtually no advertising. However, it also tells us that we would need an extensive advertising campaign if we produce close to what our plants can handle. If we get all the way up to the maximum that could be produced of either

FIGURE 10.9

The spreadsheet model that was formulated in Section 2.3 for the original Wyndor problem introduced in Section 2.2.

	A	B	C	D	E	F	G
1		**Wyndor Glass Co. Product-Mix Problem**					
2							
3			Doors	Windows			
4		Unit Profit	$300	$500			
5					Hours		Hours
6			Hours Used per Unit Produced		Used		Available
7		Plant 1	1	0	2	≤	4
8		Plant 2	0	2	12	≤	12
9		Plant 3	3	2	18	≤	18
10							
11			Doors	Windows			Total Profit
12		Units Produced	2	6			$3,600

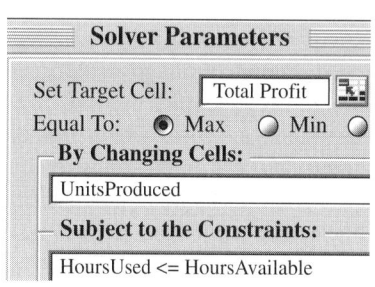

Solver Parameters

Set Target Cell: [Total Profit]

Equal To: ● Max ○ Min ○

By Changing Cells:

[UnitsProduced]

Subject to the Constraints:

[HoursUsed <= HoursAvailable]

	E
5	Hours
6	Used
7	=SUMPRODUCT(C7:D7,UnitsProduced)
8	=SUMPRODUCT(C8:D8,UnitsProduced)
9	=SUMPRODUCT(C9:D9,UnitsProduced)

	G
11	Total Profit
12	=SUMPRODUCT(UnitProfit,UnitsProduced)

Solver Options

☑ Assume Linear Model

☑ Assume Non-Negative

Range Name	Cells
HoursAvailable	G7:G9
HoursUsed	E7:E9
HoursUsedPerUnitProduced	C7:D9
TotalProfit	G12
UnitProfit	C4:D4
UnitsProduced	C12:D12

product, it now appears that we would need to lower the price a little to sell it all. Has a final decision been made yet on the production rates?

John: No, it hasn't. Based on the report from the Management Science Group, we definitely want to go ahead with both products and we are thinking in terms of production rates reasonably close to what is recommended in the report. However, now that our planning is much further along, it is clearer just what our costs will be, so we want the Management Science Group to fine-tune its analysis before we make a final decision. In fact, that's why I asked you to come see me. We would like to ask for your help.

Ann: Sure. What can I do?

John: Well, basically what we want is your updated input on what the marketing costs per week would need to be to sell each product if the production rate were to be set at each of several alternative values.

Ann: Sure, I can do that. When they started their analysis before, I was asked to estimate the marketing cost per door and per window. I told them $75 per door and $200 per window. Those looked like good estimates at the time.

John: Yes. Those cost estimates were factored in when they developed their estimated profits of $300 per door and $500 per window. Do your cost estimates still look pretty close?

Ann: No, not really. I don't think it makes sense any more to figure our marketing costs on a per door or per window basis. As I was saying before, our costs would be very small with low production rates, but would need to be very substantial with high production rates. Therefore, figuring $75 per door and $200 per window is much too large with low production rates, about right at medium production rates, and much too small at high production rates.

A linear formula is no longer adequate for estimating the marketing costs.

John: Yes, that's what I suspected. That's why we want you to forget about doing it now on a per door or per window basis and instead estimate your weekly marketing costs for each product if the production rate were to be set at each of several alternative values. This will enable the Management Science Group to perform a more precise analysis of what the production rates should be.

Ann: That makes sense. I'll pull these new estimates together right away.

After receiving these estimates, the Management Science Group plotted the weekly marketing cost for each product versus the production rate of the product. Each of these plots showed that the marketing cost increases roughly with the *square* of the production rate as this rate is increased. Therefore, a *quadratic form* was assumed to apply Excel's curve fitting procedure to each of these plots.

This curve fitting procedure estimated that the weekly marketing costs required to sustain a production rate of D doors per week would be roughly

$$\text{Marketing cost for doors} = \$25D^2$$

for any fractional or integer value of D permitted by the production constraints. Excluding marketing costs, the gross profit per door sold is about $375. Therefore, the weekly net profit would be roughly

$$\text{Net profit for doors} = \$375D - \$25D^2$$

The corresponding estimates per week for windows are

$$\text{Marketing cost for windows} = \$66\tfrac{2}{3}W^2$$

$$\text{Gross profit for windows} \quad = \$700W$$

$$\text{Net profit for windows} \quad = \$700W - \$66\tfrac{2}{3}W^2$$

The new estimates of marketing costs cause both the doors and windows to have decreasing marginal returns.

Figure 10.10 shows the resulting profit graphs for both products. Note that both curves show decreasing marginal returns, where this becomes particularly pronounced for larger values of W.

FIGURE 10.10

The smooth curves are the profit graphs for Wyndor's doors and windows for the version of its problem where nonlinear marketing costs must be considered.

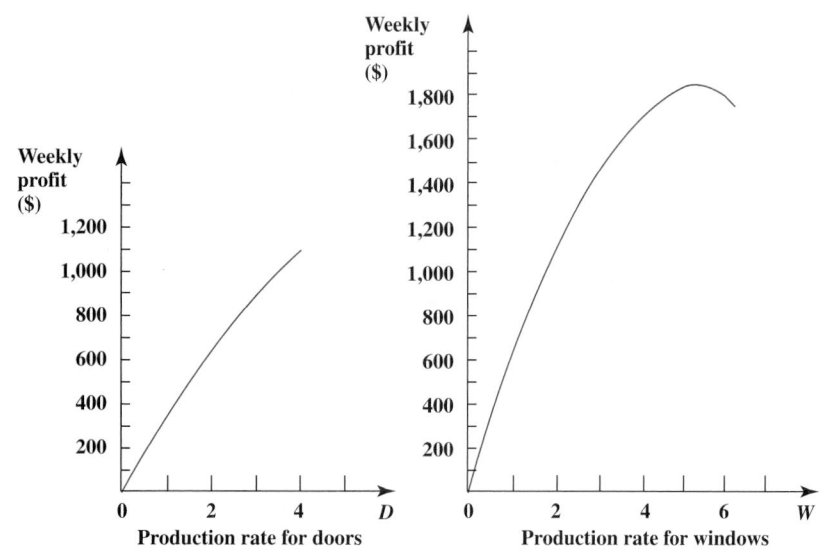

Combining the net profit for doors and for windows, the new objective function to be maximized for this problem is

$$\text{Profit} = \$375D - \$25D^2 + \$700W - \$66\frac{2}{3}W^2$$

subject to the same constraints as before. Because the terms involving D^2 and W^2 have exponents different from 1 for these decision variables, this objective function is a *nonlinear* function. Therefore, the overall problem is a *nonlinear programming* problem. Furthermore, because this objective function has a *quadratic form* (and the problem has all three characteristics listed at the beginning of this section), the overall problem is a special type of nonlinear programming problem called a **quadratic programming** problem. This is a common type of nonlinear programming problem and also a particularly convenient type to formulate and solve. Special algorithms have been developed just to solve quadratic programming problems very efficiently, so commercial management science software packages often include such an algorithm to enable solving huge problems of this type. (However, the Excel Solver only uses a general algorithm for solving any nonlinear programming problem with decreasing marginal returns.)

A quadratic programming problem has linear constraints and an objective function that has both a quadratic form and decreasing marginal returns.

A Spreadsheet Formulation

Figure 10.11 shows the formulation of a spreadsheet model for this problem. It is interesting to compare this model with the one for the original Wyndor problem in Figure 10.9. At first glance, they appear to be nearly the same. A closer examination reveals four significant differences.

First, the unit profits in row 4 of Figure 10.9 have been replaced here by the *gross* unit profits, which exclude the marketing costs.

Second, to take the marketing costs into account in calculating the target cell TotalProfit (H16), the spreadsheet in Figure 10.11 has added several output cells: GrossProfitFromSales (H12), MarketingCost (C14:D14), and TotalMarketingCost (H14).

Third, a fundamental difference lies in the equations entered into certain output cells. In Figure 10.9, the formula for TotalProfit (G12) is expressed in terms of the SUMPRODUCT function that is characteristic of linear programming when each product is the product of a data cell and a changing cell. In Figure 10.11, something else is needed for calculating the marketing cost portion of total profit because that portion of the objective function is nonlinear. For example, consider the term involving D^2 in the objective function. Because the value of D appears in DoorsProduced (C12), Excel expresses D^2 as DoorsProduced^2, where the symbol ^ indicates that the number following this symbol (2) is the exponent of the number in DoorsProduced (C12). The same approach is used for expressing W^2. Therefore, the formula for total marketing cost is

Excel Tip: When a changing cell needs to be raised to some power in a formula, the symbol ^ is placed between the changing cell and the exponent.

$$\text{Total Marketing Cost} = \text{SUM(MarketingCost)}$$
$$= 25*(\text{DoorsProduced}^2) + 66.667*(\text{WindowsProduced}^2)$$

The formula for the target cell then becomes

$$\text{TotalProfit (H16)} = \text{GrossProfitFromSales (H12)} - \text{TotalMarketingCost (H14)}$$

The fourth difference arises in the selection of the Solver options at the bottom of Figures 10.9 and 10.11. In contrast to Figure 10.9, note that the Assume Linear Model option is *not* selected in Figure 10.11, because the model is not a linear programming model.

Before solving any nonlinear programming model, you should click on the Option button and make sure that the Assume Linear Model option has not been selected.

For this particular model, clicking on the Solve button provides the optimal solution shown in UnitsProduced (C12:D12), namely,

$$D = 3.214 \quad \text{(produce an average of 3.214 doors per week)}$$

$$W = 4.179 \quad \text{(produce an average of 4.179 windows per week)}$$

FIGURE 10.11

A spreadsheet model for the Wyndor nonlinear programming problem with nonlinear marketing costs, where the changing cells UnitsProduced (C12:D12) show the optimal production rates and the target cell TotalProfit (H16) gives the resulting total profit per week.

	A	B	C	D	E	F	G	H
1		**Wyndor Problem with Nonlinear Marketing Costs**						
2								
3			Doors	Windows				
4		Unit Profit (Gross)	$375	$700				
5					Hours		Hours	
6			Hours Used per Unit Produced		Used		Available	
7		Plant 1	1	0	3.214	≤	4	
8		Plant 2	0	2	8.357	≤	12	
9		Plant 3	3	2	18	≤	18	
10								
11			Doors	Windows				
12		Units Produced	3.214	4.179			Gross Profit from Sales	$4,130
13								
14		Marketing Cost	$258	$1,164			Total Marketing Cost	$1,422
15								
16							Total Profit	$2,708

Solver Parameters

Set Target Cell: | Total Profit |

Equal To: ● Max ○ Min ○

By Changing Cells:

| UnitsProduced |

Subject to the Constraints:

| HoursUsed <= HoursAvailable |

	E
5	Hours
6	Used
7	=SUMPRODUCT(C7:D7,UnitsProduced)
8	=SUMPRODUCT(C8:D8,UnitsProduced)
9	=SUMPRODUCT(C9:D9,UnitsProduced)

	G	H
12	Gross Profit from Sales	=SUMPRODUCT(UnitProfit,UnitsProduced)
13		
14	Total Marketing Cost	=SUM(MarketingCost)
15		
16	Total Profit	=GrossProfitFromSales−TotalMarketingCost

	B	C	D
14	Marketing Cost	=25*(DoorsProduced^2)	=66.667*(WindowsProduced^2)

Solver Options

☐ Assume Linear Model
☑ Assume Non-Negative

Range Name	Cells
DoorsProduced	C12
GrossProfitFromSales	H12
HoursAvailable	G7:G9
HoursUsed	E7:E9
HoursUsedPerUnitProduced	C7:D9
MarketingCost	C14:D14
TotalMarketingCost	H14
TotalProfit	H16
UnitProfit	C4:D4
UnitsProduced	C12:D12
WindowsProduced	D12

FIGURE 10.12

Graphical display of the nonlinear programming formulation of the Wyndor problem with nonlinear marketing costs. The curves are objective function curves for some sample values of Profit and the one (Profit = $2,708) that passes through the optimal solution, $(D, W) = (3\frac{3}{14}, 4\frac{5}{28})$.

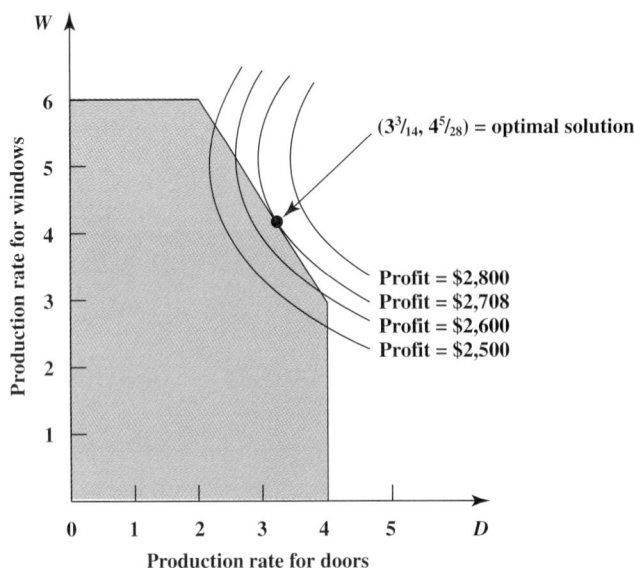

where TotalProfit (H16) shows a resulting weekly profit of $2,708. These strange values of D and W certainly are not intuitive. Figure 10.12 conveys some graphical intuition into why this answer was obtained. The feasible region is the same as for the original Wyndor problem in Chapter 2. However, instead of having objective function *lines* with which to search for an optimal solution, plotting the points that give any constant value for our nonlinear objective function now gives an objective function *curve* instead. Thus, when using the objective function to calculate Profit for various feasible and infeasible values of (D, W), each of the four curves in the figure shows all the values of (D, W) that give the fixed value of Profit indicated for that curve. (Plotting these points is a tedious and difficult process, so we will not bother with the details of how it is done.) The figure shows that increasing Profit moves the objective function curve to the right. The largest value of Profit such that the objective function curve still passes through any points in the feasible region is Profit = $2,708. Therefore, using fractions, the one feasible point that the Profit = $2,708 curve passes through,

$$(D, W) = (3\tfrac{3}{14}, 4\tfrac{5}{28})$$

is the optimal solution.

Since these are not particularly convenient fractions with which to plan production schedules, they should be adjusted slightly. The curve for Profit = $2,708 in Figure 10.12 indicates that any point on the slanting line at the boundary of the feasible region that is close to the optimal solution will provide a weekly profit very close to $2,708. For example,

$$(D, W) = (3\tfrac{1}{3}, 4)$$

gives a weekly profit of $2,706, so management prefers this more convenient production schedule.

By contrast, consider the linear programming solution in Figure 10.9, $(D, W) = (2, 6)$, that does not take the nonlinearities in the marketing costs into account. When using the current objective function that incorporates these nonlinearities, $(D, W) = (2, 6)$ provides a weekly profit of only $2,450. This illustrates the kind of improvement that can be obtained by replacing an approximate linear programming model by a more precise nonlinear programming model.

Applying Nonlinear Programming to Portfolio Selection

It now is common practice for professional managers of large stock portfolios to use computer models based partially on nonlinear programming to guide them. Because investors are concerned about both the *expected return* (gain) and the *risk* associated with their investments, nonlinear programming is used to determine a portfolio that, under certain assumptions, provides an optimal trade-off between these two factors. This approach is based largely on path-breaking research done by Harry Markowitz and William Sharpe that helped them win the 1990 Nobel Prize in economics.

One way of formulating their approach is as a nonlinear version of the *cost–benefit trade-off problems* discussed in Section 4.3. In this case, the cost involved is the risk associated with the investments. The benefit is the expected return from the portfolio of investments. Therefore, the general form of the model is

This model focuses on the trade-off between risk and expected return from the portfolio of investments.

$$\text{Minimize} \quad \text{Risk}$$

subject to

$$\text{Expected return} \geq \text{Minimum acceptable level}$$

The measure of risk used here is a basic quantity from probability theory called the *variance* of the return. Using standard formulas from probability theory, the objective function then can be expressed as a nonlinear function of the decision variables (the fractions of the total investment to invest in the respective stocks) that yields *decreasing marginal returns* for the stocks. By adding the constraint on expected return, as well as nonnegativity constraints and a constraint that the fractions of the total investment invested in the respective stocks sum to 1, we thereby obtain a simple type of nonlinear programming model for optimizing the selection of the portfolio.

To illustrate the approach, we now will focus on a small numerical example where just three stocks (securities) are being considered for inclusion in the portfolio. Thus, the decision variables are

$$S_1 = \text{Fraction of total investment invested in stock 1}$$

$$S_2 = \text{Fraction of total investment invested in stock 2}$$

$$S_3 = \text{Fraction of total investment invested in stock 3}$$

Since these fractions need to sum to 1,

$$S_1 + S_2 + S_3 = 1$$

will be included as one of the constraints of the model.

Table 10.2 gives the needed data for these three stocks. The second column provides the expected return for each of these stocks, so the expected return for the overall portfolio is

$$\text{Expected return} = (21S_1 + 30S_2 + 8S_3)\%$$

The investor's current choice of the minimum acceptable level for this quantity is

$$\text{Minimum acceptable expected return} = 18\%$$

Since the expected returns of stocks 1 and 2 exceed 18%, this minimum acceptable level will be achieved if these stocks comprise a sufficiently large portion of the portfolio.

However, stocks 1 and 2 are much riskier than stock 3. There is no certainty that the expected returns shown in Table 10.2 actually will be achieved, but there is much more uncertainty for stocks 1 and 2 than for stock 3. Each stock has an underlying *probability distribution* of what

TABLE 10.2

Data for the Stocks of the Portfolio Selection Example

Stock	Expected Return	Risk (Standard Deviation)	Pair of Stocks	Joint Risk per Stock (Covariance)
1	21%	25%	1 and 2	0.040
2	30	45	1 and 3	−0.005
3	8	5	2 and 3	−0.010

The challenge is to find the right balance between the high return but high risk from stocks 1 and 2 and the low risk but low return from stock 3.

its return will turn out to be. In each case, the *standard deviation* (i.e., the square root of the variance) of this distribution provides a measure of how spread out this distribution is, since there is roughly a two-thirds probability that the return will turn out to be within one standard deviation of the expected return. This measure of the risk of a stock is given in the third column of Table 10.2.

However, the risk for the portfolio cannot be obtained solely from the third column, since this column only gives the risk for each individual stock considered in isolation. The risk for the portfolio also is affected by whether the particular stocks tend to move up and down together (increased risk) or tend to move in opposite directions (decreased risk). In the rightmost column of Table 10.2, the *positive* joint risk for stocks 1 and 2 indicates that these two stocks have some tendency to move in the same direction. However, the *negative* joint risk for the other two pairs of stocks shows that stock 3 tends to go up when either stock 1 or 2 goes down, and vice versa. (In the terminology of probability theory, the joint risk for *each* of two stocks is the *covariance* of their returns, as given in the rightmost column of Table 10.2, so the total joint risk for two stocks is two times this covariance.)

The data in Table 10.2 typically are obtained by taking samples of the returns of the stocks from a number of previous years and then calculating the averages, standard deviations, and covariances for these samples. Adjustments in the resulting estimate of at least the expected return of a stock also may be made if it appears that the current prospects for the stock are somewhat different than in previous years. Using the formula from probability theory for calculating the overall variance from individual variances and covariances, the risk for the entire portfolio is

$$\text{Risk} = (0.25S_1)^2 + (0.45S_2)^2 + (0.05S_3)^2 + 2(0.04)S_1S_2 + 2(-0.005)S_1S_3 + 2(-0.01)S_2S_3$$

Therefore, the algebraic form of the nonlinear programming model for this example is

$$\text{Minimize} \quad \text{Risk} = (0.25S_1)^2 + (0.45S_2)^2 + (0.05S_3)^2 + 2(0.04)S_1S_2 \\ + 2(-0.005)S_1S_3 + 2(-0.01)S_2S_3$$

subject to

$$21S_1 + 30S_2 + 8S_3 \geq 18$$

$$S_1 + S_2 + S_3 = 1$$

and

$$S_1 \geq 0 \qquad S_2 \geq 0 \qquad S_3 \geq 0$$

This kind of quadratic programming model is widely used by portfolio managers.

Fortunately, the objective function for this model has decreasing marginal returns. (This is not obvious, but it has been verified that Risk, measured by the variance of the return for the entire portfolio, *always* has decreasing marginal returns for any portfolio.) Furthermore, this is a *quadratic programming* model since the objective function is quadratic (terms consisting of a coefficient times the product of two variables are allowed in a quadratic function) and the model has all three characteristics listed at the beginning of this section. Therefore, this is a particularly simple type of nonlinear programming model to solve.

Figure 10.13 shows the corresponding spreadsheet model after having applied the Solver. For ease of interpretation, the changing cells Portfolio (C14:E14) give the values of S_1, S_2, and S_3 as percentages rather than fractions. These cells indicate that the optimal solution is

$S_1 = 40.2\%$: Allocate 40.2% of the portfolio to stock 1

$S_2 = 21.7\%$: Allocate 21.7% of the portfolio to stock 2

$S_3 = 38.1\%$: Allocate 38.1% of the portfolio to stock 3

Thus, despite its relatively low return, including a substantial amount of stock 3 in the portfolio is worthwhile to counteract the high risk associated with stocks 1 and 2. ExpectedReturn (C19) indicates that this portfolio still achieves an expected return of 18 percent, which equals the minimum acceptable level. The target cell Variance (C21) gives the risk for the portfolio,

FIGURE 10.13

A spreadsheet model for the portfolio selection example of nonlinear programming, where the changing cells Portfolio (C14:E14) give the optimal portfolio and the target cell Variance (C21) shows the resulting risk.

	A	B	C	D	E	F	G	H
1	**Portfolio Selection Problem (Nonlinear Programming)**							
2								
3			Stock 1	Stock 2	Stock 3			
4		Expected Return	21%	30%	8%			
5								
6		Risk (Stand. Dev.)	25%	45%	5%			
7								
8		Joint Risk (Covar.)	Stock 1	Stock 2	Stock 3			
9		Stock 1		0.040	-0.005			
10		Stock 2			-0.010			
11		Stock 3						
12								
13			Stock 1	Stock 2	Stock 3	Total		
14		Portfolio	40.2%	21.7%	38.1%	100%	=	100%
15								
16					Minimum			
17					Expected			
18			Portfolio		Return			
19		Expected Return	18%	≥	18%			
20								
21		Risk (Variance)	0.0238					
22								
23		Risk (Stand. Dev.)	15.4%					

Range Name	Cells
Covar12	D9
Covar13	E9
Covar23	E10
Covariance	C9:E11
ExpectedReturn	C19
MinExpectedReturn	E19
OneHundredPercent	H14
Portfolio	C14:E14
SD1	C6
SD2	D6
SD3	E6
StandDev	C23
Stock1	C14
Stock2	D14
Stock3	E14
StockExpectedReturn	C4:E4
StockStandDev	C6:E6
Total	F14
Variance	C21

Solver Parameters

Set Target Cell: Variance
Equal To: ○ Max ● Min ○ Valu

By Changing Cells:
Portfolio

Subject to the Constraints:
ExpectedReturn >= MinExpectedReturn
Total = OneHundredPercent

Solver Options
☐ Assume Linear Model
☑ Assume Non-Negative

	F
13	Total
14	=SUM(Portfolio)

	B	C
19	Expected Return	=SUMPRODUCT(StockExpectedReturn,Portfolio)
20		
21	Risk (Variance)	=((SD1*Stock1)^2)+((SD2*Stock2)^2)+((SD3*Stock3)^2)+2*Covar12*Stock1*Stock2+2*Covar13*Stock1*Stock3+2*Covar23*Stock2*Stock3
22		
23	Risk (Stand. Dev.)	=SQRT(Variance)

There is a good chance that the return for the portfolio will not deviate from the expected return by more than the standard deviation of the return.

namely, the variance of the return for the entire portfolio, as 0.0238. To help interpret this quantity, StandDev (C23) calculates the corresponding standard deviation of the return for the portfolio as $\sqrt{0.0238} = 0.154 = 15.4\%$. The fact that this standard deviation is less than the expected return is encouraging, because this indicates that it is fairly unlikely that the actual return that eventually is achieved by the portfolio will turn out to be negative. The standard deviation is this small, despite the much larger standard deviations of the returns for stocks 1 and 2 given in StockStandDev (C6:E6), because of the very small standard deviation for stock 3 and the negative values in Covar13 (E9) and Covar23 (E10).

This is an example of a cost–benefit trade-off problem since it involves finding the best trade-off between cost (risk) and a benefit (expected return). Except for the form of the objective function, it is analogous to the cost–benefit trade-off problems discussed in Section 4.3. As discussed further in Chapter 5, analysis of such a problem seldom ends with finding an optimal solution for the original version of the model. The minimum acceptable level stated in the model for the benefit (or benefits) involved is a tentative policy decision. After learning the resulting cost, further analysis is needed to find the best trade-off between costs and benefits. This analysis involves varying the minimum acceptable level for the benefit and seeing what the effect is on the cost. If a lot more benefit can be obtained for relatively little cost, this probably should be done. On the other hand, if decreasing the benefit a little would save a lot of cost, the minimum acceptable level probably should be decreased.

An investor needs the kind of table and graph shown in Figure 10.14 to decide on which portfolio provides the best trade-off between expected return and risk.

One way of applying this approach to the current example is to use the Solver Table (in your MS Courseware) as described in Chapter 5 to generate a table that gives the expected return and risk provided by an optimal solution for the model for a range of values of the minimum acceptable expected return. Figure 10.14 shows such a table. In the parlance of the world of finance, the pairs of values in columns F and G are referred to as points on the *efficient frontier*. In fact,

FIGURE 10.14

An application of the Solver Table that shows the trade-off between expected return and risk when the model of Figure 10.13 is altered by varying the minimum acceptable expected return.

	A	B	C	D	E	F	G	H	I	J	K
25		**Solver Table for Portfolio Selection Problem**									
26											
27		Minimum									
28		Expected				Risk	Expected				
29		Return	Stock 1	Stock 2	Stock 3	(St. Dev.)	Return				
30			40.20%	21.70%	38.10%	15.40%	18.00%				
31		8%	7.10%	3.70%	89.10%	3.90%	9.70%				
32		10%	8.10%	4.30%	87.60%	3.90%	10.00%				
33		12%	16.20%	8.60%	75.20%	5.60%	12.00%				
34		14%	24.20%	13.00%	62.80%	8.60%	14.00%				
35		16%	32.20%	17.30%	50.50%	12.00%	16.00%				
36		18%	40.20%	21.70%	38.10%	15.40%	18.00%				
37		20%	48.20%	26.10%	25.70%	18.90%	20.00%				
38		22%	56.20%	30.40%	13.40%	22.50%	22.00%				
39		24%	64.20%	34.80%	1.00%	26.10%	24.00%				
40		26%	44.40%	55.60%	0.00%	30.80%	26.00%				
41		28%	22.20%	77.80%	0.00%	37.30%	28.00%				
42		30%	0.00%	100.00%	0.00%	45.00%	30.00%				

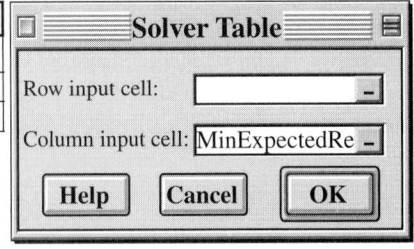

	C	D	E	F	G
28				Risk	Expected
29	Stock 1	Stock 2	Stock 3	(St. Dev.)	Return
30	=Stock1	=Stock2	=Stock3	=StandDev	=ExpectedReturn

Solver Table

Row input cell: [   ] −

Column input cell: [MinExpectedRe −]

[Help]   [Cancel]   [OK]

Range Name	Cells
ExpectedReturn	C19
MinExpectedReturn	E19
StandDev	C23
Stock1	C14
Stock2	D14
Stock3	E14

the right-hand side of Figure 10.14 shows a plot of this efficient frontier. After examining enough such points, the investor then can make a personal decision about which one provides the best trade-off between expected return and risk.

Review Questions

1. What are the three characteristics of a simple type of nonlinear programming problem that can be readily solved by the Excel Solver?

2. For this simple type of nonlinear programming problem, how does the graphical display for a two-variable problem differ from that for a two-variable linear programming problem?

3. What additional characteristic must this type of nonlinear programming problem have in order to be a quadratic programming problem?

4. When applying nonlinear programming to portfolio selection, a trade-off is being sought between which two factors?

10.3   SEPARABLE PROGRAMMING

Section 10.1 described several types of nonproportional relationships between an activity and the overall measure of performance for a problem. One such relationship is *decreasing marginal returns* and Section 10.2 has just focused on nonlinear programming problems where this type of relationship holds for all the activities. We now turn our attention to a related kind of nonproportional relationship where the activities again have decreasing marginal returns. However, the difference is that the profit or cost graph for each activity now is *piecewise linear* because it consists of a sequence of connected line segments. Figure 10.2(b) in Section 10.1 illustrated such a

For nonlinear programming problems with decreasing marginal returns where the profit or cost graphs also are piecewise linear, the separable programming technique converts the problem into an equivalent linear programming problem.

profit graph (or the graph for any other measure of performance to be maximized) and Figure 10.3(c) did the same for a cost graph (or any related graph with minimization).

There is a special technique called *separable programming* that is designed to deal with this kind of nonlinear programming problem. Thus, the total profit (or cost) is simply the sum of the profits (or costs) obtained directly from these piecewise linear profit (or cost) graphs for the individual activities. (No cross-product terms are allowed and each graph must have decreasing marginal returns.) Because of the line segments in each profit or cost graph, this technique converts the formulation of the model into a *linear programming* model. This enables solving the model extremely efficiently and then applying the powerful tools of what-if analysis for linear programming.

The next episode in the saga of the Wyndor Glass Co. problem illustrates this technique.

The Wyndor Glass Co. Problem When Overtime Is Needed

The company now is ready to begin production of its special new doors and windows, based on the planning described in Chapter 2, Chapter 5, and Section 10.2. Because of the nonlinear marketing costs discussed in Section 10.2, the current plan is to use production rates of

$$(D,W) = \left(3\frac{1}{3}, 4 \right)$$

where D and W are the number of doors and windows to be produced per week, respectively.

However, there now is a new development that might alter this production plan for the first four months.

In particular, the company has accepted a special order for hand-crafted goods to be made in plants 1 and 2 throughout the next four months. Filling this order will require borrowing certain employees from the work crews for the regular products, so the remaining workers will need to work overtime to utilize the full production capacity of each plant's machinery and equipment for these products.

Without worrying about the new estimates of nonlinear marketing costs yet, how should the original Wyndor model be modified to consider overtime?

Because of this new development, management has asked the Management Science Group to quickly update its model and check whether the current production plan still would be the most profitable one to use during the first four months. To get a quick handle on the problem, the group decides to ignore the nonlinearities in the marketing costs for now and simply modify the original spreadsheet model shown in Figure 10.9 (in the preceding section) to take overtime into account.

The constraints in this original model, HoursUsed (E7:E9) ≤ HoursAvailable (G7:G9), are still valid, where overtime would be used to fill some of the hours of production time available in plants 1 and 2 as given by cells G7 and G8. However, the objective function no longer is valid because the additional cost of using overtime work reduces the profit obtained from each unit of product produced in this way.

For the portion of the work done in plants 1 and 2, Table 10.3 shows the maximum number of units of each product that can be produced per week on regular time and on overtime. Plant 3 does not need to use overtime, so its unchanged constraint is given in parentheses at the bottom. The fourth column is the sum of the second and third columns, where these sums are implied by the original constraints for plants 1 and 2 ($D \leq 4$ and $2W \leq 12$, so $W \leq 6$). The final two columns give the estimated profit for each unit produced on regular time and on overtime (in plants 1 and 2), based on the original estimates of marketing costs rather than those developed in Section 10.2.

TABLE 10.3
Data for the Original Wyndor Problem When Overtime Is Needed

Product	Maximum Weekly Production			Profit per Unit Produced	
	Regular Time	Overtime	Total	Regular Time	Overtime
Doors	3	1	4	$300	$200
Windows	3	3	6	500	100
	(and $3D + 2W \leq 18$)				

FIGURE 10.15

Profit graphs for the Wyndor Glass Co. that show the total weekly profit from each product versus the production rate for that product when overtime is needed to exceed a production rate of three units per week. At this point, these profit graphs are based on the original estimates of marketing costs rather than the estimates of nonlinear marketing costs developed in Section 10.2.

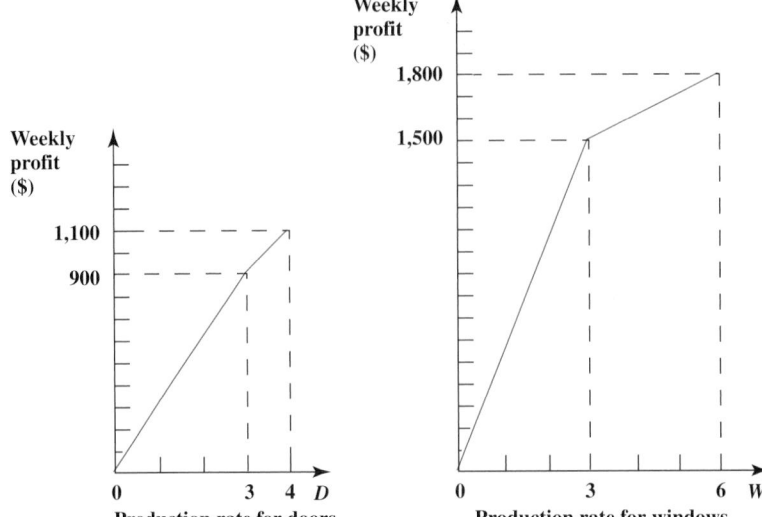

Figure 10.15 plots the weekly profit from each product versus its production rate. Note that the *slope* (steepness) of each profit graph decreases when the production rate is increased sufficiently to require overtime, because the profit per unit produced shown in Table 10.3 is less on overtime than on regular time. Thus, these two products have *decreasing marginal returns*.

Management had considered hiring some temporary workers to avoid the extra expense of using overtime. However, this would mean incurring some training costs, as well as inefficiencies from using inexperienced workers. Therefore, because this is a temporary situation where regular production can resume in four months, management has decided to go ahead and use overtime.

The model needs to provide a solution that uses overtime for a product only if all available regular time for that product has been fully utilized.

However, management does insist that the work crew for each product be fully utilized on regular time before any overtime is used. Furthermore, it feels that the current plans for the production rates should be changed temporarily if this would improve overall profitability.

Applying Separable Programming to This Problem

Since each profit graph in Figure 10.15 is not a straight line, the profit from each product is *not* proportional to its production rate. Consequently, the proportionality assumption of linear programming (discussed in Section 10.1) is violated. However, each profit graph does consist of *two* straight lines (line segments) that are connected together at the point where the slope changes. Thus, within each line segment, the profit graph looks like the proportionality assumption still holds. This suggests the following key idea.

The key idea is to have a separate decision variable for each line segment in a profit graph (or cost graph).

The Separable Programming Technique: For each activity that violates the proportionality assumption, separate its profit graph into parts, with a line segment in each part. Then, instead of using a single decision variable to represent the level of each such activity, introduce a separate new decision variable for each line segment on that activity's profit graph. Since the proportionality assumption holds for these new decision variables, formulate a linear programming model in terms of these variables.

For the Wyndor problem, these new decision variables are

D_R = Number of doors produced per week on regular time

D_O = Number of doors produced per week on overtime

W_R = Number of windows produced per week on regular time

W_O = Number of windows produced per week on overtime

The unit profits associated with these variables are given in the final two columns of Table 10.3, so these numbers become the coefficients in the objective function. The second and

FIGURE 10.16

A spreadsheet model for the Wyndor separable programming problem when overtime is needed, where the changing cells UnitsProduced (C14:D15) give the optimal production rates obtained by the Solver and the target cell TotalProfit (D18) shows the resulting total profit per week. This model is based on the profit graphs in Figure 10.15 and so does not incorporate the nonlinear marketing costs developed in Section 10.2.

	A	B	C	D	E	F	G
1		**Wyndor Problem with Overtime (Separable Programming)**					
2							
3		**Unit Profit**	Doors	Windows			
4		Regular	$300	$500			
5		Overtime	$200	$100			
6					Hours		Hours
7			Hours Used per Unit Produced		Used		Available
8		Plant 1	1	0	4	≤	4
9		Plant 2	0	2	6	≤	12
10		Plant 3	3	2	18	≤	18
11							
12			**Units Produced**			**Maximum**	
13			Doors	Windows		Doors	Windows
14		Regular	3	3	≤	3	3
15		Overtime	1	0	≤	1	3
16		Total Produced	4	3			
17							
18			Total Profit	$2,600			

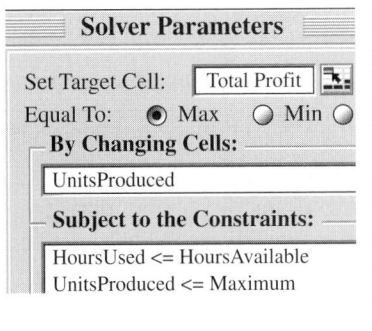

Solver Parameters

Set Target Cell: [Total Profit]

Equal To: ● Max   ○ Min ○

By Changing Cells:

[UnitsProduced]

Subject to the Constraints:

HoursUsed <= HoursAvailable
UnitsProduced <= Maximum

	E
6	Hours
7	Used
8	=SUMPRODUCT(C8:D8,TotalProduced)
9	=SUMPRODUCT(C9:D9,TotalProduced)
10	=SUMPRODUCT(C10:D10,TotalProduced)

	B	C	D
16	Total Produced	=SUM(C14:C15)	=SUM(D14:D15)

	C	D
18	Total Profit	=SUMPRODUCT(UnitProfit,UnitsProduced)

Solver Options

☑ Assume Linear Model
☑ Assume Non-Negative

Range Name	Cells
HoursAvailable	G8:G10
HoursUsed	E8:E10
HoursUsedPerUnitProduced	C8:D10
Maximum	F14:G15
TotalProduced	C16:D16
TotalProfit	D18
UnitProfit	C4:D5
UnitsProduced	C14:D15

third columns give the maximum values of these variables, so corresponding constraints are introduced into the model. The three functional constraints in the model for the original Wyndor problem also need to hold, but with D replaced by $(D_R + D_O)$ and W replaced by $(W_R + W_O)$.

We now have formulated a linear programming model to fit what was originally a nonlinear programming problem.

The resulting spreadsheet model is shown in Figure 10.16. The changing cells UnitsProduced (C14:D15) include separate cells for each of the four decision variables. The new constraints, UnitsProduced (C14:D15) ≤ Maximum (F14:G15), enforce the upper bounds on these decision variables indicated by the second and third columns of Table 10.3. The new output cells Total-Produced (C16:D16) sum the production quantities on regular time and overtime for each of the products. This then enables calculating the hours used with the equation, HoursUsed (E8:E10) = SUMPRODUCT (HoursUsedPerUnitProduced, TotalProduced). Otherwise, the model is basically the same as the original linear programming model in Figure 10.9. Note that the Assume Linear Model option has been selected because the new model also has been formulated to become a linear programming model. The proportionality assumption now is satisfied for the new decision variables. Therefore, the model can be solved very efficiently. This ability to reformulate the original model to make it fit linear programming is what makes separable programming a valuable technique.

However, there is one important factor that is not taken into account explicitly in this formulation. Recall that management insists that regular time production be fully utilized before using any overtime on each product. There are no constraints in the model that enforce this restriction. Consequently, it actually is feasible in the model to have $D_O > 0$ when $D_R < 3$, or to have $W_O > 0$ when $W_R < 3$.

Fortunately, even though such a solution is feasible in the model, it cannot be optimal. The reason is that the activities (producing the two products) have *decreasing marginal returns,* since the unit profit on overtime is less than on regular time for each product. Therefore, to maximize the total profit, an optimal solution automatically will use up all regular time for a product before starting on overtime.

The key is to have decreasing marginal returns. Without it, the linear programming model with this approach may not provide a legitimate optimal solution. This is the reason that separable programming is only applicable when the activities have decreasing marginal returns (except for those activities that satisfy the proportionality assumption).

Figure 10.16 shows the changing cells UnitsProduced (C14:D15) after using the Excel Solver to obtain an optimal solution. This optimal solution is

$$D_R = 3, D_O = 1: \quad \text{Produce 4 doors per week}$$

$$W_R = 3, W_O = 0: \quad \text{Produce 3 windows per week}$$

for a total profit of $2,600 per week given by the target cell TotalProfit (D18). This compares with a total profit of $2,567 per week for the previous plan (produce 3⅓ doors and 4 windows per week) that had been adopted before the need to use overtime arose.

Applying Separable Programming with Smooth Profit Graphs

In some applications of separable programming, the profit graphs will be *curves* rather than a series of line segments. This occurs when the marginal return from an activity decreases on a continuous basis rather than just at certain points.

For example, the solid curve in Figure 10.17 shows such a profit graph for an activity. To apply separable programming, this curve can then be approximated by a series of line segments, such as the dashed-line segments in the figure. By introducing a new decision variable for each of the line segments (and repeating this for other activities with such profit graphs), the approach just illustrated by the Wyndor example can again be used to convert the overall problem into a linear programming problem.

This is not the only way to solve problems where the activities have profit graphs with shapes similar to the one shown in Figure 10.17. Section 10.2 discusses problems of just this same type. The Excel Solver can readily solve such problems by using a nonlinear programming model that employs the formulas for the profit graphs. The advantage is that no approximation is needed, whereas separable programming uses the kind of approximation illustrated in Figure 10.17.

However, the separable programming approach also has certain advantages. One is that converting the problem into a linear programming problem tends to make it quicker to solve, which can be very helpful for large problems. Another advantage is that a linear programming formulation makes available Solver's Sensitivity Report, which is a great aid to what-if analysis, whereas the sensitivity information provided when using a nonlinear programming model is not nearly as useful. A third important advantage is that the separable programming approach only requires estimating the profit from each activity at a few points, such as the dots in Figure 10.17.

Decreasing marginal returns are needed to use the separable programming technique.

The approximation in Figure 10.17 only requires estimating the profit at the three dots rather than estimating a formula for the entire profit graph.

FIGURE 10.17

The solid curve shows a profit graph for an activity whose marginal return decreases on a continuous basis. The dashed-line segments display the kind of approximation used by separable programming.

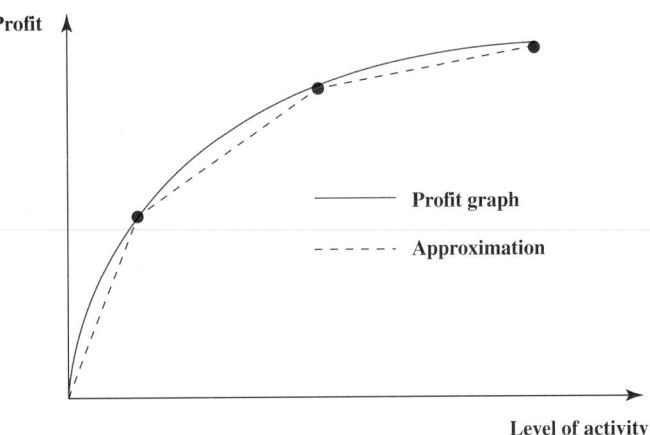

Therefore, it is not necessary to use a curve fitting method to estimate the formula for the profit graph, where this estimation would have introduced an approximation into the process.

The end of the Wyndor story (below) illustrates the application of both approaches.

The Wyndor Problem with Both Overtime Costs and Nonlinear Marketing Costs

The spreadsheet model in Figure 10.16 provides a good quick estimate of approximately what the production rates should be for the new products over the next four months. This is useful for planning purposes, but the model is a somewhat rough one because it does not take into account the new estimates of nonlinear marketing costs that were developed in Section 10.2. Therefore, the next step for Wyndor's Management Science Group is to enhance the model by incorporating these new estimates.

Recall that Ann Lester, Wyndor's vice president for marketing, now is estimating that the marketing costs will need to be $25D^2$ and $66\tfrac{2}{3}W^2$ to sustain sales of D doors and W windows per week. These costs then would need to be subtracted from the gross profit for each product (the profit excluding marketing costs) to obtain that product's profit. Since the original estimates of marketing costs had been $75 per door and $200 per window when estimating the unit profits given in Table 10.3, the group now needs to use the data shown in Table 10.4.

Based on these data, the fourth column of Table 10.5 shows the weekly profit that would be obtained by producing D doors per week for various values of D. This profit is calculated by

TABLE 10.4

Data for the Wyndor Problem with Both Overtime Costs and Nonlinear Marketing Costs

Product	Maximum Weekly Production			Gross Unit Profit		
	Regular Time	Overtime	Total	Regular Time	Overtime	Marketing Costs
Doors	3	1	4	$375	$275	$25D^2$
Windows	3	3	6	700	300	$66\tfrac{2}{3}W^2$

TABLE 10.5

Calculations of Wyndor's Weekly Profit from Producing D Doors per Week

D	Gross Profit	Marketing Costs	Profit	Incremental Profit
0	0	0	0	—
1	$ 375	$ 25	$ 350	$350
2	750	100	650	300
3	1,125	225	900	250
4	1,400	400	1,000	100

TABLE 10.6

Calculations of Wyndor's Weekly Profit from Producing *W* Windows per Week

W	Gross Profit	Marketing Costs	Profit	Incremental Profit
0	0	0	0	—
1	$ 700	$ 66⅔	$ 633⅓	$ 633⅓
2	1,400	266⅔	1,133⅓	500
3	2,100	600	1,500	366⅔
4	2,400	1,066⅔	1,333⅓	− 166⅔
5	2,700	1,666⅔	1,033⅓	−300
6	3,000	2,400	600	− 433⅓

subtracting the marketing costs in the third column from the gross profit in the second column. The rightmost column gives the incremental profit from the last increase of 1 in the value of *D*. Thus, the incremental profit is calculated by taking the profit in the same row and subtracting the profit in the preceding row. Note the large drop in the incremental profit at $D = 4$ because overtime must be used to increase *D* above 3.

Table 10.6 provides the corresponding calculations for windows. In this case, the incremental profit at $W = 4$, $W = 5$, and $W = 6$ actually is negative because of the large extra costs of the overtime that is needed to increase *W* above 3.

The solid curves in Figure 10.18 show the entire profit graphs for the doors and windows. The slope of each graph always is decreasing as the production rate increases, so both activities have decreasing marginal returns. This decrease in the slope is almost imperceptible at small production rates and then becomes more pronounced at larger rates. There also is a kink in each graph at $D = 3$ or $W = 3$ because overtime is required to increase the production rate further.

> It is very reasonable to use separable programming when the piecewise linear graphs approximate the actual profit graphs this closely.

The Management Science Group now wants to use separable programming to determine what the production rates should be to maximize total profit. For this purpose, the group uses the dashed-line segments in Figure 10.18 to obtain piecewise linear graphs that closely approximate the actual profit graphs. The one place where the approximation is not really close is when the profit graph for windows goes from $1,500, at $W = 3$, to $600, at $W = 6$ (an average decrease of $300 per unit of *W*). Since the profit decreases when *W* is increased above $W = 3$, it seems undesirable to increase *W* this much. Therefore, a particularly close approximation is not needed in this part of the graph, so only a single line segment is used between $W = 3$ and $W = 6$.

Figure 10.19 shows the separable programming spreadsheet model that is based on the piecewise linear profit graphs in Figure 10.18. This model is very similar to the separable programming spreadsheet model in Figure 10.16 that does not incorporate the new estimates of nonlinear marketing costs. The latter model is based on the piecewise linear profit graphs in Figure 10.15, each of which has only two line segments. Therefore, each of the sets of cells, UnitProfit (C4:D5) and UnitsProduced (C14:D15), has only two rows. Because each of the piecewise linear profit graphs in Figure 10.18 has four line segments, each of the corresponding sets of cells in Figure 10.19, UnitProfit (C4:D7) and UnitsProduced (C17:D20), has four rows. The numbers in UnitProfit (C4:D7) are the slopes of the corresponding line segments in Figure 10.18. These slopes come directly from the incremental profits given in Tables 10.5 and 10.6, except for cell D7. This cell is based on the line segment from $W = 3$ to $W = 6$ in Figure 10.18, which has a slope of −$300 since the profit is decreasing at the rate of $300 per unit increase in *W*. This slope of −$300 is the average of the last three incremental profits in Table 10.6. All the other line segments in Figure 10.18 run over only one unit of *D* or *W*, so the slope of each of these line segments equals the corresponding incremental profit in Table 10.5 or 10.6.

> Separable programming calculates unit profits for different parts of a profit graph by using the slopes of the line segments in the piecewise linear approximation of the profit graph.

The changing cells in Figure 10.19, UnitsProduced (C17:D20), give the optimal solution obtained by Solver. TotalProduced (C21:D21), which = SUM(UnitsProduced), gives the corresponding total production rates, namely,

$D = 4$:   Produce 4 doors per week, including 1 on overtime

$W = 3$:   Produce 3 windows per week

The target cell TotalProfit (D23) indicates that the resulting weekly profit would be $2,501. (Solver actually is incurring round-off error here since the correct weekly profit is $2,500.)

FIGURE 10.18

The solid curves show the profit graphs for Wyndor's doors and windows when both overtime costs and nonlinear marketing costs are incorporated into the problem. The dashed-line segments display the approximation used by the separable programming model in Figure 10.19.

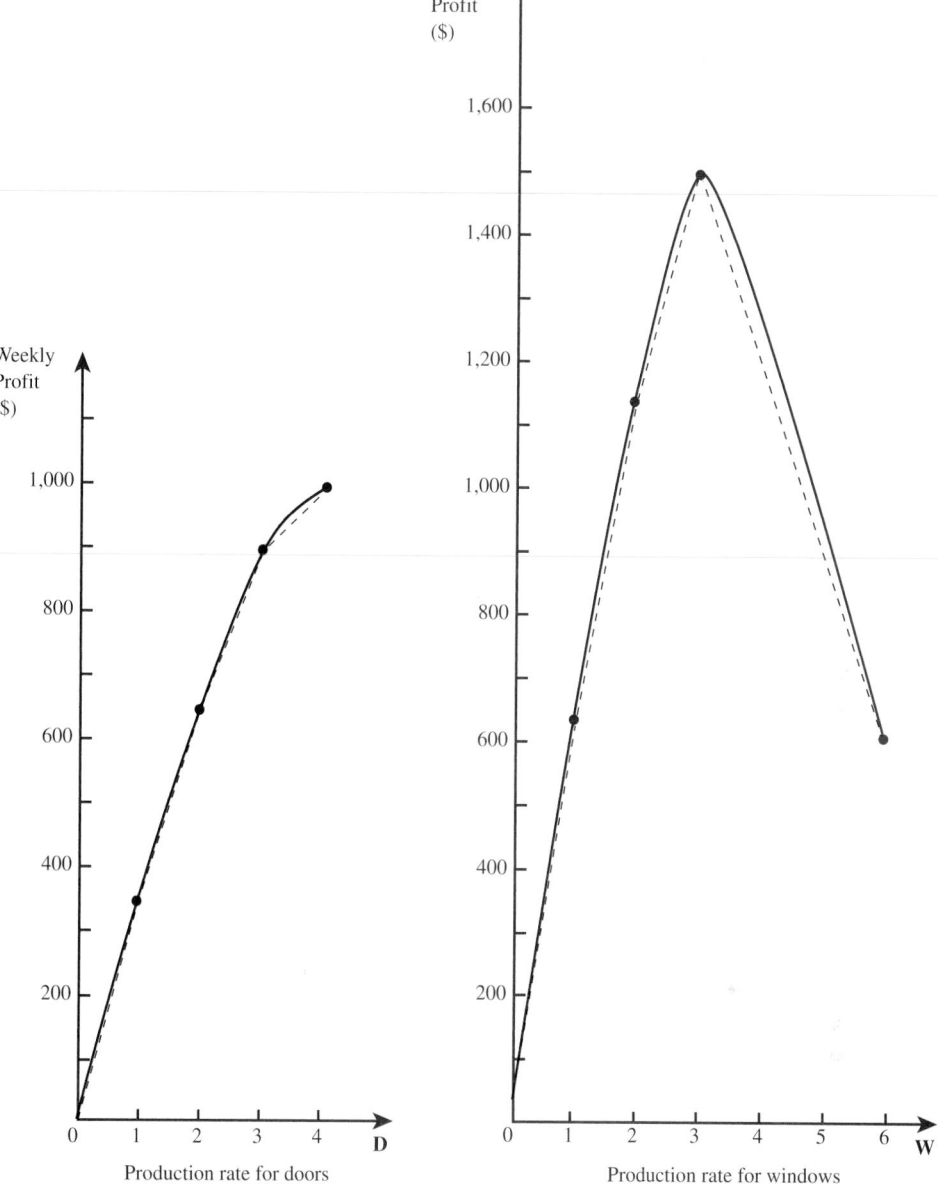

Figures 10.19 and 10.20 provide a comparison between a separable programming model and the kind of nonlinear programming model discussed in Section 10.2.

To check these results, the Management Science Group also formulates and runs the corresponding nonlinear programming model that employs the formulas for the smooth profit graphs in Figure 10.18. This spreadsheet model is shown in Figure 10.20. It is nearly the same as the one in Figure 10.11 that does not include overtime costs. The one difference is that the single row for UnitProfit (C4:D4) and for UnitsProduced (C12:D12) in Figure 10.11 now is split into two rows each, (C4:D5) and (C15:D16), to differentiate between regular time and overtime. Because of the kink in the profit graphs at $D = 3$ and $W = 3$, the pairs of rows are needed to provide separate formulas for the two parts of each profit graph on either side of the kink. TotalProduced (C17:D17) provides the same optimal solution, $(D, W) = (4, 3)$, as the separable programming model in Figure 10.19, with a total profit of \$2,500.

Based on these results, Wyndor management now adopts production rates of $(D, W) = (4, 3)$ for the next four months while overtime is needed. Following that period, the plan is to switch to $(D, W) = (3\frac{1}{3}, 4)$ because of the results obtained in Section 10.2.

This completes the Wyndor case study. One key lesson is that a management science study may involve developing more than just a single model to represent a problem. As the study goes

FIGURE 10.19

A spreadsheet model for the Wyndor separable programming problem when overtime is needed and nonlinear marketing costs also are incorporated into the problem. By summing the columns of the changing cells UnitsProduced (C17:D20), TotalProduced (C21:D21) gives the optimal production rates obtained by the Solver. Due to rounding error, the target cell TotalProfit (D23) shows a resulting weekly profit of $2,501 rather than the correct amount of $2,500.

	A	B	C	D	E	F	G
1		**Wyndor with Overtime and Marketing Costs (Separable)**					
2							
3		**Unit Profit**	Doors	Windows			
4		Regular (0–1)	$350.00	$633.33			
5		Regular (1–2)	$300.00	$500.00			
6		Regular (2–3)	$250.00	$367.67			
7		Overtime	$100.00	-$300.00			
8							
9					Hours		Hours
10			Hours Used per Unit Produced		Used		Available
11		Plant 1	1	0	4	≤	4
12		Plant 2	0	2	6	≤	12
13		Plant 3	3	2	18	≤	18
14							
15			**Units Produced**			**Maximum**	
16			Doors	Windows		Doors	Windows
17		Regular (0–1)	1	1	≤	1	1
18		Regular (1–2)	1	1	≤	1	1
19		Regular (2–3)	1	1	≤	1	1
20		Overtime	1	0	≤	1	3
21		Total Produced	4	3			
22							
23			Total Profit	$2,501			

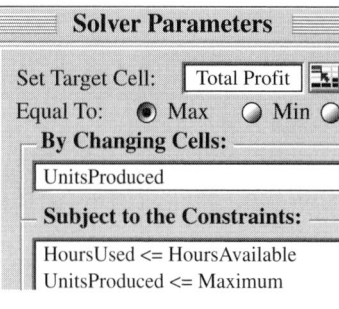

Solver Parameters

Set Target Cell: [Total Profit]

Equal To: ◉ Max ○ Min

By Changing Cells:
[UnitsProduced]

Subject to the Constraints:
HoursUsed <= HoursAvailable
UnitsProduced <= Maximum

	E
9	Hours
10	Used
11	=SUMPRODUCT(C11:D11,TotalProduced)
12	=SUMPRODUCT(C12:D12,TotalProduced)
13	=SUMPRODUCT(C13:D13,TotalProduced)

	B	C	D
21	Total Produced	=SUM(C17:C20)	=SUM(D17:D20)

	C	D
23	Total Profit	=SUMPRODUCT(UnitProfit,UnitsProduced)

Solver Options

☑ Assume Linear Model
☑ Assume Non-Negative

Range Name	Cells
HoursAvailable	G11:G13
HoursUsed	E11:E13
HoursUsedPerUnitProduced	C11:D13
Maximum	F17:G20
TotalProduced	C21:D21
TotalProfit	D23
UnitProfit	C4:D7
UnitsProduced	C17:D20

FIGURE 10.20

A spreadsheet model for the Wyndor nonlinear programming problem when overtime is needed and nonlinear marketing costs also are incorporated into the problem. TotalProduced (C17:D17) gives the optimal production rates obtained by the Solver and the target cell TotalProfit (H20) shows the resulting weekly profit. Note that this nonlinear programming formulation gives the same results (except for rounding error) as the separable programming formulation in Figure 10.19.

	A	B	C	D	E	F	G	H
1		**Wyndor With Overtime and Marketing Costs (Nonlinear Programming)**						
2								
3		**Unit Profit (Gross)**	Doors	Windows				
4		Regular	$375	$700				
5		Overtime	$275	$300				
6								
7					Hours		Hours	
8			Hours Used per Unit Produced		Used		Available	
9		Plant 1	1	0	4	≤	4	
10		Plant 2	0	2	6	≤	12	
11		Plant 3	3	2	18	≤	18	
12								
13						**Maximum**		
14		**Units Produced**	Doors	Windows		Doors	Windows	
15		Regular	3	3	≤	3	3	
16		Overtime	1	0	≤	1	3	
17		Total Produced	4	3				
18							Gross Profit from Sales	$3,500
19		Marketing Cost	$400	$600			Total Marketing Cost	$1,000
20							Total Profit	$2,500

Solver Parameters

Set Target Cell: [Total Profit]

Equal To: ● Max ○ Min ○

By Changing Cells:

[UnitsProduced]

Subject to the Constraints:

HoursUsed <= HoursAvailable
UnitsProduced <= Maximum

Solver Options

☐ Assume Linear Model
☑ Assume Non-Negative

Range Name	Cells
DoorsProduced	C17
GrossProfitFromSales	H18
HoursAvailable	G9:G11
HoursUsed	E9:E11
HoursUsedPerUnitProduced	C9:D11
MarketingCost	C19:D19
Maximum	F15:G16
TotalMarketingCost	H19
TotalProduced	C17:D17
TotalProfit	H20
UnitProfit	C4:D5
UnitsProduced	C15:D16
WindowsProduced	D17

	E
7	Hours
8	Used
9	=SUMPRODUCT(C9:D9,TotalProduced)
10	=SUMPRODUCT(C10:D10,TotalProduced)
11	=SUMPRODUCT(C11:D11,TotalProduced)

	B	C	D
17	Total Produced	=SUM(C15:C16)	=SUM(D15:D16)
18			
19	Marketing Cost	=25*(DoorsProduced^2)	=66.667*(WindowsProduced^2)

	G	H
18	Gross Profit from Sales	=SUMPRODUCT(UnitProfit,UnitsProduced)
19	Total Marketing Cost	=SUM(MarketingCost)
20	Total Profit	=GrossProfitFromSales–TotalMarketingCost

Here is one key lesson from the Wyndor case study.

on and additional relevant considerations come to light, the original model may evolve through a series of enhancements into a rather different kind of model. For example, what started as a linear programming model may end up needing to be a nonlinear programming model.

Review Questions

1. For each activity that violates the proportionality assumption, what must be the shape of its profit graph (or at least an approximation of the profit graph) in order to apply separable programming?

2. What kind of mathematical model is eventually formulated when applying the separable programming technique?

3. For problems where the activities have profit graphs with shapes similar to the one shown in Figure 10.17, what are some advantages of using the kind of approximation displayed in this figure to enable applying separable programming?

4. For these same problems, what is an advantage of instead using a nonlinear programming model that directly employs the formulas for the profit graphs?

10.4 DIFFICULT NONLINEAR PROGRAMMING PROBLEMS

We saw in Section 10.2 that even if a model has a nonlinear objective function, so long as the model has certain properties (e.g., linear constraints and maximizing an objective function with decreasing marginal returns), the Solver can easily find an optimal solution. Furthermore, we saw in Section 10.3 that in some cases separable programming can be used to model (or approximate) a nonlinear problem in such a way that *linear* programming can be used to efficiently find an optimal solution.

The standard Solver often has difficulty solving nonlinear programming models if the constraints are nonlinear or if the profit graphs for any activities are either not smooth or have increasing marginal returns.

However, nonlinear programming problems come in many guises and forms. For example, for problems where the objective is to maximize total profit, some might have *increasing* marginal returns for the profit from certain activities. Some might have nonlinear functions in the constraints. Some might have profit graphs with several disconnected curves. These other kinds of nonlinear programming problems often are much more difficult, if not impossible, to solve. The reason is that there may be many locally optimal solutions that are not globally optimal. We saw in Figures 10.7 and 10.8 how the Solver can get stuck at these locally optimal solutions without ever finding the globally optimal solution.

If there are multiple local optima, running Solver many times with different starting points can sometimes find the global optimum.

One approach for attempting to solve problems that may have multiple local optima is to run the Solver many times, each time starting with a different initial solution entered into the changing cells on the spreadsheet. For each run, Solver will start its search at the given initial solution (the starting point) and move in a direction that improves the objective function until it finds a local optimum. By trying many starting points, the goal is to find most or all of the local optima. We then pick the best solution found from all the trials. At a minimum, we are likely to end up with a solution that is better than if we just take the first local optimum that Solver finds. With luck, one of the starting points will yield the globally optimal solution.

For example, consider the model in Figure 10.7 with the corresponding profit graph in Figure 10.8. For any starting point x less than 1.5, the objective function increases by moving toward the local maximum at $x = 0.371$ (Profit = $3.19). Thus, for any starting point x less than 1.5 (including the starting point $x = 0$ tried in the leftmost spreadsheet in Figure 10.7), Solver's search will move toward and eventually converge to this local maximum. Similarly, for any starting point x between 1.5 and 4.6 (such as $x = 3$ tried in the center spreadsheet in Figure 10.7), Solver will converge to the local (and global) maximum at $x = 3.126$ (Profit = $6.13). Finally, for any starting point x greater than 4.6 (such as $x = 4.7$ tried in the rightmost spreadsheet in Figure 10.7), Solver will converge to the local maximum at $x = 5$ (Profit = $0). By trying several starting points, three different local optima are found. The best of these local optima is $x = 3.126$ with a corresponding profit of $6.13.

If there are only one or two changing cells, this approach can be done more systematically by using the Solver Table add-in that is provided in your MS Courseware. To demonstrate, we will continue to use the spreadsheet model shown in Figure 10.7. Figure 10.21 displays how Solver Table is used to try six different starting points (0, 1, 2, 3, 4, and 5) for this model by

FIGURE 10.21
An application of the Solver Table (an Excel add-in provided in your MS Courseware) to the example considered in Figures 10.7 and 10.8.

	A	B	C	D	E	F	G	H	I	J
1	**Using Solver Table to Try Different Starting Points**									
2										
3										
4					Maximum		Starting			
5		*x* =	3.126	≤	5		Point	Solution		
6							*x*	*x**	Profit	
7		Profit =$0.5x^5$-$6x^4$+$24.5x^3$-$39x^2$+$20x$						3.126	$6.13	Select the
8		=	$6.13				0	0.371	$3.19	entire table
9							1	0.371	$3.19	(G7:I13),
10							2	3.126	$6.13	before
11							3	3.126	$6.13	choosing
12							4	3.126	$6.13	Solver Table
13							5	5.000	$0.00	from the Tools menu.

Solver Table

Row input cell: [   ]

Column input cell: [x   ]

[Help] [Cancel] [OK]

	H	I
5	Solution	
6	*x**	Profit
7	=*x*	=Profit

Range Name	Cell
x	C5
Profit	C8

The Solver Table can be used to systematically re-solve a small nonlinear programming model with many different starting points.

executing the following steps. In the first row of the table, enter formulas that refer to the changing cell, *x* (C5), and the target cell, Profit (C8). The different starting points are entered in the first column of the table (G8:G13). Then, select the entire table (G7:I13) and choose the Solver Table from the Tools menu. The column input cell entered in the Solver Table dialogue box is the changing cell, *x* (C5), since this is where we want the different starting points in the first column of the table to be entered. (No row input cell is entered in this dialogue box since only a column is being used to list the starting points.) Clicking OK then causes the Solver Table to re-solve the problem for all these starting points in the first column and fill in the corresponding results (the local maximum for *x* and Profit referred to in the first row) in the other columns of the table.

This example has only one changing cell. However, the Solver Table also can be used to try multiple starting points for problems with two changing cells. This is done by using the first row and first column of the table to specify different starting points for the two changing cells. Enter an equation referring to the target cell in the upper left-hand corner of the table. Select the entire table and choose Solver Table from the Tools menu, with the two changing cells selected as the column input cell and row input cell. The Solver Table then re-solves the problem for each combination of starting points of the two changing cells and fills in the body of the table with the objective function value of the solution that is found (a local optimum) for each of these combinations. (See Section 5.4 for more details about setting up a two-dimensional Solver Table.)

For problems with more than two changing cells, this same approach still can be used to try multiple starting points for any two of the changing cells at a time. However, this becomes a very cumbersome way of trying a broad range of starting points for all the changing cells when there are more than three or four of these cells.

This approach has some major limitations.

Unfortunately, there is no guarantee in general of finding a globally optimal solution, no matter how many different starting points are tried. Also, if the profit graphs are not smooth (e.g., if they have discontinuities or kinks), as is typically the case if functions like IF, ABS, MAX, or ROUND are used, then Solver may not even be able to find local optima. Fortunately, there is another approach available to attempt to solve these difficult nonlinear problems. We explore this new approach in the next section.

1. The Solver has difficulty solving nonlinear programming problems with certain properties. List three of these properties.

2. What is a method for attempting to solve problems with multiple locally optimal solutions?

10.5   EVOLUTIONARY SOLVER AND GENETIC ALGORITHMS

The installer for Premium Solver is available in your MS Courseware.

Evolutionary Solver uses the principles of genetics, evolution, and the survival of the fittest.

Frontline Systems, the developer of the standard Solver included with Excel, has developed Premium versions of Solver. One version of Premium Solver (Premium Solver for Education) is available in your MS Courseware (but not included with standard Excel). Every version of Premium Solver, including this one, adds a new search procedure called **Evolutionary Solver** to the set of tools available in Solver. Evolutionary Solver uses an entirely different approach than the standard Solver to search for an optimal solution for a model. The philosophy of Evolutionary Solver is based on genetics, evolution, and the survival of the fittest. Hence, this type of algorithm is sometimes called a **genetic algorithm.**

The standard Solver starts with a single solution (the starting point) and then moves in directions that will improve this solution. At any point in time, standard Solver is only keeping track of a single solution (the best one found so far). In contrast, Evolutionary Solver begins by randomly generating a large set of candidate solutions, called the **population.** Throughout the solution process, Evolutionary Solver keeps track of the whole population of candidate solutions. Much like trying different starting points with the standard Solver, this attention to many candidate solutions can help avoid being trapped at a local optimum.

Each pair of parents creates offspring that resemble the parents.

After generating the population, Evolutionary Solver next creates a new **generation** of the population. The existing population of candidate solutions is paired off to create "offspring" for the next generation. Borrowing from the principles of genetics, the offspring combine some elements from each parent. For example, an offspring could combine some of the changing cell values from one parent and some from the other, while other changing cells might be averaged between the two parents.

Only the fit parents are allowed to create many offspring.

Among the population of solutions in any generation, some solutions will be good (or "fit") and some will be bad (or "unfit"). The level of fitness is determined by evaluating the objective function at each of the candidate solutions in the population. A penalty is subtracted for any solution that does not satisfy one or more of the constraints. Then, borrowing from the principles of evolution and the survival of the fittest, the "fit" members of the population are allowed to reproduce frequently (create many offspring), while the "unfit" members are not allowed to reproduce. In this way, the population eventually evolves to become more and more fit.

Random mutations occasionally occur in the offspring.

Another key feature of genetic algorithms is **mutation.** Like gene mutation in biology, Evolutionary Solver will occasionally make a random change in a member of the population. For example, the value of one changing cell might be replaced with a new random value. This mutation can create offspring that are far removed from the rest of the population. This is important, since it can help the algorithm get unstuck if it is getting trapped near a local optimum.

Evolutionary Solver keeps creating new generations of solutions until there have been no improvements in several consecutive generations. The algorithm then terminates and the best solution found so far is reported.

Now let us look at an example where Evolutionary Solver is needed to solve the problem.

Selecting a Portfolio to Beat the Market

In Section 10.2, we developed a model for finding a portfolio of stocks that minimizes the risk (variance of the return from the portfolio) subject to achieving at least some desired minimum expected return. The standard Solver could be used for that problem because the constraints were linear and the objective function was smooth and had decreasing marginal returns.

Now consider another common goal of portfolio managers—to beat the market. Figure 10.22 shows a spreadsheet model for pursuing this goal when choosing a portfolio from five large stocks traded on the New York Stock Exchange (NYSE): America Online (AOL), Boeing (BA), Ford (F), Procter & Gamble (PG), and McDonald's (MCD). The quarterly performance (return)

FIGURE 10.22

A spreadsheet model (prior to using the Premium Solver dialogue box) for selecting a portfolio that beat the market most frequently in recent quarters. A starting solution has been entered in the changing cells Portfolio (D31:H31). The target cell is NumberBeatingTheMarket (J36).

	A	B	C	D	E	F	G	H	I	J	K
1		**Beating the Market**									
2										Beat	Market
3		Quarter	Year	AOL	BA	F	PG	MCD	Return	Market?	(NYSE)
4		Q4	2001	-3.02%	16.35%	-8.54%	8.77%	-1.64%	2.38%	No	8.45%
5		Q3	2001	-37.55%	-39.56%	-28.49%	14.71%	0.30%	-18.12%	No	-12.53%
6		Q2	2001	32.00%	0.07%	-11.80%	2.54%	1.92%	4.95%	Yes	4.38%
7		Q1	2001	15.37%	-15.34%	21.28%	-19.80%	-21.91%	-4.08%	Yes	-9.32%
8		Q4	2000	-35.14%	2.55%	-7.00%	17.07%	13.37%	-1.83%	No	-0.93%
9		Q3	2000	1.46%	54.71%	3.66%	18.06%	-8.35%	13.91%	Yes	3.31%
10		Q2	2000	-21.37%	10.98%	-6.39%	0.00%	-11.87%	-5.73%	No	-0.91%
11		Q1	2000	-11.36%	-8.44%	-13.83%	-48.20%	-7.29%	-17.82%	No	-0.40%
12		Q4	1999	45.82%	-2.48%	6.10%	16.87%	-6.79%	11.90%	Yes	9.70%
13		Q3	1999	-5.40%	-2.83%	-10.96%	6.38%	5.17%	-1.53%	Yes	-8.54%
14		Q2	1999	-25.17%	29.83%	-0.44%	-10.02%	-9.24%	-3.01%	No	7.38%
15		Q1	1999	89.52%	4.21%	-3.41%	7.26%	17.98%	23.11%	Yes	1.31%
16		Q4	1998	177.96%	-4.92%	24.87%	28.38%	28.69%	51.00%	Yes	18.11%
17		Q3	1998	6.18%	-23.00%	-20.34%	-21.89%	-13.50%	-14.51%	No	-12.83%
18		Q2	1998	53.89%	-14.51%	-8.94%	7.93%	15.00%	10.67%	Yes	1.04%
19		Q1	1998	50.96%	6.51%	33.46%	5.72%	25.65%	24.46%	Yes	12.05%
20		Q4	1997	19.96%	-10.10%	7.62%	15.57%	0.26%	6.66%	Yes	2.81%
21		Q3	1997	35.61%	2.59%	18.75%	-2.21%	-1.42%	10.66%	Yes	7.42%
22		Q2	1997	30.90%	7.60%	21.12%	23.09%	2.25%	16.99%	Yes	16.14%
23		Q1	1997	27.82%	-7.39%	-2.71%	6.62%	4.13%	5.69%	Yes	1.59%
24		Q4	1996	-6.34%	12.70%	3.20%	10.39%	-4.22%	3.15%	No	6.80%
25		Q3	1996	-18.86%	8.46%	-3.47%	7.59%	1.34%	-0.99%	No	2.26%
26		Q2	1996	-21.87%	0.58%	-5.82%	6.93%	-2.60%	-4.56%	No	3.54%
27		Q1	1996	49.33%	10.53%	19.05%	2.11%	6.37%	17.48%	Yes	5.28%
28											
29				0%	0%	0%	0%	0%			
30				≤	≤	≤	≤	≤	Sum		
31			Portfolio	20.0%	20.0%	20.0%	20.0%	20.0%	100%	=	100%
32				≤	≤	≤	≤	≤			
33				100%	100%	100%	100%	100%			
34										Number of Quarters	
35										Beating the Market	
36										14	

Range Name	Cells
BeatMarket?	J4:J27
Market	K4:K27
NumberBeatingTheMarket	J36
OneHundredPercent	D33:H33
OneHundredPercent2	K31
Portfolio	D31:H31
Return	I4:I27
StockData	D4:H27
Sum	I31
ZeroPercent	D29:H29

	I	J
2		Beat
3	Return	Market?
4	=SUMPRODUCT(Portfolio,D4:H4)	=IF(Return>Market,"Yes","No")
5	=SUMPRODUCT(Portfolio,D5:H5)	=IF(Return>Market,"Yes","No")
6	=SUMPRODUCT(Portfolio,D6:H6)	=IF(Return>Market,"Yes","No")
7	=SUMPRODUCT(Portfolio,D7:H7)	=IF(Return>Market,"Yes","No")
8	:	:
9	:	:

	I
30	Sum
31	=SUM(Portfolio)

	J
34	Number of Quarters
35	Beating the Market
36	=COUNTIF(BeatMarket?,"Yes")

of each of these stocks over a six-year period (1995–2001) is shown in StockData (D4:H27). The performance of the market as a whole, as measured by the NYSE Composite Index, is shown in column K.

The objective is to find the portfolio that beat the market most frequently.

If we assume that past performance is somewhat of an indicator of the future, then picking a portfolio that beat the market most often during these six years might yield a portfolio that will more than likely beat the market in the future. Thus, the model in Figure 10.22 uses the objective of choosing the portfolio that beat the market for the largest number of quarters during this period.

The changing cells in this model are Portfolio (D31:H31), representing the percentage of the portfolio to invest in each individual stock. The return of the given portfolio for each quarter is calculated in column I. Column J then compares the return of the portfolio to the return of the market and determines whether the portfolio beat the market using the IF functions shown below the spreadsheet in Figure 10.22. The number of quarters in which the portfolio beat the market is then calculated in the target cell, NumberBeatingTheMarket (J36). As seen in the figure, a portfolio that was evenly split among the five stocks (20 percent in each) would have beaten the market in 14 of the 24 quarters during this six-year period.

The standard Solver can't handle this kind of problem.

The standard Solver would have little to no chance of solving this model. The objective function is not smooth since changes in the Portfolio can cause instantaneous (nonsmooth) jumps in the target cell (the number of quarters that the portfolio beats the market). However, the target cell remains constant for small changes in the changing cells until the change is significant enough to cause a quarter in column J to switch from Yes to No (or No to Yes). An unfortunate consequence of this is that nearly every solution is a local maximum, since very small changes in the portfolio will lead to no improvement in the target cell. Thus, Solver typically will stop its search immediately and report the initial solution as a local maximum. Since the standard Solver cannot solve this model, we will try the Evolutionary Solver.

Applying Evolutionary Solver to Portfolio Selection to Beat the Market

Installing the Premium Solver available in your MS Courseware adds a button labeled "Premium" to the Solver. Clicking this button yields the Premium Solver dialogue box shown in Figure 10.23. (The button then changes its label to "Standard," since clicking it again switches back to the standard Solver.) This dialogue box has a dropdown menu that gives a choice of which algorithm to employ. The choices are Standard GRG Nonlinear, Standard Simplex LP, and Standard Evolutionary. The first choice (GRG Nonlinear) is identical to using standard Solver *without* the "Assume Linear Model" option selected. The second choice (Simplex LP) is equivalent to using standard Solver *with* the "Assume Linear Model" option selected. The final choice (Evolutionary) employs the Evolutionary Solver that is needed for the problem considered in Figure 10.22. A major benefit of using Premium Solver instead of the standard Solver that comes with Excel is the addition of this Evolutionary Solver option. (Certain versions of Premium Solver also are faster and able to solve larger problems than the standard Solver, but Premium Solver for Education provided in your MS Courseware does not have this advantage, so it is needed only when Evolutionary Solver is required.)

Premium Solver includes Evolutionary Solver, but the standard Solver does not.

FIGURE 10.23

The Premium Solver dialogue box that is used to complete the spreadsheet model introduced in Figure 10.22. Selecting Standard Evolutionary from the dropdown menu specifies that Evolutionary Solver will be used to solve the problem.

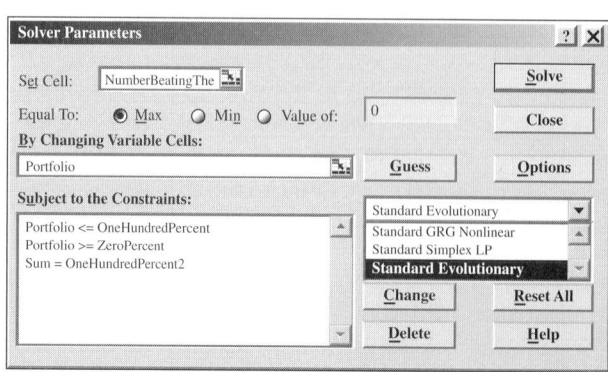

As shown in Figure 10.23, the Premium Solver dialogue box needs to specify the target cell (NumberBeatingTheMarket, or J36) and changing cells (Portfolio, or D31:H31). It also must include the constraints that (1) the portfolio needs to sum to 100 percent and (2) each individual stock must represent between 0 and 100 percent of the portfolio.

Clicking the Option button in the Premium Solver dialogue box yields the Solver Options dialogue box shown in Figure 10.24. This allows changing various parameters of the search, such as the maximum time to allow the search to continue, the size of the population, and the mutation rate. The default values for the parameters displayed in Figure 10.24 are reasonable ones for most small applications. However, feel free to experiment with these parameters. For example, increasing the population size or mutation rate may help with searches that are getting stuck.

Use the Require Bounds on Variables option whenever possible.

The Require Bounds on Variables option is selected by default. This forces all changing cells to be constrained with lower and upper limits. We strongly recommend that you use this option to place bounds on the changing cells whenever possible. This greatly narrows the area over which Evolutionary Solver needs to search and can increase the chances of finding a good solution.

Clicking the Limit Options button in the Solver Options dialogue box yields the dialogue box in Figure 10.25. This dialogue box gives additional control over when to terminate the search. Entering large values in Max Subproblems and Max Feasible Sols will allow the search to continue for a long time. A tolerance value of 0.05 and Max Time w/o Improvement of 30 means Evolutionary Solver will continue the search until it has not improved the solution by more than 5 percent within the last 30 seconds. Decreasing the tolerance and/or increasing the Max Time w/o Improvement generally will allow for longer search time.

This solution found by Evolutionary Solver is not guaranteed to be optimal, but it probably is at least close to optimal.

Clicking Solve in the Premium Solver dialogue box then causes Evolutionary Solver to begin its search. Within a minute or so, the solution shown in Figure 10.26 was found. This represents

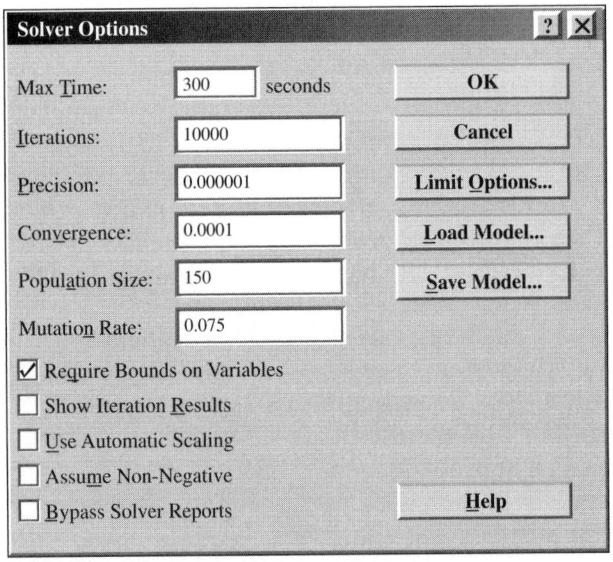

FIGURE 10.24
This Solver Options dialogue box for Premium Solver provides several parameters for Evolutionary Solver. The default values shown here are reasonable choices for most small applications.

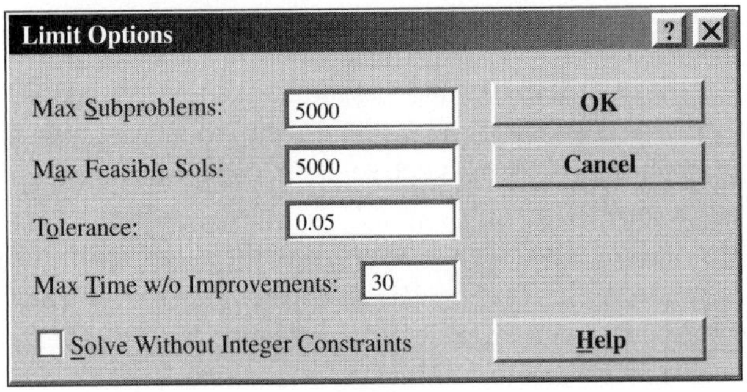

FIGURE 10.25
This Limit Options dialogue box provides additional control over when the search conducted by Evolutionary Solver should be terminated.

FIGURE 10.26

After clicking the Solve button in the Premium Solver dialogue box, Evolutionary Solver found the solution shown in the changing cells Portfolio (D31:H31) for the model formulated in Figures 10.22 and 10.23. The target cell NumberBeatingTheMarket (J36) indicates that this portfolio beat the market in 19 of these 24 quarters. Clicking Solve again probably would lead to at least a slightly different solution for the portfolio.

	A	B	C	D	E	F	G	H	I	J	K
1		**Beating the Market (Evolutionary Solver)**									
2										Beat	Market
3		Quarter	Year	AOL	BA	F	PG	MCD	Return	Market?	(NYSE)
4		Q4	2001	-3.02%	16.35%	-8.54%	8.77%	-1.64%	10.20%	Yes	8..45%
5		Q3	2001	-37.55%	-39.56%	-28.49%	14.71%	0.30%	-24.12%	No	-12.53%
6		Q2	2001	32.00%	0.07%	-11.80%	2.54%	1.92%	7.02%	Yes	4.38%
7		Q1	2001	15.37%	-15.34%	21.28%	-19.80%	-21.91%	-10.53%	No	-9.32%
8		Q4	2000	-35.14%	2.55%	-7.00%	17.07%	13.37%	-0.86%	Yes	-0.93%
9		Q3	2000	1.46%	54.71%	3.66%	18.06%	-8.35%	33.43%	Yes	3.31%
10		Q2	2000	-21.37%	10.98%	-6.39%	0.00%	-11.87%	1.31%	Yes	-0.91%
11		Q1	2000	-11.36%	-8.44%	-13.83%	-48.20%	-7.29%	-19.56%	No	-0.40%
12		Q4	1999	45.82%	-2.48%	6.10%	16.87%	-6.79%	12.11%	Yes	9.70%
13		Q3	1999	-5.40%	-2.83%	-10.96%	6.38%	5.17%	-0.78%	Yes	-8.54%
14		Q2	1999	-25.17%	29.83%	-0.44%	-10.02%	-9.24%	7.76%	Yes	7.38%
15		Q1	1999	89.52%	4.21%	-3.41%	7.26%	17.98%	22.03%	Yes	1.31%
16		Q4	1998	177.96%	-4.92%	24.87%	28.38%	28.69%	40.51%	Yes	18.11%
17		Q3	1998	6.18%	-23.00%	-20.34%	-21.89%	-13.50%	-16.81%	No	-12.83%
18		Q2	1998	53.89%	-14.51%	-8.94%	7.93%	15.00%	5.39%	Yes	1.04%
19		Q1	1998	50.96%	6.51%	33.46%	5.72%	25.65%	15.40%	Yes	12.05%
20		Q4	1997	19.96%	-10.10%	7.62%	15.57%	0.26%	2.82%	Yes	2.81%
21		Q3	1997	35.61%	2.59%	18.75%	-2.21%	-1.42%	7.78%	Yes	7.42%
22		Q2	1997	30.90%	7.60%	21.12%	23.09%	2.25%	16.24%	Yes	16.14%
23		Q1	1997	27.82%	-7.39%	-2.71%	6.62%	4.13%	3.45%	Yes	1.59%
24		Q4	1996	-6.34%	12.70%	3.20%	10.39%	-4.22%	8.06%	Yes	6.80%
25		Q3	1996	-18.86%	8.46%	-3.47%	7.59%	1.34%	2.72%	Yes	2.26%
26		Q2	1996	-21.87%	0.58%	-5.82%	6.93%	-2.60%	-2.22%	No	3.54%
27		Q1	1996	49.33%	10.53%	19.05%	2.11%	6.37%	15.88%	Yes	5.28%
28											
29				0%	0%	0%	0%	0%			
30				≤	≤	≤	≤	≤	Sum		
31			Portfolio	19.7%	52.0%	0.2%	26.6%	1.6%	100%	=	100%
32				≤	≤	≤	≤	≤			
33				100%	100%	100%	100%	100%			
34										Number of Quarters	
35										Beating the Market	
36										19	

a portfolio that beat the market in 19 of the 24 quarters over this six-year period. Is this solution optimal? Perhaps not. Unfortunately, there is no way to guarantee that we have found an optimal solution. However, it likely is a good solution (close to optimal).

Advantages and Disadvantages of Evolutionary Solver

Evolutionary Solver has two significant advantages over the standard Solver for solving difficult nonlinear programming problems. First, the complexity of the objective function does not

Evolutionary Solver can handle problems with complicated objective functions and many local optima.

impact Evolutionary Solver. As long as the function can be evaluated for a given candidate solution (in order to determine the level of fitness), it does not matter if the function has kinks or discontinuities or many local optima. Second, by evaluating whole populations of candidate solutions that aren't necessarily in the same neighborhood as the current best solution, Evolutionary Solver keeps from getting trapped at a local optimum. Furthermore, even if the whole population eventually evolves toward a solution that is only locally optimal, mutation allows for the possibility of getting unstuck. In fact, because of the random mutations, Evolutionary Solver is guaranteed to eventually find an optimal solution for any optimization problem if it runs forever, but this is impractical of course.

However, Evolutionary Solver also has several limitations.

On the other hand, it must be pointed out that Evolutionary Solver is not a panacea. First, it can take *much* longer than the standard Solver to find a final solution. With certain choices of limit options, the search for better solutions can continue for hours or even days. Second, Evolutionary Solver does not perform well on models that have many constraints. For instance, it would not perform very well on many of the models considered in Chapters 2–7, even though the standard Solver can solve these models almost instantaneously. Third, Evolutionary Solver is a random process. Running Evolutionary Solver again on the same model usually will yield a different final solution. Finally, the best solution found typically is not optimal (although it may be very close). Evolutionary Solver is not an optimizer in the same sense that the standard Solver is. It does not continuously move toward better solutions until it reaches a local optimum. Rather it is more like an intelligent search engine, trying out different random solutions. Thus, while it is quite likely to end up with a solution that is very close to optimal, it almost never returns the exact optimal solution on most types of nonlinear programming problems. (However, its chances of finding an optimal solution are much better on problems like the beat-the-market example where the target cell only takes on integer values.) Consequently, it often can be beneficial to run the standard Solver (GRG Nonlinear) after the Evolutionary Solver, starting with the final solution obtained by the Evolutionary Solver, to see if this solution can be improved by searching around its neighborhood.

Review Questions

1. Why is the algorithm used by Evolutionary Solver called a genetic algorithm?
2. What criterion does Evolutionary Solver use to choose which members of a generation are fit and which are unfit?
3. How does mutation help Evolutionary Solver?
4. What is the advantage of Premium Solver for Education over the standard Solver packaged with Excel?
5. What are two advantages that Evolutionary Solver has over the standard Solver for solving difficult nonlinear programming problems?
6. What are three disadvantages of Evolutionary Solver compared to the standard Solver?

10.6 Summary

A nonlinear programming model has the same characteristics as a linear programming model with one key exception. All the mathematical expressions (including the objective function) are linear in a linear programming model, but at least one of these expressions (often just the objective function) is nonlinear in a nonlinear programming model. When formulating the model in a spreadsheet, this means that the model becomes a nonlinear programming model if a nonlinear formula needs to be entered into the target cell (and perhaps into some other output cells). A nonlinear formula is needed for the target cell whenever there is a nonproportional relationship between the level of any of the activities and the overall measure of performance for the problem. This kind of relationship violates the proportionality assumption of linear programming.

Formulating and solving a nonlinear programming model tends to be more difficult than formulating and solving a linear programming model. For example, some nonlinear programming models have a number of locally optimal solutions where only one of these solutions is globally optimal and most of the others are greatly inferior. Unfortunately, after a starting solution is entered into the spreadsheet, the standard Excel Solver will find only one of these locally optimal solutions, with no indication of whether this is the one that also is globally optimal or perhaps one that is far from optimal. Which locally optimal solution is found depends on the choice of the starting solution.

However, when a nonlinear programming model has decreasing marginal returns, it generally is easy to solve. For this type of problem, a locally optimal solution automatically is also a globally optimal solution. Therefore, the solution found by the Excel Solver is guaranteed to be the best solution for the model (or at least one of those tied for being the best).

Some nonlinear programming problems with decreasing marginal returns can be solved in an even easier way. This occurs when the profit graphs (or cost graphs) for the activities are piecewise linear (or at least can be closely approximated by piecewise linear graphs). In this case, the separable programming technique can be applied to convert the problem into a linear programming problem, which is the easiest type of problem for the Excel Solver.

For more difficult nonlinear programming problems that might have a number of locally optimal solutions, one approach is to run the Solver many times, each time starting with a different initial solution entered into the changing cells on the spreadsheet. If there are only one or two changing cells, this approach can be done systematically by using the Solver Table add-in that is provided in your MS Courseware.

However, this method of dealing with difficult problems has two major limitations. First, it is impractical for problems with more than a few changing cells. Second, it does not work for problems with such complicated objective functions that the Solver is not even able to find local optima. If such problems don't have many constraints, another search procedure called Evolutionary Solver is likely to perform well. Using concepts from genetics, evolution, and the survival of the fittest, this procedure is able to gradually move toward the best of the local optima. Given enough search time (which may be a very long time), it frequently succeeds in finding a solution that is very close to optimal.

Glossary

curve fitting method A method for using the known values in a profit or cost graph to find the equation for the graph that best fits these data. (Section 10.1), *445*

decreasing marginal returns An activity with a profit graph has decreasing marginal returns if the slope (steepness) of this profit graph never increases but sometimes decreases as the level of the activity increases. (Section 10.1), *442*

discontinuity A spot in a graph where it is disconnected because it suddenly jumps up or down. (Section 10.1), *443*

Evolutionary Solver A search procedure provided in Premium Solver that uses concepts from genetics, evolution, and the survival of the fittest. (Section 10.5), *470*

generation A new set of candidate solutions that is created by Evolutionary Solver by pairing off members of the existing population of candidate solutions to create "offspring" for the next generation. (Section 10.5), *470*

genetic algorithm A type of algorithm that uses concepts from genetics. (Section 10.5), *470*

global maximum The highest point on an entire graph. (Section 10.1), *447*

local maximum A point at which a graph reaches its maximum within a local neighborhood of that point. (Section 10.1), *447*

mutation Similar to gene mutation in biology, this is a random change that Evolutionary Solver occasionally makes in a member of the current population. (Section 10.5), *470*

nonproportional relationship An activity has a nonproportional relationship with the overall measure of performance for a problem if the contribution of the activity to this measure is *not* proportional to the level of the activity. (Section 10.1), *442*

piecewise linear A graph is piecewise linear if it consists of a sequence of connected line segments. (Section 10.1), *443*

population The large set of candidate solutions that is randomly generated by Evolutionary Solver. (Section 10.5), *470*

proportional relationship An activity has a proportional relationship with the overall measure of performance for a problem if the contribution of the activity to this measure is proportional to the level of the activity. (Section 10.1), *441*

proportionality assumption A basic assumption of linear programming that requires the contribution of each activity to the value of the objective function to be proportional to the level of that activity. (Section 10.1), *441*

quadratic programming A special type of nonlinear programming where the objective function has both a quadratic form and decreasing marginal returns and all the constraints are linear. (Section 10.2), *452*

Learning Aids for This Chapter in Your MS Courseware

Chapter 10 Excel Files:

Constructing a Nonlinear Formula
An Example with Multiple Local Maxima

Original Wyndor Problem
Wyndor Problem with Nonlinear Marketing Costs
Portfolio Selection Example
Wyndor Problem with Overtime
Wyndor Problem with Overtime and Marketing Costs (Separable Programming)
Wyndor Problem with Overtime and Marketing Costs (Nonlinear Programming)
Beating the Market Example

Excel Add-ins:

Premium Solver for Education
Solver Table

Problems

To the left of each of the following problems (or their parts), we have inserted an E* whenever Excel should be used (unless your instructor gives you contrary instructions). An asterisk on the problem number indicates that at least a partial answer is given in the back of the book.

10.1.   The J. P. Atkins Company will soon be introducing a new product. Estimates have been made of the monthly profit that would be generated by this product for each of four alternative values of the monthly production rate, as shown below.

Production Rate	Profit
200	$ 9,500
500	22,500
800	34,000
1,000	40,000

a. Draw a profit graph for this product by plotting the profits for the four production rates and then drawing a smooth curve through the four points by hand. (Start the graph with a profit of 0 at a production rate of 0.)

b. Does the proportionality assumption of linear programming seem to be satisfied reasonably well for this product?

c. To the extent that profit is not strictly proportional to the production rate, does this product have decreasing marginal returns, increasing marginal returns, or neither?

E*   d. Use Excel's curve fitting method to (1) obtain a nonlinear formula with a quadratic form for the profit graph and then (2) construct the graph.

10.2.   Consider the following three cases for how the profit from an activity varies with the level of the activity.

Level of Activity	Profit ($)		
	Case 1	Case 2	Case 3
0	0	0	0
1	9	6	5
2	16	14	6
3	21	24	3
4	24	36	4
5	25	50	7

a. For each case, draw the profit graph by plotting the profits for the various levels of the activity and then drawing a smooth curve through the points by hand.

b. For each case, indicate whether the activity has decreasing marginal returns, increasing marginal returns, or neither.

c. How would your answers in part *b* change if the graphs plotted in part *a* were cost graphs instead of profit graphs?

E* *d.* For each case, use Excel's curve fitting method to (1) obtain a nonlinear formula with a quadratic form for the profit graph and then (2) construct the graph. For any case where the activity has neither decreasing marginal returns nor increasing marginal returns, comment on how good a fit is provided by using a quadratic form.

10.3. The Chiplet Corporation is about to launch the production and marketing of a new microchip that is more powerful than anything that is currently on the market. Not surprisingly, the profitability of this microchip will depend greatly on its reception in this highly competitive and fast-moving market. If the sales are fairly low, the company will still be able to make a respectable profit because it will have enough available production capacity to produce the microchip with its current facilities. However, if sales are somewhat higher, the company will need to expand its production facilities, which will have the effect of depressing the profit from the microchip if sales only reach a moderate level. (Fully meeting this demand would still be worthwhile because one of top management's prime goals is to continue increasing the company's market share as it points toward future generations of microchips already under development.) Fortunately, if sales reach a relatively high level, the profit from the microchip will become very substantial. The following table shows the estimated profit for various levels of sales over the short lifetime of this microchip.

Sales	Profit (millions of dollars)
0	0
100,000	15
200,000	18
300,000	13
400,000	4
500,000	1
600,000	6
700,000	30
800,000	70

a. Draw a profit graph for this microchip by plotting the profits for the various sales levels and then drawing a smooth curve that passes through (or very near) these points.

b. Does the microchip have decreasing marginal returns, increasing marginal returns, or neither?

E* *c.* Use Excel's curve fitting method to (1) obtain a nonlinear formula with a quadratic form (a polynomial of order 2) for the profit graph and then (2) construct the graph.

E* *d.* Repeat part *c* when using the Excel option of a polynomial of order 3 instead of order 2.

e. Which of the Excel options used in parts *c* and *d* does a better job of fitting the profit graph to the data?

10.4. The following table shows the estimated daily profit from a new product for several of the alternative choices for the production rate.

Production Rate (R)	Profit per Day (P)
0	0
1	$ 95
2	184
3	255
4	320

Because the profit goes up less than proportionally with the production rate (decreasing marginal returns), the management science team analyzing what this production rate (and the production rates of some other products) should be has decided to approximate the profit (P) by a simple *nonlinear function* of the production rate R.

a. One such approximation is $P = \$100R - \$5R^2$. How closely does this nonlinear function approximate the five values of P given in the table?

      b. Repeat part *a* for the approximation, $P = \$104R - \$6R^2$.

      c. Which of these two nonlinear functions provides the better fit to all the data?

E*   *d.* Use Excel's curve fitting method to (1) obtain a nonlinear formula with a quadratic form for the profit graph and then (2) construct the graph.

E*10.5.   Reconsider the portfolio selection example, including its spreadsheet model in Figure 10.13, given in Section 10.2. Note in Table 10.2 that stock 2 has the highest expected return and stock 3 has by far the lowest. Nevertheless, the changing cells Portfolio (C14:E14) provide an optimal solution that calls for purchasing far more of stock 3 than of stock 2. Although purchasing so much of stock 3 greatly reduces the risk of the portfolio, an aggressive investor may be unwilling to own so much of a stock with such a low expected return.

      For the sake of such an investor, add a constraint to the model that specifies that the percentage of stock 3 in the portfolio cannot exceed the amount specified by the investor. Then compare the expected return and risk (standard deviation of the return) of the optimal portfolio with that in Figure 10.13 when the upper bound on the percentage of stock 3 allowed in the portfolio is set at the following values.

      a. 20%

      b. 0%

      c. Use the Solver Table to systematically try all the percentages at 5% intervals from 0% to 50%.

10.6.*   A stockbroker, Richard Smith, has just received a call from his most important client, Ann Hardy. Ann has $50,000 to invest and wants to use it to purchase two stocks. Stock 1 is a solid blue-chip security with a respectable growth potential and little risk involved. Stock 2 is much more speculative. It is being touted in two investment newsletters as having outstanding growth potential, but also is considered very risky. Ann would like a large return on her investment, but also has considerable aversion to risk. Therefore, she has instructed Richard to analyze what mix of investments in the two stocks would be appropriate for her. She also informs him that her plan is to hold the stock being purchased now for three years before selling it.

      After doing some research on the historical performances of the two stocks and on the current prospects for the companies involved, Richard is able to make the following estimates. If the entire $50,000 were to be invested in stock 1 now, the profit when sold in three years would have an expected value of $12,500 and a standard deviation of $5,000. If the entire $50,000 were to be invested in stock 2 now, the profit when sold in three years would have an expected value of $20,000 and a standard deviation of $30,000. The two stocks behave independently in different sectors of the market so Richard's calculation from historical data is that the covariance of the profits from the two stocks is 0.

      Richard now is ready to use a spreadsheet model to determine how to allocate the $50,000 to the two stocks so as to minimize Ann's risk while providing an expected profit that is at least as large as her minimum acceptable value. He asks Ann to decide what her minimum acceptable value is.

      a. Without yet assigning a specific numerical value to the minimum acceptable expected profit, formulate a quadratic programming model in algebraic form for this problem.

E*   *b.* Display this model on a spreadsheet.

E*   *c.* Solve this model for four cases: Minimum acceptable expected profit = $13,000, $15,000, $17,000, and $19,000.

      d. Ann was a statistics major in college and so understands well that the *expected return* and *risk* in this model represent estimates of the *mean* and *standard deviation* of the probability distribution of the profit from the corresponding portfolio. Ann uses the notation μ and σ for the mean and standard deviation. She recalls that, for typical probability distributions, the probability is fairly high (about 0.8 or 0.9) that the return will exceed $\mu - \sigma$, and the probability is extremely high (often close to 0.999) that the profit will exceed $\mu - 3\sigma$. Calculate $\mu - \sigma$ and $\mu - 3\sigma$ for the four portfolios obtained in part *c*. Which portfolio will give Ann the highest μ among those that also give $\mu - \sigma \geq 0$?

10.7.   Reconsider the portfolio selection example given in Section 10.2. A fourth stock (stock 4) now has been found that gives a good balance between expected return and risk. Using the same units as in Table 10.2, its expected return is 17% and its risk is 18%. Its joint risk per stock with stocks 1, 2, and 3 is −0.015, −0.025, and 0.003, respectively.

      a. Still using a minimum acceptable expected return of 18%, formulate the revised quadratic programming model in algebraic form for this problem.

E*   *b.* Display and solve this model on a spreadsheet.

E*   *c.* Develop a revision of the Solver Table shown in Figure 10.14 for this revised problem.

10.8.   The management of the Albert Hanson Company is trying to determine the best product mix for two new products. Because these products would share the same production facilities, the total number of units produced of the two products combined cannot exceed two per hour. Because of uncertainty about how well these products will sell, the profit from producing each product provides decreasing marginal returns as the production rate is increased. In particular, with a production rate of R_1 units per hour, it is estimated that product 1 would provide a profit per hour of $200R_1 - \$100R_1^2$. If the production rate of product 2 is R_2 units per hour, its estimated profit per hour would be $300R_2 - \$100R_2^2$.

     a. Formulate a quadratic programming model in algebraic form for determining the product mix that maximizes the total profit per hour.

E*   *b.* Formulate and solve this model on a spreadsheet.

10.9.   The B. J. Jensen Company specializes in the production of power saws and power drills for home use. Sales are relatively stable throughout the year except for a jump upward during the Christmas season. Since the production work requires considerable work and experience, the company maintains a stable employment level and then uses overtime to increase production in November. The workers also welcome this opportunity to earn extra money for the holidays.

     B. J. Jensen, Jr., the current president of the company, is overseeing the production plans being made for the upcoming November. He has obtained the following data.

	Maximum Monthly Production*		Profit per Unit Produced	
	Regular Time	**Overtime**	**Regular Time**	**Overtime**
Power saws	3,000	2,000	$150	$50
Power drills	5,000	3,000	100	75

*Assuming adequate supplies of materials from the company's vendors.

     However, Mr. Jensen now has learned that, in addition to the limited number of labor hours available, two other factors will limit the production levels that can be achieved this November. One is that the company's vendor for power supply units will only be able to provide 10,000 of these units for November (2,000 more than his usual monthly shipment). Each power saw and each power drill requires one of these units. Second, the vendor who supplies a key part for the gear assemblies will only be able to provide 15,000 for November (4,000 more than for other months). Each power saw requires two of these parts and each power drill requires one.

     Mr. Jensen now wants to determine how many power saws and how many power drills to produce in November to maximize the company's total profit.

     a. Draw the profit graph for each of these two products.

E*   *b.* Use separable programming to formulate a linear programming model on a spreadsheet for this problem. Then solve the model. What does this say about how many power saws and how many power drills to produce in November?

10.10.*   The Dorwyn Company has two new products (special kinds of doors and windows) that will compete with the two new products for the Wyndor Glass Co. (described in Section 2.2). Using units of hundreds of dollars for the objective function, the linear programming model in algebraic form shown below has been formulated to determine the most profitable product mix.

$$\text{Maximize} \quad \text{Profit} = 4D + 6W$$

subject to

$$D + 3W \leq 8$$

$$5D + 2W \leq 14$$

and

$$D \geq 0 \quad W \geq 0$$

However, because of the strong competition from Wyndor, Dorwyn management now realizes that the company will need to make a strong marketing effort to generate substantial sales of these products. In particular, it is estimated that achieving a production and sales rate of D doors per week will require weekly marketing costs of D^3 hundred dollars (so \$100 for $D = 1$, \$800 for $D = 2$, \$2,700 for $D = 3$, etc.). The corresponding marketing costs for windows are estimated to be $2W^2$ hundred dollars. Thus, the objective function in the model should be

$$\text{Profit} = 4D + 6W - D^3 - 2W^2$$

Dorwyn management now would like to use the revised model to determine the most profitable product mix.

E*   *a.* Formulate and solve this nonlinear programming model on a spreadsheet.

b. Construct tables to show the profit data for each product when the production rate is 0, 1, 2, 3.

c. Draw a figure that plots the weekly profit points for each product when the production rate is 0, 1, 2, 3. Connect the pairs of consecutive points with (dashed) line segments.

E*   *d.* Use separable programming based on this figure to formulate an approximate linear programming model on a spreadsheet for this problem. Then solve the model. What does this say to Dorwyn management about which product mix to use?

e. Compare the solution based on a separable programming approximation in part *d* with the solution obtained in part *a* for the exact nonlinear programming model.

10.11.   The MFG Corporation is planning to produce and market three different products. Let x_1, x_2, and x_3 denote the number of units of the three respective products to be produced. The preliminary estimates of their potential profitability are as follows.

For the first 15 units produced of product 1, the unit profit would be approximately \$360. The unit profit would be only \$30 for any additional units of product 1. For the first 20 units produced of product 2, the unit profit is estimated at \$240. The unit profit would be \$120 for each of the next 20 units and \$90 for any additional units. For the first 10 units of product 3, the unit profit would be \$450. The unit profit would be \$300 for each of the next 5 units and \$180 for any additional units.

Certain limitations on the use of needed resources impose the following constraints on the production of the three products:

$$
\begin{aligned}
x_1 + x_2 + x_3 &\le 60 \\
3x_1 + 2x_2 \quad\;\; &\le 200 \\
x_1 \quad\;\; + 2x_3 &\le 70
\end{aligned}
$$

Management wants to know what values of x_1, x_2, and x_3 should be chosen to maximize the total profit.

a. Plot the profit graph for each of the three products.

E*   *b.* Use separable programming to formulate a linear programming model on a spreadsheet for this problem. Then solve the model. What is the resulting recommendation to management about the values of x_1, x_2, and x_3 to use?

10.12.   Reconsider the production scheduling problem of the Build-Em-Fast Company described in Problem 6.15. The *special restriction* for such a situation is that overtime should not be used in any particular period unless regular time in that period is completely used up. Explain why the logic of *separable programming* implies that this restriction will be satisfied automatically by any optimal solution for the transportation problem formulation of the problem.

10.13.   Suppose that separable programming has been applied to a certain problem (the "original problem") to convert it to the following equivalent linear programming model in algebraic form:

$$\text{Maximize} \quad \text{Profit} = 5x_{11} + 4x_{12} + 2x_{13} + 4x_{21} + x_{22}$$

subject to

$$
\begin{aligned}
3x_{11} + 3x_{12} + 3x_{13} + 2x_{21} + 2x_{22} &\le 25 \\
2x_{11} + 2x_{12} + 2x_{13} - x_{21} - x_{22} &\le 10
\end{aligned}
$$

and

$$0 \leq x_{11} \leq 2 \qquad 0 \leq x_{21} \leq 3$$

$$0 \leq x_{12} \leq 3 \qquad 0 \leq x_{22} \leq 1$$

$$0 \leq x_{13}$$

What was the mathematical model for the original problem? Answer this by plotting the profit graph for each of the original activities and then writing the constraints for the original problem in terms of the original decision variables.

10.14. Jim Matthews, vice president for marketing of the J. R. Nickel Company, is planning advertising campaigns for two unrelated products. These two campaigns need to use some of the same resources. Therefore, Jim knows that his decisions on the levels of the two campaigns need to be made jointly after considering these resource constraints. In particular, letting x_1 and x_2 denote the levels of campaigns 1 and 2, respectively, these constraints are $4x_1 + x_2 \leq 20$ and $x_1 + 4x_2 \leq 20$.

In facing these decisions, Jim is well aware that there is a point of diminishing returns when raising the level of an advertising campaign too far. At that point, the cost of additional advertising becomes larger than the increase in net revenue (excluding advertising costs) generated by the advertising. After careful analysis, he and his staff estimate that the net profit from the first product (including advertising costs) when conducting the first campaign at level x_1 would be $3x_1 - (x_1 - 1)^2$ in millions of dollars. The corresponding estimate for the second product is $3x_2 - (x_2 - 2)^2$.

Letting P be total net profit, this analysis led to the following nonlinear programming model for determining the levels of the two advertising campaigns:

$$\text{Maximize} \qquad P = 3x_1 - (x_1 - 1)^2 + 3x_2 - (x_2 - 2)^2$$

subject to

$$4x_1 + x_2 \leq 20$$

$$x_1 + 4x_2 \leq 20$$

and

$$x_1 \geq 0 \qquad x_2 \geq 0$$

a. Construct tables to show the profit data for each product when the level of its advertising campaign is $x_1 = 0, 1, 2, 2.5, 3, 4, 5$ (for the first product) or $x_2 = 0, 1, 2, 3, 3.5, 4, 5$ (for the second product).

b. Use these profit data to draw rough-hand a smooth profit graph for each product. (Note that these profit graphs start at negative values when $x_1 = 0$ or $x_2 = 0$ because the products would lose money if there is no advertising to support them.)

c. On the profit graph for the first product, draw an approximation of this profit graph by inserting a dashed-line segment between the profit at $x_1 = 0$ and $x_1 = 2$, between the profit at $x_1 = 2$ and $x_1 = 4$, and between the profit at $x_1 = 4$ and $x_1 = 5$. Then do the same on the profit graph for the second product with $x_2 = 0, 2, 4, 5$.

E* d. Use separable programming with the approximation of the profit graphs obtained in part *c* to formulate an approximate linear programming model on a spreadsheet for Jim Matthews's problem. Then solve this model. What does this solution say the levels of the advertising campaigns should be? What would the total net profit from the two products be?

E* e. Repeat parts *c* and *d* except using $x_1 = 0, 2, 2.5, 3, 5$ and $x_2 = 0, 3, 3.5, 4, 5$ for the approximations of the profit graphs in part *c*. (These particular approximations actually lead to the exact optimal solution for Jim Matthews's problem.)

E* f. Use Excel and its Solver to formulate and solve the original nonlinear programming model directly. Compare with the answers obtained after completing part *e*.

g. Use calculus to find the value of x_1 that maximizes $3x_1 - (x_1 - 1)^2$, the net profit from the first product. Also use calculus to find the value of x_2 that maximizes $3x_2 - (x_2 - 2)^2$, the net profit from the second product. Show that these values satisfy the constraints for the nonlinear programming model. Then compare these values with the answers obtained in parts *e* and *f*.

E*10.15. Consider the following nonlinear programming problem.

$$\text{Maximize} \quad \text{Profit} = x^5 - 13x^4 + 59x^3 - 107x^2 + 61x$$

subject to

$$0 \le x \le 5$$

   a. Formulate this problem in a spreadsheet and then use the Solver Table to solve this problem with the following starting points: $x = 0, 1, 2, 3, 4,$ and 5. Include the value of x and the profit as output cells in the Solver Table.

   b. Use Evolutionary Solver to solve this problem.

E*10.16. Consider the following nonlinear programming problem.

$$\text{Maximize} \quad \text{Profit} = 100x^6 - 1{,}359x^5 + 6{,}836x^4 - 15{,}670x^3 + 15{,}870x^2 - 5{,}095x$$

subject to

$$0 \le x \le 5$$

   a. Formulate this problem in a spreadsheet and then use the Solver Table to solve this problem with the following starting points: $x = 0, 1, 2, 3, 4,$ and 5. Include the value of x and the profit as output cells in the Solver Table.

   b. Use Evolutionary Solver to solve this problem.

E*10.17. Because of population growth, the state of Washington has been given an additional seat in the House of Representatives, making a total of ten. The state legislature, which is currently controlled by the Republicans, needs to develop a plan for redistricting the state. There are 18 major cities in the state of Washington that need to be assigned to 1 of the 10 congressional districts. The table below gives the numbers of registered Democrats and registered Republicans in each city. Each district must contain between 150,000 and 350,000 of these registered voters. Use Evolutionary Solver to assign each city to 1 of the 10 congressional districts in order to maximize the number of districts that have more registered Republicans than registered Democrats. (Hint: Use the SUMIF function.)

City	Democrat (Thousands)	Republican (Thousands)
1	152	62
2	81	59
3	75	83
4	34	52
5	62	87
6	38	87
7	48	69
8	74	49
9	98	62
10	66	72
11	83	75
12	86	82
13	72	83
14	28	53
15	112	98
16	45	82
17	93	68
18	72	98

10.18. Reconsider the portfolio optimization problem considered in Section 10.5, where the goal was to select the portfolio that beat the market for the largest number of quarters over the last six years.

E*   *a.* Using the naive solution (20 percent in each stock) as a starting point, apply Evolutionary Solver to optimize the portfolio again when considering the data for the first three years only (Q1 1996 through Q4 1998).

   b. For how many quarters does this same portfolio beat the market for the next three years (Q1 1999 through Q4 2001)?

   c. Comment on the results from parts *a* and *b*.

E*10.19.   Reconsider the portfolio optimization problem considered in Section 10.5, where the goal was to select the portfolio that beat the market for the largest number of quarters over the last six years.

   a. Use Evolutionary Solver to instead find a portfolio that did not lose money in the largest number of quarters.

   b. Use Evolutionary Solver to instead find a portfolio that yielded a return of at least 10 percent for the largest number of quarters.

10.20.   Reconsider the Wyndor Glass Co. problem introduced in Section 2.2.

E*   a. Solve this problem using the standard Solver.

E*   b. Starting with an initial solution of producing 0 doors and 0 windows, solve this problem using Evolutionary Solver.

   c. Comment on the performance of the two approaches.

Case 10-1

Continuation of the Super Grain Case Study

Reconsider the Super Grain case study introduced in Section 4.1 and continued in Section 4.5. Recall that Claire Syverson, vice president for marketing of The Super Grain Corporation, is planning an advertising campaign for the company's new breakfast cereal (Crunchy Start) with the help of a leading advertising firm, Giacomi & Jackowitz. The campaign will use three advertising media: television commercials on Saturday morning programs for children, advertisements in food- and family-oriented magazines, and advertisements in Sunday supplements of major newspapers. The problem being addressed is to determine the best mix of these advertising media.

The spreadsheet in Figure 4.6 shows the revised linear programming model that was used to address this problem. This model includes constraints on advertising expenditures, planning expenditures, and the use of cents-off coupons, as well as on managerial goals involving the numbers of young children and their parents that should be reached by the advertising. The changing cells NumberOfAds (C19:E19) show the optimal number of advertisements to place in each of the three media according to this model. The target cell TotalExposures (H19) gives an estimate of the resulting total number of exposures, where each viewing of an advertisement by some individual counts as one exposure.

The ultimate goal of the advertising campaign is to maximize the company's profits that are attained because of the resulting sales. However, it is difficult to make a direct connection between advertising exposure and profits. Therefore, the total number of exposures was chosen to be a rough surrogate for profit. This is why the target cell in Figure 4.6 (and in Figure 4.1) gives the total number of exposures instead of the total profit.

Claire is uneasy with having done this. She realizes that her assumption—that the total profit from the introduction of Crunchy Start is proportional to the total number of exposures from the advertising campaign—is only a rough approximation. The most important reason is that running too many advertisements in an advertising medium reaches a saturation level, where the impact of one more advertisement is substantially less than that for the first advertisement in that medium. Nevertheless, when the target cell gives the total number of exposures, having an individual see the advertisement one more time after being saturated counts the same (one more exposure) as seeing the advertisement for the first time.

To check the results in Figure 4.6, Claire decides to try using profit directly as the measure of performance to be recorded in the target cell. She carefully defines profit as the total profit obtained from first-time sales of Crunchy Start that occur because of the advertising campaign. Excluded from consideration are profits from impulse purchases of Crunchy Start by customers who have seen no advertisements but are attracted to this new cereal with its shiny box trumpeting its virtues sitting on a store shelf, since these sales have no relevance for evaluating the advertising campaign. Repeat purchases of Crunchy Start also are excluded from consideration because these depend mainly on the reaction to the cereal from the first purchase instead of the advertising campaign.

Claire asks Sid Jackowitz, one of the senior partners of Giacomi & Jackowitz, to develop estimates of the number of first-time purchases of Crunchy Start that should result from various numbers of advertisements in each medium. His estimates are shown in the following tables.

Number of TV Spots	Number of Sales	Number of Magazine Ads	Number of Sales	Number of Ads in Sunday Supplements	Number of Sales
1	1,000,000	5	700,000	2	1,200,000
2	1,750,000	10	1,200,000	4	2,200,000
3	2,450,000	15	1,550,000	6	3,000,000
4	2,800,000	20	1,800,000	8	3,500,000
5	3,000,000	25	2,000,000	10	3,750,000

Sid also reports that it is reasonable to assume that sales resulting from advertising in one of the media are not substantially affected by the amount of advertising in the other media since the audiences for the different media are somewhat different.

It is estimated that the company's gross profits from Crunchy Start will be 75¢ per sale. However, this gross profit excludes the advertising costs and planning costs for the advertising campaign. Therefore, Claire wants to include these costs in her definition of the total profit that should be considered for determining the best advertising mix.

a. For each of the three advertising media, draw a graph of the number of sales versus the number of advertisements by plotting the sales for the five points provided by Sid Jackowitz and then drawing a smooth curve through (or very near) these points. (Fractional advertisements are allowed by using only a portion of the available outlets.)

b. For each of the advertising media, use Excel's curve fitting method to (1) obtain a nonlinear formula for the sales graph and then (2) construct the graph. In each case, try three Excel options for the form of the graph—a polynomial of order 2 (the quadratic form), a polynomial of order 3, and the logarithmic form—and then choose the option that you feel provides the best fit.

c. Using your results from part *b,* write an expression for the total profit (as defined by Claire) in terms of the number of advertisements of each type.

d. Using your result from part *c,* revise the spreadsheet model in Figure 4.6 (available on the CD-ROM) so that it maximizes total profit instead of the total number of exposures, and then solve.

e. Use the sales tables provided by Sid Jackowitz to apply separable programming to this problem when maximizing total profit.

f. Compare your results in parts *d* and *e* with those in Figure 4.6 and then give your recommendation (with a brief explanation) for the best advertising mix. Do you feel it was worthwhile to introduce a nonlinear profit function into the model in order to refine the linear programming model used in Figure 4.6?

Case 10-2

Savvy Stock Selection

Ever since the day she took her first economics class in high school, Lydia wondered about the financial practices of her parents. They worked very hard to earn enough money to live a comfortable middle-class life, but they never made their money work for them. They simply deposited their hard-earned paychecks in savings accounts earning a nominal amount of interest. (Fortunately, there always was enough money available when it came time to pay her college bills.) She promised herself that when she became an adult, she would not follow the same financially conservative practices as her parents.

And Lydia kept this promise. She took every available finance course in her business program at college. Having landed a coveted job on Wall Street upon graduation, she now begins every morning by watching the CNN financial reports. She plays investment games on the World Wide Web, finding portfolios that maximize her return while minimizing her risk. And she reads *The Wall Street Journal* and *Financial Times.*

Lydia also reads the investment advice columns of the financial magazines. She decides to follow the current advice given by her two favorite columnists. In his monthly column, editor Jonathan Taylor recommends three stocks that he believes will rise far above market average. In addition, the well-known mutual fund guru Donna Carter advocates the purchase of three more stocks that she thinks will outperform the market over the next year.

Bigbell (ticker symbol on the stock exchange: BB), one of the nation's largest telecommunications companies, trades at a price-earnings ratio well below market average. Huge investments over the last eight months have depressed earnings considerably. However, with its new cutting-edge technology, the company is expected to significantly raise its profit margins. Taylor predicts that the stock will rise from its current price of $60 per share to $72 per share within the next year.

Lotsofplace (LOP) is one of the leading hard drive manufacturers in the world. The industry recently underwent major consolidation, as fierce price wars over the last few years were followed by many competitors going bankrupt or being bought by Lotsofplace and its competitors. Due to reduced competition in the hard drive market, revenues and earnings are expected to rise considerably over the next year. Taylor predicts a one-year increase of 42 percent in the stock of Lotsofplace from the current price of $127 per share.

Internetlife (ILI) has survived the many ups and downs of Internet companies. With the next Internet frenzy just around the corner, Taylor expects a doubling of this company's stock price from $4 to $8 within a year.

Healthtomorrow (HEAL) is a leading biotechnology company that is about to get approval for several new drugs from the Food and Drug Administration, which will help earnings to grow 20 percent over the next few years. In particular, a new drug to significantly reduce the risk of heart attacks is supposed to reap huge profits. Also, due to several new great-tasting medications for children, the company has been able to build an excellent image in the media. This public relations coup will surely have a positive effect on the sale of its over-the-counter medications. Carter is convinced that the stock will rise from $50 to $75 per share within a year.

Quicky (QUI) is a fast-food chain that has been vastly expanding its network of restaurants all over the United States. Carter has followed this company closely since it went public some 15 years ago when it had only a few dozen restaurants on the West Coast of the United States. Since then the company has expanded, and it now has restaurants in every state. Due to its emphasis on healthy foods, it is capturing a growing market share. Carter believes that the stock will continue to perform well above market average for an increase of 46 percent in one year from its current stock price of $150.

Automobile Alliance (AUA) is a leading car manufacturer from the Detroit area that just recently introduced two new models. These models show very strong initial sales, and therefore the company's stock is predicted to rise from $20 to $26 over the next year.

On the World Wide Web, Lydia found data about the risk involved in the stocks of these companies. The historical variances of return of the six stocks and their covariances are shown in the following table.

Company	BB	LOP	ILI	HEAL	QUI	AUA
Variance	0.032	0.1	0.333	0.125	0.065	0.08

Covariances	LOP	ILI	HEAL	QUI	AUA
BB	0.005	0.03	−0.031	−0.027	0.01
LOP		0.085	−0.07	−0.05	0.02
ILI			−0.11	−0.02	0.042
HEAL				0.05	−0.06
QUI					−0.02

a. At first, Lydia wants to ignore the risk of all the investments. Given this strategy, what is her optimal investment portfolio; that is, what fraction of her money should she invest in each of the six different stocks? What is the total risk of her portfolio?

b. Lydia decides that she doesn't want to invest more than 40 percent in any individual stock. While still ignoring risk, what is her new optimal investment portfolio? What is the total risk of her new portfolio?

c. Now Lydia wants to take into account the risk of her investment opportunities. For use in the following parts, formulate a quadratic programming model that will minimize her risk (measured by the variance of the return from her portfolio) while ensuring that her expected return is at least as large as her choice of a minimum acceptable value.

   d. Lydia wants to ensure that she receives an expected return of at least 35 percent. She wants to reach this goal at minimum risk. What investment portfolio allows her to do that?

   e. What is the minimum risk Lydia can achieve if she wants an expected return of at least 25 percent? Of at least 40 percent?

   f. Do you see any problems or disadvantages with Lydia's approach to her investment strategy?

Case 10-3

International Investments

Charles Rosen relaxes in a plush, overstuffed recliner by the fire, enjoying the final vestiges of his week-long winter vacation. As a financial analyst working for a large investment firm in Germany, Charles has very few occasions to enjoy these private moments since he is generally catching red-eye flights around the world to evaluate various investment opportunities. Charles pats the loyal golden retriever lying at his feet and takes a swig of brandy, enjoying the warmth of the liquid. He sighs and realizes that he must begin attending to his own financial matters while he still has the time during the holiday. He opens a folder placed conspicuously on the top of a large stack of papers. The folder contains information about an investment Charles made when he graduated from college four years ago . . .

Charles remembers his graduation day fondly. He obtained a degree in business administration and was full of investment ideas that were born while he had been daydreaming in his numerous finance classes. Charles maintained a well-paying job throughout college, and he was able to save a large portion of the college fund that his parents had invested for him.

Upon graduation, Charles decided that he should transfer the college funds to a more lucrative investment opportunity. Since he had signed on to work in Germany, he evaluated investment opportunities in that country. Ultimately, he decided to invest 30,000 German marks (DM) in so-called B bonds that would mature in seven years. Charles purchased the bonds just four years ago last week (in early January of what will be called the "first year" in this discussion). He considered the bonds an excellent investment opportunity since they offered high interest rates (see Table 1) that would rise over the subsequent seven years and because he could sell the bonds whenever he wanted after the first year. He calculated the amount that he would be paid if he sold bonds originally worth DM 100 on the last day of any of the seven years (see Table 2). The amount paid included the principal plus the interest. For example, if he sold bonds originally worth DM 100 on December 31 of the sixth year, he would be paid DM 163.51 (the principal is DM 100 and the interest is DM 63.51).

TABLE 1
Interest Rates over the Seven Years

Year	Interest Rate	Annual Percentage Yield
1	7.50%	7.50%
2	8.50	8.00
3	8.50	8.17
4	8.75	8.31
5	9.00	8.45
6	9.00	8.54
7	9.00	8.61

TABLE 2
Total Return on 100 DM

Year	DM
1	107.50
2	116.64
3	126.55
4	137.62
5	150.01
6	163.51
7	178.23

Charles did not sell any of the bonds during the first four years. Last year, however, the German federal government introduced a capital gains tax on interest income. The German government designated that the first DM 6,100 a single individual earns in interest per year would be tax-free. Any interest income beyond DM 6,100 would be taxed at a rate of 30 percent. For example, if Charles earned interest income of DM 10,100, he would be required to pay 30 percent of DM 4,000 (DM 10,100 − DM 6,100) in taxes, or DM 1,200. His after-tax income would therefore be DM 8,900.

Because of the new tax implemented last year, Charles has decided to reevaluate the investment. He knows that the new tax affects his potential return on the B bonds, but he also knows that most likely a strategy exists for maximizing his return on the bonds. He might be able to decrease the tax he has to pay on interest income by selling portions of his bonds in different years. Charles considers his strategy viable because the government requires investors to pay taxes on interest income only when they sell their B bonds. For example, if Charles were to sell one-third of his B bonds on December 31 of the sixth year, he would have to pay taxes on the interest income of DM (6,351 − 6,100).

Charles asks himself several questions. Should he keep all the bonds until the end of the seventh year? If so, he would earn 0.7823 times DM 30,000 in interest income, but he would have to pay very substantial taxes for that year. Considering these tax payments, Charles wonders if he should sell a portion of the bonds at the end of this year (the fifth year) and at the end of next year.

If Charles sells his bonds, his alternative investment opportunities are limited. He could purchase a certificate of deposit (CD) paying 4.0 percent interest, so he investigates this alternative. He meets with an investment advisor from the local branch of a bank, and the advisor tells him to keep the B bonds until the end of the seventh year. She argues that even if he had to pay 30 percent in taxes on the 9.00 percent rate of interest that the B bonds would be paying in their last year (see Table 1), this strategy would still result in a net rate of 6.30 percent interest, which is much better than the 4.0 percent interest he could obtain on a CD.

Charles concludes that he will make all his transactions on December 31, regardless of the year. Also, since he intends to attend business school in the United States in the fall of the seventh year and plans to pay his tuition for his second, third, and fourth semester with his investment, he does not plan to keep his money in Germany beyond December 31 of the seventh year.

(For the first three parts, assume that if Charles sells a portion of his bonds, he will put the money under his mattress earning zero percent interest. For the subsequent parts, assume that he could invest the proceeds of the bonds in the certificate of deposit.)

a. Formulate a separable programming model to be used in the following parts.

b. What is the optimal investment strategy for Charles?

c. What is fundamentally wrong with the advice Charles got from the investment advisor at the bank?

d. Now that Charles is considering investing in the certificate of deposit, what is his optimal investment strategy?

e. What would his optimal investment strategy for the fifth, sixth, and seventh years have been if he had originally invested DM 50,000?

f. Charles and his fiancée have been planning to get married after his first year in business school. However, Charles learns that for married couples, the tax-free amount of interest earnings each year is DM 12,200. How much money could Charles save on his DM 30,000 investment by getting married this year (the fifth year for his investment)?

g. Due to a recession in Germany, interest rates are low and are expected to remain low. However, since the American economy is booming, interest rates are expected to rise in the United States. A rise in interest rates would lead to a rise of the dollar in comparison to the mark. Analysts at Charles's investment bank expect the dollar to remain at the current exchange rate of DM 1.50 per dollar for the fifth year and then to rise to DM 1.80 per dollar by the end of the seventh year. Therefore, Charles is considering investing at the beginning of the sixth year in a two-year American municipal bond paying 3.6 percent tax-exempt interest to help pay tuition. How much money should he plan to convert into dollars by selling B bonds for this investment?

Learning objectives

After completing this chapter, you should be able to

1. Identify the kinds of managerial problems that goal programming can address.

2. Describe how a goal programming model differs from other kinds of management science models.

3. Discuss the differences between the weighted goal programming approach and the preemptive goal programming approach.

4. Determine which of these approaches seems more appropriate for a given situation.

5. Formulate and apply a weighted goal programming model from a description of the problem.

6. Formulate and apply a preemptive goal programming model from a description of the problem.

Chapter **Eleven**

Goal Programming

Goal programming provides a way of seeking a solution that comes as close as possible toward satisfying all of management's major goals for a project.

In the preceding chapters, you have seen various kinds of management science models that can address a wide variety of managerial problems. However, all these models share one common characteristic. They all have a single objective function that expresses the overall measure of performance for the problem. For example, the objective might be to maximize total profit.

Unfortunately, it is not always possible to encapsulate management's objectives into one overall measure of performance in this way. The objectives might be so disparate that there is no common basis for measuring progress toward these objectives. In this kind of situation, management might instead set numeric goals for the various objectives and then seek a solution that makes as much progress as possible toward all these goals. This is the kind of problem that goal programming addresses.

The chapter begins with a case study that demonstrates how this kind of situation can arise. You will see three members of top management championing three very different goals for a project. The CEO agrees that all three goals are important and then mediates to assess their relative importance. You also will see how the head of the Management Science Department works with top management to elicit the kind of input needed to apply goal programming.

Goal programming provides two alternative ways of formulating problems with multiple goals. One, called *weighted goal programming*, assigns weights to the goals that measure their relative importance and then seeks a solution that minimizes the weighted sum of the deviations from the goals. This approach is described in Section 11.2 in the context of the case study. The second approach, called *preemptive goal programming*, requires deciding on the order of importance of the goals. It then focuses on one goal at a time in this order. This approach is described in Section 11.3. The dialogue for the case study in Section 11.1 also introduces both approaches, including when each one is more appropriate and how management should provide the needed input, in a practical setting.

11.1 A CASE STUDY: THE DEWRIGHT CO. GOAL-PROGRAMMING PROBLEM

"What's the matter, honey? A rough day at the office?"

"Well, it really wasn't all that bad," Kathleen responds to her husband Scott. "Mainly just frustrating. Ever since I got this job as head of Dewright's Management Science Department, I have emphasized making sure that everything we do is responding to management's needs. Understand what management's objectives are for the decisions they need to make based on our studies. Then address those objectives rather than what we think the goals should be. I preach that all the time."

"So what happened?"

A management science study should focus on addressing management's goals for the study.

"Well, we've just been handed an extremely important new project, a really juicy management science study. So I made the rounds today interviewing the key people in top management to clarify just what they wanted to get out of our study. What is the basic objective for the decisions they need to make? Usually this goes pretty smoothly, with a lot of consensus about what the overriding objective should be. But not today. First I was told that we should focus on such and such as the main goal of the study. Then the next person I interviewed said no, the key goal was something completely different. Then the next guy had an entirely new slant on it. I've never seen so much disagreement. Each one was only protecting his or her own interests instead of looking at the big picture of what is best for the company as a whole. So now we're stymied. I've already selected the members of the team to work on this study. But we can't really get started until we receive much clearer direction from management. And, of course, management needs the study completed quickly. One jokester said they would like our report the day before yesterday. I laughed politely, but I felt like kicking him. Don't they realize that our output from the study can only be as good as their input!?! And that we can only act as quickly as they give us the direction we need!"

"Wow, no wonder you're frustrated," Scott responds. "It sounds like management really dropped the ball on this one."

"Yes, they did. It was clear that they hadn't talked to each other about this issue, even though they knew I would be interviewing all of them about this today. It's management's responsibility to thrash this out and come to a common understanding of what they want out of a management science study, and then give us clear direction. They really didn't do their job this time!"

"So what's the next step?"

"I've already called our CEO late this afternoon. Direction needs to come from the top. Actually, Gary was pretty sympathetic. He even volunteered that he thought his people had let me down this time."

"So did he give you the direction you need?" Scott asks Kathleen.

"No, I really wasn't asking for that at this point. He wasn't involved with requesting this management science study, so I was hitting him cold. But he understood right away what had gone wrong. Even before I could suggest it, he said that the managers involved with this project should be brought together in a meeting to thrash out what the main goals should be. He even said he would chair the meeting himself. He also wants me and key members of my team there. He says it is very important that we have a clear understanding of management's thinking on this issue. And I certainly agreed."

"Great! So it sounds to me like all you have to do is attend the meeting and listen carefully. Let them do their homework and then come to a meeting of the minds. Press them if necessary to get the clarity you need. Then you'll be off and running."

Background

The Dewright Company is one of the largest producers of power tools in the United States. The company has had its ups and downs but has managed to maintain its position as one of the market leaders for over 20 years. This is largely due to superior products produced by a skilled and loyal work force, many of whom have been with the company for most of its existence. One of management's priorities has been to maintain a relatively stable employment level to retain the high morale and loyalty of this work force.

The company has just gone through one of its leaner years. Sales were down slightly from the preceding year and earnings dipped as well (much to the discontent of the company's stockholders). One consequence is that the company now has less capital available than usual with which to invest in new product development. Management also is concerned that some downsizing may be needed if sales don't improve soon.

Fortunately, help is on the way. The company is preparing to replace its current product line with the next generation of products—specifically, three exciting new power tools with the latest state-of-the-art features, so they are expected to sell well for at least a year or two. Because of the limited amount of capital available, management needs to make some difficult choices about how much to invest in each of these products. Another concern is the effect of these decisions on the company's ability to maintain a relatively stable employment level. A competitor is known to be developing similar new products, so decisions must be made quickly.

These kinds of considerations recently led the company's president, Tasha Johnson, to call Kathleen Donaldson, head of the Management Science Department, to request an urgent management science study to analyze what the product mix should be. Tasha asked Kathleen to come see her for a briefing on management's objectives in making the product-mix decisions. Tasha also suggested that Kathleen talk with Vijay Shah (vice president for manufacturing) and Hien Nguyen (the chief financial officer).

Management's goals for the study should reflect what is best for the company as a whole rather than parochial concerns.

It is management's responsibility to thrash out its collective goals for the study from a company-wide viewpoint.

One priority is to maintain a relatively stable employment level.

The management science study will analyze what the product mix should be for the three new products.

Kathleen has just completed these interviews, with the unsatisfactory results reported to her husband.

Gary Lang, the company's CEO, now has arranged for the meeting to bring these parties together with Kathleen and key members of her team.

The Management Science Team Meets with Top Management

After some pleasantries, the meeting gets under way.

Gary Lang (CEO): I've called this meeting to clarify what we want to accomplish when we introduce these three new products. What are our main goals? I have some thoughts on that. But first I want to hear your thinking. Then we can work this out together. Once this is settled, planning can get under way to accomplish what we want accomplished. As you know, Tasha has asked Kathleen to personally head a management science team from her department to analyze how we can best meet our goals. Before the team can do that, they need some clear direction from us on just what our goals and priorities are. Kathleen, is that a fair summary of what you want to get out of this meeting?

> *The purpose of the meeting is to clarify management's goals for the management science study.*

Kathleen Donaldson (head of Management Science Department): Yes, it is, Gary. Thank you.

Gary: OK. Let's make the rounds then and get your thinking. Tasha, let's start with you.

Tasha Johnson (president): Well, as usual, I think we need to focus on the bottom line. If we do that, everything else will fall into place. After the year we just went through, we've got to get our earnings up. That's certainly the message our board of directors has been giving us. You'll recall the plan I presented at the last board meeting. To get our earnings headed up where we want them, we need to generate a total profit of at least $125 million from these three products until they're replaced by the next generation of products. And I think that's doable. I've already told Kathleen that I would like her team to find the mix of the three products that would maximize our profit. And to make sure that it is at least $125 million, as I promised the board of directors. I think that should be our main focus.

> *Generating a total profit of at least $125 million from the three new products would be very desirable.*

Gary: Thank you, Tasha. It's certainly true that the board has been pressing us to substantially improve earnings. And they were encouraged by your plan to generate profits of at least $125 million from these products. Vijay, what is your take on this issue of where our focus should be?

Vijay Shah (vice president for manufacturing): Well, I'm certainly not going to argue against making profits. But there are different ways of accomplishing that. By and large, we've been a very profitable company for over 20 years. And despite our occasional off years like last year, I think we will continue to be a very successful company as long as we don't forget what got us here. Our number one asset is our work force. They're the best in the business and we all know it. Besides our strong leadership at the top, they're our main reason for success. If we simply go scrambling after big profits in the short run to satisfy the board of directors for a little while, I think that's going to mean some downsizing. That would ruin morale! And cause all kinds of disruption. I know a lot of companies have been doing it, often to their regret, but it would be a huge mistake in our case. Let's not kill the goose that's been laying our golden eggs. We have great morale and an exceptionally efficient work force largely because we've kept them together all these years. We're going to have larger profits in the long run if we maintain a stable employment level and continue developing new products to keep them fully utilized. I told Kathleen that I thought her team should develop a plan for the current new products that would maintain our present employment level, and then profits would take care of themselves.

> *Maintaining a stable employment level enhances morale and efficiency.*

Tasha: But in this global economy, the companies that are surviving are those that downsize quickly when they need to in order to stay competitive.

Vijay: That would be shortsighted, especially in our situation.

Gary: Vijay, I do agree that we have a terrific work force and we should try to maintain it if possible. It is my hope that these three new products will enable us to do just that. We currently have 4,000 employees. We might even be able to increase that if everything falls into place. When you talk about the disadvantages of changing the employment level, how would you feel about an increase rather than a decrease?

Vijay: An increase wouldn't be so bad. But it still would cause some problems, especially since the increase probably would be temporary as these products wind down. First, we would incur the expense and disruption of training these inexperienced workers. Then we would turn around and need to lay them off because we have so little attrition here. Any layoffs are not good for morale. I think we're better off sticking pretty close to the 4,000 employees.

Decreasing the employment level would be more problematic than increasing the employment level.

Gary: OK. Thanks, Vijay. Now I'm anxious to hear from Hien, especially after our financial downturn this past year.

Hien Nguyen (chief financial officer):   Yes. You know well that we're not in a good financial situation. We seldom have been as strapped for capital as we are right now.

Gary: Unfortunately, we're going to need a lot of capital to launch these new products properly. And it is very important to the future of this company to have a good launch. I'm going to need to depend on you to work your usual magic to come up with at least the minimum amounts necessary to invest in the production facilities, marketing campaigns, and so forth, that we need for these products. How much do you think we can do?

Holding the capital investment down to no more than $55 million would be very desirable.

Hien: I've been looking into that pretty carefully. I think we can scrape together something close to $55 million. However, I wouldn't advise trying to go beyond that. If we get that overextended, I fear that our corporate bonds will be downgraded into the junk bond category. And then we would be paying through the nose in high interest rates for all our debt. So when Kathleen saw me recently, I advised her to stick with plans that would hold the capital investment down to no more than $55 million.

Gary: I hear you. OK, here is my conclusion so far. I think all three of you have raised very valid concerns. You each have enunciated a goal: Achieve a total profit from these products of at least $125 million, maintain the current employment level of 4,000 employees, and hold the capital investment down to no more than $55 million. These all are legitimate goals. I seriously doubt that we can fully achieve all of them. However, rather than selecting just one of them, I think we need to try to come as close to meeting all three goals simultaneously as we can.

The CEO wants to strive toward all the goals simultaneously.

Kathleen: I have a question.

Gary: Shoot.

Kathleen: Do you see any way of combining all three goals into a single overriding objective—one objective that would encompass all three?

Gary: Such as?

Kathleen: Well, perhaps maximizing *long-run* profit. The problems associated with either changing the employment level or overextending our capital outlays affect our profit in the long run. Can we measure these effects on long-run profits and combine them with the direct profit from the new products?

Gary: Hmmm. An interesting idea. But no, I don't think so. You're really comparing apples and oranges. There are too many intangibles involved in the impact of missing either the second or third goal. I don't see how you can develop any reasonable estimate of the long-run profit that would result from all this.

Kathleen: Yes, that was my reaction too. But yours is the one that counts. So it sounds like we should consider all three goals as separate goals, but then analyze them simultaneously.

Gary: Yes, I think so. Do you have a good way of doing this?

Kathleen: Well, I can think of two possibilities. But we need further guidance from all of you to determine the approach we should use.

Gary: Go ahead.

Kathleen: One possibility is to use a linear programming approach. You'll recall that we've conducted several linear programming studies for you recently.

Gary: Yes.

Kathleen: This would involve maximizing the total profit from the new products, subject to constraints that the second and third goals are met. But this would mean requiring that the second and third goals are completely satisfied. Would that requirement seem reasonable to you?

Tasha: No, no, no! I think the first goal is the most important. We should make sure we meet it even if that means missing the second and third goals somewhat.

Vijay: But we also should permit missing the first goal somewhat to avoid missing the other goals by a large amount.

Gary: Well, there you have it. I agree that we shouldn't require any of the goals to be completely satisfied if they can't all be satisfied simultaneously.

Kathleen: OK, fine. So formulating a linear programming model would not be appropriate to meet your needs. But now it sounds to me like the second approach would be perfect for you.

Gary: What's that?

Goal programming is designed to find the best way of striving toward several goals.

Kathleen: It's a management science technique called **goal programming.** It is designed to find the best way of striving toward several goals.

Gary: Yes, that sounds like just the ticket. So now you have what you need from us to start your study?

Kathleen: Not quite. I need to ask your indulgence for a few minutes to elicit a little more input—information we need to be able to use goal programming.

Gary: This is important. We'll take as long as you need.

Kathleen: Thank you. What we need is your collective assessment of the relative importance of these three goals.

Management needs to provide a collective assessment of the relative importance of the goals, so the CEO responds with direction from the top.

Gary: I would like to take a crack at that. I've been thinking hard about this during our discussion here. I must say that Tasha, Vijay, and Hien all have made strong cases. I think all three goals are important. However, I don't think we have any choice but to put top priority on achieving our profit goal. That is the engine that drives everything else. And our board of directors has made it very clear that this needs to be our top priority. But I also resonate with what Vijay had to say about our work force being our number one asset. However, I would divide his goal of maintaining a stable employment level into two parts—avoiding a *decrease* in the employment level and avoiding an *increase* in the employment level. I think the negative impact of laying off some of our loyal long-time employees would be much more serious than that of hiring new people and perhaps laying them off in a year or two. Therefore, I would place a pretty strong second priority on avoiding layoffs, but not on avoiding new hiring. Then sorry, Hien, but I think we can only give third priority to the goal of holding our capital investment under $55 million. We mustn't ignore your very legitimate concerns. However, we are in a hole that we need to dig out of, even if that means stretching our finances more than we normally would be willing to do. Then finally, I would put fourth priority on the second part of Vijay's goal—avoiding an increase in our employment level since it might need to be temporary.
  What do the rest of you think? Does this seem reasonable?

Tasha: Definitely.

Vijay: I can live with it.

Hien: You're the one that needs to set priorities. But we do need to be cautious about getting overextended financially.

Gary: I hear you. OK, Kathleen, what additional input do you need from us?

Kathleen: I need your advice on the following issue. Goal programming is a flexible technique that provides two different approaches to analyzing managerial problems. Which approach is appropriate for any particular problem depends on management's assessment of how big the differences are in the importance of the goals. Are all the goals quite important with only modest differences in their importance? Or are there really big differences in their importance? In the first case, the approach is to literally consider all the goals simultaneously while recognizing the modest differences in their importance. We call this approach **weighted goal programming** because it places weights on the goals to reflect their relative importance. In the second case, because of the really big differences in the importance of the goals, the approach is to begin by focusing solely on the most important goal and going as far as possible toward achieving that goal. Then it turns to the second most important goal, and then to the third one, and so forth. This approach is called **preemptive goal programming** because its focus on each goal in turn is preempting any consideration yet of less important goals. My group would be comfortable with using either approach. However, the decision on which one to use really needs to depend on your input. How big do you think the differences are in the importance of the goals? Which approach seems more appropriate for this situation?

Gary: I could see us going in either direction. It seems to me that there are clear differences in the importance of the goals. However, they all are quite important. I wouldn't say that there are very big differences in their importance. So my inclination would be to go with that first approach you mentioned.

Kathleen: Yes, the weighted goal programming approach. Since you say you could see us going in either direction, this apparently is not a clear-cut situation. Therefore, I think what we'll do is begin with the weighted goal programming approach, but then double-check our conclusions by applying the preemptive goal programming approach as well. We'll include all our results in our report and then the four of you can put your heads together to make the decision on what the product mix should be for the three new products.

Gary: I like it. Full steam ahead. Are you all set now? Does this give you everything you need?

Kathleen: Nearly. This has been extremely helpful. However, we still need your input on one more thing in order to implement the weighted preemptive programming approach. Let me explain a little more about how this approach works. It assigns penalties to not achieving goals. The more you miss a goal, the larger the penalty. The top priority goals get the largest penalties for missing them and the lowest priority goals get the smallest penalties. Then goal programming finds the set of decisions—in this case the production rates for the three products—that minimizes the total number of penalty points incurred by missing goals.

Gary: Sounds like a good approach.

Kathleen: Yes. But what this means is that we need to assign penalty weights that measure the relative seriousness of missing the respective goals. Now we could try to assign the penalty weights based on the discussion here and the priorities you have set. But that really isn't our place. These penalty weights need to reflect *your* assessment, not ours, of the relative seriousness of missing these goals.

Gary: I agree. How do we go about that?

Kathleen: Well, the first step is that we assign any old number as the penalty weight for missing one of the goals, just to establish a standard of comparison. Then you would scale this penalty weight up or down for each of the other goals, depending on whether you think the seriousness of missing that goal is larger or smaller than for missing the first goal. OK, since our top priority is the goal of achieving a total profit from these new products of at least $125 million, let's assign a penalty weight of 5 for each $1 million you undershoot this goal. In other words, if the estimated total profit resulting from the selected profit mix is

The choice between the two goal programming approaches depends on management's assessment of how big the differences are in the importance of the goals.

The decision is made to begin with the weighted goal programming approach and then to follow up with the preemptive goal programming approach.

$124 million, 5 penalty points would be assessed. If the estimated total profit is $115 million, undershooting the goal by $10 million, then 50 penalty points would be assessed. Ten times five is 50.

Gary: I get it.

Kathleen: OK. With this penalty weight of 5 as a standard of comparison, now we're ready for the hard questions. Going down your priorities, what should the penalty weight be for each 100 employees we *undershoot* the goal of maintaining the current employment level at 4,000 employees? For each $1 million we miss the goal of holding the capital investment down to no more than $55 million? For each 100 employees we *overshoot* the goal of sticking with 4,000 employees?

Gary: Hmmm. Good questions. Hmmm. Well, I think I would go 5, 4, 3, 2. Five for the first goal, and then 4, 3, 2 for your three questions.

Kathleen: Great. Understood. That gives us exactly what we need. We can launch into our study immediately now.

Gary: Very good. You understand that we'll need your report quite soon.

Kathleen: Yes, I think we can finish in a month. I'll tell you what our biggest job is going to be. Gathering data. We're going to need to get good data on the effect of each product's production rate toward meeting each of the three goals. How much profit will each product generate? How much employment level? How much capital investment is needed? We'll have to get a lot of help from various staff people.

Gary: I'll see to it that everybody makes this their top priority.

Kathleen: Then we can do it. I don't think any of us will see much of our families for the next month, but I'll make sure that we get it done in time.

Gary: Good for you, Kathleen. Thank you so much. And let us know whenever you need more input or help from any of us.

Kathleen: I will. Thank you.

The meeting concludes, except for a somewhat heated private conversation between Tasha and Vijay.

The Conclusions from This Meeting

To summarize, here are the key conclusions from this meeting.

The management science team led by Kathleen Donaldson will conduct a study to be completed within the next month. The study will focus on determining the mix of the company's three new products that would best meet management's goals. The specific decisions to be made are the production rates for the three products.

In addressing these decisions, management wants primary consideration given to three factors: total profit, stability in the work force, and the level of capital investment needed to launch these products. In particular, management has established the following goals.

Goal 1: Achieve a total profit (net present value) from these products of at least $125 million.

Goal 2: Maintain the current employment level of 4,000 employees.

Goal 3: Hold the capital investment down to no more than $55 million.

However, management realizes that it probably will not be possible to attain all these goals simultaneously, and so they evaluated the relative importance of the goals. All are important, but by small margins their order of importance is

Order of Importance: Goal 1, part of Goal 2 (avoid decreasing the employment level), Goal 3, and the other part of Goal 2 (avoid increasing the employment level).

Penalty weights are assigned by management to measure the relative seriousness of missing the respective goals.

TABLE 11.1
Penalty Weights That Measure the Relative Seriousness of Missing the Goals for the Dewright Co. Problem

Goal	Factor	Penalty Weight for Missing Goal
1	Total profit	5 (per $1 million under the goal)
2	Employment level	4 (per 100 employees under the goal)
		2 (per 100 employees over the goal)
3	Capital investment	3 (per $1 million over the goal)

TABLE 11.2
Contributions to the Goals per Unit Rate of Production of Each Product for the Dewright Co. Problem

Factor	Unit Contribution of Product			Goal
	1	2	3	
Total profit (millions of dollars)	12	9	15	≥ 125
Employment level (hundreds of employees)	5	3	4	$= 40$
Capital investment (millions of dollars)	5	7	8	≤ 55

To further quantify this ordering, **penalty weights** were assigned to indicate the relative seriousness of missing these goals. Discussions between management and Kathleen led to the choice of the penalty weights shown in Table 11.1.

Relevant Data

What the total profit, employment level, and capital investment level will be depends on the *production rates* (number of units produced per day) of the three products. Each product's contribution to each of these three quantities is *proportional* to the rate of production of the product. Therefore, for each of the three products, the management science team focuses on estimating the contribution to each of these quantities *per unit* rate of production of the product. Much of these data are not readily available, so the team has to do considerable digging with much help from knowledgeable staff. Based on the limited information it can uncover, the team then makes the best estimates that it can of each product's contribution to each of the three quantities.

Data are needed on how much each product would contribute toward reaching each goal per unit increase in the rate of production of the product.

These estimated contributions per unit rate of production are shown in Table 11.2, where the contributions are in the units indicated (in parentheses) in the first column. Thus, for example, producing one unit per day of product 1 would contribute $12 million toward total profit, 500 employees to the employment level, and $5 million to the capital investment level.

The story of how the team uses these data to complete its study continues in the next section, after we introduce the general subject of goal programming.

Review Questions

1. What is the problem that Dewright's management science team has been asked to address?
2. What are the three goals that management has established for addressing this problem?
3. What is to be minimized when using a weighted goal-programming approach?

11.2 WEIGHTED GOAL PROGRAMMING

One common characteristic of all the different kinds of management science models introduced so far (including linear programming, integer programming, and nonlinear programming) is that they have a single objective function. This implies that all the managerial objectives for the problem being studied can be encompassed within a single overriding objective, such as maximizing total profit or minimizing total cost. However, this is not always possible, as you have just seen in the Dewright case study.

When managing a for-profit organization, the managerial objectives might well include some of the following:

1. Maintain stable profits.
2. Increase market share.
3. Diversify the product line.

4. Maintain stable prices.

5. Improve worker morale.

6. Maintain family control of the business.

7. Increase company prestige.

These objectives are so different in nature that it really is not realistic to combine them into a single overriding objective. Instead, analysis of the problem of concern requires individual consideration of the separate objectives.

Weighted goal programming provides a way of striving toward several such objectives simultaneously. The basic approach is to establish a specific numeric goal for each of the objectives and then to seek a solution that balances how close this solution comes to each of these goals. Penalty weights are assigned to the objectives to measure the relative seriousness of missing their numeric goals. An objective function is formulated for each of the objectives. The overall objective is to minimize the weighted sum of deviations of these objective functions from their respective goals. Assuming that all the individual objective functions and the constraints of the problem fit the format for linear programming, the overall problem then can be formulated as a linear programming problem.

Now let us see how Dewright's management science team does this for the case study introduced in the preceding section.

> A numeric goal is established for each managerial objective and then penalty weights are assigned to measure the relative seriousness of missing these goals.

Formulation of a Weighted Goal-Programming Model for the Dewright Co. Problem

The decisions that need to be made for the Dewright Co. problem are the production rates for the three new products that will be introduced soon. Therefore, the decision variables are

P_1 = Number of units of product 1 to produce per day

P_2 = Number of units of product 2 to produce per day

P_3 = Number of units of product 3 to produce per day

Using the unit contributions given in Table 11.2, the three goals can be expressed in terms of these decision variables as

Goal 1: $12P_1 + 9P_2 + 15P_3 \geq 125$ (Total profit goal)

Goal 2: $5P_1 + 3P_2 + 4P_3 = 40$ (Employment level goal)

Goal 3: $5P_1 + 7P_2 + 8P_3 \leq 55$ (Capital investment goal)

These mathematical expressions for the goals look like linear programming constraints. However, they cannot be used as constraints in a mathematical model because constraints definitely must be satisfied whereas Dewright management already has concluded that it probably will not be possible to attain all these goals simultaneously. For a goal-programming model, the overall objective instead is to come as close as possible to satisfying all these goals simultaneously.

More precisely, using the penalty weights given in Table 11.1, let

W = Weighted sum of deviations from the goals

= Number of penalty points incurred by missing the goals

> This weighted sum of deviations from the goals will become the target cell for the spreadsheet model.

For each goal that is missed, the number of penalty points incurred is the penalty weight *times* the deviation from the goal. Therefore, the overall objective then is to choose the values of P_1, P_2, and P_3 so as to

Minimize $W = 5$ (amount under goal 1) $+ 2$ (amount over goal 2)
$+ 4$ (amount under goal 2) $+ 3$ (amount over goal 3)

where no penalty points are incurred for being over goal 1 (exceeding the target for total profit is fine) or for being under goal 3 (underexpending the capital investment budget is satisfactory).

FIGURE 11.1
A spreadsheet model for the Dewright Co. weighted goal-programming problem formulated as a linear programming problem, where the changing cells UnitsProduced (C12:E12) show the optimal production rates and the changing cells Deviations (J6:K8) show the optimal amounts over and under the goals. The target cell WeightedSumOfDeviations (M13) gives the resulting weighted sum of deviations from the goals.

	A	B	C	D	E	F	G	H	I	J	K	L	M	N	O
1	**Dewright Co. Goal Programming (Weighted)**														
2															
3						**Goals**				**Deviations**			**Constraints**		
4			**Contribution per Unit Produced**			Level				Amount	Amount		Balance		
5			Product 1	Product 2	Product 3	Achieved		Goal		Over	Under		(Level – Over + Under)		Goal
6		Goal 1 (Profit)	12	9	15	125	≥	125		0	0		125	=	125
7		Goal 2 (Employment)	5	3	4	48.33333	=	40		8.333	0		40	=	40
8		Goal 3 (Investment)	5	7	8	55	≤	55		0	0		55	=	55
9															
10															
11			Product 1	Product 2	Product 3			**Penalty**		Over	Under		Weighted Sum		
12		**Units Produced**	8.333	0	1.667			**Weights**		Goal	Goal		of Deviations		
13								Profit			5		16.667		
14								Employment		2	4				
15								Investment		3					

Solver Parameters

Set Target Cell: WeightedSum

Equal To: ○ Max ◉ Min ○

By Changing Cells:

UnitsProduced,Deviations

Subject to the Constraints:

Balance = Goal

Solver Options

☑ Assume Linear Model

☑ Assume Non-Negative

	F
4	Level
5	Achieved
6	=SUMPRODUCT(C6:E6,UnitsProduced)
7	=SUMPRODUCT(C7:E7,UnitsProduced)
8	=SUMPRODUCT(C8:E8,UnitsProduced)

	M	N	O
4	Balance		
5	(Level − Over + Under)		Goal
6	=LevelAchieved − AmountOver+AmountUnder	=	=Goal
7	=LevelAchieved − AmountOver+AmountUnder	=	=Goal
8	=LevelAchieved − AmountOver+AmountUnder	=	=Goal

Range Name	Cells
AmountOver	J6:J8
AmountUnder	K6:K8
Balance	M6:M8
Deviations	J6:K8
Goal	H6:H8
LevelAchieved	F6:F8
PenaltyWeights	J13:K15
UnitsProduced	C12:E12
WeightedSumOfDeviations	M13

	M
11	Weighted Sum
12	of Deviations
13	=SUMPRODUCT(PenaltyWeights,Deviations)

Figure 11.1 shows one way of formulating the spreadsheet model for this problem. Three of the changing cells UnitsProduced (C12:E12) display the values of the decision variables (P_1, P_2, and P_3). Given these values, the equations entered into LevelAchieved (F6:F8) provide the levels achieved toward meeting the goals expressed in columns B, G, and H.

The most subtle part of this formulation involves columns, J, K, M, and O. Deviations (J6:K8) are additional changing cells that display the decisions on the amounts over and amounts under the respective goals. WeightedSumOfDeviations (M13) is the target cell giving the value of *W*, where the Solver dialogue box specifies that the objective is to minimize this value. Using the expression for *W* given earlier, the equation entered into this target cell is the SUMPRODUCT of the data cells PenaltyWeights (J13:K15) and the changing cells Deviations (J6:K8).

This way of formulating the model makes it a linear programming model.

The Solver options selected at the bottom of Figure 11.1 specify that this model now has been formulated in a way that fits linear programming (which enables solving the model) and that all the changing cells need to be nonnegative. There are no constraints involving the output cells LevelAchieved (F6:F8) since these cell values are not required to fully satisfy the goals specified in columns B, G, and H. However, the output cells Balance (M6:M8) do need to satisfy the constraints specified by the Solver dialogue box, Balance (M6:M8) = Goal (H6:H8).

These constraints play the key role of ensuring that the changing cells Deviations (J6:K8) will equal the amounts by which LevelAchieved (F6:F8) deviate from the goals. To see why, note that the equations entered into Balance (M6:M8) are

$$\text{Balance (M6:M8)} = \text{LevelAchieved (F6:F8)} - \text{AmountOver (J6:J8)} + \text{AmountUnder (K6:K8)}$$

Therefore, the constraints that Balance (M6:M8) = Goal (H6:H8) require that

$$\text{Goal (H6:H8)} = \text{LevelAchieved (F6:F8)} - \text{AmountOver (J6:J8)} + \text{AmountUnder (K6:K8)}$$

To minimize the target cell, the smallest nonnegative values of AmountOver (J6:J8) and AmountUnder (K6:K8) that satisfy these equations will need to be chosen. Consequently, in any row where LevelAchieved deviates from Goal, either AmountOver or AmountUnder will equal this deviation (which one depends on whether it is a positive or negative deviation) and the other one will have a value of 0.

Clicking on the Solve button yields the optimal solution for all the changing cells shown in Figure 11.1. Since the units being used in the spreadsheet are those given in the first column of Table 11.2, this solution thereby provides the following:

Production rate for product 1 = 8⅓ units per day

Production rate for product 2 = 0

Production rate for product 3 = 1⅔ units per day

Total profit = $125 million

Employment level = 4,833 employees

Capital investment = $55 million

The only deviation from management's goals is the one considered least serious (exceeding the employment level goal of 4,000 employees).

Review Questions

1. What is the one common characteristic of the management science models introduced in previous chapters that is *not* possessed by goal-programming problems?

2. What is the basic approach of goal programming?

3. What is represented by the objective function in a goal-programming model?

4. What is shown by the changing cells (other than those displaying the values of the decision variables for the original problem) in the spreadsheet model for a goal-programming problem?

5. To enable solving a goal-programming problem, it can be formulated to fit what kind of spreadsheet model?

11.3 PREEMPTIVE GOAL PROGRAMMING

Goal programming provides two distinct approaches for dealing with managerial problems where multiple goals need to be considered. The approach described in the preceding section, weighted goal programming, is designed for problems where all the goals are quite important with only modest differences in importance that can be measured by assigning weights to these goals. We now turn to the other approach, preemptive goal programming.

The preemptive goal-programming approach is to list the goals in the order of their importance and then to focus on each goal one at a time in this order.

This second approach is used when there are such major differences in the importance of the goals that it is not feasible to assign meaningful weights to these goals to measure their relative importance. Therefore, the goals are instead listed in the order of their importance. Preemptive goal programming then begins by focusing solely on meeting the most important goal as closely as possible, and next doing the same for the second most important goal, and so on through the rest of the goals in order. Thus, while this approach is focusing on one of the goals, it is preempting any consideration yet of less important goals.

One advantage of this approach is that it is less difficult for management to assess the order of importance of its goals than to assign weights to the goals to measure their relative importance. It is not easy to get a handle on what the penalty weights should be for deviations from the goals when these goals are as disparate as those for the Dewright Co. problem. Assessing the order of importance is a much more concrete task. Another advantage is that the process of focusing on one goal at a time in the order of its importance is intuitive and readily understood. Management has more confidence in the output of a model when it has confidence in both the validity of its input and the process involved in obtaining the output.

Preemptive goal programming is easier to implement than weighted goal programming.

There are situations where the features of both approaches perhaps should be combined to analyze the problem. This occurs when the goals can be divided into groups where the goals within each group are of comparable importance but there are great differences between the groups in their level of importance. In this kind of situation, weighted goal programming can be used within each group in turn while preemptive goal programming is being applied to deal with each group in order of importance. However, we will not delve further into this more advanced subject.

The spreadsheet models employed by weighted goal programming and preemptive goal programming for the same problem are quite similar. The major difference is in their target cells. Rather than using the weighted sum of deviations from the goals as the target cell to be minimized, preemptive goal programming begins by minimizing only the deviation from the most important goal. When this is completed, the second step is to add a constraint that the minimal deviation achieved must continue to be met while switching to minimizing the deviation from the second most important goal. Next, a second constraint is added that the minimal deviation achieved for this second most important goal must continue to be met while switching to minimizing the deviation from the third most important goal. This process continues until all the goals have been considered.

Each time the focus turns to the next goal, the target cell changes to the deviation from that goal. Constraints require no reduction in the progress toward the goals previously considered.

Now let us continue the Dewright Co. case study to see how this approach is applied in that context.

The Application of Preemptive Goal Programming to the Dewright Co. Problem

Dewright's Management Science Department already has applied a weighted goal-programming model to the problem described in Section 11.1 and obtained the results shown in Figure 11.1. However, recall that when the head of this department (Kathleen Donaldson) and key members of her team met with top management to discuss this problem, it was agreed that the preemptive goal-programming approach would be applied as well.

During this meeting, the company's CEO (Gary Lang) had clearly identified the order of importance of the goals, as summarized below.

Priority 1: Strive to achieve a total profit (net present value) from the three new products of at least $125 million (Goal 1).

Priority 2: Strive to avoid decreasing the employment level below 4,000 employees (the under part of Goal 2).

Priority 3: Strive to hold the capital investment down to no more than $55 million (Goal 3).

Priority 4: Strive to avoid increasing the employment level above 4,000 employees (the over part of Goal 2).

Thus, this is the order in which Kathleen and her team will address the four goals.

Figure 11.2 shows the spreadsheet model for focusing on the Priority 1 goal. This model is identical to the weighted goal-programming model in Figure 11.1 except for deleting Penalty-Weights (J13:K15) and changing the target cell. Because the objective at this point is to minimize the amount under Goal 1 (a profit of at least $125 million), the target cell now is Under-Goal1 (K6). This again is a linear programming model and so is easily solved.

The changing cells in Figure 11.2 show the solution obtained after clicking on the Solve button. This actually is only one of numerous optimal solutions that will yield a value of 0 for the target cell, so the next steps will focus on identifying which of these solutions will do the best job in striving toward the lower priority goals as well.

The second step is to focus on the Priority 2 goal of minimizing UnderGoal2 (K7). However, this cell already has a value of 0 in Figure 11.2, so this goal already is fully achieved along with the Priority 1 goal by the solution shown in this figure (and many other solutions).

Thus, we can immediately go on to the third step of focusing on the Priority 3 goal (do not exceed a capital investment of $55 million). Figure 11.3 shows the revised spreadsheet model for this step. The target cell now is OverGoal3 (J8). The other key revision is the addition of the constraints, UnderGoal1 (K6) = 0 and UnderGoal2 (K7) = 0, in the Solver dialogue box (and also displayed in cells J11:K12). The changing cells in this figure show the optimal solution obtained after clicking on the Solve button. Once again, a value of 0 has been obtained in the new target cell.

The fourth and final goal is to focus on the Priority 4 goal of minimizing OverGoal2 (J7), as shown in Figure 11.4. The constraint, OverGoal3 (J8) = 0, now has been added to the constraints that were introduced at the preceding step, UnderGoal1 (K6) = 0 and UnderGoal2 (K7) = 0. Clicking on the Solve button provides the optimal solution displayed in the changing cells along with a value of 8.3333 in the target cell.

Note that this solution is the same as the one in Figure 11.3. Thus, the revised model in Figure 11.4 did not succeed in making any more progress in striving toward the Priority 4 goal. However, this solution has fully achieved the top three priority goals, so this is an excellent outcome.

Also note that the solution in Figures 11.3 and 11.4 is identical to the one in Figure 11.1 that was obtained by using weighted goal programming. This provides additional assurance that this is the solution that best meets management's needs.

Epilogue to the Dewright Co. Case Study

Exactly one month after their first meeting, Gary Lang called the same group together again to hear the report of the management science team. The night before, Kathleen Donaldson had made sure that all the parties received the team's written report via courier service. Based on both the above analysis and that in the preceding section, the report recommended that the company focus most of its efforts on producing and marketing large quantities of Product 1 ($P_1 = 8\frac{1}{3}$), while providing some diversification with a much smaller output of Product 3 ($P_3 = 1\frac{2}{3}$). Another recommendation was that any production of Product 2 be postponed indefinitely ($P_2 = 0$), but that further development work be done on this product to see if it could be made sufficiently attractive for release with the next generation of products. The report then highlighted the fact that this plan would enable meeting all of management's more important goals.

Everybody had read the written report with this wonderful news before entering the meeting. This completely changed the mood from the usual one that Kathleen encountered when presenting an oral report and recommendations to Dewright management. Gone were the usual probing and skeptical questioning of the presentation. (In the privacy of her home with her husband Scott,

At each step of the process, the current spreadsheet model always is a linear programming model.

FIGURE 11.2 A spreadsheet model formulated as a linear programming model for the first step of the Dewright Co. preemptive goal-programming problem. Since Priority 1 is to minimize the deviation under Goal 1, the target cell is UnderGoal1 (K6) for this step. The changing cells UnitsProduced (C12:E12) show the resulting production rates and the other changing cells Deviations (J6:K8) show the resulting amounts over and under the goals after clicking on the Solve button. Since Priority 2 is to minimize UnderGoal2 (K7), which already has a value of 0, the procedure next will bypass step 2 and go directly to step 3.

	A	B	C	D	E	F	G	H	I	J	K	L	M	N	O
1		**Dewright Co. Goal Programming (Preemptive Priority 1: Minimize under Goal 1)**													
2															
3											Deviations		Constraints		
4			**Contribution per Unit Produced**			Goals				Amount	Amount		Balance		
5			Product 1	Product 2	Product 3	Level Achieved		Goal		Over	Under		(Level − Over + Under)		Goal
6		Goal 1 (Profit)	12	9	15	125	≥	125		0	0		125	=	125
7		Goal 2 (Employment)	5	3	4	40	=	40		0	0		40	=	40
8		Goal 3 (Investment)	5	7	8	61.481	≤	55		6.481	0		55	=	55
9															
10											Minimize (Under Goal 1)				
11			Product 1	Product 2	Product 3								Weighted Sum		
12		**Units Produced**	3.704	0	5.370								of Deviations		

	F
4	Level
5	Achieved
6	=SUMPRODUCT(C6:E6,UnitsProduced)
7	=SUMPRODUCT(C7:E7,UnitsProduced)
8	=SUMPRODUCT(C8:E8,UnitsProduced)

	M	N	O
4	Balance		
5	(Level − Over + Under)		Goal
6	=LevelAchieved − AmountOver+AmountUnder	=	=Goal
7	=LevelAchieved − AmountOver+AmountUnder	=	=Goal
8	=LevelAchieved − AmountOver+AmountUnder	=	=Goal

Range Name	Cells
AmountOver	J6:J8
AmountUnder	K6:K8
Balance	M6:M8
Deviations	J6:K8
Goal	H6:H8
LevelAchieved	F6:F8
OverGoal1	J6
OverGoal2	J7
OverGoal3	J8
UnderGoal1	K6
UnderGoal2	K7
UnderGoal3	K8
UnitsProduced	C12:E12

Solver Parameters

Set Target Cell: UnderGoal1
Equal To: ○ Max ● Min
By Changing Cells:
UnitsProduced,Deviations

Subject to the Constraints:
Balance = Goal

Solver Options
☑ Assume Linear Model
☑ Assume Non-Negative

FIGURE 11.3 The revision of the spreadsheet model in Figure 11.2 needed to perform step 3 of the preemptive goal-programming procedure. Since Priority 3 is to minimize the deviation over Goal 3, the target cell is OverGoal3 (J8). Constraints that UnderGoal1 (K6) = 0 and UnderGoal2 (K7) = 0 also have been added to the model. The changing cells show the results after clicking on the Solve button.

	A	B	C	D	E	F	G	H	I	J	K	L	M	N	O
1		Dewright Co. Goal Programming (Preemptive Priority 3: Minimize under Goal 3)													
2															
3								Goals		Deviations			Constraints		
4				Contribution per Unit Produced									Balance		
5			Product 1	Product 2	Product 3	Level Achieved		Goal		Amount Over	Amount Under		(Level − Over + Under)		Goal
6		Goal 1 (Profit)	12	9	15	125	≥	125		0	0		125	=	125
7		Goal 2 (Employment)	5	3	4	48.3333	=	40		8.3333	0		40	=	40
8		Goal 3 (Investment)	5	7	8	55.000	≤	55		0.000	0		55	=	55
9															
10										Minimize (Over Goal 3)					
11			Product 1	Product 2	Product 3					(Under Goal 1) = 0					
12		Units Produced	8.333	0	1.667					(Under Goal 2) = 0					

	F
4	Level
5	Achieved
6	=SUMPRODUCT(C6:E6,UnitsProduced)
7	=SUMPRODUCT(C7:E7,UnitsProduced)
8	=SUMPRODUCT(C8:E8,UnitsProduced)

	M	N	O
4	Balance		
5	(Level − Over + Under)		Goal
6	=LevelAchieved − AmountOver+AmountUnder	=	=Goal
7	=LevelAchieved − AmountOver+AmountUnder	=	=Goal
8	=LevelAchieved − AmountOver+AmountUnder	=	=Goal

Range Name	Cells
AmountOver	J6:J8
AmountUnder	K6:K8
Balance	M6:M8
Deviations	J6:K8
Goal	H6:H8
LevelAchieved	F6:F8
OverGoal1	J6
OverGoal2	J7
OverGoal3	J8
UnderGoal1	K6
UnderGoal2	K7
UnderGoal3	K8
UnitsProduced	C12:E12

Solver Parameters

Set Target Cell: OverGoal3

Equal To: ○ Max ● Min

By Changing Cells:

UnitsProduced,Deviations

Subject to the Constraints:

Balance = Goal
UnderGoal1 = 0
UnderGoal2 = 0

Solver Options

☑ Assume Linear Model
☑ Assume Non-Negative

505

FIGURE 11.4 The revision of the spreadsheet model in Figure 11.3 needed to perform step 4 of the preemptive goal-programming procedure. Since Priority 4 is to minimize the deviation over Goal 2, the target cell is OverGoal2 (J7) for this step. One more constraint, OverGoal3 (J8) = 0, also has been added to the model. Since this is the final step, the changing cells show the optimal solution obtained for Dewright's preemptive goal-programming problem by clicking on the Solve button.

	A	B	C	D	E	F	G	H	I	J	K	L	M	N	O
1		**Dewright Co. Goal Programming (Preemptive Priority 4: Minimize over Goal 2)**													
2															
3				**Contribution per Unit Produced**			**Goals**			**Deviations**			**Constraints**		
4										Amount	Amount				
5			Product 1	Product 2	Product 3	Level Achieved		Goal		Over	Under		Balance (Level − Over + Under)		Goal
6		Goal 1 (Profit)	12	9	15	125	≥	125		0	0		125	=	125
7		Goal 2 (Employment)	5	3	4	48.3333	=	40		8.3333	0		40	=	40
8		Goal 3 (Investment)	5	7	8	55.000	≤	55		0.000	0		55	=	55
9															
10										Minimize (Over Goal 2)					
11			Product 1	Product 2	Product 3					(Under Goal 1) = 0					
12		**Units Produced**	8.333	0	1.667					(Under Goal 2) = 0					
13										(Over Goal 3) = 0					

	F
4	Level
5	Achieved
6	=SUMPRODUCT(C6:E6,UnitsProduced)
7	=SUMPRODUCT(C7:E7,UnitsProduced)
8	=SUMPRODUCT(C8:E8,UnitsProduced)

	M	N	O
4	Balance		
5	(Level − Over + Under)		Goal
6	=LevelAchieved − AmountOver+AmountUnder	=	=Goal
7	=LevelAchieved − AmountOver+AmountUnder	=	=Goal
8	=LevelAchieved − AmountOver+AmountUnder	=	=Goal

Range Name	Cells
AmountOver	J6:J8
AmountUnder	K6:K8
Balance	M6:M8
Deviations	J6:K8
Goal	H6:H8
LevelAchieved	F6:F8
OverGoal1	J6
OverGoal2	J7
OverGoal3	J8
UnderGoal1	K6
UnderGoal2	K7
UnderGoal3	K8
UnitsProduced	C12:E12

Solver Parameters

Set Target Cell: OverGoal2

Equal To: ○ Max ● Min

By Changing Cells:

UnitsProduced,Deviations

Subject to the Constraints:

Balance = Goal
OverGoal3 = 0
UnderGoal1 = 0
UnderGoal2 = 0

Solver Options

☑ Assume Linear Model
☑ Assume Non-Negative

Kathleen referred to these sessions as her inquisitions.) Also missing was the zealous guarding of territory by some Dewright managers that Kathleen had observed in the past. (Kathleen marveled to Scott afterward that she actually spotted Tasha and Vijay smiling at each other for the first time in months.) Vijay did suggest, with nods all around, that some of the new employees be brought in as "temps" (temporary workers) and that the development of the next generation of new products be accelerated a little to try to avoid any future layoffs of permanent employees. Otherwise, the presentation was virtually uninterrupted. Following a quick pro forma vote to approve the plan recommended by the management science team, Gary had champagne brought in. He then offered a toast to the very fine work done by Kathleen and her team.

Thus began a very good year for the Dewright Company. However, some very rocky times—and managerial changes—awaited the company further down the road. Shortly before the downturn, Kathleen left Dewright to head up her own management science consulting firm. Her firm is doing very well.

Review Questions

1. When should preemptive goal programming be used instead of weighted goal programming?

2. How does the preemptive goal-programming approach differ from the weighted goal-programming approach?

3. What is the major difference between the spreadsheet models employed by weighted goal-programming and preemptive goal programming for the same problem?

4. After considering the first goal, what additional constraint needs to be added during each step of the preemptive goal-programming approach when attention is turned to the next goal?

5. How many of the top-priority goals for the Dewright Co. problem did preemptive goal programming succeed in fully achieving?

11.4 Summary

Most management science models make the basic assumption that a single objective function is available that encompasses the overriding objective of management for the problem. However, management sometimes will instead have a variety of rather different objectives that require separate consideration. As illustrated by the Dewright Co. case study, *goal programming* provides some ways of striving toward several such objectives simultaneously.

One basic approach, called weighted goal programming, is to establish a specific numeric goal for each of the objectives and then to seek a solution that balances how close it comes to each of these goals. By introducing some new variables (changing cells) that represent the amounts over or under the respective goals, this approach leads to formulating a model where the objective is to minimize the weighted sum of the deviations from the goals.

The other basic approach, called preemptive goal programming, begins by listing the goals in the order of their importance. It then focuses on one goal at a time in this order. While focusing on a particular goal, the model uses the objective of minimizing the deviation from that goal. The model also includes constraints that require that there be no reduction in the progress toward the goals previously considered.

With either approach, the current model often can be formulated to be a linear programming model, in which case it can be solved very readily. Thus, goal programming often provides a practical way of striving toward various managerial goals simultaneously while giving higher priority to the more important goals.

Glossary

goal programming   A technique designed to find the best way of striving toward several goals. (Section 11.1), *495*

penalty weights   Values assigned to the goals of a weighted goal-programming problem that measure the relative seriousness of missing these goals. (Sections 11.1 and 11.2), *498*

preemptive goal programming   A type of goal programming that focuses on one goal at a time in order of importance while preempting any consideration yet of less important goals. (Sections 11.1 and 11.3), *496*

weighted goal programming   A type of goal programming that assigns penalty weights to the various goals and then seeks a solution that minimizes the weighted sum of the deviations from the goals. (Sections 11.1 and 11.2), *496*

Learning Aids for This Chapter in Your MS Courseware

Chapter 11 Excel Files:

Dewright, Weighted Goal Programming
Dewright Preemptive Goal Programming (three spreadsheets)

An Excel Add-in:

Premium Solver for Education

Problems

To the left of each of the following problems (or their parts), we have inserted an E* whenever Excel should be used (unless your instructor gives you contrary instructions). An asterisk on the problem number indicates that at least a partial answer is given in the back of the book.

11.1.* One of management's goals in a goal-programming problem is to maintain the company's employment level next year at its current level of 60 full-time equivalents (60 FTEs). Each FTE under this goal is considered three times as serious as each FTE over the goal. Suppose that the *amount over* appears in cell K7 of the spreadsheet model and the *amount under* appears in cell L7. (Both cells are changing cells.) What is the relationship between the coefficients of K7 and L7 in the equation entered into the target cell?

11.2. Management of the Albert Franko Co. has established goals for the market share it wants each of the company's two new products to capture in their respective markets. Specifically, management wants product 1 to capture at least 15 percent of its market and product 2 to capture at least 10 percent of its market. Three advertising campaigns are being planned to try to achieve these market shares. One is targeted directly on the first product. The second targets the second product. The third is intended to enhance the general reputation of the company and its products. Letting x_1, x_2, and x_3 be the amount of money allocated (in millions of dollars) to these respective campaigns, the resulting market share (expressed as a percentage) for the two products are estimated to be

Market share for product 1 $= 0.5x_1 + 0.2x_3$

Market share for product 2 $= 0.3x_2 + 0.2x_3$

A total of $55 million is available for the three advertising campaigns, but management wants at least $10 million devoted to the third campaign. If both market share goals cannot be achieved, management considers each 1 percent decrease in the market share from the goal to be equally serious for the two products. In this light, management wants to know how to most effectively allocate the available money to the three campaigns.

a. Describe why this problem is a weighted goal-programming problem by giving quantitative expressions for the goals and the overall objective.

E* *b.* Formulate and solve this problem as a linear programming model on a spreadsheet.

c. Interpret this solution to management in its language.

11.3.* The Research and Development Division of the Emax Corporation has developed three new products. A decision now needs to be made on which mix of these products should be produced. Management wants primary consideration given to three factors: total profit, stability in the work force, and achieving an increase in the company's earnings next year from the $75 million achieved this year. In particular, using the units given in the following table, they want to

$$\text{Maximize} \quad M = P - 6C - 3D$$

where

M = Overall measure of performance combining the three factors

P = Total (discounted) profit over the life of the new products

C = Change (in either direction) in the current level of employment

D = Decrease (if any) in next year's earnings from the current year's level

The amount of any increase in earnings does not enter into M, because management is concerned primarily with just achieving some increase to keep the stockholders happy. (It has mixed feelings about a large increase that then would be difficult to surpass in subsequent years.)

The impact of each of the new products (per unit rate of production) on each of these factors is shown in the following table:

| | **Unit Contribution of Product** | | | | |
Factor	1	2	3	Goal	(Units)
Total profit	20	15	25	Maximize	(millions of dollars)
Employment level	6	4	5	= 50	(hundreds of employees)
Earnings next year	8	7	5	≥ 75	(millions of dollars)

E*   *a.* Formulate and solve a spreadsheet model for this problem.

     b. Interpret this solution to management in its language.

11.4.   Reconsider the Dewright Co. case study as presented in Sections 11.1 and 11.2. After further reflection about the optimal solution obtained by using weighted goal programming, management now is asking some what-if questions.

     a. Gary Lang wonders what would happen if the penalty weights in the rightmost column of Table 11.1 were to be changed to 7, 4, 1, and 3, respectively. Would you expect the optimal solution to change? Why?

E*   *b.* Tasha Johnson is wondering what would happen if the total profit goal were to be increased to wanting at least $140 million (without any change in the original penalty weights). Solve the revised model with this change.

E*   *c.* Solve the revised model if both Gary's and Tasha's changes are made.

11.5.   Montega is a developing country that has 15,000,000 acres of publicly controlled agricultural land in active use. Its government currently is planning a way to divide this land among three basic crops (labeled 1, 2, and 3) next year. A certain percentage of each of these crops is exported to obtain badly needed foreign capital (dollars), and the rest of each of these crops is used to feed the populace. Raising these crops also provides employment for a significant proportion of the population. Therefore, the main factors to be considered in allocating the land to these crops are (1) the amount of foreign capital generated, (2) the number of citizens fed, and (3) the number of citizens employed in raising these crops. The following table shows how much each 1,000 acres of each crop contributes toward these factors, and the last column gives the goal established by the government for each of these factors.

| | **Contribution per 1,000 Acres of Crop** | | | |
Factor	1	2	3	Goal
Foreign capital	$3,000	$5,000	$4,000	≥ $70 million
Citizens fed	150	75	100	≥ 1,750,000
Citizens employed	10	15	12	= 200,000

In evaluating the relative seriousness of *not* achieving these goals, the government has concluded that the following deviations from the goals should be considered *equally undesirable:* (1) each $100 under the foreign-capital goal, (2) each person under the citizens-fed goal, and (3) each deviation of one (in either direction) from the citizens-employed goal.

     a. Describe why this problem is a weighted goal-programming problem by giving quantitative expressions for the goals and the overall objective.

E*   *b.* Formulate and solve this problem as a linear programming model on a spreadsheet.

     c. Interpret this solution to management in its language.

E*11.6.   Reconsider the scenario described in Problem 11.5. The unemployment rate in Montega is rising and the shortage of foreign capital is becoming a more serious problem. Therefore, the Montega government now has decided that it needs to place higher priority on increasing employment and increasing foreign capital than on its other goals. Specifically, it has established the following order of priorities for its goals.

Priority 1:	Citizens employed	$\geq 200{,}000$
Priority 2:	Foreign capital	$\geq \$70$ million
Priority 3:	Citizens fed	$\geq 1{,}750{,}000$
Priority 4:	Citizens employed	$\leq 200{,}000$

Use preemptive goal programming to determine how the government should allocate the publicly controlled agricultural land to the three basic crops.

E*11.7. The city council of Aberdeen must determine the tax policy for the city for the coming year. Four types of taxes are used to raise money:

- Property tax
- Sales tax (a surcharge on the state sales tax)
- Entertainment tax
- Utility tax (on city-owned utilities)

The city consists of three groups of people: low income, middle income, and high income. The amount of revenue (in thousands of dollars) raised from each group by setting a particular tax at a 1 percent level is given in the following table. (For example, a 3 percent sales tax will raise $1.2 million from low-income people.)

	Thousands of Dollars Collected per 1% Tax Rate			
Income Group	**Property Tax**	**Sales Tax**	**Entertainment Tax**	**Utility Tax**
Low-income	600	400	50	100
Middle-income	800	350	100	120
High-income	1,200	250	120	80

The city council has decided that the tax policy must satisfy the following restrictions.

- The tax burden on middle-income people cannot exceed $2.5 million.
- The tax burden on high-income people cannot exceed $2.3 million.
- The total revenue raised must exceed the current level of $6 million.
- The sales tax must be between 1 percent and 3 percent.

Given these restrictions, the city council has set the following three goals (listed in order of priority):

- Goal 1: Limit the tax burden on low-income people to no more than $2 million.
- Goal 2: Set the property tax rate at no less than 1 percent.
- If their tax burden becomes too high, 20 percent of the low-income people, 20 percent of the middle-income people, and 40 percent of the high-income people may consider moving. This will start to happen if the total tax burden of this subset of the population exceeds $1.5 million. Goal 3 is thus to limit the total tax burden on this group of people to no more than $1.5 million.

  a. Use preemptive goal programming to determine how the various tax rates should be set.

  b. Use weighted goal programming to determine how the various tax rates should be set when using the following penalty weights: 1 per $1,000 in excess of goal 1; 90 per 1 percent short of goal 2; and 1 per $1,000 in excess of goal 3.

E*11.8. Reconsider the scenario described in Problem 11.2. Management of the Albert Franko Co. now has decided that it should give higher priority to the goal of having product 2 capture at least 10 percent of its market than to the goal of having product 1 capture at least 15 percent of its market. Use preemptive goal programming to determine how to most effectively allocate the available money to the three advertising campaigns.

E*11.9. Reconsider the Dewright Co. case study introduced in Section 11.1. Vijay Shah (vice president for manufacturing) still feels that the top-priority goal should be retaining the employment level at 4,000 employees (avoiding a deviation in either direction) and that satisfactory profits will then follow. Therefore, he places second priority on the goal of holding the capital investment down to no more than $55 million and places only third priority on the goal of achieving a total profit of at least $125 million. Apply preemptive goal programming to the Dewright problem using this revised order of priorities.

E*11.10. The admissions committee for the Whartvard Business School will be making its decisions regarding which applicants to admit to its MBA program for the coming year. In addition to considering each applicant on his or her own merit, the committee also needs to take three policy guidelines into account. One guideline is that, although a relatively low GMAT total score should not disqualify an applicant if other factors are very positive, the average GMAT total score for the entire MBA class should be reasonably high. (About 85 percent of all individuals taking the GMAT receive a total score below 650, but Whartvard is such a selective school that it considers anything below 650 to be a low score.) A second guideline is that the number of men and number of women in the MBA class should not be too badly out of balance. The third guideline is that the class should include a substantial number of students who are at least 30 years old, since they bring considerable work experience and maturity into the mix.

The committee now has divided both the male applicants and female applicants into three categories according to whether they have high, medium, or low GMAT total scores. The following table shows the number of applicants whose age is under 30 and at least 30 in each category.

Category	Average GMAT Total Score	Number Whose Age Is under 30	Number Whose Age Is at Least 30
High men	720	120	32
High women	720	28	4
Medium men	670	104	56
Medium women	670	32	32
Low men	620	40	40
Low women	620	32	48

The admissions committee has set four goals for this entering MBA class, in the following order of priority:

Goal 1: The entering class should include at least 240 students.

Goal 2: The entering class should have an average GMAT total score of at least 690.

Goal 3: The entering class should consist of at least 35 percent women.

Goal 4: At least 120 members of the entering class should be at least 30 years old.

Based on past experience, 60 percent of all applicants who are admitted will accept admission.

Use preemptive goal programming to determine approximately how many applicants to admit from each category.

Case 11-1

A Cure for Cuba

Fulgencio Batista led Cuba with a cold heart and iron fist—greedily stealing from poor citizens, capriciously ruling the Cuban population that looked to him for guidance, and violently murdering the innocent critics of his politics. In 1958, tired of watching his fellow Cubans suffer from corruption and tyranny, Fidel Castro led a guerrilla attack against the Batista regime and wrested power from Batista in January 1959. Cubans, along with members of the international community, believed that political and economic freedom had finally triumphed on the island. The next two years showed, however, that Castro was leading a Communist dictatorship—killing his political opponents and nationalizing all privately held assets. The United States responded to Castro's leadership in 1961 by invoking a trade embargo against Cuba. The embargo forbade any country from selling Cuban products in the United States and forbade businesses from selling American products to Cuba. Cubans did not feel the true impact of the embargo until 1989 when the Soviet economy collapsed. Prior to the disintegration of the Soviet Union, Cuba had received an average of $5 billion in annual economic assistance from the Soviet Union. With the disappearance of the economy that Cuba had almost exclusively depended upon for trade, Cubans had few avenues from which to purchase food, clothes, and medicine. The avenues narrowed even further when the United States passed the Torricelli Act in 1992 that forbade American subsidiaries in third world countries from doing business with Cuba that had been worth a total of $700 million annually.

Since 1989, the Cuban economy has certainly felt the impact from decades of frozen trade. Today poverty ravages the island of Cuba. Families do not have money to purchase bare necessities, such as food, milk, and clothing. Children die from malnutrition or exposure. Disease infects the island because medicine is unavailable. Optical neuritis, tuberculosis, pneumonia, and influenza run rampant among the population.

Few Americans hold sympathy for Cuba, but Robert Baker, director of Helping Hand, leads a handful of tender souls on Capitol Hill who cannot bear to see politics destroy so many human lives. His organization distributes humanitarian aid annually to needy countries around the world. Mr. Baker recognizes the dire situation in Cuba, and he wants to allocate aid to Cuba for the coming year.

Mr. Baker wants to send numerous aid packages to Cuban citizens. Three different types of packages are available. The basic package contains only food, such as grain and powdered milk. Each basic package costs $300, weighs 120 pounds, and aids 30 people. The advanced package contains food and clothing, such as blankets and fabrics. Each advanced package costs $350, weighs 180 pounds, and aids 35 people. The supreme package contains food, clothing, and medicine. Each supreme package costs $720, weighs 220 pounds, and aids 54 people.

Mr. Baker has several goals he wants to achieve when deciding upon the number and types of aid packages to allocate to Cuba. First, he wants to aid at least 20 percent of Cuba's 11 million citizens. Second, because disease runs rampant among the Cuban population, he wants at least 3,000 of the aid packages sent to Cuba to be the supreme packages. Third, because he knows many other nations also require humanitarian aid, he wants to keep the cost of aiding Cuba below $20 million.

Mr. Baker places different levels of importance on his three goals. He believes the most important goal is keeping costs down since low costs mean that his organization is able to aid a larger number of needy nations. He decides to penalize his plan by one point for every $1 million above his $20 million goal. He believes the second most important goal is ensuring that at least 3,000 of the aid packages sent to Cuba are supreme packages since he does not want to see an epidemic develop and completely destroy the Cuban population. He decides to penalize his plan by one point for every 1,000 packages below his goal of 3,000 packages. Finally, he believes the least important goal is reaching at least 20 percent of the population since he would rather give a smaller number of individuals all they need to thrive instead of a larger number of individuals only some of what they need to thrive. He therefore decides to penalize his plan by seven points for every 100,000 people below his 20 percent goal.

Mr. Baker realizes that he has certain limitations on the aid packages that he delivers to Cuba. Each type of package is approximately the same size, and because only a limited number of cargo flights from the United States are allowed into Cuba, he is only able to send a maximum of 40,000 packages. Along with a size limitation, he also encounters a weight restriction. He cannot ship more than six million pounds of cargo. Finally, he has a safety restriction. When sending medicine, he needs to ensure that the Cubans know how to use the medicine properly. Therefore, for every 100 supreme packages, Mr. Baker must send one doctor to Cuba at a cost of $33,000 per doctor.

a. How many basic, advanced, and supreme packages should Mr. Baker send to Cuba?

b. Mr. Baker reevaluates the levels of importance he places on each of the three goals. To sell his efforts to potential donors, he must show that his program is effective. Donors generally judge the effectiveness of a program on the number of people reached by aid packages. Mr. Baker therefore decides that he must put more importance on the goal of reaching at least 20 percent of the population. He decides to penalize his plan by 10 points for every half a percentage point below his 20 percent goal. The penalties for his other two goals remain the same. Under this scenario, how many basic, advanced, and supreme packages should Mr. Baker send to Cuba? How sensitive is the plan to changes in the penalty weights?

c. Mr. Baker realizes that sending more doctors along with the supreme packages will improve the proper use and distribution of the packages' contents, which in turn will increase the effectiveness of the program. He therefore decides to send one doctor with every 75 supreme packages. The penalties for the goals remain the same as in part *b.* Under this scenario, how many basic, advanced, and supreme packages should Mr. Baker send to Cuba?

d. The aid budget is cut, and Mr. Baker learns that he definitely cannot allocate more than $20 million in aid to Cuba. Due to the budget cut, Mr. Baker decides to stay with his original policy of sending one doctor with every 100 supreme packages. How many basic, advanced, and supreme packages should Mr. Baker send to Cuba, assuming that the penalties for not meeting the other two goals remain the same as in part *a?*

e. Now that the aid budget has been cut, Mr. Baker feels that the levels of importance of his three goals differ so much that it is difficult to assign meaningful penalty weights to deviations from these goals. Therefore, he decides that it would be more appropriate to apply a preemptive goal-programming approach (which will ensure that his budget goal is fully met if possible), while retaining his original policy of sending one doctor with every 100 supreme packages. How many basic, advanced, and supreme packages should Mr. Baker send to Cuba according to this approach?

Case 11-2

Remembering September 11

Adeline Jonasson lost two close friends in the collapse of the World Trade Center on September 11, 2001. Both had been vibrant young women who left grieving husbands and children behind. What terrible losses. Not a day goes by that she doesn't think of these friends and feel the anger yet again over those senseless deaths. Now she feels a real sense of mission to do something about it. What a relief it had been to be offered a top managerial position in the newly formed Transportation Security Administration. After being told that the job would involve heading a task force on airport security, Adeline had not hesitated a moment in accepting the position. She had greatly enjoyed her career as a management science consultant in the airline industry. It was very satisfying to help several airline companies save many millions of dollars. However, she now felt a greater calling. She would be able to use her expertise in management science to help save lives. There was no way to bring her friends back, but at least she could do everything possible to prevent this from happening again.

Adeline is indeed in the right spot to carry out her mission. Shortly after the tragic events of September 11, 2001, the United States Congress enacted emergency legislation to give the Department of Transportation primary responsibility for providing security at over 400 major U.S. airports. The Transportation Security Administration was then created within the Department of Transportation to carry out this responsibility. One assignment given to Adeline's task force is to investigate what advanced security technology should be developed and used at airport checkpoints to maximize the effectiveness with which passengers can be screened within budget constraints.

Even prior to 2001, airline passengers had become familiar with the two basic types of systems used to check each passenger at a security checkpoint. One is a portal that can detect concealed weapons as the passenger walks through. The other is a screening system that scans the passenger's carry-on luggage. Various proposals have been made for advanced security technology that would improve these two systems. Adeline's task force now needs to make recommendations on which direction to go for the next generation of these systems.

The task force has been told that the functional requirement for the new portal system is that it must be able to detect even one ounce of explosives and hazardous liquids as well as metallic weapons being concealed by a passenger. The technology needed to do this includes quadrupole resonance (closely related to magnetic resonance technology used by the medical industry) and magnetic sensors. There are various ways to design the portal with this technology that would satisfactorily meet the functional requirement. However, the designs would differ greatly in the frequency with which false alarms would occur as well as in the purchase cost and maintenance cost for the portal. The frequency of false alarms is a key consideration since it substantially affects the efficiency with which the passengers can be processed. Even more importantly, a high frequency of false alarms greatly decreases the alertness of the security personnel for detecting the relatively rare terrorists who are actually concealing destructive devices.

The most basic version of the portal system that satisfactorily meets the functional requirement has an estimated purchase price of $90,000 and, on the average, would incur an annual maintenance cost of $15,000. The drawback of this version is that it would generate a false alarm for approximately 10 percent of the passengers. This false alarm rate can be reduced by using more expensive versions of the system. Each additional $15,000 in the cost of the portal system would lower the false alarm rate 1 percent and also would increase the annual maintenance cost by $1,500. The most expensive version would cost $210,000, so it would have a false alarm rate of only 2 percent of the customers as well as an annual maintenance cost of $27,000.

Regarding the new screening system for carry-on luggage, the functional requirement is that it must clearly reveal suspicious objects as small as the smallest Swiss army knife. The technology needed to do this combines X-ray imaging, a thermal neutron scanner, and computer tomography imaging (which compares the density and other physical properties of any suspicious objects with known high-risk materials). It is estimated that the most basic version that satisfactorily meets this functional requirement would cost $60,000 plus an annual maintenance cost of $9,000. As with the most basic portal system, the drawback of this version is that it doesn't sufficiently discriminate between suspicious objects that actually are destructive devices and those that are harmless. Thus, this version would generate false alarms for approximately 6 percent of the customers. In addition to wasting time and delaying passengers, such a high false alarm rate would make it very difficult for the screening operator to pay sufficient attention when the far more unusual true alarms occur. However, more expensive versions of the screening system would be considerably more discriminating. In particular, each additional $30,000 in the cost of the system would enable a reduction of 1 percent in the false alarm rate, while also increasing the annual maintenance cost by $1,200. Thus, the most expensive version, costing $150,000, would decrease the false alarm rate to 3 percent and incur an annual maintenance cost of $12,600.

The task force has been given two budgetary guidelines.

First budgetary guideline: Plan on a total expenditure of $250,000 for both the portal system and the screening system for carry-on luggage at each security checkpoint.

Second budgetary guideline: Plan on holding down the average total maintenance costs for the two systems at each security checkpoint to no more than $30,000.

These budgetary guidelines prohibit using the most expensive versions of both the portal system and the screening system for carry-on baggage. Therefore, the task force needs to determine which financially feasible combination of versions for the two systems will maximize the effectiveness with which passengers can be screened. Doing this requires first obtaining input from the top management of the Transportation Security Administration regarding what the measure of effectiveness should be and then what management's goals and priorities are for achieving substantial effectiveness and meeting the budgetary guidelines.

Fortunately, Adeline already has had extensive discussions with top management to obtain its guidance on these matters. These discussions led to the adoption of a clear policy that was approved all the way up to the Secretary of Transportation (who also informed the chairpersons of the congressional oversight committees of this action). The policy establishes the following order of priorities.

Priority 1: The functional requirement for each of the two new systems *must* be met. (This is satisfied by all the versions under consideration by the task force.)

Priority 2: The total false alarm rate for both systems should not exceed 0.1 per passenger.

Priority 3: Meet the first budgetary guideline.

Priority 4: Meet the second budgetary guideline.

Now that it has obtained all the needed managerial input, the task force is ready to begin its analysis.

a. Identify the two decisions to be made and define a decision variable for each one.

b. Describe why this problem is a preemptive goal-programming problem by giving quantitative expressions for each of the goals in terms of the decision variables defined in part *a*.

c. Draw a single two-dimensional graph where the two axes correspond to the decision variables defined in part *a*. Consider each of the goals in order of priority and use the quantitative expression obtained in part *b* for this goal to draw a plot on the graph that displays the values of the decision variables that fully satisfy this goal. After completing this for all the goals, use the graph to determine the optimal solution for this preemptive goal-programming problem.

d. Use preemptive goal programming to formulate and solve this problem on a spreadsheet.

e. If it is possible to fully satisfy all the goals except the lowest priority goal, one can quickly solve a preemptive goal-programming problem by formulating and solving a linear programming model that includes all the goals except the last one as constraints and then uses the objective function to strive toward the lowest priority goal. Formulate and solve such a linear programming model for this problem on a spreadsheet. What would be the interpretation for the preemptive goal-programming problem if this linear programming model had no feasible solutions?

f. Perform some what-if analysis by determining how far the total false alarm rate per passenger can be reduced (perhaps even below the goal) by ignoring the second budgetary guideline but fully meeting the first one.

g. What additional what-if analysis do you feel should be performed in order to provide top management with the information needed to make a sound judgment decision about the best trade-off between (1) the total false alarm rate per passenger, (2) the total expenditure for the two new security systems per security checkpoint, and (3) the total annual maintenance cost for these two systems per security checkpoint?

Learning objectives

After completing this chapter, you should be able to

1. Identify the kind of decision-making environment for which decision analysis is needed.

2. Describe the logical way in which decision analysis organizes a problem.

3. Formulate a payoff table from a description of the problem.

4. Describe and evaluate several alternative criteria for making a decision based on a payoff table.

5. Apply Bayes' decision rule to solve a decision analysis problem.

6. Formulate and solve a decision tree for dealing with a sequence of decisions.

7. Use TreePlan to construct and solve a decision tree.

8. Perform sensitivity analysis with Bayes' decision rule.

9. Determine whether it is worthwhile to obtain more information before making a decision.

10. Use new information to update the probabilities of the states of nature.

11. Use SensIt to perform sensitivity analysis when dealing with a sequence of decisions.

12. Use utilities to better reflect the values of payoffs.

13. Describe some common features in the practical application of decision analysis.

Chapter **Twelve**

Decision Analysis

The previous chapters have focused mainly on managerial decision making when the consequences of alternative decisions are known with a reasonable degree of certainty. This decision-making environment enabled formulating helpful mathematical models (linear programming, integer programming, etc.) with objective functions that specify the estimated consequences of any combination of decisions. Although these consequences usually cannot be predicted with complete certainty, they could at least be estimated with enough accuracy to justify using such models (along with sensitivity analysis, etc.).

However, managers often must make decisions in environments that are fraught with much more uncertainty. Here are a few examples.

1. A manufacturer introducing a new product into the marketplace. What will be the reaction of potential customers? How much should be produced? Should the product be test marketed in a small region before deciding upon full distribution? How much advertising is needed to launch the product successfully?

2. A financial firm investing in securities. Which are the market sectors and individual securities with the best prospects? Where is the economy headed? How about interest rates? How should these factors affect the investment decisions?

3. A government contractor bidding on a new contract. What will be the actual costs of the project? Which other companies might be bidding? What are their likely bids?

4. An agricultural firm selecting the mix of crops and livestock for the upcoming season. What will be the weather conditions? Where are prices headed? What will costs be?

5. An oil company deciding whether to drill for oil in a particular location. How likely is there to be oil in that location? How much? How deep will they need to drill? Should geologists investigate the site further before drilling?

This is the kind of decision making in the face of great uncertainty that *decision analysis* is designed to address. Decision analysis provides a framework and methodology for rational decision making when the outcomes are uncertain.

The first section introduces a case study that will be carried throughout the chapter to illustrate the various phases involved in applying decision analysis. Section 12.2 focuses on choosing an appropriate decision criterion. The next section describes how decision trees can be used to structure and analyze a decision analysis problem. Section 12.4 discusses how sensitivity analysis can be performed efficiently with the help of decision trees. The subsequent three sections deal with whether it would be worthwhile to obtain more information and, if so, how to use this information for making a sequence of decisions. Section 12.8 introduces a useful Excel add-in called SensIt for performing sensitivity analysis even when a sequence of decisions needs to be made. Section 12.9 then describes how to analyze the problem while calibrating the possible outcomes to reflect their true value to the decision maker. Finally, Section 12.10 discusses the practical application of decision analysis and summarizes a variety of applications that have been very beneficial to the organizations involved.

12.1 A CASE STUDY: THE GOFERBROKE COMPANY PROBLEM

Max Flyer is the founder and sole owner of the Goferbroke Company, which develops oil wells in unproven territory. Max's friends refer to him affectionately as a wildcatter. However, he prefers to think of himself as an entrepreneur. He has poured his life's savings into the company in the hope of making it big with a large strike of oil.

Now his chance possibly has come. His company has purchased various tracts of land that larger oil companies have spurned as unpromising even though they are near some large oil fields. Now Max has received an exciting report about one of these tracts. A consulting geologist has just informed Max that he believes there is one chance in four of oil there.

Max has learned from bitter experience to be skeptical about the chances of oil reported by consulting geologists. Drilling for oil on this tract would require an investment of about $100,000. If the land turns out to be dry (no oil), the entire investment would be lost. Since his company does not have much capital left, this loss would be quite serious.

On the other hand, if the tract does contain oil, the consulting geologist estimates that there would be enough there to generate a net revenue of approximately $800,000, leaving an approximate profit of

$$\text{Profit if find oil} = \text{Revenue if find oil} - \text{Drilling cost}$$

$$= \$800,000 - \$100,000$$

$$= \$700,000$$

Although this wouldn't be quite the big strike for which Max has been waiting, it would provide a very welcome infusion of capital into the company to keep it going until he hopefully can hit the really big gusher.

There is another option. Another oil company has gotten wind of the consulting geologist's report and so has offered to purchase the tract of land from Max for $90,000. This is very tempting. This too would provide a welcome infusion of capital into the company, but without incurring the large risk of a very substantial loss of $100,000.

Should Max sell the land instead of drilling for oil there?

Table 12.1 summarizes the decision alternatives and prospective payoffs that face Max.

So Max is in a quandary about what to do. Fortunately, help is at hand. Max's daughter Jennifer has recently earned her degree from a fine business school and now has come to work for her proud dad. He asks her to apply her business training to help him analyze the problem. Having studied management science in college, she recommends applying decision analysis. Having paid for her fine education, he agrees to give it a try.

Jennifer begins by interviewing her dad about the problem.

Jennifer: How much faith do you put in the consulting geologist's assessment that there is one chance in four of oil on this tract?

Max: Not too much. These guys sometimes seem to pull numbers out of the air. He has convinced me that there is some chance of oil there. But it could just as well be one chance in three, or one chance in five. They don't really know.

Jennifer: Is there a way of getting more information to pin these odds down better? This is an important option with the decision analysis approach.

TABLE 12.1
Prospective Profits for the Goferbroke Company

| Status of Land | Profit | |
Alternative	Oil	Dry
Drill for oil	$700,000	−$100,000
Sell the land	90,000	90,000
Chance of status	1 in 4	3 in 4

Max: Yes. We could arrange for a detailed seismic survey of the land. That would pin down the odds somewhat better. But you don't really find out until you drill. Furthermore, these seismic surveys cost you an arm and a leg. I got a quote for this tract. 30,000 bucks! Then it might say oil is likely, so we drill and we might not find anything. Then I'm out another 100,000 bucks! Losing $130,000 would almost put us out of business.

Jennifer: OK. Let's put the seismic survey on the back burner for now. Here is another key consideration. It sounds like we need to go beyond dollars and cents to look at the consequences of the possible outcomes. Losing $130,000 would hurt a lot more than gaining $130,000 would help.

Max: That's for sure!

Jennifer: Well, decision analysis has a way of taking this into account by using what are called utilities. The **utility** of an outcome measures the true value to you of that outcome rather than just the monetary value.

Max: Sounds good.

Jennifer: Now this is what I suggest we do. We'll start out simple, without considering the option of the seismic survey and without getting into utilities. I'll introduce you to how decision analysis organizes our problem and to the options it provides for the criterion to use for making your decision. You'll be able to choose the criterion that feels right to you. Then we'll look at whether it might be worthwhile to do the seismic survey and, if so, how to best use its information. After that, we'll get into the nitty gritty of carefully analyzing the problem, including incorporating utilities. I think when we finish the process and you make your decision, you'll feel quite comfortable that you are making the best one.

Max: Good. Let's get started.

Here is the tutorial that Jennifer provided her dad about the logical way in which decision analysis organizes a problem.

Decision Analysis Terminology

Decision analysis has a few special terms.

The **decision maker** is the individual or group responsible for making the decision (or sequence of decisions) under consideration. For the Goferbroke Co. problem, the decision maker is Max. Jennifer (the management scientist) can help perform the analyses, but the objective is to assist the decision maker in identifying the best possible decision from the decision maker's perspective.

The **alternatives** are the options for the decision to be made by the decision maker. Max's alternatives at this point are to drill for oil or to sell the tract of land.

The outcome of the decision to be made will be affected by random factors that are outside the control of the decision maker. These random factors determine the situation that will be found when the decision is executed. Each of these possible situations is referred to as a possible **state of nature.** For the Goferbroke Co. problem, the possible states of nature are that the tract contains oil or that it is dry (no oil).

The decision maker generally will have some information about the relative likelihood of the possible states of nature. This information may be in the form of just subjective estimates based on the experience or intuition of an individual, or there may be some degree of hard evidence involved (such as is contained in the consulting geologist's report). When these estimates are expressed in the form of probabilities, they are referred to as the **prior probabilities** of the respective states of nature. For the Goferbroke Co. problem, the consulting geologist has provided the prior probabilities given in Table 12.2. Although these are unlikely to be the true probabilities based on more information (such as through a seismic survey), they are the best available estimates of the probabilities *prior* to obtaining more information. (Later in

The utility of an outcome measures the true value to the decision maker of that outcome.

TABLE 12.2
Prior Probabilities for the First Goferbroke Co. Problem

State of Nature	Prior Probability
The tract of land contains oil	0.25
The tract of land is dry (no oil)	0.75

TABLE 12.3
Payoff Table (Profit in $1,000s) for the First Goferbroke Co. Problem

	State of Nature	
Alternative	Oil	Dry
Drill for oil	700	−100
Sell the land	90	90
Prior probability	0.25	0.75

the chapter, we will analyze whether it would be worthwhile to conduct a seismic survey, so the current problem of what to do without a seismic survey will be referred to hereafter as the *first* Goferbroke Co. problem.)

Each combination of a decision alternative and a state of nature results in some outcome. The **payoff** is a quantitative measure of the value to the decision maker of the consequences of the outcome. In most cases, the payoff is expressed as a monetary value, such as the profit. As indicated in Table 12.1, the payoff for the Goferbroke Co. at this stage is profit. (In Section 12.9, the company's payoffs will be reexpressed in terms of utilities.)

The Payoff Table

When formulating the problem, it is important to identify *all* the relevant decision alternatives and the possible states of nature. After identifying the appropriate measure for the *payoff* from the perspective of the decision maker, the next step is to estimate the payoff for each combination of a decision alternative and a state of nature. These payoffs then are displayed in a **payoff table.**

Table 12.3 shows the payoff table for the first Goferbroke Co. problem. The payoffs are given in units of thousands of dollars of profit. Note that the bottom row also shows the prior probabilities of the states of nature, as given earlier in Table 12.2.

Review
Questions

1. What are the decision alternatives being considered by Max?
2. What is the consulting geologist's assessment of the chances of oil on the tract of land?
3. How much faith does Max put in the consulting geologist's assessment of the chances of oil?
4. What option is available for obtaining more information about the chances of oil?
5. What is meant by the possible *states of nature?*
6. What is meant by *prior probabilities?*
7. What do the *payoffs* represent in a payoff table?

12.2 DECISION CRITERIA

Given the payoff table for the first Goferbroke Co. problem shown in Table 12.3, what criterion should be used in deciding whether to drill for oil or sell the land? There is no single correct answer for this question that is appropriate for every decision maker. The choice of a decision criterion depends considerably on the decision maker's own temperament and attitude toward decision making, as well as the circumstances of the decision to be made. Ultimately, Max Flyer, as the owner of the Goferbroke Co., needs to decide which decision criterion is most appropriate for this situation from his personal viewpoint.

There is no single decision criterion that is best for every situation.

Over a period of many decades (and even centuries), a considerable number of criteria have been suggested for how to make a decision when given the kind of information provided by a payoff table. All these criteria consider the payoffs in some way and some also take into account the prior probabilities of the states of nature, but other criteria do not use probabilities in any way. Each criterion has some rationale as well as some drawbacks. However, in recent decades, a substantial majority of management scientists has concluded that one of these criteria (Bayes' decision rule) is a particularly appropriate criterion for most decision makers in most situations. Therefore, after describing and discussing Bayes' decision rule in this section, the rest of the chapter will focus on how to apply this particular criterion in a variety of contexts.

Bayes' decision rule is the recommended decision criterion for most situations.

However, before turning to Bayes' decision rule, we briefly introduce three alternative decision criteria below. All of these alternative criteria are particularly simple and intuitive. At the same time, each criterion is quite superficial in the sense that it focuses on only one piece of information provided by the payoff table and ignores the rest (including the pieces considered by the other two criteria). Nevertheless, many individuals informally apply one or more of these criteria at various times in their lives. The first two make no use of prior probabilities, which can be quite reasonable when it is difficult or impossible to obtain relatively reliable values for these probabilities. Bayes' decision rule is quite different from these alternative criteria in that it makes full use of all the information in the payoff table by applying a more structured approach to decision making.

The CD-ROM includes a supplement entitled *Decision Criteria* that provides a much more detailed discussion and critique of these three alternative decision criteria as well as three others that are somewhat more complicated.

Decision Making without Probabilities: The Maximax Criterion

The **maximax criterion** is the decision criterion for the eternal optimist. It says to focus only on the *best* that can happen to us. Here is how this criterion works:

1. Identify the *maximum payoff* from any state of nature for each decision alternative.

2. Find the *maximum* of these maximum payoffs and choose the corresponding decision alternative.

The maximax criterion always chooses the decision alternative that can give the largest possible payoff.

The rationale for this criterion is that it gives an opportunity for the best possible outcome (the largest payoff in the entire payoff table) to occur. All that is needed is for the right state of nature to occur, which the eternal optimist believes is likely.

Table 12.4 shows the application of this criterion to the first Goferbroke problem. It begins with the payoff table (Table 12.3) without the prior probabilities (since these probabilities are ignored by this criterion). An extra column on the right then shows the maximum payoff for each decision alternative. Since the maximum of these maxima (700) must be the largest payoff in the entire payoff table, the corresponding decision alternative (drill for oil) is selected by this criterion.

This criterion ignores the prior probabilities.

The biggest drawback of this criterion is that it completely ignores the prior probabilities. For example, it always would say that Goferbroke should drill for oil even if the chance of finding oil were minuscule. Another drawback is that it ignores all the payoffs except the largest one. For example, it again would say that Goferbroke should drill for oil even if the payoff from selling the land were 699 ($699,000).

Decision Making without Probabilities: The Maximin Criterion

The **maximin criterion** is the criterion for the total pessimist. In contrast to the maximax criterion, it says to focus only on the *worst* that can happen to us. Here is how this criterion works:

The maximin criterion always chooses the decision alternative that provides the best guarantee for its minimum possible payoff.

1. Identify the *minimum payoff* from any state of nature for each decision alternative.

2. Find the *maximum* of these minimum payoffs and choose the corresponding decision alternative.

TABLE 12.4

Application of the Maximax Criterion to the First Goferbroke Co. Problem

Alternative	State of Nature		Maximum in Row
	Oil	Dry	
Drill for oil	700	−100	700 ← Maximax
Sell the land	90	90	90

TABLE 12.5

Application of the Maximin Criterion to the First Goferbroke Co. Problem

	State of Nature		
Alternative	**Oil**	**Dry**	**Minimum in Row**
Drill for oil	700	−100	90 ← Maximin
Sell the land	90	90	90

The rationale for this criterion is that it provides the best possible protection against being unlucky. Even if each possible choice of a decision alternative were to lead to its worst state of nature occurring, which the total pessimist thinks is likely, the choice indicated by this criterion gives the best possible payoff under these circumstances.

The application of this criterion to the first Goferbroke problem is shown in Table 12.5. The basic difference from Table 12.4 is that the numbers in the right-hand column now are the *minimum* rather than the maximum in each row. Since 90 is the maximum of these two numbers, the alternative to be chosen is to sell the land.

The drawbacks of this criterion are similar to those for the maximax criterion. Because it completely ignores prior probabilities, it always would say that Goferbroke should sell the land even if it were almost certain to find oil if it drilled. Because it ignores all the payoffs except the maximin payoff, it again would say that Goferbroke should sell the land even if the payoff from drilling successfully for oil were 10,000 ($10 million).

This criterion also ignores the prior probabilities.

Decision Making with Probabilities: The Maximum Likelihood Criterion

The **maximum likelihood criterion** says to focus on the *most likely* state of nature as follows.

1. Identify the state of nature with the largest prior probability.

2. Choose the decision alternative that has the largest payoff for this state of nature.

The maximum likelihood criterion assumes that the most likely state of nature will occur and chooses accordingly.

The rationale for this criterion is that by basing our decision on the assumption that the most likely state of nature will occur, we are giving ourselves a better chance of a favorable outcome than by assuming any other state of nature.

Table 12.6 shows the application of this criterion to the first Goferbroke Co. problem. This table is identical to the payoff table given in Table 12.3 except for also showing step 1 (select the *dry* state of nature) and step 2 (select the *sell the land* alternative) of the criterion. Since dry is the state of nature with the larger prior probability, we only consider the payoffs in its column (−100 and 90). The larger of these two payoffs is 90, so we choose the corresponding alternative, sell the land.

This criterion ignores all the payoffs except for the most likely state of nature.

This criterion has a number of drawbacks. One is that with a considerable number of states of nature, the most likely state can have a fairly low prior probability, in which case it would make little sense to base the decision solely on this one state. Another more serious drawback is that it completely ignores all the payoffs (including any extremely large payoffs and any disastrous payoffs) throughout the payoff table except those for the single most likely state of na-

TABLE 12.6

Application of the Maximum Likelihood Criterion to the First Goferbroke Co. Problem

	State of Nature	
Alternative	**Oil**	**Dry**
Drill for oil	700	−100
		Step 2:
Sell the land	90	90 ← Maximum
Prior probability	0.25	0.75
		↑
		Step 1: Maximum

ture. For example, no matter how large the payoff for finding oil, it automatically would say that Goferbroke should sell that land instead of drilling for oil whenever the dry state has a little larger prior probability than the oil state.

Decision Making with Probabilities: Bayes' Decision Rule

Bayes' decision rule directly uses the *prior probabilities* of the possible states of nature as summarized below.

1. For each decision alternative, calculate the *weighted average* of its payoffs by multiplying each payoff by the prior probability of the corresponding state of nature and then summing these products. Using statistical terminology, refer to this weighted average as the **expected payoff (EP)** for this decision alternative.

2. Bayes' decision rule says to choose the alternative with the *largest* expected payoff.

The spreadsheet in Figure 12.1 shows the application of this criterion to the first Goferbroke Co. problem. Columns B, C, and D display the payoff table first given in Table 12.3. Cells F5 and F6 then execute step 1 of the procedure by using the equations entered into these cells, namely,

F5 = SUMPRODUCT(PriorProbability, DrillPayoff)

F6 = SUMPRODUCT(PriorProbability, SellPayoff)

Since expected payoff = 100 for the drill alternative (cell F5), versus a smaller value of expected payoff = 90 for the sell the land alternative (cell F6), this criterion says to drill for oil.

Like all the others, this criterion cannot guarantee that the selected alternative will turn out to have been the best one after learning the true state of nature. However, it does provide another guarantee described below.

> On the average, Bayes' decision rule provides larger payoffs in the long run than any other criterion.

The expected payoff for a particular decision alternative can be interpreted as what the *average* payoff would become if the same situation were to be repeated numerous times. Therefore, *on the average,* repeatedly using Bayes' decision rule to make decisions will lead to larger payoffs in the long run than any other criterion (assuming the prior probabilities are valid).

FIGURE 12.1

This spreadsheet shows the application of Bayes' decision rule to the first Goferbroke Co. problem, where a comparison of the expected payoffs in cells F5:F6 indicates that the Drill alternative should be chosen because it has the largest expected payoff.

	A	B	C	D	E	F
1		**Bayes' Decision Rule for the Goferbroke Co.**				
2						
3		**Payoff Table**	**State of Nature**			Expected
4		Alternative	Oil	Dry		Payoff
5		Drill	700	-100		100
6		Sell	90	90		90
7						
8		Prior Probability	0.25	0.75		

Range Name	Cells
DrillPayoff	C5:D5
ExpectedPayoff	F5:F6
PriorProbability	C8:D8
SellPayoff	C6:D6

	F
3	Expected
4	Payoff
5	=SUMPRODUCT(PriorProbability,DrillPayoff)
6	=SUMPRODUCT(PriorProbability,SellPayoff)

Thus, if the Goferbroke Co. owned many tracts of land with this same payoff table, drilling for oil on all of them would provide an average payoff of about 100 ($100,000), versus only 90 ($90,000) for selling. As the following calculations indicate, this is the average payoff from drilling that results from having oil in an average of one tract out of every four (as indicated by the prior probabilities).

$$\text{Oil found in one tract:} \quad \text{Payoff} = 700$$

$$\text{Three tracts are dry:} \quad \text{Payoff} = 3(-100) = -300$$

$$\text{Total payoff} = 400$$

$$\text{Average payoff} = \frac{400}{4} = 100$$

However, achieving this average payoff might require going through a long stretch of dry tracts until the "law of averages" can prevail to reach 25 percent of the tracts having oil. Surviving a long stretch of bad luck may not be feasible if the company does not have adequate financing.

This criterion also has its share of critics. Here are the main criticisms.

1. There usually is considerable uncertainty involved in assigning values to prior probabilities, so treating these values as true probabilities will not reveal the true range of possible outcomes. (Section 12.4 discusses how *sensitivity analysis* can address this concern.)

2. Prior probabilities inherently are at least largely subjective in nature, whereas sound decision making should be based on objective data and procedures. (Section 12.6 describes how new information sometimes can be obtained to improve prior probabilities and make them more objective.)

By considering only expected payoffs, Bayes' decision rule fails to give special consideration to the possibility of disastrously large losses.

3. By focusing on average outcomes, expected (monetary) payoffs ignore the effect that the amount of variability in the possible outcomes should have on the decision making. For example, since Goferbroke does not have the financing to sustain a large loss, selling the land to assure a payoff of 90 ($90,000) may be preferable to an expected payoff of 100 ($100,000) from drilling. Selling would avoid the risk of a large loss from drilling when the land is dry. (Section 12.9 will discuss how utilities can be used to better reflect the value of payoffs.)

So why is this criterion commonly referred to as Bayes' decision rule? The reason is that it is often credited to the Reverend Thomas Bayes, a nonconforming 18th century English minister who won renown as a philosopher and mathematician, although the same basic idea has even longer roots in the field of economics. (Yes, some management science techniques have *very* long roots!) Bayes' philosophy of decision making still is very influential today, and some management scientists even refer to themselves as Bayesians because of their devotion to this philosophy.

Because of its popularity, the rest of the chapter focuses on procedures that are based on this criterion.

Max's Reaction

Max: So most management scientists feel that this is the right criterion to use?

Jennifer: There really is no such thing as a right or wrong criterion for everybody. An appropriate criterion for one person might not fit another at all. It really depends on the individual's own temperament and attitude toward decision making. It might also depend on the situation: how much is known about the decision alternatives and whether meaningful prior probabilities can be obtained for the possible states of nature. All that sort of thing.

Max: So where does this leave us?

Jennifer: Well, now you need to decide which criterion seems most appropriate to you in this situation.

Max:	Well, I can't say that I am very excited about any of the criteria. But it sounded like this one is a popular one.
Jennifer:	Yes, it is.
Max:	Why?

Bayes' decision rule uses all the information provided by the payoff table.

Jennifer:	Really, two reasons. First, this is the criterion that uses all the available information. The prior probabilities may not be as accurate as we would like, but they do give us valuable information about roughly how likely each of the possible states of nature is. Many management scientists feel that using this key information should lead to better decisions.
Max:	I'm not ready to accept that yet. But what is the second reason?
Jennifer:	Remember that this is the criterion that focuses on what the average payoff would be if the same situation were repeated numerous times. We called this the expected payoff. Consistently selecting the decision alternative that provides the best expected payoff would provide the most payoff to the company in the long run. Doing what is best in the long run seems like rational decision making for a manager.
Max:	Yes, that makes some sense. But before Goferbroke can get to the long run, we need to survive the short run. We can't take many more of these losses from drilling when the land is dry.
Jennifer:	You're right. Considering the short run can be really important as well. But remember that I mentioned utilities awhile ago. A little later, I'll explain how using utilities will enable us to give full consideration to the short run as well.

Review
Questions

1. How does the maximax criterion select a decision alternative? What kind of person might find this criterion appealing?

2. What are some criticisms of the maximax criterion?

3. How does the maximin criterion select a decision alternative? What kind of person might find this criterion appealing?

4. What are some criticisms of the maximin criterion?

5. Which state of nature does the maximum likelihood criterion focus on?

6. What are some criticisms of the maximum likelihood criterion?

7. How does Bayes' decision rule select a decision alternative?

8. How is the expected payoff for a decision alternative calculated?

9. What are some criticisms of Bayes' decision rule?

12.3   DECISION TREES

The spreadsheet in Figure 12.1 illustrates one useful way of performing decision analysis with Bayes' decision rule. Another enlightening way to apply this decision rule is to use a **decision tree** to display and analyze the problem graphically. The decision tree for the first Goferbroke Co. problem is shown in Figure 12.2. Starting on the left side and moving to the right side shows the progression of events. First, a decision is made as to whether to drill for oil or sell the land. If the decision is to drill, the next event is to learn whether the state of nature is that the land contains oil or is dry. Finally, the payoff is obtained that results from these events.

In the terminology of decision trees, the junction points are called **nodes** (or forks) and the lines emanating from the nodes are referred to as **branches.** A distinction is then made between the following two types of nodes.

FIGURE 12.2

The decision tree for the first Goferbroke Co. problem as presented in Table 12.3.

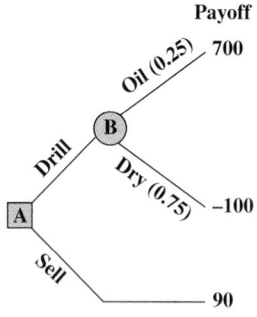

A **decision node,** represented by a *square,* indicates that a decision needs to be made at that point in the process. An **event node** (or chance node), represented by a *circle,* indicates that a random event occurs at that point.

Thus, node A in Figure 12.2 is a decision node since the decision on whether to drill or sell occurs there. Node B is an event node since a random event, the occurrence of one of the possible states of nature, takes place there. Each of the two branches emanating from this node corresponds to one of the possible random events, where the number in parentheses along the branch gives the probability that this event will occur.

A decision tree can be very helpful for visualizing and analyzing a problem. When the problem is as small as the one in Figure 12.2, using the decision tree in the analysis process is optional. However, one nice feature of decision trees is that they also can be used for more complicated problems where a sequence of decisions needs to be made. You will see this illustrated for the full Goferbroke Co. problem in Sections 12.7 and 12.9 when a decision on whether to conduct a seismic survey is made before deciding whether to drill or sell.

Spreadsheet Software for Decision Trees

Excel Tip: The TreePlan add-in can be installed either by simply opening the TreePlan file in MS Courseware or by using the installer included in MS Courseware.

We will describe and illustrate how to use TreePlan, an Excel add-in developed by Professor Michael Middleton for constructing and analyzing decision trees on a spreadsheet. The academic version is available to you as shareware in your MS Courseware. (If you want to continue to use it after this course, you will need to register and pay the shareware fee.) Like any Excel add-in, this add-in needs to be installed before it will show up in Excel.

TreePlan Tip: To change the type of a node, or to add or remove branches, click on the cell containing the node and choose Decision Tree from the Tools menu.

To begin creating a decision tree using TreePlan, select Decision Tree from the Tools menu and click on New Tree. This creates the default decision tree shown in Figure 12.3 with a single (square) decision node with two branches. It so happens that this is exactly what is needed for the first node in the Goferbroke problem (this node corresponds to node A in Figure 12.2). However, even if something else were needed, it is easy to make changes to a node in TreePlan. Simply select the cell containing the node (B5 in Figure 12.3) and choose Decision Tree from the Tools menu. This brings up a dialogue box that allows you to change the type of node (e.g., from a decision node to an event node) or add more branches.

By default, the labels for the decisions (cells D2 and D7 in Figure 12.3) are "Decision 1," "Decision 2," etc. These labels are changed by clicking on them and typing a new label. In Figure 12.3, these labels have already been changed to "Drill" and "Sell," respectively.

TreePlan Tip: To create a new node at the end of a tree, select the cell containing the terminal node and choose Decision Tree from the Tools menu. This enables you to change the terminal node into either a decision node or an event node with the desired number of branches (between 1 and 5).

If the decision is to drill, the next event is to learn whether or not the land contains oil. To create an event node, click on the cell containing the terminal node at the end of the drill branch, just to the right of the vertical line (cell F3 in Figure 12.3), and choose Decision Tree from the Tools menu. This brings up the TreePlan . . . Terminal dialogue box shown in Figure 12.4. Choose the "Change to event node" option on the left and select the two branches option on the right, and then click OK. This results in the decision tree with the nodes and branches shown in Figure 12.5 (after replacing the default labels "Event 1" and "Event 2" with "Oil" and "Dry," respectively).

Initially, each branch would show a default value of 0 for the net cash flow being generated there (the numbers appear below the branch labels: D6, D14, H4, and H9 in Figure 12.5). Also, each of the two branches leading from the event node would display default values of 0.5 for

FIGURE 12.3

The default decision tree created by TreePlan by selecting Decision Tree from the Tools menu, clicking on New Tree, and then entering the Drill and Sell labels for the two decision alternatives.

	A	B	C	D	E	F	G
1							
2				Drill			
3							0
4				0	0		
5			1				
6		0					
7				Sell			
8							0
9				0	0		

FIGURE 12.4

The TreePlan dialogue box that is used for making various kinds of changes in the decision tree.

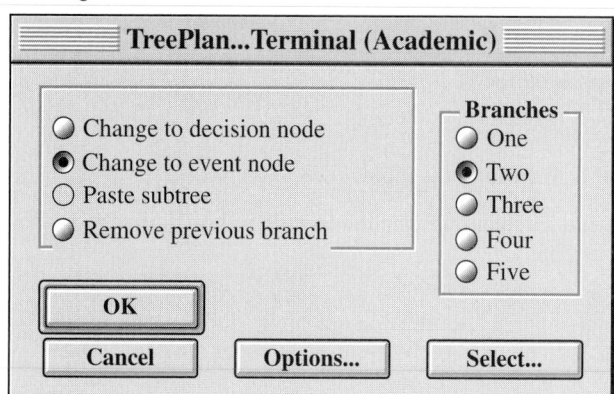

FIGURE 12.5

The decision tree constructed and solved by TreePlan for the first Goferbroke Co. problem as presented in Table 12.3, where the 1 in cell B9 indicates that the top branch (the Drill alternative) should be chosen.

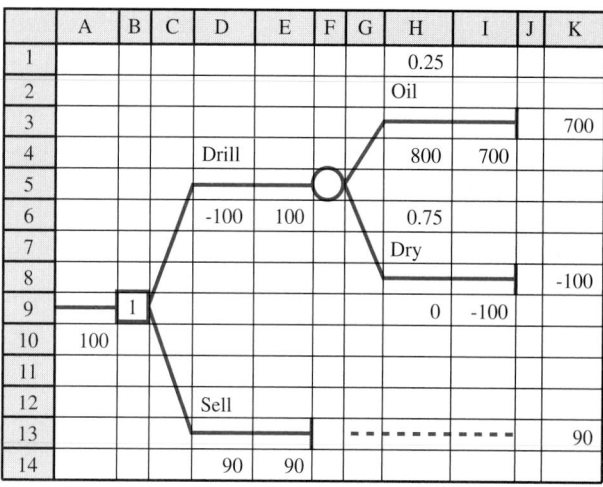

their prior probabilities (the probabilities are just above the corresponding labels: H1 and H6 in Figure 12.5). Therefore, you next should click on these default values and replace them with the correct numbers, namely,

$$D6 = -100 \quad \text{(the cost of drilling is \$100,000)}$$

$$D14 = 90 \quad \text{(the profit from selling is \$90,000)}$$

$$H1 = 0.25 \quad \text{(the prior probability of oil is 0.25)}$$

$$H4 = 800 \quad \text{(the net revenue after finding oil is \$800,000)}$$

$$H6 = 0.75 \quad \text{(the prior probability of dry is 0.75)}$$

$$H9 = 0 \quad \text{(the net revenue after finding dry is 0)}$$

as shown in the figure.

At each stage in constructing a decision tree, TreePlan automatically solves for the optimal policy with the current tree when using *Bayes' decision rule.* The number inside each decision node indicates which branch should be chosen (assuming the branches emanating from that node are numbered consecutively from top to bottom). Thus, for the final decision tree in Figure 12.5, the number 1 in cell B9 specifies that the first branch (the Drill alternative) should be chosen. The number on both sides of each terminal node is the payoff if that node is reached. The number 100 in cells A10 and E6 is the *expected payoff* (the measure of performance for Bayes' decision rule) at those stages in the process.

This description of TreePlan may seem somewhat complicated. However, we think that you will find the procedure quite intuitive when you execute it on a computer. If you spend considerable time with TreePlan, you also will find that it has many helpful features that haven't been described in this brief introduction.

> TreePlan always identifies the optimal policy for the current decision tree according to Bayes' decision rule.

Max's Reaction

Max: I like this decision tree thing. It puts everything into perspective.

Jennifer: Good.

Max: But one thing still really bothers me.

Jennifer: I think I can guess.

Max: Yes. I've made it pretty plain that I don't want to make my decision based on believing the consulting geologist's numbers. One chance in four of oil. Hah! I've seen these guys operate too much in the past. I don't mean they don't know what they're doing. They're good at spotting favorable signs for oil. The trouble comes when you ask for some numbers. They'll stare into space for awhile, and then out pops the numbers. It's just an educated guess.

Jennifer: Well, let me ask this. What is the key factor in deciding whether to drill for oil or sell the land?

Max: How likely it is that there is oil there.

Jennifer: Doesn't the consulting geologist help in determining this?

Max: Definitely. I hardly ever drill without his input.

Jennifer: So shouldn't your criterion for deciding whether to drill be based directly on this input?

Max: Yes, it should.

Jennifer: But then I don't understand why you keep objecting to using the consulting geologist's numbers.

Max: I'm not objecting to using his input. This input is vital to my decision. What I object to is using his numbers, one chance in four of oil, as being the gospel truth. That is what this Bayes' decision rule seems to do. We both saw what a close decision this was, 100 versus 90. What happens if his numbers are off some, as they probably are? This is too important a decision to be based on some numbers that are largely pulled out of the air.

Jennifer: OK, I see. Now he says that there is one chance in four of oil, a 25 percent chance. Do you think that is the right ballpark at least?

Max: Yes. I believe him that there is a decent chance of oil there.

Jennifer: If 25 percent isn't the right number, what do you think it might be?

Max: Who knows?

Jennifer: What I mean is, you have seen the consulting geologist's report and the evidence he gives to support his numbers. Based on this report and your past experience, can you give me a range for what the right number is likely to be? If not 25 percent, how much lower might it be? Or how much higher?

Max: I usually add and subtract 10 percent from whatever the consulting geologist says. So I suppose the chance of oil is likely to be somewhere between 15 percent and 35 percent.

Jennifer: Good. Now we're getting somewhere. I think I know exactly what we should do next.

Max: What's that?

Jennifer: There is a management science technique that is designed for just this kind of situation. It is called *sensitivity analysis.* It will allow us to investigate what happens if the consulting geologist's numbers are off.

Max: Great! Let's do it.

Review Questions

1. What is a *decision tree?*

2. What is a *decision node* in a decision tree? An *event node?*

3. What symbols are used to represent decision nodes and event nodes?

12.4   SENSITIVITY ANALYSIS WITH DECISION TREES

Sensitivity analysis commonly is used with various applications of management science to study the effect if some of the numbers included in the mathematical model are not correct. In this case, the mathematical model is represented by the decision tree shown in Figure 12.5. The numbers in this tree that are most questionable are the prior probabilities in cells H1 and H6, so we will initially focus the sensitivity analysis on these numbers.

It is helpful to start this process by consolidating the data and results on the spreadsheet below the decision tree, as in Figure 12.6. As indicated by the formulas at the bottom of the figure, the cells giving the results make reference to the corresponding output cells on the decision tree. Similarly, the data cells on the decision tree now reference the corresponding data cells below the tree. Consequently, the user can experiment with various alternative values in the data cells below and the results will simultaneously change in both the decision tree and the results section below the tree to reflect the new data.

Excel Tip: Consolidating the data and results on the spreadsheet makes it easier to do sensitivity analysis and also makes the model and results easier to interpret.

Consolidating the data and results offers a couple of advantages. First, it assures that each piece of data is in only one place. Each time that piece of data is needed in the decision tree, a reference is made to the single data cell below. This greatly simplifies sensitivity analysis. To change a piece of data, it needs to be changed in only one place rather than searching through the entire tree to find and change all occurrences of that piece of data.[1] A second advantage of consolidating the data and results is that it makes it easy for *anyone* to interpret the model. It is not necessary to understand TreePlan or how to read a decision tree in order to see what data were used in the model or what the suggested plan of action and expected payoff are.

The sum of the two prior probabilities must equal one, so increasing one of these probabilities automatically decreases the other one by the same amount, and vice versa. This is enforced on the decision tree in Figure 12.6 by the equation in cell H6—the probability of a dry site = H6 = 1 − ProbabilityOfOil (E22). Max has concluded that the true chances of having oil on the tract of land are likely to lie somewhere between 15 and 35 percent. In other words, the true prior probability of having oil is likely to be in the range from 0.15 to 0.35, so the corresponding prior probability of the land being dry would range from 0.85 to 0.65.

We can begin sensitivity analysis by simply trying different trial values for the prior probability of oil. This is done in Figure 12.7, first with this probability at the lower end of the range (0.15) and next with this probability at the upper end (0.35). When the prior probability of oil is only 0.15, the decision swings over to selling the land by a wide margin (an expected payoff of 90 versus only 20 for drilling). However, when this probability is 0.35, the decision is to drill by a wide margin (expected payoff = 180 versus only 90 for selling). Thus, the decision is very *sensitive* to the prior probability of oil. This sensitivity analysis has revealed that it is important to do more, if possible, to pin down just what the true value of the probability of oil is.

Using Data Tables to Do Sensitivity Analysis Systematically

A data table displays the results of selected output cells for various trial values of a data cell.

To pin down just where the suggested course of action changes, we could continue selecting new trial values of the prior probability of oil at random. However, a better approach is to systematically consider a range of values. A feature built into Excel, called data tables, is designed to perform just this sort of analysis. Data tables are used to show the results of certain output cells for various trial values of a data cell. Data tables work in the same way as the Solver Table, which was used to do sensitivity analysis for linear programming problems in Chapter 5. The only difference is that a data table does not make use of the Solver to re-solve the problem for each trial value of the data cell. (The Solver is not needed in decision analysis problems.)

To use data tables, first make a table on the spreadsheet with headings as shown in columns I, J, and K in Figure 12.8. In the first column of the table (I19:I29), list the trial values for the

---

[1]In this very simple decision tree, this advantage does not become evident since each piece of data is only used once in the tree anyway. However, in later sections, when the possibility of seismic testing is considered, some data will be repeated many times in the tree and this advantage will become more clear.

FIGURE 12.6

In preparation for performing sensitivity analysis on the first Goferbroke Co. problem, the data and results have been consolidated on the spreadsheet below the decision tree.

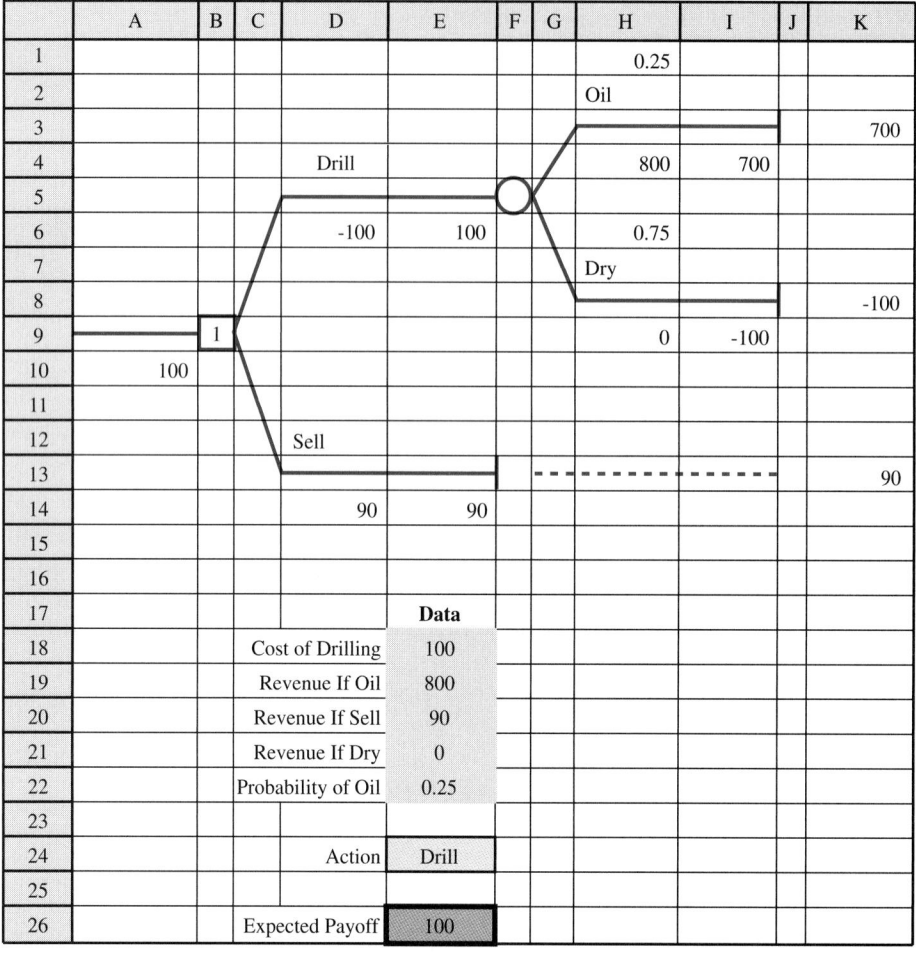

data cell (the prior probability of oil), except leave the first row blank. The headings of the next columns specify which output will be evaluated. For each of these columns, use the first row of the table (cells J18:K18) to write an equation that refers to the relevant output cell. In this case, the cells of interest are Action (E24) and ExpectedPayoff (E26), so the equations for J18:K18 are those shown below the spreadsheet in Figure 12.8.

FIGURE 12.7

Performing sensitivity analysis for the first Goferbroke Co. problem by trying alternative values (0.15 and 0.35) of the prior probability of oil.

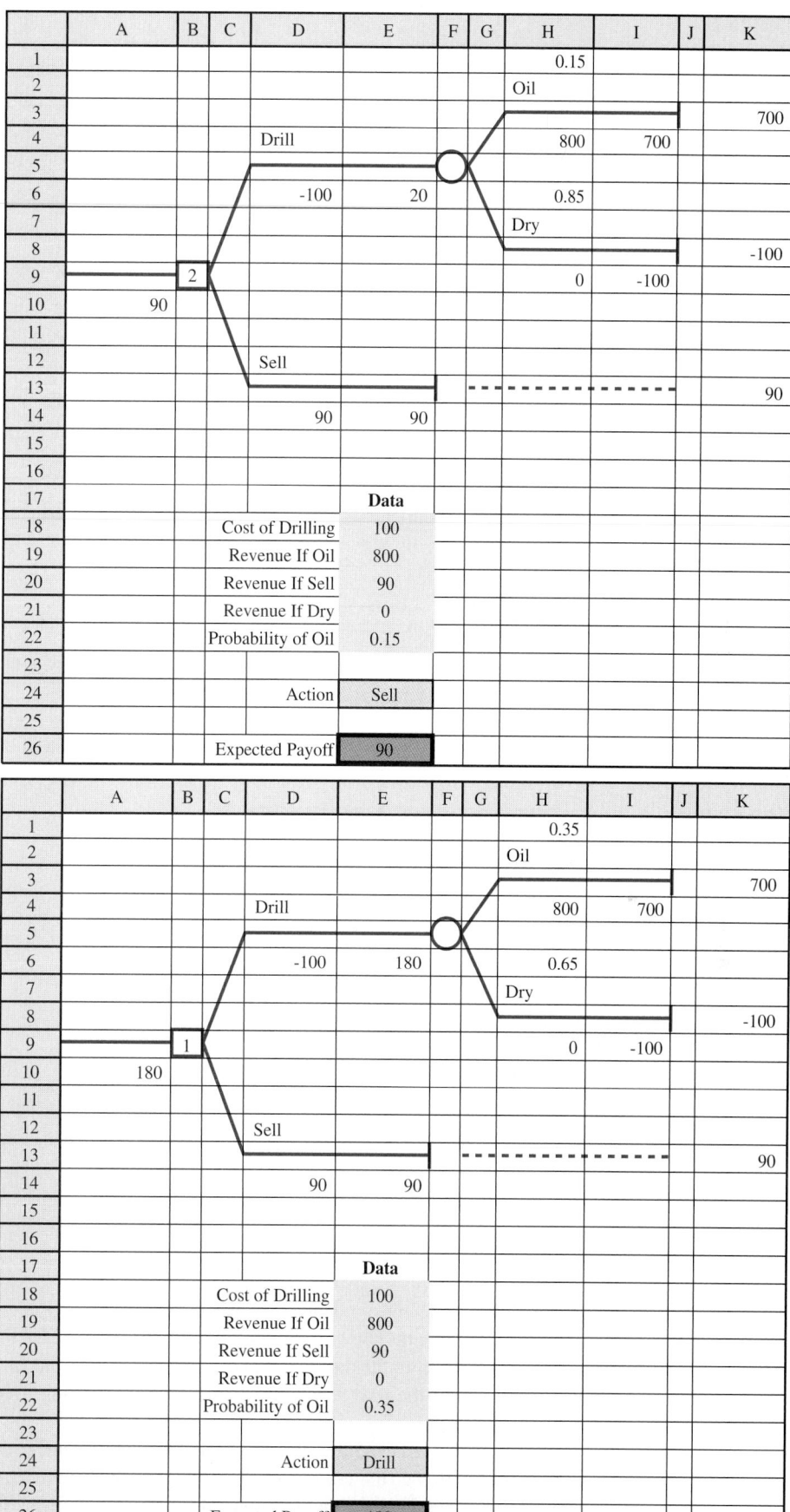

FIGURE 12.8

Expansion of the spreadsheet in Figure 12.6 to prepare for generating a data table, where the choice of E22 for the column input cell in the Table dialogue box indicates that this is the data cell that is being changed in the first column of the data table.

	A	B	C	D	E	F	G	H	I	J	K	L	M
16									Probability		Expected		
17					**Data**				of Oil	Action	Payoff		
18				Cost of Drilling	100					Drill	100	Select these	
19				Revenue If Oil	800				0.15			cells (I18:K29),	
20				Revenue If Sell	90				0.17			before	
21				Revenue If Dry	0				0.19			choosing	
22				Probability of Oil	0.25				0.21			Table from	
23									0.23			the Data	
24				Action	Drill				0.25			menu.	
25									0.27				
26				Expected Payoff	100				0.29				
27									0.31				
28									0.33				
29									0.35				

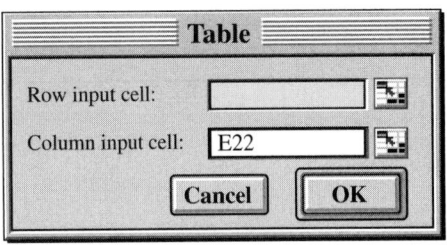

Table

Row input cell: [   ]

Column input cell: [E22]

Cancel   OK

	J	K
16		Expected
17	Action	Payoff
18	=Action	=ExpectedPayoff

Range Name	Cell
Action	E24
ExpectedPayoff	E26

FIGURE 12.9

After the preparation displayed in Figure 12.8, clicking OK generates this data table that shows the optimal action and expected payoff for various trial values of the prior probability of oil.

	I	J	K
16	Probability		Expected
17	of Oil	Action	Payoff
18		Drill	100
19	0.15	Sell	90
20	0.17	Sell	90
21	0.19	Sell	90
22	0.21	Sell	90
23	0.23	Sell	90
24	0.25	Drill	100
25	0.27	Drill	116
26	0.29	Drill	132
27	0.31	Drill	148
28	0.33	Drill	164
29	0.35	Drill	180

Next, select the entire table (I18:K29) and then choose Table from the Data menu. In the Table dialogue box (as shown at the bottom left of Figure 12.8), indicate the column input cell (E22), which refers to the data cell that is being changed in the first column of the table. Nothing is entered for the row input cell because no row is being used to list the trial values of a data cell in this case.

Clicking OK then generates the data table shown in Figure 12.9. For each trial value for the data cell listed in the first column of the table, the corresponding output cell values are calculated and displayed in the other columns of the table. (The entries in the first row of the table come from the original solution in the spreadsheet.)

This algebraic procedure finds the exact value of a prior probability where the decision shifts from one alternative to another as the prior probability increases.

Figure 12.9 reveals that the best course of action switches from Sell to Drill for a prior probability of oil somewhere between 0.23 and 0.25. Algebra can be used to solve for the exact value of this prior probability as follows.

Let p = prior probability of oil. For the alternative of drilling for oil,

$$\text{Expected payoff} = p(700) + (1 - p)(-100)$$
$$= 700p - 100 + 100p$$
$$= 800p - 100$$

Set Expected payoff = 90 (the payoff for selling the land).

$$800p - 100 = 90$$
$$800p = 190$$
$$p = \frac{190}{800} = 0.2375$$

Conclusion: Sell the land if $p < 0.2375$.

Drill for oil if $p > 0.2375$.

For a problem with more than two possible states of nature, the most straightforward approach is to focus the sensitivity analysis on only two states at a time as described above. This again would involve investigating what happens when the prior probability of one state increases as the prior probability of the other state decreases by the same amount, holding fixed the prior probabilities of the remaining states. This procedure then can be repeated for as many other pairs of states as desired.

Max's Reaction

Max: That data table paints a pretty clear picture. I think I'm getting a much better handle on the problem.

Jennifer: Good.

Max: Less than a 23¾ percent chance of oil, I should sell. If it's more, I should drill. Right?

Jennifer: That's right.

Max: That really pins it down.

Jennifer: Yes.

Max: It confirms what I suspected all along. This is a close decision, and it all boils down to picking the right number for the chances of oil. I sure wish I had more to go on than the consulting geologist's numbers.

Jennifer: You talked earlier about the possibility of paying $30,000 to get a detailed seismic survey of the land.

Max: Yes, I might have to do that. But 30,000 bucks! I'm still not sure that it's worth that much dough.

The next section describes how to find and use the expected value of perfect information.

Jennifer: I have a quick way of checking that. It's another technique I learned in my management science course. It's called finding the **expected value of perfect information (EVPI).** The expected value of perfect information is the increase in the expected payoff you would get if the seismic survey could tell you for sure if there is oil there.

Max: But it can't tell you for sure.

Jennifer: Yes, I know. But finding out for sure if oil is there is what we refer to as perfect information. So the increase in the expected payoff if you find out for sure is the expected value of perfect information. We know that's better than you actually can do with a seismic survey.

Max: Right.

Jennifer: OK, suppose we find that the expected value of perfect information is less than $30,000. Since that is better than we can do with a seismic survey, that tells us right off the bat that it wouldn't pay to do the seismic survey.

Max: OK, I get it. But what if this expected value of perfect information is more than $30,000?

Jennifer: Then you don't know for sure whether the seismic survey is worth it until you do some more analysis. This analysis takes some time, whereas it is very quick to calculate the expected value of perfect information. So it is well worth simply checking whether the expected value of perfect information is less than $30,000 and, if so, saving a lot of additional work.

Max: OK. Let's do it.

Review Questions

1. Why might it be helpful to use sensitivity analysis with Bayes' decision rule?
2. When preparing to perform sensitivity analysis, what are a couple of advantages of consolidating the data and results on the spreadsheet that contains the decision tree?
3. What is shown by a data table when it is used to perform sensitivity analysis?
4. What conclusion was drawn for the first Goferbroke Co. problem regarding how the decision should depend on the prior probability of oil?

12.5 CHECKING WHETHER TO OBTAIN MORE INFORMATION

Definitely identifying the true state of nature is referred to as *perfect information*. This represents the best outcome of seeking more information.

Prior probabilities may provide somewhat inaccurate estimates of the true probabilities of the states of nature. Might it be worthwhile for Max to spend some money for a seismic survey to obtain better estimates? The quickest way to check this is to pretend that it is possible for the same amount of money to actually determine which state is the true state of nature ("perfect information") and then determine whether obtaining this information would make this expenditure worthwhile. If having perfect information would not be worthwhile, then it definitely would not be worthwhile to spend this money just to learn more about the probabilities of the states of nature.

The key quantities for performing this analysis are

EP (without more info) = Expected payoff from applying Bayes' decision rule with the original prior probabilities
= 100 (as given in Figure 12.6)

EP (with perfect info) = Expected payoff if the decision could be made after learning the true state of nature

EVPI = Expected value of perfect information

C = Cost of obtaining more information
= 30 (cost of the seismic survey in thousands of dollars)

The expected value of perfect information is calculated as

$$\text{EVPI} = \text{EP (with perfect info)} - \text{EP (without more info)}$$

After calculating EP (with perfect info) and then EVPI, the last step is to compare EVPI with C.

If $C > \text{EVPI}$, then it is not worthwhile to obtain more information.

If $C \leq \text{EVPI}$, then it might be worthwhile to obtain more information.

To calculate EP (with perfect info), we pretend that the decision can be made *after* learning the true state of nature. Given the true state of nature, we then would automatically choose the

FIGURE 12.10
Calculation of the
expected payoff with
perfect information in cell
D11 as the
SUMPRODUCT of
PriorProbability (C9:D9)
and MaximumPayoff
(C7:D7).

	A	B	C	D	E
1		**Expected Payoff with Perfect Information**			
2					
3		**Payoff Table**	**State of Nature**		
4		Alternative	Oil	Dry	
5		Drill	700	-100	
6		Sell	90	90	
7		Maximum Payoff	700	90	
8					
9		Prior Probability	0.25	0.75	
10					
11		EP (with perfect info)		242.5	

Range Name	Cells
DryPayoff	D5:D6
MaximumPayoff	C7:D7
OilPayoff	C5:C6
PriorProbability	C9:D9

	B	C	D
7	Maximum Payoff	=MAX(OilPayoff)	=MAX(DryPayoff)

	C	D
11	EP (with perfect info)	=SUMPRODUCT(PriorProbability,MaximumPayoff)

alternative with the maximum payoff for that state. Thus, we drill if we know there is oil, whereas we sell if we know the site is dry. Figure 12.10 finds the MaximumPayoff (C7:D7) for both possible states of nature. If the site contains oil, we drill with the maximum payoff of 700. If the site is dry, we sell with the maximum payoff of 90. The prior probabilities still give the probability that each state of nature will turn out to be the true one. EP (with perfect info) is therefore the weighted average of the maximum payoff for each state, multiplying each maximum payoff by the prior probability of the corresponding state of nature. This calculation is performed in cell D11 on the spreadsheet in Figure 12.10, with the formula

$$EP \text{ (with perfect info)} = SUMPRODUCT(PriorProbability, MaximumPayoff)$$
$$= (0.25)(700) + (0.75)(90)$$
$$= 242.5$$

TreePlan also can be used to calculate EP (with perfect info) by constructing and solving the decision tree shown in Figure 12.11. The clever idea here is to *start* the decision tree with an event node whose branches are the various states of nature (oil and dry in this case). Since a decision node follows each of these branches, the decision is being made with perfect information about the true state of nature. Therefore, the expected payoff of 242.5 obtained by TreePlan in cell A11 is the expected payoff with perfect information.

Starting the decision tree with an event node whose branches are the various states of nature corresponds to starting with perfect information about the true state of nature.

Since EP (with perfect info) = 242½, we now can calculate the expected value of perfect information as

$$EVPI = EP \text{ (with perfect info)} - EP \text{ (without more info)}$$
$$= 242.5 - 100$$
$$= 142.5$$

Conclusion: EVPI > C, since 142.5 > 30. Therefore, it might be worthwhile to do the seismic survey.

Max's Reaction

Max: So you're telling me that if the seismic survey could really be definitive in determining whether oil is there, doing the survey would increase my average payoff by about $142,500?

FIGURE 12.11

By starting with an event node involving the states of nature, TreePlan uses this decision tree to obtain the expected payoff with perfect information for the first Goferbroke Co. problem.

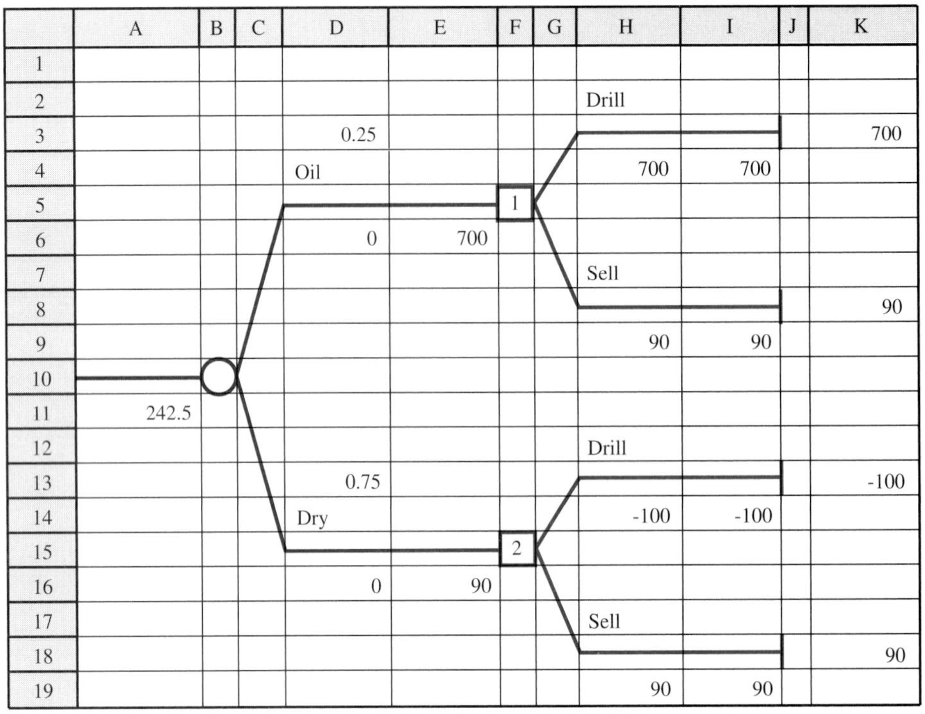

	A	B	C	D	E	F	G	H	I	J	K
1											
2								Drill			
3				0.25							700
4				Oil				700	700		
5						1					
6				0	700						
7								Sell			
8											90
9								90	90		
10		◯									
11	242.5										
12								Drill			
13				0.75							-100
14				Dry				-100	-100		
15						2					
16				0	90						
17								Sell			
18											90
19								90	90		

Jennifer: That's right.

Max: So after subtracting the $30,000 cost of the survey, I would be ahead $112,500?

Jennifer: You got it. But remember that the $112,500 is an average. That's roughly the average amount you would be ahead if you did this on many similar tracts of land. There are no guarantees on this one tract. But it does indicate that we might want to get more information.

Max: OK. Well, too bad the surveys aren't that good. In fact, they're not all that reliable.

Jennifer: Tell me more. How reliable are they?

Max: Well, they come back with seismic soundings. If the seismic soundings are favorable, then oil is fairly likely. If they are unfavorable, then oil is pretty unlikely. But you can't tell for sure.

Jennifer: OK. Suppose oil is there. How often would you get favorable seismic soundings?

Max: Oh, a little over half the time.

Jennifer: Can you give me a percentage?

Max: I can't give you an exact number. Maybe 60 percent.

Jennifer: OK, good. Now suppose that the land is dry. How often would you still get favorable seismic soundings?

Max: Too often! I've lost a lot of money drilling when the seismic survey said to and then nothing was there. That's why I don't like to spend the 30,000 bucks.

Jennifer: Sure. So it tells you to drill when you shouldn't close to half the time?

Max: No. It's not that bad. But fairly often.

Jennifer:	Can you give me a percentage?
Max:	I don't like to give those numbers. I'm no better at it than those consulting geologists.
Jennifer:	I understand. But a ballpark figure would be helpful.
Max:	OK. Maybe 20 percent.
Jennifer:	Good. Thanks. Now I think we can do some analysis to determine whether it is really worthwhile to do the seismic survey.
Max:	How do you do the analysis?
Jennifer:	Well, I'll describe the process in detail pretty soon. But here is the general idea. We'll do some calculations to determine what the chances of oil would be if the seismic soundings turn out to be favorable. Then we'll calculate the chances if the soundings are unfavorable.
Max:	You can do that?
Jennifer:	Yes, there is something called Bayes' theorem that enables us to do it.
Max:	Hmm, that Reverend Bayes fellow again?
Jennifer:	Yep.
Max:	Pretty smart guy.
Jennifer:	Yes, he was. Anyway, we'll use his theorem to improve the consulting geologist's numbers on the chances of oil for each possible outcome of the seismic survey.
Max:	Good.
Jennifer:	We called the consulting geologist's numbers prior probabilities because they were prior to obtaining more information. The improved numbers are referred to as *posterior probabilities*.

Posterior probabilities are the revised probabilities of the states of nature after doing a test or survey to improve the prior probabilities.

Max:	OK.
Jennifer:	Then we'll use these posterior probabilities to determine the average payoff, after subtracting the $30,000 cost, if we do the seismic survey. If this payoff is better than we would do without the seismic survey, then we should do it. Otherwise, not.
Max:	That makes sense.
Jennifer:	Shall we get started?
Max:	OK.

Review Questions

1. What is meant by perfect information regarding the states of nature?
2. How can the expected payoff with perfect information be calculated from the payoff table?
3. How should a decision tree be constructed to obtain the expected payoff with perfect information by solving the tree?
4. What is the formula for calculating the expected value of perfect information?
5. What is the conclusion if the cost of obtaining more information is more than the expected value of perfect information?
6. What is the conclusion if the cost of obtaining more information is less than the expected value of perfect information?
7. Which of these two cases occurs in the Goferbroke Co. problem?

12.6 USING NEW INFORMATION TO UPDATE THE PROBABILITIES

The prior probabilities of the possible states of nature often are quite subjective in nature, so they may be only very rough estimates of the true probabilities. Fortunately, it frequently is possible to do some additional testing or surveying (at some expense) to improve these estimates. These improved estimates are called **posterior probabilities.**

In the case of the Goferbroke Co., these improved estimates can be obtained at a cost of $30,000 by conducting a detailed seismic survey of the land. The possible findings from such a survey are summarized below.

Possible Findings from a Seismic Survey

FSS: Favorable seismic soundings; oil is fairly likely.

USS: Unfavorable seismic soundings; oil is quite unlikely.

To use either finding to calculate the posterior probability of oil (or of being dry), it is necessary to estimate the probability of obtaining this finding for each state of nature. During the conversation at the end of the preceding section, Jennifer elicited these estimates from Max, as summarized in Table 12.7. (Max actually only estimated the probability of favorable seismic soundings, but subtracting this number from one gives the probability of unfavorable seismic soundings.) The symbol used in the table for each of these estimated probabilities is

P(finding | state) = Probability that the indicated finding will occur, given that the state of nature is the indicated one

This kind of probability is referred to as a *conditional probability*, because it is conditioned on being given the state of nature.

Recall that the prior probabilities are

$$P(\text{Oil}) = 0.25$$

$$P(\text{Dry}) = 0.75$$

The next step is to use these probabilities and the probabilities in Table 12.7 to obtain a combined probability called a *joint probability*. Each combination of a state of nature and a finding from the seismic survey will have a joint probability that is determined by the following formula.

$$P(\text{state and finding}) = P(\text{state}) \, P(\text{finding} \mid \text{state})$$

For example, the joint probability that the state of nature is Oil *and* the finding from the seismic survey is favorable (FSS) is

$$P(\text{Oil and FSS}) = P(\text{Oil}) \, P(\text{FSS} \mid \text{Oil})$$

$$= 0.25(0.6)$$

$$= 0.15$$

Each joint probability in the third column of the probability tree diagram is the product of the probabilities in the first two columns.

The calculation of all these joint probabilities is shown in the third column of the **probability tree diagram** given in Figure 12.12. The case involved is identified underneath each branch of the tree and the probability is given over the branch. The first column gives the prior probabilities and then the probabilities from Table 12.7 are shown in the second column. Mul-

TABLE 12.7
Probabilities of the Possible Findings from the Seismic Survey, Given the State of Nature, for the Goferbroke Co. Problem

State of Nature	P(finding | state)	
	Favorable (FSS)	Unfavorable (USS)
Oil	$P(\text{FSS} \mid \text{Oil}) = 0.6$	$P(\text{USS} \mid \text{Oil}) = 0.4$
Dry	$P(\text{FSS} \mid \text{Dry}) = 0.2$	$P(\text{USS} \mid \text{Dry}) = 0.8$

FIGURE 12.12

Probability tree diagram for the Goferbroke Co. problem showing all the probabilities leading to the calculation of each posterior probability of the state of nature given the finding of the seismic survey.

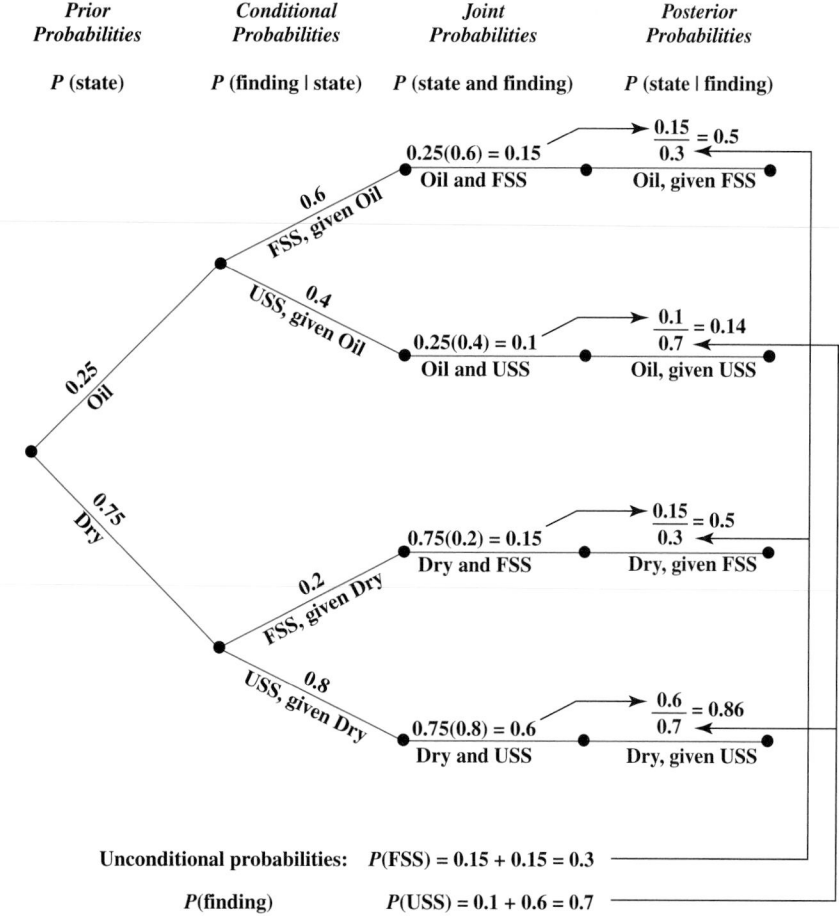

Unconditional probabilities: P(FSS) = 0.15 + 0.15 = 0.3

P(finding) P(USS) = 0.1 + 0.6 = 0.7

tiplying each probability in the first column by a probability in the second column gives the corresponding joint probability in the third column.

Having found each joint probability of both a particular state of nature and a particular finding from the seismic survey, the next step is to use these probabilities to find each probability of just a particular finding without specifying the state of nature. Since any finding can be obtained with any state of nature, the formula for calculating the probability of just a particular finding is

$$P(\text{finding}) = P(\text{Oil and finding}) + P(\text{Dry and finding})$$

For example, the probability of a favorable finding (FSS) is

$$P(\text{FSS}) = P(\text{Oil and FSS}) + P(\text{Dry and FSS})$$

$$= 0.15 + 0.15 = 0.3$$

The probability of a finding is the sum of the corresponding joint probabilities in the third column of the probability tree diagram.

where the two joint probabilities on the right-hand side of this equation are found on the first and third branches of the third column of the probability tree diagram. The calculation of both P(FSS) and P(USS) is shown underneath the diagram. (These are referred to as *unconditional* probabilities to differentiate them from the *conditional* probabilities of a finding given the state of nature, shown in the second column.)

Finally, we now are ready to calculate each *posterior probability* of a particular state of nature given a particular finding from the seismic survey. The formula involves combining the joint probabilities in the third column with the unconditional probabilities underneath the diagram as follows.

$$P(\text{state} \mid \text{finding}) = \frac{P(\text{state and finding})}{P(\text{finding})}$$

For example, the posterior probability that the true state of nature is oil, given a favorable finding (FSS) from the seismic survey, is

$$P(\text{Oil} \mid \text{FSS}) = \frac{P(\text{Oil and FSS})}{P(\text{FSS})}$$

$$= \frac{0.15}{0.3} = 0.5$$

The arrows in the probability tree diagram show where the numbers come from for calculating the posterior probabilities.

The fourth column of the probability tree diagram shows the calculation of all the posterior probabilities. The arrows indicate how each numerator comes from the corresponding joint probability in the third column and the denominator comes from the corresponding unconditional probability below the diagram.

By using the formulas given earlier for the joint probabilities and unconditional probabilities, each posterior probability also can be calculated directly from the prior probabilities (first column) and the conditional probabilities (second column) as follows.

$$P(\text{state} \mid \text{finding}) = \frac{P(\text{state}) \, P(\text{finding} \mid \text{state})}{P(\text{Oil}) \, P(\text{finding} \mid \text{Oil}) + P(\text{Dry}) \, P(\text{finding} \mid \text{Dry})}$$

For example, the posterior probability of oil, given a favorable finding (FSS), is

$$P(\text{Oil} \mid \text{FSS}) = \frac{P(\text{Oil}) \, P(\text{FSS} \mid \text{Oil})}{P(\text{Oil}) \, P(\text{FSS} \mid \text{Oil}) + P(\text{Dry}) \, P(\text{FSS} \mid \text{Dry})}$$

$$= \frac{0.25(0.6)}{0.25(0.6) + 0.75(0.2)}$$

$$= 0.5$$

This formula for a posterior probability is known as **Bayes' theorem,** in honor of its discovery by the Reverend Bayes. The clever Reverend Bayes found that any posterior probability can be found in this way for any decision analysis problem, regardless of how many states of nature it has. The denominator in the formula would contain one such term for each of the states of nature. Note that the probability tree diagram also is applying Bayes' theorem, but in smaller steps rather than a single long formula.

Table 12.8 summarizes all the posterior probabilities calculated in Figure 12.12.

After you learn the logic of calculating posterior probabilities, we suggest that you use the computer to perform these rather lengthy calculations. We have provided an Excel template (labeled Posterior Probabilities) for this purpose in this chapter's Excel files in your MS Courseware. Figure 12.13 illustrates the use of this template for the Goferbroke Co. problem. All you do is enter the prior probabilities and the conditional probabilities from the first two columns of Figure 12.12 into the top half of the template. The posterior probabilities then immediately appear in the bottom half. (The equations entered into the cells in columns E through H are similar to those for column D shown at the bottom of the figure.)

Max's Reaction

Max: So this is saying that even with favorable seismic soundings, I still only have one chance in two of finding oil.

Jennifer: Yes. Assuming you start off with the consulting geologist giving you one chance in four, that is correct.

TABLE 12.8
Posterior Probabilities of the States of Nature, Given the Finding from the Seismic Survey, for the Goferbroke Co. Problem

	P(state | finding)	
Finding	**Oil**	**Dry**
Favorable (FSS)	$P(\text{Oil} \mid \text{FSS}) = 1/2$	$P(\text{Dry} \mid \text{FSS}) = 1/2$
Unfavorable (USS)	$P(\text{Oil} \mid \text{USS}) = 1/7$	$P(\text{Dry} \mid \text{USS}) = 6/7$

FIGURE 12.13

The Posterior Probabilities template in your MS Courseware enables efficient calculation of posterior probabilities, as illustrated here for the Goferbroke Co. problem.

	A	B	C	D	E	F	G	H
1		**Template for Posterior Probabilities**						
2								
3		**Data:**		*P*(Finding | State)				
4		State of	Prior	Finding				
5		Nature	Probability	FSS	USS			
6		Oil	0.25	0.6	0.4			
7		Dry	0.75	0.2	0.8			
8								
9								
10								
11								
12		**Posterior**		*P*(State | Finding)				
13		**Probabilities:**		State of Nature				
14		Finding	*P*(Finding)	Oil	Dry			
15		FSS	0.3	0.5	0.5			
16		USS	0.7	0.14286	0.85714			
17								
18								
19								

	B	C	D
12	**Posterior**		*P*(State | Finding)
13	**Probabilities:**		State of Nature
14	Finding	*P*(Finding)	=B6
15	=D5	=SUMPRODUCT(C6:C10,D6:D10)	=C6*D6/SUMPRODUCT(C6:C10,D6:D10)
16	=E5	=SUMPRODUCT(C6:C10,E6:E10)	=C6*E6/SUMPRODUCT(C6:C10,E6:E10)
17	=F5	=SUMPRODUCT(C6:C10,F6:F10)	=C6*F6/SUMPRODUCT(C6:C10,F6:F10)
18	=G5	=SUMPRODUCT(C6:C10,G6:G10)	=C6*G6/SUMPRODUCT(C6:C10,G6:G10)
19	=H5	=SUMPRODUCT(C6:C10,H6:H10)	=C6*H6/SUMPRODUCT(C6:C10,H6:H10)

Max: No wonder I've been disappointed so often in the past when I've drilled after receiving a favorable seismic survey. I thought those surveys were supposed to be more reliable than that. So now I'm even more unenthusiastic about paying 30,000 bucks to get a survey done.

Jennifer: But one chance in two of oil. Those are good odds.

Max: Yes, they are. But I'm likely to lay out 30,000 bucks and then just get an unfavorable survey back.

Jennifer: My calculations indicate that you have about a 70 percent chance of that happening.

Max: See what I mean?

Jennifer: But even an unfavorable survey tells you a lot. Just one chance in seven of oil then. That might rule out drilling.

Max: Yes, it might not pay to drill with those odds.

Jennifer: So a seismic survey really does pin down the odds of oil a lot better. Either one chance in two or one chance in seven instead of the ballpark estimate of one chance in four from the consulting geologist.

Max: Yes, I suppose that's right. I really would like to improve the consulting geologist's numbers. It sounds like you're recommending that we do the seismic survey.

Jennifer: Well, actually, I'm not quite sure yet. We still need to do just a little more analysis. Then I think we'll have all the information you need to make a confident decision. Remember I was talking earlier about finding what the average payoff would be if we did the seismic survey and then comparing that with what we would get without the survey?

Max: Yes, I remember. But I'm still not clear on how we do that.

Jennifer: Well, what we'll do is sketch out a decision tree, showing the decision on whether to do the seismic survey and then the decision on whether to drill or sell. Then we'll work out the average payoffs for these decisions on the decision tree.

Max: OK, let's do it. I want to make a decision soon.

Review
Questions

1. What are posterior probabilities of the states of nature?
2. What are the possible findings from a seismic survey for the Goferbroke Co.?
3. What probabilities need to be estimated in addition to prior probabilities in order to begin calculating posterior probabilities?
4. What five kinds of probabilities are considered in a probability tree diagram?
5. What is the formula for calculating P(state and finding)?
6. What is the formula for calculating P(finding)?
7. What is the formula for calculating a posterior probability, P(state | finding), from P(state and finding) and P(finding)?
8. What is the name of the famous theorem for how to calculate posterior probabilities?

12.7   USING A DECISION TREE TO ANALYZE THE PROBLEM WITH A SEQUENCE OF DECISIONS

We now turn our attention to analyzing the *full* Goferbroke Co. problem with the help of a decision tree. For the full problem, there is a sequence of two decisions to be made. First, should a seismic survey be conducted? Second, after obtaining the results of the seismic survey (if it is conducted), should the company drill for oil or sell the land?

As described in Section 12.3, a decision tree provides a graphical display of the progression of decisions and random events for the problem. Figure 12.2 in that section shows the decision tree for the first Goferbroke problem where the only decision under consideration is whether to drill for oil or sell the land. Figure 12.5 then shows the same decision tree as it would be constructed and solved with TreePlan.

Constructing the Decision Tree

Now that a prior decision needs to be made on whether to conduct a seismic survey, this same decision tree needs to be expanded as shown in Figure 12.14 (before including any numbers). Recall that each *square* in the tree represents a *decision node,* where a decision needs to be made, and each *circle* represents an *event node,* where a random event will occur.

Thus, the first decision (should we have a seismic survey done?) is represented by decision node *a* in Figure 12.14. The two branches leading out of this node correspond to the two alternatives for this decision. Node *b* is an event node representing the random event of the outcome of the seismic survey. The two branches emanating from node *b* represent the two possible outcomes of the survey. Next comes the second decision (nodes *c, d,* and *e*) with its two possible choices. If the decision is to drill for oil, then we come to another event node (nodes *f, g,* and *h*), where its two branches correspond to the two possible states of nature.

The next step is to insert numbers into the decision tree as shown in Figure 12.15. The numbers under or over the branches that are *not* in parentheses are the cash flows (in thousands of

FIGURE 12.14
The decision tree for the
full Goferbroke Co.
problem (before including
any numbers) when first
deciding whether to
conduct a seismic survey.

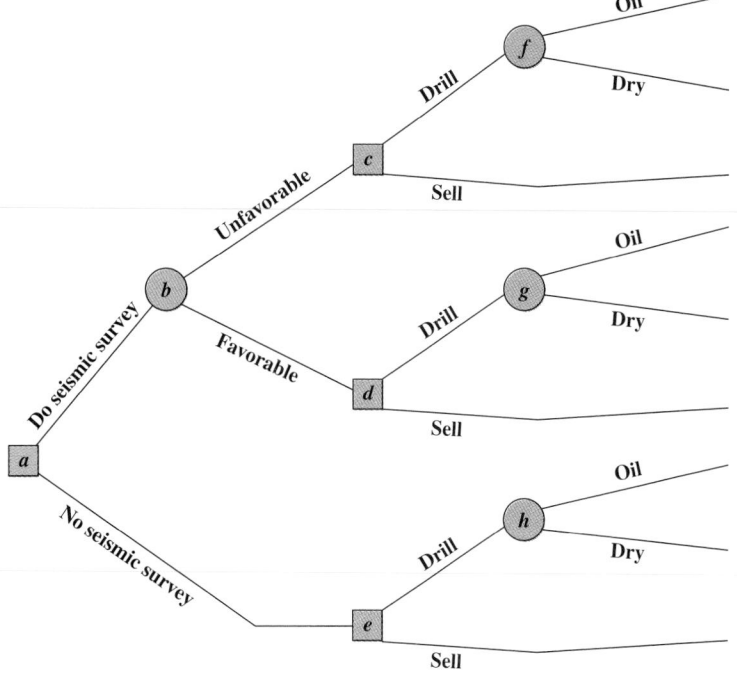

FIGURE 12.15
The decision tree in
Figure 12.14 after adding
both the probabilities of
random events and the
payoffs.

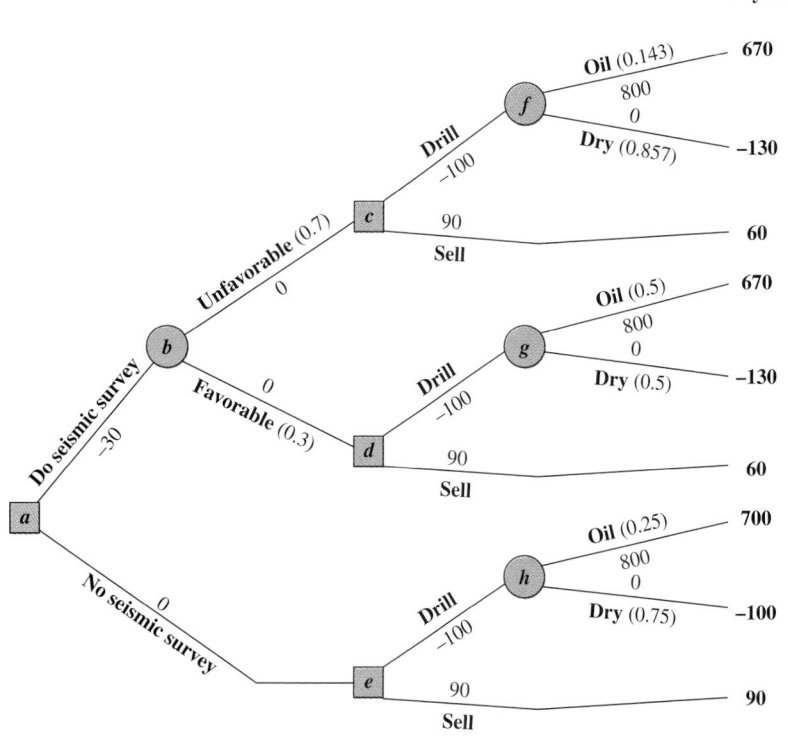

The numbers in paren-
theses are probabilities.

dollars) that occur at those branches. For each path through the tree from node *a* to a final
branch, these same numbers then are added to obtain the resulting total payoff shown in boldface to the right of that branch. The last set of numbers is the probabilities of random events.
In particular, since each branch emanating from an event node represents a possible random
event, the probability of this event occurring from this node has been inserted in parentheses
along this branch. From event node *h,* the probabilities are the *prior probabilities* of these
states of nature, since no seismic survey has been conducted to obtain more information in this

case. However, event nodes *f* and *g* lead out of a decision to do the seismic survey (and then to drill). Therefore, the probabilities from these event nodes are the *posterior probabilities* of the states of nature, given the outcome of the seismic survey, where these numbers are obtained from Table 12.8 or from cells D15:E16 in Figure 12.13. Finally, we have the two branches emanating from event node *b*. The numbers here are the probabilities of these findings from the seismic survey, Favorable (FSS) or Unfavorable (USS), as given underneath the probability tree diagram in Figure 12.12 or in cells C15:C16 of Figure 12.13.

Performing the Analysis

Having constructed the decision tree, including its numbers, we now are ready to analyze the problem by using the following procedure.

1. Start at the right side of the decision tree and move left one column at a time. For each column, perform either step 2 or step 3 depending on whether the nodes in that column are event nodes or decision nodes.

The expected payoff needs to be calculated for each event node.

2. For each event node, calculate its *expected payoff* by multiplying the expected payoff of each branch (shown in boldface to the right of the branch) by the probability of that branch and then summing these products. Record this expected payoff for each event node in boldface next to the node, and designate this quantity as also being the expected payoff for the branch leading to this node.

3. For each decision node, compare the expected payoffs of its branches and choose the alternative whose branch has the largest expected payoff. In each case, record the choice on the decision tree.

To begin the procedure, consider the rightmost column of nodes, namely, event nodes *f, g,* and *h.* Applying step 2, their expected payoffs (EP) are calculated as

$$EP = \frac{1}{7}(670) + \frac{6}{7}(-130) = -15.7 \quad \text{for node } f$$

$$EP = \frac{1}{2}(670) + \frac{1}{2}(-130) = 270 \quad \text{for node } g$$

$$EP = \frac{1}{4}(700) + \frac{3}{4}(-100) = 100 \quad \text{for node } h$$

These expected payoffs then are placed above these nodes, as shown in Figure 12.16.

Next, we move one column to the left, which consists of decision nodes *c, d,* and *e.* The expected payoff for a branch that leads to an event node now is recorded in boldface over that event node. Therefore, step 3 can be applied as follows.

Node *c:*   Drill alternative has EP $= -15.7$

Sell alternative has EP $= 60$

$60 > -15.7$, so choose the Sell alternative

Node *d:*   Drill alternative has EP $= 270$

Sell alternative has EP $= 60$

$270 > 60$, so choose the Drill alternative

Node *e:*   Drill alternative has EP $= 100$

Sell alternative has EP $= 90$

$100 > 90$, so choose the Drill alternative

A double dash indicates a rejected decision.

The expected payoff for each chosen alternative now would be recorded in boldface over its decision node, as shown in Figure 12.16. The chosen alternative also is indicated by inserting a double dash as a barrier through each rejected branch.

FIGURE 12.16

The final decision tree that records the analysis for the full Goferbroke Co. problem when using monetary payoffs.

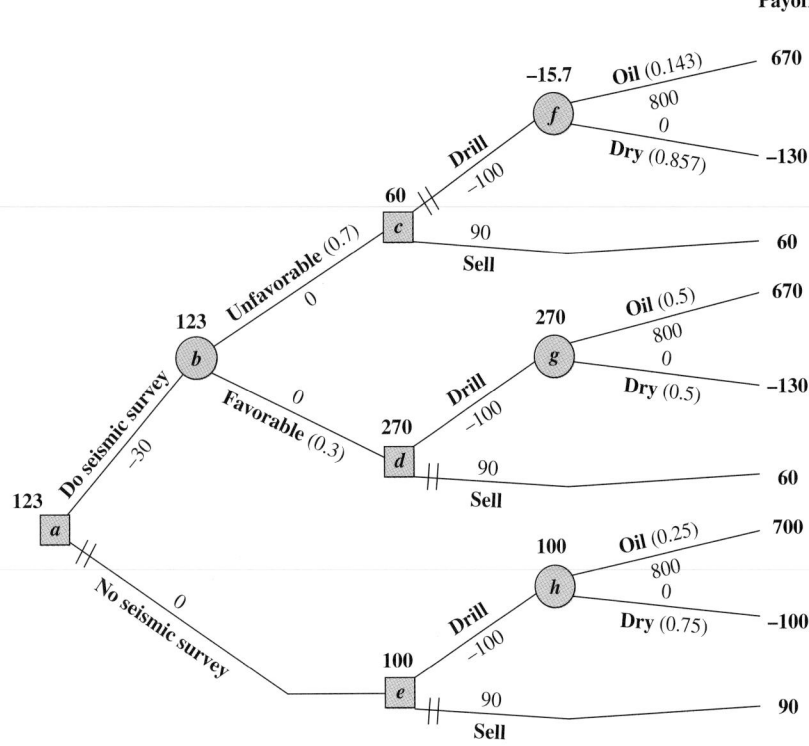

Next, moving one more column to the left brings us to node *b*. Since this is an event node, step 2 of the procedure needs to be applied. The expected payoff for each of its branches is recorded over the following decision node. Therefore, the expected payoff is

$$\text{EP} = 0.7\,(60) + 0.3(270) = 123 \qquad \text{for node } b$$

as recorded over this node in Figure 12.16.

Finally, we move left to node *a,* a decision node. Applying step 3 yields

Node *a:*   Do seismic survey has EP $= 123$

No seismic survey has EP $= 100$

$123 > 100$, so choose Do seismic survey.

This expected payoff of 123 now would be recorded over the node, and a double dash inserted to indicate the rejected branch, as already shown in Figure 12.16.

This procedure has moved from right to left for analysis purposes. However, having completed the decision tree in this way, the decision maker now can read the tree from left to right to see the actual progression of events. The double dashes have closed off the undesirable paths. Therefore, given the payoffs for the final outcomes shown on the right side, *Bayes' decision rule* says to follow only the open paths from left to right to achieve the largest possible expected payoff.

Following the open paths from left to right in Figure 12.16 yields the following optimal policy, according to Bayes' decision rule.

The open paths (no double dashes) provide the optimal decision at each decision node.

Optimal Policy

Do the seismic survey.

If the result is unfavorable, sell the land.

If the result is favorable, drill for oil.

The expected payoff (including the cost of the seismic survey) is 123 ($123,000).

FIGURE 12.17 The decision tree constructed and solved by TreePlan for the full Goferbroke Co. problem that also considers whether to do a seismic survey.

	A	B	C	D	E	F	G	H	I	J	K	L	M	N	O	P	Q	R	S
1	**Decision Tree for Goferbroke Co. Problem (with Survey)**																		
2																			
3																0.14286			
4																Oil			
5																			670
6												Drill				800	670		
7														◯					
8												-100	-15.714			0.85714			
9								0.7								Dry			
10								Unfavorable											-130
11										2						0	-130		
12								0	60										
13																			
14												Sell							
15																- - - - - - -			60
16												90	60						
17				Do Survey															
18							◯									0.5			
19				-30	123											Oil			
20																			670
21												Drill				800	670		
22														◯					
23												-100	270			0.5			
24								0.3								Dry			
25								Favorable											-130
26										1						0	-130		
27								0	270										
28																			
29		1										Sell							
30		123														- - - - - - -			60
31												90	60						
32																			
33												0.25							
34												Oil							
35																- - - - - - -			700
36								Drill				800	700						
37											◯								
38								-100	100			0.75							
39												Dry							
40				No Survey												- - - - - - -			-100
41						1						0	-100						
42				0	100														
43																			
44								Sell											
45																- - - - - - -			90
46								90	90										

Using TreePlan

Using the procedures described in Section 12.3, TreePlan can be used to construct and solve this same decision tree on a spreadsheet. Figure 12.17 shows the decision tree obtained with TreePlan. Although the form is somewhat different, note that this decision tree is completely equivalent to the one in Figure 12.16. Besides the convenience of constructing the tree directly on a spreadsheet, TreePlan also provides the key advantage of automatically solving the decision tree. Rather than relying on hand calculations as in Figure 12.16, TreePlan instantaneously calculates all the expected payoffs at each stage of the tree, as shown below and to the left of each node, as soon as the decision tree is constructed. Instead of using double dashes, TreePlan puts a number inside each decision node indicating which branch should be chosen (assuming the branches emanating from that node are numbered consecutively from top to bottom).

Max's Reaction

Max: I see that this decision tree gives me some numbers to compare alternatives. But how reliable are those numbers?

Jennifer: Well, you have to remember that these average payoffs for the alternatives at the decision nodes are based on both the payoffs on the right and the probabilities at the event nodes. These probabilities are based in turn on the consulting geologist's numbers and the numbers you gave me on how frequently you get favorable seismic soundings when you have oil or when the land is dry.

Max: That doesn't sound so good. You know what I think about the consulting geologist's numbers. And the numbers I gave you were pretty rough estimates.

Jennifer: True. So the average payoffs shown in the decision tree are only approximations. This is when some sensitivity analysis can be helpful, like we did earlier before we considered doing the seismic survey.

Max: So shouldn't we do some sensitivity analysis now?

Jennifer: Yes, it generally is a good idea to do some sensitivity analysis until you are comfortable with your decision.

Max: OK. So let's do it.

**Review
Questions**

1. What does a decision tree display?
2. What is happening at a decision node?
3. What is happening at an event node?
4. What kinds of numbers need to be inserted into a decision tree before beginning the analysis?
5. When performing the analysis, where do you begin on the decision tree and in which direction do you move for dealing with the nodes?
6. What calculation needs to be performed at each event node?
7. What comparison needs to be made at each decision node?

12.8 PERFORMING SENSITIVITY ANALYSIS ON THE PROBLEM WITH A SEQUENCE OF DECISIONS

Section 12.4 describes how the decision tree created with TreePlan (Figures 12.5 and 12.6) was used to perform sensitivity analysis for the first Goferbroke problem where the only decision being made was whether to drill for oil or sell the land (without conducting the seismic survey). The focus was on one particularly critical piece of data, the prior probability of oil, so the analysis involved checking whether the decision would change if the original value of this prior probability (0.25) were changed to various other trial values. New trial values first were considered in a trial-and-error manner (Figure 12.7) and then were investigated more systematically by constructing a data table (Figure 12.9).

Since Max Flyer wants to consider whether to have a seismic survey conducted before deciding whether to drill or sell, the relevant decision tree now is the one in Figure 12.17 instead of the one in Figure 12.5. With this sequence of decisions and the resulting need to obtain and apply posterior probabilities, conducting sensitivity analysis becomes somewhat more involved. Let's see how it is done.

Organizing the Spreadsheet

Consolidating the data and results on the spreadsheet is important for sensitivity analysis.

As was done in Section 12.4, it is helpful to begin by consolidating the data and results into one section of the spreadsheet, as shown in Figure 12.18. The data cells in the decision tree now make reference to the consolidated data cells to the right of the decision tree (cells V4:V11). Similarly, the summarized results to the right of the decision tree make reference to the output cells within the decision tree (the decision nodes in cells B29, F41, J11, and J26, as well as the expected payoff in cell A30).

The probability data in the decision tree are complicated by the fact that the posterior probabilities will need to be updated any time a change is made in any of the prior probability data. Fortunately, the template for calculating posterior probabilities (as shown in Figure 12.13) can be used to do these calculations. The relevant portion of this template (B3:H19) has been copied (using the Copy and Paste commands in the Edit menu) to the spreadsheet in Figure 12.18 (now appearing in U30:AA46). The data for the template refer to the probability data in the data cells PriorProbabilityOfOil (V9), ProbFSSGivenOil (V10), and ProbUSSGivenDry (V11), as shown in the formulas for cells V33:X34 at the bottom of Figure 12.18. The template automatically calculates the probability of each finding and the posterior probabilities (in cells V42:X43) based on these data. The decision tree then refers to these calculated probabilities when they are needed, as shown in the formulas for cells P3:P11 in Figure 12.18.

Organize the spreadsheet so that any piece of data needs to be changed in only one place.

While it takes some time and effort to consolidate the data and results, including all the necessary cross-referencing, this step is truly essential for performing sensitivity analysis. Many pieces of data are used in several places on the decision tree. For example, the revenue if Goferbroke finds oil appears in cells P6, P21, and L36. Performing sensitivity analysis on this piece of data now requires changing its value in only one place (cell V6) rather than three (cells P6, P21, and L36). The benefits of consolidation are even more important for the probability data. Changing any prior probability may cause *all* the posterior probabilities to change. By including the posterior probability template, the prior probability can be changed in one place and then all the other probabilities are calculated and updated appropriately.

After making any change in the cost data, revenue data, or probability data in Figure 12.18, the spreadsheet nicely summarizes the new results after the actual work to obtain these results is instantly done by the posterior probability template and the decision tree. Therefore, experimenting with alternative data values in a trial-and-error manner is one useful way of performing sensitivity analysis.

However, it would be desirable to have another method of performing this sensitivity analysis more systematically. Using a data table as described in Section 12.4 is one such method. However, data tables have their limitations, particularly when dealing with large problems. For example, one major limitation is that each data table can consider changes in only one or two data cells.

Excel Tip: The SensIt add-in can be used either independently or in conjunction with TreePlan. The SensIt add-in can be installed either by simply opening the SensIt file in MS Courseware or by using the installer included in MS Courseware.

Fortunately, your MS Courseware includes an Excel add-in called *SensIt* that overcomes this limitation, providing an easy way to create informative sensitivity analysis graphs that display the effect of changing *any* number of data cells. SensIt was developed by Professor Michael Middleton, who also developed TreePlan, so it is designed to be integrated with TreePlan (although it also can perform other types of sensitivity analysis that don't require the use of TreePlan).

Using SensIt to Create Three Types of Sensitivity Analysis Graphs

Installing SensIt adds a Sensitivity Analysis menu item to the Tools menu in Excel. This menu item has a submenu giving a choice of three different kinds of sensitivity analysis graphs: Plot, Spider, and Tornado (along with a Help option). Let's see how each of these types of graphs can be used to perform sensitivity analysis.

FIGURE 12.18 In preparation for performing sensitivity analysis on the full Goferbroke Co. problem, the data and results have been consolidated on the spreadsheet to the right of the decision tree.

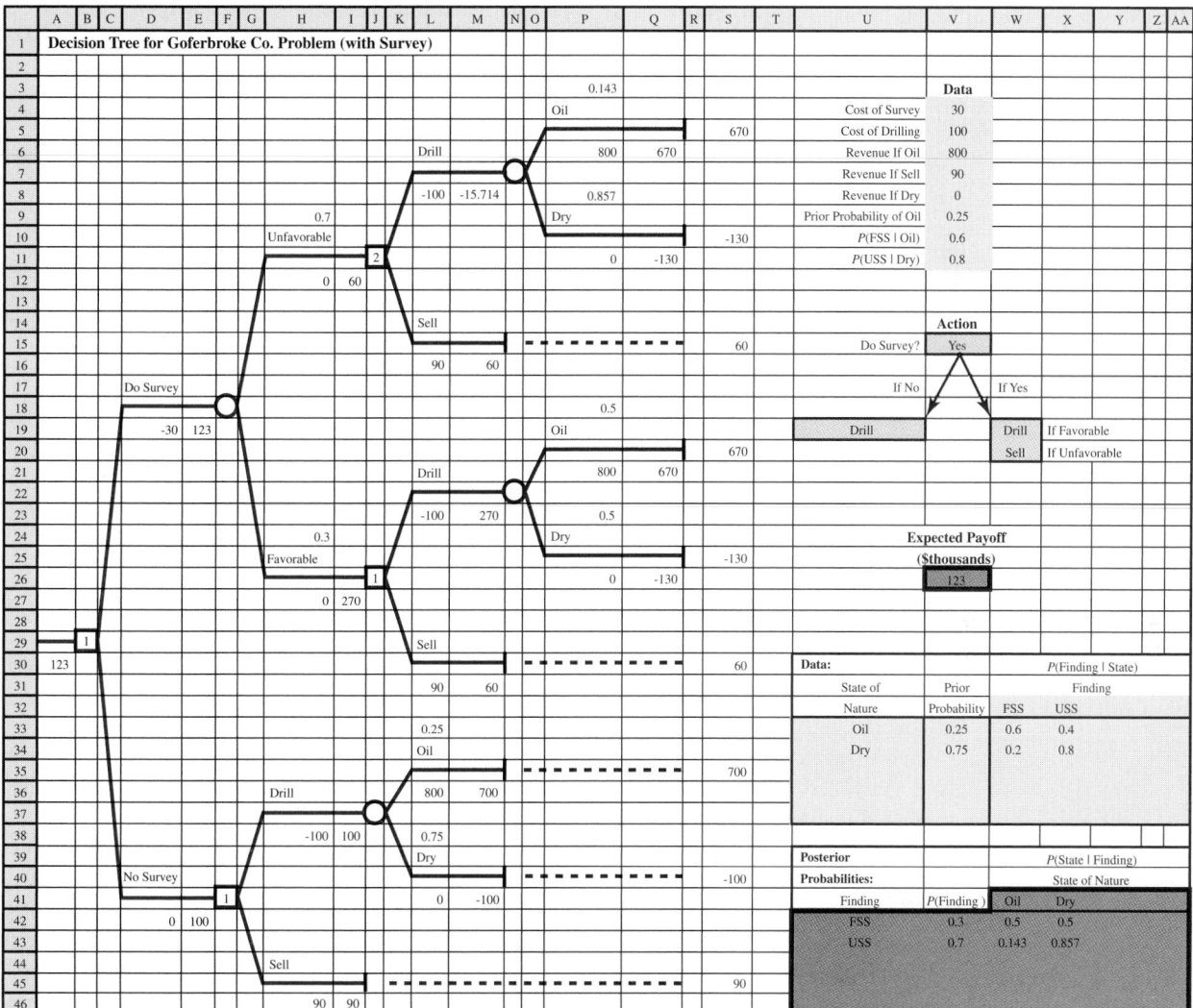

FIGURE 12.19

The dialogue box used by the Plot option of SensIt.

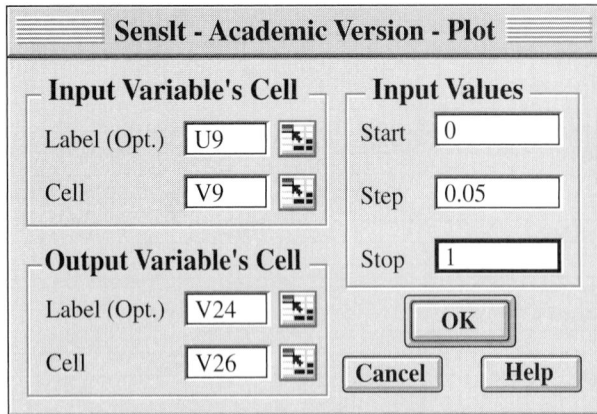

FIGURE 12.20 The graph generated by the Plot option of SensIt for the full Goferbroke Co. problem to show how the expected payoff (when using Bayes' decision rule) depends on the prior probability of oil.

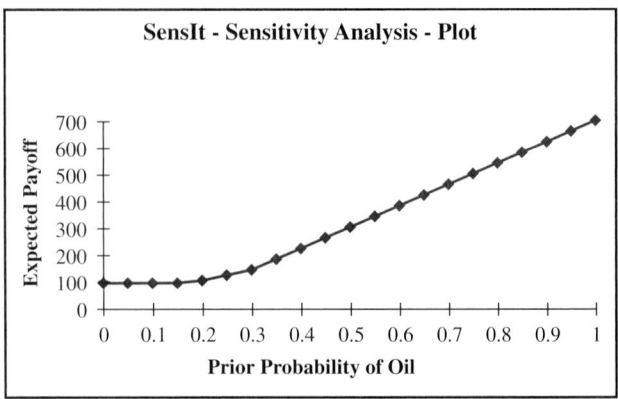

Plot is used to generate a graph that shows how an output cell varies for different values of a single data cell. Choosing this option brings up the Plot dialogue box shown in Figure 12.19. The left side of the SensIt-Plot dialogue box is used to specify the data cell that will be varied (the prior probability of oil in cell V9) and the output cell of interest (the expected payoff in cell V26). Optionally, the cells containing the labels for these cells may also be specified (cells U9 and V24, respectively). These labels are used to label the axes of the graph that is created. The right side of the SensIt-Plot dialogue box is used to specify the range of values to be considered for the single data cell (the prior probability of oil). In this case, all values between 0 and 1 (at intervals of 0.05) will be considered. Clicking OK then generates the graph shown in Figure 12.20 that reveals the relationship between the prior probability of oil and the expected payoff that results from using the optimal policy given this probability.

This graph indicates that the expected payoff starts increasing when the prior probability is a little over 0.15 and then starts increasing more rapidly when this probability is around 0.3. This suggests that the optimal policy changes at roughly these values of the prior probability. To check this out, the spreadsheet in Figure 12.18 can be used to see how the results change when the prior probability of oil is slowly increased in the vicinity of these values. This kind of trial-and-error analysis soon leads to the following conclusions about how the optimal policy depends on this probability.

Optimal Policy

Let p = Prior probability of oil.

If $p \le 0.168$, then sell the land (no seismic survey).

If 0.169 $\le p \le 0.308$, then do the survey: drill if favorable and sell if not.

If $p \ge 0.309$, then drill for oil (no seismic survey).

This sensitivity analysis has focused so far on investigating the effect if the true probability of finding oil is different from the original prior probability of 0.25. Similar analysis could be done with respect to the probabilities in cells V10:V11 of Figure 12.18. However, since there is significant uncertainty about some of the cost and revenue data in cells V4:V8, we turn next to performing sensitivity analysis with respect to these data.

Suppose we want to investigate how the expected payoff would change if one of the costs or revenues in cells V4:V7 were to change by up to *plus or minus 10 percent*. The **spider graph** (the second item in the Sensitivity Analysis submenu under the Tools menu) is used for this sort of analysis. The left side of the SensIt-Spider dialogue box (shown in Figure 12.21) is used to specify a range of data cells to be varied (the cost and revenue data in the range V4:V7) and the output cell of interest (the expected payoff in cell V26). In the right side of the SensIt-Spider dialogue box, specify the range of values to consider for the data cells in percentage

SensIt Tip: The data cells to be varied in a spider chart need to be in contiguous cells before choosing Spider in the Sensitivity Analysis submenu. Also be sure that the data cells contain the base case values.

FIGURE 12.21

The dialogue box used by the Spider option of SensIt.

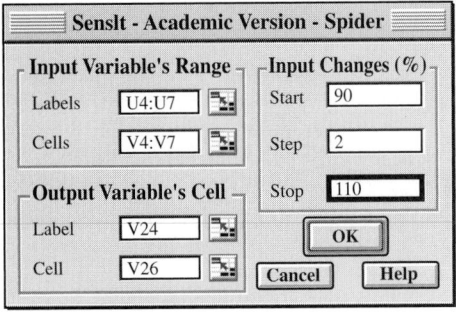

FIGURE 12.22

The spider graph generated by the Spider option of SensIt for the full Goferbroke Co. problem to show how the expected payoff (when using Bayes' decision rule) varies with changes in any one of the cost or revenue estimates.

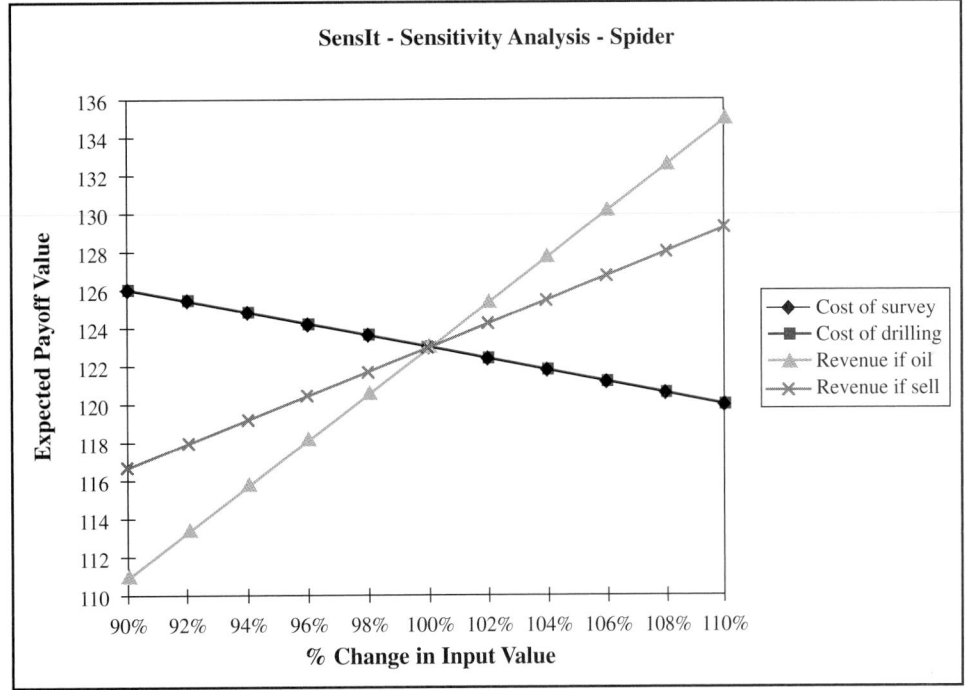

terms relative to their base value. To consider a change of plus or minus 10 percent for each data value, we consider values between 90 percent and 110 percent of the base value. Clicking OK then generates the graph shown in Figure 12.22.

Each line in the spider graph in this figure plots the expected payoff as one of the selected data cells (V4:V7) is changed from its original value by being multiplied by the percentage indicated along the bottom of the graph. (The diamonds for the *cost of survey line* are hidden under the squares for the *cost of drilling line.*) The fact that the *revenue if oil line* is the steepest one reveals that the expected payoff is particularly sensitive to the estimate of the revenue if oil is found, so any additional work on refining the estimates should focus the most attention on this one.

A limitation of SensIt's Spider graph is that it assumes that each data value varies by the same amount. For example, we considered the case where any one piece of the cost or revenue data could change by up to plus or minus 10 percent. It may be the case that some of the data are more unknown (and hence more variable) than other data. The SensIt **tornado diagram** overcomes this limitation. However, it requires some additions to the original spreadsheet (Figure 12.18). As shown in Figure 12.23, three columns are added for each data cell that will be varied, indicating the lowest value, base value, and highest value. The cost of the survey and the revenue if Max sells the land are fairly predictable (thus varying over a small range of 28–32 and 85–95, respectively), while the cost of drilling and the revenue if oil is struck are more variable (thus varying over a large range of 75–140 and 600–1,000, respectively).

A tornado diagram allows different data cells to have different degrees of variability.

FIGURE 12.23

Expansion of the spreadsheet in Figure 12.18 to prepare for generating a tornado diagram with SensIt.

	U	V	W	X	Y
		Data	Low	Base	High
3					
4	Cost of Survey	30	28	30	32
5	Cost of Drilling	100	75	100	140
6	Revenue If Oil	800	600	800	1000
7	Revenue If Sell	90	85	90	95
8	Revenue If Dry	0			
9	Prior Probability of Oil	0.25			
10	P(FSS | Oil)	0.6			
11	P(USS | Dry)	0.8			

FIGURE 12.24

The dialogue box used by the Tornado option of SensIt.

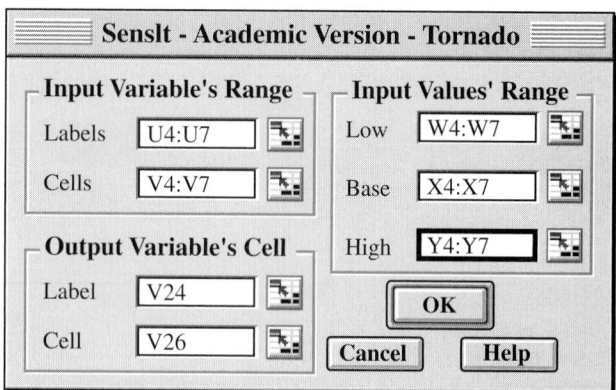

FIGURE 12.25

The tornado diagram generated by the Tornado option of SensIt for the full Goferbroke Co. problem to show how much the expected payoff (when using Bayes' decision rule) can vary over the entire range of likely values of any one of the cost or revenue estimates.

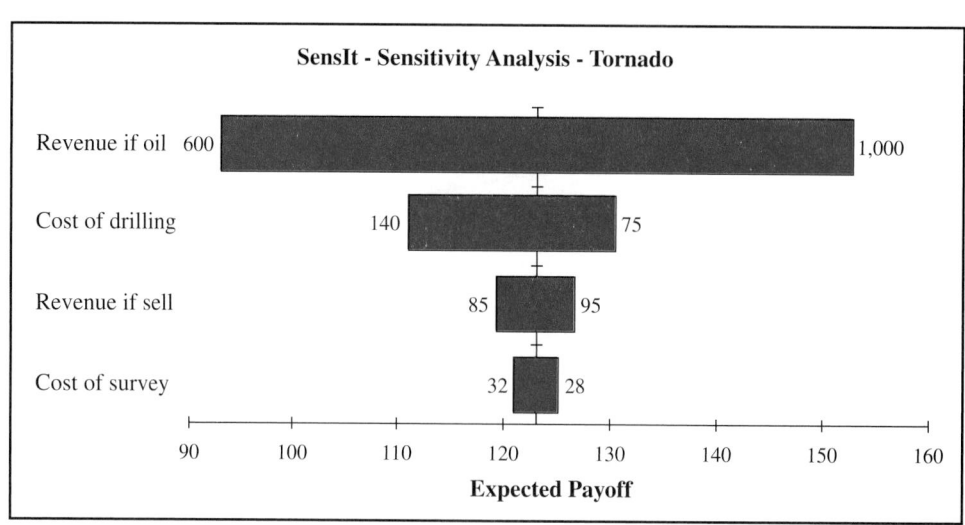

The SensIt-Tornado dialogue box (called up by choosing the third item in the Sensitivity Analysis submenu under the Tools menu) is shown in Figure 12.24. It is used to specify which data cells will be varied, which output cell will be examined, and the location of the cells specifying the range (low, base, and high) for the data cells. Clicking OK generates the chart shown in Figure 12.25. Each bar in the graph shows the range of change in the expected payoff as the corresponding cost or revenue is varied over the range of values indicated numerically at the ends of each bar. The width of each bar measures how sensitive the expected payoff is to changes in that bar's cost or revenue. Once again, *revenue if oil* stands out as causing much more sensitivity than the other costs or revenues.

Max's Reaction

Max: Very interesting. I especially liked the way we were able to use that sensitivity analysis spreadsheet to see immediately what would happen when we change some of the numbers. And there was one thing that I found particularly encouraging.

Jennifer: What was that?

Max: When we changed that prior probability of oil to nearly every other plausible value, it kept coming back with the same answer. Do the seismic survey and then drill only if the survey is favorable. Otherwise, sell. So the consulting geologist's numbers can be off by quite a bit and we still would be doing the right thing.

Jennifer: Yes, that was a key finding, wasn't it? What did you think of the sensitivity analysis involving the cost and revenue data?

Max: Those spider and tornado graph things were pretty clever. However, what they were saying didn't particularly surprise me. Sure, my payoff will depend much more on the revenue we get if we find oil than on anything else.

Jennifer: But what that is telling us is that it is especially important to try to better pin down what that revenue would be.

Max: Yes, I got that message. Unfortunately, that revenue number is particularly difficult to pin down. The geologist suggests that we should have a pretty good-sized pocket of oil there if we have anything there at all. But you never know exactly how much will be there if you're lucky enough to strike oil. And, of course, the revenue depends on the amount of oil.

Jennifer: So from where did the estimate of $800,000 in revenue come?

Max: That was based mainly on an estimate of the size of the pocket that we hope contains oil. This estimate could be off some in either direction, but it represents what we think is the most likely outcome if, in fact, any oil is there. I don't think we have any way of improving much upon this estimate.

Jennifer: Too bad. But having this kind of uncertainty in the data is pretty common in applications of decision analysis. All you can do is develop a good solid estimate of what the average revenue would be, assuming oil is found, in situations resembling this one.

Max: I think we did that.

Jennifer: Good. Then we next should do what we did with the prior probability of oil. Try various plausible values of what the revenue would be if oil is found and see if the answer remains the same about what to do. If we quickly get some different results, you should take another look at the estimate of the revenue and also think hard about these alternative courses of action before you make your decision. However, if the results basically stay the same, then we can just go with the estimate of $800,000 in revenue if oil is found.

Max: That makes sense.

Jennifer: OK, let me save you some time in doing this. Based on both the decision tree and the sensitivity results we've already gotten, I can tell you right now that the sensitivity analysis spreadsheet will give us the same results for what to do even if we make fairly substantial changes in the estimate of the revenue if oil is found. The average payoff with and without the survey (shown in cell E19 and cell E42, respectively, in Figures 12.17 and 12.18) in the decision tree indicates that the suggested policy is far from a close call. If the revenue from oil were considerably less than $800,000, then the question would become whether to do the seismic survey or simply sell the land immediately. However, the tornado diagram tells me that the revenue if oil is found could be as much as 25 percent less than the estimate of $800,000 and our average payoff from the suggested policy still would exceed the $90,000 we could get from selling the land immediately.

Max: It's pretty unlikely that the revenue would be that much less than our estimate. So I am satisfied with going ahead with $800,000 as our estimate.

Jennifer: OK. Does this mean that you are comfortable now with a decision to proceed with the seismic survey and then either drill or sell depending on the outcome of the survey?

Max: Not quite. There is still one thing that bothers me.

Jennifer:	What's that?
Max:	Suppose the seismic survey gives us a favorable seismic sounding, so we drill. If the land turns out to be dry, then I'm out 130,000 bucks! As I said at the beginning, that would nearly put us out of business. That scares me.
Jennifer:	Yes, you're right. There are about 3 chances in 20 of all that happening. But you have about the same odds of both getting a favorable seismic sounding and finding oil. If that happens, you would clear about $670,000, which would be a great boost to the company. Then there is about a 70 percent chance of obtaining unfavorable seismic soundings, in which case you would sell and clear $60,000. A nice profit. This approach is basically saying that these odds for the various possible outcomes, including the chance to clear $670,000, give you the best available gamble.
Max:	Yes, it does sound like a good gamble. I don't mind taking a small chance of a substantial loss when there is a reasonable chance of getting a much larger profit instead. That's the nature of this business. But here is my point. I currently am shorter of working capital than I normally am. Therefore, losing $130,000 now would hurt more than it normally does. It doesn't look like this approach is really taking that into account.
Jennifer:	No, you're right. It really doesn't. This approach just looks at average *monetary* values. That isn't good enough when you're dealing with such large amounts. You wouldn't be willing to flip a coin to determine whether you win or lose $130,000, right?
Max:	No, I sure wouldn't.
Jennifer:	OK, that's the tipoff. As I mentioned the first time we talked about this problem, I think the circumstances here indicate that we need to go beyond dollars and cents to look at the consequences of the possible outcomes. Fortunately, decision analysis has a way of doing this by introducing utilities.
Max:	Yes, I remember your mentioning utilities. What are they again?
Jennifer:	Well, the basic idea is that the utility of an outcome measures the true value to you of that outcome rather than just the monetary value. So by expressing payoffs in terms of utilities, the decision tree analysis would find the average utility at each node instead of the average monetary value. So now the decisions would be based on giving you the highest possible average utility. In other words, they would give the highest true value to you on the average.
Max:	Sounds reasonable. But I'm still not very clear on what these utilities are.
Jennifer:	OK, get ready and I'll give you some background on utilities next.

Considering average monetary values isn't good enough when uncomfortably large losses can occur.

Review Questions

1. When preparing to perform sensitivity analysis, how should one begin organizing the spreadsheet that contains the decision tree?
2. Performing sensitivity analysis on a certain piece of data should require changing its value in how many places on the spreadsheet?
3. What is a major limitation of using a data table to perform sensitivity analysis on a large problem?
4. How many data cells can be varied at a time when using the Plot option of SensIt?
5. Can the Spider option of SensIt consider more data cells at a time than the Plot option?
6. What is a limitation of a spider graph that is overcome by a tornado diagram?

12.9 USING UTILITIES TO BETTER REFLECT THE VALUES OF PAYOFFS

Thus far, when applying Bayes' decision rule, we have assumed that the expected payoff in *monetary terms* is the appropriate measure of the consequences of taking an action. However, in many situations where very large amounts of money are involved, this assumption is inappropriate.

For example, suppose that an individual is offered the choice of (1) accepting a 50–50 chance of winning $100,000 or (2) receiving $40,000 with certainty. Many people would prefer the $40,000 even though the expected payoff on the 50–50 chance of winning $100,000 is $50,000. A company may be unwilling to invest a large sum of money in a new product, even when the expected profit is substantial, if there is a risk of losing its investment and thereby becoming bankrupt. People buy insurance even though it is a poor investment from the viewpoint of the expected payoff.

Do these examples invalidate Bayes' decision rule? Fortunately, the answer is no, because there is a way of transforming monetary values to an appropriate scale that reflects the decision maker's preferences. This scale is called the *utility function for money.*

Utility Functions for Money

Figure 12.26 shows a typical **utility function $U(M)$ for money M.** The intuitive interpretation is that it indicates that an individual having this utility function would value obtaining $30,000 twice as much as $10,000 and would value obtaining $100,000 twice as much as $30,000. This reflects the fact that the person's highest-priority needs would be met by the first $10,000. Having this decreasing slope of the function as the amount of money increases is referred to as having a *decreasing marginal utility for money.* Such an individual is referred to as being **risk averse.**

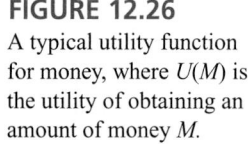
Two different individuals can have very different utility functions for money.

However, not all individuals have a decreasing marginal utility for money. Some people are **risk seekers** instead of *risk averse,* and they go through life looking for the "big score." The slope of their utility function *increases* as the amount of money increases, so they have an *increasing marginal utility for money.*

Figure 12.27 compares the shape of the utility function for money for risk-averse and risk-seeking individuals. Also shown is the intermediate case of a **risk-neutral** individual, who prizes money at its face value. Such an individual's utility for money is simply proportional to the amount of money involved. Although some people appear to be risk neutral when only small amounts of money are involved, it is unusual to be truly risk neutral with very large amounts.

It also is possible to exhibit a mixture of these kinds of behavior. For example, an individual might be essentially risk neutral with small amounts of money, then become a risk seeker with moderate amounts, and then turn risk averse with large amounts. In addition, one's attitude toward risk can shift over time depending on circumstances.

FIGURE 12.26

A typical utility function for money, where $U(M)$ is the utility of obtaining an amount of money M.

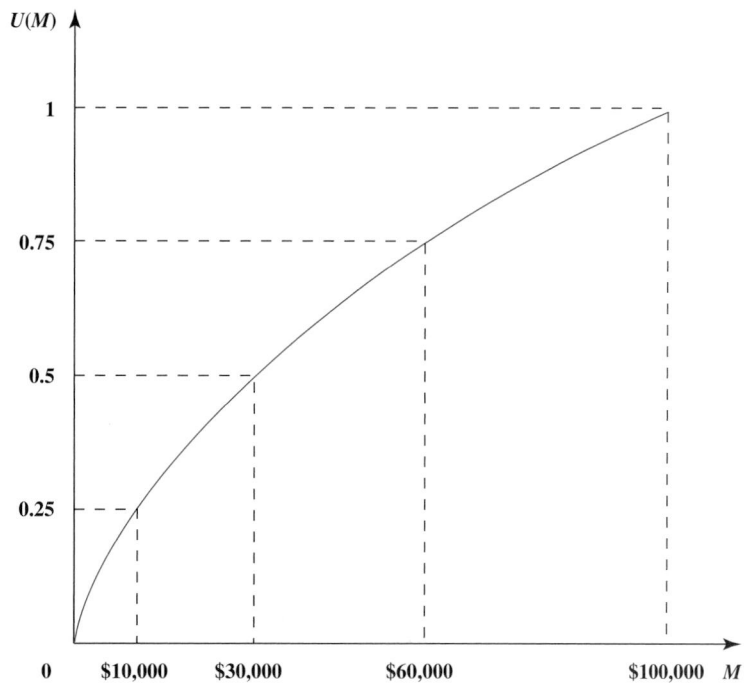

FIGURE 12.27

The shape of the utility function for money for (*a*) risk-averse, (*b*) risk-seeking, and (*c*) risk-neutral individuals.

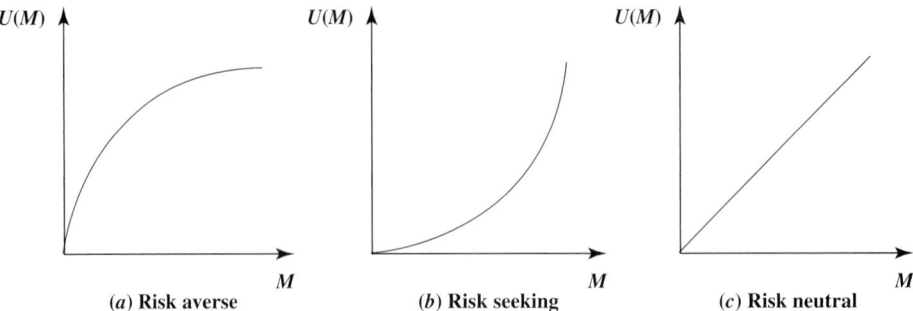

(*a*) Risk averse   (*b*) Risk seeking   (*c*) Risk neutral

Managers of a business firm need to consider the company's circumstances and the collective philosophy of top management in determining the appropriate attitude toward risk when making managerial decisions.

The fact that different people have different utility functions for money has an important implication for decision making in the face of uncertainty.

> When a *utility function for money* is incorporated into a decision analysis approach to a problem, this utility function must be constructed to fit the current preferences and values of the decision maker involved. (The decision maker can be either a single individual or a group of people.)

The key to constructing the utility function for money to fit the decision maker is the following fundamental property of utility functions.

> **Fundamental Property:** Under the assumptions of utility theory, the decision maker's *utility function for money* has the property that the decision maker is *indifferent* between two alternative courses of action if the two alternatives have the *same expected utility.*

To illustrate, suppose that the decision maker has the utility function shown in Figure 12.26. Further suppose that the decision maker is offered the following opportunity.

> **Offer:** An opportunity to obtain either $100,000 (utility = 1) with probability p or nothing (utility = 0) with probability $(1 - p)$.

Thus, by weighting the two possible utilities (1 and 0) by their probabilities, the expected utility is

$$E(\text{utility}) = p + 0\,(1 - p)$$

$$= p \text{ for this offer}$$

In all three of these cases, a decision maker with the utility function in Figure 12.26 would be indifferent between the two alternatives because they have the same expected utility.

Therefore, for *each* of the following three pairs of alternatives, the above fundamental property indicates that the decision maker is indifferent between the first and second alternatives.

1. *First alternative:* The offer with $p = 0.25$, so $E(\text{utility}) = 0.25$.
   Second alternative: Definitely obtain $10,000, so utility = 0.25.

2. *First alternative:* The offer with $p = 0.5$, so $E(\text{utility}) = 0.5$.
   Second alternative: Definitely obtain $30,000, so utility = 0.5.

3. *First alternative:* The offer with $p = 0.75$, so $E(\text{utility}) = 0.75$.
   Second alternative: Definitely obtain $60,000, so utility = 0.75.

This example also illustrates one way in which the decision maker's utility function for money can be constructed in the first place. The decision maker would be made the same hypothetical offer to obtain a large amount of money (e.g., $100,000) with probability p, or nothing otherwise. Then, for each of a few smaller amounts of money (e.g., $10,000, $30,000, and $60,000), the decision maker would be asked to choose a value of p that would make him or her *indifferent* between the offer and definitely obtaining that amount of money. The utility of the smaller amount of money then is p times the utility of the large amount. When the utility of the large amount has been set equal to 1, as in Figure 12.26, this conveniently makes the utility of the smaller amount simply equal to p. The utility values in Figure 12.26 imply that the decision maker has chosen $p = 0.25$ when $M = \$10,000$, $p = 0.5$ when $M = \$30,000$, and $p = 0.75$ when $M = \$60,000$. (Constructing the utility function in this way is an example of the *lottery procedure* described later in this section.)

The *scale* of the utility function is irrelevant. In other words, it doesn't matter whether the values of $U(M)$ at the dashed lines in Figure 12.26 are 0.25, 0.5, 0.75, 1 (as shown) or 10,000, 20,000, 30,000, 40,000, or whatever. All that matters is that these second, third, and fourth values of $U(M)$ should be 2, 3, and 4 times the first value, respectively. All the utilities can be multiplied by any positive constant without affecting which decision alternative will have the largest expected utility. Therefore, in addition to having $U(0) = 0$, the value of $U(M)$ can be set arbitrarily for one nonzero value of M (with a positive utility for a positive M and a negative utility for a negative M). For the reason described at the end of the preceding paragraph, it sometimes is convenient to set $U(M) = 1$ for the largest value of M under consideration, but this is not necessary.

It also is possible to add the same constant (positive or negative) to all the utilities without affecting which decision alternative will have the largest expected utility. However, since it is natural to think of $M = 0$ as having zero utility, we use $U(0) = 0$ throughout this chapter.

Now we are ready to summarize the basic role of utility functions in decision analysis.

When the decision maker's utility function for money is used to measure the relative worth of the various possible monetary outcomes, *Bayes' decision rule* replaces monetary payoffs by the corresponding utilities. Therefore, the optimal decision (or series of decisions) is the one that *maximizes the expected utility.*

> The objective now is to maximize the expected utility rather than the expected payoff in monetary terms.

Only utility functions for *money* have been discussed here. However, we should mention that utility functions can sometimes still be constructed when some or all of the important consequences of the decision alternatives are *not* monetary in nature. (For example, the consequences of a doctor's decision alternatives in treating a patient involve the future health of the patient.) This is not necessarily easy, since it may require making value judgments about the relative desirability of rather intangible consequences. Nevertheless, under these circumstances, it is important to incorporate such value judgments into the decision process.

Dealing with the Goferbroke Co. Problem

Recall that the Goferbroke Co. is operating without much capital, so a loss of $100,000 would be quite serious. As the owner of the company, Max already has gone heavily into debt to keep going. The worst-case scenario would be to come up with $30,000 for a seismic survey and then still lose $100,000 by drilling when there is no oil. This scenario would not bankrupt the company at this point but definitely would leave it in a precarious financial position.

On the other hand, striking oil is an exciting prospect, since earning $700,000 finally would put the company on fairly solid financial footing.

Max is the decision maker for this problem. Therefore, to prepare for using utilities to analyze the problem, it is necessary to construct Max's utility function for money, $U(M)$, where we will express the amount of money M in units of thousands of dollars.

As a starting point, it is natural to let the utility of *zero* money be zero, so $U(0) = 0$. Recall that we can also arbitrarily set the value of $U(M)$ for one nonzero value of M. We will do this for the smallest possible value of M for this problem, namely, $M = -130$ (a loss of $130,000), by setting

$$U(-130) = -150$$

Although the choice of -150 is completely arbitrary (except for being negative), this will be a convenient choice since it will happen to make $U(M)$ approximately equal to M when M is close to 0. This will enable us to better see how the utilities compare with monetary values (M) over the entire range of M.

To determine the utilities for other possible monetary payoffs, it is necessary to probe Max's attitude toward risk. Especially important are his feelings about the consequences of the worst possible loss ($130,000) and the best possible gain ($700,000), as well as how he compares these consequences. Let us eavesdrop as Jennifer probes these feelings with Max.

Interviewing Max

Jennifer: Well now, these utilities are intended to reflect your feelings about the true value to you of these various possible payoffs. Therefore, to pin down what your utilities are, we need to talk some about how you feel about these payoffs and their consequences for the company.

Max: Fine.

Jennifer: A good place to begin would be the best and worst possible cases. The possibility of gaining $700,000 or losing $130,000.

Max: Those are the big ones all right.

Jennifer: OK, suppose you drill without paying for a seismic survey and then you find oil, so your profit is about $700,000. What would that do for the company?

Max: A lot. That would finally give me the capital I need to become more of a major player in this business. I then could take a shot at finding a big oil field. That big strike I've talked about.

Jennifer: Yes, that's always been your dream, hasn't it? To get your big strike.

Max: It sure has. That's why I've gone through all those rough times all these years. It's been exciting when we got some small strikes, but scary too when we've gone through some dry patches. Fortunately, I've had some decent luck and managed to keep going. But I won't be satisfied until I get that big strike.

Jennifer: And you think that clearing $700,000 on this drill would give you a good shot at that big strike soon?

Max: A decent shot. That's all you can ask for in this business.

Jennifer: OK, good. Now let's talk about the consequences if you were to get that biggest possible loss instead. Suppose you pay for a seismic survey, then you drill and the land is dry. So you're out about $130,000. How bad would that be? What kind of future would the company have?

Max: Well, let me put it this way. It would put the company in a pretty uncomfortable financial position. I would need to work hard on getting some more financing. Then we would need to cautiously work our way out of the hole by forming some partnerships for some low-risk, low-gain drilling. But I think we could do it. I've been in that position a couple times before and come out of it. We'd be OK.

Jennifer: It sounds like you wouldn't be overly worried about such a loss as long as you have reasonable odds for a big payoff to justify this risk.

Max: That's right.

Jennifer: OK, now let's talk about those odds. What I'm going to do is set up a simpler hypothetical situation. Suppose you don't have the option of selling. So here are your alternatives. One is to drill. If you find oil, you clear $700,000. If the land is dry, you're out $130,000. The only other alternative is to do nothing, so you would neither gain nor lose anything. I know this isn't your actual situation. But let's pretend that it is.

Max: I don't understand why you want to talk about a situation that is different from what we are facing.

Jennifer: Trust me. This is going to enable us to determine your utilities.

Max: OK.

Jennifer: Now presumably if you had a 50–50 chance of either clearing $700,000 or losing $130,000, you would drill.

Max: Sure.

Jennifer: But if you had only a very small chance, say, a 10 percent chance of gaining $700,000, versus a 90 percent chance of losing $130,000, you presumably wouldn't drill.

Max: True.

Jennifer: OK, let's improve your odds a little. Suppose you have a 15 percent chance of getting the $700,000. In this case, if you look at the average payoff, you would be just a shade short of coming out even. So if you had an unlimited amount of money, you would be at just about your break-even point for going ahead and drilling.

Max: Well, I sure don't have an unlimited amount of money! I would need to do quite a bit better than breaking even on the average to justify the risk of crippling the company by losing $130,000.

Jennifer: I was guessing you would feel that way. OK, let's improve your odds some more. Suppose now that you have a 25 percent chance of gaining $700,000 versus a 75 percent chance of losing $130,000. Would you do it?

Max: I like those odds a lot better. $700,000 is over five times as large as $130,000, whereas 75 percent is only three times as large as 25 percent, so that average payoff you're always talking about must be pretty large in this case.

Jennifer: Yes, it would be over $75,000.

Max: That's a lot. Well, that $700,000 sure would give a huge boost to the future of the company. I don't relish the hard times we would go through if we lost $130,000, but yes, I think a 25 percent chance of clearing $700,000 would justify that risk. You have to take those kinds of chances in this business.

Jennifer: OK, so now we know that the point at which you would be indifferent between going ahead or not is somewhere between having a 15 percent chance and a 25 percent chance of gaining $700,000 rather than losing $130,000. Let's see if we can pin down just where your **point of indifference** is within this range from 15 percent to 25 percent. Let's try 20 percent. Would you go ahead and drill with a 20 percent chance of gaining $700,000 versus an 80 percent chance of losing $130,000?

The *point of indifference* is the point where the decision maker is indifferent between two hypothetical alternatives.

Max: Hmm. That's not so clear. What would be the average payoff in this case?

Jennifer: $36,000.

Max: Not bad. Hmm, one chance in five of gaining $700,000. That's tempting. But four chances in five of losing $130,000 with all the problems involved with that. I don't know. That's a tough one.

Jennifer: OK, let's try this. Suppose your chances of gaining $700,000 were a little better than 20 percent. Would you do it?

Max: Yes, I think so.

Jennifer: And if your chances were a little under 20 percent?

Max: Then I don't think I would do it.

Jennifer: OK. You've convinced me that your point of indifference is 20 percent. That's exactly what I needed to know.

Finding *U*(700)

Max has indeed given Jennifer just the information she needs to determine $U(700)$, Max's utility for a payoff of 700 (a gain of \$700,000). Recall that $U(-130)$ already has been set at $U(-130) = -150$. Given this value, the procedure for finding $U(700)$ is summarized below.

The decision maker (Max) is offered two alternatives, A_1 and A_2.

A_1: Obtain a payoff of 700 with probability p.
　　Obtain a payoff of -130 with probability $(1 - p)$.

A_2: Definitely obtain a payoff of 0.

Question to the decision maker: What value of p makes you *indifferent* between these two alternatives?

The decision maker's choice: $p = 0.2$.

Set E(utility for A_1) = E(utility for A_2), and solve this equation for the unknown, $U(700)$. Since $U(0) = 0$, we have E(utility for A_2) = 0. The expected utility for A_1 is

$$E(\text{utility for } A_1) = pU(700) + (1 - p)U(-130)$$

$$= 0.2U(700) + 0.8\,(-150)$$

$$= 0.2U(700) - 120$$

Because the fundamental property of utility functions says that the expected utilities for the two alternatives are the same at the decision maker's point of indifference, $p = 0.2$, we have

$$0.2U(700) - 120 = 0$$

$$0.2U(700) = 120$$

$$U(700) = 600$$

The General Procedure for Finding a Utility

The above procedure for finding $U(700)$ illustrates that the key is having the decision maker select a *point of indifference* between two alternatives where one of them (A_1) involves a *lottery*. Here is the general version of this **lottery procedure.**

Lottery Procedure

1. We are given three possible monetary payoffs—M_1, M_2, M_3 ($M_1 < M_2 < M_3$)—where the utility is known for two of them and we wish to find the utility for the third one.

2. The decision maker is offered the following two hypothetical alternatives:

    A_1: Obtain a payoff of M_3 with probability p.
    　　Obtain a payoff of M_1 with probability $(1 - p)$.
    A_2: Definitely obtain a payoff of M_2.

3. Question to the decision maker: What value of p makes you *indifferent* between these two alternatives?

4. Using this value of p, write the *fundamental property equation,*

$$E(\text{utility for } A_1) = E(\text{utility for } A_2),$$

so

$$pU(M_3) + (1 - p)U(M_1) = U(M_2).$$

5. Solve this equation for the unknown utility.

When finding $U(700)$, we actually were applying this lottery procedure with $M_1 = -130$, $M_2 = 0$, and $M_3 = 700$. When finding the next two utilities, we will have $M_3 = 0$ in the first

This fundamental property equation is the key for solving for an unknown utility.

case and then $M_1 = 0$ in the second case instead. (Although not required, it is common to include 0 as one of the three payoffs to enable focusing better on the comparison between the other two.) We also will have the middle payoff M_2 be the one with the unknown utility, although any position (smallest, middle, largest) is allowed.

Near the beginning of this section, we described how the utility function for money shown in Figure 12.26 could have been constructed by having the decision maker choose a value of p for each of three hypothetical offers. The method we were describing was, in fact, the lottery procedure. For each of these hypothetical offers, the values of the utility were known for $M_1 = 0$ and $M_3 = \$100,000$, namely, $U(0) = 0$ and $U(M_3) = 1$. The unknown utility being solved for then was $U(M_2)$, where $M_2 = \$10,000$ for the first hypothetical offer, $M_2 = \$30,000$ for the second, and $M_2 = \$60,000$ for the third. The values for $U(M_2)$ in Figure 12.26 for these values of M_2 correspond to choosing $p = 0.25$, $p = 0.5$, and $p = 0.75$ for these respective offers.

Finding $U(-100)$

We now will illustrate the lottery procedure by applying it step by step to find the utility for another of Goferbroke's possible payoffs, namely, -100 (a loss of $\$100,000$). However, we will not bother to eavesdrop this time on Jennifer's interview of Max to determine his point of indifference between the two hypothetical alternatives in this case.

We now have three payoffs ($-130, 0, 700$) with known utilities, so any two can be chosen for this procedure. The two actually selected were -130 and 0, since they can be compared to -100 somewhat more easily than can 700.

1. The three given payoffs are

   $M_1 = -130$ with $U(-130) = -150$ known

   $M_2 = -100$ with $U(-100)$ unknown

   $M_3 = 0$ with $U(0) = 0$ known

2. The two hypothetical alternatives are

   A_1: Obtain a payoff of 0 with probability p.
        Obtain a payoff of -130 with probability $(1 - p)$.
   A_2: Definitely obtain a payoff of -100.

3. Max chooses $p = 0.3$ as his point of indifference between these two alternatives.

4. The fundamental property equation is

$$pU(0) + (1 - p)\, U(-130) = U(-100)$$

   so

$$0.3\,(0) + 0.7\,(-150) = U(-100)$$

5. The solution is $U(-100) = -105$.

Finding $U(90)$

In addition to $U(0) = 0$, we now have found Max's utilities for Goferbroke's possible negative payoffs (-130 and -100) and the largest possible positive payoff (700). For our last calculation, we now will find the utility for a relatively small positive payoff (90), using 0 and 700 in the procedure as two payoffs with known utilities.

1. The three given payoffs are

   $M_1 = 0$ with $U(0) = 0$ known

   $M_2 = 90$ with $U(90)$ unknown

   $M_3 = 700$ with $U(700) = 600$ known

2. The two hypothetical alternatives are

A_1: Obtain a payoff of 700 with probability p.
    Obtain a payoff of 0 with probability $(1 - p)$.
A_2: Definitely obtain a payoff of 90.

3. Max chooses $p = 0.15$ as his point of indifference between these two alternatives.

4. The fundamental property equation is

$$pU(700) + (1 - p)\,U(0) = U(90)$$

so

$$0.15(600) + 0.85\,(0) = U(90).$$

5. The solution is $U(90) = 90$.

Constructing Max's Utility Function for Money

We now have found the utilities for five representative possible payoffs ($-130, -100, 0, 90, 700$) for Goferbroke. Plotting these values on a graph of the utility $U(M)$ versus the monetary payoff M and then drawing a smooth curve through these points gives the curve shown in Figure 12.28.

This curve is our best estimate of Max's utility function for money. The values on this curve at $M = 60$ and $M = 670$ provide the corresponding utilities, $U(60) = 60$ and $U(670) = 580$, for these last two possible payoffs. (The lottery procedure also could have been applied to find these utilities, but there is no need since these payoffs are so close to others with known utilities.) Table 12.9 gives the complete list of possible payoffs and their utilities.

For comparative purposes, the dashed line in Figure 12.28 shows the monetary value (in thousands of dollars) along the vertical axis for any payoff M along the horizontal axis. (Since this line is drawn at 45°, the value along the vertical axis always is the same as the value along the horizontal axis for any point on the line.) This dashed line would have been the utility function $U(M) = M$ if Max were completely *risk neutral*, since then monetary payoffs would be equivalent to utilities. However, note how the actual utility function $U(M)$ given by the smooth

FIGURE 12.28

Max's utility function for money as the owner of Goferbroke Co.

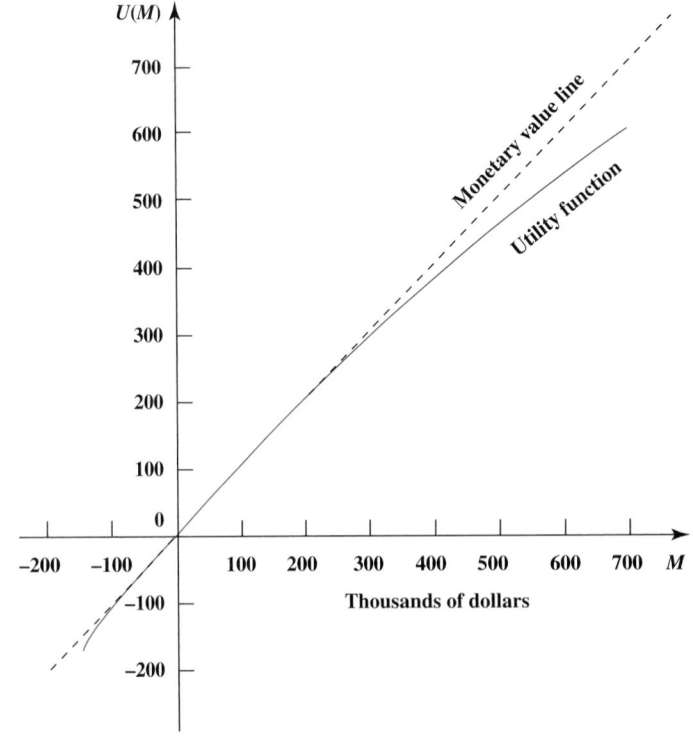

TABLE 12.9

Utilities for the
Goferbroke Co. Problem

Monetary Payoff, *M*	Utility, *U(M)*
−130	−150
−100	−105
0	0
60	60
90	90
670	580
700	600

curve essentially equals *M* for small values (positive or negative) of *M*, and then *U(M)* gradually falls off *M* for larger values of *M*. This is typical for a moderately risk-averse individual.

By nature, Max is inclined to be a risk seeker. However, the difficult financial circumstances of his company that he badly wants to keep solvent has forced him to adopt a moderately risk-averse stance in addressing his current decisions.

Summary of the Procedure for Constructing *U(M)*

Here is a summary of the general procedure that we have just followed in constructing Max's utility function *U(M)*.

Procedure for Constructing a Utility Function for Money

1. List all the possible monetary payoffs for the problem, including 0 (whether possible or not).

2. Set *U(0)* = 0 and then arbitrarily choose a utility value for one other payoff (with a negative value for a negative payoff and a positive value for a positive payoff).

3. Choose three of the payoffs where the utility is known for two of them.

4. Apply the lottery procedure to find the utility for the third payoff.

5. Repeat steps 3 and 4 for as many other representative payoffs with unknown utilities as desired.

6. Then plot the utilities found on a graph of the utility *U(M)* versus the payoff *M*. Draw a smooth curve through these points to obtain the utility function.

Using a Decision Tree to Analyze the Problem with Utilities

Now that Max's utility function for money has been constructed in Table 12.9 (and Figure 12.28), this information can be used with a decision tree as summarized below.

> The procedure for using a decision tree to analyze the problem now is *identical* to that described in Section 12.7 *except* for substituting utilities for monetary payoffs. Therefore, the value obtained to evaluate each node of the tree now is the *expected utility* there rather than the expected (monetary) payoff. Consequently, the optimal decision selected by Bayes' decision rule maximizes the expected utility for the overall problem.

Thus, using TreePlan once again, our final decision tree with utilities shown in Figure 12.29 closely resembles the one in Figure 12.17 given in Section 12.7. The nodes and branches are exactly the same, as are the probabilities for the branches emanating from the event nodes. However, the key difference from Figure 12.17 is that the monetary payoff at each terminal node now has been replaced by the corresponding utility from Table 12.9. (This was accomplished with TreePlan by entering this same utility as the "cash flow" at the terminal branch and then entering "cash flows" of 0 at all the preceding branches.) It is these utilities that have been used by TreePlan to compute the *expected utilities* given next to all the nodes.

At each terminal branch, enter the utility of that outcome as the "cash flow" there and then do not change the default value of 0 for the "cash flow" at the preceding branches.

These expected utilities lead to the same decisions as in Figure 12.17 at all decision nodes except the bottom one in cell F41. The decision at this node now switches to *sell* instead of *drill*. However, the solution procedure still leaves this node on a *closed* path, as indicated by the 1 in cell B29. Therefore, the overall optimal policy remains the same as that obtained in Figure 12.17 (do the seismic survey; sell if the result is unfavorable; drill if the result is favorable).

The approach of maximizing the expected monetary payoff used in the preceding sections was equivalent to assuming that the decision maker is neutral toward risk so that *U(M)* = *M*.

FIGURE 12.29

The final decision tree constructed and solved by TreePlan for the full Goferbroke Co. problem when using Max's utility function for money to maximize expected utility.

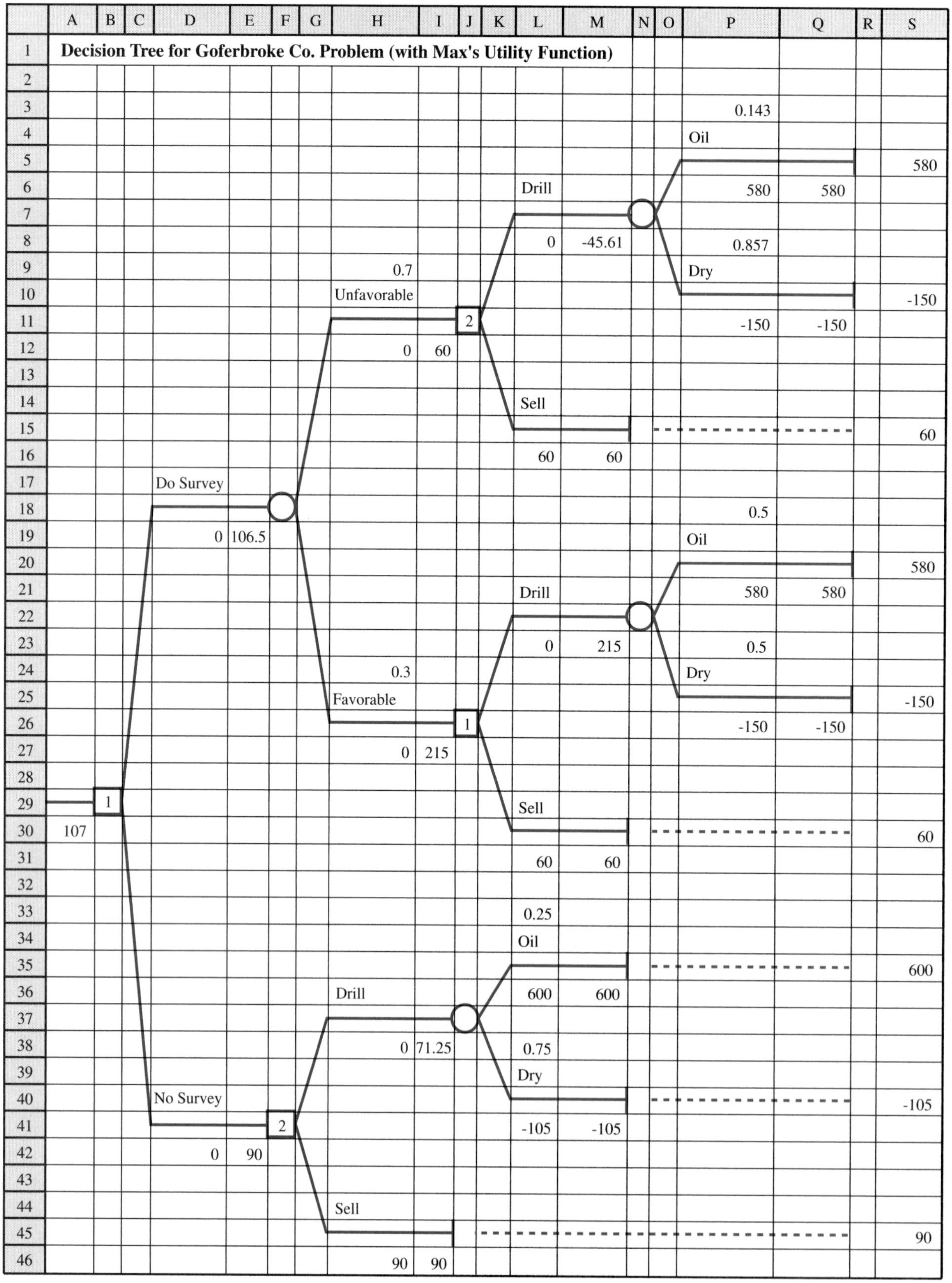

	A	B	C	D	E	F	G	H	I	J	K	L	M	N	O	P	Q	R	S
1	**Decision Tree for Goferbroke Co. Problem (with Max's Utility Function)**																		
2																			
3																0.143			
4															Oil				
5																			580
6								Drill						◯		580	580		
7																			
8										0	-45.61					0.857			
9							0.7								Dry				
10							Unfavorable												-150
11									2							-150	-150		
12									0	60									
13																			
14									Sell										
15															- - - - - - - - - - -			60
16									60	60									
17				Do Survey															
18							◯									0.5			
19					0	106.5									Oil				
20																			580
21								Drill						◯		580	580		
22																			
23										0	215					0.5			
24							0.3								Dry				
25							Favorable												-150
26									1							-150	-150		
27									0	215									
28																			
29		1										Sell							
30	107														- - - - - - - - - - -			60
31												60	60						
32																			
33												0.25							
34												Oil							
35															- - - - - - - - - - -			600
36							Drill					600	600						
37									◯										
38								0	71.25			0.75							
39												Dry							
40				No Survey											- - - - - - - - - - -			-105
41						2						-105	-105						
42					0	90													
43																			
44							Sell												
45															- - - - - - - - - - -			90
46								90	90										

The previous approach of maximizing the expected monetary payoff assumes a risk-neutral decision maker.

By using utility theory with an appropriate utility function, the optimal solution now reflects the decision maker's attitude about risk. Because Max adopted only a moderately risk-averse stance, the optimal policy did not change from before. For a somewhat more risk-averse decision maker, the optimal solution would switch to the more conservative approach of immediately selling the land (no seismic survey).

Jennifer and Max are to be commended for incorporating utilities into a decision analysis approach to his problem. Utilities help to provide a rational approach to decision making in the face of uncertainty. However, many managers are not sufficiently comfortable with the relatively abstract notion of utilities, or with working with probabilities to construct a utility function, to be willing to use this approach. Consequently, utilities are not used nearly as widely in practice as some of the other techniques of decision analysis described in this chapter, including Bayes' decision rule (with monetary payoffs) and decision trees.

Max's Reaction

Max: Whew! I haven't had to do that much hard thinking since I was in school. That management science stuff really forces you to follow a very disciplined, logical approach, doesn't it?

Jennifer: That's true. What did you think of using utilities?

Max: Well, those utilities still are a little mysterious to me. But the numbers we ended up with for the utilities made sense. I can see what this is driving at and I think these utilities do better reflect my feelings about the true value of these payoffs.

Jennifer: Good. So are you comfortable with your decisions?

Max: Yes, I am. I'm more than satisfied that we've thought it through carefully enough. And I like the fact that there are no close calls. Even if the numbers are off some, these probably are still the best decisions.

Jennifer: Right. Otherwise, I would urge you to do some more sensitivity analysis.

Max: No, I'm satisfied. It's pretty clear we should do the seismic survey. Then it certainly makes sense to drill if we get favorable seismic soundings and to sell if we don't. All this analysis has really clarified my thinking.

Jennifer: Great. That's the idea.

Max: I must say that I'm impressed with this management science stuff, even if it is a lot of work. Glad to see that all that tuition I paid for you was worthwhile.

Jennifer: I liked my management science class. A lot of it seemed very useful.

Max: Well, you've just done a great job for me applying that stuff. Thanks a lot, sweetheart.

Jennifer: You're welcome, Dad.

Another Approach for Estimating *U(M)*

The procedure described earlier for constructing *U(M)* asks the decision maker to repeatedly apply the lottery procedure, which requires him (or her) each time to make a difficult decision about which probability would make him indifferent between two alternatives. Many managers would be uncomfortable with making this kind of decision. Therefore, an alternative approach is sometimes used instead to estimate the utility function for money.

This approach assumes that the utility function has a certain mathematical form and then adjusts this form to fit the decision maker's attitude toward risk as closely as possible. For example, one particularly popular form to assume (because of its relative simplicity) is the **exponential utility function,**

$$U(M) = R\left(1 - e^{-\frac{M}{R}}\right)$$

Since *R* measures the decision maker's *risk tolerance,* the *aversion* to risk decreases as *R* increases.

where *R* is the decision maker's *risk tolerance.* This utility function has the kind of shape shown in Figure 12.27(*a*), so it is designed to fit a *risk-averse* individual. A great aversion to risk corresponds to a small value of *R* (which would cause the curve in this figure to bend sharply), whereas a small aversion to risk corresponds to a large value of *R* (which gives a much more gradual bend in the curve).

Since Max has a relatively small aversion to risk, his utility function curve in Figure 12.28 bends quite slowly. The value of *R* that would give Max's utilities of $U(670) = 580$ and $U(700) = 600$ is approximately $R = 2,250$. On the other hand, Max becomes much more risk averse when large losses are possible, since this now would threaten bankruptcy, so the value of *R* that would give his utility of $U(-130) = -150$ is only about $R = 465$.

Unfortunately, it is not possible to use two different values of *R* for the same utility function. A drawback of the exponential utility function is that it assumes a constant aversion to risk (a fixed value of *R*), regardless of how much (or how little) money the decision maker currently has. This doesn't fit Max's situation, since his current shortage of money makes him much more concerned about incurring a large loss than usual. This is why Jennifer never raised the possibility of using an exponential utility function.

In other situations where the consequences of the potential losses are not as severe, assuming an exponential utility function may provide a reasonable approximation. In such a case, here is an easy way of estimating the appropriate value of *R*. The decision maker would be asked to choose the number *R* that would make him indifferent between the following two alternatives.

A_1:   A 50–50 gamble where he would gain *R* dollars with probability 0.5 and lose *R*/2 dollars with probability 0.5.

A_2:   Neither gain nor lose anything.

Using TreePlan with an Exponential Utility Function

TreePlan includes the option of using the exponential utility function. First, the value of *R* needs to be specified on the spreadsheet. The cell containing this value then needs to be given a range name of RT (TreePlan refers to this term as the risk tolerance). Then click on the Options button in the TreePlan dialogue box, which brings up the dialogue box shown in Figure 12.30. Select the "Use Exponential Utility Function" option. Clicking OK then revises the decision tree to incorporate the exponential utility function.

Figure 12.31 shows the decision tree with a risk tolerance of $R = 1,000$ (somewhere in between the values of $R = 2,250$ and $R = 465$ that were equivalent to different regions of Max's utility function). There are now two expected payoffs calculated below and to the left of each node. The lower number represents the expected utility value at that stage in the decision tree. The upper number represents the certain payoff that is equivalent to this expected utility value. For example, cell A31 indicates that the expected value of the exponential utility function for this decision would be 0.0932. This is equivalent to a certain payoff of $98,000, as indicated in cell A30.

TreePlan Tip: The Option dialogue box lets you specify whether to use expected monetary values or the exponential utility function for applying Bayes' decision rule. The dialogue box also lets you specify whether the objective is to maximize profit (as was used throughout this chapter) or to minimize cost.

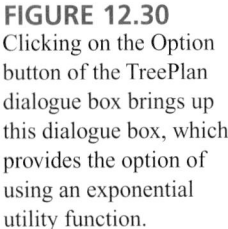

FIGURE 12.30
Clicking on the Option button of the TreePlan dialogue box brings up this dialogue box, which provides the option of using an exponential utility function.

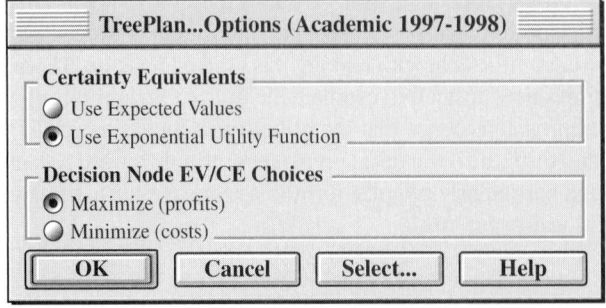

FIGURE 12.31

The final decision tree constructed and solved by TreePlan for the full Goferbroke Co. problem when using an exponential utility function.

	A	B	C	D	E	F	G	H	I	J	K	L	M	N	O	P	Q	R	S
1	**Decision Tree for Goferbroke Co. (with an Exponential Utility Function)**																		
2																			
3																0.14			
4																Oil			
5																			670
6												Drill				800	670		
7																	0.488		
8												-100	-47.981			0.86			
9								0.7					-0.0492			Dry			
10								Unfavorable											-130
11										2						0	-130		
12								0	60								-0.139		
13									0.0582										
14												Sell							
15																			60
16								90	60										
17				Do Survey									0.0582						
18																0.5			
19				-30	97.8160											Oil			
20					0.0932														670
21												Drill				800	670		
22																	0.488		
23												-100	192.047			0.5			
24								0.3					0.175			Dry			
25								Favorable											-130
26										1						0	-130		
27								0	192.047								-0.139		
28									0.175										
29		1										Sell							
30	98																		60
31	0.0932							90	60										
32													0.0582						
33									0.3										
34												Oil							
35																			700
36								Drill								800	700		
37													0.503						
38								-100	48.1147			0.8							
39									0.0470			Dry							
40				No Survey															-100
41						2							-100			0			
42				0	90								-0.105						
43					0.08607														
44								Sell											
45																			90
46								90	90										
47									0.0861										
48				RT	1,000														

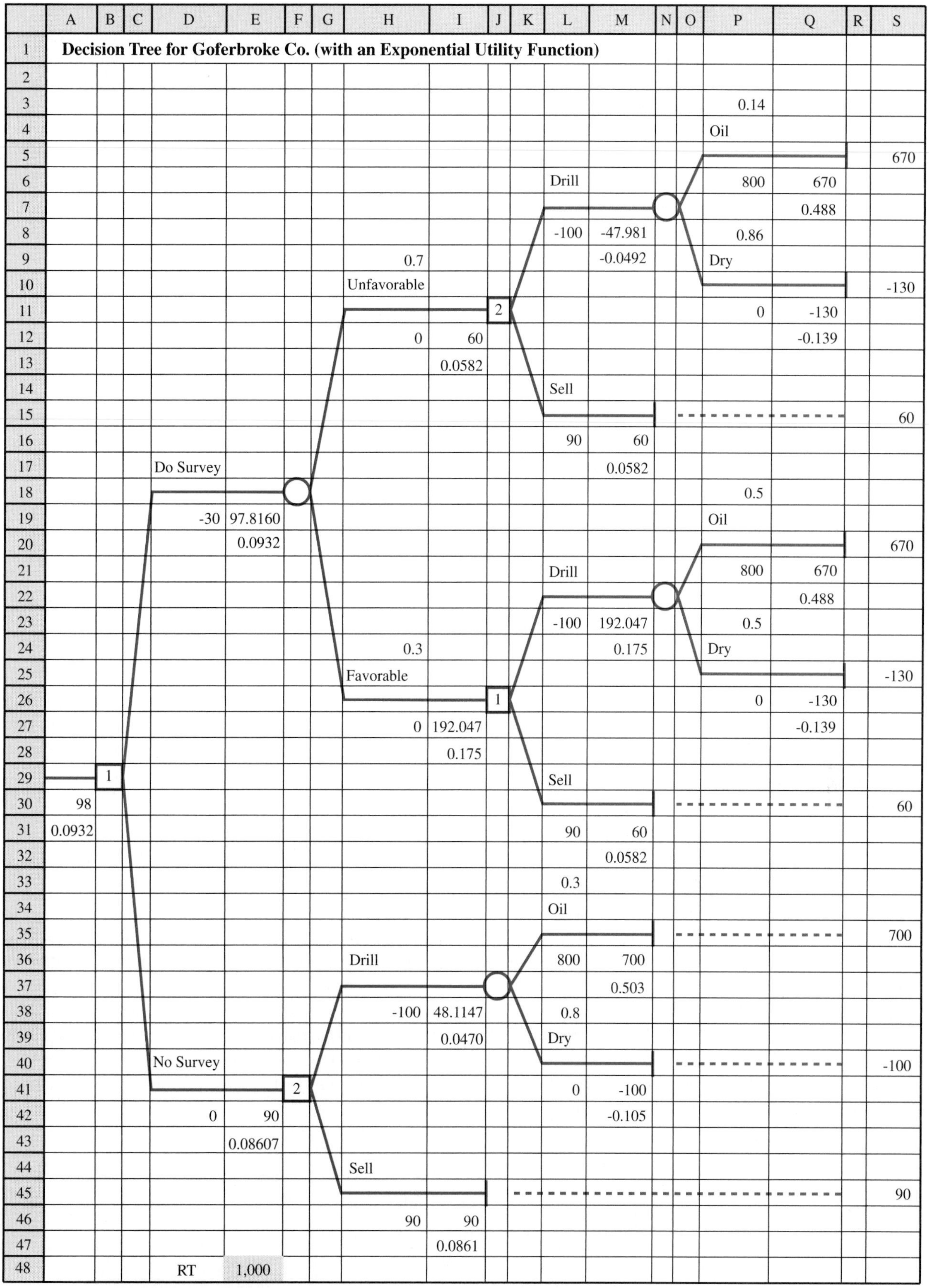

Range Name	Cells
RT	E48

The exponential utility function leads to the same decisions as in Figure 12.29. The overall optimal policy remains to do the seismic survey; sell if the result is unfavorable; drill if the result is favorable. However, the optimal policy changes when the value of R is decreased. For values of R less than 728, the optimal policy switches to not doing the survey and selling the land. Thus, a more risk-averse decision maker would make the safer decision for Goferbroke—sell the land and receive $90,000 for sure.

Review **Questions**

1. What are utilities intended to reflect?

2. What is the shape of the utility function for money for a risk-averse individual? A risk-seeking individual? A risk-neutral individual?

3. What is the fundamental property of utility functions?

4. What is the lottery when using the lottery procedure?

5. Given two hypothetical alternatives where one of them involves a probability p, what is meant by the point of indifference between these two alternatives?

6. When using utilities with a decision tree, what kind of value is obtained to evaluate each node of the tree?

7. What decisions did Max make regarding the Goferbroke Co. problem?

12.10 THE PRACTICAL APPLICATION OF DECISION ANALYSIS

In one sense, the Goferbroke Co. problem is a very typical application of decision analysis. Like other applications, Max needed to make his decisions (Do a seismic survey? Drill for oil or sell the land?) in the face of great uncertainty. The decisions were difficult because their payoffs were so unpredictable. The outcome depended on factors that were outside Max's control (does the land contain oil or is it dry?). He needed a framework and methodology for rational decision making in this uncertain environment. These are the usual characteristics of applications of decision analysis.

However, in other ways, the Goferbroke problem is not such a typical application. It was oversimplified to include only two possible states of nature (oil and dry), whereas there actually would be a considerable number of distinct possibilities. For example, the actual state might be dry, a small amount of oil, a moderate amount, a large amount, and a huge amount, plus different possibilities concerning the depth of the oil and soil conditions that impact the cost of drilling to reach the oil. Max also was considering only two alternatives for each of two decisions. Real applications commonly involve more decisions, more alternatives to be considered for each one, and many possible states of nature.

The Goferbroke Co. problem could have included many more states of nature.

Problems as tiny as the Goferbroke problem can be readily analyzed and solved by hand. However, real applications typically involve large decision trees, whose construction and analysis require the use of a software package (such as TreePlan introduced in this chapter). In some cases, the decision tree can explode in size with many thousand terminal branches. Special algebraic techniques are being developed and incorporated into the solvers for dealing with such large problems.[2]

Sensitivity analysis also can become unwieldy on large problems. Although it normally is supported by the computer software, (as with SensIt), the amount of data generated can easily overwhelm an analyst or decision maker. Therefore, some graphical techniques, such as the spider graph and tornado diagram introduced in Figures 12.22 and 12.25, have been developed to organize the data in a readily understandable way.[3]

[2]For example, see C. W. Kirkwood, "An Algebraic Approach to Formulating and Solving Large Models for Sequential Decisions under Uncertainty," *Management Science* 39 (July 1993), pp. 900–13.
[3]For further information, see T. G. Eschenbach, "Spiderplots versus Tornado Diagrams for Sensitivity Analysis," *Interfaces* 22 (November–December 1992), pp. 40–46.

Other kinds of graphical techniques also are available to complement the decision tree in representing and solving decision analysis problems. One that has become quite popular is called the **influence diagram,** and researchers continue to develop others as well.[4]

Although the Goferbroke problem only involved a single decision maker (Max) assisted by a single analyst (Jennifer), many strategic business decisions are made collectively by management. One technique for group decision making is called **decision conferencing.** This is a process where the group comes together for discussions in a decision conference with the help of an analyst and a group facilitator. The facilitator works directly with the group to help it structure and focus discussions, think creatively about the problem, bring assumptions to the surface, and address the full range of issues involved. The analyst uses decision analysis to assist the group in exploring the implications of the various decision alternatives. With the assistance of a computerized *group decision support system,* the analyst builds and solves models on the spot, and then performs sensitivity analysis to respond to what-if questions from the group.[5]

Applications of decision analysis commonly involve a partnership between the managerial decision maker (whether an individual or a group) and an analyst (whether an individual or a team) with training in management science. Some managers are not as fortunate as Max in having a staff member (let alone a daughter) like Jennifer who is qualified to serve as the analyst. Therefore, a considerable number of management consulting firms specializing in decision analysis have been formed to fill this role.

Decision analysis is widely used around the world. For proprietary reasons (among others), companies usually do not publish articles in professional journals to describe their applications of management science techniques, including decision analysis. Fortunately, such articles do filter out once in awhile, with some of them appearing in the journal called *Interfaces.* The articles about decision analysis provide valuable insights about the practical application of this technique.

Table 12.10 briefly summarizes the nature of some of the applications of decision analysis that have appeared in *Interfaces.* The rightmost column identifies the specific issue of the journal for each application. Note in the other columns the wide diversity of organizations and applications (with public utilities as the heaviest users). For each specific application, think about how uncertainties in the situation make decision analysis a natural technique to use.

If you would like to do more reading about the practical application of decision analysis, a good place to begin would be the November–December 1992 issue of *Interfaces.* This is a special issue devoted entirely to decision analysis and the related area of risk analysis. It includes many interesting articles, including descriptions of basic methods, sensitivity analysis, and decision conferencing. Also included are several of the articles on applications that are listed in Table 12.10.

Review | 1. How does the Goferbroke Co. problem compare with typical applications of decision analysis?
Questions |
| 2. What is the purpose of an influence diagram?
| 3. Who are the typical participants in a decision-conferencing process?
| 4. Where can a manager go for expert help in applying decision analysis if a qualified analyst is not available on staff?
| 5. How much is decision analysis actually used?

[4]For example, see P. P. Schnoy, "A Comparison of Graphical Techniques for Decision Analysis," *European Journal of Operational Research* 78 (October 13, 1994), pp. 1–21. Also see Z. Covaliu and R. M. Oliver, "Representation and Solution of Decision Problems Using Sequential Decision Diagrams," *Management Science* 41 (December 1995), pp. 1860–81, as well as Chapters 4 and 9 in K. T. Marshall and R. M. Oliver, *Decision Making and Forecasting* (New York: McGraw-Hill, 1995).

[5]For further information, see the two articles on decision conferencing in the November–December 1992 issue of *Interfaces,* where one describes an application in Australia and the other summarizes the experience of 26 decision conferences in Hungary.

TABLE 12.10 **Some Applications of Decision Analysis**

Organization	Nature of Application	Issue of *Interfaces*
Amoco Oil Co.	Used utilities to evaluate strategies for marketing its products through full-facility service stations.	Dec. 1982
Ohio Edison Co.	Evaluated and selected particulate emission control equipment for a coal-fired power plant.	Feb. 1983
New England Electric System	Determined an appropriate bid for the salvage rights to a grounded ship.	March–April 1984
National Weather Service	Developed a plan for responding to flood forecasts and warnings.	May–June 1984
National Forest Administrations	Planned prescribed fires to improve forest and rangeland ecosystems.	Sept.–Oct. 1984
Tomco Oil Corp.	Chose between two site locations for drilling an oil well with 74 states of nature.	March–April 1986
Personal decision	Used decision criteria without probabilities to choose between adjustable-rate and fixed-rate mortgages.	May–June 1986
U.S. Postal Service	Chose between six alternatives for a postal automation program saving $200 million.	March–April 1987 Jan.–Feb. 1988
Santa Clara University	Evaluated whether to implement a drug-testing program for intercollegiate athletes.	May–June 1990
Independent Living Center (Australia)	A decision conference developed a strategic plan for reorganizing the center.	Nov.–Dec. 1992
DuPont Corp.	Many applications to strategic planning; one added $175 million in value.	Nov.–Dec. 1992
British Columbia Hydro and Power Authority	Elicited a utility function for clarifying value trade-offs for many strategic issues.	Nov.–Dec. 1992
U.S. Department of Defense	Improved the decision process for the acquisition of weapon systems.	Nov.–Dec. 1992
Electric utility industry	Considered health and environmental risks in dealing with utility-generated solid wastes and air emissions.	Nov.–Dec. 1992
An anonymous international bank	Developed a contingency-planning program against fire and power failure for all services.	Nov.–Dec. 1992
General Motors	More than 40 major decision analysis projects over five years.	Nov.–Dec. 1992
Southern Company (electric utility)	Evaluated alternative preventive maintenance programs for motor vehicle and construction equipment fleets.	May–June 1993
ICI Americas	Selected research and development projects with little data available for assessing them.	Nov.–Dec. 1993
Federal National Mortgage Association	Used utilities to select the composition of a portfolio of home mortgage assets.	May–June 1994
Oglethorpe Power Corp.	Evaluated whether to invest in a major transmission system and how to finance it.	March–April 1995
Phillips Petroleum Co.	Evaluated oil exploration opportunities with a consistent risk-taking policy.	Nov.–Dec. 1995
Entergy Electric System	Evaluated schedules for preventive maintenance for electrical generator units.	July–Aug. 1996
Personal decision	Used decision trees, etc., to decide whether and when to have a new surgery to correct near-sightedness.	March–April 1997
Duke University	Found that a positive result on a certain medical test has a very high posterior probability of being false positive.	May–June 1999
Westinghouse Corp.	Evaluated potential research and development projects.	Nov.–Dec. 1999

12.11 Summary

Decision analysis is a valuable technique for decision making in the face of great uncertainty. It provides a framework and methodology for rational decision making when the outcomes are uncertain.

In a typical application, a decision maker needs to make either a single decision or a short sequence of decisions (with additional information perhaps becoming available between decisions). A number of alternatives are available for each decision. Uncontrollable random factors affect the payoff that would be obtained from a decision alternative. The possible outcomes of the random factors are referred to as the possible *states of nature*.

Which state of nature actually occurs will be learned only after making the decisions. However, prior to the decisions, it often is possible to estimate *prior probabilities* of the respective states of nature.

Various alternative decision criteria are available for making the decisions. A particularly popular one is *Bayes' decision rule*, which uses the prior probabilities to determine the expected payoff for each decision alternative and then chooses the one with the largest expected payoff. This is the criterion (accompanied by sensitivity analysis) that is mostly used in practice, so it is the focus of much of the chapter.

Sensitivity analysis is very helpful for evaluating the effect of having inaccurate estimates of the data for the problem, including the probabilities, revenues, and costs. Software such as SensIt is available to assist in performing sensitivity analysis.

It sometimes is possible to pay for a test or survey to obtain additional information about the probabilities of the various states of nature. Calculating the *expected value of perfect information* provides a quick way of checking whether doing this might be worthwhile.

When more information is obtained, the updated probabilities are referred to as *posterior probabilities*. A *probability tree diagram* is helpful for calculating these new probabilities.

For problems involving a sequence of decisions (including perhaps a decision on whether to obtain more information), a decision tree commonly is used to graphically display the progression of decisions and random events. The calculations for applying Bayes' decision rule then can be performed directly on the decision tree one event node or decision node at a time. Spreadsheet packages, such as TreePlan, are very helpful for constructing and solving decision trees.

When the problem involves the possibility of uncomfortably large losses, utilities provide a way of incorporating the decision maker's attitude toward risk into the analysis. Bayes' decision rule then is applied by expressing payoffs in terms of utilities rather than monetary values.

Decision analysis is widely used. Versatile software packages for personal computers have become an integral part of the practical application of decision analysis.

Glossary

alternatives   The options available to the decision maker for the decision under consideration. (Section 12.1), *519*

Bayes' decision rule   A popular criterion for decision making that uses probabilities to calculate the expected payoff for each decision alternative and then chooses the one with the largest expected payoff. (Section 12.2), *523*

Bayes' theorem   A formula for calculating a posterior probability of a state of nature. (Section 12.6), *540*

branch   A line emanating from a node in a decision tree. (Section 12.3), *525*

decision conferencing   A process used for group decision making. (Section 12.10), *569*

decision maker   The individual or group responsible for making the decision under consideration. (Section 12.1), *519*

decision node   A point in a decision tree where a decision needs to be made. (Section 12.3), *526*

decision tree   A graphical display of the progression of decisions and random events to be considered. (Sections 12.3 and 12.7), *525*

event node   A point in a decision tree where a random event will occur. (Section 12.3), *526*

expected payoff (EP)   For a decision alternative, it is the weighted average of the payoffs, using the probabilities of the states of nature as the weights. (Section 12.2), *523*

expected value of perfect information (EVPI)   The increase in the expected payoff that could be obtained if it were possible to learn the true state of nature before making the decision. (Sections 12.4 and 12.5), *533*

exponential utility function   A utility function designed to fit a risk-averse individual. (Section 12.9), *565*

influence diagram   A diagram that complements the decision tree for representing and analyzing decision tree problems. (Section 12.10), *569*

lottery procedure   The procedure for finding the decision maker's utility for a specific amount of money by comparing two hypothetical alternatives where one involves a gamble. (Section 12.9), *560*

maximax criterion   A very optimistic decision criterion that does not use prior probabilities and simply chooses the decision alternative that could give the largest possible payoff. (Section 12.2), *521*

maximin criterion   A very pessimistic decision criterion that does not use prior probabilities and simply chooses the decision alternative that provides the best guarantee for its minimum possible payoff. (Section 12.2), *521*

maximum likelihood criterion A criterion for decision making with probabilities that focuses on the most likely state of nature. (Section 12.2), *522*

node A junction point in a decision tree. (Section 12.3), *525*

payoff A quantitative measure of the outcome from a decision alternative and a state of nature. (Section 12.1), *520*

payoff table A table giving the payoff for each combination of a decision alternative and a state of nature. (Section 12.1), *520*

Plot An option provided by SensIt for generating a graph that shows how an output cell varies for different values of a single data cell. (Section 12.8), *550*

point of indifference The point where the decision maker is indifferent between the two hypothetical alternatives in the lottery procedure. (Section 12.9), *559*

posterior probabilities Revised probabilities of the states of nature after doing a test or survey to improve the prior probabilities. (Sections 12.5 and 12.6), *538*

prior probabilities The estimated probabilities of the states of nature prior to obtaining additional information through a test or survey. (Section 12.1), *519*

probability tree diagram A diagram that is helpful for calculating the posterior probabilities of the states of nature. (Section 12.6), *538*

risk-averse individual An individual whose utility function for money has a decreasing

slope as the amount of money increases. (Section 12.9), *555*

risk-neutral individual An individual whose utility for money is proportional to the amount of money involved. (Section 12.9), *555*

risk-seeking individual An individual whose utility function for money has an increasing slope as the amount of money increases. (Section 12.9), *555*

sensitivity analysis The study of how other plausible values for the probabilities of the states of nature (or for the payoffs) would affect the recommended decision alternative. (Sections 12.4 and 12.8), *529*

spider graph A graph that provides helpful comparisons for sensitivity analysis. (Section 12.8), *550*

states of nature The possible outcomes of the random factors that affect the payoff that would be obtained from a decision alternative. (Section 12.1) *519*

tornado diagram A diagram that organizes the data from sensitivity analysis in a readily understandable way. (Section 12.8), *551*

utility The utility of an outcome measures the true value to the decision maker of that outcome. (Sections 12.1 and 12.9), *519*

utility function for money, *U(M)* A plot of utility versus the amount of money *M* being received. (Section 12.9), *555*

Learning Aids for This Chapter in Your MS Courseware

Chapter 12 Excel Files:

Bayes' Decision Rule for First Goferbroke Problem
Decision Tree for First Goferbroke Problem
Data Table for First Goferbroke Problem
EP with Perfect Info for First Goferbroke Problem
Decision Tree for EVPI for First Goferbroke Problem
Template for Posterior Probabilities
Decision Tree for Full Goferbroke Problem (with SensIt Graphs)
Decision Tree for Full Goferbroke Problem with Max's Utility Function
Decision Tree for Full Goferbroke Problem with Exponential Utility Function

Excel Add-ins:

TreePlan (academic version)
SensIt (academic version)

Supplement to This Chapter on the CD-ROM:

Decision Criteria

"Ch. 12 Supplement" Excel Files:

Template for Maximax Criterion
Template for Maximin Criterion

Template for Realism Criterion
Template for Minimax Regret Criterion
Template for Maximum Likelihood Criterion
Template for Equally Likely Criterion

Problems

To the left of the following problems (or their parts), we have inserted the symbol A (for Add-in) whenever one of the Excel add-ins listed above can be used. The symbol T indicates that the Excel template for posterior probabilities can be helpful. Nearly all the problems can be conveniently formulated in a spreadsheet format, so no special symbol is used to designate this. An asterisk on the problem number indicates that at least a partial answer is given in the back of the book.

12.1. You are given the following payoff table (in units of thousands of dollars) for a decision analysis problem without probabilities.

	State of Nature		
Alternative	S_1	S_2	S_3
A_1	6	2	4
A_2	3	4	3
A_3	8	1	5

   a. Which alternative should be chosen under the maximax criterion?

   b. Which alternative should be chosen under the maximin criterion?

12.2. Follow the instructions of Problem 12.1 with the following payoff table.

	State of Nature			
Alternative	S_1	S_2	S_3	S_4
A_1	25	30	20	24
A_2	17	14	31	21
A_3	22	22	22	22
A_4	29	21	26	27

12.3. Jean Clark is the manager of the Midtown Saveway Grocery Store. She now needs to replenish her supply of strawberries. Her regular supplier can provide as many cases as she wants. However, because these strawberries already are very ripe, she will need to sell them tomorrow and then discard any that remain unsold. Jean estimates that she will be able to sell 10, 11, 12, or 13 cases tomorrow. She can purchase the strawberries for $3 per case and sell them for $8 per case. Jean now needs to decide how many cases to purchase.

   Jean has checked the store's records on daily sales of strawberries. On this basis, she estimates that the prior probabilities are 0.2, 0.4, 0.3, and 0.1 for being able to sell 10, 11, 12, and 13 cases of strawberries tomorrow.

   a. Develop a decision analysis formulation of this problem by identifying the decision alternatives, the states of nature, and the payoff table.

   b. If Jean is dubious about the accuracy of these prior probabilities and so chooses to ignore them and use the maximax criterion, how many cases of strawberries should she purchase?

   c. How many cases should be purchased if she uses the maximin criterion?

   d. How many cases should be purchased if she uses the maximum likelihood criterion?

   e. How many cases should be purchased according to Bayes' decision rule?

   f. Jean thinks she has the prior probabilities just about right for selling 10 cases and selling 13 cases, but is uncertain about how to split the prior probabilities for 11 cases and 12 cases. Reapply Bayes' decision rule when the prior probabilities of 11 and 12 cases are (*i*) 0.2 and 0.5, (*ii*) 0.3 and 0.4, and (*iii*) 0.5 and 0.2.

12.4.* Warren Buffy is an enormously wealthy investor who has built his fortune through his legendary investing acumen. He currently has been offered three major investments and he would like to choose one. The first one is a *conservative investment* that would perform very well in an improving economy and only suffer a small loss in a worsening economy. The second is a *speculative investment* that would perform extremely well in an improving economy but would do very badly in a worsening economy. The third is a *countercyclical investment* that would lose some money in an improving economy but would perform well in a worsening economy.

Warren believes that there are three possible scenarios over the lives of these potential investments: (1) an improving economy, (2) a stable economy, and (3) a worsening economy. He is pessimistic about where the economy is headed, and so has assigned prior probabilities of 0.1, 0.5, and 0.4, respectively, to these three scenarios. He also estimates that his profits under these respective scenarios are those given by the following table:

	Improving Economy	Stable Economy	Worsening Economy
Conservative investment	$ 30 million	$ 5 million	$−10 million
Speculative investment	40 million	10 million	−30 million
Countercyclical investment	−10 million	0	15 million
Prior probability	0.1	0.5	0.4

Which investment should Warren make under each of the following criteria?

a. Maximax criterion.

b. Maximin criterion.

c. Maximum likelihood criterion.

d. Bayes' decision rule.

12.5. Reconsider Problem 12.4. Warren Buffy decides that Bayes' decision rule is his most reliable decision criterion. He believes that 0.1 is just about right as the prior probability of an improving economy, but is quite uncertain about how to split the remaining probabilities between a stable economy and a worsening economy. Therefore, he now wishes to do sensitivity analysis with respect to these latter two prior probabilities.

a. Reapply Bayes' decision rule when the prior probability of a stable economy is 0.3 and the prior probability of a worsening economy is 0.6.

b. Reapply Bayes' decision rule when the prior probability of a stable economy is 0.7 and the prior probability of a worsening economy is 0.2.

c. Construct a decision tree by hand for this problem with the original prior probabilities.

A d. Use TreePlan to construct and solve a decision tree for this problem with the original prior probabilities.

A e. In preparation for performing sensitivity analysis, consolidate the data and results on the same spreadsheet as the decision tree constructed in part *d* (as was done in Figure 12.6 for the case study).

A f. Use the spreadsheet (including the decision tree) obtained in parts *d* and *e* to do parts *a* and *b*.

A g. Expanding the spreadsheet as needed, generate a data table that shows which investment Warren should make and the resulting expected profit for the following prior probabilities of a stable economy: 0, 0.1, 0.2, 0.3, 0.4, 0.5, 0.6, 0.7, 0.8, 0.9.

h. For each of the three investments, find the expected profit when the prior probability of a stable economy is 0 and then when it is 0.9 (with the prior probability of an improving economy fixed at 0.1). Plot these expected profits on a single graph that has expected profit as the vertical axis and the prior probability of a stable economy as the horizontal axis. For each of the three investments, draw a line segment connecting its two points on this graph to show how its expected profit would vary with the prior probability of a stable economy. Use this graph to describe how the choice of the investment depends on the prior probability of a stable economy.

i. Use algebra to solve for the values of this prior probability at which the choice of investment changes as the prior probability increases.

12.6.* Consider a decision analysis problem whose payoffs (in units of thousands of dollars) are given by the following payoff table:

Alternative	State of Nature	
	S_1	S_2
A_1	80	25
A_2	30	50
A_3	60	40
Prior probability	0.4	0.6

    a. Which alternative should be chosen under the maximax criterion?

    b. Which alternative should be chosen under the maximin criterion?

    c. Which alternative should be chosen under the maximum likelihood criterion?

    d. Which alternative should be chosen under Bayes' decision rule?

A   *e.* Use TreePlan to construct and solve a decision tree for this problem.

A   *f.* Expanding the spreadsheet containing this decision tree as needed, perform sensitivity analysis with the decision tree by re-solving when the prior probability of S_1 is 0.2 and again when it is 0.6.

A   *g.* Now perform this sensitivity analysis systematically by generating a data table that shows the best alternative (according to Bayes' decision rule) and the resulting expected payoff as the prior probability of S_1 increases in increments of 0.04 from 0.2 to 0.6.

12.7. You are given the following payoff table (in units of thousands of dollars) for a decision analysis problem:

Alternative	State of Nature		
	S_1	S_2	S_3
A_1	220	170	110
A_2	200	180	150
Prior probability	0.6	0.3	0.1

    a. Which alternative should be chosen under the maximax criterion?

    b. Which alternative should be chosen under the maximin criterion?

    c. Which alternative should be chosen under the maximum likelihood criterion?

    d. Which alternative should be chosen under Bayes' decision rule?

    e. Construct a decision tree by hand for this problem.

A   *f.* Use TreePlan to construct and solve a decision tree for this problem.

A   *g.* Perform sensitivity analysis with this decision tree by generating a data table that shows what happens when the prior probability of S_1 increases in increments of 0.05 from 0.3 to 0.7 while the prior probability of S_3 remains fixed at its original value. Then use algebra to solve for the value of the prior probability of S_1 at which the best alternative changes as this prior probability increases.

A   *h.* Repeat part *g* when it is the prior probability of S_2 that remains fixed at its original value.

A   *i.* Repeat part *g* when it is the prior probability of S_1 that remains fixed at its original value while the prior probability of S_2 increases in increments of 0.05 from 0 to 0.4.

    j. If you feel that the true probabilities of the states of nature should be within 10 percent of the given prior probabilities, which alternative would you choose?

12.8. Dwight Moody is the manager of a large farm with 1,000 acres of arable land. For greater efficiency, Dwight always devotes the farm to growing one crop at a time. He now needs to make a decision on which one of four crops to grow during the upcoming growing season. For each of these crops, Dwight has obtained the following estimates of crop yields and net incomes per bushel under various weather conditions.

	Expected Yield, Bushels/Acre			
Weather	Crop 1	Crop 2	Crop 3	Crop 4
Dry	20	15	30	40
Moderate	35	20	25	40
Damp	40	30	25	40
Net income per bushel	$1.00	$1.50	$1.00	$0.50

After referring to historical meteorological records, Dwight also has estimated the following prior probabilities for the weather during the growing season:

Dry   0.3

Moderate   0.5

Damp   0.2

a. Develop a decision analysis formulation of this problem by identifying the decision alternatives, the states of nature, and the payoff table.

A   b. Construct a decision tree for this problem.

c. Use Bayes' decision rule to determine which crop to grow.

d. Using Bayes' decision rule, do sensitivity analysis with respect to the prior probabilities of moderate weather and damp weather (without changing the prior probability of dry weather) by re-solving when the prior probability of moderate weather is 0.2, 0.3, 0.4, and 0.6.

12.9.   Barbara Miller makes decisions according to Bayes' decision rule. For her current problem, Barbara has constructed the following payoff table (in units of hundreds of dollars) and she now wishes to maximize the expected payoff.

	State of Nature		
Alternative	S_1	S_2	S_3
A_1	$2x$	50	10
A_2	25	40	90
A_3	35	$3x$	30
Prior probability	0.4	0.2	0.4

The value of x currently is 50, but there is an opportunity to increase x by spending some money now.

What is the maximum amount Barbara should spend to increase x to 75?

12.10.   You are given the following payoff table (in units of thousands of dollars) for a decision analysis problem:

	State of Nature		
Alternative	S_1	S_2	S_3
A_1	4	0	0
A_2	0	2	0
A_3	3	0	1
Prior probability	0.2	0.5	0.3

a. According to Bayes' decision rule, which alternative should be chosen?

b. Find the expected value of perfect information.

A   *c.* Check your answer in part *b* by recalculating it with the help of a decision tree.

       d. You are given the opportunity to spend $1,000 to obtain more information about which state of nature is likely to occur. Given your answer to part *b,* might it be worthwhile to spend this money?

12.11.*   Betsy Pitzer makes decisions according to Bayes' decision rule. For her current problem, Betsy has constructed the following payoff table (in units of dollars):

	State of Nature		
Alternative	S_1	S_2	S_3
A_1	50	100	−100
A_2	0	10	− 10
A_3	20	40	− 40
Prior probability	0.5	0.3	0.2

       a. Which alternative should Betsy choose?

       b. Find the expected value of perfect information.

A   *c.* Check your answer in part *b* by recalculating it with the help of a decision tree.

       d. What is the most that Betsy should consider paying to obtain more information about which state of nature will occur?

12.12.   Using Bayes' decision rule, consider the decision analysis problem having the following payoff table (in units of thousands of dollars):

	State of Nature		
Alternative	S_1	S_2	S_3
A_1	−100	10	100
A_2	− 10	20	50
A_3	10	10	60
Prior probability	0.2	0.3	0.5

       a. Which alternative should be chosen? What is the resulting expected payoff?

       b. You are offered the opportunity to obtain information that will tell you with certainty whether the first state of nature S_1 will occur. What is the maximum amount you should pay for the information? Assuming you will obtain the information, how should this information be used to choose an alternative? What is the resulting expected payoff (excluding the payment)?

       c. Now repeat part *b* if the information offered concerns S_2 instead of S_1.

       d. Now repeat part *b* if the information offered concerns S_3 instead of S_1.

A   *e.* Now suppose that the opportunity is offered to provide information that will tell you with certainty which state of nature will occur (perfect information). What is the maximum amount you should pay for the information? Assuming you will obtain the information, how should this information be used to choose an alternative? What is the resulting expected payoff (excluding the payment)?

       f. If you have the opportunity to do some testing that will give you partial additional information (not perfect information) about the state of nature, what is the maximum amount you should consider paying for this information?

12.13.   Reconsider the Goferbroke Co. case study, including its analysis in Sections 12.6 and 12.7. With the help of the consulting geologist, Jennifer Flyer now has obtained some historical data that provides more precise information than Max could supply on the likelihood of obtaining favorable seismic soundings on similar tracts of land. Specifically, when the land contains oil, favorable seismic soundings are obtained 80 percent of the time. This percentage changes to 40 percent when the land is dry.

      a. Revise Figure 12.12 to find the new posterior probabilities.

T   *b.* Use the corresponding Excel template to check your answers in part *a.*

      c. Revise Figure 12.16 to find the new decision tree. What is the resulting optimal policy?

A   *d.* Use TreePlan to construct and solve this new decision tree.

A12.14. Reconsider Problem 12.13. Max is skeptical that his estimates (60 percent and 20 percent) could be so far off the percentages (80 percent and 40 percent) obtained by Jennifer, so he requests that sensitivity analysis be conducted regarding these percentages.

      a. Use the spreadsheet shown in Figure 12.18 (available in one of this chapter's Excel files) to obtain the results when Jennifer's probabilities are used.

      b. Use SensIt to generate two graphs like Figure 12.20 where the horizontal axis for one is the probability in cell W33, P(FSS|Oil), and the horizontal axis for the other is the probability in cell W34, P(FSS|Dry).

      c. Generate the spider graph and tornado diagram when Jennifer's probabilities are used instead of Max's estimates.

12.15.* Vincent Cuomo is the credit manager for the Fine Fabrics Mill. He is currently faced with the question of whether to extend $100,000 of credit to a potential new customer, a dress manufacturer. Vincent has three categories for the creditworthiness of a company—poor risk, average risk, and good risk—but he does not know which category fits this potential customer. Experience indicates that 20 percent of companies similar to this dress manufacturer are poor risks, 50 percent are average risks, and 30 percent are good risks. If credit is extended, the expected profit for poor risks is $-$15,000, for average risks $10,000, and for good risks $20,000. If credit is not extended, the dress manufacturer will turn to another mill. Vincent is able to consult a credit-rating organization for a fee of $5,000 per company evaluated. For companies whose actual credit records with the mill turn out to fall into each of the three categories, the following table shows the percentages that were given each of the three possible credit evaluations by the credit-rating organization.

| | Actual Credit Record | | |
Credit Evaluation	Poor	Average	Good
Poor	50%	40%	20%
Average	40	50	40
Good	10	10	40

      a. Develop a decision analysis formulation of this problem by identifying the decision alternatives, the states of nature, and the payoff table when the credit-rating organization is not used.

      b. Assuming the credit-rating organization is not used, use Bayes' decision rule to determine which decision alternative should be chosen.

A   *c.* Find the expected value of perfect information. Does this answer indicate that consideration should be given to using the credit-rating organization?

      d. Assume now that the credit-rating organization is used. Develop a probability tree diagram to find the posterior probabilities of the respective states of nature for each of the three possible credit evaluations of this potential customer.

T   *e.* Use the corresponding Excel template to obtain the answers for part *d.*

      f. Draw the decision tree for this entire problem by hand. Use this decision tree to determine Vincent's optimal policy.

A   *g.* Use TreePlan to construct and solve this decision tree.

12.16. You are given the following payoff table (in units of dollars):

| | State of Nature | |
Alternative	S_1	S_2
A_1	400	-100
A_1	0	100
Prior probability	0.4	0.6

You have the option of paying $100 to have research done to better predict which state of nature will occur. When the true state of nature is S_1, the research will accurately predict S_1 60 percent of the time (but will inaccurately predict S_2 40 percent of the time). When the true state of nature is S_2, the research will accurately predict S_2 80 percent of the time (but will inaccurately predict S_1 20 percent of the time).

a. Given that the research is not done, use Bayes' decision rule to determine which decision alternative should be chosen.

A   *b.* Use a decision tree to help find the expected value of perfect information. Does this answer indicate that it might be worthwhile to do the research?

c. Given that the research is done, find the joint probability of each of the following pairs of outcomes: (*i*) the state of nature is S_1 and the research predicts S_1, (*ii*) the state of nature is S_1 and the research predicts S_2, (*iii*) the state of nature is S_2 and the research predicts S_1, and (*iv*) the state of nature is S_2 and the research predicts S_2.

d. Find the unconditional probability that the research predicts S_1. Also find the unconditional probability that the research predicts S_2.

e. Given that the research is done, use your answers in parts *c* and *d* to determine the posterior probabilities of the states of nature for each of the two possible predictions of the research.

T   *f.* Use the corresponding Excel template to obtain the answers for part *e*.

g. Given that the research predicts S_1, use Bayes' decision rule to determine which decision alternative should be chosen and the resulting expected payoff.

h. Repeat part *g* when the research predicts S_2.

i. Given that research is done, what is the expected payoff when using Bayes' decision rule?

j. Use the preceding results to determine the optimal policy regarding whether to do the research and the choice of the decision alternative.

A   *k.* Construct and solve the decision tree to show the analysis for the entire problem. (Using TreePlan is optional.)

12.17. An athletic league does drug testing of its athletes, 10 percent of whom use drugs. The test, however, is only 95 percent reliable. That is, a drug user will test positive with probability 0.95 and negative with probability 0.05, and a nonuser will test negative with probability 0.95 and positive with probability 0.05.

Develop a probability tree diagram to determine the posterior probability of each of the following outcomes of testing an athlete.

a. The athlete is a drug user, given that the test is positive.

b. The athlete is not a drug user, given that the test is positive.

c. The athlete is a drug user, given that the test is negative.

d. The athlete is not a drug user, given that the test is negative.

T   *e.* Use the corresponding Excel template to check your answers in the preceding parts.

12.18. Management of the Telemore Company is considering developing and marketing a new product. It is estimated to be twice as likely that the product would prove to be successful as unsuccessful. If it were successful, the expected profit would be $1,500,000. If unsuccessful, the expected loss would be $1,800,000. A marketing survey can be conducted at a cost of $100,000 to predict whether the product would be successful. Past experience with such surveys indicates that successful products have been predicted to be successful 80 percent of the time, whereas unsuccessful products have been predicted to be unsuccessful 70 percent of the time.

a. Develop a decision analysis formulation of this problem by identifying the decision alternatives, the states of nature, and the payoff table when the market survey is not conducted.

b. Assuming the market survey is not conducted, use Bayes' decision rule to determine which decision alternative should be chosen.

c. Find the expected value of perfect information. Does this answer indicate that consideration should be given to conducting the market survey?

T   *d.* Assume now that the market survey is conducted. Find the posterior probabilities of the respective states of nature for each of the two possible predictions from the market survey.

A   *e.* Use TreePlan to construct and solve the decision tree for this entire problem.

A   *f.* Use SensIt to generate a spider graph and tornado diagram with respect to the profit, loss, and cost data when each can vary as much as 25 percent in either direction from its base value.

12.19. The Hit-and-Miss Manufacturing Company produces items that have a probability p of being defective. These items are produced in lots of 150. Past experience indicates that p for an entire lot is either 0.05 or 0.25. Furthermore, in 80 percent of the lots produced, p equals 0.05 (so p equals 0.25 in 20 percent of the lots). These items are then used in an assembly, and ultimately their quality is determined before the final assembly leaves the plant. Initially the company can *either* screen each item in a lot at a cost of $10 per item and replace defective items *or* use the items directly without screening. If the latter action is chosen, the cost of rework is ultimately $100 per defective item. Because screening requires scheduling of inspectors and equipment, the decision to screen or not screen must be made two days before the screening is to take place. However, one item can be taken from the lot and sent to a laboratory for inspection, and its quality (defective or nondefective) can be reported before the screen/no-screen decision must be made. The cost of this initial inspection is $125.

 a. Develop a decision analysis formulation of this problem by identifying the decision alternatives, the states of nature, and the payoff table if the single item is not inspected in advance.

 b. Assuming the single item is not inspected in advance, use Bayes' decision rule to determine which decision alternative should be chosen.

 c. Find the expected value of perfect information. Does this answer indicate that consideration should be given to inspecting the single item in advance?

T *d.* Assume now that the single item is inspected in advance. Find the posterior probabilities of the respective states of nature for each of the two possible outcomes of this inspection.

A *e.* Construct and solve the decision tree for this entire problem.

12.20.* Silicon Dynamics has developed a new computer chip that will enable it to begin producing and marketing a personal computer if it so desires. Alternatively, it can sell the rights to the computer chip for $15 million. If the company chooses to build computers, the profitability of the venture depends on the company's ability to market the computer during the first year. It has sufficient access to retail outlets that it can guarantee sales of 10,000 computers. On the other hand, if this computer catches on, the company can sell 100,000 machines. For analysis purposes, these two levels of sales are taken to be the two possible outcomes of marketing the computer, but it is unclear what their prior probabilities are. The cost of setting up the assembly line is $6 million. The difference between the selling price and the variable cost of each computer is $600.

 a. Develop a decision analysis formulation of this problem by identifying the decision alternatives, the states of nature, and the payoff table.

 b. Construct a decision tree for this problem by hand.

A *c.* Assuming the prior probabilities of the two levels of sales are both 0.5, use TreePlan to construct and solve this decision tree. According to this analysis, which decision alternative should be chosen?

A *d.* Use SensIt to develop a graph that plots the expected payoff (when using Bayes' decision rule) versus the prior probability of selling 10,000 computers.

 e. Draw a graph that plots the expected payoff for each of the decision alternatives versus the prior probability of selling 10,000 computers.

 f. Referring to this graph, use algebra to solve for the value of the prior probability of selling 10,000 computers at the point where the two lines in the graph intersect. Explain the significance of this point.

12.21.* Reconsider Problem 12.20. Management of Silicon Dynamics now is considering doing full-fledged market research at a cost of $1 million to predict which of the two levels of demand is likely to occur. Previous experience indicates that such market research is correct two-thirds of the time.

 a. Find the expected value of perfect information for this problem.

 b. Does the answer in part *a* indicate that it might be worthwhile to perform this market research?

 c. Develop a probability tree diagram to obtain the posterior probabilities of the two levels of demand for each of the two possible outcomes of the market research.

T   *d.* Use the corresponding Excel template to check your answers in part *c.*

A12.22.*   Reconsider Problem 12.21. The management of Silicon Dynamics now wants to see a decision tree displaying the entire problem.

    a. Use TreePlan to construct and solve this decision tree.

    b. There is some uncertainty in the financial data ($15 million, $6 million, and $600) stated in Problem 12.20. Each could vary from its base value by as much as 10 percent. For each one, perform sensitivity analysis to find what would happen if its value were at either end of this range of variability (without any change in the other two pieces of data). Then do the same for the eight cases where all these pieces of data are at one end or the other of their ranges of variability.

    c. Because of the uncertainty described in part *b,* use SensIt to generate a graph that plots the expected profit over the range of variability for each piece of financial data (without any change in the other two pieces of data).

    d. Generate the corresponding spider graph and tornado diagram.

12.23.   You are given the following decision tree, where the numbers in parentheses are probabilities and the numbers on the right are payoffs at these terminal points.

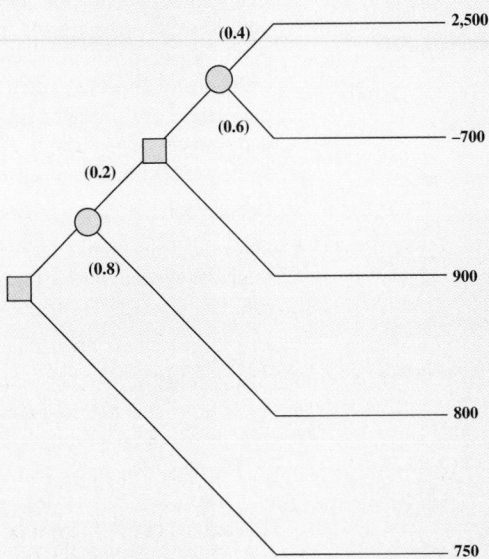

    a. Analyze this decision tree to obtain the optimal policy.

A   *b.* Use TreePlan to construct and solve the same decision tree.

12.24.   You are given the following decision tree, with the probabilities at event nodes shown in parentheses and with the payoffs at terminal points shown on the right. Analyze this decision tree to obtain the optimal policy.

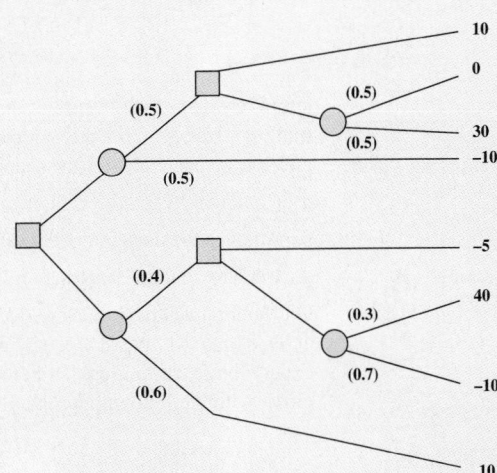

12.25.* The Athletic Department of Leland University is considering whether to hold an extensive campaign next year to raise funds for a new athletic field. The response to the campaign depends heavily on the success of the football team this fall. In the past, the football team has had winning seasons 60 percent of the time. If the football team has a winning season (W) this fall, then many of the alumni will contribute and the campaign will raise $3 million. If the team has a losing season (L), few will contribute and the campaign will lose $2 million. If no campaign is undertaken, no costs are incurred. On September 1, just before the football season begins, the Athletic Department needs to make its decision about whether to hold the campaign next year.

   a. Develop a decision analysis formulation of this problem by identifying the decision alternatives, the states of nature, and the payoff table.

   b. According to Bayes' decision rule, should the campaign be undertaken?

   c. What is the expected value of perfect information?

   d. A famous football guru, William Walsh, has offered his services to help evaluate whether the team will have a winning season. For $100,000, he will carefully evaluate the team throughout spring practice and then throughout preseason workouts. William then will provide his prediction on September 1 regarding what kind of season, W or L, the team will have. In similar situations in the past when evaluating teams that have winning seasons 50 percent of the time, his predictions have been correct 75 percent of the time. Considering that this team has more of a winning tradition, if William predicts a winning season, what is the posterior probability that the team actually will have a winning season? What is the posterior probability of a losing season? If William predicts a losing season instead, what is the posterior probability of a winning season? Of a losing season? Show how these answers are obtained from a probability tree diagram.

T   *e.* Use the corresponding Excel template to obtain the answers requested in part *d*.

   f. Draw the decision tree for this entire problem by hand. Analyze this decision tree to determine the optimal policy regarding whether to hire William and whether to undertake the campaign.

A   *g.* Use TreePlan to construct and solve this decision tree.

12.26. The comptroller of the Macrosoft Corporation has $100 million of excess funds to invest. She has been instructed to invest the entire amount for one year in either stocks or bonds (but not both) and then to reinvest the entire fund in either stocks or bonds (but not both) for one year more. The objective is to maximize the expected monetary value of the fund at the end of the second year.

   The annual rates of return on these investments depend on the economic environment, as shown in the following table:

Economic Environment	Rate of Return	
	Stocks	**Bonds**
Growth	20%	5%
Recession	−10	10
Depression	−50	20

   The probabilities of growth, recession, and depression for the first year are 0.7, 0.3, and 0, respectively. If growth occurs in the first year, these probabilities remain the same for the second year. However, if a recession occurs in the first year, these probabilities change to 0.2, 0.7, and 0.1, respectively, for the second year.

   a. Construct by hand the decision tree for this problem.

   b. Analyze the decision tree to identify the optimal policy.

A   *c.* Use TreePlan to construct and solve the decision tree.

12.27. On Monday, a certain stock closed at $10 per share. On Tuesday, you expect the stock to close at $9, $10, or $11 per share, with respective probabilities 0.3, 0.3, and 0.4. On Wednesday, you expect the stock to close 10 percent lower, unchanged, or 10 percent higher than Tuesday's close, with the following probabilities:

Today's Close	10 Percent Lower	Unchanged	10 Percent Higher
$ 9	0.4	0.3	0.3
10	0.2	0.2	0.6
11	0.1	0.2	0.7

On Tuesday, you are directed to buy 100 shares of the stock before Thursday. All purchases are made at the end of the day, at the known closing price for that day, so your only options are to buy at the end of Tuesday or at the end of Wednesday. You wish to determine the optimal strategy for whether to buy on Tuesday or defer the purchase until Wednesday, given the Tuesday closing price, to minimize the expected purchase price.

    a. Develop and evaluate a decision tree by hand for determining the optimal strategy.

A   *b.* Use TreePlan to construct and solve the decision tree.

A12.28.   Jose Morales manages a large outdoor fruit stand in one of the less affluent neighborhoods of San Jose, California. To replenish his supply, Jose buys boxes of fruit early each morning from a grower south of San Jose. About 90 percent of the boxes of fruit turn out to be of satisfactory quality, but the other 10 percent are unsatisfactory. A satisfactory box contains 80 percent excellent fruit and will earn $200 profit for Jose. An unsatisfactory box contains 30 percent excellent fruit and will produce a loss of $1,000. Before Jose decides to accept a box, he is given the opportunity to sample one piece of fruit to test whether it is excellent. Based on that sample, he then has the option of rejecting the box without paying for it. Jose wonders (1) whether he should continue buying from this grower, (2) if so, whether it is worthwhile sampling just one piece of fruit from a box, and (3) if so, whether he should be accepting or rejecting the box based on the outcome of this sampling.

    Use TreePlan (and the Excel template for posterior probabilities) to construct and solve the decision tree for this problem.

12.29.*   The Morton Ward Company is considering the introduction of a new product that is believed to have a 50–50 chance of being successful. One option is to try out the product in a test market, at a cost of $2 million, before making the introduction decision. Past experience shows that ultimately successful products are approved in the test market 80 percent of the time, whereas ultimately unsuccessful products are approved in the test market only 25 percent of the time. If the product is successful, the net profit to the company will be $40 million; if unsuccessful, the net loss will be $15 million.

    a. Discarding the test market option, develop a decision analysis formulation of the problem by identifying the decision alternatives, states of nature, and payoff table. Then apply Bayes' decision rule to determine the optimal decision alternative.

    b. Find the expected value of perfect information.

A   *c.* Now including the option of trying out the product in a test market, use TreePlan (and the Excel template for posterior probabilities) to construct and solve the decision tree for this problem.

A   *d.* There is some uncertainty in the stated profit and loss figures ($40 million and $15 million). Either could vary from its base by as much as 25 percent in either direction. For each of these two financial figures, perform sensitivity analysis to check how the results in part *c* would change if the value of the financial figure were at either end of this range of variability (without any change in the value of the other financial figure). Then do the same for the four cases where both financial figures are at one end or the other of their ranges of variability.

A   *e.* Because of the uncertainty described in part *d,* use SensIt to generate a graph that plots the expected profit over the range of variability for each of the two financial figures (without any change in the other figure).

A   *f.* Generate the corresponding spider graph and tornado diagram. Interpret each one.

A12.30.   Chelsea Bush is an emerging candidate for her party's nomination for president of the United States. She now is considering whether to run in the high-stakes Super Tuesday primaries. If she enters the Super Tuesday (S.T.) primaries, she and her advisers believe that she will either do well (finish first or second) or do poorly (finish third or worse) with probabilities 0.4 and

0.6, respectively. Doing well on Super Tuesday will net the candidate's campaign approximately $16 million in new contributions, whereas a poor showing will mean a loss of $10 million after numerous TV ads are paid for. Alternatively, she may choose not to run at all on Super Tuesday and incur no costs.

Chelsea's advisers realize that her chances of success on Super Tuesday may be affected by the outcome of the smaller New Hampshire (N.H.) primary occurring three weeks before Super Tuesday. Political analysts feel that the results of New Hampshire's primary are correct two-thirds of the time in predicting the results of the Super Tuesday primaries. Among Chelsea's advisers is a decision analysis expert who uses this information to calculate the following probabilities:

P(Chelsea does well in S.T. primaries, given she does well in N.H.) = ⅘

P(Chelsea does well in S.T. primaries, given she does poorly in N.H.) = ¼

P(Chelsea does well in N.H. primary) = ⁷⁄₁₅

The cost of entering and campaigning in the New Hampshire primary is estimated to be $1.6 million.

Chelsea feels that her chance of winning the nomination depends largely on having substantial funds available after the Super Tuesday primaries to carry on a vigorous campaign the rest of the way. Therefore, she wants to choose the strategy (whether to run in the New Hampshire primary and then whether to run in the Super Tuesday primaries) that will maximize her expected funds after these primaries.

a. Construct and solve the decision tree for this problem.

b. There is some uncertainty in the estimates of a gain of $16 million or a loss of $10 million depending on the showing on Super Tuesday. Either amount could differ from this estimate by as much as 25 percent in either direction. For each of these two financial figures, perform sensitivity analysis to check how the results in part *a* would change if the value of the financial figure were at either end of this range of variability (without any change in the value of the other financial figure). Then do the same for the four cases where both financial figures are at one end or the other of their ranges of variability.

A   *c.* Because of the uncertainty described in part *b,* use SensIt to generate a graph that plots Chelsea's expected funds after these primaries over the range of variability for each of the two financial figures (without any change in the other figure).

d. Generate the corresponding spider graph and tornado diagram. Interpret each one.

A12.31. The executive search being conducted for Western Bank by Headhunters Inc. may finally be bearing fruit. The position to be filled is a key one—vice president for Information Processing—because this person will have responsibility for developing a state-of-the-art management information system that will link together Western's many branch banks. However, Headhunters feels it has found just the right person, Matthew Fenton, who has an excellent record in a similar position for a midsized bank in New York.

After a round of interviews, Western's president believes that Matthew has a probability of 0.7 of designing the management information system successfully. If Matthew is successful, the company will realize a profit of $2 million (net of Matthew's salary, training, recruiting costs, and expenses). If he is not successful, the company will realize a net loss of $600,000.

For an additional fee of $40,000, Headhunters will provide a detailed investigative process (including an extensive background check, a battery of academic and psychological tests, etc.) that will further pinpoint Matthew's potential for success. This process has been found to be 90 percent reliable, that is, a candidate who would successfully design the management information system will pass the test with probability 0.9, and a candidate who would not successfully design the system will fail the test with probability 0.9.

Western's top management needs to decide whether to hire Matthew and whether to have Headhunters conduct the detailed investigative process before making this decision.

a. Construct the decision tree for this problem.

b. Find the probabilities for the branches emanating from the event nodes.

c. Analyze the decision tree to identify the optimal policy.

d. Now suppose that Headhunters's fee for administering its detailed investigative process is negotiable. What is the maximum amount that Western Bank should pay?

12.32. Reconsider the Goferbroke Co. case study, including the application of utilities in Section 12.9. Max Flyer now has decided that, given the company's precarious financial situation, he needs to take a much more risk-averse approach to the problem. Therefore, he has revised the utilities given in Table 12.9 as follows: $U(-130) = -200$, $U(-100) = -130$, $U(60) = 60$, $U(90) = 90$, $U(670) = 440$, and $U(700) = 450$.

    a. Analyze the revised decision tree corresponding to Figure 12.29 by hand to obtain the new optimal policy.

A   *b.* Use TreePlan to construct and solve this revised decision tree.

12.33.* You live in an area that has a possibility of incurring a massive earthquake, so you are considering buying earthquake insurance on your home at an annual cost of $180. The probability of an earthquake damaging your home during one year is 0.001. If this happens, you estimate that the cost of the damage (fully covered by earthquake insurance) will be $160,000. Your total assets (including your home) are worth $250,000.

    a. Apply Bayes' decision rule to determine which alternative (take the insurance or not) maximizes your expected assets after one year.

    b. You now have constructed a utility function that measures how much you value having total assets worth x dollars ($x \geq 0$). This utility function is $U(x) = \sqrt{x}$. Compare the utility of reducing your total assets next year by the cost of the earthquake insurance with the expected utility next year of not taking the earthquake insurance. Should you take the insurance?

12.34. For your graduation present from college, your parents are offering you your choice of two alternatives. The first alternative is to give you a money gift of $19,000. The second alternative is to make an investment in your name. This investment will quickly have the following two possible outcomes:

Outcome	Probability
Receive $10,000	0.3
Receive $30,000	0.7

Your utility for receiving M thousand dollars is given by the utility function $U(M) = \sqrt{M + 6}$. Which choice should you make to maximize expected utility?

12.35.* Reconsider Problem 12.34. You now are uncertain about what your true utility function for receiving money is, so you are in the process of constructing this utility function. So far, you have found that $U(19) = 16.7$ and $U(30) = 20$ are the utility of receiving $19,000 and $30,000, respectively. You also have concluded that you are indifferent between the two alternatives offered to you by your parents. Use this information to find $U(10)$.

12.36. You wish to construct your personal utility function $U(M)$ for receiving M thousand dollars. After setting $U(0) = 0$, you next set $U(1) = 1$ as your utility for receiving $1,000. You next want to find $U(10)$ and then $U(5)$.

    a. You offer yourself the following two hypothetical alternatives:

        A_1: Obtain $10,000 with probability p.
            Obtain 0 with probability $(1 - p)$.
        A_2: Definitely obtain $1,000.

You then ask yourself the question: What value of p makes you indifferent between these two alternatives? Your answer is $p = 0.125$. Find $U(10)$.

    b. You next repeat part *a* except for changing the second alternative to definitely receiving $5,000. The value of p that makes you indifferent between these two alternatives now is $p = 0.5625$. Find $U(5)$.

    c. Repeat parts *a* and *b*, but now use *your* personal choices for p.

12.37. You are given the following payoff table:

	State of Nature	
Alternative	S_1	S_2
A_1	25	36
A_2	100	0
A_3	0	49
Prior probability	p	$1 - p$

a. Assume that your utility function for the payoffs is $U(x)=\sqrt{x}$. Plot the expected utility of each decision alternative versus the value of p on the same graph. For each decision alternative, find the range of values of p over which this alternative maximizes the expected utility.

A   b. Now assume that your utility function is the exponential utility function with a risk tolerance of $R = 50$. Use TreePlan to construct and solve the resulting decision tree in turn for $p = 0.25$, $p = 0.5$, and $p = 0.75$.

A12.38.   Dr. Switzer has a seriously ill patient but has had trouble diagnosing the specific cause of the illness. The doctor now has narrowed the cause down to two alternatives: disease A or disease B. Based on the evidence so far, she feels that the two alternatives are equally likely.

Beyond the testing already done, there is no test available to determine if the cause is disease B. One test is available for disease A, but it has two major problems. First, it is very expensive. Second, it is somewhat unreliable, giving an accurate result only 80 percent of the time. Thus, it will give a positive result (indicating disease A) for only 80 percent of patients who have disease A, whereas it will give a positive result for 20 percent of patients who actually have disease B instead.

Disease B is a very serious disease with no known treatment. It is sometimes fatal, and those who survive remain in poor health with a poor quality of life thereafter. The prognosis is similar for victims of disease A if it is left untreated. However, there is a fairly expensive treatment available that eliminates the danger for those with disease A, and it may return them to good health. Unfortunately, it is a relatively radical treatment that always leads to death if the patient actually has disease B instead.

The probability distribution for the prognosis for this patient is given for each case in the following table, where the column headings (after the first one) indicate the disease for the patient.

	Outcome Probabilities			
	No Treatment		Receive Treatment for Disease A	
Outcome	A	B	A	B
Die	0.2	0.5	0	1.0
Survive with poor health	0.8	0.5	0.5	0
Return to good health	0	0	0.5	0

The patient has assigned the following utilities to the possible outcomes:

Outcome	Utility
Die	0
Survive with poor health	10
Return to good health	30

In addition, these utilities should be incremented by -2 if the patient incurs the cost of the test for disease A and by -1 if the patient (or the patient's estate) incurs the cost of the treatment for disease A.

Use decision analysis with a complete decision tree to determine if the patient should undergo the test for disease A and then how to proceed (receive the treatment for disease A?) to maximize the patient's expected utility.

12.39.   Consider the following decision tree, where the probabilities for each event node are shown in parentheses.

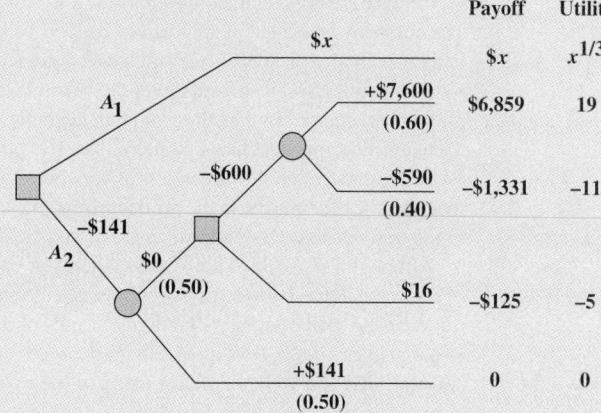

	Payoff	Utility
$x	$x	$x^{1/3}$
+$7,600 (0.60)	$6,859	19
−$590 (0.40)	−$1,331	−11
$16	−$125	−5
+$141 (0.50)	0	0

The dollar amount given next to each branch is the cash flow generated along that branch, where these intermediate cash flows add up to the total net cash flow shown to the right of each terminal branch. (The unknown amount for the top branch is represented by the variable x.) The decision maker has a utility function $U(y) = y^{1/3}$ where y is the total net cash flow after a terminal branch. The resulting utilities for the various terminal branches are shown to the right of the decision tree.

Use these utilities to analyze the decision tree. Then determine the value of x for which the decision maker is indifferent between decision alternatives A_1 and A_2.

A12.40.   Reconsider the Goferbroke Co. case study when using utilities, as presented in Section 12.9.

   a. Beginning with the decision tree shown in Figure 12.29 (available in one of this chapter's Excel files), prepare to perform sensitivity analysis by expanding and organizing the spreadsheet to (1) consolidate the data and results in one section and (2) incorporate the Excel template for posterior probabilities in another section (similar to what was done in Figure 12.18).

   b. Perform sensitivity analysis by re-solving the decision tree (after using the Excel template for posterior probabilities to revise these probabilities) when the prior probability of oil is changed in turn to 0.15, 0.2, 0.3, and 0.35.

12.41.   Select one of the applications of decision analysis listed in Table 12.10. Read the article describing the application in the indicated issue of *Interfaces*. (These articles can be downloaded at **www.mhhe.com/hillier2e/articles**.) Write a two-page summary of the application and the benefits it provided.

12.42.   Select three of the applications of decision analysis listed in Table 12.10. Read the articles describing the applications in the indicated issues of *Interfaces*. (These articles can be downloaded at **www.mhhe.com/hillier2e/articles**.) For each one, write a one-page summary of the application and the benefits it provided.

Case 12-1

Brainy Business

While El Niño is pouring its rain on northern California, Charlotte Rothstein, CEO, major shareholder, and founder of Cerebrosoft, sits in her office, contemplating the decision she faces regarding her company's newest proposed product, Brainet. This has been a particularly difficult decision. Brainet might catch on and sell very well. However, Charlotte is concerned about the risk involved. In this competitive market, marketing Brainet also could lead to substantial losses. Should she go ahead anyway and start the marketing campaign? Or just abandon the product? Or perhaps buy additional marketing research information from a local market research company before deciding whether to launch the product? She has to make a decision very soon and so, as she slowly drinks from her glass of high-protein-power multivitamin juice, she reflects on the events of the past few years.

Cerebrosoft was founded by Charlotte and two friends after they had graduated from business school. The company is located in the heart of Silicon Valley. Charlotte and her friends managed to make money in their second year in business and have continued to do so every year since. Cerebrosoft was one of the first companies to sell software over the World Wide Web and to develop PC-based software tools for the multimedia sector. Two of the products generate 80 percent of the company's revenues: Audiatur and Videatur. Each product has sold more than 100,000 units during the past year. Business is done over the Web: Customers can download a trial version of the software, test it, and if they are satisfied with what they see, they can purchase the product (by using a password that enables them to disable the time counter in the trial version). Both products are priced at $75.95 and are sold exclusively over the Web.

Although the World Wide Web is a network of computers of different types, running different kinds of software, a standardized protocol between the computers enables them to communicate. Users can surf the Web and visit computers many thousands of miles away, accessing information available at the site. Users also can make files available on the Web, and this is how Cerebrosoft generates its sales. Selling software over the Web eliminates many of the traditional cost factors of consumer products: packaging, storage, distribution, sales force, and so on. Instead, potential customers can download a trial version, take a look at it (that is, use the product) before its trial period expires, and then decide whether to buy it. Furthermore, Cerebrosoft can always make the most recent files available to the customer, avoiding the problem of having outdated software in the distribution pipeline.

Charlotte is interrupted in her thoughts by the arrival of Jeannie Korn. Jeannie is in charge of marketing for online products and Brainet has had her particular attention from the beginning. She is more than ready to provide the advice that Charlotte has requested. "Charlotte, I think we should really go ahead with Brainet. The software engineers have convinced me that the current version is robust and we want to be on the market with this as soon as possible! From the data for our product launches during the past two years, we can get a rather reliable estimate of how the market will respond to the new product, don't you think? And look!" She pulls out some presentation slides. "During that time period we launched 12 new products altogether and 4 of them sold more than 30,000 units during the first six months alone! Even better: The last two we launched even sold more than 40,000 copies during the first two quarters!" Charlotte knows these numbers as well as Jeannie does. After all, two of these launches have been products she herself helped to develop. But she feels uneasy about this particular product launch. The company has grown rapidly during the past three years and its financial capabilities are already rather stretched. A poor product launch for Brainet would cost the company a lot of money, something that isn't available right now due to the investments Cerebrosoft has recently made.

Later in the afternoon, Charlotte meets with Reggie Ruffin, a jack of all trades and the production manager. Reggie has a solid track record in his field and Charlotte wants his opinion on the Brainet project.

"Well, Charlotte, quite frankly, I think that there are three main factors that are relevant to the success of this project: competition, units sold, and cost—ah, and, of course, our pricing. Have you decided on the price yet?"

"I am still considering which of the three strategies would be most beneficial to us. Selling for $50.00 and trying to maximize revenues—or selling for $30.00 and trying to maximize market share. Of course, there is still your third alternative; we could sell for $40.00 and try to do both."

At this point, Reggie focuses on the sheet of paper in front of him. "And I still believe that the $40.00 alternative is the best one. Concerning the costs, I checked the records; basically we have to amortize the development costs we incurred for Brainet. So far we have spent $800,000 and we expect to spend another $50,000 per year for support and shipping the CDs to those who want a hardcopy on top of their downloaded software." Reggie next hands a report to Charlotte. "Here we have some data on the industry. I just received that yesterday, hot off the press. Let's see what we can learn about the industry here." He shows Charlotte some of the highlights. Reggie then agrees to compile the most relevant information contained in the report and have it ready for Charlotte the following morning. It takes him long into the night to gather the data from the pages of the report, but in the end he produces three tables, one for each of the three alternative pricing strategies. Each table shows the corresponding probability of various amounts of sales given the level of competition (severe, moderate, or weak) that develops from other companies.

TABLE 1
Probability Distribution of Unit Sales, Given a High Price ($50)

	Level of Competition		
Sales	Severe	Moderate	Weak
50,000 units	0.2	0.25	0.3
30,000 units	0.25	0.3	0.35
20,000 units	0.55	0.45	0.35

TABLE 2

Probability Distribution of Unit Sales, Given a Medium Price ($40)

Sales	Level of Competition		
	Severe	Moderate	Weak
50,000 units	0.25	0.30	0.40
30,000 units	0.35	0.40	0.50
20,000 units	0.40	0.30	0.10

TABLE 3

Probability Distribution of Unit Sales, Given a Low Price ($30)

Sales	Level of Competition		
	Severe	Moderate	Weak
50,000 units	0.35	0.40	0.50
30,000 units	0.40	0.50	0.45
20,000 units	0.25	0.10	0.05

The next morning, Charlotte is sipping from another power drink. Jeannie and Reggie will be in her office any moment now and, with their help, she will have to decide what to do with Brainet. Should they launch the product? If so, at what price?

When Jeannie and Reggie enter the office, Jeannie immediately bursts out: "Guys, I just spoke to our marketing research company. They say that they could do a study for us about the competitive situation for the introduction of Brainet and deliver the results within a week."

"How much do they want for the study?"

"I knew you'd ask that, Reggie. They want $10,000, and I think it's a fair deal."

At this point, Charlotte steps into the conversation. "Do we have any data on the quality of the work of this marketing research company?"

"Yes, I do have some reports here. After analyzing them, I have come to the conclusion that the predictions of the marketing research company are pretty good: Given that the competition turned out to be severe, they predicted it correctly 80 percent of the time, while 15 percent of the time they predicted moderate competition in that setting. Given that the competition turned out to be moderate, they predicted severe competition 15 percent of the time and moderate competition 80 percent of the time. Finally, for the case of weak competition, the numbers were 90 percent of the time a correct prediction, 7 percent of the time a 'moderate' prediction and 3 percent of the time a 'severe' prediction."

Charlotte feels that all these numbers are too much for her. "Don't we have a simple estimate of how the market will react?"

"Some prior probabilities, you mean? Sure, from our past experience, the likelihood of facing severe competition is 20 percent, whereas it is 70 percent for moderate competition and 10 percent for weak competition," says Jeannie, her numbers always ready when needed.

All that is left to do now is to sit down and make sense of all this . . .

a. For the initial analysis, ignore the opportunity of obtaining more information by hiring the marketing research company. Identify the decision alternatives and the states of nature. Construct the payoff table. Then formulate the decision problem in a decision tree. Clearly distinguish between decision and event nodes and include all the relevant data.

b. What is Charlotte's decision if she uses the maximum likelihood criterion?

c. What is Charlotte's decision if she uses Bayes' decision rule?

d. Now consider the possibility of doing the market research. Develop the corresponding decision tree. Calculate the relevant probabilities and analyze the decision tree. Should Cerebrosoft pay the $10,000 for the marketing research? What is the overall optimal policy?

Case 12-2

Smart Steering Support

On a sunny May morning, Marc Binton, CEO of Bay Area Automobile Gadgets (BAAG), enters the conference room on the 40th floor of the Gates building in San Francisco, where BAAG's offices are located. The other executive officers of the company have already gathered. The meeting has only one item on its agenda:

planning a research and development project to develop a new driver support system (DSS). Brian Huang, manager of Research and Development, is walking around nervously. He has to inform the group about the R&D strategy he has developed for the DSS. Marc has identified DSS as the strategic new product for the company. Julie Aker, vice president of Marketing, will speak after Brian. She will give detailed information about the target segment, expected sales, and marketing costs associated with the introduction of the DSS.

BAAG builds electronic nonaudio equipment for luxury cars. Founded by a group of Stanford graduates, the company sold its first product—a car routing system relying on a technology called Global Positioning Satellites (GPS)—a few years ago. Such routing systems help drivers to find directions to their desired destinations using satellites to determine the exact position of the car. To keep up with technology and to meet the wishes of its customers, the company has added a number of new features to its router during the last few years. The DSS will be a completely new product, incorporating recent developments in GPS as well as voice recognition and display technologies. Marc strongly supports this product, as it will give BAAG a competitive advantage over its Asian and European competitors.

Driver support systems have been a field of intense research for more than a decade. These systems provide the driver with a wide range of information, such as directions, road conditions, traffic updates, and so forth. The information exchange can take place verbally or via projection of text onto the windscreen. Other features help the driver avoid obstacles that have been identified by cars ahead on the road (these cars transmit the information to the following vehicles). Marc wants to incorporate all these features and other technologies into one support system that would then be sold to BAAG's customers in the automobile industry.

After all the attendees have taken their seats, Brian starts his presentation: "Marc asked me to inform you about our efforts with the driver support system, particularly the road scanning device. We have reached a stage where we basically have to make a go or no-go decision concerning the research for this device, which, as you all know by now, is a key feature in the DSS. We have already integrated the other devices, such as the GPS-based positioning and direction system. The question with which we have to deal is whether to fund basic research into the road scanning device. If this research is successful, we then will have to decide if we want to develop a product based on these results—or if we just want to sell the technology without developing a product. If we do decide to develop the product ourselves, there is a chance that the product development process might not be successful. In that case, we could still sell the technology. In the case of successful product development, we would have to decide whether to market the product. If we decide not to market the developed product, we could at least sell the product concept that was the result of our successful research and development efforts. Doing so would earn more than just selling the technology prematurely. If, on the other hand, we decide to market the driver support system, then we are faced with the uncertainty of how the product will be received by our customers."

"You completely lost me," snipes Marc.

Max, Julie's assistant, just shakes his head and murmurs, "those techno-nerds. . . ."

Brian starts to explain: "Sorry for the confusion. Let's just go through it again, step by step."

"Good idea—and perhaps make smaller steps!" Julie obviously dislikes Brian's style of presentation.

"OK, the first decision we are facing is whether to invest in research for the road scanning device."

"How much would that cost us?" asks Marc.

"Our estimated budget for this is $300,000. Once we invest that money, the outcome of the research effort is somewhat uncertain. Our engineers assess the probability of successful research at 80 percent."

"That's a pretty optimistic success rate, don't you think?" Julie remarks sarcastically. She still remembers the disaster with Brian's last project, the fingerprint-based car-security-system. After spending half a million dollars, the development engineers concluded that it would be impossible to produce the security system at an attractive price.

Brian senses Julie's hostility and shoots back: "In engineering, we are quite accustomed to these success rates—something we can't say about marketing. . . ."

"What would be the next step?" intervenes Marc.

"Hm, sorry. If the research is not successful, then we can only sell the DSS in its current form."

"The profit estimate for that scenario is $2 million," Julie throws in.

"If, however, the research effort is successful, then we will have to make another decision, namely, whether to go on to the development stage."

"If we wouldn't want to develop a product at that point, would that mean that we would have to sell the DSS as it is now?" asks Max.

"Yes, Max. Except that additionally we would earn some $200,000 from selling our research results to GM. Their research division is very interested in our work and they have offered that money for our findings."

"Ah, now that's good news," remarks Julie.

Brian continues, "If, however, after successfully completing the research stage, we decide to develop a new product, then we'll have to spend another $800,000 for that task, at a 35 percent chance of not being successful."

"So you are telling us we'll have to spend $800,000 for a ticket in a lottery where we have a 35 percent chance of not winning anything?" asks Julie.

"Julie, don't focus on the losses but on the potential gains! The chance of winning in this lottery, as you call it, is 65 percent. I believe that that's much more than with a normal lottery ticket," says Marc.

"Thanks, Marc," says Brian. "Once we invest that money in development, we have two possible outcomes: either we will be successful in developing the road scanning device or we won't. If we fail, then once again we'll sell the DSS in its current form and cash in the $200,000 from GM for the research results. If the development process is successful, then we have to decide whether to market the new product."

"Why wouldn't we want to market it after successfully developing it?" asks Marc.

"That's a good question. Basically what I mean is that we could decide not to sell the product ourselves but instead give the right to sell it to somebody else, to GM for example. They would pay us $1 million for it."

"I like those numbers!" remarks Julie.

"Once we decide to build the product and market it, we will face the market uncertainties and I'm sure that Julie has those numbers ready for us. Thanks."

At this point, Brian sits down and Julie comes forward to give her presentation. Immediately some colorful slides are projected on the wall behind her as Max operates the computer.

"Thanks, Brian. Well, here's the data we have been able to gather from some marketing research. The acceptance of our new product in the market can be high, medium, or low." Julie is pointing to some figures projected on the wall behind her. "Our estimates indicate that high acceptance would result in profits of $8.0 million and that medium acceptance would give us $4.0 million. In the unfortunate case of a poor reception by our customers, we still expect $2.2 million in profit. I should mention that these profits do not include the additional costs of marketing or R&D expenses."

"So, you are saying that in the worst case we'll make barely more money than with the current product?" asks Brian.

"Yes, that's what I am saying."

"What budget would you need for the marketing of our DSS with the road scanner?" asks Marc.

"For that we would need an additional $200,000 on top of what has already been included in the profit estimates," Julie replies.

"What are the chances of ending up with a high, medium, or low acceptance of the new DSS?" asks Brian.

"We can see those numbers at the bottom of the slide," says Julie, while she is turning toward the projection behind her. There is a 30 percent chance of high market acceptance and a 20 percent chance of low market acceptance.

At this point, Marc moves in his seat and asks: "Given all these numbers and bits of information, what are you suggesting that we do?"

a. Organize the available data on cost and profit estimates in a table.

b. Formulate the problem in a decision tree. Clearly distinguish between decision and event nodes.

c. Calculate the expected payoffs for each node in the decision tree.

d. What is BAAG's optimal policy according to Bayes' decision rule?

e. What would be the expected value of perfect information on the outcome of the research effort?

f. What would be the expected value of perfect information on the outcome of the development effort?

g. Marc is a risk-averse decision maker. In a number of interviews, his utility function for money was assessed to be

$$U(M) = \frac{1 - e^{-\frac{M}{12}}}{1 - e^{-\frac{1}{12}}}$$

where M is the company's net profit in units of hundreds of thousands of dollars (e.g., $M = 8$ would imply a net profit of $800,000). Using Marc's utility function, calculate the utility for each terminal branch of the decision tree.

h. Determine the expected utilities for all nodes in the decision tree.

i. Based on Marc's utility function, what is BAAG's optimal policy?

j. Based on Marc's utility function, what would be the expected value of perfect information on the outcome of the research effort?

k. Based on Marc's utility function, what would be the expected value of perfect information on the outcome of the development effort?

Learning objectives

After completing this chapter, you should be able to

1. Describe some important types of forecasting applications.

2. Identify two common measures of the accuracy of forecasting methods.

3. Adjust forecasting data to consider seasonal patterns.

4. Describe several forecasting methods that use the pattern of historical data to forecast a future value.

5. Apply these methods either by hand or with the software provided.

6. Compare these methods to identify the conditions when each is particularly suitable.

7. Describe and apply an approach to forecasting that relates the quantity of interest to one or more other quantities.

8. Describe several forecasting methods that use expert judgment.

9. Identify the forecasting methods that are most commonly used in practice.

Chapter **Thirteen**

Forecasting

How much will the economy grow over the next year? Where is the stock market headed? What about interest rates? How will consumer tastes be changing? What will be the hot new products?

Forecasters have answers to all these questions. Unfortunately, these answers will more than likely be wrong. Nobody can accurately predict the future every time.

Nevertheless, the future success of any business depends heavily on how savvy its management is in spotting trends and developing appropriate strategies. The leaders of the best companies often seem to have a sixth sense for when to change direction to stay a step ahead of the competition, but this sixth sense actually is guided by frequent use of the best forecasting techniques. These companies seldom get into trouble by badly misestimating what the demand will be for their products. Many other companies do. The ability to forecast well makes the difference.

When historical sales data are available, some proven **statistical forecasting methods** have been developed for using these data to forecast future demand. Such methods assume that historical trends will continue, so management then needs to make adjustments to reflect current changes in the marketplace.

Several **judgmental forecasting methods** that solely use expert judgment also are available. These methods are especially valuable when little or no historical sales data are available or when major changes in the marketplace make these data unreliable for forecasting purposes.

Forecasting product demand is just one important application of these forecasting methods. A variety of applications are surveyed in the first section.

Section 13.2 introduces a case study that will be carried through much of the chapter. Sections 13.3–13.6 focus on statistical forecasting methods and Section 13.7 on judgmental forecasting methods. The chapter then concludes by surveying forecasting practices in U.S. corporations.

13.1 SOME APPLICATIONS OF FORECASTING

We now will discuss some main areas in which forecasting is widely used. In each case, we will illustrate this use by mentioning one or more actual applications that have been described in published articles. A summary table at the end of the section will tell you where these articles can be found in case you want to read further.

Sales Forecasting

Any company engaged in selling goods needs to forecast the demand for those goods. Manufacturers need to know how much to produce. Wholesalers and retailers need to know how much to stock. Substantially underestimating demand is likely to lead to many lost sales, unhappy customers, and perhaps allowing the competition to gain the upper hand in the marketplace. On the other hand, significantly overestimating demand also is very costly due to (1) excessive inventory costs, (2) forced price reductions, (3) unneeded production or storage capacity, and (4) lost opportunities to market more profitable goods. Successful marketing and production managers understand very well the importance of obtaining good sales forecasts.

Accurate sales forecasts are needed to avoid the high cost of either underestimating or overestimating demand.

The **Merit Brass Company** is a family-owned company that supplies several thousand products to the pipe, valve, and fittings industry. In 1990, Merit Brass embarked on a modernization program that emphasized installing management science methodologies in statistical sales forecasting and finished-goods inventory management (two activities that go hand in glove). This program led to major improvements in customer service (as measured by product availability) while simultaneously achieving substantial cost reductions.

A major Spanish electric utility, **Hidroeléctrica Español,** has developed and implemented a hierarchy of management science models to assist in managing its system of reservoirs used for generating hydroelectric power. All these models are driven by forecasts of both energy demand (this company's sales) and reservoir inflows. A sophisticated statistical forecasting method is used to forecast energy demand on both a short-term and long-term basis. A hydrological forecasting model generates the forecasts of reservoir inflows.

Airline companies now depend heavily on the high fares paid by businesspeople traveling on short notice while providing discount fares to others to help fill the seats. The decision on how to allocate seats to the different fare classes is a crucial one for maximizing revenue. **American Airlines,** for example, uses statistical forecasting of the demand at each fare to make this decision.

Forecasting the Need for Spare Parts

Although effective sales forecasting is a key for virtually any company, some organizations must rely on other types of forecasts as well. A prime example involves forecasts of the need for spare parts.

Many companies need to maintain an inventory of spare parts to enable them to quickly repair either their own equipment or their products sold or leased to customers. In some cases, this inventory is huge. For example, IBM's spare-parts inventory is valued in the billions of dollars and includes many thousand different parts.

Just as for a finished-goods inventory ready for sale, effective management of a spare-parts inventory depends on obtaining a reliable forecast of the demand for that inventory. Although the types of costs incurred by misestimating demand are somewhat different, the consequences may be no less severe for spare parts. For example, the consequence for an airline not having a spare part available on location when needed to continue flying an airplane probably is at least one canceled flight.

Underestimating the need for spare parts can have dire consequences.

To support its operation of several hundred aircraft, **American Airlines** maintains an extensive inventory of spare parts. Included are over 5,000 different types of *rotatable* parts (e.g., landing gear and wing flaps) with an average value of $5,000 per item. When a rotatable part on an airplane is found to be defective, it is immediately replaced by a corresponding part in inventory so the airplane can depart. However, the replaced part then is repaired and placed back into inventory for subsequent use as a replacement part.

American Airlines uses a PC-based forecasting system called the Rotatables Allocation and Planning System (RAPS) to forecast demand for the rotatable parts and to help allocate these parts to the various airports. The statistical forecast uses an 18-month history of parts usage and flying hours for the fleet and then projects ahead based on planned flying hours.

Forecasting Production Yields

The *yield* of a production process refers to the percentage of the completed items that meet quality standards (perhaps after rework) and so do not need to be discarded. Particularly with high technology products, the yield frequently is well under 100 percent.

If the forecast for the production yield is somewhat under 100 percent, the size of the production run probably should be somewhat larger than the order quantity to provide a good chance of fulfilling the order with acceptable items. (The difference between the run size and the order quantity is referred to as the *reject allowance.*) If an expensive setup is required for each production run, or if there is only time for one production run, the reject allowance may need to be quite large. However, an overly large value should be avoided to prevent excessive production costs.

The size of the reject allowance depends on the forecast of production yield.

Obtaining a reliable forecast of production yield is essential for choosing an appropriate value of the reject allowance.

This was the case for **Albuquerque Microelectronics Operation,** a dedicated production source for radiation-hardened microchips. The first phase in the production of its microchips, the *wafer fabrication process,* was continuing to provide erratic production yields. For a given product, the yield typically would be quite small (0 to 40 percent) for the first several lots and then would gradually increase to a higher range (35 to 75 percent) for later lots. Therefore, a statistical forecasting method that considered this increasing trend was used to forecast the production yield.

Forecasting Economic Trends

With the possible exception of sales forecasting, the most extensive forecasting effort is devoted to forecasting economic trends on a regional, national, or even international level. How much will the nation's gross domestic product grow next quarter? Next year? What is the forecast for the rate of inflation? The unemployment rate? The balance of trade?

Statistical models to forecast economic trends (commonly called **econometric models**) have been developed in a number of governmental agencies, university research centers, large corporations, and consulting firms, both in the United States and elsewhere. Using historical data to project ahead, these econometric models typically consider a very large number of factors that help drive the economy. Some models include hundreds of variables and equations. However, except for their size and scope, these models resemble some of the statistical forecasting methods used by businesses for sales forecasting, and so forth.

Forecasts of economic trends guide governmental policies.

These econometric models can be very influential in determining governmental policies. For example, the forecasts provided by the U.S. Congressional Budget Office strongly guide Congress in developing the federal budgets. These forecasts also help businesses in assessing the general economic outlook.

As an example on a smaller scale, the **U.S. Department of Labor** contracted with a consulting firm to develop the *unemployment insurance econometric forecasting model* (UIEFM). The model is now in use by state employment security agencies around the nation. By projecting such fundamental economic factors as unemployment rates, wage levels, the size of the labor force covered by unemployment insurance, and so on, UIEFM forecasts how much the state will need to pay in unemployment insurance. By projecting tax inflows into the state's unemployment insurance trust fund, UIEFM also forecasts trust fund balances over a 10-year period. Therefore, UIEFM has proven to be invaluable in managing state unemployment insurance systems and in guiding related legislative policies.

Forecasting Staffing Needs

One of the major trends in the American economy is a shifting emphasis from manufacturing to *services.* More and more of our manufactured goods are being produced outside the country (where labor is cheaper) and then imported. At the same time, an increasing number of American business firms are specializing in providing a service of some kind (e.g., travel, tourism, entertainment, legal aid, health services, financial, educational, design, maintenance, etc.). For such a company, forecasting "sales" becomes forecasting the *demand for services,* which then translates into forecasting staffing needs to provide those services.

For example, one of the fastest growing service industries in the United States today is *call centers.* A call center receives telephone calls from the general public requesting a particular type of service. Depending on the center, the service might be providing technical assistance over the phone, making a travel reservation, filling a telephone order for goods, or booking services to be performed later, as well as other types of assistance. There now are more than 350,000 call centers in the United States, with over $25 billion invested to date and an annual growth rate of 20 percent.

Accurate forecasts of staffing needs enable service organizations to provide satisfactory service at the lowest possible cost.

As with any service organization, an erroneous forecast of staffing requirements for a call center has serious consequences. Providing too few agents to answer the telephone leads to unhappy customers, lost calls, and perhaps lost business. Too many agents cause excessive personnel costs.

TABLE 13.1 **Some Applications of Statistical Forecasting Methods**

Organization	Quantity Being Forecasted	Issue of *Interfaces*
Merit Brass Co.	Sales of finished goods	January–February 1993
Hidroeléctrica Español	Energy demand	January–February 1990
American Airlines	Demand for different fare classes	January–February 1992
American Airlines	Need for spare parts to repair airplanes	July–August 1989
Albuquerque Microelectronics	Production yield in wafer fabrication	March–April 1994
U.S. Department of Labor	Unemployment insurance payments	March–April 1988
United Airlines	Demand at reservations offices and airports	January–February 1986
Taco Bell	Number of customer arrivals	January–February 1998
L. L. Bean	Staffing needs at call center	November–December 1995

Section 2.1 described a major management science study that involved personnel scheduling at **United Airlines.** With over 4,000 reservations sales representatives and support personnel at its 11 reservations offices, and about 1,000 customer service agents at its 10 largest airports, a computerized planning system was developed to design the work schedules for these employees. Although several other management science techniques (including linear programming) were incorporated into this system, *statistical forecasting* of staffing requirements also was a key ingredient. This system provided annual savings of over $6 million as well as improved customer service and reduced support staff requirements.

Taco Bell is an international fast-food corporation that operates mostly through approximately 4,000 company-owned and franchised restaurants. The corporation has applied a variety of management science techniques to develop a labor-management system that each of the restaurants uses to develop work schedules and assignments for its employees. A key component of the labor-management system is *statistical forecasting* of the number of customers arriving in each 15-minute interval throughout the hours of a restaurant's operation. This system is credited with saving $13 million in labor costs while simultaneously improving the level of customer service.

L. L. Bean is a major retailer of high-quality outdoor goods and apparel. Over 70 percent of its total sales volume is generated through orders taken at the company's call center. Two 800 numbers are provided, one for placing orders and the second for making inquiries or reporting problems. Each of the company's agents is trained to answer just one of the 800 numbers. Therefore, separate statistical forecasting models were developed to forecast staffing requirements for the two 800 numbers on a weekly basis. The improved precision of these models is estimated to have saved L. L. Bean $300,000 annually through enhanced scheduling efficiency. (The case study introduced in the next section is based largely on this application.)

Other

Table 13.1 summarizes the actual applications of statistical forecasting methods presented in this section. The last column cites the issue of *Interfaces* that includes the article that describes each application in detail. (These articles can be downloaded at **www.mhhe.com/ hillier2e/articles.**)

All five categories of forecasting applications discussed in this section use the types of statistical forecasting methods presented in the subsequent sections. There also are other important categories (including forecasting weather, the stock market, and prospects for new products before market testing) that use specialized techniques that are not discussed here.

Review Questions

1. When doing sales forecasting, what are the consequences of underestimating demand? Of overestimating demand?

2. When a company leases its products to customers, what kind of forecasting is needed to provide good maintenance service to these customers?

3. What is the purpose of forecasting production yield?

4. What is the common name for statistical models used to forecast economic trends?

5. What are the consequences of an erroneous forecast of staffing needs for a call center?

13.2 A CASE STUDY: THE COMPUTER CLUB WAREHOUSE (CCW) PROBLEM

The Computer Club Warehouse (commonly referred to as CCW) sells various computer products at bargain prices by taking telephone orders (as well as website and fax orders) directly from customers. Its products include desktop and laptop computers, peripherals, hardware accessories, supplies, software (including games), and computer-related furniture. The company mails catalogs to its customers and numerous prospective customers several times per year, as well as publishing minicatalogs in computer magazines. These catalogs prominently display the 800 toll-free telephone number to call to place an order. These calls come into the company's call center.

The CCW Call Center

The call center is never closed. During busy hours, it is staffed by dozens of agents. Their sole job is to take and process customer orders over the telephone. (A second, much smaller call center uses another 800 number for callers making inquiries or reporting problems. This case study focuses on just the main call center.)

New agents receive a week's training before beginning work. This training emphasizes how to efficiently and courteously process an order. An agent is expected not to average more than five minutes per call. Records are kept and an agent who does not meet this target by the end of the probationary period will not be retained. Although the agents are well-paid, the tedium and time pressure associated with the job leads to a fairly high turnover rate.

A large number of telephone trunks are provided for incoming calls. If an agent is not free when the call arrives, it is placed on hold with a recorded message and background music. If all the trunks are in use (referred to as *saturation*), an incoming call receives a busy signal instead.

Although some customers who receive a busy signal, or who hang up after being on hold too long, will try again later until they get through, many do not. Therefore, it is very important to have enough agents on duty to minimize these problems. On the other hand, because of the high labor costs for the agents, CCW tries to avoid having so many agents on duty that they have significant idle time.

Consequently, obtaining forecasts of the demand for the agents is crucial to the company.

The Call Center Manager, Lydia Weigelt

The current manager of the call center is Lydia Weigelt. As the top student in her graduating class from business school, she was wooed by several top companies before choosing CCW. Extremely bright and hard driving, she is being groomed to enter top management at CCW in the coming years.

When Lydia was hired a little over three years ago, she was assigned to her current position in order to learn the business from the ground up. The call center is considered to be the nerve center of the entire CCW operation.

Before Lydia's arrival, the company had suffered from serious management problems with the call center. Orders were not being processed efficiently. A few were even misdirected. Staffing levels never seemed to be right. Management directives to adjust the levels kept overcompensating in the opposite direction. Data needed to get a handle on the staffing level problem hadn't been kept. Morale was low.

All that changed when Lydia arrived. One of her first moves was to install procedures for gathering the data needed to make decisions on staffing levels. The key data included a detailed record of call volume and how much of the volume was being handled by each agent. Efficiency improved substantially. Despite running a tight ship, Lydia took great pains to praise and reward good work. Morale increased dramatically.

Although gratified by the great improvement in the operation of the call center, Lydia still has one major frustration. At the end of each quarter, when she knows how many agents are not being retained at the end of their probationary period, she makes a decision on how many new agents to hire to go through the next training session (held at the beginning of each quarter). She has developed an excellent procedure for estimating the staffing level needed to cover any particular call volume. However, each time she has used this procedure to set the staffing level for the upcoming quarter, based on her forecast of the call volume, the forecast usually has turned out to be considerably off. Therefore, she still isn't getting the right staffing levels.

Better forecasts of call volume are needed.

Lydia has concluded that her next project should be to develop a better forecasting method to replace the current one.

Lydia's Current Forecasting Method

Thanks to Lydia's data-gathering procedures installed shortly after her arrival, reliable data on call volume now are available for the past three years. Figure 13.1 shows the average number of calls received per day in each of the four quarters of these years. The right side also displays these same data to show the pattern graphically. (This graph was generated from the data by choosing "Chart" under the Insert menu, selecting the Line chart type, and following the directions of the Chart Wizard.)

Forecasts need to take into account the seasonal pattern of increased sales in Quarter 4 due to Christmas purchases.

Note that the sales in Quarter 4 jump up each year due to Christmas purchases. When Lydia first joined CCW, the president told her about the "25 percent rule" that the company had traditionally used to forecast call volume (and sales).

The 25 Percent Rule: Since sales are relatively stable through the year except for a substantial increase during the Christmas season, assume that each quarter's call volume will be the same as for the preceding quarter, except for adding 25 percent for Quarter 4. Thus,

Forecast for Quarter 2 = Call volume for Quarter 1

Forecast for Quarter 3 = Call volume for Quarter 2

Forecast for Quarter 4 = 1.25(Call volume for Quarter 3)

The forecast for the next year's Quarter 1 then would be obtained from the current year's Quarter 4 by

$$\text{Forecast for next Quarter 1} = \frac{\text{Call volume for Quarter 4}}{1.25}$$

This is the forecasting method that Lydia has been using.

FIGURE 13.1
The average number of calls received per day at the CCW call center in each of the four quarters of the past three years.

	A	B	C	D	E	F	G	H	I
1		**CCW's Average Daily Call Volume**							
2									
3		Year	Quarter	Call Volume					
4		1	1	6,809					
5		1	2	6,465					
6		1	3	6,569					
7		1	4	8,266					
8		2	1	7,257					
9		2	2	7,064					
10		2	3	7,784					
11		2	4	8,724					
12		3	1	6,992					
13		3	2	6,822					
14		3	3	7,949					
15		3	4	9,650					

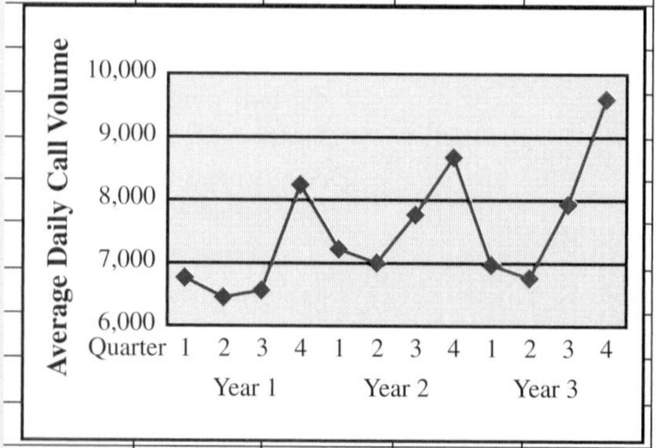

FIGURE 13.2   This spreadsheet records the results of applying the 25 percent rule over the past three years to forecast the average daily call volume for the upcoming quarter.

	A	B	C	D	E	F	G	H	I	J	K	L
1		**Lydia's Current Forecasting Method for CCW's Average Daily Call Volume**										
2												
3						**Forecasting**						
4		**Year**	**Quarter**	**Data**	**Forecast**	**Error**		**Mean Absolute Deviation**				
5		1	1	6,809				MAD =	424			
6		1	2	6,465	6,809	344						
7		1	3	6,569	6,465	104		**Mean Square Error**				
8		1	4	8,266	8,211	55		MSE =	317,815			
9		2	1	7,257	6,613	644						
10		2	2	7,064	7,257	193						
11		2	3	7,784	7,064	720						
12		2	4	8,724	9,730	1,006						
13		3	1	6,992	6,979	13						
14		3	2	6,822	6,992	170						
15		3	3	7,949	6,822	1,127						
16		3	4	9,650	9,936	286						
17		4	1		7,720							
18		4	2									
19		4	3									
20		4	4									

Range Name	Cells
Data	D5:D20
Forecast	E5:E20
ForecastingError	F5:F20

	E	F
3		**Forecasting**
4	**Forecast**	**Error**
5		
6	=D5	=ABS(D6-E6)
7	=D6	=ABS(D7-E7)
8	=1.25*D7	=ABS(D8-E8)
9	=D8/1.25	=ABS(D9-E9)
10	=D9	=ABS(D10-E10)
11	:	:
12	:	:

	H	I
5	MAD =	=AVERAGE(ForecastingError)

	H	I
8	MSE =	=SUMSQ(ForecastingError)/ COUNT(ForecastingError)

Figure 13.2 shows the forecasts that Lydia obtained with this method. Column F gives the **forecasting error** (the deviation of the forecast from what then turned out to be the true value of the call volume) in each case. Since the total of the 11 forecasting errors is 4,662, the average is

$$\text{Average forecasting error} = \frac{4,662}{11}$$

$$= 424$$

The average forecasting error is commonly called **MAD,** which stands for **mean absolute deviation.** Its formula is

MAD is simply the average of the forecasting errors.

$$\text{MAD} = \frac{\text{Sum of forecasting errors}}{\text{Number of forecasts}}$$

Thus, in this case, cell I5 gives

$$\text{MAD} = 424$$

To put this value of MAD = 424 into perspective, note that 424 is over 5 percent of the average daily call volume in most quarters. With forecasting errors ranging as high as 1,127, two of the errors are well over 10 percent. Although errors of this size are common in typical applications of forecasting, greater accuracy is needed for this particular application. Errors of 5 and 10 percent make it impossible to properly set the staffing level for a quarter. No wonder Lydia is *mad* about the poor job that the 25 percent rule is doing. A better forecasting method is needed.

Another popular measure of the accuracy of forecasting methods is called the **mean square error** and is abbreviated as **MSE.** Its formula is

> MSE is the average of the *square* of the forecasting errors.

$$\text{MSE} = \frac{\text{Sum of square of forecasting errors}}{\text{Number of forecasts}}$$

Thus, in Figure 13.2,

$$\text{MSE} = \frac{(344)^2 + (104)^2 + \cdots + (286)^2}{11}$$
$$= 317{,}815$$

> A bad forecasting error greatly increases the value of the MSE.

as given in cell I8. The advantage of squaring the forecasting errors is that it increases the weight of the large errors relative to the weight given to the small errors. Small errors are only to be expected with even the best forecasting methods and, since such errors have no serious consequences, decreasing their weight is desirable. It is the large forecasting errors that have serious consequences. Therefore, it is good to give a relatively large penalty to a forecasting method that occasionally allows large forecasting errors while rewarding a forecasting method that consistently keeps the errors reasonably small. When comparing two such methods, this can result in the former kind of method receiving the larger value of MSE even though it has the smaller MAD value. Thus, MSE provides a useful complement to MAD by providing additional information about how consistently a forecasting method avoids seriously large errors. However, the disadvantage of MSE compared to MAD is a greater difficulty in interpreting the significance of its value for an individual forecasting method. Consequently, Lydia (who is familiar with both measures) will focus most of her attention on MAD values while keeping her eye on MSE values as well.

The Plan to Find a Better Forecasting Method

Lydia remembers taking a management science course in college. She recalls that one of the topics in the course was *forecasting,* so she decides to review her textbook and class notes on this topic.

This review reminds her that she is dealing with what is called a *time series.*

A **time series** is a series of observations over time of some quantity of interest. For example, the series of observations of average daily call volume for the most recent 12 quarters, as given in Figure 13.1, constitute a time series.

She also is reminded that a variety of statistical methods are available for using the historical data from a time series to forecast a future observation in the series. Her task now is to review these methods and assess which one is best suited for her particular forecasting problem.

To assist her in this task for a few weeks, Lydia gains approval from the CCW president to contract for the services of a consultant (a former classmate) from a management science consulting firm that specializes largely in forecasting.

The next section describes their approach to the problem.

Review Questions

1. How does the Computer Club Warehouse (CCW) operate?

2. What are the consequences of not having enough agents on duty in the CCW call center? Of having too many?

3. Who is the call center manager? What is her current major frustration?

4. What is CCW's 25 percent rule?

5. What is MAD?

6. What is MSE?

7. What is a time series?

13.3   APPLYING TIME-SERIES FORECASTING METHODS TO THE CASE STUDY

Figure 13.1 in the preceding section highlights the seasonal pattern of CCW's call volumes, with a large jump up each fourth quarter due to Christmas shopping. Therefore, before considering specific forecasting methods, Lydia and the consultant begin by addressing how to deal with this seasonal pattern.

Considering Seasonal Effects

For many years, the folklore at CCW has been that the call volume (and sales) will be pretty stable over the first three quarters of a year and then will jump up by about 25 percent in Quarter 4. This has been the basis for the 25 percent rule.

To check how close this folklore still is to reality, the consultant uses the data previously given in Figure 13.1 to calculate the average daily call volume for each quarter over the past three years. For example, the average for Quarter 1 is

$$\text{Average (Quarter 1)} = \frac{6{,}809 + 7{,}257 + 6{,}992}{3}$$

$$= 7{,}019$$

These averages for all four quarters are shown in the second column of Table 13.2. Underneath this column, the *overall average* over all four quarters is calculated to be 7,529. Dividing the average for each quarter by this overall average gives the *seasonal factor* shown in the third column.

> In general, the **seasonal factor** for any period of a year (a quarter, a month, etc.) measures how that period compares to the overall average for an entire year. Specifically, using historical data, the seasonal factor is calculated to be

$$\text{Seasonal factor} = \frac{\text{Average for the period}}{\text{Overall average}}$$

This Excel template calculates seasonal factors on either a monthly or quarterly basis.

Your MS Courseware includes an Excel template for calculating these seasonal factors. Figure 13.3 shows this template applied to the CCW problem.

TABLE 13.2
Calculation of the Seasonal Factors for the CCW Problem

Quarter	Three-Year Average	Seasonal Factor
1	7,019	$\frac{7{,}019}{7{,}529} = 0.93$
2	6,784	$\frac{6{,}784}{7{,}529} = 0.90$
3	7,434	$\frac{7{,}434}{7{,}529} = 0.99$
4	8,880	$\frac{8{,}880}{7{,}529} = 1.18$

Total = 30,117

$\text{Average} = \dfrac{30{,}117}{4} = 7{,}529$

FIGURE 13.3

The Excel template in your MS Courseware for calculating seasonal factors is applied here to the CCW problem.

	A	B	C	D	E	F	G
1		**Estimating Seasonal Factors for CCW**					
2							
3				**True**			
4		**Year**	**Quarter**	**Value**		**Type of Seasonality**	
5		1	1	6,809		Quarterly	
6		1	2	6,465			
7		1	3	6,569			
8		1	4	8,266			**Estimate for**
9		2	1	7,257		**Quarter**	**Seasonal Factor**
10		2	2	7,064		1	0.9323
11		2	3	7,784		2	0.9010
12		2	4	8,724		3	0.9873
13		3	1	6,992		4	1.1794
14		3	2	6,822			
15		3	3	7,949			
16		3	4	9,650			

Range Name	Cells
SeasonalFactor	G10:G21
TrueValue	D5:D41
TypeOfSeasonality	F5

	G
8	**Estimate for**
9	**Seasonal Factor**
10	=AVERAGE(D5,D9,D13)/AVERAGE(TrueValue)
11	=AVERAGE(D6,D10,D14)/AVERAGE(TrueValue)
12	=AVERAGE(D7,D11,D15)/AVERAGE(TrueValue)
13	=AVERAGE(D8,D12,D16)/AVERAGE(TrueValue)

Note the significant differences in the seasonal factors for the first three quarters, with Quarter 3 considerably above the other two. This makes sense to Lydia, who has long suspected that back-to-school buying should give a small boost to sales in Quarter 3.

In contrast to the 25 percent rule, the seasonal factor for Quarter 4 is only 19 percent higher than that for Quarter 3. (However, the Quarter 4 factor *is* about 25 percent above 0.94, which is the *average* of the seasonal factors for the first three quarters.)

Although data on call volumes are not available prior to the most recent three years, reliable sales data have been kept. Upon checking these data several years back, Lydia finds the same seasonal patterns occurring.

Conclusion: The seasonal factors given in Table 13.2 appear to accurately reflect subtle but important differences in all the seasons. Therefore, these factors now will be used, instead of the 25 percent rule, to indicate seasonal patterns until such time as future data indicate a shift in these patterns.

The Seasonally Adjusted Time Series

It is much easier to analyze sales data and detect new trends if the data are first adjusted to remove the effect of seasonal patterns. To remove the seasonal effects from the time series shown in Figure 13.1, each of these average daily call volumes needs to be divided by the corresponding seasonal factor given in Table 13.2 and Figure 13.3. Thus, the formula is

$$\text{Seasonally adjusted call volume} = \frac{\text{Actual call volume}}{\text{Seasonal factor}}$$

Applying this formula to all 12 call volumes in Figure 13.1 gives the seasonally adjusted call volumes shown in column F of the Excel template in Figure 13.4.

FIGURE 13.4 The seasonally adjusted time series for the CCW problem obtained by dividing each actual average daily call volume in Figure 13.1 by the corresponding seasonal factor obtained in Figure 13.3.

	A	B	C	D	E	F	G	H	I	J
1		**Seasonally Adjusted Time Series for CCW**								
2										
3				**Seasonal**	**Actual**	**Seasonally Adjusted**				
4		**Year**	**Quarter**	**Factor**	**Call Volume**	**Call Volume**				
5		1	1	0.93	6,809	7,322				
6		1	2	0.90	6,465	7,183				
7		1	3	0.99	6,569	6,635				
8		1	4	1.18	8,266	7,005				
9		2	1	0.93	7,257	7,803				
10		2	2	0.90	7,064	7,849				
11		2	3	0.99	7,784	7,863				
12		2	4	1.18	8,724	7,393				
13		3	1	0.93	6,992	7,518				
14		3	2	0.90	6,822	7,580				
15		3	3	0.99	7,949	8,029				
16		3	4	1.18	9,650	8,178				

	F
3	**Seasonally Adjusted**
4	**Call Volume**
5	=E5/D5
6	=E6/D6
7	=E7/D7
8	=E8/D8
9	:
10	:

In effect, these seasonally adjusted call volumes show what the call volumes would have been if the calls that occur because of the time of the year (Christmas shopping, back-to-school shopping, etc.) had been spread evenly throughout the year instead. Compare the plots in Figures 13.4 and 13.1. After considering the smaller vertical scale in Figure 13.4, note how much less fluctuation this figure has than Figure 13.1 because of removing seasonal effects. However, this figure still is far from completely flat because fluctuations in call volume occur for other reasons besides just seasonal effects. For example, hot new products attract a flurry of calls. A jump also occurs just after the mailing of a catalog. Some random fluctuations occur without any apparent explanation. Figure 13.4 enables seeing and analyzing these fluctuations in sales volumes that are not caused by seasonal effects.

Removing seasonal effects provides a much clearer picture of trends.

The pattern in these remaining fluctuations in the **seasonally adjusted time series** (especially the pattern for the most recent data points) is particularly helpful for forecasting where the next data point will fall. Thus, in Figure 13.4, the data points fall in the range between 6,635 and 8,178, with an average of 7,529. However, the last few data points are trending upward above this average, and the last point is the highest in the entire time series. This suggests that the next data point for the upcoming quarter probably will be above the 7,529 average and may well be near or even above the last data point of 8,178.

The various **time-series forecasting methods** use different approaches to projecting forward the pattern in the seasonally adjusted time series to forecast the next data point. The main methods will be presented in this section.

After obtaining a forecast for the seasonally adjusted time series, all these methods then convert this forecast to a forecast of the actual call volume (without seasonal adjustments), as outlined below.

Outline for Forecasting Call Volume

1. Select a time-series forecasting method.

2. Apply this method to the seasonally adjusted time series to obtain a forecast of the seasonally adjusted call volume for the next quarter.[1]

3. Multiply this forecast by the corresponding seasonal factor in Table 13.2 to obtain a forecast of the actual call volume (without seasonal adjustment).

If seasonal adjustments are not needed, you can obtain your forecast directly from the original time series and then skip step 3.

The following descriptions of forecasting methods focus on how to perform step 2, that is, how to forecast the next data point for a given time series. We also include a spreadsheet in each case that applies steps 2 and 3 throughout the past three years and then calculates both MAD (the average forecasting error) and MSE (the average of the square of the forecasting errors). Lydia and the consultant are paying particular attention to the MAD values to assess which method seems best suited for forecasting CCW call volumes.

The Last-Value Forecasting Method

The **last-value forecasting method** ignores all the data points in a time series except the last one. It then uses this last value as the forecast of what the next data point will turn out to be, so the formula is simply

$$\text{Forecast} = \text{Last value}$$

Figure 13.5 shows what would have happened if this method had been applied to the CCW problem over the past three years. (We are supposing that the seasonal factors given in Table 13.2 already were being used then.) Column E gives the true values of the seasonally adjusted call volumes from column F of Figure 13.4. Each of these values then becomes the seasonally adjusted forecast for the *next* quarter, as shown in column F.

Rows 22–33 show separate plots of these values in columns E and F. Note how the plot of the seasonally adjusted forecasts follows exactly the same path as the plot of the seasonally adjusted call volumes but shifted to the right by one quarter. Therefore, each time there is a large shift up or down in the call volume, the forecasts are one quarter late in catching up with the shift.

Multiplying each seasonally adjusted forecast in column F by the corresponding seasonal factor in column K gives the forecast of the actual call volume (without seasonal adjustment) presented in column G. The difference between this forecast and the actual call volume in column D gives the forecasting error in column H.

Thus, column G is using the following formula:

$$\text{Actual forecast} = \text{Seasonal factor} \times \text{Seasonally adjusted forecast}$$

as indicated by the equations at the bottom of the figure. For example, since cell K9 gives 0.93 as the seasonal factor for Quarter 1, the forecast of the actual call volume for Year 2, Quarter 1 given in cell G10 is

$$\text{Actual forecast} = (0.93)(7,005) = 6,515$$

Since the true value of this call volume turned out to be 7,257, the forecasting error calculated in cell H10 for this quarter is

$$\text{Forecasting error} = 7,257 - 6,515 = 742$$

Summing these forecasting errors over all 11 quarters of forecasts gives a total of 3,246, so the average forecasting error given in cell K23 is

$$\text{MAD} = \frac{3,246}{11} = 295$$

---

[1]This forecast also can be projected ahead to subsequent quarters, but we are focusing on just the next quarter.

FIGURE 13.5 The Excel template in your MS Courseware for the last-value method with seasonal adjustments is applied here to the CCW problem.

	A	B	C	D	E	F	G	H	I	J	K
1		Last-Value Forecasting Method with Seasonality for CCW									
2											
3					Seasonally	Seasonally					
4				True	Adjusted	Adjusted	Actual	Forecasting			
5		Year	Quarter	Value	Value	Forecast	Forecast	Error			Type of Seasonality
6		1	1	6,809	7,322						Quarterly
7		1	2	6,465	7,183	7,322	6,589	124			
8		1	3	6,569	6,635	7,183	7,112	543		Quarter	Seasonal Factor
9		1	4	8,266	7,005	6,635	7,830	436		1	0.93
10		2	1	7,257	7,803	7,005	6,515	742		2	0.90
11		2	2	7,064	7,849	7,803	7,023	41		3	0.99
12		2	3	7,784	7,863	7,849	7,770	14		4	1.18
13		2	4	8,724	7,393	7,863	9,278	554			
14		3	1	6,992	7,518	7,393	6,876	116			
15		3	2	6,822	7,580	7,518	6,766	56			
16		3	3	7,949	8,029	7,580	7,504	445			
17		3	4	9,650	8,178	8,029	9,475	175			
18		4	1			8,178	7,606				
19		4	2								
20											
21											
22											Mean Absolute Deviation
23											MAD = 295
24											
25											Mean Square Error
26											MSE = 145,909
27											
28											
29											
30											
31											
32											
33											
34											
35											

Range Name	Cells
ActualForecast	G6:G30
ForecastingError	H6:H30
MAD	K23
MSE	K26
SeasonalFactor	K9:K20
SeasonallyAdjustedForecast	F6:F30
SeasonallyAdjustedValue	E6:E30
TrueValue	D6:D30
TypeOfSeasonality	K6

	E	F	G	H
3	Seasonally	Seasonally		
4	Adjusted	Adjusted	Actual	Forecasting
5	Value	Forecast	Forecast	Error
6	=D6/K9			
7	=D7/K10	=E6	=K10*F7	=ABS(D7-G7)
8	=D8/K11	=E7	=K11*F8	=ABS(D8-G8)
9	=D9/K12	=E8	=K12*F9	=ABS(D9-G9)
10	=D10/K9	=E9	=K9*F10	=ABS(D10-G10)
11	=D11/K10	=E10	=K10*F11	=ABS(D11-G11)
12	:	:	:	:
13	:	:	:	:

	J	K
23	MAD =	=AVERAGE(ForecastingError)

	J	K
26	MSE =	=SUMSQ(ForecastingError)/COUNT(ForecastingError)

This compares with MAD = 424 for the 25 percent rule that Lydia has been using (as described in the preceding section).

Similarly, the average of the *square* of these forecasting errors is calculated in cell K26 as

$$MSE = \frac{(124)^2 + (543)^2 + \cdots + (175)^2}{11}$$

$$= 145,909$$

This value also is considerably less than the corresponding value, MSE = 317,815, shown in Figure 13.2 for the 25 percent rule.

Except for its graph, Figure 13.5 displays one of the templates in this chapter's Excel file. In fact, your MS Courseware includes two Excel templates for each of the forecasting methods presented in this section. One template performs all the calculations for you for the case where no seasonal adjustments are needed. The second template does the same when seasonal adjustments are included, as illustrated by this figure. With all templates of the second type, you have complete flexibility for what to enter as the seasonal factors. One option is to *calculate* these factors based on historical data (as was done with another Excel template in Figure 13.3). Another is to *estimate* them based on historical experience, as with the 25 percent rule.

The 25 percent rule actually is a *last-value forecasting method* as well, but with different seasonal factors. Since this rule holds that the call volume in the fourth quarter will average 25 percent more than *each* of the first three quarters, its seasonal factors are essentially 0.94 for Quarters 1, 2, and 3 and 1.18 (25 percent more than 0.94) for Quarter 4. Thus, the lower value of MAD in Figure 13.5 is entirely due to refining the seasonal factors in Table 13.2.

Lydia is enthusiastic to see the substantial improvement obtained by simply refining the seasonal factors. However, the consultant quickly adds a note of caution. The forecasts obtained in Figure 13.5 are using the same data that were used to calculate these refined seasonal factors, which creates some bias for these factors to tend to perform better than on new data (future call volumes). Fortunately, Lydia also has checked older sales data to confirm that these seasonal factors seem quite accurate. The consultant agrees that it appears that these factors should provide a significant improvement over the 25 percent rule.

This method is a good one to use when conditions are changing rapidly.

The last-value forecasting method sometimes is called the **naive method,** because statisticians consider it naive to use just a *sample size of one* when additional relevant data are available. However, when conditions are changing rapidly, it may be that the last value is the only relevant data point for forecasting the next value under current conditions. Therefore, managers who are anything but naive do occasionally use this method under such circumstances.

The Averaging Forecasting Method

The **averaging forecasting method** goes to the other extreme. Rather than using just a sample size of one, this method uses *all* the data points in the time series and simply *averages* these points. Thus, the forecast of what the next data point will turn out to be is

Forecast = Average of all data to date

Using the corresponding Excel template to apply this method to the CCW problem over the past three years gives the seasonally adjusted forecasts shown in column F of Figure 13.6. At the bottom of the figure, the equation entered into each of the column F cells is just the average of the column E cells in the preceding rows. The middle of the figure shows a plot of these seasonally adjusted forecasts for all three years next to the true values of the seasonally adjusted call volumes. Note how each forecast lies at the average of the preceding call volumes. Therefore, each time there is a large shift in the call volume, the subsequent forecasts are very slow in catching up with the shift.

Multiplying all the seasonally adjusted forecasts in column F by the corresponding seasonal factors in column K then gives the *forecasts of the actual call volumes* shown in column G. Based on the resulting forecasting errors given in column H, the average forecasting error in this case (cell K23) is

$$MAD = 400$$

FIGURE 13.6 The Excel template in your MS Courseware for the averaging method with seasonal adjustments is applied here to the CCW problem.

	A	B	C	D	E	F	G	H	I	J	K
1		**Averaging Forecasting Method with Seasonality for CCW**									
2											
3					**Seasonally**	**Seasonally**					
4				**True**	**Adjusted**	**Adjusted**	**Actual**	**Forecasting**			
5		**Year**	**Quarter**	**Value**	**Value**	**Forecast**	**Forecast**	**Error**			**Type of Seasonality**
6		1	1	6,809	7,322						Quarterly
7		1	2	6,465	7,183	7,322	6,589	124			
8		1	3	6,569	6,635	7,252	7,180	611		**Quarter**	**Seasonal Factor**
9		1	4	8,266	7,005	7,047	8,315	49		1	0.93
10		2	1	7,257	7,803	7,036	6,544	713		2	0.90
11		2	2	7,064	7,849	7,190	6,471	593		3	0.99
12		2	3	7,784	7,863	7,300	7,227	557		4	1.18
13		2	4	8,724	7,393	7,380	8,708	16			
14		3	1	6,992	7,518	7,382	6,865	127			
15		3	2	6,822	7,580	7,397	6,657	165			
16		3	3	7,949	8,029	7,415	7,341	608			
17		3	4	9,650	8,178	7,471	8,816	834			
18		4	1			7,530	7,003				
19		4	2								
20											
21											
22											**Mean Absolute Deviation**
23											MAD = 400
24											
25											**Mean Square Error**
26											MSE = 242,876
27											
28											
29											
30											
31											
32											
33											
34											
35											

Range Name	Cells
ActualForecast	G6:G30
ForecastingError	H6:H30
MAD	K23
MSE	K26
SeasonalFactor	K9:K20
SeasonallyAdjustedForecast	F6:F30
SeasonallyAdjustedValue	E6:E30
TrueValue	D6:D30
TypeOfSeasonality	K6

	E	F	G	H
3	**Seasonally**	**Seasonally**		
4	**Adjusted**	**Adjusted**	**Actual**	**Forecasting**
5	**Value**	**Forecast**	**Forecast**	**Error**
6	=D6/K9			
7	=D7/K10	=AVERAGE(E$6:E6)	=K10*F7	=ABS(D7-G7)
8	=D8/K11	=AVERAGE(E$6:E7)	=K11*F8	=ABS(D8-G8)
9	=D9/K12	=AVERAGE(E$6:E8)	=K12*F9	=ABS(D9-G9)
10	=D10/K9	=AVERAGE(E$6:E9)	=K9*F10	=ABS(D10-G10)
11	=D11/K10	=AVERAGE(E$6:E10)	=K10*F11	=ABS(D11-G11)
12	:	:	:	:
13	:	:	:	:

	J	K
23	MAD =	=AVERAGE(ForecastingError)

	J	K
26	MSE =	=SUMSQ(ForecastingError)/COUNT(ForecastingError)

which is considerably larger than the 295 obtained for the last-value forecasting method. Similarly, the average of the square of the forecasting errors given in cell K26 is

$$MSE = 242,876$$

which also is considerably larger than the corresponding value of 145,909 for the last-value forecasting method.

Lydia is quite surprised, since she expected an average to do much better than a sample size of one. The consultant agrees that averaging should perform considerably better if conditions remain the same throughout the time series. However, it appears that the conditions affecting the CCW call volume have been changing significantly over the past three years. The call volume was quite a bit higher in Year 2 than in Year 1, and then jumped up again late in Year 3, apparently as popular new products became available. Therefore, the Year 1 values were not very relevant for forecasting under the changed conditions of Years 2 and 3. Including the Year 1 call volumes in the overall average caused *every* forecast for Years 2 and 3 to be too low, sometimes by large amounts.

The averaging forecasting method is a good one to use when conditions are very stable, which is not the case for CCW.

The Moving-Average Forecasting Method

Rather than using old data that may no longer be relevant, the **moving-average forecasting method** averages the data for only the most recent time periods. Let

n = Number of most recent periods considered particularly relevant for forecasting the next period

Then the forecast for the next period is

Forecast = Average of last n values

Lydia and the consultant decide to use $n = 4$, since conditions appear to be relatively stable for only about four quarters (one year) at a time.

With $n = 4$, the first forecast becomes available after four quarters of call volumes have been observed. Thus, the initial seasonally adjusted forecasts in cells F10:F12 of Figure 13.7 are

$$Y2, Q1: \quad \text{Seas. adj. forecast} = \frac{7{,}322 + 7{,}183 + 6{,}635 + 7{,}005}{4} = 7{,}036$$

$$Y2, Q2: \quad \text{Seas. adj. forecast} = \frac{7{,}183 + 6{,}635 + 7{,}005 + 7{,}803}{4} = 7{,}157$$

$$Y2, Q3: \quad \text{Seas. adj. forecast} = \frac{6{,}635 + 7{,}005 + 7{,}803 + 7{,}849}{4} = 7{,}323$$

Note how each forecast is updated from the preceding one by lopping off one observation (the oldest one) and adding one new one (the most recent observation).

Column F of Figure 13.7 shows all the seasonally adjusted forecasts obtained in this way with the equations at the bottom. For each of these forecasts, note in the plot how it lies at the average of the four preceding (seasonally adjusted) call volumes. Consequently, each time there is a large shift in the call volume, it takes four quarters for the forecasts to fully catch up with this shift (by which time another shift may already have occurred). Consequently, the average of the eight forecasting errors in column H is

$$MAD = 437$$

the highest of any of the methods so far, including even the 25 percent rule. The average of the square of the forecasting errors is somewhat better at

$$MSE = 238,816$$

since this is slightly lower than for the averaging method and considerably below the value for the 25 percent rule, but it is still substantially higher than for the last-value method.

Lydia is very puzzled about this surprisingly high MAD value. The moving-average method seemed like a very sensible approach to forecasting, with more rationale behind it than any of

FIGURE 13.7 The Excel template in your MS Courseware for the moving-average method with seasonal adjustments is applied here to the CCW problem.

	A	B	C	D	E	F	G	H	I	J	K
1		**Moving-Average Forecasting Method with Seasonality for CCW**									
2											
3					Seasonally	Seasonally					
4				True	Adjusted	Adjusted	Actual	Forecasting		**Number of previous**	
5		Year	Quarter	Value	Value	Forecast	Forecast	Error		**periods to consider**	
6		1	1	6,809	7,322					$n =$	4
7		1	2	6,465	7,183						
8		1	3	6,569	6,635						**Type of Seasonality**
9		1	4	8,266	7,005						Quarterly
10		2	1	7,257	7,803	7,036	6,544	713			
11		2	2	7,064	7,849	7,157	6,441	623		**Quarter**	**Seasonal Factor**
12		2	3	7,784	7,863	7,323	7,250	534		1	0.93
13		2	4	8,724	7,393	7,630	9,003	279		2	0.90
14		3	1	6,992	7,518	7,727	7,186	194		3	0.99
15		3	2	6,822	7,580	7,656	6,890	68		4	1.18
16		3	3	7,949	8,029	7,589	7,513	436			
17		3	4	9,650	8,178	7,630	9,004	646			
18		4	1			7,826	7,279				
19		4	2								
20											
21											
22											
23											
24											
25										**Mean Absolute Deviation**	
26										MAD =	437
27											
28										**Mean Square Error**	
29										MSE =	238,816
30											
31											
32											
33											
34											
35											

Range Name	Cells
ActualForecast	G6:G30
ForecastingError	H6:H30
MAD	K26
MSE	K29
NumberOfPeriods	K6
SeasonalFactor	K12:K23
SeasonallyAdjustedForecast	F6:F30
SeasonallyAdjustedValue	E6:E30
TrueValue	D6:D30
TypeOfSeasonality	K9

	E	F	G	H
3	Seasonally	Seasonally		
4	Adjusted	Adjusted	Actual	Forecasting
5	Value	Forecast	Forecast	Error
6	=D6/K12			
7	=D7/K13			
8	=D8/K14			
9	=D9/K15			
10	=D10/K12	=AVERAGE(E6:E9)	=K12*F10	=ABS(D10-G10)
11	=D11/K13	=AVERAGE(E7:E10)	=K13*F11	=ABS(D11-G11)
12	=D12/K14	=AVERAGE(E8:E11)	=K14*F12	=ABS(D12-G12)
13	=D13/K15	=AVERAGE(E9:E12)	=K15*F13	=ABS(D13-G13)
14	=D14/K12	=AVERAGE(E10:E13)	=K12*F14	=ABS(D14-G14)
15	=D15/K13	=AVERAGE(E11:E14)	=K13*F15	=ABS(D15-G15)
16	:	:	:	:
17	:	:	:	:

	J	K
26	MAD =	=AVERAGE(ForecastingError)

	J	K
29	MSE =	=SUMSQ(ForecastingError)/COUNT(ForecastingError)

the previous methods. (It uses only recent history *and* it uses multiple observations.) So why should it do so poorly?

The consultant explains that this is indeed a very good forecasting method when conditions remain pretty much the same over *n* time periods (or four quarters in this case). For example, the seasonally adjusted call volumes remained reasonably stable throughout Year 2 and the first half of Year 3. Consequently, the forecasting error dropped all the way down to 68 (cell H15) for the last of these six quarters. However, when conditions shift sharply, as with the big jump up in call volumes at the beginning of Year 2, and then again in the middle of Year 3, the next few forecasting errors tend to be very large.

Thus, the moving-average method is somewhat slow to respond to changing conditions. One reason is that it places the *same* weight on each of the last *n* values in the time series even though the older values may be less representative of current conditions than the last value observed.

The next method corrects this weighting defect.

The moving-average forecasting method is a good one to use when conditions don't change much over the number of time periods included in the average.

The Exponential Smoothing Forecasting Method

The **exponential smoothing forecasting method** modifies the moving-average method by placing the greatest weight on the last value in the time series and then progressively smaller weights on the older values. However, rather than needing to calculate a *weighted average* each time, it uses a simpler formula to obtain the same result.

This formula for forecasting the next value in the time series combines the *last value* and the *last forecast* (the one used one time period ago to forecast this last value) as follows:

$$\text{Forecast} = \alpha(\text{Last value}) + (1 - \alpha)(\text{Last forecast})$$

where α (the Greek letter alpha) is a constant between 0 and 1 called the **smoothing constant.** For example, if the last value in a time series (not the CCW time series) is 24, the last forecast is 20, and $\alpha = 0.25$, then

$$\text{Forecast} = 0.25(24) + 0.75(20)$$

$$= 21$$

Two Excel templates (one without seasonal adjustments and one with) are available in your MS Courseware for applying this formula to generate a series of forecasts (period by period) for a time series when you specify the value of α.

The choice of the value for the smoothing constant α has a substantial effect on the forecast, so the choice should be made with care. A small value (say, $\alpha = 0.1$) is appropriate if conditions are remaining relatively stable. However, a larger value (say, $\alpha = 0.3$) is needed if significant changes in the conditions are occurring relatively frequently. Because of the frequent shifts in the CCW seasonally adjusted time series, Lydia and the consultant conclude that $\alpha = 0.5$ would be an appropriate value. (The values selected for most applications are between 0.1 and 0.3, but a larger value can be used in this kind of situation.)

The more unstable the conditions, the larger the smoothing constant α needs to be (but never bigger than 1).

When making the first forecast, there is no *last forecast* available to plug into the right-hand side of the above formula. Therefore, to get started, a reasonable approach is to make an *initial estimate* of the average value anticipated for the time series. This initial estimate is used as the forecast for the first value, and then the formula is used to forecast the second value onward.

CCW call volumes have averaged just over 7,500 for the past three years, and the level of business just prior to Year 1 was comparable. Consequently, Lydia and the consultant decide to use

$$\text{Initial estimate} = 7,500$$

to begin retrospectively generating the forecasts over the past three years. Recall that the first few seasonally adjusted call volumes are 7,322, 7,183, and 6,635. Thus, using the above formula with $\alpha = 0.5$ for the second quarter onward, the first few seasonally adjusted forecasts are

Y1, Q1:   Seas. adj. forecast = 7,500

Y1, Q2:   Seas. adj. forecast = 0.5(7,322) + 0.5(7,500) = 7,411

Y1, Q3:   Seas. adj. forecast = 0.5(7,183) + 0.5(7,411) = 7,297

Y1, Q4:   Seas. adj. forecast = 0.5(6,635) + 0.5(7,297) = 6,966

To see why these forecasts are weighted averages of the time series values to date, look at the calculations for Quarters 2 and 3. Since

$$0.5(7,322) + 0.5(7,500) = 7,411$$

the forecast for Quarter 3 can be written as

$$\text{Seas. adj. forecast} = 0.5(7,183) + 0.5(7,411)$$

$$= 0.5(7,183) + 0.5[0.5(7,322) + 0.5(7,500)]$$

$$= 0.5(7,183) + 0.25(7,322) + 0.25(7,500)$$

$$= 7,297$$

Similarly, the forecast for Quarter 4 is

$$\text{Seas. adj. forecast} = 0.5(6,635) + 0.5(7,297)$$

$$= 0.5(6,635) + 0.5[0.5(7,183) + 0.25(7,322) + 0.25(7,500)]$$

$$= 0.5(6,635) + 0.25(7,183) + 0.125(7,322) + 0.125(7,500)$$

$$= 6,966$$

The exponential smoothing forecasting method places the greatest weight on the last value and then decreases the weights as the values get older.

Thus, this latter forecast places a weight of 0.5 on the last value, 0.25 on the next-to-last value, and 0.125 on the next prior value (the first one), with the remaining weight on the initial estimate. With other values of α, these weights would be α, $\alpha(1 - \alpha)$, $\alpha(1 - \alpha)^2$, and so forth.

Therefore, choosing the value of α amounts to using this pattern to choose the desired progression of weights on the time series values. With frequent shifts in the time series, a large weight needs to be placed on the most recent value, with rapidly decreasing weights on older values. However, with a relatively stable time series, it is desirable to place a significant weight on many values in order to have a large sample size.

Further insight into the choice of α is provided by an alternative form of the forecasting formula.

$$\text{Forecast} = \alpha(\text{Last value}) + (1 - \alpha)(\text{Last forecast})$$

$$= \alpha(\text{Last value}) + \text{Last forecast} - \alpha(\text{Last forecast})$$

$$= \text{Last forecast} + \alpha(\text{Last value} - \text{Last forecast})$$

where the absolute value of (Last value − Last forecast) is just the last forecasting error. Therefore, the bottom form of this formula indicates that each new forecast is adjusting the last forecast by adding or subtracting the quantity α *times* the last forecasting error. If the forecasting error usually is mainly due to random fluctuations in the time-series values, then only a small value of α should be used for this adjustment. However, if the forecasting error often is largely due to a shift in the time series, then a large value of α is needed to make a substantial adjustment quickly.

Using $\alpha = 0.5$, the Excel template in Figure 13.8 provides all the results for CCW with this forecasting method. Rows 22–32 show a plot of all the seasonally adjusted forecasts next to the true values of the seasonally adjusted call volumes. Note how each forecast lies midway between the preceding call volume and the preceding forecast. Therefore, each time there is a large shift in the call volume, the forecasts largely catch up with the shift rather quickly. The resulting average of the forecasting errors in column H is given in cell K28 as

$$\text{MAD} = 324$$

This is significantly smaller than for the previous forecasting methods, except for the value of MAD = 295 for the last-value forecasting method. The same comparison also holds for the average of the square of the forecasting errors, which is calculated in cell K31 as

$$\text{MSE} = 157,836$$

Lydia is somewhat frustrated at this point. She feels that she needs a method with average forecasting errors well below 295. Realizing that the last-value forecasting method is considered the *naive* method, she had expected that such a popular and sophisticated method as exponential smoothing would beat it easily.

FIGURE 13.8 The Excel template in your MS Courseware for the exponential smoothing method with seasonal adjustments is applied here to the CCW problem.

	A	B	C	D	E	F	G	H	I	J	K
1		Exponential Smoothing Forecasting Method with Seasonality for CCW									
2											
3					Seasonally	Seasonally					
4				True	Adjusted	Adjusted	Actual	Forecasting		Smoothing Constant	
5		Year	Quarter	Value	Value	Forecast	Forecast	Error		α =	0.5
6		1	1	6,809	7,322	7,500	6,975	166			
7		1	2	6,465	7,183	7,411	6,670	205		Initial Estimate	
8		1	3	6,569	6,635	7,297	7,224	655		Average =	7,500
9		1	4	8,266	7,005	6,966	8,220	46			
10		2	1	7,257	7,803	6,986	6,497	760		Type of Seasonality	
11		2	2	7,064	7,849	7,394	6,655	409		Quarterly	
12		2	3	7,784	7,863	7,622	7,545	239			
13		2	4	8,724	7,393	7,742	9,136	412		Quarter	Seasonal Factor
14		3	1	6,992	7,518	7,568	7,038	46		1	0.93
15		3	2	6,822	7,580	7,543	6,789	33		2	0.90
16		3	3	7,949	8,029	7,561	7,486	463		3	0.99
17		3	4	9,650	8,178	7,795	9,199	451		4	1.18
18		4	1			7,987	7,428				
19		4	2								
20											
21											
22											
23											
24											
25											
26											
27										Mean Absolute Deviation	
28										MAD =	324
29											
30										Mean Square Error	
31										MSE =	157,836
32											
33											
34											
35											

Range Name	Cells
ActualForecast	G6:G30
Alpha	K5
ForecastingError	H6:H30
InitialEstimate	K8
MAD	K28
MSE	K31
SeasonalFactor	K14:K25
SeasonallyAdjustedForecast	F6:F30
SeasonallyAdjustedValue	E6:E30
TrueValue	D6:D30
TypeOfSeasonality	K11

	E	F	G	H
3	Seasonally	Seasonally		
4	Adjusted	Adjusted	Actual	Forecasting
5	Value	Forecast	Forecast	Error
6	=D6/K14	=InitialEstimate	=K14*F6	=ABS(D6-G6)
7	=D7/K15	=Alpha*E6+(1-Alpha)*F6	=K15*F7	=ABS(D7-G7)
8	=D8/K16	=Alpha*E7+(1-Alpha)*F7	=K16*F8	=ABS(D8-G8)
9	=D9/K17	=Alpha*E8+(1-Alpha)*F8	=K17*F9	=ABS(D9-G9)
10	=D10/K14	=Alpha*E9+(1-Alpha)*F9	=K14*F10	=ABS(D10-G10)
11	=D11/K15	=Alpha*E10+(1-Alpha)*F10	=K15*F11	=ABS(D11-G11)
12	:	:	:	:
13	:	:	:	:

	J	K
28	MAD =	=AVERAGE(ForecastingError)

	J	K
31	MSE =	=SUMSQ(ForecastingError)/COUNT(ForecastingError)

The consultant is somewhat surprised also. However, he points out that the difference between MAD = 324 for exponential smoothing and MAD = 295 for last-value forecasting is really too small to be statistically significant. If the same two methods were to be applied the *next* three years, exponential smoothing might come out ahead. Lydia is not impressed.

Although he isn't ready to mention it to Lydia yet, the consultant is beginning to develop an idea for a whole new approach that might give her the forecasting precision she needs. But first he has one more time-series forecasting method to present.

To lay the groundwork for this method, the consultant explains a major reason why exponential smoothing did not fare well in this case. Look at the plot of seasonally adjusted call volumes in Figure 13.8. Note the distinct trend downward in the first three quarters, then a sharp trend upward for the next two, and finally a major trend upward for the last five quarters. Also note the large gap between the two plots (meaning large forecasting errors) by the end of each of these trends. The reason for these large errors is that exponential smoothing forecasts lag well behind such a trend because they place significant weight on values near the beginning of the trend. Although a large value of $\alpha = 0.5$ helps, exponential smoothing forecasts tend to lag further behind such a trend than last-value forecasts.

The next method adjusts exponential smoothing by also estimating the current trend and then projects this trend forward to help forecast the next value in the time series.

Exponential Smoothing with Trend

Exponential smoothing with trend uses the recent values in the time series to estimate any current upward or downward **trend** in these values. It is especially designed for the kind of time series depicted in Figure 13.9 where an upward (or downward) trend tends to continue for a considerable number of periods (but not necessarily indefinitely). This particular figure shows the estimated population of a certain state at midyear over a series of years. The line in the figure (commonly referred to as a *trend line*) shows the basic trend that the time series is following, but with fluctuations on both sides of the line. Because the basic trend is upward in

FIGURE 13.9

A time series that gives the estimated population of a certain state over a series of years. The trend line shows the basic upward trend of the population.

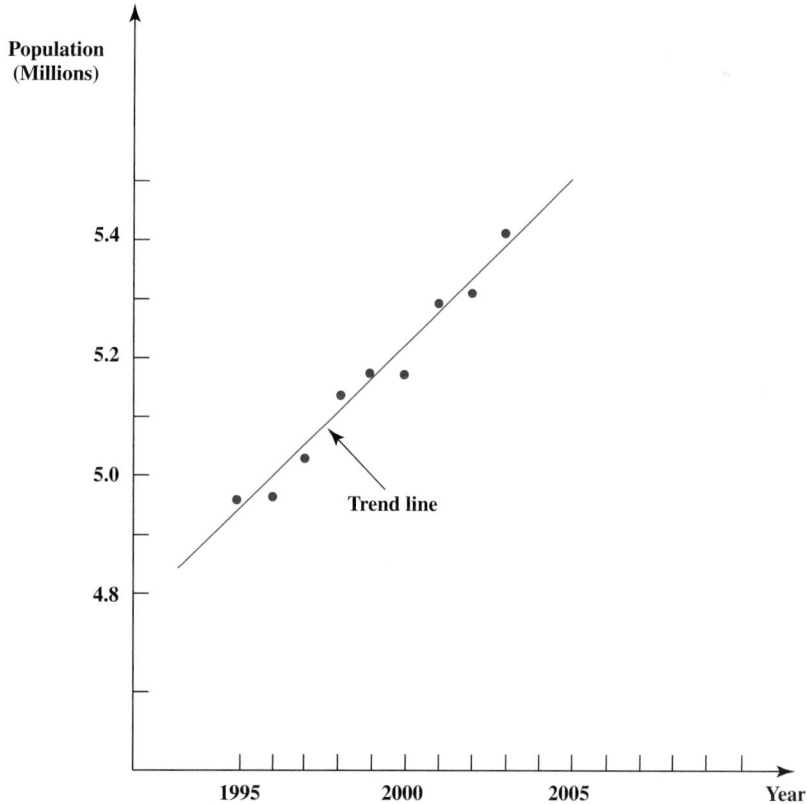

this case, forecasts based on any of the preceding forecasting methods would tend to be considerably too low. However, by developing an estimate of the current slope of this trend line, and then adjusting the forecast to consider this slope, considerably more accurate forecasts should be obtained. This is the basic idea behind exponential smoothing with trend.

Trend is defined as

Trend = Average change from one time-series value to the next if the current pattern continues

The formula for forecasting the next value in the time series, then, is modified from the preceding method by *adding the estimated trend.* Thus, the new formula is

Adding the estimated trend enables the forecast to keep up with the current trend in the data.

$$\text{Forecast} = \alpha(\text{Last value}) + (1 - \alpha)(\text{Last forecast}) + \text{Estimated trend}$$

(A separate box describes how this formula can be easily modified to forecast *beyond* the next value in the time series as well.)

Forecasting More Than One Time Period Ahead

We have focused thus far on forecasting what will happen in the *next* time period (the next quarter in the case of CCW). However, managers sometimes need to forecast further into the future. How can the various time-series forecasting methods be adapted to do this?

In the case of the last-value, averaging, moving-average, and exponential smoothing methods, the forecast for the next period also is the best available forecast for subsequent periods as well. However, when there is a *trend* in the data, it is important to take this trend into account for long-range forecasts. *Exponential smoothing with trend* provides a way of doing this. In particular, after determining the *estimated trend,* this method's forecast for *n* time periods into the future is

$$\text{Forecast for } n \text{ periods from now} = \alpha(\text{Last value}) + (1 - \alpha)(\text{Last forecast}) + n \times (\text{Estimated trend})$$

Exponential smoothing also is used to obtain and update the *estimated trend* each time. The formula is

The trend smoothing constant β is used to apply exponential smoothing to estimating the trend.

$$\text{Estimated trend} = \beta(\text{Latest trend}) + (1 - \beta)(\text{Last estimate of trend})$$

where β (the Greek letter beta) is the **trend smoothing constant,** which, like α, must be between 0 and 1. *Latest trend* refers to the trend based on just the last two values in the time series and the last two forecasts. Its formula is

$$\text{Latest trend} = \alpha(\text{Last value} - \text{Next-to-last value})$$
$$+ (1 - \alpha)(\text{Last forecast} - \text{Next-to-last forecast})$$

Getting started with this forecasting method requires making two initial estimates about the status of the time series just prior to beginning forecasting. These initial estimates are

1. Initial estimate of the *average value* of the time series if the conditions just prior to beginning forecasting were to remain unchanged without any trend.

2. Initial estimate of the *trend* of the time series just prior to beginning forecasting.

The forecast for the first period being forecasted then is

$$\text{First forecast} = \text{Initial estimate of average value} + \text{Initial estimate of trend}$$

The second forecast is obtained from the above formulas, where the *initial estimate of trend* is used as the last estimate of trend in the formula for estimated trend and the *initial estimate of average value* is used as both the next-to-last value and the next-to-last forecast in the formula for latest trend. The above formulas then are used directly to obtain subsequent forecasts.

The Excel templates for this method perform the calculations for you.

Since the calculations involved with this method are relatively involved, a computer commonly is used to implement the method. Your MS Courseware includes two Excel templates (one without seasonal adjustments and one with) for this method.

The considerations involved in choosing the trend smoothing constant β are similar to those for α. A large value of β (say, $\beta = 0.3$) is more responsive to recent changes in the trend, whereas a relatively small value (say, $\beta = 0.1$) uses more data in a significant way to estimate trend.

After trying various combinations of α and β on the CCW problem, the consultant concludes that $\alpha = 0.3$ and $\beta = 0.3$ perform about as well as any. Both values are on the high end of the typically used range (0.1 to 0.3), but the frequent changes in the CCW time series call for large values. However, lowering α from the 0.5 value used with the preceding method seems justified since incorporating trend into the analysis would help respond more quickly to changes.

When applying exponential smoothing *without* trend earlier, Lydia and the consultant chose 7,500 as the initial estimate of the average value of the seasonally adjusted call volumes. They now note that there was no noticeable trend in these call volumes just prior to the retrospective generation of forecasts three years ago. Therefore, to apply exponential smoothing with trend, they decide to use

Initial estimate of average value $= 7,500$

Initial estimate of trend $= 0$

Working with the seasonally adjusted call volumes given in several recent figures, these initial estimates lead to the following seasonally adjusted forecasts.

Y1, Q1:   Seas. adj. forecast $= 7,500 + 0 = 7,500$

Y1, Q2:   Latest trend $= 0.3(7,322 - 7,500) + 0.7(7,500 - 7,500) = -53.4$

Estimated trend $= 0.3(-53.4) + 0.7(0) = -16$

Seas. adj. forecast $= 0.3(7,322) + 0.7(7,500) - 16 = 7,431$

Y1, Q3:   Latest trend $= 0.3(7,183 - 7,322) + 0.7(7,431 - 7,500) = -90$

Estimated trend $= 0.3(-90) + 0.7(-16) = -38.2$

Seas. adj. forecast $= 0.3(7,183) + 0.7(7,431) - 38.2 = 7,318$

When the trend in the data suddenly reverses direction, it takes a little while for the estimated trend to turn around.

The Excel template in Figure 13.10 shows the results from these calculations for all 12 quarters over the past three years, as well as for the upcoming quarter. The middle of the figure shows the plots of all the seasonally adjusted call volumes and seasonally adjusted forecasts. Note how each trend up or down in the call volumes causes the forecasts to gradually trend in the same direction, but then the trend in the forecasts takes a couple quarters to turn around when the trend in call volumes suddenly reverses direction. The resulting forecasting errors in column J then give an average forecasting error (cell M30) of

$$\text{MAD} = 345$$

a little above the 324 value for regular exponential smoothing and 295 for last-value forecasting. A similar result is obtained when using the square of the forecasting errors since the mean square error given in cell M33,

$$\text{MSE} = 180,796$$

also is a little above the MSE values for these other two forecasting methods.

Table 13.3 summarizes the values of MAD and MSE for all the forecasting methods so far. Here is Lydia's reaction to the large MAD value for exponential smoothing with trend.

Lydia: I'm very discouraged. These time-series forecasting methods just aren't doing the job I need. I thought this one would. It sounded like an excellent method that also would deal with the trends we keep encountering.

Consultant: Yes, it is a very good method under the right circumstances. When you have trends that may occasionally shift some over time, it should do a great job.

Lydia: So what went wrong here?

FIGURE 13.10 The Excel template in your MS Courseware for the exponential smoothing with trend method with seasonal adjustments is applied here to the CCW problem.

	A	B	C	D	E	F	G	H	I	J	K	L	M
1		\multicolumn{12}{Exponential Smoothing with Trend Forecasting Method with Seasonality for CCW}										
2													
3					Seasonally			Seasonally					
4				True	Adjusted	Latest	Estimated	Adjusted	Actual	Forecasting		Smoothing Constant	
5		Year	Quarter	Value	Value	Trend	Trend	Value	Forecast	Error		α =	0.3
6		1	1	6,809	7,322		0	7,500	6,975	166		β =	0.3
7		1	2	6,465	7,183	-54	-16	7,430	6,687	222			
8		1	3	6,569	6,635	-90	-38	7,318	7,245	676		Initial Estimate	
9		1	4	8,266	7,005	-243	-100	7,013	8,276	10		Average =	7,500
10		2	1	7,257	7,803	-102	-100	6,910	6,427	830		Trend =	0
11		2	2	7,064	7,849	167	-20	7,158	6,442	622			
12		2	3	7,784	7,863	187	42	7,407	7,333	451		Type of Seasonality	
13		2	4	8,724	7,393	179	83	7,627	9,000	276		Quarterly	
14		3	1	6,992	7,518	13	62	7,619	7,085	93			
15		3	2	6,822	7,580	32	53	7,642	6,877	55		Quarter	Seasonal Factor
16		3	3	7,949	8,029	34	47	7,670	7,594	355		1	0.93
17		3	4	9,650	8,178	155	80	7,858	9,272	378		2	0.90
18		4	1			176	108	8,062	7,498			3	0.99
19		4	2									4	1.18

Mean Absolute Deviation — MAD = 345

Mean Square Error — MSE = 180,796

	E	F	G	H	I	J
3	Seasonally			Seasonally		
4	Adjusted	Latest	Estimated	Adjusted	Actual	Forecasting
5	Value	Trend	Trend	Forecast	Forecast	Error
6	=D6/M16		=InitialEstimateTrend	=InitialEstimateAverage+InitialEstimateTrend	=M16*H6	=ABS(D6-I6)
7	=D7/M17	=Alpha*(E6-InitialEstimateAverage)+(1-Alpha)*(H6-InitialEstimateAverage)	=Beta*F7+(1-Beta)*G6	=Alpha*E6+(1-Alpha)*H6+G7	=M17*H7	=ABS(D7-I7)
8	=D8/M18	=Alpha*(E7-E6)+(1-Alpha)*(H7-H6)	=Beta*F8+(1-Beta)*G7	=Alpha*E7+(1-Alpha)*H7+G8	=M18*H8	=ABS(D8-I8)
9	=D9/M19	=Alpha*(E8-E7)+(1-Alpha)*(H8-H7)	=Beta*F9+(1-Beta)*G8	=Alpha*E8+(1-Alpha)*H8+G9	=M19*H9	=ABS(D9-I9)
10	=D10/M16	=Alpha*(E9-E8)+(1-Alpha)*(H9-H8)	=Beta*F10+(1-Beta)*G9	=Alpha*E9+(1-Alpha)*H9+G10	=M16*H10	=ABS(D10-I10)
11	=D11/M17	=Alpha*(E10-E9)+(1-Alpha)*(H10-H9)	=Beta*F11+(1-Beta)*G10	=Alpha*E10+(1-Alpha)*H10+G11	=M17*H11	=ABS(D11-I11)
12	:	:	:	:	:	:

Range Name	Cells
ActualForecast	I6:I30
Alpha	M5
Beta	M6
ForecastingError	J6:J30
InitialEstimateAverage	M9
InitialEstimateTrend	M10
MAD	M30
MSE	M33
SeasonalFactor	M16:M27
SeasonallyAdjustedForecast	H6:H30
SeasonallyAdjustedValue	E6:E30
TrueValue	D6:D30
TypeOfSeasonality	M13

	L	M
30	MAD =	=AVERAGE(ForecastingError)

	L	M
33	MSE =	=SUMSQ(ForecastingError)/COUNT(ForecastingError)

TABLE 13.3

The Average Forecasting Error (MAD) and Mean Square Error (MSE) for the Various Time-Series Forecasting Methods When Forecasting CCW Call Volumes

Forecasting Method	MAD	MSE
CCW's 25 percent rule	424	317,815
Last-value method	295	145,909
Averaging method	400	242,876
Moving-average method	437	238,816
Exponential smoothing	324	157,836
Exponential smoothing with trend	345	180,796

Consultant: Well, look at the trends you have here in the seasonally adjusted time series. You have a fairly sharp downward trend the first three quarters and then suddenly a very sharp upward trend for a couple quarters. Then it flattens out before a big drop in the eighth quarter. Then suddenly it is going up again. It is really tough to keep up with such abrupt big shifts in the trends. This method is better suited for much more gradual shifts in the trends.

Lydia: OK. But aren't there any other methods? None of these will do.

Consultant: There is one other main time-series forecasting method. It is called the **ARIMA** method, which is an acronym for AutoRegressive Integrated Moving Average. It also is sometimes called the Box-Jenkins method, in honor of its founders. It is a very sophisticated method, but some excellent software is available for implementing it. Another nice feature is that it is well-suited for dealing with strong seasonal patterns.

The ARIMA method is another good forecasting method, but it requires much more data than CCW currently has available.

Lydia: Sounds good. So shouldn't we be trying this ARIMA method?

Consultant: Not at this point. It is such a sophisticated method that it requires a great amount of past data, say, a minimum of 50 time periods. We don't have nearly enough data.

Lydia: A pity. So what are we going to do? I haven't seen anything that will do the job.

Consultant: Cheer up. I have an idea for how we can use one of these time-series forecasting methods in a different way that may do the job you want.

Lydia: Really? Tell me more.

Consultant: Well, let me hold off on the details until we can check out whether this is going to work.

Lydia: OK. But how do we check it out?

Consultant: Well, what I would like you to do is contact CCW's marketing manager and set up a meeting between the three of us. Also, send him your data on call volumes for the past three years. Ask him to dig out his sales data for the same period and compare it to your data.

Lydia: OK. What should I tell him is the purpose of the meeting?

Consultant: Explain what we're trying to accomplish here about forecasting call volumes. Then tell him that we're trying to understand better what has been causing these sudden shifts in call volumes. He knows more about what has been driving sales up or down than anybody. We just want to pick his brain about this.

Lydia: OK. Will do.

The Meeting with the Marketing Manager

This meeting takes place a few days later. As you eavesdrop (after the preliminaries), you will find it helpful to refer to the call volume data in one of the recent spreadsheets, such as Figure 13.10.

Lydia: Did you receive the call volume data I mailed to you?

Marketing manager: Yes, I did.

Consultant: How does it compare with your own sales data for these three years?

Marketing manager: Your data track mine pretty closely. I see the same ups and downs in both sets of data.

Lydia: That makes sense, since it's the calls to my call center that generate those sales.

Marketing manager: Right.

Consultant: Now, let me check on what caused the ups and downs. Three years ago, what we labeled as Year 1 in our data, there was a definite trend down for most of the year. What caused that?

Marketing manager: Yes, I remember that year all too well. It wasn't a very good year. The new Klugman operating system had been scheduled to come out early that year. Then they kept pushing the release date back. People kept waiting. They didn't manage to get it out until the beginning of the next year, so we even missed the Christmas sales.

Lydia: But our call volume did jump up a little more than usual during that holiday season.

Marketing manager: Yes. So did sales. I remember that we came out with a new networking tool, one with faster data transfer, in time for the holiday season. It turned out to be very popular for a few months. It really bailed us out during that slow period.

Consultant: Then the Klugman operating system was released and sales jumped the next year.

Marketing manager: Right.

Lydia: What happened late in the year? We weren't as busy as we expected to be.

Marketing manager: I assume that most people already had updated to the new operating system by then. There wasn't any major change in our product mix during that period.

Consultant: Then sales moved back up the next year. Last year.

Marketing manager: Yes, last year was a rather good year. We had a couple new products that did very well. One was a new data storage device that came out early in the year. Very inexpensive. The other was a color plain-paper printer that was released in July. We were able to offer it at a very competitive price and our customers gobbled it up.

Consultant: Thanks. That really clarifies what lies behind those call volume numbers we've been working with. Now I have another key question for you. When you look at your sales data and do your own forecasting, what do you see as the key factors that drive total sales up or down?

Marketing manager: There really is just one big factor: Do we have any hot new products out there? We have well over a hundred products. But most of them just fill a small niche in the market. Many of them are old standbys that, with updates, just keep going indefinitely. All these small-niche products together provide most of our total sales. A nice stable market base. Then, in addition, we should have three or four major new products out there. Maybe a couple that have been out for a few months but still have some life left in them. Then one or two just coming out that we hope will do very well.

The one big factor that drives total sales up or down is whether the company has just released any hot new products.

Consultant: I see. A large market base and then three or four major new products.

Marketing manager: That's what we shoot for.

Consultant: Are you able to predict how well a major new product will do?

Marketing manager: I try. I've gotten better at it. I'm usually fairly close on what the initial response will be, but it is difficult to predict how long the product will hold up. I would like to have a better handle on it.

Consultant: Thanks very much for all your information. It has verified what I've been suspecting for awhile now.

Forecasting call volumes better requires coordinating directly with what is driving sales.

Lydia: What's that?

Consultant: That we really need to coordinate directly with what is driving sales in order to do a better job of forecasting call volumes.

Lydia: Good thought!

Consultant: How would the two of you feel about coordinating in developing better procedures for forecasting both sales and call volumes?

Lydia: You bet.

Marketing manager: I would need to see what you have in mind. But as I said, I would like to have a better handle on my forecasting.

Lydia: OK, let us work out some details and then we'll send you a specific proposal.

Marketing manager: Sounds good.

Lydia: Thanks again for all your help.

Marketing manager: Any time.

The marketing manager leaves.

Lydia: I'm beginning to see where you are headed with all this. And I really like it. Are you ready to give me the details yet?

Consultant: Almost. I am convinced now that what I have in mind is probably going to work. But let me first spend a little time using the marketing manager's information to put the time-series forecasting methods into better perspective for you. Then I'll give you my recommended plan.

Lydia: OK, let's do it.

We will return to this story in Section 13.5 after introducing some useful forecasting software below and in Section 13.4.

Helpful Educational Software

A helpful forecasting module is included in your Interactive Management Science Modules at **www.mhhe.com/hillier2e.** An offline version also is included in your MS Courseware on the CD-ROM.

This module includes all the time-series forecasting methods presented in this section (as well as in Section 13.6). All you need to do is select a forecasting method, enter the time-series data from which you want to obtain a forecast, and then press the Forecast button. (It does not explicitly make seasonal adjustments, so you will need to enter seasonally adjusted data if such adjustments are necessary.) In addition to listing the forecasts and forecasting errors period by period, the module also plots a graph that shows both the time-series data (in blue dots) and the resulting forecasts (in red dots).

What is unique about this software is its interactive graphing feature that immediately shows you graphically how the forecasts will change as you change any piece of data. You move your mouse onto the blue dot that corresponds to the piece of data and then drag the dot vertically to change its value. As you drag the blue dot, the red dots corresponding to the forecasts instantaneously change accordingly. The purpose is to allow you to play with the data and gain a better feeling for how the forecasts perform with various configurations of data for each of the forecasting methods. Thus, this module is designed primarily to be an educational tool rather than professional forecasting software. It is limited to dealing with small, textbook-sized problems.

In the next section, we describe another package accompanying this text that is indeed professional forecasting software.

Review Questions

1. What does a seasonal factor measure?

2. What is the formula for calculating the seasonally adjusted call volume from the actual call volume and the seasonal factor?

3. What is the formula for calculating the forecast of the actual call volume from the seasonal factor and the seasonally adjusted forecast?

4. Why is the last-value forecasting method sometimes called the *naive method?*

5. Why did the averaging forecasting method not perform very well on the case study?

6. What is the rationale for replacing the averaging forecasting method by the moving-average forecasting method?

7. How does the exponential smoothing forecasting method modify the moving-average forecasting method?

8. With exponential smoothing, when is a small value of the smoothing constant appropriate? A larger value?

9. What is the formula for obtaining the next forecast with exponential smoothing? What is added to this formula when using exponential smoothing with trend?

10. What does the marketing manager say is the one big factor that drives CCW's total sales up or down?

13.4   TIME-SERIES FORECASTING WITH CB PREDICTOR

Since CB Predictor is part of the Crystal Ball package provided in your MS Courseware, the abbreviation of Crystal Ball (CB) is included in its name.

Included in your MS Courseware is an Excel add-in called CB Predictor that is designed to perform time-series forecasting within a spreadsheet environment. CB Predictor was developed by Decisioneering, Inc., and is part of Crystal Ball 2000, Professional Edition. This entire suite of Excel add-ins is available in your MS Courseware. (This suite is a trial version that can be used for 140 days, so if you wish to keep using Crystal Ball 2000 beyond the trial period, it should be purchased from Decisioneering.)

The CB Predictor dialogue box guides you through a 10-step forecasting process.

CB Predictor will perform most of the forecasting techniques discussed in this chapter, as well as a few others. This requires entering the historical data in a spreadsheet, as shown in Figure 13.11 for the CCW problem. The next step is to select a cell within the body of the data (e.g., somewhere in column D of Figure 13.11) and choose CB Predictor from the CB Tools menu (if CB Predictor is installed as part of the Crystal Ball 2000, Professional Edition package) or from the Tools menu (if CB Predictor is installed as a standalone package). This brings up the CB Predictor dialogue box shown in Figure 13.12. This dialogue box contains four panes

FIGURE 13.11

The first step in doing time-series forecasting with CB Predictor is to enter the historical data in a spreadsheet, as shown here for the CCW problem.

	A	B	C	D
1		**Crystal Ball Predictor for CCW**		
2				
3		Year	Quarter	Call Volume
4		1	Q1	6,809
5		1	Q2	6,465
6		1	Q3	6,569
7		1	Q4	8,266
8		2	Q1	7,257
9		2	Q2	7,064
10		2	Q3	7,784
11		2	Q4	8,724
12		3	Q1	6,992
13		3	Q2	6,822
14		3	Q3	7,949
15		3	Q4	9,650

FIGURE 13.12

The CB Predictor dialogue box has the four panes (Input Data, Data Attributes, Method Gallery, and Results) displayed here, where the entries shown are for the CCW problem.

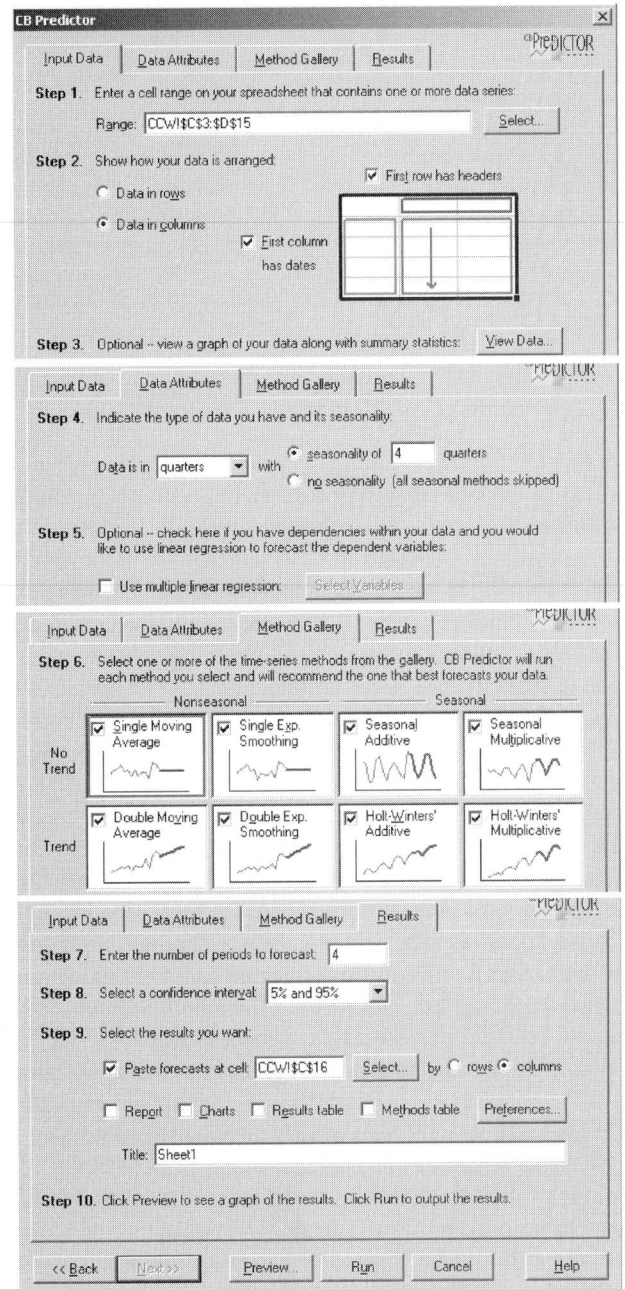

(Input Data, Data Attributes, Method Gallery, and Results) used to perform the 10-step process of forecasting with CB Predictor.

Figure 13.12 shows the entries that are needed in this dialogue box for the CCW problem. In the first pane (Input Data), CB Predictor has made a (correct) guess as to the appropriate cell range for the data (C3:D15) in Step 1. If this guess had not been correct, corrections would need to be made. Next, the arrangement of the data is specified in Step 2. For CCW, the data are in columns, the first column has dates, and the first row has headers. If desired, you can view a graph of the data in Step 3.

Click on Next or the Data Attributes tab to move to the second pane. Step 4 specifies the type of data and whether to apply seasonality. For CCW, the data are in quarters and there is seasonality over each cycle of four quarters. Step 5 is used only if you wish to perform linear regression (the subject of Section 13.6).

TABLE 13.4
The Relationship between CB Predictor Techniques and the Forecasting Techniques in Section 13.3

CB Predictor Technique	Related Technique in Section 13.3
Single moving average	Moving average
Double moving average	Not covered
Single exponential smoothing	Exponential smoothing
Double exponential smoothing	Exponential smoothing with trend
Seasonal additive	Not covered
Holt-Winters additive	Not covered
Seasonal multiplicative	Exponential smoothing with seasonality
Holt-Winters multiplicative	Exponential smoothing with seasonality and trend

In the third pane (Method Gallery), Step 6 allows you to choose the time-series forecasting methods that CB Predictor should try. Most of the techniques displayed in the Method Gallery are similar to techniques that were covered in Section 13.3, although they are given somewhat different names. (Three of the techniques were not covered.) Table 13.4 identifies the relationships between the methods in CB Predictor and the methods discussed in Section 13.3. However, each of the CB Predictor techniques that involves exponential smoothing differs from its counterpart in Section 13.3 by eliminating the need for the user to provide any inputs (seasonal factors, initial estimates, and smoothing constants) other than the raw data. Instead, CB Predictor uses the raw data to provide the best fit for all these inputs as well as the forecasts (so a considerable amount of raw data is needed to accomplish all this well). While this is very helpful for an inexperienced user, it deprives an experienced user of the opportunity to provide any desired inputs. Therefore, CB Predictor includes an option to override this feature and manually provide smoothing constants. (This is done by double-clicking on any technique in the dialogue box, which brings up a Parameters dialogue box, and then entering user-defined parameters.) CB Predictor will try all the techniques that are checked in the Method Gallery and use the one that fits the historical data the best.

In the final pane (Results), Steps 7, 8, and 9 are used to specify how many periods to forecast, the percentiles for a confidence interval, and whether to paste the forecast into the spreadsheet. Once these steps are completed, clicking on Preview can generate a preview graph of the forecast. The resulting forecast is shown in Figure 13.13. The historical data for Years 1 through 3 are shown as a light line, while the forecasts generated are shown with a dark line. In Year 4, the forecasts are displayed along with a 5 percent and 95 percent confidence interval (light lines). These light lines specify the range of values that fall within the confidence interval. Given the percentiles of 5 percent and 95 percent for the confidence interval, each piece of actual Year 4 data should have only a 5 percent chance of falling below the lower line and a 5 percent chance of rising above the upper line if the time series is not disrupted by some event.

Clicking on Run in the final pane generates the forecast for the number of periods specified in Step 7 and (if Step 9 is checked) pastes the forecast directly into the spreadsheet. The result is shown in Figure 13.14, where cells D16:D19 give the forecasts for all four quarters of Year 4.

The top right-hand side of the Preview Forecast in Figure 13.13 indicates that the technique that fits the historical data best is the Holt-Winters multiplicative method (called exponential smoothing with seasonality and trend in Section 13.3), so this is the one that provides the forecasts shown in Figure 13.14. The bottom right-hand side of Figure 13.13 also reveals the curious fact that this method concluded that the best values for all the smoothing constants—alpha, beta, and gamma (the smoothing constant for seasonal factors)—are essentially 0. This means that the forecasting method essentially uses only an initial estimate, initial trend, and initial seasonality factors (all calculated based on the first three years of data) to forecast the future, without updating these estimates using exponential smoothing. We suspect that with more historical data, the method would pick nonzero smoothing constants to take advantage of exponential smoothing.

CB Predictor uses the raw data to determine the seasonal factors, initial estimates, and smoothing constants, unless you choose to override this feature and provide these inputs yourself.

The confidence interval shows the range of likely values for the quantity being forecasted.

FIGURE 13.13

This CB Predictor preview graph for the CCW problem uses dark lines to show the forecasts generated retrospectively (Years 1 through 3) and for each quarter of the next year (Year 4). The light lines for Years 1 through 3 display the historical data, whereas the two light lines in Year 4 show a confidence interval (with percentiles of 5 percent and 95 percent) for next year's forecasts.

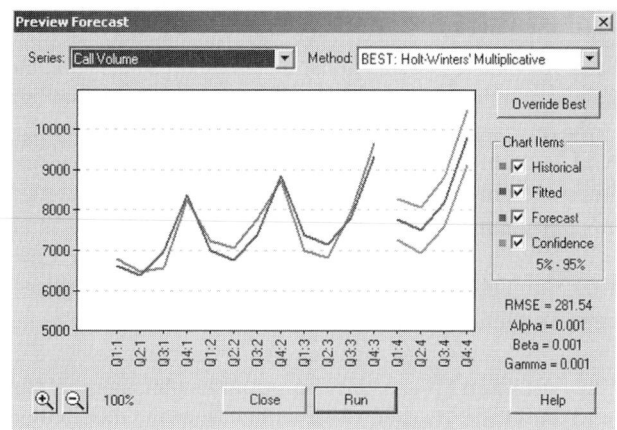

FIGURE 13.14

Using the data from Figure 13.11, cells D16:D19 give the forecast obtained by CB Predictor for each quarter of the coming year (Year 4) for the CCW problem. These are the forecasts plotted with the dark line in the Year 4 portion of the preview graph in Figure 13.13.

	A	B	C	D
1		**Crystal Ball Predictor for CCW**		
2				
3		Year	Quarter	Call Volume
4		1	Q1	6,809
5		1	Q2	6,465
6		1	Q3	6,569
7		1	Q4	8,266
8		2	Q1	7,257
9		2	Q2	7,064
10		2	Q3	7,784
11		2	Q4	8,724
12		3	Q1	6,992
13		3	Q2	6,822
14		3	Q3	7,949
15		3	Q4	9,650
16		4	**Q1**	**7,791**
17		4	**Q2**	**7,515**
18		4	**Q3**	**8,203**
19		4	**Q4**	**9,799**

Review Questions

1. How does CB Predictor differ from the techniques in Section 13.3 with regard to user inputs (seasonal factors, initial estimates, and smoothing constants)?
2. What is the meaning of a 5 percent and a 95 percent confidence interval?

13.5   THE TIME-SERIES FORECASTING METHODS IN PERSPECTIVE

Section 13.3 presented several methods for forecasting the next value of a time series in the context of the CCW case study. We now will take a step back to place into perspective just what these methods are trying to accomplish. After providing this perspective, CCW's consultant then will give his recommendation for setting up a forecasting system.

The Goal of the Forecasting Methods

It actually is something of a misnomer to talk about forecasting *the* value of the next observation in a time series (such as CCW's call volume in the next quarter). It is impossible to predict *the value* precisely, because this next value can turn out to be anything over some range. What it will be depends upon future circumstances that are beyond our control.

In other words, the next value that will occur in a time series is a *random variable.* It has some *probability distribution.* For example, Figure 13.15 shows a typical probability distribution for the CCW call volume in a future quarter in which the mean of this distribution happens to be 7,500. This distribution indicates the relative likelihood of the various possible values of the call volume. Nobody can say in advance which value actually will occur.

So what is the meaning of the single number that is selected as the "forecast" of the next value in the time series? If possible, we would like this number to be the *mean* of the distribution. The reason is that random observations from the distribution tend to cluster around the mean of the distribution. Therefore, using the mean as the forecast would tend to minimize the average forecasting error.

Unfortunately, we don't actually know what this probability distribution is, let alone its mean. The best we can do is use all the available data (past values from the time series) to estimate the mean as closely as possible.

> The goal of time-series forecasting methods is to estimate the *mean* of the underlying probability distribution of the next value of the time series as closely as possible.

Given some random observations from a single probability distribution, the best estimate of its mean is the *sample average* (the average of all these observations). Therefore, if a time series has exactly the same distribution for each and every time period, then the *averaging forecasting method* provides the best estimate of the mean.

However, other forecasting methods commonly are used instead because the distribution may be changing over time.

Problems Caused by Shifting Distributions

Section 13.3 began by considering seasonal effects. This then led to estimating CCW's seasonal factors as 0.93, 0.90, 0.99, and 1.18 for Quarters 1, 2, 3, and 4, respectively.

If the overall average daily call volume for a year is 7,500, these seasonal factors imply that the probability distributions for the four quarters of that year fall roughly as shown in Figure 13.16. Since these distributions have different means, we should no longer simply average the random observations (observed call volumes) from all four quarters to estimate the mean for any one of these distributions.

The next value in a time series cannot be forecasted with certainty because it has a probability distribution rather than a fixed value that definitely will occur.

FIGURE 13.15

A typical probability distribution of what the average daily call volume will be for CCW in a quarter when the mean is 7,500.

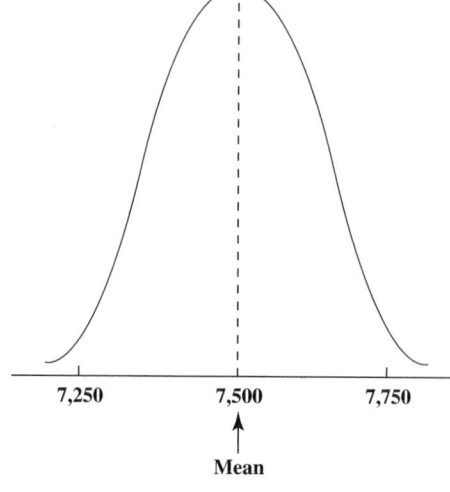

7,250   7,500   7,750

Mean

FIGURE 13.16

Typical probability distributions of CCW's average daily call volumes in the four quarters of a year in which the overall average is 7,500.

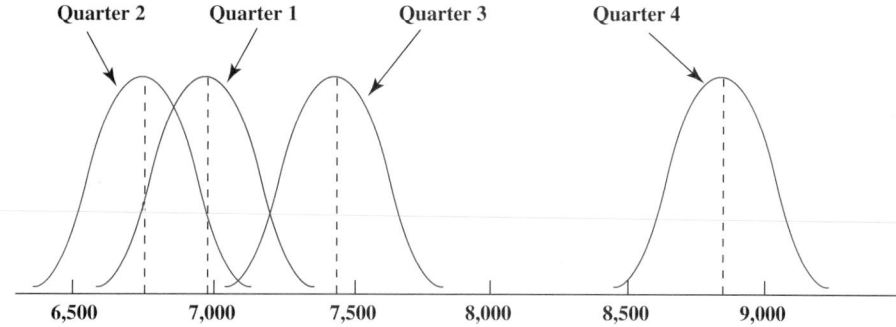

FIGURE 13.17

Comparison of typical probability distributions of CCW's average daily call volumes (seasonally adjusted) in Years 1 and 2.

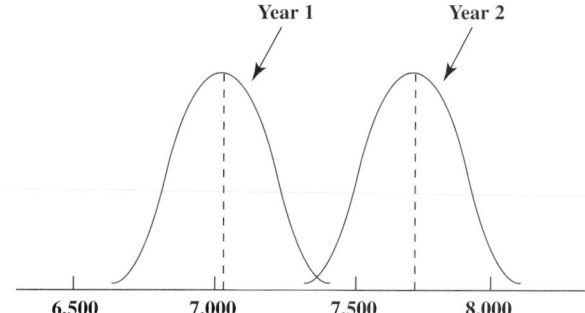

This complication is why the preceding section seasonally adjusted the time series. Dividing each quarter's call volume by its seasonal factor shifts the distribution of this seasonally adjusted call volume over to basically the distribution shown in Figure 13.15 with a mean of 7,500. This allows averaging the seasonally adjusted values to estimate this mean.

Unfortunately, even after seasonally adjusting the time series, the probability distribution may not remain the same from one year to the next (or even from one quarter to the next). For example, as CCW's marketing manager explained, total sales jumped substantially at the beginning of Year 2 when the new Klugman operating system became available. This also caused the average daily call volume to increase by about 10 percent, from just over 7,000 in Year 1 to over 7,700 in Year 2. Figure 13.17 compares the resulting distributions for typical quarters (seasonally adjusted) in the two years.

Random observations from the Year 1 distribution in this figure provide a poor basis for estimating the mean of the Year 2 distribution. Yet, except for the last-value method, *each* of the forecasting methods presented in the preceding section placed at least some weight on these observations from Year 1 to estimate the mean for *each* quarter in Year 2. This was a major part of the reason why both the average forecasting errors (MAD) and the mean square errors (MSE) were higher for these methods than for the last-value method.

Judging from the marketing manager's information, it appears that some shift in the distribution also occurred several times from just one quarter to the next. This further added to the forecasting errors.

When the probability distribution for a time series shifts frequently, recent data quickly become outdated for forecasting purposes.

Comparison of the Forecasting Methods

Section 13.3 presented five methods for forecasting the next value in a time series. Which of these methods is particularly suitable for a given application depends greatly on how *stable* the time series is.

A time series is said to be **stable** if its underlying probability distribution usually remains the same from one time period to the next. (Any shifts that do occur in the distribution are both infrequent and small.) A time series is **unstable** if both frequent and sizable shifts in the distribution tend to occur.

CCW's seasonally adjusted time series shown in Figure 13.4 (and many subsequent figures) appears to have had several shifts in the distribution, including the sizable one depicted in Figure 13.17. Therefore, this time series is an example of a relatively *unstable* one.

Here is a summary of which type of time series fits each of the forecasting methods.

The key factor in choosing a forecasting method is how stable the time series is.

Last-value method: Suitable for a time series that is so unstable that even the next-to-last value is not considered relevant for forecasting the next value.

Averaging method: Suitable for a very stable time series where even its first few values are considered relevant for forecasting the next value.

Moving-average method: Suitable for a moderately stable time series where the last few values are considered relevant for forecasting the next value. The number of values included in the moving average reflects the anticipated degree of stability in the time series.

Exponential smoothing method: Suitable for a time series in the range from somewhat unstable to rather stable, where the value of the smoothing constant needs to be adjusted to fit the anticipated degree of stability. Refines the moving-average method by placing the greatest weight on the most recent values, but is not as readily understood by managers as the moving-average method.

Exponential smoothing with trend: Suitable for a time series where the mean of the distribution tends to follow a trend either up or down, provided that changes in the trend occur only occasionally and gradually.

Unfortunately for CCW, its seasonally adjusted time series proved to be a little too unstable for any of these methods except the last-value method, which is considered to be the least powerful of these forecasting methods. Even when using exponential smoothing with trend, the changes in the trend occurred too frequently and sharply.

In light of these considerations, the consultant now is ready to present his recommendations to Lydia for a new forecasting procedure.

The Consultant's Recommendations

1. Forecasting should be done monthly rather than quarterly in order to respond more quickly to changing conditions.

2. Hiring and training of new agents also should be done monthly instead of quarterly in order to fine-tune staffing levels to meet changing needs.

3. Recently retired agents should be offered the opportunity to work part-time on an on-call basis to help meet current staffing needs more closely.

4. Since sales drive call volume, the forecasting process should begin by forecasting sales.

5. For forecasting purposes, total sales should be broken down into the major components described by the marketing manager, namely, (1) the relatively stable market base of numerous small-niche products and (2) *each* of the few (perhaps three or four) major new products whose success or failure can significantly drive total sales up or down. These major new products would be identified by the marketing manager on an ongoing basis.

Forecasting call volume should begin by separately forecasting the major components of total sales.

6. Exponential smoothing with a relatively small smoothing constant is suggested for forecasting sales of the marketing base of numerous small-niche products. However, before making a final decision on the forecasting method, retrospective testing should be conducted to check how well this particular method would have performed over the past three years. This testing also should guide selection of the value of the smoothing constant.

7. Exponential smoothing with trend, with relatively large smoothing constants, is suggested for forecasting sales of *each* of the major new products. Once again, retrospective testing

should be conducted to check this decision and to guide choosing values for the smoothing constants. The marketing manager should be asked to provide the initial estimate of anticipated sales in the first month for a new product. He also should be asked to check the subsequent exponential smoothing forecasts and make any adjustments he feels are appropriate based on his knowledge of what is happening in the marketplace.

8. Because of the strong seasonal sales pattern, seasonally adjusted time series should be used for each application of these forecasting methods.

9. After separately obtaining forecasts of actual sales for each of the major components of total sales identified in recommendation 5, these forecasts should be summed to obtain a forecast of total sales.

The next section describes how to obtain a forecast of call volume from a forecast of total sales.

10. *Causal forecasting with linear regression* (as described in the next section) should be used to obtain a forecast of *call volume* from this forecast of total sales.

Lydia accepts these recommendations with considerable enthusiasm. She also agrees to work with the marketing manager to gain his cooperation.

Read on to see how the last recommendation is implemented.

Review Questions

1. What kind of variable is the next value that will occur in a time series?
2. What is the goal of time-series forecasting methods?
3. Is the probability distribution of CCW's average daily call volume the same for every quarter?
4. What is the explanation for why the average forecasting errors were higher for the other time-series forecasting methods than for the supposedly less powerful last-value method?
5. What is the distinction between a *stable* time series and an *unstable* time series?
6. What is the consultant's recommendation regarding what should be forecasted instead of call volumes to begin the forecasting process?
7. What are the major components of CCW's total sales?

13.6 CAUSAL FORECASTING WITH LINEAR REGRESSION

We have focused so far on *time-series forecasting methods,* that is, methods that forecast the next value in a time series based on its previous values. These methods have been used retrospectively in Section 13.3 to forecast CCW's call volume in the next quarter based on its previous call volumes.

Causal Forecasting

However, the consultant's last recommendation suggests another approach to forecasting. It is really sales that drive call volume, and sales can be forecasted considerably more precisely than call volume. Therefore, it should be possible to obtain a better forecast of call volume by relating it directly to forecasted sales. This kind of approach is called *causal forecasting.*

For the CCW problem, call volume is the dependent variable and total sales is the independent variable.

Causal forecasting obtains a forecast of the quantity of interest (the **dependent variable**) by relating it directly to one or more other quantities (the **independent variables**) that drive the quantity of interest.

Table 13.5 shows some examples of the kinds of situations where causal forecasting sometimes is used. In each of the first four cases, the indicated dependent variable can be expected to go up or down rather directly with the independent variable(s) listed in the rightmost column. The last case also applies when some quantity of interest (e.g., sales of a product) tends to follow a steady trend upward (or downward) with the passage of time (the independent variable that drives the quantity of interest).

TABLE 13.5
Possible Examples of
Causal Forecasting

Type of Forecasting	Possible Dependent Variable	Possible Independent Variables
Sales	Sales of a product	Amount of advertising
Spare parts	Demand for spare parts	Usage of equipment
Economic trends	Gross domestic product	Various economic factors
CCW call volume	Call volume	Total sales
Any quantity	This same quantity	Time

FIGURE 13.18
The data needed to do
causal forecasting for the
CCW problem by relating
call volume to sales.

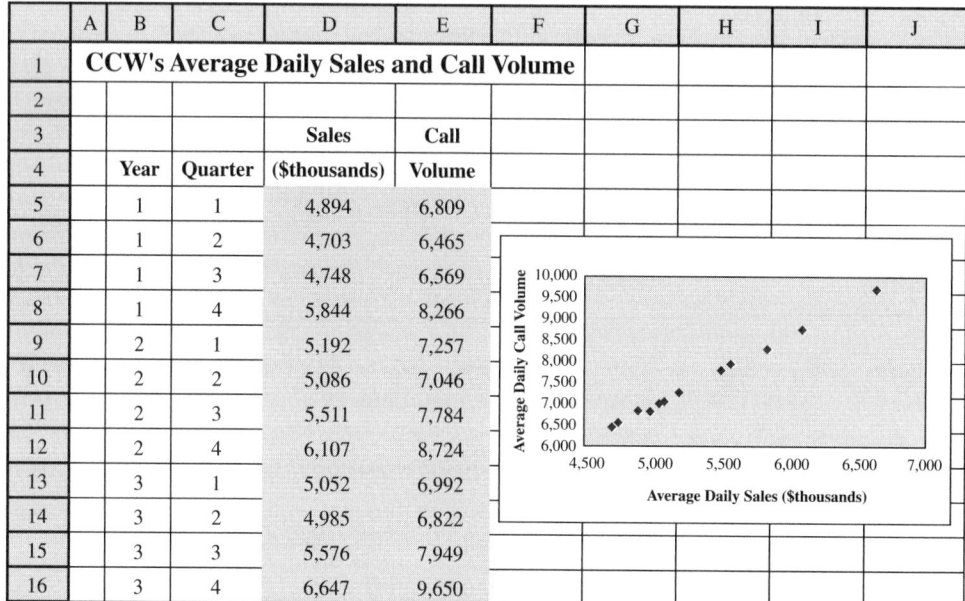

	A	B	C	D	E	F	G	H	I	J
1		CCW's Average Daily Sales and Call Volume								
2										
3				Sales	Call					
4		Year	Quarter	($thousands)	Volume					
5		1	1	4,894	6,809					
6		1	2	4,703	6,465					
7		1	3	4,748	6,569					
8		1	4	5,844	8,266					
9		2	1	5,192	7,257					
10		2	2	5,086	7,046					
11		2	3	5,511	7,784					
12		2	4	6,107	8,724					
13		3	1	5,052	6,992					
14		3	2	4,985	6,822					
15		3	3	5,576	7,949					
16		3	4	6,647	9,650					

As one specific example, Section 13.1 includes a description of American Airline's elaborate system for forecasting its need for expensive spare parts (its "rotatable" parts) to continue operating its fleet of several hundred airplanes. This system uses causal forecasting, where the demand for spare parts is the dependent variable and the number of flying hours is the independent variable. This makes sense because the demand for spare parts should be roughly proportional to the number of flying hours for the fleet.

Linear Regression

At Lydia's request, the marketing manager brought sales data for the past three years to their recent meeting. These data are summarized in Figure 13.18. In particular, column D gives the average daily sales (in units of thousands of dollars) for each of the 12 past quarters. Column E repeats the data given previously on average daily call volumes. None of the data have been seasonally adjusted.

The right side of the figure was generated by choosing Chart under the Insert menu, selecting an XY (Scatter) chart type, and following the directions of the Chart Wizard. This graph shows a plot of the data in columns D and E on a two-dimensional graph. Thus, each of the 12 points in the graph shows the combination of sales and call volume for one of the 12 quarters (without identifying which quarter).

This graph shows a close relationship between call volume and sales. Each increase or decrease in sales is accompanied by a roughly proportional increase or decrease in call volume. This is not surprising since the sales are being made through the calls to the call center.

It appears from this graph that the relationship between call volume and sales can be approximated by a straight line. Figure 13.19 shows such a line. (This line was generated by clicking on the graph in Figure 13.18, selecting Add Trendline under the Chart menu, and then

FIGURE 13.19

Figure 13.18 has been modified here by adding a trend line to the graph.

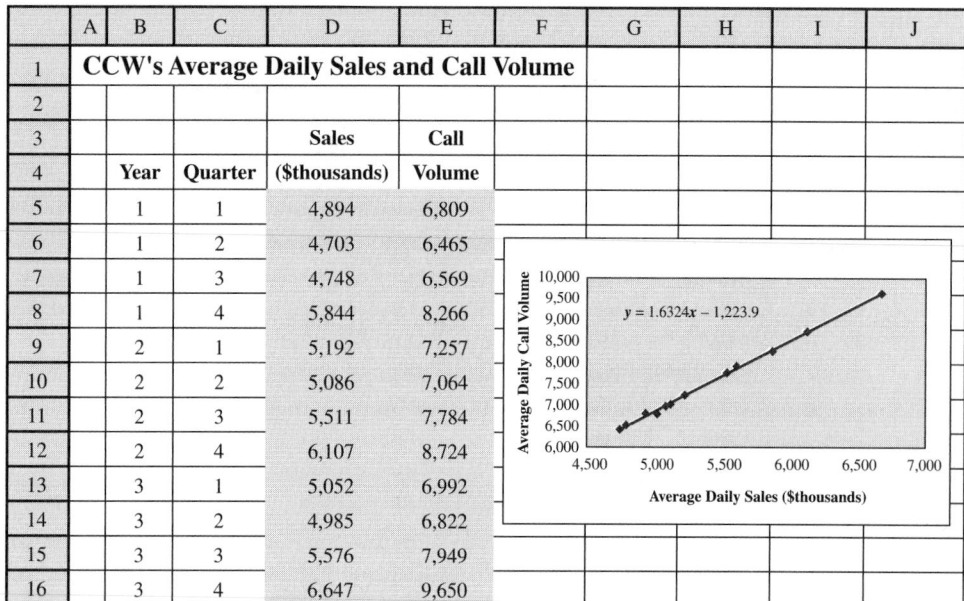

	A	B	C	D	E	F	G	H	I	J
1		**CCW's Average Daily Sales and Call Volume**								
2										
3				**Sales**	**Call**					
4		**Year**	**Quarter**	**($thousands)**	**Volume**					
5		1	1	4,894	6,809					
6		1	2	4,703	6,465					
7		1	3	4,748	6,569					
8		1	4	5,844	8,266					
9		2	1	5,192	7,257					
10		2	2	5,086	7,064					
11		2	3	5,511	7,784					
12		2	4	6,107	8,724					
13		3	1	5,052	6,992					
14		3	2	4,985	6,822					
15		3	3	5,576	7,949					
16		3	4	6,647	9,650					

selecting Linear Trend under the Options tab. The equation above the line was added by choosing Display Equation on Chart under the Options tab.) This line is referred to as a *linear regression line.*

A linear regression line estimates what the value of the dependent variable should be for any particular value of the independent variable.

When doing causal forecasting with a single independent variable, **linear regression** involves approximating the relationship between the dependent variable (call volume for CCW) and the independent variable (sales for CCW) by a straight line. This **linear regression line** is drawn on a graph with the independent variable on the horizontal axis and the dependent variable on the vertical axis. The line is constructed after plotting a number of points showing each observed value of the independent variable and the corresponding value of the dependent variable.

Thus, the linear regression line in Figure 13.19 can be used to estimate what the call volume should be for a particular value of sales. In general, the equation for the linear regression line has the form

$$y = a + bx$$

where

y = Estimated value of the dependent variable, as given by the linear regression line

a = Intercept of the linear regression line with the y-axis

b = Slope of the linear regression line

x = Value of the independent variable

The equation for a linear regression line is called the regression equation.

(If there is more than one independent variable, then this **regression equation** has a term, a constant times the variable, added on the right-hand side for *each* of these variables.) For the linear regression line in this figure, the exact values of a and b happen to be

$$a = -1,223.9 \qquad b = 1.6324$$

Figure 13.20 shows the Excel template in your MS Courseware that can be used to find these values of a and b, and so on. You need to input all the observed values of the independent variable (sales) and of the dependent variable (call volume) in columns C and D, and then the template performs all the calculations. On the right, note that you have the option of inserting a value for x (sales) in cell J10 and then the template calculates the corresponding value of y (call volume) that lies on the linear regression line. This calculation can be repeated for as many values of x as desired. In addition, column E already shows these calculations for each

FIGURE 13.20 The Excel template in your MS Courseware for doing causal forecasting with linear regression, as illustrated here for the CCW problem.

	A	B	C	D	E	F	G	H	I	J
1			Linear Regression of Call Volume vs. Sales Volume for CCW							
2										
3		Time	Independent	Dependent		Estimation	Square		Linear Regression Line	
4		Period	Variable	Variable	Estimate	Error	of Error		y = a + bx	
5		1	4,894	6,809	6,765	43.85	1,923		a =	-1,223.86
6		2	4,703	6,465	6,453	11.64	136		b =	1.63
7		3	4,748	6,569	6,527	42.18	1,780			
8		4	5,844	8,266	8,316	49.93	2,493			
9		5	5,192	7,257	7,252	5.40	29		Estimator	
10		6	5,086	7,064	7,079	14.57	212		if x =	5,000
11		7	5,511	7,784	7,772	11.66	136			
12		8	6,107	8,724	8,745	21.26	452		then y =	6,938.18
13		9	5,052	6,992	7,023	31.07	965			
14		10	4,985	6,822	6,914	91.70	8,408			
15		11	5,576	7,949	7,878	70.55	4,977			
16		12	6,647	9,650	9,627	23.24	540			
17		13								
18		14								
19		15								
20		16								
21		17								
22		18								
23		19								
24		20								
25		21								
26		22								
27		23								
28		24								
29		25								
30		26								
31		27								
32		28								
33		29								
34		30								

Range Name	Cells
a	J5
b	J6
DependentVariable	D5:D34
Estimate	E5:E34
EstimationError	F5:F34
IndependentVariable	C5:C34
SquareOfError	G5:G34
x	J10
y	J12

	E	F	G
3		Estimation	Square
4	Estimate	Error	of Error
5	=a+b*C5	=ABS(D5-E5)	=F5^2
6	=a+b*C6	=ABS(D6-E6)	=F6^2
7	=a+b*C7	=ABS(D7-E7)	=F7^2
8	=a+b*C8	=ABS(D8-E8)	=F8^2
9	=a+b*C9	=ABS(D9-E9)	=F9^2
10	:	:	:
11	:	:	:

	I	J
5	a =	=INTERCEPT(DependentVariable,IndependentVariable)
6	b =	=SLOPE(DependentVariable,IndependentVariable)

	I	J
12	then y =	=a+b*x

value of x in column C, so each cell in column E gives the estimate of call volume provided by the linear regression line for the corresponding sales level in column C. The difference between this estimate and the actual call volume in column D gives the estimation error in column F. The *square* of this error is shown in column G.

The procedure used to obtain a and b is called the **method of least squares.** This method chooses the values of a and b that *minimize* the sum of the *square of the estimation errors* given

The method of least squares chooses the values of *a* and *b* that make the sum of the resulting numbers in column G as small as possible.

in column G of Figure 13.20. Thus, the sum of the numbers in column G (22,051) is the minimum possible. Any significantly different values of *a and b* would give different estimation errors that would cause this sum to be larger.

The *average* of the square of the estimation errors in column G (1,838) has an interesting interpretation. Suppose that the sales for a quarter could be known in advance (either because of advance orders or an exact prediction). In this case, using the linear regression line to forecast call volume would give a mean square error (MSE) of 1,838. What the method of least squares has done is place the linear regression line exactly where it would minimize MSE in this situation. Note that this minimum value of MSE = 1,838 is roughly 1 percent of the MSE values given earlier in Table 13.3 for the time-series forecasting methods presented in Section 13.3.

The numbers in column F also are interesting. Averaging these numbers reveals that the *average estimation error* for the 12 quarters is only 35. This indicates that if the sales for a quarter were known in advance (or could be predicted exactly), then using the linear regression line to forecast call volume would give an average forecasting error (MAD) of only 35. This is only about 10 percent of the values of MAD obtained for the various time-series forecasting methods in Section 13.3.

For some applications of causal forecasting, the value of the independent variable will be known in advance. This is not the case here, where the independent variable is the total sales for the upcoming time period. However, the consultant is confident that a very good forecast of total sales can be obtained by following his recommendations. This forecast can then be used as the value of the independent variable for obtaining a good forecast of call volume from the linear regression line.

CCW's New Forecasting Procedure

1. Obtain a forecast of total (average daily) sales for the upcoming month by implementing the consultant's recommendations.

2. Use this forecast as the value of total sales in forecasting the average daily call volume for the upcoming month from the linear regression line identified in Figures 13.19 and 13.20.

Seasonal adjustments play a role in step 1 of this procedure, but not in step 2. Based on the consultant's recommendations presented at the end of the preceding section (see recommendation no. 8), seasonal adjustments should be incorporated into whatever forecasting method is used in step 1. However, a forecast of seasonally adjusted sales would then be converted back into a forecast of actual sales for use in step 2. By using a forecast of actual sales, the forecast of call volume obtained from the linear regression line in step 2 will be the desired forecast of actual call volume rather than seasonally adjusted call volume.

Linear regression with multiple independent variables is sometimes referred to as *multiple linear regression.*

This application of linear regression to the CCW problem involves only one independent variable (total sales) that drives the dependent variable (call volume). As mentioned at the beginning of this section, some applications of causal forecasting with linear regression involve multiple independent variables that together drive the dependent variable. For example, when using linear regression to forecast the nation's gross domestic product (the dependent variable) for the next quarter, the independent variables might include such leading indicators of future economic performance as the current level of the stock market, the current index of consumer confidence, the current index of business activity (measuring orders placed), and so forth. If there are, say, two independent variables, the regression equation would have the form

$$y = a + b_1 x_1 + b_2 x_2$$

where x_1 and x_2 are the independent variables with b_1 and b_2 as their respective coefficients. The corresponding linear regression line now would lie in a three-dimensional graph with *y* (the dependent variable) as the vertical axis and both x_1 and x_2 as horizontal axes in the other two dimensions. Regardless of the number of independent variables, the *method of least squares* still can be used to choose the value of *a*, b_1, b_2, etc., that minimizes the sum of the square of the estimation errors when comparing the values of the dependent variable at the various data points with the corresponding estimates given by the regression equation. However, we will not delve further into this more advanced topic.

The CCW Case Study a Year Later

A year after implementing the consultant's recommendations, Lydia gives him a call.

Lydia: I just wanted to let you know how things are going. And to congratulate you on the great job you did for us.

Consultant: Thanks. So my recommended forecasting procedure is performing well?

Lydia: Extremely well. Remember that the 25 percent rule was giving us MAD values over 400? And then the various time-series forecasting methods were doing almost as badly?

Consultant: Yes, I do remember. You were pretty discouraged there for awhile.

Lydia: I sure was! But I'm feeling a lot better now. I just calculated MAD for the first year under your new procedure.

Consultant: Oh. What did you get?

Lydia: 120. Only 120!

Consultant: Great. That's the kind of improvement we like to see. What do you think has made the biggest difference?

Lydia: I think the biggest factor was tying our forecasting into forecasting sales. We never had much feeling for where call volumes were headed. But we have a much better handle on what sales will be because, with the marketing manager's help, we can see what is causing the shifts.

A key to successful forecasting is to understand what is causing shifts so that they can be caught as soon as they occur.

Consultant: Yes. I think that is a real key to successful forecasting. You saw that we can get a lot of garbage by simply applying a time-series forecasting method to historical data without understanding what is causing the shifts. You have to get behind the numbers and see what is really going on, then design the forecasting procedure to catch the shifts as they occur, like we did by having the marketing manager identify the major new products that impact total sales and then separately forecasting sales for each of them.

Lydia: Right. Bringing the marketing manager in on this was a great move. He's a real supporter of the new procedure now, by the way. He says it is giving him valuable information as well.

A good forecasting procedure combines a well-constructed statistical forecasting procedure and a savvy manager who understands what is driving the numbers and so is able to make appropriate adjustments in the forecasts.

Consultant: Good. Is he making adjustments in the statistical forecasts, based on his knowledge of what is going on in the marketplace, like I recommended?

Lydia: Yes, he is. He says he isn't ready to be replaced by a computer yet.

Consultant: He sure isn't. He's a savvy guy. A good forecasting procedure needs somebody like him overseeing things and making appropriate adjustments in the forecasts. That's a great combination: a well-constructed statistical forecasting procedure and a savvy manager who understands what is driving the numbers.

Lydia: Well, it's really working. Anyway, you have a couple fans here. We really appreciate the great job you did for us.

Review Questions

1. What is causal forecasting?
2. When applying causal forecasting to the CCW problem, what is the dependent variable and what is the independent variable?
3. When doing causal forecasting with a single independent variable, what does linear regression involve?
4. What is the form of the equation for a linear regression line with a single independent variable? With more than one independent variable?

5. What is the name of the method for obtaining the value of the constants, *a* and *b*, for a linear regression line?

6. How does the MAD value for CCW's new forecasting procedure compare with that for the old procedure that used the 25 percent rule?

13.7   JUDGMENTAL FORECASTING METHODS

Judgmental forecasting methods use expert opinion to make forecasts.

We have focused so far on *statistical* forecasting methods that base the forecast on historical data. However, such methods cannot be used if no data are available, or if the data are not representative of current conditions. In such cases, **judgmental forecasting methods** can be used instead.

Even when good data are available, some managers prefer a judgmental method instead of a formal statistical method. In many other cases, a combination of the two may be used. For example, in the CCW case study, the marketing manager uses his judgment, based on his long experience and his knowledge of what is happening in the marketplace, to adjust the sales forecasts obtained from time-series forecasting methods.

Here is a brief overview of the main judgmental forecasting methods.

1. **Manager's opinion:** This is the most informal of the methods, because it simply involves a single manager using his or her best judgment to make the forecast. In some cases, some data may be available to help make this judgment. In others, the manager may be drawing solely on experience and an intimate knowledge of the current conditions that drive the forecasted quantity.

2. **Jury of executive opinion:** This method is similar to the first one, except now it involves a small group of high-level managers who pool their best judgments to collectively make the forecast. This method may be used for more critical forecasts for which several executives share responsibility and can provide different types of expertise.

The salesforce composite method uses a bottom-up approach.

3. **Salesforce composite:** This method is often used for sales forecasting when a company employs a salesforce to help generate sales. It is a *bottom-up approach* whereby each salesperson provides an estimate of what sales will be in his or her region. These estimates then are sent up through the corporate chain of command, with managerial review at each level, to be aggregated into a corporate sales forecast.

4. **Consumer market survey:** This method goes even further than the preceding one in adopting a *grass-roots approach* to sales forecasting. It involves surveying customers and potential customers regarding their future purchasing plans and how they would respond to various new features in products. This input is particularly helpful for designing new products and then in developing the initial forecasts of their sales. It also is helpful for planning a marketing campaign.

5. **Delphi method:** This method employs a panel of experts in different locations who independently fill out a series of questionnaires. However, the results from each questionnaire are provided with the next one, so each expert then can evaluate this group information in adjusting his or her responses next time. The goal is to reach a relatively narrow spread of conclusions from most of the experts. The decision makers then assess this input from the panel of experts to develop the forecast. This involved process normally is used only at the highest levels of a corporation or government to develop long-range forecasts of broad trends.

Review
Questions

1. Statistical forecasting methods cannot be used under what circumstances?

2. Are judgmental forecasting methods only used when statistical forecasting methods cannot be used?

3. How does the jury of executive opinion method differ from the manager's opinion method?

4. How does the salesforce composite method begin?

5. When is a consumer market survey particularly helpful?

6. When might the Delphi method be used?

13.8 FORECASTING IN PRACTICE

You now have seen the major forecasting methods used by managers. We conclude with a brief look at how widely the various methods are used.

To begin, consider the actual forecasting applications discussed in Section 13.1 and summarized in Table 13.1 there. Most of this table is repeated here in Table 13.6, but the rightmost column now identifies which forecasting method was used in each application. Not surprisingly, these major forecasting projects tended to choose one of the more sophisticated statistical forecasting methods. (The most sophisticated is the ARIMA method, commonly called the Box-Jenkins method, that the consultant introduced to Lydia in a conversation described near the end of Section 13.3.)

All companies need to do at least some forecasting, but their methods often are not as sophisticated as the ones applied to these major projects. Some insight into their general approach was provided by a survey conducted several years ago[2] of sales forecasting practices at 500 U.S. corporations.

Judgmental forecasting methods are used more than statistical methods.

This survey indicates that, generally speaking, *judgmental* forecasting methods are somewhat more widely used than *statistical* methods. The main reasons given for using judgmental methods were accuracy and difficulty in obtaining the data required for statistical methods. Comments also were made that upper management is not familiar with quantitative techniques, that judgmental methods create a sense of ownership, and that these methods add a common-sense element to the forecast.

Among the judgmental methods, the most popular is a *jury of executive opinion.* This is especially true for companywide or industry sales forecasts, but it also holds true by a small margin over *manager's opinion* when forecasting sales of individual products or families of products.

Statistical forecasting methods often are used in companies with high sales.

Statistical forecasting methods also are fairly widely used, especially in companies with high sales. Compared to earlier surveys, familiarity with such methods is increasing. However, many survey respondents cited better data availability as the improvement they most wanted to see in their organizations. The availability of good data is crucial for the use of these methods.

The moving-average method and linear regression are the most popular statistical forecasting methods.

The survey indicates that the *moving-average method* and *linear regression* are the most widely used statistical forecasting methods. The moving-average method is more popular for short- and medium-range forecasts (less than a year), as well as for forecasting sales of individual products and families of products. Linear regression is more popular for longer range forecasts and for forecasting either companywide or industry sales.

Judgmental forecasting methods often are used to adjust the forecasts provided by statistical methods.

Both exponential smoothing and the last-value method also receive considerable use. However, the highest dissatisfaction is with the last-value method, and its popularity is decreasing compared to earlier surveys.

When statistical forecasting methods are used, it is fairly common to also use judgmental methods to adjust the forecasts.

TABLE 13.6 The Forecasting Methods Used in the Actual Applications Presented in Section 13.1

Organization	Quantity Being Forecasted	Forecasting Method
Merit Brass Co.	Sales of finished goods	Exponential smoothing
Hidroeléctrica Español	Energy demand	ARIMA (Box-Jenkins), etc.
American Airlines	Demand for different fare classes	Exponential smoothing
American Airlines	Need for spare parts to repair airplanes	Causal forecasting with linear regression
Albuquerque Microelectronics	Production yield in wafer fabrication	Exponential smoothing with trend
U.S. Department of Labor	Unemployment insurance payments	Causal forecasting with linear regression
United Airlines	Demand at reservations offices and airports	ARIMA (Box-Jenkins)
Taco Bell	Number of customer arrivals	Moving average
L. L. Bean	Staffing needs at call center	ARIMA (Box-Jenkins)

[2]N. R. Sanders and K. B. Manrodt, "Forecasting Practices in U.S. Corporations: Survey Results," *Interfaces* 24 (March–April 1994), pp. 92–100.

As managers become more familiar with statistical methods, and more used to using the computer to compile data and implement management science techniques, we anticipate a continuing increase in the usage of statistical forecasting methods. However, there always will be an important role for judgmental methods, both alone and in combination with statistical methods.

Review Questions

1. According to the survey of sales forecasting practices mentioned in this section, are judgmental or statistical forecasting methods more widely used?

2. What does this survey indicate are the most popular judgmental forecasting methods?

3. What does this survey indicate are the most popular statistical forecasting methods?

13.9 Summary

The future success of any business depends heavily on the ability of its management to forecast well. Forecasting may be needed in several areas, including sales, the need for spare parts, production yields, economic trends, and staffing needs.

The Computer Club Warehouse (CCW) case study illustrates a variety of approaches to forecasting, some of which prove unsatisfactory for this particular application. Ultimately, it becomes necessary to get behind the CCW data to understand just what is driving the call volumes at its call center in order to develop a good forecasting system.

A time series is a series of observations over time of some quantity of interest. Several statistical forecasting methods use these observations in some way to forecast what the next value will be. These methods include the last-value method, the averaging method, the moving-average method, the exponential smoothing method, and exponential smoothing with trend.

The goal of all these methods is to estimate the mean of the underlying probability distribution of the next value of the time series as closely as possible. This may require using seasonal factors to seasonally adjust the time series, as well as identifying other factors that may cause this underlying probability distribution to shift from one time period to the next.

Another statistical forecasting approach is called causal forecasting. This approach obtains a forecast of the quantity of interest (the dependent variable) by relating it directly to one or more other quantities (the independent variables) that drive the quantity of interest. Frequently, this involves using linear regression to approximate the relationship between the dependent variable and each independent variable by a straight line.

The software accompanying this book includes Excel templates for the various statistical forecasting methods, a forecasting module in the Interactive Management Science Modules, and a commercial Excel add-in called CB Predictor for performing time-series forecasting within a spreadsheet environment.

Still another key category of forecasting methods is judgmental methods. This category involves basing the forecast on a manager's opinion, a jury of executive opinion, a salesforce composite, a consumer market survey, or the Delphi method. A survey of 500 U.S. corporations indicates that judgmental methods are used even more widely for sales forecasting than statistical methods. Frequently, both types of methods are used in complementary ways.

Glossary

ARIMA An acronym for the AutoRegressive Integrated Moving Average method, a sophisticated time-series forecasting method commonly referred to as the Box-Jenkins method. (Section 13.3), *617*

averaging forecasting method A method that uses the average of the past observations from a time series as a forecast of the next value. (Section 13.3), *606*

causal forecasting Obtaining a forecast of the dependent variable by relating it directly to one or more independent variables. (Section 13.6), *627*

consumer market survey A judgmental forecasting method that uses surveys of customers and potential customers. (Section 13.7), *633*

Delphi method A judgmental forecasting method that uses input from a panel of experts in different locations. (Section 13.7), *633*

dependent variable The quantity of interest when doing causal forecasting. (Section 13.6), *627*

econometric model A statistical model used to forecast economic trends. (Section 13.1), *595*

exponential smoothing forecasting method A method that uses a weighted average of the last value from a time series and the last forecast to obtain the forecast of the next value. (Section 13.3), *610*

exponential smoothing with trend An adjustment of the exponential smoothing forecasting method that projects the current trend forward to help forecast the next value of a time series (and perhaps subsequent values as well). (Section 13.3), *613*

forecasting error The deviation of the forecast from the realized quantity. (Section 13.2), *599*

independent variable   A quantity that drives the value of the dependent variable in causal forecasting. (Section 13.6), *627*

judgmental forecasting methods   Methods that use expert judgment to make forecasts. (Introduction and Section 13.7), *593*

jury of executive opinion   A judgmental forecasting method that involves a small group of high-level managers pooling their best judgment to collectively make the forecast. (Section 13.7), *633*

last-value forecasting method   A method that uses the last value of a time series as the forecast of the next value. (Section 13.3), *604*

linear regression   Approximating the relationship between the dependent variable and each independent variable by a straight line. (Section 13.6), *629*

linear regression line   The line that approximates the relationship between the dependent variable and each independent variable when using causal forecasting. (Section 13.6), *629*

MAD   An acronym for mean absolute deviation, the average forecasting error. (Section 13.2), *599*

manager's opinion   A judgmental forecasting method that involves using a single manager's best judgment to make the forecast. (Section 13.7), *633*

mean absolute deviation (MAD)   The average forecasting error. (Section 13.2), *599*

mean square error (MSE)   The average of the square of the forecasting errors. (Section 13.2), *600*

method of least squares   The procedure used to obtain the constants in the equation for a linear regression line. (Section 13.6), *630*

moving-average forecasting method   A method that uses the average of the last *n* observations from a time series as a forecast of the next value. (Section 13.3), *608*

MSE   An acronym for mean square error, the average of the square of the forecasting errors. (Section 13.2), *600*

naive method   Another name for the last-value forecasting method. (Section 13.3), *606*

regression equation   The equation for a linear regression line. (Section 13.6), *629*

salesforce composite   A judgmental forecasting method that aggregates the sales forecasts of the salesforce from their various regions. (Section 13.7), *633*

seasonal factor   A factor for any period of a year that measures how that period compares to the overall average for an entire year. (Section 13.3), *601*

seasonally adjusted time series   An adjustment of the original time series that removes seasonal effects. (Section 13.3), *603*

smoothing constant   A parameter of the exponential smoothing forecasting method that gives the weight to be placed on the last value in the time series. (Section 13.3), *610*

stable time series   A time series whose underlying probability distribution usually remains the same from one time period to the next. (Section 13.5), *625*

statistical forecasting methods   Methods that use historical data to forecast future quantities. (Introduction and Sections 13.2–13.6), *593*

time series   A series of observations over time of some quantity of interest. (Section 13.2), *600*

time-series forecasting methods   Methods that use the past observations in a time series to forecast what the next value will be. (Sections 13.3–13.5), *603*

trend   The average change from one time series value to the next if the current pattern continues. (Section 13.3), *613*

trend smoothing constant   A smoothing constant for estimating the trend when using exponential smoothing with trend. (Section 13.3), *614*

unstable time series   A time series that has frequent and sizable shifts in its underlying probability distribution. (Section 13.5), *625*

Summary of Key Formulas

Forecasting error = Difference between a forecasted value and the true value then obtained   (Section 13.2)

$$\text{MAD} = \frac{\text{Sum of forecasting errors}}{\text{Number of forecasts}}$$ (Section 13.2)

$$\text{MSE} = \frac{\text{Sum of square of forecasting errors}}{\text{Number of forecasts}}$$ (Section 13.2)

$$\text{Seasonal factor} = \frac{\text{Average for the period}}{\text{Overall average}}$$ (Section 13.3)

$$\text{Seasonally adjusted value} = \frac{\text{Actual value}}{\text{Seasonal factor}}$$ (Section 13.3)

Last-Value Method: (Section 13.3)

Forecast = Last value

Averaging Method: (Section 13.3)

Forecast = Average of all data to date

Moving-Average Method: (Section 13.3)

Forecast = Average of last *n* values

Exponential Smoothing Method: (Section 13.3)

Forecast = α(Last value) + $(1 - \alpha)$(Last forecast)

Exponential Smoothing with Trend: (Section 13.3)

Forecast = α(Last value) + $(1 - \alpha)$(Last forecast) + Estimated trend

Estimated trend = β(Latest trend) + $(1 - \beta)$(Last estimate of trend)

Latest trend = α(Last value − Next-to-last value) + $(1 - \alpha)$(Last forecast − Next-to-last forecast)

Linear Regression Line: (Section 13.6)

$$y = a + bx$$

Learning Aids for This Chapter in Your MS Courseware

Chapter 13 Excel Files:

Template for *Seasonal Factors*
Templates for *Last-Value Method* (with and without Seasonality)
Templates for *Averaging Method* (with and without Seasonality)
Templates for *Moving-Average Method* (with and without Seasonality)
Templates for *Exponential Smoothing Method* (with and without Seasonality)
Templates for *Exponential Smoothing with Trend* (with and without Seasonality)
Template for *Linear Regression*

An Excel Add-in:

CB Predictor (part of Crystal Ball 2000, Professional Edition)

Interactive Management Science Modules:

Module for forecasting

Problems

The first 16 problems should be done by hand without using the above templates. To the left of the subsequent problems (or their parts), we have inserted the symbol E (for Excel) to indicate that one of the above templates can be helpful. (Either CB Predictor or the forecasting module in your Interactive Management Science Modules should be used for certain problems, but this will be specified in the statement of the problem whenever needed.) An asterisk on the problem number indicates that at least a partial answer is given in the back of the book.

13.1.* The Hammaker Company's newest product has had the following sales during its first five months: 5, 17, 29, 41, 39. The sales manager now wants a forecast of sales in the next month.

   a. Use the last-value method.

   b. Use the averaging method.

   c. Use the moving-average method with the three most recent months.

   d. Given the sales pattern so far, do any of these methods seem inappropriate for obtaining the forecast? Why?

13.2. Sales of stoves have been going well for the Good-Value Department Store. These sales for the past five months have been 15, 18, 12, 17, 13. Use the following methods to obtain a forecast of sales for the next month.

   a. The last-value method.

   b. The averaging method.

   c. The moving-average method with three months.

   d. If you feel that the conditions affecting sales next month will be the same as in the last five months, which of these methods do you prefer for obtaining the forecast? Why?

13.3.* You have been forecasting sales the last four quarters. These forecasts and the true values that subsequently were obtained are shown below.

Quarter	Forecast	True Value
1	327	345
2	332	317
3	328	336
4	330	311

Calculate the forecasting error for each quarter. Then calculate MAD and MSE.

13.4. Sharon Johnson, sales manager for the Alvarez-Baines Company, is trying to choose between two methods for forecasting sales that she has been using during the past five months. During these months, the two methods obtained the forecasts shown next for the company's most important product, where the subsequent actual sales are shown on the right.

	Forecast		
Month	**Method 1**	**Method 2**	**Actual Sales**
1	5,324	5,208	5,582
2	5,405	5,377	4,906
3	5,195	5,462	5,755
4	5,511	5,414	6,320
5	5,762	5,549	5,153

a. Calculate and compare MAD for these two forecasting methods. Then do the same with MSE.

b. Sharon is uncomfortable with choosing between these two methods based on such limited data, but she also does not want to delay further before making her choice. She does have similar sales data for the three years prior to using these forecasting methods the past five months. How can these older data be used to further help her evaluate the two methods and choose one?

13.5. Figure 13.1 shows CCW's average daily call volume for each quarter of the past three years and Figure 13.4 gives the seasonally adjusted call volumes. Lydia Weigelt now wonders what these seasonally adjusted call volumes would have been had she started using seasonal factors two years ago rather than applying them retrospectively now.

a. Use only the call volumes in Year 1 to determine the seasonal factors for Year 2 (so that the "average" call volume for each quarter is just the actual call volume for that quarter in Year 1).

b. Use these seasonal factors to determine the seasonally adjusted call volumes for Year 2.

c. Use the call volumes in Years 1 and 2 to determine the seasonal factors for Year 3.

d. Use the seasonal factors obtained in part c to determine the seasonally adjusted call volumes for Year 3.

13.6. Even when the economy is holding steady, the unemployment rate tends to fluctuate because of seasonal effects. For example, unemployment generally goes up in Quarter 3 (summer) as students (including new graduates) enter the labor market. The unemployment rate then tends to go down in Quarter 4 (fall) as students return to school and temporary help is hired for the Christmas season. Therefore, using seasonal factors to obtain a seasonally adjusted unemployment rate is helpful for painting a truer picture of economic trends.

Over the past 10 years, one state's average unemployment rates (not seasonally adjusted) in Quarters 1, 2, 3, and 4 have been 6.2 percent, 6.0 percent, 7.5 percent, and 5.5 percent, respectively. The overall average has been 6.3 percent.

a. Determine the seasonal factors for the four quarters.

b. Over the next year, the unemployment rates (not seasonally adjusted) for the four quarters turn out to be 7.8 percent, 7.4 percent, 8.7 percent, and 6.1 percent. Determine the seasonally adjusted unemployment rates for the four quarters. What does this progression of rates suggest about whether the state's economy is improving?

13.7. Ralph Billett is the manager of a real estate agency. He now wishes to develop a forecast of the number of houses that will be sold by the agency over the next year.

The agency's quarter-by-quarter sales figures over the last three years are shown below.

Quarter	Year 1	Year 2	Year 3
1	23	19	21
2	22	21	26
3	31	27	32
4	26	24	28

a. Determine the seasonal factors for the four quarters.

b. After considering seasonal effects, use the last-value method to forecast sales in Quarter 1 of next year.

c. Assuming that each of the quarterly forecasts is correct, what would the last-value method forecast as the sales in each of the four quarters next year?

    d. Based on his assessment of the current state of the housing market, Ralph's best judgment is that the agency will sell 100 houses next year. Given this forecast for the year, what is the quarter-by-quarter forecast according to the seasonal factors?

13.8.* You are using the moving-average forecasting method based on the last four observations. When making the forecast for the last period, the oldest of the four observations was 1,945 and the forecast was 2,083. The true value for the last period then turned out to be 1,977. What is your new forecast for the next period?

13.9. You are using the moving-average forecasting method based on sales in the last three months to forecast sales for the next month. When making the forecast for last month, sales for the third month before were 805. The forecast for last month was 782 and then the actual sales turned out to be 793. What is your new forecast for next month?

13.10. After graduating from college with a degree in mathematical statistics, Ann Preston has been hired by the Monty Ward Company to apply statistical methods for forecasting the company's sales. For one of the company's products, the moving-average method based on sales in the 10 most recent months already is being used. Ann's first task is to update last month's forecast to obtain the forecast for next month. She learns that the forecast for last month was 1,551 and that the actual sales then turned out to be 1,532. She also learns that the sales for the 10th month before last month were 1,632. What is Ann's forecast for next month?

13.11. The J. J. Bone Company uses exponential smoothing to forecast the average daily call volume at its call center. The forecast for last month was 782, and then the actual value turned out to be 792. Obtain the forecast for next month for each of the following values of the smoothing constant: $\alpha = 0.1, 0.3, 0.5$.

13.12.* You are using exponential smoothing to obtain monthly forecasts of the sales of a certain product. The forecast for last month was 2,083, and then the actual sales turned out to be 1,973. Obtain the forecast for next month for each of the following values of the smoothing constant: $\alpha = 0.1, 0.3, 0.5$.

13.13. Three years ago, the Admissions Office for Ivy College began using exponential smoothing with a smoothing constant of 0.25 to forecast the number of applications for admission each year. Based on previous experience, this process was begun with an initial estimate of 5,000 applications. The actual number of applications then turned out to be 4,600 in the first year. Thanks to new favorable ratings in national surveys, this number grew to 5,300 in the second year and 6,000 last year.

    a. Determine the forecasts that were made for each of the past three years.

    b. Calculate MAD and MSE for these three years.

    c. Determine the forecast for next year.

13.14. Reconsider Problem 13.13. Notice the steady trend upward in the number of applications over the past three years—from 4,600 to 5,300 to 6,000. Suppose now that the Admissions Office of Ivy College had been able to foresee this kind of trend and so had decided to use exponential smoothing with trend to do the forecasting. Suppose also that the initial estimates just over three years ago had been *average value = 3,900* and *trend = 700*. Then, with any values of the smoothing constants, the forecasts obtained by this forecasting method would have been exactly correct for all three years.

    Illustrate this fact by doing the calculations to obtain these forecasts when the smoothing constant is $\alpha = 0.25$ and the trend smoothing constant is $\beta = 0.25$.

13.15.* Exponential smoothing with trend, with a smoothing constant of $\alpha = 0.2$ and a trend smoothing constant of $\beta = 0.3$, is being used to forecast values in a time series. At this point, the last two values have been 535 and then 550. The last two forecasts have been 530 and then 540. The last estimate of trend has been 10. Use this information to forecast the next value in the time series.

13.16. The Healthwise Company produces a variety of exercise equipment. Healthwise management is very pleased with the increasing sales of its newest model of exercise bicycle. The sales during the last two months have been 4,655 and then 4,935.

    Management has been using exponential smoothing with trend, with a smoothing constant of $\alpha = 0.1$ and a trend smoothing constant of $\beta = 0.2$, to forecast sales for the next month each time. The forecasts for the last two months were 4,720 and then 4,975. The last estimate of trend was 240.

    Calculate the forecast of sales for next month.

13.17.* Ben Swanson, owner and manager of Swanson's Department Store, has decided to use statistical forecasting to get a better handle on the demand for his major products. However, Ben now needs to decide which forecasting method is most appropriate for each category of product. One category is major household appliances, such as washing machines, which have a relatively stable sales level. Monthly sales of washing machines last year are shown below.

Month	Sales	Month	Sales	Month	Sales
January	23	May	22	September	21
February	24	June	27	October	29
March	22	July	20	November	23
April	28	August	26	December	28

  a. Considering that the sales level is relatively stable, which of the most basic forecasting methods—the last-value method, the averaging method, or the moving-average method—do you feel would be most appropriate for forecasting future sales? Why?

E b. Use the last-value method retrospectively to determine what the forecasts would have been for the last 11 months of last year. What are MAD and MSE?

E c. Use the averaging method retrospectively to determine what the forecasts would have been for the last 11 months of last year. What are MAD and MSE?

E d. Use the moving-average method with $n = 3$ retrospectively to determine what the forecasts would have been for the last nine months of last year. What are MAD and MSE?

  e. Use their MAD values to compare the three methods.

  f. Use their MSE values to compare the three methods.

  g. Do you feel comfortable in drawing a definitive conclusion about which of the three forecasting methods should be the most accurate in the future based on these 12 months of data?

E13.18. Reconsider Problem 13.17. Ben Swanson now has decided to use the exponential smoothing method to forecast future sales of washing machines, but he needs to decide on which smoothing constant to use. Using an initial estimate of 24, apply this method retrospectively to the 12 months of last year with $\alpha = 0.1, 0.2, 0.3, 0.4$, and 0.5. Compare MAD for these five values of the smoothing constant α. Then do the same with MSE.

13.19. Reconsider Problem 13.17. For each of the forecasting methods specified in parts *b, c,* and *d,* use the forecasting module in your Interactive Management Science Modules to obtain the requested forecasts. Then use the accompanying graph that plots both the sales data and forecasts to answer the following questions for these forecasting methods.

  a. Based on your examination of the graphs for the three forecasting methods, which method do you feel is doing the best job of forecasting with the given data? Why?

  b. Ben Swanson now has found that an error was made in determining the sales for April, but he has not yet obtained the corrected sales figure. For each of the three forecasting methods, Ben wants to know which of the original monthly forecasts would change now because of changing the sales figure for April. Answer this question by dragging vertically the blue dot that corresponds to April sales and observing which of the red dots (corresponding to monthly forecasts) move.

  c. Repeat part *a* if the sales for April change from 28 to 16.

  d. Repeat part *a* if the sales for April change from 28 to 40.

13.20. Management of the Jackson Manufacturing Corporation wishes to choose a statistical forecasting method for forecasting total sales for the corporation. Total sales (in millions of dollars) for each month of last year are shown below.

Month	Sales	Month	Sales	Month	Sales
January	126	May	153	September	147
February	137	June	154	October	151
March	142	July	148	November	159
April	150	August	145	December	166

      a. Note how the sales level is shifting significantly from month to month—first trending upward and then dipping down before resuming an upward trend. Assuming that similar patterns would continue in the future, evaluate how well you feel each of the five forecasting methods introduced in Section 13.3 would perform in forecasting future sales.

E   *b.* Apply the last-value method, the averaging method, and the moving-average method (with $n = 3$) retrospectively to last year's sales and compare their MAD values. Then compare their MSE values.

E   *c.* Using an initial estimate of 120, apply the exponential smoothing method retrospectively to last year's sales with $\alpha = 0.1, 0.2, 0.3, 0.4$, and 0.5. Compare both MAD and MSE for these five values of the smoothing constant α.

E   *d.* Using initial estimates of 120 for the average value and 10 for the trend, apply exponential smoothing with trend retrospectively to last year's sales. Use all combinations of the smoothing constants where $\alpha = 0.1, 0.3$, or 0.5 and $\beta = 0.1, 0.3$, or 0.5. Compare both MAD and MSE for these nine combinations.

       e. Which one of the above forecasting methods would you recommend that management use? Using this method, what is the forecast of total sales for January of the new year?

13.21.   Reconsider Problem 13.20. Use the lessons learned from the CCW case study to address the following questions.

       a. What might be causing the significant shifts in total sales from month to month that were observed last year?

       b. Given your answer to part *a,* how might the basic statistical approach to forecasting total sales be improved?

       c. Describe the role of managerial judgment in applying the statistical approach developed in part *b.*

13.22.   Reconsider Problem 13.20. For each of the forecasting methods specified in parts *b, c,* and *d* (with smoothing constants $\alpha = 0.5$ and $\beta = 0.5$ as needed), use the forecasting module in your Interactive Management Science Modules to obtain the requested forecasts. Then use the accompanying graph that plots both the sales data and forecasts to answer the following questions for these forecasting methods.

       a. Based on your examination of the graphs for the five forecasting methods, which method do you feel is doing the best job of forecasting with the given data? Why?

       b. Management now has been informed that an error was made in calculating the sales for April, but a corrected sales figure has not yet been obtained. Therefore, for each of the five forecasting methods, management wants to know which of the original monthly forecasts would change now because of changing the sales figure for April. Answer this question by dragging vertically the blue dot that corresponds to April sales and observing which of the red dots (corresponding to monthly forecasts) move.

       c. Repeat part *a* if the sales for April change from 150 to 125.

       d. Repeat part *a* if the sales for April change from 150 to 175.

E13.23.   Choosing an appropriate value of the smoothing constant α is a key decision when applying the exponential smoothing method. When relevant historical data exist, one approach to making this decision is to apply the method retrospectively to these data with different values of α and then choose the value of α that gives the smallest MAD. Use this approach for choosing α with each of the following time series representing monthly sales. In each case, use an initial estimate of 50 and compare $\alpha = 0.1, 0.2, 0.3, 0.4$, and 0.5.

       a. 51, 48, 52, 49, 53, 49, 48, 51, 50, 49

       b. 52, 50, 53, 51, 52, 48, 52, 53, 49, 52

       c. 50, 52, 51, 55, 53, 56, 52, 55, 54, 53

13.24.   Reconsider Problem 13.23. For each of the three cases, use CB Predictor to determine the best value of α by selecting only *single exponential smoothing* in step 6 and clicking Preview in step 10. Also obtain a forecast of the next observation in each of these time series.

E13.25.   The choice of the smoothing constants, α and β, has a considerable effect on the accuracy of the forecasts obtained by using exponential smoothing with trend. For each of the following time series, set $\alpha = 0.2$ and then compare MAD obtained with $\beta = 0.1, 0.2, 0.3, 0.4$, and 0.5. Begin with initial estimates of 50 for the average value and 2 for the trend.

 a. 52, 55, 55, 58, 59, 63, 64, 66, 67, 72, 73, 74

 b. 52, 55, 59, 61, 66, 69, 71, 72, 73, 74, 73, 74

 c. 52, 53, 51, 50, 48, 47, 49, 52, 57, 62, 69, 74

13.26.   Reconsider Problem 13.25. For each of the three cases, use CB Predictor to determine the best values of both α and β by selecting only *double exponential smoothing* in step 6 and clicking Preview in step 10. Also obtain a forecast of the next observation in each of these time series.

13.27.   The Andes Mining Company mines and ships copper ore. The company's sales manager, Juanita Valdes, has been using the moving-average method based on the last three years of sales to forecast the demand for the next year. However, she has become dissatisfied with the inaccurate forecasts being provided by this method.

 The annual demands (in tons of copper ore) over the past 10 years are 382, 405, 398, 421, 426, 415, 443, 451, 446, 464.

 a. Explain why this pattern of demands inevitably led to significant inaccuracies in the moving-average forecasts.

E   *b.* Determine the moving-average forecasts for the past seven years. What are MAD and MSE? What is the forecast for next year?

E   *c.* Determine what the forecasts would have been for the past 10 years if the exponential smoothing method had been used instead with an initial estimate of 380 and a smoothing constant of α = 0.5. What are MAD and MSE? What is the forecast for next year?

E   *d.* Determine what the forecasts would have been for the past 10 years if exponential smoothing with trend had been used instead. Use initial estimates of 370 for the average value and 10 for the trend, with smoothing constants α = 0.25 and β = 0.25.

 e. Based on the MAD and MSE values, which of these three methods do you recommend using hereafter?

 f. Use CB Predictor to compare the moving-average method, exponential smoothing method, and exponential smoothing with trend (with the best choice of smoothing constants), so that CB Predictor then can select the best of these methods for this particular series of demands. Also obtain the forecast for next year with the selected method.

13.28.   Reconsider Problem 13.27. For each of the forecasting methods specified in parts *b, c,* and *d,* use the forecasting module in your Interactive Management Science Modules to obtain the requested forecasts. After examining the accompanying graph that plots both the demand data and forecasts, write a one-sentence description for each method regarding whether its plot of forecasts tends to lie below or above or at about the same level as the demands being forecasted. Then use these conclusions to select one of the methods to recommend using hereafter.

E13.29.*   The Pentel Microchip Company has started production of its new microchip. The first phase in this production is the wafer fabrication process. Because of the great difficulty in fabricating acceptable wafers, many of these tiny wafers must be rejected because they are defective. Therefore, management places great emphasis on continually improving the wafer fabrication process to increase its *production yield* (the percentage of wafers fabricated in the current lot that are of acceptable quality for producing microchips).

 So far, the production yields of the respective lots have been 15 percent, 21 percent, 24 percent, 32 percent, 37 percent, 41 percent, 40 percent, 47 percent, 51 percent, and 53 percent. Use exponential smoothing with trend to forecast the production yield of the next lot. Begin with initial estimates of 10 percent for the average value and 5 percent for the trend. Use smoothing constants of α = 0.2 and β = 0.2.

13.30.   The Centerville Water Department provides water for the entire town and outlying areas. The number of acre-feet of water consumed in each of the four seasons of the three preceding years is shown below.

Season	Year 1	Year 2	Year 3
Winter	25	27	24
Spring	47	46	49
Summer	68	72	70
Fall	42	39	44

E   *a.* Determine the seasonal factors for the four seasons.

E   *b.* After considering seasonal effects, use the last-value method to forecast water consumption next winter.

c. Assuming that each of the forecasts for the next three seasons is correct, what would the last-value method forecast as the water consumption in each of the four seasons next year?

E   *d.* After considering seasonal effects, use the averaging method to forecast water consumption next winter.

E   *e.* After considering seasonal effects, use the moving-average method based on four seasons to forecast water consumption next winter.

E   *f.* After considering seasonal effects, use the exponential smoothing method with an initial estimate of 46 and a smoothing constant of $\alpha = 0.1$ to forecast water consumption next winter.

E   *g.* Compare both the MAD and MSE values of these four forecasting methods when they are applied retrospectively to the last three years.

13.31.   Reconsider Problem 13.7. Ralph Billett realizes that the last-value method is considered to be the naive forecasting method, so he wonders whether he should be using another method. Therefore, he has decided to use the available Excel templates that consider seasonal effects to apply various statistical forecasting methods retrospectively to the past three years of data and compare both their MAD and MSE values.

E   *a.* Determine the seasonal factors for the four quarters.

E   *b.* Apply the last-value method.

E   *c.* Apply the averaging method.

E   *d.* Apply the moving-average method based on the four most recent quarters of data.

E   *e.* Apply the exponential smoothing method with an initial estimate of 25 and a smoothing constant of $\alpha = 0.25$.

E   *f.* Apply exponential smoothing with trend with smoothing constants of $\alpha = 0.25$ and $\beta = 0.25$. Use initial estimates of 25 for the average value and 0 for the trend.

E   *g.* Compare both the MAD and MSE values for these methods. Use the one with the smallest MAD to forecast sales in Quarter 1 of next year.

h. Use the forecast in part *g* and the seasonal factors to make long-range forecasts now of the sales in the remaining quarters of next year.

E13.32.   Transcontinental Airlines maintains a computerized forecasting system to forecast the number of customers in each fare class who will fly on each flight in order to allocate the available reservations to fare classes properly. For example, consider *economy-class customers* flying in midweek on the noon flight from New York to Los Angeles. The following table shows the average number of such passengers during each month of the year just completed. The table also shows the seasonal factor that has been assigned to each month based on historical data.

Month	Average Number	Seasonal Factor	Month	Average Number	Seasonal Factor
January	68	0.90	July	94	1.17
February	71	0.88	August	96	1.15
March	66	0.91	September	80	0.97
April	72	0.93	October	73	0.91
May	77	0.96	November	84	1.05
June	85	1.09	December	89	1.08

a. After considering seasonal effects, compare both the MAD and MSE values for the last-value method, the averaging method, the moving-average method (based on the most recent three months), and the exponential smoothing method (with an initial estimate of 80 and a smoothing constant of $\alpha = 0.2$) when they are applied retrospectively to the past year.

b. Use the forecasting method with the smallest MAD value to forecast the average number of these passengers flying in January of the new year.

13.33. Reconsider Problem 13.32. The economy is beginning to boom so the management of Transcontinental Airlines is predicting that the number of people flying will steadily increase this year over the relatively flat (seasonally adjusted) level of last year. Since the forecasting methods considered in Problem 13.32 are relatively slow in adjusting to such a trend, consideration is being given to switching to exponential smoothing with trend.

Subsequently, as the year goes on, management's prediction proves to be true. The following table shows the corresponding average number of passengers in each month of the new year.

Month	Average Number	Month	Average Number	Month	Average Number
January	75	May	85	September	94
February	76	June	99	October	90
March	81	July	107	November	106
April	84	August	108	December	110

E   *a.* Repeat part *a* of Problem 13.32 for the two years of data.

E   *b.* After considering seasonal effects, apply exponential smoothing with trend to just the new year. Use initial estimates of 80 for the average value and 2 for the trend, along with smoothing constants of $\alpha = 0.2$ and $\beta = 0.2$. Compare MAD for this method to the MAD values obtained in part *a.* Then do the same with MSE.

E   *c.* Repeat part *b* when exponential smoothing with trend is begun at the beginning of the first year and then applied to both years, just like the other forecasting methods in part *a.* Use the same initial estimates and smoothing constants except change the initial estimate of trend to 0.

d. Based on these results, which forecasting method would you recommend that Transcontinental Airlines use hereafter?

e. One month later (January), the average number of passengers is 97. Use CB Predictor to apply exponential smoothing with seasonality and trend to all the data. Identify the values of the smoothing constants (including the smoothing constant for seasonal factors) that CB Predictor concludes are the best values. Also obtain forecasts (as of the end of January) of the average number of passengers in each subsequent month of the third year.

13.34. Quality Bikes is a wholesale firm that specializes in the distribution of bicycles. In the past, the company has maintained ample inventories of bicycles to enable filling orders immediately, so informal rough forecasts of demand were sufficient to make the decisions on when to replenish inventory. However, the company's new president, Marcia Salgo, intends to run a tighter ship. Scientific inventory management is to be used to reduce inventory levels and minimize total variable inventory costs. At the same time, Marcia has ordered the development of a computerized forecasting system based on statistical forecasting that considers seasonal effects. The system is to generate three sets of forecasts—one based on the moving-average method, a second based on the exponential smoothing method, and a third based on exponential smoothing with trend. The average of these three forecasts for each month is to be used for inventory management purposes.

The following table gives the available data on monthly sales of 10-speed bicycles over the past three years. The last column also shows monthly sales this year, which is the first year of operation of the new forecasting system.

Month	Past Sales Year 1	Year 2	Year 3	Current Sales This Year
January	352	317	338	364
February	329	331	346	343
March	365	344	383	391
April	358	386	404	437
May	412	423	431	458
June	446	472	459	494
July	420	415	433	468
August	471	492	518	555
September	355	340	309	387
October	312	301	335	364
November	567	629	594	662
December	533	505	527	581

E   *a.* Determine the seasonal factors for the 12 months based on past sales.

E   *b.* After considering seasonal effects, apply the moving-average method based on the most recent three months to forecast monthly sales for each month of this year.

E   *c.* After considering seasonal effects, apply the exponential smoothing method to forecast monthly sales this year. Use an initial estimate of 420 and a smoothing constant of $\alpha = 0.2$.

E   *d.* After considering seasonal effects, apply exponential smoothing with trend to forecast monthly sales this year. Use initial estimates of 420 for the average value and 0 for the trend, along with smoothing constants of $\alpha = 0.2$ and $\beta = 0.2$.

e. Compare both the MAD and MSE values obtained in parts *b, c,* and *d.*

f. Calculate the combined forecast for each month by averaging the forecasts for that month obtained in parts *b, c,* and *d.* Then calculate MAD for these combined forecasts.

g. Based on these results, what is your recommendation for how to do the forecasts next year?

h. Combining the data on past sales for years 1, 2, and 3 and the current sales for this year, use CB Predictor to compare exponential smoothing with seasonality and exponential smoothing with seasonality and trend (with the best choice of smoothing constants), so that CB Predictor then can select the best of these methods for this particular set of sales data. Also obtain the forecasts (as of the end of this year) for each month of next year with the selected method.

13.35.* Long a market leader in the production of heavy machinery, the Spellman Corporation recently has been enjoying a steady increase in the sales of its new lathe. The sales over the past 10 months are shown below.

Month	Sales	Month	Sales
1	430	6	514
2	446	7	532
3	464	8	548
4	480	9	570
5	498	10	591

Because of this steady increase, management has decided to use *causal forecasting,* with the month as the independent variable and sales as the dependent variable, to forecast sales in the coming months.

a. Plot these data on a two-dimensional graph with the month on the horizontal axis and sales on the vertical axis.

E   *b.* Find the formula for the linear regression line that fits these data.

c. Plot this line on the graph constructed in part *a.*

d. Use this line to forecast sales in month 11.

e. Use this line to forecast sales in month 20.

f. What does the formula for the linear regression line indicate is roughly the average growth in sales per month?

13.36.   Reconsider Problems 13.13 and 13.14. Since the number of applications for admission submitted to Ivy College has been increasing at a steady rate, causal forecasting can be used to forecast the number of applications in future years by letting the year be the independent variable and the number of applications be the dependent variable.

a. Plot the data for Years 1, 2, and 3 on a two-dimensional graph with the year on the horizontal axis and the number of applications on the vertical axis.

b. Since the three points in this graph line up in a straight line, this straight line is the linear regression line. Draw this line.

E   *c.* Find the formula for this linear regression line.

d. Use this line to forecast the number of applications for each of the next five years (Years 4 through 8).

e. As these next years go on, conditions change for the worse at Ivy College. The favorable ratings in the national surveys that had propelled the growth in applications turn unfavorable. Consequently, the number of applications turn out to be 6,300 in Year 4 and 6,200 in

Year 5, followed by sizable drops to 5,600 in Year 6 and 5,200 in Year 7. Does it still make sense to use the forecast for Year 8 obtained in part *d*? Explain.

E   *f.* Plot the data for all seven years. Find the formula for the linear regression line based on all these data and plot this line. Use this formula to forecast the number of applications for Year 8. Does the linear regression line provide a close fit to the data? Given this answer, do you have much confidence in the forecast it provides for Year 8? Does it make sense to continue to use a linear regression line when changing conditions cause a large shift in the underlying trend in the data?

E   *g.* Apply exponential smoothing with trend to all seven years of data to forecast the number of applications in Year 8. Use initial estimates of 3,900 for the average and 700 for the trend, along with smoothing constants of $\alpha = 0.5$ and $\beta = 0.5$. When the underlying trend in the data stays the same, causal forecasting provides the best possible linear regression line (according to the method of least squares) for making forecasts. However, when changing conditions cause a shift in the underlying trend, what advantage does exponential smoothing with trend have over causal forecasting?

13.37. Reconsider Problem 13.27. Despite some fluctuations from year to year, note that there has been a basic trend upward in the annual demand for copper ore over the past 10 years. Therefore, by projecting this trend forward, causal forecasting can be used to forecast demands in future years by letting the year be the independent variable and the demand be the dependent variable.

   a. Plot the data for the past 10 years (years 1 through 10) on a two-dimensional graph with the year on the horizontal axis and the demand on the vertical axis.

E   *b.* Find the formula for the linear regression line that fits these data.

   c. Plot this line on the graph constructed in part *a*.

   d. Use this line to forecast demand next year (Year 11).

   e. Use this line to forecast demand in Year 15.

   f. What does the formula for the linear regression line indicate is roughly the average growth in demand per year?

   g. Use the forecasting module in your Interactive Management Science Modules to generate a graph of the data and the linear regression line. Then experiment with the data to see how the linear regression line shifts as you drag any of the data points up or down.

13.38. Luxury Cruise Lines has a fleet of ships that travel to Alaska repeatedly every summer (and elsewhere during other times of the year). A considerable amount of advertising is done each winter to help generate enough passenger business for that summer. With the coming of a new winter, a decision needs to be made about how much advertising to do this year.

   The following table shows the amount of advertising (in thousands of dollars) and the resulting sales (in thousands of passengers booked for a cruise) for each of the past five years.

Amount of advertising ($1,000s)	225	400	350	275	450
Sales (thousands of passengers)	16	21	20	17	23

   a. To use causal forecasting to forecast sales for a given amount of advertising, which need to be the dependent variable and the independent variable?

   b. Plot the data on a graph.

E   *c.* Find the formula for the linear regression line that fits these data. Then plot this line on the graph constructed in part *b*.

   d. Forecast the sales that would be attained by expending $300,000 on advertising.

   e. Estimate the amount of advertising that would need to be done to attain a booking of 22,000 passengers.

   f. According to the linear regression line, about how much increase in sales can be attained on the average per $1,000 increase in the amount of advertising?

13.39.   Reconsider Problem 13.38. Use the forecasting module in your Interactive Management Science Modules to generate the linear regression line. On the resulting graph that shows this line and the five data points (as blue dots), note that the leftmost data point, the middle data point, and the rightmost data point all lie very close to the line. You can see how the linear regression line shifts as any one of these data points moves up or down by moving your mouse onto the blue dot at this point and dragging it vertically.

For each of these three data points, determine whether the linear regression line shifts above or below this point or whether it still passes essentially through it when the following change is made in one of these data points (but none of the others).

a. Change the sales from 16 to 19 when the amount of advertising is 225.

b. Change the sales from 23 to 26 when the amount of advertising is 450.

c. Change the sales from 20 to 23 when the amount of advertising is 350.

13.40. To support its large fleet, North American Airlines maintains an extensive inventory of spare parts, including wing flaps. The number of wing flaps needed in inventory to replace damaged wing flaps each month depends partially on the number of flying hours for the fleet that month, since increased usage increases the chances of damage.

The following table shows both the number of replacement wing flaps needed and the number of thousands of flying hours for the entire fleet for each of several recent months.

Thousands of flying hours	162	149	185	171	138	154
Number of wing flaps needed	12	9	13	14	10	11

a. Identify the dependent variable and the independent variable for doing causal forecasting of the number of wing flaps needed for a given number of flying hours.

b. Plot the data on a graph.

E *c.* Find the formula for the linear regression line.

d. Plot this line on the graph constructed in part *b.*

e. Forecast the average number of wing flaps needed in a month in which 150,000 flying hours are planned.

f. Repeat part *e* for 200,000 flying hours.

g. Use the forecasting module in your Interactive Management Science Modules to generate a graph of the data and the linear regression line. Then experiment with the data to see how the linear regression line shifts as you drag any of the data points up or down.

E13.41. Joe Barnes is the owner of Standing Tall, one of the major roofing companies in town. Much of the company's business comes from building roofs on new houses. Joe has learned that general contractors constructing new houses typically will subcontract the roofing work about two months after construction begins. Therefore, to help him develop long-range schedules for his work crews, Joe has decided to use county records on the number of housing construction permits issued each month to forecast the number of roofing jobs on new houses he will have two months later.

Joe has now gathered the following data for each month over the past year, where the second column gives the number of housing construction permits issued in that month and the third column shows the number of roofing jobs on new houses that were subcontracted out to Standing Tall in that month.

Month	Permits	Jobs	Month	Permits	Jobs
January	323	19	July	446	34
February	359	17	August	407	37
March	396	24	September	374	33
April	421	23	October	343	30
May	457	28	November	311	27
June	472	32	December	277	22

Use a causal forecasting approach to develop a forecasting procedure for Joe to use hereafter.

Case 13-1

Finagling the Forecasts

Mark Lawrence has been pursuing a vision for more than two years. This pursuit began when he became frustrated in his role as director of Human Resources at Cutting Edge, a large company manufacturing computers and computer peripherals. At that time, the Human Resources Department under his direction provided records and benefits administration to the 60,000 Cutting Edge employees throughout the United States, and 35 separate records and benefits administration centers existed across the country. Employees contacted these records and benefits centers to obtain information about dental plans and stock options, change tax forms and personal information, and process leaves of absence and retirements. The decentralization of these administration centers caused numerous headaches for Mark. He had to deal with employee complaints often since each center interpreted company policies differently—communicating inconsistent and sometimes inaccurate answers to employees. His department also suffered high operating costs since operating 35 separate centers created inefficiency.

His vision? To centralize records and benefits administration by establishing one administration center. This centralized records and benefits administration center would perform two distinct functions: data management and customer service. The data management function would include updating employee records after performance reviews and maintaining the human resource management system. The customer service function would include establishing a call center to answer employee questions concerning records and benefits and to process records and benefits changes over the phone.

One year after proposing his vision to management, Mark received the go-ahead from Cutting Edge corporate headquarters. He prepared his "to do" list—specifying computer and phone systems requirements, installing hardware and software, integrating data from the 35 separate administration centers, standardizing record-keeping and response procedures, and staffing the administration center. Mark delegated the systems requirements, installation, and integration jobs to a competent group of technology specialists. He took on the responsibility of standardizing procedures and staffing the administration center.

Mark had spent many years in human resources and therefore had little problem with standardizing record-keeping and response procedures. He encountered trouble in determining the number of representatives needed to staff the center, however. He was particularly worried about staffing the call center since the representatives answering phones interact directly with customers—the 60,000 Cutting Edge employees. The customer service representatives would receive extensive training so that they would know the records and benefits policies backwards and forwards—enabling them to answer questions accurately and process changes efficiently. Overstaffing would cause Mark to suffer the high costs of training unneeded representatives and paying the surplus representatives the high salaries that go along with such an intense job. Understaffing would cause Mark to continue to suffer the headaches from customer complaints—something he definitely wanted to avoid.

The number of customer service representatives Mark needed to hire depended on the number of calls that the records and benefits call center would receive. Mark therefore needed to forecast the number of calls that the new centralized center would receive. He approached the forecasting problem by using judgmental forecasting. He studied data from one of the 35 decentralized administration centers and learned that the decentralized center had serviced 15,000 customers and had received 2,000 calls per month. He concluded that since the new centralized center would service four times the number of customers—60,000 customers—it would receive four times the number of calls—8,000 calls per month.

Mark slowly checked off the items on his "to do" list, and the centralized records and benefits administration center opened one year after Mark had received the go-ahead from corporate headquarters.

Now, after operating the new center for 13 weeks, Mark's call center forecasts are proving to be terribly inaccurate. The number of calls the center receives is roughly three times as large as the 8,000 calls per month that Mark had forecasted. Because of demand overload, the call center is slowly going to hell in a handbasket. Customers calling the center must wait an average of five minutes before speaking to a representative, and Mark is receiving numerous complaints. At the same time, the customer service representatives are unhappy and on the verge of quitting because of the stress created by the demand overload. Even corporate headquarters has become aware of the staff and service inadequacies, and executives have been breathing down Mark's neck demanding improvements.

Mark needs help, and he approaches you to forecast demand for the call center more accurately.

Luckily, when Mark first established the call center, he realized the importance of keeping operational data, and he provides you with the number of calls received on each day of the week over the last 13 weeks. The data (shown next) begins in week 44 of the last year and continues to week 5 of the current year.

	Monday	**Tuesday**	**Wednesday**	**Thursday**	**Friday**
Week 44	1,130	851	859	828	726
Week 45	1,085	1,042	892	840	799
Week 46	1,303	1,121	1,003	1,113	1,005
Week 47	2,652	2,825	1,841	0	0
Week 48	1,949	1,507	989	990	1,084
Week 49	1,260	1,134	941	847	714
Week 50	1,002	847	922	842	784
Week 51	823	0	0	401	429
Week 52/1	1,209	830	0	1,082	841
Week 2	1,362	1,174	967	930	853
Week 3	924	954	1,346	904	758
Week 4	886	878	802	945	610
Week 5	910	754	705	729	772

Mark indicates that the days where no calls were received were holidays.

a. Mark first asks you to forecast daily demand for the next week using the data from the past 13 weeks. You should make the forecasts for all the days of the next week now (at the end of week 5), but you should provide a different forecast for each day of the week by treating the forecast for a single day as being the actual call volume on that day.

   1. From working at the records and benefits administration center, you know that demand follows "seasonal" patterns within the week. For example, more employees call at the beginning of the week when they are fresh and productive than at the end of the week when they are planning for the weekend. You therefore realize that you must account for the seasonal patterns and adjust the data that Mark gave you accordingly. What is the seasonally adjusted call volume for the past 13 weeks?

   2. Using the seasonally adjusted call volume, forecast the daily demand for the next week using the last-value forecasting method.

   3. Using the seasonally adjusted call volume, forecast the daily demand for the next week using the averaging forecasting method.

   4. Using the seasonally adjusted call volume, forecast the daily demand for the next week using the moving-average forecasting method. You decide to use the five most recent days in this analysis.

   5. Using the seasonally adjusted call volume, forecast the daily demand for the next week using the exponential smoothing forecasting method. You decide to use a smoothing constant of 0.1 because you believe that demand without seasonal effects remains relatively stable. Use the daily call volume average over the past 13 weeks for the initial estimate.

b. After one week, the period you have forecasted passes. You realize that you are able to determine the accuracy of your forecasts because you now have the actual call volumes from the week you had forecasted. The actual call volumes are shown below.

	Monday	**Tuesday**	**Wednesday**	**Thursday**	**Friday**
Week 6	723	677	521	571	498

For each of the forecasting methods, calculate the mean absolute deviation for the method and evaluate the performance of the method. When calculating the mean absolute deviation, you should use the actual forecasts you found in part *a* above. You should not recalculate the forecasts based on the actual values. In your evaluation, provide an explanation for the effectiveness or ineffectiveness of the method.

You realize that the forecasting methods that you have investigated do not provide a great degree of accuracy, and you decide to use a creative approach to forecasting that combines the statistical and judgmental approaches. You know that Mark had used data from one of the 35 decentralized records and benefits administration centers to perform his original forecasting. You therefore suspect that call volume data exists for this decentralized center. Because the decentralized centers performed the same functions as the new centralized center currently performs, you decide that the call volumes from the decentralized center will help you forecast the call volumes for the new centralized center. You simply need to understand how the decentralized volumes relate to the new centralized volumes. Once you understand this relationship, you can use the call volumes from the decentralized center to forecast the call volumes for the centralized center.

You approach Mark and ask him whether call center data exist for the decentralized center. He tells you that data exist, but data do not exist in the format that you need. Case volume data—not call volume data—exist. You do not understand the distinction, so Mark continues his explanation. There are two types of demand data—case volume data and call volume data. Case volume data count the actions taken by the representatives at the call center. Call volume data count the number of calls answered by the representatives at the call center. A case may require one call or multiple calls to resolve it. Thus, the number of cases is always less than or equal to the number of calls.

You know you only have case volume data for the decentralized center, and you certainly do not want to compare apples and oranges. You therefore ask if case volume data exist for the new centralized center. Mark gives you a wicked grin and nods his head. He sees where you are going with your forecasts, and he tells you that he will have the data for you within the hour.

c. At the end of the hour, Mark arrives at your desk with two data sets: weekly case volumes for the decentralized center and weekly case volumes for the centralized center. You ask Mark if he has data for daily case volumes, and he tells you that he does not. You therefore first have to forecast the weekly demand for the next week and then break this weekly demand into daily demand.

The decentralized center was shut down last year when the new centralized center opened, so you have the decentralized case data spanning from week 44 of two years ago to week 5 of last year. You compare this decentralized data to the centralized data spanning from week 44 of last year to week 5 of this year. The weekly case volumes are shown in the table below.

	Decentralized Case Volume	**Centralized Case Volume**
Week 44	612	2,052
Week 45	721	2,170
Week 46	693	2,779
Week 47	540	2,334
Week 48	1,386	2,514
Week 49	577	1,713
Week 50	405	1,927
Week 51	441	1,167
Week 52/1	655	1,549
Week 2	572	2,126
Week 3	475	2,337
Week 4	530	1,916
Week 5	595	2,098

1. Find a mathematical relationship between the decentralized case volume data and the centralized case volume data.

2. Now that you have a relationship between the weekly decentralized case volume and the weekly centralized case volume, you are able to forecast the weekly case volume for the new center. Unfortunately, you do not need the weekly case volume; you need the daily call volume. To calculate call volume from case volume, you perform further analysis and determine that each case generates an average of 1.5 calls. To calculate daily call volume from weekly call volume, you decide to use the seasonal factors as conversion factors. Given the following case volume data from the decentralized center for week 6 of last year, forecast the daily call volume for the new center for week 6 of this year.

	Week 6
Decentralized case volume	613

3. Using the actual call volumes given in part *b,* calculate the mean absolute deviation and evaluate the effectiveness of this forecasting method.

d. Which forecasting method would you recommend Mark use and why? As the call center continues its operation, how would you recommend improving the forecasting procedure?

Learning objectives

After completing this chapter, you should be able to

1. Describe the elements of a queueing model.

2. Identify the characteristics of the probability distributions that are commonly used in queueing models.

3. Give many examples of various types of queueing systems that are commonly encountered.

4. Identify the key measures of performance for queueing systems and the relationships between these measures.

5. Describe the main types of basic queueing models.

6. Determine which queueing model is most appropriate from a description of the queueing system being considered.

7. Apply a queueing model to determine the key measures of performance for a queueing system.

8. Describe how differences in the importance of customers can be incorporated into priority queueing models.

9. Describe some key insights that queueing models provide about how queueing systems should be designed.

10. Apply economic analysis to determine how many servers should be provided in a queueing system.

Chapter **Fourteen**

Queueing Models

In Great Britain, waiting lines are referred to as *queues,* so this term has been adopted by management scientists.

Queues (waiting lines) are a part of everyday life. We all wait in queues to buy a movie ticket, make a bank deposit, pay for groceries, mail a package, obtain food in a cafeteria, start a ride in an amusement park, and so on. We have become accustomed to considerable amounts of waiting, but still we get annoyed by unusually long waits.

However, having to wait is not just a petty personal annoyance. The amount of time that a nation's populace wastes by waiting in queues is a major factor in both the quality of life there and the efficiency of the nation's economy. For example, before its dissolution, the USSR was notorious for the tremendously long queues that its citizens frequently had to endure just to purchase basic necessities. Even in the United States today, it has been estimated that Americans spend 37,000,000,000 hours per year waiting in queues. If this time could be spent productively instead, it would amount to nearly 20 million person-years of useful work each year!

Even this staggering figure does not tell the whole story of the impact of causing excessive waiting. Great inefficiencies also occur because of other kinds of waiting than people standing in line. For example, making machines wait to be repaired may result in lost production. Vehicles (including ships and trucks) that need to wait to be unloaded may delay subsequent shipments. Airplanes waiting to take off or land may disrupt later travel schedules. Delays in telecommunication transmissions due to saturated lines may cause data glitches. Causing manufacturing jobs to wait to be performed may disrupt subsequent production. Delaying service jobs beyond their due dates may result in lost future business.

Making customers, employees, or jobs wait very long in a queue can have serious consequences for any business.

Queueing theory is the study of waiting in all these various guises. It uses *queueing models* to represent the various types of *queueing systems* (systems that involve queues of some kind) that arise in practice. Formulas for each model indicate how the corresponding queueing system should perform, including the average amount of waiting that will occur, under a variety of circumstances.

Queueing models often are used to determine how much service capacity should be provided to a queue to avoid excessive waiting.

Therefore, these queueing models are very helpful for determining how to operate a queueing system in the most effective way. Providing too much service capacity to operate the system involves excessive costs. But not providing enough service results in excessive waiting and all its unfortunate consequences. The models enable finding an appropriate balance between the cost of service and the amount of waiting.

The first three sections of this chapter describe the elements of queueing models, give various examples of important queueing systems to which these models can be applied, and present measures of performance for these queueing systems. Section 14.4 then introduces a case study that will be carried through most of the chapter. Three subsequent sections present the most important queueing models in the context of analyzing the case study. Section 14.8 summarizes some key insights from the case study for designing queueing systems. After describing how economic analysis can be used to determine the number of servers to provide in a queueing system, the chapter then concludes by describing some award-winning applications of queueing models.

14.1 ELEMENTS OF A QUEUEING MODEL

We begin by describing the basic type of queueing system assumed by the queueing models in this chapter.

A Basic Queueing System

Figure 14.1 depicts a typical **queueing system. Customers** arrive individually to receive some kind of service. If an arrival cannot be served immediately, that customer joins a **queue** (waiting line) to await service. (The queue does not include the customers who are currently being served.) One or more **servers** at the service facility provide the service. Each customer is individually served by one of the servers and then departs. You can see a demonstration of a queueing system in action by viewing the Waiting Line module in your Interactive Management Science Modules at **www.mhhe.com/hillier2e** or on the CD-ROM.

The customers coming to some queueing systems are vehicles or machines or jobs instead of people.

For some queueing systems, the customers are *people.* However, in other cases, the customers might be *vehicles* (e.g., airplanes waiting to take off on a runway), *machines* (e.g., machines waiting to be repaired), or other *items* (e.g., jobs waiting for a manufacturing operation).

A server commonly is an individual person. However, it might instead be a crew of people working together to serve each customer. The server can also be a machine, a vehicle, an electronic device, and so forth.

In most cases, the queue is just an ordinary waiting line. However, it is not necessary for the customers to be standing in line in front of a physical structure that constitutes the service facility. They might be sitting in a waiting room. They might even be scattered throughout an area waiting for a server to come to them (e.g., stationary machines needing repair).

The next section presents many more examples of important queueing systems that fit Figure 14.1 and the above description. All the queueing models in this chapter also are based on this figure.

However, we also should mention that more complicated kinds of queueing systems sometimes do arise in practice. For example, a server might serve a group of customers simultaneously. Customers also might arrive in a group rather than individually. Impatient customers might leave before receiving service. The queueing system might include multiple queues, one for each server, with customers occasionally switching queues. It might include multiple service facilities, where some customers need to go to more than one of the facilities to obtain all the required service. (This last type of queueing system is referred to as a *queueing network.*) Such queueing systems also are quite important, but we will not delve into the more complicated queueing models that have been developed to deal with them. The next two chapters will describe another technique (computer simulation) that often is used to analyze complex queueing systems.

An Example

Herr Cutter is a German barber who runs a one-man barber shop. Thus, his shop is a basic queueing system for which he is the only server.

Herr Cutter opens his shop at 8:00 A.M. each weekday morning. Table 14.1 shows his queueing system in action over the beginning of a typical morning. For each of his first five customers, the table indicates when the customer arrived, when his haircut began, how long the haircut took, and when the haircut was finished.

FIGURE 14.1

A basic queueing system, where each customer is indicated by *C* and each server by *S*. Although this figure shows four servers, some queueing systems (including the example in this section) have only a single server.

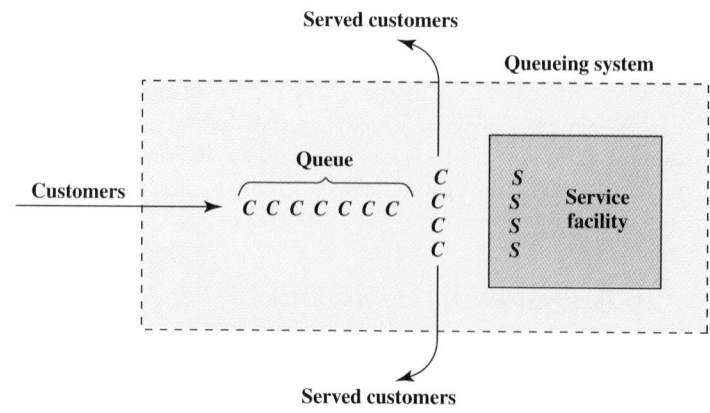

TABLE 14.1
The Data for Herr Cutter's First Five Customers

Customer	Time of Arrival	Haircut Begins	Duration of Haircut	Haircut Ends
1	8:03	8:03	17 minutes	8:20
2	8:15	8:20	21 minutes	8:41
3	8:25	8:41	19 minutes	9:00
4	8:30	9:00	15 minutes	9:15
5	9:05	9:15	20 minutes	9:35
6	9:43	—	—	—

FIGURE 14.2
The evolution of the number of customers in Herr Cutter's barber shop over the first 100 minutes (from 8:00 to 9:40), given the data in Table 14.1.

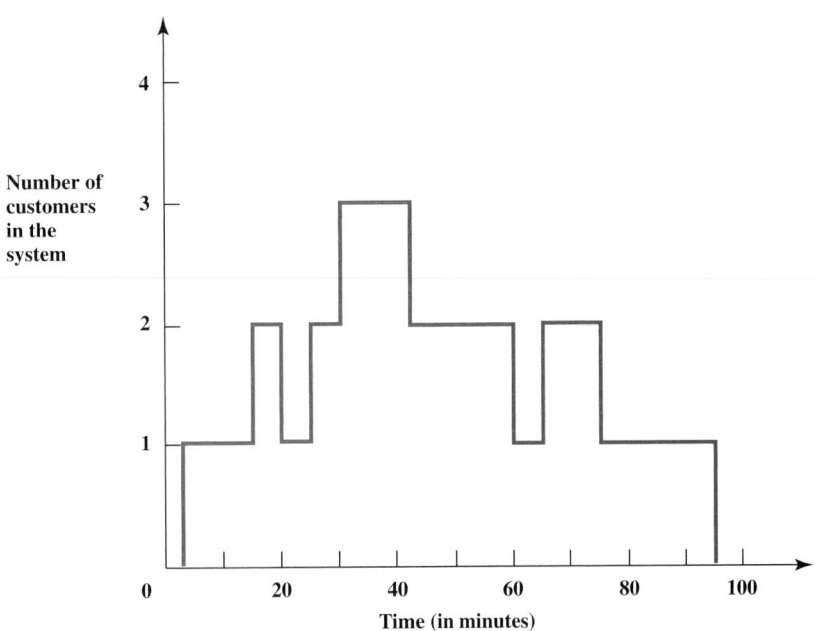

Figure 14.2 plots the number of customers in this queueing system over the first 100 minutes. This number includes both the customers waiting to begin a haircut and the one already under way. Thus, the number of customers in the queue (only those waiting to begin) is one less (except that this number is zero when the number of customers in the queueing system is zero).

Referring to this example, let us now look at the kinds of assumptions that the queueing models make about the different parts of a basic queueing system.

Arrivals

The times between consecutive arrivals to a queueing system are called the **interarrival times.** For Herr Cutter's barber shop, the second column of Table 14.1 indicates that the interarrival times on this particular morning are 12 minutes, 10 minutes, 5 minutes, 35 minutes, and 38 minutes.

*The times between consecutive arrivals to a queueing system (called **interarrival times**) commonly are highly variable.*

This high variability in the interarrival times is common for queueing systems. As with Herr Cutter, it usually is impossible to predict just how long until the next customer will arrive.

However, after gathering a lot more data such as in the second column of Table 14.1, it does become possible to do two things:

1. Estimate the *expected number* of arrivals per unit time. This quantity is normally referred to as the **mean arrival rate.** (The symbol for this quantity is λ, which is the Greek letter lambda.)

2. Estimate the *form* of the probability distribution of interarrival times.

The mean of this distribution actually comes directly from item 1. Since

$$\lambda = \text{Mean arrival rate for customers coming to the queueing system}$$

the mean of the probability distribution of interarrival times is

$$\frac{1}{\lambda} = \text{Expected interarrival time}$$

For example, after gathering more data, Herr Cutter finds that 300 customers have arrived over a period of 100 hours.[1] Therefore, the estimate of λ is

$$\lambda = \frac{300 \text{ customers}}{100 \text{ hours}} = 3 \text{ customers per hour on the average}$$

The corresponding estimate of the expected interarrival time is

$$\frac{1}{\lambda} = \frac{1}{3} \text{ hour between customers on the average}$$

Most queueing models assume that the *form* of the probability distribution of interarrival times is an *exponential distribution,* as explained below.

The Exponential Distribution for Interarrival Times

Figure 14.3 shows the shape of an exponential distribution, where the height of the curve at various times represents the relative likelihood of those times occurring. Note in the figure how the highest points on the curve are at very small times and then the curve drops down "exponentially" as time increases. This indicates a high likelihood of small interarrival times, well under the mean. However, the long tail of the distribution also indicates a small chance of a very large interarrival time, much larger than the mean. All this is characteristic of interarrival times observed in practice. Several customers may arrive quickly. Then there may be a long pause until the next arrival.

This variability in interarrival times makes it impossible to predict just when future arrivals will occur. When the variability is as large as for the exponential distribution, this is referred to as having *random arrivals.*

> For most queueing systems, the servers have no control over when customers will arrive. In this case, the customers generally arrive *randomly.* Having *random arrivals* means that arrival times are completely unpredictable in the sense that the chance of an arrival in the next minute always is just the same (no more and no less) as for any other minute. It does not matter how long it has been since the last arrival occurred. The only distribution of interarrival times that fits having random arrivals is the exponential distribution.

FIGURE 14.3

The shape of an exponential distribution, commonly used in queueing models as the distribution of interarrival times (and sometimes as the distribution of service times as well).

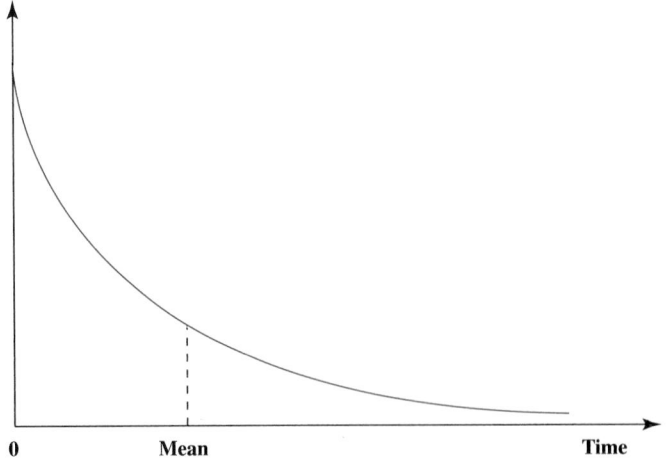

[1] The count of 300 arrivals includes those customers who enter the barber shop but decide not to stay because the wait would be too long. The effect of these immediate departures is analyzed in the supplement to this chapter on the CD-ROM.

14.1 *Elements of a Queueing Model* **657**

Interarrival times have an exponential distribution when the customers arrive randomly. In this case, the time of the next arrival always is completely uninfluenced by when the last arrival occurred (called the lack-of-memory property).

The fact that the probability of an arrival in the next minute is completely uninfluenced by when the last arrival occurred is called the **lack-of-memory property** (or the *Markovian property*). This is a strange property, because it implies that the probability distribution of the *remaining time from now* until the next arrival occurs always is the same, regardless of whether the last arrival occurred just now or a long time ago. Therefore, this distribution of the remaining time from now is the same as the distribution of the *total interarrival time* given in Figure 14.2. (This is what causes the probability of an arrival in the next minute to always be the same.) Although this concept of a lack-of-memory property takes some getting used to, it is an integral part of what is meant by having random arrivals.

The Queue

The queue is where customers wait before being served. For Herr Cutter's barber shop, the customers in the queue sit in chairs (other than the barber's chair) while waiting to begin a haircut.

Because there are two ways of counting the customers, queueing models distinguish between them with the following terminology.

> The **number of customers in the queue** (or *queue size* for short) is the number of customers waiting for service to begin. The **number of customers in the system** is the number in the queue *plus* the number currently being served.

The queue does not include the customers who are already being served.

For example, Figure 14.1 shows 7 customers in the queue plus 4 more being served by the 4 servers, so a total of 11 customers are in the system. Since Herr Cutter is the only server for his queueing system, the number of customers in his queue is one less than the number of customers in the system shown in Figure 14.2 (except that the number in the queue is zero when the number in the system is zero).

The **queue capacity** is the maximum number of customers that can be held in the queue. An **infinite queue** is one in which, for all practical purposes, an unlimited number of customers can be held there. When the capacity is small enough that it needs to be taken into account, then the queue is called a **finite queue.** During those times when a finite queue is full, any arriving customers will immediately leave.

Herr Cutter's queue actually is a finite queue. The queue capacity is three since he provides only three chairs (other than the barber's chair) for waiting. (He has found that his customers typically are unwilling to wait for a haircut when there already are three customers waiting in front of them.)

All the queueing models in this chapter assume an infinite queue, so no limit is placed on the number of customers that can be held in the queue.

Unless specified otherwise, queueing models conventionally assume that the queue is an *infinite* queue. (All the models in this chapter make this assumption, but the chapter supplement on the CD-ROM introduces a model that assumes a finite queue. This model is used to analyze Herr Cutter's barber shop.)

The **queue discipline** refers to the order in which members of the queue are selected to begin service. The most common is *first-come, first-served* (FCFS). However, other possibilities include *random selection,* some *priority procedure,* or even *last-come, first-served.* (This last possibility occurs, for example, when jobs brought to a machine are piled on top of the preceding jobs and then the machine operator takes the next job to be performed off the top of the pile.)

Section 14.7 will focus on priority queueing models. Otherwise, the queueing models throughout the chapter make the conventional assumption that the queue discipline is first-come, first-served.

Service

For a basic queueing system, each customer is served individually by one of the servers. A system with more than one server is called a *multiple-server system,* whereas a *single-server system* has just one server (as for Herr Cutter's barber shop).

When a customer enters service, the elapsed time from the beginning to the end of the service is referred to as the **service time.** Service times generally vary from one customer to the next. However, basic queueing models assume that the service time has a particular probability distribution, independent of which server is providing the service.

The symbol used for the *mean* of the service-time distribution is

$$\frac{1}{\mu} = \text{Expected service time}$$

where μ is the Greek letter mu. The interpretation of μ itself is

μ = Expected number of service completions per unit time for a single
continuously busy server

where this quantity is called the **mean service rate.** For example, Herr Cutter's expected time to give a haircut is

$$\frac{1}{\mu} = 20 \text{ minutes} = \frac{1}{3} \text{ hour per customer}$$

so his mean service rate is

$$\mu = 3 \text{ customers per hour}$$

Different queueing models provide a choice of service-time distributions, as described next.

Some Service-Time Distributions

The most popular choice for the probability distribution of service times is the **exponential distribution,** which has the shape already shown in Figure 14.3. The main reason for this choice is that this distribution is *much* easier to analyze than any other. Although this distribution provides an excellent fit for *interarrival times* for most situations, this is much less true for *service times.* Depending on the nature of the queueing system, the exponential distribution can provide either a reasonable approximation or a gross distortion of the true service-time distribution. Caution is needed.

As suggested by Figure 14.3, the exponential distribution implies that many of the service times are quite short (considerably less than the mean) but occasional service times are very long (far more than the mean). This accurately describes the kind of queueing system where many customers have just a small amount of business to transact with the server but occasional customers have a lot of business. For example, if the server is a bank teller, many customers have just a single check to deposit or cash, but occasional customers have many transactions.

However, the exponential distribution is a poor fit for the kind of queueing system where service consists basically of a fixed sequence of operations that require approximately the same time for every customer. For example, this describes the situation where the server is an ATM machine. Although there may be small variations in service times from one customer to the next, these times generally are just about the same.

For the latter kind of queueing system, a much better approximation would be to assume **constant service times,** that is, the same service time for every customer. (This also is referred to as having a *degenerate distribution* for service times.)

The exponential and degenerate distributions represent two rather extreme cases regarding the amount of variability in the service times. A standard measure of the amount of variability is the *standard deviation* of the distribution, denoted by σ. For example, a value of σ that is nearly as large as the mean $(1/\mu)$ of a service-time distribution is a large standard deviation indicating a high degree of variability. For the two distributions considered above, the standard deviations are

$\sigma = \text{Mean}$ for the exponential distribution

$\sigma = 0$ for the degenerate distribution (constant service times)

For some queueing systems, the service times have much less variability than implied by the exponential distribution, so queueing models that use other distributions should be considered.

For many queueing systems, the amount of variability in the service times falls somewhere between those for the exponential and degenerate distributions. Another service-time distribution that fills this middle ground is the **Erlang distribution.** (It is named after A. K. Erlang, a Danish mathematician in the early twentieth century whose work for the Copenhagen Telephone Company in analyzing the waiting of telephone calls began the development of queue-

The Erlang distribution provides a more realistic service-time distribution for many queueing systems.

ing theory.) This distribution has a parameter k, called the *shape parameter,* that determines the standard deviation σ. In particular,

$$\sigma = \frac{1}{\sqrt{k}} \text{ mean}$$

where k is allowed to be any positive integer ($k = 1,2,3, \ldots$). Figure 14.4 shows the shape of this distribution for several values of k.

When $k = 1$, this figure indicates that the shape of the Erlang distribution is the same as for the exponential distribution. This is no coincidence, because the two distributions actually are the same for $k = 1$. For larger values of k, the figure shows that the high point of the distribution (called the *mode*) no longer is at 0. In fact,

$$\text{Mode} = \left(\frac{k-1}{k} \right) \text{ mean}$$

Thus, as k increases, the mode moves closer and closer to the mean and, simultaneously, the spread (standard deviation) of the distribution decreases. When $k = \infty$, so $\sigma = 0$, the Erlang distribution coincides with the degenerate distribution. Consequently, both of the previous service-time distributions can be thought of as special cases of the Erlang distribution.

Certain queueing models use still other service-time distributions, but these three are the most important.

Table 14.2 compares the standard deviation of these three service-time distributions for several values of k. Note that quadrupling k decreases the standard deviation by a factor of ½.

When choosing a service-time distribution for a queueing model to redesign a queueing system that is already in operation, a good approach is to take some observations of the actual service times. The sample average provides an estimate of the mean of the distribution. Similarly, the square root of the sample variance estimates the standard deviation. The right column of Table 14.2 then can be used to determine the distribution and (for the Erlang distribution) the integer value of k that gives the column value closest to this estimate of the standard deviation.

When designing a new queueing system, it becomes necessary to estimate what the mean and standard deviation of the service-time distribution will be, based on previous experience with similar systems.

If the standard deviation is expected to be reasonably close to the mean, practitioners normally choose the exponential distribution because of its convenience.

FIGURE 14.4

The shape of several Erlang distributions with the same mean but with different values of the shape parameter k.

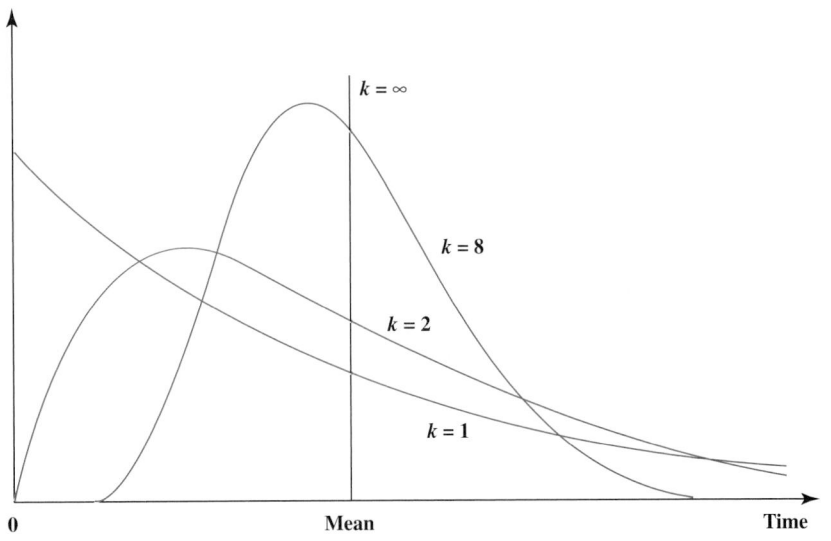

TABLE 14.2
The Relationship between the Standard Deviation and the Mean for Service-Time Distributions

Distribution	Standard Deviation
Exponential	mean
Degenerate (constant)	0
Erlang, any k ($k = 1, 2, \ldots$)	$\dfrac{1}{\sqrt{k}}$ mean
Erlang, $k = 2$	$\dfrac{1}{\sqrt{2}}$ mean
Erlang, $k = 4$	$\dfrac{1}{2}$ mean
Erlang, $k = 8$	$\dfrac{1}{2\sqrt{2}}$ mean
Erlang, $k = 16$	$\dfrac{1}{4}$ mean

Labels for Queueing Models

To identify which probability distribution is being assumed for service times (and for interarrival times), a queueing model for a basic queueing system conventionally is labeled as follows:

$$\underset{\uparrow}{\text{—}} / \overset{\downarrow}{\text{—}} / \text{—} \leftarrow \text{Number of servers}$$

Distribution of service times (top arrow); Distribution of interarrival times (bottom arrow)

The symbols used for the possible distributions (for either service times or interarrival times) are

M = Exponential distribution (Markovian)

D = Degenerate distribution (constant times)

E_k = Erlang distribution (shape parameter = k)

The first symbol identifies the distribution of interarrival times and the second symbol identifies the distribution of service times.

For example, the $M/M/1$ model is the single-server model that assumes that both interarrival times and service times have an exponential distribution. The $M/M/2$ model is the corresponding model with two servers. Letting s be the symbol that represents the number of servers, the $M/M/s$ model is the corresponding model that permits any number of servers. Similarly, the $M/D/s$ model has exponential interarrival times, constant service times, and any desired number of servers. The $M/E_k/2$ model has exponential interarrival times, Erlang service times (with any desired value of k), and two servers.

Interarrival times also can have either a degenerate or Erlang distribution instead of an exponential distribution. The $D/M/s$ model has constant interarrival times, exponential service times, and any desired number of servers. The $E_k/M/2$ model has Erlang interarrival times, exponential service times, and two servers.

All the queueing models mentioned above will be considered at least briefly later in the chapter, along with results on how well such queueing systems perform.

There even are queueing models (with limited results) that permit choosing *any* probability distribution for the interarrival times or for the service times. The symbols used in these cases are

GI = General independent interarrival-time distribution (any arbitrary distribution allowed)

G = General service-time distribution (any arbitrary distribution allowed)

Thus, the $GI/M/s$ model allows any interarrival-time distribution (with independent interarrival times), exponential service times, and any desired number of servers. The $M/G/1$ model has exponential interarrival times and one server but allows any service-time distribution. (We will touch later on just the latter model.)

Summary of Model Assumptions

To summarize, we list below the assumptions generally made by queueing models of a basic queueing system. Each of these assumptions should be taken for granted unless a model explicitly states otherwise.

1. Interarrival times are independent and identically distributed according to a specified probability distribution.

2. All arriving customers enter the queueing system and remain there until service has been completed.

3. The queueing system has a single *infinite queue,* so that the queue will hold an unlimited number of customers (for all practical purposes).

4. The queue discipline is first-come, first-served.

5. The queueing system has a specified number of servers, where each server is capable of serving any of the customers.

6. Each customer is served individually by any one of the servers.

7. Service times are independent and identically distributed according to a specified probability distribution.

Review *Questions*

1. What might the customers of a queueing system be other than people?

2. What might the server of a queueing system be other than an individual person?

3. What is the relationship between the mean arrival rate and the mean of the probability distribution of interarrival times?

4. What is the shape of the exponential distribution?

5. What is the relationship between the mean and the standard deviation of the exponential distribution?

6. What is meant by customers arriving *randomly?* Which distribution of interarrival times corresponds to random arrivals?

7. What is the distinction between the number of customers in the queue and the number in the system?

8. What is the conventional assumption made by most queueing models about the queue capacity? About the queue discipline?

9. What is the relationship between the mean of the service-time distribution and the mean service rate for a single continuously busy server?

10. What are the three most important service-time distributions? How do their standard deviations compare?

11. What information is provided by the three parts of the label for queueing models?

14.2 SOME EXAMPLES OF QUEUEING SYSTEMS

Our description of queueing systems in the preceding section may appear relatively abstract and applicable to only rather special practical situations. On the contrary, queueing systems are surprisingly prevalent in a wide variety of contexts. To broaden your horizons on the applicability of queueing models, let us take a brief look at a variety of examples of real queueing systems.

One important class of queueing systems that we all encounter in our daily lives is **commercial service systems,** where outside customers receive service from commercial organizations. The first column of Table 14.3 lists a sampling of typical commercial service systems. Each of these is a queueing system whose customers and servers are identified in the second and third columns.

Most of these examples involve the customers coming to the server at a fixed location, where a physical queue forms if customers need to wait to begin service. However, for the plumbing

A commercial service system is a queueing system where a commercial organization provides a service to customers from outside the organization.

TABLE 14.3
Examples of Commercial Service Systems That Are Queueing Systems

Type of System	Customers	Server(s)
Barber shop	People	Barber
Bank teller service	People	Teller
ATM machine service	People	ATM machine
Checkout at a store	People	Checkout clerk
Plumbing services	Clogged pipes	Plumber
Ticket window at a movie theater	People	Cashier
Check-in counter at an airport	People	Airline agent
Brokerage service	People	Stockbroker
Gas station	Cars	Pump
Call center for ordering goods	People	Telephone agent
Call center for technical assistance	People	Technical representative
Travel agency	People	Travel agent
Automobile repair shop	Car owners	Mechanic
Vending services	People	Vending machine
Dental services	People	Dentist
Roofing services	Roofs	Roofer

TABLE 14.4
Examples of Internal Service Systems That Are Queueing Systems

Type of System	Customers	Server(s)
Secretarial services	Employees	Secretary
Copying services	Employees	Copy machine
Computer programming services	Employees	Programmer
Mainframe computer	Employees	Computer
First-aid center	Employees	Nurse
Faxing services	Employees	Fax machine
Materials-handling system	Loads	Materials-handling unit
Maintenance system	Machines	Repair crew
Inspection station	Items	Inspector
Production system	Jobs	Machine
Semiautomatic machines	Machines	Operator
Tool crib	Machine operators	Clerk

An internal service system is a queueing system where the customers receiving service are internal to the organization providing the service.

A transportation service system is a queueing system involving transportation so that either the customers or the server(s) are vehicles.

services and roofing services examples, the server comes to the customers, so the customers in the queue are geographically dispersed. In several other cases, the service is performed over the telephone, perhaps after some customers have been placed on hold (the queue).

Organizations also have their own **internal service systems,** where the customers receiving service are internal to the organization. As the examples in Table 14.4 indicate, these too are queueing systems. In some cases, the customers are employees of the organizations. In other examples, the customers are loads to be moved, machines to be repaired, items to be inspected, jobs to be performed, and so forth.

Transportation service systems provide another important category of queueing systems. Table 14.5 gives some examples. For several of the cases, the vehicles involved are the customers. For others, each vehicle is a server. A few of the examples go beyond the basic kind of queueing system described in the preceding section. In particular, the airline service and elevator service examples involve a server that serves a group of customers simultaneously rather than just one at a time. The queue in the parking lot example has zero capacity because arriving cars (customers) go elsewhere to park if all the parking spaces are occupied (all the servers are busy).

There are many additional examples of important queueing systems that may not fit nicely into any of the above categories. For example, a judicial system is a queueing network, where the courts are service facilities, the judges (or panels of judges) are the servers, and the cases waiting to be tried are the customers. Various health care systems, such as hospital emergency

TABLE 14.5
Examples of Transportation Service Stations That Are Queueing Systems

Type of System	Customers	Server(s)
Highway tollbooth	Cars	Cashier
Truck loading dock	Trucks	Loading crew
Port unloading area	Ships	Unloading crew
Airplanes waiting to take off	Airplanes	Runway
Airplanes waiting to land	Airplanes	Runway
Airline service	People	Airplane
Taxicab service	People	Taxicab
Elevator service	People	Elevator
Fire department	Fires	Fire truck
Parking lot	Cars	Parking space
Ambulance service	People	Ambulance

rooms, also are queueing systems. For example, x-ray machines and hospital beds can be viewed as servers in their own queueing systems. The initial applications of queueing theory (thanks to A. K. Erlang with the Copenhagen Telephone Company) were to telephone engineering, and the general area of telecommunications continues to be a very important area of application. Furthermore, we all have our own personal queues—homework assignments, books to be read, and so forth. Queueing systems do indeed pervade many areas of society.

Review Questions

1. What are commercial service systems? Also give a new example (not included in Table 14.3) of such a system, including identifying the customers and server.

2. What are internal service systems? Also give a new example (not included in Table 14.4) of such a system, including identifying the customers and server.

3. What are transportation service systems? Also give a new example (not included in Table 14.5) of such a system, including identifying the customers and server.

14.3 MEASURES OF PERFORMANCE FOR QUEUEING SYSTEMS

Managers who oversee queueing systems are mainly concerned with two types of measures of performance:

1. How many customers typically are waiting in the queueing system?

2. How long do these customers typically have to wait?

These measures are somewhat related, since how long a customer has to wait is partially determined by how many customers are already there when this customer arrives. Which measure is of greater concern depends on the situation.

Choosing a Measure of Performance

Having customers wait in an internal service system causes lost productivity.

When the customers are internal to the organization providing the service (internal service systems), the first measure tends to be more important. In this situation, forcing customers to wait causes them to be unproductive members of the organization during the wait. For example, this is the case for machine operators waiting at a tool crib or for machines that are down waiting to be repaired. Having such customers wait causes *lost productivity,* where the amount of lost productivity is directly related to the number of waiting customers. The active members of the organization may be able to fill in for one or two idle members, but not for more.

Making customers wait too long in a commercial service system may result in lost profit from lost future business.

Commercial service systems (where outside customers receive service from commercial organizations) tend to place greater importance on the second measure. For such queueing systems, an important goal is to keep customers happy so they will return again. Customers are more concerned with how long they have to wait than with how many other customers are there. The consequence of making customers wait too long may be *lost profit from lost future business.*

Defining the Measures of Performance

The two measures of performance commonly are expressed in terms of their *expected values* (in the statistical sense). To do this, it is necessary to clarify whether we are counting customers only while they are in the queue (i.e., before service begins) or while they are anywhere in the queueing system (i.e., either in the queue or being served). These two ways of defining the two types of measures thereby give us four measures of performance. These four measures and their symbols are shown below.

L = Expected **number of customers in the system,** including those being served (the symbol L comes from *Line Length*)

These are four key measures of performance for any queueing system.

L_q = Expected **number of customers in the queue,** which excludes customers being served

W = Expected **waiting time in the system** (includes service time) for an individual customer (the symbol W comes from *Waiting* time)

W_q = Expected **waiting time in the queue** (excludes service time) for an individual customer

These definitions assume that the queueing system is in a **steady-state condition,** that is, the system is in its normal condition after operating for some time. During the initial *startup period* after a queueing system opens up with no customers there, it takes awhile for the expected number of customers to reach its normal level. After essentially reaching this level, the system is said to be in a steady-state condition. (This condition also rules out such abnormal operating conditions as a temporary "rush hour" jump in the mean arrival rate.)

The choice of whether to focus on the entire queueing system (L or W) or just on the queue (L_q or W_q) depends on the nature of the queueing system. For a hospital emergency room or a fire department, the queue (the time until service can begin) probably is more important. For an internal service system, the entire queueing system (the total number of members of the organization that are idle there) may be more important.

Relationships between L, W, L_q, and W_q

The only difference between W and W_q is that W includes the expected service time and W_q does not. Therefore, since $1/\mu$ is the symbol for the expected service time (where μ is called the *mean service rate*),

$$W = W_q + \frac{1}{\mu}$$

For example, if

W_q = ¾ hour waiting in the queue on the average

$\dfrac{1}{\mu}$ = ¼ hour service time on the average

then

$$W = \text{¾ hour} + \text{¼ hour}$$

$$= 1 \text{ hour waiting in the queueing system on the average}$$

This is a very handy formula for immediately obtaining either L or W from the other one.

Perhaps the most important formula in queueing theory provides a direct relationship between L and W. This formula is

$$L = \lambda W$$

where

λ = Mean arrival rate for customers coming to the queueing system

This is called **Little's formula,** in honor of the eminent management scientist John D. C. Little (a long-time faculty member at MIT), who provided the first rigorous proof of the formula in 1961.

To illustrate the formula, suppose that

$W = 1$ hour waiting in the queueing system on the average

$\lambda = 3$ customers per hour arrive on the average

It then follows that

$$L = (3 \text{ customers/hour})(1 \text{ hour})$$

$$= 3 \text{ customers in the queueing system on the average}$$

Here is an intuitive way to view Little's formula. Since L is the expected number of customers in the queueing system at any time, a customer looking back at the system after completing service should see L customers there on the average. With a first-come, first-served queue discipline, all L customers there normally would have arrived during this customer's waiting time in the queueing system. This waiting time is W on the average. Since λ is the expected number of arrivals per unit time, λW is the expected number of arrivals during this customer's waiting time in the system. Therefore, $L = \lambda W$.

Professor Little's proof that $L = \lambda W$ also applies to the relationship between L_q and W_q. Therefore, another version of Little's formula is

$$L_q = \lambda W_q$$

For example, if

$W_q = \frac{3}{4}$ hour waiting in the queue on the average

$\lambda = 3$ customers per hour arrive on the average

then

$$L_q = (3 \text{ customers/hour})(\tfrac{3}{4} \text{ hour})$$

$$= 2\tfrac{1}{4} \text{ customers in the queue on the average}$$

Combining the above relationships also gives the following direct relationship between L and L_q.

These expressions show the relationships between all four measures of performance.

$$L = \lambda W = \lambda \left(W_q + \frac{1}{\mu} \right)$$

$$= L_q + \frac{\lambda}{\mu}$$

For example, if $L_q = 2\tfrac{1}{4}$, $\lambda = 3$, and $\mu = 4$, then

$$L = 2\tfrac{1}{4} + \tfrac{3}{4} = 3 \text{ customers in the system on the average}$$

These relationships are extremely important because they enable all four of the fundamental quantities—L, W, L_q, and W_q—to be immediately determined as soon as one is found analytically. This situation is fortunate because some of these quantities often are much easier to find than others when a queueing model is solved from basic principles.

Using Probabilities as Measures of Performance

Managers frequently are interested in more than what happens *on the average* in a queueing system. In addition to wanting L, L_q, W, and W_q not to exceed target values, they also may be concerned with *worst-case scenarios*. What will be the *maximum* number of customers in the system (or in the queue) that will only be exceeded a small fraction of the time (that is, with a small probability)? What will be the *maximum* waiting time of customers in the system (or in the queue) that will only be exceeded a small fraction of the time? A manager might specify that the queueing system should be designed in such a way that these maximum numbers do not exceed certain values.

Meeting such a goal requires using the steady-state *probability distribution* of these quantities (the number of customers and the waiting time). For example, suppose that the goal is to have no more than three customers in the system at least 95 percent of the time. Using the notation

P_n = Steady-state probability of having exactly n customers in the system
(for $n = 0, 1, 2, \ldots$)

meeting this goal requires that

$$P_0 + P_1 + P_2 + P_3 \geq 0.95$$

Since waiting times vary from customer to customer, $\mathcal{W}$ has a probability distribution, whereas W is the mean of this distribution.

Similarly, suppose that another goal is that the waiting time in the system should not exceed two hours for at least 95 percent of the customers. Let the *random variable* $\mathcal{W}$ be the waiting time in the system for an individual customer while the system is in a steady-state condition. (Thus, W is the expected value of this random variable.) Using the probability distribution for this random variable, meeting the goal requires that

$$P(\mathcal{W} \leq 2 \text{ hours}) \geq 0.95$$

If the goal is stated in terms of the waiting time in the *queue* instead, then a different random variable $\mathcal{W}_q$ representing this waiting time would be used in the same way.

Formulas are available for calculating at least some of these probabilities for several of the queueing models considered later in the chapter. Excel templates in your MS Courseware will perform these calculations for you.

Review Questions

1. Which type of measure of performance of queueing systems tends to be more important when the customers are internal to the organization?
2. Which type of measure of performance tends to be more important for commercial service systems?
3. What are the four basic measures of performance based on expected values? What are their symbols?
4. What is meant by a queueing system being in a steady-state condition?
5. What is the formula that relates W and W_q?
6. What is Little's formula that relates L and W? That relates L_q and W_q?
7. What is the formula that relates L and L_q?
8. What kinds of probabilities can also be used as measures of performance of queueing systems?

14.4   A CASE STUDY: THE DUPIT CORP. PROBLEM

The Dupit Corporation is a long-time leader in the office photocopier marketplace. One reason for this leadership position is the service the company provides its customers. Dupit has enjoyed a reputation of excellent service and intends to maintain that reputation.

Some Background

Dupit has a service division that is responsible for providing high-quality support to the company's customers by promptly repairing the Dupit machines when needed. This work is done on the customer's site by the company's *service technical representatives,* more commonly known as **tech reps.**

Each tech rep currently is assigned his or her own territory for servicing the machines.

Each tech rep is given responsibility for a specified territory. This enables providing personalized service, since a customer sees the same tech rep on each service call. The tech rep generally feels like a one-person territory manager and takes pride in this role.

John Phixitt is the Dupit senior vice president in charge of the service division. He has spent his entire career with the company and actually began as a tech rep. While in this initial position, John took classes in the evening for several years to earn his business degree. Since then, he has moved steadily up the corporate ladder. He is well respected for his sound judgment and his thorough understanding of the company's business from the ground up.

John's years as a tech rep impressed upon him the importance of the tech rep's role as an ambassador of the company to its customers. He continues to preach this message regularly. He has established high personnel standards for becoming and remaining a tech rep and has built up the salaries accordingly. The morale in the division is quite high, largely through his efforts.

John also emphasizes obtaining regular feedback from a random sample of the company's customers on the quality of the service being provided. He likes to refer to this as keeping his ear to the ground. The customer feedback is channeled to both the tech reps and management for their information.

Another of John's themes is the importance of not overloading the tech reps. When he was a tech rep himself, the company policy had been to assign each tech rep enough machines in his or her territory that the tech rep would be active repairing machines 90 percent of the time (during an eight-hour working day). The intent was to maintain a high utilization of expensive personnel while providing some slack so that customers would not have to wait very long for repairs. John's own experience was that this did not work very well. He did have his idle periods about 10 percent of the time, which was helpful for catching up on his paperwork and maintaining his equipment. However, he also had frequent busy periods with many repair requests, including some long ones, and a large backlog of unhappy customers waiting for repairs would build up.

> Tech reps need considerable slack time to ensure providing prompt service to customers.

Therefore, when he was appointed to his current position, one of his first moves was to make the case to Dupit top management that tech reps needed to have more slack time to ensure providing prompt service to customers. A major part of his argument was that customer feedback indicated that the company was failing to deliver on the second and third parts of the company slogan given below.

1. High-quality products.

2. High-quality service.

3. All delivered efficiently.

The company president had been promoting this slogan for years and so found this argument persuasive. Despite continuing pressure to hold costs down, John won approval for changing company policy regarding tech reps as summarized below.

> Each tech rep's territory currently has approximately 150 machines, which requires a tech rep to be busy on service calls approximately 75 percent of the time.

Current Policy: Each tech rep's territory should be assigned enough machines so that the tech rep will be active repairing machines (or traveling to the repair site) approximately 75 percent of the time. When working continuously, each tech rep should be able to repair an average of four machines per day (an average of two hours per machine, including travel time). Therefore, to minimize customer waiting times, the goal is to have an average of three repair calls per working day. Since the company's machines now are averaging 50 work days between needing repairs, the target is to assign approximately 150 machines to each tech rep's territory.

Under this policy, the company now has nearly 10,000 tech reps, with a total payroll (including benefits) of approximately $600 million per year.

The Issue Facing Top Management

A long succession of very successful products has helped Dupit maintain its position as a market leader for many years. Furthermore, its latest product has been a particularly big winner. It is a color printer-copier that collates, staples, and so on, as well as having faxing capabilities. Thus, it is a state-of-the-art, all-in-one copier for the modern office. Sales have even exceeded the optimistic predictions made by the vice president for marketing.

However, the success of this product also has brought problems. The fact that the machine performs so many key functions makes it a vital part of the purchaser's office. The owner has great difficulty in getting along without it for even a few hours when it is down requiring

The company's new color printer-copier is such a vital part of each purchaser's office that a much higher level of service is required to reduce downtime.

repair. Consequently, even though the tech reps are giving the same level of service as they have in the past, complaints about intolerable waits for repairs have skyrocketed.

This crisis has led to an emergency meeting of top management, with John Phixitt the man on the spot. He assures his colleagues that service has not deteriorated in the least. There is agreement that the company is a victim of its own success. The new machine is so valuable that a much higher level of service is required.

After considerable discussion about how to achieve the needed service, Dupit's president suggests the following four-step approach to dealing with the problem.

1. Agree on a tentative new standard for the level of service that needs to be provided.

2. Develop some proposals for alternative approaches that might achieve this standard.

3. Have a management science team work with John Phixitt to analyze these alternative approaches in detail to evaluate the effectiveness and cost of each one.

4. Reconvene this group of top management to make a final decision on what to do.

The group agrees.

Discussion then turns to what the new standard should be for the level of service. John proposes that this standard should specify that a customer's average waiting time before the tech rep can respond to the request for a repair should not exceed some maximum quantity. The customer relations manager agrees and argues that this average waiting time should not exceed two hours (versus about six hours now). The group agrees to adopt two hours as the tentative standard, pending further analysis by the management science team.

The proposal is to reduce average waiting times before the repair process begins from six hours to two hours.

> **Proposed New Service Standard:** The average waiting time of customers before the tech rep begins the trip to the customer site to repair the machine should not exceed two hours.

Alternative Approaches to the Problem

After further discussion of various ideas about how to meet this service standard, the meeting concludes. The president asks the participants who had proposed some approach to think further about their idea. If they conclude that their idea should be a particularly sound approach to the problem, they are to send him a memorandum supporting that approach.

The president subsequently receives four memoranda supporting the approaches summarized below.

Approach Suggested by John Phixitt: Modify the current policy by decreasing the percentage of time that tech reps are expected to be active repairing machines. This involves simply decreasing the number of machines assigned to each tech rep and adding more tech reps. This approach would enable continuing the mode of operation for the service division that has served the company so well in the past while increasing the level of service to meet the new demands of the marketplace.

Approach Suggested by the Vice President for Engineering: Provide new state-of-the-art equipment to the tech reps that would substantially reduce the time required for the longer repairs. Although expensive, this would significantly reduce the average repair time. Perhaps more importantly, it would greatly reduce the variability of repair times, which might decrease average waiting times for repairs.

Approach Suggested by the Chief Financial Officer: Replace the current one-person tech rep territories by larger territories that would be served by multiple tech reps. Having teams of tech reps to back each other up during busy periods might decrease average waiting times for repairs enough that the company would not need to hire additional tech reps.

Approach Suggested by the Vice President for Marketing: Give owners of the new printer-copier priority for receiving repairs over the company's other customers. Since the complaints about slow service are coming mainly from these owners, this approach might give them the service they require while still giving adequate service to other customers.

Queueing models will be used to analyze each of the four proposed approaches.

The president is pleased to have four promising approaches to consider. As previously agreed, his next step is to set up a team of management scientists (three from the company plus an outside consultant) to work with John Phixitt in analyzing these approaches in detail. They are to report back to top management with their results and recommendations in six weeks.

Before reading further, we suggest that you think about these four alternative approaches and decide which one seems most promising. You then will be able to compare your conclusions with the results from the management science study.

The Management Science Team's View of the Problem

The management science team quickly recognizes that *queueing theory* will be a key technique for analyzing this problem. In particular, each tech rep's territory can be viewed as including the basic queueing system described below.

The Queueing System for Each Tech Rep

1. **The customers:** The machines needing repair.

2. **Customer arrivals:** The calls to the tech rep on his or her cellular telephone requesting repairs.

3. **The queue:** The machines waiting for repair to begin at their sites.

4. **The server:** The tech rep.

5. **Service time:** The total time the tech rep is tied up with a machine, either traveling to the machine site or repairing the machine. (Thus, a machine is viewed as leaving the queue and entering service when the tech rep begins the trip to the machine site.)

With the approach suggested by the chief financial officer (enlarge the territories with multiple tech reps for each territory), this single-server queueing system would be changed to a multiple-server queueing system.

The management science team now needs to decide which specific queueing model is most appropriate for analyzing each of the four approaches. You will see this story unfold in the next few sections while we are presenting various important queueing models.

Review
Questions

1. What is the company's current policy regarding the workload for tech reps?
2. What is the issue currently facing top management?
3. What is the proposed new service standard?
4. How many alternative approaches have been suggested for dealing with the issue facing top management?
5. Who now will be analyzing these approaches?
6. In the queueing system interpretation of this problem, what are the customers? The server?

14.5   SOME SINGLE-SERVER QUEUEING MODELS

Using the background on the elements of queueing models presented in Section 14.1, this section focuses on models of basic queueing systems having just one server. Key symbols introduced in Section 14.1 that will continue to be used here (and throughout the remainder of the chapter) are

λ = Mean arrival rate for customers coming to the queueing system

= Expected number of arrivals per unit time

μ = Mean service rate (for a continuously busy server)

= Expected number of service completions per unit time

Also recall that $1/\lambda$ is the *expected interarrival time* (the average time between the arrival of consecutive customers) and $1/\mu$ is the *expected service time* for each customer.

A new symbol for this section is

$$\rho = \frac{\lambda}{\mu}$$

The utilization factor plays a key role in the efficiency of a queueing system.

where ρ is the Greek letter rho. This quantity ρ is referred to as the **utilization factor,** because it represents the average fraction of time that the server is being utilized serving customers.

In the Dupit Corp. case study, under the company's current policy, a typical tech rep experiences

λ = 3 customers (machines needing repair) arriving per day on the average

μ = 4 service completions (repair completions) per day on the average when the tech rep is continuously busy

Since

$$\rho = \frac{3}{4} = 0.75$$

the tech rep is active repairing machines 75 percent of the time.

For each of the queueing models, we will consider the measures of performance introduced in Section 14.3. Because of the relationships between the four basic measures—L, L_q, W, and W_q—including Little's formula given in that section, recall that all four quantities can be calculated easily as soon as one of their values has been determined. Therefore, we sometimes will be focusing on just one of these measures of performance for the following models.

The *M/M/*1 Model

Using the labels for queueing models given near the end of Section 14.1, recall that the first symbol (M) in the $M/M/1$ label identifies the probability distribution of *interarrival times,* the second symbol (M) indicates the distribution of *service times,* and the third symbol (1) gives the number of servers. Since M is the symbol used for the *exponential distribution,* the $M/M/1$ model makes the following assumptions.

Assumptions

1. *Interarrival times* have an exponential distribution with a mean of $1/\lambda$. (See Figure 14.3 and the description of this distribution in Section 14.1.)

2. *Service times* have an exponential distribution with a mean of $1/\mu$.

3. The queueing system has 1 server.

As discussed in Section 14.1, the first assumption corresponds to having customers arrive *randomly.* Consequently, this assumption commonly is a valid one for real queueing systems.

The second assumption also is a reasonable one for those queueing systems where many service times are quite short (well under the mean) but occasional service times are very long. Some queueing systems fit this description, but some others do not even come close.

Although the second assumption is sometimes questionable, this model is widely used because it provides so many useful results.

Along with its multiple-server counterpart (considered in Section 14.6), the $M/M/1$ model is the most widely used queueing model. (It is even sometimes used for queueing systems that don't fit the second assumption very well.) A key reason is that this model has the most results readily available. Because the formulas are relatively simple, we give them for all the measures of performance below. (All these measures assume that the queueing system is in a *steady-state condition.*)

Using $\rho = \lambda/\mu$, two equivalent formulas for the *expected number of customers in the system* are

$$L = \frac{\rho}{1 - \rho} = \frac{\lambda}{\mu - \lambda}$$

Because of Little's formula ($L = \lambda W$), the *expected waiting time in the system* is

$$W = \frac{1}{\lambda} L = \frac{1}{\mu - \lambda}$$

Therefore, the *expected waiting time in the queue* (excludes service time) is

$$W_q = W - \frac{1}{\mu} = \frac{1}{\mu - \lambda} - \frac{1}{\mu} = \frac{\mu - (\mu - \lambda)}{\mu(\mu - \lambda)}$$

$$= \frac{\lambda}{\mu(\mu - \lambda)}$$

Applying the other version of Little's formula again ($L_q = \lambda W_q$), the *expected number of customers in the queue* (excludes customers being served) is

$$L_q = \lambda W_q = \frac{\lambda^2}{\mu(\mu - \lambda)} = \frac{\rho^2}{1 - \rho}$$

Even the formulas for the various probabilities are relatively simple. The probability of having exactly n customers in the system is

$$P_n = (1 - \rho)\rho^n \qquad \text{for } n = 0, 1, 2, \dots$$

Thus,

$$P_0 = 1 - \rho$$

$$P_1 = (1 - \rho)\rho$$

$$P_2 = (1 - \rho)\rho^2$$

.

.

.

The probability that the *waiting time in the system* exceeds some amount of time t is

$$P(W > t) = e^{-\mu(1 - \rho)t} \qquad \text{for } t \geq 0$$

The corresponding probability that the *waiting time in the queue* exceeds t is

$$P(W_q > t) = \rho e^{-\mu(1 - \rho)t} \qquad \text{for } t \geq 0$$

Since this waiting time in the queue is 0 if there are no customers in the system when an arrival occurs,

$$P(W_q = 0) = P_0 = 1 - \rho$$

All these formulas assume that the server has a manageable utilization factor ($\rho = \lambda/\mu$), that is, that

$$\rho < 1$$

(*All* single-server queueing models make this same assumption.) When $\rho > 1$, so that the mean arrival rate λ exceeds the mean service rate μ, the server is not able to keep up with the arrivals so the queueing system never reaches a steady-state condition. (This is even technically true when $\rho = 1$.)

The Excel template for the *M/M/s* model can be applied to this *M/M/*1 model by setting $s = 1$.

There is an Excel template for the *M/M/s* model in your MS Courseware that will calculate all these measures of performance for you if you wish. All you have to do is set $s = 1$ and then specify the values of λ and μ. Since λ and μ are the *estimated* values of the mean arrival rate and mean service rate, respectively, you then can conduct sensitivity analysis on λ and μ by rerunning the template for various other possible values. All this can be done in a matter of seconds.

In addition, an animated demonstration of an *M/M/s* queueing system in action—showing customers arriving, waiting in the system, and departing when their service is completed—is provided by the Waiting Line module in your Interactive Management Science Modules at **www.mhhe.com/hillier2e** or on the CD-ROM. After setting the values of s, λ, and μ and then viewing the queueing system in action (repeatedly if desired), the module will calculate *estimates* of L, L_q, W, and W_q by using the averages for the customers that have arrived so far. If the queueing system were to run an extremely long time, these estimates would be very close to the exact values for these measures of performance that are provided by the Excel template for this model.

Applying the *M/M/*1 Model to the Case Study under the Current Policy

The Dupit management science team begins its study by gathering some data on the experiences of some representative tech reps. They determine that the company's current policy regarding tech rep workloads (they are supposed to be busy repairing machines 75 percent of the time) is operating basically as intended. Although there is some variation from one tech rep to the next, they typically are averaging about three calls requesting repairs per day. They also are averaging about two hours per repair (including a little travel time), and so can average four repairs for each eight-hour working day that they are continuously repairing machines. This verifies that the best estimates of the daily rates for a typical tech rep's queueing system (where the tech rep is the server and the machines needing repairs are the customers) are a mean arrival rate of $\lambda = 3$ customers per day and a mean service rate of $\mu = 4$ customers per day (so $\rho = \lambda/\mu = 0.75$), just as assumed under the current policy. (Other time units, such as *hourly* rates rather than *daily* rates, could be used for λ and μ, but it is essential that the *same* time units be used for both.)

> Under the current policy, each tech rep is the server for his or her own queueing system where the machines needing repair are the customers.

The team also concludes that the customer arrivals (calls requesting repairs) are occurring *randomly,* so the first assumption of the *M/M/*1 model (an exponential distribution for interarrival times) is a good one for this situation. The team is less comfortable with the second assumption (an exponential distribution for service times), since the *total service time* (travel time plus repair time) never is extremely short as allowed by the exponential distribution. However, many service times are at least fairly short (well under the mean) and occasional service times are very long, which does fit the exponential distribution reasonably well. Furthermore, calculations with the data gathered on service times indicate that the standard deviation of the service-time distribution is just about as large as the mean (they are equal for the exponential distribution). Therefore, the team decides that it is reasonable to use the *M/M/*1 model to represent a typical tech rep's queueing system under the current policy.

> The *M/M/*1 model with $\lambda = 3$ and $\mu = 4$ provides a reasonable representation of each tech rep's queueing system.

The Excel template in Figure 14.5 shows the results from applying the various formulas for this model to this queueing system. Look first at the results at the top of column G. The expected number of machines needing repairs is $L = 3$. When excluding any machine that is currently being repaired, the expected number of machines waiting to begin service is $L_q = 2.25$. The expected waiting time of a machine, measured from when the service request is submitted to the tech rep until the repair is completed, is $W = 1$ day. When excluding the repair time, the expected waiting time to begin service is $W_q = 0.75$ day. (These results are treating a machine as moving from the queue into service when the tech rep begins the trip to the site of the machine.)

While gathering data, the management science team found that the average waiting time of customers until service begins on their failed machines is approximately six hours of an eight-hour workday (i.e., ¾ of a workday). The fact that this time agrees with the value of W_q yielded by the model gives further credence to the validity of the model for this application.

Now look at the results in column G for P_n (the probability of having exactly n customers in the system). With $P_0 = 0.25$, the tech rep will only be busy repairing machines 75 percent of the time (as indicated by the utilization factor of $\rho = 0.75$). Since $P_0 + P_1 + P_2 = 0.58$, the tech rep will have no more than two machines needing repair (including the one being worked on) well over half the time. However, he or she also will have *much* larger backlogs with some frequency. For example, $P_0 + P_1 + P_2 + \ldots + P_7 = 0.9$, which indicates that the tech rep will have *at least* eight machines needing repair (about two days' work or more) 10 percent of the time. With all the randomness inherent in such a queueing system (the great variability in

FIGURE 14.5 This spreadsheet shows the results from applying the *M/M*/1 model with λ = 3 and μ = 4 to the Dupit case study under the current policy. The equations for the *M/M*/1 model have been entered into the corresponding output cells, as shown at the bottom of the figure.

	A	B	C	D	E	F	G
1				*M/M*/1 Queueing Model for the Dupit Corp. Problem			
2							
3			**Data**				**Results**
4		λ =	3	(mean arrival rate)		*L* =	3
5		μ =	4	(mean service rate)		L_q=	2.25
6		*s* =	1	(# servers)			
7						W =	1
8		Pr(*W* > *t*) =	0.368			W_q=	0.75
9		when *t* =	1				
10						ρ =	0.75
11		Prob(*W$_q$* > *t*) =	0.276				
12		when *t* =	1			*n*	P_n
13						0	0.2500
14						1	0.1875
15						2	0.1406
16						3	0.1055
17						4	0.0791
18						5	0.0593
19						6	0.0445
20						7	0.0334
21						8	0.0250
22						9	0.0188
23						10	0.0141

Range Name	Cells
L	G4
Lambda	C4
L_q	G5
Mu	C5
n	F13:F38
P_0	G13
P_n	G13:G38
Rho	G10
s	C6
Time1	C9
Time2	C12
W	G7
W_q	G8

	B	C
8	Pr(*W*>*t*) =	=EXP(-Mu*(1-Rho)*C9)

	B	C
11	Prob(*W$_q$*>*t*) =	=Rho*EXP(-Mu*(1-Rho)*C12)

	F	G
4	*L* =	=Lambda/(Mu-Lambda)
5	L_q =	=Lambda)^2/(Mu*(Mu-Lambda)
6		
7	W =	=1/(Mu-Lambda)
8	W_q=	=Lambda/(Mu*(Mu-Lambda))
9		
10	ρ =	=Lambda/Mu
11		
12	*n*	P_n
13	0	=1-Rho
14	1	=(1-Rho)*Rho^n
15	2	=(1-Rho)*Rho^n
16	3	:
17	4	:

All the results from the *M/M*/1 model indicate that unacceptably long delays in repairing failed machines will occur too frequently under the current policy.

both interarrival times and service times), these very big backlogs (and many unhappy customers) will occur occasionally despite the tech rep only having a utilization factor of 0.75.

Finally, look at the results in cells C8:C12. By setting *t* = 1, the probability that a customer has to wait more than one day (eight work hours) before a failed machine is operational again is given as $P(W > 1 \text{ day}) = 0.368$. The probability of waiting more than one day before the repair begins is $P(W_q > 1 \text{ day}) = 0.276$.

Upon being shown all these results, John Phixitt comments that he understands better now why the complaints have been pouring in. No owner of such a vital machine as the new printer-copier should be expected to go more than a day (or even most of a day) before it is repaired.

Applying the *M/M/*1 Model to John Phixitt's Suggested Approach

The management science team now is ready to begin analyzing each of the suggested approaches for lowering to two hours (¼ workday) the average waiting time before service begins. Thus, the new constraint is that

$$W_q \leq \tfrac{1}{4} \text{ day}$$

The first approach, suggested by John Phixitt, is to modify the current policy by lowering a tech rep's utilization factor sufficiently to meet this new service requirement. This involves decreasing the number of machines assigned to each tech rep from about 150 to some smaller number. Since each machine needs repair about once every 50 work days on the average, decreasing the number of machines in a tech rep's territory results in decreasing the mean arrival rate λ from 3 to

> To meet the proposed new service standard that $W_q \leq \tfrac{1}{4}$ day, John Phixitt suggests reducing the number of machines assigned to each tech rep from 150 to some smaller number.

$$\lambda = \frac{\text{Number of machines assigned to tech rep}}{50}$$

With μ fixed at four, this decrease in λ will decrease the utilization factor, $\rho = \lambda/\mu$.

Since decreasing λ decreases W_q, the largest value of λ that has $W_q \leq$ ¼ day is the one that makes W_q equal to ¼ day. The easiest way to find this λ is by trial and error with the Excel template, trying various values of λ until one is found where $W_q = 0.25$. Figure 14.6 shows the template that gives this value of W_q by setting λ = 2. (By using the formula for W_q, it also is possible to solve algebraically to find λ = 2.)

Decreasing λ from three to two would require decreasing the target for the number of machines assigned to each tech rep from 150 to 100. This 100 is the *maximum* number that would satisfy the requirement that $W_q \leq$ ¼ day. With λ = 2 and μ = 4, the utilization factor for each tech rep would be only

> The *M/M/*1 model indicates that the number of machines assigned to each tech rep would need to be reduced to 100 with John Phixitt's approach.

$$\rho = \frac{\lambda}{\mu} = \frac{2}{4} = 0.5$$

Recall that the company's payroll (including benefits) for its nearly 10,000 tech reps currently is about $600 million annually. Decreasing the number of machines assigned to each tech rep from 150 to 100 would require hiring nearly 5,000 more tech reps to cover all the ma-

FIGURE 14.6

This application of the spreadsheet in Figure 14.5 shows that, when μ = 4, the *M/M/*1 model gives an expected waiting time to begin service of W_q = 0.25 day (the largest value that satisfies Dupit's proposed new service standard) when λ is changed from λ = 3 to λ = 2.

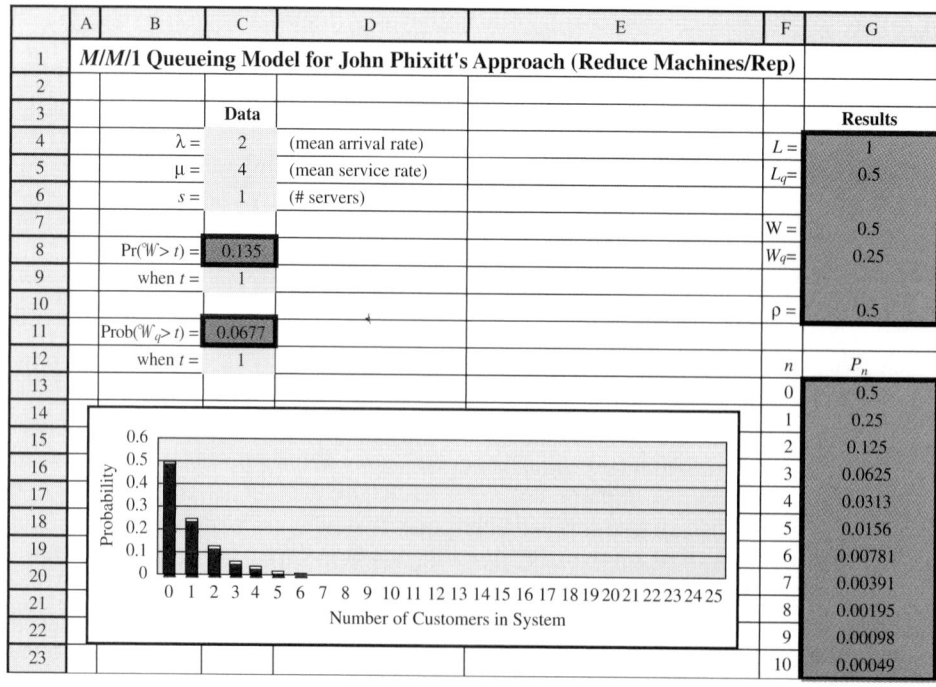

	A	B	C	D	E	F	G
1		*M/M/*1 Queueing Model for John Phixitt's Approach (Reduce Machines/Rep)					
2							
3			**Data**				**Results**
4		λ =	2	(mean arrival rate)		L =	1
5		μ =	4	(mean service rate)		L_q=	0.5
6		s =	1	(# servers)			
7						W =	0.5
8		Pr(W > t) =	0.135			W_q=	0.25
9		when t =	1				
10						ρ =	0.5
11		Prob(W_q > t) =	0.0677				
12		when t =	1			n	P_n
13						0	0.5
14						1	0.25
15						2	0.125
16						3	0.0625
17						4	0.0313
18						5	0.0156
19						6	0.00781
20						7	0.00391
21						8	0.00195
22						9	0.00098
23						10	0.00049

chines. The additional payroll cost would be about $270 million annually. (It is a little less than half the current payroll cost because the new tech reps would have less seniority than the current ones.) However, the management science team estimates that the additional costs of hiring and training the new tech reps, covering their work expenses, providing them with equipment, and adding more field service managers to administer them would be equivalent to about $30 million annually.

> **Total Additional Cost of the Approach Suggested by John Phixitt:** Approximately $300 million annually.

The *M/G/*1 Model

This queueing model differs from the *M/M/*1 model only in the second of its assumptions summarized below.

Assumptions

1. *Interarrival times* have an exponential distribution with a mean of $1/\lambda$.

2. *Service times* can have *any* probability distribution. It is not even necessary to determine the form of this distribution. You just need to estimate the mean ($1/\mu$) and standard deviation (σ) of the distribution.

You now need to also estimate σ, the standard deviation of the service-time distribution.

3. The queueing system has one server.

Thus, this is an extremely flexible model that only requires the common situation of *random arrivals* (equivalent to the first assumption) and a single server, plus estimates of λ, μ, and σ.

Using $\rho = \lambda/\mu$, here are the available formulas for this model.

$$P_0 = 1 - \rho$$

$$L_q = \frac{\lambda^2\sigma^2 + \rho^2}{2(1 - \rho)}$$

$$L = L_q + \rho$$

$$W_q = \frac{L_q}{\lambda}$$

$$W = W_q + \frac{1}{\mu}$$

These steady-state measures of performance require only that $\rho < 1$, which allows the queueing system to reach a steady-state condition.

To illustrate the formulas, suppose that the service-time distribution is the exponential distribution with mean $1/\mu$. Then, since the standard deviation σ is

$$\sigma = \text{mean} = \frac{1}{\mu} \quad \text{for the exponential distribution}$$

the formula for L_q indicates that

$$L_q = \frac{\lambda^2\left(\dfrac{1}{\mu^2}\right) + \rho^2}{2(1 - \rho)} = \frac{\rho^2 + \rho^2}{2(1 - \rho)}$$

$$= \frac{\rho^2}{(1 - \rho)}$$

just as for the *M/M/*1 model. Having $\sigma = 1/\mu$ also causes the formulas for L, W_q, and W to reduce algebraically to those given earlier for the *M/M/*1 model. In fact, the *M/M/*1 model is just the special case of the *M/G/*1 model where $\sigma = 1/\mu$. (However, the *M/M/*1 model yields some results that are not available from the *M/G/*1 model.)

TABLE 14.6   The Values of σ and L_q for the *M/G/*1 Model with Various Service-Time Distributions

Distribution	Mean	σ	Model	L_q
Exponential	$\dfrac{1}{\mu}$	$\dfrac{1}{\mu}$	*M/M/*1	$\dfrac{\rho^2}{1-\rho}$
Degenerate (constant service times)	$\dfrac{1}{\mu}$	0	*M/D/*1	$\dfrac{1}{2}\dfrac{\rho^2}{1-\rho}$
Erlang, with shape parameter *k* (*k* = 1, 2, . . .)	$\dfrac{1}{\mu}$	$\dfrac{1}{\sqrt{k}}\dfrac{1}{\mu}$	*M/E$_k$/*1	$\dfrac{k+1}{2k}\dfrac{\rho^2}{1-\rho}$

Table 14.6 gives the value of the standard deviation σ for each of the service-time distributions discussed in Section 14.1. The fourth column shows the label for the special case of the *M/G/*1 model with this service-time distribution. The rightmost column then indicates to what the L_q formula for the *M/G/*1 model reduces for this special case. Individual Excel templates are available in your MS Courseware for calculating both L_q and the other available results for each of these special cases listed in the fourth column. In addition, a template is available for the general *M/G/*1 model.

Note in the third column of the table that the value of σ for the Erlang distribution lies in the inclusive range between the values for the other two distributions (as do most real queueing systems). The value of *k* determines just where σ lies in this range. (The Erlang distribution with *k* = 1 is identical to the exponential distribution.) The rightmost column shows that the value of L_q with the Erlang distribution also lies within the inclusive range between the values obtained with the other service-time distributions.

The L_q formula for the *M/G/*1 model is an enlightening one, because it reveals even more clearly than the table what effect the variability of the service-time distribution has on this measure of performance. With fixed values of λ, μ, and ρ, decreasing this variability (i.e., decreasing σ) definitely decreases L_q. The same thing happens with *L, W,* and W_q. Thus, the consistency of the server has a major bearing on the performance of the queueing system. Given the choice between two servers with the same average speed (the same value of 1/μ), the one with less variability (smaller σ) definitely should be preferred over the other one. (We will discuss this further in Section 14.8.)

Decreasing the variability of the service-time distribution has the beneficial effect of decreasing L_q, L, W, and W_q.

Considering the complexity involved in analyzing a model that permits *any* service-time distribution, it is remarkable that such a simple formula can be obtained for L_q. This formula is one of the most important results in queueing theory because of its ease of use and the prevalence of *M/G/*1 queueing systems in practice. This equation for L_q (or its counterpart for W_q) commonly is referred to as the Pollaczek-Khintchine formula, named after two pioneers in the development of queueing theory who derived the formula independently in the early 1930s.

Applying the *M/G/*1 Model to the Approach Suggested by the Vice President for Engineering

Dupit's vice president for engineering has suggested providing the tech reps with new state-of-the-art equipment that would substantially reduce the time required for the longer repairs. This would decrease the average repair time a little, and also would substantially decrease the variability of the repair times.

The new state-of-the-art equipment suggested by the vice president for engineering would substantially reduce both the mean and the standard deviation of the service-time distribution.

After gathering more information from this vice president and analyzing it further, the management science team makes the following estimates about the effect of this approach on the service-time distribution.

The mean would decrease from ¼ day to ⅓ day.

The standard deviation would decrease from ¼ day to ¹⁄₁₀ day.

FIGURE 14.7

This Excel template for the *M/G*/1 model shows the results from applying this model to the approach suggested by Dupit's vice president for engineering to use new state-of-the-art equipment.

	A	B	C	D	E	F	G
1			**M/G/1 Model for VP of Engineering's Approach (New Equipment)**				
2							
3			**Data**				**Results**
4		$\lambda =$	3	(mean arrival rate)		$L =$	1.163
5		$1/\mu =$	0.2	(expected service time)		$L_q=$	0.563
6		$\sigma =$	0.1	(standard deviation)			
7		$s =$	1	(# servers)		$W =$	0.388
8						$W_q=$	0.188
9							
10						$\rho =$	0.6
11							
12						$P_0 =$	0.4

Range Name	Cell
L	G4
Lambda	C4
L_q	G5
OneOverMu	C5
Rho	G10
s	C7
Sigma	C6
W	G7
W_q	G8

	F	G
4	$L =$	=L_q+Rho
5	$L_q=$	=((Lambda)^2)*(Sigma^2)+(Rho^2))/(2*(1-Rho))
6		
7	$W =$	=W_q+OneOverMu
8	$W_q=$	=L_q/Lambda
9		
10	$\rho =$	=Lambda*OneOverMu
11		
12	$P_0 =$	=1-Rho

Thus, the standard deviation would decrease from equaling the previous mean (as for the exponential distribution) to being just half the new mean (as for the Erlang distribution with shape parameter $k = 4$). Since $\mu = 1/\text{mean}$, we now have $\mu = 5$ instead of $\mu = 4$.

With $\sigma = 0.1$, the Excel template for the *M/G*/1 model yields the results shown in Figure 14.7. Note that $W_q = 0.188$ day. This big reduction from $W_q = 0.75$ day under the current policy (as given in Figure 14.5) is largely due to the big decrease in σ. If the service-time distribution continued to be an exponential distribution, then increasing μ from 4 to 5 would decrease W_q from 0.75 day to 0.3 day. The additional reduction from 0.3 day to 0.188 day is because of the large reduction in the variability of service times.

The *M/G*/1 model indicates that the proposed new service standard would be met easily by this approach.

Recall that the proposed new service standard is $W_q \le 0.25$ day. Therefore, the approach suggested by the vice president for engineering would satisfy this standard.

Unfortunately, the management science team also determines that this approach would be expensive, as summarized below.

Total Additional Cost of the Approach Suggested by the Vice President for Engineering: A one-time cost of approximately $500 million (about $50,000 for new equipment per tech rep).

Review Questions

1. What are represented by the symbols λ and μ? By $1/\lambda$ and $1/\mu$? By ρ?

2. What are the assumptions of the *M/M*/1 model?

3. For which measures of performance (both expected values and probabilities) are formulas available for the *M/M*/1 model?

4. Which values of ρ correspond to the server in a single-server queueing system having a manageable utilization factor that allows the system to reach a steady-state condition?

5. Under Dupit's current policy, what is the average waiting time of customers until service begins on their failed machines?

6. How much more would it cost Dupit to reduce this average waiting time to ¼ workday by decreasing the number of machines assigned to each tech rep?

7. How does the *M/G*/1 model differ from the *M/M*/1 model?

8. Which service-time distribution is assumed by the *M/D*/1 model? By the *M/E$_k$*/1 model?

9. For the *M/G*/1 model, what is the effect on L_q, L, W, and W_q of decreasing the standard deviation of the service-time distribution?

10. What is the total additional cost of the approach suggested by Dupit's vice president for engineering?

14.6 SOME MULTIPLE-SERVER QUEUEING MODELS

Many queueing systems have more than one server, so we now turn our attention to multiple-server queueing models. In particular, we will discuss what results are available for the multiple-server counterparts of the single-server models introduced in the preceding section.

Recall that the third symbol in the label for a queueing model indicates the number of servers. For example, the *M/M*/2 model has two servers. The *M/M/s* model allows the choice of any number of servers, where *s* is the symbol for this number.

Also recall that $\rho(=\lambda/\mu)$ was the symbol used for the *utilization factor* for the server in a single-server queueing system. With multiple servers, the formula for this symbol changes to

$$\rho = \frac{\lambda}{s\mu} \qquad \textbf{(utilization factor)}$$

where λ continues to be the mean arrival rate (so $1/\lambda$ still is the expected interarrival time) and μ continues to be the mean service rate for a single continuously busy server (so $1/\mu$ still is the expected service time). The models assume that all the servers have the same service-time distribution, so μ is the same for every server. Since

λ = Expected number of arrivals per unit time

$s\mu$ = Expected number of service completions per unit time when all *s* servers are
　　　continuously busy

As with single-server queueing models, the utilization factor ρ still is the average fraction of time that the individual servers are being utilized serving customers.

it follows that $\rho = \lambda/s\mu$ is indeed the average fraction of time that individual servers are being utilized serving customers.

In order for the servers to have a manageable utilization factor, it is again necessary that

$$\rho < 1$$

All the models make this assumption to enable the queueing system to reach a steady-state condition.

Of the four previously considered single-server models (*M/M*/1, *M/G*/1, *M/D*/1, and *M/E$_k$*/1), the *M/G*/1 model is the only one whose multiple-server counterpart yields no useful analytical results. Combining the complication of multiple servers with the complication of allowing the choice of any service-time distribution is too much to handle.

We begin with the *M/M/s* model, including its application to the Dupit case study. We then mention the limited results available for the *M/D/s* and *M/E$_k$/s* models.

The *M/M/s* Model

Except for the last one, the assumptions are the same as for the *M/M*/1 model.

Assumptions

1. Interarrival times have an exponential distribution with a mean of $1/\lambda$.

2. Service times have an exponential distribution with a mean of $1/\mu$.

3. Any number of servers (denoted by *s*) can be chosen for the queueing system.

Explicit formulas are available for all the measures of performance (including the probabilities) considered for the *M/M*/1 model. However, when $s > 1$, the formulas are too tedious to want to do by hand. Therefore, you should use the Excel template for the *M/M/s* model (as

FIGURE 14.8

Values of L for the *M/M/s* model for various values of s, the number of servers.

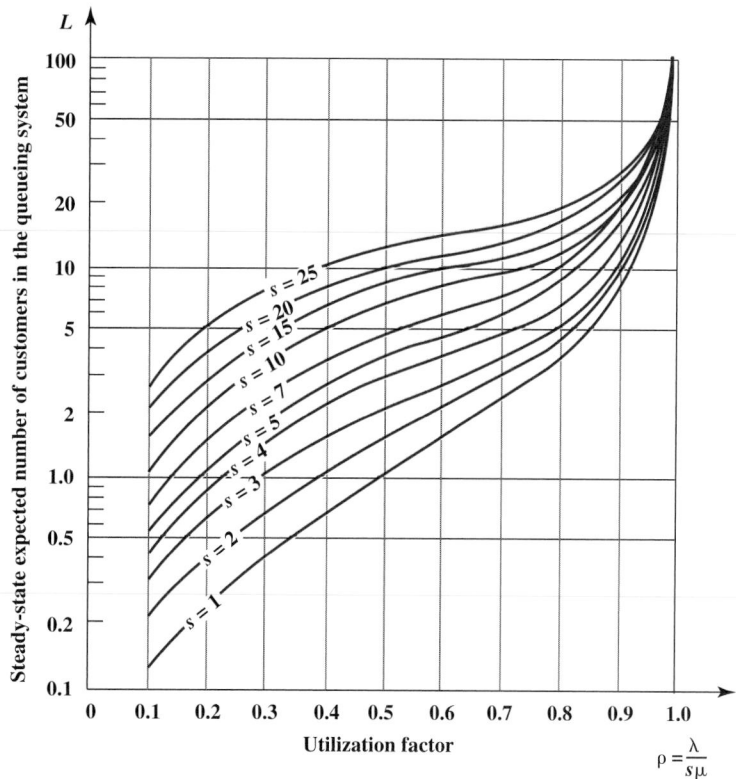

The Excel template for the *M/M/s* model provides all the measures of performance that were described in Section 14.5 for the *M/M/1* model.

demonstrated earlier in Figures 14.5 and 14.6) to generate all these results. (You also can see a demonstration of the *M/M/s* queueing system in action by viewing the Waiting Line module in your Interactive Management Science Modules at **www.mhhe.com/hillier2e** or on the CD-ROM.)

Another alternative is to use Figure 14.8, which shows the values of L versus the utilization factor for various values of s. (Be aware that the vertical axis uses a logarithmic scale, so you need to refer to the notches to determine the value along this axis.) By estimating L from this graph, you then can use Little's formula ($L = \lambda W$ and $L_q = \lambda W_q$), plus $W = W_q + \frac{1}{\mu}$ to calculate W, W_q, and L_q.

Applying These Models to the Approach Suggested by the Chief Financial Officer

Dupit's chief financial officer has suggested combining the current one-person tech rep territories into larger territories that would be served jointly by multiple tech reps. The hope is that, without changing the total number of tech reps, this reorganization might decrease W_q sufficiently from its current value ($W_q = 0.75$ day) to satisfy the proposed new service standard ($W_q \le 0.25$ day).

Let us first try it with *two* tech reps assigned to each territory.

A Territory with Two Tech Reps

Number of machines:	300	(versus 150 before)
Mean arrival rate:	$\lambda = 6$	(versus $\lambda = 3$ before)
Mean service rate:	$\mu = 4$	(same as before)
Number of servers:	$s = 2$	(versus $s = 1$ before)
Utilization factor:	$\rho = \dfrac{\lambda}{s\mu} = 0.75$	(same as before)

FIGURE 14.9

This Excel template for the *M/M/s* model shows the results from applying this model to the approach suggested by Dupit's chief financial officer with two tech reps assigned to each territory.

	A	B	C	D	E	F	G
1		**M/M/s Model for CFO's Approach (Combine into Teams of Two)**					
2							
3			**Data**				**Results**
4		$\lambda =$	6	(mean arrival rate)		$L =$	3.429
5		$\mu =$	4	(mean service rate)		$L_q=$	1.929
6		$s =$	2	(# servers)			
7						$W =$	0.571
8		$\Pr(W > t) =$	0.169			$W_q=$	0.321
9		when $t =$	1				
10						$\rho =$	0.75
11		$\text{Prob}(W_q > t) =$	0.087				
12		when $t =$	1			n	P_n
13						0	0.1429
14						1	0.2143
15						2	0.1607
16						3	0.1205
17						4	0.0904
18						5	0.0678
19						6	0.0509
20						7	0.0381
21						8	0.0286
22						9	0.0215
23						10	0.0161

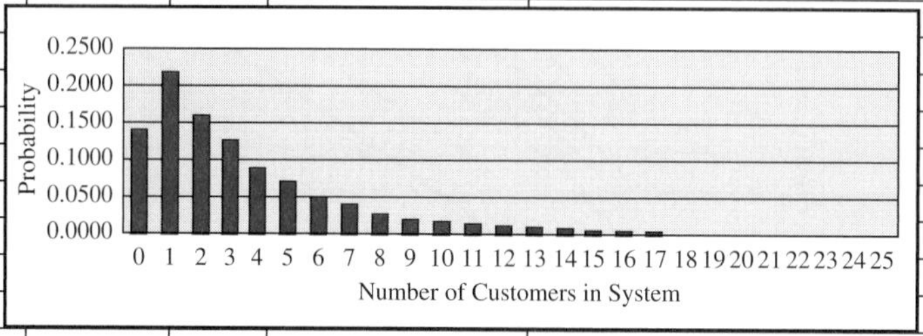

(chart: Probability vs. Number of Customers in System, y-axis 0.0000 to 0.2500)

Applying the Excel template for the *M/M/s* model with these data yields the results shown in Figure 14.9, including $W_q = 0.321$ day. (The equations entered into the output cells are not given in this figure because they are very complicated, but they can be viewed in this chapter's Excel file that contains this template.)

This is a very big improvement over the current value of $W_q = 0.75$ day, but it does not quite satisfy the service standard of $W_q \leq 0.25$ day. So let us next see what would happen if *three* tech reps were assigned to each territory.

A Territory with Three Tech Reps

Number of machines:	450	(versus 150 before)
Mean arrival rate:	$\lambda = 9$	(versus $\lambda = 3$ before)
Mean service rate:	$\mu = 4$	(same as before)
Number of servers:	$s = 3$	(versus $s = 1$ before)
Utilization factor:	$\rho = \dfrac{\lambda}{s\mu} = 0.75$	(same as before)

With this utilization factor, Figure 14.8 indicates that L is very close to 4. Using 4 as the approximate value, and applying the relationships given in Section 14.3 (Little's formula, etc.),

$$W = \frac{L}{\lambda} = \frac{4}{9} = 0.44 \text{ day}$$

$$W_q = W - \frac{1}{\mu} = 0.44 - 0.25 = 0.19 \text{ day}$$

The *M/M/s* model indicates that the proposed new service standard would be comfortably satisfied by combining three one-person tech rep territories into a single larger territory that would be served jointly by all three tech reps.

More precisely, the Excel template in Figure 14.10 gives $L = 3.953$ and $W_q = 0.189$ day. Since a workday is eight hours, this expected waiting time converts to just over one hour and 30 minutes.

Consequently, three-person territories would easily satisfy the proposed new service standard of $W_q \leq 0.25$ workday (two hours). Even considering that these larger territories would modestly increase the travel times for the tech reps, they still would comfortably satisfy the service standard.

Table 14.7 summarizes the data and values of W_q for territories with one, two, and three tech reps. Note how sharply W_q decreases as the number of tech reps (servers) increases without

FIGURE 14.10

This Excel template modifies the results in Figure 14.9 by assigning three tech reps to each territory.

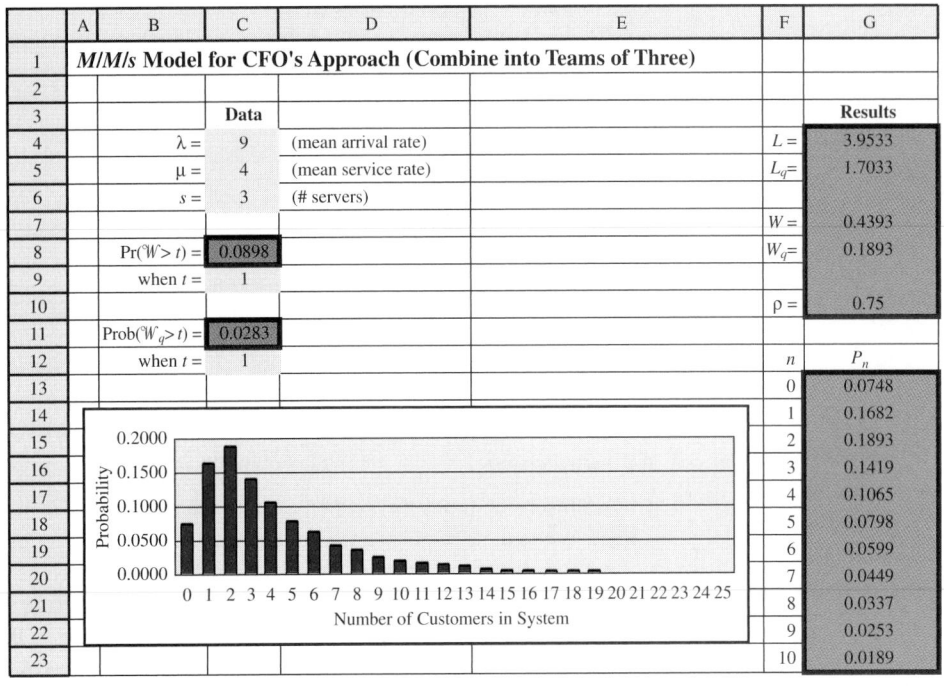

TABLE 14.7

Comparison of W_q Values with Territories of Different Sizes for the Dupit Problem

Number of Tech Reps	Number of Machines	λ	μ	s	ρ	W_q
1	150	3	4	1	0.75	0.75 workday (6 hours)
2	300	6	4	2	0.75	0.321 workday (2.57 hours)
3	450	9	4	3	0.75	0.189 workday (1.51 hours)

changing the utilization factor. In fact, W_q for $s = 2$ is well under *half* that for $s = 1$, and W_q for $s = 3$ is about a *fourth* of that for $s = 1$.

These results suggest that further enlarging the territories by assigning four or more tech reps to each one would decrease W_q even further. However, there also are disadvantages to enlarging the territories. One is the possibility of a significant increase in the average time required for a tech rep to travel to the site of a failed machine. When combining only two or three one-person tech rep territories into a single joint territory, the average travel times should not increase much since the tech reps can effectively coordinate in dividing up the repair jobs based on the proximity of the jobs to the current locations of the tech reps. However, this becomes more difficult with even more tech reps in an even larger territory, so occasional travel times might become excessive. Since time traveling to a repair site is part of the total time a tech rep must devote to a repair, the *mean service rate* μ may decrease slightly from the four repairs per day assumed in Table 14.7 when the number of tech reps is more than three. For any given number of tech reps, decreasing μ increases W_q. Therefore, it is unclear how much further W_q can be decreased, if at all, by increasing the number of tech reps per territory beyond three.

Assigning a large number of tech reps to each territory has a number of practical drawbacks as well. Coordination between tech reps becomes more difficult. Customers lose the feeling of receiving personalized service when they are visited by so many different tech reps. Furthermore, tech reps lose the pride of ownership in managing their own territory and dealing with "their" customers. Personal or professional conflicts between tech reps also can arise when they share the same territory, and the opportunities for such conflicts increase with larger teams.

For all these reasons, John Phixitt concludes that normally assigning three tech reps to each territory would provide the best trade-off between minimizing these disadvantages of large territories and reducing W_q to a satisfactory level.

Combining too many tech reps into a very large territory can cause excessive travel times, among other problems.

Conclusion: The approach suggested by the chief financial officer would indeed satisfy the proposed new service standard ($W_q \leq 0.25$ day) if each three contiguous one-person tech rep territories are combined into a larger territory served jointly by the same three tech reps. Since the total number of tech reps does not change, there would be no significant additional cost from implementing this approach other than the disadvantages of larger territories just cited. To minimize these disadvantages, the territories should not be enlarged any further than having three tech reps per territory.

The *M/D/s* Model

The service times in many queueing systems have much less variability than is assumed by the *M/M/s* model. In some cases, there may be no variability (or almost no variability) at all in the service times. The *M/D/s* model is designed for these cases.

Assumptions: Same as for the *M/M/s* model, except now all the service times are the *same*. This *constant service time* is denoted by $1/\mu$. (This is referred to as having a *degenerate* service-time distribution, which provides the symbol *D* for the model label.)

Constant service times arise when exactly the same work is being performed to serve each customer. When the servers are *machines,* there may literally be no variability at all in the service times. The assumption of constant service times also can be a reasonable approximation with *human servers* if they are performing the same routine task for all customers.

> Just as for single-server queueing systems, eliminating the variability of service times substantially increases the efficiency of multiple-server queueing systems.

Table 14.6 in the preceding section reveals that, when $s = 1$, the value of L_q for the *M/D/1* model is only *half* that for the *M/M/1* model. Similar differences in L_q between the two models also occur when $s > 1$ (especially with larger values of the utilization factor ρ). Substantial differences between the models also occur for W_q, W, and L.

These large differences emphasize the importance of using the model that best fits the queueing system under study. Because the *M/M/s* model is the most convenient one, it is common practice to routinely use this model for most applications. However, doing so when there is little or no variability in the service times causes a large error in some measures of performance.

The procedures for calculating the various measures of performance for the *M/D/s* model are far more complicated than for the *M/M/s* model, so no Excel template is available in the case when $s > 1$. However, special projects have been conducted to calculate the measures. Figure 14.11 shows the values of L versus ρ for many values of s. The other main measures (W, W_q, and L_q) then can be obtained from L by using Little's formula, and so forth (as described in Section 14.3).

The *M/E_k/s* Model

When the service times have some variability, but less so than for the exponential distribution, the *M/E_k/s* model provides a welcome middle ground between the *M/M/s* and *M/D/s* models.

Assumptions: Same as for the *M/M/s* model, except now service times have an Erlang distribution with a mean of $1/\mu$ and shape parameter k ($k = 1,2, \ldots$). (See Section 14.1 and Figure 14.4 there for a description of this distribution.)

As indicated in Table 14.6 in the preceding section, the standard deviation σ for the Erlang distribution with shape parameter k is

> When σ is considerably less than the mean, using the *M/E_k/s* model with an appropriate value of k will provide much more accurate results than the *M/M/s* model.

$$\sigma = \frac{1}{\sqrt{k}} \text{ mean} = \frac{1}{\sqrt{k}} \frac{1}{\mu}$$

The ability to choose any positive integer value for k provides considerable flexibility to match σ in this model quite closely to the anticipated standard deviation for the queueing system under study.

The procedures for obtaining the measures of performance for the *M/E_k/s* model are even more complicated than for the *M/D/s* model. However, considerable numerical results have been generated.[2] Figure 14.12 compares the values of L for three values of k for the case of

---

[2]Extensive tables and graphs for both the *M/E_k/s* and *M/D/s* models are available in F. S. Hillier and O. S. Yu, with D. Avis, L. Fossett, F. Lo, and M. Reiman, *Queueing Tables and Graphs* (New York: 1981), Elsevier North-Holland.

FIGURE 14.11

Values of L for the $M/D/s$ model for various values of s, the number of servers.

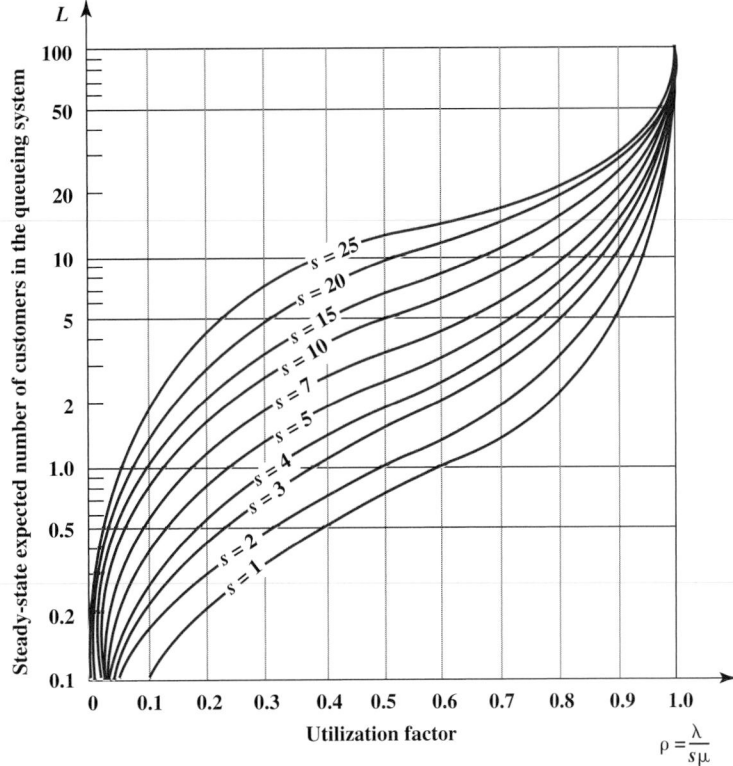

FIGURE 14.12

Values of L for the $M/E_k/2$ model for various values of the shape parameter k.

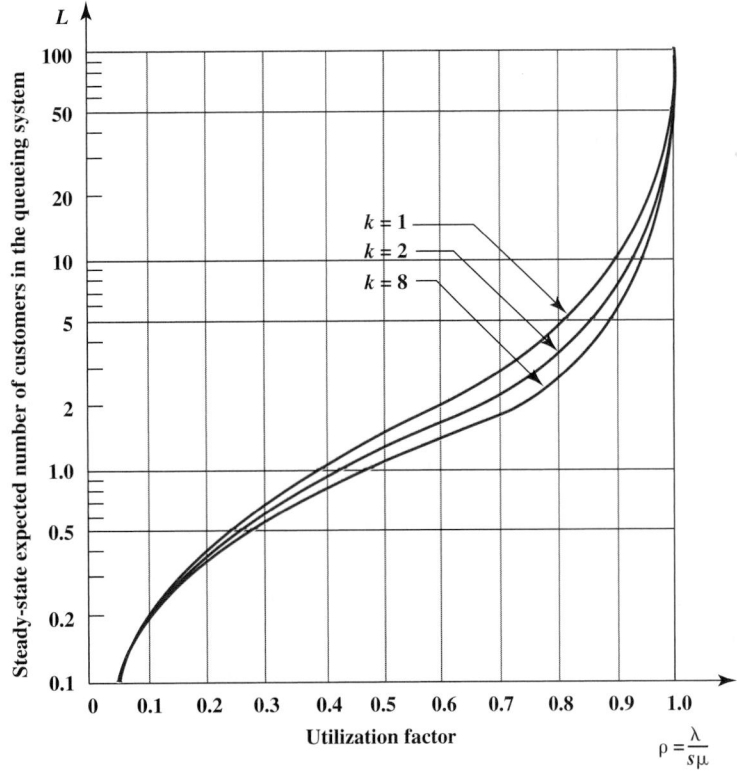

two servers ($s = 2$). The values of W, W_q, and L_q then can be obtained from L. (The percentage differences in the values of $L_q = L - \lambda/\mu$ between the cases of $k = 1$, $k = 2$, and $k = 8$ are considerably larger than these differences in L shown in the figure.)

Review Questions

1. For multiple-server queueing models, what is the formula for the utilization factor ρ? What is the interpretation of ρ in terms of how servers use their time?

2. Which values of ρ correspond to the servers having a manageable utilization factor that allows the system to reach a steady-state condition?

3. Are there any measures of performance that can be calculated for the *M/M/*1 model but not the *M/M/s* model?

4. How many one-person tech rep territories need to be combined into a larger territory in order to satisfy Dupit's proposed new service standard?

5. Compare the *M/M/s*, *M/D/s*, and *M/E_k/s* models in terms of the amount of variability in the service times.

14.7   PRIORITY QUEUEING MODELS

Priority queueing models are used when high-priority customers are served ahead of others who have waited longer.

All the queueing models presented so far assume that the customers are served on a first-come, first-served basis. Not all queueing systems operate that way. In some systems, the more important customers are served ahead of others who have waited longer. Management may want certain special customers to be given priority over others. In some cases, the customers in the queueing system are jobs to be performed, and the different deadlines for the jobs dictate the order in which these customers are served. Rush jobs need to be done before routine jobs.

A *hospital emergency room* is an example of a queueing system where priorities automatically are used. An arriving patient who is in critical condition naturally will be treated ahead of a routine patient who was already there waiting.

The models for such queueing systems generally make the following general assumptions.

General Assumptions

1. There are two or more categories of customers. Each category is assigned to a **priority class.** Customers in priority class 1 are given priority for receiving service over customers in priority class 2. If there are more than two priority classes, customers in priority class 2 then are given priority over customers in priority class 3, and so on.

2. After deferring to higher priority customers, the customers within each priority class are served on a first-come, first-served basis. Thus, within a priority class, priority for receiving service is based on the time already spent waiting in the queueing system.

There actually are two types of priorities, as described below.

Nonpreemptive priorities: Once a server has begun serving a customer, the service must be completed without interruption even if a higher priority customer arrives while this service is in process. However, once service is completed, if there are customers in the queue, priorities are applied to select the one to begin service. In particular, the one selected is that member of the *highest* priority class represented in the queue who has waited longest.

Preemptive priorities: The lowest priority customer being served is *preempted* (ejected back into the queue) whenever a higher priority customer enters the queueing system. A server is thereby freed to begin serving the new arrival immediately. Whenever a server does succeed in *finishing* a service, the next customer to begin receiving service is selected just as described above for nonpreemptive priorities. (The preempted customer becomes the member of its priority class in the queue who has waited longest, so it hopefully will get back into service soon and, perhaps after additional preemptions, will eventually finish.)

This section includes a basic queueing model for each of these two types of priorities.

A Preemptive Priorities Queueing Model

Along with the general assumptions about priorities given above, this model makes the following assumptions.

Additional Assumptions

1. Preemptive priorities are used as just described. (Let n denote the number of priority classes.)

2. For priority class i ($i = 1, 2, \ldots, n$), the *interarrival times* of customers in that class have an *exponential* distribution with a mean of $1/\lambda_i$.

3. All *service times* have an *exponential* distribution with a mean of $1/\mu$, regardless of the priority class involved.

4. The queueing system has a single server.

This model fits the *M/M/*1 model except for also having preemptive priorities.

Thus, except for the complication of using preemptive priorities, the assumptions are the same as for the *M/M/*1 model.

Since λ_i is the mean arrival rate for customers in priority class i ($i = 1, 2, \ldots, n$), $\lambda = (\lambda_1 + \lambda_2 + \ldots + \lambda_n)$ is the overall mean arrival rate for all customers. Therefore, the *utilization factor* for the server is

$$\rho = \frac{\lambda_1 + \lambda_2 + \cdots + \lambda_n}{\mu}$$

As with the previous models, $\rho < 1$ is required to enable the queueing system to reach a steady-state condition for all priority classes.

The reason for using priorities is to *decrease* the waiting times for high-priority customers. This is accomplished at the expense of *increasing* the waiting times for low-priority customers.

Assuming $\rho < 1$, formulas are available for calculating the main measures of performance (L, W, L_q, and W_q) for *each* of the priority classes. An Excel template in your MS Courseware quickly performs all these calculations for you.

A Nonpreemptive Priorities Queueing Model

Along with the general assumptions given earlier, this model makes the following assumptions.

Additional Assumptions

1. Nonpreemptive priorities are used as described earlier in the section. (Again, let n be the number of priority classes.)

2. and 3. Same as for the preemptive priorities queueing model.

4. The queueing system can have any number of servers.

This model fits the *M/M/s* model except for also having nonpreemptive priorities.

Except for using nonpreemptive priorities, these assumptions are the same as for the *M/M/s* model.

The utilization factor for the servers is

$$\rho = \frac{\lambda_1 + \lambda_2 + \cdots + \lambda_n}{s\mu}$$

Again, $\rho < 1$ is needed to enable the queueing system to reach a steady-state condition for all the priority classes.

As before, an Excel template is available in your MS Courseware to calculate all the main measures of performance for *each* of the priority classes.

Applying the Nonpreemptive Priorities Queueing Model to the Approach Suggested by the Vice President for Marketing

Now we come to the last of the four approaches being investigated by Dupit's management science team. The vice president for marketing has proposed giving the printer-copiers priority over other machines for receiving service. In other words, whenever a tech rep finishes a repair, if there are *both* printer-copiers and other machines still waiting to be repaired, the tech rep *always* should choose a printer-copier (the one that has waited longest) to be repaired next, even if other machines have waited longer.

The rationale for this proposal is that the printer-copier performs so many vital functions that its owners cannot tolerate being without it as long as other machines. Indeed, nearly all the complaints about excessive waiting for repairs have come from these owners even though other machines wait just as long. Therefore, the vice president for marketing feels that the proposed new service standard ($W_q \leq 2$ hours) only needs to be applied to the printer-copiers. Giving them priority for service hopefully will result in meeting this standard while still providing satisfactory service to other machines.

The suggestion of the vice president for marketing is to apply the proposed new service standard to the printer-copiers only and then to give them nonpreemptive priority over the other machines.

To investigate this, the management science team is applying the nonpreemptive priorities queueing model. There are two priority classes.

Priority class 1: Printer-copiers.

Priority class 2: Other machines.

Therefore, a distinction is made between these two types of arriving customers (machines needing repairs) for the queueing system in each tech rep territory. To determine the *mean arrival rate* for each of these two priority classes (denoted by λ_1 and λ_2, respectively), the team has ascertained that about a third of the machines assigned to tech reps currently are printer-copiers. Each printer-copier requires service with about the same frequency (approximately once every 50 workdays) as other machines. Consequently, since the *total* mean arrival rate for all the machines in a one-person tech rep territory typically is three machines per day,

$$\lambda_1 = 1 \text{ customer (printer-copier) per workday} \qquad \text{(now)}$$

$$\lambda_2 = 2 \text{ customers (other machines) per workday} \qquad \text{(now)}$$

However, the proportion of the machines that are printer-copiers is expected to gradually increase until it peaks at about *half* in a couple of years. At that point, the mean arrival rates will have changed to

$$\lambda_1 = 1.5 \text{ customers (printer-copiers) per workday} \qquad \text{(later)}$$

$$\lambda_2 = 1.5 \text{ customers (other machines) per workday} \qquad \text{(later)}$$

The *mean service rate* for each tech rep is unchanged by applying priorities, so its best estimate continues to be $\mu = 4$ customers per workday. Under the company's current policy of one-person tech rep territories, the queueing system for each territory has a single server ($s = 1$). Since $(\lambda_1 + \lambda_2) = 3$ both now and later, the value of the utilization factor will continue to be

$$\rho = \frac{\lambda_1 + \lambda_2}{s\mu} = \frac{3}{4}$$

Figure 14.13 shows the results obtained by applying the Excel template for the nonpreemptive priorities model to this queueing system *now* ($\lambda_1 = 1$ and $\lambda_2 = 2$). Figure 14.14 does the same under the conditions expected *later* ($\lambda_1 = 1.5$ and $\lambda_2 = 1.5$).

The management science team is particularly interested in the values of W_q, the expected waiting time in the queue, given in the last column of these two figures. These values are summarized in Table 14.8, where the first row comes from Figure 14.13 and the second comes from Figure 14.14.

For the printer-copiers, note that $W_q = 0.25$ workday now, which barely meets the proposed new service standard of $W_q \leq 0.25$ workday, but this expected waiting time would deteriorate later to 0.3 workday. Thus, this approach falls a little short. Furthermore, the expected waiting time before service begins for the other machines would go from $W_q = 1$ workday now to $W_q = 1.2$ workdays later. This large increase from the average waiting times being experienced under the current policy of $W_q = 0.75$ workday (as given in Figure 14.5) is likely to alienate a considerable number of customers.

Table 14.7 in the preceding section demonstrated what a great impact combining one-person tech rep territories into larger territories has on decreasing expected waiting times.

FIGURE 14.13

This Excel template applies the nonpreemptive priorities queueing model to the Dupit problem *now* under the approach suggested by the vice president for marketing to give priority to the printer-copiers.

	A	B	C	D	E	F	G
1		**Nonpreemptive Priorities Model for VP of Marketing's Approach**					
2		**(Current Arrival Rates)**					
3							
4		$n =$	2	(# of priority classes)			
5		$\mu =$	4	(mean service rate)			
6		$s =$	1	(# servers)			
7							
8							
9			λ_i	L	L_q	W	W_q
10		Priority Class 1	1	0.5	0.25	0.5	0.25
11		Priority Class 2	2	2.5	2	1.25	1
12							
13							
14							
15							
16		$\lambda =$	3				
17		$\rho =$	0.75				

FIGURE 14.14

The modification of Figure 14.13 that applies the same model to the *later* version of the Dupit problem.

	A	B	C	D	E	F	G
1		**Nonpreemptive Priorities Model for VP of Marketing's Approach**					
2		**(Future Arrival Rates)**					
3							
4		$n =$	2	(# of priority classes)			
5		$\mu =$	4	(mean service rate)			
6		$s =$	1	(# servers)			
7							
8							
9			λ_i	L	L_q	W	W_q
10		Priority Class 1	1.5	0.825	0.45	0.55	0.3
11		Priority Class 2	1.5	2.175	1.8	1.45	1.2
12							
13							
14							
15							
16		$\lambda =$	3				
17		$\rho =$	0.75				

Since assigning nonpreemptive priorities doesn't help enough (especially later), let's also try combining one-person tech rep territories into larger joint territories.

Therefore, the management science team decides to investigate combining this approach with applying nonpreemptive priorities.

Combining pairs of one-person tech rep territories into single two-person tech rep territories doubles the mean arrival rates for both priority classes (λ_1 and λ_2) for each new territory. Since the number of servers also doubles (from $s = 1$ to $s = 2$) without any change in μ (the mean service rate for each server), the utilization factor ρ remains the same. These values now and later are shown in the third and fourth rows of Table 14.8. Applying the nonpreemptive priorities queueing model then yields the expected waiting times given in the last two columns.

These large reductions in the W_q values from the $s = 1$ case result in rather reasonable waiting times. Both now and later, W_q for printer-copiers is only about *half* of the maximum under the proposed new service standard ($W_q \leq 2$ hours). Although W_q for the other machines is somewhat over this maximum both now and later, these waiting times also are somewhat under the average waiting times currently being experienced (6 hours) without many complaints from members of this priority class. John Phixitt's reaction is favorable. He feels that the service standard

TABLE 14.8   Expected Waiting Times* when Nonpreemptive Priorities Are Applied to the Dupit Problem

s	When	λ_1	λ_2	μ	ρ	W_q for Printer-Copiers	W_q for Other Machines
1	Now	1	2	4	0.75	0.25 workday (2 hrs.)	1 workday (8 hrs.)
1	Later	1.5	1.5	4	0.75	0.3 workday (2.4 hrs.)	1.2 workdays (9.6 hrs.)
2	Now	2	4	4	0.75	0.107 workday (0.86 hr.)	0.429 workday (3.43 hrs.)
2	Later	3	3	4	0.75	0.129 workday (1.03 hrs.)	0.514 workday (4.11 hrs.)
3	Now	3	6	4	0.75	0.063 workday (0.50 hr.)	0.252 workday (2.02 hrs.)
3	Later	4.5	4.5	4	0.75	0.076 workday (0.61 hr.)	0.303 workday (2.42 hrs.)

*These times are obtained in units of *workdays,* consisting of eight hours each, and then converted to hours.

Two-person tech rep territories with priorities reduce waiting times to satisfactory levels.

of $W_q \leq 2$ hours really was proposed with the printer-copiers in mind and that the other members of top management probably will also be satisfied with the values of W_q shown in the third and fourth rows of Table 14.8.

Since the analytical results reported in Table 14.7 were so favorable for three-person tech rep territories without priorities, the management science team decides to investigate this option *with priorities* as well. The last two rows of Table 14.8 show the results for this case. Note that these W_q values for $s = 3$ are even smaller than for $s = 2$. In fact, even the W_q values for other machines nearly satisfy the proposed new service standard at this point. However, John Phixitt points out that three-person territories have substantial disadvantages compared to two-person territories. One is longer travel times to machine sites. Another is that customers would feel that service is considerably less personalized when they are seeing three different tech reps coming for repairs instead of just two. Another perhaps more important disadvantage is that three tech reps would have considerably more difficulty coordinating their work than two. John does not feel that the decreases in W_q values for $s = 3$ are worth these (and related) disadvantages.

Three-person tech rep territories with priorities reduce waiting times even further but have substantial disadvantages compared to two-person territories.

Conclusion: Since the high-priority need is to improve service for the printer-copiers, strong consideration should be given to giving these machines priority over others for receiving repairs. However, the waiting times for both printer-copiers and other machines will remain unsatisfactory if the current one-person tech rep territories continue to be used. Enlarging to two-person territories would reduce these waiting times to levels that appear to be satisfactory, without any significant additional (monetary) costs. Enlarging the territories even further probably would not be worthwhile in light of the disadvantages of large territories.

Management's Conclusions

Having been assigned by Dupit's president to study the four suggested approaches to the company's problem, the management science team and John Phixitt were asked to report back to the top management group dealing with the problem in six weeks. They now do so by sending their report to each member of the group. The report presents their conclusions (as stated above and in the preceding sections) on each of the four approaches they were asked to investigate. Also included are the projected measures of performance (such as in Tables 14.7 and 14.8) for these approaches.

Table 14.9 summarizes the four approaches as they now have been refined by the management science team.

At this point, the president reconvenes his top management group (including John Phixitt). The meeting begins with a brief (and well-rehearsed) presentation by the head of the management science team summarizing the analysis and conclusions of the team. The presentation is interrupted frequently by comments and questions from the group. The president next asks John Phixitt to present his recommendations.

Although the first two proposals retain the many advantages of one-person territories, both proposals are too costly, so the choice is between the third and fourth proposals.

John begins by emphasizing the many advantages of the current system of one-person territories. The first two proposals in Table 14.9 would enable continuing this system, but at a very high cost. He then concedes that he has concluded that the cost would be too high and that the time has come to modify the system in order to efficiently deliver the service that the marketplace now is demanding. (A brief discussion reveals strong agreement from the group on this point.)

TABLE 14.9

The Four Approaches Being Considered by Dupit Management

Proposer	Proposal	Additional Cost
John Phixitt	Maintain one-person territories, but reduce number of machines assigned to each from 150 to 100	$300 million per year
Vice president for engineering	Keep current one-person territories, but provide new state-of-the-art equipment to the tech reps	One-time cost of $500 million
Chief financial officer	Change to three-person territories	None, except disadvantages of larger territories
Vice president for marketing	Change to two-person territories, with priority given to the printer-copiers for repairs	None, except disadvantages of larger territories

This leaves the third and fourth proposals in Table 14.9 under consideration. John repeats the arguments he had given earlier to the management science team about the important advantages of two-person territories over three-person territories. He then points out that the fourth proposal not only would provide two-person territories but also would result in the printer-copiers having smaller average waiting times for repairs than under the third proposal. When the customer relations manager objects that the average waiting times of *other machines* would not meet the proposed new service standard (a maximum of two hours), John emphasizes that these waiting times still would decrease substantially from current levels and that the owners of these machines aren't even complaining now. In conclusion, John recommends adoption of the fourth proposal.

Some minor concerns are raised in the subsequent discussion, including the possibility that owners of other machines might feel that they are being treated as second-class customers. However, John indicates that the new policy would not be publicized, but, if discovered, could be easily justified to a customer. The group soon concurs with John's recommendation.

Decision: Adopt the fourth proposal in Table 14.9.

Finally, John points out that there currently are a relatively few one-person territories that are so sparsely populated that combining them into two-person territories would cause excessive travel times for the tech reps. Since this would defeat the purpose of the new policy, he suggests adopting the second proposal for these territories and then using the experience with the new equipment to make future decisions on which equipment to provide to all tech reps as service demands further increase. The group agrees.

Decision: As an exception to the new policy, the second proposal in Table 14.9 is adopted just for current one-person territories that are particularly sparsely populated. The experience with the new equipment will be closely monitored to help guide future equipment purchase decisions for all tech reps.

The president thanks John Phixitt and the management science team for their outstanding work in pointing the way toward what appears to be an excellent resolution of a critical problem for the company. John graciously states that the real key was the insights obtained by the management science team by making effective use of the appropriate queueing models. The president smiles and makes a mental note to seek John's advice more often.

Review Questions

1. How does using priorities differ from serving customers on a first-come, first-served basis?
2. What is the difference between nonpreemptive priorities and preemptive priorities?
3. Except for using preemptive priorities, the assumptions of the preemptive priorities model are the same as for which basic queueing model?
4. Except for using nonpreemptive priorities, the assumptions of the nonpreemptive priorities model are the same as for which basic queueing model?
5. For these models, which values of the utilization factor ρ enable the queueing system to reach a steady-state condition for all priority classes?

6. When applying the nonpreemptive priorities queueing model to the Dupit case study, what are the two priority classes?

7. For this application, what is the conclusion about the minimum number of tech reps per territory needed to reduce waiting times for repairs to levels that appear to be satisfactory?

8. What is the decision of Dupit's top management regarding which of the four proposed approaches will be adopted (except for particularly sparsely populated territories)?

14.8   SOME INSIGHTS ABOUT DESIGNING QUEUEING SYSTEMS

The Dupit case study illustrates some key insights that queueing models provide about how queueing systems should be designed. This section highlights these insights in a broader context.

There are four insights presented here. Each one was first seen when analyzing one of the four approaches proposed for the Dupit problem. After summarizing each insight, we will briefly review its application to the case study and then describe the insight in general terms.

> **Insight 1:** When designing a single-server queueing system, beware that giving a relatively high utilization factor (workload) to the server provides surprisingly poor measures of performance for the system.[3]

This insight arose in Section 14.5 when analyzing John Phixitt's suggested approach of decreasing the utilization factor ρ for each tech rep sufficiently to meet the proposed new service standard (a maximum average waiting time for repairs of two hours). The current $\rho = 0.75$ gave average waiting times of six hours, which falls far short of this standard. It was necessary to decrease ρ all the way down to $\rho = 0.5$ to meet this standard.

To further demonstrate this insight, we have used the Excel template for the *M/M/s* model (previously shown in Figures 14.9 and 14.10), with $s = 1$ and $\mu = 1$ (so the utilization factor ρ equals λ), to generate the data table in Figure 14.15. Here are the steps to follow to do this. First make a table with the column headings shown in columns I, J, and K in Figure 14.15. In the first column of the table (I5:I16), list the trial values for the data cell (the mean arrival rate, or equivalently, the utilization factor), except leave the first row blank. The headings of the next columns specify which output will be evaluated. For each of these columns, use the first row of the table (cells J4:K4) to write an equation that refers to the relevant output cell. In this case, the cells of interest are the expected number of customers in the system (L) and in the queue (L_q), so the equations for J4:K4 are those shown below the spreadsheet in Figure 14.15.

Next, select the entire table (I4:K16) and then choose Table from the Data menu. In the Table dialogue box (as shown at the bottom left-hand side of Figure 14.15), indicate the column input cell (Lambda or C4), which refers to the data cell that is being changed in the first column of the table. Nothing is entered for the row input cell because no row is being used to list the trial values of a data cell in this case.

Clicking OK then generates the data table shown in Figure 14.15. For each trial value for the data cell listed in the first column of the table, the corresponding output cell values are calculated and displayed in the other columns of the table. (The numbers in the first row of the table come from the original solution in the spreadsheet.)

> The average number of customers waiting in a queueing system (L) increases rapidly with even small increases in the utilization factor ρ, so ρ should be kept well under 1.

Note in this data table how rapidly L_q and L increase with even small increases in ρ. For example, L triples when ρ is increased from 0.5 to 0.75, and then triples again when increasing ρ from 0.75 to 0.9. As ρ is increased above 0.9, L_q and L grow astronomically. (Although this data table has been generated with $\mu = 1$, the same values of L_q and L would be obtained with any other value of μ as well when the numbers in the first column are the utilization factor $\rho = \lambda/\mu$.)

Managers normally strive for a high utilization factor for their employees, machines, equipment, and so on. This is an important part of running an efficient business. A utilization factor of 0.9 or higher would be considered desirable. However, all this should change when the

---

[3]The one exception is a queueing system that has *constant* (or nearly constant) interarrival times and service times. Such a system will perform very well with a high utilization factor.

FIGURE 14.15
This data table demonstrates Insight 1 in Section 14.8.

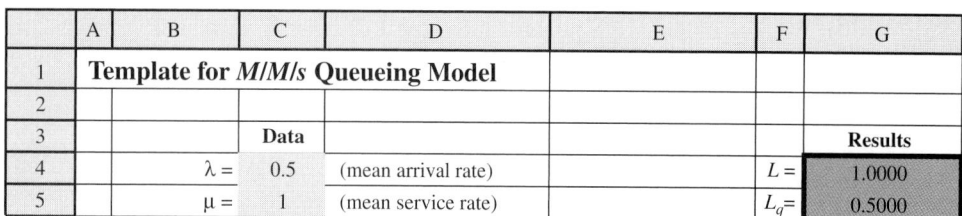

	A	B	C	D	E	F	G
1				Template for *M/M/s* Queueing Model			
2							
3			Data				Results
4		$\lambda =$	0.5	(mean arrival rate)		$L =$	1.0000
5		$\mu =$	1	(mean service rate)		$L_q=$	0.5000

	H	I	J	K	L	M	N	O
1		Data Table Demonstrating the Effect of Increasing ρ on L_q and L for *M/M/1*						
2								
3		$\lambda = \rho$	L	L_q				
4			1	0.5				
5		0.01	0.010	0.000				
6		0.25	0.333	0.083				
7		0.5	1	0.5				
8		0.6	1.5	0.9				
9		0.7	2.333	1.633				
10		0.75	3	2.25				
11		0.8	4	3.2				
12		0.85	5.667	4.817				
13		0.9	9	8.1				
14		0.95	19	18.05				
15		0.99	99	98.01				
16		0.999	999	998.001				
17								
18			Select entire table (I4:K16), before					
19			choosing Table from the Data menu.					
20								

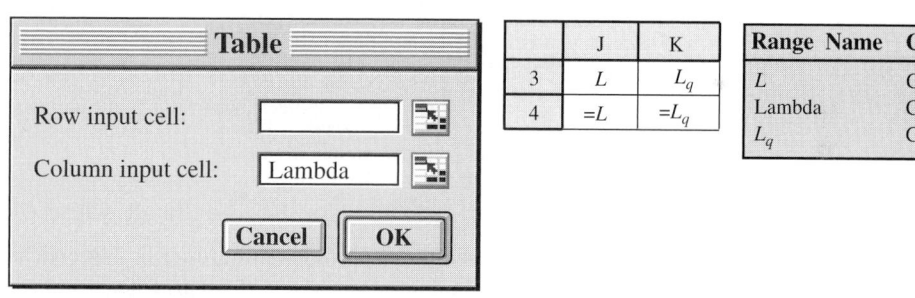

	J	K
3	L	L_q
4	$=L$	$=L_q$

Range Name	Cell
L	G4
Lambda	C4
L_q	G5

employee or machine or piece of equipment is the server in a single-server queueing system that has considerable variability in its interarrival times and service times (such as for an *M/M/1* system). For most such systems, the cognizant manager would consider it unacceptable to *average* having nine customers wait in the system ($L = 9$ with $\rho = 0.9$). If so, a utilization factor somewhat less (perhaps much less) than 0.9 would be needed. For example, we just mentioned that meeting Dupit's proposed service standard with John Phixitt's original suggested approach required reducing the utilization factor all the way down to $\rho = 0.5$.

Insight 2: Decreasing the *variability* of service times (without any change in the mean) improves the performance of a single-server queueing system substantially. (This also tends to be true for multiple-server queueing systems, especially with higher utilization factors.)

This insight was found in the Dupit study while analyzing the proposal by the vice president for engineering to provide new state-of-the-art equipment to all the tech reps. As described at the end of Section 14.5, this approach would decrease both the *mean* and *standard deviation* of the service-time distribution. Decreasing the mean also decreased the utilization

FIGURE 14.16

This data table demonstrates Insight 2 in Section 14.8.

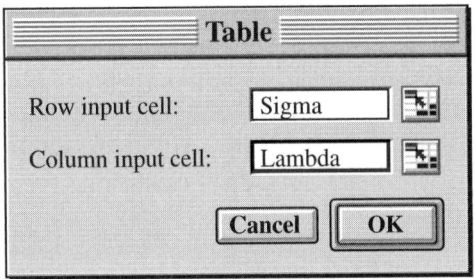

	A	B	C	D	E	F	G	H	I
1				**Template for the *M/G/*1 Queueing Model**					
2									
3			**Data**				**Results**		
4		$\lambda =$	0.5	(mean arrival rate)		$L =$	0.8125		
5		$1/\mu =$	1	(expected service time)		$L_q =$	0.3125		
6		$\sigma =$	0.5	(standard deviation)					
7		$s =$	1	(# servers)		$W =$	1.625		
8						$W_q =$	0.625		
9									
10						$\rho =$	0.5		
11									
12						$P_0 =$	0.5		
13									
14		**Data Table Demonstrating the Effect of Decreasing σ on L_q for *M/G/*1**							
15									
16				Body of Table Shows L_q Values					
17									
18					σ				
19			0.3125	1	0.5	0			
20			0.5	0.500	0.313	0.250	Select entire table (C19:F23), before choosing Table from the Data menu.		
21		$\rho (=\lambda)$	0.75	2.250	1.406	1.125			
22			0.9	8.100	5.063	4.050			
23			0.99	98.010	61.256	49.005			

Table

Row input cell: Sigma

Column input cell: Lambda

Cancel   OK

	C
19	$=L_q$

Range Name	Cell
Lambda	C4
L_q	G5
Sigma	C6

factor, which decreased the expected waiting time W_q. Decreasing the standard deviation σ (which measures the amount of variability) then provided an *additional* 37.5 percent reduction in W_q. Insight 2 refers to this latter substantial improvement in W_q (and in the other measures of performance).

The two-way data table in Figure 14.16 demonstrates the effect on L_q of decreasing the standard deviation σ of the service-time distribution for any *M/G/*1 queueing system. (This table was generated from the Excel template introduced in Figure 14.7 for the *M/G/*1 model.)

To create this two-way data table, make a table with column and row headings as shown in rows 19–23 of the spreadsheet in Figure 14.16. In the upper left-hand corner of the table (C19), write an equation that refers to the output cell for which you are interested in seeing the results ($= L_q$ or G5). In the first column of the table (column C, below the equation in cell C19), insert all the different values for the first changing data cell (λ). In the first row of the table (row 19, to the right of the equation in cell C19), insert all the different values for the second changing data cell (σ).

Next, select the entire table (C19:F23) and then choose Table from the Data menu. In the Table dialogue box (shown at the bottom left-hand side of Figure 14.16), indicate which data cells are being changed simultaneously. The column input cell refers to the data cell whose various values are indicated in the first column of the table (Lambda, or cell C4), while the row input cell refers to the data cell whose various values are indicated in the first row of the table (Sigma, or cell C6).

The data table shown in Figure 14.16 is then generated automatically by clicking OK. For each pair of values of the input cell indicated in the first row and column of the table, Excel determines the corresponding value of the output cell referred to in the upper left-hand corner of the table. These values are then filled into the body of the table.

Before generating this data table, the mean of the service-time distribution has been set in cell C5 at $1/\mu = 1$ (which makes $\rho = \lambda$), so the column headings of $\sigma = 1$, $\sigma = 0.5$, and $\sigma = 0$ correspond to $\sigma = $ mean, $\sigma = 0.5$ mean, and $\sigma = 0$, respectively. Therefore, as you read the values of L_q in the table from left to right, σ decreases from equaling the mean of the distribution (as for the $M/M/1$ model) to being *half* the mean (as for the $M/E_k/1$ model with $k = 4$) and then to $\sigma = 0$ (as for the $M/D/1$ model). If the mean were to be changed to some value different from 1, the same values of L_q still would be obtained for each value of the utilization factor $\rho = \lambda/\mu$ listed in cells C20:C23 as long as the values of σ for the respective columns are $\sigma = $ mean, $\sigma = 0.5$ mean, and $\sigma = 0$.

In each row of this table, the value in the $\sigma = 0$ column is only *half* that in the $\sigma = 1$ column, so completely eliminating the variability of the service times gives a large improvement. However, the value in the $\sigma = 0.5$ column is only 62.5 percent of that in the $\sigma = 1$ column, so even cutting the variability in half provides most of the improvement from completely eliminating the variability. Therefore, whatever can be done to reduce the variability even modestly is going to improve the performance of the system significantly.

> *If service times are highly variable, eliminating this variability can reduce L_q by about half.*

> **Insight 3:** *Multiple-server* queueing systems can perform satisfactorily with somewhat higher utilization factors than can single-server queueing systems. For example, *pooling servers* by combining separate single-server queueing systems into one multiple-server queueing system (without changing the utilization factor) greatly improves the measures of performance.

This insight was gained during the Dupit study while investigating the proposal by the chief financial officer to combine one-person territories into larger territories served jointly by multiple tech reps. Table 14.7 in Section 14.6 summarizes the great impact that this approach would have on improving average waiting times to begin repairs (W_q). In particular, W_q for two-person territories is well under *half* that for one-person territories, and W_q for three-person territories is about a *fourth* of that for one-person territories, even though the utilization factor is the same for all these cases.

These dramatic improvements are not unusual. In fact, it has been found that pooling servers as described below *always* provides similar improvements.

> *Here is a way to reduce waiting times dramatically.*

> **The Impact of Pooling Servers:** Suppose you have a number (denoted by n) of identical single-server queueing systems that fit the $M/M/1$ model. Suppose you then combine these n systems (without changing the utilization factor) into a single queueing system that fits the $M/M/s$ model, where the number of servers is $s = n$. This change *always* improves the value of W_q by *more* than dividing by n, that is,

$$W_q(\text{for combined system}) \; < \; \frac{W_q(\text{for each single-server system})}{n}$$

Although this inequality is not guaranteed to hold if these queueing systems do not fit the $M/M/1$ and $M/M/s$ models, the improvement in W_q by combining systems still will be very substantial for other models as well.

> **Insight 4:** Applying *priorities* when selecting customers to begin service can greatly improve the measures of performance for high-priority customers.

This insight became evident during the Dupit study while investigating the proposal by the vice president for marketing to give higher (nonpreemptive) priority to repairing the printer-copiers than to repairing other machines. Table 14.8 in the preceding section gives the values of W_q for the printer-copiers and for the other machines under this proposal. Comparing these values to those in Table 14.7 without priorities shows that giving priority to the printer-copiers would reduce their waiting times now dramatically (but would also increase the waiting times for the

> *Applying priorities can reduce waiting times dramatically for high-priority customers but will increase waiting times for low-priority customers.*

other machines). Later, as printer-copiers become a larger proportion of the machines being serviced (half instead of a third), the reduction in their waiting times would not be quite as large.

For other queueing systems as well, the impact of applying priorities depends somewhat on the proportion of the customers in the respective priority classes. If the proportion in the top priority class is small, the measures of performance for these customers will improve tremendously. If the proportion is large, the improvement will be more modest.

Preemptive priorities give an even stronger preference to high-priority customers than do the *nonpreemptive* priorities used for the Dupit problem. Therefore, applying preemptive priorities improves the measures of performance for customers in the top priority class even more than applying nonpreemptive priorities.

Review Questions

1. What is the effect of giving a relatively large utilization factor (workload) to the server in a single-server queueing system?

2. What happens to the values of L_q and L for the *M/M/*1 model when ρ is increased well above 0.9?

3. What is the effect of decreasing the variability of service times (without any change in the mean) on the performance of a single-server queueing system?

4. For an *M/G/*1 queueing system, does cutting the variability (standard deviation) of service times in half provide most of the improvement that would be achieved by completely eliminating the variability?

5. What is the effect of combining separate single-server queueing systems into one multiple-server queueing system (without changing the utilization factor)?

6. What is the effect of applying priorities when selecting customers to begin service?

7. Do preemptive priorities or nonpreemptive priorities give the greater improvement in the measures of performance for customers in the top priority class?

14.9 ECONOMIC ANALYSIS OF THE NUMBER OF SERVERS TO PROVIDE

When designing a queueing system, a key question often is how many servers to provide. Providing too many causes excessive costs. Providing too few causes excessive waiting by the customers. Therefore, choosing the number of servers involves finding an appropriate trade-off between the cost of the servers and the amount of waiting.

In many cases, the consequences to an organization of making its customers wait can be expressed as a **waiting cost.** This is especially true when the customers are *internal* to the organization, such as the employees of a company. Making one's own employees wait causes *lost productivity,* which results in *lost profit.* This lost profit is the waiting cost.

A manager is interested in minimizing the total cost. Let

TC = Expected total cost per unit time

SC = Expected service cost per unit time

WC = Expected waiting cost per unit time

Then the objective is to choose the number of servers so as to

$$\text{Minimize} \quad \text{TC} = \text{SC} + \text{WC}$$

When each server costs the same, the **service cost** is

$$\text{SC} = C_s s$$

where

C_s = Cost of a server per unit time

s = Number of servers

When the waiting cost is proportional to the amount of waiting, this cost can be expressed as

$$\text{WC} = C_w L$$

FIGURE 14.17

The shape of the cost curves for determining the number of servers to provide.

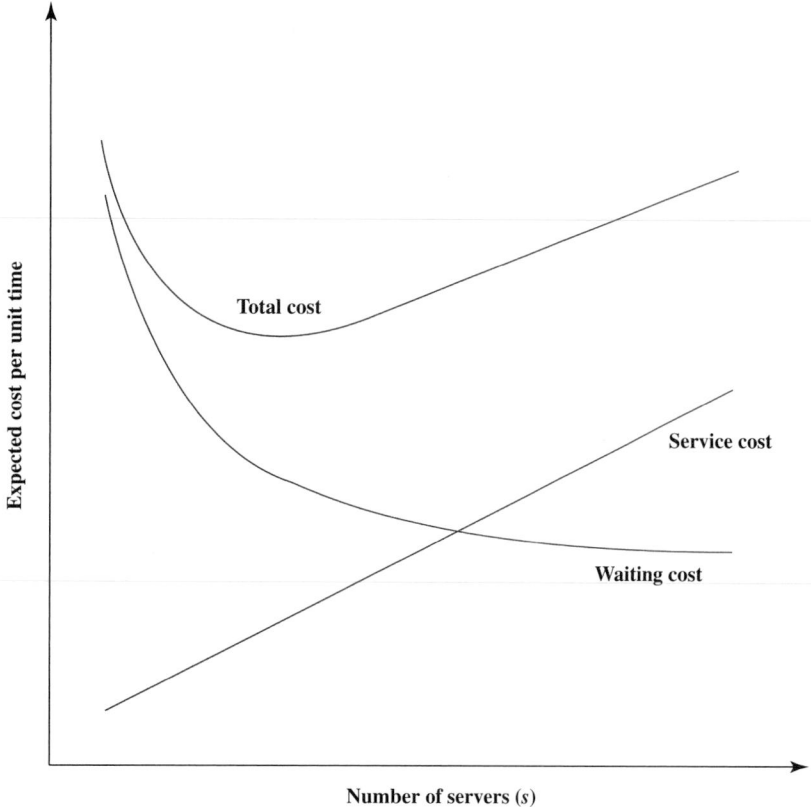

where

C_w = Waiting cost per unit time for each customer in the queueing system

L = Expected number of customers in the queueing system

Therefore, after estimating the constants C_s and C_w, the goal is to choose the value of s so as to

$$\text{Minimize} \qquad \text{TC} = C_s s + C_w L$$

By choosing the queueing model that fits the queueing system, the value of L can be obtained for various values of s. Increasing s decreases L, at first rapidly and then gradually more slowly.

Figure 14.17 shows the general shape of the SC, WC, and TC curves versus the number of servers s. (For better conceptualization, we have drawn these as smooth curves even though the only feasible values of s are $s = 1, 2, \ldots$). By calculating TC for consecutive values of s until TC stops decreasing and starts increasing instead, it is straightforward to find the number of servers that minimizes total cost. The following example illustrates this process.

Calculate TC for consecutive values of s until TC stops decreasing to find the optimal number of servers.

An Example

The Acme Machine Shop has a tool crib for storing tools required by the shop mechanics. Two clerks run the tool crib. The tools are handed out by the clerks as the mechanics arrive and request them and are returned to the clerks when they are no longer needed. There have been complaints from supervisors that their mechanics have had to waste too much time waiting to be served at the tool crib, so it appears that there should be *more* clerks. On the other hand, management is exerting pressure to reduce overhead in the plant, and this reduction would lead to *fewer* clerks. To resolve these conflicting pressures, a management science study is being conducted to determine just how many clerks the tool crib should have.

The tool crib constitutes a queueing system, with the clerks as its servers and the mechanics as its customers. After gathering some data on interarrival times and service times, the management science team has concluded that the queueing model that fits this queueing system best is the *M/M/s* model. The estimates of the mean arrival rate λ and the mean service rate (per server) μ are

$$\lambda = 120 \text{ customers per hour}$$

$$\mu = 80 \text{ customers per hour}$$

so the utilization factor for the two clerks is

$$\rho = \frac{\lambda}{s\mu} = \frac{120}{2(80)} = 0.75$$

The total cost to the company of each tool crib clerk is about \$20 per hour, so $C_s = \$20$. While a mechanic is busy, the value to the company of his or her output averages about \$48 per hour, so $C_w = \$48$. Therefore, the management science team now needs to find the number of servers (tool crib clerks) s that will

$$\text{Minimize} \quad TC = \$20s + \$48L$$

An Excel template has been provided in your MS Courseware for calculating these costs with the *M/M/s* model. All you need to do is enter the data for the model along with the unit service cost C_s, the unit waiting cost C_w, and the number of servers s you want to try. The template then calculates SC, WC, and TC. This is illustrated in Figure 14.18 with $s = 3$ for this example. By repeatedly entering alternative values of s, the template then can reveal which value minimizes TC in a matter of seconds.

Your MS Courseware includes an Excel template that will calculate TC for you.

FIGURE 14.18

This Excel template for using economic analysis to choose the number of servers with the *M/M/s* model is applied here to the Acme Machine Shop example with $s = 3$.

	A	B	C	D	E	F	G
1		**Economic Analysis of Acme Machine Shop Example**					
2							
3			**Data**				**Results**
4		$\lambda =$	120	(mean arrival rate)		$L =$	1.736842105
5		$\mu =$	80	(mean service rate)		$L_q=$	0.236842105
6		$s =$	3	(# servers)			
7						$W =$	0.014473684
8		$\text{Pr}(W > t) =$	0.02581732			$W_q=$	0.001973684
9		when $t =$	0.05				
10						$\rho =$	0.5
11		$\text{Prob}(W_q > t) =$	0.00058707				
12		when $t =$	0.05			n	P_n
13						0	0.210526316
14		**Economic Analysis:**				1	0.315789474
15		$C_s =$	\$20.00	(cost/server/unit time)		2	0.236842105
16		$C_w =$	\$48.00	(waiting cost/unit time)		3	0.118421053
17						4	0.059210526
18		Cost of Service	\$60.00			5	0.029605263
19		Cost of Waiting	\$83.37			6	0.014802632
20		Total Cost	\$143.37			7	0.007401316

	B	C
18	Cost of Service	$= C_s * s$
19	Cost of Waiting	$= C_w * L$
20	Total Cost	=CostOfService+CostOfWaiting

Range Name	Cell
CostOfService	C18
CostOfWaiting	C19
C_s	C15
C_w	C16
L	G4
s	C6
TotalCost	C20

FIGURE 14.19
This data table compares the expected hourly costs with various alternative numbers of clerks assigned to the Acme Machine Shop tool crib.

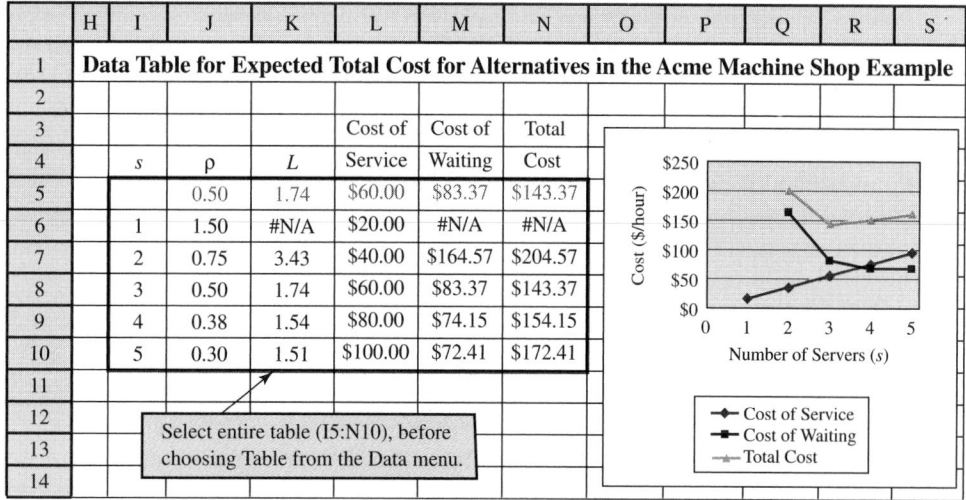

	H	I	J	K	L	M	N	O	P	Q	R	S
1			**Data Table for Expected Total Cost for Alternatives in the Acme Machine Shop Example**									
2												
3					Cost of	Cost of	Total					
4		s	ρ	L	Service	Waiting	Cost					
5			0.50	1.74	$60.00	$83.37	$143.37					
6		1	1.50	#N/A	$20.00	#N/A	#N/A					
7		2	0.75	3.43	$40.00	$164.57	$204.57					
8		3	0.50	1.74	$60.00	$83.37	$143.37					
9		4	0.38	1.54	$80.00	$74.15	$154.15					
10		5	0.30	1.51	$100.00	$72.41	$172.41					
11												
12				Select entire table (I5:N10), before								
13				choosing Table from the Data menu.								
14												

	J	K	L	M	N
3			Cost of	Cost of	Total
4	ρ	L	Service	Waiting	Cost
5	=Rho	=L	=CostOfService	=CostOfWaiting	=TotalCost

Range Name	Cell
CostOfService	C18
CostOfWaiting	C19
L	G4
Rho	G10
s	C6
TotalCost	C20

Figure 14.19 shows a data table that has been generated from this template by repeating these calculations for $s = 1, 2, 3, 4,$ and 5. (See Section 14.8 for more information about generating data tables.) Since the utilization factor for $s = 1$ is $\rho = 1.5$, a single clerk would be unable to keep up with the customers (as indicated by #N/A in cells K6 and M6:N6), so this option is ruled out. All larger values of s are feasible, but $s = 3$ has the smallest total cost. Furthermore, $s = 3$ would decrease the current total cost for $s = 2$ by $62 per hour. Therefore, despite management's current drive to reduce overhead (which includes the cost of tool crib clerks), the management science team recommends that a third clerk be added to the tool crib. Note that this recommendation would decrease the utilization factor for the clerks from an already modest 0.75 all the way down to 0.5. However, because of the large improvement in the productivity of the mechanics (who are much more expensive than the clerks) through decreasing their time wasted waiting at the tool crib, management adopts the recommendation.

A low utilization factor of 0.5 is best for the tool crib clerks because this greatly reduces the time wasted by expensive mechanics waiting at the tool crib.

Review Questions

1. What is the trade-off involved in choosing the number of servers for a queueing system?
2. What is the nature of the waiting cost when the customers for the queueing system are the company's own employees?
3. When the waiting cost is proportional to the amount of waiting, what is an expression for the waiting cost?
4. What does the Acme Machine Shop example demonstrate about the advisability of always maintaining a relatively high utilization factor for the servers in a queueing system?

14.10   SOME AWARD-WINNING APPLICATIONS OF QUEUEING MODELS

Section 1.3 describes the prestigious Franz Edelman Awards for Management Science Achievement that are awarded annually. A rather substantial number of these awards have been given for innovative applications of queueing models. We briefly describe some of these applications next.

One of the early first-prize winners (November 1975 issue, Part 2, of *Interfaces*) was the **Xerox Corporation.** The company had recently introduced a major new duplicating system that was proving to be particularly valuable for its owners. Consequently, these customers were demanding that Xerox's tech reps reduce the waiting times to repair the machines. A management science team then applied queueing models to study how best to meet the new service requirements. This resulted in replacing the previous one-person tech rep territories by larger three-person tech rep territories. This change had the dramatic effect of both substantially reducing the average waiting times of the customers and increasing the utilization of the tech reps by over 50 percent.

Yes, the Dupit case study is based on this award-winning application (with some new enhancements). Although this application occurred many years ago, the case study demonstrates that the same principles for how to apply queueing models are equally valid today.

In Sections 2.1 and 4.8, we described an award-winning application by **United Airlines** (January 1986 issue of *Interfaces*) that resulted in annual savings of over $6 million. This application involved scheduling the work assignments of United's 4,000 reservations sales representatives and support personnel at its 11 reservations offices and the 1,000 customer service agents at its 10 largest airports. After determining how many employees were needed at each location during each half hour of the week, we discussed in these earlier sections how linear programming was applied to design the work schedules for all the employees to meet these service requirements most efficiently. However, we never mentioned how these service requirements on the number of employees needed each half hour were determined.

We now are in a position to point out that these service requirements were determined by applying *queueing models*. Each specific location (e.g., the check-in counters at an airport) constitutes a queueing system with the employees as the servers. After forecasting the mean arrival rate during each half hour of the week, queueing models were used to find the minimum number of servers that would provide satisfactory measures of performance for the queueing system.

L. L. Bean, Inc., the large telemarketer and mail-order catalog house, relied mainly on queueing models for its award-winning study of how to allocate its telecommunications resources. (The article describing this study is in the January 1991 issue of *Interfaces,* and other articles giving additional information are in the November 1989 and March–April 1993 issues of this journal.) The telephone calls coming in to its call center to place orders are the customers in a large queueing system, with the telephone agents as the servers. The key questions being asked during the study were the following.

1. How many telephone trunk lines should be provided for incoming calls to the call center?

2. How many telephone agents should be scheduled at various times?

3. How many hold positions should be provided for customers waiting for a telephone agent? (Note that the limited number of hold positions causes the system to have a *finite queue.*)

For each interesting combination of these three quantities, queueing models provide the measures of performance of the queueing system. Given these measures, the management science team carefully assessed the cost of lost sales due to making some customers either incur a busy signal or be placed on hold too long. By adding the cost of the telemarketing resources, the team then was able to find the combination of the three quantities that minimized the expected total cost. This resulted in cost savings of $9 to $10 million per year.

New York City has a long-standing tradition of using management science techniques in planning and operating many of its complex urban service systems. Starting in the late 1960s, award-winning studies involving queueing models have been conducted for its Fire Department and its Police Department. (Fires and police emergencies are the customers in these respective queueing systems.) Subsequently, major management science studies (including several more involving queueing models) have been conducted for its Department of Sanitation, Department of Transportation, Department of Health and Hospitals, Department of Environmental Protection, Office of Management and Budget, and Department of Probation. Because of the success of these studies, many of these departments now have their own in-house management science groups.

The Dupit case study is adapted from this award-winning application of queueing models at the Xerox Corporation.

United Airlines applied queueing models to determine how many servers should be provided at each ground location where customers are being served.

This application of queueing models saves L. L. Bean $9 to $10 million per year.

The award-winning study in New York City that we will describe here involves its *arrest-to-arraignment system*. This system consists of the process from when individuals are arrested until they are arraigned (the first court appearance before an arraignment judge, who determines whether there was probable cause for the arrest). Before the study, the city's arrestees (the customers in a queueing system) were in custody waiting to be arraigned for an average of 40 hours (occasionally more than 70 hours). These waiting times were considered excessive, because the arrestees were being held in crowded, noisy conditions that were emotionally stressful, unhealthy, and often physically dangerous. Therefore, a two-year management science study was conducted to overhaul the system. Both queueing models and computer simulation (the subject of the next chapters) were used. This led to sweeping operational and policy changes that *simultaneously* reduced average waiting times until arraignment to 24 hours or less and provided annual savings of $9.5 million. (See the January–February 1993 issue of *Interfaces* for details.)

The first prize in the 1993 competition was won by **AT&T** for a study that (like the preceding one) also combined the use of queueing models and computer simulation (see the January–February 1994 issue of *Interfaces*). The models are of both AT&T's telecommunication network and the call center environment for the typical business customers of AT&T that have such centers. The purpose of the study was to develop a user-friendly PC-based system that AT&T's business customers could use to guide them in how to design or redesign their call centers. Since call centers comprise one of the United States's fastest growing industries, this system had been used about 2,000 times by AT&T's business customers by 1992. This resulted in more than $750 million in annual profits for these customers.

Hewlett-Packard (HP) is a leading multinational manufacturer of electronic equipment. In 1993, the company installed a mechanized assembly-line system for manufacturing ink-jet printers at its plant in Vancouver, Washington, to meet the exploding demand for such printers. It soon became apparent that the system installed would not be fast enough or reliable enough to meet the company's production goals. Therefore, a joint team of management scientists from HP and the Massachusetts Institute of Technology (MIT) was formed to study how to redesign the system to improve its performance.

As described in the January–February 1998 issue of *Interfaces,* the HP/MIT team quickly realized that the assembly-line system could be modeled as a special kind of queueing system where the customers (the printers to be assembled) go through a series of servers (assembly operations) in a fixed sequence. A special queueing model for this kind of system quickly provided the analytical results that were needed to determine how the system should be redesigned to achieve the required capacity in the most economical way. The changes included adding some buffer storage space at strategic points to better maintain the flow of work to the subsequent stations and to dampen the effect of machine failures. The new design increased productivity about 50 percent and yielded incremental revenues of approximately $280 million in printer sales as well as additional revenue from ancillary products. This innovative application of the special queueing model also provided HP with a new method for creating rapid and effective system designs subsequently in other areas of the company.

In case you would like to read more about any of these applications, we have cited the issue of *Interfaces* in which a full descriptive article appears. With the exception of the Xerox article, all of these articles also can be downloaded at **www.mhhe.com/hillier2e/articles.**

There have been many other award-winning applications of queueing models, as well as numerous additional articles describing other successful applications. However, the several examples presented in this section hopefully have given you a feeling for the kinds of applications that are occurring and for the impact they can have.

Review Questions

1. What change in tech rep territories was made as a result of the award-winning application of queueing models at the Xerox Corporation?

2. What was found by using queueing models in the award-winning study at United Airlines?

3. Decisions needed to be made on which three quantities in the award-winning study at L. L. Bean, Inc.?

4. Who are the customers in the queueing system that was studied in the award-winning application in New York City?

5. How much additional annual profit was obtained by the business customers of AT&T who used its system to guide the design or redesign of their call centers?

6. What special kind of queueing system was analyzed in the award-winning application at Hewlett-Packard?

14.11 Summary

Queueing systems are prevalent throughout society. The adequacy of these systems can have an important effect on the quality of life and the productivity of the economy.

Key components of a queueing system are the *arriving customers,* the *queue* in which they wait for service, and the *servers* that provide the service. A queueing model representing a queueing system needs to specify the number of servers, the distribution of interarrival times, and the distribution of service times. An *exponential* distribution usually is chosen for the distribution of interarrival times because this corresponds to the common phenomenon of arrivals occurring randomly. An exponential distribution sometimes provides a reasonable fit to the service-time distribution as well, and is a particularly convenient choice in terms of ease of analysis. Other probability distributions sometimes used for the service-time distribution include the *degenerate* distribution (constant service times) and the *Erlang* distribution.

Key measures of the performance of queueing systems are the expected values of the number of customers in the queue or in the system (the latter adds on customers currently being served) and of the waiting time of a customer in the queue or in the system. General relationships between these expected values, including Little's formula, enable all four values to be determined immediately as soon as one has been found. In addition to the expected values, the probability distributions of these quantities are sometimes used as measures of performance as well.

This chapter's case study has the top management of the Dupit Corporation grappling with a difficult issue. The company's customers now are demanding a much higher level of service in promptly repairing the photocopiers (and particularly a new printer-copier) purchased from the company. Dupit already is spending $600 million per year servicing these machines. Each tech rep territory includes a queueing system with the tech rep as the server and the machines needing repairs as the customers. A management science team finds that the $M/M/1$ model, the $M/G/1$ model, the $M/M/s$ model, and a nonpreemptive priorities model enable analyzing the alternative approaches to redesigning this queueing system. This analysis leads to top management adopting a policy of combining pairs of one-person tech rep territories into two-person territories that give priority to repairing the new printer-copiers. This provides the needed level of service without a significant increase in cost.

Other queueing models discussed in the chapter include the $M/D/1$ and $M/D/s$ models, the $M/E_k/1$ and $M/E_k/s$ models, and a preemptive priorities model. A supplement to this chapter on the CD-ROM also introduces the finite queue variation and the finite calling population variation of the $M/M/s$ model.

Section 14.8 presents four key insights that queueing models provide about how queueing systems should be designed. Each of these insights also is illustrated by the Dupit case study.

The chapter concludes with a description of six award-winning applications of queueing models. Each of these applications has led to annual savings of many millions of dollars.

Glossary

commercial service system   A queueing system where a commercial organization provides a service to customers from outside the organization. (Section 14.2), *661*

constant service times   Every customer has the same service time. (Section 14.1), *658*

customers   A generic term that refers to whichever kind of entity (people, vehicles, machines, items, etc.) is coming to the queueing system to receive service. (Section 14.1), *654*

Erlang distribution   A common service-time distribution whose shape parameter k specifies the amount of variability in the service times. Figure 14.4 shows its shape. (Section 14.1), *658*

exponential distribution   The most popular choice for the probability distribution of both interarrival times and service times. Its shape is shown in Figure 14.3. (Section 14.1), *658*

finite queue   A queue that can hold only a limited number of customers. (Section 14.1), *657*

infinite queue   A queue that can hold an essentially unlimited number of customers. (Section 14.1), *657*

interarrival time   The elapsed time between consecutive arrivals to a queueing system. (Section 14.1), *655*

internal service system   A queueing system where the customers receiving service are internal to the organization providing the service. (Section 14.2), *662*

lack-of-memory property   When referring to arrivals, this property is that the time of the next arrival is completely uninfluenced by when the last arrival occurred. Also called the Markovian property. (Section 14.1), *657*

Little's formula The formula $L = \lambda W$, or $L_q = \lambda W_q$. (Section 14.3), *665*

mean arrival rate The expected number of arrivals to a queueing system per unit time. (Section 14.1), *655*

mean service rate The expected number of service completions per unit time for a single continuously busy server. (Section 14.1), *658*

nonpreemptive priorities Priorities for selecting the next customer to begin service when a server becomes free. However, these priorities do not affect customers who already have begun service. (Section 14.7), *684*

number of customers in the queue The number of customers who are waiting for service to begin. (Sections 14.1, 14.3), *657*

number of customers in the system The total number of customers in the queueing system, either waiting for service to begin or currently being served. (Sections 14.1, 14.3), *657*

preemptive priorities Priorities for serving customers that include ejecting the lowest priority customer being served back into the queue in order to serve a higher priority customer that has just entered the queueing system. (Section 14.7), *684*

priority classes Categories of customers that are given different priorities for receiving service. (Section 14.7), *684*

queue The waiting line in a queueing system. The queue does not include customers who are already being served. (Section 14.1), *654*

queue capacity The maximum number of customers that can be held in the queue. (Section 14.1), *657*

queue discipline The rule for determining the order in which members of the queue are selected to begin service. (Section 14.1), *657*

queueing system A place where customers receive some kind of service from a server, perhaps after waiting in a queue. (Section 14.1), *654*

server An entity that is serving the customers coming to a queueing system. (Section 14.1), *654*

service cost The cost associated with providing the servers in a queueing system. (Section 14.9), *694*

service time The elapsed time from the beginning to the end of a customer's service. (Section 14.1), *657*

steady-state condition The normal condition that a queueing system is in after operating for some time with a fixed utilization factor less than one. (Section 14.3), *664*

tech rep An abbreviated name for the service technical representatives in the Dupit case study. (Section 14.4), *666*

transportation service system A queueing system involving transportation, so that either the customers or the server(s) are vehicles. (Section 14.2), *662*

utilization factor The average fraction of time that the servers are being utilized serving customers. (Sections 14.5, 14.6), *670*

waiting cost The cost associated with making customers wait in a queueing system. (Section 14.9), *694*

waiting time in the queue The elapsed time that an individual customer spends in the queue waiting for service to begin. (Section 14.3), *664*

waiting time in the system The elapsed time that an individual customer spends in the queueing system both before service begins and during service. (Section 14.3), *664*

Key Symbols

λ = Mean arrival rate (Section 14.1)

μ = Mean service rate (Section 14.1)

s = Number of servers (Section 14.1)

L = Expected number of customers in the system (Section 14.3)

L_q = Expected number of customers in the queue (Section 14.3)

W = Expected waiting time in the system (Section 14.3)

W_q = Expected waiting time in the queue (Section 14.3)

ρ = Utilization factor for the servers (Sections 14.5 and 14.6)

Learning Aids for This Chapter in Your MS Courseware

Chapter 14 Excel Files:

Template for M/M/s Model

Template for M/G/1 Model

Template for M/D/1 Model

Template for M/E$_k$/1 Model

Template for Nonpreemptive Priorities Model
Template for Preemptive Priorities Model
Template for M/M/s Economic Analysis of Number of Servers

Interactive Management Science Modules:

Waiting Line Module

Supplement to This Chapter on the CD-ROM:

The Finite Queue and Finite Calling Population Variations of the M/M/s Model

Supplement to Chapter 14 Excel Files:

Template for Finite Queue Variation of M/M/s Model
Template for Finite Calling Population Variation of M/M/s Model

Problems

To the left of the following problems (or their parts), we have inserted the symbol E (for Excel) whenever one of the above templates can be helpful. An asterisk on the problem number indicates that at least a partial answer is given in the back of the book.

14.1. Consider a typical hospital emergency room.

   a. Describe why it is a queueing system.

   b. What is the *queue* in this case? Describe how you would expect the queue discipline to operate.

   c. Would you expect *random arrivals?*

   d. What are *service times* in this context? Would you expect much variability in the service times?

14.2. Identify the customers and the servers in the queueing system in each of the following situations.

   a. The checkout stand in a grocery store.

   b. A fire station.

   c. The toll booth for a bridge.

   d. A bicycle repair shop.

   e. A shipping dock.

   f. A group of semiautomatic machines assigned to one operator.

   g. The materials-handling equipment in a factory area.

   h. A plumbing shop.

   i. A job shop producing custom orders.

   j. A secretarial word processing pool.

14.3.* For each of the following statements about using the exponential distribution as the probability distribution of interarrival times, label the statement as true or false and then justify your answer by referring to a specific statement in the chapter.

   a. It is the only distribution of interarrival times that fits having random arrivals.

   b. It has the lack-of-memory property because it cannot remember when the next arrival will occur.

   c. It provides an excellent fit for interarrival times for most situations.

14.4. For each of the following statements about using the exponential distribution as the probability distribution of service times, label the statement as true or false and then justify your answer by referring to a specific statement in the chapter.

   a. It generally provides an excellent approximation of the true service-time distribution.

   b. Its mean and variance are always equal.

   c. It represents a rather extreme case regarding the amount of variability in the service times.

14.5. For each of the following statements about the queue in a queueing system, label the statement as true or false and then justify your answer by referring to a specific statement in the chapter.

   a. The queue is where customers wait in the queueing system until their service is completed.

   b. Queueing models conventionally assume that the queue can hold only a limited number of customers.

   c. The most common queue discipline is first-come, first-served.

14.6. Midtown Bank always has two tellers on duty. Customers arrive to receive service from a teller at a mean rate of 40 per hour. A teller requires an average of two minutes to serve a customer. When both tellers are busy, an arriving customer joins a single line to wait for service. Experience has shown that customers wait in line an average of one minute before service begins.

   a. Describe why this is a queueing system.

   b. Determine the basic measures of performance—W_q, W, L_q, and L—for this queueing system. (*Hint:* We don't know the probability distributions of interarrival times and service times for this queueing system, so you will need to use the relationships between these measures of performance to help answer the question.)

14.7. Mom-and-Pop's Grocery Store has a small adjacent parking lot with three parking spaces reserved for the store's customers. During store hours, when the lot is not full, cars enter the lot and use one of the spaces at a mean rate of two per hour. When the lot is full, arriving cars leave and do not return. For $n = 0, 1, 2, 3$, the probability P_n that exactly n spaces currently are being used is $P_0 = 0.2$, $P_1 = 0.3$, $P_2 = 0.3$, $P_3 = 0.2$.

   a. Describe how this parking lot can be interpreted as being a queueing system. In particular, identify the customers and the servers. What is the service being provided? What constitutes a service time? What is the queue capacity? (*Hint:* See Table 14.5.)

   b. Determine the basic measures of performance—L, L_q, W, and W_q—for this queueing system. (*Hint:* You can use the given probabilities to determine the average number of parking spaces that are being used.)

   c. Use the results from part *b* to determine the average length of time that a car remains in a parking space.

14.8.* Newell and Jeff are the two barbers in a barber shop they own and operate. They provide two chairs for customers who are waiting to begin a haircut, so the number of customers in the shop varies between 0 and 4. For $n = 0, 1, 2, 3, 4$, the probability P_n that exactly n customers are in the shop is $P_0 = \frac{1}{16}$, $P_1 = \frac{4}{16}$, $P_2 = \frac{6}{16}$, $P_3 = \frac{4}{16}$, $P_4 = \frac{1}{16}$.

   a. Use the formula $L = 0P_0 + 1P_1 + 2P_2 + 3P_3 + 4P_4$ to calculate L. How would you describe the meaning of L to Newell and Jeff?

   b. For each of the possible values of the number of customers in the queueing system, specify how many customers are in the queue. For each of the possible numbers in the queue, multiply by its probability, and then add these products to calculate L_q. How would you describe the meaning of L_q to Newell and Jeff?

   c. Given that an average of four customers per hour arrive and stay to receive a haircut, determine W and W_q. Describe these two quantities in terms meaningful to Newell and Jeff.

   d. Given that Newell and Jeff are equally fast in giving haircuts, what is the average duration of a haircut?

14.9. Explain why the utilization factor ρ for the server in a single-server queueing system must equal $1 - P_0$, where P_0 is the probability of having 0 customers in the system.

14.10. The Friendly Neighbor Grocery Store has a single checkout stand with a full-time cashier. Customers arrive randomly at the stand at a mean rate of 30 per hour. The service-time distribution is exponential, with a mean of 1.5 minutes. This situation has resulted in occasional long lines and complaints from customers. Therefore, because there is no room for a second checkout stand, the manager is considering the alternative of hiring another person to help the cashier by bagging the groceries. This help would reduce the expected time required to process a customer to 1 minute, but the distribution still would be exponential.

   The manager would like to have the percentage of time that there are more than two customers at the checkout stand down below 25 percent. She also would like to have no more than 5 percent of the customers needing to wait at least five minutes before beginning service, or at least seven minutes before finishing service.

   a. Use the formulas for the *M/M/*1 model to calculate L, W, W_q, L_q, P_0, P_1, and P_2 for the current mode of operation. What is the probability of having more than two customers at the checkout stand?

E *b.* Use the Excel template for this model to check your answers in part *a*. Also, find the probability that the waiting time before beginning service exceeds five minutes, and the probability that the waiting time before finishing service exceeds seven minutes.

   c. Repeat part *a* for the alternative being considered by the manager.

E *d.* Repeat part *b* for this alternative.

   e. Which approach should the manager use to satisfy her criteria as closely as possible?

14.11.* The 4M Company has a single turret lathe as a key work center on its factory floor. Jobs arrive randomly at this work center at a mean rate of two per day. The processing time to perform each job has an exponential distribution with a mean of ¼ day. Because the jobs are bulky, those not being worked on are currently being stored in a room some distance from the machine. However, to save time in fetching the jobs, the production manager is proposing to add enough in-process storage space next to the turret lathe to accommodate three jobs in addition to the one being processed. (Excess jobs will continue to be stored temporarily in the distant room.) Under this proposal, what proportion of the time will this storage space next to the turret lathe be adequate to accommodate all waiting jobs?

a. Use available formulas to calculate your answer.

E b. Use an Excel template to obtain the information needed to answer the question.

14.12. Jerry Jansen, materials handling manager at the Casper-Edison Corporation's new factory, needs to decide whether to purchase a small tractor-trailer train or a heavy-duty forklift truck for transporting heavy goods between certain producing centers in the factory. Calls for the materials-handling unit to move a load would come essentially at random at a mean rate of four per hour. The total time required to move a load has an exponential distribution, where the expected time would be 12 minutes for the tractor-trailer train and 9 minutes for the forklift truck. The total equivalent uniform hourly cost (capital recovery cost plus operating cost) would be $50 for the tractor-trailer train and $150 for the forklift truck. The estimated cost of idle goods (waiting to be moved or in transit) because of increased in-process inventory is $20 per load per hour.

Jerry also has established certain criteria that he would like the materials-handling unit to satisfy in order to keep production flowing on schedule as much as possible. He would like to average no more than half an hour for completing the move of a load after receiving the call requesting the move. He also would like the time for completing the move to be no more than one hour 80 percent of the time. Finally, he would like to have no more than three loads waiting to start their move at least 80 percent of the time.

E a. Obtain the various measures of performance if the tractor-trailer train were to be chosen. Evaluate how well these measures meet the above criteria.

E b. Repeat part a if the forklift truck were to be chosen.

c. Compare the two alternatives in terms of their expected total cost per hour (including the cost of idle goods).

d. Which alternative do you think Jerry should choose?

E14.13. Suppose a queueing system fitting the $M/M/1$ model has $W = 120$ minutes and $L = 8$ customers. Use these facts (and the formula for W) to find λ and μ. Then find the various other measures of performance for this queueing system.

14.14.* The Seabuck and Roper Company has a large warehouse in southern California to store its inventory of goods until they are needed by the company's many furniture stores in that area. A single crew with four members is used to unload and/or load each truck that arrives at the loading dock of the warehouse. Management currently is downsizing to cut costs, so a decision needs to be made about the future size of this crew.

Trucks arrive randomly at the loading dock at a mean rate of one per hour. The time required by a crew to unload and/or load a truck has an exponential distribution (regardless of crew size). The mean of this distribution with the four-member crew is 15 minutes. If the size of the crew were to be changed, it is estimated that the mean service rate of the crew (now $\mu = 4$ customers per hour) would be *proportional* to its size.

The cost of providing each member of the crew is $20 per hour. The cost that is attributable to having a truck not in use (i.e., a truck standing at the loading dock) is estimated to be $30 per hour.

a. Identify the customers and servers for this queueing system. How many servers does it currently have?

E b. Find the various measures of performance of this queueing system with four members on the crew. (Set $t = 1$ hour in the Excel template for the waiting-time probabilities.)

E c. Repeat b with three members.

E d. Repeat part b with two members.

e. Should a one-member crew also be considered? Explain.

f. Given the previous results, which crew size do you think management should choose?

g. Use the cost figures to determine which crew size would minimize the expected total cost per hour.

14.15.   Jake's Machine Shop contains a grinder for sharpening the machine cutting tools. A decision must now be made on the speed at which to set the grinder.

The grinding time required by a machine operator to sharpen the cutting tool has an exponential distribution, where the mean $1/\mu$ can be set at 1 minute, 1.5 minutes, or 2 minutes, depending upon the speed of the grinder. The running and maintenance costs go up rapidly with the speed of the grinder, so the estimated cost per minute is $1.60 for providing a mean of 1 minute, $0.90 for a mean of 1.5 minutes, and $0.40 for a mean of 2 minutes.

The machine operators arrive randomly to sharpen their tools at a mean rate of one every two minutes. The estimated cost of an operator being away from his or her machine to the grinder is $0.80 per minute.

E   a. Obtain the various measures of performance for this queueing system for each of the three alternative speeds for the grinder. (Set $t = 5$ minutes in the Excel template for the waiting-time probabilities.)

b. Use the cost figures to determine which grinder speed minimizes the expected total cost per minute.

E14.16.   The Centerville International Airport has two runways, one used exclusively for takeoffs and the other exclusively for landings. Airplanes arrive randomly in the Centerville air space to request landing instructions at a mean rate of 10 per hour. The time required for an airplane to land after receiving clearance to land has an exponential distribution with a mean of three minutes, and this process must be completed before giving clearance to land to another airplane. Airplanes awaiting clearance must circle the airport.

The Federal Aviation Administration has a number of criteria regarding the safe level of congestion of airplanes waiting to land. These criteria depend on a number of factors regarding the airport involved, such as the number of runways available for landing. For Centerville, the criteria are (1) the average number of airplanes waiting to receive clearance to land should not exceed one, (2) 95 percent of the time, the actual number of airplanes waiting to receive clearance to land should not exceed four, (3) for 99 percent of the airplanes, the amount of time spent circling the airport before receiving clearance to land should not exceed 30 minutes (since exceeding this amount of time often would require rerouting the plane to another airport for an emergency landing before its fuel runs out).

a. Evaluate how well these criteria are currently being satisfied.

b. A major airline is considering adding this airport as one of its hubs. This would increase the mean arrival rate to 15 airplanes per hour. Evaluate how well the above criteria would be satisfied if this happens.

c. To attract additional business (including the major airline mentioned in part b), airport management is considering adding a second runway for landings. It is estimated that this eventually would increase the mean arrival rate to 25 airplanes per hour. Evaluate how well the above criteria would be satisfied if this happens.

14.17.*   Consider the $M/G/1$ model. What is the effect on L_q and W_q if $1/\lambda$, $1/\mu$, and σ are all reduced by half?

14.18.   Consider the $M/G/1$ model with $\lambda = 0.2$ and $\mu = 0.25$.

E   a. Use the Excel template for this model to generate a data table that gives the main measures of performance—L, L_q, W, W_q—for each of the following values of σ: 4, 3, 2, 1, 0.

b. What is the ratio of L_q with $\sigma = 4$ to L_q with $\sigma = 0$? What does this say about the importance of reducing the variability of the service times?

c. Calculate the reduction in L_q when σ is reduced from 4 to 3, from 3 to 2, from 2 to 1, and from 1 to 0. Which is the largest reduction? Which is the smallest?

E   d. Use trial and error with the template to see approximately how much μ would need to be increased with $\sigma = 4$ to achieve the same L_q as with $\mu = 0.25$ and $\sigma = 0$.

E   e. Use the template to generate a data table that gives the value of L_q with $\sigma = 4$ when μ increases in increments of 0.01 from 0.25 to 0.35.

E   f. Use the template to generate a two-way data table that gives the value of L_q for the various combinations of values of μ and σ where $\mu = 0.22, 0.24, 0.26, 0.28, 0.3$ and $\sigma = 4, 3, 2, 1, 0$.

14.19.   Consider the following statements about the $M/G/1$ queueing model, where σ^2 is the variance of service times. Label each statement as true or false, and then justify your answer.

a. Increasing σ^2 (with fixed λ and μ) will increase L_q and L, but will not change W_q and W.

    b. When the choice is between a tortoise (small μ and σ^2) and a hare (large μ and σ^2) to be the server, the tortoise always wins by providing a smaller L_q.

    c. With λ and μ fixed, the value of L_q with an exponential service-time distribution is twice as large as with constant service times.

14.20.   Marsha operates an espresso stand. Customers arrive randomly at a mean rate of 30 per hour. The time needed by Marsha to serve a customer has an exponential distribution with a mean of 75 seconds.

E   *a.* Use the Excel template for the $M/G/1$ model to find L, L_q, W, and W_q.

E   *b.* Suppose Marsha is replaced by an espresso vending machine that requires exactly 75 seconds to operate for each customer. Find L, L_q, W, and W_q.

    c. What is the ratio of L_q in part *b* to L_q in part *a?*

E   *d.* Use trial and error with the template to see approximately how much Marsha would need to reduce her expected service time to achieve the same L_q as with the espresso vending machine.

E   *e.* Use the template to generate a data table that gives the value of L_q when Marsha is serving with the following values (in seconds) for her expected service time: 75, 70, 65, 64, 63, 62, 61, 60.

14.21.*   The production of tractors at the Jim Buck Company involves producing several subassemblies and then using an assembly line to assemble the subassemblies and other parts into finished tractors. Approximately three tractors per day are produced in this way. An in-process inspection station is used to inspect the subassemblies before they enter the assembly line. At present, there are two inspectors at the station, and they work together to inspect each subassembly. The inspection time has an exponential distribution, with a mean of 15 minutes. The cost of providing this inspection system is $40 per hour.

    A proposal has been made to streamline the inspection procedure so that it can be handled by only one inspector. This inspector would begin by visually inspecting the exterior of the subassembly, and she would then use new efficient equipment to complete the inspection. Although this process with just one inspector would slightly increase the mean of the distribution of inspection times from 15 minutes to 16 minutes, it also would reduce the variance of this distribution to only 40 percent of its current value. The cost would be $30 per hour.

    The subassemblies arrive randomly at the inspection station at a mean rate of three per hour. The cost of having the subassemblies wait at the inspection station (thereby increasing in-process inventory and possibly disrupting subsequent production) is estimated to be $20 per hour for each subassembly.

    Management now needs to make a decision about whether to continue the status quo or adopt the proposal.

E   *a.* Find the main measures of performance—L, L_q, W, W_q—for the current queueing system.

E   *b.* Repeat part *a* for the proposed queueing system.

    c. What conclusions can you draw about what management should do from the results in parts *a* and *b?*

    d. Determine and compare the expected total cost per hour for the status quo and the proposal.

14.22.   Antonio runs a shoe repair store by himself. Customers arrive randomly to bring a pair of shoes to be repaired at a mean rate of one per hour. The time Antonio requires to repair each *individual* shoe has an exponential distribution with a mean of 15 minutes. According to statistical theory, this implies that the time required to repair a *pair* of shoes has an Erlang distribution with a mean of 30 minutes and a shape parameter of $k = 2$.

    a. Calculate the average number of pairs of shoes in the shop.

    b. Calculate the average amount of time from when a customer drops off a pair of shoes until they are repaired and ready to be picked up.

E   *c.* Use the Excel template for the $M/G/1$ model to check your answers in parts *a* and *b*.

E   *d.* Repeat part *c* with the Excel template for the $M/E_k/1$ model.

14.23.*   The maintenance base for Friendly Skies Airline has facilities for overhauling only one airplane engine at a time. Therefore, to return the airplanes to use as soon as possible, the policy has been to stagger the overhauling of the four engines of each airplane. In other words, only one engine is overhauled each time an airplane comes into the shop. Under this policy, airplanes have arrived randomly at a mean rate of one per day. The time required for an engine overhaul (once work has begun) has an exponential distribution with a mean of ½ day.

A proposal has been made to change the policy so that all four engines are overhauled consecutively each time an airplane comes into the shop. This would mean that each plane would need to come to the maintenance base only one-fourth as often. Since the time required to overhaul one engine has an exponential distribution, statistical theory indicates that the time required to overhaul four engines has an Erlang distribution with a mean four times as large and with a shape parameter of $k = 4$.

Management now needs to decide whether to continue the status quo or adopt the proposal. The objective is to minimize the average amount of flying time lost by the entire fleet per day due to engine overhauls.

E   *a.* Compare the two alternatives with respect to the average amount of flying time lost by an airplane each time it comes to the maintenance base.

E   *b.* Compare the two alternatives with respect to the average number of airplanes losing flying time due to being at the maintenance base.

        c. Which of these two comparisons is the appropriate one for making management's decision? Explain.

E14.24. The Security & Trust Bank employs four tellers to serve its customers. Customers arrive randomly at a mean rate of two per minute. However, business is growing and management projects that the mean arrival rate will be three per minute a year from now. The transaction time between the teller and customer has an exponential distribution with a mean of one minute.

Management has established the following guidelines for a satisfactory level of service to customers. The average number of customers waiting in line to begin service should not exceed one. At least 95 percent of the time, the number of customers waiting in line should not exceed five. For at least 95 percent of the customers, the time spent in line waiting to begin service should not exceed five minutes.

        a. Use the *M/M/s* model to determine how well these guidelines are currently being satisfied.

        b. Evaluate how well the guidelines will be satisfied a year from now if no change is made in the number of tellers.

        c. Determine how many tellers will be needed a year from now to completely satisfy these guidelines.

E14.25. Consider the *M/M/s* model. For each of the following two cases, generate a data table that gives the values of L, L_q, W, W_q, and $P\{W > 5\}$ for the following mean arrival rates: 0.5, 0.9, and 0.99 customers per minute.

        a. Suppose there is one server and the expected service time is one minute. Compare L for the cases where the mean arrival rate is 0.5, 0.9, and 0.99 customers per minute, respectively. Do the same for L_q, W, W_q, and $P\{W > 5\}$. What conclusions do you draw about the impact of increasing the utilization factor ρ from small values (e.g., $\rho = 0.5$) to fairly large values (e.g., $\rho = 0.9$) and then to even larger values very close to 1 (e.g., $\rho = 0.99$)?

        b. Now suppose there are two servers and the expected service time is two minutes. Follow the instructions for part *a*.

E14.26. Consider the *M/M/s* model with a mean arrival rate of 10 customers per hour and an expected service time of five minutes. Use the Excel template for this model to print out the various measures of performance (with $t = 10$ and $t = 0$, respectively, for the two waiting-time probabilities) when the number of servers is one, two, three, four, and five. Then, for each of the following possible criteria for a satisfactory level of service (where the unit of time is one minute), use the printed results to determine how many servers are needed to satisfy this criterion.

        a. $L_q \leq 0.25$

        b. $L \leq 0.9$

        c. $W_q \leq 0.1$

        d. $W \leq 6$

        e. $P\{W_q > 0\} \leq 0.01$

        f. $P\{W > 10\} \leq 0.2$

        g. $\sum_{n=0}^{s} P_n \geq 0.95$

14.27. Greg is making plans to open a new fast-food restaurant soon. He is estimating that customers will arrive randomly at a mean rate of 150 per hour during the busiest times of the day. He is planning to have three employees directly serving the customers. He now needs to make a decision about how to organize these employees.

Option 1 is to have three cash registers with one employee at each to take the orders and get the food and drinks. In this case, it is estimated that the average time to serve each customer would be one minute, and the distribution of service times is assumed to be exponential.

Option 2 is to have one cash register with the three employees working together to serve each customer. One would take the order, a second would get the food, and the third would get the drinks. Greg estimates that this would reduce the average time to serve each customer down to 20 seconds, with the same assumption of exponential service times.

Greg wants to choose the option that would provide the best service to his customers. However, since Option 1 has three cash registers, both options would serve the customers at a mean rate of three per minute when everybody is busy serving customers, so it is not clear which option is better.

E
a. Use the main measures of performance—L, L_q, W, W_q—to compare the two options.

b. Explain why these comparisons make sense intuitively.

c. Which measure do you think would be most important to Greg's customers? Why? Which option is better with respect to this measure?

E14.28.*
In the Blue Chip Life Insurance Company, the deposit and withdrawal functions associated with a certain investment product are separated between two clerks. Deposit slips arrive randomly at Clerk Clara's desk at a mean rate of 16 per hour. Withdrawal slips arrive randomly at Clerk Clarence's desk at a mean rate of 14 per hour. The time required to process either transaction has an exponential distribution with a mean of three minutes. In order to reduce the expected waiting time in the system for both deposit slips and withdrawal slips, the Actuarial Department has made the following recommendations: (1) Train each clerk to handle both deposits and withdrawals; (2) put both deposit and withdrawal slips into a single queue that is accessed by both clerks.

a. Determine the expected waiting time in the system under current procedures for each type of slip. Then combine these results (multiply W for deposit slips by $\frac{16}{30}$, multiply W for withdrawal slips by $\frac{14}{30}$, and add these two products) to calculate the expected waiting time in the system for a random arrival of either type of slip.

b. If the recommendations are adopted, determine the expected waiting time in the system for arriving slips.

c. Now suppose that adopting the recommendations would result in a slight increase in the expected processing time. Use the Excel template for this model to determine by trial and error the expected processing time (within 0.01 minute) that would cause the expected waiting time in the system for a random arrival to be essentially the same under current procedures and under the recommendations.

E14.29.
People's Software Company has just set up a call center to provide technical assistance on its new software package. Two technical representatives are taking the calls, where the time required by either representative to answer a customer's questions has an exponential distribution with a mean of eight minutes. Calls are arriving randomly at a mean rate of 10 per hour.

By next year, the mean arrival rate of calls is expected to decline to five per hour, so the plan is to reduce the number of technical representatives to one then. Determine L, L_q, W, and W_q for both the current queueing system and next year's system. For each of these four measures of performance, which system yields the smaller value?

14.30.
The McAllister Company factory currently has two tool cribs, each with a single clerk, in its manufacturing area. One tool crib handles only the tools for the heavy machinery; the second one handles all other tools. However, for each crib, the mechanics arrive randomly to obtain tools at a mean rate of 24 per hour, and the expected service time is two minutes.

Because of complaints that the mechanics coming to the tool cribs have to wait too long, it has been proposed that the two tool cribs be combined so that either clerk can handle either kind of tool as the demand arises. It is believed that the mean arrival rate to the combined two-clerk tool crib would double to 48 per hour and that the expected service time would continue to be two minutes. However, information is not available on the *form* of the probability distribution for service times, so it is not clear which queueing model would be most appropriate.

E
a. Compare the status quo and the proposal with respect to the total expected number of mechanics at the tool crib(s) and the expected waiting time (including service) for each me-

chanic. Do this by tabulating these data for the four queueing models where the distribution of service times is (1) exponential, (2) Erlang with shape parameter $k = 2$, (3) Erlang with shape parameter $k = 8$, and (4) degenerate (constant service times). Use available Excel templates, as well as Figures 14.11 and 14.12, as needed.

b. Given these results, which alternative should be chosen?

c. Which of the four insights presented in Section 14.8 is illustrated by these results?

14.31. The Southern Railroad Company has been subcontracting for the painting of its railroad cars as needed. However, management has decided that the company can save money by doing this work itself. A decision now needs to be made to choose between two alternative ways of doing this.

Alternative 1 is to provide two paint shops, where painting is done by hand (one car at a time in each shop), for a total hourly cost of $70. The painting time for a car would be six hours. Alternative 2 is to provide one spray shop involving an hourly cost of $100. In this case, the painting time for a car (again done one at a time) would be three hours. For both alternatives, the cars arrive randomly with a mean rate of 1 every 5 hours. The cost of idle time per car is $100 per hour.

a. Use Figure 14.11 to estimate L, L_q, W, and W_q for Alternative 1.

E *b.* Find these same measures of performance for Alternative 2.

c. Determine and compare the expected total cost per hour for these alternatives.

14.32. The car rental company, Try Harder, has been subcontracting for the maintenance of its cars in St. Louis. However, due to long delays in getting its cars back, the company has decided to open its own maintenance shop to do this work more quickly. This shop will operate 42 hours per week.

Alternative 1 is to hire two mechanics (at a cost of $1,500 per week each), so that two cars can be worked on at a time. The time required by a mechanic to service a car has an Erlang distribution with a mean of five hours and a shape parameter of $k = 8$.

Alternative 2 is to hire just one mechanic (for $1,500 per week) but to provide some additional special equipment (at a capitalized cost of $1,250 per week) to speed up the work. In this case, the maintenance work on each car is done in two stages, where the time required for each stage has an Erlang distribution with the shape parameter $k = 4$, where the mean is two hours for the first stage and one hour for the second stage. This implies that the probability distribution of the total time for both stages has a mean of three hours and a variance equal to the sum of the variances of the times for the individual stages. However, the form of this distribution is unknown. (It is not Erlang.)

For both alternatives, the cars arrive randomly at a mean rate of 0.3 cars per hour (during work hours). The company estimates that its net lost revenue due to having its cars unavailable for rental is $150 per week per car.

a. Use Figure 14.12 to estimate L, L_q, W, and W_q for Alternative 1.

E *b.* Find these same measures of performance for Alternative 2.

c. Determine and compare the expected total cost per week for these alternatives.

14.33.* Southeast Airlines is a small commuter airline serving primarily the state of Florida. Its ticket counter at the Orlando airport is staffed by a single ticket agent. There are two separate lines— one for first-class passengers and one for coach-class passengers. When the ticket agent is ready for another customer, the next first-class passenger is served if there are any in line. If not, the next coach-class passenger is served. Service times have an exponential distribution with a mean of three minutes for both types of customers. During the 12 hours per day that the ticket counter is open, passengers arrive randomly at a mean rate of 2 per hour for first-class passengers and 10 per hour for coach-class passengers.

a. What kind of queueing model fits this queueing system?

E *b.* Find the main measures of performance—L, L_q, W, and W_q—for both first-class passengers and coach-class passengers.

c. What is the expected waiting time before service begins for first-class customers as a fraction of this waiting time for coach-class customers?

d. Determine the average number of hours per day that the ticket agent is busy.

14.34. The County Hospital emergency room always has one doctor on duty. In the past, having just a single doctor there has been sufficient. However, because of a growing tendency for emergency cases to use these facilities rather than go to a private doctor, the number of emergency room visits has been steadily increasing. By next year, it is estimated that patients will arrive randomly at a mean rate of two per hour during peak usage hours (the early evening). Therefore, a proposal has been made to assign a second doctor to the emergency room next year during those hours. Hospital management (an HMO) is resisting this proposal, but has asked a management scientist (you) to analyze whether a single doctor will continue to be sufficient next year.

The patients are not treated on a first-come, first-served basis. Rather, the admitting nurse divides the patients into three categories: (1) *critical* cases, where prompt treatment is vital for survival; (2) *serious* cases, where early treatment is important to prevent further deterioration; and (3) *stable* cases, where treatment can be delayed without adverse medical consequences. Patients are then treated in this order of priority, where those in the same category are normally taken on a first-come, first-served basis. A doctor will interrupt treatment of a patient if a new case in a higher priority category arrives. Approximately 10 percent of the patients fall into the first category, 30 percent into the second, and 60 percent into the third. Because the more serious cases will be sent to the hospital for further care after receiving emergency treatment, the average treatment time by a doctor in the emergency room actually does not differ greatly among these categories. For all of them, the treatment time can be approximated by an exponential distribution with a mean of 20 minutes.

Hospital management has established the following guidelines. The average waiting time in the emergency room before treatment begins should not exceed 2 minutes for critical cases, 15 minutes for serious cases, and 2 hours for stable cases.

 a. What kind of queueing model fits this queueing system?

E b. Use this model to determine if the management guidelines would be satisfied next year by continuing to have just a single doctor on duty.

 c. Use the formula for W_q for the $M/M/1$ model to determine if these guidelines would be satisfied if treatment were given on a first-come, first-served basis instead.

E d. The mean arrival rate of two patients per hour during peak usage hours next year is only an estimate. Perform sensitivity analysis by repeating part *b* if this mean arrival rate were to turn out to be 2.25 patients per hour instead.

E14.35. The Becker Company factory has been experiencing long delays in jobs going through the turret lathe department because of inadequate capacity. The head of this department contends that five machines are required, as opposed to the three machines that he now has. However, because of pressure from management to hold down capital expenditures, only one additional machine will be authorized unless there is solid evidence that a second one is necessary.

This shop does three kinds of jobs, namely, government jobs, commercial jobs, and standard products. Whenever a turret lathe operator finishes a job, he starts a government job if one is waiting; if not, he starts a commercial job if any are waiting; if not, he starts on a standard product if any are waiting. Jobs of the same type are taken on a first-come, first-served basis.

Although much overtime work is required currently, management wants the turret lathe department to operate on an eight-hour, five-day-per-week basis. The probability distribution of the time required by a turret lathe operator for a job appears to be approximately exponential, with a mean of 10 hours. Jobs come into the shop randomly at a mean rate of six per week for government jobs, four per week for commercial jobs, and two per week for standard products. (These figures are expected to remain the same for the indefinite future.)

Management feels that the average waiting time before work begins in the turret lathe department should not exceed 0.25 (working) days for government jobs, 0.5 days for commercial jobs, and 2 days for standard products.

 a. Determine how many additional turret lathes need to be obtained to satisfy these management guidelines.

 b. It is worth about $750, $450, and $150 to avoid a delay of one additional (working) day in a government, commercial, and standard job, respectively. The incremental capitalized cost of providing each turret lathe (including the operator and so on) is estimated to be $250 per working day. Determine the number of additional turret lathes that should be obtained to minimize the expected total cost.

E14.36. When describing economic analysis of the number of servers to provide in a queueing system, Section 14.9 introduces a cost model where the objective is to minimize $TC = C_s s + C_w L$. The purpose of this problem is to enable you to explore the effect that the relative sizes of C_s and C_w have on the optimal number of servers.

Suppose that the queueing system under consideration fits the $M/M/s$ model with $\lambda = 8$ customers per hour and $\mu = 10$ customers per hour. Use the Excel template for economic analysis with the $M/M/s$ model to find the optimal number of servers for each of the following cases.

    a. $C_s = \$100$ and $C_w = \$10$.

    b. $C_s = \$100$ and $C_w = \$100$.

    c. $C_s = \$10$ and $C_w = \$100$.

    d. For each of these three cases, generate a data table that compares the expected hourly costs with various alternative numbers of servers.

E14.37.* Jim McDonald, manager of the fast-food hamburger restaurant McBurger, realizes that providing fast service is a key to the success of the restaurant. Customers who have to wait very long are likely to go to one of the other fast-food restaurants in town next time. He estimates that each minute a customer has to wait in line before completing service costs him an average of 30¢ in lost future business. Therefore, he wants to be sure that enough cash registers always are open to keep waiting to a minimum. Each cash register is operated by a part-time employee who obtains the food ordered by each customer and collects the payment. The total cost for each such employee is $9 per hour.

During lunchtime, customers arrive randomly at a mean rate of 66 per hour. The time needed to serve a customer is estimated to have an exponential distribution with a mean of two minutes.

Determine how many cash registers Jim should have open during lunchtime to minimize his expected total cost per hour.

E14.38. The Garrett-Tompkins Company provides three copy machines in its copying room for the use of its employees. However, due to recent complaints about considerable time being wasted waiting for a copier to become free, management is considering adding one or more additional copy machines.

During the 2,000 working hours per year, employees arrive randomly at the copying room at a mean rate of 30 per hour. The time each employee needs with a copy machine is believed to have an exponential distribution with a mean of five minutes. The lost productivity due to an employee spending time in the copying room is estimated to cost the company an average of $25 per hour. Each copy machine is leased for $3,000 per year.

Determine how many copy machines the company should have to minimize its expected total cost per hour.

Case 14-1

Queueing Quandary

A Sequel to Case 13.1

Never dull. That is how you would describe your job at the centralized records and benefits administration center for Cutting Edge, a large company manufacturing computers and computer peripherals. Since opening the facility six months ago, you and Mark Lawrence, the director of Human Resources, have endured one long roller-coaster ride. Receiving the go-ahead from corporate headquarters to establish the centralized records and benefits administration center was definitely an up. Getting caught in the crossfire of angry customers (all employees of Cutting Edge) because of demand overload for the records and benefits call center was definitely a down. Accurately forecasting the demand for the call center provided another up.

And today you are faced with another down. Mark approaches your desk with a not altogether attractive frown on his face.

He begins complaining immediately, "I just don't understand. The forecasting job you did for us two months ago really allowed us to understand the weekly demand for the center, but we still have not been able to get a grasp on the staffing problem. We used both historical data and your forecasts to calculate the average weekly demand for the call center. We transformed this average weekly demand into average hourly demand by dividing the weekly demand by the number of hours in the workweek. We then staffed the center to meet this average hourly demand by taking into account the average number of calls a representative is able to handle per hour.

But something is horribly wrong. Operational data records show that over 35 percent of the customers wait over four minutes for a representative to answer the call! Customers are still sending me numerous complaints, and executives from corporate headquarters are still breathing down my neck! I need help!"

You calm Mark down and explain to him that you think you know the problem: The number of calls received in a certain hour can be much greater (or much less) than the average because of the stochastic nature of the demand. In addition, the number of calls a representative is able to handle per hour can be much less (or much greater) than the average depending upon the types of calls received.

You then tell him to have no fear; you have the problem under control. You have been reading about the successful application of queueing theory to the operation of call centers, and you decide that the queueing models you learned about in school will help you determine the appropriate staffing level.

a. You ask Mark to describe the demand and service rate. He tells you that calls are randomly received by the call center and that the center receives an average of 70 calls per hour. The computer system installed to answer and hold the calls is so advanced that its capacity far exceeds the demand. Because the nature of a call is random, the time required to process a call is random, where the time frequently is small but occasionally can be much longer. On average, however, representatives can handle six calls per hour. Which queueing model seems appropriate for this situation? Given that slightly more than 35 percent of customers wait over four minutes before a representative answers the call, use this model to estimate how many representatives Mark currently employs.

b. Mark tells you that he will not be satisfied unless 95 percent of the customers wait only one minute or less for a representative to answer the call. Given this customer service level and the average arrival rates and service rates from part *a,* how many representatives should Mark employ?

c. Each representative receives an annual salary of $30,000, and Mark tells you that he simply does not have the resources available to hire the number of representatives required to achieve the customer service level desired in part *b.* He asks you to perform sensitivity analysis. How many representatives would he need to employ to ensure that 80 percent of customers wait one minute or less? How many would he need to employ to ensure that 95 percent of customers wait 90 seconds or less? How would you recommend Mark choose a customer service level? Would the decision criteria be different if Mark's call center were to serve external customers (not connected to the company) instead of internal customers (employees)?

d. Mark tells you that he is not happy with the number of representatives required to achieve a high customer service level. He therefore wants to explore alternatives to simply hiring additional representatives. The alternative he considers is instituting a training program that will teach representatives to more efficiently use computer tools to answer calls. He believes that this alternative will increase the average number of calls a representative is able to handle per hour from six calls to eight calls. The training program will cost $2,500 per employee per year since employees' knowledge will have to be updated yearly. How many representatives will Mark have to employ and train to achieve the customer service level desired in part *b?* Do you prefer this alternative to simply hiring additional representatives? Why or why not?

e. Mark realizes that queueing theory helps him only so much in determining the number of representatives needed. He realizes that the queueing models will not provide accurate answers if the inputs used in the models are inaccurate. What inputs do you think need reevaluation? How would you go about estimating these inputs?

Case 14-2

Reducing In-Process Inventory

Jim Wells, vice president for manufacturing of the Northern Airplane Company, is exasperated. His walk through the company's most important plant this morning has left him in a foul mood. However, he now can vent his temper at Jerry Carstairs, the plant's production manager, who has just been summoned to Jim's office.

"Jerry, I just got back from walking through the plant, and I am very upset."

"What is the problem, Jim?"

"Well, you know how much I have been emphasizing the need to cut down on our in-process inventory."

"Yes, we've been working hard on that," responds Jerry.

"Well, not hard enough!" Jim raises his voice even higher. "Do you know what I found by the presses?"

"No."

"Five metal sheets still waiting to be formed into wing sections. And then, right next door at the inspection station, 13 wing sections! The inspector was inspecting one of them, but the other 12 were just sitting there. You know we have a couple hundred thousand dollars tied up in each of those wing sections. So between the presses and the inspection station, we have a few million bucks' worth of terribly expensive metal just sitting there. We can't have that!"

The chagrined Jerry Carstairs tries to respond. "Yes, Jim, I am well aware that that inspection station is a bottleneck. It usually isn't nearly as bad as you found it this morning, but it is a bottleneck. Much less so for the presses. You really caught us on a bad morning."

"I sure hope so," retorts Jim, "but you need to prevent anything nearly this bad happening even occasionally. What do you propose to do about it?"

Jerry now brightens noticeably in his response. "Well, actually, I've already been working on this problem. I have a couple proposals on the table and I have asked a management scientist on my staff to analyze these proposals and report back with recommendations."

"Great," responds Jim, "glad to see you are on top of the problem. Give this your highest priority and report back to me as soon as possible."

"Will do," promises Jerry.

Here is the problem that Jerry and his management scientist are addressing. Each of 10 identical presses is being used to form wing sections out of large sheets of specially processed metal. The sheets arrive randomly at a mean rate of seven per hour. The time required by a press to form a wing section out of a sheet has an exponential distribution with a mean of one hour. When finished, the wing sections arrive randomly at an inspection station at the same mean rate as the metal sheets arrived at the presses (seven per hour). A single inspector has the full-time job of inspecting these wing sections to make sure they meet specifications. Each inspection takes her 7½ minutes, so she can inspect eight wing sections per hour. This inspection rate has resulted in a substantial average amount of in-process inventory at the inspection station (i.e., the average number of wing sheets waiting to complete inspection is fairly large), in addition to that already found at the group of machines.

The cost of this in-process inventory is estimated to be $8 per hour for each metal sheet at the presses or each wing section at the inspection station. Therefore, Jerry Carstairs has made two alternative proposals to reduce the average level of in-process inventory.

Proposal 1 is to use slightly less power for the presses (which would increase their average time to form a wing section to 1.2 hours), so that the inspector can keep up with their output better. This also would reduce the cost for each machine (operating cost plus capital recovery cost) from $7.00 to $6.50 per hour. (By contrast, increasing to maximum power would increase this cost to $7.50 per hour while decreasing the average time to form a wing section to 0.8 hours.)

Proposal 2 is to substitute a certain younger inspector for this task. He is somewhat faster (albeit with some variability in his inspection times because of less experience), so he should keep up better. (His inspection time would have an Erlang distribution with a mean of 7.2 minutes and a shape parameter $k = 2$.) This inspector is in a job classification that calls for a total compensation (including benefits) of $19 per hour, whereas the current inspector is in a lower job classification where the compensation is $17 per hour. (The inspection times for each of these inspectors are typical of those in the same job classifications.)

You are the management scientist on Jerry Carstair's staff who has been asked to analyze this problem. He wants you to "use the latest management science techniques to see how much each proposal would cut down on in-process inventory and then make your recommendations."

a. To provide a basis of comparison, begin by evaluating the status quo. Determine the expected amount of in-process inventory at the presses and at the inspection station. Then calculate the expected total cost per hour of the in-process inventory, the presses, and the inspector.

b. What would be the effect of proposal 1? Why? Make specific comparisons to the results from part *a*. Explain this outcome to Jerry Carstairs.

c. Determine the effect of proposal 2. Make specific comparisons to the results from part *a*. Explain this outcome to Jerry Carstairs.

d. Make your recommendations for reducing the average level of in-process inventory at the inspection station and at the group of machines. Be specific in your recommendations, and support them with quantitative analysis like that done in part *a*. Make specific comparisons to the results from part *a*, and cite the improvements that your recommendations would yield.

Case 14-3

KeyCorp[4]

KeyCorp, with over 1,300 branches from Maine to Alaska, was one of the largest bank holding companies in the United States. Building from a long history of strong financial performance, KeyCorp's vision was to become the first choice of those seeking world-class financial products and services. However, increased competition from conventional banks, and nonbank competitors who operated under fewer regulations, forced KeyCorp to rethink and restructure its retail branch franchise.

Electronic banking continued to gain in consumer acceptance, but branch banking continued to dominate the financial services industry. The branch teller was the primary bank contact, representing 95 percent of customer contacts at KeyCorp branches. Because of the volume of customers and transactions, and the costs associated with this service, branch managers had to continuously improve branch productivity. A fundamental problem facing KeyCorp's branch managers was figuring out how to improve customer service (defined primarily as reduced customer wait time) while still providing cost-effective staffing.

KeyCorp Executive Vice President Robert G. Jones emphasized the importance of continuously improving customer service: "We have 150 million moments of truth taking place every year . . . and it takes every one of us at KeyCorp to make those moments of truth come out in the customers' favor."

THE COMPANY AND THE INDUSTRY

Headquartered in Cleveland, Ohio, KeyCorp recorded record earnings of $854 million in 1994, with assets of $66.8 billion and equity capital of $4.7 billion at the end of the year. The consumer banking franchise, which comprised over 1,300 branches across 14 states and affiliate offices in 25 states, ranked in the top five in size within the United States. Through its full-service commercial banks and specialized subsidiaries, KeyCorp provided such services as consumer banking, investment management and trust, corporate finance, security brokerage, and private banking, as well as customized financial services to individuals, investors, and small, medium, and large corporations.

KeyCorp possessed a long history of superior financial performance, ranking it in the top five in both ROA and ROE among its peers. KeyCorp's performance was even more impressive because the banking industry was in a state of uncertain evolution. Industry consolidation, increased competition, regulatory constraints, and increasing pressures on profitability presented industry leaders with a multitude of major challenges. Over the past 15 years, banking had seen a consolidation from over 200 major banks to fewer than 50. After the next five years, industry experts projected there would be fewer than a dozen major banks nationwide.

In contrast, banking regulations had not changed materially since the 1930s when new rules were introduced to solve the problems of the Great Depression. As a result, the regulations fell short in aiding the industry with respect to the global competition of the 1990s. Regulations continued to limit the rate at which banks could enter new lines of business and offer new products and limited the banking industry's ability to compete with nonbanking entities such as Merrill Lynch and American Express. In addition, there was further competitive pressure from alternative delivery competitors, such as Microsoft with its popular PC-based home financial program, which opened the floodgates for home banking services.

Bankers faced increased competition within their traditional ranks, antiquated rules, and new, less regulated aggressive competitors. To meet these challenges, KeyCorp had to evolve from a traditional bank into a provider of financial services.

THE CUSTOMER SERVICE PROBLEM

In response to the increased competition, KeyCorp introduced First Choice 2000, which would ultimately reconfigure its distribution system from branch banking to such alternatives as ATMs, telephone banking, and PC banking. However, despite the increasing popularity of electronic banking, branch banking

[4]This is one of the INFORMS Teaching Cases that have been prepared to provide material for class discussion. This particular case was prepared by Binu Koshy under the supervision of Professor Peter Bell, Richard Ivey School of Business, The University of Western Ontario, Canada. Copyright 1998, by the Institute for Operations Research and the Management Sciences. Reproduced by permission of INFORMS, the copyright owner.

continued to dominate the industry. While the industry continued to evolve, KeyCorp had to focus on delivering quality service to its customers. Quality service included friendly, accurate tellers and fast, efficient service.

KeyCorp's branches were currently an indispensable component of the consumer franchise and would continue to play an integral role as the corporation grew. Rethinking and restructuring the retail branch franchise were critical to KeyCorp becoming a world-class provider of financial services. Two hundred ten million customer transactions were performed by branch tellers at KeyCorp every year, representing 63 percent of its total customer transactions. A survey performed by KeyCorp pointed to customer waiting times as the most frequently cited reason for customer dissatisfaction. The high volume of customers and transactions, and the costs associated with this service, led branch managers to want to continually enhance branch productivity, but if service was to be improved by reducing customer waiting times, then staffing levels and costs had to be tightly controlled. Given the dynamics of consolidation, increased competition, and the bank's continued expansion through merger and acquisition, KeyCorp wanted to control service quality rather than allow it to fall victim to industry events, and to do that it wanted to apply a systems approach.

KeyCorp viewed the management of customer service as a holistic system with all components working together toward a common goal. It emphasized the interrelationships among the component parts of the system, affirming that modifying one component would affect the others and ultimately the final outcome. KeyCorp set out the following goals for a new system:

- To empower line managers to manage those elements of service under their control while at the same time isolating and stabilizing those variables outside their control.

- To create a measurement and feedback system that was continuous and could change with the organization.

- To automate the collection of data.

- To generate fact-based output.

- To foster competition among branches and create pride and ownership in superior results.

Unlike many industries, banking was a human system. Service was provided by and consumed by human beings with the result that the environment was unpredictable and, if not managed properly, could quickly become unstable. To deal with this, KeyCorp aimed to provide managers with information to enable them to respond to the variations that inevitably occurred in this people-intensive service business. KeyCorp thought that this would foster ownership in both the approach and the results.

ELIMINATING TRANSACTION-PROCESSING IMPEDIMENTS OUTSIDE THE CONTROL OF BRANCH MANAGERS

KeyCorp management, agreeing that it was not possible to manage that which was impossible to measure, set out to break down the elements of each customer session with a branch teller. This would allow them to identify each area of opportunity to improve performance, and to identify which activities were within the control of the branch manager and which were not.

Accordingly, KeyCorp developed the Performance Capture System to collect data about each discrete component of the customer session, defined as time spent at the teller window. This system provided KeyCorp with the ability to measure individual transactions on a continuous basis, by capturing the beginning and ending times for each discrete component of the transaction: host-response time, network-response time, teller-controlled time, customer-controlled time, and branch-hardware time. KeyCorp was now able to dissect transactions into their most basic components and compare categories of transactions, allowing it to identify those components that offered the greatest opportunity for improvement. KeyCorp could also collect data on customer-session times down to the level of an individual transaction for a given teller on a particular day at a specific time.

The first transaction report published in April 1992 was based on 15,000 service sessions in five branches over 36 business days and revealed a 246-second average customer processing time, which was thought to be unacceptable.

KeyCorp performed a preliminary analysis, which defined a service objective of 90 percent of customers who had to wait less than five minutes on all days. The analysis also estimated the change in teller staffing needed to deliver service at the targeted level in a cost-effective and consistent manner and indicated that it would require an additional 502 tellers (a 30 percent increase) at a cost of over $10 million annually to meet the 90 percent objective. KeyCorp would either have to increase the pool of tellers or reduce processing time. Adding tellers was impractical for reasons of cost and because the branches simply could not physically accommodate the required increase in staff; therefore, improved management of staff and reengineering of the customer session were required if the new service quality objective was to be met.

Analysis of the detailed transaction data identified an unacceptable response time on the part of the host computer for processing an information request from the teller system, and an unacceptable network response time (the time it takes to transmit an information request from the branch modem to the host modem), even though the average host and network response times were apparently low (2.0 seconds and 2.8 seconds respectively per request). There were large variations from the average with cases of upwards of 60 seconds per request.

The first step KeyCorp took to reduce the 246-second customer session time was to reengineer the transaction process. This stabilized and streamlined the operating environment and reduced transaction-processing time by 66 seconds, or 27 percent. After eliminating or reducing all the transaction-processing impediments outside the control of branch managers, KeyCorp challenged its branch managers to better manage teller productivity and customer wait time. KeyCorp asked them to focus on two areas:

1. Improving teller proficiency and productivity.

2. Scheduling tellers so that they were available when customer traffic required them.

THE TELLER PRODUCTIVITY SYSTEM

KeyCorp management introduced the teller productivity module to the branch management in July 1992. This module used the data captured by the Performance Capture System to allow branch managers to identify the number of customers being served at any time, the associated transactions processed, and the time required to process each. The data module compiled the data and provided branch managers with four reports to help them in staffing, scheduling, and identifying tellers who needed additional training.

REPORT P1

The teller processing proficiency summary provided details on the number of customers each teller served, the total number of transactions processed, and the average number of transactions per customer. The report also compared the teller's average transaction-processing time for a given set of transactions to the top quartile processing time of all tellers for the same set of transactions.

Report P1—Teller Processing Proficiency Summary Report

Bank—District
Branch #—Name
Month Year

Teller	Customers Served	Transactions Processed	Average Number of Transactions/ Customers	Average Time per (Sec) Customer	Average Time per (Sec) Transaction	Average Processing Time/Transaction Actual	Average Processing Time/Transaction Top Quartile	Average Processing Time/Transaction Proficiency
Drive up	5,524	7,704	1.39	82	59	44	60	134
Lobby	7,465	11,971	1.60	149	93	76	77	101
Total	12,989	19,675	1.51	120	79	64	70	110
11122333	1,342	1,984	1.48	127	86	69	76	110
***	***	***	***	***	***	***	***	***
***	***	***	***	***	***	***	***	***
77788999	3,802	5,302	1.39	79	57	43	59	138

REPORT P2

The transaction type processing time summary provided managers with information about the most frequently processed transactions at their branches and the associated processing times. By sorting this information in descending order according to frequency of transaction, managers could better understand the needs of their branch customers and identify opportunities for software enhancements and strategies to move transactions from tellers to such alternatives as ATMs. Using reports P1 and P2, the manager had the tools to manage teller proficiency and productivity.

Report P2—Transaction Type Processing Time Summary

Bank—District
Branch #—Name
Month Year

Trancode	Transaction Description	Transactions Processed	Average Time per (Sec)	
			Actual	Top Quartile
0003	DDA deposit	9,504	80	80
0010	Cash on U.S. check	3,898	70	66
0091	Inquiry	2,317	76	71
0002	Cash not on U.S. check	1,579	58	53
0084	Installment loan payment	322	81	79
***	***	***	***	***
***	***	***	***	***
0074	Loc direct advance	1	213	91
Total		19,675	79	76

REPORT P3

Managers needed a forecast of patterns of peak and slow customer activity to schedule tellers. Report P3, the summary of customers and transactions by day, provided daily transaction volumes by day of the week and by calendar day to facilitate effective staffing for such peak days as payday, social security check-cashing day, and other high-volume days.

Report P3—Summary of Customers and Transactions by Day

Bank—District
Branch #—Name
Month Year

Weekday	Date	Customers Served	Transactions Processed	Average Number of Transactions/Customer	Average Time per (Sec)	
					Transaction	Customer
Thursday	09/01/94	672	1,035	1.54	78	120
Friday	09/02/94	966	1,426	1.48	78	115
***	***	***	***	***	***	***
***	***	***	***	***	***	***
Friday	09/30/94	954	1,472	1.54	76	117
Total		12,989	19,675	1.51	79	120

REPORT P4

Report P4 showed the average number of customers and transactions processed every half hour for a specific weekday. It also showed the average time taken to process a transaction and the average time for a customer session. Using reports P3 and P4, branch managers could determine daily schedules to match staffing levels with the anticipated transaction volumes.

KeyCorp believed that the teller productivity module provided branch managers with tools to measure and manage teller proficiency and to anticipate customer arrivals so that they could achieve the targeted level of service.

Report P4—Customer and Transaction Volumes by Weekday by Half Hour

**Bank—District
Branch #—Name
Month Year**

Time Interval	Average Number of Customers Served	Average Number of Transactions	Average Number of Transactions/ Customer	Average Time per (Sec)	
				Transaction	Customer
08:30 A.M.–08:59 A.M.	8	12	1.48	81	119
09:00 A.M.–09:29 A.M.	26	35	1.38	78	107
***	***	***	***	***	***
***	***	***	***	***	***
05:30 P.M.–05:59 P.M.	32	50	1.55	79	122
Total	899	1,334	1.48	78	115

A SYSTEM TO MONITOR CUSTOMER WAITING TIMES

KeyCorp next wanted to monitor customer waiting times to see if the defined service objective of 90 percent of customers waiting less than five minutes on all days was being met. In order to do this, KeyCorp collected two more sets of data. First, it collected data regarding queue lengths. In the first attempt to do this, the teller would set a mechanical kitchen timer to ring every 30 minutes, at which prompting the teller would record the number of customers standing in line. This primitive approach was soon replaced by a statistical prompt screen that automatically appeared on the teller's main menu screen (that is, between transactions) at the beginning of each half-hour interval. Once the number of customers in the queue was entered, the screen disappeared until the next half-hour interval.

Second, KeyCorp collected data on the average number of tellers working in each half hour interval. For example, this number could be 3.5 for the interval between 11:00 and 11:30 A.M. if three tellers worked the full half hour and a fourth started at 11:15, or if four tellers were working at 11:00, one left for lunch at 11:25, and another left to perform administrative duties at 11:20.

If KeyCorp was to establish separate service level targets for individual branches by day of week or by calendar day or for any combination, customer waiting times would need to be determined and reported. How could KeyCorp determine the expected customer waiting-time experience at KeyCorp branches for specific time intervals and determine whether the defined service objective was being met?

a. Address the following general issue: How can KeyCorp provide a report for branch managers that details customer waiting times and reviews branch performance against KeyCorp's service objectives?

b. Discuss the following specific questions:

1. Could KeyCorp collect customer waiting time data directly?

2. How can waiting times be estimated from the available data?

3. What assumptions are necessary to make these estimates?

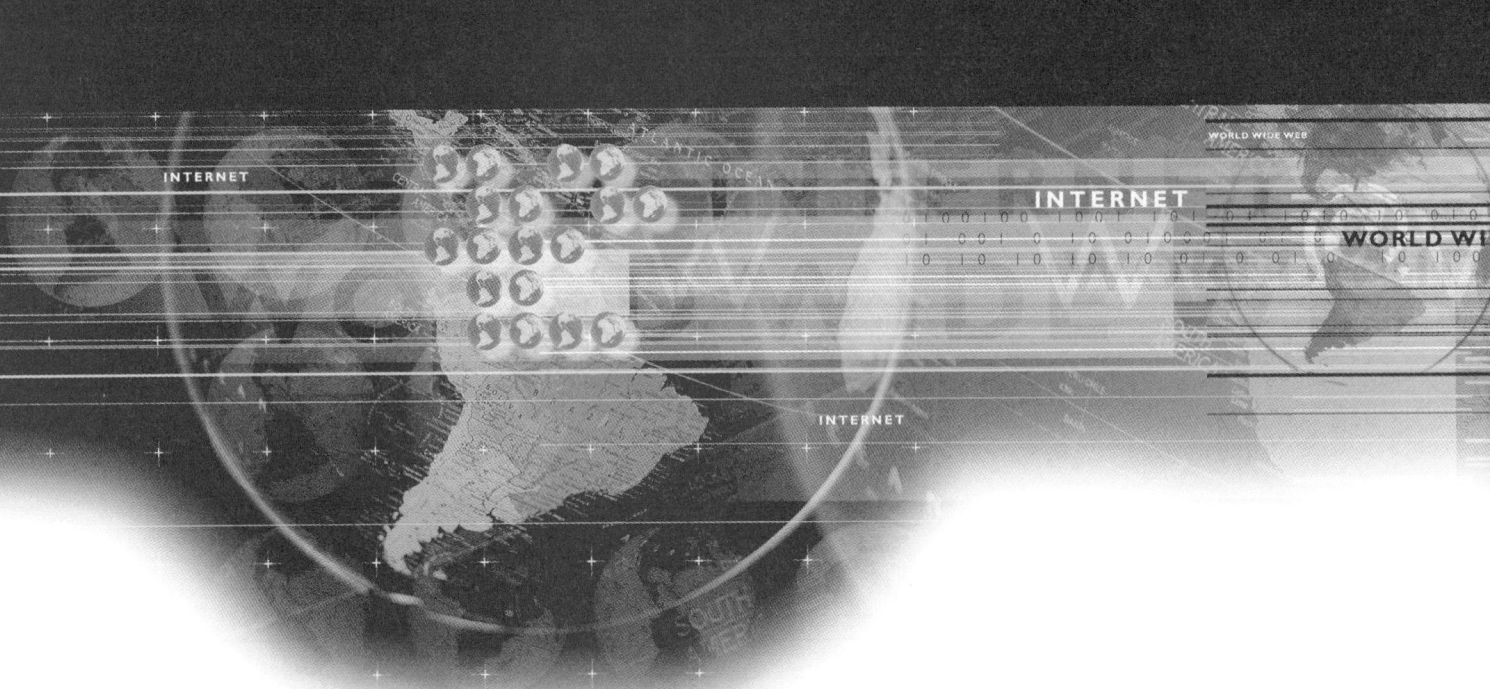

Learning objectives

After completing this chapter, you should be able to

1. Describe the basic concept of computer simulation.

2. Describe the role computer simulation plays in many management science studies.

3. Use random numbers to generate random events that have a simple discrete distribution.

4. Apply the inverse transformation method to generate random observations from any probability distribution.

5. Use Excel to perform basic computer simulations on a spreadsheet.

6. Use the Queueing Simulator to perform computer simulations of basic queueing systems and interpret the results.

7. Describe and use the building blocks of a simulation model for a stochastic system.

8. Identify some common types of applications of computer simulation.

9. Outline the steps of a major computer simulation study.

Chapter **Fifteen**

Computer Simulation: Basic Concepts

In this chapter, we now are ready to focus on the last of the key techniques of management science. *Computer simulation* ranks very high among the most widely used of these techniques. Furthermore, because it is such a flexible, powerful, and intuitive tool, it is continuing to rapidly grow in popularity. Many managers consider it one of their most valuable decision-making aids.

This technique involves using a computer to *imitate* (simulate) the operation of an entire process or system. For example, computer simulation is frequently used to perform risk analysis on financial processes by repeatedly imitating the evolution of the transactions involved to generate a profile of the possible outcomes. Computer simulation also is widely used to analyze systems that will continue operating indefinitely. For such systems, the computer randomly generates and records the occurrences of the various events that drive the system just as if it were physically operating. Because of its speed, the computer can simulate even years of operation in a matter of seconds. Recording the performance of the simulated operation of the system for a number of alternative designs or operating procedures then enables evaluating and comparing these alternatives before choosing one. For many processes and systems, all this now can be done with spreadsheet software.

The first section of this chapter describes and illustrates the essence of computer simulation. The case study for this chapter (a revisit of Herr Cutter's barber shop from the preceding chapter) is discussed and analyzed in Sections 15.2 and 15.3. The following section then presents a variety of common applications of computer simulation and Section 15.5 outlines the overall procedure for applying computer simulation. Chapter 16 will expand further on the application of computer simulation by describing how to apply Crystal Ball, a prominent Excel add-in for efficiently performing fairly complicated computer simulations on spreadsheets.

By imitating the operation of a proposed system, a computer can simulate years of operation in a matter of seconds and then record the performance.

15.1 THE ESSENCE OF COMPUTER SIMULATION

The technique of *simulation* has long been an important tool of the designer. For example, simulating airplane flight in a wind tunnel is standard practice when a new airplane is designed. Theoretically, the laws of physics could be used to obtain the same information about how the performance of the airplane changes as design parameters are altered, but, as a practical matter, the analysis would be too complicated to do it all. Another alternative would be to build real airplanes with alternative designs and test them in actual flight to choose the final design, but this would be far too expensive (as well as unsafe). Therefore, after some preliminary theoretical analysis is performed to develop a rough design, simulating flight in a wind tunnel is a vital tool for experimenting with specific designs. This simulation amounts to imitating the performance of a real airplane in a controlled environment in order to estimate what its actual performance will be. After a detailed design is developed in this way, a prototype model can be built and tested in actual flight to fine-tune the final design.

The Role of Computer Simulation

Computer simulation plays essentially this same role in many management science studies. However, rather than designing an airplane, the management science team is concerned with developing a design or operating procedure for some system. In many cases, the system is a *stochastic system,* as defined below.

> A **stochastic system** is a system that evolves over time according to one or more probability distributions. For example, the queueing systems described in the preceding chapter are stochastic systems because both the interarrival times and service times occur according to probability distributions.

Computer simulation uses probability distributions to randomly generate the various events that occur in a system.

Computer simulation imitates the operation of such a system by using the corresponding probability distributions to *randomly generate* the various events that occur in the system (e.g., the arrivals and service completions in a queueing system). However, rather than literally operating a physical system, the computer is just recording the occurrences of the *simulated* events and the resulting performance of this simulated system.

When computer simulation is used as part of a management science study, commonly it is preceded and followed by the same steps described earlier for the design of an airplane. In particular, some preliminary analysis is done first (perhaps with approximate mathematical models) to develop a rough design of the system (including its operating procedures). Then computer simulation is used to experiment with specific designs to estimate how well each will perform. After a detailed design is developed and selected in this way, the system probably is tested in actual use to fine-tune the final design.

When dealing with relatively complex systems, computer simulation tends to be a relatively expensive procedure. To get started, a detailed model must be formulated to describe the operation of the system of interest and how it is to be simulated. Then considerable time often is required to develop and debug the computer programs needed to run the simulation. Next, many long computer runs may be needed to obtain good estimates of how well all the alternative designs of the system would perform. Finally, all these data should be carefully analyzed before drawing any final conclusions. This entire process typically takes a lot of time and effort. Therefore, computer simulation should not be used when a less-expensive procedure is available that can provide the same information.

Computer simulation can predict the performance of proposed systems that are too complex to be analyzed by other mathematical models.

Computer simulation typically is used when the stochastic system involved is too complex to be analyzed satisfactorily by the kinds of mathematical models (e.g., queueing models) described in the preceding chapters. One of the main strengths of a mathematical model is that it abstracts the essence of the problem and reveals its underlying structure, thereby providing insight into the cause-and-effect relationships within the system. Therefore, if the modeler is able to construct a mathematical model that is both a reasonable approximation of the problem and amenable to solution, this approach usually is superior to computer simulation. However, many problems are too complex to permit this approach. Thus, computer simulation often provides the only practical approach to a problem.

Now let us look at a few examples to illustrate the basic ideas of computer simulation. These examples have been kept considerably simpler than the usual application of this technique in order to highlight the main ideas more readily. This also will enable us to obtain analytical solutions for the performance of the systems involved to compare with the estimates of the performance provided by computer simulation.

Example 1: A Coin-Flipping Game

You are the lucky winner of a sweepstakes contest. Your prize is an all-expense-paid vacation at a major hotel in Las Vegas, including some chips for gambling in the hotel casino.

Upon entering the casino, you find that, in addition to the usual games (blackjack, roulette, etc.), they are offering an interesting new game with the following rules.

Rules of the Game

1. Each play of the game involves repeatedly flipping an unbiased coin until the *difference* between the number of heads tossed and the number of tails is three.

2. If you decide to play the game, you are required to pay $1 for each flip of the coin. You are not allowed to quit during a play of the game.

3. You receive $8 at the end of each play of the game.

Thus, you win money if the number of flips required is fewer than eight, but you lose money if more than eight flips are required. Here are some examples (where H denotes a head and T a tail).

HHH	3 flips	You win $5
THTTT	5 flips	You win $3
THHTHTHTTTT	11 flips	You lose $3

How would you decide whether to play this game?

Many people would base this decision on *simulation,* although they probably would not call it by that name. In this case, simulation amounts to nothing more than playing the game alone many times until it becomes clear whether it is worthwhile to play for money. Half an hour spent in repeatedly flipping a coin and recording the earnings or losses that would have resulted might be sufficient. This is a true simulation because you are *imitating* the actual play of the game without actually winning or losing any money.

Since the topic of this chapter is *computer* simulation, let us see now how a computer can be used to perform this same *simulated experiment.* Although a computer cannot flip coins, it can *simulate* doing so. It accomplishes this by generating a sequence of *random numbers,* as defined below.

A number is a **random number** between 0 and 1 if it has been generated in such a way that *every* possible number within this interval has an equal chance of occurring. For example, if numbers with four decimal places are being used, every one of the 10,000 numbers between 0.0000 and 0.9999 has an equal chance of occurring. Thus, a random number between 0 and 1 is a *random observation* from a *uniform* distribution between 0 and 1. (Hereafter, we will delete the phrase *between 0 and 1* when referring to these random numbers.)

An easy way to generate random numbers is to use the RAND() function in Excel. For example, the lower left-hand corner of Figure 15.1 indicates that = RAND() has been entered into cell C13 and then copied into the range C14:C62. (The parentheses need to be included with this function, but nothing is inserted between them.) This causes Excel to generate the random numbers shown in cells C13:C62 of the spreadsheet. (Rows 27–56 have been hidden to save space in the figure.)

The probabilities for the outcome of flipping a coin are

$$P(\text{heads}) = \tfrac{1}{2} \qquad P(\text{tails}) = \tfrac{1}{2}$$

Therefore, to simulate the flipping of a coin, the computer can just let any half of the possible random numbers correspond to heads and the other half correspond to tails. To be specific, we will use the following correspondence.

0.0000 to 0.4999   correspond to   heads

0.5000 to 0.9999   correspond to   tails

By using the formula

= IF(RandomNumber < 0.5, "Heads", "Tails")

in each of the column D cells in Figure 15.1, Excel inserts Heads if the random number is less than 0.5 and inserts Tails otherwise. Consequently, the first 11 random numbers generated in column C yield the following sequence of heads (H) and tails (T):

HTTTHHHTHHH

Random numbers play a key role in performing computer simulations, so Excel uses the RAND() function to generate them.

FIGURE 15.1 A spreadsheet model for a computer simulation of the coin-flipping game (Example 1).

	A	B	C	D	E	F	G
1		**Coin-Flipping Game**					
2							
3			Required Difference	3			
4			Cash at End of Game	$8			
5							
6				**Summary of Game**			
7			Number of Flips	11			
8			Winnings	−$3			
9							
10							
11			Random		Total	Total	
12		Flip	Number	Result	Heads	Tails	Stop?
13		1	0.3039	Heads	1	0	
14		2	0.7914	Tails	1	1	
15		3	0.8543	Tails	1	2	
16		4	0.6902	Tails	1	3	
17		5	0.3004	Heads	2	3	
18		6	0.0383	Heads	3	3	
19		7	0.3883	Heads	4	3	
20		8	0.6052	Tails	4	4	
21		9	0.2231	Heads	5	4	
22		10	0.4250	Heads	6	4	
23		11	0.3729	Heads	7	4	Stop
24		12	0.7983	Tails	7	5	NA
25		13	0.2340	Heads	8	5	NA
26		14	0.0082	Heads	9	5	NA
57		45	0.7539	Tails	26	19	NA
58		46	0.2989	Heads	27	19	NA
59		47	0.6427	Tails	27	20	NA
60		48	0.2824	Heads	28	20	NA
61		49	0.2124	Heads	29	20	NA
62		50	0.6420	Tails	29	21	NA

Range Name	Cells
CashAtEndOfGame	D4
Flip	B13:B62
NumberOfFlips	D7
RandomNumber	C13:C62
RequiredDifference	D3
Result	D13:D62
Stop?	G13:G62
TotalHeads	E13:E62
TotalTails	F13:F62
Winnings	D8

	C	D
6		**Summary of Game**
7	Number of Flips	=COUNTBLANK(Stop?)+1
8	Winnings	=CashAtEndOfGame−NumberOfFlips

	C	D	E	F
11	Random		Total	Total
12	Number	Result	Heads	Tails
13	=RAND()	=IF(RandomNumber<0.5,"Heads","Tails")	=IF(Results="Heads",1,0)	=Flip-TotalHeads
14	=RAND()	=IF(RandomNumber<0.5,"Heads","Tails")	=E13+IF(Results="Heads",1,0)	=Flip-TotalHeads
15	=RAND()	=IF(RandomNumber<0.5,"Heads","Tails")	=E14+IF(Results="Heads",1,0)	=Flip-TotalHeads
16	⋮	⋮	⋮	⋮
17	⋮	⋮	⋮	⋮

	G
12	Stop?
13	
14	
15	=IF(ABS(TotalHeads-TotalTails)>=RequiredDifference,"Stop","")
16	=IF(G15="",IF(ABS(TotalHeads-TotalTails)>=RequiredDifference,"Stop",""),"NA")
17	=IF(G16="",IF(ABS(TotalHeads-TotalTails)>=RequiredDifference,"Stop",""),"NA")
18	⋮
19	⋮

at which point the game stops because the number of heads (seven) exceeds the number of tails (four) by three. Cells D7 and D8 record the total number of flips (11) and resulting winnings ($8 − $11 = −$3).

Thus, Figure 15.1 records the computer simulation of one complete play of the game. To virtually ensure that the game will be completed, 50 flips of the coin have been simulated. Columns E and F record the cumulative number of heads and tails after each flip. The equations entered into the column G cells leave each cell blank until the difference in the numbers of heads and tails reaches 3, at which point Stop is inserted into the cell. Thereafter, NA (for Not Applicable) is inserted instead.

Such simulations of plays of the game can be repeated as often as desired with this spreadsheet. Each time, Excel will generate a new sequence of random numbers and so a new sequence of heads and tails. (Excel will repeat a sequence of random numbers only if you select the range of numbers you want to repeat, copy this range with the Copy command, select Paste Special from the Edit menu, choose the Values option, and click on OK.)

Computer simulations normally are repeated many times to obtain a more reliable estimate of an average outcome. Figure 15.2 shows how a data table can be used to trick Excel into repeating the simulation 14 times. You first make a table with the column headings shown in columns J, K, and L. The first column of the table (J7:J20) is used to label the 14 plays of the game, leaving the first row blank. The headings of the next two columns specify which output will be evaluated. For each of these two columns, use the first row of the table (cells K6:L6) to write an equation that refers to the relevant output cell. In this case, the cells of interest are the number of flips and the winnings, so the equations for K6:L6 are those shown to the right of the spreadsheet in Figure 15.2.

The next step is to select the entire table (J6:L20) and then choose Table from the Data menu. In the Table dialogue box (as shown on the right-hand side of Figure 15.2), choose any

FIGURE 15.2

A data table that records the results of performing 14 replications of a computer simulation with the spreadsheet in Figure 15.1.

	I	J	K	L	M
1		**Data Table for Coin-Flipping Game**			
2		**(14 Replications)**			
3					
4			Number		
5		Play	of Flips	Winnings	
6			3	$5	
7		1	9	−$1	
8		2	5	$3	
9		3	7	$1	
10		4	11	−$3	
11		5	5	$3	
12		6	3	$5	
13		7	3	$5	
14		8	11	−$3	
15		9	7	$1	
16		10	15	−$7	
17		11	3	$5	
18		12	7	$1	
19		13	9	−$1	
20		14	5	3	
21					
22		Average	7.14	$0.86	

Select the whole table (J6:L20), before choosing Table from the Data menu.

Range Name	Cell
NumberOfFlips	D7
Winnings	D8

	K	L
4	Number	
5	of Flips	Winnings
6	=NumberOfFlips	=Winnings

Table

Row input cell: [ ]

Column input cell: [E4]

[Cancel] [OK]

	J	K	L
22	Average	=AVERAGE(K7:K20)	=AVERAGE(L7:L20)

blank cell for the column input cell (for example, E4) but do not enter anything for the row input cell. Clicking OK then generates the data table shown in Figure 15.2.

The first thing Excel does while generating the data table is to enter the numbers in the first column of the table (J7:J20), one at a time, into the column input cell (E4), which has no direct impact on the simulation. However, each time a new number is entered into the column input cell, Excel recalculates the entire original spreadsheet (Figure 15.1) in cells C13:G62 and then enters the resulting numbers in the output cells, NumberOfFlips (D7) and Winnings (D8), into the corresponding row of the data table. In essence, we have tricked Excel into repeating the simulation 14 times, each time generating new random numbers in column C to perform a completely new simulation.

Cell K22 shows that this sample of 14 plays of the game gives a sample average of 7.14 flips. The sample average provides an *estimate* of the true *mean* of the underlying probability distribution of the number of flips required for a play of the game. Hence, this sample average of 7.14 would seem to indicate that, on the average, you should win about $0.86 (cell L22) each time you play the game. Therefore, if you do not have a relatively high aversion to risk, it appears that you should choose to play this game, preferably a large number of times.

However, *beware!* One common error in the use of computer simulation is that conclusions are based on overly small samples, because statistical analysis was inadequate or totally lacking. It is very important to use a qualified statistician to help design the experiments to be performed with computer simulation. In this case, careful statistical analysis (using confidence intervals, etc.) would indicate that hundreds of simulated plays of the game would be needed before any conclusions should be drawn about whether you are likely to win or lose by playing this game numerous times.

> At least hundreds of simulated plays of this game are needed to obtain a reasonably reliable estimate of an average outcome.

It so happens that the true mean of the number of flips required for a play of this game is nine. (This mean can be found analytically, but not easily.) Thus, in the long run, you actually would average losing about $1 each time you played the game. Part of the reason that the above simulated experiment failed to draw this conclusion is that you have a small chance of a very large loss on any play of the game, but you can never win more than $5 each time. However, 14 simulated plays of the game were not enough to obtain any observations far out in the tail of the probability distribution of the amount won or lost on one play of the game. Only one simulated play gave a loss of more than $3, and that was only $7.

Figure 15.3 gives the results of running the simulation for 1,000 plays of the game (with rows 17–1,000 not shown). Cell K1008 records the average number of flips as 8.97, very close to the true mean of 9. With this number of replications, the average winnings of −$0.97 in cell L1008 now provide a reliable basis for concluding that this game will not win you money in the long run. (You can bet that the casino already has used computer simulation to verify this fact in advance.)

Example 2: Corrective Maintenance versus Preventive Maintenance

The Heavy Duty Company has just purchased a large machine for a new production process. The machine is powered by a motor that occasionally breaks down and requires a major overhaul. Therefore, the manufacturer of the machine also provides a second standby motor. The two motors are rotated in use, with each one remaining in the machine until it is removed for an overhaul and replaced by the other one.

Given the planned usage of the machine, its manufacturer has provided the company with information about the *durability* of the motors (the number of days of usage until a breakdown occurs). This information is shown in the first two columns of Table 15.1. The first column lists the number of days the current machine has been in use. For each of these days, the second column then gives the probability that the breakdown will occur on that day. Since these probabilities are 0 except for days 4, 5, and 6, the breakdown always occurs on the fourth, fifth, or sixth day.

Fortunately, the time required to overhaul a motor never exceeds three days, so a replacement motor always is ready when a breakdown occurs. When this happens, the remainder of

FIGURE 15.3

This data table improves the reliability of the computer simulation recorded in Figure 15.2 by performing 1,000 replications instead of only 14.

	I	J	K	L	M
1		**Data Table for Coin-Flipping Game**			
2		**(1,000 Replications)**			
3					
4			Number		
5		Play	of Flips	Winnings	
6			5	$3	
7		1	3	$5	
8		2	3	$5	
9		3	7	$1	
10		4	11	–$3	
11		5	13	–$5	
12		6	7	$1	
13		7	3	$5	
14		8	7	$1	
15		9	3	$5	
16		10	9	–$1	
1001		995	5	$3	
1002		996	27	–$19	
1003		997	7	$1	
1004		998	3	$5	
1005		999	9	–$1	
1006		1,000	17	–$9	
1007					
1008		Average	8.97	–$0.97	

TABLE 15.1

The Probability Distribution of Breakdowns for Heavy Duty's Motors, and the Corresponding Random Numbers

Day	Probability of a Breakdown	Corresponding Random Numbers
1, 2, 3	0	
4	0.25	0.0000 to 0.2499
5	0.5	0.2500 to 0.7499
6	0.25	0.7500 to 0.9999
7 or more	0	

the day (plus overtime if needed) is used to remove the failed motor and install the replacement motor, so the machine then is ready to begin operation again at the beginning of the next day. The average costs incurred during each *replacement cycle* (the time from when a replacement of a motor begins until just before another replacement is needed) are summarized below.

Cost of a Replacement Cycle That Begins with a Breakdown

Replace a motor	$ 2,000
Lost production during replacement	5,000
Overhaul a motor	4,000
Total	$11,000

Using Computer Simulation

Computer simulation can be used to estimate what the *average daily cost* will be for replacing the motors as needed. This requires using random numbers to determine when breakdowns occur in the *simulated* process. Using the probabilities in the second column of Table 15.1, 25 percent of the possible random numbers need to correspond to a breakdown on day 4, 50 percent

FIGURE 15.4   A spreadsheet model for a computer simulation of performing corrective maintenance on the Heavy Duty Co. motors.

	A	B	C	D	E	F	G	H	I	J	K
1		**Heavy Duty Company Corrective Maintenance Simulation**									
2											
3			Random	Time Since Last	Cumulative		Cumulative		**Distribution of**		
4		Breakdown	Number	Breakdown	Day	Cost	Cost		**Time between Breakdowns**		
5		1	0.7142	5	5	$11,000	$11,000				Number
6		2	0.4546	5	10	$11,000	$22,000		Probability	Cumulative	of Days
7		3	0.3142	5	15	$11,000	$33,000		0.25	0	4
8		4	0.1722	4	19	$11,000	$44,000		0.5	0.25	5
9		5	0.0932	4	23	$11,000	$55,000		0.25	0.75	6
10		6	0.3645	5	28	$11,000	$66,000				
11		7	0.1636	4	32	$11,000	$77,000		Breakdown Cost	$11,000	
12		8	0.7572	6	38	$11,000	$88,000				
13		9	0.3067	5	43	$11,000	$99,000				
14		10	0.9520	6	49	$11,000	$110,000				
30		26	0.8548	6	131	$11,000	$286,000				
31		27	0.7464	5	136	$11,000	$297,000				
32		28	0.9781	6	142	$11,000	$308,000				
33		29	0.6584	5	147	$11,000	$319,000			Average Cost per Day	
34		30	0.8829	6	153	$11,000	$330,000			$2,157	

	C	D	E	F	G
3	Random	Time Since Last	Cumulative		Cumulative
4	Number	Breakdown	Day	Cost	Cost
5	=RAND()	=VLOOKUP(RandomNumber,$J$7:$K$9,2)	=TimeSinceLastBreakdown	=BreakdownCost	=Cost
6	=RAND()	=VLOOKUP(RandomNumber,$J$7:$K$9,2)	=E5+TimeSinceLastBreakdown	=BreakdownCost	=G5+Cost
7	=RAND()	=VLOOKUP(RandomNumber,$J$7:$K$9,2)	=E6+TimeSinceLastBreakdown	=BreakdownCost	=G6+Cost
8	:	:	:	:	:
9	:	:	:	:	:

Range Name	Cells
AverageCostPerDay	J34
Breakdown	B5:B34
BreakdownCost	J11
Cost	F5:F34
CumulativeCost	G5:G34
CumulativeDay	E5:E34
RandomNumber	C5:C34
TimeSinceLastBreakdown	D5:D34

	J
33	Average Cost per Day
34	=CumulativeCost/CumulativeDay

to a breakdown on day 5, and the remaining 25 percent to a breakdown on day 6. The rightmost column of Table 15.1 shows the natural way of doing this.

Excel provides a convenient VLOOKUP function for implementing this correspondence between a random number and the associated event. Figure 15.4 illustrates how it works. One step is to create the table shown in columns I, J, and K, where columns K and I come directly from the first two columns of Table 15.1. Column J gives the cumulative probability *prior* to the number of days in column K, so J8 = I7 and J9 = I7 + I8. Cells J7:K9 then constitute the lookup table for the VLOOKUP function. The bottom of the figure displays how the VLOOKUP command has been entered into the column D cells. The first argument of this function indicates that the cell in the same row of RandomNumber (C5:C34) provides the random number being used. The second argument gives the range for the lookup table. The third argument (2) indicates that column 2 of the lookup table is providing the number being entered into this cell in column D. The choice of the number in column 2 of the lookup table is based on where the random number falls within the ranges between rows in column 1 of this table. In particular, the three possible choices are

if	$0 \leq$ RAND() < 0.25	choose 4 days
if	$0.25 \leq$ RAND() < 0.75	choose 5 days
if	$0.75 \leq$ RAND() < 1	choose 6 days

which is precisely the correspondence indicated in Table 15.1.

By generating 30 simulated breakdowns in this way in column D of Figure 15.4, columns E, F, and G then show the resulting cumulative number of days, the estimated cost for each replacement cycle, and the cumulative cost for the corresponding replacement cycles. (In a more detailed computer simulation, random numbers also could be used to generate the exact costs with each simulated breakdown.) Since the total number of days in this simulation (cell E34) is 153 and the cumulative cost (cell G34) is $330,000, the average daily cost is calculated in cell J34 as

$$\text{Average cost per day} = \frac{\$330,000}{153} = \$2,157$$

Comparisons with Example 1

Comparing this computer simulation with the ones run for the coin-flipping game reveal a couple of interesting differences. One is that the IF function was used to generate each simulated coin flip from a random number (see the equations entered into the column D cells in Figure 15.1), whereas the VLOOKUP function has just been used here to generate the simulated results. Actually, the VLOOKUP function could have been used instead for the coin flips, but the IF function was more convenient. Conversely, a nested IF function could have been used instead for the current example, but the VLOOKUP function was more convenient. In general, we prefer using the IF function to generate a random observation from a probability distribution that has only two possible values, whereas we prefer the VLOOKUP function when the distribution has more than two possible values.

A second difference arose in the way the replications of the two computer simulations were recorded. For the coin-flipping game, simulating a single play of the game involved using the spreadsheet with 62 rows shown in Figure 15.1. Therefore, to record many replications, this same spreadsheet was used to generate the data table in Figure 15.2, which summarized the results of each replication in a single row. For the current example, no separate data table was needed because each replication could be executed and displayed in a single row of the original spreadsheet in Figure 15.4.

However, one similarity between the two examples is that we purposely kept each one sufficiently simple that an analytical solution is available to compare with the simulation results. In fact, it is quite straightforward to obtain the analytical solution for the current version of the Heavy Duty Co. problem. Using the probabilities in Table 15.1, the *expected* number of days until a breakdown occurs is

$$E \text{ (time until a breakdown)} = 0.25(4 \text{ days}) + 0.5(5 \text{ days}) + 0.25(6 \text{ days})$$

$$= 5 \text{ days}$$

Therefore, the *expected value* (in the statistical sense) of the cost per day is

$$E \text{ (cost per day)} = \frac{\$11,000}{5 \text{ days}} = \$2,200 \text{ per day}$$

The average cost of $2,157 per day obtained by computer simulation (cell J34 of Figure 15.4) is an estimate of this true expected value.

The fact that computer simulation actually was not needed to analyze this version of the Heavy Duty Co. problem illustrates a possible pitfall with this technique. Computer simulation is easy enough to use that there occasionally is a tendency to rush into using this technique when a bit of careful thought and analysis first could provide all the needed information more precisely (and perhaps more quickly) than computer simulation. In other cases, starting with a simple analytical model sometimes can provide important insights as a prelude to using computer simulation to refine the analysis with a more precise formulation of the problem.

Some Preventive Maintenance Options

The goal of preventive maintenance is to provide maintenance early enough to prevent a breakdown.

So far, we have assumed that the company will use a *corrective maintenance* policy. This means that the motor in the machine will be removed and overhauled only after it has broken down. However, many companies use a *preventive maintenance* policy instead. Such a policy in this case would involve *scheduling* the motor to be removed (and replaced) for an overhaul at a certain time even if a breakdown has not occurred. The goal is to provide maintenance early enough to prevent a breakdown. Scheduling the overhaul also enables removing and replacing the motor at a convenient time when the machine would not be in use otherwise, so that no production is lost. For example, by paying overtime wages for the removal and replacement, this work can be done after the normal workday ends so that the machine will be ready by the beginning of the next day. One possibility is to do this at the end of day 3, which would definitely be in time to prevent a breakdown. Other options are to do it at the end of day 4 or day 5 (if a breakdown has not yet occurred) in order to prevent disrupting production with a breakdown in the very near future. Computer simulation can be used to evaluate and compare each of these options (along with a corrective maintenance policy) when analytical solutions are not available.

Consider the option of removing (and replacing) the motor for an overhaul at the end of day 3. The average cost each time this is done happens to be the following.

Cost of a Replacement Cycle That Begins without a Breakdown

Replace a motor on overtime	$3,000
Lost production during replacement	0
Overhaul a motor before a breakdown	3,000
Total	$6,000

Since this total cost of $6,000 occurs every three days, the expected cost per day of this option would be

$$E \text{ (cost per day)} = \frac{\$6,000}{3 \text{ days}} = \$2,000 \text{ per day}$$

Since this cost has been obtained analytically, computer simulation is not needed in this case.

Now consider the remaining two options of removing (and replacing) the motor after day 4 or after day 5 if a breakdown has not yet occurred. Since it is somewhat more difficult to find the expected cost per day analytically for these options, we now will use computer simulation. For either case, the average cost during a replacement cycle depends on whether the replacement began before or after a breakdown occurred. As outlined earlier, these average costs are

Cost of a replacement cycle that begins with a breakdown   = $11,000

Cost of a replacement cycle that begins without a breakdown = $ 6,000

Figure 15.5 shows the use of computer simulation for the option of scheduling the replacement of each motor after four days. The times until 30 consecutive motors would have broken down without the replacements are obtained from column D (except rows 15–29 are hidden). The cases where this time is four (indicating a breakdown *during* day 4) correspond to a motor breaking down before it is replaced. (This occurs in rows 6, 9, 13–14 and in five of the hidden rows.) The first cycle concludes with the replacement of the first motor after four days, as shown in row 5. Column G gives the cumulative number of days at the end of each cycle. Column F indicates whether each cycle ends with a breakdown or with a replacement that is soon enough to avoid a breakdown, and column H gives the resulting cost. Column I then cumulates

Heavy Duty Company Preventive Maintenance Simulation (Replace After 4 Days)

Cycle	Random Number	Time Until Breakdown	Scheduled Time Until Replacement	Event That Concludes Cycle	Cumulative Day	Cost	Cumulative Cost
1	0.7861	6	4	Replacement	4	$6,000	$6,000
2	0.0679	4	4	Breakdown	8	$11,000	$17,000
3	0.9296	6	4	Replacement	12	$6,000	$23,000
4	0.4430	5	4	Replacement	16	$6,000	$29,000
5	0.1223	4	4	Breakdown	20	$11,000	$40,000
6	0.4530	5	4	Replacement	24	$6,000	$46,000
7	0.3972	5	4	Replacement	28	$6,000	$52,000
8	0.9289	6	4	Replacement	32	$6,000	$58,000
9	0.2195	4	4	Breakdown	36	$11,000	$69,000
10	0.0706	4	4	Breakdown	40	$11,000	$80,000
26	0.8720	6	4	Replacement	104	$6,000	$201,000
27	0.8902	6	4	Replacement	108	$6,000	$207,000
28	0.3839	5	4	Replacement	112	$6,000	$213,000
29	0.7404	5	4	Replacement	116	$6,000	$219,000
30	0.7264	5	4	Replacement	120	$6,000	$225,000

Distribution of Time between Breakdowns

Probability	Cumulative	Number of Days
0.25	0	4
0.5	0.25	5
0.25	0.75	6

Breakdown Cost	$11,000
Replacement Cost	$6,000
Replace After	4 days

Average Cost per Day	$1,875

	Random Number	Time Until Breakdown	Scheduled Time Until Replacement
5	=RAND()	=VLOOKUP(RandomNumber,$L$7:$M$9,2)	=ReplaceAfter
6	=RAND()	=VLOOKUP(RandomNumber,$L$7:$M$9,2)	=ReplaceAfter
7	=RAND()	=VLOOKUP(RandomNumber,$L$7:$M$9,2)	=ReplaceAfter
8	:	:	:
9	:	:	:

	Event That Concludes Cycle
5	=IF(TimeUntilBreakdown<=ScheduledTimeUntilReplacement,"Breakdown","Replacement")
6	=IF(TimeUntilBreakdown<=ScheduledTimeUntilReplacement,"Breakdown","Replacement")
7	=IF(TimeUntilBreakdown<=ScheduledTimeUntilReplacement,"Breakdown","Replacement")
8	:
9	:

	Cumulative Day	Cost
3	Cumulative	
4	Day	Cost
5	=MIN(D5,E5)	=IF(Event="Breakdown",BreakdownCost,ReplacementCost)
6	=G5+MIN(D6,E6)	=IF(Event="Breakdown",BreakdownCost,ReplacementCost)
7	=G6+MIN(D7,E7)	=IF(Event="Breakdown",BreakdownCost,ReplacementCost)
8	:	:
9		

	Cumulative Cost
3	Cumulative
4	Cost
5	=Cost
6	=I5+Cost
7	=I6+Cost
8	:
9	:

	Average Cost per Day
33	Average Cost per Day
34	=CumulativeCost/CumulativeDay

Range Name	Cells
AverageCostPerDay	L34
BreakdownCost	L11
Cost	H5:H34
CumulativeCost	I5:I34
CumulativeDay	G5:G34
Cycle	B5:B34
Event	F5:F34
RandomNumber	C5:C34
ReplaceAfter	L14
ReplacementCost	L12
ScheduledTimeUntilReplacement	E5:E34
TimeUntilBreakdown	D5:D34

these costs. Since the 30 cycles last 120 days (cell G34) and have a total cost of $225,000 (cell I34), this simulation yields

$$\text{Average cost per day} = \frac{\$225,000}{120} = \$1,875$$

as the *estimate* of the expected cost per day (which actually is $1,812 per day) for this option.

Figure 15.6 shows the corresponding simulation for the option of scheduling the replacement of each motor after five days. Thus, if the time until a breakdown would be on the sixth day (as indicated in column D), the replacement is made in time to avoid the breakdown (as indicated in column F). Since most of the times in column D are four or five instead, most of the cycles conclude with a breakdown. This leads to a much higher total cost for the 30 cycles of $300,000, along with a somewhat longer total time of 141 days. Therefore, the *estimate* of the expected cost per day for this option is

$$\text{Average cost per day} = \frac{\$300,000}{141} = \$2,128$$

(The true expected cost per day is $2,053.)

Based on all the above results, the clear choice for the least expensive option is the one that schedules the replacement of each motor after four days, since its estimated expected cost per day is only $1,875. Although this estimate based on the simulation in Figure 15.5 overestimates the true expected cost per day by $63, this option still is the least expensive one by a wide margin.

In practice, the simulation runs usually would be considerably longer than those shown in Figures 15.4, 15.5, and 15.6 in order to obtain more precise estimates of the true costs for the alternative options. The simulations typically also would include more details, such as when during a day a breakdown occurs and the resulting cost of lost production that day.

Longer and more detailed simulation runs are commonly conducted.

Both Examples 1 and 2 used random numbers to generate random observations from *discrete* probability distributions. Many computer simulations require generating random observations from *continuous* distributions instead. We next describe a general method for doing this with *either* continuous or discrete distributions.

Generating Random Observations from a Probability Distribution

The method for generating these observations is called the **inverse transformation method.** To explain and apply the method, we will use the following notation.

r is a random number.

$F(x)$ is the *cumulative distribution function* (CDF) of the distribution from which we wish to generate a random observation. Thus, for each possible value of x, $F(x)$ is the probability of being less than or equal to x.

For example, Figure 15.7 shows a random number, $r = 0.5271$, and also plots $F(x)$ versus x for an arbitrary probability distribution.

Generating each random observation then requires the following two steps.

The Inverse Transformation Method

1. Generate a random number r.

2. Find the value of x such that $F(x) = r$. This value of x is the desired random observation from the probability distribution.

The random observation in Figure 15.7 is the value of x such that $F(x) = r$.

Figure 15.7 illustrates the graphical application of this method. After locating the value of r along the vertical axis, a horizontal dashed line is drawn over to $F(x)$. When this line hits the $F(x)$ curve, a vertical dashed line then is dropped down to the horizontal axis. This point on the horizontal axis is the desired random observation because it is the value of x such that $F(x) = r$.

Although the probability distribution shown in Figure 15.7 is a *continuous* distribution, the inverse transformation method also can be used to generate random observations from *discrete* distributions. For example, consider the discrete distribution given in Table 15.1 for

FIGURE 15.6 A revision of Figure 15.5 to schedule the replacement of the motors after five days instead of four.

Heavy Duty Company Preventive Maintenance Simulation (Replace After 5 Days)

Cycle	Random Number	Time Until Breakdown	Scheduled Time Until Replacement	Event That Concludes Cycle	Cumulative Day	Cost	Cumulative Cost
1	0.0558	4	5	Breakdown	4	$11,000	$11,000
2	0.0690	4	5	Breakdown	8	$11,000	$22,000
3	0.1889	4	5	Breakdown	12	$11,000	$33,000
4	0.9471	6	5	Replacement	17	$6,000	$39,000
5	0.9173	6	5	Replacement	22	$6,000	$45,000
6	0.3541	5	5	Breakdown	27	$11,000	$56,000
7	0.7035	5	5	Breakdown	32	$11,000	$67,000
8	0.0350	4	5	Breakdown	36	$11,000	$78,000
9	0.5755	5	5	Breakdown	41	$11,000	$89,000
10	0.8910	6	5	Replacement	46	$6,000	$95,000
26	0.7386	5	5	Breakdown	122	$11,000	$261,000
27	0.2648	5	5	Breakdown	127	$11,000	$272,000
28	0.6239	5	5	Breakdown	132	$11,000	$283,000
29	0.9988	6	5	Replacement	137	$6,000	$289,000
30	0.0061	4	5	Breakdown	141	$11,000	$300,000

Distribution of Time between Breakdowns

Probability	Cumulative	Number of Days
0.25	0	4
0.5	0.25	5
0.25	0.75	6

Breakdown Cost	$11,000
Replacement Cost	$6,000
Replace After	5 days

Average Cost per Day $2,128

FIGURE 15.7

Illustration of the inverse transformation method for obtaining a random observation from a given probability distribution.

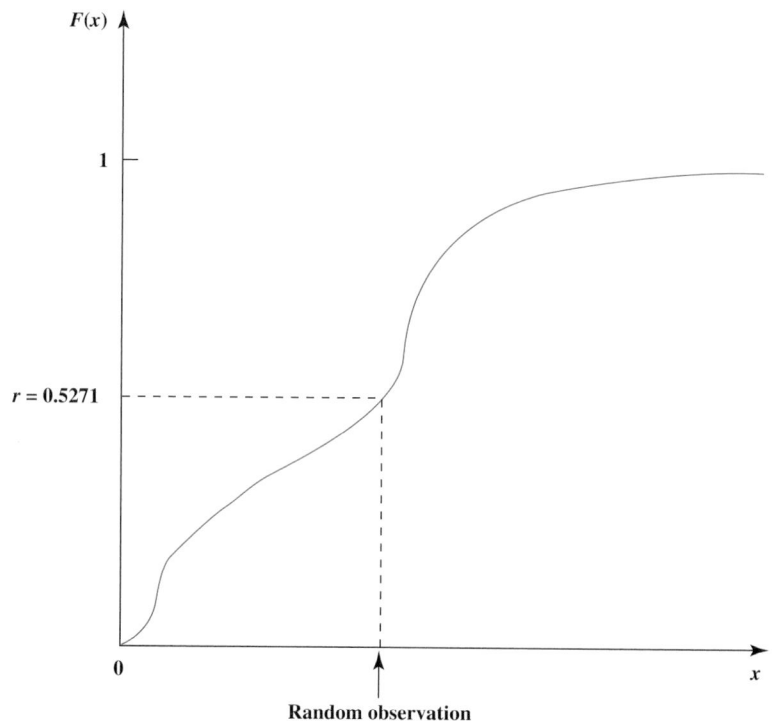

FIGURE 15.8

Applying the inverse transformation method to obtain a random observation from the discrete probability distribution for Example 2 given in Table 15.1.

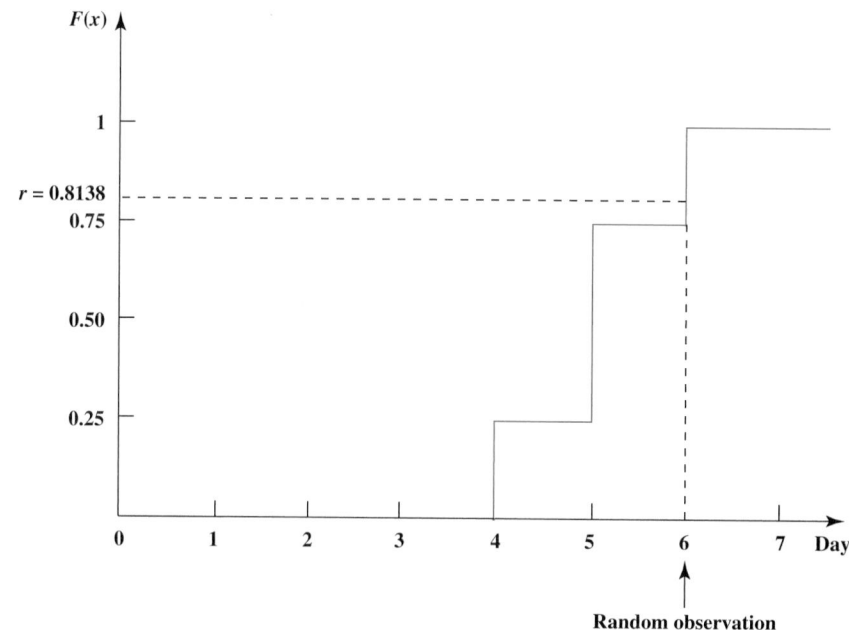

Example 2. Since the probability that a motor will break down on days 4, 5, and 6 is 0.25, 0.5, and 0.25, respectively, the CDF of this distribution is the one shown in Figure 15.8. A random number of $r = 0.8138$, for example, then generates the random observation that the breakdown occurs on day 6.

Excel's VLOOKUP function is designed specifically for applying the inverse transformation method to any discrete distribution. This function also can be applied to a continuous distribution by entering an extensive *lookup table* that closely approximates the distribution.

For certain common continuous distributions, the equation that $F(x) = r$ has an analytical solution for x. In such cases, the inverse transformation method enables Excel to quickly generate random observations from these distributions. Two examples of such distributions are the uniform distribution and the exponential distribution. We will illustrate the method with these two distributions in the next section in the context of a case study.

Unfortunately, when $F(x)$ is a relatively complicated function, the inverse transformation method becomes more difficult to apply *analytically*. One example is the *normal distribution*. The option of using the VLOOKUP function after entering an extensive *lookup table* always is available for such a distribution. However, the normal distribution is such an important one that more convenient special methods have been developed to generate random observations from this distribution. In particular, Excel uses the function

$$\text{NORMINV(RAND(), } \mu, \sigma)$$

to do this after you substitute the numerical values for the mean μ and standard deviation σ of the distribution.

This is a very handy Excel function to generate a random observation from a normal distribution.

Several Excel add-ins have been developed to extend the simulation capabilities of the standard Excel package, including providing special functions to immediately generate random observations from a wide variety of probability distributions. Two of these (Crystal Ball and RiskSim) are included in your MS Courseware. Crystal Ball will be featured in the next chapter. RiskSim is shareware developed by Professor Michael Middleton. Although not as elaborate or powerful as Crystal Ball, RiskSim is easy to use and is well documented on the CD-ROM. (If you want to continue to use it after this course, you should register and pay the shareware fee.) Like any Excel add-ins, these add-ins need to be installed before they will show up in Excel.

Review Questions

1. How does computer simulation imitate the operation of a stochastic system?
2. Why does computer simulation tend to be a relatively expensive procedure?
3. When is computer simulation typically used despite being relatively expensive?
4. What is a random number? For what purpose is it used?
5. What is the purpose of the inverse transformation method? What are its two steps?

15.2   A CASE STUDY: HERR CUTTER'S BARBER SHOP (REVISITED)

If you have already studied the preceding chapter, you hopefully recall the brief description in Section 14.1 of Herr Cutter's barber shop as an example of a basic kind of queueing system. (A queueing system is a place where customers receive some kind of service from a server, perhaps after waiting in a line called a queue.) As indicated there, Herr Cutter is a German barber who runs a one-man barber shop. He opens his shop at 8:00 A.M. each weekday morning. His customers arrive randomly at an average rate of two customers per hour. He requires an average of 20 minutes for each haircut.

The case study concerns the problem described below.

The Decision Facing Herr Cutter

Herr Cutter has run his barber shop in the same location for nearly 25 years. Although his parents had wanted him to follow in his father's footsteps as a medical doctor, he has never regretted his decision to follow this more modest career path. He enjoys the relaxed working environment, the regular hours, and the opportunity to visit with his customers.

Over the years, he has built up a loyal clientele. He is a fine barber who takes pride in his work. As his business has increased, his customers now often need to wait awhile (sometimes over half an hour) to begin a haircut. However, his long-time customers are willing to do so.

The shop is in a growing city. As the pace of life has increased, Herr Cutter has noticed that new customers are much less likely to return than in the early years, especially if they have had to wait very long. He attributes this to a decreasing tolerance for waiting. However, since he is not gaining many new regular customers, his volume of business has leveled off at a steady average of two customers per hour.

The decision facing Herr Cutter is whether to add an associate to share the workload in the barber shop.

As he has grown older, Herr Cutter has wondered increasingly about whether he should add an associate to share the workload. He also would enjoy the company, as well as the additional flexibility. A second barber should reduce the waiting times of the customers considerably, so an additional benefit would be that the total volume of business for the shop should increase somewhat.

However, what has always held him back from adding an associate is the fear of decreasing his personal income from the business. He needs to be putting away considerable money toward retirement and really can't afford a significant decrease in his already modest income. Given the salary and commission he would need to pay an associate, business would need to almost double just to maintain his current level of income. (We will spell out the financial details in the next section when the analysis takes place.) He is doubtful that business would increase nearly this much.

But now opportunity has come knocking on the door. A fellow barber (and friend) in the city has decided to retire and close his shop. This friend has had the same associate for several years, and he now has invited Herr Cutter to hire this fine young man. The friend highly recommends him, and also points out that the associate would bring considerable business with him.

So now Herr Cutter is in a quandary as to whether he should take the plunge in hiring this associate.

Fortunately, help is at hand for making this decision. This friend has shown Herr Cutter an interesting recent article in *The Barber's Journal.* The article describes a study that has been done of barber shops and how long customers now are willing to wait for haircuts to begin. The article concludes with two rules of thumb.

First Rule of Thumb: In a well-run barber shop with a long-established clientele, these loyal customers are willing to tolerate an average waiting time of about 20 minutes until the haircut begins.

Herr Cutter feels that this description fits his situation. He has never tried to estimate the waiting times of his customers, but guesses that an average of 20 minutes sounds about right.

Second Rule of Thumb: In a well-run barber shop, new customers are willing to tolerate an average waiting time of about 10 minutes before the haircut begins. (With longer waits, they tend to take their business elsewhere in the future.)

Again, Herr Cutter feels that this rule of thumb agrees with his own experience.

This second rule of thumb has given Herr Cutter a good idea about how to view his decision. With his current clientele, adding an associate probably would reduce their average waiting time to less than 10 minutes. This prompt service then should help to gradually attract and retain new customers (including some of the associate's customers from the barber shop that is closing). According to the rule of thumb, the level of business should increase until it reaches the point where the average waiting time before the haircut begins has increased to about 10 minutes. Estimating the level of business at that point would indicate the new level of income to the shop and his share of that income. The dilemma is that he does not see how to estimate this level of business in advance.

With an associate, the level of business should reach the point where the average waiting time to begin a haircut is about 10 minutes.

Herr Cutter asks for advice from his nephew Fritz (a university student majoring in business) about how to resolve this dilemma. Fritz excitedly responds that he thinks he knows just the right approach to use. Computer simulation.

Fritz recently took a course in management science. In fact, he has a copy of MS Courseware, including its Queueing Simulator for simulating queueing systems like his uncle's barber shop. Although not as sophisticated as expensive commercial software packages for performing computer simulations, Fritz explains to his uncle how this routine can indeed provide a good estimate in advance of what the level of business would be with an associate.

Fritz proposes spending a little time with his uncle to gather some data and develop a *simulation model* in preparation for performing the computer simulations. His first simulation will be of the barber shop under its current mode of operation (without an associate) to estimate the current average waiting time. Comparing the results from this simulation with what is actually happening in the barber shop also will help to test the validity of the simulation model. If necessary,

The Financial Factors

Here are the main financial factors (converted from German currency to American dollars) for addressing this decision.

$$\text{Revenue} = \$15 \text{ per haircut}$$

$$\text{Average tip} = \$2 \text{ per haircut}$$

$$\text{Cost of maintaining the shop} = \$50 \text{ per working day}$$
(with or without an associate)

$$\text{Salary of an associate} = \$120 \text{ per working day}$$

$$\text{Commission for an associate} = \$5 \text{ per haircut given by the associate}$$

In addition to his salary and commission, the associate would keep his own tips. Otherwise, the revenue would go to Herr Cutter.

The shop opens at 8:00 A.M. and closes its door to new customers at 5:00 P.M., so it admits customers for nine hours. Herr Cutter and any associate eat their sack lunches and take other breaks only during times when no customers are waiting. Thus, any customer who wants to enter the shop at any time during the nine hours is welcomed by a barber on duty.

Analysis of Continuing without an Associate

As indicated in the preceding section (and depicted in Figure 15.10), the current distribution of interarrival times has a mean of 30 minutes. Thus, Herr Cutter is averaging two customers per hour, or an average of 18 customers per working day. Therefore, after subtracting the cost of maintaining the shop, his average net income per working day is

$$\text{Net daily income} = (\$15 + \$2)(18 \text{ customers}) - \$50$$

$$= \$306 - \$50$$

$$= \$256$$

Herr Cutter's nephew Fritz is helping his uncle analyze his decision by using the Queueing Simulator in your MS Courseware to run computer simulations of the barber shop. This routine is specifically designed to efficiently run long simulations for a variety of queueing systems. It operates basically as illustrated in Figure 15.13, but with more flexibility as to the type of system and with far more output, as outlined below.

The Queueing Simulator is available in one of this chapter's Excel files.

Features of the Queueing Simulator

1. Can run computer simulations of various kinds of basic queueing systems described in Section 14.1.

2. Can have any number of servers up to a maximum of 25.

3. Can use any of the following probability distributions for either interarrival times or service times:

   a. Constant time (also called the degenerate distribution).

   b. Exponential distribution (described in Sections 14.1 and 15.2).

   c. Translated exponential distribution (the sum of a constant time and a time from an exponential distribution).

   d. Uniform distribution.

   e. Erlang distribution (described in Section 14.1).

4. Provides estimates of various key measures of performance described in Section 14.3 for queueing systems, namely,

L = Expected number of customers in the system, including those being served

L_q = Expected number of customers in the queue, which excludes customers being served

W = Expected waiting time in the system (includes service time) for an individual customer

W_q = Expected waiting time in the queue (excludes service time) for an individual customer

P_n = Probability of exactly n customers in the system (for $n = 0, 1, 2, \ldots, 10$)

(If you have not previously studied Chapter 14 to learn about queueing systems, you might find it helpful to see the live demonstration of a queueing system in action that is provided by the Waiting Line module in your Interactive Management Science Modules at **www.mhhe.com/ hillier2e.** An offline version also is included in your MS Courseware on the CD-ROM.)

Largely to help test the validity of his simulation model (described in the preceding section), Fritz is beginning by simulating the current operation of the shop. Although Figure 15.13 already did this for roughly a week of simulated operation (100 customer arrivals), he now wishes to simulate several years of operation (100,000 arrivals).

Figure 15.15 shows the output that Fritz obtains from this computer simulation. If you wish, you can duplicate this simulation run by using the Queueing Simulator yourself. You should obtain very similar results, although they will be slightly different because different random numbers are used each time.

The measures of performance in column E are the same as those described for any queueing system in Section 14.3. Column F gives the **point estimate,** the single number that is the best estimate of the measure from this simulation run. Using statistical theory, columns G and H then provide a 95 percent **confidence interval** for each measure. Thus, there is a 95 percent chance that the *true* value of the measure lies within this interval. Because the simulation run was so long (100,000 arrivals), each of these confidence intervals is quite narrow.

A confidence interval is an interval within which the true value of a measure of performance is likely to lie.

FIGURE 15.15

The output obtained by using the Queueing Simulator in one of this chapter's Excel files to perform a computer simulation of Herr Cutter's barber shop (without an associate) over a period of 100,000 customer arrivals.

	A	B	C	D	E	F	G	H
1		Queueing Simulator for Herr Cutter's Barber Shop						
2								
3		Number of Servers	1			Point	95% Confidence Interval	
4						Estimate	Low	High
5		**Interarrival Times**			$L =$	1.358	1.332	1.385
6		Distribution	Exponential		$L_q =$	0.689	0.666	0.712
7		Mean	30		$W =$	40.582	39.983	41.180
8					$W_q =$	20.577	19.980	21.174
9								
10		**Service Times**			$P_0 =$	0.330	0.326	0.335
11		Distribution	Uniform		$P_1 =$	0.310	0.307	0.313
12		Minimum	15		$P_2 =$	0.183	0.180	0.185
13		Maximum	25		$P_3 =$	0.0942	0.0920	0.0963
14					$P_4 =$	0.0451	0.0433	0.0469
15		**Length of Simulation Run**			$P_5 =$	0.0206	0.0192	0.0220
16		Number of Arrivals	100,000		$P_6 =$	0.00950	0.00849	0.0105
17					$P_7 =$	0.00432	0.00360	0.00503
18					$P_8 =$	0.00219	0.00163	0.00274
19		Run Simulation			$P_9 =$	0.000876	0.000540	0.00121
20					$P_{10} =$	0.000372	0.000165	0.000579

Testing the Validity of the Simulation Model

When starting a management science study that will use computer simulation, it is a good idea to first run the simulation model on a simple version of the system for which analytical results are available (if such a version exists). Comparing the results from this simulation run with the analytical results then provides a good test of the validity of the simulation model.

Fritz recalls that the $M/G/1$ queueing model presented in Section 14.5 provides some exact analytical results for the same queueing system that has been assumed for the simulation run in Figure 15.15. This queueing model uses four parameters:

λ = Mean arrival rate

   = $\frac{1}{30}$ customer per minute   (from Figure 15.10)

μ = Mean service rate

   = $\frac{1}{20}$ customer per minute   (from Figure 15.9)

$$\rho = \frac{\lambda}{\mu} = \frac{1/30}{1/20} = \frac{2}{3}$$

σ = Standard deviation of the distribution of service times

Because the standard deviation of the uniform distribution from 0 to 1 is $1/\sqrt{12}$, the standard deviation of the service-time distribution given in Figure 15.9 is

$$\sigma = \frac{10}{\sqrt{12}} = 2.887$$

After entering these values of λ, $1/\mu$, and σ, the Excel template for the $M/G/1$ model in the Chapter 14 portion of your MS Courseware yields the results shown in Figure 15.16. Note how

Since a queueing model is available for the single-server version of the system, Fritz will use its results to test the validity of his simulation model.

FIGURE 15.16

This Excel template for the $M/G/1$ model shows the basic measures of performance for Herr Cutter's barber shop without an associate.

	A	B	C	D	E	F	G
1		**Analytical *M/G/1* Queueing Results for Herr Cutter**					
2							
3			**Data**				**Results**
4		$\lambda =$	0.0333	(Mean arrival rate)		$L =$	1.344
5		$1/\mu =$	20	(Expected service time)		$L_q=$	0.678
6		$\sigma =$	2.887	(Standard deviation)			
7		$s =$	1	(# servers)		$W =$	40.356
8						$W_q=$	20.356
9							
10						$\rho =$	0.666
11							
12						$P_0=$	0.334

Range Name	Cell
L	G4
Lambda	C4
L_q	G5
OneOverMu	C5
Rho	G10
s	C7
Sigma	C6
W	G7
W_q	G8

	F	G
4	$L =$	=L_q+Rho
5	$L_q=$	=((Lambda^2)*(Sigma^2)+(Rho^2))/(2*(1-Rho))
6		
7	$W =$	=W_q+OneOverMu
8	$W_q=$	=L_q/Lambda
9		
10	$\rho =$	=Lambda*OneOverMu
11		
12	$P_0=$	=1-Rho

each of these exact results for the measures of performance fall well within the corresponding 95 percent confidence interval in Figure 15.15. This provides some reassurance that the simulation model and the computer simulation are operating as intended.

To further test the validity of the simulation model, Fritz shows the results in column F of Figure 15.15 to Herr Cutter and asks whether these numbers seem consistent with what he has been experiencing in the barber shop. Although Herr Cutter has not been keeping such data, his impression is that the numbers seem about right. He also points out that the average waiting time of about 20 minutes before beginning a haircut is consistent with the first rule of thumb in the article in *The Barber's Journal* (described at the beginning of the preceding section).

To make sure that no big mistake has been made when constructing a simulation model, its results should be checked for reasonableness by someone familiar with the system being simulated.

Unfortunately, no queueing model yielding useful analytical results is available for the *two-server* queueing system that corresponds to Herr Cutter's barber shop *with* an associate. (None of the multiple-server queueing models presented in Chapter 14 allow a service-time distribution even close to the one in this barber shop.) Therefore, it will be necessary to use computer simulation to obtain good estimates of how the barber shop would perform with an associate. However, after the above testing of the validity of his simulation model, Fritz now is confident that this model will indeed provide good estimates.

Fritz does recognize that his simulation model (just like the $M/G/1$ queueing model) makes two simplifying assumptions that are only approximations of how the barber shop actually operates. (These assumptions are incorporated into the Queueing Simulator.)

Simplifying Assumptions

1. The system (barber shop) has an *infinite queue,* so arriving customers always enter the system regardless of how many customers already are there. (In reality, Herr Cutter has found that arriving customers normally do not stay if three customers already are there waiting to begin a haircut, so he now only provides three chairs for waiting customers.)

2. Once started, the system operates continually without ever closing and reopening. (In reality, the barber shop closes its door at 5:00 P.M. each working day and reopens at 8:00 A.M. the next day.)

To evaluate the effect of the first assumption, Fritz notes that the results in Figure 15.15 estimate that

$$P_0 + P_1 + P_2 + P_3 + P_4 = 0.330 + 0.310 + 0.183 + 0.094 + 0.045$$

$$= 0.962$$

Thus, the simulation run exceeds the actual maximum of four customers in the barber shop (one receiving a haircut and three waiting to begin) less than 4 percent of the time. The effect of exceeding the actual maximum so infrequently is to slightly inflate the estimates of L, L_q, W, and W_q above their true values for the barber shop. Thus, the numbers in Figure 15.15 provide conservative estimates (which are preferable to overly optimistic estimates). If Herr Cutter does add an associate, he would provide three additional chairs for waiting customers. There also would be less waiting to begin a haircut, so having arriving customers not stay would become very unusual. Therefore, the first simplifying assumption seems very reasonable for simulating the barber shop with an associate.

Simplifying assumptions that provide conservative estimates are preferable to those that lead to overly optimistic estimates.

The effect of the second simplifying assumption also is to slightly inflate the estimates of L, L_q, W, and W_q above their true values. The reason is that the barber shop begins empty each morning and then gradually builds up to a steady-state condition, whereas the simulation model has the shop operating in a steady-state condition for all but the very beginning of the simulation run. Fortunately, adding an associate would tend to keep the number of customers in the shop down to minimal levels, even in a steady-state condition (which would be nearly reached early in the day). Therefore, the estimation errors from using this assumption to simulate the shop with an associate should be reasonably small.

By obtaining a more expensive computer simulation package and devoting additional preparation time, Fritz would be able to closely simulate the actual operation of the barber shop without making these two approximations. A key advantage of computer simulation is the ability to incorporate as many realistic features into the model as desired.

However, just as with the mathematical model for any other management science technique, there always is a trade-off between the amount of realism incorporated into a model and the ease with which the model can be used. A simulation model does not need to be a completely realistic representation of the real system. Many simulation models err on the side of being overly realistic rather than overly idealistic. An overly realistic model includes unimportant details that do not significantly affect the estimates obtained from the simulation runs. Such a model often is very difficult to debug, and may never be completely debugged. It also is likely to require a great deal of programming and computer time to obtain a small amount of information. The goal should be to incorporate only the important features of the system into the model in order to generate reasonably accurate information that will enable management to make well-informed decisions in a timely fashion.

Fritz feels that his current simulation model meets this goal.

Analysis of the Option of Adding an Associate

As described near the beginning of Section 15.2, Herr Cutter and his nephew Fritz have agreed on a plan for analyzing the option of adding an associate. They assume that the probability distribution of service times (the times required to give a haircut) for the associate would be the same as for Herr Cutter. Based on the second rule of thumb given in Section 15.2, they also are assuming that adding the associate would (1) reduce the average waiting time before a haircut begins to less than 10 minutes and (2) then gradually attract new business until this average waiting time reaches about 10 minutes. The level of business (say, the average number of customers per day) determines the mean of the probability distribution of interarrival times. Therefore, a number of computer simulations will be run with different means of this distribution to determine which mean would result in an average waiting time of about 10 minutes. Given the corresponding level of business, a financial analysis can then be conducted.

As depicted in Figure 15.10 in the preceding section, the current mean (without an associate) of the distribution of interarrival times is 30 minutes. Therefore, proceeding by trial and error, Fritz tries the series of means shown in the first column of Table 15.2. To quickly hone in on the neighborhood for the right mean, he uses the Queueing Simulator to run computer simulations of only moderate length, namely, 10,000 arrivals each (roughly half a year of simulated operation). The point estimates of W_q (the average waiting time until a haircut begins) in the second column indicate that the mean that gives a true value of W_q of 10 minutes should be somewhere close to 14.3 minutes. The 95 percent confidence intervals for W_q in the rightmost column further suggest that this mean should be within about half a minute of 14.3 minutes.

To check this further, Fritz next does a long simulation run (100,000 arrivals) with a mean of 14.3 minutes for the interarrival-time distribution. The complete results for all the measures of performance are shown in Figure 15.17. The point estimate of W_q (and most of the 95 percent confidence interval for W_q) now is slightly over 10. However, Fritz also recalls that the two simplifying assumptions discussed in the preceding subsection cause this estimate to slightly overstate the true value of W_q for the barber shop. Therefore, he concludes that 14.3 minutes is the best available estimate of the mean that would result in an average waiting time of about 10 minutes.

Although some software packages enable adding many realistic features into a simulation model, unimportant details that make the model overly complex should be avoided.

The level of business is expected to increase to the point where the average waiting time to begin a haircut is 10 minutes, so computer simulations will be run to estimate this level of business.

TABLE 15.2

The Estimates of W_q Obtained by Using the Queueing Simulator to Simulate Herr Cutter's Barber Shop with an Associate for 10,000 Arrivals for Different Means of the Distribution of Interarrival Times

Mean of Interarrival Times	Point Estimate of W_q	95 Percent Confidence Interval for W_q
20 minutes	3.33 minutes	3.05 to 3.61 minutes
15 minutes	8.10 minutes	6.98 to 9.22 minutes
14 minutes	10.80 minutes	9.51 to 12.08 minutes
14.2 minutes	9.83 minutes	8.83 to 10.84 minutes
14.3 minutes	9.91 minutes	8.76 to 11.05 minutes

FIGURE 15.17

The results obtained by using the Queueing Simulator to perform a computer simulation of Herr Cutter's barber shop with an associate over a period of 100,000 customer arrivals.

	A	B	C	D	E	F	G	H
1		Queueing Simulator for Herr Cutter's Barber Shop with an Associate						
2								
3		Number of Servers	2			Point	95% Confidence Interval	
4						Estimate	Low	High
5		**Interarrival Times**			$L =$	2.126	2.090	2.163
6		Distribution	Exponential		$L_q =$	0.719	0.689	0.748
7		Mean	14.3		$W =$	30.212	29.833	30.591
8					$W_q =$	10.211	9.834	10.588
9								
10		**Service Times**			$P_0 =$	0.163	0.160	0.166
11		Distribution	Uniform		$P_1 =$	0.266	0.262	0.270
12		Minimum	15		$P_2 =$	0.233	0.230	0.235
13		Maximum	25		$P_3 =$	0.1541	0.1518	0.1564
14					$P_4 =$	0.0877	0.0855	0.0898
15		**Length of Simulation Run**			$P_5 =$	0.0467	0.0448	0.0487
16		Number of Arrivals	100,000		$P_6 =$	0.02417	0.02264	0.0257
17					$P_7 =$	0.01282	0.01162	0.01401
18					$P_8 =$	0.00634	0.00546	0.00722
19		**Run Simulation**			$P_9 =$	0.003208	0.002530	0.00389
20					$P_{10} =$	0.001546	0.001076	0.002017

Fritz realizes that he could spend more time running long computer simulations with means slightly different from 14.3 minutes in order to pin down this estimate even better. However, he already knows from the confidence intervals in Table 15.2 that 14.3 minutes is at least very close. Furthermore, given the slight inaccuracies known to be in the simulation model due to the two simplifying assumptions, there is no point in trying to obtain an estimate of the mean that is more precise than the model is. This would only give a false sense of accuracy. He is content that 14.3 minutes provides a very adequate and conservative estimate of the mean for purposes of analysis.

A conservative estimate is that the level of business will increase to the point where customers are arriving at an average of one every 14.3 minutes.

Based on this estimate, Fritz concludes that having his uncle add an associate should gradually increase the level of business to around the point where

$$\text{Average interarrival time} = 14.3 \text{ minutes}$$

which would yield

$$\text{Mean arrival rate} = \frac{60}{14.3} \text{ customers per hour}$$

$$= 4.2 \text{ customers per hour}$$

$$= 4.2(9) \text{ customers per day}$$

$$= 37.8 \text{ customers per day}$$

This level of business would be more than double the current average of 18 customers per day for the shop. Herr Cutter would plan to divide the customers equally with the associate, so each would average 18.9 customers per day.

Therefore, using the cost factors given at the beginning of this section, Herr Cutter's average net income per working day would become

$$\text{Net daily income} = 37.8(\$15) \quad \text{(shop revenue)}$$

$$+ 18.9(\$2) \quad \text{(his tips)}$$

$$- \$50 \quad \text{(shop maintenance)}$$

$$- \$120 \quad \text{(associate's salary)}$$

$$- 18.9(\$5) \quad \text{(associate's commission)}$$

$$= \$567 + \$37.80 - \$50 - \$120 - \$94.50$$

$$= \$340.30$$

This compares with Herr Cutter's current net daily income of $256. Thus, it is estimated that the change in his net daily income from adding an associate would eventually become

$$\text{Change in net daily income} = \$340.30 - \$256$$

$$= \$84.30$$

Thus, he actually would increase his income significantly.

When presenting this analysis to his uncle, Fritz emphasizes that this $84.30 figure is just an *estimate* of what will happen *after* the level of business gradually increases to its new level. It may take awhile, even a year or two, to reach this new level. Meanwhile, Herr Cutter's income may start off less than it has been before gradually increasing. Furthermore, the optimistic conclusion of a substantial increase in income eventually is based largely on the rather shaky premise that the second rule of thumb in the article in *The Barber's Journal* will prove to be valid and applicable to his shop. This premise leads to an estimate that his level of business would more than double eventually. Achieving this big increase in business would seem realistic only if the associate is able to bring a considerable number of customers with him from his current shop and then the two of them are able to attract many additional new customers.

> This estimate of increased income needs to be interpreted carefully.

Herr Cutter feels confident that they can accomplish this. This associate was highly recommended by his friend. Furthermore, he feels that his own skill as a barber already would have attracted many new customers if he didn't already have as much business as he could handle alone. In this growing city, the opportunity is there. He also likes the fact that adding an associate would enable him to improve the level of service for his current loyal clientele by substantially decreasing their average waiting time before beginning a haircut. Finally, he also sees many personal advantages to having a good associate that cannot be measured in monetary terms. Therefore, he wouldn't mind a temporary decrease in income as long as he probably would at least equal his current income level in a year or two. Actually increasing his income would be a pleasant bonus.

> Herr Cutter decides to hire the associate.

On these grounds, Herr Cutter decides to hire the associate. He also thanks his nephew for the invaluable help that Fritz's computer simulations provided him in making his decision.

Review Questions

1. What did Fritz simulate in his first simulation run? For what purpose?
2. What are the two types of estimates of a measure of performance obtained by the Queueing Simulator?
3. What were the two ways with which Fritz tested the validity of his simulation model?
4. Does Fritz's simulation model make any simplifying assumptions? Is it necessary for a simulation model to be a completely realistic representation of the real system?
5. Does Fritz's analysis estimate that Herr Cutter's income will eventually increase or decrease (compared to its current level) if he adds an associate?

15.4   SOME COMMON TYPES OF APPLICATIONS

Computer simulation is an exceptionally versatile technique. It can be used (with varying degrees of difficulty) to investigate virtually any kind of stochastic system, as well as simpler systems involving probability distributions. This versatility has made computer simulation the most widely used management science technique for studies dealing with such systems, and its popularity is continuing to increase. The ability of Excel and Excel add-ins to perform many of these computer simulations has given further impetus to the use of this technique.

Because of the tremendous diversity of its applications, it is impossible to enumerate all the specific areas in which computer simulation has been used. However, we will briefly describe here some particularly important categories of applications.

The first three categories concern types of stochastic systems considered in other chapters. It is common to use the kinds of mathematical models described in those chapters to analyze simplified versions of the system and then to apply computer simulation to refine the results.

Design and Operation of Queueing Systems

Section 14.2 gives several dozen examples of commonly encountered queueing systems that illustrate how such systems pervade many areas of society. Many mathematical models are available (including several presented in Chapter 14) for analyzing relatively simple types of queueing systems. Unfortunately, these models can only provide rough approximations at best of more complicated queueing systems. However, computer simulation is well-suited for dealing with even very complicated queueing systems, so many of its applications fall into this category.

For example, this chapter's case study is of this type. Although a mathematical model (the $M/G/1$ model) is available to provide some of the measures of performance of Herr Cutter's barber shop under its current mode of operation (without an associate), this is not the case for the option of adding an associate. Therefore, computer simulation was needed for the key part of the study.

Because applications in this category are so pervasive, the Queueing Simulator in your MS Courseware has been designed specifically for simulating queuing systems.

Among the six award-winning applications of queueing models presented in Section 14.10, two of these also made heavy use of computer simulation. One was the study of **New York City's** arrest-to-arraignment system that led to great improvements in the efficiency of this system plus annual savings of $9.5 million. The other was **AT&T's** development of a PC-based system to help its business customers design or redesign their call centers, resulting in more than $750 million in annual profit for these customers.

Many applications in this category combine the use of both queueing models and computer simulation.

Have you ever eaten at a **Taco Bell** restaurant? If so, you were the beneficiary of an award-winning application of computer simulation (described in the January–February 1998 issue of *Interfaces*). You were one of the customers in a complicated kind of queueing system where each group of customers is being served simultaneously by several servers (including those preparing the different types of food). Because this system is too complicated to be analyzed with an available queueing model, computer simulation is used instead to determine how much labor is needed to provide the desired level of customer service during the different hours of operation. This information then is fed into an integer programming model that optimally schedules and allocates crew members to minimize payroll. Forecasting techniques are used to predict customer arrivals as input to the computer simulation. This integrated set of management science techniques (called the Labor-Management System) is used throughout the roughly 4,000 restaurants owned or franchised by the Taco Bell Company. This management science application has achieved labor savings of approximately $13 million per year while also improving the quality and consistency of customer service, among other benefits.

Managing Inventory Systems

One of the supplements on the CD-ROM (see Chapter 19) discusses the management of inventory systems when the products involved have uncertain demand. Two mathematical models are presented to guide the management of basic systems of this type. Section 19.6 then describes the kinds of larger inventory systems that commonly arise in practice. Although mathematical models sometimes can help analyze these more complicated systems, computer simulation often plays a key role as well.

Various possible redesigns of the company's supply chain were evaluated by simulating their operation.

As one example, an article in the April 1996 issue of *OR/MS Today* describes a management science study of this kind that was done for the **IBM PC Company** in Europe. Facing unrelenting pressure from increasingly agile and aggressive competitors, the company had to find a way to greatly improve its performance in quickly filling customer orders. The management science team analyzed how to do this by simulating various redesigns of the company's entire *supply chain* (the network of facilities that spans procurement, manufacturing, and distribution, including all the inventories accumulated along the way). This led to major changes in the design and operation of the supply chain (including its inventory systems) that greatly improved the company's competitive position. Direct cost savings of $40 million per year also were achieved.

Estimating the Probability of Completing a Project by the Deadline

One of the key concerns of a project manager is whether his or her team will be able to complete the project by the deadline. Section 8.4 describes how the PERT three-estimate approach can be used to obtain a rough estimate of the probability of meeting the deadline with the current project plan. That section also describes three simplifying approximations made by this approach to be able to estimate this probability. Unfortunately, because of these approximations, the resulting estimate always is overly optimistic, and sometimes by a considerable amount.

Many project managers use computer simulation to estimate the probability of meeting the deadline for completion with the current project plan or with a possible new plan.

Consequently, it is becoming increasingly common now to use computer simulation to obtain a better estimate of this probability. This involves generating random observations from the probability distributions of the duration of the various activities in the project. By using the project network, it then is straightforward to simulate when each activity begins and ends, and so when the project finishes. By repeating this simulation thousands of times (in one computer run), a very good estimate can be obtained of the probability of meeting the deadline. (You will see an example in Section 16.3.)

Design and Operation of Manufacturing Systems

Surveys consistently show that a large proportion of the applications of computer simulation involve manufacturing systems. Many of these systems can be viewed as a queueing system of some kind (e.g., a queueing system where the machines are the servers and the jobs to be processed are the customers). However, various complications inherent in these systems (e.g., occasional machine breakdowns, defective items needing to be reworked, and multiple types of jobs) go beyond the scope of the usual queueing models. Such complications are no problem for computer simulation.

Here are a few examples of the kinds of questions that might be addressed.

1. How many machines of each type should be provided?

2. How many materials-handling units of each type should be provided?

These questions are typical of those addressed by computer simulation.

3. Considering their due dates for completion of the entire production process, what rule should be used to choose the order in which the jobs currently at a machine should be processed?

4. What are realistic due dates for jobs?

5. What will be the bottleneck operations in a new production process as currently designed?

6. What will be the throughput (production rate) of a new production process?

Design and Operation of Distribution Systems

Any major manufacturing corporation needs an efficient *distribution system* for distributing its goods from its factories and warehouses to its customers. There are many uncertainties involved in the operation of such a system. When will vehicles become available for shipping the goods? How long will a shipment take? What will be the demands of the various customers? By generating random observations from the relevant probability distributions, computer simulation can readily deal with these kinds of uncertainties. Thus, it is used quite often to test various possibilities for improving the design and operation of these systems.

One award-winning application of this kind is described in the January–February 1991 issue of *Interfaces*. **Reynolds Metals Company** spends over $250 million annually to deliver its products and receive raw materials. Shipments are made by truck, rail, ship, and air across a network of well over a hundred shipping locations including plants, warehouses, and suppliers. A combination of mixed binary integer programming (Chapter 9) and computer simulation was

Annual freight costs were reduced by over $7 million.

used to design a new distribution system with central dispatching. The new system both improved on-time delivery of shipments and reduced annual freight costs by over $7 million.

The study for the IBM PC Company in Europe mentioned earlier (under "Managing Inventory Systems") also encompassed the design and operation of distribution systems as well.

Financial Risk Analysis

By generating thousands of scenarios for how an investment will turn out, computer simulation provides a risk profile for the investment.

Financial risk analysis was one of the earliest application areas of computer simulation, and it continues to be a very active area. For example, consider the evaluation of a proposed capital investment with uncertain future cash flows. By generating random observations from the probability distributions for the cash flow in each of the respective time periods (and considering relationships between time periods), computer simulation can generate thousands of scenarios for how the investment will turn out. This provides a *probability distribution* of the return (e.g., net present value) from the investment. This distribution (sometimes called the *risk profile*) enables management to assess the risk involved in making the investment. (You will see an example in Section 16.5.)

A similar approach enables analyzing the risk associated with investing in various securities, including the more exotic financial instruments such as puts, calls, futures, stock options, and so on.

Health Care Applications

Computer simulation also can generate thousands of scenarios for how a human disease evolves.

Health care is another area where, like the evaluation of risky investments, analyzing future uncertainties is central to current decision making. However, rather than dealing with uncertain future cash flows, the uncertainties now involve such things as the evolution of human diseases.

Here are a few examples of the kinds of computer simulations that have been performed to guide the design of health care systems.

1. Simulating the use of hospital resources when treating patients with coronary heart disease.

2. Simulating health expenditures under alternative insurance plans.

3. Simulating the cost and effectiveness of screening for the early detection of a disease.

4. Simulating the use of the complex of surgical services at a medical center.

5. Simulating the timing and location of calls for ambulance services.

6. Simulating the matching of donated kidneys with transplant recipients.

7. Simulating the operation of an emergency room.

Applications to Other Service Industries

Like health care, other service industries also have proven to be fertile fields for the application of computer simulation. These industries include government services, banking, hotel management, restaurants, educational institutions, disaster planning, the military, amusement parks, and many others. In many cases, the systems being simulated are, in fact, queueing systems of some type.

The January–February 1992 issue of *Interfaces* describes an award-winning application in this category. The **U.S. Postal Service** had identified *automation technology* as the only way it would be able to handle its increasing mail volume while remaining price competitive and satisfying service goals. Extensive planning over several years was required to convert to a largely automated system that would meet these goals. The backbone of the analysis leading to the adopted plan was performed with a comprehensive simulation model called META (Model for Evaluating Technology Alternatives). This model was first applied extensively at the national level, and then it was moved down to the local level for detailed planning. The resulting plan required a cumulative capital investment of $12 billion, but also was projected to

Labor savings of over $4 billion per year were projected.

achieve labor savings of over $4 billion per year. Another consequence of this highly successful application of computer simulation was that the value of management science tools now is recognized at the highest levels of the Postal Service. Management science techniques continue to be used by the planning staff both at headquarters and in the field divisions.

New Applications

More new innovative applications of computer simulation are being made each year. Many of these applications are first announced publicly at the annual Winter Simulation Conference, held each December in some U.S. city. Since its beginning in 1967, this conference has been an institution in the computer simulation field. It now is attended by nearly a thousand participants, divided roughly equally between academics and practitioners. Hundreds of papers are presented to announce both methodological advances and new innovative applications.

Review
Questions

1. This chapter's case study falls into which category of computer simulation applications?

2. What was simulated in the management science study done for the IBM PC Company in Europe?

3. What is the quantity being estimated when computer simulation is used to supplement the PERT three-estimate approach?

4. What is an example of the kind of question that might be addressed when simulating a manufacturing system?

5. What was being designed when computer simulation was applied in the award-winning application at Reynolds Metal Company?

6. What can computer simulation provide to enable management to assess the risk involved in making a capital investment with uncertain future cash flows?

7. What is an example of the kind of computer simulation that has been performed to guide the design of health care systems?

8. What was being planned during the award-winning application of computer simulation performed for the U.S. Postal Service? What were the projected labor savings from the resulting plan?

15.5   OUTLINE OF A MAJOR COMPUTER SIMULATION STUDY

Thus far, this chapter has focused mainly on the *process* of performing a computer simulation and some applications from doing so. We now place this material into broader perspective by briefly outlining all the typical steps involved in a major management science study that is based on applying computer simulation. (Nearly the same steps also apply when the study is applying other management science techniques instead.)

We should emphasize that some applications of computer simulation do not require all the effort described in the following steps. The advent of Excel and Excel add-ins for efficiently performing basic computer simulations on a spreadsheet now often enables conducting the study with far less time and expense than previously possible. Managers now can sometimes perform the studies that previously were done by management science specialists.

However, major applications of computer simulation still require the extended effort of management science teams, as described below.

Step 1: Formulate the Problem and Plan the Study

The management science team needs to begin by meeting with management to address the following kinds of questions.

These are key questions that management should answer to initiate any management science study.

1. What is the problem that management wants studied?

2. What are the overall objectives for the study?

3. What specific issues should be addressed?

4. What kinds of alternative system configurations should be considered?

5. What measures of performance of the system are of interest to management?

6. What are the time constraints for performing the study?

In addition, the team also needs to meet with engineers and operational personnel to learn the details of just how the system would operate. (The team generally will also include one or more members with a firsthand knowledge of the system.) If a current version of the system is in operation, the team will observe the system to identify its components and the linkages between them.

For the case study involving Herr Cutter's barber shop, the components of this queueing system are the arriving customers, the queue, and the barber(s) as the server(s). Because this was a small informal study, the management science team consisted of just Herr Cutter's nephew Fritz, with Herr Cutter as the lone member of management.

Before concluding this step, the head of the management science team also needs to plan the overall study in terms of the number of people, their responsibilities, the schedule, and a budget for the study.

Step 2: Collect the Data and Formulate the Simulation Model

The types of data needed depend on the nature of the system to be simulated. For Herr Cutter's barber shop, the key pieces of data were the distribution of *interarrival times* and the distribution of *service times* (times needed to give a haircut). For a single-product inventory system, the team would need the distribution of *demand* for the product and the distribution of the *lead time* between placing an order to replenish inventory and receiving the amount ordered. For a PERT project network where the activity durations are uncertain, distributions of the *durations of the activities* are needed. For a manufacturing system involving machines that occasionally break down, the team needs to determine the distribution of the *time until a machine breaks down* and the distribution of *repair times*.

Computer simulations should use probability distributions of the relevant quantities rather than averages.

In each of these examples, note that it is the *probability distributions* of the relevant quantities that are needed. In order to generate representative scenarios of how a system will perform, it is essential for a computer simulation to generate *random observations* from these distributions rather than simply using averages.

Generally, it will only be possible to *estimate* these distributions. This is done after taking direct observations from an existing version of the system under study, or from a similar system. If no such system exists, other possible sources of information include industrial engineering time studies, engineering records, operating manuals, machine specifications, and interviews with individuals who have experience with similar kinds of operations.

A simulation model often is formulated in terms of a *flow diagram* that links together the various components of the system. Operating rules are given for each component, including the probability distributions that control when events will occur there. The model only needs to contain enough detail to capture the essence of the system. For a large study, it is a good idea to begin by formulating and debugging a relatively simple version of the model before adding important details.

Step 3: Check the Accuracy of the Simulation Model

Before constructing a computer program, the management science team should engage the people most intimately familiar with how the system will operate in checking the accuracy of the simulation model. This often is done by performing a structured walk-through of the conceptual model, using an overhead projector, before an audience of all the key people. Typically at such meetings, several erroneous model assumptions will be discovered and corrected, a few new assumptions will be added, and some issues will be resolved about how much detail is needed in the various parts of the model.

In addition to helping to ensure the accuracy of the simulation model, this process tends to provide the key people with some sense of ownership of the model and the study.

Step 4: Select the Software and Construct a Computer Program[1]

There are four major classes of software used for computer simulations. One is *spreadsheet software.* Section 15.1 described how Excel is able to perform some basic computer simulations on a spreadsheet. In addition, some excellent Excel add-ins now are available to enhance this kind of spreadsheet modeling. Chapter 16 focuses on the use of one of these add-ins in your MS Courseware.

The other three classes of software for computer simulations are intended for more extensive applications where it is no longer convenient to use spreadsheet software. One such class is a *general-purpose programming language,* such as C, FORTRAN, PASCAL, BASIC, and so on. Such languages (and their predecessors) often were used in the early history of the field because of their great flexibility for programming any sort of simulation. However, because of the considerable programming time required, they are not used nearly as much now.

The third class is a **general-purpose simulation language.** These languages provide many of the features needed to program a simulation model, and so may reduce the required programming time substantially. They also provide a natural framework for simulation modeling. Although less flexible than a general-purpose programming language, they are capable of programming almost any kind of simulation model. However, some degree of expertise in the language is needed.

Prominent general-purpose simulation languages include the current version of GPSS, SIMSCRIPT, SLAM, and SIMAN. The initial versions of these languages date back to 1961, 1963, 1979, and 1983, respectively, but all have stood the test of time.

A key development in the 1980s and 1990s has been the emergence of the fourth class of software, called **applications-oriented simulators** (or just **simulators** for short). Each of these simulators is designed for simulating fairly specific types of systems, such as certain types of manufacturing, computer, and communications systems. Some are very specific (e.g., for oil and gas production engineering, nuclear power plant analysis, or cardiovascular physiology). Their *goal* is to be able to construct a simulation "program" by the use of menus and graphics, without the need for programming. They are relatively easy to learn and have modeling constructs closely related to the system of interest.

A simulator can be wonderful if the system you wish to simulate fits right into the prescribed category for the simulator. However, the prescription of allowable system features tends to be fairly narrow. Therefore, the major drawback of many simulators is that they are limited to modeling only those system configurations that are allowed by their standard features. Some simulators do allow the option of incorporating routines written in a general-purpose programming language to handle nonstandard features. This option is frequently needed when simulating relatively complex systems.

Another key development in recent years has been the development of **animation** capabilities for displaying computer simulations in action. In an animation, key elements of a system are represented in a computer display by icons that change shape, color, or position when there is a change in the state of the simulation system. (One example of an animation of a computer simulation of a queueing system is provided by the Waiting Line module in your Interactive Management Science Modules at **www.mhhe.com/hillier2e** or on the CD-ROM.) Most simulation software vendors now offer a version of their software with animation capabilities. Furthermore, the animation is becoming increasingly elaborate, including even three-dimensional capabilities in some cases.

The major reason for the popularity of animation is its ability to communicate the essence of a simulation model (or of a computer simulation run) to managers and other key personnel. This greatly increases the credibility of the computer simulation approach. In addition, animation can be helpful in debugging the computer program for a computer simulation program.

General-purpose simulation languages often are used for large computer simulation studies.

Animation capabilities for displaying computer simulations in action are very useful for communicating the essence of a simulation model to managers and other key personnel.

---

[1]This subsection does not attempt to enumerate or describe the individual simulation software packages that currently are available. For details about 58 such packages, see the Buyer's Guide to Simulation Software on pp. 41–50 of the May 2001 issue of *IIE Solutions.*

Step 5: Test the Validity of the Simulation Model

After the computer program has been constructed and debugged, the next key step is to test whether the simulation model incorporated into the program is providing valid results for the system it is representing. Specifically, will the measures of performance for the real system be closely approximated by the values of these measures generated by the simulation model?

This question usually is difficult to answer because most versions of the "real" system do not currently exist. Typically, the purpose of computer simulation is to investigate and compare various proposed system configurations to help choose the best one.

However, some version of the real system may currently be in operation. If so, its performance data should be compared with the corresponding output measures generated by pilot runs of the simulation model.

In some cases, a mathematical model may be available to provide results for a simple version of the system. If so, these results also should be compared with the simulation results.

For example, in the case study, the barber shop currently is in operation with Herr Cutter as the only barber. Therefore, as described in Section 15.3 (see the subsection entitled "Testing the Validity of the Simulation Model"), Fritz compared the results from an applicable queueing model with a simulation of this current version of the barber shop. (Because this was a small informal simulation study, he and Herr Cutter did not take the time to gather detailed performance data for the actual operation of the shop.)

A field test of a small prototype of the proposed system is sometimes used to collect real data to compare with the simulation results and to fine-tune the design.

When no real data are available to compare with simulation results, one possibility is to conduct a *field test* to collect such data. This would involve constructing a small prototype of some version of the proposed system and placing it into operation. This prototype might also be used after the simulation study has been completed to fine-tune the design of the system before the real system is installed.

Another useful validation test is to have knowledgeable operational personnel check the credibility of how the simulation results change as the configuration of the simulated system is changed. Even when no basis exists for checking the reasonableness of the measures of performance obtained for a particular version of the system, some conclusions often can be drawn about how the *relative* performance of the system should change as its parameters are changed.

Watching animations of simulation runs is another way of checking the validity of the simulation model. Once the model is operating properly, animations also generate interest and credibility in the simulation study for both management and operational personnel.

Step 6: Plan the Simulations to Be Performed

At this point, you need to begin making decisions as to which system configurations to simulate. This often is an evolutionary process, where the initial results for a range of configurations help you to hone in on which specific configurations warrant detailed investigation.

Decisions also need to be made now on such issues as the lengths of simulation runs. Keep in mind that computer simulation does not produce *exact* values for the measures of performance of a system. Instead, each simulation run can be viewed as a *statistical experiment* that is generating *statistical observations* of the performance of the simulated system. These observations are used to produce *statistical estimates* of the measures of performance. Increasing the length of a run increases the precision of these estimates.

Each simulation run generates statistical observations of the performance of the simulated system, so statistical theory should guide the planning of the runs.

The statistical theory for designing statistical experiments conducted through computer simulation is little different than for experiments conducted by directly observing the performance of a physical system.[2] Therefore, the services of a professional statistician (or at least an experienced simulation analyst with a strong statistical background) can be invaluable at this step.

Step 7: Conduct the Simulation Runs and Analyze the Results

The output from the simulation runs now provides statistical estimates of the desired measures of performance for each system configuration of interest. In addition to a *point estimate* of

---

[2]For details about the relevant statistical theory, see Chapters 9–12 in A. M. Law and W. W. Kelton, *Simulation Modeling and Analysis,* 2nd ed. (New York: McGraw-Hill, 1991).

each measure, a *confidence interval* normally should be obtained to indicate the range of likely values of the measure (just as was done for the case study).

These results might immediately indicate that one system configuration is clearly superior to the others. More often, they will identify the few strong candidates to be the best one. In the latter case, some longer simulation runs would be conducted to better compare these candidates. Additional runs also might be used to fine-tune the details of what appears to be the best configuration.

After identifying the few best system configurations, longer simulation runs should be used to select the single best one and to fine-tune its design.

Step 8: Present Recommendations to Management

After completing its analysis, the management science team needs to present its recommendations to management. This usually would be done through both a written report and a formal oral presentation to the managers responsible for making the decisions regarding the system under study.

Both the written report and the oral presentation should highlight the recommendations and the rationale for those recommendations.

The report and presentation should summarize how the study was conducted, including documentation of the validation of the simulation model. A demonstration of the *animation* of a simulation run might be included to better convey the simulation process and add credibility. Numerical results that provide the rationale for the recommendations need to be included.

Management usually involves the management science team further in the initial implementation of the new system, including the indoctrination of the affected personnel.

Review Questions

1. When beginning a computer simulation study, with whom should a management science team meet to address some key questions and then to learn the details of how the system would operate?

2. What kind of diagram is often used to formulate a simulation model?

3. Who should the team engage to help check the accuracy of the simulation model?

4. What is the difference between a general-purpose simulation language and an applications-oriented simulator?

5. When using animation to display a computer simulation in action, how are the key elements of the system represented?

6. What is the specific question being addressed when testing the validity of a simulation model?

7. A simulation run can be viewed as what kind of statistical experiment?

8. What kinds of estimates are obtained from simulation runs?

9. What are the two ways in which a management science team usually presents its recommendations to management?

15.6 Summary

Computer simulation is one of the most popular management science techniques because it is such a flexible, powerful, and intuitive tool. It involves using a computer to *imitate* (simulate) the operation of an entire process or system. For a system that evolves over time according to one or more probability distributions, random observations are generated from these distributions to generate the various events that occur in the simulated system over time. (The inverse transformation method uses *random numbers* to generate these random observations.) This provides a relatively quick way of investigating how well a proposed system configuration would perform without incurring the great expense of actually constructing and operating the system. Therefore, many alternative system configurations can be investigated and compared in advance before choosing the one to use.

Herr Cutter's barber shop provides a case study of how computer simulation was able to provide the needed information to decide whether to change this stochastic system by adding a second barber. Like so many others, this stochastic system is a *queueing system*, but one that is too complicated to be analyzed solely by using queueing models.

This case study also illustrates the building blocks of a *simulation model* that represents the system to be simulated and describes how the simulation will be performed. One key building block is a *simulation clock*, which is the variable in the computer program that records the amount of simulated time that has elapsed so far. The *next-event time-advance procedure* advances the time on the simulation clock by repeatedly moving from the current event to the next event that will occur in the simulated system.

In a matter of seconds or minutes, a computer simulation can simulate even years of operation of a typical system. Each simulation run generates a series of statistical observations about the performance of the system over the period of time simulated. These observations then are used to estimate the interesting measures of performance of the system. Both a *point estimate* and a *confidence interval* can be obtained for each measure.

Because of its exceptional versatility, computer simulation has been applied to a wide variety of areas. Some of these applications have involved investigating the kinds of stochastic systems introduced in other chapters, such as queueing systems, inventory systems, and PERT projects. Other prominent areas of application include manufacturing systems, distribution systems, financial risk analysis, health care systems, and other systems in service industries.

Some computer simulation studies can be done relatively quickly by a single individual, who might be the manager concerned with the problem. For a more extensive study, however, the manager might want to assign a staff member, or even a full-fledged management science team, to the project. A major management science study based on computer simulation requires a series of important steps before the team is ready to obtain results from simulation runs. A series of questions must be addressed to management to properly define the problem from their viewpoint. Collecting good data generally is a difficult and time-consuming process. Another big task is formulating the simulation model, checking its accuracy, and then testing the validity of the model for closely approximating the system being simulated. One of the team's most important decisions is the choice of the software to be used. Several excellent *general-purpose simulation languages* are available. *Simulators* designed for simulating rather specific types of systems also have come on the market. Most simulation software vendors also now offer a version of their software with *animation* capabilities. Animation is very useful for illustrating the results of computer simulation for managers and other key personnel, which can add much credibility to the study.

Even after the computer program is ready to go, the management science team needs to design the statistical experiments to be conducted through computer simulation. Then the simulation runs can be conducted and the results analyzed. Finally, the team usually needs to both prepare a written report and make a formal oral presentation to present its recommendations to management.

Glossary

animation A computer display with icons that shows what is happening in a computer simulation. (Section 15.5), *757*

applications-oriented simulator A software package designed for simulating a fairly specific type of stochastic system. (Section 15.5), *757*

confidence interval An interval within which the true value of a measure of performance is likely to lie. (Section 15.3), *746*

general-purpose simulation language A general-purpose language for programming almost any kind of simulation model. (Section 15.5), *757*

inverse transformation method A method for generating random observations from a probability distribution. (Section 15.1), *732*

next-event time advance A procedure for advancing the time on the simulation clock by repeatedly moving from the current event to the next event that will occur in the simulated system. (Section 15.2), *741*

point estimate The single number that provides the best estimate of a measure of performance. (Section 15.3), *746*

random number A random observation from the uniform distribution over the interval from 0 to 1. (Section 15.1), *723*

simulation clock A variable in the computer program that records how much simulated time has elapsed so far. (Section 15.2), *741*

simulation model A representation of the system to be simulated that also describes how the simulation will be performed. (Section 15.2), *741*

simulator The common short name for *applications-oriented simulator* (defined above). (Section 15.5), *757*

state of the system The key information that defines the current status of the system. (Section 15.2), *741*

stochastic system A system that evolves over time according to one or more probability distributions. (Section 15.1), *722*

Learning Aids for This Chapter in Your MS Courseware

Chapter 15 Excel Files:

Coin-Flipping Game Example
Heavy Duty Co. Examples (3)
Herr Cutter's Barber Shop Case Study

Queueing Simulator
Template for M/G/1 Queueing Model

Excel Add-ins:

Crystal Ball (to be featured in the next chapter)
RiskSim

Routine:

Queueing Simulator (in an Excel file)

Interactive Management Science Modules:

Waiting Line Module

Problems

The symbols to the left of some of the problems (or their parts) have the following meaning:

E*: Use Excel.
Q*: Use the Queueing Simulator.

An asterisk on the problem number indicates that at least a partial answer is given in the back of the book.

15.1.* Use the random numbers in cells C13:C18 of Figure 15.1 to generate six random observations for each of the following situations.

   a. Throwing an unbiased coin.

   b. A baseball pitcher who throws a strike 60 percent of the time and a ball 40 percent of the time.

   c. The color of a traffic light found by a randomly arriving car when it is green 40 percent of the time, yellow 10 percent of the time, and red 50 percent of the time.

15.2. Reconsider the coin-flipping game introduced in Section 15.1 and analyzed with computer simulation in Figures 15.1, 15.2, and 15.3.

   a. Simulate one play of this game by repeatedly flipping your own coin until the game ends. Record your results in the format shown in columns B, D, E, F, and G of Figure 15.1. How much would you have won or lost if this had been a real play of the game?

E*   *b.* Revise the spreadsheet model in Figure 15.1 by using Excel's VLOOKUP function instead of the IF function to generate each simulated flip of the coin. Then perform a computer simulation of one play of the game.

E*   *c.* Use this revised spreadsheet model to generate a data table with 14 replications like Figure 15.2.

E*   *d.* Repeat part *c* with 1,000 replications (like Figure 15.3).

15.3. Each time an unbiased coin is flipped three times, the probability of getting 0, 1, 2, and 3 heads is ⅛, ⅜, ⅜, and ⅛, respectively. Therefore, with eight groups of three flips each, *on the average,* one group will yield no heads, three groups will yield one head, three groups will yield two heads, and one group will yield three heads.

   a. Using your own coin, flip it 24 times divided into eight groups of three flips each, and record the number of groups with no head, with one head, with two heads, and with three heads.

   b. Use random numbers in the order in which they are given in column C of Figure 15.4 and then in cells C5:C13 of Figure 15.5 to simulate the flips specified in part *a* and record the information indicated in part *a.*

E*   *c.* Formulate a spreadsheet model for performing a computer simulation of three flips of the coin and recording the number of heads. Perform one replication of this simulation.

E*   *d.* Use this spreadsheet to generate a data table with eight replications of the simulation. Compare this frequency distribution of the number of heads with the probability distribution of the number of heads with three flips.

E*   *e.* Repeat part *d* with 800 replications.

15.4. The weather can be considered a stochastic system, because it evolves in a probabilistic manner from one day to the next. Suppose for a certain location that this probabilistic evolution satisfies the following description:

   The probability of rain tomorrow is 0.6 if it is raining today. The probability of its being clear (no rain) tomorrow is 0.8 if it is clear today.

   a. Use the random numbers in cells C17:C26 of Figure 15.1 to simulate the evolution of the weather for 10 days, beginning the day after a clear day.

E*   *b.* Now use a computer with the random numbers generated by Excel to perform the simulation requested in part *a* on a spreadsheet.

15.5.* The game of craps requires the player to throw two dice one or more times until a decision has been reached as to whether he (or she) wins or loses. He wins if the first throw results in a sum of seven or 11 or, alternatively, if the first sum is 4, 5, 6, 8, 9, or 10 and the same sum reappears before a sum of seven has appeared. Conversely, he loses if the first throw results in a sum of 2, 3, or 12 or, alternatively, if the first sum is 4, 5, 6, 8, 9, or 10 and a sum of 7 appears before the first sum reappears.

E*   *a.* Formulate a spreadsheet model for performing a computer simulation of the throw of two dice. Perform one replication.

E*   *b.* Perform 25 replications of this simulation.

   c. Trace through these 25 replications to determine the number of times the simulated player would have won the game of craps when each play starts with the next throw after the previous play ends.

15.6. Jessica Williams, manager of kitchen appliances for the Midtown Department Store, feels that her inventory levels of stoves have been running higher than necessary. Before revising the inventory policy for stoves, she records the number sold each day over a period of 25 days, as summarized below.

Number sold	2	3	4	5	6
Number of days	4	7	8	5	1

   a. Use these data to estimate the probability distribution of daily sales.

   b. Calculate the mean of the distribution obtained in part *a*.

   c. Describe how random numbers can be used to simulate daily sales.

   d. Use the random numbers 0.4476, 0.9713, and 0.0629 to simulate daily sales over three days. Compare the average with the mean obtained in part *b*.

E*   *e.* Formulate a spreadsheet model for performing a computer simulation of the daily sales. Perform 300 replications and obtain the average of the sales over the 300 simulated days.

15.7.* Apply the inverse transformation method as indicated below to generate three random observations from the uniform distribution between -10 and 40 by using the following random numbers: 0.0965, 0.5692, 0.6658.

   a. Apply this method graphically.

   b. Apply this method algebraically.

   c. Write the equation that Excel would use to generate each such random observation.

15.8. Eddie's Bicycle Shop has a thriving business repairing bicycles. Trisha runs the reception area where customers check in their bicycles to be repaired and then later pick up their bicycles and pay their bills. She estimates that the time required to serve a customer on each visit has a uniform distribution between three minutes and eight minutes.

   Apply the inverse transformation method as indicated below to simulate the service times for five customers by using the following five random numbers: 0.6505, 0.0740, 0.8443, 0.4975, 0.8178.

   a. Apply this method graphically.

   b. Apply this method algebraically.

   c. Calculate the average of the five service times and compare it to the mean of the service-time distribution.

E*   *d.* Use Excel to generate 500 random observations and calculate the average. Compare this average to the mean of the service-time distribution.

15.9.* Reconsider Eddie's Bicycle Shop described in the preceding problem. Forty percent of the bicycles require only a minor repair. The repair time for these bicycles has a uniform distribution between zero and one hour. Sixty percent of the bicycles require a major repair. The repair time for these bicycles has a uniform distribution between one hour and two hours. You now need to estimate the mean of the overall probability distribution of the repair times for all bicycles by using the following alternative methods.

a. Use the random numbers 0.7256, 0.0817, and 0.4392 to simulate whether each of three bicycles requires minor repair or major repair. Then use the random numbers 0.2243, 0.9503, and 0.6104 to simulate the repair times of these bicycles. Calculate the average of these repair times to estimate the mean of the overall distribution of repair times.

b. Draw the cumulative distribution function (CDF) for the overall probability distribution of the repair times for all bicycles. (*Hint:* This CDF = 0.4 at one hour.)

c. Use the inverse transformation method with the latter three random numbers given in part *a* to generate three random observations from the overall distribution considered in part *b*. Calculate the average of these observations to estimate the mean of this distribution.

d. Repeat part *c* with the complements of the random numbers used there, so the new random numbers are 0.7757, 0.0497, and 0.3896.

e. Combine the random observations from parts *c* and *d* and calculate the average of these six observations to estimate the mean of the overall distribution of repair times. (This is referred to as the *method of complementary random numbers.*)

f. The true mean of the overall probability distribution of repair times is 1.1. Compare the estimates of this mean obtained in parts *a, c, d,* and *e.* For the method that provides the closest estimate, give an intuitive explanation for why it performed so well.

E*   g. Formulate a spreadsheet model to apply the method of complementary random numbers described in part *e*. Use 300 random numbers to generate 600 random observations from the distribution considered in part *b* and calculate the average of these random observations. Compare this average with the true mean of the distribution.

15.10. The employees of General Manufacturing Corp. receive health insurance through a group plan issued by Wellnet. During the past year, 40 percent of the employees did not file any health insurance claims, 40 percent filed only a small claim, and 20 percent filed a large claim. The small claims were spread uniformly between 0 and $2,000, whereas the large claims were spread uniformly between $2,000 and $20,000.

Based on this experience, Wellnet now is negotiating the corporation's premium payment per employee for the upcoming year. You are a management science analyst for the insurance carrier, and you have been assigned the task of estimating the average cost of insurance coverage for the corporation's employees.

Follow the instructions of Problem 15.9, where the size of an employee's health insurance claim (including zero if no claim was filed) now plays the role that the repair time for a bicycle did in Problem 15.9. (For part *f,* the true mean of the overall probability distribution of the size of an employee's health insurance claim is $2,600.)

15.11. Richard Collins, manager and owner of Richard's Tire Service, wishes to use computer simulation to analyze the operation of his shop. One of the activities to be included in the computer simulation is the installation of automobile tires (including balancing the tires). Richard estimates that the cumulative distribution function (CDF) of the probability distribution of the time (in minutes) required to install a tire has the graph shown below.

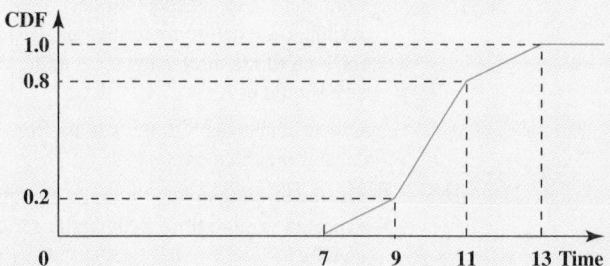

a. Use the inverse transformation method to generate five random observations from this distribution when using the following five random numbers: 0.2655, 0.3472, 0.0248, 0.9205, 0.6130.

b. Use a nested IF function to write an equation that Excel can use to generate each random observation from this distribution.

15.12.*Consider the probability distribution whose cumulative distribution function is

$$F(x) = x^2 \qquad \text{if } 0 \le x \le 1$$

Suppose you need to generate random observations from this distribution to help perform a computer simulation.

a. Derive an expression for each random observation in terms of the random number r.

b. Generate five random observations for this distribution by using the following random numbers: 0.0956, 0.5629, 0.6695, 0.7634, 0.8426.

c. The inverse transformation method was applied to generate the following three random observations from this distribution: 0.09, 0.64, 0.49. Identify the three random numbers that were used.

d. Write an equation that Excel can use to generate each random observation from this distribution.

15.13. The William Graham Entertainment Company will be opening a new box office where customers can come to make ticket purchases in advance for the many entertainment events being held in the area. Computer simulation is being used to analyze whether to have one or two clerks on duty at the box office.

While simulating the beginning of a day at the box office, the first customer arrives five minutes after it opens and then the interarrival times for the next four customers (in order) are three minutes, nine minutes, one minute, and four minutes, after which there is a long delay until the next customer arrives. The service times for these first five customers (in order) are eight minutes, six minutes, two minutes, four minutes, and seven minutes.

a. For the alternative of a single clerk, draw a figure like Figure 15.14 that shows the evolution of the number of customers at the box office over this period.

b. Use this figure to estimate the usual measures of performance—L, L_q, W, W_q, and the P_n (as defined in Section 14.3)—for this queueing system.

c. Repeat part *a* for the alternative of two clerks.

d. Repeat part *b* for the alternative of two clerks.

15.14. The Rustbelt Manufacturing Company employs a maintenance crew to repair its machines as needed. Management now wants a computer simulation study done to analyze what the size of the crew should be, where the crew sizes under consideration are two, three, and four. The time required by the crew to repair a machine has a uniform distribution over the interval from zero to twice the mean, where the mean depends on the crew size. The mean is four hours with two crew members, three hours with three crew members, and two hours with four crew members. The time between breakdowns of some machine has an exponential distribution with a mean of five hours. When a machine breaks down and so requires repair, management wants its average waiting time before repair begins to be no more than three hours. Management also wants the crew size to be no larger than necessary to achieve this.

a. Develop a simulation model for this problem by describing its six basic building blocks listed in Section 15.2 as they would be applied to this situation.

E*   b. Formulate a spreadsheet model to perform a computer simulation to estimate the average waiting time before repair begins. Perform this simulation over a period of 100 breakdowns for each of the three crew sizes under consideration. What do these results suggest the crew size should be?

Q*   c. Use the Queueing Simulator to perform this computer simulation over 10,000 breakdowns for each of the three crew sizes.

E*   d. Use the Excel template for the $M/G/1$ queueing model in this chapter's Excel file to obtain the expected waiting time analytically for each of the three crew sizes. Which crew size should be used?

15.15. Refer to the first 100 minutes of the computer simulation of the current operation of Herr Cutter's barber shop presented in Figure 15.13 and summarized in Figure 15.14. Now consider the alternative of adding an associate. Perform a simulation of this alternative by hand by using exactly the same interarrival times (in the same order) and exactly the same service times (in the same order) as in Figure 15.13.

a. Determine the new waiting time before beginning a haircut for each of the 5 customers who arrive in the first 100 minutes. Use these results to estimate W_q, the expected waiting time before the haircut.

    b. Plot the new version of Figure 15.14 to show the evolution of the number of customers in the barber shop over these 100 minutes.

15.16. While performing a computer simulation of a single-server queueing system, the number of customers in the system is zero for the first 10 minutes, one for the next 17 minutes, two for the next 24 minutes, one for the next 15 minutes, two for the next 16 minutes, and one for the next 18 minutes. After this total of 100 minutes, the number becomes 0 again. Based on these results for the first 100 minutes, perform the following analysis (using the notation for queueing models introduced in Section 14.3).

    a. Draw a figure like Figure 15.14 showing the evolution of the number of customers in the system.

    b. Develop estimates of P_0, P_1, P_2, P_3.

    c. Develop estimates of L and L_q.

    d. Develop estimates of W and W_q.

15.17. A major banking institution, Best Bank, plans to open a new branch office in Littletown. Preliminary estimates suggest that two tellers (and teller windows) should be provided, but this decision now awaits further analysis.

    Marketing surveys indicate that the new Littletown bank will attract enough business that customers requiring teller service will enter the bank at the rate of about one per minute on the average. Thus, the average time between consecutive customer arrivals is estimated to be one minute.

    No parking is available near the bank, so a special parking lot for bank customers only will be provided. A parking lot attendant will be on duty to validate each customer's parking before he or she leaves the car to enter the bank. This validation process takes at least 0.5 minutes, so the *minimum* time between consecutive arrivals of customers into the bank is 0.5 minutes. The amount by which the interarrival time exceeds 0.5 minutes is estimated to have an *exponential* distribution with a mean of 0.5 minutes. Therefore, the total interarrival time has a *translated exponential* distribution with a mean of (0.5 + 0.5) = 1.0 minute. (A translated exponential distribution is just an exponential distribution with a constant added.)

    Based on past experience in other branch offices, it is known that the time required by a teller to serve a customer will vary widely from customer to customer, but the average time is about 1.5 minutes. This experience also indicates that service time has approximately an *Erlang* distribution with a mean of 1.5 minutes and a shape parameter of $k = 4$, which provides a standard deviation of 0.75 minute (half that for an exponential distribution with the same mean).

    These data suggest that two tellers should be able to keep up with the customers quite well. However, management wants to be sure that customers will not frequently encounter a long waiting line and an excessive wait before receiving service. Therefore, computer simulation will be used to study these measures of performance.

Q*   *a.* Use the Queueing Simulator with 5,000 customer arrivals to estimate the usual measures of performance for this queueing system if two tellers are provided.

Q*   *b.* Repeat part *a* if three tellers are provided.

Q*   *c.* Now perform some sensitivity analysis by checking the effect if the level of business turns out to be even higher than projected. In particular, assume that the average time between customer arrivals turns out to be only 0.9 minutes (0.5 minutes plus a mean of only 0.4 minutes). Evaluate the alternatives of two tellers and three tellers under this assumption.

    d. Suppose *you* were the manager of this bank. Use your computer simulation results as the basis for a managerial decision on how many tellers to provide. Justify your answer.

15.18.* Hugh's Repair Shop specializes in repairing German and Japanese cars. The shop has two mechanics. One mechanic works on only German cars and the other mechanic works on only Japanese cars. In either case, the time required to repair a car has an exponential distribution with a mean of 0.2 days. The shop's business has been steadily increasing, especially for German cars. Hugh projects that, by next year, German cars will arrive randomly to be repaired at a mean rate of four per day, so the time between arrivals will have an exponential distribution with a mean of 0.25 days. The mean arrival rate for Japanese cars is projected to be two per day, so the distribution of interarrival times will be exponential with a mean of 0.5 days.

    For either kind of car, Hugh would like the average waiting time in the shop before the repair is completed to be no more than 0.5 days.

E*   *a.* Formulate a spreadsheet model to perform a computer simulation to estimate what the average waiting time until repair is completed will be next year for either kind of car.

E*   b. Perform this simulation for German cars over a period of 100 car arrivals.

E*   c. Repeat part b for Japanese cars.

Q*   d. Use the Queueing Simulator to do parts b and c with 10,000 car arrivals in each case.

Q*   e. Hugh is considering hiring a second mechanic who specializes in German cars so that two such cars can be repaired simultaneously. (Only one mechanic works on any one car.) Use the Queueing Simulator with 10,000 arrivals of German cars to evaluate this option.

Q*   f. Another option is to train the two current mechanics to work on either kind of car. This would increase the mean repair time by 10 percent, from 0.2 days to 0.22 days. Use the Queueing Simulator with 20,000 arrivals of cars of either kind to evaluate this option.

E*   g. Because both the interarrival-time and service-time distributions are exponential, the $M/M/1$ and $M/M/s$ queueing models introduced in Sections 14.5 and 14.6 can be used to evaluate all the above options analytically. Use the template for the $M/M/s$ queueing model (with $s = 1$ or 2) in an Excel file for Chapter 14 to determine W, the expected waiting time until repair is completed for each of the cases considered in parts b through f. For each case, compare the estimate of W obtained by computer simulation with the analytical value. What does this say about the number of car arrivals that should be included in the computer simulation?

      h. Based on the above results, which option would you select if you were Hugh? Why?

15.19. Vistaprint produces monitors and printers for computers. In the past, only some of them were inspected on a sampling basis. However, the new plan is that they all will be inspected before they are released. Under this plan, the monitors and printers will be brought to the inspection station one at a time as they are completed. For monitors, the interarrival time will have a uniform distribution between 10 and 20 minutes. For printers, the interarrival time will be a constant 15 minutes.

The inspection station has two inspectors. One inspector works on only monitors and the other one inspects only computers. In either case, the inspection time has an exponential distribution with a mean of 10 minutes.

Before beginning the new plan, management wants an evaluation made of how long the monitors and printers will be held up waiting at the inspection station.

E*   a. Formulate a spreadsheet model to perform a computer simulation to estimate the average waiting times (both before beginning inspection and after completing inspection) for either the monitors or the printers.

E*   b. Perform this simulation for the monitors over a period of 100 arrivals.

E*   c. Repeat part b for the printers.

Q*   d. Use the Queueing Simulator to repeat parts b and c with 10,000 arrivals in each case.

Q*   e. Management is considering the option of providing new inspection equipment to the inspectors. This equipment would not change the mean time to perform an inspection but it would decrease the variability of the times. In particular, for either product, the inspection time would have an Erlang distribution with a mean of 10 minutes and shape parameter $k = 4$. Use the Queueing Simulator to repeat part d under this option. Compare the results with those obtained in part d.

Q* 15.20. Consider the case study introduced in Section 15.2. After observing the operation of the barber shop, Herr Cutter's nephew Fritz is concerned that his uncle's estimate that the time required to give a haircut has a uniform distribution between 15 and 25 minutes appears to be a poor approximation of the actual probability distribution of haircut times. Based on the data he has gathered, Fritz's best estimate is that the actual distribution is an Erlang distribution with a mean of 20 minutes and a shape parameter of $k = 8$.

      a. Repeat the simulation run that Fritz previously used to obtain Figure 15.15 (with a mean of 30 minutes for the interarrival-time distribution) except substitute this new distribution of haircut times.

      b. Repeat the simulation run that Fritz previously used to obtain Figure 15.17 (with a mean of 14.3 minutes for the interarrival-time distribution) except substitute this new distribution of haircut times.

15.21. For the Dupit Corp. case study introduced in Section 14.4, the management science team was able to apply a variety of queueing models by making the following simplifying approximation. Except for the approach suggested by the vice president for engineering, the team assumed that the total time required to repair a machine (including travel time to the machine site) has an exponential distribution with a mean of two hours (¼ workday). However, the team was somewhat uncomfortable in making this assumption because the total repair times are never extremely short, as allowed by the exponential distribution. There always is some travel time and then some setup time to start the actual repair, so the total time generally is at least 40 minutes (⅒ workday).

A key advantage of computer simulation over mathematical models is that it is not necessary to make simplifying approximations like this one. For example, one of the options available in the Queueing Simulator is to use a *translated* exponential distribution, which has a certain *minimum* time and then the *additional* time has an exponential distribution with some mean. (Commercial packages for computer simulation have an even greater variety of options.)

Use computer simulation to refine the results obtained by queueing models as given by the Excel templates in the figures indicated below. Use a translated exponential distribution for the repair times where the *minimum* time is ½ workday and the *additional* time has an exponential distribution with a mean of ⅙ workday (80 minutes). In each case, use a run size of 25,000 arrivals and compare the point estimate obtained for W_q (the key measure of performance for this case study) with the value of W_q obtained by the queueing model.

Q*   *a.* Figure 14.5.

Q*   *b.* Figure 14.6.

Q*   *c.* Figure 14.9.

Q*   *d.* Figure 14.10.

        e. What conclusion do you draw about how sensitive the results from a computer simulation of a queueing system can be to the assumption made about the probability distribution of service times?

Case 15-1

Planning Planers

This was the first time that Carl Schilling had been summoned to meet with the bigwigs in the fancy executive offices upstairs. And he hopes it will be the last time. Carl doesn't like the pressure. He has had enough pressure just dealing with all the problems he has been encountering as the foreman of the planer department on the factory floor. What a nightmare this last month has been!

Fortunately, the meeting had gone better than Carl had feared. The bigwigs actually had been quite nice. They explained that they needed to get Carl's advice on how to deal with a problem that was affecting the entire factory. The origin of the problem is that the planer department has had a difficult time keeping up with its workload. Frequently there are a number of workpieces waiting for a free planer. This waiting has seriously disrupted the production schedule for subsequent operations, thereby greatly increasing the cost of in-process inventory as well as the cost of idle equipment and resulting lost production. They understood that this problem was not Carl's fault. However, they needed to get his ideas on what changes were needed in the planer department to relieve this bottleneck. Imagine that! All these bigwigs with graduate degrees from the fanciest business schools in the country asking advice from a poor working slob like him who had barely made it through high school. He could hardly wait to tell his wife that night.

The meeting had given Carl an opportunity to get two pet peeves off his chest. One peeve is that he has been telling his boss for months that he really needs another planer, but nothing ever gets done about this. His boss just keeps telling him that the planers he already has aren't being used 100 percent of the time, so how can adding even more capacity be justified? Doesn't his boss understand about the big backlogs that build up during busy times?

Then there is the other peeve—all those peaks and valleys of work coming to his department. At times, the work just pours in and a big backlog builds up. Then there might be a long pause when not much comes in so the planers stand idle part of the time. If only those departments that are feeding castings to his department could get their act together and even out the work flow, many of his backlog problems would disappear.

Carl was pleased that the bigwigs were nodding their heads in seeming agreement as he described these problems. They really appeared to understand. And they seemed very sincere in thanking him for his good advice. Maybe something is actually going to get done this time.

Here are the details of the situation that Carl and his "bigwigs" are addressing. The company has two planers for cutting flat smooth surfaces in large castings. The planers currently are being used for two purposes. One is to form the top surface of the *platen* for large hydraulic lifts. The other is to form the mating surface of the final drive *housing* for a large piece of earth-moving equipment. The time required to perform each type of job varies somewhat, depending largely upon the number of passes that must be made. In particular, for each platen or each housing, the time required by a planer has a translated exponential distribution, where the minimum time is 10 minutes and the additional time beyond 10 minutes has an exponential distribution with a mean of 10 minutes. (A distribution of this type is one of the options in the Queueing Simulator in this chapter's Excel file.)

Castings of both types arrive one at a time to the planer department. For the castings for forming platens, the arrivals occur randomly with a mean rate of two per hour. For the castings for forming housings, the arrivals again occur randomly with a mean rate of two per hour.

Based on Carl Schilling's advice, management has asked a management scientist (you) to analyze the following two proposals for relieving the bottleneck in the planer department:

Proposal 1: Obtain one additional planer. The total incremental cost (including capital recovery cost) is estimated to be $30 per hour. (This estimate takes into account the fact that, even with an additional planer, the total running time for all the planers will remain the same.)

Proposal 2: Eliminate the variability in the interarrival times of the castings, so that the castings would arrive regularly, one every 15 minutes, alternating between platen castings and housing castings. This would require making some changes in the preceding production processes, with an incremental cost of $60 per hour.

These proposals are not mutually exclusive, so any combination can be adopted.

It is estimated that the total cost associated with castings having to wait to be processed (including processing time) is $200 per hour for each platen casting and $100 per hour for each housing casting, provided the waits are not excessive. To avoid excessive waits for either kind of casting, all the castings are processed as soon as possible on a first-come, first-served basis.

Management's objective is to minimize the expected total cost per hour.

Use computer simulation to evaluate and compare all the alternatives, including the status quo and the various combinations of proposals. Then make your recommendation to management.

Are there any other alternatives you would recommend considering?

Case 15-2

Reducing In-Process Inventory (Revisited)

Reconsider Case 14.2. The current and proposed queueing systems in this case were to be analyzed with the help of queueing models to determine how to reduce in-process inventory as much as possible. However, these same queueing systems also can be effectively analyzed by applying computer simulation with the help of the Queueing Simulator in your MS Courseware.

Use computer simulation to perform all the analysis requested in this case.

Learning objectives

After completing this chapter, you should be able to

1. Describe the role of Crystal Ball in performing computer simulations.

2. Use Crystal Ball to perform various basic computer simulations that cannot be readily performed with the standard Excel package.

3. Interpret the results generated by Crystal Ball when performing a computer simulation.

4. Use a Crystal Ball feature that enables stopping a simulation run after achieving the desired level of precision.

5. Describe the characteristics of many of the probability distributions that can be incorporated into a computer simulation when using Crystal Ball.

6. Use a Crystal Ball procedure that identifies the continuous distribution that best fits historical data.

7. Use a Crystal Ball feature that generates both a decision table and a trend chart as an aid to decision making.

8. Use a Crystal Ball tool called OptQuest that automatically searches for an optimal solution for a simulation model.

Chapter **Sixteen**

Computer Simulation with Crystal Ball

The preceding chapter presented the basic concepts of computer simulation. Its emphasis throughout was on the use of spreadsheet modeling to perform basic computer simulations. Except for the use of the Queueing Simulator to deal with queueing systems, all of the computer simulations in Chapter 15 were executed using nothing more than the standard Excel package.

Although the standard Excel package has some basic simulation capabilities, an exciting development in recent years has been the development of powerful Excel add-ins that greatly extend these capabilities. An especially popular one is *Crystal Ball,* developed by Decisioneering, Inc. Decisioneering has generously provided Crystal Ball 2000 (Professional Edition) on a 140-day trial basis to be included with the MS Courseware on the CD-ROM. In addition to its strong functionality for performing computer simulations, this advanced version of Crystal Ball also includes two other modules. One is CB Predictor, which is used for generating forecasts from time-series data, as described and illustrated in Section 13.4. The other is OptQuest, which enhances Crystal Ball by using its output from a series of simulation runs to automatically search for an optimal solution for a simulation model.

This chapter focuses on describing and illustrating the advances in spreadsheet simulation modeling that are made possible by Crystal Ball, including its OptQuest module. (Other Excel add-ins for spreadsheet simulation modeling provide some of the same functionality.) Section 16.1 begins with a case study that will be revisited in Sections 16.7–16.9. Sections 16.2–16.6 present several other examples of important business problems that can be effectively addressed by using computer simulations with Crystal Ball. Section 16.7 focuses on how to choose the right probability distributions as inputs for a computer simulation. Section 16.8 then describes how decision tables (which work much like data tables or like Solver Table in your MS Courseware) can be constructed and applied to make a decision about the problem being simulated. Finally, Section 16.9 discusses and illustrates the powerful optimization tool provided by OptQuest.

16.1 A CASE STUDY: FREDDIE THE NEWSBOY'S PROBLEM

This case study concerns a newsstand in a prominent downtown location of a major city. The newsstand has been there longer than most people can remember. It has always been run by a well-known character named Freddie. (Nobody seems to know his last name.) His many customers refer to him affectionately as Freddie the newsboy, even though he is considerably older than most of them.

Freddie sells a wide variety of newspapers and magazines. The most expensive of the newspapers is a large national daily called the *Financial Journal.* Our case study involves this newspaper.

Freddie's Problem

The day's copies of the *Financial Journal* are brought to the newsstand early each morning by a distributor. Any copies unsold at the end of the day are returned to the distributor the next morning. However, to encourage ordering a large number of copies, the distributor does give a small refund for unsold copies.

Here are Freddie's cost figures.

Freddie pays $1.50 per copy delivered.

Freddie charges $2.50 per copy.

Freddie's refund is $0.50 per unsold copy.

Partially because of the refund, Freddie always has taken a plentiful supply. However, he has become concerned about paying so much for copies that then have to be returned unsold, particularly since this has been occurring nearly every day. He now thinks he might be better off ordering only a minimal number of copies and saving this extra cost.

To investigate this further, Freddie has been keeping a record of his daily sales. This is what he has found.

- Freddie sells anywhere between 40 and 70 copies on any given day.

- The frequency of the numbers between 40 and 70 are roughly equal.

Freddie's problem involves determining the order quantity that will maximize his average daily profit.

Freddie needs to determine how many copies to order per day from the distributor. His objective is to maximize his average daily profit.

If you have previously studied inventory management in an operations management course, you might recognize this problem as being an example of what is now called either the *newsboy problem* or the *newsvendor problem*. In fact, we use a basic inventory model to analyze a simplified version of this same case study in Chapter 19 (one of the supplementary chapters on the CD-ROM). However, we will use computer simulation to analyze this problem in this chapter.

A Spreadsheet Model for This Problem

Figure 16.1 shows a spreadsheet model for this problem. Given the data cells C4:C6, the decision variable is the order quantity to be entered in cell C9. (The number 60 has been entered arbitrarily in this figure as a first guess of a reasonable value.) The bottom of the figure shows the equations used to calculate the output cells C15:C17. These output cells are then used to calculate the output cell Profit (C19).

The only uncertain input quantity in this spreadsheet is the day's demand in cell C12. This quantity can be anywhere between 40 and 70. Since the frequency of the numbers between 40 and 70 are about the same, the probability distribution of the day's demand can be reasonably assumed to be a *uniform distribution* between 40 and 70, as indicated in cells D12:F12. Rather than enter a single number permanently into SimulatedDemand (C12), what Crystal Ball does is enter this probability distribution into this cell. (Before turning to Crystal Ball, an arbitrary number 55 has been entered temporarily into this cell in Figure 16.1.) By using Crystal Ball to generate a *random observation* from this probability distribution, the spreadsheet can calculate the output cells in the usual way. Each time this is done is referred to as a **trial** by Crystal Ball. By running the number of trials specified by the user (typically hundreds or thousands), the computer simulation thereby generates the same number of random observations of the values in the output cells. Crystal Ball records this information for the output cell(s) of particular interest (Freddie's daily profit) and then, at the end, displays it in a variety of convenient forms that reveal an estimate of the underlying probability distribution of Freddie's daily profit. (More about this later.)

A day's demand for the Financial Journal appears to have a uniform distribution between 40 and 70.

Since the uniform distribution is a continuous distribution, the value in SimulatedDemand (C12) may take on *any* value between 40 and 70, including noninteger values. However, the actual demand on any particular day must be an *integer* number of copies of the *Financial*

FIGURE 16.1

A spreadsheet model for applying computer simulation to the case study that involves Freddie the newsboy. The assumption cell is SimulatedDemand (C12), the forecast cell is Profit (C19), and the decision variable is OrderQuantity (C9).

	A	B	C	D	E	F
1		**Freddie the Newsboy**				
2						
3			**Data**			
4		Unit Sale Price	$2.50			
5		Unit Purchase Cost	$1.50			
6		Unit Salvage Value	$0.50			
7						
8			**Decision Variable**			
9		Order Quantity	60			
10						
11			**Simulation**		Minimum	Maximum
12		Simulated Demand	55	*Uniform*	40	70
13		Demand (rounded)	55			
14						
15		Sales Revenue	$137.50			
16		Purchasing Cost	$90.00			
17		Salvage Value	$2.50			
18						
19		Profit	$50.00			

	B	C
11		**Simulation**
12	Simulated Demand	55
13	Demand (rounded)	=ROUND(SimulatedDemand,0)
14		
15	Sales Revenue	=UnitSalePrice*MIN(OrderQuantity,Demand)
16	Purchasing Cost	=UnitPurchaseCost*OrderQuantity
17	Salvage Value	=UnitSalvageValue*MAX(OrderQuantity-Demand,0)
18		
19	Profit	=SalesRevenue-PurchasingCost+SalvageValue

Range Name	Cell
Demand	C13
OrderQuantity	C9
Profit	C19
PurchasingCost	C16
SalesRevenue	C15
SalvageValue	C17
SimulatedDemand	C12
UnitPurchaseCost	C5
UnitSalePrice	C4
UnitSalvageValue	C6

Excel Tip: The Excel function ROUND(x, 0) rounds the value x to the nearest integer. The zero specifies how many digits after the decimal point should be included when rounding.

Journal. Therefore, the Excel ROUND function is used to round off SimulatedDemand (C12) to the nearest integer to obtain the actual demand in cell C13. This is why Demand (C13) is used instead of SimulatedDemand (C12) in the equations used to calculate SalesRevenue (C15) and SalvageValue (C17).

The Application of Crystal Ball

Four steps must be taken to use the spreadsheet in Figure 16.1 to perform the computer simulation with Crystal Ball. They are:

1. Define the random input cells.

2. Define the output cells to forecast.

3. Set the run preferences.

4. Run the simulation.

We now describe each of these four steps in turn.

Define the Random Input Cells

Crystal Ball Tip: Before defining an assumption cell, the cell *must* contain a value. Any number can be entered, since it will not be used during the actual simulation. When a simulation run is completed, Crystal Ball restores the same value.

A random input cell is an input cell that has a random value (such as the daily demand for the *Financial Journal*). Therefore, an assumed probability distribution must be entered into the cell instead of permanently entering a single number. The only random input cell in Figure 16.1 is SimulatedDemand (C12). Crystal Ball refers to each such random input cell as an **assumption cell.**

The following procedure is used to define an assumption cell.

FIGURE 16.2

The Crystal Ball toolbar.

	Define Assumption
	Define Decision
	Define Forecast
	Select Assumptions
	Select Decisions
	Select Forecasts
	Copy Data
	Paste Data
	Clear Data
	Run Preferences
	Start Simulation
	Stop Simulation
	Reset Simulation
	Single Step
	Forecast Windows
	Overlay Chart
	Trend Chart
	Sensitivity Chart
	Create Report
	Extract data
	Crystal Ball Help

The Distribution Gallery includes 17 probability distributions.

Crystal Ball Tip: Rather than entering raw numbers, use cell references for the distribution parameters (e.g., type =E12 and =F12 as shown in Figure 16.4). This allows changes to be made directly on the spreadsheet rather than having to dig into Crystal Ball dialogue boxes.

Procedure for Defining an Assumption Cell

1. Select the cell by clicking on it.

2. If the cell does not already contain a value, enter *any* number into the cell.

3. Click on the first button (the Define Assumption button) in the Crystal Ball toolbar shown in Figure 16.2 (or choose Define Assumption from the Cell menu).

4. Select a probability distribution to enter into the cell by clicking on this distribution in the Distribution Gallery shown in Figure 16.3.

5. Click on OK (or double click on the distribution) to bring up a dialogue box for the selected distribution.

6. Use this dialogue box to enter the parameters for the distribution, preferably by referring to the cells in the spreadsheet that contain the values of these parameters. If desired, a name also can be entered for the assumption cell. (If the cell already has a name next to it or above it on the spreadsheet, that name will appear in the dialogue box.)

7. Click on OK.

The **Distribution Gallery** mentioned in step 4 provides a wide variety of 17 probability distributions from which to choose. Figure 16.3 displays 12 of these distributions, but five more also are available by clicking on the More button. (Section 16.7 will focus on the question of how to choose the right distribution.)

In Freddie's case, double clicking on the uniform distribution in the Distribution Gallery brings up the Uniform Distribution dialogue box shown in Figure 16.4, which is used to enter the parameters of the distribution. For each of the parameters (Min and Max), we refer to the data cells in E12 and F12 on the spreadsheet by typing the formulas shown in Figure 16.4. When cell references are used in this way, a choice needs to be made between the "Static" option and the "Dynamic" option by clicking on one of the buttons just below the display of the distribution. The **static option** means that each cell reference is only evaluated once, at the beginning of the simulation run, and then each parameter value (Min and Max) at that point is used for all the trials of the simulation. This is fine when the parameter value in each cell never changes, which is the case in this example, so the static option has been selected in Figure 16.4. The **dynamic option** means that each cell reference is evaluated for each separate trial, which would be needed if the parameter value in each cell might change because it depends on another assumption cell. (This arises in the example featured in Section 16.6.)

Define the Output Cells to Forecast

Crystal Ball refers to the output of a computer simulation as a *forecast,* since it is forecasting the underlying probability distribution for the performance of the system (now being simulated) when it actually is in operation. Thus, each output cell that is being used by a computer simulation to forecast a measure of performance is referred to as a **forecast cell.** The spread-

FIGURE 16.3

The Crystal Ball Distribution Gallery dialogue box. In addition to the 12 distributions displayed here, five more distributions can be accessed by clicking on the More button.

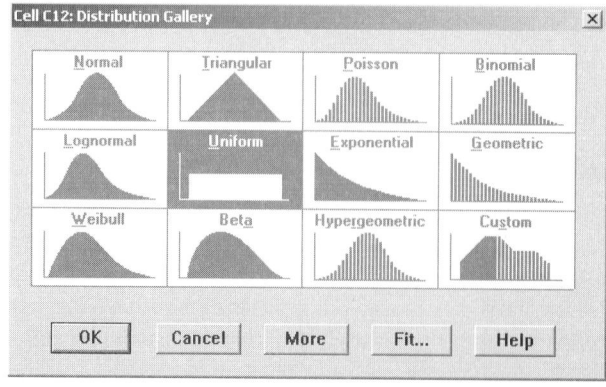

FIGURE 16.4

The Crystal Ball Uniform Distribution dialogue box. It is being used here to enter a uniform distribution with the parameters in cells E12 and F12 into the assumption cell SimulatedDemand (C12) in the spreadsheet model in Figure 16.1.

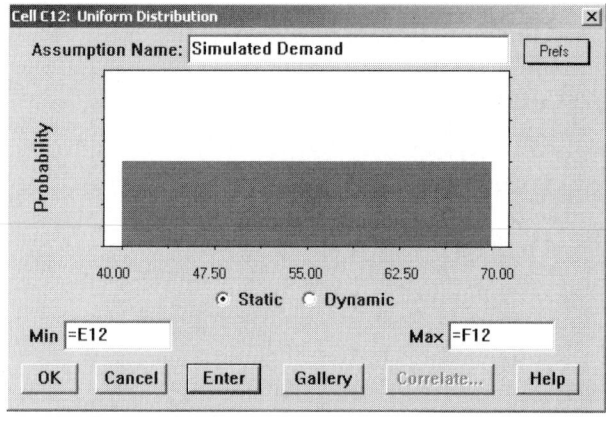

FIGURE 16.5

The Crystal Ball Define Forecast dialogue box. It is being used here to define the forecast cell Profit (C19) in the spreadsheet model in Figure 16.1.

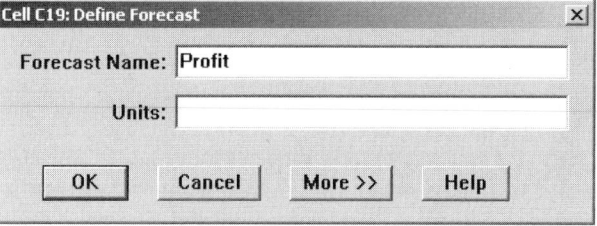

sheet model for a computer simulation does not include a target cell, but a forecast cell plays roughly the same role.

The measure of performance of interest to Freddie the newsboy is his daily profit from selling the *Financial Journal,* so the only forecast cell in Figure 16.1 is Profit (C19). The following procedure is used to define such an output cell as a forecast cell.

Procedure for Defining a Forecast Cell

1. Select the cell by clicking on it.

2. Click on the third button (the Define Forecast button) in the Crystal Ball toolbar shown in Figure 16.2 (or choose Define Forecast from the Cell menu), which brings up the Define Forecast dialogue box (as shown in Figure 16.5 for Freddie's problem).

3. This dialogue box can be used to define a name and (optionally) units for the forecast cell. (If a range name already has been assigned to the cell, that name will appear in the dialogue box.)

4. Click on OK.

Set the Run Preferences

The third step—setting run preferences—refers to such things as choosing the number of trials to run and deciding on other options regarding how to perform the computer simulation. This step begins by clicking on the Run Preferences button on the Crystal Ball toolbar or choosing Run Preferences from the Run menu. The Run Preferences dialogue box has the six tabs shown on the right-hand side of Figure 16.6. By clicking on these buttons, you can enter or change any of the specifications controlled by that tab for how to run the computer simulation. For example, Figure 16.6 shows the version of the dialogue box that is obtained by selecting the Trials tab. This figure indicates that 500 has been chosen as the maximum number of trials for the computer simulation. (The second option in the Run Preferences Trials dialogue box—Stop If Specified Precision Is Reached—will be described later.)

Run the Simulation

At this point, the stage is set to begin running the computer simulation. To start, you only need to click on the Start Simulation button (see the middle of Figure 16.2) or choose Run Simulation

FIGURE 16.6

The Crystal Ball Run Preferences dialogue box after selecting the Trials tab.

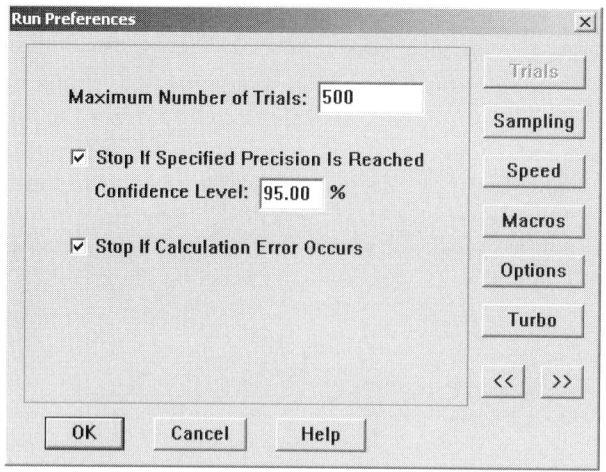

Crystal Ball Tip: If the forecast window does not display during the simulation run, then this option has been turned off in the expanded Define Forecast dialogue box (shown later in Figure 16.10), but it can be turned back on by clicking on that option.

Crystal Ball Tip: To display the mean line on the frequency chart, as in Figure 16.7, choose this option in "Chart . . ." under the Preferences menu.

from the Run menu. However, if a computer simulation has been run previously, you should first click on the Reset Simulation button or choose Reset Simulation from the Run menu to reset the simulation before starting a new one.

Once started, a forecast window displays the results of the computer simulation as it runs. Figure 16.7 shows the forecast for Profit (Freddie's daily profit from selling the *Financial Journal*) after all 500 trials have been completed. The default view of the forecast is the frequency chart shown in the figure. The height of the vertical lines in the frequency chart indicates the relative frequency of the various profit values that were obtained during the simulation run. For example, consider the tall vertical line at $60. The right-hand side of the chart indicates a frequency of 175 there, which means that 175 of the 500 trials led to a profit of $60. Thus, the left-hand side of the chart indicates that the estimated probability of a profit of $60 is 175/500 = 0.350. This is the profit that results whenever the demand equals or exceeds the order quantity of 60. The remainder of the time, the profit was scattered fairly evenly between $20 and $60. These profit values correspond to trials where the demand was between 40 and 60 units, with lower profit values corresponding to demands closer to 40 and higher profit values corresponding to demands closer to 60. The mean of the 500 profit values is $46.67, as indicated by the *mean line* (the dashed vertical line) at this point.

The statistics table in Figure 16.7 is obtained by choosing Statistics from the View menu. These statistics summarize the outcome of the 500 trials of the computer simulation. These 500 trials provide a sample of 500 random observations from the underlying probability distribution of Freddie's daily profit. The most interesting statistics about this sample provided by the table include the *mean* of $46.67, the *median* of $50.00 (indicating that $50 was the middle profit value from the 500 trials when listing the profits from smallest to largest), the *mode* of $60 (meaning that this was the profit value that occurred most frequently), and the *standard deviation* of $13.36. The information near the bottom of the table regarding the *range* of profit values also is particularly useful.

In addition to the frequency chart and statistics table presented in Figure 16.7, the View menu provides some other useful ways of displaying the results of a simulation run, including a percentiles table, a cumulative chart, and a reverse cumulative chart. These alternative displays are shown in Figure 16.8. The percentiles table is based on listing the profit values generated by the 500 trials from smallest to largest, dividing this list into 10 equal parts (50 values in each), and then recording the value at the end of each part. Thus, the value 10 percent through the list is $26, the value 20 percent through the list is $32, and so forth. (For example, the intuitive interpretation of the 10 percent percentile of $26 is that 10 percent of the trials have profit values less than or equal to $26 and the other 90 percent of the trials have profit values greater than or equal to $26, so $26 is the dividing line between the smallest 10 percent of the values and the largest 90 percent.) The cumulative chart provides similar (but more detailed) information about this same list of the smallest-to-largest profit values. The horizontal

In general, the *x* percent percentile is the dividing line between the smallest *x* percent of the values and the rest of the values.

FIGURE 16.7   The frequency chart and statistics table provided by Crystal Ball to summarize the results of running the simulation model in Figure 16.1 for the case study that involves Freddie the newsboy.

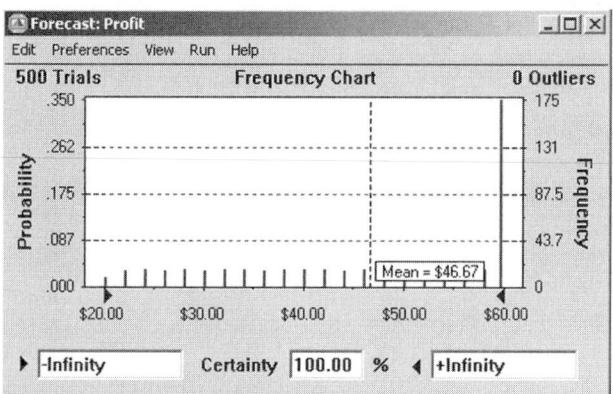
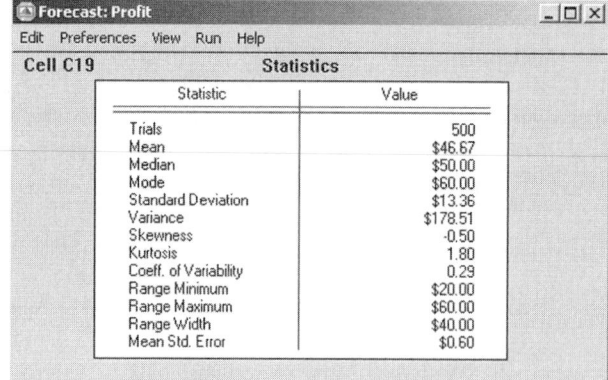

FIGURE 16.8   Three more forms in which Crystal Ball displays the results of running the simulation model in Figure 16.1 for the case study that involves Freddie the newsboy.

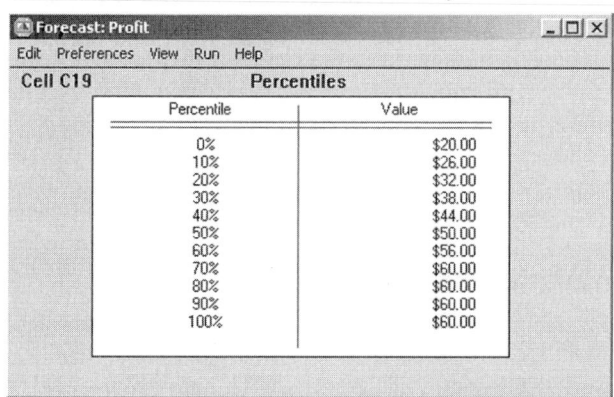
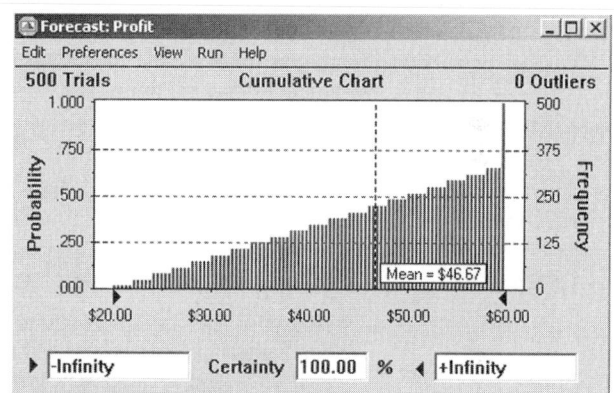

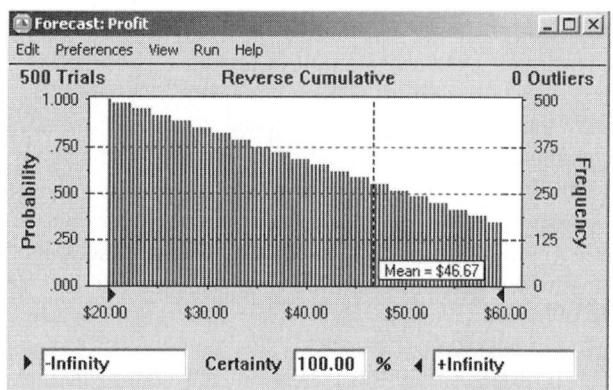

axis shows the entire range of values from the smallest possible profit value ($20) to the largest possible profit value ($60). For each value in this range, the chart cumulates the number of actual profits generated by the 500 trials that are less than or equal to that value. This number equals the frequency shown on the right or, when divided by the number of trials, the probability shown on the left. The reverse cumulative chart is constructed in the same way as the cumulative chart except for the following crucial difference. For each value in the range from $20 to $60, the reverse cumulative chart cumulates the number of actual profits generated by the 500 trials that are *greater* than or equal to that value.

FIGURE 16.9

After setting a lower bound of $40 for desirable profit values, the Certainty box below this frequency chart reveals that 68.40 percent of the trials in Freddie's simulation run provided a profit at least this high.

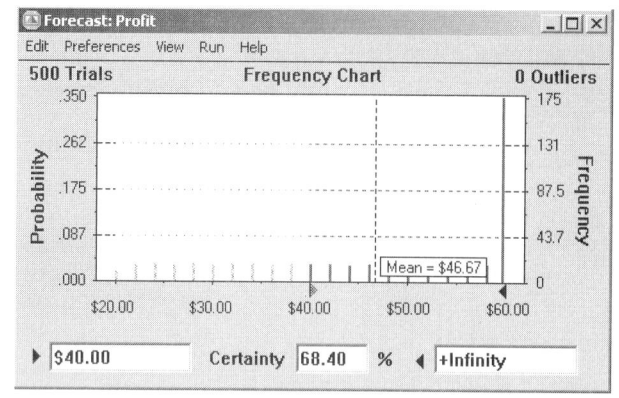

Figure 16.9 illustrates another of the many helpful ways provided by Crystal Ball for extracting helpful information from the results of a simulation run. Freddie the newsboy feels that he has had a reasonably successful day if he obtains a profit of at least $40 from selling the *Financial Journal.* Therefore, he would like to know the percentage of days that he could expect to achieve this much profit if he were to adopt the order quantity currently being analyzed (60). An estimate of this percentage (68.40 percent) is shown in the Certainty box below the frequency chart in Figure 16.9. Crystal Ball can provide this percentage in two ways. First, the user can drag the triangle on the left just under the chart (originally at $20 in Figure 16.7) to the right until it is at $40 (as in Figure 16.9). Alternatively, $40 can be typed directly into the box in the lower left-hand corner. If desired, the probability of obtaining a profit between any two values also could be estimated immediately by dragging the two triangles to those values.

The Certainty box gives the percentage of the trials that generated values between the values in the adjacent boxes.

How Accurate Are the Simulation Results?

An important number provided by Figure 16.7 is the mean of $46.67. This number was calculated as the *average* of the 500 random observations from the underlying probability distribution of Freddie's daily profit that were generated by the 500 trials. This *sample average* of $46.67 thereby provides an *estimate* of the *true mean* of this distribution. The true mean might deviate somewhat from $46.67. How accurate can we expect this estimate to be?

The *mean standard error* specifies how close the mean obtained in a simulation run is likely to be to the true mean.

The answer to this key question is provided by the *mean standard error* of $0.60 given at the bottom of the statistics table in Figure 16.7. In particular, the true mean can readily deviate from the sample mean by any amount up to the mean standard error, but most of the time (approximately 68 percent of the time), it will not deviate by more than that. Thus, the interval from $46.67 − $0.60 = $46.07 to $46.67 + $0.60 = $47.27 is a 68 percent *confidence interval* for the true mean. Similarly, a larger confidence interval can be obtained by using an appropriate multiple of the mean standard error to subtract from the sample mean and then to add to the sample mean. For example, the appropriate multiple for a 95 percent confidence interval is 1.965, so such a confidence interval ranges from $46.67 − 1.965($0.60) = $45.49 to $46.67 + 1.965($0.60) = $47.85. (This multiple of 1.965 will change slightly if the number of trials is different from 500.) Therefore, it is very likely that the true mean is somewhere between $45.49 and $47.85.

If greater precision is required, the mean standard error normally can be reduced by increasing the number of trials in the simulation run. However, the reduction tends to be small unless the number of trials is increased substantially. For example, cutting the mean standard error in half requires approximately quadrupling the number of trials. Thus, a surprisingly large number of trials may be required to obtain the desired degree of precision.

Since the number of trials required to obtain the desired degree of accuracy cannot be predicted very well in advance of the simulation run, the temptation is to specify an extremely large number of trials. This specified number may turn out to be many times as large as necessary and thereby cause an excessively long computer run. Fortunately, Crystal Ball has a special method of precision control for stopping the simulation run early as soon as the desired precision has

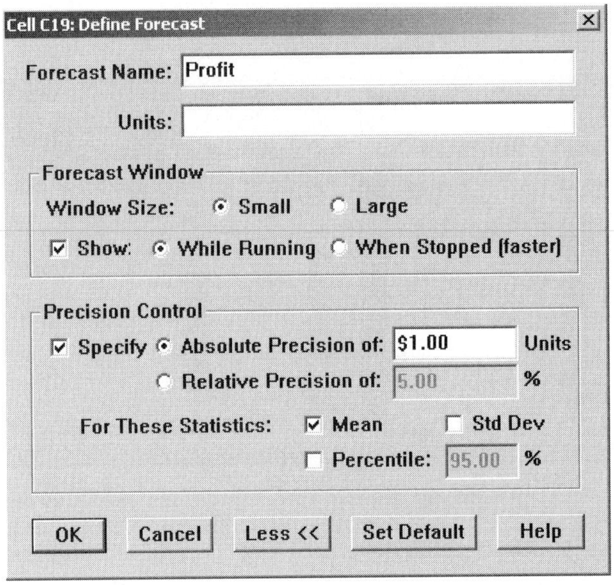

FIGURE 16.10
This Expanded Define Forecast dialogue box is being used to specify how much precision is desired in Freddie's simulation run.

been reached. This method is triggered by choosing the second option ("Stop If Specified Precision Is Reached") in the Run Preferences Trials dialogue box shown in Figure 16.6. The specified precision is entered in the Expanded Define Forecast dialogue box displayed in Figure 16.10. (This dialogue box is brought up by clicking on the More button in the Define Forecast dialogue box shown in Figure 16.5.) The lower right-hand side of Figure 16.10 indicates that the precision control is being applied to the mean (but not to the standard deviation or to a specified percentile) and that a 95 percent confidence interval is being used. The width of half of the confidence interval, measured from its midpoint to either end, is considered to be the precision that has been achieved. The desired precision can be specified in either absolute terms (using the same units as for the confidence interval) or in relative terms (expressed as a percentage of the midpoint of the confidence interval).

The middle of the dialogue box in Figure 16.10 indicates that the decision was made to specify the desired precision in absolute terms as $1. The 95 percent confidence interval for the mean after 500 trials was found to be $46.67 plus-or-minus $1.18, so $1.18 is the precision that was achieved after all these trials. Crystal Ball also calculates the confidence interval (and so the current precision) periodically to check whether the current precision is under $1, in which case the run would be stopped. However, this never happened, so Crystal Ball allowed the simulation to run until the maximum number of trials (500) was reached.

To obtain the desired precision, the simulation would need to be restarted to generate additional trials. This is done by entering a larger number (such as 1,000) for the maximum number of trials (including the 500 already obtained) in the Run Preferences dialogue box (shown in Figure 16.6) and then clicking on the Start Simulation button on the Crystal Ball toolbar. Figure 16.11 shows the results of doing this. The first row indicates that the desired precision was obtained after only 250 additional trials, for a total of 750 trials. (The default value for the frequency of checking the precision is every 50 trials, so the precision of $1 actually was reached somewhere between 700 and 750 trials.) Because of the additional trials, some of the statistics have changed slightly from those given in Figure 16.7. For example, the best estimate of the mean now is $46.61, with a precision of $0.96. Thus, it is very likely (95 percent confidence) that the true value of the mean is within $0.96 of $46.61.

750 trials were needed to have 95 percent confidence that the true value of the mean is within $1 of the mean obtained in the simulation run.

95% confidence interval: $45.65 ≤ Mean ≤ $47.57

The precision also is given for the current estimates of the median and the standard deviation, as well as for the estimates of the percentiles given in the percentiles table. Therefore, a 95 percent confidence interval also can be calculated for each of these quantities by adding and subtracting its precision from its estimate.

FIGURE 16.11 The results obtained after continuing Freddie's simulation run until the precision specified in Figure 16.10 is achieved.

Cell C19	Statistics	
Statistic	Value	Precision
Trials	750	
Mean	$46.61	$0.96
Median	$50.00	$2.65
Mode	$60.00	
Standard Deviation	$13.47	$0.43
Variance	$181.42	
Skewness	-0.49	
Kurtosis	1.78	
Coeff. of Variability	0.29	
Range Minimum	$20.00	
Range Maximum	$60.00	
Range Width	$40.00	
Mean Std. Error	$0.49	

* Statistics shown in color are tested for $1.00 precision at 95.00% confidence

Cell C19	Percentiles	
Percentile	Value	Precision
0%	$20.00	
10%	$26.00	$1.44
20%	$32.00	$1.93
30%	$38.00	$2.04
40%	$44.00	$2.39
50%	$50.00	$2.65
60%	$56.00	$2.35
70%	$60.00	$0.00
80%	$60.00	$0.00
90%	$60.00	$0.00
100%	$60.00	

* Statistics shown in color are tested for $1.00 precision at 95.00% confidence

Freddie's Conclusions

The results presented in Figures 16.7 and 16.11 were from a simulation run that fixed Freddie's daily order quantity at 60 copies of the *Financial Journal* (as indicated in cell C9 of the spreadsheet in Figure 16.1). Freddie wanted this order quantity tried first because it seems to provide a reasonable compromise between being able to fully meet the demand on many days (about two-thirds of them) while often not having many unsold copies on those days. However, the results obtained do not reveal whether 60 is the *optimal* order quantity that would maximize his average daily profit. Many more simulation runs with other order quantities will be needed to determine (or at least estimate) the optimal order quantity. Section 16.8 will describe how this search for the optimal order quantity can be done for Freddie with the help of a decision table and a trend chart. Section 16.9 then describes how the OptQuest module in your Crystal Ball software package uses a powerful optimization technique to search systematically for the optimal order quantity. That presentation will bring the case study to a close.

Freddie now has 95 percent confidence that an order quantity of 60 would provide an average daily profit between $45.65 and $47.57 in the long run.

Although there is still much more to come, Freddie already has learned from Figure 16.11 that an order quantity of 60 would provide a nice average daily profit of approximately $46.61. This is only an estimate, but Freddie also has learned from the 95 percent confidence interval that the average daily profit probably would turn out to be somewhere between $45.65 and $47.57.

However, these profit figures provided by computer simulation are based on the assumption in the spreadsheet model (see cells D12:F12 in Figure 16.1) that demand has a uniform distribution between 40 and 70. Therefore, these profit figures will be correct only if this assumption is a valid one. More work is needed to either verify that this assumed distribution is the appropriate one or to identify another probability distribution that provides a better fit to the data of daily demands that Freddie actually has been experiencing. This issue will be explored further in Section 16.7.

Computer simulation with Crystal Ball is an extremely versatile tool that can address a myriad of managerial issues. Therefore, before continuing the case study in Sections 16.7–16.9, we turn in the intervening sections to presenting five additional examples of the application of computer simulation with Crystal Ball.

Review Questions

1. What is the decision that Freddie the newsboy needs to make?
2. What is an *assumption cell* when using Crystal Ball?
3. What is entered into the assumption cell in Freddie's spreadsheet model?
4. What is a *forecast cell* when using Crystal Ball?
5. What is entered into the forecast cell in Freddie's spreadsheet model?
6. What kind of information is provided by a frequency chart when using Crystal Ball?
7. What are the key statistics provided by the statistics table when using Crystal Ball?

8. What is the significance of the *mean standard error* of the results from a computer simulation?

9. What provision does Crystal Ball provide for perhaps stopping a simulation run before the specified number of trials have been completed?

10. What has Freddie the newsboy learned so far about what his order quantity should be?

16.2 BIDDING FOR A CONSTRUCTION PROJECT: A PRELUDE TO THE RELIABLE CONSTRUCTION CO. CASE STUDY

Managers frequently must make decisions whose outcomes will be greatly affected by the corresponding decisions being made by the management of competitor firms. For example, marketing decisions often fall into this category. To illustrate, consider the case in which a manager must determine the price for a new product being brought to market. How well this decision works out will depend greatly on the pricing decisions being made nearly simultaneously by other firms marketing competitive new products. Similarly, the success of a decision on how soon to market a product under development will be determined largely by whether this product reaches the market before competitive products are released by other firms.

When a decision must be made before learning the corresponding decisions being made by competitors, the analysis needs to take into account the uncertainty surrounding what competitors' decisions will be. Computer simulation provides a natural way of doing this by using assumption cells to represent competitors' decisions.

The following example illustrates this process by considering a situation where the decision being made is the bid to submit on a construction project while three other companies are simultaneously preparing their own bids.

The Reliable Construction Co. Bidding Problem

The case study carried throughout Chapter 8 involves the Reliable Construction Co. and its project to construct a new plant for a major manufacturer. That chapter describes how the project manager (David Perty) made extensive use of PERT/CPM models to help guide his management of the project.

As the opening sentence of Section 8.1 indicates, this case study begins as the company has just made the winning bid of $5.4 million to do this project. We now will back up in time to describe how the company's management used computer simulation with Crystal Ball to guide its choice of $5.4 million as its bid for the project. You will not need to review the case study in Chapter 8 to follow this example.

This section reveals how the company chose the bid of $5.4 million, which won the contract.

Reliable's first step in this process was to estimate what the company's total cost would be if it were to undertake the project. This was determined to be $4.55 million. (This amount excludes the penalty for missing the deadline for completion of the project, as well as the bonus for completion well before the deadline, since management considers either event to be relatively unlikely.) There also is an additional cost of approximately $50,000 for preparing the bid, including estimating the project cost and analyzing the bidding strategies of the competition.

Three other construction companies also were invited to submit bids for this project. All three have been long-standing competitors of the Reliable Construction Co., so the company has had a great deal of experience in observing their bidding strategies. A veteran analyst in the bid preparation office has taken on the task of estimating what bid each of these competitors will submit. Since there is so much uncertainty in this process, the analyst has determined that each of these estimates needs to be in the form of a probability distribution. Competitor 1 is known to use a 30 percent profit margin above the total (direct) cost of a project in setting its bid. However, competitor 1 also is a particularly unpredictable bidder because of an inability to estimate the true costs of a project with much accuracy. Its actual profit margin on past bids has ranged from as low as minus 5 percent to as high as 60 percent. Competitor 2 uses a 25 percent profit margin and is somewhat more accurate than competitor 1 in estimating project costs, but it still has set bids in the past that have missed this profit margin by as much as 15 percent in either direction. On the other hand, competitor 3 is unusually accurate in estimating project costs (as is the Reliable Construction Co.). Competitor 3 also is adept at adjusting its bidding strategy, so it is equally likely to set its profit margin anywhere between 20 and 30 percent, depending on its assessment of the competition, its current backlog of work, and various other factors. Therefore, the estimated probability distributions of the bids that the three competitors will submit, expressed as a percentage of Reliable's assessment of the total project cost, are as follows.

Competitor 1: A triangular distribution with a minimum value of 95 percent, a most likely value of 130 percent, and a maximum value of 160 percent.

Competitor 2: A triangular distribution with a minimum value of 110 percent, a most likely value of 125 percent, and a maximum value of 140 percent.

Competitor 3: A uniform distribution between 120 percent and 130 percent.

A Spreadsheet Model for Applying Computer Simulation

Figure 16.12 shows the spreadsheet model that has been formulated to evaluate any possible bid that Reliable might submit. Since there is uncertainty about what the competitors' bids will be, this model needs CompetitorBids (C8:E8) to be *assumption cells,* so the above probability distributions are entered into these cells. As described in the preceding section, this is done by selecting each cell in turn, entering any number into the cell, choosing Define Assumption from the Cell menu (or clicking on the first button in the Crystal Ball toolbar), and then clicking on the appropriate distribution in the Distribution Gallery, which brings up the dialogue box for that distribution. Figure 16.13 shows the Triangular Distribution dialogue box that has been used to set the parameter values (Min, Likeliest, and Max) for competitor 1, and competitor 2 would be handled similarly. These parameter values for competitor 1 come from cells C18:C20, where the parameters in percentage terms (cells C13:C15) have been converted to dollars by multiplying them by OurProjectCost (C4). The Uniform Distribution dialogue box, such as the one shown in Figure 16.4 in the preceding section, is used instead to set the parameter values for cell E8.

> The bids that other companies will submit are uncertain, so they need to be assumption cells.

MinimumCompetitorBid (C23) records the smallest of the competitors' bids for each trial of the computer simulation. The company wins the bid on a given trial only if the quantity entered into OurBid (C25) is less than the smallest of the competitors' bids. The IF function entered into WinBid? (C27) then returns a 1 if this occurs and a 0 otherwise.

Since management wants to maximize the expected profit from the entire process of determining a bid (if the bid wins) and then doing the project, the forecast cell in this model is Profit (C29). The profit achieved on a given trial depends on whether the company wins the bid. If not, the profit actually is a loss of $50,000 (the bid cost). However, if the bid wins, the profit is the amount by which the bid exceeds the sum of the project cost and the bid cost. The equation entered into Profit (C29) performs this calculation for whichever case applies.

> The objective is to determine the bid that would maximize the resulting expected profit.

Here is a summary of the key cells in this model.

Assumption cells:	CompetitorBids (C8:E8)
Decision variable:	OurBid (C25)
Forecast cell:	Profit (C29)

The Simulation Results

To evaluate a possible bid of $5.4 million entered into OurBid (C25), a computer simulation of this model ran for 500 trials. Figure 16.14 shows the results in the form of a frequency chart and a statistics table, while Figure 16.15 displays the corresponding percentiles table and cumulative chart. Using units of millions of dollars, the profit on each trial has only two possible values, namely, a loss shown as −0.050 in these figures (if the bid loses) or a profit of 0.800 (if the bid wins). The frequency chart indicates that this loss of $50,000 occurred on 181 of the 500 trials whereas the profit of $800,000 occurred on the other 319 trials. This resulted in a mean profit of 0.492 ($492,000) from all 500 trials, as well as the other statistics recorded in

FIGURE 16.12   A spreadsheet model for applying computer simulation to the Reliable Construction Co.'s contract bidding problem. The assumption cells are CompetitorBids (C8:E8), the forecast cell is Profit (C29), and the decision variable is OurBid (C25).

	A	B	C	D	E
1		**Reliable Construction Co. Contract Bidding**			
2					
3		**Data**			
4		Our Project Cost ($million)	4.550		
5		Our Bid Cost ($million)	0.050		
6					
7		**Competitor Bids**	Competitor 1	Competitor 2	Competitor 3
8		Bid ($million)	5.839	5.688	5.688
9					
10		Distribution	*Triangular*	*Triangular*	*Uniform*
11					
12		Competitor Distribution Parameters (Proportion of Our Project Cost)			
13		Minimum	95%	110%	120%
14		Most Likely	130%	125%	
15		Maximum	160%	140%	130%
16					
17		Competitor Distribution Parameters ($million)			
18		Minimum	4.323	5.005	5.460
19		Most Likely	5.915	5.688	
20		Maximum	7.280	6.370	5.915
21					
22		**Minimum Competitor**			
23		**Bid ($million)**	5.688		
24					
25		**Our Bid ($million)**	5.400		
26					
27		**Win Bid?**	1	(1=yes, 0=no)	
28					
29		**Profit ($million)**	0.800		

Range Name	Cells
CompetitorBids	C8:E8
MinimumCompetitorBid	C23
OurBid	C25
OurBidCost	C5
OurProjectCost	C4
Profit	C29
WinBid?	C27

	B	C	D	E
18	Minimum	=OurProjectCost*C13	=OurProjectCost*D13	=OurProjectCost*E13
19	Most Likely	=OurProjectCost*C14	=OurProjectCost*D14	
20	Maximum	=OurProjectCost*C15	=OurProjectCost*D15	=OurProjectCost*E15

	B	C
22	**Minimum Competitor**	
23	**Bid ($million)**	=MIN(C8:E8)
24		
25	**Our Bid ($million)**	5.4
26		
27	**Win Bid?**	=IF(OurBid<MinimumCompetitorBid,1,0)
28		
29	**Profit ($million)**	=WinBid?*(OurBid-OurProjectCost)-OurBidCost

the statistics table. In Figure 16.15, note how the possibility of only two profit values results in only these values appearing in the percentiles table and also results in having a flat cumulative chart until the upper value is reached.

By themselves, these results do not show that $5.4 million is the best bid to submit. We still need to estimate with additional simulation runs whether a larger expected profit could be obtained with another bid value. Section 16.8 will describe how doing this with a decision table leads to choosing $5.4 million as the bid. This turned out to be the winning bid for the Reliable Construction Co., which then led into the case study for Chapter 8.

This story will continue in Section 16.8.

FIGURE 16.13

The Triangular Distribution dialogue box. It is being used here to enter a triangular distribution with the parameters in cells C18:C20 into the assumption cell C8 in the spreadsheet model in Figure 16.12.

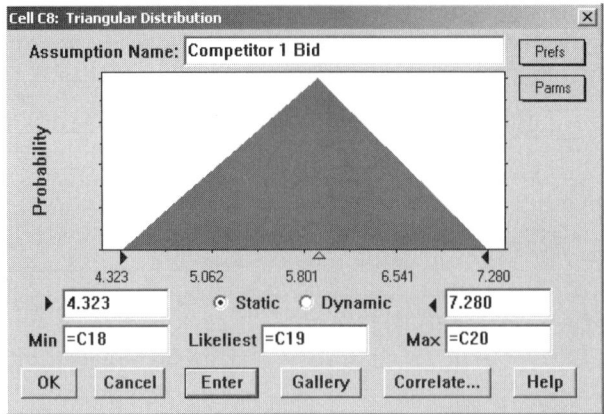

FIGURE 16.14 The frequency chart and statistics table that summarize the results of running the simulation model in Figure 16.12 for the Reliable Construction Co. contract bidding problem.

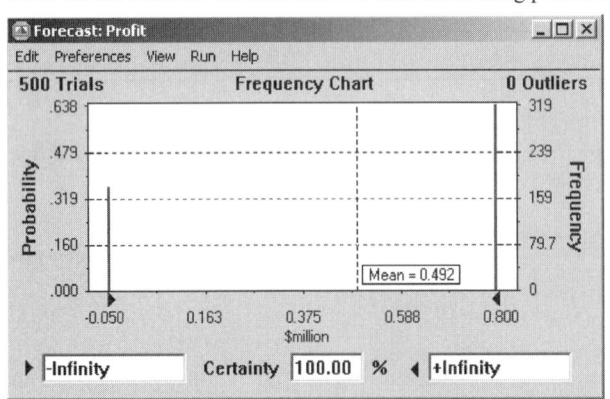
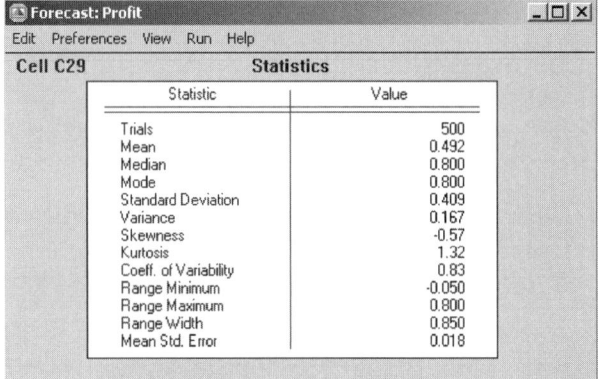

FIGURE 16.15 Further results for the Reliable Construction Co. contract bidding problem.

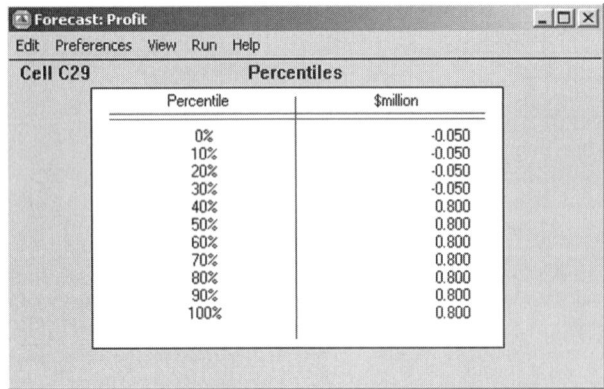
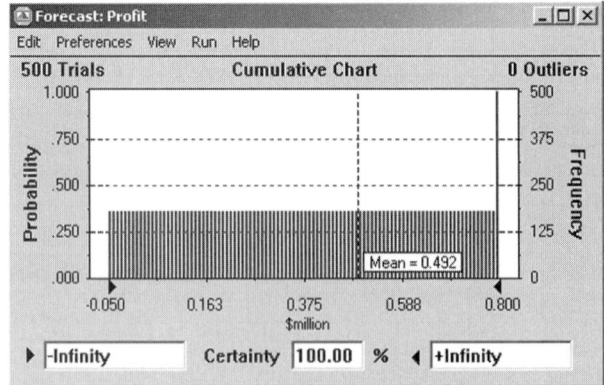

Review Questions

1. What is the project for which the Reliable Construction Co. is submitting a bid?

2. The bids of the competitors are being estimated in what form?

3. What are the quantities in the assumption cells in this example's spreadsheet model for applying computer simulation?

4. What quantity appears in the forecast cell for this spreadsheet model?

5. What are the possible outcomes on each trial of this computer simulation?

16.3   PROJECT MANAGEMENT: REVISITING THE RELIABLE CONSTRUCTION CO. CASE STUDY

Computer simulation improves upon a PERT/CPM method for estimating the probability of completing a project by the deadline.

One of the most important responsibilities of a project manager is to meet the deadline that has been set for the project. Therefore, a skillful project manager will revise the plan for conducting the project as needed to ensure a strong likelihood of meeting the deadline. But how does the project manager estimate the probability of meeting the deadline with any particular plan? Section 8.4 described one method provided by PERT/CPM. We now will illustrate how computer simulation provides a better method.

This example illustrates a common role for computer simulation—refining the results from a preliminary analysis conducted with approximate mathematical models. You also will get a first look at assumption cells where the random inputs are *times*. Another interesting feature of this example is its use of a special kind of Crystal Ball chart called the *sensitivity chart*. This chart will provide a key insight into how the project plan should be revised.

The Problem Being Addressed

Like the example in the preceding section, this one also revolves around the Reliable Construction Co. case study introduced in Section 8.1 and continued throughout Chapter 8. However, rather than preceding the part of the story described in Chapter 8, this example arises in the middle of the case study. In particular, Section 8.4 discussed how a PERT/CPM procedure was used to obtain a rough approximation of the probability of meeting the deadline for the Reliable Construction Co. project. It then was pointed out that computer simulation could be used to obtain a better approximation. We now are in a position to describe how this is done.

Here are the essential facts about the case study that are needed for the current example. The Reliable Construction Company has just made the winning bid to construct a new plant for a major manufacturer. However, the contract includes a large penalty if construction is not completed by the deadline 47 weeks from now. Therefore, a key element in evaluating alternative construction plans is the *probability of meeting this deadline* under each plan. There are 14 major activities involved in carrying out this construction project, as listed on the right-hand side of Figure 16.16 (which repeats Figure 8.1 for your convenience). The project network in this figure depicts the precedence relationships between the activities. Thus, there are six sequences of activities (paths through the network), all of which must be completed to finish the project. These six sequences are listed below.

The deadline for completing the project is 47 weeks from now.

Path 1:	Start → A → B → C → D → G → H → M → Finish
Path 2:	Start → A → B → C → E → H → M → Finish
Path 3:	Start → A → B → C → E → F → J → K → N → Finish
Path 4:	Start → A → B → C → E → F → J → L → N → Finish
Path 5:	Start → A → B → C → I → J → K → N → Finish
Path 6:	Start → A → B → C → I → J → L → N → Finish

The numbers next to the activities in the project network represent the *estimates* of the number of weeks the activities will take if they are carried out in the normal manner with the usual crew sizes, and so forth. Adding these times over each of the paths (as was done in Table 8.2) reveals that path 4 is the *longest path,* requiring a total of 44 weeks. Since the project is finished as soon as its longest path is completed, this indicates that the project can be completed in 44 weeks, 3 weeks before the deadline.

Now we come to the crux of the problem. The times for the activities in Figure 16.16 are only estimates, and there actually is considerable uncertainty about what the duration of each activity will be. Therefore, the duration of the entire project could well differ substantially from the estimate of 44 weeks, so there is a distinct possibility of missing the deadline of 47 weeks. What is the *probability* of missing this deadline? To estimate this probability, we need to learn more about the probability distribution of the duration of the project.

FIGURE 16.16

The project network for the Reliable Construction Co. project.

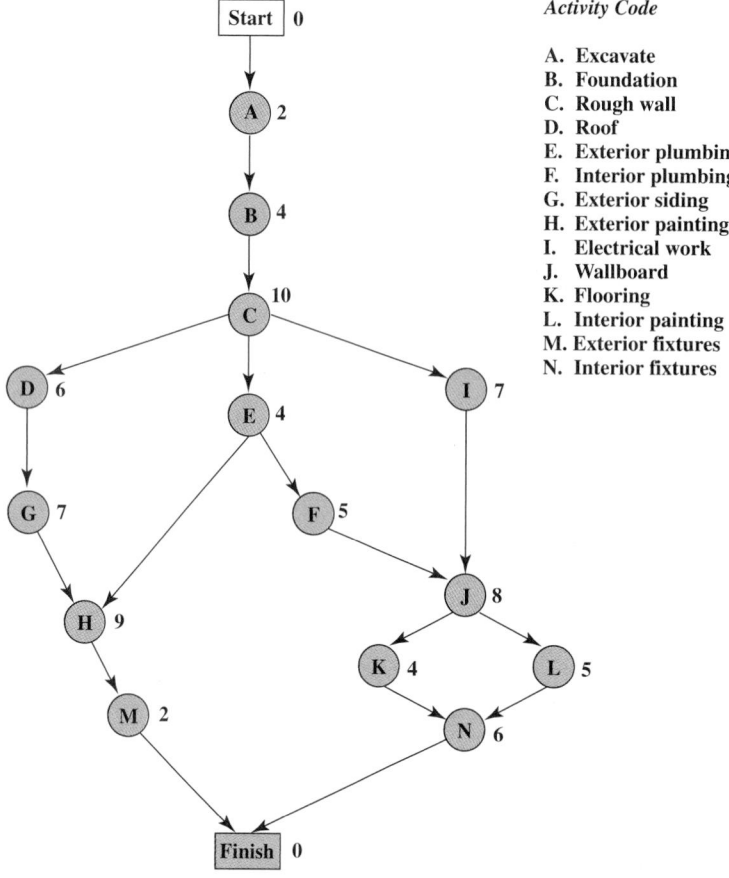

Activity Code

A. **Excavate**
B. **Foundation**
C. **Rough wall**
D. **Roof**
E. **Exterior plumbing**
F. **Interior plumbing**
G. **Exterior siding**
H. **Exterior painting**
I. **Electrical work**
J. **Wallboard**
K. **Flooring**
L. **Interior painting**
M. **Exterior fixtures**
N. **Interior fixtures**

FIGURE 16.17

The shape of a triangular distribution for the duration of an activity, where the minimum lies at the optimistic estimate *o*, the most likely value lies at the most likely estimate *m*, and the maximum lies at the pessimistic estimate *p*.

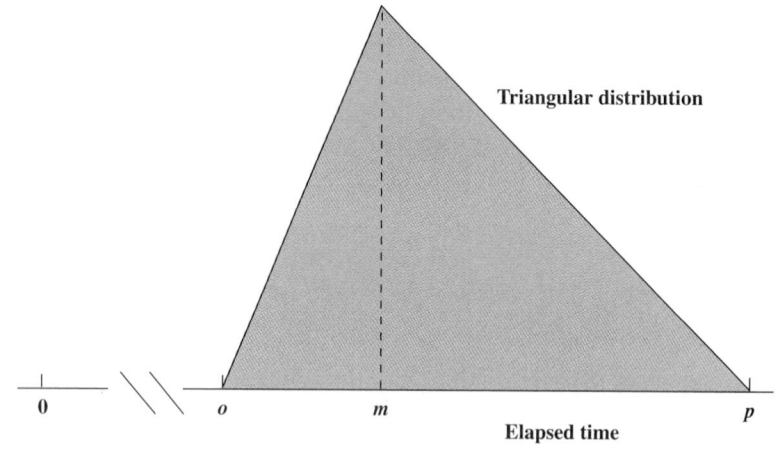

Triangular distribution

0   *o*   *m*   *p*

Elapsed time

This is the reason for the PERT three-estimate approach described in Section 8.4. This approach involves obtaining three estimates—a *most likely estimate,* an *optimistic estimate,* and a *pessimistic estimate*—of the duration of each activity. (Table 8.4 lists these estimates for all 14 activities for the project under consideration.) These three quantities are intended to estimate the most likely duration, the minimum duration, and the maximum duration, respectively. Using these three quantities, PERT assumes (somewhat arbitrarily) that the form of the probability distribution of the duration of an activity is a *beta distribution.* By also making three simplifying approximations (described in Section 8.4), this leads to an analytical method for roughly approximating the probability of meeting the project deadline.

Computer simulation has two key advantages over analytical methods like PERT/CPM.

One key advantage of computer simulation is that it does not need to make most of the simplifying approximations that may be required by analytical methods. Another is that there is great flexibility about which probability distributions to use. It is not necessary to choose an analytically convenient one.

When dealing with the duration of an activity, computer simulations commonly use a *triangular distribution* as the distribution of this duration. A triangular distribution for the duration of an activity has the shape shown in Figure 16.17, where *o, m,* and *p* are the labels for the optimistic estimate, the most likely estimate, and the pessimistic estimate, respectively. For each *assumption cell* containing this distribution, a Triangular Distribution dialogue box (such as the one shown in Figure 16.13) is used to enter the values of *o, m,* and *p* by entering their respective cell references into the Min, Likeliest, and Max boxes.

A Spreadsheet Model for Applying Computer Simulation

Figure 16.18 shows a spreadsheet model for simulating the duration of the Reliable Construction Co. project. The values of *o, m,* and *p* in columns D, E, and F are obtained directly from

FIGURE 16.18

A spreadsheet model for applying computer simulation to the Reliable Construction Co. project scheduling problem. The assumption cells are cells H6:H15 and H17:H19. The forecast cell is ProjectCompletion (I21).

	A	B	C	D	E	F	G	H	I
1		**Simulation of Reliable Construction Co. Project**							
2									
3								Activity	
4			Immediate	Time Estimates			Start	Time	Finish
5		Activity	Predecessor	*o*	*m*	*p*	Time	*(triangular)*	Time
6		A	—	1	2	3	0	2	2
7		B	A	2	3.5	8	2	4.5	6.5
8		C	B	6	9	18	6.5	11	17.5
9		D	C	4	5.5	10	17.5	6.5	24
10		E	C	1	4.5	5	17.5	3.5	21
11		F	E	4	4	10	21	6	27
12		G	D	5	6.5	11	24	7.5	31.5
13		H	E, G	5	8	17	31.5	10	41.5
14		I	C	3	7.5	9	17.5	6.5	24
15		J	F, I	3	9	9	27	7	34
16		K	J	4	4	4	34	4	38
17		L	J	1	5.5	7	34	4.5	38.5
18		M	H	1	2	3	41.5	2	43.5
19		N	K, L	5	5.5	9	38.5	6.5	45
20									
21								Project Completion	45

	G	H	I
3		Activity	
4	Start	Time	Finish
5	Time	*(triangular)*	Time
6	0	2	=AStart+ATime
7	=AFinish	4.5	=BStart+BTime
8	=BFinish	11	=CStart+CTime
9	=CFinish	6.5	=DStart+DTime
10	=CFinish	3.5	=EStart+ETime
11	=EFinish	6	=FStart+FTime
12	=DFinish	7.5	=GStart+GTime
13	=MAX(EFinish,GFinish)	10	=HStart+HTime
14	=CFinish	6.5	=IStart+ITime
15	=MAX(FFinish,IFinish)	7	=JStart+JTime
16	=JFinish	4	=KStart+KTime
17	=JFinish	4.5	=LStart+LTime
18	=HFinish	2	=MStart+MTime
19	=MAX(KFinish,LFinish)	6.5	=NStart+NTime
20			
21		Project Completion	=MAX(MFinish,NFinish)

Range Name	Cell
AFinish	I6
AStart	G6
ATime	H6
BFinish	I7
BStart	G7
BTime	H7
CFinish	I8
CStart	G8
CTime	H8
DFinish	I9
DStart	G9
DTime	H9
EFinish	I10
EStart	G10
ETime	H10
FFinish	I11
FStart	G11
FTime	H11
GFinish	I12
GStart	G12
GTime	H12
HFinish	I13
HStart	G13
HTime	H13
IFinish	I14
IStart	G14
ITime	H14
JFinish	I15
JStart	G15
JTime	H15
KFinish	I16
KStart	G16
KTime	H16
LFinish	I17
LStart	G17
LTime	H17
MFinish	I18
MStart	G18
MTime	H18
NFinish	I19
NStart	G19
NTime	H19
ProjectCompletion	I21

FIGURE 16.19

A triangular distribution with parameters D6:F6 is being entered into the first assumption cell H6 in the spreadsheet model in Figure 16.18.

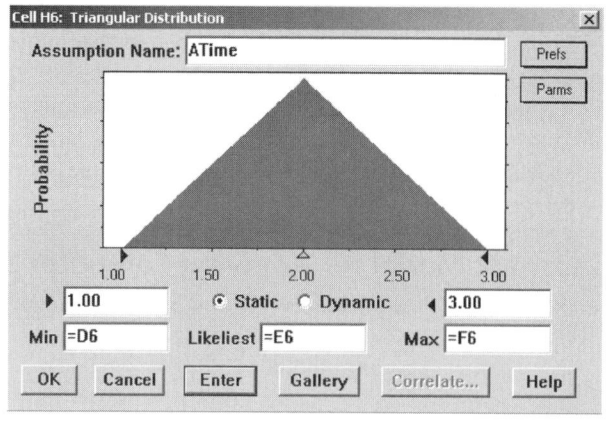

Variable activity times need to be assumption cells.

Table 8.4. The equations entered into the cells in columns G and I give the start times and finish times for the respective activities. For each trial of the simulation, the maximum of the finish times for the last two activities (M and N) gives the duration of the project (in weeks), which goes into the forecast cell ProjectCompletion (I21).

Since the activity times generally are variable, the cells H6:H19 all need to be *assumption cells* with the one exception of cell H16. Since $o = m = p = 4$ for activity K, its activity time actually is a constant 4, so this constant is entered into cell H16. (Crystal Ball would give an error message if cell H16 were specified to be an assumption cell with a triangular distribution where Min = Likeliest = Max.) Figure 16.19 shows the Triangular Distribution dialogue box after it has been used to specify the parameters for the first assumption cell H6. Rather than repeating this process for all the other assumption cells, it is quicker to simply copy and paste the parameters for the other assumption cells. This is begun by selecting cell H6 and clicking on the Copy Data button in the Crystal Ball toolbar (the seventh button from the left) or choosing Copy Data from the Cell menu. Then select the cells in which to paste the data (H7:H15 and H17:H19) and choose Paste Data (either by clicking this button on the Crystal Ball toolbar or by choosing this item from the Cell menu). Since the cell references in Figure 16.19 are relative references (no $ signs), the row numbers will update appropriately to refer to the data cells in the correct row during this copy-and-paste process. For example, the cell references for the parameters of the triangular distribution in cell H7 will update to = D7, = E7, and = F7.

Here is a summary of the key cells in this model.

Assumption cells: Cells H6:H15 and H17:H19

Forecast cell: ProjectCompletion (I21)

The Simulation Results

We now are ready to undertake a computer simulation of the spreadsheet model in Figure 16.18. Using the Run Preferences dialogue box to specify 1,000 trials, Figure 16.20 shows the results in the form of a frequency chart, a statistics table, and a percentiles table. These results show a very wide range of possible project durations. Out of the 1,000 trials, both the statistics table and percentiles table indicate that one trial had a duration as short as 35.38 weeks while another was as long as 58.09 weeks. The frequency chart indicates that the duration that occurred most frequently during the 1,000 trials is close to 47 weeks (the project deadline), but that many other durations up to a few weeks either shorter or longer than this also occurred with considerable frequency. The mean is 46.11 weeks, which is much too close to the deadline of 47 weeks to leave much margin for slippage in the project schedule. (The small mean standard error of 0.12 weeks reported at the bottom of the statistics table shows that the sample average of 46.11 weeks from the 1,000 trials probably is extremely close to the true mean of the underlying probability distribution of project duration.) The 70 percent percentile of 48.00 weeks in the percentiles table reveals that 30 percent of the trials missed the deadline by at least a week.

FIGURE 16.20 The frequency chart, statistics table, and percentiles table that summarize the results of running the simulation model in Figure 16.18 for the Reliable Construction Co. project scheduling problem.

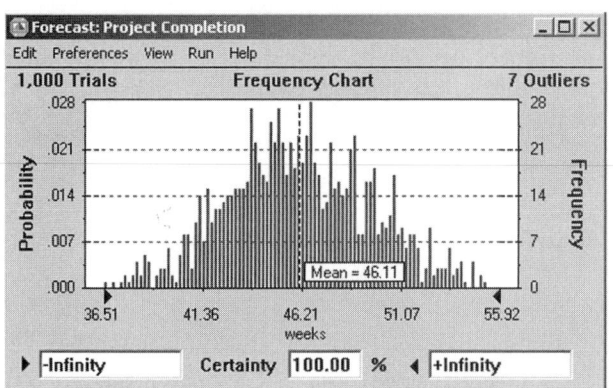

Forecast: Project Completion		
Cell I21	Statistics	
Statistic	Value	
Trials	1,000	
Mean	46.11	
Median	45.94	
Mode	...	
Standard Deviation	3.64	
Variance	13.24	
Skewness	0.11	
Kurtosis	2.96	
Coeff. of Variability	0.08	
Range Minimum	35.38	
Range Maximum	58.09	
Range Width	22.72	
Mean Std. Error	0.12	

Forecast: Project Completion

Cell I21 — Percentiles

Percentile	weeks
0%	35.38
10%	41.58
20%	43.09
30%	44.09
40%	45.07
50%	45.94
60%	46.82
70%	48.00
80%	49.32
90%	50.81
100%	58.09

A statistic of special interest to Reliable's management is the probability of meeting the deadline of 47 weeks under the current project plan. (Remember that the contract includes a severe penalty of $300,000 for missing this deadline.) The 60 percent percentile of 46.82 weeks in the percentiles table suggests that slightly over 60 percent of the trials made the deadline, but nothing else in Figure 16.20 pins down this percentage any closer. Figure 16.21 shows that all you need to do to identify the exact percentage is to type the deadline of 47.00 in the box in the lower right-hand corner of either the frequency chart or the cumulative chart. The Certainty box then reveals that exactly 61.50 percent of the trials (so 615 of the 1,000 trials) met the deadline.

If the simulation run were to be repeated with another 1,000 trials, this percentage probably would change a little. However, with such a large number of trials, the difference in the percentages should be slight. Therefore, the probability of 0.615 provided by the Certainty boxes in Figure 16.21 is a close estimate of the true probability of meeting the deadline under the assumptions of the spreadsheet model in Figure 16.18. Note how much smaller this relatively precise estimate is than the rough estimate of 0.84 obtained by the PERT three-estimate approach in Section 8.4. Thus, the simulation estimate provides much better guidance to management in deciding whether the project plan should be changed to improve the chances of meeting the deadline. This illustrates how useful computer simulation can be in refining the results obtained by approximate analytical results.

Computer simulation provides a close estimate of the probability of meeting the project deadline (0.615) that is much smaller than the rough PERT/CPM estimate (0.84).

A Key Insight Provided by the Sensitivity Chart

Given such a low probability (0.615) of meeting the project deadline, Reliable's project manager (David Perty) will want to revise the project plan to improve the probability substantially. Crystal Ball has another tool, called the *sensitivity chart,* that provides strong guidance in identifying which revisions in the project plan would be most beneficial. To generate a sensitivity chart, the "Calculate Sensitivity" option must have been selected in the Options tab of the Run

FIGURE 16.21 After entering the project deadline of 47 weeks into the box in the lower right-hand corner, the Certainty box for both of these charts reveals that 61.50 percent of the trials resulted in the project being completed by the deadline.

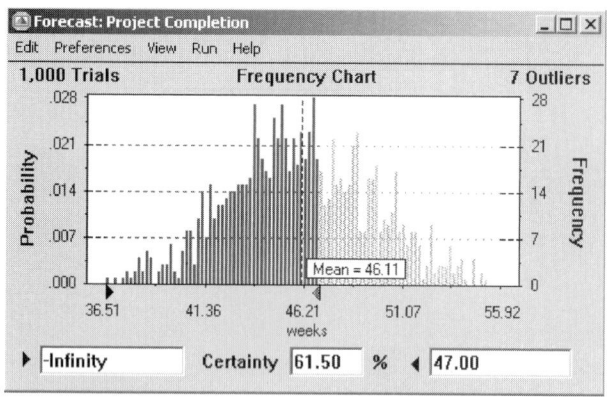
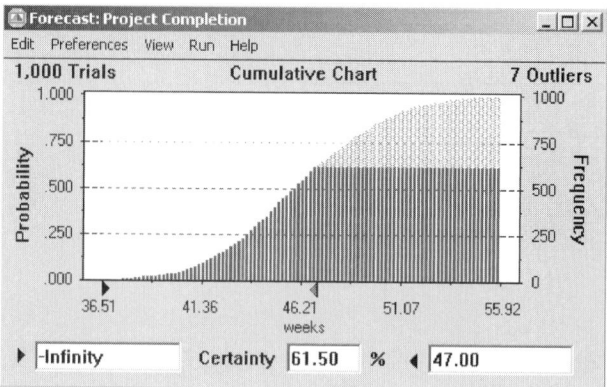

FIGURE 16.22

After selecting the Options tab, the Run Preferences dialogue box is used here to select the Calculate Sensitivity option in preparation for generating a sensitivity chart.

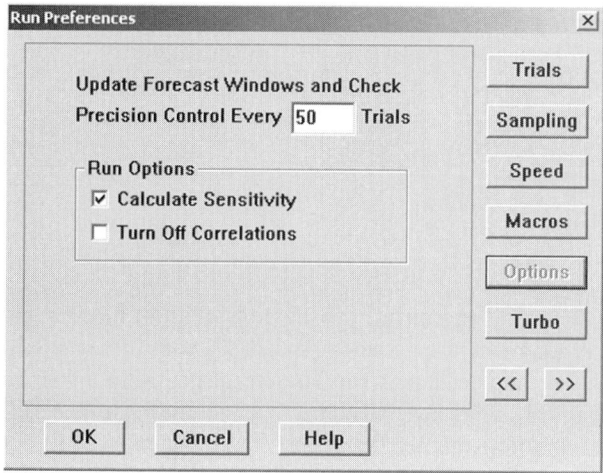

FIGURE 16.23 This sensitivity chart shows how strongly various activity times in the Reliable Construction Co. project are influencing the project completion time.

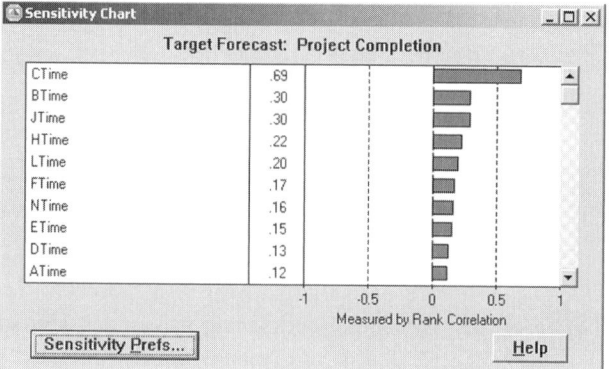

Preferences dialogue box, as shown in Figure 16.22, *before* running the simulation. (The number 50 in the upper box is a default value that is unrelated to the sensitivity chart.) Figure 16.23 displays the resulting sensitivity chart that is opened by clicking on the Sensitivity Chart button in the Crystal Ball toolbar (or by choosing Open Sensitivity Chart from the Run menu). Using range names, the first column identifies various assumption cells (activity times) in column H of the spreadsheet model in Figure 16.18. The other key cell in the spreadsheet model that is considered in this sensitivity chart (as indicated at the top of the chart) is the forecast cell ProjectCompletion (I21) that gives the duration of the project. For each assumption cell listed in the first column of the sensitivity chart, the corresponding entry in the second column gives the correlation coefficient (based on rank values) between this assumption cell and the forecast cell. The right side then graphs these same correlation coefficients in block form. The ten rows in Figure 16.23 are listed in descending order of the correlation coefficients.

A correlation coefficient between two variables measures the strength of the relationship between those variables. Thus, each correlation coefficient in Figure 16.23 measures how strongly that activity time is influencing the project completion time. The higher the correlation coefficient, the stronger is this influence. Therefore, the activities with the highest correlation coefficients are those where the greatest effort should be made to reduce their activity times.

Figure 16.23 indicates that CTime has a far higher correlation coefficient than the times for any of the other activities. An examination of Figures 16.16 and 16.18 suggests why. Figure 16.16 shows that activity C precedes *all* the other activities except activities A and B, so any delay in completing activity C would delay the start time for all these other activities. Furthermore, cells D8:F8 in Figure 16.18 indicate that CTime is highly variable, with an unusually large spread of 9 weeks between its most likely estimate and its pessimistic estimate, so long delays beyond the most likely estimate may well occur.

The sensitivity chart reveals that reducing the time for activity C would most improve the chances of completing the project before the deadline.

This very high correlation coefficient for CTime suggests that the best way to reduce the project completion time is to focus on reducing this activity time (and its variability). This can be accomplished by revising the project plan to assign activity C more personnel, better equipment, stronger supervision, and so forth. Crystal Ball's sensitivity chart clearly highlights this insight into where the project plan needs to be revised.

Review
Questions

1. What is the project that is being considered in this section's example?

2. A PERT/CPM procedure can obtain only a rough approximation of a certain key quantity, so computer simulation is used to obtain a much closer estimate of the quantity. What is this quantity?

3. Computer simulations commonly use which kind of probability distribution as the distribution of the duration of an activity?

4. What are the three estimates provided by the PERT three-estimate approach that give the parameters of this distribution of the duration of an activity?

5. What can be done to quickly enter these parameters into all the assumption cells after using the dialogue box for the distribution of the duration of only the first activity?

6. What quantity appears in the forecast cell of the spreadsheet model for this example?

7. What needs to be done to identify the exact percentage of trials of a computer simulation of this spreadsheet model that will result in meeting the project completion deadline?

8. What kind of chart is used to highlight where a project plan needs to be revised to best improve the chances of meeting the project deadline?

16.4   CASH FLOW MANAGEMENT: REVISITING THE EVERGLADE GOLDEN YEARS COMPANY CASE STUDY

Many applications of computer simulation involve scenarios that evolve far into the future. Since nobody can predict the future with certainty, computer simulation is needed to take future uncertainties into account. For example, businesses typically have great uncertainty about what their future cash flows will be. An attempt often is made to predict these future cash flows as a first step toward making decisions about what should be done (e.g., arranging for loans) to meet cash flow needs. However, effective cash management requires going a step further to consider the effect of the uncertainty in the future cash flows. This is where computer simulation comes in, with assumption cells being used for the cash flows in various future periods. This process is illustrated by the following example.

The Everglade Cash Flow Management Problem

The case study analyzed in Chapter 3 involves the Everglade Golden Years Company (which operates upscale retirement communities) and its efforts to manage its cash flow problems. In particular, because of both a temporary decline in business and some current or future construction costs, the company is facing some negative cash flows in the next few years as well as in some more distant years. As first provided in Table 3.1, Table 16.1 shows the projected net cash flows over the next 10 years (2003 to 2012). The company has some new retirement communities opening within the 10 years, so it is anticipated (or at least hoped) that a large positive cash flow will occur in 2012. Therefore, the problem confronting Everglade management is how to best arrange Everglade's financing to tide the company over until its investments in new retirement communities can start to pay off.

TABLE 16.1
Projected Net Cash Flows for the Everglade Golden Years Company over the Next Ten Years

Year	Projected Net Cash Flow (millions of dollars)
2003	−8
2004	−2
2005	−4
2006	3
2007	6
2008	3
2009	−4
2010	7
2011	−2
2012	10

Chapter 3 describes how a decision was made to combine taking a long-term (10-year) loan now (the beginning of 2003) and a series of short-term (1-year) loans as needed to maintain a positive cash balance of at least $500,000 (as dictated by company policy) throughout the 10 years. Assuming no deviation from the projected cash flows shown in Table 16.1, linear programming was used to optimize the size of both the long-term loan and the short-term loans so as to maximize the company's cash balance at the beginning of 2013 when all of the loans have been paid off. Figure 3.5 in Chapter 3 shows the complete spreadsheet model after using the Excel Solver to obtain the optimal solution. For your convenience, Figure 3.5 is repeated here as Figure 16.24. The changing cells, LTLoan (D11) and STLoan (E11:E20), give the sizes of the long-term loan and the short-term loans at the beginning of the various years. The target cell EndBalance (J21) indicates that the resulting cash balance at the end of the 10 years (the beginning of 2013) would be $2.92 million. Since this is the cell that is being maximized, any other plan for the sizes of the loans would result in a smaller cash balance at the end of the 10 years.

The drawback of the linear programming solution in Figure 16.24 is that it does not assess the effect of the great uncertainty regarding future cash flows, so computer simulation is needed to do this.

Obtaining the "optimal" financing plan presented in Figure 16.24 is an excellent first step in developing a final plan. However, the drawback of the spreadsheet model in Figure 16.24 is that it makes no allowance for the inevitable deviations from the projected cash flows shown in Table 16.1. The actual cash flow for the first year (2003) probably will turn out to be quite close to the projection. However, it is difficult to predict the cash flows in even the second and third years with much accuracy, let alone up to 10 years into the future. Computer simulation is needed to assess the effect of these uncertainties.

A Spreadsheet Model for Applying Computer Simulation

Figure 16.25 shows the modification of the spreadsheet model in Figure 16.24 that is needed to apply computer simulation. One key difference is that the constants in CashFlow (C11:C20) in Figure 16.24 have turned into random inputs in CashFlow (F12:F21) in Figure 16.25. Thus, the latter cells, CashFlow (F12:F21), are *assumption cells.* (The numbers appearing in these cells have been entered arbitrarily as a first step in defining these assumption cells.) As indicated in cells D9:E9, the assumption has been made that each of the cash flows has a triangular distribution. Estimates have been made of the three parameters of this distribution (minimum, most likely, and maximum) for each of the years, as presented in cells C12:E21.

The uncertain future cash flows need to be assumption cells.

The number 6.65 entered into LTLoan (G12) is the size of the long-term loan (in millions of dollars) that was obtained in Figure 16.24. However, because of the variability in the cash flows, it no longer makes sense to lock in the sizes of the short-term loans that were obtained in STLoan (E11:E20) in Figure 16.24. It is better to be flexible and adjust these sizes based on the actual cash flows that occur in the preceding years. If the balance at the beginning of a year (as calculated in BalanceBeforeSTLoan [L12:L22]) already exceeds the required minimum balance of $0.50 million, then there is no need to take any short-term loan at that point. However, if the balance is not this large, then a sufficiently large short-term loan should be taken to bring the balance up to $0.50 million. This is what is done by the equations entered into STLoan (M12:M22) that are shown at the bottom of Figure 16.25.

FIGURE 16.24 The spreadsheet model that used linear programming in Chapter 3 (Figure 3.5) to analyze the Everglade Golden Years Company cash flow management problem without taking the uncertainty in future cash flows into account.

	A	B	C	D	E	F	G	H	I	J	K	L
1	**Everglade Cash Flow Management Problem When Applying Linear Programming**											
2												
3		LT Rate	7%									
4		ST Rate	10%									
5												
6		Start Balance	1			(all cash figures in millions of dollars)						
7		Minimum Cash	0.5									
8												
9			Cash	LT	ST	LT	ST	LT	ST	Ending		Minimum
10		Year	Flow	Loan	Loan	Interest	Interest	Payback	Payback	Balance		Balance
11		2003	-8	6.65	0.85					0.50	≥	0.5
12		2004	-2		3.40	-0.47	-0.09		-0.85	0.50	≥	0.5
13		2005	-4		8.21	-0.47	-0.34		-3.40	0.50	≥	0.5
14		2006	3		6.49	-0.47	-0.82		-8.21	0.50	≥	0.5
15		2007	6		1.61	-0.47	-0.65		-6.49	0.50	≥	0.5
16		2008	3		0	-0.47	-0.16		-1.61	1.27	≥	0.5
17		2009	-4		3.70	-0.47	0		0	0.50	≥	0.5
18		2010	7		0	-0.47	-0.37		-3.70	2.97	≥	0.5
19		2011	-2		0	-0.47	0		0	0.50	≥	0.5
20		2012	10		0	-0.47	0		0	10.03	≥	0.5
21		2013				-0.47	0	-6.65	0	2.92	≥	0.5

Range Name	Cells
CashFlow	C11:C20
EndBalance	J21
EndingBalance	J11:J21
LTLoan	D11
LTRate	C3
MinimumBalance	L11:L21
MinimumCash	C7
StartBalance	C6
STLoan	E11:E20
STRate	C4

Solver Parameters

Set Target Cell: EndBalance

Equal To: (•) Max ( ) Min ( )

By Changing Cells:

LTLoan,STLoan

Subject to the Constraints:

EndingBalance >= MinimumBalance

Solver Options

☑ Assume Linear Model

☑ Assume Non-Negative

	F	G	H	I	J	K	L
9	LT	ST	LT	ST	Ending		Minimum
10	Interest	Interest	Payback	Payback	Balance		Balance
11					=StartBalance+SUM(C11:I11)	≥	=MinimumCash
12	=–LTRate*LTLoan	=–STRate*E11		=–E11	=J11+SUM(C12:I12)	≥	=MinimumCash
13	=–LTRate*LTLoan	=–STRate*E12		=–E12	=J12+SUM(C13:I13)	≥	=MinimumCash
14	=–LTRate*LTLoan	=–STRate*E13		=–E13	=J13+SUM(C14:I14)	≥	=MinimumCash
15	=–LTRate*LTLoan	=–STRate*E14		=–E14	=J14+SUM(C15:I15)	≥	=MinimumCash
16	=–LTRate*LTLoan	=–STRate*E15		=–E15	=J15+SUM(C16:I16)	≥	=MinimumCash
17	=–LTRate*LTLoan	=–STRate*E16		=–E16	=J16+SUM(C17:I17)	≥	=MinimumCash
18	=–LTRate*LTLoan	=–STRate*E17		=–E17	=J17+SUM(C18:I18)	≥	=MinimumCash
19	=–LTRate*LTLoan	=–STRate*E18		=–E18	=J18+SUM(C19:I19)	≥	=MinimumCash
20	=–LTRate*LTLoan	=–STRate*E19		=–E19	=J19+SUM(C20:I20)	≥	=MinimumCash
21	=-LTRate*LTLoan	=–STRate*E20	=–LTLoan	=–E20	=J20+SUM(C21:I21)	≥	=MinimumCash

FIGURE 16.25 A spreadsheet model for applying computer simulation to the Everglade Golden Years Company cash flow management problem. The assumption cells are CashFlow (F12:F21) and the forecast cell is EndBalance (N22).

Everglade Cash Flow Management Problem When Applying Simulation

	Value
LT Rate	7%
ST Rate	10%
Start Balance	1
Minimum Cash	0.5

(all cash figures in millions of dollars)

Year	Cash Flow (Triangular Distribution) Minimum	Most Likely	Maximum	Simulated Cash Flow	LT Loan	LT Interest	ST Interest	LT Payback	ST Payback	Balance Before ST Loan	ST Loan	Ending Balance		Minimum Balance
2003	-9	-8	-7	-8.00	6.65		-0.09		-0.85	-0.35	0.85	0.50	≥	0.50
2004	-4	-2	1	-1.67		-0.47	-0.31		-3.07	-2.57	3.07	0.50	≥	0.50
2005	-7	-4	0	-3.67		-0.47	-0.75		-7.51	-7.01	7.51	0.50	≥	0.50
2006	0	3	7	1.33		-0.47	-0.54		-5.39	-4.89	5.39	0.50	≥	0.50
2007	3	6	9	6.00		-0.47	-0.04		-0.39	0.11	0.39	0.50	≥	0.50
2008	1	3	5	3.00		-0.47	0		0	2.60	0.00	2.60	≥	0.50
2009	-6	-4	-2	-4.00		-0.47	-0.24		-2.36	-1.86	2.36	0.50	≥	0.50
2010	4	7	12	7.67		-0.47	0		0	5.10	0.00	5.10	≥	0.50
2011	-5	-2	4	-1.00		-0.47	0		0	3.64	0.00	3.64	≥	0.50
2012	5	10	18	11.00		-0.47	0		0	14.17	0.00	14.17	≥	0.50
2013						-0.47	0	-6.65	0	7.05		7.05	≥	0.50

Range Names

Range Name	Cells
BalanceBeforeSTLoan	L12:L22
CashFlow	F12:F21
EndBalance	N22
EndingBalance	N12:N22
LTLoan	G12
LTRate	C3
MinimumBalance	P12:P22
MinimumCash	C7
StartBalance	C6
STLoan	M12:M22
STRate	C4

Formulas (columns H–K)

	LT Interest	ST Interest	LT Payback	ST Payback
12		=-STRate*M12		=-M12
13	=-LTRate*LTLoan	=-STRate*M13		=-M13
14	=-LTRate*LTLoan	=-STRate*M14		=-M14
15	=-LTRate*LTLoan	=-STRate*M15		=-M15
16	=-LTRate*LTLoan	=-STRate*M16		=-M16
17	=-LTRate*LTLoan	=-STRate*M17		=-M17
18	=-LTRate*LTLoan	=-STRate*M18		=-M18
19	=-LTRate*LTLoan	=-STRate*M19		=-M19
20	=-LTRate*LTLoan	=-STRate*M20		=-M20
21	=-LTRate*LTLoan	=-STRate*M21		=-M21
22	=-LTRate*LTLoan	=-STRate*M21	=-LTLoan	=-M21

Formulas (columns L–P)

	Before ST Loan	ST Loan	Ending Balance		Minimum Balance
12	=StartBalance+SUM(F12:K12)	=MAX(MinimumBalance-BalanceBeforeSTLoan,0)	=BalanceBeforeSTLoan+STLoan	≥	=MinimumCash
13	=N12+SUM(F13:K13)	=MAX(MinimumBalance-BalanceBeforeSTLoan,0)	=BalanceBeforeSTLoan+STLoan	≥	=MinimumCash
14	=N13+SUM(F14:K14)	=MAX(MinimumBalance-BalanceBeforeSTLoan,0)	=BalanceBeforeSTLoan+STLoan	≥	=MinimumCash
15	=N14+SUM(F15:K15)	=MAX(MinimumBalance-BalanceBeforeSTLoan,0)	=BalanceBeforeSTLoan+STLoan	≥	=MinimumCash
16	=N15+SUM(F16:K16)	=MAX(MinimumBalance-BalanceBeforeSTLoan,0)	=BalanceBeforeSTLoan+STLoan	≥	=MinimumCash
17	=N16+SUM(F17:K17)	=MAX(MinimumBalance-BalanceBeforeSTLoan,0)	=BalanceBeforeSTLoan+STLoan	≥	=MinimumCash
18	=N17+SUM(F18:K18)	=MAX(MinimumBalance-BalanceBeforeSTLoan,0)	=BalanceBeforeSTLoan+STLoan	≥	=MinimumCash
19	=N18+SUM(F19:K19)	=MAX(MinimumBalance-BalanceBeforeSTLoan,0)	=BalanceBeforeSTLoan+STLoan	≥	=MinimumCash
20	=N19+SUM(F20:K20)	=MAX(MinimumBalance-BalanceBeforeSTLoan,0)	=BalanceBeforeSTLoan+STLoan	≥	=MinimumCash
21	=N20+SUM(F21:K21)	=MAX(MinimumBalance-BalanceBeforeSTLoan,0)	=BalanceBeforeSTLoan+STLoan	≥	=MinimumCash
22	=N21+SUM(F22:K22)	=MAX(MinimumBalance-BalanceBeforeSTLoan,0)	=BalanceBeforeSTLoan+STLoan	≥	=MinimumCash

The target cell EndBalance (J21) in Figure 16.24 becomes the forecast cell EndBalance (N22) in Figure 16.25. On any trial of the computer simulation, if the simulated cash flows in CashFlow (F12:F21) in Figure 16.25 are more favorable than the projected cash flows given in Table 16.1 (as is the case for the current numbers in Figure 16.25), then EndBalance (N22) in Figure 16.25 would be larger than EndBalance (J21) in Figure 16.24. However, if the simulated cash flows are less favorable than the projections, then EndBalance (N22) in Figure 16.25 might even be a negative number. For example, if all the simulated cash flows are close to the corresponding minimum values given in cells C12:C21, then the required short-term loans will become so large that paying off the last one at the beginning of 2013 (along with paying off the long-term loan then) will result in a very large negative number in EndBalance (N22). This would spell serious trouble for the company. Computer simulation will reveal the relative likelihood of this occurring versus a favorable outcome.

A key question is the likelihood of achieving a positive cash balance at the end of the 10 years.

Here is a summary of the key cells in this model.

> **Assumption cells:** CashFlow (F12:F21)
>
> **Forecast cell:** EndBalance (N22)

The Simulation Results

Figure 16.26 shows the results from applying computer simulation with 500 trials. Because Everglade management is particularly interested in learning how likely it is that the current financing plan would result in a positive cash balance at the end of the 10 years, the number 0 has been entered into the lower left-hand box in the frequency chart. The Certainty box in the lower middle box then indicates that 88 percent of the trials resulted in a positive cash balance at the end. Furthermore, both the frequency chart and the cumulative chart show that many of these positive cash balances are reasonably large, with some exceeding $10 million. The overall mean is $6.70 million.

The Certainty box in the frequency chart reveals that 88 percent of the trials resulted in a positive cash balance at the end of the 10 years.

On the other hand, it is worrisome that 12 percent of the trials resulted in a negative cash balance at the end. Although huge losses were rare, most of these negative cash balances were quite significant, ranging from $1 million to $3 million.

Conclusions

Everglade management is pleased that the simulation results indicate that the proposed financing plan is likely to lead to a favorable outcome at the end of the 10 years. At the same time, management feels that it would be prudent to take steps to reduce the 12 percent chance of an unfavorable outcome.

One possibility would be to increase the size of the long-term loan, since this would reduce the sizes of the higher interest short-term loans that would be needed in the later years if the cash flows are not as good as currently projected. This possibility is investigated in Problem 16.19.

FIGURE 16.26   The frequency chart and cumulative chart that summarize the results of running the simulation model in Figure 16.25 for the Everglade Golden Years cash flow management problem.

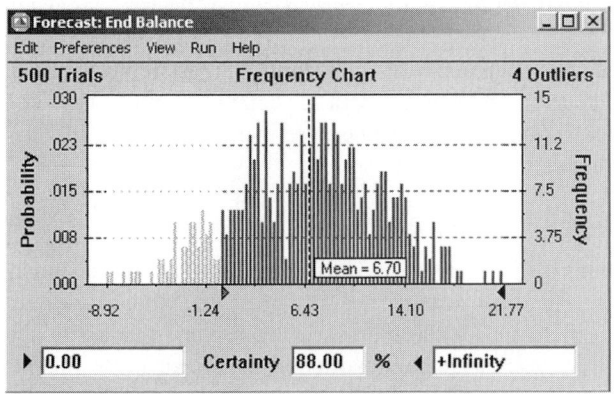
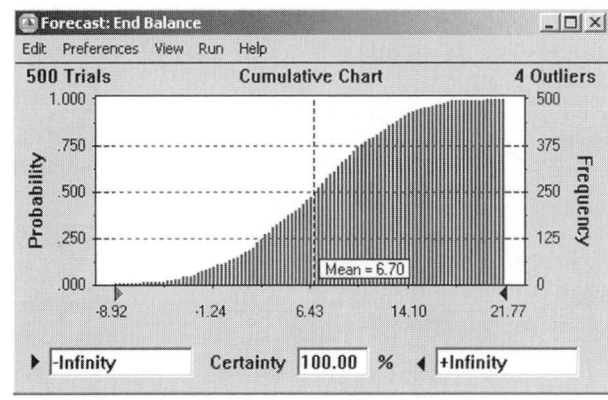

The scenarios that would lead to a negative cash balance at the end of the 10 years are those where the company's retirement communities fail to achieve full occupancy because of over-estimating the demand for this service. Therefore, Everglade management concludes that it should take a more cautious approach in moving forward with its current plans to build more retirement communities over the next 10 years. In each case, the final decisions regarding the start date for construction and the size of the retirement community should be made only after obtaining and carefully assessing a detailed forecast of the trends in the demand for this service.

After adopting this policy, Everglade management approves the financing plan that is incorporated into the spreadsheet model in Figure 16.25. In particular, a 10-year loan of $6.65 million will be taken now (the beginning of 2003). In addition, a one-year loan will be taken at the beginning of each year from 2003 to 2012 if it is needed to bring the cash balance for that year up to the level of $500,000 required by company policy.

A more cautious expansion plan is needed to improve the chances of ending with a positive cash balance.

Review *Questions*

1. What is the cash flow management problem that is currently confronting the management of the Everglade Golden Years Company?

2. Which management science technique was previously used to address this cash flow management problem before applying computer simulation?

3. What aspect of the problem does computer simulation take into account that this prior management science technique could not?

4. What are the quantities in the assumption cells in this example's spreadsheet model for applying computer simulation?

5. How are the sizes of the short-term loans determined in this spreadsheet model?

6. What can happen in a trial of the computer simulation that would result in a negative cash balance at the end of 10 years?

7. What percentage of the trials actually resulted in a negative cash balance at the end of 10 years?

8. What policy did Everglade management adopt to reduce the possibility of having a negative cash balance at the end of 10 years?

16.5   FINANCIAL RISK ANALYSIS: REVISITING THE THINK-BIG DEVELOPMENT CO. PROBLEM

One of the earliest areas of application of computer simulation, dating back to the 1960s, was *financial risk analysis*. This continues today to be one of the most important areas of application.

When assessing any financial investment (or a portfolio of investments), the key trade-off is between the *return* from the investment and the *risk* associated with the investment. Of these two quantities, the less difficult one to determine is the return that would be obtained if everything evolves as currently projected. However, assessing the risk is relatively difficult. Fortunately, computer simulation is ideally suited to perform this risk analysis by obtaining a **risk profile,** namely, a *frequency distribution* of the return from the investment. The portion of the frequency distribution that reflects an unfavorable return clearly describes the risk associated with the investment.

The following example illustrates this approach in the context of real estate investments. Like the Everglade example in the preceding section, you will see computer simulation being used to refine prior analysis done by linear programming because this prior analysis was unable to take the uncertainty in future cash flows into account.

The Think-Big Financial Risk Analysis Problem

As introduced in Section 4.2, the Think-Big Development Co. is a major investor in commercial real estate development projects. It has been considering taking a share in three large construction projects—a high-rise office building, a hotel, and a shopping center. In each case, the partners in the project would spend three years with the construction, then retain ownership for three years while establishing the property, and then sell the property in the seventh year. By

TABLE 16.2
The Estimated Cash Flows for 100 Percent of the Hotel and Shopping Center Projects

Hotel Project		Shopping Center Project	
Year	Cash Flow ($1,000,000s)	Year	Cash Flow ($1,000,000s)
0	−80	0	−90
1	Normal (−80, 5)	1	Normal (−50, 5)
2	Normal (−80, 10)	2	Normal (−20, 5)
3	Normal (−70, 15)	3	Normal (−60, 10)
4	Normal (+30, 20)	4	Normal (+15, 15)
5	Normal (+40, 20)	5	Normal (+25, 15)
6	Normal (+50, 20)	6	Normal (+40, 15)
7	Uniform (+200, 844)	7	Uniform (160, 600)

using estimates of expected cash flows, Section 4.2 describes how linear programming has been applied to obtain the following proposal for how big a share Think-Big should take in each of these projects.

Proposal

Do not take any share of the high-rise building project.

Take a 16.50 percent share of the hotel project.

Take a 13.11 percent share of the shopping center project.

This proposal is estimated to return a *net present value* (NPV) of $18.11 million to Think-Big.

However, Think-Big management understands very well that such decisions should not be made without taking risk into account. These are very risky projects since it is unclear how well these properties will compete in the marketplace when they go into operation in a few years. Although the construction costs during the first three years can be estimated fairly roughly, the net incomes during the following three years of operation are very uncertain. Consequently, there is an extremely wide range of possible values for each sale price in year 7. Therefore, management wants *risk analysis* to be performed in the usual way (with computer simulation) to obtain a *risk profile* of what the total NPV might actually turn out to be with this proposal.

Management needs a risk profile of the proposal to assess whether the likelihood of a sizable profit justifies the risk of possible large losses.

To perform this risk analysis, Think-Big staff now has devoted considerable time to estimating the amount of uncertainty in the cash flows for each project over the next seven years. These data are summarized in Table 16.2 (in units of millions of dollars) for a 100 percent share of each project. Thus, when taking a smaller percentage share of a project, the numbers in the table should be reduced proportionally to obtain the relevant numbers for Think-Big. In years 1 through 6 for each project, the probability distribution of cash flow is assumed to be a *normal distribution,* where the first number shown is the estimated *mean* and the second number is the estimated *standard deviation* of the distribution. In year 7, the income from the sale of the property is assumed to have a *uniform distribution* over the range from the first number shown to the second number shown.

To compute NPV, a cost of capital of 10 percent per annum is being used. Thus, the cash flow in year n is divided by 1.1^n before adding these discounted cash flows to obtain NPV.

A Spreadsheet Model for Applying Computer Simulation

A spreadsheet model has been formulated for this problem in Figure 16.27. There is no uncertainty about the immediate (Year 0) cash flows appearing in cells D6 and D16, so these are data cells. However, because of the uncertainty for Years 1–7, cells D7:D13 and D17:D23 containing the simulated cash flows for these years need to be assumption cells. (The numbers in these cells in Figure 16.27 happen to be mean values that were entered merely to start the process of defining these assumption cells.) Table 16.2 specifies the probability distributions and their parameters that have been estimated for these cash flows, so the form of the distributions has been recorded in cells E7:E13 and E17:E23 while entering the corresponding parameters in cells F7:G13 and F17:G23. Figure 16.28 shows the Normal Distribution dialogue

Crystal Ball Tip: After entering the parameters for an assumption cell, you can have Crystal Ball display the mean in this cell by choosing this option under Preferences in the Cell menu.

FIGURE 16.27

A spreadsheet model for applying computer simulation to the Think-Big Development Co. financial risk analysis problem. The assumption cells are cells D7:D13 and D17:D23, the forecast cell is NetPresentValue (D37), and the decision variables are HotelShare (H28) and ShoppingCenterShare (H29).

	A	B	C	D	E	F	G	H
1		**Simulation of Think-Big Development Co. Problem**						
2								
3				**Project Simulated**				
4				**Cash Flow**				
5		**Hotel Project:**		**($millions)**				
6		Construction Costs:	Year 0	-80				
7			Year 1	-80	*Normal*	-80	5	(mean, st. dev.)
8			Year 2	-80	*Normal*	-80	10	(mean, st. dev.)
9			Year 3	-70	*Normal*	-70	15	(mean, st. dev.)
10		Revenue per Share	Year 4	30	*Normal*	30	20	(mean, st. dev.)
11			Year 5	40	*Normal*	40	20	(mean, st. dev.)
12			Year 6	50	*Normal*	50	20	(mean, st. dev.)
13		Selling Price per Share	Year 7	522	*Uniform*	200	844	(min,max)
14								
15		**Shopping Center Project**						
16		Construction Costs:	Year 0	-90				
17			Year 1	-50	*Normal*	-50	5	(mean, st. dev.)
18			Year 2	-20	*Normal*	-20	5	(mean, st. dev.)
19			Year 3	-60	*Normal*	-60	10	(mean, st. dev.)
20		Revenue per Share	Year 4	15	*Normal*	15	15	(mean, st. dev.)
21			Year 5	25	*Normal*	25	15	(mean, st. dev.)
22			Year 6	40	*Normal*	40	15	(mean, st. dev.)
23		Selling Price per Share	Year 7	387.5	*Uniform*	160	615	(min,max)
24								
25				**Think-Big's**				
26				**Simulated Cash Flow**				
27				**($millions)**				**Share**
28			Year 0	-24.999			Hotel	16.50%
29			Year 1	-19.755		Shopping Center		13.11%
30			Year 2	-15.822				
31			Year 3	-19.416		Cost of Capital		10%
32			Year 4	6.917				
33			Year 5	9.878				
34			Year 6	13.494				
35			Year 7	136.931				
36								
37		Net present Value ($millions)		18.120				

	C	D
25		**Total Simulated**
26		**Cash Flow**
27		**($millions)**
28	Year 0	=HotelShare*D6+ShoppingCenterShare*D16
29	Year 1	=HotelShare*D7+ShoppingCenterShare*D17
30	Year 2	=HotelShare*D8+ShoppingCenterShare*D18
31	Year 3	=HotelShare*D9+ShoppingCenterShare*D19
32	Year 4	=HotelShare*D10+ShoppingCenterShare*D20
33	Year 5	=HotelShare*D11+ShoppingCenterShare*D21
34	Year 6	=HotelShare*D12+ShoppingCenterShare*D22
35	Year 7	=HotelShare*D13+ShoppingCenterShare*D23
36		
37	Net Present Value ($millions)	=CashFlowYear0+NPV(CostOfCapital,CashFlowYear1To7)

Range Name	Cells
CashFlowYear0	D28
CashFlowYear1To7	D29:D35
CostOfCapital	H31
HotelShare	H28
NetPresentValue	D37
ShoppingCenterShare	H29

FIGURE 16.28

A normal distribution with parameters F7:G7 is being entered into the first assumption cell D7 in the spreadsheet model in Figure 16.27.

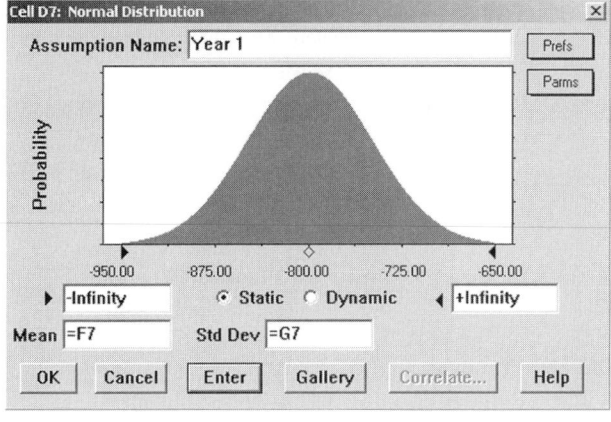

box that is used to enter the parameters (mean and standard deviation) for the normal distribution into the first assumption cell D7 by referencing cells F7 and G7. The parameters for the other normal distributions are then copied and pasted into the corresponding assumption cells. The Uniform Distribution dialogue box (like the one displayed earlier in Figure 16.4) is used in a similar way to enter the parameters (minimum and maximum) for this kind of distribution into the assumption cells D13 and D23.

The simulated cash flows in cells D6:D13 and D16:D23 are for 100 percent of the hotel project and the shopping center project, respectively, so Think-Big's share of these cash flows needs to be reduced proportionally based on its shares in these projects. The proposal being analyzed is to take the shares shown in cells H28:H29. The equations entered into cells D28:D35 (see the bottom of Figure 16.27) then gives Think-Big's total cash flow in the respective years for its share of the two projects.

Excel Tip: The NPV (*discount rate, cash flows*) function calculates the net present value of a stream of *future* cash flows at regular intervals (e.g., annually) in a range of cells (*cash flows*) using the specified *discount rate* per interval.

Think-Big's management wants to obtain a risk profile of what the total net present value (NPV) might be with this proposal. Therefore, the forecast cell is NetPresent Value (D37).

Here is a summary of the key cells in this model.

Assumption cells: Cells D7:D13 and D17:D23

Decision variables: HotelShare (H28) and ShoppingCenterShare (H29)

Forecast cell: NetPresentValue (D37)

The Simulation Results

The frequency chart provides the risk profile for the proposal.

Using the Run Preferences dialogue box to specify 1,000 trials, Figure 16.29 shows the results of applying computer simulation to the spreadsheet model in Figure 16.27. The frequency chart in Figure 16.29 provides the risk profile for the proposal since it shows the relative likelihood of the various values of NPV, including those where NPV is negative. The mean is $18.116 million, which is very attractive. However, the 1,000 trials generated an extremely wide range of NPV values, all the way from about −$22 million to over $60 million. Thus, there is a significant chance of incurring a huge loss. By entering 0 into the box in the lower left-hand corner of the frequency chart, the Certainty box indicates that 81 percent of the trials resulted in a profit (a positive value of NPV). This also gives the bad news that there is about a 19 percent chance of incurring a loss of some size. The lightly shaded portion of the chart to the left of 0 shows that most of the trials with losses involved losses up to about $10 million, but that quite a few trials had losses that ranged from $10 million to $20 million.

The percentiles table in Figure 16.29 also provides management with some specific numbers for better assessing the risk. The 10 percent percentile of −6.813 indicates a 10 percent chance of incurring a loss greater than $6.8 million. On the other hand, the 90 percent percentile of 40.669 indicates a 10 percent chance of achieving a huge profit (NPV) exceeding $40.6 million.

Armed with all this information, a managerial decision now can be made about whether the likelihood of a sizable profit justifies the significant risk of incurring a loss and perhaps even

FIGURE 16.29 The frequency chart and percentiles table that summarize the results of running the simulation model in Figure 16.27 for the Think-Big Development Co. financial risk analysis problem. The Certainty box under the frequency chart reveals that 81 percent of the trials resulted in a positive value of the net present value.

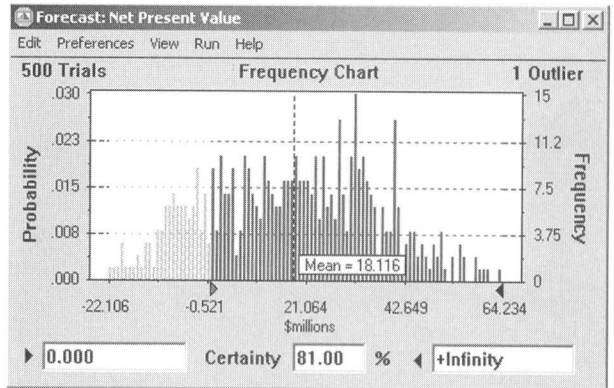
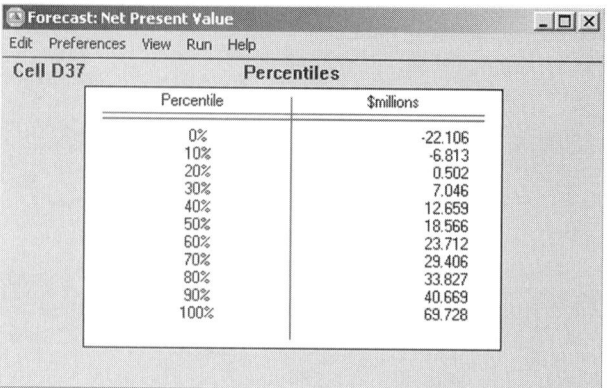

a very substantial loss. Thus, the role of computer simulation is to provide the information needed for making a sound decision, but it is management that uses its best judgment to make the decision.

Review Questions

1. What is a *risk profile* for an investment (or a portfolio of investments)?

2. What is the investment proposal that the management of the Think-Big Development Co. needs to evaluate?

3. What are the estimates that need to be made to prepare for applying computer simulation to this example?

4. What quantities appear in the assumption cells of the spreadsheet model for this example?

5. What quantity appears in the forecast cell for this example?

6. Does computer simulation indicate a significant chance of incurring a loss if Think-Big management approves the investment proposal?

16.6 REVENUE MANAGEMENT IN THE TRAVEL INDUSTRY

One of the most prominent areas for the application of management science in recent years has been in improving *revenue management* in the travel industry. Revenue management refers to the various ways of increasing the flow of revenues through such devices as setting up different fare classes for different categories of customers. The objective is to maximize total income by setting fares that are at the upper edge of what the different market segments are willing to pay and then allocating seats appropriately to the various fare classes.

As the example in this section will illustrate, one key area of revenue management is *overbooking,* that is, accepting a slightly larger number of reservations than the number of seats available. There usually are a small number of no-shows, so overbooking will increase revenue by essentially filling the available seating. However, there also are costs incurred if the number of arriving customers exceeds the number of available seats. Therefore, the amount of overbooking needs to be set carefully so as to achieve an appropriate trade-off between filling seats and avoiding the need to turn away customers who have a reservation.

A new overbooking model increased annual revenues for American Airlines by about $225 million.

American Airlines was the pioneer in making extensive use of management science for improving its revenue management. The guiding motto was "selling the right seats to the right customers at the right time." This work won the 1991 Franz Edelman Award as that year's best application of management science anywhere throughout the world. As described in an article in the January–February 1992 issue of *Interfaces,*[1] this application was credited with increas-

---

[1] This article can be downloaded at **www.mhhe.com/hillier2e/articles**.

ing annual revenues for American Airlines by over $500 million. Nearly half of these increased revenues came from the use of a new overbooking model.

Following this breakthrough at American Airlines, other airlines quickly stepped up their use of management science in similar ways. These applications to revenue management then spread to other segments of the travel industry (train travel, cruise lines, rental cars, hotels, etc.) around the world. Our example below involves overbooking by an airline company.

The Transcontinental Airlines Overbooking Problem

Transcontinental Airlines has a daily flight (excluding weekends) from San Francisco to Chicago that is mainly used by business travelers. There are 150 seats available in the single cabin. The average fare per seat is $300. This is a nonrefundable fare, so no-shows forfeit the entire fare. The fixed cost for operating the flight is $30,000, so more than 100 reservations are needed to make a profit on any particular day.

For most of these flights, the number of requests for reservations considerably exceeds the number of seats available. The company's management science group has been compiling data on the number of reservation requests per flight for the past several months. The average number has been 195, but with considerable variation from flight to flight on both sides of this average. Plotting a frequency chart for these data suggests that they roughly follow a bell-shaped curve. Therefore, the group estimates that the number of reservation requests per flight has a *normal distribution* with a mean of 195. A calculation from the data estimates that the standard deviation is 30.

The company's policy is to accept 10 percent more reservations than the number of seats available on nearly all its flights, since roughly 10 percent of all its customers making reservations end up being no-shows. However, if its experience with a particular flight is much different from this, then an exception is made and the management science group is called in to analyze what the overbooking policy should be for that particular flight. This is what has just happened regarding the daily flight from San Francisco to Chicago. Even when the full quota of 165 reservations has been reached (which happens for most of the flights), there usually are a significant number of empty seats. While gathering its data, the management science group has discovered the reason why. Only 80 percent of the customers who make reservations for this flight actually show up to take the flight. The other 20 percent forfeit the fare (or, in most cases, allow their company to do so) because their plans have changed.

Now that the data have been gathered, the management science group decides to begin its analysis by investigating the option of increasing the number of reservations to accept for this flight to 190. If the number of reservation requests for a particular day actually reaches this level, then this number should be large enough to avoid many, if any, empty seats. Furthermore, this number should be small enough that there will not be many occasions when a significant number of customers need to be bumped from the flight because the number of arrivals exceeds the number of seats available (150). Thus, 190 appears to be a good first guess for an appropriate trade-off between avoiding many empty seats and avoiding bumping many customers.

When a customer is bumped from this flight, Transcontinental Airlines arranges to put the customer on the next available flight to Chicago on another airline. The company's average cost for doing this is $150. In addition, the company gives the customer a voucher worth $200 for use on a future flight. The company also feels that an additional $100 should be assessed for the intangible cost of a loss of goodwill on the part of the bumped customer. Therefore, the total cost of bumping a customer is estimated to be $450.

The management science group now wants to investigate the option of accepting 190 reservations by using computer simulation to generate frequency charts for the following three measures of performance for each day's flight:

1. The profit.

2. The number of filled seats.

3. The number of customers denied boarding.

An unusually high 20 percent no-show rate requires developing a special overbooking policy for this particular flight.

A Spreadsheet Model for Applying Computer Simulation

Having three measures of performance means that the simulation model needs three forecast cells.

Figure 16.30 shows a spreadsheet model for this problem. Because there are three measures of interest here, the spreadsheet model needs three forecast cells. These forecast cells are Profit (F23), NumberOfFilledSeats (C20), and NumberDeniedBoarding (C21). The decision variable ReservationsToAccept (C13) has been set at 190 for investigating this current option. Some basic data have been entered near the top of the spreadsheet in cells C4:C7.

FIGURE 16.30

A spreadsheet model for applying computer simulation to the Transcontinental Airlines overbooking problem. The assumption cells are SimulatedTicketDemand (C10) and NumberThatShow (C17). The forecast cells are Profit (F23), NumberOfFilledSeats (C20), and NumberDeniedBoarding (C21). The decision variable is ReservationsToAccept (C13).

	A	B	C	D	E	F
1		**Airline Overbooking**				
2						
3			**Data**			
4		Available Seats	150			
5		Fixed Cost	$30,000			
6		Avg. Fare / Seat	$300			
7		Cost of Bumping	$450			
8						
9					Mean	Standard Dev.
10		Ticket Demand	195	*Normal*	195	30
11		Demand (rounded)	195			
12						
13		Reservations to Accept	190			
14						
15					Tickets	Probability
16					Purchased	to Show Up
17		Number That Show	152	*Binomial*	190	80%
18						
19						
20		Number of Filled Seats	150		Ticket Revenue	$45,000
21		Number Denied Boarding	2		Bumping Cost	$900
22					Fixed Cost	$30,000
23					Profit	$14,100

	B	C
11	Demand (rounded)	=ROUND(SimulatedTicketDemand,0)

	E
15	Tickets
16	Purchased
17	=MIN(Demand,ReservationsToAccept)

Range Name	Cell
AvailableSeats	C4
AverageFare	C6
BumpingCost	F21
CostOfBumping	C7
Demand	C11
FixedCost	C5
NumberDeniedBoarding	C21
NumberOfFilledSeats	C20
NumberThatShow	C17
Profit	F23
ReservationsToAccept	C13
SimulatedTicketDemand	C10
TicketRevenue	F20
TicketsPurchased	E17

	B	C
20	Number of Filled Seats	=MIN(AvailableSeats,NumberThatShow)
21	Number Denied Boarding	=MAX(0,NumberThatShow–AvailableSeats)

	E	F
20	Ticket Revenue	=AverageFare*NumberOfFilledSeats
21	Bumping Cost	=CostOfBumping*NumberDeniedBoarding
22	Fixed Cost	=FixedCost
23	Profit	=TicketRevenue–BumpingCost–FixedCost

Each trial of the computer simulation will correspond to one day's flight. There are two random inputs associated with each flight, namely, the number of customers requesting reservations (abbreviated as Ticket Demand in cell B10) and the number of customers who actually arrive to take the flight (abbreviated as Number That Show in cell B17). Thus, the two assumption cells in this model are SimulatedTicketDemand (C10) and NumberThatShow (C17).

Since the management science group has estimated that the number of customers requesting reservations has a normal distribution with a mean of 195 and a standard deviation of 30, this information has been entered into cells D10:F10. The Normal Distribution dialogue box (shown earlier in Figure 16.28) then has been used to enter this distribution with these parameters into SimulatedTicketDemand (C10). Because the normal distribution is a continuous distribution, whereas the number of reservations must have an integer value, Demand (C11) uses Excel's ROUND function to round the number in SimulatedTicketDemand (C10) to the nearest integer.

The random input for the second assumption cell NumberThatShow (C17) depends on two key quantities. One is TicketsPurchased (E17), which is the minimum of Demand (C11) and ReservationsToAccept (C13). The other key quantity is the probability that an individual making a reservation actually will show up to take the flight. This probability has been set at 80 percent in cell F17 since this is the *average* percentage of those who have shown up for the flight in recent months.

However, the *actual* percentage of those who show up on any particular day may vary somewhat on either side of this average percentage. Therefore, even though NumberThatShow (C17) would be expected to be fairly close to the product of cells E17 and F17, there will be some variation according to some probability distribution. What is the appropriate distribution for this assumption cell? Section 16.7 will describe the characteristics of various distributions. The one that has the characteristics to fit this assumption cell turns out to be the *binomial distribution.*

As indicated in Section 16.7, the binomial distribution gives the distribution of the number of times a particular event occurs out of a certain number of opportunities. In this case, the *event* of interest is a passenger showing up to take the flight. The *opportunity* for this event to occur arises when a customer makes a reservation for the flight. These opportunities are conventionally referred to as *trials* (not to be confused with a trial of a computer simulation). The binomial distribution assumes that the trials are statistically independent and that, on each trial, there is a fixed probability (80 percent in this case) that the event will occur. The parameters of the distribution are this fixed probability and the number of trials.

Figure 16.31 displays the Binomial Distribution dialogue box that enters this distribution into NumberThatShow (C17) by referencing the parameters in cells F17 and E17. Note that the "Dynamic" button has been selected just above the Trials box. This selection means that the cell references in the Prob. and Trials boxes will be evaluated for each trial of the computer simulation rather than just once at the beginning of the simulation run (the static option). This

These characteristics of the binomial distribution are just what is needed for the assumption cell NumberThatShow (C17).

Choosing the "Dynamic" option is mandatory here because one of the parameters of the distribution may change on each new trial.

FIGURE 16.31

A binomial distribution with parameters F17 and E17 is being entered into the assumption cell NumberThatShow (C17). The "Dynamic" option has been chosen because the value in cell E17 may change with each new trial of the simulation.

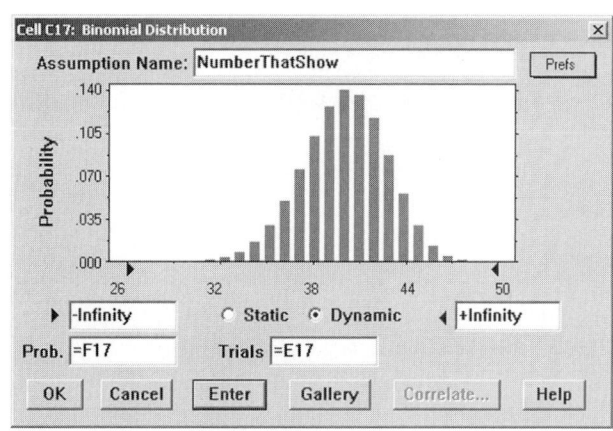

is necessary here because the number of trials for the binomial distribution (the number of tickets purchased given in cell E17) may change on each new trial of the computer simulation.

The equations entered into all the output cells and forecast cells are given at the bottom of Figure 16.30.

Here is a summary of the key cells in this model.

Assumption cells: SimulatedTicketDemand (C10) and NumberThatShow (C17)

Decision variable: ReservationsToAccept (C13)

Forecast cells: Profit (F23), NumberOfFilledSeats (C20), and NumberDeniedBoarding (C21)

The Simulation Results

Figure 16.32 shows the frequency chart obtained for each of the three forecast cells after applying computer simulation for 500 trials to the spreadsheet model in Figure 16.30, with ReservationsToAccept (C13) set at 190.

The profit results estimate that the mean profit per flight would be $6,821. However, this mean is a little less than the profits that had the highest frequencies. The reason is that a small number of trials had profits far below the mean, including even a few that incurred losses, which dragged the mean down somewhat. By entering 0 into the lower left-hand box, the Certainty box reports that 94.40 percent of the trials resulted in a profit for that day's flight.

The frequency chart for NumberOfFilledSeats (C20) indicates that 220 of the 500 trials resulted in all 150 seats being filled. Furthermore, most of the remaining trials had at least

FIGURE 16.32 The frequency charts that summarize the results for the respective forecast cells—Profit (F23), NumberOfFilledSeats (C20), and NumberDeniedBoarding (C21)—from running the simulation model in Figure 16.30 for the Transcontinental Airlines overbooking problem. The Certainty box below the first frequency chart reveals that 94.4 percent of the trials resulted in a positive profit.

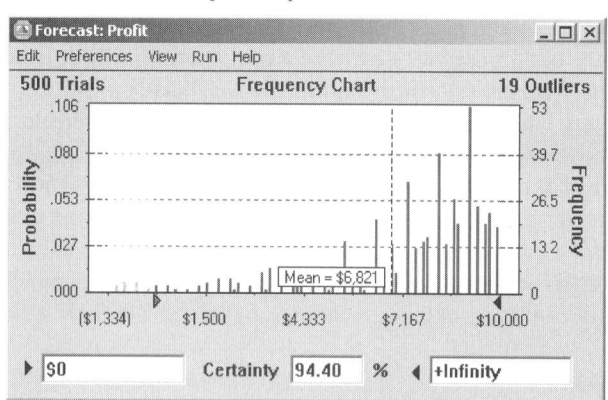

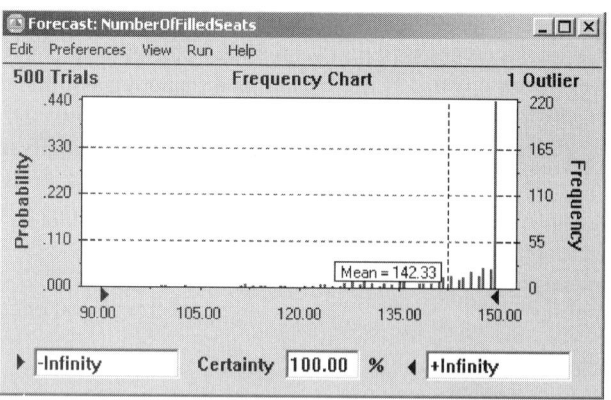

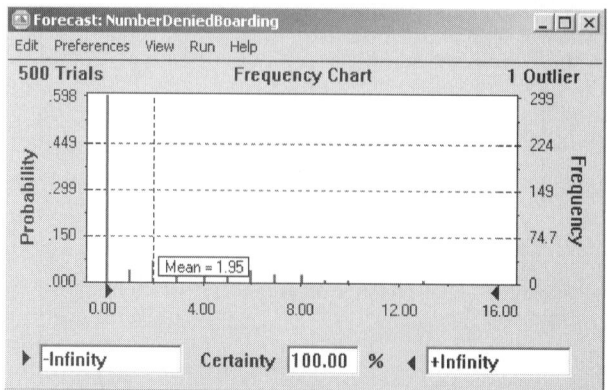

140 seats filled. The fact that the mean of 142.33 is so close to 150 shows that a policy of accepting 190 reservations would do an excellent job of filling seats.

The price that would be paid for filling seats so well is that a few customers would need to be bumped from some of the flights. The frequency chart for NumberDeniedBoarding (C21) indicates that this occurred on 201 of the 500 trials (since $500 - 299 = 201$). On nearly all of these trials, the number ranged between one and eight. Considering that no customers were denied boarding on 299 of the trials, the mean number is only 1.95.

We will return to this example in Section 16.8 to further evaluate how many reservations to accept.

Although these results suggest that a policy of accepting 190 reservations would be an attractive option for the most part, they do not demonstrate that this is necessarily the best option. Additional simulation runs are needed with other numbers entered in ReservationsTo Accept (C13) to pin down the optimal value of this decision variable. We will demonstrate how to do this efficiently with the help of a decision table in Section 16.8.

Review Questions

1. What is meant by *revenue management* in the travel industry?
2. In the pioneering application of management science to revenue management at American Airlines, what increase in annual revenues was achieved?
3. What problem is being addressed by the management science group at Transcontinental Airlines in this section's example?
4. What trade-off must be considered in addressing this problem?
5. What is the decision variable for this problem?
6. What quantities appear in the forecast cells of the spreadsheet model for this problem?
7. What quantities appear in the assumption cells of the spreadsheet model?
8. What are the parameters of a binomial distribution?
9. Why must the "Dynamic" option be chosen in the Binomial Distribution dialogue box for the current spreadsheet model?
10. Did the simulation results obtained in this section determine how many reservations should be accepted for the flight under consideration?

16.7   CHOOSING THE RIGHT DISTRIBUTION

As mentioned in Section 16.1, Crystal Ball's Distribution Gallery provides a wealth of choices. Any of 17 probability distributions can be selected as the one to be entered into any assumption cell. In the preceding sections, we have illustrated the use of four of these distributions (the uniform, triangular, normal, and binomial distributions). However, not much was said about *why* any particular distribution was chosen.

In this section, we focus on the issue of how to choose the right distribution. We begin by surveying the characteristics of many of the 17 distributions and how these characteristics help to identify the best choice. We next describe a special feature of Crystal Ball for creating a custom distribution when none of the other 16 choices in the Distribution Gallery will do. We then return to the case study presented in Section 16.1 to illustrate another special feature of Crystal Ball. When historical data are available, this feature will identify which of the available continuous distributions provides the best fit to these data while also estimating the parameters of this distribution. If you do not like this choice, it will even identify which of the distributions provides the second best fit, the third best fit, and so on.

Characteristics of the Available Distributions

The probability distribution of any random variable describes the relative likelihood of the possible values of the random variable. A *continuous* distribution is used if *any* values are possible, including both integer and fractional numbers, over the entire range of possible values. A *discrete* distribution is used if only certain specific values (e.g., only the integer numbers over some range) are possible. However, if the only possible values are integer numbers over a relatively broad range, a continuous distribution may be used as an approximation by rounding any fractional value to the nearest integer. (This approximation was used in cells C12:C13 of the spreadsheet model in Figure 16.1 and in cells C10:C11 of the spreadsheet model in Figure 16.30.) Crystal Ball's Distribution Gallery includes both continuous and discrete distributions. We will begin by looking at the continuous distributions.

The right-hand side of Figure 16.33 shows the dialogue box for three popular continuous distributions from the Distribution Gallery. The dark figure in each dialogue box displays a typical *probability density function* for that distribution. The height of the probability density function at the various points shows the relative likelihood of the corresponding values along the horizontal axis. Each of these distributions has a most likely value where the probability density function reaches a peak. Furthermore, all the other relatively high points are near the peak. This indicates that there is a tendency for one of the central values located near the most likely value to be the one that occurs. Therefore, these distributions are referred as *central-tendency distributions.* The characteristics of each of these distributions are listed on the left-hand side of Figure 16.33.

The Normal Distribution

The normal distribution is widely used by both management scientists and others because it describes so many natural phenomena. (Because of its importance, Appendix A provides a

FIGURE 16.33

The characteristics and dialogue boxes for three popular central-tendency distributions in Crystal Ball's Distribution Gallery: (1) the normal distribution, (2) the triangular distribution, and (3) the lognormal distribution.

Popular Central-Tendency Distributions

Normal Distribution:
- Some value most likely (the mean)
- Values close to mean more likely
- Symmetric (as likely above as below mean)
- Extreme values possible, but rare

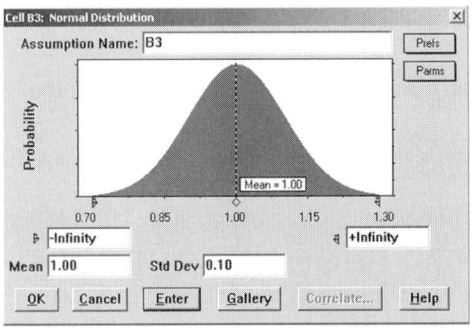

Triangular Distribution:
- Some value most likely
- Values close to most likely value more common
- Can be asymmetric
- Fixed upper and lower bound

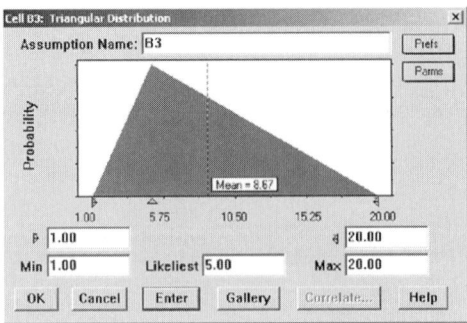

Lognormal Distribution:
- Some value most likely
- Positively skewed (below mean more likely)
- Values cannot fall below zero
- Extreme values (high end only) possible, but rare

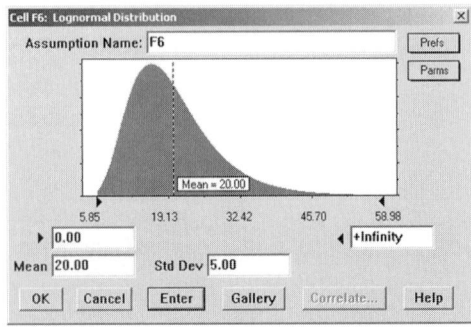

table for this distribution.) One reason that it arises so frequently is that the sum of many random variables tends to have a normal distribution (approximately) even when the individual random variables do not. Using this distribution requires estimating the mean and the standard deviation. The mean coincides with the most likely value because this is a symmetric distribution. Thus, the mean is a very intuitive quantity that can be readily estimated, but the standard deviation is not. About two-thirds of the distribution lies within one standard deviation of the mean. Therefore, if historical data are not available for calculating an estimate of the standard deviation, a rough estimate can be elicited from a knowledgeable individual by asking for an amount such that the random value will be within that amount of the mean about two-thirds of the time.

One danger with using the normal distribution for some applications is that it can give negative values even when such values actually are impossible. Fortunately, it can give negative values with significant frequency only if the mean is less than three standard deviations. For example, consider the situation where a normal distribution was entered into an assumption cell in Figure 16.30 to represent the number of customers requesting a reservation. A negative number would make no sense in this case, but this was no problem since the mean (195) was much larger than three standard deviations ($3 \times 30 = 90$) so a negative value essentially could never occur. (When normal distributions were entered into assumption cells in Figure 16.27 to represent cash flows, the means were small or even negative, but this also was no problem since cash flows can be either negative or positive.)

The normal distribution allows negative values, which is not appropriate for some applications.

The Triangular Distribution

A comparison of the shapes of the triangular and normal distributions in Figure 16.33 reveals some key differences. One is that the triangular distribution has a fixed minimum value and a fixed maximum value, whereas the normal distribution allows rare extreme values far into the tails. Another is that the triangular distribution can be asymmetric (as shown in the figure), because the most likely value does not need to be midway between the bounds, whereas the normal distribution always is symmetric. This provides additional flexibility to the triangular distribution. Another key difference is that all its parameters (the minimum value, most likely value, and maximum value) are intuitive ones, so they are relatively easy to estimate.

The parameters of a triangular distribution are relatively easy to estimate because they are so intuitive.

These advantages have made the triangular distribution a popular choice for computer simulations. They are the reason why this distribution was used in previous examples to represent competitors' bids for a construction contract (in Figure 16.12), activity times (in Figure 16.18), and cash flows (in Figure 16.25).

However, the triangular distribution also has certain disadvantages. One is that, in many situations, rare extreme values far into the tails are possible, so it is quite artificial to have fixed minimum and maximum values. This also makes it difficult to develop meaningful estimates of the bounds. Still another disadvantage is that a curve with a gradually changing slope, such as the bell-shaped curve for the normal distribution, should describe the true distribution more accurately than the straight line segments in the triangular distribution.

The Lognormal Distribution

The lognormal distribution shown at the bottom of Figure 16.33 combines some of the advantages of the normal and triangular distributions. It has a curve with a gradually changing slope. It also allows rare extreme values on the high side. At the same time, it does not allow negative values, so it automatically fits situations where this is needed. This is particularly advantageous when the mean is less than three standard deviations and the normal distribution should not be used.

The lognormal distribution has a long tail to the right but does not allow negative values to the left.

This distribution always is "positively skewed," meaning that the long tail always is to the right. This forces the most likely value to be toward the left side (so the mean is on its right), so this distribution is less flexible than the triangular distribution. Another disadvantage is that it has the same parameters as the normal distribution (the mean and the standard deviation), so the less intuitive one (the standard deviation) is difficult to estimate unless historical data are available.

When a positively skewed distribution that does not allow negative values is needed, the lognormal distribution provides an attractive option. That is why this distribution frequently is used to represent stock prices or real estate prices.

FIGURE 16.34

The characteristics and dialogue box for the uniform distribution in Crystal Ball's Distribution Gallery.

Uniform Distribution

Uniform Distribution:
- Fixed minimum and maximum value
- All values equally likely

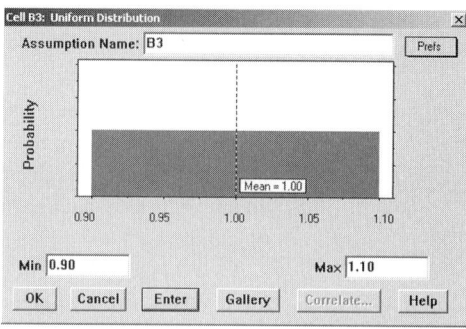

The Uniform Distribution

Although the preceding three distributions are all central-tendency distributions, the uniform distribution shown in Figure 16.34 definitely is not. It has a fixed minimum value and a fixed maximum value. Otherwise, it says that no value between these bounds is any more likely than any other. Therefore, this distribution has more variability than the central-tendency distributions with the same range of possible values (excluding rare extreme values).

This distribution is a particularly convenient one because it has only two parameters (the minimum value and the maximum value) and both are very intuitive. It receives considerable use for this reason. Earlier in this chapter, the uniform distribution was used to represent the demand for a newspaper (in Figure 16.1), the bid for a construction project by one competitor (in Figure 16.12), and the future sale price for real estate property (in Figure 16.27).

The uniform distribution is easy to use but usually is only a rough approximation of the true distribution.

The disadvantage of this distribution is that it usually is only a rough approximation of the true distribution. It is uncommon for either the minimum value or the maximum value to be just as likely as any other value between these bounds while any value barely outside these bounds is impossible.

The Weibull and Beta Distributions

We will describe the Weibull and beta distributions together because, as suggested by their similar shapes in Figure 16.35, these two distributions have similar characteristics. In contrast to the uniform distribution, both are central-tendency distributions. In contrast to the normal, lognormal, and uniform distributions, both also are three-parameter distributions. The three parameters provide great flexibility in adjusting the shape of the curve to fit the situation. This enables making the distribution positively skewed, symmetric, or negatively skewed as desired. This flexibility is the key advantage of these distributions. Another advantage is that they have a minimum value, so negative values can be avoided. The location parameter sets the minimum value for the Weibull distribution whereas Crystal Ball always sets the minimum value at 0 for the beta distribution. (If a positive minimum value is desired instead for the beta distribution, you can simply add this constant to any random observation from the distribution.) The Weibull distribution allows rare extreme values to the right, whereas the beta distribution has a fixed maximum value.

The Weibull and beta distributions are flexible enough to fit many situations, but they usually require historical data in order to calculate good estimates of their parameters.

Certain parameters, such as the location parameter mentioned above for the Weibull distribution, have an intuitive interpretation. In particular, the scale parameter for both distributions simply sets the width of the distribution (excluding rare extreme values in the case of the Weibull distribution). However, neither the shape parameter for the Weibull distribution nor the alpha and beta parameters for the beta distribution are particularly intuitive. Therefore, these distributions are mainly used only when historical data are available for calculating estimates of these parameters. (One exception is the innovative use of the beta distribution by the PERT three-estimate approach described in Section 8.4, which uses the minimum, most likely, and maximum values to calculate approximate values of the mean and standard deviation.) With historical data available, the choice between these two distributions (and other options as

FIGURE 16.35

The characteristics and dialogue boxes for two three-parameter distributions in Crystal Ball's Distribution Gallery: (1) the Weibull distribution and (2) the beta distribution.

Three-Parameter Distributions

Weibull Distribution:

- Random value above some number (location)
- Shape > 0 (usually ≤ 10)
- Shape < 3 becomes more positively skewed (below mean more likely) until it resembles exponential distribution (equivalent at Shape = 1)
- Symmetrical at Shape = 3.25, becomes more negatively skewed above that
- Scale defines width

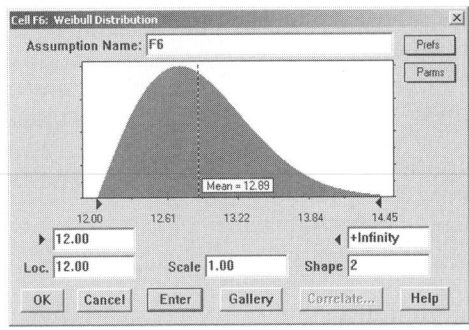

Beta Distribution:

- Random value between 0 and some positive number (scale)
- Shape specified using two positive values (alpha, beta)
- Alpha < beta: positively skewed (below mean more likely)
- Beta < alpha: negatively skewed

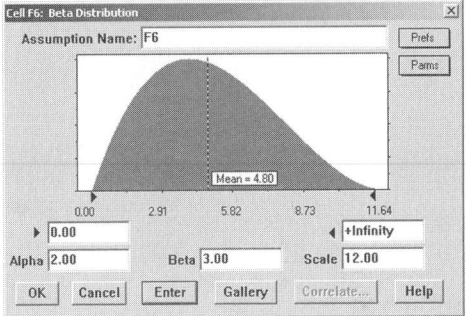

well) then can be based on which one provides the best fit with the data after obtaining statistical estimates of its parameters. We will describe a little later how Crystal Ball can do all of this for you.

The Exponential Distribution

If you have studied Chapter 14 on queueing models, you hopefully will recall that the most commonly used queueing models assume that the time between consecutive arrivals of customers to receive a particular service has an exponential distribution. The reason for this assumption is that, in most such situations, the arrivals of customers are random events and the exponential distribution is the probability distribution of the time between random events. Section 14.1 describes this property of the exponential distribution in some detail.

As first depicted in Figure 14.3, this distribution has the unusual shape shown in Figure 16.36. In particular, the peak is at 0 but there is a long tail to the right. This indicates that the most likely times are short ones well below the mean but that very long times also are possible. This is the nature of the time between random events.

Since the only parameter is the rate at which the random events occur on the average, this distribution is a relatively easy one to use.

The Poisson Distribution

Although the exponential distribution (like all the preceding ones) is a continuous distribution, the Poisson distribution is a discrete distribution. The only possible values are nonnegative integers: 0, 1, 2, · · ·. However, it is natural to pair this distribution with the exponential distribution for the following reason. If the time between consecutive events has an exponential distribution (i.e., the events are occurring at random), then the number of events that occur within a certain period of time has a Poisson distribution. This distribution has some other applications as well.

When considering the number of events that occur within a certain period of time, the "Rate" to be entered into the one parameter field in the dialogue box should be the average number of events that occur within that period of time.

FIGURE 16.36

The characteristics and dialogue boxes for two distributions that involve random events. These distributions in Crystal Ball's Distribution Gallery are (1) the exponential distribution and (2) the Poisson distribution.

Distributions for Random Events

Exponential Distribution:

- Widely used to describe time between random events (e.g., time between arrivals)
- Events are independent
- Rate = average number of events per unit time (e.g., arrivals per hour)

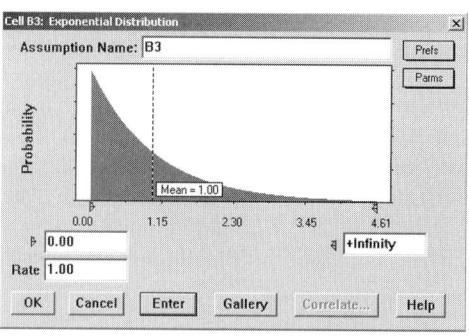

Poisson Distribution:

- Describes the number of times an event occurs during a given period of time or space
- Occurrences are independent
- Any number of events is possible
- Rate = average number of events during period of time (e.g., arrivals per hour), assumed constant over time

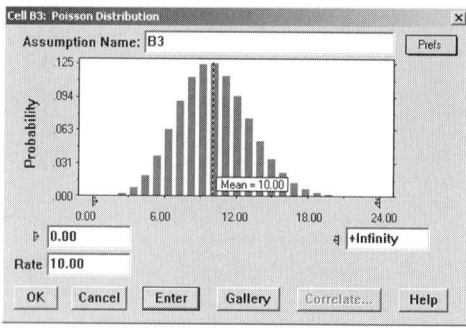

FIGURE 16.37

The characteristics and dialogue box for the binomial distribution in Crystal Ball's Distribution Gallery.

Distribution for Number of Times an Event Occurs

Binomial Distribution:

- Describes number of times an event occurs in a fixed number of trials (e.g., number of heads in 10 flips of a coin)
- For each trial, only two outcomes possible
- Trials independent
- Probability remains same for each trial

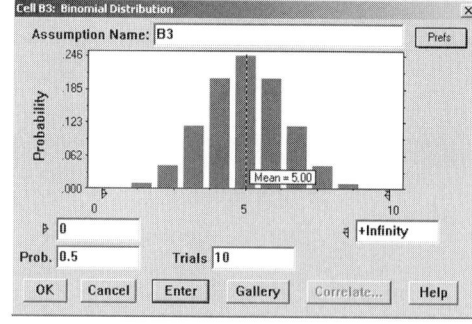

The Binomial Distribution

The binomial distribution also is a discrete distribution whose possible values are the nonnegative integers, as shown in Figure 16.37. It gives the probability distribution of the number of times a particular *event* occurs, given the number of independent opportunities (called *trials*) for the event to occur, where the probability of the event occurring remains the same from trial to trial. For example, if the event of interest is getting heads on the flip of a coin, the binomial distribution (with Prob. = 0.5) gives the distribution of the number of heads in a given number of flips of the coin. Each flip constitutes a trial where there is an opportunity for the event (heads) to occur with a fixed probability (0.5).

You have seen another example in the preceding section when the binomial distribution was entered into the assumption cell NumberThatShow (C17) in Figure 16.30. In this airline overbooking example, the events are customers showing up for the flight and the trials are customers making reservations, where there is a fixed probability that a customer making a reservation actually will arrive to take the flight.

FIGURE 16.38

The characteristics and dialogue boxes for two distributions that involve the number of trials until events occur. These distributions in Crystal Ball's Distribution Gallery are (1) the geometric distribution and (2) the negative binomial distribution.

Distributions for Number of Trials Until Event Occurs

Geometric Distribution:

- Describes number of trials until an event occurs (e.g., number of times to spin roulette wheel until you win)
- Probability same for each trial
- Continue until succeed
- Number of trials unlimited

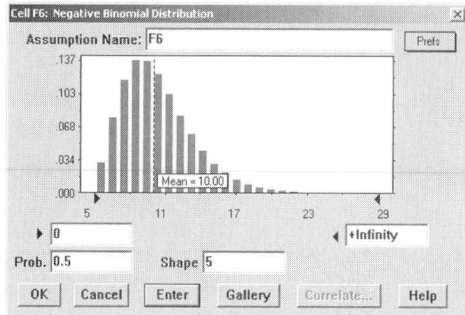

Negative Binomial Distribution:

- Describes number of trials until an event occurs *n* times
- Same as geometric when Shape = *n* = 1
- Probability same for each trial
- Continue until *n*th success
- Number of trials unlimited

The only parameters for this distribution are the number of trials and the probability of the event occurring on a trial.

The Geometric and Negative Binomial Distributions

These two distributions displayed in Figure 16.38 are related to the binomial distribution because they again involve trials where there is a fixed probability on each trial that the event will occur. The *geometric distribution* gives the distribution of the number of trials until the event occurs for the first time. After entering a positive integer into the Shape field in its dialogue box, the *negative binomial distribution* gives the distribution of the number of trials until the event occurs the number of times specified in the Shape field. Thus, shape is a parameter for this distribution and the fixed probability of the event occurring on a trial is a parameter for both distributions.

To illustrate these distributions, suppose you are again interested in the event of getting heads on a flip of a coin (a trial). The geometric distribution (with Prob. = 0.5) gives the distribution of the number of flips until the first head occurs. If you want five heads, the negative binomial distribution (with Prob. = 0.5 and Shape = 5) gives the distribution of the number of flips until heads have occurred five times.

Similarly, consider a production process with a 50 percent yield, so each unit produced has an 0.5 probability of being acceptable. The geometric distribution (with Prob. = 0.5) gives the distribution of the number of units that need to be produced to obtain one acceptable unit. If a customer has ordered five units, the negative binomial distribution (with Prob. = 0.5 and Shape = 5) gives the distribution of the production run size that is needed to fulfill this order.

To reach the negative binomial distribution in Crystal Ball's Distribution Gallery dialogue box, the More button needs to be clicked. All the other distributions discussed so far appear on the front screen of this dialogue box (as shown earlier in Figure 16.3).

Other Distributions

The Distribution Gallery includes six additional distributions: the custom, hypergeometric, gamma, logistic, Pareto, and extreme value distributions. The More button needs to be clicked on the dialogue box to reach the last four of these distributions (along with the negative binomial distribution).

The custom distribution is an especially useful one because it enables you to design your own distribution when none of the other 16 distributions in the Distribution Gallery will do. The next subsection will focus on how this is done.

The remaining five distributions are not widely used in computer simulations, so they will not be discussed further.

The Custom Distribution

Of the 17 probability distributions included in the Distribution Gallery, 16 of them are standard types that might be discussed in a course on probability and statistics. In most cases, one of these standard distributions will be just what is needed for an assumption cell. However, unique circumstances occasionally arise where none of the standard distributions fit the situation. This is where the 17th member of the Distribution Gallery, called the "custom distribution," enters the picture.

The custom distribution actually is not a probability distribution until you make it one. Rather, choosing this member of the Distribution Gallery triggers a process that enables you to custom-design your own probability distribution to fit almost any unique situation you might encounter. In designing your distribution, you are given the choice of entering individual discrete values, a range of discrete values with equal probabilities, or a continuous distribution. The three examples displayed in Figure 16.39 illustrate these respective options.

In the first example, a company is developing a new product but it is unclear which of three production processes will be needed to produce the product. The unit production cost will be $10, $12, or $14, depending on which process is needed. The probabilities for these individual discrete values of the cost are the following.

20 percent chance of $10

50 percent chance of $12

30 percent chance of $14

The top part of Figure 16.39 shows how to enter this distribution. Each discrete value and probability (expressed as a decimal number) is entered, one at a time, in the Value and Prob. boxes while leaving the other two boxes blank. Clicking on Enter each time clears the parameter entry boxes so that the next value and probability can be entered.

The middle of Figure 16.39 illustrates how to enter a range of discrete values with equal probabilities. In this example, a single die is being rolled, so the possible values are 1, 2, 3, 4, 5, or 6. These values are equally likely, so the probability distribution is the following.

Range of discrete values: 1, 2, 3, 4, 5, 6

Probability of each value: $\frac{1}{6}$

This distribution could be entered as in the first example. However, it is much quicker to simply enter the lower end of the range of values (1) in the Value box, the upper end of the range of values (6) in the Value2 box, the total probability for the entire set of values (1) in the Prob. box, the increase from one discrete value to the next (1) in the Step box, and then click on Enter.

The third option is to enter a continuous distribution, as shown at the bottom of Figure 16.39. The distribution for this example has the following characteristics.

Range of values: 4,000 to 6,000

Total probability over this range: 1

The values become slightly less likely as they increase

This distribution is entered by entering the lower end of the range of values (4,000) in the Value box, the upper end of the range of values (6,000) in the Value2 box, and the total probability over this range of values (1) in the Prob. box. The Step box is left blank. The last step before clicking on Enter is to drag the upper right-hand corner of the graph downward to reflect the decreasing likelihood of values as they increase. (If the value of the total probability changes during this dragging process, click on Rescale to reset this value.)

(margin note) Choosing the custom distribution from the Distribution Gallery enables you to custom-design your own distribution to fit a special situation.

FIGURE 16.39

Following the instructions on the left, these dialogue boxes illustrate in turn how Crystal Ball's custom distribution can enable you to custom-design your own distribution in three ways: (1) enter a set of discrete values and their probabilities, (2) enter a range of discrete values with equal probabilities, and (3) enter a continuous distribution with a straight top.

Custom Distribution

Set of Discrete Values (Custom Distribution):

- Enter set of values with varying probabilities
- For each discrete value, enter "Value" and "Prob." (leave other boxes blank)
- Clicking Enter clears boxes for entering next discrete value

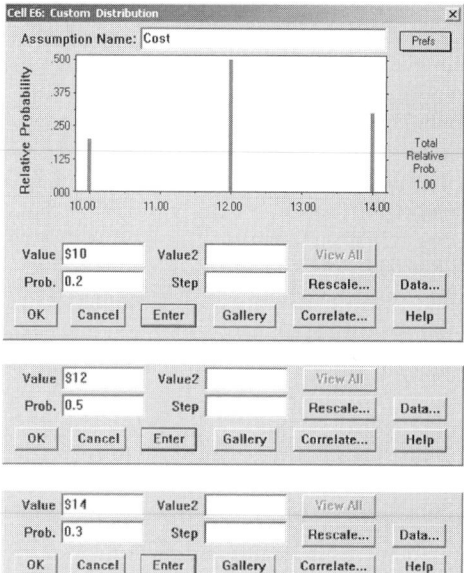

Range of Discrete Values (Custom Distribution):

- Enter range of discrete values, each equally likely
- Enter lower and upper end of range in "Value" and "Value2"
- Enter the total probability for the whole set in "Prob."
- Enter the distance between discrete values in "Step"

Continuous Distribution (Custom Distribution):

- Enter the lower and upper end of range in "Value" and "Value2"
- Enter the total probability for the range in "Prob."
- Leave "Step" blank for a continuous distribution
- Drag the corners of the distribution graph up or down to change the relative probabilities throughout the range
- Dragging corners may affect the total probability; Clicking on "Rescale" allows you to reset the total probability

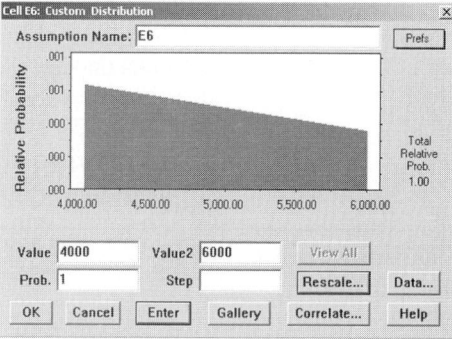

A limitation of this dragging process is that the top of the graph (which shows the probability density function for the distribution) remains a straight line after the dragging is completed. Therefore, this process does not enable you to put any curves into the graph that might be needed for some continuous distributions. However, Crystal Ball does allow you to input multiple portions of the distributions separately by entering the range and total probability for each portion one at a time, which better enables you to approximate continuous distributions that have curves.

It also is possible to enter combinations of the three options (a set of discrete values, a range of discrete values, and a continuous distribution) just described. This process is illustrated in

FIGURE 16.40

Following the instructions on the left, this dialogue box for the custom distribution demonstrates combining two of the options in Figure 16.39: (1) enter a discrete value at $0 and (2) enter a uniform distribution between $600,000 and $1,000,000.

Combinations with the Custom Distribution

Combination (Custom Distribution):

- Any combination of discrete values, ranges of discrete values, or continuous distributions can be entered
- Input each element (as described in Figure 16.39), click on Enter, input next element, etc.
- If the cumulative probabilities do not add to 1, clicking on "Rescale" allows you to proportionally adjust all of the probabilities so they sum to 1

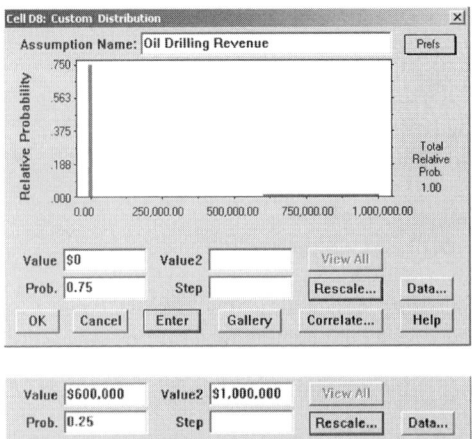

Figure 16.40. The example in this case is a variation of the probability distribution of the revenue from drilling for oil in the Goferbroke Company case study introduced in Section 12.1. In that case study, there was a probability of 0.75 of not finding oil (so a revenue of $0) and a probability of 0.25 of finding oil, in which case the revenue would be $800,000. However, there actually is some uncertainty about how much revenue would be received if oil were found, so the following distribution would be more realistic.

Revenue of $0 has probability 0.75

A range of revenue values: $600,000 to $1,000,000

The values over this range are equally likely

Probability of a value in this range: 0.25

This distribution combines a single discrete value at $0 with a continuous portion between $600,000 and $1,000,000. Therefore, we apply the instructions at the top of Figure 16.39 by entering $0 into the Value box and 0.75 into the Prob. box, and then clicking on Enter. We next follow the instructions at the bottom of Figure 16.39 by entering $600,000 into the Value box, $1,000,000 into the Value2 box, and 0.25 into the Prob. box before clicking on Enter again. All these entries are shown in Figure 16.40.

Identifying the Continuous Distribution That Best Fits Historical Data

If you don't know which continuous distribution should be chosen for an assumption cell, Crystal Ball can do it for you if historical data are available.

We now have at least mentioned all 17 types of probability distributions in the Distribution Gallery and have described the characteristics of many of them. This brings us to the question of how to identify which distribution is best for a particular assumption cell. When historical data are available, Crystal Ball provides a powerful feature for doing this with the continuous distributions by using the Fit button on the Distribution Gallery dialogue box. We will illustrate this feature next by returning to the case study presented in Section 16.1.

Recall that one of the most popular newspapers that Freddie the newsboy sells from his newsstand is the daily *Financial Journal*. Freddie purchases copies from his distributor early each morning. Since excess copies left over at the end of the day represent a loss for Freddie, he is trying to decide what his order quantity should be in the future. This led to the spreadsheet model in Figure 16.1 that was shown earlier in Section 16.1. This model includes the assumption cell SimulatedDemand (C12). To get started, a uniform distribution between 40 and 70 has been entered into this assumption cell.

To better guide his decision on what the order quantity should be, Freddie has been keeping a record of the *demand* (the number of customers requesting a copy) for this newspaper

FIGURE 16.41

Cells F4:F63 contain the historical demand data that have been collected for the case study involving Freddie the newsboy that was introduced in Section 16.1. Columns B and C come from the simulation model for this case study in Figure 16.1.

	A	B	C	D	E	F
1		**Freddie the Newsboy**				Historical
2						Demand
3			**Data**		Day	Data
4		Unit Sale Price	$2.50		1	62
5		Unit Purchase Cost	$1.50		2	45
6		Unit Salvage Value	$0.50		3	59
7					4	65
8			**Decision Variable**		5	50
9		Order Quantity	60		6	64
10					7	56
11			**Simulation**		8	51
12		Simulated Demand	55		9	55
13		Demand (rounded)	55		10	61
14					11	40
15		Sales Revenue	$137.50		12	47
16		Purchasing Cost	$90.00		13	63
17		Salvage Value	$2.50		14	68
18					15	67
19		Profit	$50.00		16	67
20					17	68
58					55	41
59					56	42
60					57	64
61					58	45
62					59	59
63					60	70

each day. Figure 16.41 shows a portion of the data he has gathered over the last 60 days in cells F4:F63, along with part of the original spreadsheet model from Figure 16.1. These data indicate a lot of variation in sales from day to day—ranging from about 40 copies to 70 copies. However, it is difficult to tell from these numbers which distribution in the Distribution Gallery best fits these data.

Crystal Ball provides the following procedure for addressing this issue.

Procedure for Fitting the Best Continuous Distribution to Data

1. Gather the data needed to identify the best distribution to enter into an assumption cell.

2. Enter the data into the spreadsheet containing your simulation model.

3. Select the cell that you want to define as an assumption cell that contains the distribution that best fits the data.

4. Choose Define Assumption from the Crystal Ball toolbar (shown in Figure 16.2), which brings up the Distribution Gallery dialogue box.

5. Click the Fit button on this dialogue box, which brings up the first Fit Distribution dialogue box.

6. Use the Range box in this dialogue box to enter the range of the historical data in your worksheet.

7. Click the Next button in this dialogue box, which brings up the second Fit Distribution dialogue box.

8. Use this dialogue box to specify which continuous distributions are being considered for fitting. (Discrete distributions are not considered in this procedure.)

9. Also use this dialogue box to select which ranking method should be used to evaluate how well a distribution fits the data. (The default is the chi-square test, since this is the most popular choice.)

10. Click OK, which brings up the comparison chart that identifies the distribution (including its parameter values) that best fits the data.

11. If desired, the Next Distribution button can be clicked repeatedly for identifying the other types of distributions (including their parameter values) that are next in line for fitting the data well.

12. After choosing the distribution (from steps 10 and 11) that you want to use, click the Accept button while that distribution is showing. This will enter the appropriate parameters into the dialogue box for this distribution. Clicking OK then enters this distribution into the assumption cell.

Since Figure 16.41 already includes the needed data in cells F4:F63, applying this procedure to Freddie's problem begins by selecting SimulatedDemand (C12) as the cell we want to define as an assumption cell that contains the distribution that best fits the data. Then applying steps 4 and 5 brings up the first Fit Distribution dialogue box displayed in Figure 16.42. The range F4:F63 of the data in Figure 16.41 is entered into the Range box of this dialogue box. Clicking the Next button then brings up the second Fit Distribution dialogue box displayed in Figure 16.42. When deciding which continuous distributions should be considered for fitting, the default option of considering all the continuous distributions in the Distribution Gallery has been selected here. The default choice of the chi-square test also has been selected for the ranking method. Clicking OK then brings up the comparison chart displayed in Figure 16.43. The vertical lines show the frequency chart for the data in Figure 16.41. The right side of the comparison chart identifies the best-fitting distribution as being the uniform distribution with parameters Minimum = 39.49 and Maximum = 70.51.

This finding confirms the choice made in Freddie's original spreadsheet model in Figure 16.1 to enter the uniform distribution into the assumption cell SimulatedDemand (C12). Figure 16.43 provides a slight refinement in the parameter values of Minimum = 40 and Maximum = 70 entered into cells E12:F12 of Figure 16.1 by setting these parameter values at Minimum = 39.49 and Maximum = 70.51 instead. Because the simulated demand is rounded to the nearest integer in Demand (C13) in Figure 16.41, this refinement will give both 40 and 70 the same probability as each of the intermediate integers.

FIGURE 16.42

The first Fit Distribution dialog box specifies the range of the data in Figure 16.41 for the case study. The second Fit Distribution dialogue box specifies which continuous distributions will be considered (all) and which ranking method will be used (the chi-square test) to evaluate how well each of the distributions fit the data.

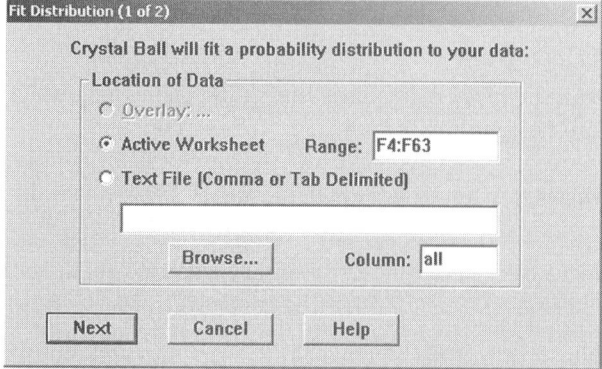
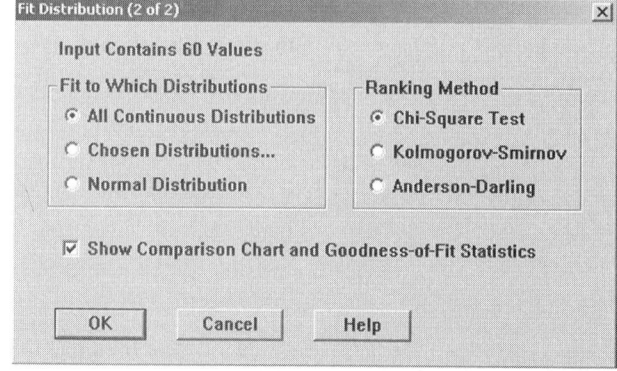

FIGURE 16.43

On the right, this comparison chart identifies the continuous distribution that provides the best fit with the historical demand data in Figure 16.41. This distribution then is plotted (the horizontal line) so that it can be compared with the frequency distribution of the historical demand data.

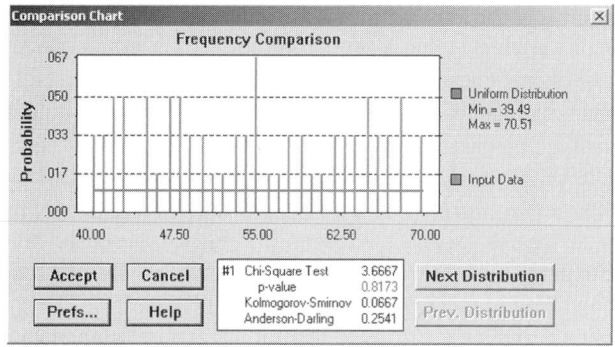

If step 11 is used, the procedure identifies the logistic distribution (with Mean = 54.39 and Scale = 5.60) as the one that provides the second best fit. The normal distribution (with Mean = 54.48 and Standard Deviation = 9.14) provides the third best fit. However, there is no reason to prefer either of these distributions over the uniform distribution in this case, so the procedure is completed by entering the uniform distribution identified in Figure 16.43 into SimulatedDemand (C12) in Figure 16.41.

Review Questions

1. How many probability distributions are available in Crystal Ball's Distribution Gallery?
2. What is the difference between a continuous distribution and a discrete distribution?
3. What is a possible danger with choosing the normal distribution to enter into an assumption cell?
4. What are some advantages of choosing the triangular distribution instead?
5. How does the lognormal distribution compare with the normal and triangular distributions?
6. Why is the uniform distribution sometimes a convenient choice for an assumption cell?
7. What would be the key advantage of choosing either the Weibull distribution or a beta distribution for an assumption cell?
8. The binomial distribution gives the probability distribution of what?
9. What does choosing the custom distribution from the Distribution Gallery enable you to do?
10. What procedure does Crystal Ball provide for helping to identify the best distribution to enter into an assumption cell?

16.8   DECISION MAKING WITH DECISION TABLES

Many simulation models include at least one decision variable. For example, here are some of the decision variables encountered in this chapter.

> **The case study:**   OrderQuantity (C9) in Figure 16.1
>
> **Bidding example:**   OurBid (C25) in Figure 16.12
>
> **Overbooking example:**   ReservationsToAccept (C13) in Figure 16.30

In each of these cases, you have seen how well computer simulation with Crystal Ball can *evaluate* a particular value of the decision variable by providing a wealth of output for the forecast cell(s). However, in contrast to many of the management science techniques presented in previous chapters (including linear programming and decision analysis), this approach has not identified an *optimal solution* for the decision variable(s). Fortunately, Crystal Ball provides a special feature called the **Decision Table tool** that systematically applies computer simulation to identify at least an approximation of an optimal solution for problems with only one or two decision variables. In this section, we describe this valuable tool and illustrate it by applying it in turn to the three decision variables listed above.

An intuitive approach for doing this would be to use trial and error. Try different values of the decision variable(s), run a simulation for each, and see which one provides the best estimate of the chosen measure of performance. This is what the Decision Table tool does, but it does it in a systematic way. Its dialogue boxes enable you to quickly specify what you want to do. Then, after you click one button, all the desired simulations are run and the results soon are displayed nicely in the Decision Table. If desired, you also can view some charts, including an enlightening *trend chart,* which provide additional details about the results.

> The Decision Table tool systematically applies computer simulation over a range of values of one or two decision variables and then displays the results in a table.

If you have previously used either an Excel data table or the Solver Table that is included in your MS Courseware for performing sensitivity analysis systematically, the Decision Table works in much the same way. In particular, the layout for a Decision Table with either one or two decision variables is similar to that for either a one-dimensional Solver Table (introduced in Section 5.3) or a two-dimensional Solver Table (introduced in Section 5.4). Two is the maximum number of decision variables that can be varied simultaneously in a Decision Table.

Let us begin by returning to this chapter's case study to apply the Decision Table tool.

Application of the Decision Table Tool to the Case Study

Recall that Freddie the newsboy wants to determine what his daily order quantity should be for copies of the *Financial Journal.* Figures 16.1–16.11 in Section 16.1 show the application of computer simulation for evaluating the option of using an order quantity of 60. The final estimate of the average daily profit that would be obtained with this order quantity is $46.61. As indicated in Figure 16.41, the number of copies that Freddie's customers want to purchase varies widely from day to day. The comparison chart in Figure 16.43 has concluded that the probability distribution that best describes this variability is the uniform distribution between 39.49 and 70.51 (and then rounding to the nearest integer). Given such a high degree of variability, it is unclear where the order quantity should be set within the range between 40 and 70. Could an average daily profit larger than $46.61 be obtained by choosing an order quantity different from 60? Which order quantity between 40 and 70 would maximize the average daily profit?

> Before applying the Decision Table to any problem, the one or two decision variables being investigated must be defined.

To address these questions, it would seem sensible to begin by trying a sampling of possible order quantities, say, 40, 45, 50, 55, 60, 65, and 70. To do this with the Decision Table tool, the first step is to define the decision variable being investigated, namely, OrderQuantity (C9) in Figure 16.1, by using the following procedure.

Procedure for Defining a Decision Variable

1. Select the cell containing the decision variable by clicking on it.

2. If the cell does not already contain a value, enter *any* number into the cell.

3. Click on the second button (the Define Decision button) in the Crystal Ball toolbar (or choose Define Decision from the Cell menu), which brings up the Define Decision Variable dialogue box (as shown in Figure 16.44 for Freddie's problem).

4. Enter the lower limit and the upper limit of the range of values to be simulated for the decision variable.

5. Click on either Continuous or Discrete to define whether the decision variable is continuous or discrete.

6. If Discrete is selected in step 5, use the Step box to specify the difference between the successive possible values (not just those to be simulated) of the decision variable. (The default value is 1.)

7. Click on OK.

Figure 16.44 shows the application of this procedure to Freddie's problem. Since simulations will be run for order quantities ranging from 40 to 70, these limits for the range have been entered on the left. The order quantity can have any integer value within this range, so this is indicated on the right.

Now we are ready to choose Decision Table from the Crystal Ball Tools menu. This brings up the sequence of three dialogue boxes shown in Figure 16.45.

FIGURE 16.44

This Define Decision Variable dialogue box specifies the characteristics of the decision variable OrderQuantity (C9) in the simulation model in Figure 16.1 for the case study that involves Freddie the newsboy.

Cell C9: Define Decision Variable

Name: Order Quantity

Variable Bounds

Lower: 40

Upper: 70

Variable Type

○ Continuous

● Discrete

Step: 1

OK   Cancel   Help

FIGURE 16.45   To prepare for generating a Decision Table, these three dialogue boxes specify (1) which forecast cell will be the target cell, (2) which one or two decision variables will be varied, and (3) the running options. The choices made here are for the case study that involves Freddie the newsboy.

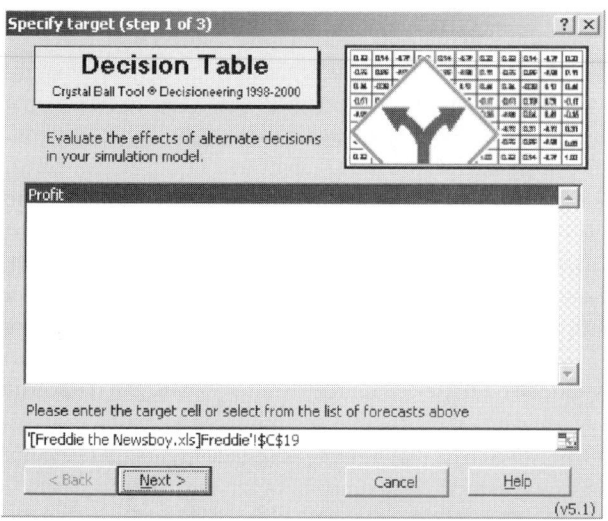

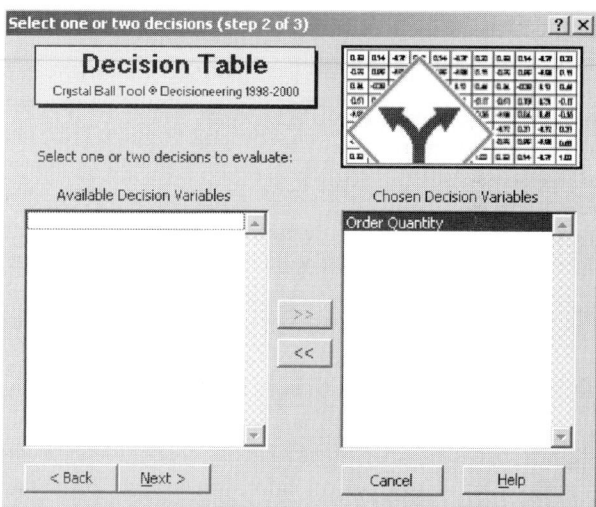

Specify target (step 1 of 3)

Decision Table

Crystal Ball Tool ⊕ Decisioneering 1998-2000

Evaluate the effects of alternate decisions in your simulation model.

Profit

Please enter the target cell or select from the list of forecasts above

'[Freddie the Newsboy.xls]Freddie'!$C$19

< Back   Next >   Cancel   Help

(v5.1)

Select one or two decisions (step 2 of 3)

Decision Table

Crystal Ball Tool ⊕ Decisioneering 1998-2000

Select one or two decisions to evaluate:

Available Decision Variables   Chosen Decision Variables

Order Quantity

>>

<<

< Back   Next >   Cancel   Help

Specify options (step 3 of 3)

Decision Table

Crystal Ball Tool ⊕ Decisioneering 1998-2000

Simulation Control

Test 7   values for Order Quantity

Run each simulation for 500   trials (maximum)

While Running

○ Show forecasts as defined

● Show only target forecast

○ Hide all forecasts

< Back   Start   Cancel   Help

The Step 1 dialogue box is used to choose one of the forecast cells listed there to be the target cell for the Decision Table. Freddie's spreadsheet model in Figure 16.1 has only one forecast cell, Profit (C19), so select it and then click on the Next button.

Initially, the left-hand side of the Step 2 dialogue box includes a list of all the cells that have been defined as decision variables. This consists of the single decision variable, OrderQuantity

(C9), for Freddie's problem. The purpose of this dialogue box is to choose which one or two decision variables to vary for the Decision Table. This is done by selecting these decision variables on the left side and then clicking on the double right arrows (>>) between the two boxes, which brings these decision variables to the right side. Figure 16.45 shows the result of doing this with Freddie's decision variable.

After specifying the number of values of a decision variable to consider, Crystal Ball distributes the values evenly over the range of values specified in the Define Decision Variable dialogue box.

The Step 3 dialogue box is used to specify the options for the Decision Table. The first entry box records the number of values of the decision variable for which simulations will be run. Crystal Ball then distributes the values evenly over the range of values specified in the Define Decision Variable dialogue box (Figure 16.44). For Freddie's problem, the range of values is 40 to 70, so entering 7 into the first entry box in the Step 3 dialogue box results in choosing 40, 45, 50, 55, 60, 65, and 70 as the seven values of the order quantity for which simulations will be run. After selecting the run size for each simulation and specifying what you want to see while the simulations are running, the last step is to click the Start button.

After Crystal Ball runs the simulations, the Decision Table is created in a new spreadsheet as shown in Figure 16.46. For each of the order quantities shown at the top, row 2 gives the mean of the values of the target cell, Profit (C19), obtained in all the trials of that simulation run. Cells D2:F2 reveal that an order quantity of 55 achieved the largest mean profit of $47.49, while order quantities of 50 and 60 essentially tied for the second largest mean profit.

This is a one-dimensional Decision Table because the problem has only one decision variable. For problems where two decision variables have been defined and selected, the resulting Decision Table will be a two-dimensional table, with one variable changing in the rows and the other in the columns.

The sharp drop off in mean profits on both sides of these order quantities virtually guarantees that the optimal order quantity lies between 50 and 60 (and probably close to 55). To pin this down better, the logical next step would be to generate another Decision Table that considers all integer order quantities between 50 and 60. You are asked to do this in Problem 16.14.

The upper left-hand corner of the Decision Table provides three options for obtaining more detailed information about the results of the simulation runs for the cells that you select. One option is to view the forecast chart of interest, such as a frequency chart or cumulative chart, by choosing a forecast cell in row 2 and then clicking on the Forecast Charts button. Another option is to see the results of two or more simulation runs together. This is done by selecting a set of forecast cells, say, cells E2:F2 in Figure 16.46, and then clicking on the Overlay Chart button. The resulting overlay chart is shown in Figure 16.47. The dark lines show the frequency chart for cell E2 (an order quantity of 55) while the light lines do the same for cell F2 (an order quantity of 60), so the results for these two cases can be compared side by side. (On a color monitor, you will see different colors being used to distinguish between the different cases.)

The third option is to select all the forecast cells of interest (cells B2:H2 in Figure 16.46) and then click on the Trend Chart button. This generates an interesting chart, called the *trend chart,* shown in Figure 16.48. The key points along the horizontal axis are the seven vertical grid lines that correspond to the seven cases (order quantities of 40, 45, . . . 70) for which the simulations were run. The vertical axis gives the profit values obtained in the trials of these simulation runs. The bands in the chart summarize information about the frequency distribution of the profit values from each simulation run. (On a color monitor, the bands appear in color—light blue for the center band, red for the adjacent pair of bands, green for the next pair, and dark blue for the outer pair of bands.) These bands are centered on the *medians* of the frequency distributions. In other words, the center of the middle band (the lightest one) gives the profit value such that half of the trials gave a larger value and half gave a smaller value. This middle band contains the middle 10 percent of the profit values (so 45 percent are on each side of the band). Similarly, the middle three bands contain the middle 25 percent of the profit val-

FIGURE 16.46

The Decision Table for the case study introduced in Section 16.1.

	A	B	C	D	E	F	G	H
1	Trend Chart / Overlay Chart / Forecast Charts	Order Quantity (40)	Order Quantity (45)	Order Quantity (50)	Order Quantity (55)	Order Quantity (60)	Order Quantity (65)	Order Quantity (70)
2		$40.00	$44.17	$46.66	$47.49	$46.64	$44.14	$39.97
3		1	2	3	4	5	6	7

FIGURE 16.47

The overlay chart that compares the frequency distributions for order quantities of 55 and 60 for Freddie's problem.

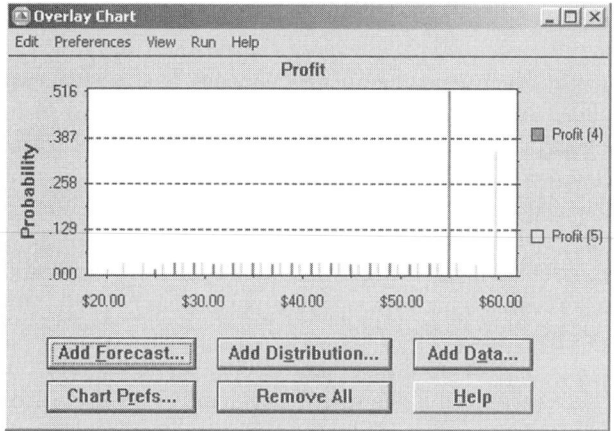

FIGURE 16.48

The trend chart that shows the trend in the range of various portions of the frequency distribution as the order quantity increases for Freddie's problem.

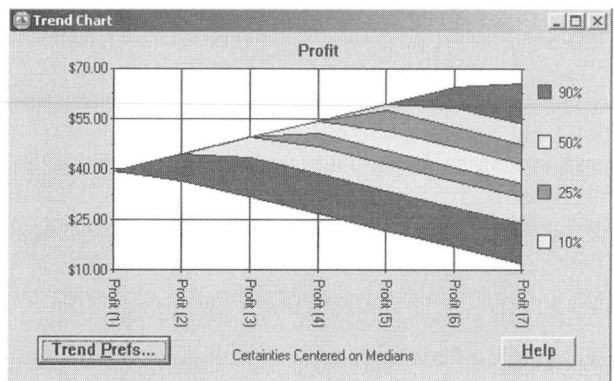

ues, the middle five bands contain the middle 50 percent of the profit values, and all seven bands contain the middle 90 percent of the profit values. (These percentages are listed to the right of the trend chart.) Thus, 5 percent of the profit values generated in the trials of each simulation run lie above the top band and 5 percent lie below the bottom band.

The trend chart received its name because it shows the trends graphically as the value of the decision variable (the order quantity in this case) increases. In Figure 16.48, for example, consider the middle band (which gets hidden in the narrow part of the chart on the left). In going from the third order quantity (50) to the fourth one (55), the middle band is trending upward, but then it is trending downward thereafter. Thus, the median value of the profit values generated in the respective simulation runs increases as the order quantity increases until the median reaches its peak at an order quantity of 55, after which the median trends downward. Similarly, most of the other bands also are trending downward as the order quantity increases above 55. This suggests that an order quantity of 55 is a particularly attractive one in terms of its entire frequency distribution and not just its mean value. The fact that the trend chart is spreading out as it moves to the right provides the further insight that the variability of the profit values increases as the order quantity is increased. Although the largest order quantities provide some chance of particularly high profits on occasional days, they also give some likelihood to obtaining an unusually low profit on any given day. This risk profile may be relevant to Freddie if he is concerned about the variability of his daily profits.

We return to this case study again in the next section when another special Crystal Ball feature, called OptQuest, is used to search for the optimal order quantity.

> A trend chart shows the trends graphically as the value of a decision variable increases.

Application of the Decision Table Tool to the Reliable Construction Co. Bidding Problem

We turn now to the application of the Decision Table tool to the Reliable Construction Co. bidding problem presented in Section 16.2. Since the procedure for how to generate a Decision

Table already has been presented in the preceding subsection, our focus here is on summarizing the results.

Recall that the management of the company is concerned with determining what bid it should submit for a project that involves constructing a new plant for a major manufacturer. Therefore, the decision variable in the spreadsheet model in Figure 16.12 is OurBid (C25). The Define Decision Variable dialogue box in Figure 16.49 is used to further describe this decision variable. Management feels that the bid should be in the range between $4.8 million and $5.8 million, so these are the numbers (in units of millions of dollars) that are entered into the entry boxes for Variable Bounds in this dialogue box. Because the bid can be *any* amount (down to the cent) within this range, the variable has been classified as a continuous variable on the right-hand side of the dialogue box.

Management wants to choose the bid that would maximize its expected profit. Consequently, the forecast cell in the spreadsheet model is Profit (C29). In the Decision Table dialogue box for Step 1 shown in Figure 16.50, this forecast cell has been selected to be the target cell. In the Step 2 dialogue box, the decision variable OurBid (C25) already has been brought over to the right-hand side as the variable to be considered. The decision has been made in the Step 3 dialogue box to test six values for this decision variable. The six values automatically are distributed evenly over the range specified in Figure 16.49, so simulations will be run for bids of 4.8, 5.0, 5.2, 5.4, 5.6, and 5.8 (in millions of dollars). The Step 3 dialogue box also has been used to specify that each simulation will run for 500 trials.

> A bid of $5.4 million was the winning bid for the Reliable Construction Co. in the case study for Chapter 8.

Figure 16.51 shows the resulting Decision Table. A bid of $5.4 million gives the largest mean value of the profits obtained on the 500 trials of the simulation run. This mean value of $501,000 in cell E2 should be a close estimate of the expected profit from using this bid. The case study in Chapter 8 begins with the company having just won the contract by submitting this bid.

Problem 16.17 asks you to refine this analysis by generating a Decision Table that considers all bids between $5.2 million and $5.6 million in multiples of $0.05 million. (It also asks you to use the OptQuest technique presented in the next section to search for the precise optimal bid.)

Application of the Decision Table Tool to the Transcontinental Airlines Overbooking Problem

As described in Section 16.6, Transcontinental Airlines has a popular daily flight from San Francisco to Chicago with 150 seats available. The number of requests for reservations usually exceeds the number of seats by a considerable amount. However, even though the fare is nonrefundable, an average of only 80 percent of the customers who make reservations actually show up to take the flight, so it seems appropriate to accept more reservations than can be flown. At the same time, significant costs are incurred if customers with reservations are not allowed to take the flight. Therefore, the company's management science group is analyzing what number of reservations should be accepted to maximize the expected profit from the flight.

> The decision variable in Figure 16.30 is ReservationsToAccept (C13).

In the spreadsheet model in Figure 16.30, the decision variable is ReservationsToAccept (C13) and the forecast cell is Profit (F23). The management science group wants to consider integer values of the decision variable over the range between 150 and 200, so the Define Deci-

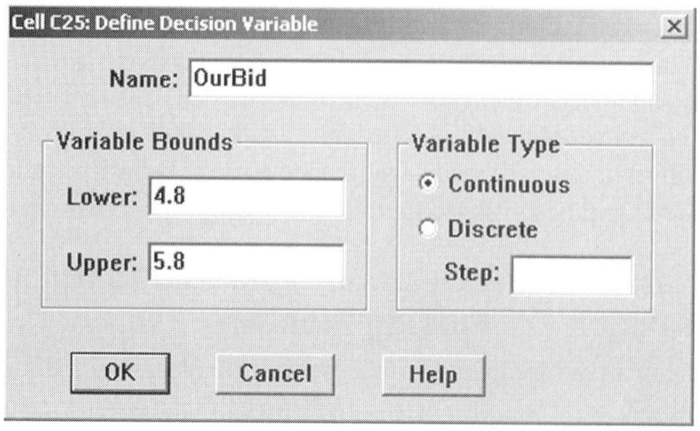

FIGURE 16.49

This dialogue box specifies the characteristics of the decision variable OurBid (C25) in Figure 16.12 for the Reliable Construction Co. contract bidding problem.

FIGURE 16.50 The three Decision Table dialogue boxes for the Reliable Construction Co. contract bidding problem.

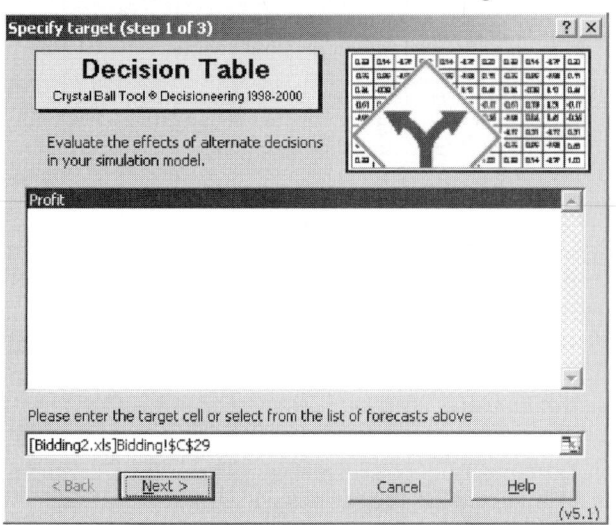

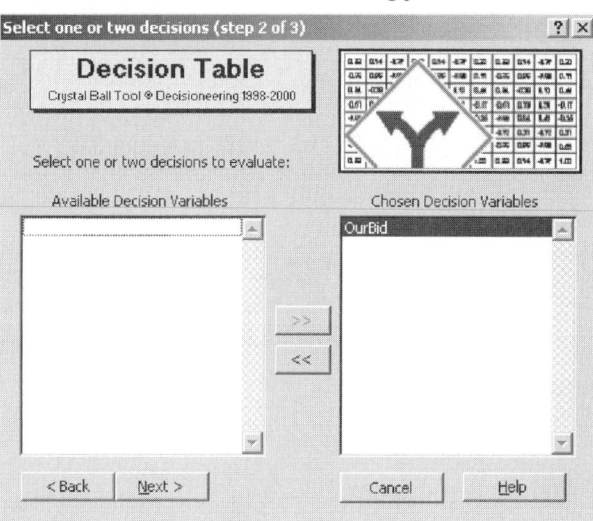

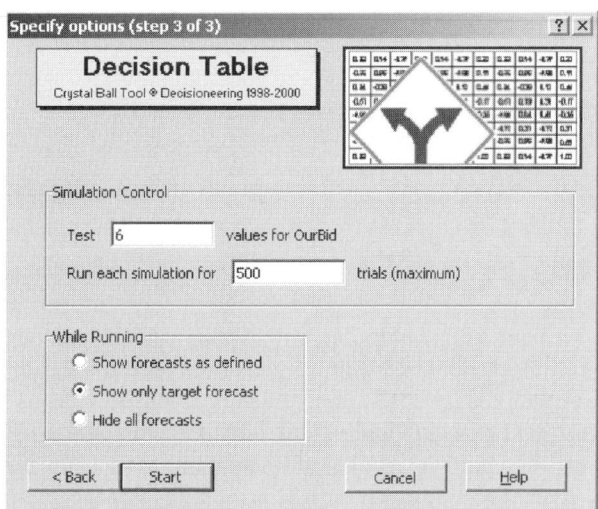

FIGURE 16.51

The Decision Table for the Reliable Construction Co. contract bidding problem described in Section 16.2.

	A	B	C	D	E	F	G
	Trend Chart	OurBid (4.800)	OurBid (5.000)	OurBid (5.200)	OurBid (5.400)	OurBid (5.600)	OurBid (5.800)
	Overlay Chart						
1	Forecast Charts						
2		0.188	0.357	0.476	0.501	0.252	0.010
3		1	2	3	4	5	6

sion Variable dialogue box is used in the usual way to specify these bounds on the variable and to define the variable as being discrete. The three Decision Table dialogue boxes also are used in the usual way. In the Step 3 dialogue box, the decision is made to test 11 values of ReservationsToAccept (C13), so simulations will be run for values in intervals of five between 150 and 200. The number of trials for each simulation run also is set at 500 in this dialogue box.

The results are shown in Figure 16.52. The Decision Table in the figure reveals that the mean of the profit values obtained in the respective simulation runs climbs rapidly as ReservationsToAccept (C13) increases until the mean reaches a peak of $7,014 at 185 reservations, after which it starts to drop. Only the means at 180 and 190 reservations are close to this peak, so it seems clear that the most profitable number of reservations lies somewhere between 180 and 190. (Now that the range of numbers that need to be considered has been

FIGURE 16.52   The Decision Table and trend chart for the Transcontinental Airlines overbooking problem described in Section 16.6.

	A	B	C	D	E	F	G	H	I	J	K	L
1	Trend Chart / Overlay Chart / Forecast Charts	ReservationsToAccept (150)	ReservationsToAccept (155)	ReservationsToAccept (160)	ReservationsToAccept (165)	ReservationsToAccept (170)	ReservationsToAccept (175)	ReservationsToAccept (180)	ReservationsToAccept (185)	ReservationsToAccept (190)	ReservationsToAccept (195)	ReservationsToAccept (200)
2		$788	$1,888	$2,963	$3,999	$4,990	$5,897	$6,638	$7,014	$6,821	$6,256	$5,554
3		1	2	3	4	5	6	7	8	9	10	11

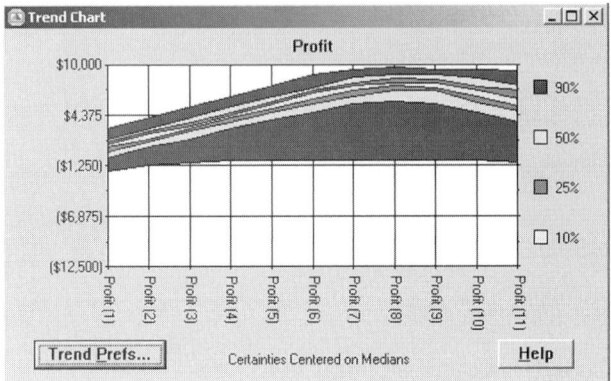

narrowed down this far, Problem 16.20 asks you to continue that analysis by generating a Decision Table that considers all integer values over this range, as well as by applying OptQuest to search for the optimal number of reservations to accept.)

The trend chart in Figure 16.52 provides additional insight. All seven bands in this chart trend upward until the number of reservations to accept reaches approximately 185; then they start trending slowly downward. This indicates that the *entire* frequency distribution from the respective simulation runs keeps shifting upward until the eighth run (the one for 185 reservations) and then starts shifting downward. Also note that the width of the entire set of seven bands increases until about the eighth simulation run and then remains about the same thereafter. This indicates that the amount of variability in the profit values also increases until about the eighth simulation run and then remains about the same thereafter.

Review Questions

1. What does the Decision Table tool enable you to do that a single simulation run with one value of the decision variable(s) does not?

2. What are the advantages of using the Decision Table tool instead of simply using trial and error to try different values of the decision variable(s) and running a simulation for each?

3. What is the maximum number of decision variables that can be varied simultaneously in a Decision Table?

4. What procedure needs to be used before choosing Decision Table from the Crystal Ball Tools menu?

5. After choosing Decision Table from this menu, what is the purpose of the Step 1 dialogue box?

6. What is the purpose of the Step 2 dialogue box?

7. What is the purpose of the Step 3 dialogue box?

8. What does an overlay chart show?

9. What kind of information is summarized by the bands in a trend chart?

10. After a Decision Table has been used to narrow down the range of values of a decision variable that need to be considered, how can another Decision Table be used to better approximate the optimal value of the decision variable?

16.9 OPTIMIZING WITH OPTQUEST

In the preceding section, you saw how the Decision Table tool sometimes can be used to find at least a close approximation of an optimal solution. The three examples presented there illustrate the kind of problem where the Decision Table tool can do this well. All three examples had only a *single* decision variable. (Remember that a Decision Table can consider a maximum of only two decision variables.) Furthermore, in two of these examples (the case study involving Freddie the newsboy and the airline overbooking example), the single decision variable was a *discrete* variable that had only a moderate number of possible values that needed consideration (namely, integers over a reasonably small range). This enabled using a Decision Table to identify a small range of values that provided the best solutions. If desired, a second Decision Table then could have been generated to evaluate *every* possible value of the decision variable within this small range.

However, this approach does not work as well when the single decision variable is either a continuous variable or a discrete variable with a large range of possible values. It also is more difficult with two decision variables. It is not feasible at all for larger problems with more than two decision variables and numerous possible solutions. Many problems in practice fall into these categories.

Although the Decision Table can consider at most two decision variables, OptQuest can handle any number of decision variables.

Fortunately, Crystal Ball includes another module called **OptQuest** that automatically searches for an optimal solution for simulation models with any number of decision variables. (This module currently is included in only the Professional Edition of Crystal Ball, which is the version included in your MS Courseware.) Based on years of research in both optimization and artificial intelligence, OptQuest provides a powerful search engine for conducting an intelligent and efficient search for the best solution. (The ideas are similar to those described in Section 10.5 for genetic algorithms.) The search is conducted by executing a series of simulation runs for a series of leading candidates to be an actual optimal solution, where the results of each run are used to determine the most promising remaining candidate to try next. Opt-Quest cannot guarantee that the best solution it finds will literally be an optimal solution. However, given enough time, it often will find an optimal solution and, if not, it usually will find a solution that is close to optimal. For problems with only a few discrete decision variables, it frequently will find an optimal solution fairly early in the process and then spend the rest of the time ruling out other candidate solutions. Thus, although OptQuest cannot tell when it has found an optimal solution, it can estimate (within the range of precision provided by simulation runs) that the other leading candidates are not better than the best solution found so far.

Although OptQuest often will find an optimal solution, this cannot be guaranteed.

To illustrate how to use OptQuest, we begin with a problem that it can handle extremely easily, namely, the case study with Freddie the newsboy. After summarizing the overall procedure, we then turn to a more challenging example involving the selection of projects.

Application of OptQuest to the Case Study

In the preceding section, the Decision Table generated in Figure 16.46 indicated that Freddie the newsboy should order between 50 and 60 copies of the *Financial Journal* each day. Now let us see how OptQuest can estimate which specific order quantity would maximize his average daily profit.

Before opening OptQuest, the initial steps are the same as described in Section 16.1 for preparing to begin a single simulation run. Thus, after formulating the simulation model in a spreadsheet, as shown in Figure 16.1, Crystal Ball is used to define the assumption cell SimulatedDemand (C12) and the forecast cell Profit (C19), including specifying the precision control for the forecast cell (as in Figure 16.10). The Run Preferences dialogue boxes also are used in the usual way. These definitions and run preferences set in Crystal Ball are the ones that will be used by OptQuest.

The dialogue boxes in Figure 16.53 show the run preferences that are recommended for most applications of OptQuest. The Trials box in the upper left-hand portion of the figure indicates that the maximum number of trials for each simulation run has been set at 500. This number represents a trade-off between two worthy goals. One goal is to achieve a high degree of precision by having a large number of trials in each simulation run. The conflicting goal is

FIGURE 16.53 These three dialogue boxes show the run preferences that are recommended for most applications of OptQuest.

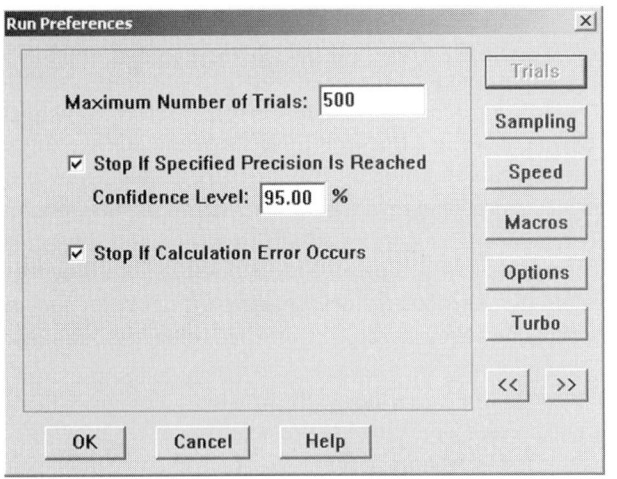
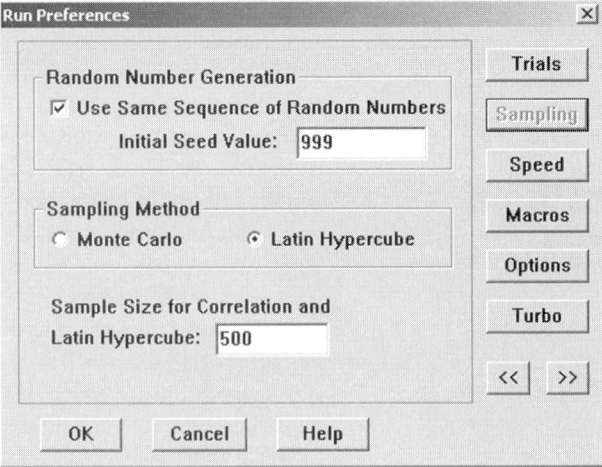
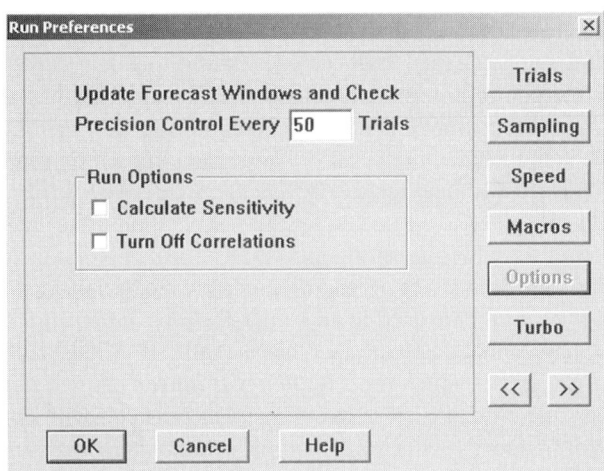

to leave time for a large number of simulation runs so that a large number of optimal solution candidates can be evaluated. When the key statistic being obtained from each simulation run is the *mean* of the values in the forecast cell, 500 trials provides a good trade-off between these two goals because the mean tends to stabilize sufficiently by this number of trials. However, when the key statistic of interest is one that is more difficult to estimate precisely, such as a percentile at a tail end of the frequency distribution (or even the maximum or minimum value in this distribution), then a larger number of trials (at least 1,000) should be used.

In the Run Preferences Sampling dialogue box shown in the upper right-hand portion of Figure 16.53, the option of using the same sequence of random numbers (with an initial seed value of 999) for every simulation run should be chosen. This enables the pattern of the random numbers to affect every simulation run in the same way, which increases the precision when comparing the results from different simulation runs. The Latin Hypercube sampling method also is recommended. This method ensures a representative sampling from the entire probability distribution entered into each assumption cell, which improves the quality of the results (especially the mean) from each simulation run.

The option of using the same sequence of random numbers for every simulation run provides more precise comparisons.

The Run Preferences Options dialogue box in the lower portion of Figure 16.53 is used to specify how frequently the precision control should be checked. The default choice of every 50 trials is a good one because this enables OptQuest to stop a simulation run relatively soon after its results so far indicate that the current solution has very little chance of being better than the best solution found so far.

FIGURE 16.54

These four OptQuest dialogue boxes are used to (1) select the decision variables to vary and set their bounds, (2) specify any constraints, (3) specify the objective for the optimization, and (4) control the running time. The choices made here are for the case study that involves Freddie the newsboy.

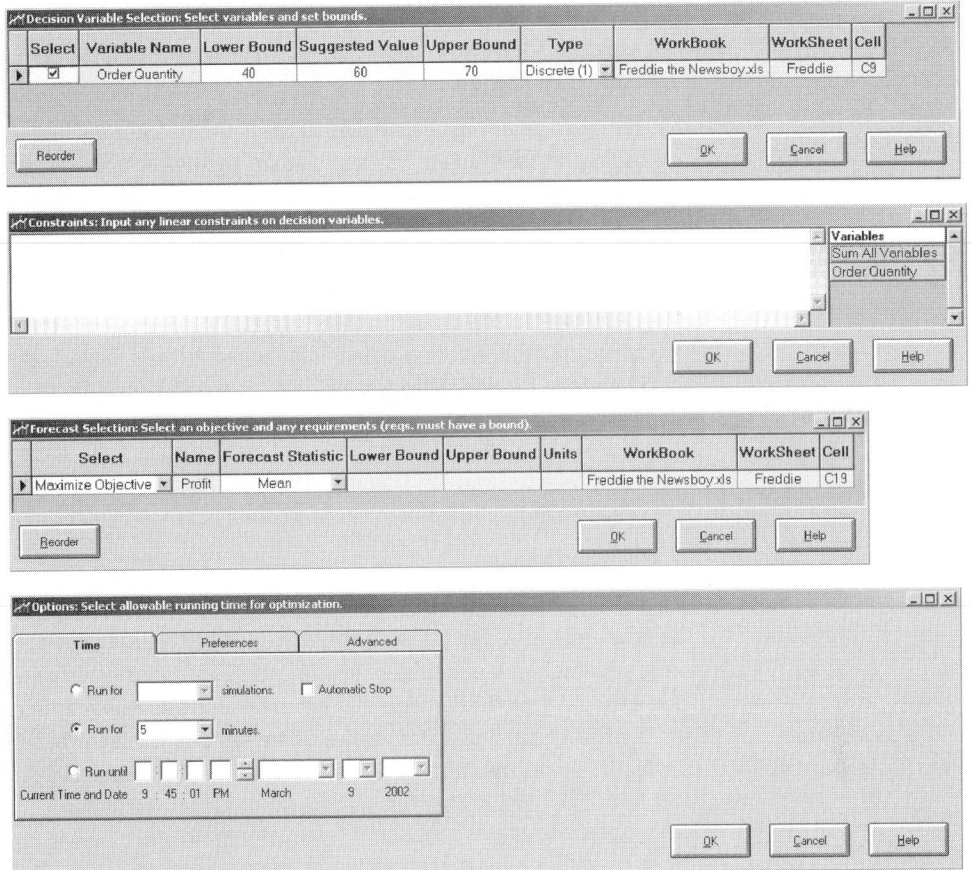

The final step before opening OptQuest is to define the decision variables for the problem by using the procedure presented in Section 16.8. In this case, the only decision variable is OrderQuantity (C9). Figure 16.44 (in Section 16.8) shows the dialogue box that was used to define this variable, including setting its bounds at 40 and 70.

We now are ready to open OptQuest. This is done by choosing OptQuest from the Crystal Ball Tools menu and then selecting New under the File menu. This brings up in succession the four dialogue boxes shown in Figure 16.54.

The first dialogue box is used to select the decision variables to vary (by clicking in the Select column) and to set their bounds in the third and fifth columns. All the decision variables that have been defined will be listed here, along with their bounds, variable type, and (if discrete) step size. All this information for Freddie's single decision variable comes from the Define Decision Variable dialogue box in Figure 16.44. The entry of 60 in the Suggested Value column comes from the value that was used in the previous simulation run in Section 16.1. The entries in the Bound columns and the Suggested Value column should be checked at this point to see if you want to change them. OptQuest will consider only values between the bounds, so setting the bounds as tightly as possible without eliminating the optimal value will speed up the search for an optimal solution. OptQuest will use the suggested value for the first simulation run, so a best guess for this value also will tend to speed up the search. To better illustrate what OptQuest can do without the help of a Decision Table, we will ignore the results in Section 16.8 and stick with the values shown in the first dialogue box in Figure 16.54.

Clicking on OK then leads to the Constraints dialogue box. This box is used to type in any relevant constraints of the kind used in linear programming. Freddie's problem does not have any such constraints, so we leave this dialogue box blank and click on OK. (Our next example will illustrate the inclusion of a constraint.)

The purpose of the Forecast Selection box is to specify the objective for the optimization. This requires several steps.

1. The Name column of the Forecast Selection dialogue box lists all forecast cells that have been defined. Decide which one you want to optimize and click in the same row of the Forecast Statistic column.

2. The drop-down menu in the Forecast Statistic column lists many possible statistics (including Mean, Median, Mode, Standard Deviation, and Certainty). Select the one you want to optimize.

3. From the drop-down menu in the Select column, select either Maximize Objective (to maximize the selected statistic) or Minimize Objective (to minimize the selected statistic).

4. If you wish to add the requirement that a solution should not be considered if a particular statistic for this solution either falls below a lower bound or above an upper bound, then (1) click in the selected forecast row, (2) select Duplicate from the Edit menu (which creates a duplicate of this forecast row), (3) use the duplicate row to select Requirement from the drop-down menu in the Select column, (4) select the statistic of interest from the Forecast Statistic drop-down menu, and (5) enter either the lower bound or upper bound (whichever one the statistic needs to observe) in the corresponding column.

5. Click on OK.

For Freddie's problem, the only forecast cell is Profit (C19). Figure 16.54 indicates that he wants to maximize the mean of this forecast cell. Step 4 above could have been used, for example, to eliminate any order quantities whose variability (standard deviation) of his daily profits is too high, but Freddie did not choose to add this requirement.

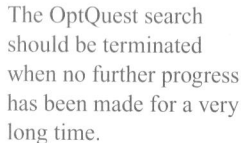
The OptQuest search should be terminated when no further progress has been made for a very long time.

The Options dialogue box shown at the bottom of Figure 16.54 is used to control how long to run the optimization (5 minutes for Freddie's problem). The Automatic Stop option can be selected, if desired, to stop the optimization early if the process has not found a better solution for a significant number of simulations. However, you also can terminate the search manually by selecting Stop in the Run menu (or by pressing <Esc> or clicking on the Stop icon) when you see that no further progress is being made.

Whenever desired, you can modify the choices made in any of the four dialogue boxes in Figure 16.54 by choosing Decision Variables, Constraints, Forecasts, or Options under the Tools menu (or by clicking the corresponding button on the OptQuest toolbar).

At this point, clicking on OK in the Options dialogue box and selecting Start from the Run menu begins the search for an optimal solution. While the search is running, you can view the progress in the Status and Solutions window. Figure 16.55 shows this window at the conclusion of the search. On the left, the solutions area indicates that the first simulation was run with

FIGURE 16.55
The optimization results provided by OptQuest for the case study introduced in Section 16.1. The best solution found for Freddie the newsboy is to use an order quantity of 55.

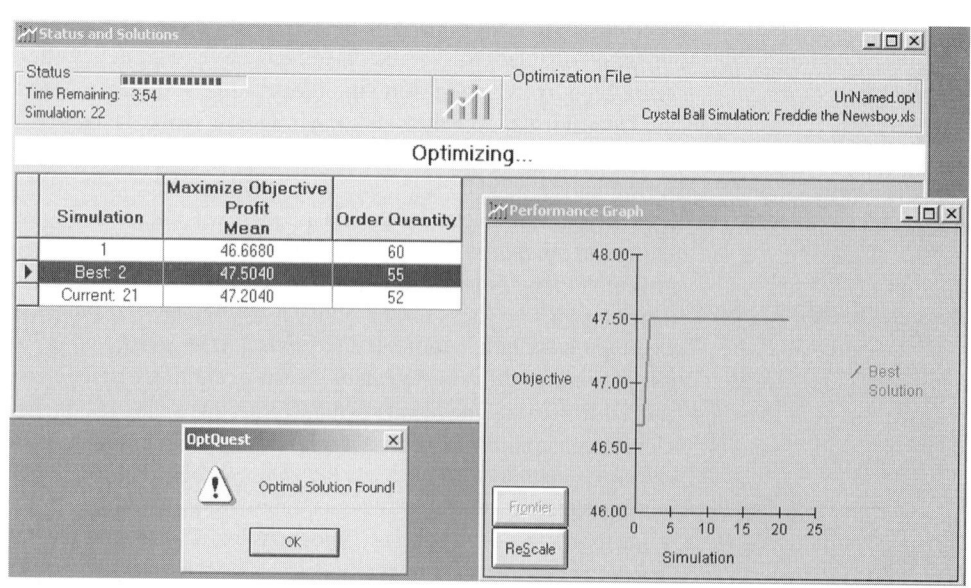

the suggested value of the order quantity (60) given in the top dialogue box in Figure 16.54. This run provided a mean profit of $46.6680. OptQuest tried an order quantity of 55 next on simulation 2, which provided a mean profit of $47.5040. The subsequent simulation runs (including the last one listed in the table) tried other order quantities but could not improve on this mean profit, so simulation 2 is highlighted in the table as the best one. Thus, an order quantity of 55 has been found to be (in all likelihood) the optimal solution for Freddie's problem.

The performance graph on the right-hand side of Figure 16.55 plots the best mean profit value found so far throughout the search process. After this graph remained flat for so many simulations from simulation 2 onward, OptQuest determined that no other order quantity would yield a mean profit better than $47.5040, so the optimization was terminated and OptQuest reported that an optimal solution had been found.

The final step is to select the best solution and then choose Copy to Excel from the Edit menu to transfer this solution to your spreadsheet model. This also will automatically display the frequency distribution from the simulation run that provided the best solution. If desired, you can see the summary statistics from this run as well by selecting Statistics from the View menu.

The following is a summary of the entire procedure for applying OptQuest, as just illustrated for Freddie's problem.

Procedure for Applying OptQuest

1. Formulate your simulation model on a spreadsheet.

2. Use Crystal Ball to complete your formulation by defining your assumption cells, forecast cells, and decision variables, as well as setting your run preferences.

3. Choose OptQuest from the Crystal Ball Tools menu and select New under the File menu.

4. Use the Decision Variable Selection dialogue box to select your decision variables.

5. Use the Constraints dialogue box to specify your constraints (if any).

6. Use the Forecast Selection dialogue box to specify the objective.

7. Use the Options dialogue box to specify the running time.

8. Select Start from the Run menu to run the optimization.

9. Choose Copy to Excel from the Edit menu to copy your results to your spreadsheet model.

Application of OptQuest to a Project Selection Example

We now turn to a more challenging example that involves applying OptQuest. This example is based on Case 6.3 at the end of Chapter 6. Here are the essential facts.

Tazer Corp., a pharmaceutical manufacturing company, is beginning the search for a new breakthrough drug. The following five potential research and development projects have been identified for attempting to develop such a drug.

Project Up: Develop a more effective antidepressant that does not cause serious mood swings.

Project Stable: Develop a drug that addresses manic depression.

Project Choice: Develop a less intrusive birth control method for women.

Project Hope: Develop a vaccine to prevent HIV infection.

Project Release: Develop a more effective drug to lower blood pressure.

In contrast to Case 6.3, Tazer management now has concluded that the company cannot devote enough money to research and development to undertake all of these projects. Only $1.2 billion is available, which will be enough for only two or three of the projects. The second column of Table 16.3 shows the amount needed (in millions of dollars) for each of these projects. The third column estimates each project's probability of being successful. If a project is successful, it

TABLE 16.3
Data for the Tazer Project Selection Problem

Project	R&D Investment ($millions)	Success Rate	Revenue ($millions) If Successful	
			Mean	Standard Deviation
Up	$400	50%	$1,400	$400
Stable	300	35	1,200	400
Choice	600	35	2,200	600
Hope	500	20	3,000	900
Release	200	45	600	200

The objective is to choose the projects that will maximize the expected profit while satisfying the budget constraint.

is quite uncertain how much revenue will be generated by the drug. The estimate of the amount of revenue (in millions of dollars) is that it has a *normal distribution* with the mean and standard deviation given in the last two columns of the table.

Tazer management now wants to determine which of these projects should be undertaken to maximize the expected total profit from the resulting revenues (if any). Because of the great uncertainty in what the total profit will turn out to be, management also would like to have a reasonably high probability of achieving a satisfactory total profit (at least $100 million).

Figure 16.56 shows a simulation model on a spreadsheet for this problem. The data in Table 16.3 have been transferred directly into the data cells C7:F11. The cells in the next column, Success? (G7:G11), are assumption cells that will have a value of 0 or 1 for each trial of a simula-

FIGURE 16.56   A spreadsheet model for applying computer simulation to the Tazer Corp. project selection problem. The assumption cells are Success? (G7:G11) and Revenue (H7:H11), the decision variables are Decisions (J7:J11), and the forecast cell is TotalProfit (I13).

	A	B	C	D	E	F	G	H	I	J
1		**Budget-Constrained Project Selection**								
2										
3					Estimated Revenue					
4			R&D		$millions If Successful					
5			Investment	Success	(Normal Distribution)			Revenue ($millions)		
6		Project	($millions)	Rate	Mean	St. Dev.	Success?	(If Successful)	Profit	Decisions
7		Up	400	50%	1,400	400	0.5	1,400	0.00	0
8		Stable	300	35%	1,200	400	0.35	1,200	0.00	0
9		Choice	600	35%	2,200	600	0.35	2,200	0.00	0
10		Hope	500	20%	3,000	900	0.2	3,000	0.00	0
11		Release	200	45%	600	200	0.45	600	0.00	0
12										
13		Invested	0					Total profit ($millions)	0.00	
14			<=							
15		Budget	1,200							

	B	C
13	Invested	=SUMPRODUCT(RandDInvestment,Decisions)

Range Name	Cells
Budget	C15
Decisions	J7:J11
Invested	C13
Profit	I7:I11
RandDInvestment	C7:C11
Revenue	H7:H11
Success?	G7:G11
TotalProfit	I13

	I
6	Profit
7	=Decisions*(Success?*Revenue–RandDInvestment)
8	=Decisions*(Success?*Revenue–RandDInvestment)
9	=Decisions*(Success?*Revenue–RandDInvestment)
10	=Decisions*(Success?*Revenue–RandDInvestment)
11	=Decisions*(Success?*Revenue–RandDInvestment)

	H	I
13	Total profit ($millions)	=SUM(Profit)

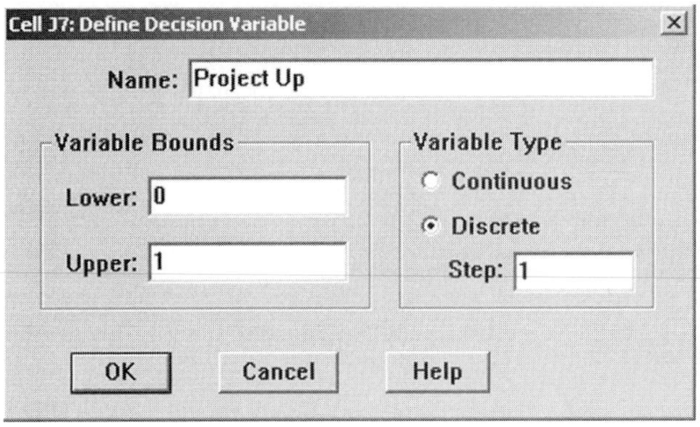

FIGURE 16.57

This Define Decision Variable dialogue box specifies the characteristics of the first decision variable Project Up in the simulation model in Figure 16.56. The other decision variables are defined in the same way.

The cells in column G, Success? (G7:G11), are assumption cells that indicate whether the corresponding projects fail (a value of 0) or succeed (a value of 1) on each trial of a simulation run.

tion run. This value indicates whether the corresponding project would fail (a value of 0) or succeed (a value of 1) on that trial if it were to be undertaken. Thus, the probability distribution entered into each of these assumption cells needs to be a *binomial distribution* (as described in Section 16.7), where the parameters are that the number of trials for this distribution is 1 and the probability of a success on this trial is given in column D. The cells in column H, Revenue (H7:H11), also are assumption cells. The probability distribution for each is a *normal distribution* with the parameters given in columns E and F.

The cells in column J, Decisions (J7:J11), are the decision variables for the model. Each of these decision variables is a *binary variable,* that is, a variable whose only possible values are 0 and 1. For example, the Define Decision Variable dialogue box in Figure 16.57 shows how the decision variable in cell J7 is defined in this way by giving it bounds of 0 and 1 and then specifying that it is a discrete variable with a step size of 1. The other four decision variables are defined in the same way. For each project listed in column B, the corresponding decision variable in column J has the following interpretation.

$$
\text{Decision Variable} = \begin{cases} 1, & \text{If approve the project} \\ 0, & \text{If reject the project} \end{cases}
$$

Budget (C15) gives the maximum amount that can be invested in these research and development projects. The output cell Invested (C13) records the total amount invested in the projects, given the decisions regarding which ones are approved. The equation entered into this cell is shown under the spreadsheet on the left-hand side of Figure 16.56. The limited budget means that the decision variables must satisfy the constraint that

$$
\text{Invested (C13)} \leq \text{Budget (C15)}
$$

The revenues in the assumption cells Revenue (H7:H11) are received only if the corresponding projects are approved and then are successful.

The output cells Profit (I7:I11) give the profit (revenue minus investment) from each project on each trial of a simulation run. The profit from a project is 0 if the project is rejected. If it is approved, the revenue is 0 if the project is not successful (as indicated by a 0 in the corresponding row of column G). If the project is successful (as indicated by a 1 in its row of column G), the revenue on that trial will be the random value that appears in the corresponding row of column H. Therefore, the equations entered into Profit (I7:I11) are those shown in the lower right-hand corner of Figure 16.56. Also note that SUM(Profit) gives the value in the *forecast cell* TotalProfit (I13).

After using Crystal Ball to define the assumption cells and forecast cell in the usual way (along with the decision variables), opening OptQuest brings up in succession the four dialogue boxes displayed in Figure 16.58.

The second column of the Decision Variable Selection dialogue box lists the five decision variables, using the names given them in the Define Decision Variable dialogue box. Since we don't yet know the best value for any of them, all five decision variables have been selected in the Select column to instruct the search procedure to consider their alternative values (0 or 1). The entries of 0 in the Suggested Value column come from the arbitrary entries of 0 in Decisions (J7:J11) in the spreadsheet model shown in Figure 16.56. Entering a better guess for a

FIGURE 16.58

These four OptQuest dialogue boxes show the choices needed to apply OptQuest to the Tazer Corp. project selection problem formulated in Figure 16.56.

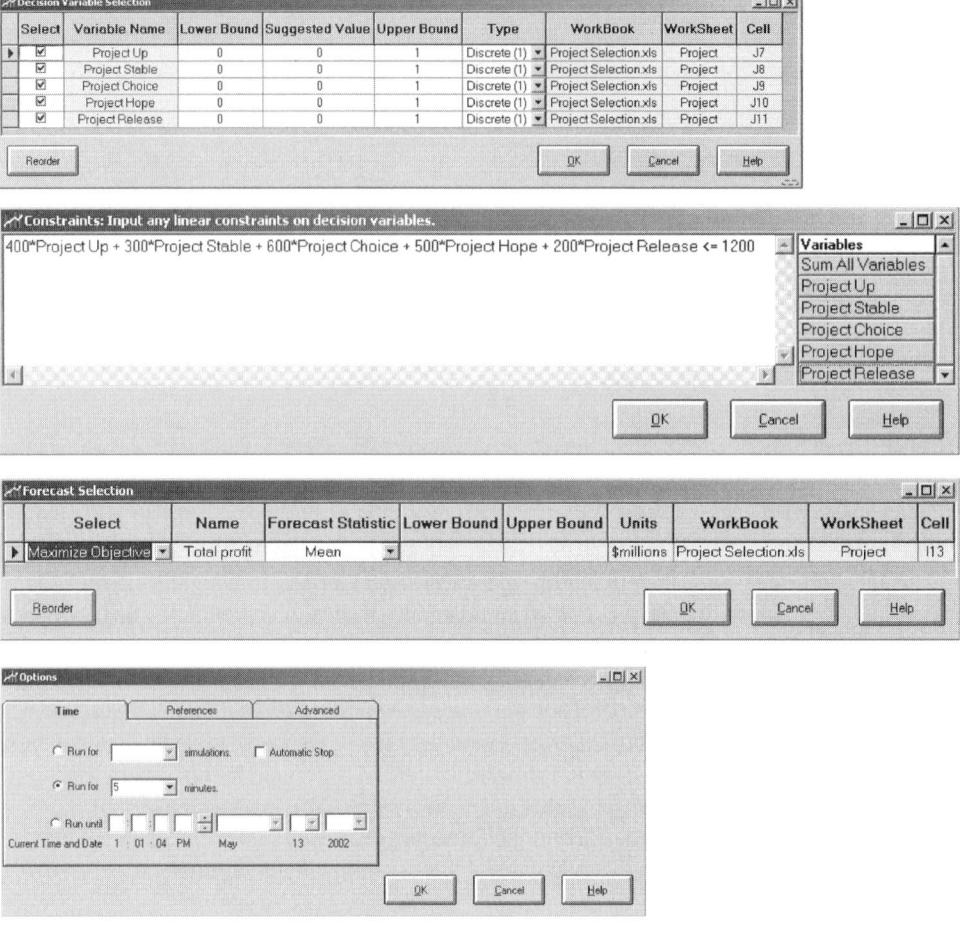

good solution in the Suggested Value column would speed up OptQuest, but we'll stick with the values of 0 to give OptQuest more of a challenge.

In addition to the bounds on the individual decision variables, the limited budget imposes another constraint on the decision variables. This constraint needs to be typed into the Constraints dialogue box in the format of a linear programming constraint, as shown in Figure 16.58. An asterisk * is used to indicate multiplication. Cell references are not allowed when entering constraints in OptQuest. Therefore, you need to either type the decision variable names or click on the corresponding buttons on the right-hand side of the dialogue box to have OptQuest enter these names for you where needed. You also need to type <= for less-than-or-equal. (Other constraints can have >= or = instead.)

Only constraints that would fit linear programming can be added in the Constraints dialogue box.

Tazer management is seeking a solution that maximizes the mean of TotalProfit (I13) in Figure 16.56, so this objective is entered into the Forecast Selection dialogue box in Figure 16.58. A run time of 5 minutes has been specified in the Options dialogue box.

Figure 16.59 summarizes the results obtained by OptQuest during this run. Simulation 1 used the values of the decision variables that had been entered in the Suggested Value column of the Decision Variable Selection dialogue box. The table in Figure 16.59 indicates that OptQuest then found improved solutions with simulations 4, 5, 6, 11, 16, and 17. Many subsequent simulations failed to find any further improvement, as depicted graphically by the long flat line at the top of the performance chart. At that point, OptQuest determined that no better solutions were available, so the optimization was terminated. The highlighted row in the table shows the best solution that was found. Consequently, the conclusion is that this solution

Choose Project Up, Project Choice, and Project Release

Mean of total profit = $551,330 million

is, in all likelihood, the optimal solution.

FIGURE 16.59

The optimization results provided by OptQuest for the Tazer Corp. project selection problem. The best solution found is to approve Project Up, Project Choice, and Project Release.

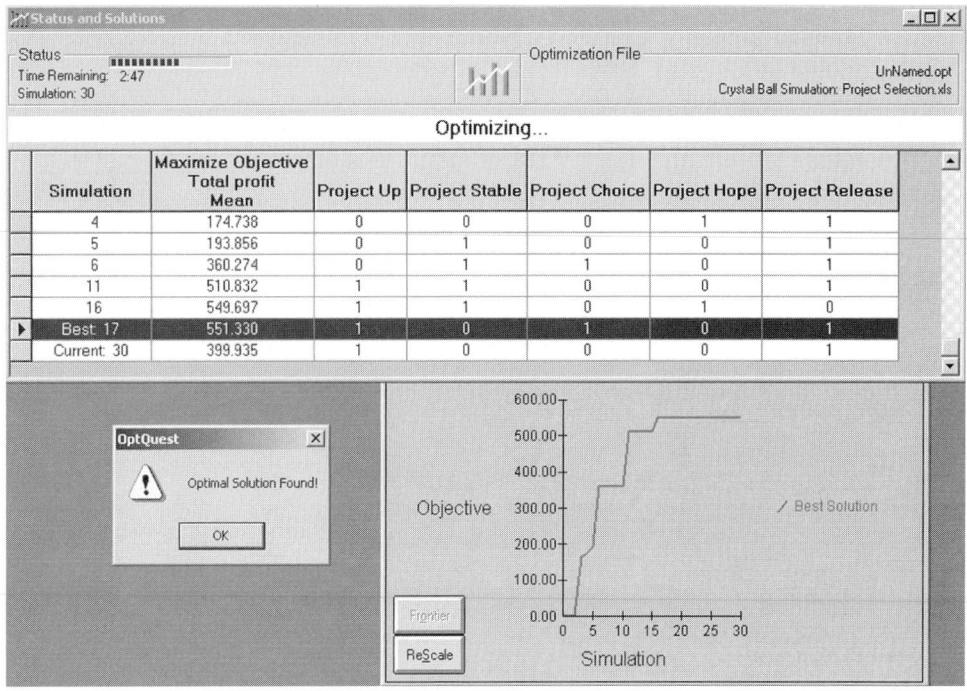

FIGURE 16.60

The frequency chart for the best solution found in Figure 16.59. The Certainty box shows the percentage of the trials that provided a profit of at least $100 million.

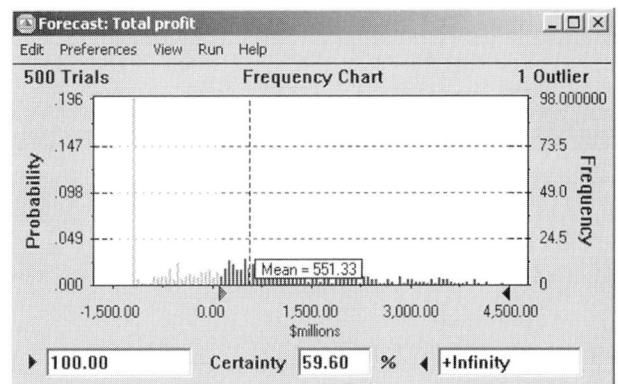

Figure 16.60 shows the frequency chart that was obtained with the simulation run that used the best solution. This chart shows a high degree of variability in the profit values obtained during the various trials of the simulation run. There is a substantial probability of actually incurring a loss from the selected research and development projects (which is fairly common in this industry). In fact, 98 of the 500 trials resulted in a loss of $1.2 billion because all three projects failed. Fortunately, there also is a good chance of reaping extremely big profits. Because Tazer management would like to have a high probability of obtaining a total profit of at least $100 million, this quantity has been entered in the box in the lower left-hand corner. The Certainty box indicates that 59.60 percent of the trials did at least this well.

Tazer management had hoped to have a higher probability of obtaining a total profit of at least $100 million. Therefore, the question is raised whether there might be another combination of research and development projects that would increase this probability.

Tazer management also would be interested in a solution that maximizes the probability of obtaining a satisfactory profit of at least $100 million.

To address this question, choose Forecasts under the Tools menu in OptQuest (or click the corresponding button on the OptQuest toolbar). This brings up the Forecast Selection dialogue box shown in the upper part of Figure 16.61. Rather than maximizing the mean, use the pull-down menu in the Forecast Statistic column to choose Certainty. This brings up the Certainty dialogue box in the lower part of Figure 16.61. Enter a lower bound of 100. Since units of millions of dollars are being used, this changes the objective in the Forecast Selection dialogue

FIGURE 16.61 The choices made in this Forecast Selection dialogue box and this Certainty dialogue box will enable OptQuest to maximize the probability that Tazer Corp. will obtain a profit of at least $100 million from its choice of research and development projects.

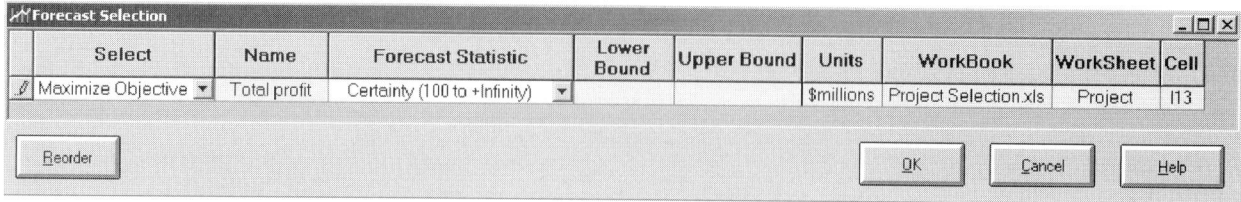

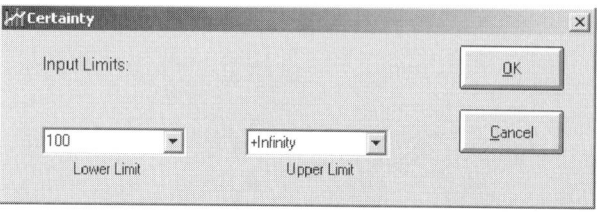

FIGURE 16.62

The optimization results provided by OptQuest for the revision of the Tazer Corp. project selection problem that uses the objective specified in Figure 16.61. The best solution found is to approve Project Up, Project Stable, and Project Release.

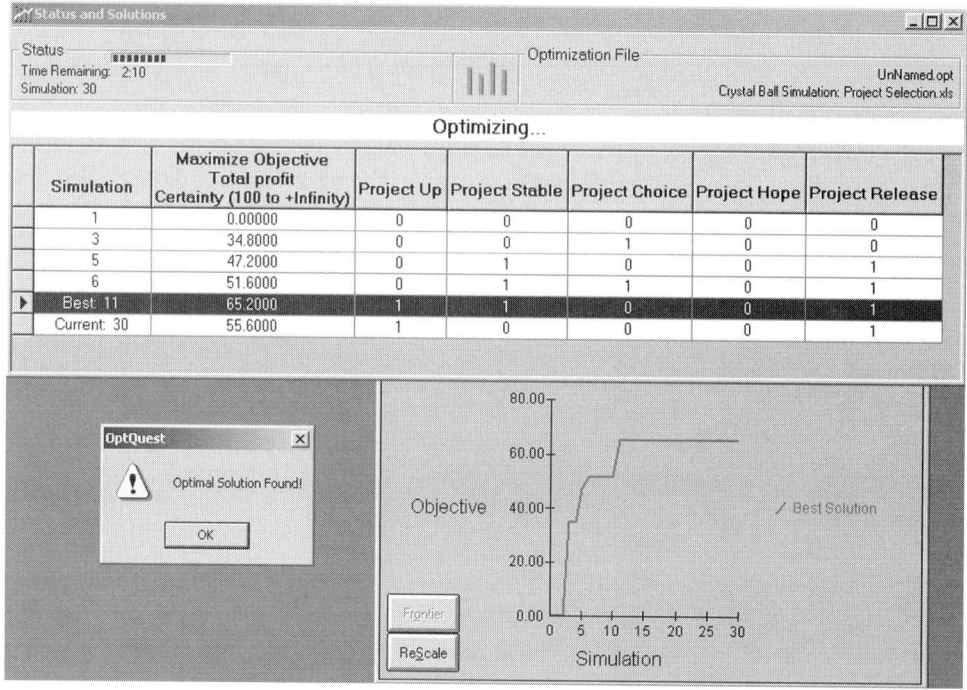

box (as displayed in the figure) to finding the solution that maximizes the *probability* (certainty) that the total profit will be at least $100 million.

Rerunning OptQuest with this new objective leads to the results shown in Figure 16.62. Simulations 3, 5, 6, and 11 all succeeded in improving on the best previous solution. The performance chart depicts the progress made. The best solution found by the end of the run (simulation 11) had 65.2 percent of the trials providing a total profit of at least $100 million. This solution is

Choose Project Up, Project Stable, and Project Release

Certainty of total profit ≥ $100 million: 65.2%

By substituting Project Stable for the much more expensive Project Choice from the best solution found in Figure 16.59, this more conservative solution has managed to boost the estimated probability of achieving a satisfactory total profit from 59.6 percent to 65.2 percent.

FIGURE 16.63

The frequency chart for the profit values obtained in the simulation run that provided the best solution in Figure 16.62. The Certainty box shows the percentage of the trials that provided a profit of at least $100 million.

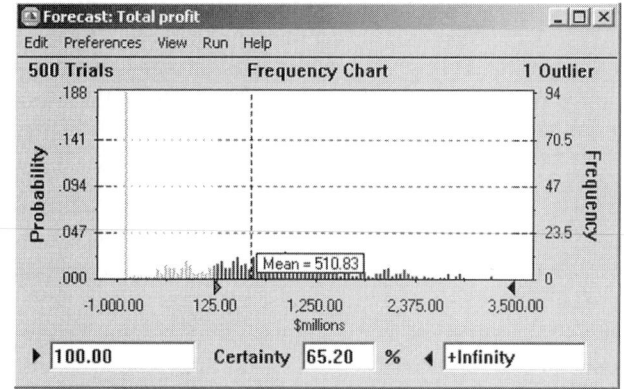

However, after copying the best solution in Figure 16.62 to Excel and displaying the results for this simulation run, the frequency chart in Figure 16.63 reveals a disadvantage of this conservative solution. The mean of the total profit from this solution was only $510.83 million versus $551.33 million for the best solution found in Figure 16.59 when the objective was to maximize this quantity. At the same time, the conservative solution has reduced the maximum possible loss from $1.2 billion to $900 million.

In conclusion, OptQuest has provided Tazer management with two different kinds of solutions from which to choose, along with considerable information about each. One appears to be the best high-risk, high-reward solution that is available because it maximizes the total profit that would be obtained on the average. The other appears to be the best available conservative solution because it maximizes the chances of obtaining a satisfactory profit. By evaluating the trade-off between risk and reward, management now can make a judgment decision about which solution to use.

Review Questions

1. What does OptQuest search for in a simulation model with decision variables?
2. What kinds of problems can OptQuest deal with that the Decision Table tool cannot?
3. Does OptQuest always find an optimal solution?
4. What initial steps need to be completed before opening OptQuest?
5. What is the purpose of the Decision Variable Selection dialogue box?
6. What is the purpose of the Constraints dialogue box?
7. What is the purpose of the Forecast Selection dialogue box?
8. What is the purpose of the Options dialogue box?
9. When running OptQuest, what information is provided in the Status and Solutions window?
10. When running OptQuest, when is it reasonable to terminate the run manually?
11. The decision variables for the project selection example needed to be of what kind?

16.10 Summary

Increasingly, spreadsheet software is being used to perform computer simulations. As described in the preceding chapter, the standard Excel package sometimes is sufficient to do this. In addition, some Excel add-ins now are available that greatly extend these capabilities. Crystal Ball is an especially powerful add-in of this kind.

When using Crystal Ball, each input cell that has a random value is referred to as an *assumption cell*. The procedure for defining an assumption cell includes selecting one of 17 types of probability distributions from a Distribution Gallery to enter into the cell. When historical data are available, Crystal Ball also has a procedure for identifying which continuous distribution fits the data best.

An output cell that is used to forecast a measure of performance is called a *forecast cell*. Each trial of a simulation run generates a value in each forecast cell. When the simulation run is completed, Crystal Ball provides the results in a variety of useful forms, including a frequency distribution, a statistics table, a percentiles table, and a cumulative chart.

When a simulation model has one or two decision variables, Crystal Ball provides a *Decision Table tool* that systematically applies computer simulation to identify at least an approximation of an optimal solution. A *trend chart* also provides additional insights to aid in decision making.

In addition, the Professional Edition of Crystal Ball includes a powerful optimization module called OptQuest that is based on years of research in optimization and artificial intelligence. This module efficiently uses a series of simulation runs to search for an optimal solution for a simulation model with any number of decision variables.

The availability of such powerful software now enables managers to add computer simulation to their personal tool kit of management science techniques for analyzing some key managerial problems. A variety of examples in this chapter illustrate some of the many possibilities for important applications of computer simulation.

Glossary

assumption cell   An input cell that has a random value so that an assumed probability distribution must be entered into the cell instead of permanently entering a single number. (Section 16.1), *773*

Decision Table tool   A Crystal Ball module that systematically applies computer simulation over a range of values of one or two decision variables and then displays the results in a table. (Section 16.8), *817*

Distribution Gallery   Crystal Ball's gallery of 17 probability distributions from which one is chosen to enter into any assumption cell. (Sections 16.1 and 16.7), *774*

dynamic option   When cell references are entered into any of the parameter fields in the dialogue box for a distribution, choosing the dynamic option causes each of these cell references to be evaluated for each separate trial of the simulation run. (Section 16.1), *774*

forecast cell   An output cell that is being used by a computer simulation to forecast a measure of performance. (Section 16.1), *774*

OptQuest   A Crystal Ball module that automatically searches for an optimal solution for a simulation model with any number of decision variables. (Section 16.9), *825*

risk profile   A frequency distribution of the return from an investment. (Section 16.5), *796*

static option   When cell references are entered into any of the parameter fields in the dialogue box for a distribution, choosing the static option causes each of these cell references to be evaluated only once, at the beginning of the simulation run, so the parameter values at that point are used for all trials of the simulation. (Section 16.1), *774*

trial   A single application of the process of generating a random observation from each probability distribution entered into the spreadsheet and then calculating the output cells in the usual way and recording the results of interest. (Section 16.1), *772*

Learning Aids for This Chapter in Your MS Courseware

Chapter 16 Excel Files:

Freddie the Newsboy Case Study
Reliable Co. Bidding Example
Reliable Co. Project Scheduling Example
Everglade Co. Cash Flow Linear Programming
Everglade Co. Cash Flow Management Example
Think-Big Co. Financial Risk Analysis Example
Transcontinental Airlines Overbooking Example
Tazer Corp. Project Selection Example
Sales Data 1
Sales Data 2

An Excel Add-in:

Crystal Ball 2000 Professional Edition

Problems

Crystal Ball should be used for all of the following problems. An asterisk on the problem number indicates that a partial answer is given in the back of the book.

16.1.   The results from a simulation run are inherently random. This problem will demonstrate this fact and investigate the impact of the number of trials on this randomness. Consider the case study involving Freddie the newsboy that was introduced in Section 16.1. The spreadsheet model is available on your MS Courseware CD-ROM. Make sure that the "Use Same Sequence of Random Numbers" option is *not* checked and that the Monte-Carlo Sampling Method is selected in the Sampling tab of Run Preferences. Use an order quantity of 60.

    a. Set the number of trials to 100 in Run Preferences and run the simulation of Freddie's problem five times. Note the mean profit for each simulation run.

    b. Repeat part *a* except set the number of trials to 1,000 in Run Preferences.

    c. Compare the results from part *a* and part *b* and comment on any differences.

16.2. Consider the Reliable Construction Co. project scheduling example presented in Section 16.3. Recall that computer simulation was used to estimate the probability of meeting the deadline and that Figure 16.21 revealed that the deadline was met on 61.50 percent of the trials from one simulation run. As discussed while interpreting this result, the percentage of trials on which the project is completed by the deadline will vary from simulation run to simulation run. This problem will demonstrate this fact and investigate the impact of the number of trials on this randomness. The spreadsheet model is available on your MS Courseware CD-ROM. Make sure that the "Use Same Sequence of Random Numbers" option is *not* checked and that the Monte-Carlo Sampling Method is selected in the Sampling tab of Run Preferences.

    a. Set the number of trials to 100 in Run Preferences and run the simulation of the project five times. Note the mean completion time and the percentage of trials on which the project is completed within the deadline of 47 weeks for each simulation run.

    b. Repeat part *a* except set the number of trials to 1,000 in Run Preferences.

    c. Compare the results from part *a* and part *b* and comment on any differences.

16.3.* Consider the historical data contained in the Excel File "Sales Data 1" on your MS Courseware CD-ROM. Use Crystal Ball to fit all continuous distributions to these data.

    a. Which distribution provides the closest fit to the data? What are the parameters of the distribution?

    b. Which distribution provides the second-closest fit to the data? What are the parameters of the distribution?

16.4. Consider the historical data contained in the Excel File "Sales Data 2" on your MS Courseware CD-ROM. Use Crystal Ball to fit all continuous distributions to these data.

    a. Which distribution provides the closest fit to the data? What are the parameters of the distribution?

    b. Which distribution provides the second-closest fit to the data? What are the parameters of the distribution?

16.5. The Aberdeen Development Corporation (ADC) is reconsidering the Aberdeen Resort Hotel project. It would be located on the picturesque banks of Grays Harbor and have its own championship-level golf course.

    The cost to purchase the land would be $1 million, payable now. Construction costs would be approximately $2 million, payable at the end of year 1. However, the construction costs are uncertain. These costs could be up to 20 percent higher or lower than the estimate of $2 million. Assume that the construction costs would follow a triangular distribution.

    ADC is very uncertain about the annual operating profits (or losses) that would be generated once the hotel is constructed. Its best estimate for the annual operating profit that would be generated in years 2, 3, 4, and 5 is $700,000. Due to the great uncertainty, the estimate of the standard deviation of the annual operating profit in each year also is $700,000. Assume that the yearly profits are statistically independent and follow the normal distribution.

    After year 5, ADC plans to sell the hotel. The selling price is likely to be somewhere between $4 and $8 million (assume a uniform distribution). ADC uses a 10 percent discount rate for calculating net present value. (For purposes of this calculation, assume that each year's profits are received at year-end.) Use Crystal Ball to perform 1,000 trials of a computer simulation of this project on a spreadsheet.

    a. What is the mean net present value (NPV) of the project? (*Hint:* The NPV (rate, cash stream) function in Excel returns the NPV of a stream of cash flows assumed to start one year from now. For example, NPV(10%, C5:F5) returns the NPV at a 10% discount rate when C5 is a cash flow at the end of year 1, D5 at the end of year 2, E5 at the end of year 3, and F5 at the end of year 4.)

    b. What is the estimated probability that the project will yield an NPV greater than $2 million?

    c. ADC also is concerned about cash flow in years 2, 3, 4, and 5. Use Crystal Ball to generate a forecast of the distribution of the *minimum* annual operating profit (undiscounted) earned in any of the four years. What is the mean value of the minimum annual operating profit over the four years?

d. What is the probability that the annual operating profit will be at least $0 in all four years of operation?

16.6. Ivy University is planning to construct a new building for its business school. This project will require completing all of the activities in the following table. For most of these activities, a set of predecessor activities must be completed before the activity begins. For example, the foundation cannot be laid until the building is designed and the site prepared.

Activity	Predecessors
A. Secure funding	—
B. Design building	A
C. Site preparation	A
D. Foundation	B,C
E. Framing	D
F. Electrical	E
G. Plumbing	E
H. Walls and roof	F, G
I. Finish construction	H
J. Landscaping	H

Obtaining funding likely will take approximately six months (with a standard deviation of one month). Assume that this time has a normal distribution. The architect has estimated that the time required to design the building could be anywhere between 6 and 10 months. Assume that this time has a uniform distribution. The general contractor has provided three estimates for each of the construction tasks—an optimistic scenario (minimum time required if the weather is good and all goes well), a most likely scenario, and a pessimistic scenario (maximum time required if there are weather and other problems). These estimates are provided in the table that follows. Assume that each of these construction times has a triangular distribution. Finally, the landscaper has guaranteed that his work will be completed in five months.

Construction Time Estimates (months)

Activity	Optimistic Scenario	Most Likely Scenario	Pessimistic Scenario
C. Site preparation	1.5	2	2.5
D. Foundation	1.5	2	3
E. Framing	3	4	6
F. Electrical	2	3	5
G. Plumbing	3	4	5
H. Walls and roof	4	5	7
I. Do the finish work	5	6	7

Use Crystal Ball to generate 1,000 trials of a computer simulation for this project. Use the results to answer the following questions.

a. What is the mean project completion time?

b. What is the probability that the project will be completed in 36 months or less?

c. Generate a sensitivity chart. Based on this chart, which activities have the largest impact on the variability in the project completion time?

16.7.* Reconsider Problem 8.12, which involves estimating both the duration of a project and the probability that it will be completed by the deadline. Assume now that the duration of each activity has a triangular distribution that is based on the three estimates shown in Problem 8.12. Use Crystal Ball to perform 1,000 trials of a computer simulation of the project on a spreadsheet.

a. What is the mean project completion time?

b. What is the probability that the project can be completed within 22 months?

c. Generate a sensitivity chart. Based on this chart, which two activities have the largest impact on the variability in the project completion time?

16.8. Reconsider Problem 15.10. To obtain a close estimate of the average cost of insurance coverage for the corporation's employees, use Crystal Ball with a spreadsheet to perform 500 iterations of a computer simulation of an employee's health insurance experience. Generate a frequency chart and a statistics table.

16.9. Reconsider the Heavy Duty Co. problem that was presented as Example 2 in Section 15.1. For each of the following three options in parts *a* through *c,* obtain an estimate of the expected cost per day by using Crystal Ball to perform 1,000 trials of a computer simulation of the problem on a spreadsheet. Generate a frequency chart and a statistics table.

a. The option of not replacing a motor until a breakdown occurs.

b. The option of scheduling the replacement of a motor after four days (but replacing it sooner if a breakdown occurs).

c. The option of scheduling the replacement of a motor after five days (but replacing it sooner if a breakdown occurs).

d. An analytical result of $2,000 per day is available for the expected cost per day if a motor is replaced every three days. Comparing this option and the above three, which one appears to minimize the expected cost per day?

16.10. The Avery Co. factory has been having a maintenance problem with the control panel for one of its production processes. This control panel contains four identical electromechanical relays that have been the cause of the trouble. The problem is that the relays fail fairly frequently, thereby forcing the control panel (and the production process it controls) to be shut down while a replacement is made. The current practice is to replace the relays only when they fail. The average total cost of doing this has been $3.19 per hour. To attempt to reduce this cost, a proposal has been made to replace all four relays whenever any one of them fails to reduce the frequency with which the control panel must be shut down. Would this actually reduce the cost?

The pertinent data are the following. For each relay, the operating time until failure has approximately a uniform distribution from 1,000 to 2,000 hours. The control panel must be shut down for one hour to replace one relay or for two hours to replace all four relays. The total cost associated with shutting down the control panel and replacing relays is $1,000 per hour plus $200 for each new relay.

Use computer simulation on a spreadsheet to evaluate the cost of the proposal and compare it to the current practice. Use Crystal Ball to perform 1,000 trials (where the end of each trial coincides with the end of a shutdown of the control panel) and determine the average cost per hour.

16.11. For one new product produced by the Aplus Company, bushings need to be drilled into a metal block and cylindrical shafts need to be inserted into the bushings. The shafts are required to have a radius of at least 1.0000 inch, but the radius should be as little larger than this as possible. With the proposed production process for producing the shafts, the probability distribution of the radius of a shaft has a triangular distribution with a minimum of 1.0000 inch, a most likely value of 1.0010 inches, and a maximum value of 1.0020 inches. With the proposed method of drilling the bushings, the probability distribution of the radius of a bushing has a normal distribution with a mean of 1.0020 inches and a standard deviation of 0.0010 inches. The clearance between a bushing and a shaft is the difference in their radii. Because they are selected at random, there occasionally is interference (i.e., negative clearance) between a bushing and a shaft to be mated.

Management is concerned about the disruption in the production of the new product that would be caused by this occasional interference. Perhaps the production processes for the shafts and bushings should be improved (at considerable cost) to lessen the chance of interference. To evaluate the need for such improvements, management has asked you to determine how frequently interference is likely to occur with the currently proposed production processes.

Estimate the probability of interference by using Crystal Ball to perform 500 trials of a computer simulation on a spreadsheet.

16.12. Refer to the financial risk analysis example presented in Section 16.5, including its results shown in Figure 16.29. Think-Big management is quite concerned about the risk profile for the proposal. Two statistics are causing particular concern. One is that there is nearly a 20 percent chance of losing money (a negative NPV). Second, there is a 10 percent chance of losing at least a full third ($6 million) as much as the mean gain ($18 million). Therefore, management is wondering whether it would be more prudent to go ahead with just one of the two projects. Thus, in addition to option 1 (the proposal), option 2 is to take a 16.50 percent share of the hotel project only (so no participation in the shopping center project) and option 3 is to take a 13.11 percent share of the shopping center only (so no participation in the hotel project). Management wants to choose one of the three options. Risk profiles now are needed to evaluate the latter two.

   a. Generate a frequency chart and a percentiles table for option 2 after performing a computer simulation with 1,000 trials for this option.

   b. Repeat part *a* for option 3.

   c. Suppose *you* were the CEO of the Think-Big Development Co. Use the results in Figure 16.29 for option 1 along with the corresponding results obtained for the other two options as the basis for a managerial decision on which of the three options to choose. Justify your answer.

16.13. Reconsider Problem 15.5 involving the game of craps. Now the objective is to estimate the probability of winning a play of this game. If the probability is greater than 0.5, you will want to go to Las Vegas to play the game numerous times until you eventually win a considerable amount of money. However, if the probability is less than 0.5, you will stay home.

   You have decided to perform computer simulation on a spreadsheet to estimate this probability. Use Crystal Ball to perform the number of trials (plays of the game) indicated below.

   a. 100 trials.

   b. 1,000 trials.

   c. 10,000 trials.

   d. The true probability is 0.493. Based upon the above simulation runs, what number of trials appears to be needed to give reasonable assurance of obtaining an estimate that is within 0.007 of the true probability?

16.14. Consider the case study involving Freddie the newsboy that was introduced in Section 16.1. The spreadsheet model is available on your MS Courseware CD-ROM. The Decision Table generated in Section 16.8 (see Figure 16.46) for Freddie's problem suggests that 55 is the best order quantity, but this table only considered order quantities that were a multiple of 5. Refine the search by generating a Decision Table for Freddie's problem that considers all integer order quantities between 50 and 60.

16.15.* Michael Wise operates a newsstand at a busy intersection downtown. Demand for the Sunday *Times* averages 300 copies with a standard deviation of 50 copies (assume a normal distribution). Michael purchases the papers for $0.75 and sells them for $1.25. Any papers left over at the end of the day are recycled with no monetary return.

   a. Suppose that Michael buys 350 copies for his newsstand each Sunday morning. Use Crystal Ball to perform 500 trials of a computer simulation on a spreadsheet. What will be Michael's mean profit from selling the Sunday *Times?* What is the probability that Michael will make at least $0 profit?

   b. Generate a Decision Table to consider five possible order quantities between 250 and 350. Which order quantity maximizes Michael's mean profit?

   c. Generate a trend chart for the five order quantities considered in part *b.*

   d. Use OptQuest to find the order quantity that maximizes Michael's mean profit.

16.16. Susan is a ticket scalper. She buys tickets for Los Angeles Lakers games before the beginning of the season for $100 each. Since the games all sell out, Susan is able to sell the tickets for $150 on game day. Tickets that Susan is unable to sell on game day have no value. Based on past experience, Susan has predicted the probability distribution for how many tickets she will be able to sell, as shown in the following table.

Tickets	Probability
10	0.05
11	0.10
12	0.10
13	0.15
14	0.20
15	0.15
16	0.10
17	0.10
18	0.05

   a. Suppose that Susan buys 14 tickets for each game. Use Crystal Ball to perform 500 trials of a computer simulation on a spreadsheet. What will be Susan's mean profit from selling the tickets? What is the probability that Susan will make at least $0 profit? (*Hint:* Use the Custom Distribution to simulate the demand for tickets.)

   b. Generate a Decision Table to consider all nine possible quantities of tickets to purchase between 10 and 18. Which purchase quantity maximizes Susan's mean profit?

   c. Generate a trend chart for the nine purchase quantities considered in part *b.*

   d. Use OptQuest to find the purchase quantity that maximizes Susan's mean profit.

16.17. Consider the Reliable Construction Co. bidding problem discussed in Section 16.2. The spreadsheet model is available on your MS Courseware CD-ROM. The Decision Table generated in Section 16.8 (see Figure 16.51) for this problem suggests that $5.4 million is the best bid, but this table only considered bids that were a multiple of $0.2 million.

   a. Refine the search by generating a Decision Table for this bidding problem that considers all bids between $5.2 million and $5.6 million in multiples of $0.05 million.

   b. Use OptQuest to find the bid that maximizes Reliable Construction Co.'s mean profit. Assume that the bid may be any value between $4.8 million and $5.8 million.

16.18. Road Pavers, Inc., (RPI) is considering bidding on a county road construction project. RPI has estimated that the cost of this particular job would be $5 million. The cost of putting together a bid is estimated to be $50,000. The county also will receive four other bids on the project from competitors of RPI. Past experience with these competitors suggests that each competitor's bid is most likely to be 20 percent over cost, but could be as low as 5 percent over or as much as 40 percent over cost. Assume a triangular distribution for each of these bids.

   a. Suppose that RPI bids $5.7 million on the project. Use Crystal Ball to perform 500 trials of a computer simulation on a spreadsheet. What is the probability that RPI will win the bid? What is RPI's mean profit?

   b. Generate a Decision Table to consider eight possible bids between $5.3 million and $6 million and forecast RPI's mean profit. Which bid maximizes RPI's mean profit?

   c. Generate a trend chart for the eight bids considered in part *b.*

   d. Use OptQuest to find the bid that maximizes RPI's mean profit.

16.19. Consider the Everglade cash flow problem analyzed in Section 16.4. The spreadsheet model is available on your MS Courseware CD-ROM.

   a. Generate a Decision Table to consider five possible long-term loan amounts between $0 million and $20 million and forecast Everglade's mean ending balance. Which long-term loan amount maximizes Everglade's mean ending balance?

   b. Generate a trend chart for the five long-term loan amounts considered in part *a.*

   c. Use OptQuest to find the long-term loan amount that maximizes Everglade's mean ending balance.

16.20. Consider the airline overbooking problem discussed in Section 16.6. The spreadsheet model is available on the MS Courseware CD-ROM packaged with the textbook. The Decision Table generated in Section 16.8 (see Figure 16.52) for this problem suggests that 185 is the best number of reservations to accept in order to maximize profit, but the only numbers considered were a multiple of five.

   a. Refine the search by generating a Decision Table for this overbooking problem that considers all integer values for the number of reservations to accept between 180 and 190.

   b. Generate a trend chart for the 11 forecasts considered in part *a.*

   c. Use OptQuest to find the number of reservations to accept that maximizes the airline's mean profit. Assume that the number of reservations to accept may be any integer value between 150 and 200.

16.21. Flight 120 between Seattle and San Francisco is a popular flight among both leisure and business travelers. The airplane holds 112 passengers in a single cabin. Both a discount 7-day advance fare and a full-price fare are offered. The airline's management is trying to decide (1) how many seats to allocate to its discount 7-day advance fare and (2) how many tickets to issue in total.

   The discount ticket sells for $150 and is nonrefundable. Demand for the 7-day advance fares is typically between 50 and 150, but is most likely to be near 90. (Assume a triangular distribution.) The full-price fare (no advance purchase requirement and fully refundable prior to check-in time) is $400. Excluding customers who purchase this ticket and then cancel prior to check-in time, demand is equally likely to be anywhere between 30 and 70 for these tickets (with essentially all of the demand occurring within one week of the flight). The average no-show rate is 5 percent for the nonrefundable discount tickets and 15 percent for the refundable full-price tickets. If more ticketed passengers show up than there are seats available, the extra passengers must be bumped. A bumped passenger is rebooked on another flight and given a voucher for a free ticket on a future flight. The total cost to the airline for bumping a passenger is $600. There is a fixed cost of $10,000 to operate the flight.

There are two decisions to be made. First, prior to one week before flight time, how many tickets should be made available at the discount fare? Too many and the airline risks losing out on potential full-fare passengers. Too few and the airline may have a less-than-full flight. Second, how many tickets should be issued in total? Too many and the airline risks needing to bump passengers. Too few and the airline risks having a less-than-full flight.

a. Suppose that the airline makes available a maximum of 75 tickets for the discount fare and a maximum of 120 tickets in total. Use Crystal Ball to generate a 1,000 trial forecast of the distribution of the profit, the number of seats filled, and the number of passengers bumped.

b. Generate a two-dimensional Decision Table that gives the mean profit for all combinations of the following values of the two decision variables: (1) the maximum number of tickets made available at the discount fare is a multiple of 10 between 50 and 90 and (2) the maximum number of tickets made available for either fare is 112, 117, 122, 127, or 132.

c. Use OptQuest to try to determine the maximum number of discount fare tickets and the maximum total number of tickets to make available so as to maximize the airline's expected profit.

Case 16-1

Action Adventures

The Adventure Toys Company manufactures a popular line of action figures and distributes them to toy stores at the wholesale price of $10 per unit. Demand for the action figures is seasonal, with the highest sales occurring before Christmas and during the spring. The lowest sales occur during the summer and winter months.

Each month the monthly "base" sales follow a normal distribution with a mean equal to the previous month's actual "base" sales and with a standard deviation of 500 units. The actual sales in any month are the monthly base sales multiplied by the seasonality factor for the month, as shown in the table below. Base sales in December 2002 were 6,000, with actual sales equal to $(1.18)(6,000) = 7,080$. It is now January 1, 2003.

Month	Seasonality Factor	Month	Seasonality Factor
January	0.79	July	0.74
February	0.88	August	0.98
March	0.95	September	1.06
April	1.05	October	1.10
May	1.09	November	1.16
June	0.84	December	1.18

Cash sales typically account for about 40 percent of monthly sales, but this figure has been as low as 28 percent and as high as 48 percent in some months. The remainder of the sales are made on a 30-day interest-free credit basis, with full payment received one month after delivery. In December 2002, 42 percent of sales were cash sales and 58 percent were on credit.

The production costs depend upon the labor and material costs. The plastics required to manufacture the action figures fluctuate in price from month to month, depending on market conditions. Because of these fluctuations, production costs can be anywhere from $6 to $8 per unit. In addition to these variable production costs, the company incurs a fixed cost of $15,000 per month for manufacturing the action figures. The company assembles the products to order. When a batch of a particular action figure is ordered, it is immediately manufactured and shipped within a couple of days.

The company utilizes eight molding machines to mold the action figures. These machines occasionally break down and require a $5,000 replacement part. Each machine requires a replacement part with a 10 percent probability each month.

The company has a policy of maintaining a minimum cash balance of at least $20,000 at the end of each month. The balance at the end of December 2002 (or equivalently, at the beginning of January 2003) is $25,000. If required, the company will take out a short-term (one-month) loan to cover expenses and maintain the minimum balance. The loans must be paid back the following month with interest (using the current month's loan interest rate). For example, if March's annual interest rate is 6 percent (so 0.5 percent per month) and a $1,000 loan is taken out in March, then $1,005 is due in April. However, a new loan can be taken out each month.

Any balance remaining at the end of a month (including the minimum balance) is carried forward to the following month and also earns savings interest. For example, if the ending balance in March is $20,000 and March's savings interest is 3 percent per annum (so 0.25 percent per month), then $50 of savings interest is earned in April.

Both the loan interest rate and the savings interest rate are set monthly based upon the prime rate. The loan interest rate is set at prime + 2%, while the savings interest rate is set at prime − 2%. However, the loan interest rate is capped at (can't exceed) 9 percent and the savings interest rate will never drop below 2 percent.

The prime rate in December 2002 was 5 percent per annum. This rate depends upon the whims of the Federal Reserve Board. In particular, for each month there is a 70 percent chance it will stay unchanged, a 10 percent chance it will increase by 25 basis points (0.25 percent), a 10 percent chance it will decrease by 25 basis points, a 5 percent chance it will increase by 50 basis points, and a 5 percent chance it will decrease by 50 basis points.

a. Formulate a simulation model on a spreadsheet to track the company's cash flows from month to month. Indicate the probability distributions (both the type and the parameters) for the assumption cells directly on the spreadsheet. Use Crystal Ball to simulate 1,000 trials for the year 2003 and paste your results in the spreadsheet.

b. Adventure Toys management wants information about what the company's net worth might be at the end of 2003, including the likelihood that the net worth will exceed $0. (The net worth is defined here as the ending cash balance *plus* savings interest and account receivables *minus* any loans and interest due.) Display the results of your simulation run from part *a* in the various forms that you think would be helpful to management in analyzing this issue.

c. Arrangements need to be made to obtain a specific credit limit from the bank for the short-term loans that might be needed during 2003. Therefore, Adventure Toys management also would like information regarding the size of the maximum short-term loan that might be needed during 2003. Display the results of your simulation run from part *a* in the various forms that you think would be helpful to management in analyzing this issue.

Case 16-2

Pricing under Pressure

Elise Sullivan moved to New York City in September to begin her first job as an analyst working in the Client Services Division of FirstBank, a large investment bank providing brokerage services to clients across the United States. The moment she arrived in the Big Apple after receiving her undergraduate business degree, she hit the ground running—or, more appropriately, working. She spent her first six weeks in training, where she met new FirstBank analysts like herself and learned the basics of FirstBank's approach to accounting, cash flow analysis, customer service, and federal regulations.

After completing training, Elise moved into her bullpen on the 40th floor of the Manhattan FirstBank building to begin work. Her first few assignments have allowed her to learn the ropes by placing her under the direction of senior staff members who delegate specific tasks to her.

Today, she has an opportunity to distinguish herself in her career, however. Her boss, Michael Steadman, has given her an assignment that is under her complete direction and control. A very eccentric, wealthy client and avid investor by the name of Emery Bowlander is interested in purchasing a European call option that provides him with the right to purchase shares of Fellare stock for $44.00 on the first of February—12 weeks from today. Fellare is an aerospace manufacturing company operating in France, and Mr. Bowlander has a strong feeling that the European Space Agency will award Fellare with a contract to build a portion of the International Space Station some time in January. In the event that the European Space Agency awards the contract to Fellare, Mr. Bowlander believes the stock will skyrocket, reflecting investor confidence in the capabilities and growth of the company. If Fellare does not win the contract, however, Mr. Bowlander believes the stock will continue its current slow downward trend. To guard against this latter outcome, Mr. Bowlander does not want to make an outright purchase of Fellare stock now.

Michael has asked Elise to price the option. He expects a figure before the stock market closes so that if Mr. Bowlander decides to purchase the option, the transaction can take place today.

Unfortunately, the investment science course Elise took to complete her undergraduate business degree did not cover options theory; it only covered valuation, risk, capital budgeting, and market efficiency. She remembers from her valuation studies that she should discount the value of the option on February 1 by the appropriate interest rate to obtain the value of the option today. Because she is discounting over a 12-week period, the formula she should use to discount the option is (Value of the Option/ $[1 + \text{Weekly Interest Rate}]^{12}$). As a starting point for her calculations, she decides to use an annual interest rate of 8 percent. But she now needs to decide how to calculate the value of the option on February 1.

Elise knows that on February 1, Mr. Bowlander will take one of two actions: either he will exercise the option and purchase shares of Fellare stock or he will not exercise the option. Mr. Bowlander will exercise the option if the price of Fellare stock on February 1 is above his exercise price of $44.00. In this case, he purchases Fellare stock for $44.00 and then immediately sells it for the market price on February 1. Under this scenario, the value of the option would be the difference between the stock price and the exercise price. Mr. Bowlander will not exercise the option if the price of Fellare stock is below his exercise price of $44.00. In this case, he does nothing, and the value of the option would be $0.

The value of the option is therefore determined by the value of Fellare stock on February 1. Elise knows that the value of the stock on February 1 is uncertain and is therefore represented by a probability distribution of values. Elise recalls from a management science course in college that she can use computer simulation to estimate the mean of this distribution of stock values. Before she builds the simulation model, however, she needs to know the price movement of the stock. Elise recalls from a probability and statistics course that the price of a stock can be modeled as following a random walk and either growing or decaying according to a lognormal distribution. Therefore, according to this model, the stock price at the end of the next week is the stock price at the end of the current week multiplied by a growth factor. This growth factor is expressed as the number e raised to a power that is equal to a normally distributed random variable. In other words:

$$s_n = e^N s_c$$

where

s_n = The stock price at the end of next week

s_c = The stock price at the end of the current week

N = A random variable that has a normal distribution

To begin her analysis, Elise looks in the newspaper to find that the Fellare stock price for the current week is $42.00. She decides to use this price to begin her 12-week analysis. Thus, the price of the stock at the end of the first week is this current price multiplied by the growth factor. She next estimates the mean and standard deviation of the normally distributed random variable used in the calculation of the growth factor. This random variable determines the degree of change (volatility) of the stock, so Elise decides to use the current annual interest rate and the historical annual volatility of the stock as a basis for estimating the mean and standard deviation.

The current annual interest rate is $r = 8$ percent, and the historical annual volatility of the aerospace stock is 30 percent. But Elise remembers that she is calculating the *weekly* change in stock—*not* the *annual* change. She therefore needs to calculate the weekly interest rate and weekly historical stock volatility to obtain estimates for the mean and standard deviation of the weekly growth factor. To obtain the weekly interest rate w, Elise must make the following calculation:

$$w = (1 + r)^{(1/52)} - 1$$

The historical weekly stock volatility equals the historical annual volatility divided by the square root of 52. She calculates the mean of the normally distributed random variable by subtracting one-half of the square of the weekly stock volatility from the weekly interest rate w. In other words:

$$\text{Mean} = w - 0.5(\text{Weekly Stock Volatility})^2$$

The standard deviation of the normally distributed random variable is simply equal to the weekly stock volatility.

Elise is now ready to build her simulation model.

a. Build a simulation model in a spreadsheet to calculate the value of the option in today's dollars. Use Crystal Ball to run three separate simulations to estimate the value of the call option and hence the price of the option in today's dollars. For the first simulation, run 100 trials of the simulation. For the second simulation, run 500 trials of the simulation. For the third simulation, run 1,000 trials of the simulation. For each simulation, record the price of the option in today's dollars.

b. Elise takes her calculations and recommended price to Michael. He is very impressed, but he chuckles and indicates that a simple, closed-form approach exists for calculating the value of an option: the Black-Scholes formula. Michael grabs an investment science book from the shelf above his desk and reveals the very powerful and very complicated Black-Scholes formula:

$$V = N[d_1] \, P - N[d_2] \, PV[K]$$

where

$$d_1 = \frac{\ln[P/PV[K]]}{\sigma\sqrt{t}} + \frac{\sigma\sqrt{t}}{2}$$

$$d_2 = d_1 - \sigma\sqrt{t}$$

$N[x]$ = The Excel function NORMSDIST (x) where

$$x = d_1 \text{ or } x = d_2$$

P = Current price of the stock

K = Exercise price

$PV[K]$ = Present value of exercise price = $\dfrac{K}{(1 + w)^t}$

t = Number of weeks to exercise date

σ = Weekly volatility of stock

Use the Black-Scholes formula to calculate the value of the call option and hence the price of the option. Compare this value to the value obtained in part *a*.

c. In the specific case of Fellare stock, do you think that a random walk as described above completely describes the price movement of the stock? Why or why not?

Appendix A

Table for the Normal Distribution

The table in this appendix can be used to find any desired probabilities from a normal distribution. To do this, you need to identify the values of the following parameters of the distribution.

μ = Mean of the distribution

σ = Standard deviation of the distribution

FINDING PROBABILITIES WHEN $\mu = 0$ AND $\sigma = 1$

When $\mu = 0$ and $\sigma = 1$, probabilities can be read immediately from the table. In particular, for any specific value of $z \geq 0$, suppose you want to know the probability that the value of a random observation from the distribution will be less than or equal to z. The table gives this probability

$$F(z) = \text{Prob } \{\text{Value} \leq z\}$$

by reading the number in the table that corresponds to the value of z. For example, if $z = 1.25$, look in the 1.2 row and the 0.5 column to read the probability .8944. Thus,

$$F(1.25) = \text{Prob } \{\text{Value} \leq 1.25\} = 0.8944$$

Because the normal curve is symmetrical about the mean and the total area under the curve is 1, the probabilities for other ranges of values also can be obtained easily. For example,

Prob $\{\text{Value} > 1.25\} = 1 - F(1.25) = 1 - 0.8944 = 0.1056$

Prob $\{\text{Value} < -1.25\} = \text{Prob } \{\text{Value} > 1.25\} = 0.1056$

Prob $\{-1.25 \leq \text{Value} \leq 1.25\} = \text{Prob } \{\text{Value} \leq 1.25\} - \text{Prob } \{\text{Value} < -1.25\}$
$$= 0.8944 - 0.1056 = 0.7888$$

FINDING PROBABILITIES FOR OTHER VALUES OF μ AND σ

When you don't have both $\mu = 0$ and $\sigma = 1$, one quick calculation is needed before using the table. In particular, for a specific value of x, suppose you want to know the probability that the value of a random observation from the distribution will be less than or equal to x. The first step is to calculate

$$z = \frac{x - \mu}{\sigma}$$

Then the desired probability is

$$\text{Prob } \{\text{Value} \leq x\} = F(z)$$

where F(z) is read from the table in the usual way.

To illustrate, suppose that $\mu = 10$, $\sigma = 4$, and $x = 15$. Since

$$z = \frac{15 - 10}{4} = 1.25$$

the desired probability is

$$\text{Prob } \{\text{Value} \leq 15\} = F(1.25) = 0.8944$$

Similarly,

$$\text{Prob } \{\text{Value} > 15\} = 1 - F(1.25) = 1 - 0.8944 = 0.1056$$

If $x = 5$ instead, then

$$z = \frac{5 - 10}{4} = -1.25$$

so the corresponding probability is

$$P \{\text{Value} \leq 5\} = F(-1.25) = 1 - F(1.25)$$
$$= 1 - 0.8944 = 0.1056$$

Therefore,

$$\text{Prob } \{5 \leq \text{Value} \leq 15\} = \text{Prob } \{\text{Value} \leq 15\} - \text{Prob } \{\text{Value} < 5\}$$
$$= 0.8944 - 0.1056 = 0.7888$$

Probabilities for various other ranges of values can be obtained in the same way.

Table for the Normal Distribution

Areas under the standardized normal curve, from $-\infty$ to $+z$

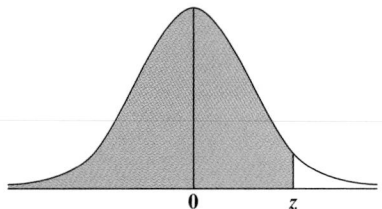

z	.00	.01	.02	.03	.04	.05	.06	.07	.08	.09
.0	.5000	.5040	.5080	.5120	.5160	.5199	.5239	.5279	.5319	.5359
.1	.5398	.5438	.5478	.5517	.5557	.5596	.5636	.5675	.5714	.5753
.2	.5793	.5832	.5871	.5910	.5948	.5987	.6026	.6064	.6103	.6141
.3	.6179	.6217	.6255	.6293	.6331	.6368	.6406	.6443	.6480	.6517
.4	.6554	.6591	.6628	.6664	.6700	.6736	.6772	.6808	.6844	.6879
.5	.6915	.6950	.6985	.7019	.7054	.7088	.7123	.7157	.7190	.7224
.6	.7257	.7291	.7324	.7357	.7389	.7422	.7454	.7486	.7517	.7549
.7	.7580	.7611	.7642	.7673	.7703	.7734	.7764	.7794	.7823	.7852
.8	.7881	.7910	.7939	.7967	.7995	.8023	.8051	.8078	.8106	.8133
.9	.8159	.8186	.8212	.8238	.8264	.8289	.8315	.8340	.8365	.8389
1.0	.8413	.8438	.8461	.8485	.8508	.8531	.8554	.8577	.8599	.8621
1.1	.8643	.8665	.8686	.8708	.8729	.8749	.8770	.8790	.8810	.8830
1.2	.8849	.8869	.8888	.8907	.8925	.8944	.8962	.8980	.8997	.9015
1.3	.9032	.9049	.9066	.9082	.9099	.9115	.9131	.9147	.9162	.9177
1.4	.9192	.9207	.9222	.9236	.9251	.9265	.9279	.9292	.9306	.9319
1.5	.9332	.9345	.9357	.9370	.9382	.9394	.9406	.9418	.9429	.9441
1.6	.9452	.9463	.9474	.9484	.9495	.9505	.9515	.9525	.9535	.9545
1.7	.9554	.9564	.9573	.9582	.9591	.9599	.9608	.9616	.9625	.9633
1.8	.9641	.9649	.9656	.9664	.9671	.9678	.9686	.9693	.9699	.9706
1.9	.9713	.9719	.9726	.9732	.9738	.9744	.9750	.9756	.9761	.9767
2.0	.9772	.9778	.9783	.9788	.9793	.9798	.9803	.9808	.9812	.9817
2.1	.9821	.9826	.9830	.9834	.9838	.9842	.9846	.9850	.9854	.9857
2.2	.9861	.9864	.9868	.9871	.9875	.9878	.9881	.9884	.9887	.9890
2.3	.9893	.9896	.9898	.9901	.9904	.9906	.9909	.9911	.9913	.9916
2.4	.9918	.9920	.9922	.9925	.9927	.9929	.9931	.9932	.9934	.9936
2.5	.9938	.9940	.9941	.9943	.9945	.9946	.9948	.9949	.9951	.9952
2.6	.9953	.9955	.9956	.9957	.9959	.9960	.9961	.9962	.9963	.9964
2.7	.9965	.9966	.9967	.9968	.9969	.9970	.9971	.9972	.9973	.9974
2.8	.9974	.9975	.9976	.9977	.9977	.9978	.9979	.9979	.9980	.9981
2.9	.9981	.9982	.9982	.9983	.9984	.9984	.9985	.9985	.9986	.9986
3.0	.9987	.9987	.9987	.9988	.9988	.9989	.9989	.9989	.9990	.9990
3.1	.9990	.9991	.9991	.9991	.9991	.9992	.9992	.9992	.9993	.9993
3.2	.9993	.9993	.9994	.9994	.9994	.9994	.9994	.9995	.9995	.9995
3.3	.9995	.9995	.9995	.9996	.9996	.9996	.9996	.9996	.9996	.9997
3.4	.9997	.9997	.9997	.9997	.9997	.9997	.9997	.9997	.9997	.9998

Appendix B

Partial Answers to Selected Problems

CHAPTER 2

2.8. *d.* Fraction of 1st = 0.667, fraction of 2nd = 0.667. Profit = \$6,000.

2.13. *a.* If $x_2 = 0$, then $x_1 = 2$. If $x_1 = 0$, then $x_2 = 4$.

    c. Slope = -2.

    d. $x_2 = -2x_1 + 4$.

2.16. *a.*

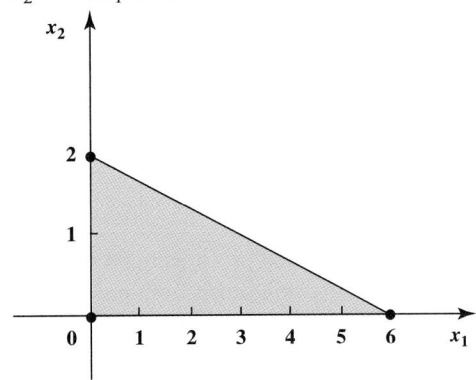

2.21. *b.*

	Slope-Intercept Form	Slope	x_2 Intercept
Profit = 6	$x_2 = -\frac{2}{3}x_1 + 2$	$-\frac{2}{3}$	2
Profit = 12	$x_2 = -\frac{2}{3}x_1 + 4$	$-\frac{2}{3}$	4
Profit = 18	$x_2 = -\frac{2}{3}x_1 + 6$	$-\frac{2}{3}$	6

2.25. $x_2 = -\frac{8}{5}x_1 + 8$.

2.29. *b.* $x_1 = 13$, $x_2 = 5$. Profit = \$31.

2.40. *b.* $x_1 = 2$, $x_2 = 4$. Cost = \$110.

CHAPTER 3

3.2. *d.* 0 end tables, 40 coffee tables, 30 dining room tables. Profit = \$10,600.

3.4. *e.* 19% participation in Project A, 0% participation in Project B, and 100% participation in Project C. Ending Balance = \$59.5 million.

3.6. *d.* 4 FT (8AM–4PM), 4 FT (12PM–8PM), 4 FT (4PM–midnight), 2 PT (8AM–12PM), 0 PT (12PM–4PM), 4 PT (4PM–8PM), 2 PT (8PM–midnight). Total cost per day = $1,728.

CHAPTER 4

4.2. *c.* 3.333 of Activity 1, 3.333 of Activity 2. Profit = $166.67.

4.5. *d.* 26 of Product 1, 54.76 of Product 2, 20 of Product 3. Profit = $2,904.76.

4.10. *d.* 1.14 kg of corn, 2.43 kg of alfalfa. Cost = $2.42.

4.15. *b.* Cost = $410,000.

Shipment Quantities	Customer 1	Customer 2	Customer 3
Factory 1	300	0	100
Factory 2	0	200	300

4.17. *c.* $60,000 in Investment A (year 1), $84,000 in Investment A (year 3), $117,600 in Investment D (year 5). Total accumulation in year 6 = $152,880.

4.20. *a.* Profit = $13,330.

Cargo Placement	Front	Center	Back
Cargo 1	0	5	10
Cargo 2	7.333	4.167	0
Cargo 3	0	0	0
Cargo 4	4.667	8.333	0

CHAPTER 5

5.1. *f.* Allowable range for unit profit from producing toys: $2.50 to $5.00.
Allowable range for unit profit from producing subassemblies: −$3.00 to −$1.50.

5.4. *f.* (*Part a*)
Optimal solution does not change (within allowable increase of $10).

(*Part b*)
Optimal solution does change (outside of allowable decrease of $5).

(*Part c*)
By the 100% rule for simultaneous changes in the objective function, the optimal solution may or may not change.

C_{8AM}: $160 → $165   % of allowable increase = $100 \left(\dfrac{165 - 160}{10} \right) = 50\%$

C_{4PM}: $180 → $170   % of allowable decrease = $100 \left(\dfrac{180 - 170}{5} \right) = \underline{200\%}$

Sum = 250%

5.8. *a.* Produce 2,000 toys and 1,000 sets of subassemblies. Profit = $3,500.

b. The shadow price for subassembly A is $0.50, which is the maximum premium that the company should be willing to pay.

5.12. *a.* The total expected number of exposures could be increased by 3,000 for each additional $1,000 added to the advertising budget.

b. This remains valid for increases of up to $250,000.

e. By the 100% rule for simultaneous changes in right-hand sides, the shadow prices are still valid. Using units of thousands of dollars,

$$C_A: \quad \$4,000 \to \$4,100 \quad \% \text{ of allowable increase} = 100 \left(\frac{4,100 - 4,000}{250} \right) = 40\%$$

$$C_P: \quad \$1,000 \to \$1,100 \quad \% \text{ of allowable increase} = 100 \left(\frac{1,100 - 1,000}{450} \right) = \underline{22\%}$$

$$\text{Sum} = 62\%$$

CHAPTER 6

6.5. 3 pints from Harry today, 4 pints from Dick tomorrow. Total cost = $19.50.

6.19. *b.* A-2, B-4, C-3, D-1. Total cost = $20.

6.22. *b.* David—backstroke, Tony—breaststroke, Chris—butterfly, Carl—freestyle. Total time = 126.20 seconds.

CHAPTER 7

7.1. *c.* 0 S1-D1, 10 S1-D2, 30 S1-D3, 30 S2-D1, 30 S2-D2, 0 S2-D3. Total cost = $580.

7.4. *c.* $2,187,000.

7.7. Maximum flow = 15.

7.12. *b.* Replace after year 1. Total cost = $29,000.

7.15. Links: B-C, E-F, C-D, A-B, C-F, E-G. Total cost = $18,000.

CHAPTER 8

8.2. *c.* AFK, AGHIJ, BCHIJ.

8.5. *c.* BEJM, CGLN.

8.8. ABCEFJKN. Total duration = 26 weeks.

8.10. $\mu = 37$, $\sigma^2 = 9$.

8.14. *b.* ACEF. Length = 51 days.

 c. 0.9772.

 d. 0.9192.

8.20. *b.* Crash B 1 week, C 2 weeks, D 1 week, and E 2 weeks. $7,834 is saved.

8.21. Crash A 2 weeks, B 1 week, G 1 week, and H 1 week. Total cost = $217.

8.24. *d.*

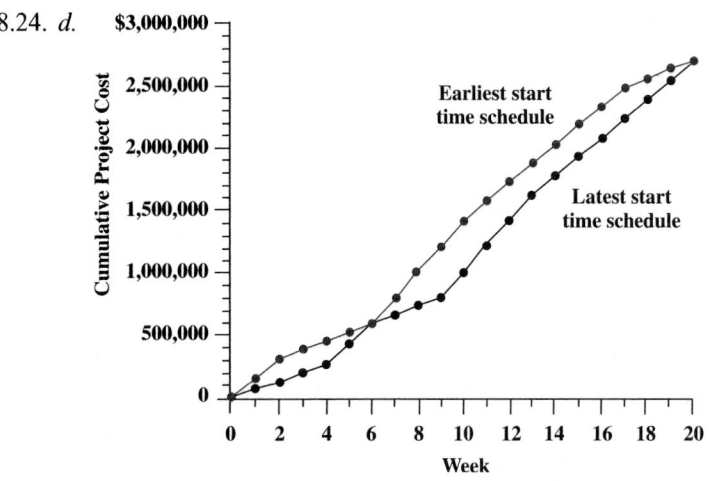

e. The project manager should focus attention on activity D since it is not yet finished and is running over budget.

CHAPTER 9

9.3.   a. Optimal solution: $(x_1, x_2) = (2,3)$, $P = 13$.

9.5.   a. 14 long-range, 0 medium-range, 16 short-range. Profit = $95.6 million.

9.9.   b. Marketing and dishwashing by Eve, cooking and laundry by Steven. Total time = 18.4 hours.

9.13. Produce 2,000 of product 2. Total revenue = $80,000.

9.17. Produce 45 of product 1, 31 of product 2.

9.19. Optimal path = OADT. Total distance = 10 miles.

CHAPTER 10

10.6.   c. Invest $46,667 in Stock 1 and $3,333 in Stock 2 for $13,000 expected profit.

Invest $33,333 in Stock 1 and $16,667 in Stock 2 for $15,000 expected profit.

10.10. d. Dorwyn should produce 1 window and 1 door.

CHAPTER 11

11.1. The coefficient for L7 is three times as large as the coefficient for K7.

11.3. a. Produce 15 units of product 3.

CHAPTER 12

12.4.   a. Speculative investment.

d. Counter-cyclical investment.

12.6.   b. A_3

c. A_2

12.11. a. A_1

b. $18.

12.15. c. EVPI = $3,000. The credit-rating organization should not be used.

12.20. c. Choose to build computers (expected payoff is $27 million).

f. They should build when $p \leq 0.722$ and sell when $p > 0.722$.

12.21. a. EVPI = $7.5 million.

c. P(Sell 10,000 | Predict Sell 10,000) = 0.667.

P(Sell 100,000 | Predict Sell 100,000) = 0.667.

12.22. a. The optimal policy is to do no market research and build the computers.

12.25. c. $800,000.

f, g. Leland University should hire William. If he predicts a winning season, then they should hold the campaign. If he predicts a losing season, then they should not hold the campaign.

12.29. a. Choose to introduce the new product (expected payoff is $12.5 million).

b. $7.5 million.

c. The optimal policy is not to test but to introduce the new product.

f. Both charts indicate that the expected profit is sensitive to both parameters, but is somewhat more sensitive to changes in the profit if successful than to changes in the loss if unsuccessful.

12.33. *a.* Choose not to buy insurance (expected payoff is $249,840).

    b. Choose to buy insurance (expected utility is 499.82).

12.35. 9.

CHAPTER 13

13.1. *a.* 39.

    b. 26.

    c. 36.

13.3. MAD = 15.

13.8. 2,091.

13.12. When $\alpha = 0.1$, forecast = 2,072.

13.15. 552.

13.17. *b.* MAD = 5.18.

    c. MAD = 3.

    d. MAD = 3.93.

13.29. 62 percent.

13.35. *b.* $y = 410 + 17.6x$.

    d. 604.

CHAPTER 14

14.3. *a.* True.

    b. False.

    c. True.

14.8. *a.* $L = 2$

    b. $L_q = 0.375$

    c. $W = 30$ minutes, $W_q = 5.625$ minutes.

14.11. *a.* 96.9% of the time.

14.14. *b.* $L = 0.333$

    g. Two members.

14.17. L_q is unchanged and W_q is reduced by half.

14.21. *a.* $L = 3$

    d. TC (status quo) = $85/hour.

       TC (proposal) = $73/hour.

14.23. *a.* One day with current policy, 3.25 days under proposed policy.

    b. One airplane with current policy, 0.8125 airplanes under proposed policy.

14.28. *a.* 0.211 hours.

    c. Approximately 3.43 minutes.

14.33. *c.* 0.4.

    d. 7.2 hours.

14.37. Jim should operate 4 cash registers. Expected cost per hour = $80.59.

CHAPTER 15

15.1. *b.* Let the numbers 0.0000 to 0.5999 correspond to strikes and the numbers 0.6000 to 0.9999 correspond to balls. The random observations for pitches are 0.3039 = strike, 0.7914 = ball, 0.8543 = ball, 0.6902 = ball, 0.3004 = strike, 0.0383 = strike.

15.5. *a.* Here is a sample replication.

Summary of Results:

Win? (1=Yes, 0=No)	0
Number of Tosses =	3

Simulated Tosses

Toss	Die 1	Die 2	Sum
1	4	2	6
2	3	2	5
3	6	1	7
4	5	2	7
5	4	4	8
6	1	4	5
7	2	6	8

Results

Win?	Lose?	Continue?
0	0	Yes
0	0	Yes
0	1	No
NA	NA	No
NA	NA	No
NA	NA	No
NA	NA	No

15.7. *b.* $F(x) = 0.0965$ when $x = -5.18$.
$F(x) = 0.5692$ when $x = 18.46$.
$F(x) = 0.6658$ when $x = 23.29$.

15.9. *a.* Let the numbers 0.0000 to 0.3999 correspond to a minor repair and 0.4000 to 0.9999 correspond to a major repair. The average repair time is then $(1.224 + 0.950 + 1.610)/3 = 1.26$ hours.

c. The average repair time is 1.28 hours.

e. The average repair time is 1.09 hours.

15.12. *a.* $x = \sqrt{r}$

d. $= \text{SQRT(RAND())}$.

15.18. *b.* The average waiting time should be approximately 1 day.

c. The average waiting time should be approximately 0.33 days.

CHAPTER 16

16.3. *a.* Triangular distribution (Min = 293.51, Likeliest = 501.00, Max = 599.72).

16.7. *a.* The mean project completion time should be approximately 33 months.

c. Activities B and J have the greatest impact on the variability in the project completion time.

16.15. *a.* Mean profit should be around $107, with about a 96.5% chance of making at least $0.

CHAPTER 17

17.16. *a.* Optimal Solution: $(x_1, x_2) = (0.667, 0.667)$ and Profit = $6,000$.

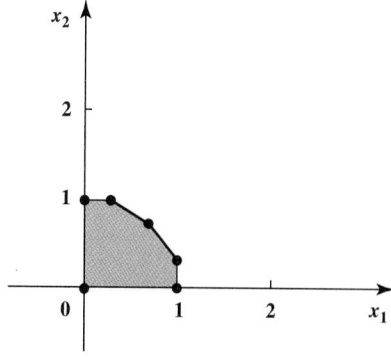

Note: Corner points will be called A, B, C, D, E, and F going clockwise from (0,1).

b. Corner Point   A: F and B are adjacent.

                  B: A and C are adjacent.

                  C: B and D are adjacent.

                  D: C and E are adjacent.

                  E: D and F are adjacent.

                  F: E and A are adjacent.

17.20.

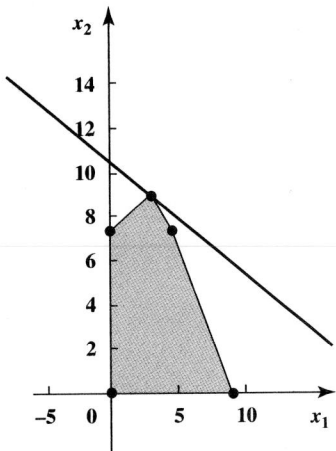

Corner Point	Profit $= 10x_1 + 20x_2$	Next Step
(0, 0)	0	Check (0, 7.5) and (9, 0)
(0, 7.5)	150	Move to (0, 7.5)
(9, 0)	90	Check (3, 9)
(3, 9)	210	Move to (3, 9)
		Check (4.5, 7.5)
(4.5, 7.5)	195	Stop, (3, 9) is optimal

CHAPTER 18

18.1.   *a.*

Data		
D =	676	(demand/year)
K =	$75	(setup cost)
h =	$600.00	(unit holding cost)
L =	3.5	(lead time in days)
WD =	365	(working days/year)

Results	
Reorder Point =	6.5
Annual Setup Cost =	$10,140
Annual Holding Cost =	$1,500
Total Variable Cost =	$11,640

Decision		
Q =	5	(order quantity)

d.

Data		
$D =$	676	(demand/year)
$K =$	$75	(setup cost)
$h =$	$600.00	(unit holding cost)
$L =$	3.5	(lead time in days)
WD $=$	365	(working days/year)

Results	
Reorder Point $=$	6.48
Annual Setup Cost $=$	$3,900
Annual Holding Cost $=$	$3,900
Total Variable Cost $=$	$7,800

Decision		
$Q =$	13	(order quantity)

The results are the same as those obtained in part *c*.

f. Number of orders per year $= 52$

$$ROP = 6.5 - \text{Inventory level when each order is placed}$$

g. The optimal policy reduces the total variable inventory cost by $3,840 per year, which is a 33% reduction.

18.6. *a.* $h = \$3$ per month which is 15% of the acquisition cost.

c. Reorder point is 10.

d. ROP $= 5$ hammers which adds $20 to his TVC (5 hammers $\times$ $4 holding cost).

18.9. *c.*

Quantity	Basic EOQ Model	EOQ Model with Planned Shortages
Order quantity	244.95	316.23
Maximum shortage	0	126.49
Maximum inventory level	244.95	189.74
Reorder point	0	-126.49
Annual setup cost	$2,449.49	$1,897.37
Annual holding cost	$2,449.49	$1,138.42
Annual shortage cost	0	$758.95
Total variable cost	$4,898.98	$3,794.73

18.17. *a.*

Data		
$D =$	6000	(demand/year)
$R =$	24,000	(production rate)
$K =$	$7,500	(unit setup cost)
$h =$	$120.00	(unit holding cost)

Results	
Annual Setup Cost $=$	$45,000.00
Annual Holding Cost $=$	$45,000.00
Total Variable Cost $=$	$90,000.00

Decision		
$Q =$	1,000	(production lot size)

b. Production run duration $= 0.5$ months.

Time interval between production runs $= 2$ months.

c. Maximum inventory level $= 750$. This is less than the production lot size since monitors are being withdrawn from inventory while a production run is going on.

CHAPTER 19

19.3. *a.* Optimal service level = 0.667.

  c. Q* = 500.

  d. The probability of running short is 33.3%.

  e. Optimal service level = 0.833.

19.6. *a.* This problem can be interpreted as an inventory problem with uncertain demand for a perishable product with eurotraveler's checks as the product. Once Stan gets back from his trip the checks are not good anymore so they are a perishable product. He can redeposit the amount into his savings account but will incur a fee of lost interest. Stan must decide how many checks to buy without knowing how many he will need.

$$C_{under} = \text{Value of 1 day} - \text{Cost of 1 day} - \text{Cost of 1 check} = \$49$$
$$C_{over} = \text{Cost of check} + \text{Lost interest} = \$3$$

  b. Purchase 4 additional checks.

  c. Optimal service level = 0.94.

  Buy 4 additional checks.

19.10. *a.* Q = 60.

  b. R = 60.

  d. Safety Stock = 10.

  e. If demand during the delivery time exceeds 60 (the order quantity), then the reorder point will be hit again before the order arrives, triggering another order.

19.15. *b.* Ground Chuck: R = 145.

  Chuck Wagon: R = 829.

  c. Ground Chuck: Safety Stock = 45.

  Chuck Wagon: Safety Stock = 329.

  f. Ground Chuck: $39,378.71.

  Chuck Wagon: $41,958.61.

  Jed should choose Ground Chuck as their supplier.

  g. If Jed would like to use the beef within a month of receiving it, then Ground Chuck is the better choice. The order quantity with Ground Chuck is roughly one month's supply, whereas with Chuck Wagon the optimal order quantity is roughly three month's supply.

Index

Student CD Content

- Quizzes
- Spreadsheets
- Solver Table
- Enrichment Modules
- Software
  - Crystal Ball
  - Premium Solver
  - MS Project 2002
  - Interactive Management Science Modules
  - TreePlan
  - Sensit
  - RiskSim
- Link to OMC Website